HANDBOOKS

ALASKA

DON PITCHER

ARCTIC
ALASKA
Arctic Circle
Chukchi Sea
RUSSIA
Noatak National Preserve
Cape Krusenstern National Monument
Kobuk Valley National Park
Kotzebue
Bering Strait
Bering Land Bridge National Preserve
Selawik
Nome
St. Lawrence Island
RUSSIA
U.S.A.
Innoko
National
Wildlife
Refuge
Yukon
Bering Sea
Holy Cross
Yukon Delta National Wildlife Refuge
St. Matthew Island
Bethel
Nunivak Island
Togiak National Wildlife Refuge
Dillingham
King Salmon
St. Paul Island
Pribilof Islands
St. George Island
Becharof National Wildlife Refuge
Alaska Peninsula
Aniakchak National Monument and Preserve
0
100 mi
0
100 km
Izembek National Wildlife Refuge
Alaska Peninsula National Wildlife Refuge
Alaska Maritime National Wildlife Refuge
Unalaska
The Aleutian Islands

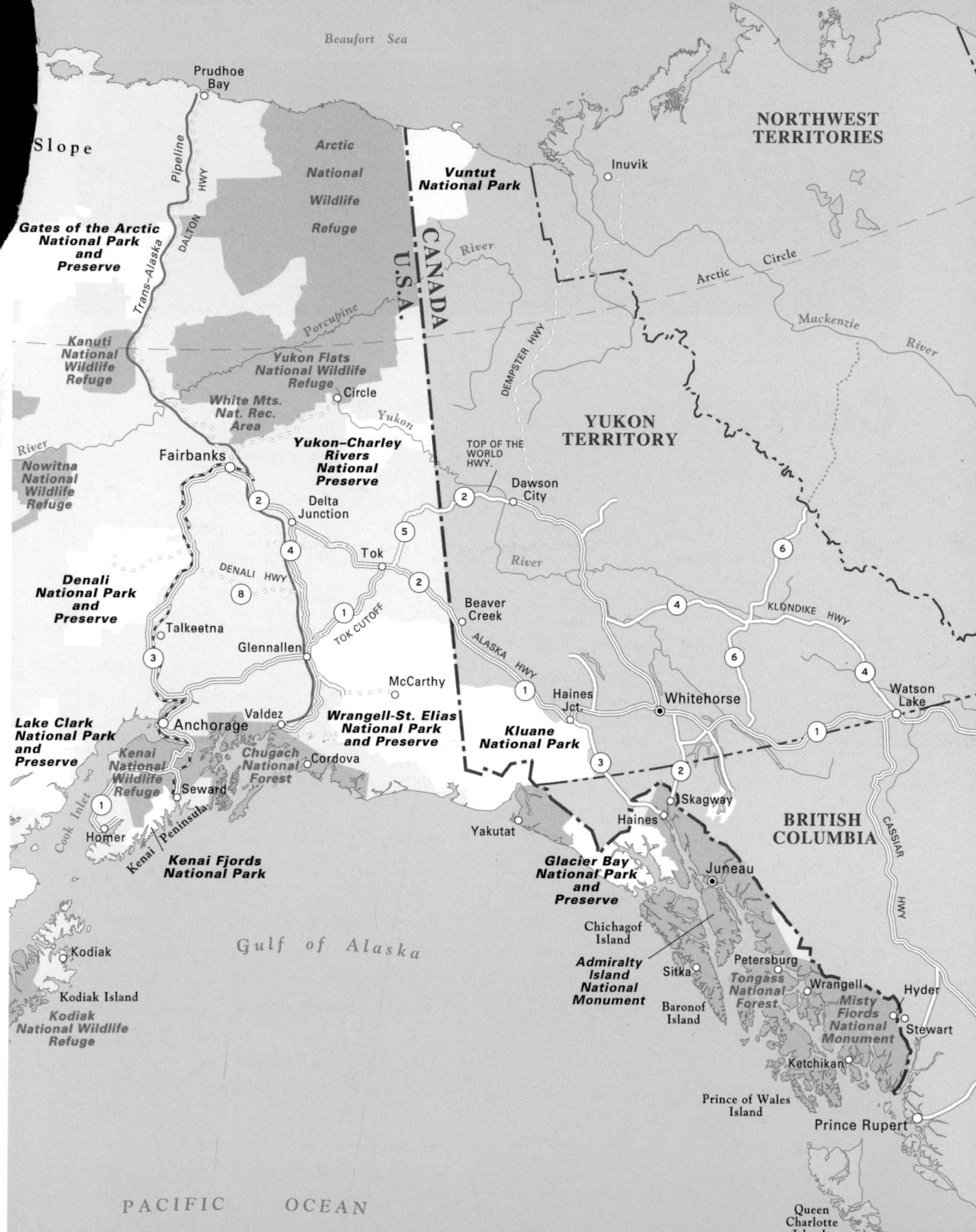
OCEAN
Beaufort Sea
Prudhoe Bay
Slope
Pipeline
DALTON HWY
Trans-Alaska
Arctic National Wildlife Refuge
Vuntut National Park
NORTHWEST TERRITORIES
Inuvik
Gates of the Arctic National Park and Preserve
CANADA
U.S.A.
River
Porcupine
Arctic Circle
Mackenzie River
Kanuti National Wildlife Refuge
Yukon Flats National Wildlife Refuge
Circle
DEMPSTER HWY
White Mts. Nat. Rec. Area
Yukon
YUKON TERRITORY
River
Nowitna National Wildlife Refuge
Fairbanks
Yukon–Charley Rivers National Preserve
TOP OF THE WORLD HWY.
Dawson City
Delta Junction
Tok
River
DENALI HWY
Denali National Park and Preserve
Beaver Creek
KLONDIKE HWY
TOK CUTOFF
Talkeetna
Glennallen
ALASKA HWY
McCarthy
Haines Jct.
Whitehorse
Watson Lake
Lake Clark National Park and Preserve
Anchorage
Valdez
Wrangell-St. Elias National Park and Preserve
Kluane National Park
Kenai National Wildlife Refuge
Chugach National Forest
Cordova
Seward
Skagway
Haines
BRITISH COLUMBIA
Cook Inlet
Homer
Kenai Peninsula
Yakutat
CASSIAR HWY
Kenai Fjords National Park
Glacier Bay National Park and Preserve
Juneau
Chichagof Island
Gulf of Alaska
Kodiak
Admiralty Island National Monument
Sitka
Petersburg
Tongass National Forest
Wrangell
Hyder
Kodiak Island
Baronof Island
Misty Fiords National Monument
Stewart
Kodiak National Wildlife Refuge
Ketchikan
Prince of Wales Island
Prince Rupert
PACIFIC OCEAN
Queen Charlotte Islands

Contents

List of Maps

MOON ALASKA
Avalon Travel
a member of the Perseus Books Group
1700 Fourth Street
Berkeley, CA 94710, USA
www.moon.com

Editor: Shaharazade Husain
Series Manager: Kathryn Ettinger
Copy Editor: Christopher Church
Graphics and Production Coordinator:
Domini Dragoone
Cover Designer: Domini Dragoone
Map Editor: Mike Morgenfeld
Cartographers: Kat Bennett, Mike Morgenfeld
Indexer: Jean Mooney

ISBN: 978-1-59880-350-1
ISSN: 1547-0261

Printing History
1st Edition – 1983
10th Edition – May 2010
5 4 3 2 1

Front cover photo: Bull moose in Chugach State Park © Getty Images/Photodisc/Eastcott Momatluk.
Title page photo: Totem poles and Beaver Clan House in Saxman village near Ketchikan © Don Pitcher.
Front color images: All photos © Don Pitcher.

Printed in Canada by Friesens

KEEPING CURRENT

If you have a favorite gem you'd like to see included in the next edition, or see anything that needs updating, clarification, or correction, please drop us a line. Send your comments via email to feedback@moon.com, or use the address above.

MAP SYMBOLS

- Expressway
- Primary Road
- Secondary Road
- Unpaved Road
- Trail
- Ferry
- Railroad
- Pedestrian Walkway
- Stairs
- Highlight
- City/Town
- State Capital
- National Capital
- Point of Interest
- Accommodation
- Restaurant/Bar
- Other Location
- Campground
- Airfield
- Airport
- Mountain
- Unique Natural Feature
- Waterfall
- Park
- Trailhead
- Skiing Area
- Golf Course
- Parking Area
- Archaeological Site
- Church
- Gas Station
- Glacier
- Mangrove
- Reef
- Swamp

CONVERSION TABLES

°C = (°F - 32) / 1.8
°F = (°C x 1.8) + 32
1 inch = 2.54 centimeters (cm)
1 foot = 0.304 meters (m)
1 yard = 0.914 meters
1 mile = 1.6093 kilometers (km)
1 km = 0.6214 miles
1 fathom = 1.8288 m
1 chain = 20.1168 m
1 furlong = 201.168 m
1 acre = 0.4047 hectares
1 sq km = 100 hectares
1 sq mile = 2.59 square km
1 ounce = 28.35 grams
1 pound = 0.4536 kilograms
1 short ton = 0.90718 metric ton
1 short ton = 2,000 pounds
1 long ton = 1.016 metric tons
1 long ton = 2,240 pounds
1 metric ton = 1,000 kilograms
1 quart = 0.94635 liters
1 US gallon = 3.7854 liters
1 Imperial gallon = 4.5459 liters
1 nautical mile = 1.852 km

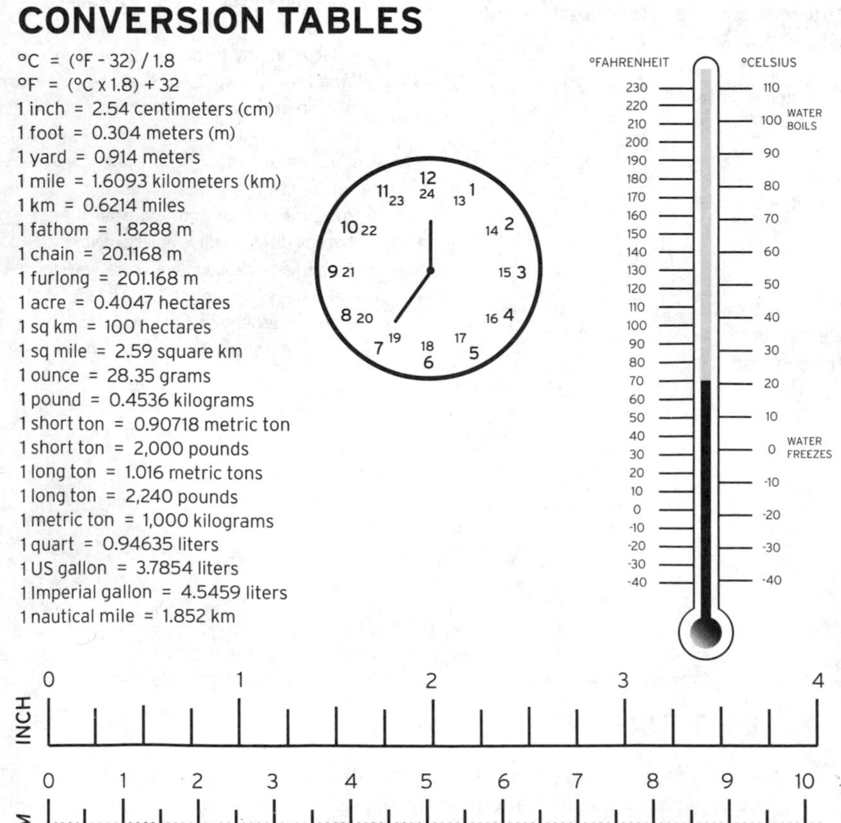

Discover Alaska

There is something about Alaska that has always stirred the imagination. From the first migrants who crossed the Bering land bridge during the ice ages, to today's travelers escaping the madness of city life, Alaska draws people from the world over to see its wonders: dramatic mountains and immense glaciers, rivers thick with brown bears, northern lights dancing across a velvety winter sky.

Alaska is a place apart – both physically and culturally – from the rest of the United States. In Alaska, the term *wilderness* does not refer to a small enclave of the natural world surrounded by shopping malls, traffic jams, and suburban sprawl. The Great Land is so huge, so wild, so underpopulated that it's almost incomprehensible: it falls right off the edge of your imagination. Here, like nowhere else on earth, human developments will always be dwarfed by the vastness of the land.

One characteristic of Alaska that comes as a surprise to first-time visitors is its diversity. It isn't just the high mountains and forested valleys of Interior Alaska, but also vast rain forests carpeting the islands of the Inside Passage, the wildlife-rich tundra stretching to the horizon on the Yukon Delta, the active volcanoes of the Aleutian Islands where earthquakes are an almost daily occurrence, and even a surfing beach that extends 70 miles along the Gulf of Alaska. You could spend an

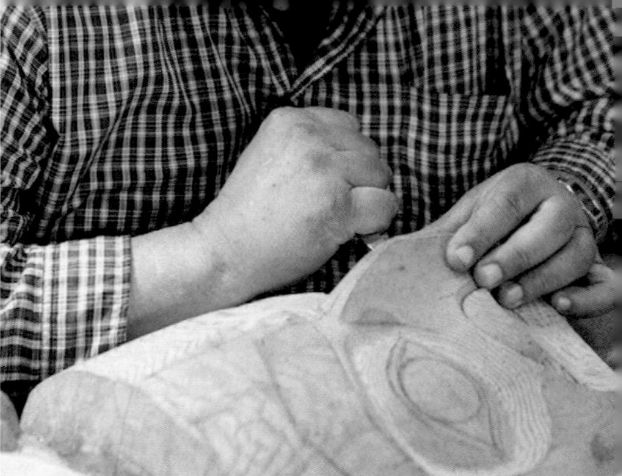

evening in Anchorage dining on king crab and sampling French wines, and the next day take a one-hour floatplane ride to a cabin where the only sounds are singing loons and droning mosquitoes.

Alaska has not just the continent's tallest mountain (20,320-foot Mt. McKinley) but entire ranges where unnamed peaks rim the valleys. One of the most spectacular areas – Wrangell-St. Elias National Park – covers an astounding 13 million acres, with three mountain ranges, many volcanoes, a glacier larger than Rhode Island, massive rivers, and nine of the 16 highest mountains in North America. Admiralty Island in Southeast Alaska has the highest brown bear density of any place on earth, with thick spruce forests, gorgeous alpine country, graceful bays, and one tiny Native Alaskan village on the southwestern shore. Located above the Arctic Circle, Kobuk Valley National Park has sand dunes topping 250 feet in height and covering 25 square miles. If you haven't been to Alaska before, you're in for a treat. If you have, you will almost certainly want to return.

Planning Your Trip

For many visitors, planning an Alaskan adventure entails going to a travel agent or website and booking an all-inclusive voyage on the HMS *Geezer,* where everything is packaged neatly for mass-market vacationers. Cruises *do* provide an introduction to the state, but people who really want to see Alaska need to get off the megaships and get away from the canned bus tours, shops selling made-in-China totems, and "eco-adventures" where you paddle a kayak around the harbor. Independent travelers have a slightly more difficult time arranging a trip to Alaska, but they will be rewarded a hundredfold with a more authentic experience. With the right planning, an Alaskan adventure can be the trip of a lifetime.

The type of travel you arrange, of course, depends on your interests, budget, and how much time you have. Retirees driving the Alaska Highway have very different needs from families riding the ferry to Juneau or mountaineers heading out on a grand wilderness adventure. Sit down with this book and see what works for you.

Getting around such a vast state forces visitors to put transportation at the core of planning, especially when ferry and train travel are involved. Don't schedule your trip too tightly since weather delays or mechanical problems may appear at the most inopportune moment. Leave some time in your schedule to relax, even if you have just a week. Those with specific must-see destinations such as bear-viewing flights, bus tours into Denali National Park, or

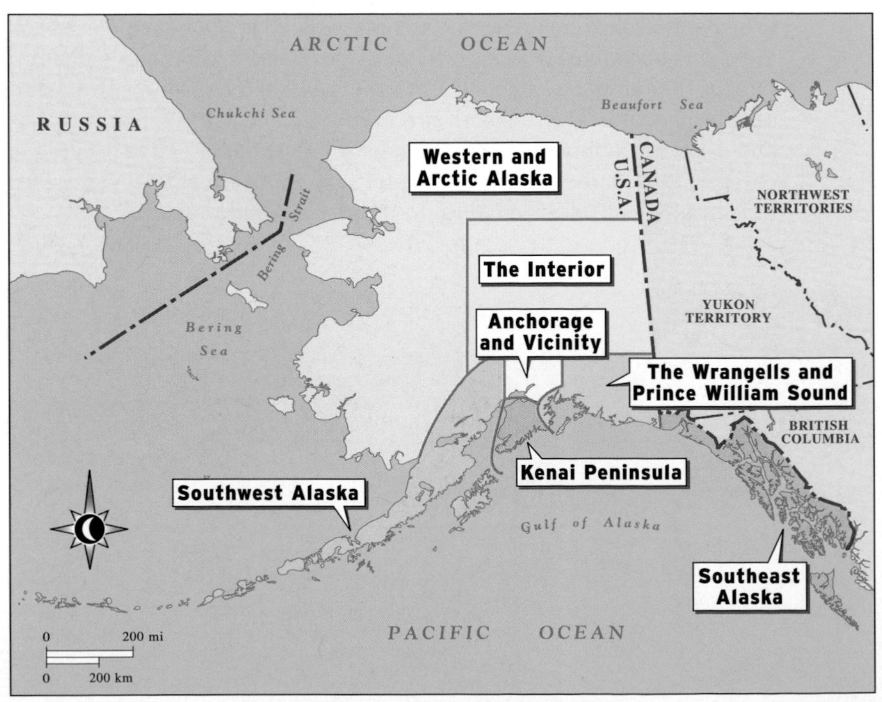

three-day sea kayaking trips should be sure to make reservations well ahead of time. Lodging places in such prime spots as Brooks Camp within Katmai National Park may fill up a year ahead of the peak summer season.

A good starting point when planning a trip to Alaska is the *Alaska State Vacation Planner,* distributed by the Alaska Travel Industry Association (907/929-2200 or 800/862-5275, www.travelalaska.com).

▸ WHERE TO GO

Southeast Alaska

Southeast is Alaska's "Panhandle," a coastal region dissected by the Inside Passage, much of it within massive **Tongass National Forest.** The southernmost town, rainy **Ketchikan** is famous for totem poles and cliff-walled Misty Fiords National Monument. **Juneau** is both the state capital and a major destination for travelers. Nearby are the fjords and glaciers within Tracy Arm and **Glacier Bay National Park.** Other towns have their own flavor, including **Petersburg**'s Norwegian heritage, the picture-perfect setting for **Sitka,** and **Skagway**'s gold-rush history.

Anchorage and Vicinity

Anchorage is home to nearly half the state's population, an international airport, and a multitude of cultural amenities. Hanging baskets of flowers and colorful gardens decorate Town Square in front of the Performing Arts Center. Especially notable are the **Anchorage Museum,** the largest in the state, and the **Alaska Native Heritage Center.** A paved trail skirts the shoreline, and great day-hiking is a short drive away within **Chugach State Park.** Head south along **Turnagain Arm,** with its enormous tides and beluga whales, to **Portage Glacier** and the ski resort town of **Girdwood.**

Kenai Peninsula

The Kenai Peninsula is perfect for quick escapes from Anchorage. Two primary roads—Seward Highway and Sterling Highway—cross the peninsula, which is dominated by **Chugach National Forest,**

iceberg in Tracy Arm, Tongass National Forest, near Juneau

Kenai National Wildlife Refuge, and Kenai Fjords National Park. The last of these is based in Seward, where you can join boat or kayak trips or visit the Alaska SeaLife Center. Kenai and Soldotna are bases for Kenai River fishing. The hip town of Homer is a premier destination for fishing, sea kayaking, and hiking, with notable lodges, restaurants, and art galleries.

The Wrangells and Prince William Sound

This section of Alaska encompasses the Copper River Valley, Wrangell Mountains, and Prince William Sound. Glenn Highway crosses the northern edge, passing Matanuska Glacier before dropping to the town of Glennallen. The Richardson Highway heads north to Tok and south over Thompson Pass to Valdez, terminus of the Trans-Alaska Pipeline. Wrangell-St. Elias National Park—the country's largest—lies at the heart of this region, with picturesque red mining buildings at Kennicott as the main attraction. State ferries connect the Prince William Sound communities of Cordova and Whittier.

IF YOU HAVE . . .

- **ONE WEEK:** Fly to Anchorage and visit Denali National Park and the Kenai Peninsula.
- **TWO WEEKS:** Take the ferry from Bellingham up the Inside Passage to Ketchikan, Petersburg, Wrangell, Juneau, Sitka, Haines, and Skagway.
- **THREE WEEKS:** Fly to Anchorage, drive to Denali National Park, Fairbanks, and Wrangell-St. Elias National Park, take the ferry from Valdez to Whittier, visit Seward and Homer, take the ferry to Kodiak Island.

The Interior

Interior Alaska is best known for Denali National Park, with caribou, brown bears, wolves, and other wildlife, plus amazing Alaska Range vistas. The town of Talkeetna provides a base for flightseeing trips to Mt. McKinley, North America's tallest peak. In Fairbanks, the second largest city in Alaska, don't miss the University of Alaska Museum of the North, Pioneer Park, and nearby Chena Hot

grizzly bear in Denali National Park

boats in Kodiak harbor

Springs. The Dalton Highway pushes north across the Arctic Circle, paralleling the Trans-Alaska Pipeline over the Brooks Range all the way to Prudhoe Bay.

Southwest Alaska

Southwest Alaska encompasses a ruggedly beautiful mix of lush islands, active volcanoes, and wild, wild country from Kodiak out the Alaska Peninsula to the Aleutians. The weather—dominated by rain, fog, and wind—is notoriously challenging for travelers. Kodiak Island has forests on the northeast end near the town of Kodiak that give way to tundra. The island is famous for its massive brown bears. Bear viewing flights depart for remote parts of the island or to Katmai National Park on the Alaska Peninsula. The Pribilof Islands are known for seabirds, seals, and other wildlife.

Western and Arctic Alaska

This is true bush Alaska, where the marshy tundra, powerful rivers, and high mountains are virtually untouched by human developments. Commercial salmon fishing dominates around Bristol Bay, but visitors come to see walrus at Round Island or to explore Wood-Tikchik State Park. Farther north is the old gold-mining town of Nome and the little-traveled Arctic, with a handful of settlements, including Barrow and Kaktovik (polar bears). Intrepid adventurers hike spectacular Gates of the Arctic National Park or float rivers in Arctic National Wildlife Refuge.

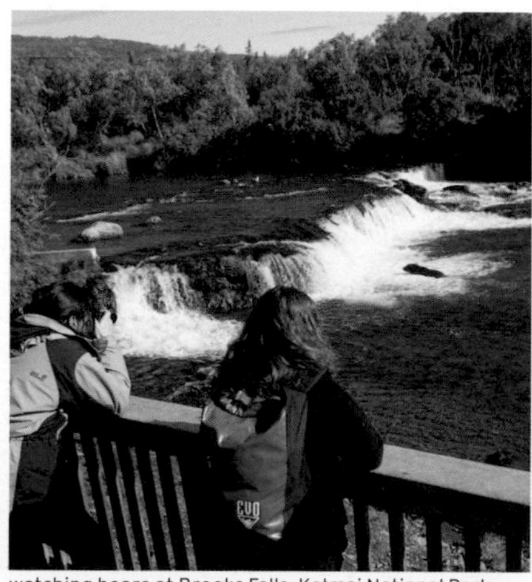
watching bears at Brooks Falls, Katmai National Park

▸ WHEN TO GO

Alaska is primarily a summer destination, and the vast majority of the 1.5 million annual visitors travel **mid-May–mid-September,** with the peak in **July–August.** The advantages of summer travel are obvious: long days, warmer weather, all the attractions are operating, and children are out of school, not to mention the return of salmon and the emergence of bears and other wildlife. Because of Alaska's northern location, spring arrives late, and much of the state does not green up until mid-May. The road into Denali National Park is closed by snow until late May, and the landscape can be bleak before leaves emerge. Summer has its drawbacks too, including mosquitoes, high lodging prices, and crowded venues.

forget-me-not, Alaska's state flower

Fall comes early. Autumn colors (primarily yellows on the aspen, birch, and willows, with reds and oranges in alpine areas) typically peak in early September across Interior Alaska, and a couple of weeks later for Southcentral Alaska. Days shorten dramatically by October—en route to the December 21 winter solstice—but longer nights also make Alaska's famous **northern lights** visible. Winter visitors come to view them, and to watch such events as the **Iditarod** and **Yukon Quest.** Interior Alaska can be bitterly cold in winter, but Anchorage and points south are typically milder, especially by mid-February.

Spring (especially April) is the ugly season, at least until the trees leaf out. Most winter activities are closed, and the summer fun hasn't cranked up, so do what Alaskans do and head to Hawaii instead.

Brilliant auroras light up the winter sky over the Arctic village of Bettles.

A bright summer day lights up a church in the village of Karluk on Kodiak Island.

▸ BEFORE YOU GO

It pays to do some planning before your trip to Alaska, especially if you're heading into remote bush parts of the state. This is a massive state, and unless you have months of time and a big bank account, you're wise to pick one region to explore. Ferry travelers to Southeast Alaska will need to develop their travels around the ferry schedule since several days may pass before the next ferry arrives. Many travelers fly into Anchorage and launch out from there by rental car, RV, train, or bus. Lodging, meals, and travel will eat a big hole in your budget, but you can avoid some expenses by camping and finding places where you can cook your own meals. Book well ahead for bus trips into Denali National Park and for lodging around the park. Do your research by reading this book, checking out the websites of places you might want to visit, and requesting a copy of the *Alaska State Vacation Planner.*

What to Take

Summer visitors will want to bring a light waterproof jacket and rain pants plus a sweater or polypropylene pullover for warmth. Hiking boots are recommended if you plan to spend any time in the backcountry, but good running shoes are fine for many purposes. Hikers in Southeast Alaska will need rubber boots and heavy-duty rain gear.

Winter visitors should be prepared for the cold and bring appropriate winter wear for extreme conditions, especially anyone planning a trip to Fairbanks, where temperatures are often well below zero, sometimes plummeting to -40°F. Southcentral winters are milder, with Anchorage temperatures often in the teens or single digits in January. Juneau and other Southeast Alaska towns have relatively mild winters with a mix of rain and snow.

Explore Alaska

▸ BEST OF ALASKA

This trip is perfect if you only have a week and want a taste of Alaska. It uses Anchorage as a base, while mixing travel by train, bus, car, boat, and air.

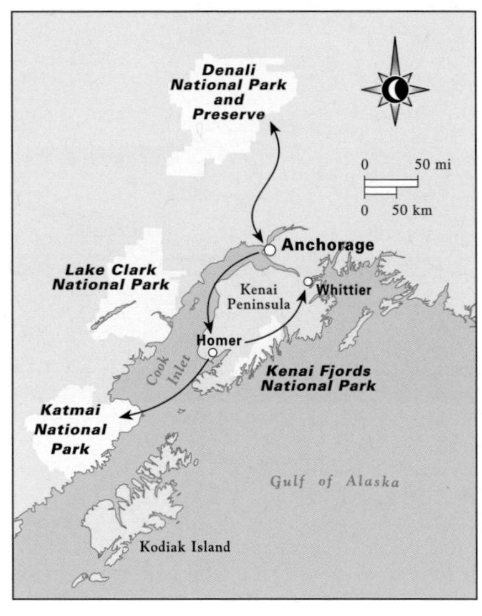

Day 1

Fly into Anchorage, settle into your hotel, and then cruise downtown to check out the flowers, gift shops, and visitors center. Enjoy a fine seafood dinner at Simon & Seaforts, where you can sip an 11 P.M. cocktail as the sun arcs across the summer sky over Cook Inlet.

Day 2

Hop on the 8 A.M. Alaska Railroad northbound train, arriving in Denali National Park eight hours later. (The luxurious GoldStar railcars cost more, but they have open-air viewing platforms to take in the grand scenery along the way.) Stay at one of the hotels just outside the park entrance; Denali Bluffs Hotel or Denali Crow's Nest are good choices.

Day 3

Join an all-day bus tour into Denali National Park. It's eight hours round-trip to the visitors center at Eielson (with fine views of Mt. McKinley when it's visible), or 11 hours if you want to go all the way out to Wonder Lake and back. This tour is the highlight of many Alaska visitors' trips, and you're likely to see grizzlies, moose, caribou, Dall sheep, and the occasional wolf along the way.

Day 4

After a morning visit to the Denali Visitors Center and a short hike, take the noon train back south, getting to Anchorage that evening. It won't get dark, so you might as well take a stroll out on the scenic Tony Knowles Coastal Trail.

Day 5

Rent a car and drive 225 miles down the Kenai Peninsula to the town of Homer. There's plenty to see and do, from sea kayaking and beachcombing to shopping and fine dining at Homestead Restaurant or Wasabi's. If you're looking for a spectacular bay vista, stay at the appropriately named Halcyon Heights B&B.

Day 6

This is a day that could go in three completely different directions. If you have the cash, hop on one of the all-day bear-viewing flights to Katmai National Park. Sea kayaking

BEAR-VIEWING

Bear-viewing is a booming business in Alaska, and visitors never forget their first sighting. Most folks choose a package trip to areas where the bears have become somewhat habituated to the presence of humans – but there are more adventurous opportunities as well.

BROWN BEARS

The most famous places to see and photograph brown (grizzly) bears are **Denali National Park** in Interior Alaska, **Brooks Camp** within Katmai National Park and Preserve, and at nearby **McNeil River State Game Sanctuary.** Some boats and planes also offer bear-viewing day trips to coastal **Lake Clark National Park.**

On Kodiak Island, bear-viewing centers around **Frazer Lake** within the Kodiak National Wildlife Refuge, but most of the bear-viewing flights out of Kodiak actually head to the Katmai coast.

In Southeast Alaska, the most popular area is **Pack Creek** on Admiralty Island, though you will also see brown bears at **Fish Creek** near Hyder, and a few at Anan Creek near Wrangell.

In addition to the official bear-viewing areas, quite a few air-taxi operators fly out of Anchorage, Homer, Kodiak, Soldotna, and King Salmon on daylong trips in search of brown bears. Most of these head to the outer coast of Katmai National Park and Preserve for $550-625 per person.

BLACK BEARS

The best Alaskan places to see black bears (and some brownies) are **Anan Creek** near Wrangell and **Margaret Creek Fish Ladder** near Ketchikan, both within **Tongass National Forest.**

POLAR BEARS

In Alaska, polar bears are most common within the **Arctic National Wildlife Refuge** and are occasional visitors to **Barrow** and the village of **Kaktovik,** particularly during the fall whaling seasons when fresh carcasses provide a food source. Local operators – including a boat-based tour in Kaktovik – take visitors to see and photograph the bears. These are powerful and dangerous creatures, and passenger vehicles do not really provide protection from a bear attack.

If you're really looking for polar bears, head to Churchill in Manitoba, Canada, where special tundra-buggy vehicles provide safe platforms for viewing and photography.

young brown bears on Kodiak Island

is a less expensive option, and True North Adventures has an all-day trip that includes a water taxi to Yukon Island, where you join a guided kayak adventure. The third option is to hop on an early morning **halibut fishing charter boat.** You're almost certain of getting your limit, and fish over 100 pounds are occasionally pulled in. Coal Point Seafood will process, freeze, and ship your catch.

Days 7-8

Head out early and drive back north to **Whittier.** (It is 191 miles from Homer to Whittier; allow at least four hours' travel time plus any tunnel delays.) In Whittier, take a leisurely five-hour **glacier tour** to **Blackstone Bay.** Seals lounge on the icebergs, and several active glaciers are visible at once. Spend the night at Alyeska Hotel in Girdwood and then continue on to Anchorage the next morning, or return to Anchorage late and fly out the next day. You'll want more time for your next Alaskan adventure!

Blackstone Glacier

▸ ALASKA'S HEARTLAND

This trip provides the chance to see the highlights of Southcentral and Interior Alaska, and could easily be extended to three weeks or shortened to one week. It is especially popular with families, since flights into Anchorage are relatively cheap with lots of car or RV rental options available.

Day 1

Fly into **Anchorage,** get a rental car, then find your hotel and settle in. (If you haven't already, make reservations for your trip to Denali on Day 4.) If you have time, you may want to get oriented by heading to the downtown visitors center. Or if the weather cooperates, take a walk along the **Coastal Trail;** it offers great vistas across **Cook Inlet** and is readily accessible from downtown.

Day 2

Drop by New Sagaya's for an espresso, croissant, and sack lunch. Spend the day exploring the **Anchorage Museum** and the **Alaska Native Heritage Center,** or heading out for a short hike in **Chugach State Park.** Overnight in Anchorage again.

Day 3

Get an early start since this is a long day. Drive north on the Parks Highway, stopping in **Talkeetna** (115 miles) for lunch. If you want to add a **one-hour flightseeing** trip over the park (recommended), you should probably spend the night in Talkeetna, adding another day to your trip. Otherwise, continue north to the Denali Park area (150 miles from Anchorage) where a range of lodging and camping options are available.

Day 4

This is your day to explore **Denali National Park** by tour bus, but advance reservations are absolutely necessary for this all-day adventure (many people book several months ahead of time to be sure of a space). Many buses turn around at Eielson Visitors Center, where you'll get a fine view of **Mt. McKinley** (if it isn't obscured by clouds), but you could also ride to **Wonder Lake** and back (11 long hours) or take a shorter wildlife-focused tour. Return to your hotel or campsite for a second night.

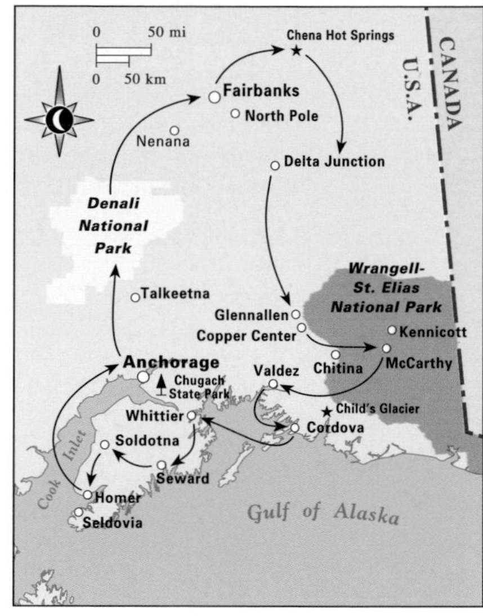

Day 5

Drive north on the Parks Highway, stopping in Nenana for a quick visit before rolling into **Fairbanks** (125 miles) for the night. Head to the new **Morris Thompson Cultural and Visitors Center** for an introduction, and then over to **Pioneer Park** to see the historical buildings, ride the kiddie train, do a bit of shopping, or take in a musical comedy show. Stick around for dinner at the Alaska Salmon Bake.

Day 6

Set aside a couple of hours to see the **University of Alaska Museum of the North** and other nearby sights, including the **Large Animal Research Station** (musk ox and caribou) and **Creamer's Field** (great

caribou in Denali National Park

TOP TEN ALASKA TOWNS

Wild places are the heart and soul of Alaska, but a number of small towns merit a visit, especially if you're looking to see how real folks live. Here are a few of the author's favorite places.

TALKEETNA

Number one on the *Northern Exposure* meter, funky Talkeetna is a haven for climbers en route to Mt. McKinley and flightseeing trips over the park. The town has several excellent restaurants and good lodging choices.

SKAGWAY

It gets thousands of cruise ship tourists daily in the summer, but this picturesque and walkable town remains an authentic dose of the past. Famed Chilkoot Trail is nearby, and a narrow-gauge railroad climbs over the pass into Yukon.

CORDOVA

Accessible only by air or ferry, this compact Prince William Sound fishing town has a spectacular drive-up glacier, not to mention the acclaimed Copper River red salmon.

SITKA

Steeped in Russian and Native Alaskan history, Sitka has a gem-like setting and all sorts of outdoor options, from whale-watching to mountain hiking.

HOMER

This road's-end Kenai Peninsula town has it all: glaciers, fishing, sea kayaking, fine restaurants and lodging, art galleries, a hip populace, and a to-die-for setting.

HAINES

One of the few Southeast towns connected by highway to the mainland, Haines has historic buildings at Fort Seward and a salmon-filled river that attracts hundreds of eagles in winter.

NOME

Just 190 miles from the Siberian coast, this is the end of the Iditarod Trail and home to active gold mines, unusual wildlife, and wonderful backcountry roads across the tundra.

Yakutat sunset

YAKUTAT

Primarily a destination for fly-fishers in search of steelhead, this remote settlement surprises with amazing beaches, towering glaciers, and big-wave surfing.

McCARTHY

At the end of a rough 60-mile dirt road within Wrangell-St. Elias National Park, this tiny settlement has quaint lodging places and restaurants. Just up the road are the picture-perfect buildings of long-abandoned Kennecott Mine.

GUSTAVUS

There isn't much to Gustavus itself, but it's right on the edge of Glacier Bay National Park, with several high-end lodges, great kayaking, whale-watching, and trips up the bay.

WASILLA

OK, this one makes 11 towns. Shop at the same Wal-Mart as Sarah Palin. Enjoy the traffic jams, strip malls, and fast-growing suburbs. But you can't see Russia from here.

birding). Two fun—though touristy—options are an afternoon Riverboat Discovery tour and a visit to Gold Dredge No. 8.

Day 7

Check out of your hotel and get an early start. Drive to Chena Hot Springs for a soak in the wonderful outdoor pool and a tour of the Ice Museum (don't miss this), before turning south on the Richardson Highway. Make a short stop at Santa Claus House in the town of North Pole, and bed down in Delta Junction, home to historic Rika's Roadhouse.

Day 8

Head south on the Richardson Highway through beautiful country around Summit Lake, where there are several nice day hikes, and on to Glennallen for a gas-and-groceries stop before ending the day in quiet Copper Center (165 miles). Stay at the historic Copper Center Lodge and head over to the Wrangell-St. Elias National Park Visitors Center for an introduction to this part of Alaska.

Day 9

Drive to the little town of Chitina (50 miles) with its century-old buildings, dirt streets, and fish wheels before continuing out a scenic 60-mile dirt road to McCarthy in the heart of Wrangell–St. Elias. (Many rental car companies prohibit driving on this road, but a shuttle service is available.) Surprisingly fine food and lodging can be found in McCarthy and nearby Kennicott, where you can tour the old copper mine buildings or take a glacier hike. You could easily add several days to your trip in this fascinating area.

Day 10

Drive back out to the main (Richardson) highway and head south to Valdez, with short stops at Worthington Glacier and Keystone Canyon en route. Valdez is only 180 miles, but plan to take at least six hours. Catch the fast ferry to Cordova, an out-of-the-way fishing town, and bed down for the night; a good place is Cordova Rose Lodge.

Day 11

Drive the 50-mile Copper River Highway (gravel) to the Million Dollar Bridge and Childs Glacier, where you could spend several hours just watching enormous chunks of ice calving into the Copper River. Excellent hiking is available, along with lovely

Ice Museum in Chena Hot Springs

bald eagle over Kenai Mountains

campsites if you don't want to spend the night back in Cordova.

Day 12

Take the morning ferry to Whittier and drive through the tunnel to Portage and then south to Seward (90 miles) where you can visit the Alaska SeaLife Center and enjoy dinner at Ray's Waterfront or Exit Glacier Salmon Bake. Hotels, B&Bs, and in-town campsites are all available.

Day 13

Take a half-day boat tour around Resurrection Bay or a hike to Exit Glacier, and then head north in the afternoon to Soldotna (150 miles). Bring your fishing pole if you want to join the throngs of anglers catching red salmon on the Kenai and Russian Rivers. The Aspen Hotel and the Kenai River Lodge both offer riverside accommodations in Soldotna.

Day 14

Turning south, the Sterling Highway ends in Homer, where the Homer Spit, Islands and Ocean Center, Pratt Museum, and art galleries are all big draws. You'll find lots of fine restaurants and lodging places, or you can pitch a tent on the Spit (but make sure it's anchored well against the wind).

Day 15

Take a Kachemak Bay tour to Gull Island and Halibut Cove or a day trip to Seldovia, returning to Homer for the evening. Other options include halibut charter fishing or the budget choice: trying your luck at the Fishing Hole.

Day 16

It's a five-hour drive to Anchorage, but if you get going early enough you could still have fun along the way or in the big city on those long summer days. If you have kids along, take them to H2Oasis Indoor Waterpark as a treat. Couples should head to Marx Bros. Café for the ultimate Alaskan dining experience.

▸ NORTHERN EXPOSURE

This trip begins and ends in Fairbanks, with long day trips launching out to adventures in all directions, including the Dalton Highway all the way to Prudhoe Bay. Several airlines have flights into Fairbanks, or you can start from Anchorage and take the train or a rental car north.

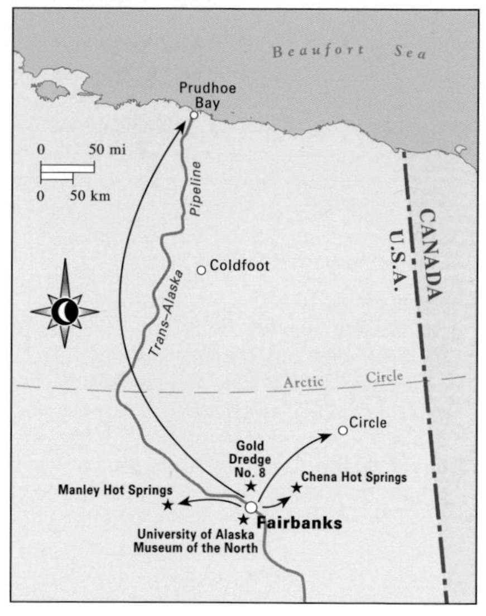

Days 1-2

Fairbanks is a good base for day trips into surrounding areas and has an abundance of lodging and dining options. Stay at the budget-priced Golden North Motel, or find more upscale accommodations at Sophie Station Hotel. Fans of Thai food will enjoy a visit to Lemongrass Thai Cuisine, and Lavelle's Bistro serves gourmet meals in a classy setting. While in Fairbanks, be sure to see the **University of Alaska Museum of the North,** Pioneer Park, Large Animal Research Station, and **Creamer's Field** (great birding).

Day 3

It's an easy 1.5-hour drive to **Chena Hot Springs,** where indoor and outdoor pools are available, along with a year-round **Ice Museum** that houses amazingly intricate carved pieces by a world-renowned ice sculptor. Several streams offer good fishing in the area, and the resort has lodging, food, and campsites.

Day 4

Today's long day trip goes out the paved-and-gravel **Steese Highway** to Circle, 161 miles each way from Fairbanks. Heading north, you may want to stop in the settlement of Fox to take a tour of historic **Gold Dredge No. 8** and to see the **Trans-Alaska Pipeline.** The road climbs over scenic Cleary Summit, down to the old gold settlement of Chatanika (interesting mining artifacts), to **Davidson Ditch Historical Site** (good for gold panning), over Twelvemile Summit (nice alpine hike), and finally to the Yukon River town of Circle. There are no accommodations in Circle, so consider camping at Upper Chatanika or Cripple Creek for the night. Hikers can just take the road to Twelvemile Summit for a fun day hike and then return to Fairbanks (170 miles round-trip) for an easier day.

Day 5

Take a break from travel to spend time in Fairbanks, **shopping downtown,** enjoying a **canoe float** down the Chena River, or visiting the **Tanana Valley Farmers Market** (held Wednesdays and Saturdays) for local arts and crafts, baked goods, and other treats.

Day 6

Another long trip into the country, this time on the 150-mile **Elliott Highway** northwest of

A KODIAK ADVENTURE

Alaska's "Emerald Isle," **Kodiak Island** is a world unto itself. Located 250 air miles southwest of Anchorage, the island is best known for its enormous brown bears, but also features everything from gourmet restaurants to missile launches. Visitors typically fly into Kodiak from Anchorage, but a more scenic route is via the **state ferry** from Homer, which passes around the remote **Barren Islands.**

brown bear cub

KODIAK SIGHTS

Start with the **Baranov Museum,** in town, with its remarkable gift shop selling fine Russian china and nesting dolls, followed by the old **Russian Orthodox Church,** the **Alutiiq Museum,** and the recently opened **Kodiak National Wildlife Refuge Visitors Center.** When the weather cooperates (or if you've got good rain gear), a hike up **Pyramid Peak** provides fine views.

For adventure outside of town, rent a car to explore the many miles of backcountry roads spanning out from Kodiak. **Chiniak Highway** heads south of town to **Pasagshak Bay** (good salmon fishing), past a rocket launch complex and grazing bison to **Fossil Beach** with its fossilized shells and sandy shoreline.

Be sure to see the **Kodiak brown bears** for which the island is so famous. Local air taxis offer half-day floatplane trips (around $550) to salmon streams on Kodiak or to the coast of Katmai National Park.

ACCOMMODATIONS AND FOOD

If you have the time (and cash), book one of the Kodiak National Wildlife Refuge cabins for a few nights. Access is by floatplane, and you'll be entirely on your own, so come prepared for a true wilderness experience.

Budget travelers may opt to camp at **Fort Abercrombie State Park,** a great place to hike in the moss-draped rainforest or to explore rocky shoreline for nesting puffins.

For a relaxing dining experience in a beautiful setting, hop onboard a **Galley Gourmet dinner and wildlife cruise.** If you're staying on land, don't miss the fresh sushi at **The Old Power House Restaurant.**

Fairbanks. The main attractions here are access to hiking trails in the White Mountains and Manley Hot Springs at the end of the road, the last 80 miles of which are gravel. The historic Manley Roadhouse—here since 1906—has rustic accommodations and homemade food.

Days 7-8

Time to head north, way north up the Dalton Highway, where flat tires and broken windshields are common occurrences. Don't try this in a standard rental car; Arctic Outfitters has vehicles set up specifically for travel on the "Haul Road," which parallels the Trans-Alaska Pipeline to the oilfields at Prudhoe Bay. A less stressful trip is to join one of the bus tours—some combine bus travel up with a flight back—from Fairbanks to the Arctic Circle (200 miles) or Prudhoe Bay/Deadhorse (500 miles). Lodging is available in Fairbanks and Coldfoot (where most buses stop for the night).

▸ FERRYING THROUGH THE INSIDE PASSAGE

Alaska's Inside Passage consists of thousands of islands spread in a long "Panhandle" hanging from the rest of the state. Most towns here are off the road system, with access by air or sea. Cruise ships are the most popular way to visit Southeast Alaska, but the Alaska Marine Highway ferry system is a wonderful alternative for independent travelers. There are all sorts of possible routes, and your options depend on how much time you have, the ferry schedule, and, of course, money. The routing below begins and ends in Seattle.

Alaska-bound ferries depart from Bellingham, Washington, and passengers flying into Seattle will need to take a shuttle bus from Sea-Tac Airport. The ferries run daily during summer and have comfortable cabins, reasonably priced dining, and a Forest Service naturalist onboard, but budget travelers can spread out their sleeping bags in the solarium.

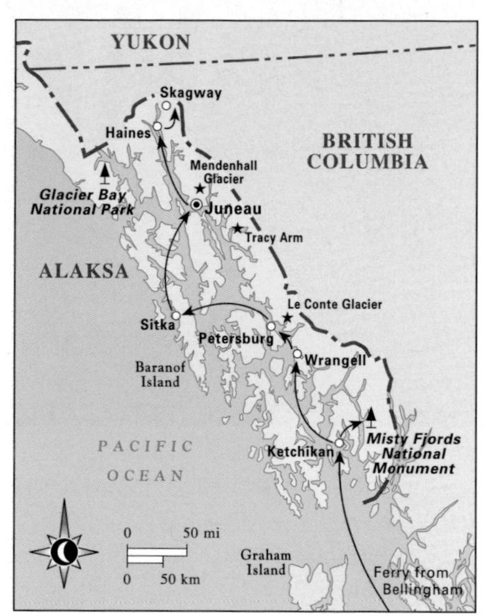

Days 1-2

It's a 36-hour ferry ride from Bellingham to the first Alaska stop, Ketchikan, famous for its rain forests, totem poles, and picturesque waterside setting. The town has good bus service, but a rental car makes it easy to get around in the rain, especially if you're heading out on the road or camping at Ward Lake. Local attractions include historic Creek Street, famous for its buildings on pilings that once housed the local red-light district, a fine Forest Service visitors center, and gorgeous collections of totem poles at Saxman, Totem Heritage Center, and Totem Bight State Historical Park.

Day 3

Take a day trip to spectacular Misty Fiords National Monument, accessible by boat tours, floatplane trips, or a combination of the two.

Days 4-5

Hop back on the ferry for the five-hour ride to Wrangell with its cozy harbor centered around Chief Shakes Island. The big attraction here is the Stikine River, and several companies have half-day jet-boat trips up the river to an active glacier and a relaxing riverside hot spring. Also popular are trips to see black bears at Anan Creek.

Days 6-7

Next up is the ferry ride though scenic Wrangell Narrows to Petersburg, where snow-capped mountains create a backdrop for this pretty town known for its Norwegian heritage. Day trips to LeConte Glacier are popular.

Days 8-9

Take the ferry north and west to remote Sitka, located on the Pacific Ocean side of Baranof Island. The town hosts the Alaska

Viking boat replica *Valhalla* in Petersburg

Raptor Center, Sitka National Historical Park (totem poles, Native Alaskan arts, and the old Russian Bishop's house), and other interesting sights, but it also has fun hiking trails, good fishing, and one of the finest restaurants in Southeast Alaska, Ludvig's Bistro.

Days 10-11

The fast ferry *Fairweather* provides frequent service connecting Sitka with the next stop, Juneau, considered by many the nation's loveliest state capital. The city is home to the Alaska State Museum, a scenic tramway up Mt. Roberts, a busy salmon hatchery, and easily accessible Mendenhall Glacier. One could easily spend several days checking out the sights, hiking a couple of trails, taking a day trip by floatplane to Taku Glacier Lodge or a helicopter flight onto Juneau Icefield, or just enjoying the fine dining, funky bars, rainforest zip lines, and other adventures. There are enough roads and out-of-the-way places in Juneau to justify renting a car.

Day 12

Take an all-day boat tour to Tracy Arm on board the *Adventure Bound* boat to see an active glacier up close and personal, or tack on a couple of days for a side trip to Glacier Bay National Park. The latter requires a flight from Juneau to Gustavus, followed by an all-day boat tour into this spectacular bay. Lodging and food are available (Gustavus Inn is especially nice), or you could pitch a tent at the Park Service campground.

Day 13

Haines is the next ferry stop, with the old white clapboard buildings of Fort Seward as a focal point. The Chilkat River is popular for summertime floats and wintertime eagle viewing. Stay at Hotel Halsingland—in one of the old fort buildings—and walk down the hill to Fireweed Restaurant for meals.

Day 14

A private ferry service provides fast connections between Haines and Skagway, an amazingly busy town packed with thousands of cruise ship passengers all summer. The town's downtown contains more than a dozen buildings within Klondike Gold Rush National Historical Park, and the narrow-gauge trains from the White Pass & Yukon Route Railroad take visitors on an incredible ride to the summit of the pass at the Canadian border. The town is the starting point for the difficult Chilkoot Trail, a four-day trudge up the route traversed by the miners more than a century ago. Skagway has several fine restaurants (try Stowaway Café) and comfortable B&Bs.

Day 15

It's the end of the line, so turn back south to Juneau on the ferry (or hop on one of the frequent flights from Skagway). You could return by ferry all the way to Bellingham, but an Alaska Air flight from Juneau gets you home quicker.

SOUTHEAST ALASKA

For many people, the name Alaska conjures up images of bitterly cold winters and sunshine-packed summers, of great rivers, enormous snowcapped mountains, and open tundra reaching to the horizon. If that's your vision of the state, you've missed its Garden of Eden, the Southeast. Almost entirely boxed in by British Columbia, Southeast Alaska's "Panhandle" or Inside Passage stretches 500 miles along the North American coast. Everything about this beautiful lush country is water-based: the rain that falls on the land, the glaciers that drop from giant ice fields, and the ocean that surrounds it all. Gray-blue clouds play a constant game of hide-and-seek with the verdant islands; deep fjords drive in between snow-covered summits; waterfalls plummet hundreds of feet through the evergreen forests to feed rivers rich in salmon; brown bears prowl the creeks in search of fish; bald eagles perch on treetops beside the rugged rocky coastline; and great blue glaciers press down toward the sea.

Nearly 95 percent of the Southeast is federal property, most of it within Tongass National Forest and Glacier Bay National Park. The Panhandle is composed of a mountainous mainland and hundreds of islands, varying from rocky reefs that barely jut out of the sea at low tide to some of the largest islands in North America. Collectively, these islands are called the Alexander Archipelago. This ragged shoreline stretches for more than 11,000 miles and includes over 1,000 named islands, the largest being Prince of Wales, Chichagof, Baranof, Admiralty, Revillagigedo,

HIGHLIGHTS

Totem Bight State Historical Park: Ketchikan is home to several notable totem pole collections, but Totem Bight takes the prize with a gorgeous waterside setting, historic clan house, and lush forests (page 35).

Misty Fiords National Monument: Almost always encased in clouds, this wilderness has spectacular cliffs that plummet into deep fiords. Tours by air and boat are offered from Ketchikan (page 46).

The Stikine River: Jet-boat trips from Wrangell are the main attraction for visitors to this mighty river with its hidden glaciers and relaxing hot springs (page 72).

Sitka National Historical Park: This gem of a park encompasses Sitka's rich Tlingit and Russian heritage with historic buildings, totems bordering a wooded trail, and the chance to watch Native Alaskan artisans at work (page 87).

Mendenhall Glacier: Southeast Alaska's best-known drive-up glacier, Mendenhall has fine hiking trails and a fascinating visitors center. It's just a few miles north of Juneau (page 108).

Tracy Arm-Fords Terror Wilderness: Almost unknown outside Alaska, this wilderness area is a popular destination for day tours by boat from Juneau. It's a great place to watch ice calving from the glacier or to see seals resting atop icebergs (page 124).

Glacier Bay National Park and Preserve: Made famous by John Muir, this national park has towering mountains, thundering glaciers, abundant wildlife, fun day trips, and memorable sea kayaking adventures (page 131).

Fort Seward: Looking more like a New England village than a fort, this picture-perfect collection of historic Haines buildings now houses a variety of artistic, commercial, and cultural endeavors (page 142).

Klondike Gold Rush National Historical Park: The town of Skagway's gold rush heritage is preserved in a dozen classic – and immaculately restored – downtown buildings that now hum with visitors all summer (page 153).

White Pass & Yukon Route Railroad: Originally built to haul miners into the Klondike and gold back out, this narrow-gage railroad now fills with travelers and hikers. It may be the most scenic train ride in the country (page 153).

LOOK FOR TO FIND RECOMMENDED SIGHTS, ACTIVITIES, DINING, AND LODGING.

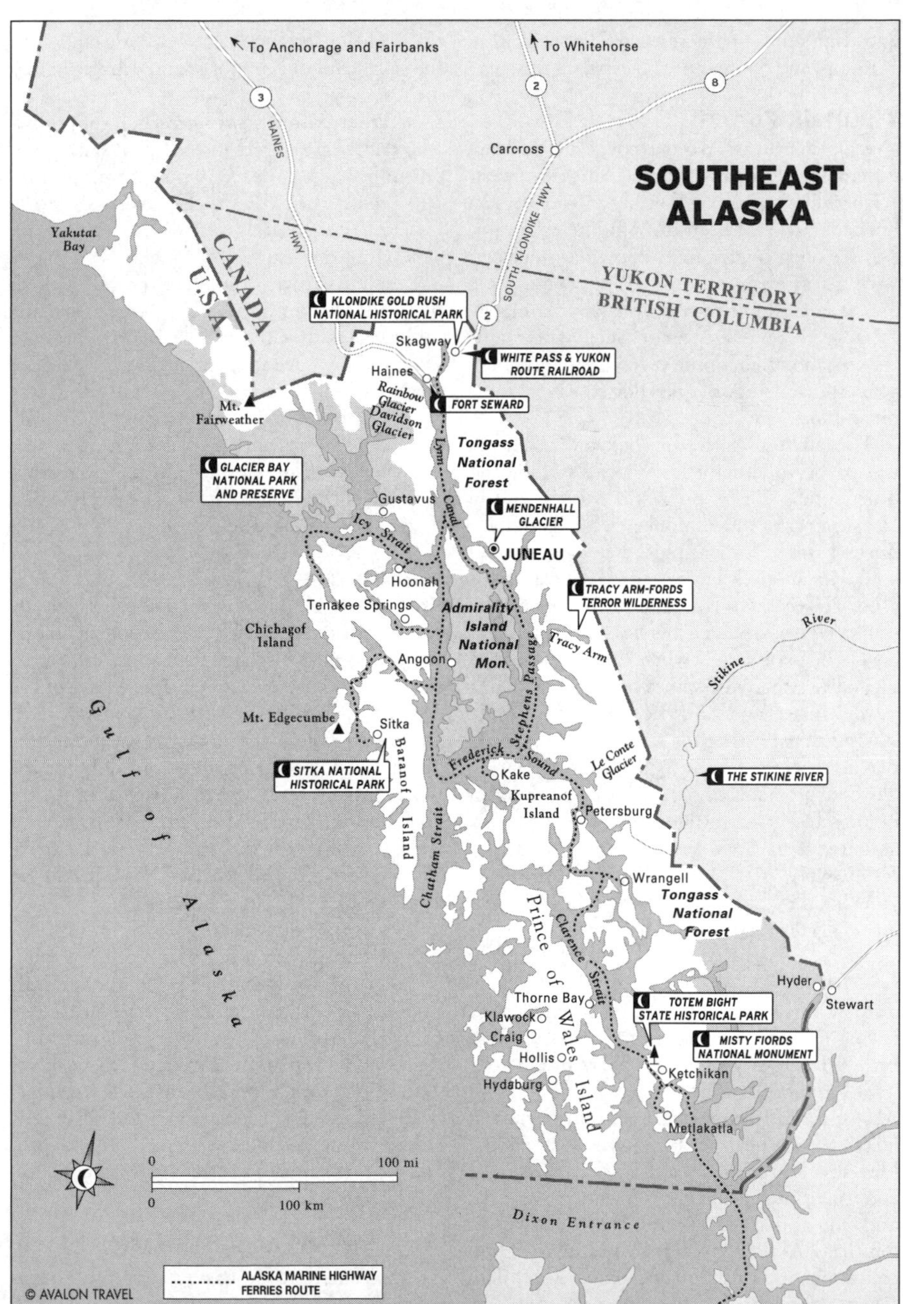

SOUTHEAST ALASKA
To Anchorage and Fairbanks
To Whitehorse
HAINES HWY
SOUTH KLONDIKE HWY
Carcross
YUKON TERRITORY
BRITISH COLUMBIA
CANADA
U.S.A.
Yakutat Bay
KLONDIKE GOLD RUSH NATIONAL HISTORICAL PARK
Skagway
WHITE PASS & YUKON ROUTE RAILROAD
Haines
Rainbow Glacier
Davidson Glacier
FORT SEWARD
Mt. Fairweather
Tongass National Forest
GLACIER BAY NATIONAL PARK AND PRESERVE
Lynn Canal
Gustavus
MENDENHALL GLACIER
Icy Strait
JUNEAU
Hoonah
TRACY ARM-FORDS TERROR WILDERNESS
Tenakee Springs
Admiralty Island National Mon.
Chichagof Island
Tracy Arm
Stephens Passage
River
Stikine
Angoon
Gulf of Alaska
Mt. Edgecumbe
Sitka
Baranof Island
Frederick Sound
Le Conte Glacier
SITKA NATIONAL HISTORICAL PARK
Kake
THE STIKINE RIVER
Kupreanof Island
Petersburg
Chatham Strait
Wrangell
Tongass National Forest
Prince of Wales Island
Clarence Strait
Hyder
Stewart
Thorne Bay
TOTEM BIGHT STATE HISTORICAL PARK
Klawock
Craig
MISTY FIORDS NATIONAL MONUMENT
Hollis
Ketchikan
Hydaburg
Metlakatla
0
100 mi
0
100 km
Dixon Entrance
ALASKA MARINE HIGHWAY FERRIES ROUTE
© AVALON TRAVEL

and Kupreanof—names that reflect the British, Russians, and Spaniards who explored the area.

The Rain Forest

Much of Southeast Alaska is covered with dense rain forests of Sitka spruce (the state tree), western hemlock, Alaska yellow cedar, and western red cedar. Interspersed through these rain forests are open boggy areas known as muskegs, with a scattering of stunted lodgepole pines and cedars. Above the tree line (approximately 2,500 feet) are rocky peaks covered with fragile flowers and other alpine vegetation. Shorelines often sport a fringe of grass dotted with flowers during the summer.

The rain forests here are choked with a dense understory of huckleberry, devil's club, and other shrubs. Berry lovers will enjoy a feast in late summer as the salmonberries, red and blue huckleberries, and thimbleberries all ripen. If you're planning a hike, learn to recognize **devil's club,** a lovely abundant plant with large maple-shaped leaves and red berries. Barbed spines cover the plants, and when touched they feel like a bee sting. The spines become embedded in your fingers and are difficult to remove, often leaving a nasty sting for several days. If you're planning a cross-country hike, wear leather gloves to protect your hands. Surprisingly, mosquitoes and other biting insects are not nearly as abundant in Southeast Alaska as they are in, for example, Alaska's Interior. They can make your life miserable some of the time, however, especially during no-see-um season.

Climate

Tourist brochures invariably show happy folks cavorting around gleaming glaciers under a brilliant blue sky. Photographers might wait weeks to capture all three elements: Southeast Alaska is rain country. Expect rain or mist at least half of the time. In much of the region, blue-sky days come once a week, if that. The cool maritime climate brings rain in summer, and rain and snow in winter. Most towns in Southeast Alaska get 80 inches or more of precipitation, and of the major towns, Ketchikan takes top honors with 162 inches per year. The tiny fishing settlement of Port Alexander on the south end of Baranof Island drowns in 220 inches per year.

Weather patterns vary greatly in Southeast Alaska; Skagway gets just 22 inches per year, but only a few miles away, precipitation tops 160 inches annually on the peaks bordering Canada. Fortunately, the driest months are generally June–August.

Residents learn to tolerate the rain, which they call "liquid sunshine." You won't see many umbrellas, but heavy rain gear and red rubber XtraTuf boots are appropriate dress for almost any occasion. If you ask, locals will admit to a grudging appreciation for the rain; it not only creates the lush green countryside and provides ample stream-flow for the vital salmon runs, it also keeps the region safe from overcrowding by the drier-minded set.

The People

Southeast Alaska has only 70,000 people. Nearly half live in Juneau, with the rest spread among nearly two-dozen isolated towns and settlements strung along the Inside Passage. Much of the economy is based on fishing, logging, government, and tourism. The towns are dependent on the sea for their survival, not only for the fish it provides but also as a way to transport huge log rafts to the mills. Fully 95 percent of the goods brought to Southeast Alaska arrive by barge or ship, and most of the visitors arrive aboard cruise ships or state ferries.

The Southeast corresponds almost exactly to the ancestral homeland of the Tlingit (KLINK-it) Indians, and signs of their culture—both authentic and visitor-oriented—are common. Almost every town has at least one totem pole, and some have a dozen or more. Tlingit artwork generally includes carvings, beadwork, sealskin moccasins, and silver jewelry. It *doesn't* include the *ulus,* Eskimo dolls, and other paraphernalia frequently sold in local tourist shops.

PLANNING YOUR TIME

All the major Inside Passage towns are separated by water or mountainous coastlines, with

© DON PITCHER

Devil's club is a ubiquitous plant in the rainforests of Southeast Alaska.

planes, state ferries, and cruise ships providing the connections. This limitation is a blessing in disguise: A long ferry ride north allows time to soak up the scenery and plan adventures in the next port. Anyone traveling with a vehicle is limited to ferry travel, while others can mix and match ferries or plane flights with local car rentals when needed. Cruise ships, of course, offer the "leave the drive to us" version. Plan on at least a week in Southeast Alaska—and preferably more—unless you are simply taking the Alaska Air jet to Sitka (or another town) and stopping for a few days of exploration.

Rain-soaked Ketchikan is the southernmost port and a very popular destination for travelers of all ages and incomes. Downtown's Creek Street forms a picturesque stop, while totem poles and Tlingit (KLINK-it) culture are the big draws at Saxman and **Totem Bight State Historical Park.** Day trips by air or sea to **Misty Fiords National Monument** provide a great introduction to a dramatic wilderness of high cliffs and deep inlets.

Nearby Metlakatla and Prince of Wales Island are off-the-beaten-path destinations, and to the north lie the fishing towns of Wrangell and Petersburg, with the mighty **Stikine River** (popular for jet-boat trips) heading into the mountains of British Columbia. Stop in the old Native Alaskan and Russian town of Sitka with its gemlike setting, **Sitka National Historical Park,** and the Alaska Raptor Center. Juneau is not just the state capital and third largest city but also home to a fun tramway up Mt. Roberts, the Alaska State Museum, and famous **Mendenhall Glacier.** Boat tours to the deep fjords and calving glaciers of **Tracy Arm** are popular day trips from Juneau, as are boat tours (and kayaking trips) into magnificent **Glacier Bay.** The quiet town of Haines is home to **Fort Seward,** where century-old homes surround the old parade grounds. The touristy town of Skagway has a gold-rush aura courtesy of the many buildings preserved within **Klondike Gold Rush National Historical Park.** Especially popular here are narrow-gauge train rides aboard the **White Pass & Yukon Route Railroad.**

GETTING THERE

Visitors come to Southeast Alaska by three primary means: cruise ship, jet, and ferry (the Alaska Marine Highway). Cruise ships are easily the most popular method—more than 800,000 people travel this way each year—but also the most expensive and the least personal. Cruise options include the more expensive small-ship voyages that take you to less-traveled spots.

The second option, air, is more popular with independent travelers. **Alaska Airlines** (800/426-0333, www.alaskaair.com) has daily flights from Seattle, with service to Juneau, Ketchikan, Wrangell, Petersburg, Sitka, Gustavus, and other Alaskan cities. Floatplanes connect these towns to smaller places and provide access to even the most remote corners of the Inside Passage, such as Elfin Cove, Tokeen, and Port Alexander.

The Ferry System

Only three Southeast towns (Haines, Skagway, and Hyder) are connected by road to the rest of the continent. All the others, including Juneau, the state capital, are accessible only by boat or plane. This lack of roads—hopefully they will never be built—has led to an efficient public ferry system, the best in the western hemisphere and the longest in the world. Most ferries sail between Prince Rupert, British Columbia, and Skagway, stopping along the way in the major towns. There is also weekly service from Bellingham, Washington, all the way to Skagway, a three-day voyage. In the larger towns, summer service runs almost daily, but in the smallest settlements, ferries may be up to two weeks apart. Get schedules and make reservations from the **Alaska Marine Highway** (907/465-3941 or 800/642-0066, www.dot.state.ak.us/amhs). Since most travel in Southeast Alaska centers on the ferry schedules, it's wise to check the ferry schedule before making any solid travel plans. Reservations for the summer can be made as early as December, and travelers taking a vehicle should book as early as possible to be sure of getting a space.

The **Inter-Island Ferry Authority** (907/826-4848 or 866/308-4848, www.interislandferry.com) has a vehicle and passenger ferry that connects Prince of Wales Island with Ketchikan.

Ketchikan

After the 36-hour ferry ride up from Bellingham, Ketchikan is many first-timers' introduction to Alaska. Along the way they've heard tales from sourdoughs (and those who claim to be), talked to Forest Service naturalists, and watched the logging towns and lush green islands of British Columbia float past. As the ferry pulls into busy Tongass Narrows, an air of expectancy grows among the newcomers, who are about to take their first steps in Alaska.

The state's fourth-largest city (pop. 8,000, plus another 5,000 in nearby areas), Ketchikan bills itself as "Alaska's First City," and even its zip code, 99901, seems to bear this out. Quite a few ferry passengers don't bother to stop here, instead hurrying on toward Juneau and points north. Because downtown is two miles away, they only have time for a superficial bus tour or a walk to the grocery store for provisions. But with its great scenery, fine local trails, the world's largest collection of totem poles, a bustling downtown, and the famous Misty Fiords nearby, Ketchikan certainly deserves a longer stay.

The Setting

Located 90 miles north of Prince Rupert, British Columbia, Ketchikan clings to a steep slope along Tongass Narrows, on Revillagigedo

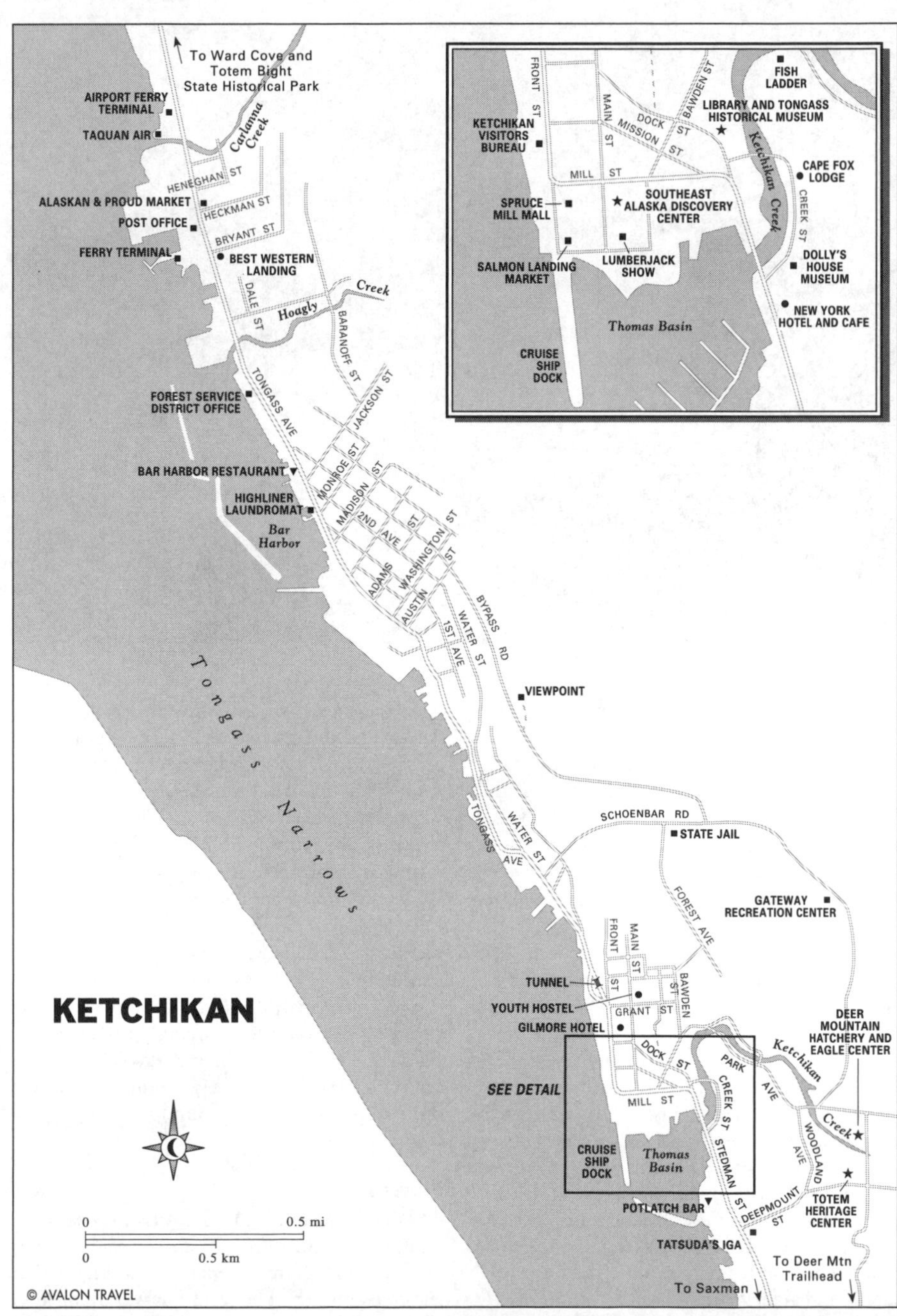
KETCHIKAN
To Ward Cove and Totem Bight State Historical Park
AIRPORT FERRY TERMINAL
TAQUAN AIR
Carlanna Creek
HENEGHAN ST
ALASKAN & PROUD MARKET
HECKMAN ST
POST OFFICE
BRYANT ST
FERRY TERMINAL
BEST WESTERN LANDING
DALE ST
Hoagly Creek
BARANOFF ST
FOREST SERVICE DISTRICT OFFICE
TONGASS AVE
JACKSON ST
BAR HARBOR RESTAURANT
MONROE ST
MADISON ST
HIGHLINER LAUNDROMAT
Bar Harbor
2ND AVE
WASHINGTON ST
ADAMS
AUSTIN
BYPASS RD
1ST AVE
WATER ST
VIEWPOINT
Tongass Narrows
SCHOENBAR RD
STATE JAIL
FOREST AVE
GATEWAY RECREATION CENTER
FRONT ST
MAIN ST
BAWDEN ST
TUNNEL
YOUTH HOSTEL
GRANT ST
GILMORE HOTEL
DOCK ST
PARK AVE
Ketchikan Creek
DEER MOUNTAIN HATCHERY AND EAGLE CENTER
SEE DETAIL
MILL ST
CREEK ST
STEDMAN ST
WOODLAND AVE
CRUISE SHIP DOCK
Thomas Basin
POTLATCH BAR
DEEPMOUNT ST
TOTEM HERITAGE CENTER
TATSUDA'S IGA
To Deer Mtn Trailhead
To Saxman
0 0.5 mi
0 0.5 km
FISH LADDER
LIBRARY AND TONGASS HISTORICAL MUSEUM
KETCHIKAN VISITORS BUREAU
MISSION ST
CAPE FOX LODGE
SPRUCE MILL MALL
SOUTHEAST ALASKA DISCOVERY CENTER
SALMON LANDING MARKET
LUMBERJACK SHOW
DOLLY'S HOUSE MUSEUM
NEW YORK HOTEL AND CAFE

© DON PITCHER

Ketchikan

(ruh-VEE-ya-he-HAY-do) Island; locals shorten the name to "Revilla." Fortunately, it doesn't bear the one-time viceroy of Mexico's full name: Don Juan Vicente de Güemes Pacheco de Pedilla y Horcasitas, Count of Revilla Gigedo. Locals call the town "three miles long and three blocks wide." It forms a continuous strip of development along the waterfront from the ferry terminal to beyond Thomas Basin. Because of this, Tongass Avenue—the only through street—has long been one of the busiest in the entire state. A hilltop bypass opened a few years back, but traffic is still very heavy on Tongass Avenue.

Much of Ketchikan is built on fill, on pilings over the water, or on hillsides with steep winding ramps for streets. Fishing boats jam the three boat harbors (there are almost as many boats as cars in Ketchikan), and the canneries and cold-storage plants run at full throttle during the summer. Floatplanes are constantly taking off from the narrows, cruise ships crowd the docks, and tourists explore the downtown shops and attractions.

Ketchikan is one of the rainiest places in Alaska, getting upward of 13 feet per year, or an average of half an inch per day. Luckily, May–August are the driest months, but expect to get wet nevertheless. Locals adapt with "Ketchikan sneakers" (red rubber boots) and Helly Hansen rain gear; umbrellas are the mark of a tourist. Residents pride themselves on almost never canceling baseball games, and they enjoy weekend picnics at Ward Lake in a downpour. Weather prediction is easy in Ketchikan: If you can't see the top of Deer Mountain, it's raining; if you can, it's *going* to rain. For an only-in-Ketchikan sight, check out the Valley Park Grade School on Schoenbar Road. This unique school was built atop its own playground, creating an escape from the rain.

History

The name Ketchikan comes from *kitcxan,* a Tlingit word meaning "where the eagle's wings are," a reference to the shape of a sand spit at the creek mouth. The sand spit was dredged in the 1930s to create Thomas Basin Boat Harbor. Rumor has it that several bodies were found then, and suspicious fingers were pointed toward the denizens of nearby Creek Street, the local red-light district.

One of Southeast Alaska's youngest major towns, Ketchikan began when the first of many salmon canneries at the mouth of Ketchikan Creek opened in 1885. By the 1930s it had become the "Salmon Capital of the World" (13 canneries), and Alaska's largest town. Overfishing caused salmon populations to crash in the 1940s, and the fishing industry was supplanted in the 1950s by a new pulp mill that turned the town into a major logging center.

For several decades Ketchikan's pulp mill was the biggest employer in Southeast Alaska, processing spruce and hemlock for the production of rayon and cellophane. The pulp mill closed in 1997, just as Ketchikan's economy shifted full-bore into tourism.

The big story today for Ketchikan—as in Juneau and Skagway—is cruise ships. More than 800,000 cruise ship travelers step onto Ketchikan's docks annually, with four or five ships tied up along Tongass Narrows most summer days. The rough old downtown with its sawmill, flophouses, and bars has been transformed into rows of jewelry stores (63 at last count!) staffed by employees from the Caribbean, and trinket shops selling plastic totem poles and stuffed animals made in China. Crossing guards at the intersections, horse-drawn wagon rides, amphibious "duck" tours, a pseudo-logging show, and thousands of cruise shippies add to what Edward Abbey labeled "industrial tourism." It makes the cash registers ring, at least for those businesses willing to accept kickback deals with the cruise lines in exchange for promotion on board the ships. Fortunately, the cruise ships generally depart by early evening, allowing locals and overnight visitors to rediscover this fascinating town.

SIGHTS

Visitors Center

The **Ketchikan Visitors Bureau** (131 Front St., 907/225-6166 or 800/770-3300, www.visit-ketchikan.com) is right on the downtown dock. It's open whenever cruise ships are docked, which means daily 6:30 A.M.–6 P.M. most days May–September, and Monday–Friday 8 A.M.–5 P.M. the rest of the year. Pick up their free map, which includes a walking tour of local sites. The building also houses booths for local tour companies. A smaller visitors center is located along the promenade just north of the tunnel.

Southeast Alaska Discovery Center

A great place to start your exploration of Ketchikan is the Southeast Alaska Discovery Center (50 Main St., 907/228-6220, www.fs.fed.us/r10, Mon.–Sat. 8 A.M.–5 P.M., Sun. 8 A.M.–4 P.M. May–Sept., Tues.–Sat. 10 A.M.–4:30 P.M. Oct.–Apr., $5 adults, children under 15 free). Operated by the U.S. Forest Service, it's filled with impressive exhibits—including a full-scale rain forest—that offer an educational portrait of the land and people of Southeast Alaska. A variety of wildlife videos are available, along with nature programs. The staff will help you with information on the outdoors, and the big bookshop features books, trail guides, and maps.

Logging Show

Located on Mill Street next to the cruise ship dock, the **Spruce Mill Complex** is the tourist shopping center for downtown Ketchikan, with retail stores, souvenir shops, galleries, and restaurants. Ketchikan's old spruce mill stood on this site for many years, so it is perhaps fitting to find **The Great Alaskan Lumberjack Show** (907/225-9050 or 888/320-9049, www.lumberjacksports.com, 3 shows daily—rain or shine—May–Sept., $34 adults, $17 children) here. This cornball one-hour exhibition of old-time logging skills features ax throwing, bucksawing, springboard chopping, logrolling, and a speedy 50-foot tree climb. Covered grandstands protect the audience from the inevitable rain. If you're looking for a cheesy Disneyfied imitation of old-time logging, this may be your ticket.

Tongass Historical Museum

The cramped Tongass Historical Museum (629 Dock St., 907/225-5600, www.city.ketchikan.ak.us, daily 8 A.M.–5 P.M. May–Sept., Wed.–Fri. 1–5 P.M., Sat. 10 A.M.–4 P.M., Sun. 1–4 P.M. Oct.–Apr., $2) shares the library building. The museum contains local historical items with changing exhibits that include examples of Native Alaskan culture and commercial fishing. Look around for the model of a clan house, the 200-year-old Chilkat blanket, the dance paddle inlaid with abalone shell, the bentwood boxes, and the amusing totem pole with President Truman's features.

Creek Street

Ketchikan's best-known and most-photographed section features wooden houses on pilings along Ketchikan Creek. A boardwalk connects the buildings and affords views of salmon and steelhead in the creek. Now a collection of tourist shops, Creek Street once housed the red-light district; during Prohibition it was the only place to buy booze. Jokesters call it "the only place where both salmon and men came up from the sea to spawn." By 1946 more than 30 "female boardinghouses" operated here. Prostitution on Creek Street was stopped in 1954, and the house of Dolly Arthur was eventually turned into the **Dolly's House Museum** (907/225-2279, daily May–Sept., $5). Inside are antiques, liquor caches, and risqué photos. Born in 1888, Dolly moved to Ketchikan in 1919 and worked at the world's oldest profession for many decades. When she died in 1975 her obituary was featured in newspapers across the West. Dolly's is fun to tour with grandmothers who would never otherwise step foot in such a place, and the fascinating collection of memorabilia makes it well worth a visit. It's open whenever large cruise ships are in port.

A **funicular car** ($2; free if you hike up and ride down) connects Creek Street with Cape Fox Lodge, where you'll discover impressive vistas over Ketchikan and Tongass Narrows.

© DON PITCHER

Dolly's House Museum on Creek Street

Other Downtown Sights

Outside the library and museum is **Raven Stealing the Sun Totem,** and not far away stands the **Chief Johnson Pole** (an older version is inside the Totem Heritage Center). Tiny Whale Park occupies the intersection across from the Forest Service office and is home to the **Chief Kyan Totem,** reputed to reward those who touch it by bringing money within a day. It's worth a try, but don't immediately head to Las Vegas on the basis of this claim.

Check out some of Ketchikan's many long aerobic **stairways** up to hillside homes and outstanding vistas. The best ones start from the tunnel at Front and Grant Streets, and from the intersection of Main and Pine Streets. If you have a bike (or better yet, a skateboard), you may want to test your mettle on Schoenbar Road, the route blasted out of a steep hillside behind town. By the way, the Front Street **tunnel** is said to be the only one in the world that you can drive through, around, and over—or so claims the *Guinness Book of World Records.* A pretty **promenade** follows the shore north from here, with cedar benches, stained glass pieces, and colorful flowers.

Picturesque **Thomas Basin Boat Harbor** is just across the bridge over Creek Street. Walk out on Thomas Street, past the Potlatch Bar (good for a game of pool or a beer with local fishers), and out along the jetty for a fine view back toward town.

Totem Heritage Center

One of the highlights of the Ketchikan area, the Totem Heritage Center (907/225-5900, www.city.ketchikan.ak.us, daily 8 A.M.–5 P.M. May–Sept., Mon.–Fri. 1–5 P.M. Oct.–Apr., $5 adults, children under 12 free) is a quarter-mile walk up Deermount Street. The center was established in 1976 to preserve a collection of 33 original totem poles and house posts retrieved from abandoned village sites. Unlike other totems in the area, these works are not brightly painted copies or restorations, but were carved more than a century ago to record Tlingit and Haida events and legends. Guides answer your questions and put on a short video about the totem recovery program. Surrounding the building is a short trail with signs identifying local plants. Out front is the Fog-Woman pole by noted carver Nathan Jackson.

Deer Mountain Hatchery and Eagle Center

This small hatchery along Ketchikan Creek is just across a footbridge from the Totem Heritage Center. Signboards illustrate the process of breeding and rearing king salmon, coho salmon, and steelhead; visitors can feed the young fish. The hatchery is run by the **Ketchikan Indian Council** (907/228-5530, www.kictribe.org, daily 8 A.M.–4:30 P.M. May–Sept.), with educational tours and a video on the salmon life cycle. A large enclosure houses two eagles with permanent injuries—you might even see them catching salmon. Tours are $10, or $15 for a combination hatchery tour and eagle center presentation.

King salmon arrive from the Pacific Ocean to spawn at the hatchery late in the summer; look for them in the creek. A **fish ladder** to help them get past the falls is visible from the Park Avenue bridge. If too many fish return to spawn, the state opens Ketchikan Creek to dip-net fishing by locals, creating an astounding scene. Thousands of pink salmon (humpback salmon, or "humpies") also spawn in the creek each summer. Another good place to see spawning humpies is **Hoadly Creek,** a half-mile south of the ferry terminal.

Totem Bight State Historical Park

Located eight miles northwest of the ferry terminal, Totem Bight (907/247-8574, www.alaskastateparks.org, free) has 15 Haida and Tlingit totems and a realistic replica of a clan house, complete with a brightly painted facade and cedar-scented interior. Be sure to pick up the brochure describing the poles and their meanings. The totems, carved 1938–1941, are modeled after older poles. They are surrounded by a stand of young hemlock trees and a gorgeous view across Tongass Narrows. Drop by the gift shop for details on the poles or the informative weekly tours. Access to Totem Bight is easy and cheap: city buses ($1 each way) stop at Totem Bight hourly on weekdays.

Saxman

This Native Alaskan village, ironically named for a white schoolteacher, is a 2.5-mile walk via a paved path, a $1 city bus ride, or a $12 taxi ride south of Ketchikan. Saxman (pop. 400) is crowded with the largest collection of standing totem poles in the world—more than two dozen. Most were brought from their original sites in the 1930s and restored by Native Alaskan Civilian Conservation Corps (CCC) workers; others came from a second restoration project in 1982. The oddest pole is topped with a figure of Abraham Lincoln and commemorates the settlement of a war begun by the U.S. revenue cutter *Lincoln*. Probably the most photographed is the Rock Oyster Pole, which tells the story of a man who drowned after his hand became caught in a large oyster. Behind the poles is a cedar **Beaver Clan House,** open most days.

Adjacent to the totem park is a **carving**

TOTEM POLES

These largest of wooden sculptures were carved in cedar by the Tlingit, Haida, Tsimshian, Kwakiutl, and Bella Bella peoples of the Pacific Northwest. Their history is not completely known, but early explorers found poles in villages throughout Southeast Alaska. Apparently, totem-pole carving reached its heyday in the late 19th century with the arrival of metal woodworking tools. The animals, birds, fish, and marine mammals on the poles were totems that represented a clan, and in combination, conveyed a message.

Totem poles were very expensive and time-consuming to produce; a clan's status could be determined in part by the size and elaborateness of its poles. In a society without written words to commemorate people or events, the poles served a variety of purposes. Some totem poles told a family's history, others told local legends, and still others served to ridicule an enemy or debtor. In addition, totems were used to commemorate the dead, with a special niche at the back to hold the ashes of a revered ancestor.

Totem poles were never associated with religion, yet early missionaries destroyed many, and as recently as 1922 the Canadian government outlawed the art in an attempt to make the indigenous people more submissive. Realizing that a rich heritage was being lost because of neglect, skilled Native Alaskan carvers worked with the Civilian Conservation

Corps during the 1930s to restore older totems and create new ones. Today, active carving and restoration programs are taking place in Saxman, Ketchikan, Sitka, and Haines. Other good places to find totems include the Southeast Alaska towns of Hydaburg, Klawock, Kasaan, Juneau, Wrangell, and Kake.

shed (free admission) where you'll find local artisans completing totems, masks, and other pieces. You're welcome to drop in whenever a carver is at work, which is most weekdays in the summer. Renowned carver Nathan Jackson can often be found working here. Interested in having a pole carved? Expect to pay at least $2,000 per linear foot.

Cape Fox Tours (907/225-4846, www.capefoxtours.com, $45) leads 1.5-hour tours that include a visit to the carving shed, a video on Tlingit culture, and a performance by the Cape Fox Dancers. Get tickets at the Ketchikan Visitors Center or the **Saxman Village Store** (907/225-4421), which sells a mix of wares. Half the shop is dedicated to inexpensive imports, but the other side is more noteworthy, with high-quality locally made totems, masks, paddles, jewelry, and carved pieces, including an $8,000 bentwood box. Two blocks downhill is the **Saxman Arts Co-op** (907/225-4166), with historic photos and local pieces.

ENTERTAINMENT AND EVENTS

A local theater group, First City Players (907/225-4792, www.firstcityplayers.org), puts on the lighthearted melodrama ***Fish Pirate's Daughter*** Friday and Saturday evenings in July. The show has been running since 1966, and tickets cost $40 with an all-you-can eat Dungeness crab dinner. Performances take place at the Ted Ferry Civic Center behind Cape Fox Lodge.

Catch a movie downtown at the **Coliseum Twin Theater** (405 Mission St., 907/225-2294, www.ketchikanmovies.com).

Ketchikan's live music scene changes frequently, but something is always happening downtown; just follow your ears. **First City Saloon** (830 Water St., 907/225-1494) tends to bring in the better bands and is the main dance spot in town. The **Arctic Bar** (907/225-4709, www.arcticbar.com), near the Front Street tunnel, is more rock-oriented and has a pleasant patio that hangs over Tongass Narrows. Shock your friends back home with one of their risqué baseball caps or shirts; they call it "home of the happy bears." If Dave Rubin and his rockin' Potlatch Band are playing at the **Potlatch Bar** (907/225-4855), next to Thomas Basin, make tracks in that direction; you won't regret it. The finest bar views are from **Cape Fox Lodge,** overlooking town above Creek Street. It's a nice place to get romantic.

On Friday evenings, head to **Ketchikan Coffee Company** (207 Stedman St., 907/225-8646, www.ketchikancoffee.com) in the New York Hotel for music jam sessions and great food.

Ketchikan's fun **4th of July** celebration includes the usual parade and fireworks (if the rain lets up). In the first week of August, check out the **Blueberry Arts Festival,** complete with slug races, pie-eating contests, a fun run, arts and crafts exhibitions, and folk music. Ketchikan also has king and silver salmon fishing derbies and a halibut derby each summer. The **Winter Arts Faire** on the weekend after Thanksgiving is a good time to buy local arts and crafts. **Festival of the North** arrives in February, complete with music, art shows, and workshops for the entire month.

SHOPPING

The **Spruce Mill Mall** is the primary focal point for downtown shopping. Cruise ships dock directly in front, disgorging their passengers to feed the hungry cash registers of such places as Caribbean Gems or Tanzanite International. Needless to say, locals would never step foot in these jewelry stores owned and staffed by "outsiders" cashing in on the tourists. Fortunately, many of the other downtown shops—including a number of places in Salmon Landing Marketplace—are locally owned and worth a visit.

Locals do much of their shopping at **Plaza Mall** (www.ketchikanplaza.com), centering around a Safeway and a McDonald's, and the **Wal-Mart** (907/247-2156) five miles north of town. There are free summertime shuttles from downtown to Wal-Mart; they're mainly for cruise ship workers, but are also popular with cheapskate travelers.

Arts and Crafts

A surprisingly creative town, Ketchikan is home to a number of fine artists. The first Friday of each month brings gallery openings, events, and music. The center of Ketchikan's art action is the historic 5-Star Building on Creek Street, where artist Ray Troll holds down the fort at **Soho Coho** (5 Creek St., 907/225-5954 or 800/888-4070, www.trollart.com), with his weird and fishy T-shirts and prints. Other artists—including the wonderfully prolific printmaker Evon Zerbetz—also display works here. The same building houses **Alaska Eagle Arts** (907/225-8365 or 800/308-2787, www.marvinoliver.com), which has colorful T-shirts, jewelry, and prints along with samples of the stunning Native Alaskan designs by world-famous sculptor and printmaker Marvin Oliver.

Other downtown galleries worth a visit include **Exploration Gallery** (633 Mission St., 907/225-4278, www.explorationgallery.com), **Blue Heron Gallery** (123 Stedman St., 907/225-1982, www.blueheronalaska.com), **Eagle Spirit Gallery** (310 Mission St., 907/225-6626 or 866/867-0976, www.eaglespiritalaska.com), **Scanlon Gallery** (318 Mission St., 907/247-4730 or 888/228-4730, www.scanlongallery.com), and **Crazy Wolf Studio** (607 Mission St., 907/225-9653 or 888/331-9653, www.crazywolfstudio.com).

The Ketchikan Area Arts and Humanities Council (716 Totem Way, 907/225-2211, www.ketchikanarts.org) produces the ***Ketchikan Arts Guide*** with brief bios of local artists plus descriptions of galleries, museums, and other places to find creative works. In the winter, their **Monthly Grind** brings fun events the third Saturday of each month at the Saxman Tribal House.

RECREATION

The Ketchikan area is blessed with an abundance of hiking trails and remote wilderness cabins maintained by the U.S. Forest Service. If you arrive in Ketchikan unprepared for a cabin stay, **Alaska Wilderness Outfitting** (907/225-7335, www.latitude56.com) rents outboard motors, coolers, stoves, and dishes (but not sleeping bags). It even has a "cabin outfit" set up with the supplies you'll need at a Forest Service cabin.

Take in a **panoramic view of Ketchikan** from the short trail that climbs from the highpoint along Bypass Road (Forest Ave.). The road takes off from the south end of Schoenbar Road.

The city's **Gateway Recreation Center** (601 Schoenbar Rd., 907/225-9579, $5) is open daily and has an indoor track, a fitness room, basketball, racquetball, and various classes. At the **Ketchikan High School swimming pool** (2610 4th Ave., 907/225-2010), a swim, sauna, and shower cost $5.

Zip-Lines

Eight miles south of town at Herring Cove is the **Alaska Rainforest Sanctuary** (907/225-5503, www.alaskarainforest.com), where a former lumber mill serves as headquarters for two different sets of exciting zip-lines. The **Rain Forest Canopy Trek** includes eight zip-lines (the longest is 850 feet) and three sky-bridges through the treetops, while the **Bear Creek Zip-line** has seven zip-lines, a long sky-bridge, rappelling, and a steep 250-foot hillside slide. Guided tours cost $179 and take 3.5 hours. Children must be taller than 50 inches. A gift shop and totem carving area are at the old mill site, and a boardwalk leads along the creek—a good place to watch black bears fishing for salmon most summer evenings. The sanctuary also has guided rain forest walks ($80), mainly for cruise ship passengers.

A smaller zip-line operated by **Southeast Exposure** (907/225-8829, www.southeastexposure.com) is 14 miles north of town. The course covers eight cable spans and a rope bridge plus a climbing wall for $99. This is a low-key family-run operation. Free transportation is often available from Ketchikan.

Deer Mountain

The best hike from Ketchikan is up to the 3,000-foot summit of Deer Mountain (6 miles round-trip). Begin by heading 0.5 miles uphill

© DON PITCHER

Rain Forest Canopy Trek

from Deermount and Fair Streets. Take the first left—the road to Ketchikan Lakes, source of the city's drinking water—and then an immediate right to the trailhead. The trail climbs along an excellent but strenuous path through dense Sitka spruce and western hemlock forests. There's an incredible view in all directions from the top of Deer Mountain, but right into July you'll have to cross snowbanks to reach the summit. (Rain gear works fine for sledding down again.)

Just before the final climb to the peak, a trail to the left leads around the north slope and on to tiny **Blue Lake** and **John Mountain** (3,238 feet). Entirely above the tree line, this section can be hazardous for inexperienced hikers. Carry a map and compass since it's easy to become disoriented if the clouds drop down. Ambitious hikers can do a 12-mile trek over the top, ending at Beaver Falls powerhouse, at the end of South Tongass Highway. Free **shelter cabins** (no reservations) are atop Deer Mountain and at Blue Lake; get current trail info at the Discovery Center.

Ward Lake Area

Several good trails are near the Forest Service campground at Ward Lake, eight miles north of downtown via Revilla Road. The 1.3-mile **Ward Lake Nature Trail** is an easy loop with interpretive signs and good summertime fishing for steelhead and salmon. **Ward Creek Trail** starts across from the day-use area and follows the creek 2.5 miles to Last Chance Campground. It's built to be wheelchair accessible, with a couple of short spur paths leading to platforms over this beautiful creek.

Perseverance Trail climbs two miles to Perseverance Lake following a "stairway-to-heaven" boardwalk, passing through several muskegs along the way. Beyond this, you can take the **Minerva Mountain Trail** all the way to Carlanna Lake. Contact the Forest Service for details on the latter since this is a newly built trail.

Settler's Cove State Recreation Site, 16 miles north of Ketchikan, has a one-mile trail through the rain forest, with a pretty waterfall and spawning pink salmon in midsummer. Offshore is Back Island, home to the U.S. Navy's Southeast Alaska Acoustic Measurement Facility, where submarines are tested to help them operate silently. The subs themselves are rarely seen.

Nearby Cabins

The Naha River watershed, 20 miles north of Ketchikan, contains one of the finest trail and cabin systems in Southeast Alaska. The river once supported astounding runs of sockeye salmon and is still a popular salmon, steelhead, and trout fishing area for locals. At one time the town of **Loring** (established 1888) at its mouth had the world's largest fish cannery and was the main point of entry into Alaska. Today, it is a tiny settlement of retirees and vacation homes. **Heckman Lake,** six miles upriver, supported the world's largest and most costly salmon hatchery in the early 1900s. All that remains are overgrown ruins.

The pleasant six-mile **Naha River Trail** begins at Naha Bay, follows the shore of Roosevelt Lagoon, then climbs gently up to Jordon and

Heckman Lakes. At the mouth of Roosevelt Lagoon is an interesting salt chuck where the direction of water flow changes with the tides. Covered picnic tables are nearby. More picnic tables are two miles up the trail at a small waterfall—a good place to watch black bears catching salmon late in the summer. There's a Forest Service cabin on Jordan Lake and two cabins on Heckman Lake (one is wheelchair accessible); all three have rowboats and cost $35. Reservations ($10 fee) can be made at 518/885-3639, 877/444-6777, or www.recreation.gov. Access to the Naha area is by sea kayak, floatplane, or skiff. Contact **Knudsen Cove Marina** (907/225-8500 or 800/528-2486, www.knudsoncovemarina.com) for skiff rentals or drop-offs.

Lake Shelokum, 40 miles north of Ketchikan, has a free three-sided shelter near a hot spring. A two-mile trail stretches from the shelter to Bailey Bay, passing the scenic lake and an impressive waterfall. Other cabins well worth visiting include **Lake McDonald, Reflection Lake, Helm Creek,** and **Blind Pass.** Get details at the Discovery Center in Ketchikan.

Sea Kayaking

The Discovery Center has detailed information on sea kayaking in the waters near Ketchikan, including Misty Fiords and a circumnavigation of Revilla Island. **Southeast Sea Kayaks** (907/225-1258 or 800/287-1607, www.kayakketchikan.com) leads a variety of kayak trips, including a 2.5-hour paddle along Tongass Narrows ($94) and a 4-hour trip ($159) that includes a boat ride to a quiet cove and the chance to explore by kayak. An all-day trip to Misty Fiords ($559) includes the boat ride over and back, lunch, and four hours of paddling.

Located 13 miles north of town at Knudson Cove, **Southeast Exposure** (907/225-8829, www.southeastexposure.com) has a range of trips that are especially popular with cruise ship passengers, starting with a $65 paddle to Eagle Island. Bike tours and zip-line adventures are also available. Both Southeast Sea Kayaks and Southeast Exposure also offer multiday trips to Misty Fiords, kayak rentals, and water taxis.

Fishing and Boating

Many Ketchikan companies offer charter fishing trips in search of salmon or halibut; see the visitors bureau for a complete listing. Rent skiffs and fishing gear to head out on your own from **Knudsen Cove Marina** (13 miles north of town, 907/247-8500 or 800/528-2486, www.knudsoncovemarina.com). If you're just looking to try your luck with all the locals who fish from the Creek Street bridge, rent a pole from the little stand that's a block away, across from the Federal Building. **Mountain Point,** 5.5 miles south of Ketchikan, is a good spot to try your luck at salmon fishing from the shore.

Alaska Tours Undersea (907/247-8889 or 877/461-8687, www.alaskaunderseatours.com) is a rather bizarre semisubmersible vessel with big windows that extend six feet below the waterline. Ninety-minute tours are $52 adults, $32 children when cruise ships are in port, or $35 adults, $20 children when they aren't. (Jeez, I wonder if cruise ship passengers pay more because some giant corporation gets a substantial booking fee?)

ACCOMMODATIONS

For an up-to-date listing of local lodging places, visit the Ketchikan Visitors Bureau website (www.visit-ketchikan.com).

Hostel

Downtown in the basement of the Methodist church at Grant and Main Streets is the **Ketchikan Youth Hostel** (907/225-3319, www.ktnumc.com, June–Aug., $17 pp). It's open 6 P.M.–9 A.M., and the doors are locked at 11 P.M. If your ferry will be getting in after that, call the hostel in advance and they'll open for you. The hostel isn't fancy—we're talking simple cots—but it is friendly and clean, with kitchen facilities and showers. It is a good place to meet other budget travelers. There's a four-night maximum stay, and reservations are recommended.

Hotels and Motels

Built in the 1930s and now on the National Register of Historic Places, the centrally located **Gilmore Hotel** (326 Front St., 907/225-9423 or 800/275-9423, www.gilmorehotel.com) exudes an old-fashioned ambience but has been updated with modern furnishings. Rates are reasonable: $95 d for cramped guest rooms, $125 d for larger ones with two beds and a water view. Amenities include courtesy van service, a continental breakfast, Wi-Fi, parking, and a full-service restaurant (Annabelle's). Rooms over the bar may get noisy at night, and smoking is still allowed in some rooms.

Cozy **New York Hotel** (207 Stedman St., 907/225-0246 or 866/225-0246, www.thenewyorkhotel.com) has been painstakingly restored to its Roaring '20s heyday. It has a great location—facing the harbor, and just a few steps off Creek Street—and the downstairs café is one of the best in town. It also has complimentary airport and ferry shuttles. The eight guest rooms in the historic main building are small but nicely furnished, and cost $139 s or d with private baths and queen beds. Also available are six luxury suites with covered waterside decks along Creek Street for $159–219 d, plus $15 for each additional guest. Several of the suites feature lofts with spiral stairs, kitchenettes, and jetted tubs. Book early for these popular suites.

The Narrows Inn (907/247-2600 or 888/686-2600, www.narrowsinn.com) sits four miles north of Ketchikan along Tongass Narrows. Guest rooms ($145–170 d) are small but modern, bright, and nicely appointed. In-room fridges and microwaves, plus Wi-Fi and a continental breakfast, are included. Waterside rooms (ask for room 1209) have small balconies where you can watch the parade of boats and planes, and three larger suites ($230–245 d) are available. A steak and seafood restaurant is also on the premises, and the staff is very accommodating.

Ketchikan's largest lodging place, **Best Western Landing** (3434 Tongass Ave., 907/225-5166 or 800/428-8304, www.landinghotel.com, $200–240 d) sits right across from the ferry terminal. The 107 guest rooms are newly refurbished and include microwaves and fridges. Also on the premises are two restaurants, a fitness center, a courtesy van, and free Wi-Fi.

At the top end of Ketchikan's lodging spectrum is the elaborate **Cape Fox Lodge** (800 Venetia Way, 907/225-8001 or 866/225-8001, www.capefoxlodge.com, $199–209 d, 2-room suite $249 d). This attractive hilltop hotel overlooks Tongass Narrows and has spacious rooms with fridges, microwaves, and Wi-Fi. A funicular car takes guests to the Cape Fox from Creek Street.

Fishing Lodges

Many fishing lodges can be found in the Ketchikan area, particularly on nearby Prince of Wales Island; see www.visit-ketchikan.com for a complete listing.

Located 17 miles north of Ketchikan, **Salmon Falls Resort** (907/225-2752 or 800/247-9059, www.salmonfallsresort.com, mid-May–mid-Sept.) has modern rooms and a dramatic shore-side setting. Three-night guided fishing packages are $4,300 for two people.

Yes Bay Lodge (907/225-7906 or 800/999-0784, www.yesbay.com) is a remote fishing lodge near Lake McDonald on the Cleveland Peninsula north of Ketchikan. The setting is wonderful, and the fishing is great, most notably in a famous steelhead stream adjacent to the property. Rates start at $6,400 d for a four-night all-inclusive package.

Also check out **Naha Bay Outdoor Adventures** (907/247-4453, www.nahabayoutdooradventures.com), a 20-minute boat ride from Knudson Cove Marina. Naha has good fishing, hiking, sea kayaking, and more, starting at $600 d for three nights.

Bed-and-Breakfasts

You'll find links to Ketchikan B&Bs at www.visit-ketchikan.com, or contact **Ketchikan Reservation Service** (907/247-5337 or 800/987-5337, www.ketchikan-lodging.com) or **Alaska Travelers Accommodations**

(907/247-7117 or 800/928-3308, www.alaskatravelers.com) for assistance in booking a B&B, a room, a cabin, or a guest house.

Captain's Quarters B&B (325 Lund St., 907/225-4912, www.captainsquartersbb.com, $105–115 d) has three rooms with private baths, harbor views, and continental breakfasts; children are not allowed.

Two miles north of the ferry terminal, **Black Bear Inn B&B** (907/225-4343, www.stayinalaska.com, $160 d) is an elegant, recently built four-bedroom house with an outdoor hot tub, plenty of privacy, and tall windows facing Tongass Narrows. A separate apartment ($220 d) on the top floor has its own entrance and porch, and a private cabin ($195 d) is also available. Make-it-yourself breakfast is provided.

On a steep hill a few blocks from downtown, **Eagle Heights B&B** (1626 Water St., 907/225-1760, www.eagleheightsbb.com) is an impressive 1940s home overlooking Tongass Narrows. A guest room ($105 d) and two suites ($125–135 d) have private baths, Wi-Fi, and continental breakfasts.

Lundberg's South Shore Inn (907/225-0909, www.innsalaska.com, $145 d, includes continental breakfast) has a private two-bedroom apartment with a kitchenette, a woodstove, a large deck, and a private beach. This very comfortable home is seven miles southeast of town near Mountain Point.

Located four miles south of town and right on the water, **Anchor Inn by the Sea** (907/247-7117 or 800/928-3308, www.alaskatravelers.com/anchor.htm, $135–160 d) is a fine option for families, with three large suites with kitchenettes. All of these feature private baths and entrances. A five-night minimum stay is required.

Along picturesque George Inlet eight miles south of Ketchikan, **Waypoint Inn at Herring Bay** (907/225-8605, www.waypointinn.com, $175 d) is a studio apartment with a full kitchen and a big deck for relaxing. There is a minimum four-night stay. The owners also have a comfortable in-town home with two separate units ($135–175 d).

Alaska's Hidden Cove Vacation Rentals (907/225-7934, www.akhiddencove.com) has two lovely places north of town: a three-bedroom home ($285 d) and a one-bedroom suite ($125 d); a four-night minimum stay is required.

Red Fish Cottage (907/247-7117 or 800/928-3308, www.alaskatravelers.com, $165 d) is a gorgeous little place perched on a steep hillside a short walk from downtown. Bedroom and living room windows look over Tongass Narrows, and the unit includes a fireplace, a flat screen TV, a kitchen, a sofa bed, and a deck. The cottage was built in the 1920s and lovingly refurbished in 2008. A five-night minimum stay is required. This is a wonderful getaway spot for couples.

CAMPING

There are no campsites in town, but the Forest Service operates two summer-only campgrounds ($10) in the scenic Ward Lake area—a world away from the craziness of downtown Ketchikan when cruise ships are in port. Get there by heading five miles north from the ferry terminal and turning right up Revilla Road. Ward Cove is a good place to see eagles, so stop for a look before heading to the lake. The most popular camping area is scenic **Signal Creek Campground,** along Ward Lake. Another 1.5 miles north is **Last Chance Campground.** Both campgrounds have running water and can be reserved (518/885-3639 or 877/444-6777, www.recreation.gov).

Settler's Cove State Recreation Site (16 miles north of the ferry, $10) has campsites beneath the trees. The beach is a popular spot for summer picnics, and a rain forest trail leads to a small waterfall.

Clover Pass Resort (907/247-2234 or 800/410-2234, www.cloverpassresort.com, mid-May–Sept.), 15 miles north of Ketchikan, has RV hookups ($31–36) plus a restaurant on the premises. RVers often park for free in the **Wal-Mart** lot.

FOOD

Breakfast and Lunch

Housed within the historic New York Hotel, **Ketchikan Coffee Company** (207 Stedman

St., 907/225-8646, www.ketchikancoffee.com, Sun.–Wed. 7 A.M.–4 P.M., Thurs.–Sat. 7 A.M.–4 P.M. and 7–11 P.M. summer, Sat.–Thurs. 7 A.M.–3 P.M., Fri. 7 A.M.–3 P.M. and 7–10 P.M. winter, $7–14) has big windows facing Thomas Basin Harbor and a menu of espresso, pastries, and bagels for breakfast, along with lunchtime paninis, smoked salmon chowder, spanakopita, tuna sandwiches, and black-bean burritos. If you're around on a Thursday evening in winter, don't miss classic films projected on the wall. Wi-Fi and computer rentals are available for a fee.

Located right across from the ferry terminal, **The Landing Restaurant** (3434 Tongass Ave., 907/225-5166, www.landinghotel.com), fills with locals and travelers in search of a filling breakfast.

Find the best local chicken sandwiches, salmon burgers, halibut and chips, and hamburgers at the tiny **Burger Queen** (907/225-6060, Mon. 11 A.M.–3 P.M., Tues.–Sat. 11 A.M.–7 P.M., $9–17) just north of the Front Street tunnel. **McDonald's** is in the Plaza Mall 0.75 miles south of the ferry, and the local **Subway** (415 Dock St.) is downtown.

If you're out on the road heading north, drop by the little red caboose called **Rose's** (4761 N. Tongass Hwy., 907/225-8377, $4–8) for halibut cheeks, burgers, shakes, and the best fries in town.

Dinner

Upstairs in the Spruce Mill Mall, **Steamers** (907/225-1600, daily May–late Sept., $15–40) is a large and noisy tourist restaurant where you'll find fresh seafood, pasta, and steaks along with 31 brews—half of them Alaskan beers—on draft. The featured attraction is crab, but all the seafood is good, and servings are ample. Try the teriyaki lemon salmon, prime rib, or blackened halibut tacos. Make reservations for a window seat facing Tongass Narrows, although the view is usually blocked by one of the cruise ships.

Ocean View Restaurant (1831 Tongass Ave., 907/225-7566, www.oceanviewmex.com, daily 11 A.M.–11 P.M., dinner entrées $11–21) is a favorite of locals, and with good reason. The food is varied and nicely prepared, the atmosphere is classy (but noisy), prices are reasonable, and delivery is free. The menu encompasses pasta (including halibut fettuccine), steaks, seafood, burgers, and the best pizzas in town, but fajitas, burritos, chile rellenos, house-made guacamole, and other Mexican dishes are the real attraction. All meals come with chips, salsa, and Mexican tunes from the speakers. Most luncheon specials are $9–10, but you can also get a taco or enchilada for $4. There's a full bar with margaritas and other drinks and a covered outside deck facing the Tongass Narrows for summer dining.

Next to the footbridge at the north end of Creek Street, **Good Fortune Chinese Restaurant** (907/225-1818) has upstairs seating overlooking the water. It's decent and reasonable, including an $8 lunch of sweet-and-sour pork or spicy kung pao chicken. À la carte dinners are $11–15, and service is quick and friendly.

Fine Dining

With its 1920s-style decor, **Annabelle's Keg and Chowder House** (326 Front St., 907/225-6009, www.gilmorehotel.com, daily 10 A.M.–10 P.M. summer, daily 11 A.M.–9 P.M. winter, dinner entrées $19–32) wins the "best atmosphere" prize among Ketchikan restaurants. The menu features seafood (including four kinds of chowders), steaks, salads, and sandwiches, along with prime rib on weekends. There are daily specials, cocktails, and free Wi-Fi. Located in the historic Gilmore Hotel, this is a good place to impress a friend.

Bar Harbor Restaurant (2813 Tongass Ave., 907/225-2813, www.barharborrestaurant-ktn.com, lunch daily 11 A.M.–1:30 P.M., dinner Sun.–Thurs. 5–8 P.M., Fri.–Sat. 5–9 P.M., dinner $18–26) fills a tiny building south of the ferry terminal, and the back deck provides outdoor dining with a view of this busy harbor if it isn't raining too hard. The food is dependably good and includes such specialties as scallops a la Paula, bleu steak salad, crab cakes, and weekend prime rib. Reservations are recommended for both lunch and dinner.

Héen Kahídi Restaurant and Lounge (800 Venetia Way, 907/225-8001, www.capefoxlodge.com, daily 7 A.M.–9 P.M., $24–39), inside Cape Fox Lodge, serves seafood and steak dinners—try the pepper steak or halibut Olympia—in a quiet and romantic setting. Reserve ahead to get a window seat for an evening sunset over town.

Located 17 miles north of Ketchikan, **Salmon Falls Resort** (907/225-2752 or 800/247-9059, www.salmonfallsresort.com, daily 5–9 P.M. May–Sept.) is a large octagonal restaurant specializing in steaks and seafood, with blackened halibut, king crab, steaks, lobster, and other filling fare for $22–33. The building vaults 40 feet overhead, with views across Clover Passage and an impressive waterfall nearby.

Fish House (907/225-4055 or 877/732-9453, www.alaskafreshketch.com, daily 10 A.M.–3 P.M. May–Sept., $9–14) has a little storefront next to the Lumberjack Show downtown. Drop by for outstanding fish and chips, salmon chowder, fish cakes, halibut and bacon sandwiches, and blueberry-rhubarb bread pudding. The owners also do five-course "Chef's Table" gourmet dinners daily if you want to learn from the pros.

Groceries and Sweets

The closest grocery store to the ferry is **Alaskan & Proud Market** (907/225-1279 or 800/770-8258, www.alaskaandproud.com) right across the road, while **Safeway,** 0.75 miles south of the ferry, has a salad bar and the biggest selection of groceries. **Tatsuda's IGA** (633 Stedman St., 907/225-4125) is on the south edge of town.

Salmon Etc. (907/225-6008 or 800/354-7256 outside Alaska, www.salmonetc.com) has two locations: on Creek Street and downtown at 322 Mission Street. It sells high-quality canned, smoked, or frozen salmon, halibut, crab, clams, and other sea critters.

KetchiCandies (315 Mission St., 907/225-0900 or 800/225-0970, www.ketchicandies.com) makes hand-dipped chocolates, and they will ship your purchases.

INFORMATION AND SERVICES

The two primary information centers are the Ketchikan Visitors Bureau (131 Front St., 907/225-6166 or 800/770-3300, www.visit-ketchikan.com) and the Southeast Alaska Discovery Center (50 Main St., 907/228-6220, www.fs.fed.us/r10, Mon.–Sat. 8 A.M.–5 P.M., Sun. 8 A.M.–4 P.M. May–Sept., Tues.–Sat. 10 A.M.–4:30 P.M. Oct.–Apr.). Forest Service offices for **Ketchikan and Misty Fiords** ranger districts (3031 Tongass Ave., 907/225-2148, www.fs.fed.us/r10/tongass) are 0.5 miles south of the ferry terminal.

Showers are available at **Highliner Laundromat** (2703 Tongass Ave.) and **Thomas Wash Basin** (989 Stedman St., 907/247-9274), which also has Wi-Fi and a snack bar with espresso. A better option is to head up Madison Street to the **high school swimming pool** (2610 4th Ave., 907/225-2010), where a swim, sauna, and shower cost $5.

Get fast cash from ATMs at First Bank and Wells Fargo downtown, and at the Safeway and A&P grocery stores.

The main **post office** is next to the ferry terminal on the north end of town, and a branch post office is downtown in the Great Alaskan Clothing Company (422 Mission St.).

Ketchikan General Hospital (3100 Tongass Ave., 907/225-5171, www.peacehealth.org) is the largest in southern Southeast Alaska.

Books and Internet

Ketchikan's woefully small **public library** (629 Dock St., 907/225-3331, www.firstcitylibraries.org, Sun. 1–5 P.M., Mon.–Wed. 10 A.M.–8 P.M., Thurs.–Sat. 10 A.M.–6 P.M.) is a great place to relax, with big windows overlooking Ketchikan Creek. Unfortunately, this may be the only Alaskan library where the computer terminals are off-limits to nonresidents (they'd be overwhelmed by cruise ship folks).

A book-lover's bookstore, **Parnassus Bookstore** (5 Creek St., 907/225-7690, www.

ketchikanbooks.com) is upstairs above Soho Coho on Creek Street. Parnassus stocks an especially impressive collection of Alaskan, Native American, and women's books. The other bookshop is **Waldenbooks** (907/225-8120) in Plaza Mall.

Surf the Web for a fee at **Seaport CyberStation** (Salmon Landing Mall, 907/247-4615 or 888/295-0965, www.seaportel.com). Several places have free Wi-Fi; try Ketchikan Coffee Company, Annabelle's Restaurant, and Thomas Wash Basin.

GETTING THERE

Ferry

Ketchikan's ferry terminal is two miles northwest of downtown and is open Monday–Friday 9 A.M.–4:30 P.M. and when ships are in port. Call 907/225-6182 or 907/225-6181 for recorded arrival and departure times. During the summer, ferries provide almost-daily runs to Prince Rupert, Metlakatla, Wrangell, and points north. Ferry service to Bellingham is once per week. Contact the **Alaska Marine Highway** (907/465-3941 or 800/642-0066, www.dot.state.ak.us/amhs) for the current schedule and prices.

The **Inter-Island Ferry Authority** (907/826-4848 or 866/308-4848, www.interislandferry.com) operates from the same building, with daily service to Hollis on Prince of Wales Island.

Air

Ketchikan Airport is on Gravina Island, directly across Tongass Narrows from the ferry terminal. The airport has a café, cocktails, and Wi-Fi ($6 per hour). In 2005, Ketchikan became a national laughingstock when Alaska's congressional delegation rammed through a bill that included funding for a pair of bridges to the otherwise-uninhabited island. The notorious "bridge to nowhere" became a national symbol of pork barrel politics before the funding was hurriedly cut off. The incident received additional scrutiny when Sarah Palin ran on the 2008 Republican ticket claiming to have opposed the bridge, a half-truth at best. There really isn't a need for bridges since an **airport ferry** (907/225-6800, $5 one-way plus $6 for vehicles) operates every 30 minutes daily 6:15 A.M.–9:30 P.M. The ferry leaves the airport side on the hour and half-hour, and leaves the Ketchikan side of the channel at 15 and 45 minutes past the hour.

If you're heading downtown and don't have a rental car, Rich Schuerger of **Tongass Water Taxi** (907/225-8294) takes you directly from the airport to Thomas Basin in the heart of Ketchikan for $19 s or $27 d. He meets most flights and can be found next to the baggage claim.

Alaska Airlines (800/426-0333, www.alaskaair.com) has flights from Ketchikan to Juneau, Petersburg, Sitka, Wrangell, and other cities in Alaska and the Lower 48. Three air-taxi operators, **ProMech Air** (907/225-3845 or 800/860-3845, www.promechair.com), **Pacific Airways** (907/225-3500 or 877/360-3500, www.flypacificairways.com), and **Taquan Air** (907/225-8800 or 800/770-8800, www.taquanair.com), have daily service to Prince of Wales Island and Metlakatla.

ProMech, Pacific Airways, and Taquan also do flightseeing trips around Ketchikan. Other air-taxi operators include **Carlin Air** (907/225-3036 or 888/594-3036, www.carlinair.com), **Family Air Tours** (907/247-1305 or 800/380-1305, www.familyairtours.com), **Island Wings Air Service** (907/225-2444 or 888/854-2444, www.islandwings.com), **Misty Fjords Air and Outfitting** (1285 Tongass Ave., 907/225-5155 or 877/228-4656, www.mistyfjordsair.com), **Alaska Seaplane Tours** (907/225-1974 or 866/858-2327, www.alaskaseaplanetours.com), **Seawind Aviation** (907/225-1206 or 877/225-1203, www.seawindaviation.com), and **Southeast Aviation** (907/225-2900 or 888/359-6478, www.southeastaviation.com). Especially popular is a two-hour flightseeing trip to Misty Fiords National Monument that includes a landing on a lake for around $230. Some of these companies include a half-hour on land as part of the tour, providing a good chance to stretch your legs and take in the wild country.

GETTING AROUND

The Bus (907/225-8726, www.borough.ketchikan.ak.us, $1) runs throughout Ketchikan, south to Saxman, and north to Totem Bight approximately every 20 minutes daily 7 A.M.–7 P.M. Schedules are available at the visitors bureau and ferry terminal, or just find a bus stop and wait.

The local taxi companies are **Alaska Cab Co.** (907/225-2133), **Sourdough Cab** (907/254-7286, www.ketchikantaxicabtours.com; recommended), and **Yellow Taxi** (907/225-5555). They charge about $12 from the ferry to downtown, $13 from downtown to Saxman, or $75 per hour for tours (up to 6 people).

Tours

The downtown visitors bureau houses booths from companies promoting two-hour city tours ($40–50). Most of these—including an embarrassing "Duck Tour"—are for cruise ship travelers. Also popular are two-hour waterfront paddle-wheel boat cruises offered by **Alaska Travel Adventures** (907/247-5295 or 800/791-2673, www.bestofalaskatravel.com, $59 adults, $39 children) and visits to Saxman village from **Cape Fox Tours** (907/225-4846, www.capefoxtours.com, $45).

Car Rentals

Because Ketchikan's sights are so spread out, renting a car is a good idea. Rental rates with unlimited miles start around $65 (including tax) from **Alaska Car Rental** (a.k.a. E-Z Rent-A-Car 2828 N. Tongass Ave., 907/225-5000 or 800/662-0007, www.akcarrental.com) and **Budget** (4950 N. Tongass Ave., 907/225-6004 or 800/478-2438, www.budget.com). Both companies have cars at the airport and on the Ketchikan side of Tongass Narrows; it's an $11 ferry ride each way to transport a vehicle.

Vicinity of Ketchikan

MISTY FIORDS NATIONAL MONUMENT

The 2.2-million-acre Misty Fiords National Monument is the largest national forest wilderness in the United States, covering the east side of Revillagigedo Island, the adjacent mainland all the way to the Canadian border, and the long narrow Behm Canal that separates the island and the mainland. Misty contains a diversity of gorgeous scenery—glaciers, rain forests, narrow fjords, and rugged mountains—but is best known for the spectacular cliffs that rise as high as 3,000 feet from the ocean. Almost unknown until its establishment in 1978, Misty Fiords is today one of the highlights of an Alaskan trip for many visitors. Be forewarned, however, it's an expensive highlight.

The name "Misty" comes from the wet and cloudy conditions that predominate throughout the summer. Rainfall averages almost 160 inches per year, so be sure to bring rubber boots and rain gear. Because of all this rain the land exhibits a verdant beauty, even when clouds drape the mountain slopes.

Flightseeing and Boat Tours

On any given summer day, flightseeing planes constantly take off from Tongass Narrows for trips over the monument. Two-hour flightseeing trips cost around $230 (including a water landing) and are offered by all the local air taxis.

Another excellent way to see Misty is by boat from either **Alaska Travel Adventures** (907/247-5295 or 800/791-2673, www.bestofalaskatravel.com, 5.5 hours, $158 adults, $105 children) or **Allen Marine Tours** (907/225-8100 or 877/686-8100, www.allenmarinetours.com, 4.5 hours, $159 adults, $109 children). Both companies operate catamaran cruises into Misty Fiords in the summer. Along the way, the boats pass towering cliffs, peaceful coves, and dramatic New Eddystone Rock, which juts straight out of the water from a tiny island in the midst of Behm Canal. The tours turn

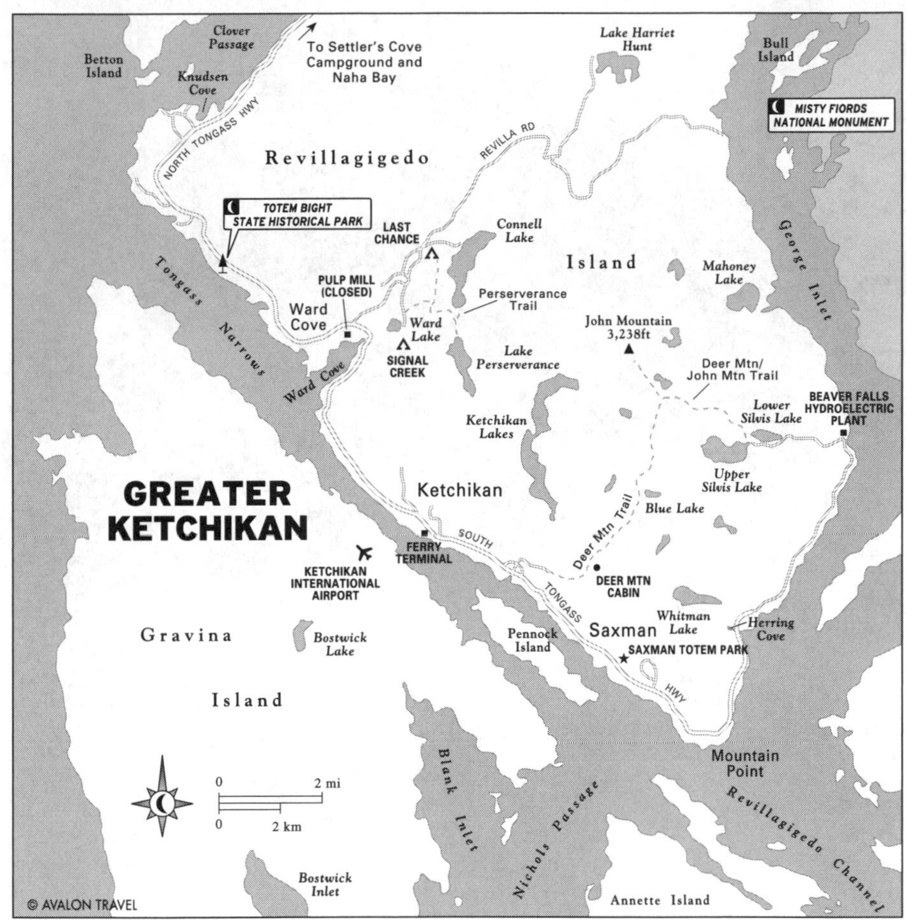

around in Rudyerd Bay before returning to Ketchikan. There's an onboard naturalist, and a filling lunch is included. When the weather cooperates, this is one of the best side trips you can take anywhere in Alaska. Alaska Travel Adventures also offers a faster 3.5-hour trip—most folks choose this version—that includes a flightseeing return trip to Ketchikan or vice versa for $329 adults or $289 children.

Sea Kayaking Tours

The best way to see Misty Fiords is from a kayak. You can paddle there from Ketchikan, but only if you're experienced and adequately prepared. Two Ketchikan companies offer guided multiday sea kayaking trips in Misty Fiords: **Southeast Sea Kayaks** (907/225-1258 or 800/287-1067, www.kayakketchikan.com) and **Southeast Exposure** (907/225-8829, www.southeastexposure.com). Both companies also rent kayaks and set up transportation into Misty for those who prefer to paddle independently. Kayakers should be warned that flightseeing planes and cruise ships may impact your wilderness experience in Rudyerd Bay, but other areas get far less use.

floatplane and cruise ship, Tongass Narrows

Hiking and Cabins

Misty Fiords National Monument has 14 recreation cabins (518/885-3639 or 877/444-6777, www.recreation.gov, $35). Those near magnificent **Rudyerd Bay** are very popular, and reservations must be made months in advance. There are also 10 trails that take you from saltwater to scenic lakes, most with cabins or free three-sided shelters. Two of the best trails lead up to shelters at Punchbowl and Nooya Lakes. The 0.75-mile **Punchbowl Lake Trail** switchbacks up from Rudyerd Bay, passing spectacular Punchbowl Creek Waterfall on the way. Punchbowl is one of the finest short hikes in Southeast Alaska, and there's a canoe and skiff at the lake. Both brown and black bears may be encountered on any of these trails, so be certain to make plenty of noise and to hang all food.

Before heading out on any overnight trips into Misty, talk with staff at the District Office (1817 Tongass Ave., 907/225-2148, www.fs.fed.us/r10/tongass). They can provide information on trail conditions, campsites, and what to expect. Be sure to request a copy of their Misty Fiords map.

METLAKATLA

Twelve miles southwest of Ketchikan on the western shore of Annette Island is the community of Metlakatla (pop. 1,500). Metlakatla (meaning "saltwater channel" in Tsimshian) is Alaska's only Indian reservation, a status that was reaffirmed in 1971 when its residents refused to join other Native American groups under the Alaska Native Claims Settlement Act. This quiet, conservative town—the only predominantly Tsimshian settlement in Alaska—has a strong religious heritage and the air of a pioneer village. Large frame houses occupy big corner lots, while vacant lots yield abundant berry crops. There seems to be a church on every corner—eight in all, none of them Catholic. Metlakatla boasts a flourishing cannery, a cold-storage facility, a fish hatchery, a rock quarry, and a sawmill. Most of Annette Island is wooded mountainous terrain reaching up to 3,500 feet, but the town of Metlakatla spreads out across a large, relatively flat portion of the island that contains many muskegs and lakes. Although Metlakatla is only a dozen miles from Ketchikan, it gets 118 inches of precipitation per year, 44 inches less than Ketchikan.

History

In 1887, a Tsimshian Indian group left Canada in search of religious freedom in Alaska. They discovered an abandoned Tlingit settlement on Annette Island offering a sheltered bay, gently sloping beaches, and a beautiful nearby waterfall. Under the direction of Anglican missionary William Duncan (who established a similar community in Metlakatla, Canada), 823 Tsimshian followers began clearing a town site. The converts took new Christian names, dressed in suits, and abandoned much of their cultural heritage. At Metlakatla, Alaska, the settlers established a sawmill to produce lumber for the construction of houses and the first cannery.

The most ambitious building erected was a 1,000-seat church, "The Westminster Abbey of Alaska." It burned down in 1948 but was replaced by a replica six years later. In 1891 the U.S. Congress granted the Tsimshians the entire 86,000-acre island as a reservation, a right they jealously guard to this day. Duncan maintained his hold over most aspects of life here until 1913 when a government school opened. (Duncan's paternalism extended in other directions too: Rumors persist that the bachelor fathered many Metlakatla children.) He opposed the school, preferring that education remain in the hands of his church. The ensuing conflict led to intervention by the U.S. Department of the Interior in 1915, which seized the sawmill, cannery, and other facilities that had been under his personal control. Duncan died three years later, but his memory is still revered by many, and his influence can still be seen in the healthy little Indian settlement of today. For a fascinating account of Father Duncan and the two Metlakatlas, read Peter Murray's *The Devil and Mr. Duncan.*

During World War II, the U.S. Army constructed a major military base seven miles from Metlakatla on Annette Island. The base included observation towers (to search for Japanese subs), a large airfield, hangars, communications towers, shore batteries, and housing for 10,000 personnel. At the time the airport was built, it was the most expensive ever constructed by the government—everything kept sinking out of sight into the muskeg. Until the construction of an airport on Gravina Island in 1973, this airfield was used for jet service to Ketchikan, forcing passengers to land on Annette and fly by floatplane to Ketchikan. With the area's notorious weather, delays were common; many times it took longer to get the last dozen miles to Ketchikan than the 600 miles from Seattle to Annette Island.

Sights

Father Duncan's Cottage (907/886-8687) —where the missionary lived from 1894 until his death in 1918—is open as a museum when cruise ships are in port or by appointment. The old photographs of Metlakatla and the fascinating assortment of personal items owned by Duncan make a stop here a must. Unique items housed within these walls include old glass fire extinguishers, an 1890 flag with 38 stars, and the second Edison phonograph ever made. Operated by a sewing machine treadle, it was given to Duncan by Edison. Duncan's tiny bed (he stood just over five feet tall), old medical books, and medicines line the walls. The rather run-down **William Duncan Memorial Church** (built in 1954) stands at the corner of 4th Avenue and Church Street. Duncan's grave is on the left side.

A traditional **longhouse** (Mon.–Fri. afternoon summer) has been erected on the waterfront to stimulate local arts and crafts and to help recover the cultural traditions lost because of Duncan's missionary zeal. The back of the building has three totem poles, and the front is decorated with Tsimshian designs. Native dance performances take place when cruise ships are in port. Inside is a small library and a model of one of the floating fish traps that were used on the island for many years. An adjacent **Artists Village,** open when cruise ships are in port, has booths selling locally made crafts.

Metlakatla Tours (907/886-8687, www.metlakatlatours.net) leads tours that include the Duncan house, artists village, and a dance performance at the longhouse. These often fill with cruise ship folks, but space may be available if you call ahead.

Locals celebrate the establishment of Metlakatla each year on **Founder's Day,** August 7. As with most other American towns, Metlakatla also has a parade and other events on the 4th of July.

Recreation

Unlike almost everywhere else in Alaska, there are no bears on Annette Island, a relief to those who fear encounters with bruins. A short hiking trail runs from the corner of Milton Street and Airport Road on the southeast edge of town along **Skaters Lake,** a large pond where native plants and ducks can be observed. **Yellow Hill,** a 540-foot-tall fragment of 150-million-year-old sandstone, is unique in Southeast Alaska. The rock is rich in iron and magnesium, giving it a lovely desert-like yellow color set off by gnarled old lodgepole pines. An easy boardwalk trail (20 minutes each way) leads up to its summit, where you can catch panoramic vistas of the western side of Annette along with the snowcapped peaks of nearby Prince of Wales Island. Get there by walking or hitching 1.5 miles south from town on Airport Road to the signed trailhead on the right side. Some people claim to see George Washington's profile in a nearby mountain visible from Yellow Hill.

Two trails access alpine lakes in the mountains east of Metlakatla. The **Chester Lake Trail** starts at the end of the road, 0.25 mile beyond the ferry terminal. From the trail there are views over the impressive **Chester Lake Falls,** which first attracted Duncan's flock to Annette Island. The trail climbs steeply up steps and a slippery path along a waterline used for power generation. Plan on 45 minutes to reach beautiful Chester Lake, where there's a small dam. From this point, the country is above the tree line and it's possible to climb along several nearby ridges for even better views. Good camping sites are available, but be careful coming up the steep slippery path with a pack.

Farther afield and not quite as scenic is the **Purple Lake Trail.** Take Airport Road four miles south of town and turn left near the Quonset huts at the unmarked Purple Mountain Road. Follow it two miles to the power plant. The unmarked trail heads directly up a steep jeep road. After a 30-minute climb you reach a saddle, and from there you can head up adjacent ridges into the alpine area or drop down to Purple Lake (10 minutes). Another place worth a look is the aptly named **Sand Dollar Beach** on the southwest end of the island. Ask locally for directions.

The flat country around Metlakatla contains a labyrinth of dirt roads built during World War II, and if you have a mountain bike or car, they're well worth exploring. You'll find abandoned structures of all types: huge communications towers, strangely quiet empty hangars, old gun emplacements, and a major airport with no planes. From the south end of the road network are excellent views of Prince of Wales and Duke Islands, as well as the open sea beyond Dixon Entrance. This is the southernmost road in Alaska.

Accommodations and Food

Metlakatla Inn (3rd Ave. and Lower Milton St., 907/886-3456, www.metlakatlainn.com, $89 s or d) has a half-dozen standard motel rooms with microwaves, fridges, Wi-Fi, flat-screen TVs, and a guest computer. Meals and car rentals are available.

Tuck'em Inn (907/886-1074, www.alaskanow.com/tuckem-inn, $85 s, $95 d) has six comfortable and well-kept bedrooms in two houses on the same street. Some units have private baths, and all include small fridges and microwaves plus light breakfast fixings. The owners also operate a full-service restaurant (Mon.–Fri. 11 A.M.–7 P.M., Sat. 9:30 A.M.–7 P.M.) with dinners that range from $6 burgers to $24 steaks.

Get huge portions of burgers, fish-and-chips, and other greasy fare at the **Mini Mart** (907/886-3000). No wonder half the local population seems obese! There's a little espresso stand near the floatplane dock, or head to **Leask's Market** for groceries. Check the bulletin board here for such items as hand-carved fossil ivory or fresh Ooligan grease (if you don't know what it is, you probably won't like it). Metlakatla is a dry town, so alcoholic beverages are not allowed.

Services

For local information, drop by the **municipal building** (907/886-4868) or visit www.metlakatla.com on the Web. Camping is discouraged, and visitors who want to stay on Annette Island more than five days must obtain a special permit from the city. A local sponsor is required, and fishing is not allowed. The **Lepquinum Wellness Center,** next to the high school, houses an Olympic-size swimming pool, plus a weight room, a racquetball court, a sauna, and showers. Out front is **Raven and the Tide Woman Totem,** with a descriptive plaque.

Getting There

The state ferry *Lituya* provides daily runs between Metlakatla and Ketchikan, stopping at the **ferry terminal** (907/465-3941 or 800/642-0066, www.alaska.gov/ferry) 1 mile east of town. The military finished a 14-mile dirt road across the northern end of the island in 2007. A new ferry dock will eventually be built at the end of the road, providing much faster service to Ketchikan.

ProMech Air (907/225-3845 or 800/860-3845, www.promechair.com) and **Taquan Air** (907/225-8800 or 800/770-8800, www.taquanair.com) have daily floatplane service between Ketchikan and Metlakatla for $95 round-trip.

HYDER AND STEWART

The twin towns of Hyder, Alaska, and Stewart, British Columbia, lie at the head of the long narrow Portland Canal that separates Canada and the United States. The area's remoteness has kept it one of the relatively undiscovered gems of the entire Pacific Northwest coast. Most people arrive via the extraordinary 41-mile drive down Highway 37A from Meziadin Junction into Stewart, passing beautiful lakes, majestic glaciers, high waterfalls, spectacular mountain peaks, the narrow Bear River Canyon, and finally the mountain-rimmed, water-trimmed towns.

The town of Stewart (pop. 800) lies at the mouth of the Bear River, while tiny Hyder (pop. 90) is two miles down the road next to the mouth of the Salmon River. They are as different as two towns could possibly be. Stewart is the "real" town, with a hospital, churches, schools, a museum, a pharmacy, a bank, and the other necessities of life; it bills itself as Canada's northernmost ice-free port. In contrast, Hyder, "the friendliest ghost town in Alaska," makes the most of its flaky reputation. Between the two settlements lies an international boundary that seems of little importance; border checks are only made when reentering Canada, and locals get waved through. Residents send their kids to school in British Columbia. Everyone uses Canadian currency and the Canadian phone system (area code 250). You can, however, mail letters from a post office in either country, saving postage and the hassles of shipping parcels internationally. Hyder is officially on Alaska time, but everyone except the postmaster sets their watches one hour later, to Pacific standard time.

History

In 1793, Captain George Vancouver, searching for the fabled Northwest Passage, turned into Portland Canal. For days his men worked their boats up the narrow fjord, but when they reached its end after so many miles he was "mortified with having devoted so much time to so little purpose." Over a century later the area finally began to develop. In 1896, Captain

David Gilliard of the Army Corps of Engineers (for whom Gilliard Cut in the Panama Canal was later named) explored the region and left behind four stone storehouses, Alaska's first masonry buildings. Prospectors soon arrived and found an incredible wealth of gold, silver, and other minerals in the nearby mountains. Stewart received its name from two of its earliest settlers, Robert and John Stewart. The adjacent Alaskan town was initially named Portland City, but postal authorities, wary of yet another Portland, vetoed it. Instead, the town was named after Frederick B. Hyder, a Canadian mining engineer.

Gold fever and the prospect of a transcontinental Canadian railway terminus attracted more than 10,000 newcomers to the area. The steep mountainous terrain was difficult to build on; much of Hyder was constructed on pilings driven into the mudflats. The planned railroad made it only a few miles out of town, but in 1919 prospectors struck it rich. Until its 1948 closure, the Premier Gold and Silver Mine was the largest gold mine in North America. After it shut down, the local population dwindled to less than 1,000 until development of the Granduc copper mine in the 1960s. To reach the rich Leduc ore vein, workers dug the longest tunnel ever built from one end—10 miles. A devastating avalanche in 1965 buried 40 men in a tunnel entrance, killing 27 of them. The mine operated until 1984 when it was closed down and dismantled, and the site was restored to a relatively natural condition.

The spectacular Stewart-Hyder area has served as the location for several Hollywood movies: *Insomnia, Bear Island, The Thing, Iceman,* and *Leaving Normal.* Recent years have also seen sporadic promises of new gold, silver, coal, or asbestos mines, but times have been hard of late. As one local told me, "The Moose Park Graveyard is full of people still waiting for Hyder to boom."

Sights

Stewart/Hyder International Chamber of Commerce operates the **Stewart Visitors Information Centre** (250/636-9224 or 888/366-5999, www.stewart-hyder.com, daily 9 A.M.–6 P.M. mid-May–Sept.) in Stewart, at the west end of 5th Avenue.

Housed in a Fire Hall from 1910, the **Stewart Historical Society Museum** (Columbia St. and 6th Ave., 250/636-2568, daily 10 A.M.–7 P.M. July–Aug., C$5) has wildlife specimens on the first floor as well as numerous historical items both upstairs and out front.

On the U.S. side of the international border stands a tiny **stone storehouse** built in 1896 by Captain Gilliard. The building looks like an old jail and once served that purpose, but for much of its life it was a shoe repair shop. On the mudflats in front of Hyder are hundreds of old pilings, remnants of what was once a town of 1,000 people. The straight row of pilings in front of Stewart is all that remains of the aborted transcontinental railroad.

About five miles out of Hyder (turn right at the end of the main drag) is **Fish Creek Wildlife-Viewing Area.** Late July–mid-September the creek is filled with pink salmon, along with some of the world's largest chum salmon—some weighing as much as 35 pounds. A viewing platform provides an excellent vantage point for watching brown (and a few black) bears that feast on the salmon. Forest Service (250/636-2367) staff are on hand to ensure the safety of bear-watchers and to answer questions; see bear photos at www.fishcreek.org.

The road beyond Fish Creek is well worth driving, but before heading out, be sure to ask about road conditions and snow levels; travel by RV is not recommended. Just 0.25 miles beyond Fish Creek are remains of an old brothel operated by Dolly, Ketchikan's best-known madam. Continuing north, the road follows the Salmon River, passes the remains of a covered bridge that once provided access to a remote mine, then begins a tortuous climb, reentering Canada along the way. The first glimpses of stunning **Salmon Glacier** come into view 17 miles from Hyder, but the views improve as the ever-narrowing road climbs above the tree line to a lookout point 23 miles from town.

Beyond the glacier is **Tide Lake,** site of the world's greatest recorded annual snowfall: 88 feet in 1971.

Gorgeous **Bear Glacier,** 20 miles east of Stewart on Highway 37A, should not be missed. Like its more famous cousin, Juneau's Mendenhall, it is a "drive-up glacier" with the highway passing close to its base. The small lake in front is often filled with icebergs.

FISH TRAPS

The floating fish trap was developed in 1907 and quickly proved an amazingly efficient way to catch salmon. The traps were constructed with heavy wire netting that directed migrating salmon into progressively smaller enclosures. All one had to do was wait. The traps were hated by most Alaskans because they were owned by "outsiders" who could afford the high construction and maintenance costs, and because their efficiency took jobs from local fishers. Their efficiency also robbed many streams of needed brood stock.

For many years these traps brought in over half of Southeast Alaska's salmon catch. Locals got even by stealing fish from the traps, and those who did often became folk heroes. As a territory, Alaska had no say in its own affairs, but when statehood came in 1959, the first act of the state legislature was to outlaw all fish traps. Only the Annette Island Reservation (which manages all waters within 3,000 feet of the island, and sets its own fish and game regulations) was allowed to continue operating the floating fish traps after statehood, but the last of these was closed in the 1990s.

Accommodations

Ripley Creek Inn (5th Ave., Stewart, 250/636-2344, www.ripleycreekinn.homestead.com) in Stewart is the finest local lodging choice, with several dozen guest rooms scattered over five buildings. The three main units (Ripley Creek Inn, Kate Ryan Building, and Crow's Landing) are C$85–125 d, with large and nicely furnished guest rooms that include Wi-Fi and access to the sauna and exercise room. The lobby houses **Toastworks Museum,** an offbeat collection of some 600 antique kitchen appliances. The owners also run Bayview Hotel, with simple but clean rooms (C$50–75 d, no phones).

A comfortable home in the center of Hyder, **Kathy's Korner B&B** (250/636-2393, www.theinnkeeper.com/bnb/8841, May–Sept., $90 d) has three guest rooms with shared baths, continental breakfasts, and a large deck. Children are not permitted.

King Edward Hotel/Motel (250/636-9160 or 800/663-3126, www.kingedwardhotel.com, C$69–109 d) also has hotel rooms in Stewart. In Hyder, **Sealaska Inn** (250/636-9006 or 888/393-1199, www.sealaskainn.com) has seasonal motel rooms for C$64 s or C$69 d, and hostel-style rooms with a bath down the hall for C$36 s or C$42 d.

Camping

Stewart's city-run **Rainey Creek Campground** (250/636-2537 or 888/366-5999, mid-May–mid-Sept., tents C$12, RVs C$15–21) is quietly situated on the edge of town and has a cookhouse, firewood, and pay showers. Park RVs at **Camp Run-A-Muck** (250/636-9006 or 888/393-1199, www.sealaskainn.com, mid-May–mid-Sept., RVs C$20, tents C$12) in Hyder, or **Bear River RV Park** (250/636-9205, www.stewartbc.com/rvpark, RVs C$25, tents C$14) in Stewart.

Food and Drink

Several places serve meals in Stewart, but your best bet is **Bitter Creek Café** (5th Ave., 250/636-2166, www.bittercreek.homestead.com, daily 4:30–8:30 P.M. late May–Sept., closed Sun. in June, dinner entrées C$13–30) with everything from prawn fajitas to prime rib, along with homemade breads, desserts, espresso, and nightly specials. An outside deck is a good place for a beer on a summer day. Inside, a 1930 Pontiac is the centerpiece for an eccentric collection of antiques.

Get morning espresso and pastries—along with a few microwaved options—inside the Toastworks Museum at Ripley Creek Inn (5th Ave., Stewart, 250/636-2344, www.ripleycreekinn.homestead.com, daily 7:30–11 A.M. summer).

Hyder has three bars for fewer than 100 inhabitants, and getting "Hyderized" at the **Glacier Inn** (250/636-9248) is an experience that attracts folks from all over the world. It's cheap and lasts a lifetime (you even get an official card), but could also prove expensive if you fail the test. Warning: It involves a strong distilled spirit called Everclear. The walls of the Glacier Inn are papered with thousands of dollars in signed bills left by drinkers, creating the "world's most expensive wallpaper." The tradition began when prospectors would tack a dollar bill on the wall, in case they were broke on their next trip into town.

Operating out of a converted school bus in Hyder, **Alaska Premier Seafood** (250/636-9011, www.hyderalaska.com) serves fresh seafood: halibut burgers, steak and shrimp, and grilled salmon. **Sealaska Inn,** also in Hyder, serves pizzas and pasta and has free Wi-Fi.

Services

There is **no cell phone coverage** in the Hyder-Stewart area.

The U.S. Forest Service has a summertime office and information center in Hyder; stop in for details on bear-viewing up the road. For swimming, showers, and a weight room, head to **Stewart High School pool** on 9th Avenue. The public library is also at the high school. There are no U.S. banks in the area, but Stewart has a branch of the Canadian Imperial Bank of Commerce with an ATM. Showers and washing machines can be found at the Camp Run-A-Muck RV park.

Canada Day (July 1) and Independence Day (July 4) provide the opportunity for a four-day party in Stewart and Hyder. **International Days,** as it's called, features parades, pancake breakfasts, crafts, and culminates in a fireworks display in Hyder as darkness falls on the 4th.

Getting There and Around

There is no ferry service to Hyder, but **Taquan Air Service** (250/636-9150 or 907/225-8800, www.taquanair.com) flies every Monday and Thursday from Ketchikan. This is also the only time mail goes in or out of the Hyder post office. **Seaport Limousine** (250/636-2622, www.seaportnorthwest.com) has vans between Terrace, British Columbia, and Stewart, as well as guided tours of the area, including to Fish Creek and Salmon Glacier.

Prince of Wales Island

With more miles of roads than the rest of Southeast Alaska combined, a beautifully wild coastline, deep U-shaped valleys, rugged snow-topped mountains, hidden caves, and a wealth of wildlife, you might expect the country's third-largest island (after Kodiak and Hawaii) to be a major tourist attraction. But Prince of Wales Island (POW) has thus far remained off the tourist path for a number of reasons, the primary one being logging. Much of the land has been heavily logged, with huge clearcuts gouged out of the hillsides, particularly along the extensive road network. Logging has slowed markedly in recent years as the Forest Service shifts to a more diverse land-management policy, and as the Native Alaskan corporations run out of trees to cut.

Actually, POW's notoriety is its saving grace as well: The towns are authentically Alaskan, with no pretext of civility for the tourists. The 4,500 or so people who live here are friendly, and the roads offer good opportunities for a variety of recreation—including mountain biking—not available elsewhere in the Southeast. The island is very popular with hunters, and the roads provide easy access to

many bays for fishing. Black bears and deer are common sights, and wolves are occasionally seen. As logging has declined on POW, tourism—especially from those looking to catch halibut and salmon—has increased. Most of the main roads are now paved, and a ferry provides daily service between Ketchikan and Hollis.

Prince of Wales Island's largest settlement is Craig, on the west coast, but Klawock, Thorne Bay, and Hydaburg each have several hundred people. Rainfall on POW ranges 60–200 inches per year, depending on local topographic conditions. As an aside, this is one of four Prince of Wales Islands on the planet. The others are in Canada's Northwest Territories, in Australia, and in Malaysia.

Located in Klawock, the **Prince of Wales Chamber of Commerce** (907/755-2626, www.princeofwalescoc.org, Mon.–Fri. 8 A.M.–4 P.M. year-round) is a good source for local info, and their website features links to many island lodging places and fishing resorts.

CRAIG

Just across a short bridge from the western shore of POW Island, the town of Craig (pop. 1,100) overflows Craig Island. Named after Craig Miller—founder of an early fish cannery here—it was originally even more prosaically called "Fish Egg," for the herring eggs that are considered a Tlingit delicacy. Fishing and logging are the mainstays of Craig's economy, giving it a likable feeling. The town has two fish-processing plants and a number of sportfishing lodges. There are no real "sights" in town, but as you enter Craig you pass the **Healing Heart Totem Pole.** Black bears and

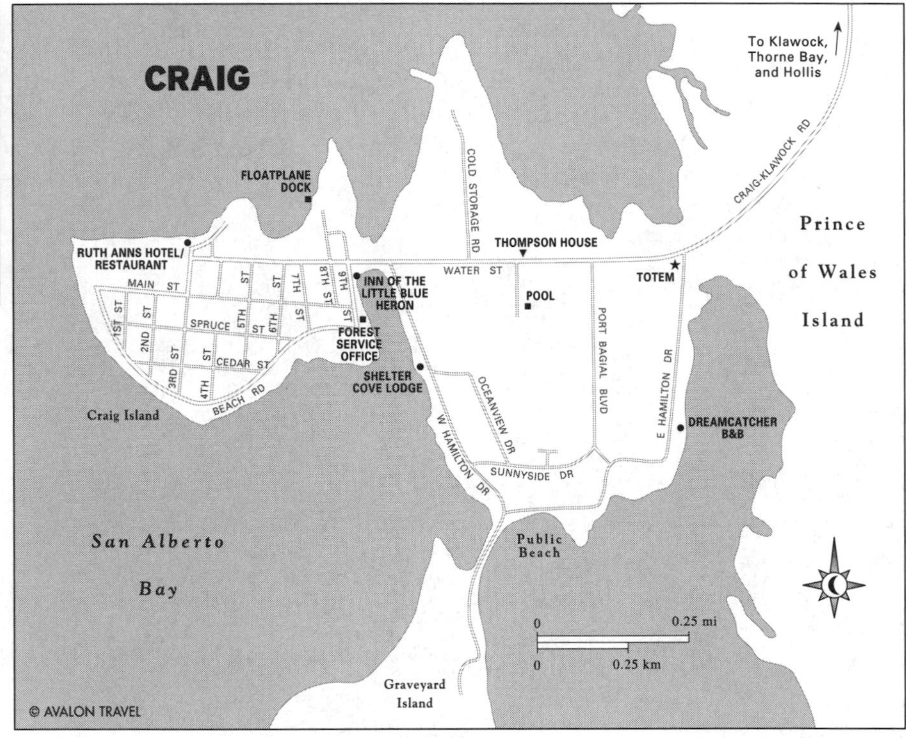

bald eagles are often seen at the dump, a mile north of town.

Hidden in the J. T. Brown Industrial Park a mile north of town is **Stone Arts of Alaska** (907/826-3571, www.stoneartsofalaska.com), an unpretentious stone yard and gallery space where you can watch Gary McWilliams as he works on one-of-a-kind pieces—all created from stones he collected in Southeast Alaska. The gallery and stone yard are open daily in the summer and include both functional pieces (tables, benches, bowls, and garden art) and fine art—the finest of which sell for upward of $40,000.

Accommodations

Find quaint cozy guest rooms (some with microwaves and fridges) at **Ruth Ann's Hotel** (907/826-3378, $100–127 d), and a honeymoon suite ($147 d) that includes a private hot tub. Most rooms have Wi-Fi access. The guest rooms are across the street from Ruth Ann's Restaurant.

At **Inn of the Little Blue Heron** (907/826-3608, www.littleblueheroninn.com), three guest rooms ($79–115 d) include private baths and fridges along with Wi-Fi. The back deck overlooks the boat harbor, and a continental breakfast is served. Also available is a new two-bedroom waterfront home ($295) that sleeps four guests.

Located above Wheelhouse Coffee Roasters, **Water Street Apartments** (907/826-2333, $135 s, $145 d) consists of three efficiency units with small kitchens and Wi-Fi.

Dreamcatcher B&B (1405 E. Hamilton Dr., 907/826-2238, www.dreamcatcher-bedandbreakfast.com, $105 d) is a modern home with wraparound decks facing the bay. The three attractive guest rooms have Wi-Fi and private baths, and a continental breakfast is served.

If you have the money and like to fish, **Waterfall Resort** (907/225-9461 or 800/544-5125, www.waterfallresort.com) will put you in seventh (or eighth) heaven. Located on the south end of POW in a beautifully refurbished fish cannery, Waterfall is popular with the elite crowd. Pampered guests stay in tiny Cape Cod–style cottages along a remote stretch of coast and are treated to great fishing with a personal fishing guide, plus three sumptuous meals daily. It's not cheap: Two people should be ready to drop $8,000 for three nights, but this does include floatplane fare from Ketchikan and all expenses.

Right in Craig, **Shelter Cove Lodge** (907/826-2939 or 888/826-3474, www.sheltercovelodge.com) has package lodging-and-fishing trips from a modern and comfortable lodge, starting around $2,650 per person for three days of fishing.

RainCountry RV Park (907/826-3632, $34) is on JS Drive.

Food

Meal prices are high on POW; your best bet may be to stock up in Ketchikan or at the grocery store in Craig, **Thompson House** (907/826-3394), which has a deli. The historic **J. T. Brown's General Store** (907/826-3290) is a classic heart-of-town place with groceries, fishing gear, and other supplies.

For fresh-roasted coffees, espresso, and pastries—plus books, gifts, computer rentals, and free Wi-Fi—head to **Wheelhouse Coffee Roasters** (907/826-2333), across from the grocery store on Cold Storage Road. This is a fine spot to hang out.

Right next door in another historic structure is **Ruth Ann's Restaurant** (907/826-3377, daily 8 A.M.–9 P.M.), a classy place with an old-time atmosphere. You'll find good food three meals a day with a front-row view of the harbor. The diverse menu includes seafood, chicken, and steaks for dinner, plus burgers, salads, halibut, fish-and-chips, and sandwiches for lunch. Dinner reservations are advised if you want a window seat. The building also houses a popular but minuscule bar. Dinner entrées start around $14 and range up to $47 for king crab.

Also downtown is **Dockside Café** (907/826-5544, daily 5:30 A.M.–3 P.M.), with reasonable breakfasts plus tasty lunches and fresh-baked pies. Dockside opens at 5:30 A.M. and is packed with smokers for the first hour or so, although smoking isn't allowed later in the day. Steak and eggs ($15) are the most expensive item.

Near the grocery store, **Annie Betty's Bakery-Café** (907/826-2299, Mon.–Fri. 7 A.M.–5:30 P.M., Sat. 8 A.M.–5:30 P.M., Sun. 10 A.M.–4 P.M., under $7) serves paninis, smoothies, ice cream, and espresso, along with homemade breads, cinnamon rolls, muffins, cookies, and doughnuts.

Craig's fine-dining experience, **Shelter Cove Lodge** (703 Hamilton Dr., 907/826-2939 or 888/826-3474, www.sheltercovelodge.com, daily 4–9 P.M. mid-June–Aug., $23–28) has tall windows facing the boat harbor, and a dinner-only menu of fine seafood, steaks, ribs, pasta, and nightly specials.

Very good pizzas—including a pesto and artichoke version—can be had at **Papa's Pizza** (907/826-2244, Mon.–Fri. 11 A.M.–9 P.M., Sat.–Sun. 11 A.M.–10 P.M.), which also serves chicken and lasagna. Small pizzas start at $8 and range up to $21 for the family size.

Services

Located along the south boat harbor, the Forest Service's **Craig District Office** (907/826-3271, www.fs.fed.us/r10/tongass) has maps and recreational information, including a listing of more charter fishing operators. **ATMs** can be found at the Wells Fargo and First Bank offices in Craig, and at the Thompson House grocery store. **Craig Clinic** (907/755-3257) has a doctor on staff.

Craig has an indoor **swimming pool** (907/826-2794) complete with a water slide, a hot tub, a sauna, and a weight room. **Log Cabin Sporting Goods** (1 Easy St., 907/826-2205 or 888/265-0375) sells outdoor gear.

KLAWOCK

Six miles from Craig is the Tlingit village of Klawock (pop. 800), home to the oldest cannery in Alaska (1878), along with a bustling sawmill, a state fish hatchery, and POW's only airport; all other POW settlements have floatplane service. Klawock is best known for its 21-pole **Totem Park,** which dominates the center of town. In the 1930s these brightly painted poles—all originals—were moved from the old abandoned village of Tuxekan (20 miles north) and restored. The **Prince of Wales Hatchery** (907/755-2231, www.powhasalmon.org, tours Mon.–Sat. 1–5 P.M. summer, free) in Klawock raises coho and sockeye salmon and has a 250-gallon aquarium filled with coho fry. **Stan Snider Park** is a pleasant picnic spot beneath the trees.

Practicalities

Log Cabin Resort and RV Park (907/755-2205 or 800/544-2205, www.logcabinresortandrvpark.com, May–Sept.) has a variety of lodging options, starting with basic cabins ($95 d) that share a bathhouse. Three suites with kitchenettes in the modern main lodge are $160 d, and a separate log house with a full kitchen is $160 d or $190 for five guests. RV sites ($27) are also available, along with canoe and skiff rentals, and charter fishing.

Although primarily geared to weekly fishing packages, **Southeast Retreat Lodge** (907/755-2994, www.southeastretreat.com) has a furnished apartment with a full kitchen for $275 for up to four people, including use of a 4WD vehicle and a continental breakfast. The lodge sits along Salt Lake.

Fireweed Lodge (907/755-2930, www.fireweedlodge.com) is a full-service fishing lodge in Klawock, and **Changing Tides Inn** (907/755-2305, www.changingtidesinn.com) provides weekly stays in a waterside location.

B&T's Cafe (907/755-2986, Tues.–Sat. 11 A.M.–7 P.M.) serves all-American fare, including burgers, steaks, and chicken. There's always a $10 dinner special available. Get groceries and baked goods from **Alaska Commercial Company** (907/755-2722, www.alaskacommercial.com).

OTHER TOWNS

Thorne Bay

In the 1980s Thorne Bay (pop. 500; www.thornebayalaska.net) was a booming logging town, home to the world's largest logging camp. The mill is long closed, and most of the logging is gone, forcing locals to shift to fishing and tourism to survive. Thorne Bay isn't the most beautiful place, but it does have all the basics, including a grocery store, gas, lodging, a large and underpopulated school, and a Forest Service district office (907/828-3304, www.fs.fed.us/r10/tongass).

McFarland's Floatel B&B (907/828-3335 or 888/828-3335, www.mcfarlandsfloatel.com, Apr.–Oct.) has modern two-bedroom log cabins ($295) that sleep four. There are no TVs or phones, but the units do include full kitchens, baths, and Wi-Fi. Car and skiff rentals are also available.

Right in town, **Welcome Inn B&B** (907/828-3950, www.lodginginnalaska.com, $85 s, $115 d) has three guest rooms and full breakfasts. Two businesses offer fishing packages that include lodging, a vehicle, and your own skiff: **Adventure Alaska Southeast** (907/828-3907 or 877/499-3474, www.fishorhunt.com) and **The Landing at Otter Cove** (907/247-3528 or 888/424-5445, www.thelandingatottercove.com). **Boardwalk Lodge** (907/828-3918 or 800/764-3918, www.boardwalklodge.com) is a luxurious fishing lodge near Thorne Bay, with access by boat or air.

Ten miles north of town on Forest Highway 30 is **Sandy Beach Picnic Area,** an attractive sandy beach (rare in Southeast Alaska) where you can pitch a tent. The road is narrow and slippery after a rain.

There are no restaurants in Thorne Bay, but **Port's Tackle Shop** (907/828-3994) serves hot dogs and espresso, or head to **Thorne Bay Market** (907/828-3306) for groceries. Amazingly, Thorne Bay lacks a bar, although you can purchase alcohol from **Riptide Liquor Store** (907/828-3353).

Thorne River, near Thorne Bay

Hydaburg

Hydaburg (pop. 400), 42 miles south of Craig, is the largest Haida settlement in Alaska. The Haida Indians are relative newcomers to the state, arriving in this Tlingit land around 1700. Originally from Canada's Queen Charlotte Islands, the Haida were given parts of POW in compensation for the accidental killing of a Haida chief by the Tlingits. Hydaburg was established in 1911 when three nearby Haida villages combined into one. Hydaburg has the prettiest setting on POW, situated along scenic Sukkwan Strait. Most of the houses, however, are very plain Bureau of Indian Affairs–style boxes. The newly paved road to Hydaburg was only completed in 1983, opening the town to the outside world. In town is a nice row of totems restored by the Civilian Conservation Corps in the 1930s, along with a newer one erected in 1991. For food, head to **AC Haida Market** (907/285-3311, daily 10 A.M.–7 P.M.). Ask locally for rooms to rent.

Kasaan

The Tlingit village of Kasaan (pop. 50) is a rough 16-mile drive off the main road between Klawock and Thorne Bay. This is a wonderful out-of-the-way settlement, and just a 15-minute walk from the community hall are a beautiful **clan house** and a number of totem poles set in the woods. The poles were mostly carved in the 1930s and 1940s, and the clan house belonged to Chief Son-i-hat, who is buried nearby. (Try to ignore the logging that has been allowed almost right up to the graves.) Older totems are in the abandoned village of Old Kasaan, accessible only by boat.

Logging and Fishing Villages

Several tiny communities (mostly former logging camps) are along the road network on the north end of POW Island.

The little settlement of **Coffman Cove** (pop. 200) is 53 miles north of Klawock. Visitors will find a general store (The Riggin Shack, 907/329-2213) with groceries, gas, and other essentials. Coffman Cove boasts several

© DON PITCHER

totem pole in Kasaan

lodging options, all on the Web at www.coffmancovealaska.com. They include **Coffman Cove Cabins** (907/329-2251) with cute cabins ($40 pp), and **Oceanview RV Park & Campground** (907/329-2032, tents $20, RVs $30), which has beach-front campsites, a coin laundry, and showers.

Sixty-five miles north of Klawock is **Whale Pass** (pop. 60), with a general store and gas. Find lodging at **Northend Cabin** (907/846-5315) and **Bear Valley Lodge** (907/247-8512 or 800/936-9600, www.bearvalleylodgealaska.com).

On the far northern end of POW are a couple of minuscule fishing/retirement villages. A long boardwalk connects the homes of **Port Protection** (pop. 50), where **Wooden Wheel Cove Lodge** (907/489-2288 or 888/489-9288, www.woodenwheellodge.com) has fishing-lodge accommodations with a three-night minimum. **Point Baker** (pop. 50) is home to a small general store and the nation's only floating post office.

RECREATION

Hiking, Camping, and Cabins

There are only a few trails on POW. One of the best and most accessible is the 1.5-mile **One Duck Trail** southwest of Hollis. The trailhead is on the east side of the Hydaburg Road, two miles south of the junction with the Craig–Hollis Road. The path climbs sharply to an Adirondack shelter (free) on the edge of the alpine zone where the scenery is grand and the hiking is easy. Be sure to wear rubber boots since the trail can be mucky.

The **Soda Lake Trail** (marked) begins approximately 14 miles south of the junction along the Hydaburg Road. This 2.5-mile trail leads to a pungent collection of bubbling soda springs covering several acres. There are colorful tufa deposits (primarily calcium carbonate) similar to those in Yellowstone, but on a vastly smaller scale. **Control Lake,** at the junction of the Thorne Bay and Big Salt Lake Roads, has a nice cabin ($45) with a rowboat. There are 20 other Forest

Service cabins (reservations 518/885-3639 or 877/444-6777, www.recreation.gov, $10 fee) scattered around POW, most accessible only by floatplane or boat.

For world-class steelhead and salmon fishing, reserve one of the four cabins in the Karta River area north of Hollis. The five-mile-long **Karta River Trail** connects Karta Bay to the **Salmon Lake Cabin** ($35) and provides panoramic views of surrounding mountains. This is part of the 40,000-acre **Karta Wilderness.**

You can camp almost anywhere on POW's National Forest land, but avoid trespassing on Native Alaskan lands (these are generally quite easy to identify since the trees have been razed for miles in all directions). **Eagle's Nest Campground** ($8) is just east of the intersection of the Klawock–Thorne Bay Road and Coffman Cove Road. Also here is a pleasant pair of lakes (Balls Lakes—named for...well, you figure it out) with a short path down to tent platforms overlooking the water. This is a good place for canoeing. **Harris River Campground** ($8) is 19 miles west of Hollis on the road to Klawock.

Spelunking

Prince of Wales Island has the best-known and probably the most extensive system of caves in Alaska, and spelunkers keep discovering more.

In **El Capitan Cave** explorers found a treasure trove of bones from black bears, brown bears, river otters, and other mammals, the oldest dating back more than 12,000 years. The cave is located on the north end of the island at Mile 51 near Whale Pass. Free two-hour Forest Service tours (907/828-3304, www.fs.fed.us/r10/tongass) are offered three times a day in the summer. Bring flashlights, warm clothing, and hiking boots; hard hats are provided. Reservations are required at least two days in advance; Children under age 7 are not allowed.

Three miles south of El Capitan is another underground wonder. A stream flows out of Cavern Lake, and then underground for a few hundred feet before emerging from **Cavern Lake Cave.** You can wade up the water into the cave for 150 feet or so.

Canoeing

The **Sarkar Canoe Trail** is an easy 15-mile loop route with boardwalk portages connecting seven lakes. The trailhead is at the south end of Sarkar Lake, on the northwest side of POW off Forest Road 20.

A more strenuous route is the 34-mile-long **Honker Divide Canoe Route.** This paddle-and-portage route begins near Coffman Cove at the bridge over Hatchery Creek on Forest Road 30, and works up Hatchery Creek to Honker Lake, which has a Forest Service cabin ($35). You may need to pull the canoe up shallow sections of the creek. The route then continues over Honker Divide on a 1-mile-long portage to the upper Thorne River before heading downstream all the way to Thorne Bay. There is a 2-mile portage to avoid dangerous rapids and falls. The route is strenuous and should only be attempted by experienced canoeists. For more information on either of these routes, contact the Thorne Bay Ranger District (907/828-3304, www.fs.fed.us/r10/tongass).

Sea Kayaking

With its hundreds of miles of rugged coastline and numerous small islands, inlets, and bays, POW offers tremendous opportunities for sea kayakers. One of the wildest areas is the 98,000-acre **South Prince of Wales Wilderness,** but access is difficult, and much of the area is exposed to fierce ocean storms. Nearby **Dall Island** has exploring possibilities, but parts of it have been logged. On beaches exposed to the open sea, you'll occasionally find beautiful Japanese glass fishing floats that have washed ashore.

Three other wilderness areas along POW's outer coast—**Maurelle Islands, Warren Island,** and **Coronation Island**—offer remote and rarely visited places to see whales, sea otters, and nesting colonies of seabirds. You're likely to see a few fishers but nobody else.

TONGASS NATIONAL FOREST

Three times larger than any other national forest in the country, Southeast Alaska's Tongass National Forest is America's rainforest masterpiece. Within these 17 million acres are magnificent coastal forests, dozens of glaciers, snowcapped peaks, an abundance of wildlife, hundreds of verdant islands, and a wild beauty that has long since been lost elsewhere.

Originally named Alexander Archipelago Forest Reserve in 1902, the area became Tongass National Forest in 1907 by proclamation of President Theodore Roosevelt. It was later enlarged to include most of the Panhandle. For more information, visit the Forest Service Tongass website (www.fs.fed.us/r10/tongass) or contact the Southeast Alaska Discovery Center (907/228-6220, www.alaskacenters.gov) in Ketchikan.

RECREATION

The Tongass is a paradise for those who love the outdoors. It has dozens of scenic hiking trails and over 1,000 miles of logging roads accessible by mountain bike (if you don't mind the clear-cuts and can avoid the logging trucks and flying gravel). The islands contain hundreds of crystal-clear lakes, many with Forest Service cabins on them. Fishing enthusiasts will enjoy catching salmon, cutthroat trout, and other fish from these lakes, the ocean, and the thousands of streams that empty into bays.

The Inside Passage is composed of a wonderful maze of semiprotected waterways, a sea kayaker's dream come true. Particularly popular with kayakers are Misty Fiords National Monument, Admiralty Island National Monument, Glacier Bay National Park, and the waters around Sitka and Juneau, but outstanding sea kayaking opportunities can be found throughout Southeast Alaska. If you have a sea kayak, access is easy, since they can be carried on the ferries (for an extra charge). Ask the Forest Service recreation staff in the local district offices for information on nearby routes and conditions.

WILDERNESS AREAS

Less than 5 percent of the Tongass has been logged or otherwise developed, so it isn't necessary to visit an official wilderness area to see truly wild country. However, 21 wilderness areas total well over 5 million acres in the national forest, offering outstanding recreational opportunities. The largest are **Misty Fiords National Monument** (2.1 million acres) near Ketchikan and **Admiralty Island National Monument** (956,000 acres) near Juneau. Other major wildernesses include **Tracy Arm-Fords Terror** (653,000 acres) south of Juneau, **Stikine-LeConte** (449,000 acres) near Wrangell, **Russell Fiord** (349,000 acres) near Yakutat, **South Baranof** (320,000 acres) south of Sitka, and **West Chichagof-Yakobi** (265,000 acres) near Pelican.

GETTING THERE

Ferry

The **Inter-Island Ferry Authority** (907/826-4848 or 866/308-4848, www.interislandferry.com) operates the MV *Prince of Wales,* a vehicle and passenger ferry with daily round-trips between Ketchikan and the tiny spot called Hollis (no services other than phones and toilets). It's 25 miles from Hollis to Klawock, the nearest town. Reservations are strongly recommended for vehicles on this ferry.

Shoo Teen Taxi Service (907/965-4949) provides shuttle vans from the ferry in Hollis to and from Craig ($35 pp). Call a day ahead for reservations.

Air

On a rainy midsummer day when the clouds were almost to the water, I sat in Craig waiting to fly back to Ketchikan. The weather looked marginal to me, but when I asked at the air-taxi counter if they were flying, the woman glanced outside and nonchalantly responded, "Oh sure, it looks pretty good today." We flew. Three air-taxi operators, **ProMech Air** (907/225-3845 or

Several wilderness areas, such as the remote islands off the west coast of Prince of Wales (Coronation, Maurelle, and Warren Islands), are exposed to the open ocean and are inaccessible for much of the year, even by floatplane. Others, such as the Stikine-LeConte, Admiralty Island, Russell Fiord, and Petersburg Creek-Duncan Salt Chuck Wilderness Areas are relatively accessible. There are developed trails or canoe and kayak routes within the Misty Fiords, Admiralty Island, Stikine-LeConte, Tebenkof Bay, and Petersburg Creek-Duncan Salt Chuck Wilderness Areas.

FOREST SERVICE CABINS

Tongass National Forest has 150 public recreation cabins scattered throughout Southeast Alaska, providing a wonderful way to see the *real* Alaska. Most cabins are rustic one-room Pan Adobe log structures, 12 by 14 feet in size, with bunk space for 4-6 people. They generally have a woodstove with cut firewood (some have oil stoves), an outhouse, and rowboats at cabins along lakes. You'll need to bring your own bedding, cookstove, cooking and eating utensils, Leatherman or Swiss Army knife, food, playing cards, candles, flashlight, matches, and mousetraps. (Some of this will probably be there, but it's better to be sure by bringing your own.) Cabins have no cell phone coverage, so you're generally on your own when it comes to emergencies.

Many Forest Service cabins can only be reached by floatplane. These flights can be very expensive, but even those on a tight budget should plan to spend some time at one of these cabins. A few can be reached by hiking from towns (Ketchikan, Petersburg, Juneau, and Skagway), cutting out the expensive flight. If you're considering a flightseeing trip anyway, make it to one of these remote cabins where you get to see what the country is really like. This is one splurge you won't regret.

CABIN RESERVATIONS

The Forest Service charges $25-50 per night for these cabins, with all fees going toward their maintenance. Reservations are on a first-come, first-served basis up to six months in advance; some of the most popular cabins are even chosen by lottery. The Forest Service publishes brochures describing recreation facilities, and can also supply Tongass National Forest maps showing cabin locations. Both the **Forest Service Information Center** (907/586-8751) at Centennial Hall in Juneau and the **Southeast Alaska Discovery Center** (907/228-6220) in Ketchikan, can provide cabin information, as can the ranger district offices scattered around the Southeast. Make reservations and find additional information at 518/885-3639, 877/444-6777, or www.recreation.gov.

800/860-3845, www.promechair.com), **Pacific Airways** (907/225-3500 or 877/360-3500, www.flypacificairways.com), and **Taquan Air** (907/225-8800 or 800/770-8800, www.taquanair.com) have daily floatplane service from Ketchikan to Craig, Hollis, and Thorne Bay. Taquan also flies to smaller settlements scattered across the island, including Coffman Cove, Naukati, Point Baker, Point Protection, and Whale Pass. **Harris Aircraft Services** (907/966-3050 or 877/966-3050, www.harrisaircraft.com) flies most days between Sitka and Klawock.

GETTING AROUND

For a good road map, pick up the ***Prince of Wales Road Guide*** at Forest Service offices in Ketchikan, Craig, or Thorne Bay. In the last few years the roads have improved dramatically, and the most-used sections are now paved and in good condition, including roads connecting Hollis, Craig, Klawock, Thorne Bay, and Coffman Cove. Some 1,500 miles of rough gravel roads, most built for logging operations, remain on POW, providing lots of interesting mountain bike rides—if you don't mind the old clear-cuts and soggy weather.

Rent cars in Craig from **Wilderness Car Rental** (907/755-2691 or 800/949-2205, www.wildernesscarrental.com) or **Shaub-Ellison Tire & Fuel** (907/826-3450). **Hollis Adventure Rentals** (907/530-7040, www.harentals.com) has vehicle rentals at the ferry dock in Hollis, and also rents skiffs, kayaks, canoes, fishing poles, and camping gear.

Wrangell

Quiet, friendly, and conservative, the settlement of Wrangell (pop. 1,700) sits on an island near the mouth of the Stikine River. The streets are full of folks in pickup trucks, their dogs hanging out the back and country tunes on the radio. Wrangell is quite unlike its neighbor, prim and proper Petersburg. Wrangell's inner harbor resonates with salmon- and shrimp-processing plants, fishing boats, and seaplanes, while totem poles guard historic Chief Shakes Island. Surrounding the harbor are old buildings on piles, wooded hillsides, and snowcapped mountains. Wrangell is compact enough that visitors can hoof it around to the most interesting sites in an hour or two and still have time to buy beer for the ferry. To see the area right, however, you should spend a couple of days, or longer if you're interested in exploring the mighty Stikine River.

HISTORY

Redoubt St. Dionysius

The third-oldest community in Alaska, Wrangell is the only one to have been governed by four nations: Tlingit, Russia, Britain, and the United States. Tlingit legends tell of an ancient time when advancing glaciers forced them to abandon their coastal life and move to what is now British Columbia. As the ice retreated after the last ice age, the Stikine River was their entryway back to the newly reborn land. When the Tlingits discovered that the river suddenly disappeared under a glacier, they sent old women to explore, expecting never to see them again. One can only imagine their astonishment when the women returned to lead canoes full of people out to the coast.

For many centuries the Tlingits lived in the Stikine River area, paddling canoes upstream to catch salmon and trade with interior tribes. Similarly, the river figured strongly in Wrangell's founding. Russians began trading with Stikine Indians in 1811; by 1834 the British were trying to move in on their lucrative fur-trading monopoly. To prevent this, Lieutenant Dionysius Zarembo and a band of men left New Archangel (the present-day Sitka) to establish a Russian fort near the mouth of the Stikine River. The settlement, later to become Wrangell, was originally named Redoubt St. Dionysius. When the British ship *Dryad* anchored near the river, the Russians boarded the vessel and refused to allow access to the Stikine. The *Dryad* was forced to return south, but a wedge had been driven in Russia's Alaskan empire. Five years later, the Hudson's Bay Company acquired a long-term lease to the coastline from the Russian government. Redoubt St. Dionysius became Fort Stikine, and the Union Jack flew from town flagpoles.

Gold Fever

The discovery of gold on Stikine River gravel bars in 1861 brought a boom to Fort Stikine. Hundreds of gold-seekers arrived, but the deposit proved relatively small, and most prospectors soon drifted on to other areas. With the transfer of Alaska to American hands in 1867, Fort Stikine was renamed Wrangell, after Baron Ferdinand Petrovich von Wrangel, governor of the Russian-American Company. Its population dwindled until 1872 when gold was again discovered in the Cassiar region of British Columbia. Thousands of miners quickly flooded the area, traveling on steamboats up the Stikine. Wrangell achieved notoriety as a town filled with hard-drinking rabble-rousers,

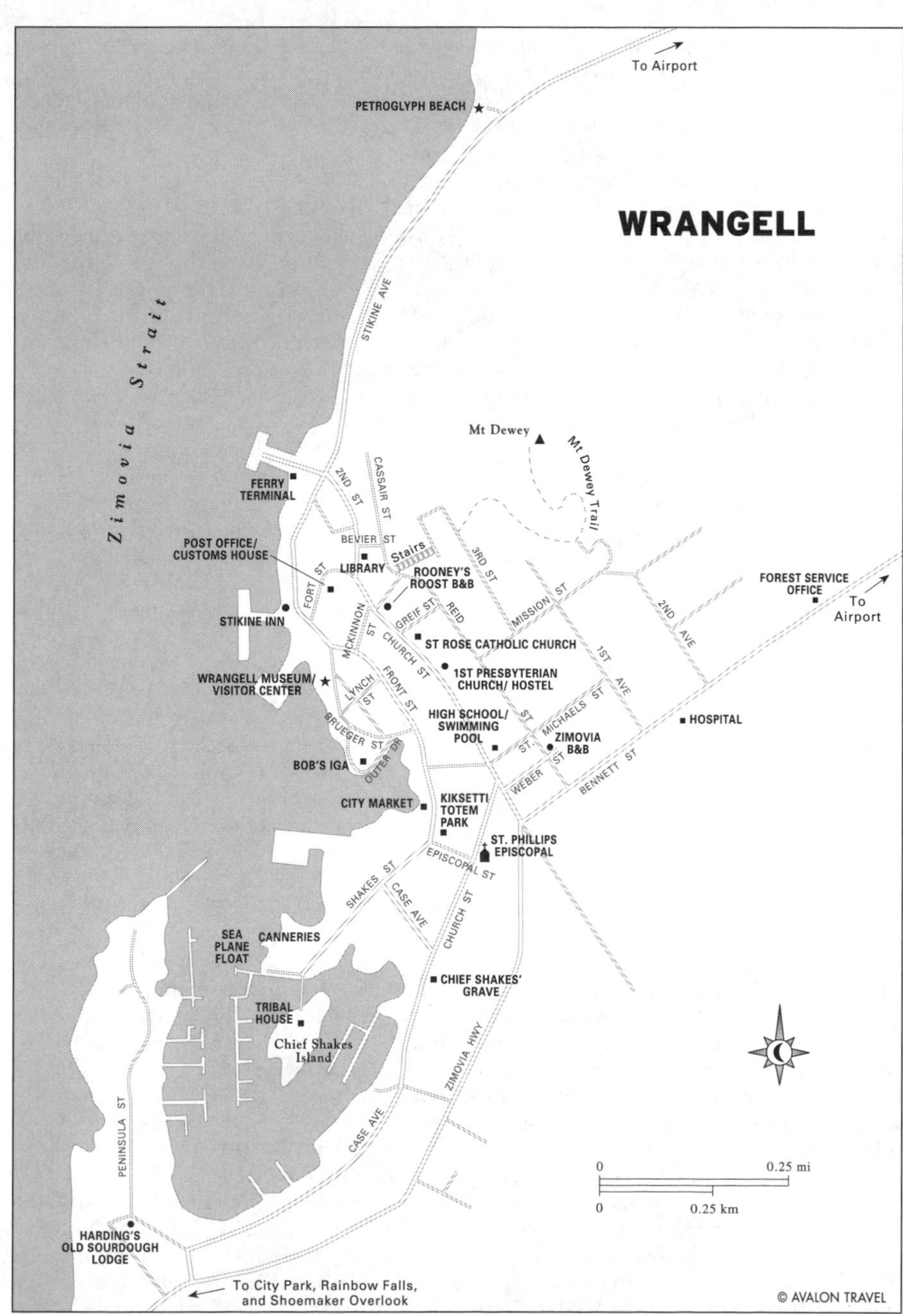
WRANGELL
To Airport
PETROGLYPH BEACH
Zimovia Strait
STIKINE AVE
Mt Dewey
Mt Dewey Trail
FERRY TERMINAL
2ND ST
CASSAIR ST
BEVIER ST
Stairs
3RD ST
POST OFFICE/ CUSTOMS HOUSE
LIBRARY
ROONEY'S ROOST B&B
FORT ST
STIKINE INN
MCKINNON ST
GREIF ST
REID
MISSION ST
2ND AVE
FOREST SERVICE OFFICE
To Airport
ST ROSE CATHOLIC CHURCH
CHURCH ST
1ST PRESBYTERIAN CHURCH/ HOSTEL
1ST AVE
WRANGELL MUSEUM/ VISITOR CENTER
LYNCH ST
FRONT ST
HIGH SCHOOL/ SWIMMING POOL
ST. MICHAELS ST
ZIMOVIA B&B
HOSPITAL
BRUEGER ST
OUTER DR
BOB'S IGA
WEBER ST
BENNETT ST
CITY MARKET
KIKSETTI TOTEM PARK
ST. PHILLIPS EPISCOPAL
EPISCOPAL ST
SHAKES ST
CASE AVE
CHURCH ST
SEA PLANE FLOAT
CANNERIES
CHIEF SHAKES' GRAVE
TRIBAL HOUSE
Chief Shakes Island
ZIMOVIA HWY
CASE AVE
PENINSULA ST
0
0.25 mi
0
0.25 km
HARDING'S OLD SOURDOUGH LODGE
To City Park, Rainbow Falls, and Shoemaker Overlook
© AVALON TRAVEL

gamblers, and shady ladies. When the naturalist John Muir visited in 1879 he called it

> *the most inhospitable place at first sight I had ever seen...a lawless draggle of wooden huts and houses, built in crooked lines, wrangling around the boggy shore of the island for a mile or so in the general form of the letter S, without the slightest subordination to the points of the compass or to building laws of any kind.*

By the late 1880s the second gold rush had subsided, and lumbering and fishing were getting started as local industries. The Klondike gold rush of the late 1890s brought another short-lived boom to Wrangell as the Stikine was again tapped for access to interior Canada, but Skagway's Chilkoot Trail became the preferred route. With its rowdy days behind, Wrangell settled into the 20th century as a home to logging and fishing operations, still mainstays of the local economy. Rebuilt after destructive fires in 1906 and 1952, much of downtown is now on rock-fill and pilings. Today, Wrangell is searching for a more prosperous future—and tourism is right at the forefront of that quest—while getting by on the remaining industries: fishing, construction, and small timber operations. It's an easy-going, slow-paced, and friendly town and a good place to unwind.

SIGHTS

Wrangell is home to the oldest Protestant church building in Alaska, the **First Presbyterian Church,** as well as the oldest Roman Catholic parish, **St. Rose of Lima Catholic Church.** Appropriately located on Church Street, both were founded in 1879. The large red neon cross atop the Presbyterian church is one of only two in the world used as a navigational aid (the other is in Rio de Janeiro).

Keep your eyes open for local kids selling **garnets** for $0.25 to $10, depending on the size. They put up tables at the museum and on the cruise ship dock when ships are in port. These imperfect but attractive stones come from a garnet ledge along the Stikine River, deeded to the Boy Scouts in 1962 by a former mayor. At one time the mine was owned by the Alaska Garnet Mining and Manufacturing Company, the world's first women-only corporation.

Chief Shakes Island

This is the centerpiece of picturesque Wrangell harbor. A footbridge at the bottom of Front Street near Wrangell's cannery and cold-storage plant gives access to the island. Here you'll find the **Tribal House of the Bear** (907/874-2023, www.shakesisland.com), a Native Alaskan log house built in 1939–1940 by the Civilian Conservation Corps (CCC). Inside are various artifacts, including beautifully carved house posts that date from 1835. The house is only open for tours when cruise ships are in port, or by appointment. Surrounding the house are seven totems, reproductions of older poles from the area. Shakes Island is especially beautiful at night, surrounded by the town and harbor.

The Shakes lineage was established more than three centuries ago, after the Stikine Tlingits defeated Niska invaders and then forced the vanquished chief, We-Shakes, to give away his name in exchange for peace. Head off the island to **Chief Shakes V's gravesite,** opposite the Hansen Boat Shop on Case Avenue. A white fence surrounds it, and two carved killer whales watch silently. (Surprisingly, Chief Shakes isn't really buried in this grave.)

Several impressive totem poles, carved by the CCC, stand in front of the library on 2nd Street. Wrangell's small **Kiksetti Totem Park,** next to the City Market along Front Street, has four poles that were carved without the aid of power tools.

Wrangell Museum and Visitor Center

Given the size of Wrangell, its museum (296 Outer Dr., 907/874-3770, Mon.–Sat. 10 A.M.–5 P.M. May–Sept. and when cruise ships are in port, Tues.–Sat. 1–5 P.M. the rest of the year, $5 adults, $3 seniors and children

© DON PITCHER

Tribal House of the Bear on Chief Shakes Island

ages 6–12, younger children free, $12 families) is a delightful surprise. Housed in the spacious and modern Nolan Center, professional exhibits take you through Wrangell's rich past with an in-depth look at the Tlingit, Russian, British, and American peoples who all called this place home. Petroglyphs, Native Alaskan baskets, old photographs, and local relics are crowded into this provocative museum. Of particular interest are the original house posts from the Chief Shakes house. Carved in the 1740s—before contact with Europeans—they are the oldest Tlingit house posts in existence. The gift shop has a fine selection of books.

Also within the Nolan Center is the **Wrangell Visitors Center** (907/874-3901 or 800/367-9745, www.wrangellalaska.org, Mon.–Fri. 8 A.M.–5 P.M. and when cruise ships are in port). You can pick up brochures here if the museum is open, and a computer and Wi-Fi are available for a fee.

Petroglyphs

Hundreds of ancient petroglyphs (rock carvings) are found on Wrangell Island, but precisely who carved them or when is uncertain. They may date back more than 8,000 years. The best nearby carvings are only a 20-minute walk from town. To get there, turn left (north) from the ferry terminal and walk 0.7 miles to a small parking area on the left. A newly built boardwalk provides access to the beach, where you will find a dozen petroglyph rocks along upper parts of the beach, especially those on the right side, facing the water. One of the best, a killer whale, lies on the edge of a grassy lawn to the right of the path. Most petroglyphs face seaward and are near the high-tide line. They may be covered by water if the tide is over 10 feet. To protect the originals, the state has set up several stone reproductions of the petroglyphs along the boardwalk for those who want to make rubbings. Rubbings are made by

THE PETROGLYPH MYSTERY

Petroglyphs (ancient rock carvings) are found along the West Coast from Kodiak to the Columbia River, although the greatest concentration is between Sitka and Puget Sound. The coastal type is very different from the petroglyphs of the interior plateau and central Oregon, but has similarities to carvings in the Amur River region of Siberia. Although a single style can be followed down the coast, no one knows who carved the petroglyphs, when they were carved, or why. Contemporary Native Alaskans have no knowledge of them. Many petroglyphs – such as those in Wrangell – face west and were carved on rocks below the high-tide mark. Were they territorial boundary signs? Greetings to returning salmon? Sacred places? As with Stonehenge, we can only speculate. Some have posited that the petroglyphs were just the idle doodles of some ancient graffiti artist. This is unlikely not only from a cultural perspective but also because of the difficulty of pecking out a design on these hard fine-grained rocks using only stone tools.

© DON PITCHER

petroglyphs along the shore in Wrangell

placing rice paper—available in local stores—over the copies and rubbing the surface with crayons, ferns, or charcoal. Other petroglyphs are in the Wrangell Museum and in front of the library. Do not make rubbings of the originals.

Mt. Dewey

An excellent half-mile boardwalk and trail wind up Mt. Dewey (actually more of a hill) from 3rd Street behind the high school. It's a steep 15-minute climb up to the top, where a platform provides a vantage point over Wrangell. You could probably find a place to camp up here in a pinch. On a wild stormy night in 1879, John Muir did just that. He also decided to build a huge bonfire atop the hill, however, its flames dancing off the clouds. Muir later wrote, "Of all the thousands of campfires I have elsewhere built none was just like this one, rejoicing in triumphant strength and beauty in the heart of the rain-laden gale." To the Native Alaskan people below, however, the fire ignited fears of evil spirits, and as Muir's partner noted, "the Tlingits ever afterward eyed Muir askance, as a mysterious being whose ways and motives were beyond all conjecture."

ANAN CREEK WILDLIFE-VIEWING SITE

Anan Creek, 30 miles south of Wrangell on the mainland's Cleveland Peninsula, is a fine place to watch black and brown bears catching salmon and steelhead. A 0.5-mile boardwalk leads from saltwater to an observation platform above the creek, and a three-sided blind sits closer to the falls, where most of the action takes place. The best time to visit is the peak of the pink salmon run, mid-July–mid-August. Forest Service personnel are at the trailhead and observation area to provide information. No food is allowed along these trails, and flash photography is discouraged. The creek is shaded by tall trees, and it's often raining, making photography a challenge.

Because of Anan Creek's popularity, permits ($10) are required, and a maximum of 60 visitors are allowed per day in July–August. If you're traveling on your own, get the permit from the Forest Service office in Wrangell (907/874-2323, www.fs.fed.us/r10/tongass). If you're in a guided group, the guide already has your permit.

The Forest Service's **Anan Bay Cabin** (518/885-3639 or 877/444-6777, www.recreation.gov, $45) is just 1 mile away on a good trail, but reserve early since it's often booked months in advance.

Many visitors to Anan Creek arrive on flights by **Sunrise Aviation** (907/874-2319 or 800/874-2311, www.sunriseflights.com) from Wrangell or **Taquan Air** (907/225-8800 or 800/770-8800, www.taquanair.com) from Ketchikan.

A number of companies offer guided boat trips to Anan Creek, including **Alaska Vistas** (907/874-3006 or 866/874-3006, www.alaskavistas.com), **Alaska Waters** (907/874-2378 or 800/347-4462, www.alaskawaters.com), **Alaska Charters and Adventures** (907/874-4157 or 888/993-2750, www.alaskaupclose.com), and **Breakaway Adventures** (907/874-2488 or 888/385-2488, www.breakawayadventures.com). Expect to pay $210–265 per person for a trip that includes 4–5 hours on the ground at Anan (plus 1 hour or so each way in transit). If you're more experienced in the wilderness, Breakaway also offers unguided tours to Anan for $107 per person for all day.

Those with a sea kayak may want to paddle along the east side of Wrangell Island to Anan Bay. En route, be sure to visit scenic **Berg Bay,** an area rich in moose, mountain goats, grizzlies, deer, geese, and other wildlife. A Forest Service cabin ($45) is available here, and a trail leads from the cabin along Berg Creek several miles into a cirque basin with old mine ruins.

EVENTS

Wrangell's **Stikine River Birding Festival** in early May celebrates the arrival of spring with natural history presentations, bird-watching tours, and more. Mid-May–mid-June, pull out your fishing pole for the **King Salmon Derby**—top prize is $6,000. The main summer event is the town's **July 4th** celebration, with a parade, a logging show, log rolling contests, a tug of war, live music, and fireworks. All this is funded by a handful of teenagers and their families who run downtown food booths in June.

RECREATION

Rain Walker Expeditions (907/874-2549, www.rainwalkerexpeditions.com) rents bikes, canoes, and kayaks from the Breakaway office across from Stikine Inn. Owner Marie Oboczky leads informative nature hikes and bus tours lasting from two hours to all day. They're fun and geared to your area of interest, whether it's petroglyphs or rain forests.

A paved **walking and biking path** runs from Wrangell for six miles to the trailhead for Rainbow Falls at Shoemaker Bay.

Alaska Vistas (907/874-3006 or 866/874-3006, www.alaskavistas.com) guides sea kayaking day trips and multiday adventures in the Wrangell area. They also rent canoes and kayaks and offer water taxi shuttles for do-it-yourselfers heading to Forest Service cabins or into the wilderness.

Klondike Bike (502 Wrangell Ave., 907/874-2453, www.klondikebike.com) has quality mountain bikes for rent if you want to explore the many miles of old logging roads.

Muskeg Meadows Golf Course (907/874-4653, www.wrangellalaskagolf.com) is an attractive nine-hole course with putting greens, a pro shop, and driving range.

Wrangell's **swimming pool** (907/874-2444) is at the high school. Fishing and sightseeing **charters** are available through a number of local outfits; get brochures from the visitor center.

Boat Tours

Wrangell is the primary starting point for fun and fast jet-boat tours to watch bears at Anan Creek or to motor up the mighty Stikine River. Three companies also offer excellent jet-boat trips to LeConte Glacier and Petersburg: **Breakaway Adventures** (907/874-3455 or 888/385-2488, www.breakawayadventures.com), **Alaska Waters** (907/874-2378 or 800/347-4462, www.alaskawaters.com), and **Alaska Vistas** (907/874-3006 or 866/874-3006, www.alaskavistas.com). Expect to pay $205–240 per person for the all-day tour that includes a two-hour stop in Petersburg.

Hiking

Scenic **Rainbow Falls Trail,** a moderately steep 0.75-mile hike (710 stair steps!), begins across the road from Shoemaker Bay Campground, five miles south of town. More ambitious bodies can continue three miles up the trail to **Shoemaker Overlook** (1,500 feet). The trail accesses large ridgetop muskeg areas and ends at a three-sided Adirondack-style shelter offering a panoramic vista of Zimovia Strait. The trail and shelter provide an excellent opportunity for an overnight camping trip. The trail is steep and often muddy but has a boardwalk in places.

Logging roads crisscross most of Wrangell Island, providing cycling opportunities for mountain bike enthusiasts—if you enjoy seeing cut-over land. Those with wheels may want to visit several areas on the island. **Long Lake Trail,** 28 miles southeast of Wrangell along Forest Road 6271, is a 0.5-mile boardwalk that ends at an Adirondack shelter complete with a rowboat, a fire grill, and an outhouse. In the same vicinity is a 300-foot path to **Highbrush Lake,** where you'll find a small boat in which to practice your rowing skills. Individuals with disabilities may want to try fishing at **Salamander Creek,** 23 miles south of town on Forest Road 6265, where ramps lead right up to a pad along the creek. There is good fishing for king salmon here, along with three campsites. For information on cabins and other trails around Wrangell, visit the Forest Service's **Wrangell Ranger District Office** (525 Bennett St., 907/874-2323, www.fs.fed.us/r10/tongass).

Cabins

There are 21 different Forest Service cabins (518/885-3639 or 877/444-6777, www.recreation.gov, $45) near Wrangell, including several in the Stikine River region. The closest is at **Virginia Lake,** accessible by floatplane. Another nearby cabin is at **Kunk Lake,** across Zimovia Strait from the south end of the Wrangell Island road system. Access is by kayak, or skiff if you can get someone to run you across. A 1.5-mile trail climbs to a three-sided shelter at the lake. From here it's a relatively easy climb into high-elevation muskeg and alpine areas that cross Etolin Island.

ACCOMMODATIONS

Housed within the Presbyterian church, Wrangell's **Youth Hostel** (220 Church St., 907/874-3534, late May–early Sept., $16 pp) is clean and well-managed but nothing fancy, with air mattresses for sleeping as well as kitchen and shower facilities. A family room is available if you call ahead. The hostel is open all day.

Centrally located and with many rooms facing picturesque Zimovia Strait, **Stikine Inn** (107 Stikine Ave., 907/874-3388 or 888/874-3388, www.stikineinn.com) has a variety of newly updated lodging options. Standard guest rooms cost $115–143 s or $134–151 d, and suites are $152–165 for up to six people.

With its quiet edge-of-the-woods location,

Zimovia B&B (319 Webber St., 907/874-2626 or 866/946-6842, www.zimoviabnb.com, $100 d) is a cedar-shingled home just a few blocks from downtown. The two guest rooms each have private baths and entrances, and one includes a sauna. Breakfast features home-baked pastries, and the owners provide a complimentary tour plus transport around town.

Rooney's Roost B&B (206 McKinnon St., 907/874-2026, www.rooneysroost.com) has five comfortable guest rooms for just $75 d with a shared bath or $95 d with private baths. The attractive home is centrally located, and a gourmet breakfast is included. The owners are friendly too.

Located two miles south of town, **Grand View B&B** (907/874-3225, www.grandviewbnb.com, $105 s or $115 d, no credit cards) is a newly built beachfront home along the Zimovia Strait. Three guest rooms have private baths and queen beds. Amenities include a kitchen and living room, Wi-Fi, and private entrances. Owner Judy Baker serves a filling hot breakfast each morning. Transportation from town is provided.

CAMPING

There is free tent camping (no RVs) at **City Park** just beyond the ball field, two miles south of the ferry on the water side of Zimovia Highway. The official limit is 24 hours, but this isn't strictly enforced. Showers are available at a coin laundry near Chief Shakes Island, and at the high school swimming pool.

You'll find additional camping at the city-run **Shoemaker Bay Recreational Area** (907/874-2444, year-round, RVs $25 with electricity, tents free), five miles south of town and right alongside the highway. RVers get a pass to the city pool for showers and a free swim, and the area is near trails to Rainbow Falls and Shoemaker Overlook. The Forest Service's free **Nemo Campground** is 14 miles south of town and up Forest Roads 16 and 6267; from here there are impressive views across Zimovia Strait.

Alaska Waters RV Park (241 Berger St., 907/874-2378 or 800/347-4462, www.alaskawaters.com, RVs $25) is on the south side of the harbor.

FOOD

For breakfast, head to **Diamond C Restaurant** (223 Front St., 907/874-3677, daily 6 A.M.–3 P.M., $9–11).

With panoramic views across Zimovia Strait and the best meals in town, **Stikine Inn Restaurant** (107 Stikine Ave., 907/874-3388 or 888/874-3388, www.stikineinn.com, daily 11 A.M.–9:30 P.M. summer, daily 11 A.M.–8 P.M. winter, dinner entrées $15–30) is your best bet in Wrangell. It's open for lunch and dinner and serves big portions of fresh shrimp, halibut, salmon, steaks, burgers, pasta, salads, sandwiches, and other fare. A cozy room doubles as a morning espresso bar (great lattes) and smoke-free lounge, with a flat-screen TV and a fireplace. In addition to the Stikine Inn, you can find espresso—and use the free Wi-Fi—at the summer-only **Java Junkie** next to the downtown dock.

Zak's Café (316 Front St., 907/874-3355, Mon.–Sat. 11 A.M.–8 P.M.) offers a good variety of food: pasta, stir-fries, and steaks for dinner ($14–22) and lunchtime salads, sandwiches, and wraps ($7–10). The setting is simple and clean, with fast service.

Bob's IGA (Outer Dr., 907/874-2341) has a deli with inexpensive sandwiches. **City Market** (Front St., 907/874-3336) is Wrangell's other grocery store. Both are closed on Sunday and at 6 P.M. other nights.

Locals hang out in the smoke-filled **Marine Lounge** (274 Shakes St., 907/874-3005)—a.k.a. the Hungry Beaver—which has the best pizzas in town, along with various pub grub. Tell them to go light on the cheese. It's one of the few late-night place for food.

SERVICES

The Forest Service's **Wrangell Ranger District Office** (525 Bennett St., 907/874-2323, www.fs.fed.us/r10/tongass) is 0.75 miles from town on the left side of the road. It has information on local hiking trails, the Stikine River, and nearby recreation cabins.

Adjacent to the Stikine Inn is **River's Edge Fine Arts and Gifts** (907/874-3508, www.marineartist.com), selling locally made clothing, carved wooden bowls, pottery, and jewelry, plus the distinctive marine art of owner Brenda Schwartz-Yeager.

The **Irene Ingle Public Library** (124 2nd Ave., 907/674-3535, Mon. and Fri. 10 A.M.–5 P.M., Tues.–Thurs. 1–5 P.M. and 7–9 P.M., Sat. 9 A.M.–5 P.M.) houses a good collection of books about Alaska and a couple of petroglyphs out front, along with computers for Web access. Head to the Nolan Center theater for weekend movies.

Located out on Airport Road, the **Wrangell Medical Center** (310 Bennett St., 907/874-7000, www.wrangellmedicalcenter.com) has physicians on staff.

GETTING THERE AND AROUND

Wrangell's **ferry terminal** (907/874-3711) is right in town. **Alaska Marine Highway** (907/465-3941 or 800/642-0066, www.dot.state.ak.us/amhs) ferries head both north and south almost daily during the summer, but the terminal is open only for vessel arrivals and departures.

The airport is 1.5 miles from town on Bennett Street. **Alaska Airlines** (800/426-0333, www.alaskaair.com) has daily flights from Wrangell to Juneau, Ketchikan, Petersburg, and Sitka. **Sunrise Aviation** (907/874-2319 or 800/874-2311, www.sunriseflights.com) provides flightseeing trips and charter flights to nearby Forest Service cabins and Anan Creek. They often have seat-fare rates if someone else has already set up a charter; this can be a fast and reasonable way to fly to Petersburg or Prince of Wales.

Rent cars at the airport from **Practical Rent-A-Car** (907/874-3975). Both **Northern Lights Taxi** (907/874-4646) and **Star Cab** (907/874-3622) charge $7 from the airport to town.

THE STIKINE RIVER

Seven miles north of Wrangell is the Stikine River, one of the top 10 wild rivers of Canada and the fastest navigable river in North America. The river begins its 330-mile journey to the sea high inside British Columbia's Spatsizi Wilderness Park. The 55-mile-long **Grand Canyon of the Stikine,** just above Telegraph Creek, British Columbia, has thousand-foot walls enclosing fierce white water. River travel is easier below Telegraph Creek all the way to Wrangell between the high peaks of the coast range and past glaciers and forested hills. At one spot on the river, 21 different glaciers are visible! These glaciers dump tons of silt into the river, coloring it a milky gray; at the mouth of the Stikine the sea takes on this color for miles in all directions. So much for the advertisements about "glacially pure" water.

© DON PITCHER

Mist rises from the rain forest along the Stikine River.

Each spring, upward of 1,500 bald eagles flock to the river mouth to eat "hooligan" (eulachon), an oily fish that spawns here late March–early May. The fish also attract hundreds of thousands of gulls and kittiwakes, plus harbor seals, Steller sea lions, and even killer whales.

River Tours

Several Wrangell charter boat operators provide

fun jet-boat trips up the Stikine River with a lunch break at Shakes Glacier and fast runs up the back sloughs. Three of the larger operators are **Breakaway Adventures** (907/874-3455 or 888/385-2488, www.breakawayadventures.com), **Alaska Waters** (907/874-2378 or 800/347-4462, www.alaskawaters.com), and **Alaska Vistas** (907/874-3006 or 866/874-3006, www.alaskavistas.com). All of these do a great job of showing the sights, but the Breakaway and Alaska Vistas trips are cheaper ($175 versus $200 for a 5–6-hour trip) and sometimes include a soak at Chief Shakes Hot Springs. Alaska Waters uses a larger 22-person boat with an onboard restroom. For the quick version, Breakaway offers a four-hour trip to the glacier for $125 per person. Late-season trips are more likely to get closer to Chief Shakes Glacier, but increased calving in recent years (global warming?) has made it more difficult for boats to approach the face of the glacier. Despite this, you will certainly get up-close views of the icebergs.

Running the River

The Stikine River is a popular destination for kayakers, canoeists, and river rafters. (It's even more popular with local jet-boaters, so don't expect peace and quiet in the lower reaches.) Most folks choose to float down the river after being transported up from Wrangell by boat or plane. You will need to go through Customs (907/874-3415) at the Wrangell airport if you cross the border. In addition, a Canadian agent is frequently stationed along the river just across the border. The Forest Service publishes a helpful guide to canoeing or kayaking the Stikine River; it's available from the **Wrangell Ranger District** (907/874-2323, www.fs.fed.us/r10/tongass).

Stikine Riversong Lodge (250/235-3196, www.stikineriversong.com) in Telegraph Creek, 160 miles upriver from Wrangell, has lodging, supplies, and a pleasant café. The owners also offer river tours, canoe and kayak rentals, and will help you set up trips down the Stikine.

In Wrangell, rent kayaks and canoes from **Rain Walker Expeditions** (907/874-2549, www.rainwalkerexpeditions.com), **Breakaway Adventures** (907/874-3455 or 888/385-2488, www.breakawayadventures.com), or **Alaska Waters** (907/874-2378 or 800/347-4462, www.alaskawaters.com); they can also provide jet-boat transportation to Telegraph Creek. The latter company offers fun four-day safaris to the wild upper reaches of the river, with meals and lodging included for $1,700 per person; fall is the prettiest time to visit. **Alaska Vistas** (907/874-3006 or 866/874-3006, www.alaskavistas.com) leads 11-day raft trips down the Stikine River.

Camping and Cabins

The lower Stikine is a multichanneled silt-laden river nearly a mile wide in places. The route is spectacular, wildlife crowds the banks, campsites are numerous, and 13 Forest Service cabins (518/885-3639 or 877/444-6777, www.recreation.gov, $45) are available. One of the finest is the **Mount Rynda Cabin** along crystal-clear Andrew Creek, a spawning area for king salmon. You may also want to stay in one of the two extremely popular cabins near **Chief Shakes Hot Springs.** At the springs you'll discover beautifully maintained wooden hot tubs (one enclosed to protect you from the mosquitoes); these are great places to soak those aching muscles. The area gets mighty busy on summer weekends, so you probably won't have it to yourself, and things can get rowdy after the locals pop a few beers. Escape the crowds at the main hot springs by finding your own undeveloped springs nearby.

The upper portion of the Stikine is a vastly different river, with less noise and development than on the U.S. side of the border and a drier, colder climate. The vegetation reflects this. The historic settlement of **Telegraph Creek** is accessible by road from the rest of British Columbia, or you can charter a small plane or jet-boat from Wrangell. The upper river above Telegraph Creek is some of the wildest white water anywhere; canoeists and kayakers intent on running the river would do best to begin at Telegraph Creek.

Petersburg

Southeast Alaska's picture-postcard town, Petersburg (pop. 3,200) sits at the northern tip of Mitkof Island along Wrangell Narrows. Great white walls of snow and ice serve as a dramatic backdrop for the town. "Peter's Burg" was named after Peter Buschmann, who built a sawmill here in 1897, followed by a cannery three years later. With ample supplies of fish, timber, and glacial ice, the cannery proved an immediate success—32,750 cases of salmon were shipped that first season. Unlike boom-and-bust Wrangell, the planned community of Petersburg has kept pace with its expanding fishing base. A number of the present inhabitants are descended from Norwegian fishers, who found that the place reminded them of their native land. The language is still occasionally heard on Petersburg's streets, and Norwegian *rosemaling* (floral painting) can be found on shutters of the older homes.

Petersburg is a prosperous and squeaky-clean town with green lawns, tidy homes, and a hardworking heritage that may appear a bit cliquish to outsiders. The country around Petersburg is filled with opportunities for exploration by those who love the outdoors, but this off-the-beaten-path community still views tourism with a degree of skepticism. Although Petersburg has a lumber mill, fishing remains the main activity, with salmon, halibut, herring, crab, and shrimp all landed. The odor of fish hangs in the air, and bumper stickers proclaim "Friends don't let friends eat farmed salmon." With four canneries, Petersburg has the largest concentration in Southeast Alaska, and it is also home to a large halibut fleet.

© DON PITCHER

three generations in Norwegian costume

Wrangell Narrows

Between Wrangell and Petersburg, the ferry passes through tortuous Wrangell Narrows, a 46-turn nautical obstacle course that resembles a pinball game played by ships. This is one of the highlights of the Inside Passage trip and is even more exciting at night when the zigzag course is lit up like a Christmas tree. Be up front to see it. The larger cruise ships are too big to negotiate these shallow waters between Kupreanof and Mitkof Islands, thus sparing Petersburg from the tourist blitz and glitz that most other Southeast towns endure.

SIGHTS

In Town

Petersburg's main attraction is its gorgeous harbor and spectacular setting. The sharply pointed peak visible behind Petersburg is **Devil's Thumb,** a 9,077-foot mountain 30 miles away on the U.S.-Canada border. Built in 1912, the large **Sons of Norway Hall** (907/772-4575) stands on pilings over scenic Hammer Slough and is adorned with traditional Norwegian *rosemaling* designs. Next to Sons of Norway is the surprisingly small ***Valhalla,*** a replica of the original Viking boat. It was built in 1976 and sailed in the parade of ships at the bicentennial

celebration in New York Harbor. A memorial to fishers lost at sea stands next to the Sons of Norway Hall. Walk up the wooden street along **Hammer Slough** to see old homes hanging over this tidal creek. The boat harbors usually have several Steller sea lions cruising around.

Patti-Wagon Tours (907/772-4837) leads tours of the Trident Seafoods plant with a ride along Wrangell Narrows.

The **Petersburg Visitors Information Center** (corner of 1st St. and Fram St., 907/772-4636 or 866/484-4700 message only, www.petersburg.org, Sun. noon–4 P.M., Mon.–Sat. 9 A.M.–5 P.M. May–Sept., Mon.–Fri. 10 A.M.–2 P.M. Oct.–Apr.) has a helpful staff, lots of brochures, plus details on local attractions and Tongass National Forest recreation.

Clausen Memorial Museum (2nd St. and Fram St., 907/772-3598, www.clausenmuseum.net, Mon.–Sat. 10 A.M.–5 P.M. May–early Sept., call for winter hours, $3, children under 13 free) has exhibits on commercial fishing—including the world's largest king salmon (a 126-pound monster) and chum salmon (36 pounds)—plus the Cape Decision lighthouse lens, a 200-year-old Tlingit dugout canoe, a bentwood box, and other historical exhibits.

Sons of Norway Hall and replica Viking boat *Valhalla* along Hammer Slough

Outside is *The Fisk,* a fishy sculpture and fountain by Carson Boysen.

Nearby

A good place to watch for the American national bird is **Eagle's Roost Park,** north of the Petersburg Fisheries cannery. Upward of 30 eagles can be seen along here when the tide is low. Whales, seals, and sea lions are frequent sights in Frederick Sound near **Sandy Beach Park** north of town. Covered picnic tables and a playground add to the allure, and by late summer, pink salmon spawn in the tiny creek that flows through the park. Hike to the west side of Sandy Beach Park to discover ancient petroglyphs on the rocks. Icebergs from LeConte Glacier are common along the north side of Frederick Sound and sometimes drift across to Petersburg, especially in winter.

Heading out on the Road

South of town the main road is paved for 18 miles, with a gravel road continuing another 16 miles to the southeast end of Mitkof Island. From this point you have excellent views of the nearby mouth of the Stikine River and the white-capped peaks of the Coast Range. Canoeists and kayakers (with transportation) may want to start their trip up the Stikine from here rather than at Wrangell.

Approximately eight miles out is a small turnoff to **Falls Creek,** a pleasant picnic spot. Stop here to look at the fish ladder, built in 1959 and used by coho and pink salmon as well as steelhead.

Located 15 miles south of town, the **Blind River Rapids Trail** is an easy half-mile boardwalk that leads through the muskeg to a three-sided shelter overlooking the saltwater rapids. Bring your fishing pole. The trail loops back through the muskeg for a total distance of nearly one mile.

A **trumpeter swan observatory** is set up on Blind Slough 16 miles south of Petersburg. A dozen or so of these majestic birds overwinter here, and other waterfowl abound during spring and fall migrations. The state-run **Crystal Lake Fish Hatchery** (907/772-

4772), 18 miles south of Petersburg, produces king and coho salmon. The kings return in June–July, while the coho come back to spawn mid-August–September. Blind Slough flows away from the hatchery and is a great place to explore by canoe or kayak. The water gets swimmably warm by midsummer, and picnic tables sit among the trees. The Forest Service's Ohmer Creek Campground is three miles farther down the road. Also popular for swimming is **Man Made Hole,** an old quarry at Mile 20, with a picnic shelter and fishing.

LECONTE GLACIER

LeConte Glacier, the southernmost tidewater glacier in North America, dips into LeConte Bay on the mainland, 25 miles east of Petersburg. Part of the vast Stikine Ice Field, its glacial ice was once used by local fishers to keep their catches cold on the way to market in Seattle. Today, locals use it to cool their drinks. LeConte Bay is home to 2,000 harbor seals. The entire area is included within the 448,841-acre **Stikine-LeConte Wilderness.**

There are no Forest Service cabins in LeConte Bay, but an excellent one is on **Mallard Slough** (518/885-3639 or 877/444-6777, www.recreation.gov, $45), near its entrance. A 1.5-mile trail connects the cabin and Le Conte Bay, where you're likely to find icebergs high and dry at low tide. A fine trip for experienced sea kayakers is to head up the Stikine River from Wrangell and then into LeConte Bay, 10 miles north, before crossing Frederick Sound and continuing on to Petersburg. The total distance is approximately 50 miles (longer if you explore the Stikine River or LeConte Bay).

Getting There

The visitors center has a complete listing of boat charters for glacier sightseeing, whale-watching, and fishing. Reliable companies include **Kaleidoscope Cruises** (907/772-3736 or 800/868-4373, www.petersburglodgingandtours.com) and **Whale Song Cruises** (907/772-9393, www.whalesongcruises.com). Other companies also head to LeConte Glacier from Wrangell.

Kupreanof Flying Service (907/772-3396, www.kupreanof.com), **Nordic Air** (907/772-3535), **Pacific Wing** (907/772-4258, www.pacificwing.com), and **Temsco Helicopters** (907/772-4780 or 877/789-9501, www.temscoair.com) all offer flightseeing tours over the glacier.

EVENTS AND ENTERTAINMENT

Petersburg's **Little Norway Festival,** held each year on the weekend nearest Norwegian Independence Day (May 17), is the town's biggest event. The three-day festivities include a parade, traditional Scandinavian costumes, crafts, music, a pageant, and a big seafood feast on the beach. American **Independence Day** (July 4) is another time for fun, with a parade, blindfolded rowboat races, and fireworks. The annual king salmon derby in late May is always popular with locals.

The **Petersburg Canned Salmon Classic** is a contest to guess the number of cans of salmon packed by local canneries each year; $2,000 goes to the person who comes closest. It's awarded in early August.

Live music, booze, cigarette smoke, and a clientele of local toughs make for good fights in **Kito's Kave** (Sing Lee Alley, 907/772-3207). The nautically themed **Harbor Bar** (Nordic Dr., 907/772-4526) is a good place to meet local fishers over a beer.

RECREATION

Contact **Tongass Kayak Adventures** (907/772-4600, www.tongasskayak.com) for sea kayaking around the harbor and up Petersburg Creek. Guided four-hour trips are $85. All-day trips to LeConte Glacier include a water taxi and 10 hours of paddling near the glacier for $225. The company also runs multiday kayaking tours to LeConte Glacier, the Stikine River, and Tebenkof Bay, and rents kayaks for do-it-yourselfers. **Scandia House** (110 Nordic Dr., 907/772-4281 or 800/722-5006, www.scandiahousehotel.com) and **Doyle's Boat Rentals** (907/772-4439 or 877/442-4010, www.doylesboatrentals.com) have skiff rentals if you want to explore nearby waters or do a bit of fishing.

Petersburg and Mitkof Island are relatively bike-friendly (if the weather cooperates), with many miles of old logging roads traversing the landscape. **Zoom Bikes** (400 N. Nordic St., 907/772-2546, www.zoombikeshop.com) rents quality mountain bikes for $25 per day in the summer.

Stop by the **Forest Service district office** (Nordic Dr. and Haugen Dr.) for detailed maps of local hiking trails and 25 nearby cabins (877/444-6777, www.recreation.gov, $45). A pleasant walk takes off from Nordic Drive, three miles from town and just beyond Sandy Beach, and continues down a mile-long boardwalk to **Frederick Point.** Along the way, you get a taste of muskeg, rain forest, and a creek that's packed with salmon in August. You can return to town along the beach.

Located on the high school campus, the modern **Petersburg Aquatic Center** (209 Charles W St., 907/772-3304) has lap swimming and an adjacent community gym that contains a weight room and racquetball courts.

A short in-town boardwalk leads through the muskeg from the top of Excel Street to the senior center on 12th Street. The center is crowded with flowers outside, along with a menagerie of ducks, rabbits, geese, turkeys, and chickens. Right across the street is the Forest Service's area office. In addition, the half-mile **Hungry Point Trail** traverses the muskeg from Hungry Point to the ball field. A paved **bike path** parallels the highway for two miles south from the ferry terminal.

Ravens Roost Cabin

Petersburg has one of the few Forest Service cabins in Southeast Alaska that can be reached by hiking from town. The Ravens Roost cabin lies 1,600 feet above sea level at the end of a four-mile trail that starts near the airport. The trail crosses muskeg for the first mile and becomes very steep (and often mucky) for the next mile through the forest before breaking into open muskeg again along a ridge. Here the trail is in better condition, and you are treated to grand views of Devil's Thumb and the surrounding country. The path ends at a two-level Forest Service cabin with space for up to eight people. Allow three hours for the hike up, and be sure to make advance reservations for the cabin through the Forest Service (877/444-6777, www.recreation.gov).

Three Lakes Recreation Area

Very popular with locals for picnicking, fishing, and berry picking is the beautiful Three Lakes Recreation Area, 22 miles southeast of town along Forest Service Road 6235. You can hitch there, but it's a long hike back to town if your thumb is numb. Each lake has a rowboat and picnic table, and you may want to camp nearby at the old three-sided shelter built by the Civilian Conservation Corps along tiny **Shelter Lake.** An easy three-mile boardwalk loop trail connects the lakes, and a boardwalk trail continues from Sand Lake to nearby Ideal Cove, 1.5 miles away. The three main lakes (Sand, Hill, and Crane) are named after the sandhill cranes that announce each spring.

Kupreanof Trails and Cabins

On nearby Kupreanof Island, the Petersburg Mountain and Petersburg Lake trails provide good hiking and great views. Both paths begin at Bayou Point directly across Wrangell Narrows. Contact **Petersburg Creek Charters** (907/772-2425, www.alaska.net/~psgcreek) for a water taxi from town. A number of Forest Service cabins are available on Kupreanof.

For **Petersburg Mountain Trail,** walk north (right) up the road 1.5 miles to the trail marker. Be prepared for a very steep, muddy, and brushy path rising 3,000 feet in a distance of only 2.5 miles. From the top, however, you'll be rewarded with outstanding views of the entire Petersburg area.

Petersburg Lake Trail provides an easy 6.5-mile hike to a Forest Service cabin on Petersburg Lake within the 46,777-acre **Petersburg Creek-Duncan Salt Chuck Wilderness.** Check with the Forest Service for current conditions for both of these trails.

From Petersburg Lake it's possible to continue another 10.5 miles along a primitive trail to the Forest Service's Salt Chuck East Cabin. The trail is nearly level the entire distance and offers spectacular views of Portage Mountain.

On the south end of Kupreanof Island is **Kah Sheets Lake,** where the Forest Service has a very popular A-frame cabin. It's a 30-minute flight from Petersburg. A three-mile trail leads from the lake to Kah Sheets Bay, where you can fish for coho and sockeye salmon. A second Forest Service cabin sits along the bay.

West Point Cabin, in Portage Bay on the north end of Kupreanof Island, is a great spot to watch for whales, and the beach makes for good hiking.

Thomas Bay Area

Several of the most popular local Forest Service cabins are in the country around Thomas Bay, on the mainland approximately 20 miles from Petersburg. Spectacular Baird and Patterson Glaciers feed into this bay. Reserve months ahead to ensure a spot. **Cascade Creek Cabin** is on the saltwater and is accessible by either air or charter boat. Backpackers will love **Cascade Creek Trail,** one of the best (and steepest) paths in the Southeast. This three-mile path climbs 3,000 feet from the cabin to Falls Lake, passing cascading water much of the way. A three-sided shelter (free) sits along the shore of Falls Lake, and there's good fishing for rainbow trout. Hikers can continue two more miles up the trail beyond Falls Lake to Swan Lake. **Swan Lake Cabin** is on the opposite end of the lake from the trailhead and offers great views of the rocky mountain country. Contact the Petersburg Forest Service office for details on trail conditions and access.

ACCOMMODATIONS

For a complete list of local lodging choices, see the Petersburg Chamber of Commerce website (www.petersburg.org) or try www.petersburgalaska.com.

The best deal in town is **Alaska Island Hostel** (805 Gjoa St., 907/772-3632 or 877/772-3632, www.alaskaislandhostel.com, adults $23, children $12, May–early Sept.), where Ryn Schneider makes everyone welcome. There are separate men's and women's dorms (4 bunks per room), along with a kitchen, laundry, and free Internet access. Children under age 6 are not allowed, and check-in is 5–8 P.M.

Petersburg's largest lodging place, **Tides Inn** (307 N. 1st. St., 907/772-4288 or 800/665-8433, www.tidesinnalaska.com, $90–110 s, $100–120 d) has clean and well-maintained guest rooms, Wi-Fi, a guest computer, continental breakfast, and friendly owners. Most rooms include fridges and microwaves.

Scandia House (110 Nordic Dr., 907/772-4281 or 800/722-5006, www.scandiahousehotel.com) is a modern building with 33 brightly furnished guest rooms. Standard guest rooms (some with kitchenettes) go for $120–150 d; full suites with in-room hot tubs and king beds cost $185 d. A courtesy van and Wi-Fi are available.

The Lucky Loon (907/772-2345, www.theluckyloon.com) is a private beach house three miles south of town. Amenities include a covered deck, baths, a full kitchen, laundry, and Wi-Fi. It sleeps up to five for $200 per day with a three-day minimum.

Located along Frederick Sound just north of town, **A Guest House at Water's Edge** (705 Sandy Beach Rd., 907/772-3736 or 800/868-4373, www.petersburglodgingandtours.com) is a quiet and peaceful home with two guest rooms, a full kitchen, baths, bikes, Wi-Fi, and courtesy shuttles. The house sleeps four guests ($175 pp or $150 d) with a three-night minimum. The owners—35-year residents—also lead ecotours through Kaleidoscope Cruises.

A number of fishing lodges line the Wrangell Narrows, but the nicest is **Rocky Point Resort** (907/772-4420, www.rockypointresortak.com), midway along the channel.

Bed-and-Breakfasts

One of Petersburg's older homes, built in the 1920s, **Broom Hus B&B** (411 S. Nordic Dr., 907/772-3459, www.broomhus.com, May–Oct., $95 d) has a downstairs apartment with a full kitchen and a pleasant back deck. A continental breakfast is served.

Das Hagedorn Haus—The Hawthorne House (400 2nd St., 907/772-3775, www.dashagedornhaus.com, $80 s, $90 d)—is similar, with an attractive basement apartment. The owners prepare a full breakfast and provide a computer and Wi-Fi.

A short walk from the ferry terminal, **Nordic House B&B** (1106 Nordic Dr., 907/772-3620, www.nordichouse.net, $82–105 s, $92–105 d) is a comfortable and attractive home with a glassed-in deck overlooking the harbor along with Wi-Fi. Six guest rooms have private or shared baths, and a light breakfast is served. A separate apartment with a full kitchen costs $140 for up to four guests.

Waterfront B&B (1004 S. Nordic Dr., 907/772-9300, www.waterfrontbedandbreakfast.com, $110–121 d) stands on pilings along the shore just north of the ferry terminal. Five guest rooms include private baths and share a sitting room and large waterside deck; a full home-cooked breakfast and Wi-Fi are included.

Other places to check out include **Feathered Nest B&B** (907/772-3090, www.featherednestbandb.com, $100 s, $110 d), **Morning Mist B&B** (907/772-3557, www.alaska.net/~mornmist, $70 s, $80 d), and **Sea Level B&B** (907/772-3240, www.sealevelbnb.com, $110–140 d).

CAMPING

Those with a vehicle or willing to try hitching should head south 22 miles to the Forest Service's **Ohmer Creek Campground** ($6). This is a quiet place in a flower-filled meadow along Blind Slough, with water available. Not far away is the 0.25-mile-long wheelchair-accessible Ohmer Creek Trail, complete with interpretive signs. This is a beautiful old-growth rain forest walk, with steelhead fishing in the spring.

Twin Creek RV Park (907/772-3244, www.twincreekrv.com, RVs $28, tents $15) is seven miles south of town, and **The Trees RV Park** (907/772-2502, RVs $30) is 10 miles out, with an adjacent store and Laundromat.

FOOD

Open seasonally, **Tina's Kitchen** (907/772-2090, Sun. 11 A.M.–7 P.M., Mon.–Sat. 11 A.M.–8 P.M. summer, $8–11) occupies a little downtown stand next to Scandia House with amazingly tasty Baja-style halibut-cheek tacos, plus chicken teriyaki, shrimp burgers, burritos, and even Philly steak sandwiches. Eat at the picnic tables out front or inside the party tent with heaters.

A latte joint, **Java Hus** (907/772-2626, Sun. 7 A.M.–4 P.M., Mon.–Sat. 6 A.M.–5 P.M.) is inside Scandia House. A better bet is **Common Ground** (904 S. Nordic Dr., 907/772-2299, Sun. 7 A.M.–4 P.M., Mon.–Sat. 6 A.M.–5:30 P.M.), a little drive-through with an adjacent roaster. It's 0.5 miles north of the ferry terminal.

For fresh bread, croissants, cinnamon rolls, scones, giant cookies, quiche, and the cheapest coffee in town, check out **Emily's Bakery** (1000 S. Mitkof Hwy., 907/772-4555, Mon.–Fri. 8 A.M.–4 P.M.), a few steps toward town from the ferry. Get there early or the shelves may be bare.

Given the importance of fishing in the local economy, it comes as no surprise that Petersburg has a number of places offering fresh seafood. **Coastal Cold Storage Fish Market** (306 N. Nordic Dr., 907/772-4177, Sun. 6 A.M.–2 P.M., Mon.–Sat. 6 A.M.–6 P.M., $5–12) serves tasty halibut beer bits, shrimp burgers, Reubens, king crab sandwiches, chowders, and other lunch fare, plus Ole and Lena omelets for a Norwegian breakfast. You can also buy fresh fish, scallops, crab (cooked if you like), and other seafood—including, of course, lutefisk.

Tonka Seafoods (907/772-3662 or 888/560-3662, www.tonkaseafoods.com) specializes in premium smoked, canned, or fresh salmon, rockfish, and halibut. The retail store, across from the Sons of Norway Hall on Sing Lee Alley, is open weekdays, and tours may be available.

Open for three meals a day, **Rooney's Northern Lights Restaurant** (203 Sing Lee Alley, 907/772-2900, daily 6 A.M.–8 P.M., dinner $15–26) has windows facing the harbor and dependably good meals, including fish baskets, Petersburg peel-and-eat shrimp, and a three-berry cobbler for dessert.

Prices for food and other items are higher in Petersburg than in other Southeast Alaska towns. Two local grocers have all the supplies: **Hammer & Wikan** (1300 Howkan Dr., 907/772-4246, www.hammerandwikan.com, Sun. 8 A.M.–7 P.M., Mon.–Sat. 7 A.M.–8 P.M.), with a full deli and a bakery, and the downtown **Trading Union** (907/772-3881, Mon.–Fri. 8 A.M.–7 P.M., Sat.–Sun. 10 A.M.–5 P.M.).

SHOPPING

Sing Lee Alley Books (907/772-4440, Mon.–Sat.), next to the Sons of Norway Hall, has an excellent collection of Alaskan books and other choice reading material. **Cubby Hole** (14 Sing Lee Alley, 907/772-2717) sells Norwegian-style handicrafts decorated with *rosemaling* designs.

Wild Celery (400 N. Nordic Dr., 907/772-2471) is the local art gallery. Get beautiful Norwegian and Icelandic sweaters at **Lee's Clothing** (207 Nordic Dr., 907/772-4229).

SERVICES

Get cash 24 hours a day from ATMs at First Bank and Wells Fargo. The post office (907/772-3121) is out near the airport on Haugen Drive, and the **Petersburg Public Library** (907/772-3349, www.psglib.org, Mon.–Thurs. noon–9 P.M., Fri.–Sat. 10 A.M.–5 P.M., closed Sat.–Sun.) is crowded into the upstairs of the municipal building on Nordic Drive. Check your email on the computers or use their free Wi-Fi.

Coin-op showers are downtown at the harbormaster's office and at **Glacier Laundry** on Nordic Drive. For a better deal, paddle over to the **Aquatic Center** (209 Charles W St., 907/772-3304, $3), with a lap pool, a water slide, plus an adjacent community gym with a weight room, a climbing wall, and racquetball courts. **Petersburg Medical Center** (2nd St. and Fram St., 907/772-4299) is the local hospital.

GETTING THERE AND AROUND

Petersburg is strung out along Wrangell Narrows, with the **ferry terminal** (907/772-3855) a mile south of the town center. During the summer, ferries run almost daily both northbound and southbound from Petersburg. They usually stop for an hour or two, long enough to walk into town or at least check out the nearby harbor. The ferry terminal opens two hours before ship arrivals and generally stays open a half-hour after it departs. For reservations and schedules, contact the **Alaska Marine Highway** (907/465-3941 or 800/642-0066, www.dot.state.ak.us/amhs).

Metro Cab (907/772-2700) and **Midnight Rides** (907/772-2222) charge $6 for transport from the airport or ferry to town.

Rent cars from **Allstar Rent-A-Car** (907/772-4281 or 800/722-5006, www.scandiahousehotel.com) at Scandia House or **Avis** (907/772-4716 or 800/331-1212, www.tidesinnalaska.com) inside Tides Inn.

Petersburg Airport is a mile southeast of town on Haugen Drive. **Alaska Airlines** (907/772-4255 or 800/426-0333, www.alaskaair.com) has daily service to other Southeast Alaska towns and the Lower 48. **Pacific Wing** (907/772-9258, www.pacificwing.com), **Kupreanof Flying Service** (907/772-3396, www.kupreanof.com), and **Nordic Air** (907/772-3535) all provide air charter service to Forest Service cabins. **Temsco Helicopters** (907/772-4780 or 877/789-9501, www.temscoair.com) offers helicopter flightseeing. **Sunrise Aviation** (907/874-2319 or 800/874-2311, www.sunriseflights.com) often has seat fares to Wrangell.

KAKE

The little Tlingit village of Kake (pop. 700) lies along the northwest shore of Kupreanof Island, halfway between Petersburg and Sitka. Kake's claim to fame is the **world's tallest totem pole,** exhibited at the 1970 World's Fair in Osaka, Japan. This 132-foot pole is unique in that it contains figures representing all the

Tlingit clans on a single pole. Kake is also the starting point for sea kayak trips into two large wilderness areas on nearby Kuiu Island. Also of interest is the quaint **Kake Presbyterian Church.** Built in 1929, it is the oldest public building in town.

History

During the 1800s the Kake tribe had a reputation as one of the fiercest in the Southeast. Richard Meade recorded the following incident:

> *In 1855 a party of Kakes, on a visit south to Puget Sound, became involved in some trouble there, which caused a United States vessel to open fire on them, and during the affair one of the Kake chiefs was killed. This took place over 800 miles from the Kake settlements on Kupreanof Island. The very next year the tribe sent a canoe-load of fighting men all the way from Clarence Straits in Russian America to Whidby's Island in Washington Territory, and attacked and beheaded an ex-collector – not of internal revenue, for that might have been pardonable – but of customs, and returned safely with his skull and scalp to their villages. Such people are, therefore, not to be despised, and are quite capable of giving much trouble in the future unless wisely and firmly governed."*

John Muir later described a visit to a Kake village where human bones were scattered all over the ground, reminders of previous battles: "Chief Yana Taowk seemed to take pleasure in kicking the Sitka bones that lay in his way, and neither old nor young showed the slightest trace of superstitious fear of the dead at any time." Needless to say, the people of Kake treat outsiders in a friendlier manner today.

Practicalities

Keex' Kwaan Lodge (907/785-3434, www.kakealaska.com, $134 s, $153 d) is a comfortable modern lodge where most rooms include two queen beds, fridges, microwaves, and Wi-Fi.

Nugget Inn (907/785-6469, daily 9 A.M.–6:30 P.M. May–Sept., Thurs.–Tues. 9 A.M.–2 P.M. winter, entrées $18–26) serves meals three times a day in the summer, including fresh fish and crab (when available), deep-fried chicken, burgers, and New York steaks. It's on the right when you exit the ferry. Upstairs are three tiny rooms with one ($75) or two ($84) twin beds, TVs, and a bath down the hall.

Get groceries from **SOS Value-Mart** (907/785-6444), 0.25 miles from the ferry. Kake has a liquor store, but no bank. The gas station (on the left from the ferry) has an ATM, but it's often out of cash.

Camping facilities are not available, and much of the land around Kake is privately owned, but camping is permitted on Forest Service land, two miles south of town. Kake is one of the drier towns in the Southeast, with only 50 inches per year of precipitation. The town has a fish hatchery and cold-storage plant but no Forest Service office. Ask at the Forest Service office in Petersburg about the Cathedral Falls, Goose Lake, and Hamilton River Trails. **Big John Cabin** on Big John Bay is accessible via the road network from Kake.

The **Alaska Marine Highway** (800/642-0066, www.dot.state.ak.us/amhs) ferry visits Kake twice a week, heading both east to Petersburg and west to Sitka. It docks 1.5 miles from the center of town. There is a covered shelter area, but no phone. The ferry usually stops just long enough to load and unload cars (a half-hour or so).

Wings of Alaska (907/789-0790, www.wingsofalaska.com), has daily service between Kake and Juneau, while **Harris Aircraft Services** (907/966-3050 or 877/966-3050, www.harrisaircraft.com) flies to Sitka most days.

KUIU ISLAND

If you have the time, equipment, and skill, nearby Kuiu Island (pronounced Q-U) provides excellent kayaking and canoeing opportunities. Two wilderness areas encompass the south and west sides of Kuiu; other parts have been heavily logged. Dozens of interesting islands, islets, and coves crowd the west side of Kuiu in the 67,000-acre **Tebenkof Bay Wilderness,** while the south end includes the 60,000-acre **Kuiu Wilderness.** The Forest Service publishes a detailed map of Kuiu Island with descriptions of all portages and routes. Get a copy of ***Kuiu Island/Tebenkof Bay Canoe/Kayak Routes*** from Petersburg Ranger District (907/772-3871, www.fs.fed.us/r10/tongass).

Experienced kayakers will enjoy the paddle between Kake and Petersburg around the south end of Kupreanof Island. There is open water in places, but a good portion of the route is protected, and the state ferry makes it easy to get between Kake and Petersburg.

PORT ALEXANDER

Southeast Alaska's most remote settlement, tiny Port Alexander (pop. 50) sits near the southern tip of rugged Baranof Island. In the 1920s—heyday of the salmon canneries—the town buzzed with 2,000 workers. Today, Port Alexander is quiet and lovely, with boardwalks, a general store, a post office, and a one-teacher school. It's also very rainy, averaging an incredible 220 inches of the wet stuff per year.

There's a small fleet of long-liners and trollers, along with two sportfishing places: **Laughing Raven Lodge** (800/768-7752, www.portalexander.com) and **Fishermen's Inn** (907/568-2399 or 480/225-2217, www.fisherssinn.com). **Harris Aircraft Services** (907/966-3050 or 877/966-3050, www.harrisaircraft.com) flies several times per week between Sitka and Port Alexander.

Sitka

With its gem-like island-dotted setting, Sitka (pop. 9,000) is everybody's favorite Southeast Alaska town. On a typical summer day you'll see fishing boats heading out to sea from the four harbors around Sitka Sound, and cruise ships steaming by, their decks crowded with tourists as they pass Mt. Edgecumbe, the Fuji-like snowcapped volcano that adorns Sitka's outer waters. Back in town, other visitors glance inside the Russian church that dominates Sitka's center, wander along totem-pole-lined paths in peaceful Sitka National Historical Park, and climb the sharply rising wooded peaks behind town. The people who make this their home are similarly diverse, ranging from beer-guzzling fishers barely making ends meet to wealthy retirees from California who are pushing housing prices into the stratosphere. The gorgeous setting makes Sitka a detour well worth the effort. Be forewarned, however, to expect rain—the town soaks in 94 inches per year. By the way, Sitka lays claim to being the "biggest city in America"; its boundaries encircle Baranof Island, fully 4,710 square miles (New York City covers only 301 square miles).

Peril Strait

Located on the western shore of Baranof Island, "Sitka-by-the-Sea" is Southeast Alaska's most remote ferry stop, and the only major Inside Passage town to front on the Pacific Ocean. Getting to Sitka by ferry requires a long detour through the scenic but treacherous Peril Strait that separates Baranof and Chichagof Islands—a great place to watch for eagles perched on trees along the shore. During larger tides, fierce currents prevent ferries from going through, and the ships must time their passage to coincide with a high or low slack tide. The passage narrows to only 300 feet in one spot (24 feet deep). When the tide is really cooking, the buoys are often bent far over by the wild currents. This has one side benefit: The ferry is forced to stay for three hours or so in Sitka, long enough for you to get a taste of this fascinating town. But to see this pretty place better, be sure to stay awhile.

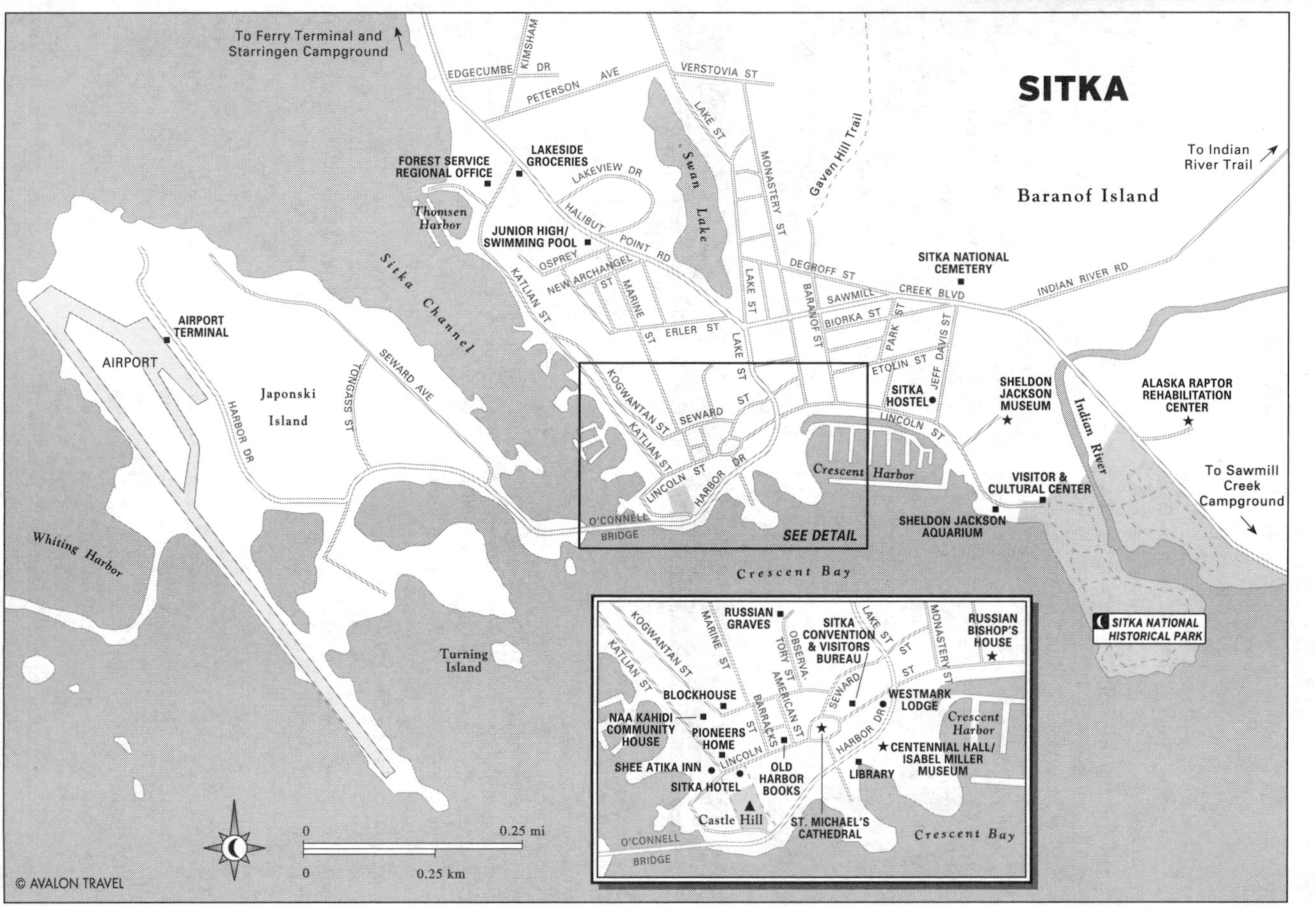

SITKA
Baranof Island
To Ferry Terminal and Starringen Campground
To Indian River Trail
To Sawmill Creek Campground
EDGECUMBE DR
KIMSHAM
PETERSON AVE
VERSTOVIA ST
LAKE ST
Swan Lake
Gaven Hill Trail
MONASTERY ST
FOREST SERVICE REGIONAL OFFICE
LAKESIDE GROCERIES
LAKEVIEW DR
HALIBUT POINT RD
Thomsen Harbor
JUNIOR HIGH/ SWIMMING POOL
OSPREY
NEW ARCHANGEL ST
MARINE ST
KATLIAN ST
DEGROFF ST
SAWMILL
CREEK BLVD
BARANOF ST
BIORKA ST
PARK ST
ERLER ST
ETOLIN ST
JEFF DAVIS ST
SITKA NATIONAL CEMETERY
INDIAN RIVER RD
Sitka Channel
AIRPORT TERMINAL
AIRPORT
Japonski Island
HARBOR DR
TONGASS ST
SEWARD AVE
KOGWANTAN ST
SEWARD ST
LINCOLN ST
HARBOR DR
O'CONNELL BRIDGE
SEE DETAIL
Crescent Harbor
SITKA HOSTEL
SHELDON JACKSON MUSEUM
Indian River
ALASKA RAPTOR REHABILITATION CENTER
VISITOR & CULTURAL CENTER
SHELDON JACKSON AQUARIUM
Whiting Harbor
Crescent Bay
Turning Island
SITKA NATIONAL HISTORICAL PARK
0 0.25 mi
0 0.25 km
© AVALON TRAVEL
KOGWANTAN ST
KATLIAN ST
MARINE ST
RUSSIAN GRAVES
OBSERVATORY ST
AMERICAN ST
BARRACKS ST
LAKE ST
SITKA CONVENTION & VISITORS BUREAU
MONASTERY ST
RUSSIAN BISHOP'S HOUSE
BLOCKHOUSE
NAA KAHIDI COMMUNITY HOUSE
PIONEERS HOME
SEWARD ST
WESTMARK LODGE
Crescent Harbor
HARBOR DR
CENTENNIAL HALL/ ISABEL MILLER MUSEUM
LINCOLN
SHEE ATIKA INN
SITKA HOTEL
OLD HARBOR BOOKS
LIBRARY
Castle Hill
ST. MICHAEL'S CATHEDRAL
O'CONNELL BRIDGE
Crescent Bay

Sitka Channel and Sitka

HISTORY

Russian America

First established as a base for collecting sea otter pelts, Sitka has a long and compelling history. In 1799, Alexander Baranov—head of the Russian American Company—founded the settlement under a charter from the czar. Baranov (also spelled Baranof) built his original fort, Redoubt St. Michael, near the present Alaska ferry terminal, only to see it destroyed in a Tlingit attack in 1802. There is evidence that the British, long enemies of the Russians, assisted the Tlingits in the fort's destruction. Two years later, Baranov returned with 120 soldiers and 800 Aleuts in 300 *baidarkas,* defeating the Tlingits in what was to become the last major resistance by any Northwest Coast Indians. The Russians rebuilt the town, then called New Archangel, on the present site and constructed a stockade enclosing what is now downtown Sitka. New Archangel soon became the capital of Russian America and a vital center for the sea otter and fur seal trade with China. Although the Tlingits were invited back in 1821 (Native leaders say the Russians begged them to return), the groups coexisted uneasily. Tlingits built their houses just outside the stockade, facing a battery of eight Russian cannons.

Once labeled the "Paris of the North Pacific," New Archangel quickly became the Northwest's most cosmopolitan port. By 1840 it was already home to a library of several thousand volumes, a museum, a meteorological observatory, two schools, a hospital, an armory, two orphanages, and dozens of other buildings. The wealthier citizens lived in elaborate homes filled with crystal and fine lace, but as in czarist Russia itself, the opulence of Sitka did not extend beyond a select few. Slave-like working and living conditions were forced on the Aleut sea otter hunters.

America Takes Over

An emotional ceremony at Sitka in 1867 marked the passage of Alaska from Russian to American hands, and most of the Russians, including many third-generation Sitkans, returned to their motherland. Even today, there are locals who speak Russian. Although the town served as Alaska's first capital city for three decades, its importance declined rapidly under the Americans, and it was almost a ghost town by the turn of the 20th century. The territorial government was moved to the then-booming mining town of Juneau in 1900.

During World War II, Sitka became a major link in the defense of Alaska against Japan. Hangars remain from the large amphibious air base just across the bridge on Japonski Island (Fort Ray), and the barracks that once housed 3,500 soldiers were turned into Mt. Edgecumbe High School, Alaska's only boarding high school for Native Alaskans. The boarding school is now fully integrated.

Sitka's largest employer until 1993 was a Japanese-owned pulp mill five miles east of town. The mill closed mainly because of the high cost of production and competition from mills elsewhere. Before it closed, the mill gained national attention for dumping large quantities of cancer-causing dioxin into nearby Silver Bay, and for being one of the primary forces behind the clear-cut logging of Tongass National Forest. Many Sitkans still work in the fishing and tourism industries, or for the government. The mill's closure did not have nearly the devastating effect the prophets of doom had predicted; in fact Sitka seems to be doing just fine, fueled by tourism and the arrival of retirees. Large cruise ships are in port most summer days, but things aren't nearly as bad (yet) as in Juneau, Ketchikan, or Skagway.

SIGHTS

The Centennial Building houses a small information desk and brochure rack, or drop by the **Sitka Convention & Visitors Bureau** (upstairs at 303 Lincoln St., 907/747-5940, www.sitka.org, Mon.–Fri. 8 A.M.–5 P.M.).

One of the finest views of Sitka is from the walkway along the distinctive cable-stayed girder-span bridge that connects Sitka with Japonski Island. On a clear day you'll have a hard time deciding which direction to look: The mountains of Baranof Island rise up behind the town, while the perfect volcanic cone of **Mt. Edgecumbe** (3,000 feet) on Kruzof Island dominates the opposite vista. Beside the old post office on Lincoln Street a stairway leads up to **Castle Hill,** a tiny state park commemorating the spot where the ceremony transferring Alaska to the United States was held on October 18, 1867. The Kiksadi Indians inhabited this hill for many generations before the Russians' arrival. After defeating the Kiksadi, Alexander Baranov built his castle-like house here, but the building burned down in 1894. The splendid view makes Castle Hill a must.

The most prominent downtown feature is the large yellow **Alaska Pioneers Home,** built in 1934 and housing elderly Alaskans with 15 or more years' state residence. The ***Prospector*** statue out front was based on William "Skagway Bill" Fonda, an Alaskan pioneer. Across the road is a **totem pole** bearing the Russian coat of arms, three old English anchors, and a couple of Indian petroglyphs. Adjacent to the Pioneers Home is **Sheet'Ka Kwaan Naa Kahidi Community House,** based on traditional longhouse designs and offering Native Alaskan dance performances in summer. Two tall house screens dominate the interior.

Atop a small hill just west of the Pioneer Home stands a reconstructed **Russian blockhouse** from the stockade that kept the Indians restricted to the area along Katlian Street. It's open Sunday afternoons during the summer. **Kogwantan and Katlian Streets,** directly below the blockhouse, are a picturesque mixture of docks, fish canneries, shops, and old houses, one with its exterior entirely covered in Tlingit designs. The main **Finnish Lutheran Cemetery,** 400 graves dating as far back as 1848, is behind the blockhouse at the end of Princess Street. The grave of the Russian **Princess Maksoutoff** is here, and nearby are more Russian graves, including that of Iahov Netsvetov, a Russian Orthodox saint. Cemetery buffs might also be interested in the small **Sitka National Cemetery,** accessible via Jeff Davis Street beside Sheldon Jackson College. It's the oldest national cemetery west of the Mississippi. Built in 1900, the **Geodetic Survey House** (210 Seward St., Tues.–Thurs. 9 A.M.–4 P.M.) houses displays on Mt. Edgecumbe and Tongass National Forest.

St. Michael's Cathedral

The most striking symbol of Russian influence in Sitka is St. Michael's Cathedral (907/747-8120), right in the center of town. Built in 1848, the building burned down in 1966 but was replaced by a replica a decade later. The original Russian artifacts and icons, including the Sitka Madonna (purportedly a miraculous healer), were saved from the fire and have been returned to their original setting in this, the mother church for all of Alaska's 20,000 Russian Orthodox. During the summer, the church ($2) is open Monday–Friday 9 A.M.–4 P.M. or whenever a large cruise ship is in port. It's open by appointment at other times but is not open to tourists during religious services.

Sitka Historical Museum

Tucked away inside Centennial Hall, this small museum (330 Harbor Dr., 907/747-6455, www.sitkahistory.org, Mon.–Fri. 8:30 A.M.–5 P.M., Sat.–Sun. 10 A.M.–4 P.M. summer, $1) houses local artifacts and an interesting scale model of Sitka in 1867—the year Alaska became a U.S. territory. Out front is a 50-foot carved and painted replica of a **Tlingit war canoe.**

Russian Bishop's House

Administered by the National Park Service, the Russian Bishop's House (907/747-6281, www.nps.gov/sitk, daily 9 A.M.–3 P.M. May–Sept.) is Sitka's oldest building and one of just four Russian structures still standing in North America. Built in 1842, it was home to Ivan Veniaminov, bishop of Alaska and later head of the entire Russian Orthodox church hierarchy in Moscow. The first floor houses exhibits describing the building and its occupants, as well as the exploits of Russia's American colony. The second floor has been fully restored to its 1853 appearance and is filled with original furnishings and artifacts. Access to the second floor is part of a half-hour tour ($4) led by park interpreters.

Sheldon Jackson Museum

Farther along the waterfront are the distinctive brown and white buildings of **Sheldon Jackson College.** Established in 1878 as a place to train Native Alaskans, this was the oldest educational institution in the state. It closed in 2007. Still open is the outstanding Sheldon Jackson Museum (907/747-8981, www.museums.state.ak.us, daily 9 A.M.–5 P.M. mid-May–mid-Sept., Tues.–Sat. 10 A.M.–4 P.M. mid-Sept.–mid-May, $4, students free). Dr. Sheldon Jackson (1834–1909) worked as both a Presbyterian missionary and as the first General Agent for Education in Alaska. His extensive travels throughout the territory 1888–1898 allowed him to acquire thousands of Eskimo, Athabascan, Tlingit, Haida, and Aleut artifacts. To protect this priceless collection, a fireproof museum (the first concrete structure in Alaska) was built here in 1895. The museum houses a remarkable selection of kayaks, hunting tools, dogsleds, baskets, bentwood boxes, Eskimo masks, and other artifacts. Be sure to check out the drawers of artifacts beneath the display cases. Also here is a small gift shop selling quality Alaskan jewelry, crafts, and note cards. Native Alaskan artisans are often at work inside the museum during the summer.

Across the street is the **Sheldon Jackson Aquarium** (907/747-8878, www.sjhatchery.org, daily 8 A.M.–5 P.M. summer only, free), with an 800-gallon saltwater aquarium and three touch tanks to get up close to tide pool creatures.

Sitka National Historical Park

For many, the highlight of a visit to Sitka is Sitka National Historical Park, at the mouth of Indian River where the Tlingits and Russians fought their final battle in 1804.

© DON PITCHER

Chilkat blanket weaving, Sitka National Historical Park

The Indians kept the invaders at bay for a week, but with their ammunition exhausted and resupply efforts thwarted, they abandoned the fortress and silently withdrew to Peril Strait. The visitors and Native Alaskan cultural center (907/747-8061, www.nps.gov/sitk, daily 8 A.M.–5 P.M. summer, and Mon.–Fri. 8 A.M.–5 P.M. the rest of the year, $4) includes an informative small museum on Tlingit culture. In summertime, Native Alaskan craft workers can be seen producing bead blankets, jewelry, and wood carvings in the workshop. The 10-minute historical video *Battle of Sitka* is very informative, and rangers offer daily historical walks in the summer.

Quite a few historical totems are housed in one large room, and outside are 15 more totems, most of which were carved for the 1904 St. Louis World's Fair. The totems line a one-mile trail through the lush second-growth spruce forest, with outstanding views of Sitka Sound along the way. You'll find spawning pink salmon in Indian River (near the 1804 battleground) late in the summer. The park is a peaceful place where mysterious totems in the trees, the strident calls of ravens and eagles, and the lapping of waves combine to enhance the beauty.

Alaska Raptor Center

Located off Sawmill Creek Road, this impressive facility (907/747-8662 or 800/643-9425, www.alaskaraptor.org, $12 adults, $6 children under 12) has two dozen or so bald eagles and other birds of prey—including owls, hawks, falcons, and ravens—at any given time. Most are recovering from gunshots, car accidents, or encounters with power lines. Of the birds brought in, one-third recover sufficiently to be released back into the wild. Most of the others end up in captive breeding or educational programs in the Lower 48. Get to the center by walking out of town along Sawmill Creek Road a couple hundred feet beyond the Indian River bridge. The access road takes off to your left a short distance beyond this. A more scenic route is to follow the trails through Sitka National Historical Park or along the Indian River behind Sheldon Jackson College. It's an easy 10-minute walk from Sitka National Historical Park, or 20 minutes from the center of town. The Community Ride Bus ($2) takes you within two blocks of the center.

A focal point is the 20,000-square-foot flight-training center that replicates the rain forest environment outside; visitors watch the eagles through one-way glass. Staff use the enclosure to teach eagles survival skills prior to their release. Out back is a deck overlooking a large enclosure, called a mews, where eagles unable to survive in the wild are kept. Additional mews with hawks, owls, and other birds are along a rain forest path. The gift shop sells all sorts of eagle paraphernalia.

Visitors get the chance to meet one of the birds up close, and are given a half-hour tour and video. The center is open daily 8 A.M.–4 P.M. year-round, and there's always someone on hand whenever a cruise ship is in town. No winter tours.

Whale Park

Six miles out Sawmill Creek Road is Whale Park, consisting of a roadside turnout with interpretive signs and a boardwalk to an overlook where there's a good chance of seeing whales during the fall and winter months. Offshore hydrophones broadcast the sounds of passing whales (if they are around).

ENTERTAINMENT AND EVENTS

Cultural Performances

When cruise ships are in town, Herrigan Centennial Hall auditorium comes alive with half-hour performances of traditional Russian, Ukrainian, and Moldavian dance by the 30-member all-female **New Archangel Dancers** (907/747-5516, www.newarchangeldancers.com, $8). The troupe has toured extensively, including visits to Japan, Canada, Mexico, and even the Russian motherland.

For a very different form of dance, the **Sheet'Ka Kwaan Naa Kahidi Dancers** (907/747-7290, $8 adults, $5 children) give Tlingit performances in full regalia through the summer months. These excellent half-hour productions are offered when cruise ships are in port. Most folks see them as part of a bus tour given by Tribal Tours. Performances take place in the imposing Sheet'Ka Kwaan Naa Kahidi Community House, next to the Pioneers Home on Katlian Street.

Nightlife

Fishers and would-be crewmembers hang out at the sometimes-rowdy **Pioneer Bar** (Katlian St., 907/747-3456). The P-Bar's walls are crowded with hundreds of photos of local fishing boats, and the blackboard often has "crew wanted" ads.

Inside the Sitka Hotel, **Victoria's Pourhouse** (907/747-9301) has a gigantic TV, beer on tap, a smoke-free setting, and free Wi-Fi. **Ernie's Old Time Saloon** (130 Lincoln St., 907/747-3334) features live music most weekends and a couple of offbeat stuffed animals, including a "sidehill" salmon.

Events

For three weeks in June, the renowned **Sitka Summer Music Festival** (907/747-6744, www.sitkamusicfestival.org) attracts musicians from all over the world. Chamber music concerts are given several evenings per week in Centennial Hall, but the most fun is the annual BoatParty Concert (reserve early). Concert tickets may be hard to come by, but you can always visit rehearsals for free. Another cultural event, the **Sitka Symposium** (907/747-3794, www.islandinstitutealaska.org) in late June, attracts nationally known poets and writers.

In late May, visitors can join locals in the **Sitka Salmon Derby,** where the top fish is often a 60-pound-plus king salmon. **July 4th** features a parade, races, a softball tournament, live music, dancing, and fireworks. On Labor Day weekend, the **Mudball Classic Softball Tournament** attracts teams from around the nation for fun in the muck.

As the town where Alaska was officially transferred from Russian to American hands, Sitka is also the place to be on **Alaska Day.** A celebration of "Seward's Folly" is held each October 18 with dances (including a remarkable performance by the New Archangel Dancers), traditional Russian costumes, a parade, and a reenactment of the brief transfer ceremony.

In early November, the **Sitka Whalefest** (907/747-7964, www.sitkawhalefest.org) attracts biologists and those who love whales and other marine mammals to a series of scientific seminars, whale-watching tours, concerts, crafts, and exhibits.

RECREATION

Sitka is a popular destination for **sportfishing;** drop by the Sitka Convention and Visitors Bureau office (upstairs at 303 Lincoln St., 907/747-5940, www.sitka.org, Mon.–Fri. 8 A.M.–5 P.M.) for a handout listing more than 30 charter boats.

The protected waters near Sitka provide excellent kayak access to many Forest Service cabins and trails. **Sitka Sound Ocean Adventures** (907/752-0660, www.ssoceanadventures.com)

guides kayak day trips (from $69 for 2 hours) from the harbor and rents kayaks to do it yourself. **Esther G Sea Taxi** (907/747-6481, www.puffinsandwhales.com) provides kayaker and hiker drop-offs if you're heading out.

Island Fever Diving and Sports (805 Halibut Point Rd., 907/747-7871, www.islandfeverdiving.com) sets up snorkeling excursions using dry suits. They also lead day hikes and mountain bike rides on Kruzof Island, home of Mt. Edgecumbe. **BJ Boat Rentals** (907/738-6375) rents skiffs, fishing poles, and other gear if you want to head out on your own fishing adventure.

Rent quality mountain bikes from **Yellow Jersey Cycle Shop** (329 Harbor Dr., 907/747-6317, www.yellowjerseycycles.com) downtown.

The Forest Service's **Sitka Ranger District Office** (204 Siginaka Way, 907/747-4220, www.fs.fed.us/r10/tongass) has up-to-date information on the more than 40 miles of local trails, ranging from gentle nature walks to treks that take you high up onto nearby peaks.

Indian River Trail

One of the finest of Sitka's trails, this is an easy valley hike within walking distance of town. The route follows a clear salmon stream through the rain forest, with a chance to see brown bears and deer. Begin by heading out Sawmill Creek Road and turning left onto Indian River Road. Continue past the gate about 0.5 miles to the city's water pump house. The gentle trail leads from here up along the Indian River and a tributary to the right as far as a lovely 80-foot waterfall in a V-shaped valley. The last mile of the trail is not well maintained. Allow six hours round-trip to cover the 5.5-mile trail.

Gavan Hill Trail

This "stairway to heaven" walkway starts at the end of Baranof Street and climbs three miles to the top of 2,650-foot Gavan Hill. (Bear right at the junction with Cross Trail just under a mile up.) Gavan Hill Trail then switchbacks to a long ridge that opens onto subalpine meadows before a steep final climb up the last 200 feet of elevation. From here, it's relatively easy to follow rock cairns through the alpine area, connecting to the Harbor Mountain Trail. This makes an outstanding loop hike with impressive vistas of Sitka Sound.

Harbor Mountain Trail

One of the easiest and most scenic ways to get into the alpine area is via Harbor Mountain Trail. Built by the Army during World War II, the road originally provided access to a lookout post for invading Japanese ships and submarines (none were ever seen, though a whale was once mistakenly bombed). Head four miles out on Halibut Point Road and turn right onto Harbor Mountain Road. The gravel road climbs five miles up the mountain to an elevation of 2,000 feet. Snow blocks the road until June, but you can park at the gate and walk up if you don't mind hiking on snow. On sunny days the view over Sitka Sound is breathtaking. Those without a car or mountain bike should be able to hitch a ride up with locals.

A trail begins at the parking area on top and switchbacks up a side hill before leveling out in the subalpine meadows. A spur trail heads to an overlook here, but the main trail turns right and continues past the ruins of wartime lookout buildings. Beyond this, rock cairns follow the ridge, and the path eventually connects with the Gavan Hill Trail back to town. A small hut provides a camping place approximately three miles in.

Mt. Verstovia Trail

On a clear day, get spectacular views of Sitka Sound and Mt. Edgecumbe from the Mt. Verstovia Trail, a strenuous climb to this pointy peak overlooking Sitka. The steep 2.5-mile trail begins on the west side of the Kiksadi Club, two miles east of town on Sawmill Creek Road. The trail is brushy and poorly maintained, and inexperienced hikers have gotten lost. You'll pass some old Russian charcoal pits (signposted) only 0.25 miles from the trailhead. The route switchbacks to a ridge, which you follow to the shoulder of Mt. Verstovia.

The true summit is farther northeast along the ridge. Allow four hours for the return trip as far as the shoulder (2,000 feet), six hours round-trip to the top (2,550 feet).

Beaver Lake Trail

This family friendly mile-long trail begins at the bridge in Sawmill Creek Campground seven miles east of town. The path gains 250 feet in elevation as it climbs through the forest and out onto a boardwalk over the muskeg to Beaver Lake. The lake has been stocked with grayling and is one of the only places to catch these fish in Southeast Alaska. There are fishing platforms along the lakeshore.

Mt. Edgecumbe

Mt. Edgecumbe, a 3,000-foot volcanic cone that looks like Mt. Fuji, can be climbed via a 6.5-mile trail that starts on the southeast shore of Kruzof Island. The last mile is above the tree line and runs through red volcanic ash. The island is 10 miles west of Sitka and can be reached by kayak (beware of ocean swells) or by arranging for a skiff drop-off. Stay in Fred's Creek Cabin at the trailhead or in the free three-sided shelter halfway up. Panoramic views can be had from atop this dormant volcano.

Cabins

The Forest Service has 24 cabins (518/885-3639 or 877/444-6777, www.recreation.gov, $45) in the Sitka area, most accessed by floatplane or water taxi from Sitka.

Redoubt Lake Cabin is at the end of a six-mile trail that starts in Silver Bay (10 miles southeast of Sitka). The cabin is also accessible by sea kayak from town, and a short portage takes you to Redoubt Lake.

The wheelchair-accessible **Lake Eva Cabin** is 27 miles northeast of Sitka on Baranof Island. **Plotnikof Lake Cabin** sits in the heart of the spectacularly rugged South Baranof Wilderness Area, a 45-minute flight from Sitka.

Baranof Lake Cabin looks across this blue-green lake to a waterfall. A trail at the end of the lake leads 0.5 miles to the little settlement

© DON PITCHER

Sitka Sound and Mt. Edgecumbe

of **Baranof Warm Springs,** where a privately owned hot spring is available.

Brent's Beach Cabin is on the eastern shore of Kruzof Island, 15 miles northwest of Sitka. There's a white-sand beach out front (rare in Southeast Alaska), and interesting caves and lava domes just up the shore.

The **Allan Point Cabin,** 16 miles north of Sitka, is an impressive two-story log cabin that commands a fine view across Nakwasina Sound from its location on the northeast end of Halleck Island. The equally spacious **Samsing Cove Cabin** sleeps 10 comfortably and is just six miles south of Sitka.

ACCOMMODATIONS

The Sitka Convention and Visitors Bureau produces a pamphlet and website (www.sitka.org) that detail hotels, motels, B&Bs, fishing lodges, wilderness lodges, private apartments, and houses. Unfortunately, Sitka no longer has a hostel. Add a 12 percent tax to all Sitka lodging rates.

Hotels and Motels

Built in 1939, the 50-room **Sitka Hotel** (118 Lincoln St., 907/747-3288, www.sitkahotel.net, $99 s, $105 d) is a reasonable heart-of-town option, but request a newer room since the old ones are basic and smoky. There's a good restaurant (Victoria's) and lounge downstairs, along with free Wi-Fi. Sitka Hotel exudes an old-time ambience, but it can be noisy, so it's not for everyone.

Cascade Inn (2035 Halibut Point Rd., 907/747-6804 or 800/532-0908, www.cascadeinnsitka.com) has standard guest rooms ($125–140 d) and kitchenettes ($160 d); add $20 for each extra guest. The building is two miles out of town toward the ferry, and all guest rooms feature private balconies facing the water. There is also Wi-Fi and a sauna, and a convenience store downstairs.

Conveniently located in the heart of town, **Shee Atika Totem Square Inn** (201 Katlian St., 907/747-3693 or 866/300-1353, www.totemsquare.com, $154 d) features a harborside setting, continental breakfast, an exercise room, and Wi-Fi.

Sitka's most distinctive lodging option is **Rockwell Lighthouse** (907/747-3056), a three-bedroom home built in the shape of a lighthouse on an island less than a mile from town. Skiff access is provided. With its nautical decor, curving interior staircase up into the lighthouse, and picture-perfect setting, you'll be signing up for lighthouse duty after a night or two. The entire house sleeps up to four people for $200, but call a year ahead for reservations in midsummer. Credit cards are not accepted, and a two-night minimum stay is required in summer (though you will want more time).

Bed-and-Breakfasts

Ann's Gavan Hill B&B (415 Arrowhead St., 907/747-8023, www.annsgavanhill.com) features six guest rooms with three shared baths, a hot tub on the covered side deck, filling homemade breakfasts, a guest computer, and a relaxed Alaskan atmosphere. One room is wheelchair accessible, and the rates are reasonable at $75 s or $95 d.

Helga's B&B (907/747-5497, www.sitkaalaskalodging.com, $90 s, $100 d) is a large beachside home three miles out on Halibut Point Road. The three guest rooms have Wi-Fi and private baths. Breakfast is a bit minimal (muffins, coffee, and juice) but the guest rooms contain microwaves and fridges.

Alaska Ocean View B&B (1101 Edgecumbe Dr., 907/747-8310 or 888/811-6870, www.sitka-alaska-lodging.com, $99–169 s, $119–189 d) is a lovely home with fabulous Sitka Sound vistas. Two guest rooms and a suite have private baths. Amenities include organic breakfasts, in-room fireplaces, Wi-Fi, a pond, and a covered hot tub on the patio.

Annahootz B&B (111 Jeff Davis St., 907/747-6498 or 800/746-6498, www.sitka.org/annahootz, $110 d) has two guest rooms with private baths, Wi-Fi, microwaves, and stocked fridges for make-it-yourself breakfasts.

Also of note is **Baranof Island B&B** (410

Charteris St., 907/747-8306, www.baranofislandbandb.com, $95 d), where two guest rooms share a bath. The large home has a private entrance, queen beds, Wi-Fi, a guest living room, and continental breakfasts.

For luxurious and modern lodging right along the water, stay at **Otter's Cove B&B** (3211 Halibut Point Rd., 907/747-4529, www.ottercovebandb.com, $130–150 d), with three spotless guest rooms, delicious homemade breakfasts, private baths, Wi-Fi, and a backyard (watch for the eagles) containing a fire pit and grill.

Vacation Rentals and Lodges

Sitka has 20 or so homes, apartments, and cabins that are rented out to travelers, including **Frank & Gloria's Place** (907/747-8711, www.sitkadream.com, $145 d), **Chocolate Moose** (907/747-5159, $125 d), and **Cottages on Monastery** (907/747-8123, www.cottagesonmonastery.com, $125–150 d).

A number of Sitka-area lodges provide all-inclusive fishing, meal, and lodging packages. These include **Baranof Wilderness Lodge** (530/579-3394 or 800/613-6551, www.flyfishalaska.com), **Dove Island Lodge** (907/747-5660 or 888/318-3474, www.aksitkasportfishing.com), **Quest Alaska Lodges** (605/229-8685, www.questalaskalodges.com), and **Wild Strawberry Lodge** (907/747-3232 or 800/770-2628, www.wildstrawberrylodge.com).

CAMPING

There are no campgrounds near downtown Sitka, but the Forest Service provides camping at each end of the road. The outstanding **Starrigavan Campground** (www.recreation.gov, $14–16) is seven miles northwest of town and 0.75 miles beyond the ferry terminal. Starrigavan is open all year, but there are no services October–April. All sites are wheelchair accessible. Campsites to the left of the road face onto a rocky beach, while those to the right border Starrigavan Creek, where you can watch spawning coho salmon in late summer. Starrigavan fills up with RVs in July–August, but there are six walk-in sites on the ocean side of the campground. Starrigavan also has an **artesian well** with wonderfully fresh spring water. Sitkans often drive out to fill big bottles for themselves.

The Forest Service's **Starrigavan Creek cabin** (www.recreation.gov, $50) sits amid the campsites. Constructed from logs cut on the site in 2008, this two-story cabin is wheelchair accessible and has a simple kitchen, a woodstove, and room for six. Book well ahead for this very special lodging option.

The 0.25-mile boardwalk **Estuary Life Trail** (wheelchair accessible) leads along the edge of the marsh from the campground and connects with a 0.75-mile **Forest and Muskeg Trail.** Placards describe points along this easy trail. On the road between the ferry and the campground are interpretive display signs marking the site of **Old Sitka**—burned by the Tlingits in 1802.

Quiet and little-used **Sawmill Creek Campground** (free, no water) is up Blue Lake Road, six miles east of town. The campground is a bit remote, making it hard to reach on foot, and the rough road is not recommended for RVs.

Park RVs at the city-run **Sealing Cove RV Park** (907/747-3439, April–Sept., $21 with hookups) on Japonski Island. **Sitka Sportsman's RV Park** (907/747-6033, $20) is adjacent to the ferry terminal on Halibut Point Road.

FOOD

Breakfast and Lunch

A delightful place to spend time is **Backdoor Café** (907/747-8856, Mon.–Fri. 6:30 A.M.–5 P.M., Sat. 6:30 A.M.–2 P.M., closed Sun., $4–7), an espresso shop behind Old Harbor Books on Lincoln Street. Backdoor is the literary and greenie hangout, and also serves daily lunch specials and pastries. This is the definitive Sitka meeting place.

Tucked downstairs in the Raven Radio building at the base of the bridge, **Larkspur Café** (2 Lincoln St., 907/966-2326, www.larkspurcafe.blogspot.com, Sun. 10 A.M.–3 P.M., Wed.–Sat. 11 A.M.–10 P.M., $8–15) has a menu that changes often, with fresh seafood (of course), local berries and produce in season, wonderful soups and chowders, paninis, salads, espresso, beer, wine, and occasional live music.

Victoria's (118 Lincoln St., 907/747-9301, daily 6 A.M.–9 P.M., $10–22), in the Sitka Hotel, is a decent breakfast and lunch spot but also serves a full dinner menu. Pop open your laptop for free Wi-Fi. A few doors up the street is a pharmacy that houses **Harry's Soda Shop** (907/747-8006, www.whitesalaska.com) for malts, shakes, banana splits, and homemade ice cream.

All-American

Get burgers, milk shakes, and other fast food—plus hearty breakfasts—at **Lane 7 Snack Bar** (236 Katlian St., 907/747-6310, www.lane7.com, Mon.–Sat.). **Subway** probably has the cheapest meal deal in town; it's behind the Westmark on Seward Street. Of course, there's always the **McDonald's** a mile out on Halibut Point Road for industrial-strength junk food. With the harbor-and-mountains view, this McD's certainly has one of the most impressive vistas in the entire corporate chain.

While waiting for your flight, stop by the airport's **Nugget Restaurant** (907/966-2480) for a slice of their locally famous pies.

International

Pizza Express (236 Lincoln St., 907/966-2428) serves authentic Mexican food (around $11) and decent pizzas. They're directly across from the Russian Orthodox church.

If you like Japanese food in an unpretentious setting, **Little Tokyo** (315 Lincoln St., 907/747-5699, Mon.–Sat.) is one of the best deals in town. In addition to fresh sushi, they offer a filling bento box dinner (miso soup, pot stickers, sushi, salad, and teriyaki chicken) for just $11.

Fine Dining

Van Winkle & Sons (205 Harbor Dr., 907/747-7652, lunch Mon.–Fri., dinner nightly, dinner entrées $15–27), near the bridge, has seafood, pasta, and prime rib but is best known for halibut fish-and-chips. This is the real thing, Alaskan style. The upstairs setting is quiet and romantic.

On the water three miles out of town, **Channel Club** (2906 Halibut Point Rd., 907/747-7440, www.sitkachannelclub.com, Sun.–Thurs. 5–9 P.M., Fri.–Sat. 5–10 P.M. summer, Tues.–Sat. 5–9 P.M. winter, entrées $24–32) serves seafood, steaks, prime rib (their signature dish), a big salad bar (included with most meals), and great appetizers. Call for a free shuttle from town.

Sitka's culinary gem, **Ludvig's Bistro** (256 Katlian St., 907/966-3663, www.ludvigsbistro.com, daily 4–10 P.M. May–Sept. only) ranks among the top cafés in Alaska. It's small, stylish, and noisy, with a creative Mediterranean-meets-Alaska menu. You'll find Caesar salads, daily chowders, fresh seafood specials, and pasta. Ludvig's is two blocks down Katlian, which is too far for most of the cruise ship folks to walk. Reservations are recommended, but singles will usually find space at the wine bar. Entrées run $20–33, or you can choose a selection of small tapas dishes for $17 each. The restaurant also has a seasonal **soup cart** located near the base of the bridge weekdays 11 A.M.–2 P.M. serving clam chowder and baguette sandwiches for $8–11.

Groceries and Produce

Sea Mart (907/747-6266, www.seamart.com), two miles from town along Halibut Point Road, has a salad bar, a deli, a bakery, a food court, and Sitka's most complete selection of groceries. Closer to town is **Lakeside Grocery** (705 Halibut Point Rd., 907/747-3317).

The **Sitka Farmers Market** (www.sitkalocalfoodsnetwork.org) takes place at the ANB Hall (235 Katlian St.) every other Saturday 10 A.M.–2 P.M. in the summer, with local produce, crafts, artworks, music, and food, including grilled fish.

SHOPPING

Sitka's specialty is Russian art, especially colorful nesting eggs, painted icons, and other traditional works. Several shops sell Russian crafts downtown; walk around until you find something you like. More noteworthy is **Sitka Rose Gallery** (907/747-3030 or 888/236-1536, www.sitkarosegallery.com) in a historic century-old home next to the Russian Bishop's House on Lincoln Street. Inside, find a mix of quality Native Alaskan art and Alaskan paintings, sculpture, and jewelry. The same building houses **WinterSong Soap Company** (907/747-8949 or 888/819-8949, www.wintersongsoap.com), where colorful scented soaps are handcrafted on the premises.

Located five miles east of town, **Theobroma Chocolate Company** (907/966-2349 or 888/985-2345, www.theobromachocolate.com) manufactures gourmet chocolates in a building next to the old pulp mill. You can watch them creating and packaging the chocolates, or sample unusual varieties—try the Dark Midnight Espresso, Sitka Crunch, or one of the salmon- or halibut-shaped chocolates.

Fairweather Gallery & Gifts (209 Lincoln St., 907/747-8677, www.fairweatherprints.com) is a great place to buy "wearable art" in the form of exquisite hand-painted dresses, tops, and scarves. It has the most unique T-shirts in town, plus a backroom art gallery. A few doors up the street is **Artist Cove Gallery** (241 Lincoln St., 907/747-6990, www.artistcovegallery.com). The Sheldon Jackson Museum (907/747-8981, www.museums.state.ak.us) sells Native Alaskan crafts.

Old Harbor Books (201 Lincoln St., 907/747-8808, www.oldharborbooks.com) has an outstanding collection of books on Alaska (and beyond), along with a pleasant coffee shop in the back.

The **Sitka Public Library** (907/747-8708, www.cityofsitka.com, Mon.–Fri. 10 A.M.–9 P.M., Sat.–Sun. 1–9 P.M.), next to Centennial Hall downtown, has a free paperback exchange with plenty of titles, plus a phone for local calls. Check your email on the computers, use their Wi-Fi, or borrow binoculars to watch whales, seals, and porpoises from the library windows that overlook the bay. Curved benches out back make a pleasant lunch spot when it isn't raining.

SERVICES

The **Forest Service** office (907/747-6671 or 907/747-6685 for recorded info) is in the orange-red building at 204 Siginaka Way.

Get showers at **Baranof Laundromat** (1211 Sawmill Creek Rd.) and **Sitka Laundry Center,** across from McDonald's on Halibut Point Road. A better deal is the public **swimming pool** (601 Halibut Point Rd., 907/747-8670) in Blatchley Middle School, where you can swim, sauna, and shower.

Sitka's main post office is on Sawmill Creek Road, 1.5 miles south of town, but a substation is downtown at 338 Lincoln Street. For medical emergencies, head to **Sitka Community Hospital** (209 Moller Ave., 907/747-3241, www.sitkahospital.org).

GETTING THERE

Ferry

Alaska Marine Highway (907/465-3941 or 800/642-0066, www.dot.state.ak.us/amhs) ferries reach Sitka several times a week during the summer, but the schedule is confusing, with various ships plying different routes. When it's operational—and this can be frustratingly uncommon—the high speed *Fairweather* makes a quick 4.5-hour connection between Juneau and Sitka, but be sure to confirm the ferry's departure time so you don't end up sitting in the ferry terminal. The terminal (907/747-8737) is open two hours before ship arrivals and is located seven miles north of town. **Sitka Tours shuttle buses** (907/747-8443) are available for $10 round-trip, and a taxi runs around $20 each way. Other options include tours and hitching—easy and often faster than the buses, both into and out of town.

Air

The airport is on Japonski Island, just under a mile from town by road. **Alaska Airlines** (907/966-2926 or 800/426-0333, www.alaskaair.com) flies to Juneau twice a day, plus nonstop to Seattle in the summer. Note that these flights can be canceled or delayed when the weather gets particularly adverse, a common winter experience.

Mt. Edgecumbe, Sitka

Harris Aircraft Services (907/966-3050 or 877/966-3050, www.harrisaircraft.com) has service several times a week to Angoon, Kake, Klawock, and Port Alexander, plus flightseeing and charters. **Air Excursions** (907/697-2375 or 800/354-2479, www.airexcursions.com) doesn't have scheduled service but typically flies between Sitka and other Southeast Alaska towns several times a day in the summer.

For transit into town, **Airport shuttles** (907/747-8443, $10 round trip) meet Alaska Airlines flights, or get a ride (around $10 one-way) with **Hank's Taxi & Tours** (907/747-8888, www.hankstours.com), **Sitka Cab** (907/747-5001), or **More Taxi and Tours** (907/738-3210, www.moorebusi.com).

GETTING AROUND

The city's **Community Ride Bus** (907/747-7103, http://publictransit.sitkatribe.org) has hourly service on weekdays, taking you from downtown out on Halibut Point Road and Sawmill Creek Road for $2 each way.

Transit Trolley (907/747-7290, www.sitkatribe.org, $10 day pass) buses cruise around Sitka, stopping at all the major sightseeing destinations. Buses operate weekdays and when cruise ships are in port.

Rent cars (starting at $55 per day plus 20 percent tax) at the airport from **North Star Rent-A-Car** (907/966-2552 or 800/722-6927, www.northstarrentacar.com) or **Avis** (907/966-2404 or 800/478-2847, www.avis.com). Book ahead for the busy summer months.

Tours

The ferry terminal is seven miles from town, but despite the distance you'll have time for a quick "ferry stopover tour," even if you don't stay. Many folks ride the **Sitka Tours** buses (907/747-8443, $10 round-trip) that meet the ferries and stop at the cathedral and Sitka National Historical Park. They also offer historic and nature walks geared to cruise ship travelers.

Tribal Tours (907/747-3770 or 888/270-

8687, www.sitkatours.com, $44 adults, $34 children), provides a Tlingit slant to tours of Sitka's sights. The 2.5-hour bus tours include a traditional dance performance at the Tribal Community House, plus visits to most local sights.

St. Lazaria Islands National Wildlife Refuge is a great place to see tufted puffins, storm petrels, auklets, whales, seals, and Steller sea lions. **Sitka's Secrets** (907/747-5089, www.sitkasecret.com) has three-hour cruises to the refuge and to other parts of Sitka Sound for $120 per person.

Allen Marine Tours (907/747-8100 or 888/747-8101, www.allenmarinetours.com) offers a 2.5-hour "Wildlife Quest" ($79 adults, $49 children) on Tuesday, Thursday, and Saturday evenings all summer. If sea conditions aren't too rough, these include time at St. Lazaria Island and Salisbury Sound. A naturalist is on board.

For something completely different, **Sea Life Discovery Tours** (907/966-2301 or 877/966-2301, www.sealifediscoverytours.com, May–Sept., $86 adults, $60 children) operates a semisubmersible vessel with large underwater windows plus a camera for close-up views on the monitor as a diver heads to deeper waters. Two-hour tours are a fun way to view kelp forests, fish, crabs, sea urchins, anemones, starfish, and other creatures without getting wet. The same folks also run ATV treks and speedy "ocean raft" tours; see www.greenlingenterprises.com for details.

Chichagof Island

HOONAH

The largest Tlingit village in the Southeast, Hoonah (pop. 900) nestles in Port Frederick, 20 miles south of Glacier Bay. Port Frederick has served as a home for the Tlingits since the last ice age drove them out of Glacier Bay and across Icy Strait to the north coast of Chichagof Island. There they found a protected bay they called Huna, meaning "place where the north wind doesn't blow." The Northwest Trading Company opened a store here in 1880, and missionaries added a church and school the following year. A cannery opened in 1912 and operated until 1953. The attractively restored old cannery still stands a mile north of town at the entrance to Port Frederick, but the old village and many priceless Tlingit cultural items were destroyed in a fire in 1944. The people rebuilt their village on the ashes.

Today Hoonah is far from being the prettiest town in Alaska. The weathered clapboard houses are unpainted, and junk cars pile up in the yards. It's the sort of town where the eagle calls blend with the sounds of motorboats and mufflerless dump trucks. There are dogs in almost every house and children playing on every porch. Life in Hoonah follows a slow pace: Residents half-complain that they are unable to go anywhere without meeting someone who wants to talk the hours away. Hoonah's economy is a blend of commercial fishing, a bit of logging, and traditional activities such as deer hunting, fishing, and berry picking.

The impressive cliff faces of **Elephant Mountain** (2,775 feet) guard the southern flank of Hoonah. Unfortunately, two Native corporations, Huna Totem and Sealaska, have logged much of their land near town, selling off their centuries-old heritage for short-term gain. Hoonah is now surrounded by a spiderweb of logging roads on both Native Alaskan and Forest Service land, making this a good place to explore by mountain bike, if you're prepared for all the clear-cuts.

Icy Strait Point

In the last decade Hoonah plunged into cruise ship tourism. The picturesque cannery building at Port Frederick (Icy Strait Point, 907/945-3141, www.icystraitpoint.com) has been restored, and cruise passengers (plus a few independent travelers) get a look at the way canneries operated in the 1930s. There are Native cultural presentations, whale-watching excursions, kayaking, charter fishing, mountain biking, and the real attraction: **Ziprider** ($100), the world's longest cable ride. It starts with a bus ride to the top of the mountain behind town. Then you buckle into a seat for a 60-mph blast that plummets down the slope. This exhilarating ride only lasts 90 seconds, but it seems like an eternity if you're afraid of heights. Icy Strait Point is generally open Sunday–Wednesday in the summer, and when cruise ships are in port.

Recreation

If you have a car, the 0.25-mile **Bear Paw Lake Trail,** 18 miles south of town on Road 8508, leads to a good lake where you can catch trout or coho salmon. Kayakers and canoeists may want to paddle the 40 miles from Hoonah to Tenakee Springs. The route goes to the head of Port Frederick, where there is a 100-yard portage into Tenakee Inlet. Neka Estuary in Port Frederick is a good place to see bears. A Forest Service cabin is available at nearby **Salt Lake Bay,** but a considerable amount of logging has beaten you there. Ask at the **Forest Service Hoonah District Office** (907/945-3631, www.fs.fed.us/r10/tongass) for details on these and other possible kayak trips in the area, including to **Neka Hot Spring,** 16 miles west of Hoonah.

Practicalities

Icy Strait Lodge (907/945-3636, www.icystraitnow.com, $95–105 d) is the main lodging place in town, with a dozen guest rooms plus a good restaurant (daily 8 A.M.–1:30 P.M. and 5–9 P.M., $11–27) with pizzas, burgers, steaks, and seafood. In addition, several Icy Strait Point places serve food in the summer.

Hoonah has two small grocery stores, two bars, a liquor store, a variety store, an ATM, and a laundry, plus showers at the harbor. A few miles southwest of town is the only agricultural commune in Southeast Alaska, Mt. Bether Bible Center.

Getting There

Hoonah's **ferry terminal** (907/945-3293) is 0.5 miles from town. Across from the ferry terminal is a tiny but interesting old cemetery. Ferries arrive four days a week, stopping for approximately an hour—long enough for a quick jog into town and back. Make reservations through Alaska Marine Highway (907/465-3941 or 800/642-0066, www.dot.state.ak.us/amhs).

Both **Wings of Alaska** (907/789-0790, www.wingsofalaska.com) and **Air Excursions** (907/697-2375 or 800/354-2479, www.airexcursions.com) have frequent flights between Juneau and Hoonah.

PELICAN AND VICINITY

If you're looking for a place to get away from it all, it's hard to get more remote than the tiny picturesque fishing village of Pelican (pop. 150) inside narrow Lisianski Inlet on the western shore of Chichagof Island. During the summer, Pelican's population doubles with the seasonal arrival of fishers. The town received its name from *The Pelican,* a fishing boat owned by the town's founder; there are no pelicans in Alaska.

Locals drive four-wheelers down the boardwalk connecting Pelican's restaurants, bars, general store, coin laundry, and cold-storage plant (closed in recent years). Showers are available at the coin laundry, or try the steam baths at the liquor store (no joke). The **Pelican Visitors Association** (907/735-2460, www.pelican.net) has info on local businesses.

Tiny Pelican has achieved notoriety as a party town, particularly when festivities reach their peak at the **Boardwalk Shuffle** in early May, with two days of live music—including a filthy-song contest—and some major-league boogying. This is not for the faint of heart. Lodging is in dorms at the old cannery, and Allen Marine makes a special boat run from Juneau for the event. If you miss the shuffle, don't miss the **4th of July,** with more fun and lots of competitive games, plus a little parade.

Accommodations

Lisianski Inlet Lodge (805/451-3153 or 800/962-8441, www.pelicanalaskafishing.com, May–mid-Sept.), two miles west of Pelican, offers a pricey but idyllic setting for a splurge. Package trips are $3,000 per person for five nights, including lodging, meals, fishing, and guide service.

Overlooking the harbor, **Chicobi Charters** (907/735-2233, www.chicobicharters.net) has a four-bedroom unit with a full kitchen and a living room. It sleeps up to six for $220, or $150 for two people.

Alaska Seaplane Service (907/735-2244 or 800/478-3360, www.flyalaskaseaplanes.com) rents out a one-bedroom boardwalk apartment called the Paddlehouse for $125 d plus $25 per additional guest.

Food and Drink

Infamous **Rosie's Bar and Grill** (907/735-2288, www.rosesbarandgrill.com) is a good place for drinking and pub grub, including burgers, chicken dinners, oysters, and BLTs. The ceiling is plastered with signed dollar bills, but you may get a surprise when you put yours up. If you haven't heard stories about Rosie's, you haven't been to Pelican. It's the sort of place where they sometimes black the windows out on the 4th of July—and for good reason.

Lisianski Inlet Café (907/735-2282, Mon.–Sat. 7 A.M.–3 P.M. Apr.–Sept., $7–12) is open for tasty breakfasts and lunches in the summer, with big omelets, sandwiches, and a killer borscht. The bar is a hopping place.

Getting There and Around

Ferry service to Pelican arrives only once or twice a month. The *LeConte* usually stays for two hours and then turns around for the return trip to Juneau. Get details from Alaska Marine Highway (800/642-0066, www.dot.state.ak.us/amhs),

Alaska Seaplane Service (907/735-2244 or 800/478-3360, www.flyalaskaseaplanes.com) has daily flights to Pelican from Juneau.

Several locals run fishing and sightseeing boat charters, and they will be happy to run you and your kayak out to such local destinations as White Sulfur Springs.

West Chichagof-Yakobi Wilderness

On the northwestern shore of Chichagof Island is the wildly rugged 264,747-acre West Chichagof–Yakobi Wilderness. Brown bears, marten, and deer are common, with sea otters and Steller sea lions in the waters. The coast is deeply indented with many small bays, lagoons, and inlets. It also supports areas of distinctive open spruce forest with grassy glades. Except for White Sulfur Springs, this wilderness gets little recreational use because of its remoteness and the storms that frequently make it a dangerous place for small boats and kayaks.

One of the most popular (make reservations well in advance) Forest Service cabins in Southeast Alaska is at **White Sulfur Springs,** accessible by boat, sea kayak, helicopter, or floatplane. The springs are a 20-mile kayak trip from Pelican. Much of the trip is through the protected waters of Lisianski Inlet and Strait, but the last five miles are exposed to the open ocean and require great caution. The cabin has a wonderful hot springs bathhouse overlooking Bertha Bay just 50 feet away. Note, however, that the springs are free and open to the public, so fishers, kayakers, and others from nearby Pelican will probably disturb your solitude.

Elfin Cove

This tiny fishing settlement (pop. 50 year-round, 200 in summer) tops the north end of Chichagof Island and is considered one of Alaska's prettiest towns. The setting is hard to beat: right on the edge of the wild waters of Cross Sound, yet protected within a narrow harbor. Elfin Cove has two general stores, lodging facilities, plus showers and a sauna during the summer.

The waters of Cross Sound and Icy Strait separate Chichagof Island from Glacier Bay

National Park. This is one of the best areas to see whales in Southeast Alaska, especially near Point Adolphus. Charter boats offer day trips from Glacier Bay to Elfin Cove during the summer months. Also nearby is the 23,000-acre **Pleasant-Lemesurier-Inian Islands Wilderness.**

It's pretty easy to see what makes the village tick, with 10 fishing lodges in such a small place, including **Tanaku Lodge** (www.tanaku.com), **Elfin Cove Lodge** (www.elfincove.com), **The Cove Lodge** (www.covelodge.com), and **Eagle Charters & Lodge** (www.eaglecharters.com). The last of these operates the only gift shop in town.

There is no state ferry service, but small cruise ships visit Elfin Cove several times a week in the summer, and **Alaska Seaplane Service** (907/789-3331 or 800/478-3360, www.flyalaskaseaplanes.com) has scheduled flights from Juneau.

TENAKEE SPRINGS

Residents of the tiny hamlet of Tenakee Springs (pop. 100 in summer, half that in winter) include retirees, back-to-the-earthers living off the grid, and a handful of fishers. Many Juneau folks have second homes here. Tenakee's houses stand on stilts along the shoreline; some have "long-drop" outhouses over the water (or beach, if the tide is out). Locals joke that at least the bathrooms get "flushed" twice a day by the tides. Tenakee has only one street, a dirt path barely wide enough for Tenakee's three vehicles (its oil truck, fire truck, and dump truck). Everyone else walks or uses four-wheelers and bicycles.

The town has struggled in recent years. When the K-12 school enrollment dropped to just seven students in 2009, locals went on Craigslist to recruit new families to move to Tenakee. They succeeded—at least temporarily—in keeping the school above the state's 10-student minimum. Find details at the **Tenakee Springs Business Association's** website, www.tenakeespringsak.com.

Tenakee is best known for its hot (107°F) **mineral springs,** housed in a building right beside the dock. The springs feed a small concrete pool with an adjacent changing room. There are separate hours for men (2–6 P.M. and 10 P.M.–9 A.M.) and women (6–10 P.M. and 9 A.M.–2 P.M.), but after midnight the rules tend to relax a bit. If the ferry is in town for more than a half-hour, be sure to take a quick dip in the pool.

Practicalities

You can pitch your tent two miles east of town along Indian River, but be sure to hang your food, since brown bears are sometimes a problem. Trails extend out of town for several miles in both directions along the shore. The trail south of town reaches eight miles to an old cannery and a homestead at Coffee Cove.

Beside the dock is **Snyder Mercantile Co.** (907/736-2205), a classic bush Alaska store with groceries, supplies, the latest gossip, and great folks. Built in 1899, the building is undergoing a major renovation, with a waterside restaurant and upstairs hotel rooms expected by 2011.

The other main feature of town is the Shamrock building, housing **Rosie's Blue Moon Café,** (lunch and dinner daily). You'll find chop suey, chicken, and steak on the limited menu, but almost everyone opts for Rosie Floresca's famous cheeseburgers ($7), served with freshly cut fries. There is no bar in town (it burned down a few years back), but there's a little liquor store across from the general store, and Rosie's serves beer and wine.

The Shamrock building also has a coin laundry in the back, and next door is **Party Time Bakery** (907/736-2262, daily 8 A.M.–2 P.M. summer, $6–10), open seasonally for cinnamon rolls, coffee, and bacon-and-egg breakfasts as well as daily soup specials and grilled sandwiches at lunch.

On the edge of town, **Tenakee Hot Springs Lodge** (907/364-3640, www.tenakeehotspringslodge.com, $90 s, $150 d) has five guest rooms sharing three baths; meals are available for guests. Call the Mercantile (907/736-2205) for a list of local cabin rentals. **Fishing Bear Charters** (907/736-2350, www.fishingbearcharters.com) has charters and ecotours.

Getting There

Tenakee is a popular weekend vacation spot for both Juneauites and travelers. The ferry ***LeConte*** arrives in Tenakee twice a week with a schedule that makes it possible to stop over the weekend before returning to Juneau. There is no ferry terminal, and cars cannot be offloaded. The ferry usually stays in town for just 30 minutes, barely long enough to get off the boat for a walk around. Get details from Alaska Marine Highway (800/642-0066, www.dot.state.ak.us/amhs).

Alaska Seaplane Service (907/789-3331 or 800/478-3360, www.flyalaskaseaplanes.com) has flights most days between Tenakee Springs and Juneau, or get a charter from **Ward Air** (907/789-9150, www.wardair.com).

Juneau

America's most beautiful state capital, Juneau (pop. 30,000) is a thriving slice of civilization surrounded by rugged Inside Passage scenery. The city perches on a thin strip of land at the mouth of Gold Creek, and behind it rise the precipitous summits of Mt. Juneau and Mt. Roberts. Out front, Gastineau Channel separates it from Douglas Island and the town of Douglas. The city abounds with cultural and artistic attractions, and the adjacent wild country provides a broad sampling of Southeast Alaska, from glacially capped mountains to protected coves where sea kayakers relax.

Juneau is the only state capital with no roads leading in or out. A government town, nearly half the local jobs are at state, federal, or city agencies. Tourism provides another mainstay for the local economy, fed by an annual influx of more than 700,000 visitors, primarily aboard luxury cruise ships. On summer days, up to five different ships tie up simultaneously, disgorging thousands of passengers. (To avoid the worst of the rush, get here before July or after August.) Juneau has a small fishing fleet and provides workers for a silver mine on nearby Admiralty Island.

Juneau may be small in population, but its boundaries extend to the Canadian border, covering 3,100 square miles. Less than half of Juneau's population actually lives downtown. The rest are spread into Douglas (across the channel), Mendenhall Valley (10 miles northwest), and other surrounding areas. As might be expected, these areas exhibit diverse personalities. Even the weather varies, with an average of 92 inches of rain each year downtown, but only 55 inches in Mendenhall Valley.

Downtown Juneau is marked by a mix of modern government offices and older wooden structures, many dating from the early 1900s. Across the bridge are Douglas Island and its bedroom community of Douglas. The town now consists of a few shops, but at its peak in 1915, when the Treadwell Gold Mine was operating, Douglas housed 15,000 miners. The road north from downtown Juneau is Southeast Alaska's only divided highway. Heading north, you first reach Mendenhall Valley, Juneau's version of suburbia: three shopping malls, a slew of fast fooderies, and hundreds of pseudorustic split-level homes and condos. But you can also see something most suburbs don't have: a drive-up glacier spilling out from the massive Juneau Ice Field. The road continues north from Mendenhall Valley for another 30 miles, passing Auke Lake, the ferry terminal, and scattered homes along the way, ending at scenic Echo Cove.

HISTORY

Gold in the Hills

In October 1880, two prospectors—Joe Juneau and Richard Harris—arrived at what would later be called Gold Creek. Along its banks was a small Tlingit fishing camp of the Auke tribe. Chief Kowee showed the prospectors

SOUTHEAST ALASKA

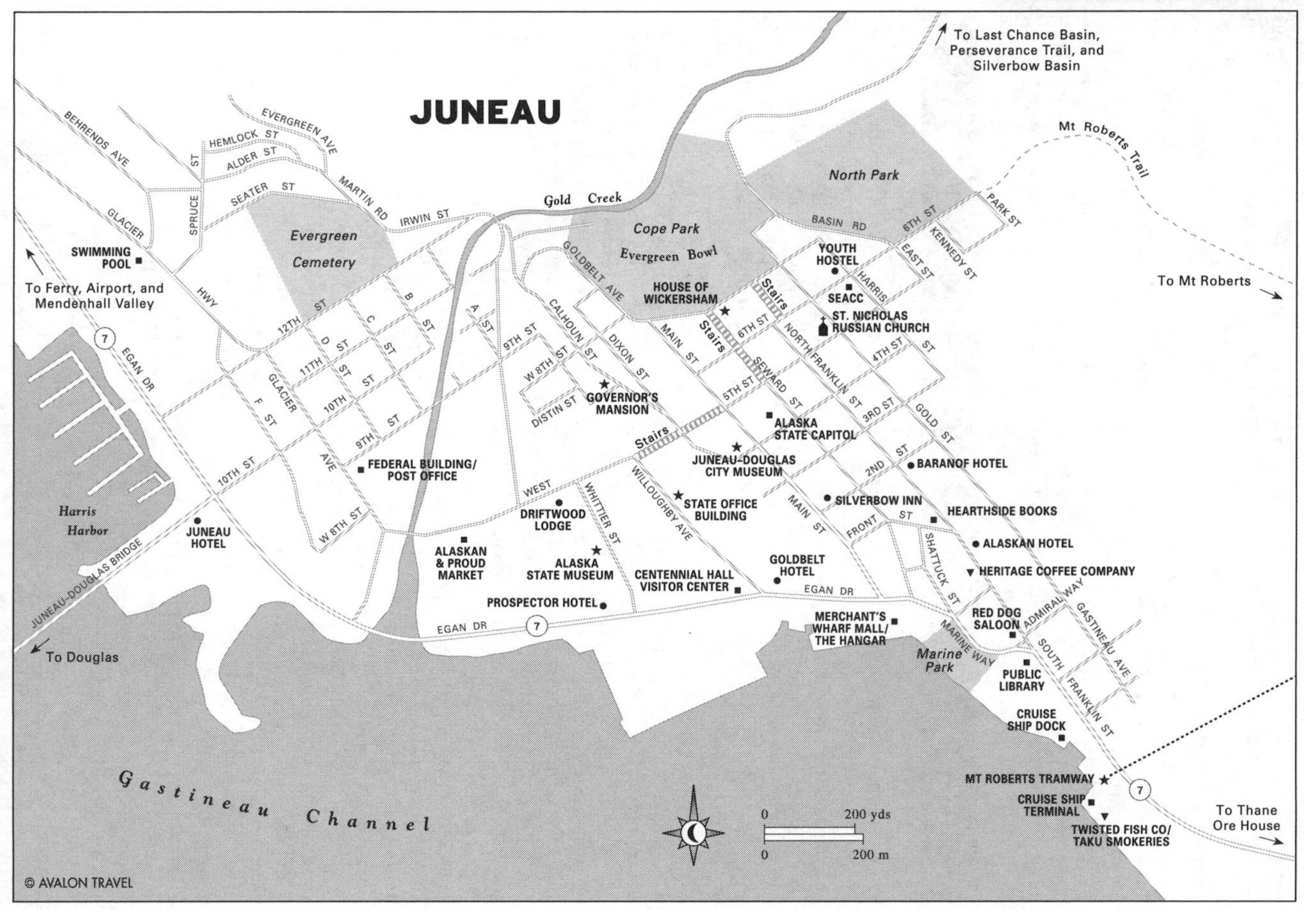

JUNEAU
To Last Chance Basin, Perseverance Trail, and Silverbow Basin
Mt Roberts Trail
To Mt Roberts
To Thane Ore House
North Park
Cope Park
Evergreen Bowl
Gold Creek
Evergreen Cemetery
Marine Park
Harris Harbor
Gastineau Channel
To Ferry, Airport, and Mendenhall Valley
To Douglas
YOUTH HOSTEL
SEACC
ST. NICHOLAS RUSSIAN CHURCH
HOUSE OF WICKERSHAM
GOVERNOR'S MANSION
ALASKA STATE CAPITOL
JUNEAU-DOUGLAS CITY MUSEUM
STATE OFFICE BUILDING
BARANOF HOTEL
SILVERBOW INN
HEARTHSIDE BOOKS
ALASKAN HOTEL
HERITAGE COFFEE COMPANY
RED DOG SALOON
PUBLIC LIBRARY
CRUISE SHIP DOCK
MT ROBERTS TRAMWAY
CRUISE SHIP TERMINAL
TWISTED FISH CO/ TAKU SMOKERIES
MERCHANT'S WHARF MALL/ THE HANGAR
GOLDBELT HOTEL
CENTENNIAL HALL VISITOR CENTER
ALASKA STATE MUSEUM
PROSPECTOR HOTEL
DRIFTWOOD LODGE
ALASKAN & PROUD MARKET
FEDERAL BUILDING/ POST OFFICE
JUNEAU HOTEL
SWIMMING POOL
Stairs
PARK ST
KENNEDY ST
6TH ST
EAST ST
BASIN RD
HARRIS
4TH ST
GOLD ST
3RD ST
2ND ST
NORTH FRANKLIN ST
SEWARD ST
5TH ST
6TH ST
MAIN ST
FRONT ST
SHATTUCK ST
ADMIRAL WAY
GASTINEAU AVE
SOUTH FRANKLIN ST
MARINE WAY
EGAN DR
WILLOUGHBY AVE
WHITTIER ST
GOLDBELT AVE
DIXON ST
CALHOUN ST
W 8TH ST
DISTIN ST
9TH ST
WEST
A ST
B ST
C ST
D ST
IRWIN ST
MARTIN RD
EVERGREEN AVE
HEMLOCK ST
ALDER ST
SEATER ST
SPRUCE ST
12TH ST
11TH ST
10TH ST
9TH ST
W 8TH ST
GLACIER AVE
F ST
GLACIER HWY
10TH ST
BEHRENDS AVE
JUNEAU-DOUGLAS BRIDGE
7
0 200 yds
0 200 m
© AVALON TRAVEL

gold flakes in the creek, and the resulting discovery turned out to be one of the largest gold deposits ever found. Harris and Juneau quickly staked a 160-acre town site. The first boatloads of prospectors arrived the next month, and almost overnight a town sprouted along the shores of Gastineau Channel. Three giant hard-rock gold mines were developed in the area, eventually producing some 7 million ounces of gold, worth *$4 billion* at today's prices. Compare that to the $7.2 million the United States paid Russia for Alaska only 13 years before the discovery.

The **Alaska Juneau (AJ) Mine** proved the most successful, operating for more than 50 years. Built in Last Chance Basin behind Juneau, its three tunnels connected the ore source to the crushing and recovery mill site on Gastineau Channel. Inside the mine was a maze of tunnels that eventually reached over 100 miles in length. Because the ore was low grade—it could take 28 tons of ore to yield one ounce of gold—enormous quantities of rock had to be removed. At its peak, the mill (still visible just south of town) employed 1,000 workers to process 12,000 tons of ore per day. Tailings from the mill were used as the fill on which much of downtown Juneau was constructed. (Franklin Street was originally built on pilings along the shore.) The AJ closed down in 1944 because of wartime labor shortages, and it never reopened.

The **Perseverance Mine** operated 1885–1921, with a two-mile tunnel carrying ore from Gold Creek to the mill four miles south of Juneau. It eventually ran into low-grade ore and was forced to close.

The best known Juneau-area mine was the **Treadwell,** on Douglas Island. The Treadwell Complex consisted of four mines and five stamping mills to process the ore. It employed some 2,000 male workers who were paid $100 a month, some of the highest wages anywhere in the world at the time. The men enjoyed such amenities as a swimming pool, Turkish baths, tennis courts, a bowling alley, a gymnasium, and a 15,000-volume library. The giant Treadwell stamping mills where the ore was pulverized made so much noise that people in downtown Douglas had to shout to be heard. Everything changed on April 21, 1917, when the ground atop the mines suddenly began to collapse, swallowing first the gymnasium and swimming pool, then the fire hall. Sea water rushed in, filling the tunnels as the miners ran for their lives. Amazingly, all of them apparently escaped alive. (The only missing miner was reportedly later seen in a nearby tavern before he skipped town.) Only one of the four mines was not destroyed in the collapse, and that one closed five years later.

Later Years

Juneau became the capital of Alaska in 1906 as a result of its rapid growth and the simultaneous decline of Sitka. Several attempts have been made to move the capital closer to the state's present power center, Anchorage. In 1976, Alaskan voters approved a new site just north of Anchorage, but six years later, when expectations for petro-billions had subsided into reality, voters thought better of the move and refused to fund it. Juneauites breathed a sigh of relief and went on a building spree that only ended with the sudden drop in state oil revenue from the 1986 oil-price plummet. Recent years have seen ever-increasing cruise ship tourism. Locals are starting to tire of the influx and its impact on the town; in 1999 they slapped a head tax on every cruise passenger who steps off in Juneau. By the way, Fridays are usually a light day for cruise ship traffic, so time your downtown visits accordingly.

SIGHTS

Juneau is jam-packed with things to see and do, from glaciers to salmon bakes and tram rides. It's the sort of place that travelers love. Many interesting places are right downtown—including two museums, numerous historic buildings, unusual shops, and even a library with a view. Farther afield are dozens of hiking trails, several easily accessible glaciers, and such attractions as an informative fish hatchery, a brewery, old mining buildings, a stone

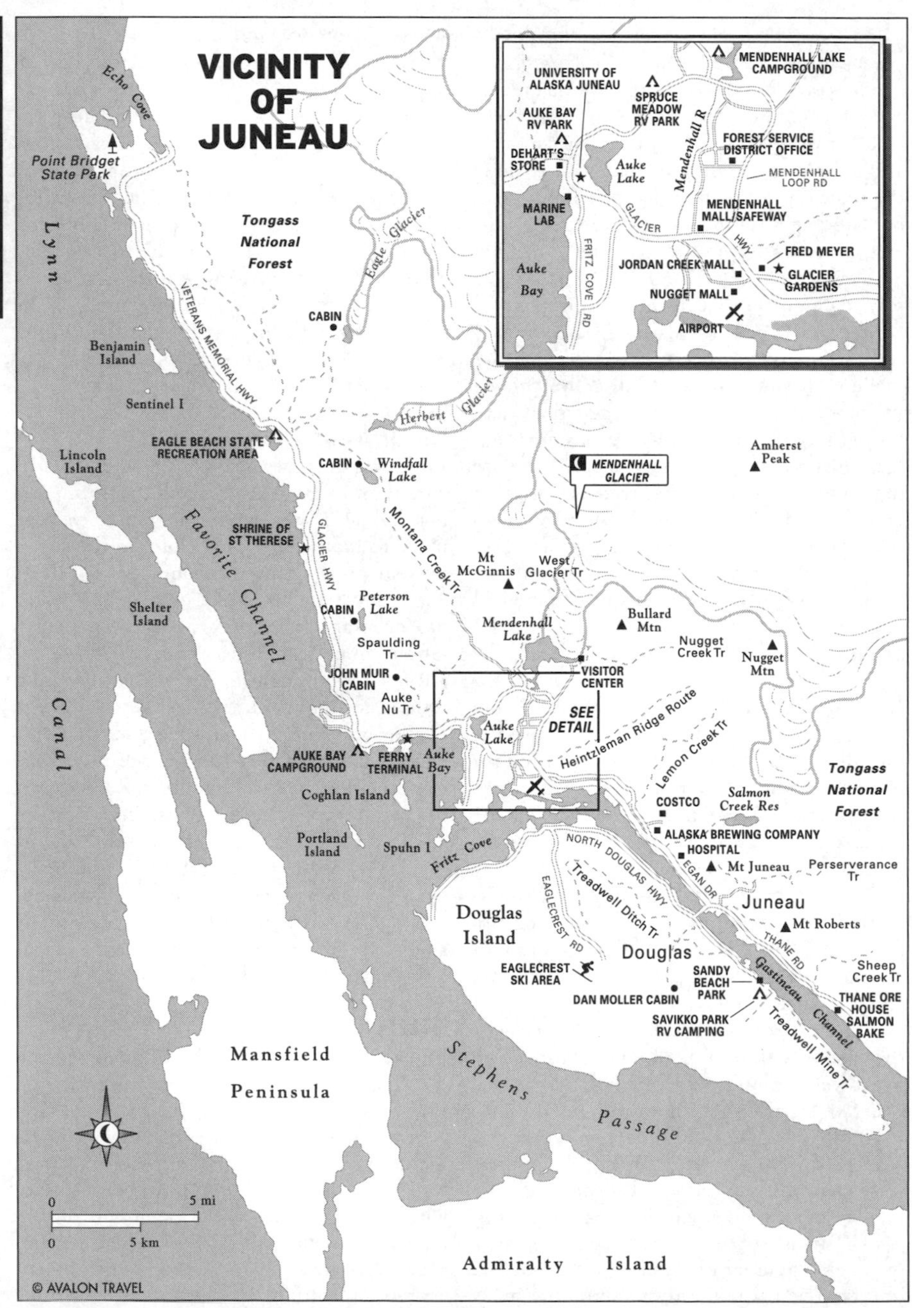
VICINITY OF JUNEAU
Echo Cove
Point Bridget State Park
Lynn Canal
Tongass National Forest
Eagle Glacier
CABIN
VETERANS MEMORIAL HWY
Benjamin Island
Sentinel I
Herbert Glacier
EAGLE BEACH STATE RECREATION AREA
Lincoln Island
CABIN
Windfall Lake
Montana Creek Tr
Favorite Channel
SHRINE OF ST THERESE
GLACIER HWY
Mt McGinnis
West Glacier Tr
Shelter Island
CABIN
Peterson Lake
Mendenhall Lake
Bullard Mtn
Spaulding Tr
Nugget Creek Tr
Nugget Mtn
JOHN MUIR CABIN
VISITOR CENTER
Auke Nu Tr
SEE DETAIL
Auke Lake
Heintzleman Ridge Route
Lemon Creek Tr
AUKE BAY CAMPGROUND
FERRY TERMINAL
Auke Bay
Coghlan Island
COSTCO
Salmon Creek Res
Tongass National Forest
ALASKA BREWING COMPANY
Portland Island
Spuhn I
Fritz Cove
NORTH DOUGLAS HWY
HOSPITAL
Mt Juneau
Perserverance Tr
EGAN DR
EAGLECREST RD
Treadwell Ditch Tr
Juneau
Douglas Island
Mt Roberts
Douglas
THANE RD
EAGLECREST SKI AREA
SANDY BEACH PARK
Sheep Creek Tr
DAN MOLLER CABIN
Gastineau Channel
THANE ORE HOUSE SALMON BAKE
SAVIKKO PARK RV CAMPING
Treadwell Mine Tr
Mansfield Peninsula
Stephens Passage
0 5 mi
0 5 km
Admiralty Island
© AVALON TRAVEL
Amherst Peak
MENDENHALL GLACIER
MENDENHALL LAKE CAMPGROUND
UNIVERSITY OF ALASKA JUNEAU
SPRUCE MEADOW RV PARK
AUKE BAY RV PARK
Mendenhall R
FOREST SERVICE DISTRICT OFFICE
DEHART'S STORE
Auke Lake
MENDENHALL LOOP RD
MARINE LAB
GLACIER HWY
MENDENHALL MALL/SAFEWAY
FRITZ COVE RD
FRED MEYER
Auke Bay
JORDAN CREEK MALL
GLACIER GARDENS
NUGGET MALL
AIRPORT

church, and much more. Even on a rainy day, you'll find something fun in Juneau.

Information

Juneau's info spot is the **Centennial Hall Visitor Center** (101 Egan Dr., 907/586-2201 or 888/581-2201, www.traveljuneau.com, daily 8 A.M.–5 P.M. May–Sept., Mon.–Fri. 8:30 A.M.–4 P.M. Oct.–Apr.). Ask for the "Juneau Walking Tour" map on a nice day, or pick out a video for a rainy-day diversion.

Three other information kiosks in Juneau have brochures and may be staffed in the summer. Find them at Marine Park, the airport, and the Cruise Ship Terminal. Other useful online info sources for Juneau include www.juneauempire.com, www.capitalcityweekly.com, www.juneau.com, and the city website, www.juneau.org.

Alaska State Museum

Anyone new to town should not miss the Alaska State Museum (395 Whittier St., 907/465-2901, www.museums.state.ak.us, daily 8:30 A.M.–5:30 P.M. mid-May–late Sept., Tues.–Sat. 10 A.M.–4 P.M. late Sept.–mid-May, $5, under age 18 free). Inside, you'll find an impressive collection of Native Alaskan artifacts (including wildly creative Yup'ik Eskimo spirit masks) and exhibits relating to the Russian-American period and other aspects of Alaskan history. The museum also houses a gallery of contemporary fine arts and brings in special exhibits each summer. But the highlight is the circular stairwell, which houses a full-size bald eagle nest and other Alaskan wildlife.

Juneau-Douglas City Museum

The fine Juneau-Douglas City Museum (4th St. and Main St., 907/586-3572, www.juneau.org/parksrec/museum, Mon.–Fri. 9 A.M.–5 P.M., Sat.–Sun. 10 A.M.–5 P.M. May–Sept., Tues.–Sat. 10 A.M.–4 P.M. Oct.–Apr., $4 adults, children free) houses an interesting collection of maps, artifacts, photos, and videos from Juneau's rich gold-mining history. Be sure to check out the three-dimensional model of Perseverance Mine with its intricate maze of tunnels. Other features include a 19th-century store, a hands-on history room that's popular with kids, and a small gift shop. Join guided **walking tours** of historic Juneau—60 downtown buildings that were built before 1904 still remain—in the summer for $10, including museum admission.

© DON PITCHER

Mt. Roberts Tramway, with Juneau and Gastineau Channel in the background

Mt. Roberts Tramway

The Mt. Roberts Tramway (907/463-3412 or 888/461-8726, www.goldbelttours.com, Mon.–Fri. 8 A.M.–9 P.M., Sat.–Sun. 9 A.M.–9 P.M. May–Sept.) provides a fast way into the high country above Juneau. The tram starts at the cruise ship dock on the south end of town and climbs 1,800 feet up the mountain, providing panoramic views of the surrounding land and water. The six-minute ride ends at an observation deck surrounded by tall Sitka spruce trees. Facilities here include a nature center, a restaurant, gift shops, and a theater where you can watch an award-wining 20-minute film about Tlingit culture. The tram costs $27 adults, $14 children ages 6–12, and free for children under age 6. If you hike up, the ride down is only $5. Tickets are good all day, but the lines can get very long in late afternoon as cruise ship passengers rush back down to avoid missing their ship departures. Because of the elevation, snow typically covers the ground until mid-June or later, and trails may not be accessible.

Gastineau Guiding (907/586-2666, www.stepintoalaska.com) leads easy "town, tram, and trek" hikes that include a short bus tour of town, a tram ride up Mt. Roberts, and a one-hour hike for $74 adults, $38 children. Or you can save your cash and simply strike out on your own along scenic alpine trails. Be sure to look for several live spruce trees carved with traditional Tlingit designs.

State Office Building

Enter the State Office Building (SOB) from Willoughby Avenue and take the elevator up to the 8th floor. Here you'll discover a 1928 Kimball organ, a lovingly preserved totem pole from the 1880s, the Alaska State Library, and a panoramic view from the big **observation deck** (great for bag lunches). The airy lobby is also a pleasant place to stay dry on a rainy day; Friday at noon you'll enjoy the added bonus of an **organ recital.**

Governor's Mansion

Just up Calhoun Avenue from the SOB is the large white Governor's Mansion. Built in 1912 in the New England colonial style, it overlooks much of Juneau from its hilltop location. The mansion is not open to the public. Out front is a **totem pole** carved in 1939–1940. Near its base are the figures of a mosquito and a man, representing the Tlingit tale of the cannibalistic giant, Guteel, and his capture by hunters in a pit. The hunters built a fire to kill him, but just before he died he warned, "Even though you kill me, I'll continue to bite you." His ashes swirled into the air, becoming the mosquitoes that fulfill Guteel's promise.

More than 20 other totems are scattered around downtown. Most are recent carvings, but some date to the 19th century. Pick up the *Totem Pole Walking Tour* brochure from the Juneau-Douglas City Museum (4th St. and Main St.) to find them all.

State Capitol

Back on 4th Street is the marble Alaska State Capitol. Completed in 1931, it was originally the federal office building and post office. The building is not at all like a traditional state capitol, and from the outside it could easily be mistaken for an aging Midwestern bank, complete with wide steps and marble columns. Free tours (907/465-2479 for reservations) of the bank—oops, capitol—are every 30 minutes Monday–Friday 9 A.M.–4:30 P.M. and Saturday 10 A.M.–4 P.M. mid-May–mid-September. Historical photos line the 2nd floor. You may sit in on the legislature when it's in session January–March. The antics of the legislature are always a hoot, especially after the FBI raided their offices in 2006 and found ball caps brazenly labeled "Corrupt Bastard's Club." It makes me proud to be an Alaskan.

Last Chance Mining Museum

Behind town, Basin Road climbs 1.5 miles to the old AJ Gold Mine. The former compressor building here has been turned into the Last Chance Mining Museum (907/586-5338, www.gastineauchannel.blogspot.com, daily 9:30 A.M.–12:30 P.M., 3:30–6:30 P.M. mid-May–late Sept., $4, children free), which houses mining paraphernalia and a 3-D map of the ore body.

Historic Downtown

Dozens of historic buildings fill the heart of downtown Juneau. Get a brochure describing them from the Juneau-Douglas City Museum (4th St. and Main St.). One of Juneau's most photographed sights is the onion-domed **St. Nicholas Russian Orthodox Church** (5th St. and Gold St., 907/586-6790, www.juneau.org/parksrec/museum, Sun. 1–4 P.M., Mon.–Fri. 9 A.M.–5 P.M., Sat. 10 A.M.–2 P.M. mid-May–Sept., tours $2), built in 1894. Inside are icons and artwork, some dating from the 1700s. For a more evocative experience, attend a service (Sat. 6 P.M. and Sun. 10 A.M.).

© DON PITCHER

Franklin Street in downtown Juneau

Marine Park, along Shattuck Way, with its lively mix of people and picturesque views, is a good place to relax after your tour of downtown. Directly across the street a bright mural depicts the Haida creation legend.

Evergreen Cemetery, between 12th and Seater Streets on the north side of town, has the graves of Juneau's founders, Joe Juneau and Richard Harris, along with a marker near the spot where Chief Kowee was cremated.

House of Wickersham

Built in 1889, the House of Wickersham (213 7th St., 907/586-9001, www.alaskastateparks.org, Tues.–Sat. 10 A.M.–4 P.M. mid-May–Sept.) offers a good view of Juneau and the surrounding country, and visitors are provided a fine tour. This was the home of Judge James Wickersham (1857–1939), a man who had a major impact on Alaskan history. As Alaska's longtime delegate to Congress, in 1916 he introduced the first statehood bill—43 years before it passed—and was instrumental in the establishment of the territorial legislature, McKinley National Park, the University of Alaska, and the Alaska Railroad. Be sure to take a gander at the Native Alaskan ivory carvings that Judge Wickersham collected from around the state.

Macaulay Salmon Hatchery

The impressive Douglas Island Pink and Chum (DIPAC) salmon hatchery (2697 Channel Dr., 907/463-4810 or 877/463-2486, www.dipac.net, Mon.–Fri. 10 A.M.–6 P.M., Sat.–Sun. 10 A.M.–5 P.M. May–Sept., by appointment Oct.–Apr., $3 adults, $2 children under 13) is three miles north of town. Here you can learn about salmon spawning and commercial fishing, watch fish moving up one of the state's largest fish ladders, and check out the saltwater aquariums and underwater viewing windows. The facility includes shops and a visitors center where tours are offered. It's a fascinating place and well worth the entrance fee. The king, coho, and chum salmon return mid-June–September, and during that time you can try your hand at fishing out front.

Glacier Gardens

This unique private botanical garden (7600 Glacier Hwy., 907/790-3377, www.glaciergardens.com, daily 9 A.M.–6 P.M. May–Sept., $22 adults, $16 ages 6–12, under 6 free) is eight miles north of downtown Juneau. The gardens are spread over 50 acres of hillside forest and include hiking trails, waterfalls, ponds, and "flower tower" cascades of blooms from upside-down trees. Motorized carts (some set up to carry wheelchairs) transport visitors along four miles of paved paths to an overlook 500 feet up the mountainside, with views across the Mendenhall Wetlands. The city bus stops out front.

Alaskan Brewing Company

For something completely different, take the city bus to Anka Street in Lemon Creek and walk two blocks to Shaune Drive. Follow it a block to the Alaskan Brewing Company building (907/780-5866, www.alaskanbeer.com, tours every 30 minutes daily 11 A.M.–6P.M.

May–Sept., Thurs.–Sun. 11 A.M.–5 P.M. the rest of the year; free). You're given a sample of various beers at the end of the tour. The brewery has developed into one of the country's finest, with its beers winning top prizes at national and international festivals. The brewery gift shop sells T-shirts, hats, and other items.

Mendenhall Glacier

Southeast Alaska's best-known drive-up ice cube, Mendenhall Glacier is without a doubt Juneau's most impressive sight. This moving river of ice pushes down from the 1,500-square-mile **Juneau Ice Field** (the fifth largest in North America) and is 12 miles long and up to 1.5 miles wide. Since 1750 the glacier has been receding, and it is now several miles farther up Mendenhall Valley. It is retreating at about 150 feet each year, but still calving icebergs into Mendenhall Lake.

The **Mendenhall Glacier Visitors Center** (907/789-6640, www.fs.fed.us/r10/tongass, daily 8 A.M.–7:30 P.M. May–mid-Sept., Thurs.–Sun. 10 A.M.–4 P.M. mid-Sept.–Apr., $3, children free) provides panoramic views of the glacier from the floor-to-ceiling windows. Use the spotting scopes to check the slopes of nearby Bullard Mountain for mountain goats. Walk through the interpretive exhibits, slip into the theater for an excellent 11-minute film on the glacier, or buy a couple of glacier postcards in the bookstore. Forest Service naturalists lead walks on nearby trails and can answer your questions. Walk up at least one of these excellent paths if you want to come away with a deeper appreciation of Mendenhall Glacier.

Although it's 13 miles northwest of town, the glacier is easily accessible by city bus. Have the driver let you off when the bus turns left a mile up Mendenhall Loop Road. It's a one-mile walk up the road from here to the glacier. Buses run both directions around Mendenhall Loop Road. On the way back you can catch a bus heading either direction since both eventually drop you off downtown.

Mighty Great Trips (907/789-5460, www.mightygreattrips.com) provides transportation from downtown to the glacier for $14 round trip, and offers a 2.5-hour tour that includes time at the glacier for $27. Most other tour companies also offer tours to Mendenhall.

University and Auke Lake

The campus of the University of Alaska Southeast, which has 2,600 students, is a dozen miles northwest of Juneau on beautiful Auke Lake. The view across the lake to Mendenhall Glacier makes it one of the most attractive campuses anywhere. Also here is **Chapel by the Lake,** a popular place for weddings, with a dramatic backdrop of mountains and the Mendenhall Glacier. Across the highway, **Auke Bay Fisheries Lab** (Mon.–Fri. 8 A.M.–4:30 P.M.) has a small saltwater aquarium and fisheries displays.

Glacier Highway

If you have a vehicle, the 40-mile drive north from Juneau provides a wonderful escape. Twenty-three miles out is a quaint Catholic chapel built in 1939, the **Shrine of St. Therese** (907/780-6112, www.shrineofsainttherese.org). The cobblestone chapel is hidden away on a small bucolic wooded island connected to the mainland by a 400-foot causeway. Named for Alaska's patron saint, St. Thérèse of Lisieux, the chapel is open all the time, with Sunday service at 1 P.M. To the right as you face the shrine is the columbarium and gardens, with concentric circles of stones forming a cross. This is a wonderful quiet place to soak up the scenery, listen for humpback whales, or try your hand at fishing for salmon from the shore. The trail to Peterson Lake is nearby, and cabins are available for rent.

Eagle Beach (at Mile 28, parking $5) is a popular day-use area with picnic tables and panoramic vistas of the snowcapped Chilkat Range. Pull out your binoculars to look for whales in Lynn Canal. Stop at **Point Bridget State Park** (Mile 38) for a pleasant hike. The road ends at scenic **Echo Cove,** a launching point for boats and kayaks.

Taku Glacier Lodge

Historic Taku Glacier Lodge (907/586-6275, www.wingsairways.com, early May–Sept., no overnight visits) sits just across Taku Inlet from the glacier of the same name. This classic log structure was built in 1923, and short nature trails lead into the surrounding country. Black bears and eagles are frequent visitors (the bears were Juneau garbage bears that would have been shot if they had not been brought here). Visits to the lodge cost $260 adults, $220 children and include a half-hour scenic flight over Taku Glacier along with two hours at the lodge and a filling salmon lunch or dinner. Flights depart the Juneau waterfront up to five times per day between 9 A.M. and 5 P.M. The lodge is oriented to the cruise-ship crowd, so expect to see lots of other folks if you go on a day when several ships are docked.

ENTERTAINMENT AND EVENTS

Nightlife

Juneau has an active nightlife with plenty of live music almost every evening. The famous **Red Dog Saloon** (South Franklin St., 907/463-3658, www.reddogsaloon.com) has sawdust on the floor and honky-tonk music in the air every day and night during the summer, starting at 2 P.M. Be sure to look for Wyatt Earp's gun; he checked it in when passing through on June 17, 1900, but his ship left for Nome before the Marshall's office reopened, so it remained unclaimed. This is where cruise ship tourists and crewmembers drink.

A block up the street, inside the Alaskan Hotel, is the **Alaskan Bar** (167 S. Franklin St., 907/586-1000, www.thealaskanhotel.com), a quieter place with blues or folk music on weekends as well as Thursday night jam sessions. It's always packed with locals, who head here in summer to escape the Red Dog crowds. The Alaskan has Victorian decor, and you can hear lawyers and lobbyists talk shop from any seat in the place during the legislative session.

Billiards aficionados fill the seven tables upstairs inside **Viking Lounge** (218 Front St., 907/586-2159). Downstairs in the back is a classy disco with occasional live music and

Red Dog Saloon

the best dance floor in Juneau. Across the street is **Imperial Bar** (907/586-1960), popular with the young crowd on weekends, when live bands perform. More music is around the corner at the **Rendezvous** (184 S. Franklin St., 907/586-1270), with very loud rock and a lowlife crowd.

The Hangar (2 Marine Way, 907/586-5018, www.hangaronthewharf.com), on the wharf, has music to make you kick up your rain boots on Friday and Saturday nights. It is especially popular with state government workers on weeknights, with over 100 brews on tap or in bottles. Get here early for the window seats facing the water. **The Island Pub** (1102 2nd St., 907/364-1595, www.theislandpub.com) is a classy smoke-free bar in Douglas with live bands most Friday and Saturday nights.

Out near the airport, **The Sandbar** (2525 Industrial Blvd., 907/789-3411) has a large dance floor and rock or country music on weekends. Also out in Mendenhall Valley is **Marlintini's Lounge** (9121 Glacier Hwy., 907/789-0799, www.myspace.com/marlintinis), which mixes karaoke on weeknights with rock bands and $10 pitchers of beer Thursday–Saturday nights.

Performing Arts and Music

On Friday evenings 7–8:30 P.M. in the summer, Marine Park in downtown Juneau comes alive with free **Concerts in the Park** (907/586-2787), ranging from classical to Middle Eastern folk. The **Juneau Symphony** (907/586-4676, www.juneausymphony.org) has monthly concerts October–April at various local venues. **Perseverance Theatre** (907/364-2421, www.perseverancetheatre.org) is a respected Douglas-based group that puts on plays September–May.

Movies

Local movie houses are the **20th Century Twin Theatre** (222 Front St., 907/586-4055) downtown and **Glacier Cinemas** (9091 Cinema Dr., 907/789-9191, www.grossalaska.com) in Mendenhall Valley. **Silverbow Inn** (120 2nd St., 907/586-9866 or 800/586-4146, www.silverbowinn.com) screens free classic flicks at 8 P.M. Monday–Wednesday in the back room, or head to **Goldtown Nickelodeon** (174 S. Franklin St., 907/586-2875, www.goldtownnick.110mb.com) for indie and art-house films.

Events

Call 907/586-5866 for a recording of upcoming events and activities in Juneau. If you're around in April, don't miss the free weeklong **Alaska Folk Festival** (907/463-3316, www.juneau.com/aff), which attracts musicians from Alaska and the Northwest. You can attend workshops and dance to some of the hottest folk and bluegrass bands. It is lots of fun and completely authentic.

In late May, culture comes to town with the **Juneau Jazz & Classics** (907/463-3378, www.jazzandclassics.org), a 10-day series of performances and workshops by local musicians and nationally acclaimed guest artists.

During even-numbered years (2010 and 2012) Juneau is home to a colorful **Native Celebration** (907/463-4844, www.sealaskaheritage.org) that attracts hundreds of participants from across the state. There are performances, crafts, and an incredible grand procession through the heart of town. Celebration takes place on the first weekend of June.

As in almost every Alaskan town, June 21, the **summer solstice,** is a time for celebration in Juneau; there's always some sort of party that long day and short night. **July 4th** is Juneau's day to play. Parades and a big fireworks show (see them from Douglas Island for the most impressive backdrop) are joined by dog Frisbee-catching and watermelon-eating contests, along with a sand castle contest at Sandy Beach Park.

Those who like to fish should throw in their lines at the annual **Golden North Salmon Derby** (www.goldennorthsalmonderby.org) in early August. A top prize of $15,000 in cash makes it *the* big summer event for locals.

SHOPPING

Most locals do their shopping out in Mendenhall Valley at Nugget Mall (www.nuggetmalljuneau.com), Fred Meyer (near the airport), or at either Costco or Wal-Mart in Lemon Creek.

Foggy Mountain Shop (134 N. Franklin St., 907/586-6780, www.foggymountainshop.com) sells camping gear, topographic maps, and sports equipment. It also rents skis and snowshoes. The best place for rugged rain gear, boots, and outdoor clothes is **Nugget Alaskan Outfitter** (Nugget Mall, 907/789-0956 or 800/478-6848, www.nuggetoutfitter.com). While there, check out the mall's nine-foot-tall stuffed brown bear. Best kid's store? Visit **Imagination Station** (174 S. Franklin St., 907/586-8697, www.alaskantoys.com).

Galleries

Be sure to check out the monthly **First Friday Art Walks,** with art openings and snacks at local galleries. **Wm. Spear Designs** (upstairs at 174 S. Franklin St., 907/586-2209, www.wmspear.com) has the complete collection of colorful enameled pins by this local artisan with an international reputation. A former lawyer, Spear's work covers the spectrum from UFOs to dinosaurs. It's definitely worth a stop.

Rie Muñoz Gallery (2101 Jordan Ave., 907/789-7411, www.riemunoz.com), near the airport, features works by several of Alaska's best-known artists. Muñoz's works are famous for their bold colors and fanciful designs of Alaskans at work and play.

The cooperatively run **Juneau Artists Gallery** (175 S. Franklin St., 907/586-9891, www.juneauartistsgallery.com) features a wide range of artwork, including paintings, pottery, jewelry, and photography.

Annie Kaill's Fine Art and Craft Gallery (244 Front St., 907/586-2880, www.annieandcojuneau.com) is packed with whimsical gifts, pottery, jewelry, and fine art.

For Native Alaskan and other fine Alaskan art—plus changing exhibits in the back rooms—visit **Alaska State Museum Gift Shop** (124 Seward St., 907/523-8431).

Native Alaskan Arts

Juneau is a good place to purchase Native Alaskan artworks, and one of the best is downstairs at the airport: **Hummingbird Hollow Gift Shop** (907/789-4672, www.hummingbirdhollow.net) has fair prices and authentic Alaskan work, with a big choice of Tlingit, Haida, Yup'ik, and Eskimo pieces. **Raven's Journey** (439 S. Franklin St., 907/463-4686), across from the tram, is another reputable shop with authentic Native Alaskan and Canadian art.

Scads of other galleries and gift shops sell artworks and trinkets. The quality varies widely, but much of it is overpriced, particularly anything by a Native Alaskan artisan. Unfortunately, the romanticized paintings, carvings, and sculpture depicting these original Alaskans hunting seals in kayaks or carving totem poles meets head-on a much sadder picture of inebriated Native Alaskans leaning against the windows of downtown Juneau bars.

The Literary Scene

Juneauites enjoy several fine public libraries. Located on the top floor of the parking garage on South Franklin Street, the award-winning **Juneau Main Library** (907/586-5249, www.juneau.lib.ak.us/library, Mon.–Thurs. 11 A.M.–9 P.M., Fri. noon–6 P.M., Sat.–Sun. noon–5 P.M.) provides a wonderful view of all the activity in Gastineau Channel from the outside walkway. Visitors may want to stop by the freebie shelves near the entrance for a trashy novel to read. Over on the 8th floor of the State Office Building, the **Alaska State Library** (907/465-2921, www.library.state.ak.us, Mon.–Fri. 10 A.M.–4:30 P.M.) is a good place to track down historical documents and photos.

Hearthside Books (254 Front St., 907/586-1726, www.hearthsidebooks.com) is a packed downtown bookshop; it also has a larger store (907/789-2750) in the Nugget Mall near the airport. **The Observatory** (299 N. Franklin St., 907/586-9676, www.observatorybooks.com) sells used books—including the largest collection of out-of-print Alaskana—plus first editions and antiquarian maps. Also worthy of a visit is **Rainy Retreat Books** (113 Seward St., 907/463-2665, www.juneaubooks.com), with over 10,000 used and rare titles.

HIKING AND CABINS

The Juneau area has an amazing wealth of hiking paths leading into the surrounding mountains. For a complete listing, pick up a copy of ***Juneau Trails*** from the Centennial Hall Visitors Center (101 Egan Dr., 907/586-8751). This is also the place to go for hiking and cabin information in Juneau. Rubber boots are recommended for all these trails, though you could get by with leather boots on some of the paths when the weather is dry.

Guided Hikes

The **City Parks and Recreation Department** (907/586-5226 or 24-hour line 907/586-0428, www.juneau.lib.ak.us/parksrec) leads free day hikes into areas around Juneau every Wednesday (adults only) and Saturday all summer.

Gastineau Guiding (907/586-2666, www.stepintoalaska.com) has hikes in the Juneau area, including a three-hour rain forest nature walk on Douglas Island ($72 adults, $46 children), and a considerably more challenging four-hour "guide's choice" hike ($79 adults, $50 children). Or you can join an older crowd for an easy "town, tram, and trek" ($74 adults, $38 children) that includes a 20-minute bus tour, a tram ride up Mt. Roberts, and a one-hour hike. The half-day "whales and rain forest trails" trip ($189 adults, $139 children) combines a whale-watching boat tour and a Mendenhall Glacier hike, or join a photo safari ($195) for tips from a professional photographer on land and sea.

Mendenhall Glacier Trails

The Mendenhall area is laced with trails, including a couple of paved interpretive paths that swarm with visitors all summer. The relatively easy **East Glacier Loop Trail** (3.5 miles) also begins near the center and provides good views of the glacier. A more challenging hike splits off from this trail and follows Nugget Creek uphill to an Adirondack shelter. Vegetation along the East Glacier Trail consists of brush and trees established since the glacier's recent retreat, while trees along the Nugget Creek Trail are much older.

My favorite Mendenhall trail is the **West Glacier Trail** (7 miles round-trip), which begins from the end of Montana Creek Road, just beyond the Mendenhall Lake Campground; there are incredible views of the glacier and icefalls en route. Experienced ice-climbers use the path to access the glacier itself. Finally, for the really ambitious, there's a primitive route up 3,228-foot **Mt. McGinnis** from the end of the West Glacier Trail, an additional four miles (6 hours) round-trip. This trail is generally covered with snow until late summer, but offers panoramic vistas of the entire Juneau area—on clear days.

Up Gold Creek

Some of the finest hiking around Juneau is found in the old gold mining areas up beyond the end of Basin Road, a pleasant half-hour walk from town. The area is amazingly quiet and scenic, particularly given its proximity to hectic downtown Juneau. You'll hear birds singing, see waterfalls, and feel the land enveloping you. One could easily spend several days exploring this scenic area. In Last Chance Basin, 1.5 miles up Basin Road, are the fascinating remains of the **AJ Mine.** A number of paths lead around the compressor building (which houses the Last Chance Mining Museum), a locomotive repair shop, and a variety of remains from the heyday of gold mining. For more details of the area, pick up the *Last Chance Basin Walking Tour* brochure from the Juneau-Douglas City Museum (4th St. and Main St.).

Perseverance Trail leads past Last Chance Basin to Silverbow Basin, site of the Perseverance Mine, three miles away. The **Mt. Juneau Trail** branches off from Perseverance Trail 0.5 miles up. It's very steep and only suitable for experienced hikers, but offers unparalleled vistas across Gastineau Channel. Plan on seven hours round-trip. Directly across from the Mt. Juneau trailhead is a short path down to Ebner Falls. Continue another mile out on Perseverance Trail to the **Granite Creek Trail** (1.5 miles each way), which follows the creek up past several waterfalls into the alpine area. Just before Silverbow Basin, yet another side trail leads right to the Glory Hole, which is connected to the AJ Mine by a tunnel. Old mining ruins are at the end of the trail, but signs warn of potential hazards from toxic tailings at the mine site.

Douglas

The remains of the **Treadwell Mine,** destroyed by the collapse and flood of 1917, offer a fascinating peek into the past. Pick up the *Treadwell Mine Historic Trail* brochure from the Juneau-Douglas City Museum (4th St. and Main St.) for a description of the area. The trail starts from the south end of St. Ann's Avenue in Douglas and passes the crumbling remains of old buildings. Get there by catching the hourly Douglas bus ($1.50) in Juneau and riding it to the end of the line at Sandy Beach. Keep right on the main trail to reach the **Treadwell Glory Hole,** once the entrance to a network of shafts under Gastineau Channel but now full of water and wrecked cars. A waterfall drops into the hole. Return to the fork in the trail and continue down to the shore to see remains of more buildings and pieces of old mining machinery. Mine tailings dumped into Gastineau Channel created an attractive sandy beach along the shore here (Sandy Beach Park). Just to the south is a steep-sided pit where the mine collapsed in 1917. Walk back along the beach and past the Small Boat Harbor to Douglas Post Office, where you can catch a bus back to Juneau.

Climbing Mt. Roberts

The most convenient way to get a panoramic view of Juneau and Gastineau Channel is by taking the tram ($27 round-trip) to the summit of Mt. Roberts, directly behind town. A more aerobic way is to take the 2.5-mile rain forest trail that begins at the east end of 6th Street. This enjoyable climb attracts many locals, especially on summer weekends, when you'll even encounter Ironman-type joggers. After a strenuous hike you're suddenly surrounded by hundreds of folks—some barely ambulatory—who have ridden the tram from their cruise ships to commune with nature and visit the gift shop, restaurant, espresso stand, and theater. It's a bit disconcerting, but that's the new Alaskan "wilderness experience" made easy for everyone. Beyond the tram station, well-maintained trails climb uphill past Native Alaskan–carved trees to spectacular viewpoints and a large wooden cross just above the tree line at 2,030 feet. There may be snow above this point until late July.

Once you get beyond the cross, the crowds quickly thin and then virtually disappear. The trail continues up to 3,666-foot **Gastineau Peak,** six miles from town, then on along the ridge to the summit of **Roberts Peak** (3,819 feet), nine miles from your starting point. Experienced hikers with a map and compass may want to continue along the ridge, eventually connecting up with other trails in the area. Weather conditions change rapidly on these ridgetops, so be aware of incoming clouds, and never hike into fog.

Point Bridget State Park

Point Bridget is a delightful park along the edge of Lynn Canal, 38 miles north of Juneau and near Echo Cove. It's a great place to hike if you have the wheels to get there. Several paths lace this 2,850-acre park, including the **Point Bridget Trail** (7 miles round-trip) that takes hikers out to a fine vantage point across Lynn Canal to the Chilkat Mountains. Sea lions, harbor seals, and humpback whales are often seen from here. Before heading out, pick up a park map from the Department of Natural Resources (400 Willoughby Ave., 907/465-4563, www.alaskastateparks.org). Three cozy public-use cabins ($35) each sleep eight.

Cabins

The Juneau area has four popular Forest Service cabins that can be reached by hiking trails or on skis in winter. Some of these book up six months in advance. For more details on all Forest Service cabins in the area, contact Centennial Hall Visitor Center (101 Egan Dr., 907/586-2201 or 888/581-2201) or the district office in Mendenhall Valley (8510 Mendenhall Loop Rd., 907/586-8800, www.fs.fed.us/r10/tongass).

Located on a scenic alpine ridge, the **John Muir Cabin** overlooks Auke Bay and the surrounding islands. Get there by following the **Spaulding Trail** for 0.5 miles, turning left onto the **Auk Nu Trail,** and continuing another 2.5 miles to the cabin. The trail starts from a parking area on the right side of the road 12 miles northwest of town and just beyond the Auke Bay Post Office.

The **Peterson Lake Cabin** lies at the end of a 4.5-mile trail. Although it's mostly boardwalk, rubber boots are strongly recommended. The trailhead is on the right, 24 miles northwest of town, and just beyond the Shrine of St. Therese. Experienced hikers or cross-country skiers with a map and compass may want to cross the alpine ridges from Peterson Lake to the John Muir Cabin (2.5 miles away), where they can head back along the Auke Nu and Spaulding Trails.

The **Dan Moller Cabin** on Douglas Island lies at the end of a three-mile trail. Get there by taking the Douglas bus to West Juneau. Get off the bus on Cordova Street and hike three blocks up the street. Turn left onto Pioneer Avenue; the trail begins from a small parking lot next to 3185 Pioneer Avenue. One of the most popular wintertime skiing trails in the area, it leads up to the beautiful alpine country of central Douglas Island.

Eagle Glacier Cabin faces this magnificent glacier, and is accessed via the **Amalga (Eagle Glacier) Trail** that begins 28 miles north of town. The path is relatively easy to hike, passes the cabin at the 5.5-mile point, and ends at the Eagle Glacier, 7.5 miles from the trailhead. The cabin faces across a lake to the glacier, offering some of the most dramatic vistas anywhere. Wear rubber boots for the oft-muddy trail.

Windfall Lake Cabin is a modern cabin with a gorgeous setting on this lake north of Juneau. It's accessible via a three-mile trail from Herbert River Road.

Two trail-accessible cabins (reservations 907/465-4563, www.alaskastateparks.org, $35) are in Point Bridget State Park, at Mile 39 of the Glacier Highway. The 12-person **Cowee Meadows Cabin** is a three-mile hike (or wintertime ski) from the road, and the **Blue Mussel Beach Cabin** is four miles and has a wonderful bay vista.

In addition to these hike-in cabins, there are five other Forest Service cabins on the mainland around Juneau, plus another 15 on nearby Admiralty Island. Access to these cabins is by floatplane or sometimes by sea kayak. The **Berners Bay Cabin** is just eight kayak miles from the north end of Glacier Highway. The location is grand, with fine vistas across the bay, good fishing, a beautiful waterfall, and lots to explore on the two-mile-wide river delta just north. Book this cabin early.

Two close and extremely popular cabins (they fill up several months in advance) are on **Turner Lake,** 20 miles east of Juneau. There is great fishing for cutthroat trout and incredible waterfall-draped rock faces on all sides. The flight in takes you near the enormous Taku Glacier, an added bonus.

RECREATION

Cycle Alaska (907/321-2453, www.cycleak.com) rents quality mountain bikes and has a variety of trips, including fun "bike and brew" tours through Mendenhall Valley with a van ride to the Alaskan Brewing Co. for some sampling afterward. Owner John McConnochie is one of the most experienced cyclists in the area. Bikes are also available from **Driftwood Lodge** (435 W. Willoughby Ave., 907/586-2280 or 800/544-2239, www.driftwoodalaska.com).

The **Augustus Brown Swimming Pool** (1619 Glacier Ave., 907/586-5325, www.juneau.org/parkrec/pool) at the high school has two pools, a co-ed sauna, and workout equipment. Rock climbers will enjoy a visit to the **Rock Dump** (1310 Eastaugh Way, 907/586-4982, www.rockdump.com, day pass $13), an indoor climbing facility south of Juneau off Thane Road.

Alaska Club (2841 Riverside Dr., 907/789-2181, www.thealaskaclub.com) features exercise equipment, indoor racquetball and tennis courts, a sauna, and a hot tub. A second downtown location (641 W. Willoughby Ave., 907/586-5773) has more limited facilities. Nonmembers pay $10 per day.

Golfers should head to **Mendenhall Golf Course** (907/789-1221), a nine-hole course near the airport, where $25 gets you the full package. It is not quite up to Arizona standards, but where else would you have a glacier backdrop?

Sea Kayaking

For an adventurous intro to sea kayaking, join trips by **Above & Beyond Alaska** (907/364-2333, www.beyondak.com), which range from short trips from nearby beaches to overnight adventures in Berner's Bay. The company also provides water taxi drop-offs for kayakers at local bays and cabins. **Alaska Travel Adventures** (907/789-0052 or 800/478-0052, www.alaskaadventures.com, $89) has three-hour kayak paddles from the north end of Douglas Island, but these are mainly for the cruise ship crowd.

Rent kayaks from **Alaska Boat & Kayak Rental** (907/789-6886, www.juneaukayak.com) at Auke Bay boat harbor, 12 miles north of Juneau. Guided trips and water taxi services are also available. **Adventure Bound Alaska** (907/463-2509 or 800/228-3875, www.adventureboundalaska.com) provides kayak drop-offs in Tracy Arm.

Floating the Mendenhall River

Experienced rafters and canoeists sometimes float the Mendenhall River, but be sure to ask the Forest Service for the details. The river is not particularly treacherous, but a number of people have died in independent boating accidents. For a guided float, join the cruise ship folks on a raft from **Alaska Travel Adventures** (907/789-0052 or 800/478-0052, www.alaskaadventures.com, $109 adults, $73 children). These four-hour floats include lunch and transportation from downtown.

Fish, Whales, and Birds

The visitors center offers a listing of Juneau's many **charter boat** operators. All sorts of options are available, from half-day fishing and whale-watching ventures to two-week cruises around Southeast Alaska. If you want to do it on your own, rent a skiff from **Panhandle Powerboats** (907/789-5767, www.panhandle-powerboats.com).

A number of companies specialize in whale-watching day trips out of Juneau, including **Orca Enterprises** (907/789-6801 or 888/733-6722, www.alaskawhalewatching.com), **Dolphin Whale Watching Tours** (907/463-3422 or 800/719-3422, www.dolphintours.com), and **Juneau Sportfishing & Sightseeing** (907/586-1887, www.juneausportfishing.com). Find their brochures, along with other operators, at the visitors center. Each company promotes its advantages, from speedy boats to small and personalized adventures. I've found that folks with the fastest boats tend to rush out, stop briefly to see whales, and then hurry on to another spot, rather than simply enjoying the chance to see whales. The best whale-watching is typically in Icy Strait near Glacier Bay, too far for Juneau area whale-watching boats, but an outstanding option is Adventure Bound Alaska (907/463-2509 or 800/228-3875, www.adventureboundalaska.com), with all-day trips from Juneau to Tracy Arm.

The **Juneau Audubon Society** website (www.juneau-audubon-society.org) provides a checklist of regional birds and places to go birding.

Skiing and Snowboarding

Come wintertime, **Eaglecrest Ski Area** (907/790-2000, www.skijuneau.com, Thurs.–Mon. early Dec.–Mar., adults $38–43) on Douglas Island provides excellent skiing opportunities—when the weather cooperates. Thirty ski trails are available with a vertical drop of 1,400 feet. Call 907/586-5330 for current snow conditions. A bus provides weekend-only transport to Eaglecrest ($6 each way). Just downhill from the ski area are three miles of groomed cross-country trails (free).

The City Parks and Recreation Department (907/586-5226, www.juneau.lib.ak.us/parksrec) leads **guided cross-country ski tours** in the winter if there's enough snow. These take place every Wednesday (adults only) and Saturday.

February–April, **Alaska Powder Descents** (907/364-2333, www.alaskapowder.com) guides spectacular heli-skiing and snowboarding trips into the Juneau Ice Field and Chilkat Mountains; the cost is around $800 for a full day's skiing.

Flightseeing and Glacier Landings

Flightseeing and charter flights are available from **Ward Air** (907/789-9150 or 800/478-9150, www.wardair.com), a long-established company with a good safety record and an excellent local reputation. Glacier Bay flightseeing can also be booked, but they're expensive due to the distance. Wait until you visit Haines, Skagway, or Gustavus, where the cost and flying time to the park are lower.

Several companies offer helicopter glacier tours to spectacular Juneau Ice Field, with landings on crevasse-free portions of the glaciers. These flights remain controversial in Juneau, primarily because of the constant din they create in Mendenhall Valley. Flights operate May–September, but trips that include dogsledding start later and end earlier due to snow conditions.

Era Helicopters (907/586-2030 or 800/843-1947, www.flightseeingtours.com) lands on Norris or Taku Glacier. A one-hour trip with a 20-minute walk is $279. It also offers a longer two-hour trip ($489) that includes a dogsled ride.

Temsco Helicopters (907/789-9501 or 877/789-9501, www.temscoair.com) has a one-hour flight ($259) that spends 25 minutes on Mendenhall Glacier. Other flight options include a "pilot's choice" 90-minute flight ($379) with two glacier landings, and a 1.5-hour trip ($479) that includes a 25-minute dogsled ride.

Coastal Helicopters (907/789-5600 or 800/789-5610, www.coastalhelicopters.com) charges $245 for a 60-minute trip, or $380 for a 90-minute trip; both include 15 minutes on Herbert Glacier or Gilkey Glacier. Also popular are dogsled tours on Herbert Glacier. These include an hour on the ice with the dogs and 30 minutes of flying time for $450.

Northstar Trekking (907/790-4530 or 866/590-4530, www.glaciertrekking.com) specializes in Mendenhall Glacier hikes of varying lengths, starting with a flight plus a one-hour hike for $359, up to three hours on the ice with the chance to learn basic ice climbing for $499. Clients are fully outfitted with mountaineering gear and crampons.

All four of these companies include transportation from downtown Juneau to their landing pads and also provide chartered flights to the glaciers for heli-hiking or skiing. Warning: Helicopters can be dangerous, and a number of fatal crashes have taken place around Juneau. Be sure to ask about safety procedures before stepping on board.

Glacier Hikes

Travelers looking for something more challenging than a helicopter glacier tour should check out **Above & Beyond Alaska** (907/364-2333, www.beyondak.com). Their seven-hour Mendenhall Glacier trek ($189) involves a hike to the west side of the glacier and time on the ice exploring its features, including the ice caves; crampons, a helmet, and an ice ax are provided. Another trek teaches basic ice-climbing skills, and custom overnight trips are also available. This trek is recommended, but you need to be in good physical condition.

Zip-Lines

Juneau is home to two high-adventure (literally) zip-lines. Locally owned **Alaska Zipline Adventures** (907/321-0947, www.alaskazip.com) operates at Eaglecrest Ski Area on north Douglas Island, with a high suspension skybridge and seven zip-lines that drop through the rain forest and across a creek. The cost is $139 adults, $99 ages 10–12 for a fun 3.5-hour adventure, including a shuttle van from town. Owners Matt and Rachel DeSpain also offer a variety of combination trips that include zip-line and various other adventures, from whale-watching to bike rides. Alaska Zipline's focus includes an ecofriendly attitude, from the recycled materials used in the tree houses to the hydroelectric-powered lodge.

A second company, **Alaska Canopy Adventures** (907/523-2920, www.alaskacanopy.com, May–Sept.), operates on the site of the old Treadwell Gold Mine on Douglas Island. Participants take a short jet-boat ride over from Juneau and then hop on an off-road vehicle to climb to the starting point in a platform high up a tree. A series of nine zip-lines (one 800 feet long) takes you through the forest and eventually over the "glory hole" 200 feet below before ending in a rappel to the ground from the last tree platform. Two suspension sky-bridges link other sections, providing treetop views of the rain forest. The cost is $179 per person for a 3.5-hour tour.

ACCOMMODATIONS

A full range of options is available to travelers staying in Juneau, but you should make reservations well in advance for arrivals in July–August, when everything in town is sometimes booked. See the Juneau Convention and Visitors Bureau website (www.traveljuneau.com) for links to many local hotels, motels, B&Bs, lodges, and resorts. If you aren't bringing a vehicle up on the ferry, be sure to ask whether your lodging place includes pickup; it could save you the $30 taxi fare. Add 12 percent tax to all rates listed below.

Hostel

Alaska's finest hostel, **Juneau International Hostel** (614 Harris St., 907/586-9559, www.juneauhostel.org, $10) is in a lovely old home just a few blocks uphill from downtown. In addition to dorm space for 46 people, the hostel has a comfortable community room with kitchen facilities as well as a washer and dryer. It does not have a TV, but Wi-Fi and a guest computer are available. The hostel is open year-round, but is closed daily 9 A.M.–5 P.M. The doors are locked at midnight, putting a damper on your nightlife. The maximum stay is three nights. Rooms are clean, and the managers are friendly, but common areas are often crowded. Reserve ahead in summer, or get here early to be certain of a place.

Hotels and Motels

In town: The **Alaskan Hotel** (167 S. Franklin St., 907/586-1000 or 800/327-9347, www.thealaskanhotel.com) has reasonably priced downtown Juneau lodging in a historic setting. Built in 1913, this is Juneau's oldest lodging place, with 45 small but surprisingly charming guest rooms. Bare-bones units with a shared bath and no TV cost $60 s or d, and nicer ones with private baths and TVs are $90 s or d; some of these include fridges and microwaves. Larger kitchenette units ($120) sleep four. Try to get a room away from the bar and not on the second floor since these can get noisy when bands are playing. During the Folk Festival each April the Alaskan is the heart of the music scene, with impromptu jams in the halls and downstairs at all hours. The Alaskan is a classic—and rustic—place, so it may not please people expecting the latest in accouterments. Wi-Fi is available in the lobby and bar.

The newest local lodging place, **Juneau Hotel** (1200 W. 9th St., 907/586-5666, www.juneauhotels.net), is an all-suites hotel with separate bedrooms (1 queen $149 d, 2 queens $179 d) and full kitchens. It's next to the Juneau-Douglas bridge.

Driftwood Lodge (435 W. Willoughby Ave., 907/586-2280 or 800/544-2239, www.driftwoodalaska.com) is convenient to town, with dated guest rooms (some with kitchenettes) for $94 d; one-bedroom units with kitchens cost $100 d, and two-bedroom units that sleep four are $110. The Driftwood provides a courtesy van to the airport or ferry terminal, and a guest computer.

Baranof Hotel (127 N. Franklin St., 907/586-2660 or 800/544-0970, www.

westmarkhotels.com) is a nine-story downtown classic with a dark lobby and a romantic restaurant. It's a favorite haunt of state legislators and lobbyists in the winter, and 20 of the guest rooms have kitchenettes ($229 d). Other guest rooms are $189 d, but units range widely; ask for a remodeled one. There's a guest computer in the lobby and Wi-Fi. The higher levels offer the best views and the least street noise.

The seven-story **Goldbelt Hotel Juneau** (51 W. Egan Dr., 907/586-6900 or 888/478-6909, www.goldbelttours.com, $179–189 d) has a convenient downtown location, modern guest rooms with two doubles or one king bed, Wi-Fi, a good restaurant (The Zen), and free airport shuttle. Ask for a room facing the water.

A Beachside Luxury Inn (907/463-5531 or 888/879-0858, www.beachsidevilla.com) is across the bridge in Douglas, with a fine waterside location facing Juneau. This isn't a B&B but has similar amenities, with lavishly appointed, immaculate guest rooms and a secluded location. Four guest rooms ($169–199 d) have kitchenettes (one features a unique waterfall tub), and the suite ($239 d) is really an apartment with a full kitchen and a Jacuzzi tub. All units include private entrances and Wi-Fi.

Mendenhall Valley and the airport: Several of Juneau's newer hotels are clustered around the airport in Mendenhall Valley. These lack the charm of the historic downtown places, and you will probably want a rental car to get around. Of course, they are also close to Mendenhall Glacier and offer the predictability of corporate lodging.

A recommended family place is **Frontier Suites Airport Hotel** (9400 Glacier Hwy., 907/790-6600 or 800/544-2250, www.frontiersuites.com, $159–189 d). It has a wide variety of rooms, all with full kitchens (including dishes), and some with jetted tubs. Three family units contain bunks. A free shuttle to the ferry and nearby airport is provided.

Super 8 Motel (2295 Trout St., 907/789-4858 or 800/800-8000, www.super8.com, $123 d) has reasonable rates, plus a continental breakfast, Wi-Fi, and courtesy shuttle. Some guest rooms include fridges and microwaves.

Also near the airport is **Grandma's Feather Bed** (2358 Mendenhall Loop Rd., 907/789-5566 or 888/781-5005, www.grandmasfeatherbed.com, $199 d), a 14-unit motel with spacious rooms, whirlpool tubs, and a hot breakfast. Nearby (and with same owners) is **Best Western Country Lane Inn** (9300 Glacier Hwy., 907/789-5005 or 888/781-5005, www.countrylaneinn.com, $169–199 d), with standard motel rooms and a continental breakfast. Both places have guest computers, Wi-Fi, and a courtesy shuttle to downtown, the ferry, or the airport.

Newly renovated, **Extended Stay Deluxe** (1800 Shell Simmons Dr., 907/790-6435 or 888/559-9846, www.extendedstay.com, $150–160 d)—just a block from the airport and nine miles from downtown—has an indoor swimming pool, a hot tub, an exercise room, in-room kitchenettes, continental breakfast, Wi-Fi, and a free shuttle to town and the ferry.

Lighthouses and Cabins

For something really different, spend a night or two at **Sentinel Island Lighthouse** (907/586-5338, www.gastineauchannel.blogspot.com, $50 pp) a few miles north of Juneau. Built in 1935, the art deco tower has bunks (bring sleeping bags), and guests can also stay in the keeper's house, which contains a kitchen. There are no good places to leave a boat overnight on Sentinel Island, so access is by kayak, charter boat drop-off, or helicopter. The island has two active eagle nests and sits right across from a Steller sea lion haul-out.

Two other lighthouses currently being restored will eventually open to the public: **Point Retreat Lighthouse** (www.aklighthouse.org), on the northern tip of Admiralty Island west of Juneau, and **Five Fingers Lighthouse** (www.5fingerlighthouse.com), in Frederick Sound 75 miles south of Juneau.

Located 23 miles north of Juneau, the **Shrine of St. Therese** (907/780-6112, www.shrineofsainttherese.org) has a surprising collection of rental cabins. The rustic cabins ($40 s, $45 d) have woodstoves but no kitchens, and you'll need to use the nearby bathrooms. A historic 1938 log cabin ($85 d) has two bedrooms plus a kitchenette and a private bath. Three larger places are available, including a lodge that can sleep 22 guests! Particularly noteworthy is Little Flower Retreat ($180 d plus $15 per additional guest), a modern two-bedroom home built on pilings over the water. You don't have to swear allegiance to the pope, but guests must abide by the contemplative spirit of this unique and peaceful place; whales are sometimes heard just offshore.

Bed-and-Breakfasts

Couples may want to spend the extra money to stay at one of more than 40 Juneau B&Bs. Accommodations run the gamut from old miner's cabins to gorgeous hillside homes. Pick up the *Juneau Visitors Guide* brochure at the visitors center for a listing of local places, or check the rack for flyers from many B&Bs. Two good Web resources for Juneau B&Bs are the Juneau Convention and Visitors Bureau (www.traveljuneau.com) and the **B&B Association of Alaska INNside Passage Chapter** (www.accommodations-alaska.com).

Downtown B&Bs: Best known for its bagels and other baked goods, **Silverbow Inn** (120 2nd St., 907/586-4146 or 800/586-4146, www.silverbowinn.com, $134–199 d) also has 11 bright guest rooms, each with a private bath, a phone, a TV, and Wi-Fi. The least-expensive rooms are small, but one spacious newer unit has a jetted tub. There's a rooftop deck with a hot tub, a sauna, and views of the harbor. Guests are served a tasty breakfast each morning, along with evening cheese and wine. There is a two-night minimum stay in midsummer.

Built in 1906 and beautifully restored to its foursquare glory, **Alaska's Capital Inn** (113 W. 5th St., 907/586-6507 or 888/588-6507, www.alaskacapitalinn.com, $259–339 d) offers sumptuous heart-of-Juneau lodging with commanding views of the city. Four guest rooms are filled with period antiques—including an 1879 pump organ and maplewood floors from a 1920s YMCA—and the entire top level has been transformed into a very private suite with a gas fireplace, a jetted tub, and a king-size sleigh bed. Two smaller garden-side rooms have private entrances, and most rooms also feature claw-foot tubs. Amenities include a flower-filled yard with a gazebo-enclosed hot tub, Wi-Fi and a guest computer, a wonderful five-course Alaskan breakfast, plus evening wine and treats. There is a two-night minimum stay in the summer.

B&Bs farther afield: Located on a small pond and surrounded by flower gardens, **Pearson's Pond Luxury Inn and Garden Spa** (4541 Sawa Circle, 907/789-3772 or 888/658-6328, www.pearsonspond.com, $349–449 s, $399–499 d) is a sumptuous home with two hot tubs and sauna, a three-level deck, five guest rooms, computers, Wi-Fi, flat-screen TVs, and Mendenhall Glacier vistas. Premium rooms include large spa tubs, rain showers, balconies, and canopy beds. Borrow a bike to ride, paddle a kayak around the pond, or just enjoy the relaxing setting. A full hot breakfast is served in the summer. There's a two-night minimum stay in summer, but many guests book a week or more. Children are not permitted, but two condos ($250 nightly with a six-night minimum) are perfect for small families.

On the north end of Douglas Island, six miles from Juneau and close to the Eaglecrest Ski Area, **Fireweed House B&B** (907/586-3885 or 800/586-3885, www.fireweedhouse.com) has a scenic and very peaceful setting. Accommodations (all with private baths and jetted tubs) include a room in the main house ($189 d) and an apartment with a kitchen ($219 d). A separate two-bedroom guesthouse ($399 for 4 people, 3-night minimum) sits on a quiet two-acre site away from the other buildings and has its own hot tub. A filling breakfast with quiche, fruit, muffins, and more is brought to your room so you can get up as late as you wish. Kids are welcome, and Wi-Fi is available.

A lovely waterside home on Douglas Island, **Gill's Horizon** (907/586-2829, www.gillshorizon.com, Mar.–Nov.) is eight miles from Juneau. Guests stay in the apartment suite ($169 d) and will appreciate the covered waterside hot tub, private beach, lush grounds, driving range, and even a pair of nesting eagles. The fridge is stocked with everything from bacon and eggs to snacks and beer. Larger groups can add on an extra room for $95. There is a three-night minimum stay.

Auke Lake B&B (11595 Mendenhall Loop Rd., 907/790-3253, www.admiraltytours.com) occupies a prime piece of shoreline on this picturesque lake. The 5,000-square-foot home has a deck with a hot tub for relaxing, two suites ($135 d), and a rather small guest room ($115 d), all with private baths, fridges, and a light breakfast. Borrow the kayak to paddle around the lake.

CAMPING

The Forest Service maintains two summer-only campgrounds in the Juneau area, but neither is close to town. Hugging the shore of Mendenhall Lake, **Mendenhall Lake Campground** (www.recreation.gov for reservations) has glacier views and access to several hiking trails. You will find backpacker units and vehicle sites ($10) along with RV sites with full hookups ($26–28). From the ferry terminal, turn right and go two miles to De Hart's Store, then left onto Loop Road. Follow it three miles to Montana Creek Road, then another 0.75 miles to the campground.

Auke Village Campground ($10) is 16 miles north on Glacier Highway and another two miles out on Point Louisa. The area is secluded, with a nice beach and views of nearby islands. If you lack a vehicle, the nearest city bus stop is four miles away.

Eagle Beach State Recreation Area (Mile 28, 907/586-2506, mid-May–mid-Sept., $10) has rustic campsites (no water). Nearby is a picnic area with all-encompassing views of the Chilkat Range.

RV Campgrounds

The city of Juneau has four RV spaces at **Savikko Park** (907/586-5255) on Douglas Island. They are free, but there are no hookups, tents are not permitted, and stays are limited to three days.

Auke Bay RV Park (907/789-9467, year-round, $26 full hookups, no tents) is 1.5 miles southeast of the ferry terminal. Reservations are recommended.

Spruce Meadow RV Park (10200 Back Loop Rd., 907/789-1990, www.juneaurv.com, year-round, $32 RVs, $20 tents) is four miles from the ferry terminal. In addition, RVs can generally overnight at Nugget Mall near the airport for free, but there are no facilities, of course.

FOOD

Breakfast and Lunch

A bit out of the way, **Sandpiper Café** (429 Willoughby Ave., 907/586-3150, daily 6 A.M.–2 P.M., $7–13) is *the* breakfast place in Juneau, with big portions of pancakes, omelets, French toast, eggs Benedict, bagel and lox, plus lunchtime soups, ostrich burgers, Reubens, and other favorites.

Heritage Coffee (174 S. Franklin St., 907/586-1087 or 800/478-5282, www.heritagecoffee.com, Sun. 7 A.M.–4 P.M., Mon.–Fri. 6:30 A.M.–5:30 P.M., Sat. 7 A.M.–5 P.M.) is easily the most popular and crowded Juneau espresso-and-pastries shop, and remains open until 11 P.M. most summer nights. They have a second shop at 216 2nd Street.

Valentine's Coffee House & Bakery (111 Seward St., 907/463-5144, www.valentinescoffeehouse.com, Mon.–Fri. 7 A.M.–7 P.M., Sat.–Sun. 9 A.M.–7 P.M. summer, Mon.–Fri. 7 A.M.–7 P.M., Sat. 9 A.M.–7 P.M. winter, $4–20) is away from the action, with a lunch menu of focaccia sandwiches, salads, calzones, and pizzas; there is also free Wi-Fi.

Alaska's oldest bakery, **Silverbow Inn Bakery** (120 2nd St., 907/586-4146, www.silverbowinn.com, Sun. 8 A.M.–4 P.M., Mon.–Fri. 6:30 A.M.–8 P.M., Sat. 7 A.M.–6 P.M., $4–9) is great for a hot bagel (try one with cream cheese and lox), soup, salad, or latte. Pastries, fresh-baked breads, cookies, and free Wi-Fi add to the allure. The atmosphere is homespun and funky, and the side-street location keeps the crowds away.

Downtown near the library, **Paradise Bakery & Café** (245 Marine Way, 907/586-2253, Mon.–Fri. 7 A.M.–3 P.M., Sat.–Sun.

8 A.M.–3 P.M., $5–9) is popular with locals and stray tourists who happen upon this cute little spot. Chef Joan Deering is best known for her "Berries in Paradise" bread pudding and other treats, but also serves a choice of brunch items, including thick bacon-and-egg sandwiches and breakfast burritos.

Best doughnuts in town? Drop by **Breeze Inn** (2200 Trout St., 907/523-4300, www.breezein.com) near the airport; it's open 24 hours a day and is also popular for takeout sandwiches.

Local Favorites

The Hangar (2 Marine Way, Merchant's Wharf, 907/586-5018, www.hangaronthewharf.com, daily 11 A.M.–10 P.M., $9–30) is an extremely popular waterfront pub with seafood, steaks, pasta, burgers, sandwiches, and salads, but I usually keep it simple with halibut fish-and-chips and an Alaskan Amber. Historic photos line the walls, and you can head upstairs for a game of pool. It's a great place to watch the sun go down while enjoying one of the 24 brews on tap. *Loud, energetic,* and *fun* are the operative terms.

Farther afield is **Hot Bite** (907/790-2483) at Auke Bay Harbor. The menu includes charbroiled burgers (the best in town), halibut and chips, grilled portobello mushroom sandwiches, milk shakes, and other tasty bites. Service can be slow since it's all made to order.

If you're out for a romantic meal, Juneau's **Zephyr Restaurant** (200 Seward St., 907/780-2221, daily 4–11 P.M., entrées $18–32) is an excellent choice, with chandeliers, candlelit tables, and live piano jazz on weekends. House specialties include pancetta-encrusted lamb, roasted chicken with polenta and sautéed chard, as well as asparagus and parmesan ravioli. There's also a late-night menu with lighter fare starting around $12.

Pizza

Juneau's best-known pizza joint since 1973 is **Bullwinkle's** (907/586-2400, www.bullwinklespizza.com, daily 11 A.M.–11 P.M.), directly across from the State Office Building on Willoughby Avenue and also in Mendenhall Valley next to Super Bear Market. Daily lunch pizza specials start at $5, and the popcorn is always free. You'll get better and more authentic pizza—including pizza by the slice—from **Pizzeria Roma** (Merchant's Wharf, 907/463-5020, www.hangaronthewharf.com).

Over in Douglas, **The Island Pub** (1102 2nd St., 907/364-1595, www.theislandpub.com, daily 11:30 A.M.–10 P.M.) serves pizzas ($13–20), sandwiches, and wraps in a great smoke-free setting with big windows facing Juneau.

International

In business since 1974, **Olivia's de Mexico** (downstairs at 222 Seward St., 907/586-6870, Mon.–Fri. 11 A.M.–9 P.M., Sat. 5–9 P.M., $12–18) serves big portions of traditional Mexican food in a basement setting.

Located across from the Auke Bay boat harbor, **Chan's Thai Kitchen** (907/789-9777, Sun. 4:30–8 P.M., Tues.–Sat. 4:30–8:30 P.M., closed Mon.) is popular with locals looking to spice up their lives. The food is dependably fine, but the place gets packed most nights, so be ready to wait. Spring rolls, chicken coconut soup, and any of the curries are all recommended. They have delicious Thai iced tea too.

For surprisingly good Japanese sushi and Chinese in a proletarian setting, head to the Korean American–owned **Seong's Sushi Bar** (740 W. 9th St., 907/586-4778, Mon.–Fri. 10 A.M.–9 P.M., Sat. 4–9 P.M.) across from the Federal Building. Lunches (around $9) are the real attraction, with big plates of chicken sukiyaki, broccoli beef, or shrimp with veggies.

Another locals' favorite is **Dragon Inn** (5000 Glacier Hwy., 907/780-4616, daily 11 A.M.–3 P.M. and 4–9:30 P.M.), in Lemon Creek three miles north of town, serving dim sum appetizers, seafood with pan-fried noodles, sautéed eggplant in garlic sauce, and more. Lunches are around $9.

Pel' Meni (on Marine Way in Merchant's Wharf, 907/586-0177, Sun.–Thurs. until 1:30 A.M., Fri.–Sat. until 3:30 A.M.) is a tiny

Russian eatery where the house specialty is $6 dumplings made with sirloin steak and topped with a spicy curry and cilantro sauce. This night-owl hangout is popular with teens.

Seafood

Juneau has two excellent salmon bakes with all-you-can-eat dinners and free bus transport from town. Both are open May–September. Housed in a rustic waterside building four miles south of town, **Thane Ore House Salmon Bake** (907/586-3442, www.thaneorehouse.com) charges $24 for a big dinner of king or sockeye salmon, beer-battered halibut, barbecue ribs, baked beans, cornbread, and unusual salads. Outside tables are perfect for those rare sunny days.

Gold Creek Salmon Bake (907/789-0052 or 800/323-5757, www.alaskaadventures.com, $39 adults, $26 children) has a similar menu north of town near the hospital.

Housed in a little stand next to the library on South Franklin Street, **Tracy's King Crab Shack** (907/723-1811, www.kingcrabshack.com, daily 10:30 A.M.–7 P.M. May–Sept., $8–20) has a couple of stools out front and a perpetual queue of tourists and locals. Try the crab bisque or crab cakes for something simple, or settle into a bucket of king crab claws if you're hungry (and have $40 to drop). The food is fresh and delicious.

Get high-quality smoked salmon at **Taku Smokeries** (550 S. Franklin St., 907/463-3474 or 800/582-5122, www.takustore.com) a few blocks south of town. Drop by for a sample or to watch through the windows as they process the fish. On the water side of the Taku Smokeries building is **Twisted Fish Co.** (907/463-5033, www.hangaronthewharf.com, daily 11 A.M.–10 P.M. May–Sept., $12–29), where the decor is playful and the food is contemporary. Big windows open onto Gastineau Channel, where floatplanes and cruise ships create a busy scene. Watch the crew in the open kitchen as they prepare wild berry halibut burgers, baked salmon in puff pastry, eight-inch pizzas, ginger ahi tuna, and a tasty clam chowder. It's noisy and fun. (The owners also operate three other nearby restaurants, including the equally popular Hangar.)

Groceries

You'll find no-frills grocery shopping at the big **Fred Meyer** (907/789-6503), nine miles northwest of town along Glacier Highway. Other grocers out in Mendenhall Valley are **Safeway** (3033 Vintage Blvd., 907/790-5500) and **Super Bear Supermarket** (Mendenhall Mall, 907/789-0173).

In town, head to friendly **Alaskan & Proud Market** (615 Willoughby Ave., 907/586-3101 or 800/478-2118, www.alaskaandproud.com)—better known as A&P, but not to be confused with the East Coast chain—for a complete selection of fresh produce and meats. Safeway, A&P, and Fred Meyer are all open 24 hours a day. You might also try the somewhat-downsized **Costco** (5225 Commercial Way, 907/780-6740) in Lemon Creek, though most visitors won't find much need for cases of tuna fish or 50-pound bags of charcoal.

The local natural foods market downtown, **Rainbow Foods** (224 4th St., 907/586-6476, www.rainbow-foods.org, Sun. noon–6 P.M., Mon.–Fri. 9 A.M.–5 P.M., Sat. 10 A.M.–6 P.M.) has a healthy and tasty lunchtime buffet ($8 per pound) with salads, soups, veggie dishes, and pizza slices; it is great for a fast lunch without a lot of fat.

SERVICES

The main **post office** is in the downtown Federal Building at 9th Street and Willoughby Avenue, and a branch post office is at 1455 South Franklin Street. **Bartlett Regional Hospital** (907/796-8900, www.bartletthospital.org), halfway between Juneau and Mendenhall Valley, is the largest medical facility in Southeast Alaska. For nonemergencies, contact **Juneau Urgent Care** (8505 Old Dairy Rd., 907/790-4111, www.juneauurgentcare.com).

A number of local places (including most coffeehouses) have wireless Internet access, or head to the Juneau Public Library for free computers and Wi-Fi.

Coin-operated showers can be found at **Harbor Washboard** (1114 Glacier Ave., 907/586-1133), **Zach Gordon Youth Center** (396 Whittier St., 907/586-2635), the **Alaskan Hotel** (167 S. Franklin St., 907/586-1000), and out of town at **Auke Bay Boat Harbor** (907/789-0819). A better deal is the high school **swimming pool** (1619 Glacier Ave., 907/586-5325), where your entrance buys access to a shower, a pool, a sauna, and weight-lifting equipment. Plus you get to check out the pallid-skinned Juneauites. Coin laundries include Harbor Washboard along with **The Dungeon** (4th St. and Franklin St., 907/586-2805) and **Mendenhall Laundromat** (Mendenhall Mall, 907/789-9781).

Southeast Alaska Conservation Council

The Southeast Alaska Conservation Council, or SEACC (419 6th St., 907/586-6942, www.seacc.org), has material on regional environmental issues, plus activist T-shirts. This is the primary environmental group in Southeast Alaska and has a reputation as a highly effective organization both locally and in Washington, D.C. Members receive a quarterly newsletter and periodic notices of important environmental issues. You can join for $25 per year.

GETTING THERE

Ferry

Juneau's Alaska Marine Highway **ferry terminal** (907/465-3940) is 14 miles northwest of town at Auke Bay. Ferries arrive and depart daily during the summer, headed north to both Haines and Skagway, southwest to Sitka, and south to other Alaskan towns. Arrivals are sometimes very late at night, so be ready to stumble off in a daze. Ferries generally stay 1–2 hours in Auke Bay. The *Fairweather* is a high-speed passenger and vehicle ferry with frequent service from Juneau to Sitka and Petersburg. Unfortunately, the ferry suffers from frequent breakdowns, so check ahead to make sure it's on schedule. The other state ferries are larger and slower. Several covered picnic tables are behind the terminal, where you can crash if you have an early-morning departure. Make ferry reservations through Alaska Marine Highway (907/465-3941 or 800/642-0066, www.dot.state.ak.us/amhs).

A cab ride to town will set you back $35–40, but hitching to town is relatively easy during the day. You can also walk the two miles from the ferry terminal to De Hart's Store, where hourly city buses will pick you up.

Alaska Fjordlines (907/766-3395 or 800/320-0146, www.alaskafjordlines.com) operates a high-speed catamaran with daily summertime runs from Yankee Cove (33 miles north of Juneau) to Skagway and Haines. Although primarily for day tours from Skagway or Juneau, it can also be used for one-way transportation north: $100 adults, $80 children; reservations are recommended.

Air

Juneau airport (www.juneau.org/airport) is nine miles northwest of downtown. Express **city buses** ($1.50) arrive hourly in front of the airport between 8 A.M.–5 P.M. On weekends or later hours (until 11:15 P.M.) you can catch the regular city bus—which is very slow—behind Nugget Mall, a half-mile away. Taxis cost $25–30 to downtown. Inside the terminal, take a look at the glass cases with various stuffed critters, including a huge polar bear (upstairs).

A good place to see waterfowl and eagles is the **Mendenhall Wetlands** that surround the airport. An overlook provides a view from Egan Highway on the way into Juneau.

Alaska Airlines (800/426-0333, www.alaskaair.com) has daily flights into Juneau from Seattle and on to Anchorage. Alaska's jets also connect Juneau with other Southeast towns and points north to Gustavus, Yakutat, and Cordova.

Options abound for small-plane service to communities around Juneau. **Wings of Alaska** (907/789-0790, www.wingsofalaska.com) has daily flights to Gustavus, Haines, Hoonah, Kake, and Skagway. **Alaska Seaplane Service** (907/789-3331 or 800/478-3360, www.flyalaskaseaplanes.com) offers serves

Angoon, Elfin Cove, Pelican, and Tenakee. **Air Excursions** (907/697-2375 or 800/354-2479, www.airexcursions.com) has the cheapest flights to Gustavus from Juneau. Flightseeing and charter flights are also available from these companies as well as **Wings Airways** (907/586-6275, www.wingsairways.com).

Air Excursions (907/697-2375 or 800/354-2479, www.airexcursions.com) doesn't have scheduled service but typically has seat fares between Juneau and the towns of Gustavus, Hoonah, Haines, Sitka, Skagway, and Tenakee Springs on a regular basis.

GETTING AROUND

Tours

Mighty Great Trips (907/789-5460, www.mightygreattrips.com) runs 2.5-hour summertime tours that include Juneau and Mendenhall Glacier for $27. Other bus tour companies include **Gray Line of Alaska** (907/586-3773 or 888/452-1737, www.graylinealaska.com), **Last Frontier Tours** (907/789-0742 or 888/396-8687, www.lastfrontiertours.com), and **Princess Tours** (907/463-3900 or 800/774-6237, www.princess.com). Princess operates excellent three-hour trips ($100) to the historic AJ Mine south of town, with detailed tours inside the mine, plenty of historical info, and the chance to pan for gold.

For something different, hop onboard the **Juneau Steamboat Co.** (907/723-0372, www.juneausteamboat.com), a little wood-fired boat modeled after ones used a century ago; 1.5-hour tours of Gastineau Channel depart the downtown dock and cost $40.

City Buses

Capital Transit buses (907/789-6901, www.juneau.org/capitaltransit, $1.50) operate daily and connect Juneau, Douglas, and Mendenhall Valley. Buses to and from Mendenhall Valley run every 30 minutes 7 A.M.–10:30 P.M. (Sun. 9 A.M.–5:30 P.M.), with both regular and express service (weekdays only). Bus service to Douglas is hourly. Pick up route maps and schedules from the various visitors centers, the ferry terminal, or the airport.

Trolley

The **Juneau Trolley Car Company** (907/586-7433, www.juneautours.org, Sun.–Tues. and Thurs. 8 A.M.–6 P.M. May–Sept., day pass $19 adults, $12 children) covers most of downtown. This red trolley features a 45-minute narrated tour, and you can get on and off at various points along the way.

Taxis

The local taxi companies are **Alaska Taxi & Tours** (907/780-6400), **Capital Cab** (907/586-2772), **Juneau Taxi & Tours** (907/790-4511), and **Evergreen Taxi** (907/586-2121, www.evergreentaxi.com). From the airport to downtown the charge is typically $25–30. A cab ride from downtown to the ferry terminal (14 miles) will cost upward of $35–40, but it might be worth it if you get several people together. Taxi tours are $55 per hour.

Car Rentals

With nearly 100 miles of roads in the Juneau area, renting a car is a smart idea. Be sure to call 2–3 weeks ahead of a midsummer arrival or you may find every car already rented. Four national chains have offices at the airport: **Avis** (907/789-9450 or 800/478-2847), **Budget** (907/790-1086), **Hertz** (907/789-9494 or 800/654-3131), and **National** (907/789-9814 or 800/478-2847). A mile from the airport, **Rent-A-Wreck** (907/789-4111 or 888/843-4111, www.juneaualaska.com) has older vehicles and lower rates.

TRACY ARM-FORDS TERROR WILDERNESS

Located 50 miles southeast of Juneau, the 653,000-acre Tracy Arm–Fords Terror Wilderness contains country that rivals Glacier Bay National Park but costs half as much to reach. The wilderness consists of a broad bay that splits into two long glacially carved arms—Tracy Arm and Endicott Arm. (Fords Terror splits off as a separate channel halfway up Endicott Arm.) Within Tracy Arm, steep-walled granite canyons plummet 2,000 feet into incredibly deep and narrow fjords. We're

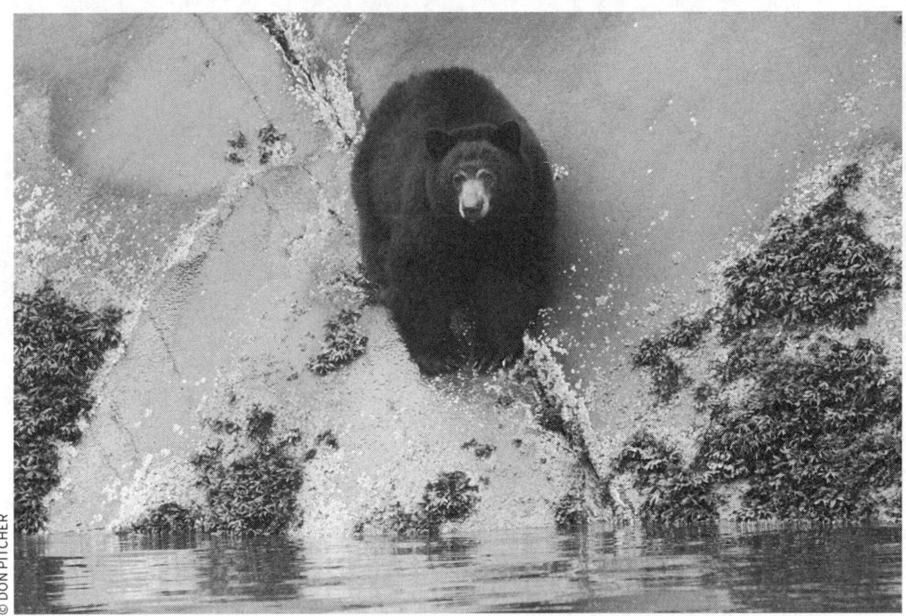

© DON PITCHER

black bear along Tracy Arm, Tracy Arm-Fords Terror Wilderness, near Juneau

talking rocks to the waterline here. The fjords wind past waterfalls to massive glaciers, their icebergs dotted with hundreds of harbor seals. Humpback whales are a common sight, as are killer whales. Look closely on the mountain slopes and you're bound to see mountain goats, especially near North Sawyer Glacier. John Muir noted that the fjord was

> *shut in by sublime Yosemite cliffs, nobly sculptured, and adorned with waterfalls and fringes of trees, bushes, and patches of flowers, but amid so crowded a display of novel beauty it was not easy to concentrate the attention long enough on any portion of it without giving more days and years than our lives can afford.*

Modern-day visitors come away equally impressed.

Two glaciers—Sawyer and South Sawyer—cap the end of Tracy Arm. Sawyer Glacier is retreating up the bay at 85 feet per year, while South Sawyer is losing over 300 feet per year. South Sawyer is larger and more interesting, but ice often blocks access. Other treats include get-wet visits to waterfalls and the chance to view seals lounging on the ice. Contact the Forest Service Information Center in Juneau (907/586-8751, www.fs.fed.us/r10/tongass) for details on Tracy Arm.

Boat Trips

Visit Tracy Arm on board **Adventure Bound Alaska** (907/463-2509 or 800/228-3875, www.adventureboundalaska.com, May–Sept.) vessels. Owner Steve Weber has been doing this for more than 15 years and knows the best places to see mountain goats, seals, and whales. The company operates two boats in mid-season, the 56-foot *Adventure Bound* and the 65-foot *Captain Cook.* The boats typically stop for at least an hour at the face of one of the glaciers, providing a fantastic opportunity to witness the calving of icebergs. All-day cruises are offered every summer day for $150 adults, $95 children ages 5–17; younger children are not permitted. Fresh sandwiches, drinks, and

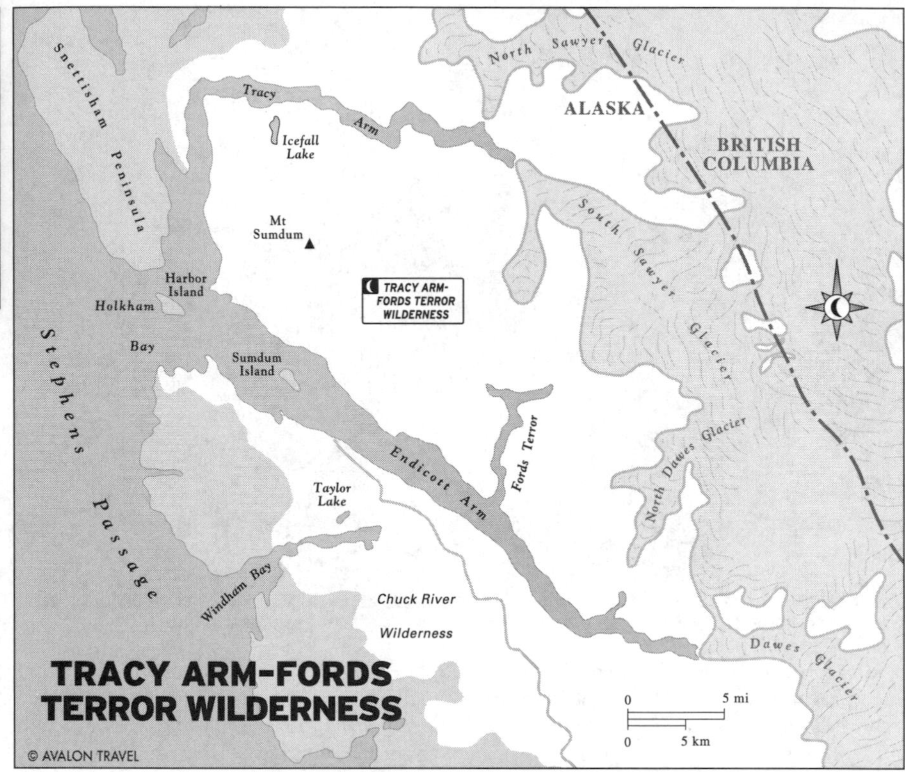

snacks are available on board for a few bucks more, and kayak drop-offs are available. This trip is highly recommended.

On Your Own

There are no trails in the Tracy Arm–Fords Terror Wilderness, but experienced sea kayakers—this definitely *isn't* for beginners—discover spectacular country to explore. Unfortunately, kayakers in Tracy Arm should be prepared for a constant parade of giant cruise ships leaving large wakes and plenty of engine noise to contend with. (Sound travels a long way over the water. Wilderness rangers report being startled to suddenly hear loudspeakers announcing, "Margaritas will be served at 16:30 in the aft lounge.") You can, however, escape the boats by hiking up ravines into the high country, or by heading into the less-congested waters of Endicott Arm, where cruise ships and powerboats rarely stray. **Adventure Bound Alaska** (907/463-2509 or 800/228-3875, www.adventureboundalaska.com) provides kayaker drop-offs, and rentals are available through **Alaska Boat & Kayak Rental** (907/789-6886, www.juneaukayak.com).

If you plan to go into Tracy Arm in a kayak, check ahead with the Forest Service's **Juneau Ranger District** (907/586-8751, www.fs.fed.us/r10/tongass) for good campsites. As you approach the glaciers at the upper end of Tracy, these become harder to find. Many boaters anchor in No Name Cove near the entrance to Tracy Arm. Kayakers will probably prefer to head to the middle part of the fjord and away from the motorboats. Ambitious folks (with a topo map) may want to try the steep half-mile

© DON PITCHER

A Tracy Arm visitor gets a close-up view of glacial ice.

cross-country climb up to **Icefall Lake** (1,469 feet above sea level).

Massive **Dawes Glacier** jams the top of Endicott Arm with thousands of bergs of all sizes and shapes, making it tough to get close to the face of the glacier. **Fords Terror** is a turbulent but spectacular inlet that angles away from Endicott Arm. Tidal changes create wild water conditions near the entrance, so kayakers and boaters need to take special precautions. Only run the narrows at slack tides, when the water is relatively calm. (The narrows are named for the terror felt by H. R. Ford, who rowed into the inlet one day in 1889 when the water was calm, but nearly died fighting the currents, whirlpools, and icebergs on the way back out.) Fords Terror has no tidewater glaciers, but numerous hanging glaciers and craggy peaks are visible.

Chuck River Wilderness

Twelve miles south of Tracy Arm is **Windham Bay,** entrance to the Chuck River Wilderness. This small wild area receives very little use but offers good fishing for salmon and a chance to explore the ruins of the Southeast's oldest mining community, Windham Bay. You can hike up the mile-long **Taylor Creek Trail** from Windham Bay to Taylor Lake.

Endicott River Wilderness

Although it encompasses 94,000 acres, this is one of the least-visited wilderness areas in the United States. Located some 60 miles northwest of Juneau, the wilderness borders on Glacier Bay National Park and includes the Endicott River watershed along the eastern slope of the Chilkat Range. The country is spruce and hemlock forests mixed with alders. Trails are nonexistent, and access from Lynn Canal is virtually impossible. Visit the Forest Service's **Juneau Ranger District** office (907/586-8751, www.fs.fed.us/r10/tongass) for more on this decidedly off-the-beaten-track area.

Admiralty Island

Just 20 miles west of Juneau lies the northern end of **Admiralty Island National Monument** (907/586-8800, www.fs.fed.us/r10/tongass) and the massive Kootznahoo Wilderness. At nearly 1 million acres, the wilderness covers 90 percent of Admiralty, making it the only large island in Southeast Alaska that has not been extensively logged or developed. The Tlingit name for Admiralty is Kootznahoo ("bear fortress"). The island is aptly named: It has perhaps 1,500 brown bears, giving it one of the highest bear densities anywhere on earth. Eagles are extraordinarily abundant along the shoreline, and the cries of loons haunt Admiralty's lakes. This is truly one of the gemstones of Southeast Alaska.

ANGOON

Located along Admiralty's southwestern shore, the Tlingit village of Angoon (pop. 600) is the island's lone settlement. It sits astride a peninsula guarding the entrance to Kootznahoo Inlet, an incredible wonderland of small islands and saltwater passages. Locals have cable TVs and microwave ovens, but smokehouses sit in front of many homes, and you'll hear older people speaking Tlingit. Angoon weather generally lives up to its reputation as Southeast Alaska's "Banana Belt"; yearly rainfall averages only 38 inches, compared to three times that in Sitka, only 40 miles away. By the way, the word *hooch* originated from the potent whiskey distilled by the "Hoosenoo" Indians of Admiralty in the 19th century. Today, Angoon is a dry town with a reputation as a place where traditional ways are encouraged.

History

The village of Angoon still commemorates an infamous incident that took place more than a century ago. While working for the Northwest Trading Company, a local shaman was killed in a seal-hunting accident. The villagers demanded 200 blankets as compensation and two days off to honor and bury the dead man. To ensure payment, they seized two hostages. Unaware of Tlingit traditions, the company manager fled to Sitka and persuaded a U.S. Navy boat to "punish them severely." On October 26, 1882, the town was shelled, destroying most of the houses. All the villagers' canoes were smashed and sunk, and all their winter supplies burned. Six children died from the smoke and the people nearly starved that winter. In a U.S. Congressional investigation two years later, the shelling was called "the greatest outrage ever committed in the United States upon any Indian tribe." Finally, in 1973, the government paid $90,000 in compensation for the shelling, but the Navy has never formally apologized.

Sights

Even if you don't stay overnight in Angoon, get off the ferry and walk across the road and down to the beach. From here you can look up to a small **cemetery** with old gravestones and fenced-in graves. Another interesting cemetery is near the end of the peninsula 0.5 miles behind the **Russian Orthodox church** in town. A number of rustic old houses line the shore, one with killer whales painted on the front. A hundred feet uphill from the post office are five memorial **totems** topped by representations of different local clans. Near Angoon Trading you get a great view of the narrow passage leading into **Kootznahoo Inlet,** where tides create dangerous rapids.

Accommodations and Food

Built in 1937, **Favorite Bay Inn B&B** (907/788-3123 or 800/423-3123, www.whalerscovelodge.com, $139 s, $209 d) is on the edge of town near the boat harbor. Five guest rooms share three baths; a full breakfast is included. The owners also run **Whaler's Cove Sportfishing Lodge** (June–Sept.) with multiday packages for anglers in search of salmon and halibut. Guests of Favorite Bay Inn can also have other meals at Whaler's Cove: $15 for lunch or $35 for dinner. Canoe, kayaks, and skiff rentals are available, and the lodge offers natural history tours.

Angoon Trading (907/788-3111, www.angoontrading.com) sells a limited and rather expensive selection of groceries and supplies, along with a selection of Native artworks. Whaler's Cove Sportfishing Lodge serves meals, but make reservations if you aren't a guest.

Getting There

The state ferry ***LeConte*** (800/642-0066, www.dot.state.ak.us/amhs) connects Angoon with Juneau twice a week, staying just long enough to unload and load vehicles. The dock (no ferry terminal) is 2.5 miles out of town, so you won't see Angoon up close unless you disembark, but "taxis" will run visitors into town.

Alaska Seaplane Service (907/789-3331 or 800/478-3360, www.flyalaskaseaplanes.com) has daily floatplane service between Angoon and Juneau, while **Harris Aircraft Services** (907/966-3050 or 877/966-3050, www.harrisaircraft.com) flies most days between Sitka and Angoon.

PACK CREEK

Located a short flight from Juneau along the west side of Seymour Canal, Pack Creek is one of Alaska's premier brown bear–viewing areas. The creek fills with spawning humpback and chum salmon during July and August, and they attract the bears, which in turn attract the people. Most visitors arrive on day trips from Juneau on the local air taxis. Others come aboard kayaks and boats, or with commercially guided groups. Pack Creek is jointly managed and staffed by the U.S. Forest Service and the Alaska Department of Fish and Game. Special regulations apply to travel and camping in the area, and it's only open for visits 9 A.M.–9 P.M.

Bear-Watching

The number of bears varies greatly through the summer, but most visitors see at least one bear, and often several. Plan to spend a full day—or longer—to increase your odds and to soak in the beauty of the area. Binoculars or a spotting scope are helpful, and photographers should be sure to bring extra digital storage cards and long lenses. Rubber boots and rain gear are strongly recommended for anyone visiting Pack Creek. Food and drinks must be stowed in a special bear-resistant box, and neither is allowed in the viewing areas.

There are two primary bear-viewing areas along Pack Creek. The most accessible is a sandy spit of land right at the mouth of the creek and a short beach hike from where floatplanes land and boats tie up. A bit more challenging is a beautiful one-mile trail that leads through an old-growth rain forest to a viewing tower. The tower has room for eight people and is an excellent place to watch bears as they pass directly below you.

Forest Service or Fish and Game rangers at Pack Creek will be happy to answer your questions, so it isn't necessary to come with a guide (unless you can't otherwise get in). They will not, however, accompany you to the observation tower.

Rules and Regulations

If you travel independently, you will need to obtain a permit and set up a charter with a local air taxi. Guided visitors are provided with transportation and permits, but the fee is much higher. Because of its popularity with both bears and people—and the potential for conflicts between the two—Pack Creek has stringent and rather confusing rules. Permits are required June 1–September 10, and only 24 people per day are allowed during the peak of the bear-viewing season (July 5–Aug. 25).

Reservations cost $50 adults, $25 seniors and children and can be postmarked as early as February 20 for the following summer. Apply early to be sure of getting a permit for the peak season. Of the 24 permits, 4 are held for late arrivals and are available 3 days in advance of your visit. These are in high demand, however, and are chosen by lottery from the applicants who show up. An unlimited number of shoulder-season permits (June 1–July 4 and Aug. 26–Sept. 10, $20 adults, $10 seniors and children) are available, but bear activity is lower. Get additional details from the **Forest Service in Juneau** (907/586-8800, www.fs.fed.us/r10/tongass).

Getting to Pack Creek

Most visitors to Pack Creek arrive by floatplane on day trips from Juneau, landing next to the south sand spit. The following companies fly to Pack Creek: **Alaska Fly 'n' Fish Charters** (907/790-2120, www.alaskabyair.com), **Alaska Seaplane Service** (907/789-3331 or 800/478-3360, www.flyalaskaseaplanes.com), and **Ward Air** (907/789-9150, www.wardair.com). The costs vary depending on how many people are on the flight, but with four in a group the price drops to $210 per person round-trip (but you'll need to get your own permit).

Guided Trips

Several guide companies offer trips to Pack Creek, and they are likely to have space available at the last minute. They're a good option if you can't get a permit—and if you have the cash. **Alaska Discovery** (510/594-6000 or 800/586-1911, www.akdiscovery.com) offers all-inclusive three-day kayak and camping trips to Pack Creek for $1,300 (including air fare).

Alaska Fly 'n' Fish Charters (907/790-2120, www.alaskabyair.com) offers guided day trips to Pack Creek; $600 for a 5.5-hour tour includes air transport from Juneau. Two companies have excellent multiday boat trips that include a day at Pack Creek: **All Aboard Yacht Charters** (360/898-7300 or 800/767-1024, www.alaskacharters.com) and **Dolphin Charters** (510/527-9622 or 800/472-9942, www.dolphincharters.com).

Kayaking

The bear-viewing area along Pack Creek is only a tiny portion of **Seymour Canal.** This is a wonderful place to explore by sea kayak, with lush country, relatively protected waters, and the chance to see eagles, brown bears, and other wildlife. **Alaska Boat & Kayak Rental** (907/789-6886, www.juneaukayak.com) has kayak rentals and can set up a water taxi to Oliver Inlet, where an ingenious mile-long boat tramway makes it easy to bring kayaks across to upper Seymour Canal. Alaska State Parks maintains the **Oliver Inlet Cabin** (www.alaskastateparks.org, $25) at the northern tip of Seymour Canal.

In Seymour you'll find many coves and islands to explore, and have a chance to observe bears that are protected from hunting. If you're adventurous, climb up the nearby peaks for fantastic views of the entire area. A three-sided shelter (free) is available in **Windfall Harbor.** Bears can be a real problem in Seymour Canal, so be sure to select your camping spots very carefully, preferably on a small island, and hang all food.

Camping

Camping is not allowed on Admiralty Island near the mouth of Pack Creek, but it is permitted on Windfall Island, where you're far less likely to have encounters with the bears. The island is 0.25 miles from Pack Creek. Independent travelers may be able to rent a sea kayak on Windfall from Alaska Discovery (advance reservation required) to reach Pack Creek or to explore the area.

Cross-Admiralty Canoe Route

Admiralty Island is ideally suited for people who enjoy canoeing or sea kayaking. Kootznahoo Inlet reaches back behind Angoon through a labyrinth of islands and narrow passages before opening into expansive Mitchell Bay. From there you can continue to Salt Lake or Kanalku Bay, or begin the Cross-Admiralty Canoe Route—a chain of scenic lakes connected by portages, one of which is over three miles long. Using this 42-mile route you should reach Seymour Canal in 4–6 days (the record is 12 hours). Along the way are six Forest Service cabins ($35) and six Adirondack shelters (free), so you won't have to sleep out in the rain all the time. For more specific canoe-route information, contact the office of **Admiralty Island National Monument** (907/586-8790, www.fs.fed.us/r10/tongass) in Juneau.

Glacier Bay National Park and Preserve

America's national parks are this country's version of Mecca, places where hordes of pilgrims are drawn in search of fulfillment that seems to come from experiencing these shrines of the natural world. Since Glacier Bay's discovery by John Muir in 1879, the spectacles of stark rocky walls, deep fjords, and giant rivers of ice calving massive icebergs into the sea have never ceased to inspire and humble visitors.

Established as a national park in 1925, Glacier Bay received major additions in the Alaska National Interest Lands Conservation Act of 1980. The park and preserve now cover more than 3.3 million acres and contain half a dozen glaciers that reach the ocean, making this one of the largest concentrations of tidewater glaciers on earth. These glaciers originate in the massive snowcapped Fairweather Range, sliding down the slopes and carving out giant troughs that become fjords when the glaciers retreat. **Mt. Fairweather,** rising 15,320 feet, is Southeast Alaska's tallest peak. On a clear day, it is prominently visible from park headquarters, 72 miles away. The vegetation of Glacier Bay varies from a 200-year-old spruce and hemlock forest at Bartlett Cove to freshly exposed moraine where tenacious plant life is just starting to take hold. Wildlife is abundant in the park: Humpback whales, harbor porpoises, harbor seals, and bird rookeries can be seen from excursion boats and kayaks. Black bears are fairly common.

HISTORY

Glacier Bay has not always looked as it does today. When Captain George Vancouver sailed through Icy Strait in 1794, he found a wall of ice more than 4,000 feet thick and 20 miles wide. Less than 100 years later when Hoonah Indian guides led John Muir into the area in 1879, he discovered that the glaciers had retreated nearly 50 miles, creating a new land and a giant bay splitting into two deep fjords on its upper end. The bay was shrouded by low clouds, but Muir, anxious to see farther into the country, climbed a peak on its western shore:

> *All the landscape was smothered in clouds and I began to fear that as far as wide views were concerned I had climbed in vain. But at length the clouds lifted a little, and beneath their gray fringes I saw the berg-filled expanse of the bay, and the feet of the mountains that stand about it, and the imposing fronts of five huge glaciers, the nearest being immediately beneath me. This was my first general view of Glacier Bay, a solitude of ice and snow and newborn rocks, dim, dreary, mysterious. I held the ground I had so dearly won for an hour or two, sheltering myself from the blast as best I could, while with benumbed fingers I sketched what I could see of the landscape, and wrote a few lines in my notebook. Then, breasting the snow again, crossing the shifting avalanche slopes and torrents, I reached camp about dark, wet and weary and glad.*

Today's traveler is less likely to take such pains to see this grand place.

The rapid retreat of the glaciers over the last 200 years has caused the land to rebound, much like a sponge that has been squeezed and then re-forms. The process is astoundingly rapid by geological standards; around Bartlett Cove the land is rising nearly two inches per year, and even faster farther up the bay. Ask the park rangers to point out some of the changes in vegetation because of this rebound effect.

VISITING GLACIER BAY

The vast majority of the over 350,000 visitors who come to Glacier Bay each year arrive aboard cruise ships, two of which are allowed in each day; they're given a talk by a Park Service naturalist as the ship heads up the west arm of the bay and never set foot on the land itself. Most other visitors stay in Glacier

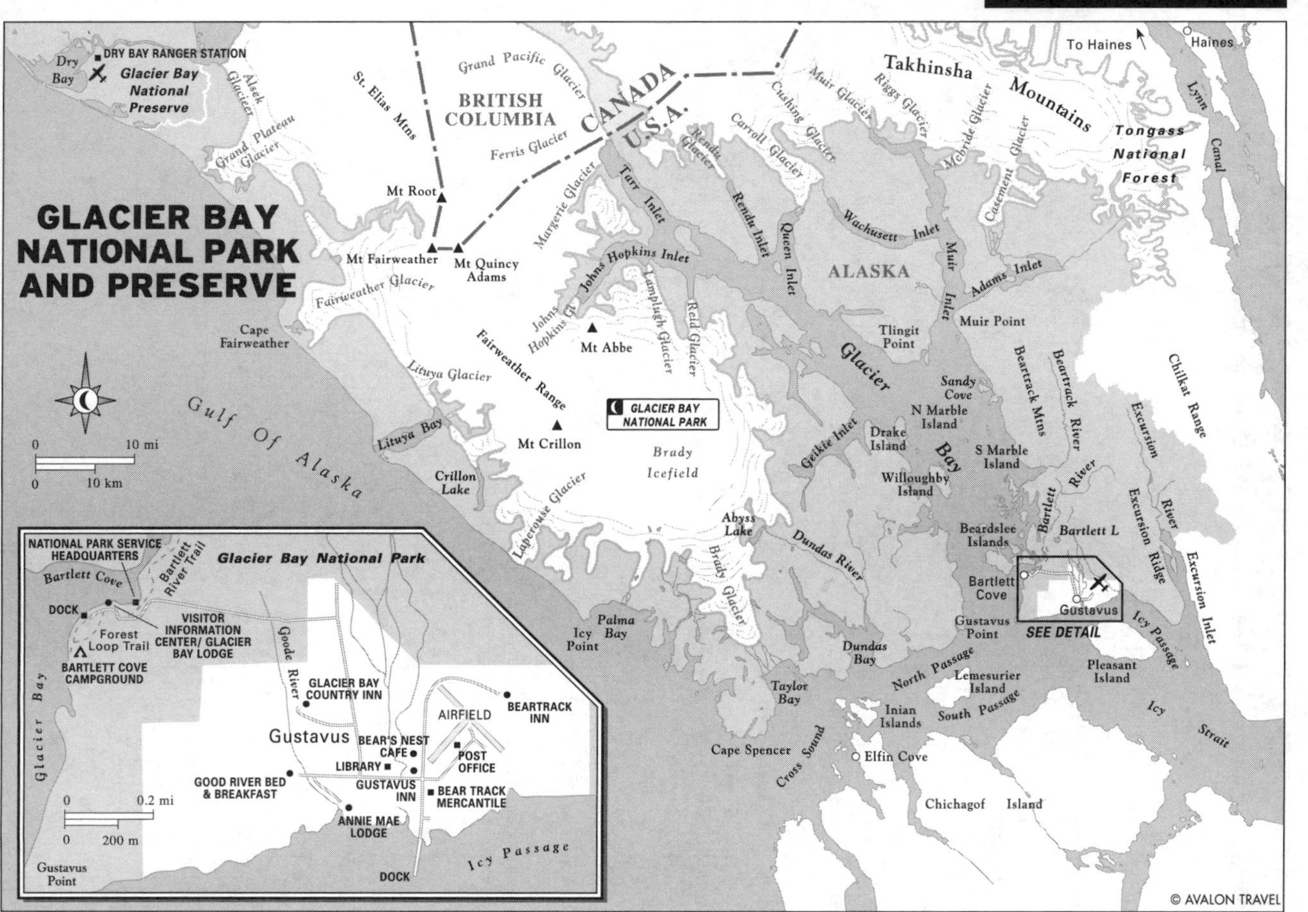
GLACIER BAY NATIONAL PARK AND PRESERVE
DRY BAY RANGER STATION
Dry Bay
Glacier Bay National Preserve
Alsek Glacier
Grand Plateau Glacier
St. Elias Mtns
BRITISH COLUMBIA
Grand Pacific Glacier
Ferris Glacier
CANADA
U.S.A.
Mt Root
Mt Fairweather
Mt Quincy Adams
Fairweather Glacier
Cape Fairweather
Margerie Glacier
Tarr Inlet
Johns Hopkins Inlet
Johns Hopkins Gl
Mt Abbe
Lamplugh Glacier
Reid Glacier
Rendu Glacier
Rendu Inlet
Carroll Glacier
Queen Inlet
Cushing Glacier
Muir Glacier
Riggs Glacier
Takhinsha Mountains
Mcbride Glacier
Casement Glacier
Wachusett Inlet
Muir Inlet
Adams Inlet
ALASKA
To Haines
Haines
Lynn Canal
Tongass National Forest
Fairweather Range
Lituya Glacier
Lituya Bay
Gulf Of Alaska
0 10 mi
0 10 km
Mt Crillon
Crillon Lake
GLACIER BAY NATIONAL PARK
Brady Icefield
Laperouse Glacier
Tlingit Point
Muir Point
Glacier Bay
Sandy Cove
N Marble Island
Drake Island
S Marble Island
Willoughby Island
Geikie Inlet
Beartrack Mtns
Beartrack River
Chilkat Range
Excursion River
Excursion Ridge
Excursion Inlet
Bartlett River
Bartlett L
Beardslee Islands
Bartlett Cove
Gustavus
SEE DETAIL
Gustavus Point
Icy Passage
Pleasant Island
Icy Strait
Abyss Lake
Dundas River
Brady Glacier
Icy Point
Palma Bay
Dundas Bay
Taylor Bay
North Passage
Lemesurier Island
Inian Islands
South Passage
Cape Spencer
Cross Sound
Elfin Cove
Chichagof Island
© AVALON TRAVEL
NATIONAL PARK SERVICE HEADQUARTERS
Bartlett River Trail
Glacier Bay National Park
Bartlett Cove
DOCK
VISITOR INFORMATION CENTER/ GLACIER BAY LODGE
Forest Loop Trail
BARTLETT COVE CAMPGROUND
Goode River
GLACIER BAY COUNTRY INN
AIRFIELD
BEARTRACK INN
Gustavus
BEAR'S NEST CAFE
LIBRARY
POST OFFICE
GOOD RIVER BED & BREAKFAST
GUSTAVUS INN
BEAR TRACK MERCANTILE
ANNIE MAE LODGE
Glacier Bay
0 0.2 mi
0 200 m
Icy Passage
DOCK
Gustavus Point

Bay Lodge at Bartlett Cove or in nearby luxury lodges in the town of Gustavus, venturing out only to cruise past the glaciers on a tour boat. The tiny percentage who come to actually see and touch their national park—rather than view it in a naturalist's slide show—are often prevented from doing so by prohibitive costs. It is somewhat ironic that the park is most accessible to those who would rather look out on its glaciers from their stateroom windows.

The nearest tidewater glacier is 40 miles from park headquarters in Bartlett Cove. To see these glaciers, you'll spend at least $400 plus food and lodging for a fast two-day trip from Juneau. A visit to Glacier Bay is a wonderful experience, but there are few options for the budget traveler, and you should probably make other plans if you're pinched for cash; consider a day trip from Juneau to Tracy Arm instead.

The park concessionaire, **Glacier Bay Lodge & Tours/Aramark** (907/264-4600 or 888/229-8687, www.visitglacierbay.com) operates the ***Fairweather Express II,*** which heads up the west arm of Glacier Bay daily in the summer, departing at 7:30 A.M. and returning at 3:30 P.M. Tours on this high-speed catamaran cost $193 adults, $96 children under 13. A light lunch is served, and a Park Service naturalist is on board to provide information on wildlife, geology, and cultural history along the route. The boat typically visits Margerie and Grand Pacific Glaciers before July, and heads up to Johns Hopkins Glacier later in the summer.

For a more personal touch, former backcountry ranger Mike Nigro runs **Gustavus Marine Charters** (907/697-2233, www.gustavusmarinecharters.com), with multiday ecotours into the park aboard his 42-foot boat with space for six.

Park Information

The Park Service maintains a **visitors center** (daily 11 A.M.–9 P.M. summer) upstairs in the Glacier Bay Lodge at Bartlett Cove. A small museum here contains natural history and geology exhibits. Naturalists lead interpretive walks every day, once-a-week summer camps for children, plus evening talks and slide shows in the auditorium. The park's **backcountry office** (daily 8 A.M.–5 P.M. summer) is near the boat dock, a short hike from the lodge. Stop here before heading into the park on an overnight trip. For additional details, contact **Glacier Bay National Park** (907/697-2230, www.nps.gov/glba).

HIKING

There are several enjoyable walks in the Bartlett Cove area. The mile-long **Forest Loop Trail** connects the lodge, boat dock, and campground, providing an excellent introduction to the area. **Bartlett River Trail** (4 miles round-trip) leads from park headquarters to the mouth of the river and has opportunities to observe wildlife. Salmon can be seen moving up the river in August. For a satisfying beach walk, head south along the shore from the campground. If you're ambitious, it is possible to walk to **Point Gustavus** (6 miles) or on to **Goode River** (13 miles). Follow the river upstream 1 mile to Gustavus, where you can walk or hitch back along the road. Beach walking is easiest at low tide; the backcountry office has tide charts. Note that none of these trails goes anywhere near the tidewater glaciers for which the park is famous, and there are no developed trails anywhere in the park's backcountry.

SEA KAYAKING

Guided Trips

Glacier Bay Sea Kayaks (907/697-2257, www.glacierbayseakayaks.com) has all-day ($95) and half-day ($150) kayak trips from the Bartlett Cove dock in the summer. These are a good way to learn the basics of sea kayaking, and they include a kayak and gear, a guide, food, and boots.

Alaska Discovery (510/594-6000 or 800/586-1911, www.akdiscovery.com) leads multiday kayak trips into Glacier Bay and nearby waters, including a three-day Point Adolphus whale-watching adventure ($995) and a five-day paddle into the heart of Glacier Bay National Park ($2,400 plus airfare from Juneau).

Spirit Walker Expeditions (907/697-2266 or 800/529-2537, www.seakayakalaska.com) runs excellent sea kayak trips, including day tours ($150) out of Gustavus up to seven-day trips ($2,650) among remote islands off Chichagof Island. The company does not generally tour within Glacier Bay National Park.

On Your Own

The finest way to explore Glacier Bay is by kayak. Some folks bring their own folding kayaks on the plane, but most people rent them from Kara Berg of **Glacier Bay Sea Kayaks** (907/697-2257, www.glacierbaysea-kayaks.com) in Bartlett Cove. Kayak rentals include a two-person boat, paddles, life vests, spray skirts, flotation bags, and a brief lesson. Reservations are a must during midsummer. The company also rents rain gear and rubber boots and will help set up your trip, including making all-important boat reservations to get up the bay.

Several focal points attract kayakers within Glacier Bay. The **Beardslee Islands,** in relatively protected waters near Bartlett Cove, make an excellent 2–3-day kayak trip and do not require any additional expenses. Beyond the Beardslees, Glacier Bay becomes much less protected, and you should plan on spending at least a week up-bay if you paddle there. (It is 50 miles or more to the glaciers.) Rather than attempting to cross this open water, most kayakers opt for a drop-off. The locations change periodically, so ask at the backcountry office in Bartlett Cove for specifics.

Muir Inlet (the east arm of Glacier Bay) is preferred by many kayakers because it is a bit more protected and is not used by the cruise ships or most tour boats. The **West Arm** is more spectacular—especially iceberg-filled Johns Hopkins Inlet—but you'll have to put up with a constant stream of large and small cruise ships. If the boat operators have their way, even more ships can be expected in future years.

The *Fairweather Express II* does camper and sea kayaker drop-offs in Glacier Bay ($223 round trip). For details, contact **Glacier Bay Lodge & Tours** (907/264-4600 or 888/229-8687, www.visitglacierbay.com).

Talk with Park Service personnel in Bartlett Cove before heading out on any hiking or kayaking trip. You'll need to be in Gustavus airport by 3 P.M. the day before to go through all the hoops (getting to Bartlett Cove, renting the kayak, going through the Park Service camping and bear safety session, and getting your kayak on board the *Fairweather Express II*). This means you cannot take the evening Alaska Airlines flight; it arrives too late in the day.

CAMPING

An excellent free campground at Bartlett Cove comes complete with bear-proof food storage caches, outhouses, and a three-sided shelter with a woodstove (great for drying your gear after a kayak trip up the bay). The campground is only 0.5 miles from Glacier Bay Lodge and usually has space. Running water is available next to the backcountry office. All cooking must be done below the high-tide line (where the odors are washed away every six hours) to reduce the chance of bear problems. You can store things for free in the shed next to the backcountry office.

Backcountry Camping

No trails exist anywhere in Glacier Bay's backcountry, but Park Service rangers can provide details on hiking and camping up the bay. Camping is allowed in most park areas. Exceptions are the Marble Islands—closed because of their importance to nesting seabirds—and a few other areas closed because of the potential for bear incidents. A gas stove is a necessity for camping, since wood is often unavailable.

Free permits (available at the backcountry office) are recommended before you head out. Park naturalists provide camper orientations each evening, including information on how and where to go, bear safety, and minimum-impact camping procedures. Bears have killed two people within the park in the past decade or so, and to lessen the chance of this happening, free

...-proof containers are loaned to all kayakers and hikers. A small storage shed beside the backcountry office is a good place to store unneeded gear while you're up the bay. Firearms are not allowed in Glacier Bay.

TATSHENSHINI AND ALSEK RIVERS

Along the western edge of Glacier Bay National Park flows the Tatshenshini River, considered one of the world's premier wilderness rafting routes. Bears, moose, mountain goats, and Dall sheep are all visible along the way. The river rolls through Class III white water and spectacular canyons along the way to its juncture with the Alsek River. **Alaska Discovery** (510/594-6000 or 800/586-1911, www.akdiscovery.com) has several trips each summer down this spectacular route, as well as down the more remote Alsek. A 12-day river-rafting trip on the Alsek isn't cheap at $4,100, but the price includes a van ride from Haines to the put-in point at Dalton Post in Yukon, and a spectacular helicopter portage around the Class VI rapids of Turnback Canyon. One of the real treats of this trip is paddling past the seven-mile-wide Alsek Glacier. The trip begins in Haines and ends in Yakutat.

Other good companies offering Alsek and Tatshenshini trips include **Chilkat Guides** (907/766-2491 or 888/292-7789, www.raftalaska.com) and **Canadian River Expeditions** (867/668-3180 or 800/297-6927, www.canriver.com). Contact the park (907/697-2230, www.nps.gov/glba) for details on running the rivers.

GUSTAVUS AND VICINITY

There are two basic centers for visitors to Glacier Bay. **Bartlett Cove,** inside the park, has Park Service Headquarters, a campground, the Glacier Bay Lodge (with a bar, a restaurant, and the park service visitors center), and a boat dock. Ten miles away (a $14 shuttle-bus ride) and outside the park boundaries is the community of **Gustavus** (pop. 370). Here you will find the airport, the main boat dock, a general store, B&Bs, and luxury lodges.

Practicalities

The town of Gustavus consists of equal parts park employees, fishers, and folks dependent on the tourism trade. It's one of the only places in Southeast Alaska that has enough flat country to raise cattle, and the only Southeast Alaska town of any size without service from the state ferry system (though this may change in 2011). Be sure to check out the historic—and still working—1937 gas pumps decorated with the old Mobil flying horse at **Gustavus Dray** (907/697-2481), which also sells antiques and gifts. Across the street is **Fireweed Gallery** (907/697-2325) and Homeshore Café. Gustavus is also home to the nine-hole **Mt. Fairweather Golf Course** (907/697-3080, www.gustavus.com/activities/golf.html).

The **Gustavus Visitors Association** (907/697-2454, www.gustavusak.com) has information and links to local lodging and other businesses; also try www.gustavus.com. Find free **Wi-Fi** at the **Gustavus Library** (907/697-2350, www.gustavus.lib.ak.us), in Glacier Bay Lodge, and at Homeshore Café. There are no ATMs in Gustavus, so be sure to bring cash with you from Juneau.

Fishing and Whale-Watching

Fishing, primarily for halibut and salmon, is a big attraction for many visitors, and most of the lodges offer package deals for anglers. Get a list of charter boat operators from the Park Service or at www.gustavusalaska.org. Most of these companies also run whale-watching trips, and some can carry sea kayaks on board.

Flightseeing

One of the best ways to see the park is from the air. Both **Air Excursions** (907/697-2375 or 800/354-2479, www.airexcursions.com) and **Fjord Flying Service** (907/697-2377, www.puffintravel.com/fjord.htm) provide flightseeing trips over the park. Other companies offer Glacier Bay flightseeing from Juneau, Haines, and Skagway, but prices are generally higher since you need to fly farther.

Accommodations

Located within Glacier Bay National Park is **Glacier Bay Lodge** (907/264-4600 or 888/229-8687, www.visitglacierbay.com, late May–mid-Sept., $171–196 d). The shore-side lodge is surrounded by tall trees at Bartlett Cove (park headquarters), and has a restaurant, informal deck dining, a pleasant bar, plus a big stone fireplace that makes a cozy place to sit on a rainy evening—even if you're not a guest. Guests stay in plain-vanilla units with double or twin beds and private baths. Many guests opt for a package that includes a night's lodging, an all-day tour of Glacier Bay, three meals, and transportation to and from Gustavus for $422 per person. Laundry facilities, coin-operated showers, and gear storage are available for campers. The lodge rents a few mountain bikes and fishing poles.

Glacier Bay Lodge provides the only in-park accommodations, but far nicer options are available in nearby Gustavus. Most of these provide free transport to and from the Gustavus airport or boat dock, along with clunker bikes to ride on the roads. All of these will also set up tours, fishing, sea kayaking, and other activities.

Honeymooners or others looking to splurge will love a visit to **Gustavus Inn** (907/697-2254 or 800/649-5220, www.gustavusinn.com, mid-May–mid-Sept.), the most famous local lodging place. Built in 1928 as the centerpiece for a homestead, the farmhouse was transformed into Gustavus Inn in 1965. Owners David and Jo Ann Lesh have created a delightful country place with a picturesque garden that provides fresh vegetables all summer. Gourmet meals are served family style in the spacious garden-side dining room. Lodging and meals cost $840 d for one night or $1,250 d for two nights, with private baths and Wi-Fi (a rarity in Gustavus).

Modern **Beartrack Inn** (907/697-3017 or 888/697-2284, www.beartrackinn.com, mid-May–mid-Sept.) occupies a 57-acre spread six miles out a rough dirt road from Gustavus. This luxuriously furnished 15,000-square-foot log inn has a central lobby with a fireplace, large windows fronting on Icy Strait, a big deck and grassy front lawn, plus 14 spacious guest rooms. A number of packages are available for stays of one ($1,150 d) to seven ($5,120 d) nights, including transportation from Juneau, lodging, and sumptuous meals; activities are extra.

Glacier Bay Country Inn (907/697-2288 or 800/628-0912, www.glacierbayalaska.com, mid-May–mid-Sept.) combines a rambling log structure with modern amenities. Guests stay in five well-appointed cabins ($490 d) or the main lodge ($436 d) and are treated to three gourmet meals per day. A variety of package options are also offered.

Annie Mae Lodge (907/697-2346 or 800/478-2346, www.anniemae.com, mid-May to mid-Sept.) is a quiet two-story lodge in a meadow-and-forest setting along the Goode River. The 11 guest rooms cost $120 s or $170 d with a shared bath and $145–150 s or $185–200 d with a private bath, including three big meals and round-trip transportation from Juneau.

Good River Bed & Breakfast (907/697-2241, www.glacier-bay.us, June–late Aug., $130–140 d) has four guest rooms with shared baths in an attractive three-story log home, plus a private but rustic log cabin with an outhouse. A full breakfast and free bikes are included.

Cottonwood Lodge & Cabin Rental (907/697-2227, www.cottonwoodlodge.net, $125 d) has newly built cabins in a secluded setting. The cabins have two queen beds, covered decks, and full kitchens, making them perfect for families. There is a two-night minimum stay.

Another fine option for longer visits is **Aimee's Guest House** (907/697-2330, www.glacierbayalaska.net, $100–150 d), with a meadow vista from the porch and two apartments, each with a full kitchen and other amenities. There's a three-night minimum stay.

Close to the center of town, **Blue Heron B&B** (907/697-2337, www.blueheronbnb.net) fronts on a flower-filled garden and meadow. Two private and comfortable cabins are $185 d, or stay in the main home for $110 s or $145 d. Breakfast is home-cooked and memorable.

Food

Located at four corners (near the gas station), **Homeshore Café** (907/697-2822, Tues.–Sat. 11:30 A.M.–2 P.M., 5–8 P.M. summer) is popular for lunchtime sandwiches, salads, and homemade soups, plus evening pizzas ($20–27) to eat in or take away.

Espresso aficionados head to the **Wings** (907/697-2201, daily 7 A.M.–3 P.M. mid-May–mid-Sept., Mon.–Sat. 8 A.M.–2 P.M. winter, $4–6) inside the Wings of Alaska airport terminal. It has an odd location, but this is a delightful little coffee shop with lattes, doughnuts (flown in from Juneau), and fresh lunchtime sandwiches.

Open for lunch and dinner, **Bear's Nest Café** (907/697-2440, www.gustavus.com/bearsnest, daily 11 A.M.–8 P.M. June–Aug., dinner entrées $22–32) specializes in locally caught salmon, halibut, and crab, along with salads and daily specials. Save room for a slice of their rhubarb-strawberry pie. Saturday night brings open-mike jam sessions.

An outstanding dinner option is **Gustavus Inn** (907/697-2255 or 800/649-5220, www.gustavusinn.com, $40), where a few spots are held for those who aren't overnighting. Reservations are required. **Glacier Bay Country Inn** (907/697-2288 or 800/628-0912, www.glacierbayalaska.com) serves nightly meals ($35) at 6 and 8 P.M. in the summer.

Glacier Bay Lodge (907/697-4000, daily 6 A.M.–10 P.M., dinner entrées $18–30) in Bartlett Cove serves so-so meals; try the Dungeness crab, seafood chowder, or sweet potato fries. There's casual dining on the outside deck, where a lighter menu ($10–15) is also available.

Open daily in the summer, the small grocery store at Gustavus, **Beartrack Mercantile** (907/697-2358), has a great little deli and sells essentials for a price, though it's cheaper to bring food from Juneau. **Pep's Packing** (907/697-2295) sells locally caught salmon if you have access to a barbecue. Glacier Bay Lodge has a full bar, or you can purchase booze at **Snug Harbor Liquor Store** (907/723-8874).

Getting There

State ferry service to Gustavus does not exist as of this writing but is expected to begin in 2011; get the latest at www.dot.state.ak.us/amhs.

Glacier Bay Lodge & Tours/Aramark (907/264-4600 or 888/229-8687, www.visitglacierbay.com) provides twice-weekly summertime boat access to Bartlett Cove from Juneau. The *Fairweather Express II* has departures in both directions on Friday and Sunday evenings for $82 adults, $41 children. Service is not dependable, and the boat often runs late. Dinner whale-watching tours ($139 adults, $64 children) are also available three times per week June–mid-August.

Many visitors fly by jet from Juneau to Gustavus on **Alaska Airlines** (800/426-0333, www.alaskaair.com), but book ahead to be sure of getting on these popular afternoon flights. The trip takes only 15 minutes in the air, so the flight attendants don't even have time to throw bags of pretzels at you.

More rewarding are flights by **Wings of Alaska** (907/789-0790, www.wingsofalaska.com), **Air Excursions** (907/697-2375 or 800/354-2479, www.airexcursions.com), or **Fjord Flying Service** (907/697-2377, www.puffintravel.com/fjord.htm). They offer more personal service to Juneau, and the small planes fly lower, providing excellent on-the-way sightseeing for around $190 round-trip. Wings of Alaska has scheduled flights, while Air Excursions and Fjord Flying fly to Juneau whenever enough folks want to go (typically several times per day).

Note that it's illegal to transport white gas and other potentially explosive fuels in any commercial aircraft, so be sure your gas stove and fuel bottles are empty before you reach the airport. Purchase fuel in Bartlett Cove next to the visitor center or in Gustavus at Beartrack Mercantile. Also, you can't carry "bear mace" on the jets, although floatplanes will sometimes carry it in their floats.

Getting Around

The airport in Gustavus is 10 miles from Park Headquarters at Bartlett Cove. A

shuttle bus meets all Alaska Airlines flights, transporting you to Bartlett Cove for $14 per person each way. Hitching is possible, but traffic can be downright scarce in tiny Gustavus. **TLC Taxi** (907/697-2239) provides passenger and kayak transport in the Gustavus area and meets air taxis and Alaska Airlines jets.

Bud's Rent-A-Car (907/697-2403) has a dozen beater rental cars, and you don't even need to fill up the tank at the end. Of course, it's also pretty hard to put many miles on around here. Check out his nonexistent license plates; in their place it simply says "Bud's Rent-A-Car" in big red letters. Apparently the state doesn't require license plates in Gustavus because it's so difficult to get in or out. Most local lodging places have loaner bikes, and Glacier Bay Lodge in Bartlett Cove rents bikes and fishing poles.

Haines

The pleasant and friendly town of Haines (pop. 1,400) provides a transition point between the lush greenery of the Southeast and the more rugged beauty of Yukon and Alaska's Interior. As the ferry sails north to Haines on the Lynn Canal—at 1,600 feet deep, it's the longest and deepest fjord in North America—the Inside Passage gets narrower, and you sense that this unique waterway, and your passage on it, are coming to an end. To the east, waterfalls tumble off the mountainsides, while to the west, glaciers lumber down from the ice fields of the Chilkat Range. The long river of ice you see 40 minutes before Haines is **Davidson Glacier. Rainbow Glacier,** also on the left, hangs from a cliff just beyond. Both originate from the same ice field that forms part of Glacier Bay National Park.

Haines lies 90 miles north of Juneau, straddling a narrow peninsula between Chilkoot and Chilkat Inlets. Its mountain-ringed setting seems to define the word *spectacular:* From the ferry you catch a glimpse of the white Victorian buildings of Fort Seward in front of the 6,500-foot Cathedral Peaks. Haines has a wealth of outdoor experiences, almost as many for those without cash as for those with. Plenty of hiking trails run up surrounding peaks, camping is right next to town, and travelers will discover a pleasant mix of working stiffs, fishers, and artisans. It could serve as the poster child for what most folks expect in an Alaskan town: cozy, homespun, and earthy—the kind of place where the local radio station broadcasts birthday wishes, road updates for drivers heading over the pass, and bush messages for folks without a phone.

Unlike nearby Skagway, where a tidal wave of tourists inundates the town daily, Haines only sees a few large cruise ships. Most Haines visitors arrive by ferry and head on up the highway (or vice versa), but Haines is also becoming a popular weekend getaway for Canadians from Whitehorse. With "only" 60 inches of precipitation a year, the weather here is decidedly drier than points farther south.

HISTORY

Long before the arrival of Europeans to the Haines area, the Tlingit people of the Chilkoot and Chilkat tribes established villages nearby. Fish were plentiful, as were game animals and berries. The area's "mother village" was Klukwan, 20 miles up the Chilkat River, but another large Chilkoot village nestled near Chilkoot Lake, and a summer camp squatted just northwest of present-day Haines. The Chilkat people were renowned for their beautiful blankets woven from mountain-goat wool and dyed with an inventive mixture of copper nuggets, urine, lichen, and spruce roots. The blankets were (and are) worn during dance ceremonies. Today they are also exceedingly valuable.

In 1879 the naturalist John Muir and the

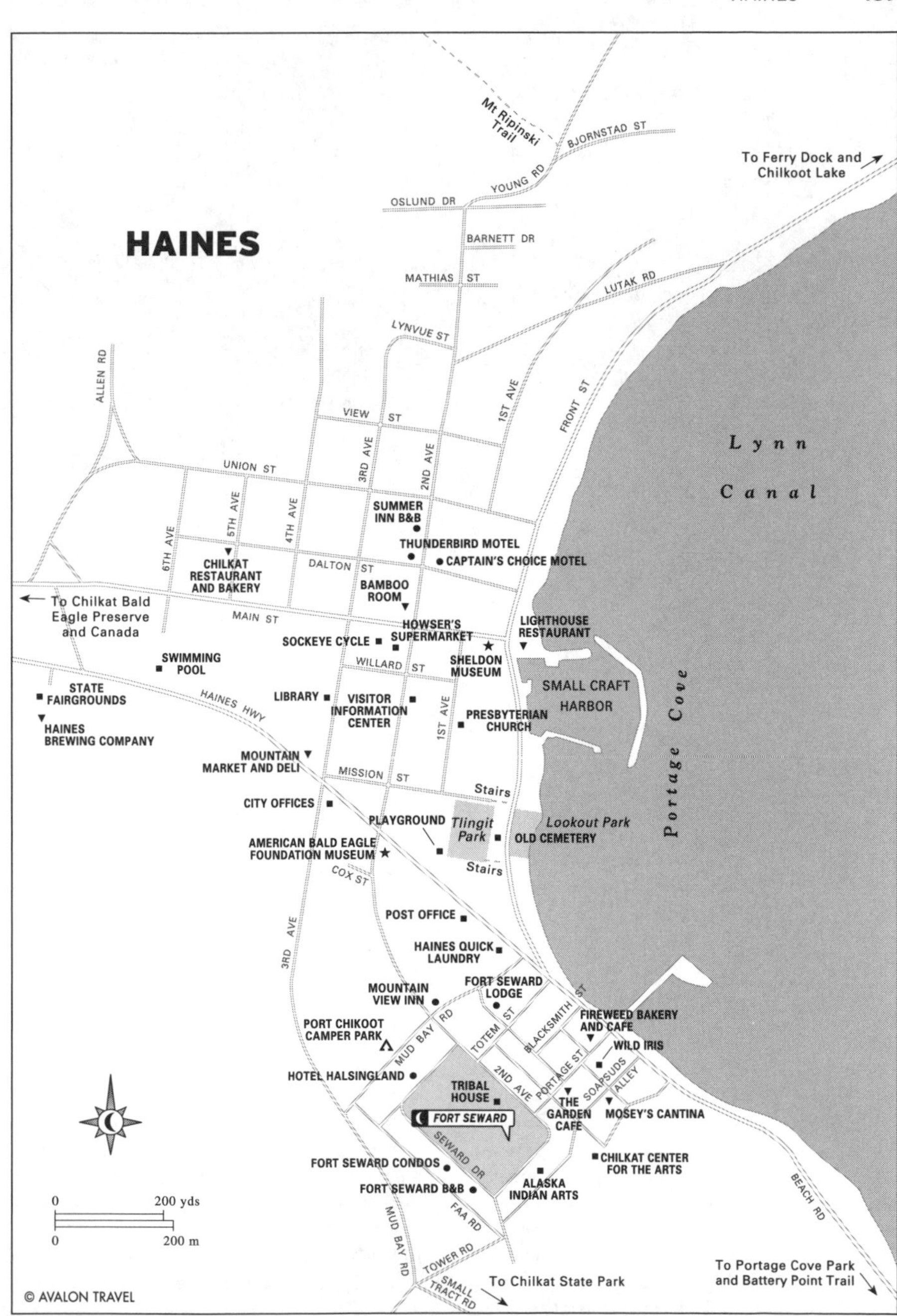
HAINES
Mt Ripinski Trail
BJORNSTAD ST
To Ferry Dock and Chilkoot Lake
YOUNG RD
OSLUND DR
BARNETT DR
MATHIAS ST
LUTAK RD
LYNVUE ST
ALLEN RD
1ST AVE
FRONT ST
VIEW ST
Lynn Canal
UNION ST
3RD AVE
2ND AVE
5TH AVE
4TH AVE
6TH AVE
SUMMER INN B&B
THUNDERBIRD MOTEL
CAPTAIN'S CHOICE MOTEL
CHILKAT RESTAURANT AND BAKERY
DALTON ST
BAMBOO ROOM
To Chilkat Bald Eagle Preserve and Canada
MAIN ST
HOWSER'S SUPERMARKET
LIGHTHOUSE RESTAURANT
SOCKEYE CYCLE
SWIMMING POOL
WILLARD ST
SHELDON MUSEUM
STATE FAIRGROUNDS
SMALL CRAFT HARBOR
HAINES HWY
LIBRARY
VISITOR INFORMATION CENTER
HAINES BREWING COMPANY
PRESBYTERIAN CHURCH
Portage Cove
MOUNTAIN MARKET AND DELI
MISSION ST
Stairs
CITY OFFICES
PLAYGROUND
Tlingit Park
Lookout Park
OLD CEMETERY
AMERICAN BALD EAGLE FOUNDATION MUSEUM
Stairs
COX ST
POST OFFICE
HAINES QUICK LAUNDRY
FORT SEWARD LODGE
MOUNTAIN VIEW INN
PORT CHIKOOT CAMPER PARK
MUD BAY RD
TOTEM ST
BLACKSMITH ST
FIREWEED BAKERY AND CAFE
WILD IRIS
PORTAGE ST
SOAPSUDS ALLEY
HOTEL HALSINGLAND
2ND AVE
TRIBAL HOUSE
THE GARDEN CAFE
MOSEY'S CANTINA
FORT SEWARD
SEWARD DR
FORT SEWARD CONDOS
CHILKAT CENTER FOR THE ARTS
FORT SEWARD B&B
ALASKA INDIAN ARTS
BEACH RD
0
200 yds
0
200 m
FAA RD
MUD BAY RD
TOWER RD
SMALL TRACT RD
To Chilkat State Park
To Portage Cove Park and Battery Point Trail
© AVALON TRAVEL

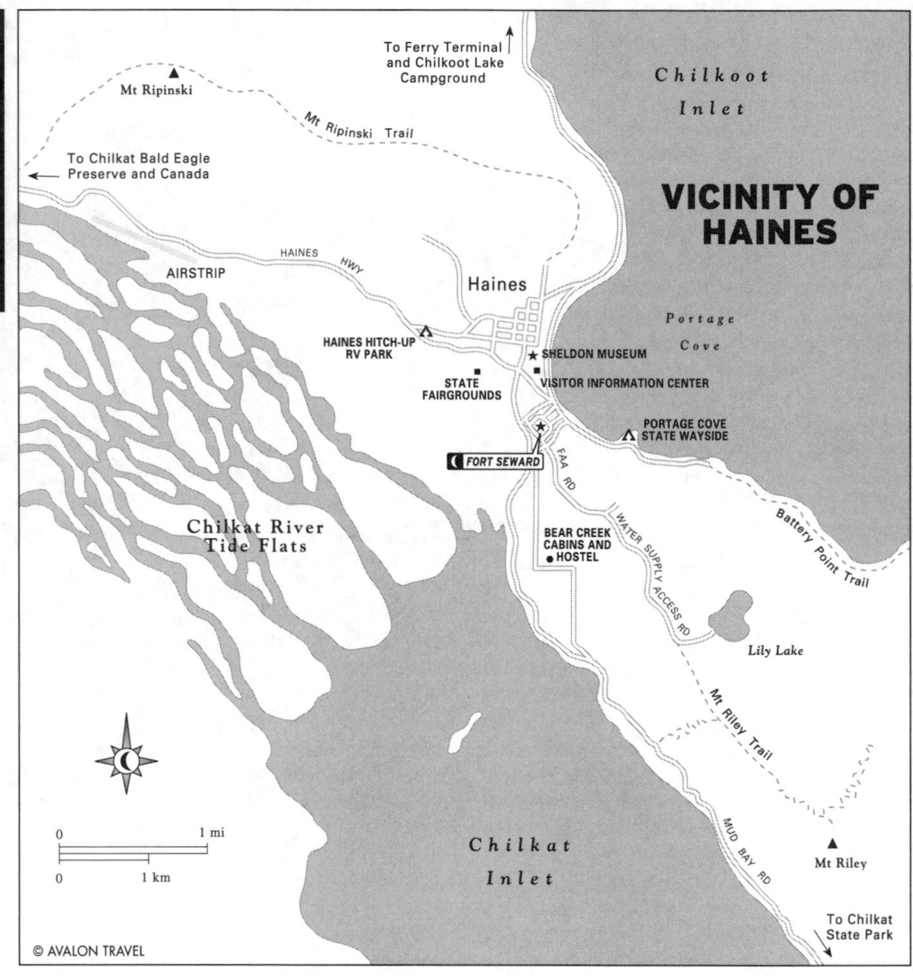

Presbyterian minister Samuel Hall Young reached the end of Lynn Canal. The Reverend Dr. Young was looking for potential mission sites to convert the Native Alaskans to Christianity. Muir was along for the canoe ride, wanting a chance to explore this remote territory. While there, they met with members of the Chilkat tribe at a settlement called Yendestakyeh. Both men gave speeches before the people, but the Chilkats were considerably more interested in Muir's "brotherhood of man" message than Dr. Young's proselytizing. Muir wrote:

> *Later, when the sending of a missionary and teacher was being considered, the chief said they wanted me, and, as an inducement, promised that if I would come to them they would always do as I directed, follow my councils, give me as many wives as I liked, build a church and school, and*

pick all the stones out of the paths and make them smooth for my feet.

Two years later the mission was established by two Presbyterian missionaries (Muir had other plans), and the village was renamed Haines, in honor of Mrs. F. E. H. Haines of the Presbyterian Home Missions Board. She never visited her namesake.

During the Klondike gold rush, an adventurer and shrewd businessman named Jack Dalton developed a 305-mile toll road that began across the river from Haines and followed an old Indian trade route into Yukon. He charged miners $150 each to use his Dalton Trail; armed men never failed to collect. To maintain order among the thousands of miners, the U.S. Army established Fort William H. Seward at Haines. Named for Alaska's "patron saint," it was built between 1900 and 1904 on 100 acres of land deeded to the government by the Haines mission. Renamed Chilkoot Barracks in 1923 in commemoration of Chilkoot Pass, it was the only military base in all of Alaska until 1940.

In 1942–1943 the Army built the 150-mile Haines Highway from Haines to Haines Junction as an emergency evacuation route from Alaska in case of invasion by the Japanese. After World War II, the post was declared excess government property and sold to a veterans' group that hoped to form a business cooperative. The venture failed, but many stayed on, making homes in the stately old officers' quarters. The site became a National Historic Landmark in 1978, and its name was changed back to Fort Seward.

Today the town of Haines has a diversified economy that includes fishing (there are no canneries, however), tourism, and government jobs. Haines has also recently become something of a center for the arts, attracting artists and crafts workers of all types, from creators of stained glass to weavers of Chilkat blankets.

SIGHTS

The **Haines Visitors Information Center** (907/766-2234 or 800/458-3579 message only, www.haines.ak.us, Mon.–Fri. 8 A.M.–6 P.M., Sat.–Sun. 9 A.M.–4 P.M. mid-May–Sept., Mon.–Fri. 8 A.M.–5 P.M. Oct.–mid-May) is on 2nd Avenue near Willard Street. Packs can generally be left here while you walk around town. Stop in for a listing of local charter fishing boats if you want to catch salmon or halibut.

Museums

Located on Main Street in the center of town, the **Sheldon Museum** (907/766-2366, www.sheldonmuseum.org, Mon.–Fri. 10 A.M.–5 P.M., Sat.–Sun. 1–4 P.M. mid-May–mid-Sept. and when cruise ships are in port, Mon.–Fri. 1–4 P.M. winter, $3 adults, under age 13 free) houses a fine collection of items from the gold rush, such as Jack Dalton's sawed-off shotgun and Tlingit artifacts—including Chilkat blankets, a gorgeous carved ceremonial hat from the Murrelet clan, and a model of a tribal house. Upstairs, you can watch the excellent Audubon Society video about the Chilkat Bald Eagle Preserve, or see a slide show about local history.

The strangest sight in Haines has to be the **Hammer Museum** (108 Main St., 907/766-2374, www.hammermuseum.org, Mon.–Fri. 10 A.M.–5 P.M. mid-May–early Nov., $3, under age 13 free). Collector and hammer expert Dave Pahl displays some 1,500 types of hammers, from cobbler's hammers to those used by 19th-century bankers. The oldest—OK, it's basically a shaped rock—was used in the building of Egypt's pyramids. Be sure to read the funny story of how Pahl's dog was saved by a hammer-shaped piece of wood.

The **American Bald Eagle Foundation** (907/766-3094, www.baldeagles.org, $3 adults, $1 ages 8–12, younger children free) sits at the intersection of Haines Highway and 2nd Avenue. Inside you'll find a collection of stuffed animals and a video about eagles. Outside is a mews containing live bald eagles that could not survive in the wild. Don't miss talks by founder Dave Olerud, who provides an introduction to eagles and their role in the web of life. The facility is open Monday–Friday 9 A.M.–6 P.M., Saturday–Sunday 1–5 P.M. May–August, with

© DON PITCHER

Hammer Museum in Haines

shortened hours the rest of September and during the Eagle Festival in early November, and closed the rest of the year.

Fort Seward

Circled around a grassy parade ground, the graceful buildings of historic Fort Seward are backdropped by snow-capped mountains. Along the top of the hill is **"Officers' Row,"** the white century-old homes that once housed captains, lieutenants, and their families. Today, the buildings are used as private residences, bed-and-breakfasts, and the Hotel Halsingland.

A reconstructed **Tlingit tribal house**—decorated inside and out with colorful carvings—sits within the parade grounds, and the nonprofit **Alaska Indian Arts** (907/766-2160, www.alaskaindianarts.com) operates from the old hospital building on the southeast side of Fort Seward. Inside you'll find master woodcarvers, silversmiths, blanket weavers, and other crafts workers, plus a gallery. It's officially open weekdays year-round, but may not be staffed when a cruise ship isn't in port. The **Haines Visitors Bureau** (2nd Ave. near Willard St., 907/766-2234, www.haines.ak.us) has a free detailed historical guide and walking tour of Fort Seward.

Other Sights

Lookout Park, next to the harbor, is a great place to watch the fishing boats, eagles, and scenery. Bring a lunch. Behind it is a small cemetery with Tlingit graves dating from the 1880s. An old building, all that remains of **Yendestakyeh,** is just beyond the airport, 3.5 miles from town. The mission bell (1880) that once called the Tlingit people to worship now sits out in front of the Presbyterian church on 2nd Avenue.

Walt Disney's *White Fang* was filmed next to Haines in 1990, and the **Dalton City** gold rush town created for the movie is at the Southeast Alaska State Fairgrounds. Wander around the buildings or poke your head inside Alaska's smallest brewery, **Haines Brewing Company** (907/766-3823, www.hainesbrewing.com), for a sample of Paul Wheeler's Lookout Stout, Eldred Rock Red, IPA, and seasonal beers. Haines bars have them on tap. Locals especially rave about the stout—at least until they taste the Bigger Hammer Barley Wine.

CHILKAT BALD EAGLE PRESERVE

Each fall, the Chilkat River north of Haines becomes home to the largest eagle gathering on earth. Throughout the summer, water flows into a massive underground reservoir created by gravel deposits at the confluence of the Tsirku, Klehini, and Chilkat Rivers north of Haines. When fall arrives this water percolates upward, keeping river temperatures above freezing. These warm waters attract an unusual late run of spawning chum and silver salmon. The dying salmon attract bears, wolves, gulls, magpies, ravens, and up to 3,500 bald eagles along a four-mile stretch of river just below the Tlingit village of **Klukwan** (pop. 140). Covering 48,000 acres, the Chilkat Bald Eagle

© DON PITCHER

Fort Seward and the Chilkat Range

Preserve (907/766-2292, www.dnr.state.ak.us) protects this unique gathering of eagles.

During the peak of the salmon run (Nov.–Jan.), black cottonwoods along the river are filled with hundreds of birds, and many more line the braided riverbanks. The area is very popular with photographers, but be sure to stay off the flats to avoid disturbing these majestic birds. During the summer, local eagle populations are much lower, but with 80 active nests and up to 400 resident eagles on the river, you're guaranteed to see some eagles.

A state campground ($10) is at **Mosquito Lake,** five miles north of Klukwan and three miles off the highway. Tours by van or boat go through the bald eagle preserve, and the Alaska Bald Eagle Festival in mid-November brings more tours and educational workshops.

ENTERTAINMENT AND EVENTS

If you hit the bar at **Fort Seward Lodge** (907/766-2009), be sure to ask for a Roadkill, the flaming house drink that's guaranteed to set your innards on fire. Fishers school up at two Front Street bars: **Harbor Bar** (907/766-2444), with occasional live bands, and **Fogcutter Bar** (907/766-2555).

Events

The **Great Alaska Craftbeer & Homebrew Festival** (www.seakfair.org/beerfestival.php) in mid-May is a fine opportunity to taste regional microbrews.

Around the summer solstice in June, the **Kluane to Chilkat International Bike Relay** (www.kcibr.org) attracts more than 1,100 cyclists for an exciting 160-mile relay race that ends in Haines. Other solstice events include live music and dancing at the fairgrounds.

July 4th brings a parade, a barbecue, a pie-eating contest, soapbox derby races, a race up Mt. Ripinski, and other fun events.

Every year during the last week of July thousands of visitors from all over Alaska and Yukon flock to Haines for the five-day-long **Southeast Alaska State Fair** (www.seakfair.org). Events include a logging show, a farmers market, a parade, pig races, a dog show, exhibits, and evening concerts by nationally known artists. Don't miss this one!

The **Alaska Bald Eagle Festival** (www.baldeaglefest.org) in early November—peak time for eagle-viewing on the Chilkat Preserve—features scientific talks, workshops, and evening entertainment. The highlight comes with the dramatic release of formerly injured eagles back into the wild.

SHOPPING

The best local gallery is **Wild Iris Shop** (Portage St., 907/766-2300), run by Fred Shields, with jewelry, trade beads, carved ivory, and photos. Find it a block up from the Port Chilkoot Dock and just down from the fort. His front garden overflows with flowers all summer.

Extreme Dreams (907/766-2097, www.extremedreams.com) has the unusual watercolors, block prints, and textiles of John and Sharon Svenson in a gorgeous setting seven miles out on Mud Bay Road. Another interesting Mud Bay Road gallery is nearby, **Catotti & Goldberg Studio** (907/766-2707, www.artstudioalaska.com), where you can see the paintings of Donna Catotti and Rob Goldberg. Although he isn't Native Alaskan, Tresham Gregg makes distinctive wood carvings and prints using Tlingit-inspired designs. Find them in his **Sea Wolf Gallery** (907/766-2540, www.tresham.com) near the center of Fort Seward.

For quality outdoor gear, head to **Alaska Backcountry Outfitters** (111 2nd Ave., 907/766-2876, www.alaskanaturetours.net). Get Alaskan and other books—plus toys and maps—from **The Babbling Book** (907/766-3356), at 223 Main Street next to Howser's.

Haines is home to one of several birch syrup producers in Alaska—**Birch Boy Products** (907/767-5660 or 877/769-5660, www.birchboy.com). The syrup is sold locally in gift shops. Don't expect the smoothness of maple syrup; birch syrup has a bit of a bite to it, but is quite good on ice cream and when blended with sugar syrup.

RECREATION

The Haines area has a number of excellent hikes, ranging from the easy (Battery Point) to the strenuous (Mt. Ripinski). For more details, pick up the *Haines Is for Hikers* pamphlet from the visitors center (2nd Ave. near Willard St., 907/766-2234, www.haines.ak.us).

One of Alaska's premier adventure programs, **Alaska Mountain Guides and Climbing School** (907/766-3366 or 800/766-3396, www.alaskamountainguides.com), is headquartered in Haines and has a wide range of trips that include sea kayaking along with rock and ice climbing. Sea kayak rentals are available.

Haines is increasingly becoming a destination for heli-skiers, with phenomenal snow and relatively mild weather. Local heli-ski companies are **Southeast Alaska Backcountry Adventures** (907/766-2009 or 877/617-3418, www.skiseaba.com) and **Alaska Heliskiing** (907/767-5745 or 877/754-4242, www.alaska-heliskiing.com).

Mt. Riley

Three trails lead to the top of 1,760-foot Mt. Riley, from which you get a panoramic view of Lynn Canal, Davidson and Rainbow Glaciers, the Chilkat River, Taiya Inlet, and 360 degrees of snowcapped peaks. The shortest and steepest route (2 miles) starts three miles southeast of Haines on Mud Bay Road. A small parking area is opposite the trailhead. You can also follow FAA Road from behind Fort Seward to another trail. This one is four miles long and follows the city water supply route for two miles before splitting off to join the more direct trail.

Battery Point

An easy and relatively level four-mile path starts from the end of the road at Portage Cove and follows the shore to a campsite at Kelgaya Point and across pebbly beaches to Battery Point.

Mt. Ripinski

The full-day hike up and down Mt. Ripinski (3,610 feet) offers unparalleled views of mountains and inland waterways, but it's strenuous and long (10 miles round-trip). You may want to camp in the alpine country and make this a two-day hike. From Haines, take Young Road north until it intersects with a jeep road that follows a buried pipeline around the mountain. The trail begins about a mile along this dirt road and climbs through a spruce and hemlock forest to muskeg and finally the alpine area at 2,500 feet. You can continue along the ridge to the north summit (3,160 feet) or on to the main peak. Return the same way, or via a steep path that takes you down to a saddle and then to the Haines Highway, seven miles northwest of Haines. Mt. Ripinski is covered with snow until midsummer, so be prepared. Don't go in bad weather, and do stay on the trail in the alpine areas.

Seduction Point

For a gentle, long, and very scenic beach walk, head to Chilkat State Park campground, seven miles southeast of Haines on Mud Bay Road. Seduction Point is on the end of the peninsula separating Chilkoot and Chilkat Inlets, a five-mile hike from the campground. The trail alternates between the forest and the beach, and it's a good idea to check the tides to make sure that you're able to hike the last beach stretch at low tide. This hike also makes a fine overnight camping trip.

ACCOMMODATIONS

The Haines Convention and Visitors Bureau website (www.haines.ak.us) has detailed info and links to local lodging places. Although most Haines-area hotels and B&Bs have Wi-Fi, there's a charge to use it. Exceptions are mentioned below.

Hostel

The youth hostel in Haines, **Bear Creek Cabins and Hostel** (907/766-2259, www.bearcreekcabinsalaska.com, mid-May–mid-Oct.), is 1.5 miles south of town on Small Tract Road. Dorm spaces are $20, and the six private cabins are $68 d. Bear Creek has kitchen facilities and Wi-Fi. The hostel is a clean and friendly place to stay, but reservations are advised in the summer.

Hotels and Motels

A beautiful old Victorian hotel that originally served as the commanding officer's quarters at Fort Seward, **Hotel Halsingland** (907/766-2000 or 800/542-6363, www.hotelhalsingland.com, late Apr.–mid-Nov.) is a step back in time to a quieter, more gracious era. In addition to the standard guest rooms ($119 d) with private baths, the hotel includes a couple of small but inexpensive shared-bath guest rooms ($69 d). Owner Jeff Butcher updated the hotel with Wi-Fi and other amenities while retaining its original charm. The restaurant is one of the finest in town, and there's a free shuttle to the airport or ferry.

Fort Seward Lodge (907/766-2009 or 800/617-3418, Feb.–Nov.) is located in another of the Fort Seward structures: This one once housed the fort's post exchange store, bowling alley, and gym. Guest rooms are simple but clean and have Wi-Fi; none have phones. Those with private baths are $95 s or $110 d. Tiny guest rooms with a bath down the hall and no television cost $50 s or $75 d. Also available are a couple of units with full kitchenettes for $125 d. A variety of outdoor packages—including fly-fishing and heli-skiing—are available.

Head a mile out of town on Beach Road to **Beach Roadhouse** (907/766-3060 or 866/736-3060, www.beachroadhouse.com, Feb.–Nov.), with a mix of kitchenette units ($105–115 d) containing one or two queen beds, along with small cabins ($145 d or $165 for 4 people) with full kitchens and Lynn Canal vistas. A guest computer and Wi-Fi are available.

Adjacent to Fort Seward, **Mountain View Inn** (Mud Bay Rd., 907/766-2900 or 800/478-2902, www.mtviewinn.net, $109 d) has seven kitchenette units and Wi-Fi. The Alaska Mountain Guides and Climbing School is based here.

Thunderbird Motel (216 Dalton St., 907/766-2131 or 800/327-2556, www.thunderbird-motel.com) has standard rooms with fridges and microwaves ($100 s, $110 d) and full kitchenettes ($140 for up to 4 people).

On Haines Highway as you head out of town, **Eagle's Nest Motel** (907/766-2891 or 800/354-6009, www.alaskaeagletours.com, $92 s, $103 d) has comfortable guest rooms and reasonable prices, along with Wi-Fi and breakfast snacks. Pets are $10 extra.

Housed within a historic officer's row building, **Fort Seward Condos** (907/766-2708, www.fortsewardcondos.com, $150–165 d) are one- and two-bedroom units with full kitchens; there is a two-night minimum stay.

The nicest local motel, **Captain's Choice Motel** (108 2nd St., 907/766-3111 or 800/478-2345, www.capchoice.com) has standard guest rooms for $119 s or $129 d, along with suites (these sleep six comfortably) for $172. All rooms contain small fridges and microwaves; continental breakfast and a courtesy van are available.

Eleven miles from town near **Chilkoot River Lodge** (907/766-2654, www.chilkootriverlodge.com) is a large, newly built structure atop a bluff near Chilkoot Lake. The three guest rooms ($150 d) have private baths, and during the summer guests can sit on the covered porch to watch brown bears fishing for salmon in the river.

Bed-and-Breakfasts

Fort Seward B&B (907/766-2856 or 800/615-6676, www.fortsewardalaska.com, open mid-Apr.–mid-Oct., $115–145 d) is a beautifully maintained historic home built for the fort's chief surgeon. Four of the seven guest rooms have private baths, and two can be combined into a family suite for $275. Guests are served a filling breakfast with sourdough pancakes; there is also free Wi-Fi.

Built in 1912 by a member of Soapy Smith's gang, **Summer Inn B&B** (2nd Ave. and Main St., 907/766-2970, www.summerinnbnb.com, $80 s, $100 d) is a cozy home near the center of town. Five guest rooms share three baths, and a big breakfast is served each morning.

Other options include **Haines Bear Lodge B&B** (907/957-1035 or 812/371-5507, www.hainesbearlodge.com, $150 d), **Chilkat Eagle B&B** (907/766-2763, www.eagle-bb.com, $80 d), and **Tanani Bay B&B** (907/766-3750, www.tananibaybnb.com, $125 d).

CAMPING

The best campsite near Haines is at **Portage Cove State Wayside** ($5), just 0.75 miles from town. Water and outhouses are available, but there is no overnight parking; the site is for hikers and cyclists only. The location is quiet and attractive, and eagles hang around.

If you have a vehicle, stay at one of the two other excellent state-run campgrounds, both with drinking water, toilets, and picnic shelters. **Chilkat State Park** ($10), seven miles southeast of Haines, has a fine hiking trail to Seduction Point; and **Chilkoot Lake State Recreation Site** ($10), five miles northwest of the ferry, has good fishing and a lovely view over this turquoise-blue lake. More camping is at **Mosquito Lake State Park** ($10), 27 miles north of Haines.

RV Parks

Located behind Hotel Halsingland, **Port Chilkoot Camper Park** (907/766-2000 or 800/542-6363, www.hotelhalsingland.com, May–Sept., tents $10, RVs $25) has attractively wooded campsites, showers, and a coin laundry.

Salmon Run Adventures RV Campground (907/766-3240, www.salmonrunadventures.com, RVs or tents $18, no hookups, June–mid-Oct.), seven miles out Lutak Road, also offers showers for $3. Another option is **Haines Hitch-Up RV Park** (851 Main St., 907/766-2882, www.hitchuprv.com, RVs $39, no tents). RVers also park at the gravel lot on Main Street named **Oceanside RV Park** (907/766-2437, www.oceansiderv.com, RVs $32).

FOOD

For a town of this size, Haines has surprisingly good food, and the prices won't ruin your credit rating. Get filling meals, friendly service, and an unpretentious setting at the **Bamboo Room** (2nd Ave., 907/766-2800,

© DON PITCHER
food cache near Haines

www.bamboopioneer.net). Breakfasts are a standout, but the Bamboo also fills up at lunch and dinner when the menu features burgers, fried chicken, halibut fish-and-chips, and other greasy fare. Check the board for today's specials.

Fort Seward Lodge Restaurant and Bar (907/766-2009 or 800/617-3418, Wed.–Sun. 8 A.M.–noon and 5–9 P.M. Feb.–Nov., entrées $15–30) serves breakfasts and dinners. The main attractions are prime rib Sundays and all-you-can-eat Dungeness crab feasts ($30) nightly in the summer.

Chilkat Restaurant and Bakery (5th Ave. and Dalton St., 907/766-3653, Mon.–Thurs. 7 A.M.–3:30 P.M., Fri.–Sat. 7 A.M.–8 P.M. mid-Mar.–mid-Nov.) bakes pastries, bagels, pies, and doughnuts daily, and serves tasty breakfasts and lunches (including homemade soups, burgers, and sandwiches) in a relaxing setting. The owners are from Thailand, and they've added spicy Thai lunch specials Thursday–Saturday.

When I'm in Haines on a chilly winter morning I beeline to the perpetually busy **Mountain Market & Deli** (3rd St. and Haines Hwy., 907/766-3340, Sun. 8 A.M.–5:30 P.M., Mon.–Sat. 7 A.M.–5:30 P.M., $6–12) for a steaming mocha and a breakfast burrito. Fresh baked goods fill the displays, and the lunch menu encompasses turkey club wraps, paninis, deli sandwiches, and salads. A natural foods market here sells organic produce. The building also houses **Mountain Spirits** (907/766-3350), with a fine wine selection and a notable choice of scotches; the owner managed a distillery in Scotland for years. There are great cheeses too.

Get groceries from **Howser's IGA Supermarket** (Main St., 907/766-2040). Ask around the boat harbor to see who's selling fresh fish, crab, or prawns if you want to cook your own. A summertime **Farmers Market** takes place at the fairgrounds every other Saturday 10 A.M.–1 P.M.

Fort Seward Eateries

Housed in one of Fort Seward's historic buildings, ☾ **Fireweed Restaurant** (Blacksmith Rd., 907/766-3838, lunch Wed.–Sat. 11:30 A.M.–3 P.M., dinner Tues.–Sat. 4:30–9 P.M. Apr.–Sept., closed Sun.–Mon., $11–25) serves delicious meals in a convivial setting. It's packed most summer evenings with a hip young crowd. There's a wraparound deck with a couple of tables outside, plus an earthy interior where the scents of freshly baked bread and the daily specials fill the air. The bar serves as the de facto brewpub for Haines Brewery, and the menu encompasses salads, sandwiches, pizzas with homemade sauce (by the pie or slice), seafood, soups, and daily specials. Fireweed is highly recommended, but don't come here in a hurry. This is slow food that's worth the wait. Return on Saturday nights for open-mike music sessions.

The restaurant at **Hotel Halsingland** (907/766-2000 or 800/542-6363, www.hotelhalsingland.com, 5:30–9 P.M. mid-May–mid-Sept., entrées $22–28) is a pleasant place for an evening out, with a fine-dining menu that stars halibut Provençal, Caesar salads, braised lamb shank, and angus steaks. Herbs come from the back garden.

Dejon Delights Smokery (Portage Rd., 907/766-2505 or 800/539-3608, www.dejondelights.com) at Fort Seward has freshly smoked salmon for sale or will smoke fish that you catch.

Hidden away on Soap Suds Alley near Fort Seward, **Mosey's Cantina** (907/766-2320, www.moseyscantina.com, Mon.–Sat. 11:30 A.M.–2:30 P.M. and 5–9 P.M. Mar.–mid-Oct., dinner $12–18) is a colorful and fun Mexican eatery. The owners head to New Mexico each winter for 1,000 pounds of fire-roasted chilies, core ingredients in the chile verde, shrimp enchiladas, Baja seafood tacos, and smothered burritos. Tortilla chips are fresh from the fryer, and the salsas are made fresh daily.

SERVICES

Check your email at the modern **Haines Public Library** (111 3rd Ave., 907/766-2545, www.haineslibrary.org, Mon.–Tues. 10 A.M.–9 P.M., Wed.–Thurs. noon–9 P.M., Fri. 10 A.M.–6:30 P.M., Sat.–Sun. 12:30–4:30 P.M.). The post office is on Haines Highway near Fort Seward. Get cash from ATMs inside Howser's Supermarket and the First National Bank of Alaska.

Showers are available at **Port Chilkoot Camper Park,** behind Hotel Halsingland, and **Haines Quick Laundry,** across from Fort Seward Lodge. Another option is the fine **swimming pool** (907/766-2666), next to the high school, where the entrance fee gets you a shower and swim.

The unique **Valley of the Eagles Golf Links** (907/766-2401, www.hainesgolf.com) is a mile north of town on tidelands occasionally covered by larger tides. The setting is dramatic, and you might even see the occasional moose or bear.

GETTING THERE

Ferry

The Haines **ferry terminal** (907/766-2111) is 3.5 miles north of town on Lutak Highway. Ferries arrive in Haines almost every day during the summer, heading both north to Skagway and south to Juneau. They generally stop for 1.5 hours. For information call **Alaska Marine Highway** (907/465-3941 or 800/642-0066, www.dot.state.ak.us/amhs).

Alaska Fjordlines (907/766-3395 or 800/320-0146, www.alaskafjordlines.com) operates a high-speed catamaran with daily summertime runs from Skagway to Haines and then on to Juneau. The boat leaves Haines at 8:45 A.M., arrives in Juneau at 11 A.M., and then heads back at 5:30 P.M., reaching Haines at 7:30 P.M. The cost is $155 adults, $125 children round-trip, including a bus to downtown Juneau. A light breakfast and dinner are included, and the boat stops for wildlife and photo opportunities. One-way trips ($100 adults, $80 children) and overnight stays in Juneau are allowed; reservations are recommended.

Haines-Skagway Fast Ferry (907/766-2100 or 888/766-2103, www.hainesskagwayfastferry.com, early May–late Sept., round-trip $68 adults, $34 children) has high-speed catamaran service between Skagway and Haines, with several departures each day.

Air

The airport is 3.5 miles west of town on the Haines Highway. The flight between Juneau and Haines is pretty spectacular; on clear days you'll be treated to views of glaciers along both sides of Lynn Canal. **Wings of Alaska** (907/789-0790, www.wingsofalaska.com) has scheduled daily service to Juneau and Skagway. There are no scheduled flights for **Air Excursions** (907/697-2375 or 800/354-2479, www.airexcursions.com), but they typically fly between Haines and Juneau several times a day.

Mountain Flying Service (907/766-3007 or 800/766-4007, www.flyglacierbay.com), a few doors up from the visitors center, offers charters and flightseeing trips over Glacier Bay starting at $160 per person for one hour. A longer trip ($299) includes two hours in the air and a beach landing within the park, providing the chance to see bears and other wildlife.

Drake Olson of **Fly Drake** (907/723-9475, www.flydrake.com) isn't your standard bush pilot: A competitive auto racer and winner of the 1985 Porsche Cup, he is also an accomplished backcountry skier and mountaineer. He can land on beaches, glaciers, or remote air strips to get you into the wild places. Trips start at $160 per person for a one-hour flight to Glacier Bay.

GETTING AROUND

Tours

The visitors center (2nd Ave. near Willard St., 907/766-2234, www.haines.ak.us) has a complete listing of local guide companies and charter boat operators. **Alaska Nature Tours** (210 Main St., 907/766-2876, www.alaskanaturetours.net) leads educational three-hour bus-and-hiking trips to the eagle-viewing area along the Chilkat River and Chilkoot Lake for $69 adults, $54 children; a four-hour tour with lunch is $69 adults, $64 children, and a four-hour rain forest hike with lunch is $69 adults, $64 children. During August–September they also offer evening bear-viewing trips, and winter ski trips are available. Their outdoor shop, Backcountry Outfitter, rents skis, snowboards, and snowshoes.

Keet Gooshi Tours (907/766-2168 or 877/776-2168, www.keetgooshi.com, $75) is a Native Alaskan–owned company with 2.5-hour van tours that take in the Bald Eagle Preserve and the village of Klukwan, including an introduction to traditional culture.

River Trips

Chilkat Guides (907/766-2491 or 888/292-7789, www.raftalaska.com, $94 adults, $66 children) guides an excellent four-hour float trip down the Chilkat River. This is a leisurely raft trip (no white water) with good views of the Chilkat Mountains, glaciers, and roosting eagles. They also guide multiple-night adventures around Alaska. **River Adventures** (907/766-2050 or 800/478-9827, www.jetboatalaska.com) runs half-day jet-boat tours up the Chilkat, and **Chilkoot Lake Tours** (907/766-3779, www.alaskaeagletours.com) has two-hour pontoon boat tours of this turquoise lake for $85.

Glacier Valley Wilderness Adventures (907/767-5522, www.glaciervalleyadventures.net) offers a variety of trips that include a flight into a gold mining camp at the base of DeBlondeau Glacier followed by a rafting or jet-boat trip down the Tsirku River, then past the Chilkat Bald Eagle Preserve to Haines. Overnight accommodations are also available in a cabin or tent at the base camp.

Car and Bike Rentals

Rent cars from **Captain's Choice Motel** (907/766-3111 or 800/478-2345, www.capchoice.com), **Eagle's Nest Car Rental** (907/766-2891 or 800/354-6009, www.alaskaeagletours.com), or **Hotel Halsingland** (Avis, 907/766-2000 or 800/542-6363, www.hotelhalsingland.com). Eagle's Nest has the cheapest rates, starting at $50 per day with 100 free miles. Cars from Halsingland/Avis start at $85 with unlimited miles, and you can drive one-way and leave the car elsewhere (including Anchorage or Fairbanks) for an extra fee.

Rent good mountain bikes from **Sockeye Cycle** (907/766-2869, www.cyclealaska.com), a fine little bike shop just down from Fort Seward. A variety of bike tours are also offered.

Heading North

The paved highway north from Haines is the most direct route to Fairbanks (665 miles) and Anchorage (775 miles). For cyclists it's much easier than the Klondike Highway out of Skagway. If you're thinking of driving to Skagway from Haines, think again. It's only 15 water or air miles away, but 359 road miles. Take the ferry! There is **no bus service** out of Haines.

Crossing the Border

The Canadian border is 42 miles north of Haines. Both Canadian and U.S. Customs are open 7 A.M.–11 P.M. Alaska time (8 A.M.–midnight Pacific time). No handguns are allowed across the Canadian border.

Skagway

Occupying a narrow plain along the mouth of the Skagway River at the head of Lynn Canal, Skagway (year-round pop. 800; twice that in the summer) is a triangle-shaped town that seems to drive a wedge into the sheer slopes that lead to White Pass. The name of this northern terminus of the Inside Passage is derived from an Indian word meaning "home of the north wind." During the Klondike gold rush, the town was the gateway to both the Chilkoot and White Pass Trails, a funnel through which thousands of frenzied fortune-seekers passed. Today, the boardwalks, frontier storefronts, restored interiors, gift shops, historic films and slide shows, and old-time cars and costumes, all in the six-block town center, give it the flavor for which it has been famous for nearly a century. Skagway survives on the thousands of visitors and adventurers who come each summer to continue on the trail that led to gold. This is the most popular cruise port in Alaska, and the Skagwegians are inundated with over 7,000 cruise ship visitors on a typical midsummer day; up to five ships can dock at once. Today, over 800,000 travelers spend time in Skagway each year, the vast majority stepping off these megaships.

Independent travelers often leave Skagway with mixed feelings, and some regard it as a schmaltzy shadow of its former self. To some extent this is true, but the town also has genuine charm, and when the cruise ships sail away each night, the locals come out to play. Skagway is compact enough to walk around easily and is filled with all sorts of characters. Besides, if the downtown scene isn't to your taste, it's easy to escape into the surrounding mountains or to head up the Chilkoot Trail, where only the hardy stray. One way to avoid most of the crowds is to get here before mid-May or after mid-September. Come in the winter and you'll have it almost to yourself.

Skagway's weather is considerably drier than other parts of Southeast Alaska. It gets only 27 inches of precipitation per year, and alders, willows, and cottonwoods carpet the adjacent hillsides. It is especially colorful in mid-September when the leaves are turning. The driest time is before July; after that, rain is more likely.

HISTORY

Klondike Gold

An enormous amount of Alaskan history was compressed into the final decade of the 19th century at Skagway. In August 1896, on the day that George Carmack struck it rich on Bonanza Creek, Skagway consisted of a single cabin, constructed eight years previously by Captain William Moore but only occupied sporadically by the transient pioneer. News of the Klondike strike hit Seattle in July 1897; within a month 4,000 people huddled in a haphazard tent city surrounding Moore's lone cabin, and "craft of every description, from ocean-going steamers to little more than floating coffins, were dumping into the makeshift village a crazily mixed mass of humanity." Almost immediately, Frank Reid surveyed and plotted the town site, and the stampeders grabbed 1,000 lots, many within Moore's homestead. There was no law to back up either claims or counterclaims, and reports from the time describe Skagway as "the most outrageously lawless quarter" on the globe.

Into this breach stepped Jefferson Randall "Soapy" Smith, Alaska's great bad man. A notorious con artist from Colorado, Soapy Smith oversaw a mind-bogglingly extensive system of fraud, theft, armed robbery, prostitution, gambling, and even murder. He had his own spy network, secret police, and army to enforce the strong-arm tactics. Finally, a vigilance committee held a meeting to oppose Soapy. Frank Reid, the surveyor, stood guard. Soapy approached. Guns blazed. Smith, shot in the chest, died instantly, at age 38. Of Soapy, the newspaper reported, "At 9:30 o'clock Friday night the checkered career of 'Soapy' Smith was brought to a sudden end by a 38 caliber

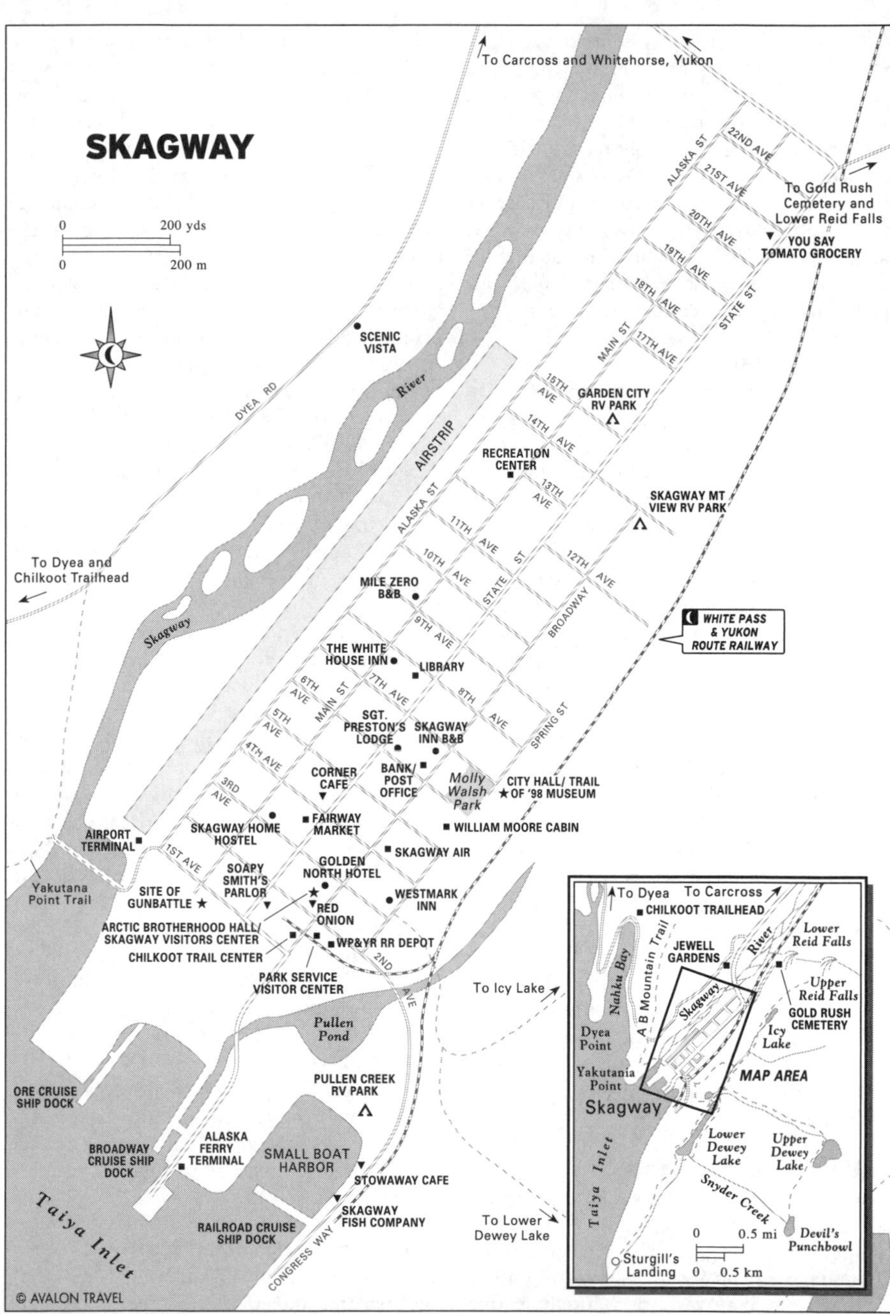
SKAGWAY
0
200 yds
0
200 m
To Carcross and Whitehorse, Yukon
To Gold Rush Cemetery and Lower Reid Falls
YOU SAY TOMATO GROCERY
22ND AVE
21ST AVE
20TH AVE
19TH AVE
18TH AVE
17TH AVE
ALASKA ST
STATE ST
MAIN ST
15TH AVE
GARDEN CITY RV PARK
14TH AVE
SCENIC VISTA
River
DYEA RD
AIRSTRIP
RECREATION CENTER
13TH AVE
SKAGWAY MT VIEW RV PARK
ALASKA ST
11TH AVE
10TH AVE
12TH AVE
STATE ST
BROADWAY
To Dyea and Chilkoot Trailhead
MILE ZERO B&B
WHITE PASS & YUKON ROUTE RAILWAY
Skagway
9TH AVE
THE WHITE HOUSE INN
LIBRARY
6TH AVE
7TH AVE
8TH AVE
MAIN ST
5TH AVE
SGT. PRESTON'S LODGE
SKAGWAY INN B&B
SPRING ST
4TH AVE
CORNER CAFE
BANK/ POST OFFICE
Molly Walsh Park
CITY HALL/ TRAIL OF '98 MUSEUM
3RD AVE
SKAGWAY HOME HOSTEL
FAIRWAY MARKET
WILLIAM MOORE CABIN
AIRPORT TERMINAL
1ST AVE
SKAGWAY AIR
Yakutana Point Trail
SOAPY SMITH'S PARLOR
GOLDEN NORTH HOTEL
SITE OF GUNBATTLE
WESTMARK INN
RED ONION
ARCTIC BROTHERHOOD HALL/ SKAGWAY VISITORS CENTER
WP&YR RR DEPOT
CHILKOOT TRAIL CENTER
2ND AVE
PARK SERVICE VISITOR CENTER
To Icy Lake
Pullen Pond
ORE CRUISE SHIP DOCK
PULLEN CREEK RV PARK
BROADWAY CRUISE SHIP DOCK
ALASKA FERRY TERMINAL
SMALL BOAT HARBOR
STOWAWAY CAFE
SKAGWAY FISH COMPANY
To Lower Dewey Lake
RAILROAD CRUISE SHIP DOCK
Taiya Inlet
CONGRESS WAY
To Dyea
To Carcross
CHILKOOT TRAILHEAD
Lower Reid Falls
JEWELL GARDENS
River
Nahku Bay
A B Mountain Trail
Skagway
Upper Reid Falls
GOLD RUSH CEMETERY
Dyea Point
Icy Lake
Yakutania Point
MAP AREA
Skagway
Lower Dewey Lake
Upper Dewey Lake
Taiya Inlet
Snyder Creek
0
0.5 mi
0
0.5 km
Devil's Punchbowl
Sturgill's Landing

bullet from a revolver in the unerring right hand of City surveyor Frank H. Reid . . ." Reid was shot in the groin and died in agony a week later. His gravestone reads, "He gave his life for the honor of Skagway." More recent evidence has been less kind to Frank Reid's reputation. It turns out that he had been a prime suspect in an Oregon murder, and as a surveyor for the railroad he was deeply involved in the theft of William Moore's homestead lands. Some locals say both men got what they deserved.

Over the Top

Skagway was the jumping-off point for **White Pass,** which crossed the Coastal Range to Lake Bennett and the Yukon headwaters. This trail, billed as the "horse route," was the choice of prosperous prospectors who could afford pack animals to carry the requisite "ton of goods." But it was false advertising at best, and death-defying at worst. The mountains were so precipitous, the trail so narrow and rough, and the weather so wild that the stampeders turned merciless; all 3,000 horses and mules that stepped onto the trail in 1897–1898 were doomed to a proverbial fate worse than death. Indeed, stampeders swore that horses leaped off the cliffs on purpose, committing suicide on the "Dead Horse Trail."

The famous **Chilkoot Trail,** which started in Dyea (die-EE), 15 miles from Skagway, was the "poor man's route." Stampeders had to backpack their year's worth of supplies 33 miles to Lake Lindeman, which included 40 trips up and down the 45-degree "Golden Stairs" to the 3,550-foot pass. This scene, recorded in black and white, is one of the most dramatic and enduring photographs of the Days of '98. At Lindeman, the stampeders built wooden boats for the sometimes treacherous journey to the gold fields at Dawson.

Building the Railroad

The late 19th century was a time when the railroad was king, and the sudden rush of prospectors to the gold fields attracted entrepreneurs intent on figuring a way to build a railroad from Skagway over White Pass. Into this breach stepped Michael J. Heney, an Irish Canadian contractor with a genius for vision, fund-raising, management, and commanding the loyalty of his workers. Heney punched through the 110-mile narrow-gauge White Pass & Yukon Route Railway to Lake Bennett by July of 1899, and then on to Whitehorse a year later. The route, so treacherous to pack animals, was no less malevolent to the railroad builders. They worked suspended from the steep slopes by ropes, often in 50-below temperatures and raging Arctic blizzards, for $3 per day. Completion of the railroad ensured the constant flow of passengers and freight to the gold fields—as well as Skagway's survival. For the next four decades, the railroad was virtually the only way into Yukon.

During World War II, the White Pass & Yukon Route hauled much of the construction equipment and personnel to build the Alaska Highway. In the 1970s the railroad shifted to hauling lead, zinc, and silver ore concentrate from a big mine in Yukon. The concentrate was shipped from Skagway for processing in Asia. When metal prices plummeted in 1982, the mine closed, and train traffic halted. (One legacy of this mine is the presence of lead and other toxins in the waters off Skagway.) But just as mining was ending, Alaska's current gold rush arrived in the form of cruise ships. The White Pass & Yukon Route reopened for excursion travel in 1988, and it is once again not only Skagway's favorite attraction but one of the only operating narrow-gauge railroads in North America. Today, over 300,000 passengers ride the train each summer.

SIGHTS

Downtown Skagway is made up of seven blocks on Broadway, along which are most of the sights. The ferry terminal is at the bottom of Broadway; a three-minute hike and you're in the heart of beautiful downtown Skagway.

Arctic Brotherhood Hall

You can't miss Arctic Brotherhood (AB) Hall between 2nd and 3rd Streets—the only example of turn-of-the-century Alaska driftwood-stick architecture, and probably the most-photographed building in Alaska. Thousands of pieces of wood—8,841 to be exact—decorate the exterior. The brotherhood was organized aboard the vessel *City of Seattle,* which waited out the winter of 1899 in Skagway Harbor. The order spread, and local chapters were established in most Alaskan towns, with dues paid solely in nuggets.

The AB Hall now houses the **Skagway Visitors Information Center** (907/983-2854 or 888/762-1898 message, www.skagway.com, daily 8 A.M.–6 P.M. May–Sept., Mon.–Fri. 8 A.M.–5 P.M. Oct.–Apr.). It has the standard brochures, plus helpful walking-tour and hiking maps. Stop in and take Buckwheat to lunch, but be sure to ask about his travels with Martha Stewart. Tell him I sent you.

Klondike Gold Rush National Historical Park

More than a dozen historic downtown buildings are owned and managed by the National Park Service as Klondike Gold Rush National Historical Park in commemoration of the 1898 stampede of miners to Canada's Yukon. Most of the restored structures are leased to private businesses. (The park is actually split into two pieces, with one visitors center in Skagway, and a second in Seattle, where nearly all the miners began their journey.)

The old White Pass & Yukon administration building houses the **Klondike Gold Rush National Historical Park Visitors Center** (907/983-2921, www.nps.gov/klgo, daily 8 A.M.–6 P.M. early May–late Sept., closed late Sept.–early May). Don't miss *Days of Adventure, Dreams of Gold,* a 30-minute film shown hourly. Ranger talks typically take place at 10 A.M. and 3 P.M., and 45-minute walking tours of old Skagway are offered five times a day—sign up early in the day to be sure of a space. Additional programs and daily tours to Dyea are also offered; see the event schedule for details. There's no charge for any of these talks. Personnel behind the desk have the latest weather and transportation information, and they can probably answer that burning question you've been carrying around all day.

Across Broadway and next to the tracks, the historic Martin Itjen House contains the **Chilkoot Trail Center,** where rangers can provide details on hiking in the footsteps of the miners. This 32-mile trail starts from the old Dyea town site, nine miles from Skagway, and climbs over Chilkoot Pass (3,535 feet) before dropping down to Bennett, British Columbia.

Just up 2nd Street is **Soapy Smith's Parlor** (www.soapysmith.net), the saloon from which the infamous blackguard supervised his various nefarious offenses. The building is now owned by the National Park Service but is not yet open to the public.

The original **Captain William Moore cabin** (5th Ave. and Spring St., daily 10 A.M.–5 P.M. summer, free), which was moved under pressure from the early stampeders to its present location, has been completely refurbished by the Park Service. Its interior walls are papered with newspapers from the 1880s.

Be sure to step inside another Park Service building, the old **Mascot Saloon** (3rd Ave. and Broadway, open daily summer, free) with exhibits depicting the saloon and life in the Days of '98.

White Pass & Yukon Route Railroad

Adjacent to the Park Visitors Center is the **White Pass & Yukon Route Depot** (2nd St., 907/983-2217 or 800/343-7373, www.whitepassrailroad.com), built in the 1990s to closely resemble the town's many historic structures. Narrow-gauge White Pass & Yukon Route trains depart from the depot several times a day early May–late September; there is no winter service.

White Pass Summit Excursion trains leave Skagway daily at 8:15 A.M., 12:45 P.M., and 4:30 P.M. May–late September and cost $103. These go to the summit of White Pass and back, a round-trip of 40 miles that takes three hours. The tracks follow along the east side of the Skagway River, with vistas that get better and better as the train climbs. Tour guides point out the sights and explain the railroad's history. Be sure to sit on the left side from Skagway and the right side on the return for the best views. The diesel smoke is lighter toward the rear of the train.

The White Pass & Yukon Route has two photogenic old **steam engines**—one built in 1920, the other from 1947—that huff and puff out of town most days, with video cameras rolling in all directions. For most runs the steam engine is replaced by a diesel engine on the edge of town to save it from wear and tear on the strenuous climb.

The railroad's special four-hour **Fraser Meadows Steam Excursions** ($133 adults, $67 children) is a real treat for train lovers. Pulled by a steam engine, these trains leave Friday and Sunday only at noon and stop in the mountains just beyond the White Pass Summit to let passengers out for a chance to take photos as the engine rolls by with steam billowing. The train returns back down the mountain to Skagway at 4 P.M.

Also available is a **Skagway-Whitehorse rail-and-bus connection** that costs $116 adults, $58 children each way. Trains depart Skagway daily at 8 A.M., with passengers transferring to buses at Fraser, British Columbia, before continuing on to Whitehorse, Yukon, arriving at noon. The buses leave Whitehorse daily at 12:30 P.M., connect with the train in Fraser, and reach Skagway at 5:15 P.M. You can take the train one-way from Skagway to Fraser with a bus back to Skagway for $125 adults, $63 children. Also available is a once-daily train between Skagway and Carcross for $228 adults, $148 children one-way. Trains stop for a hot lunch (included) at Lake Bennett. A passport is required for trips where you get off the train in Canada.

The **Chilkoot Trail Hikers Service** provides a shuttle late May–mid-September from Lake Bennett (the end of the trail) to Fraser ($50) or Skagway ($95). The schedule changes each year, so check to make sure a train will be there once you reach Lake Bennett.

Skagway Museum

This excellent collection is housed in the beautifully restored City Hall (700 Spring St., 907/983-2420, Sun. 10 A.M.–4 P.M., Mon.–Fri. 9 A.M.–5 P.M., Sat. 10 A.M.–5 P.M. summer, hours vary off-season, $2 adults, $1 students, under age 13 free), a block off Broadway. Check out the old gambling equipment, the "Moorish queen" from the Chicago World's Fair of 1893, the Native Alaskan artifacts that include a 19th-century Tlingit canoe and an amazing seal-gut parka, the colorful duck neck-feather quilt, and Soapy Smith's derringer. Several videos are available if you want to know more about the characters in Skagway's past.

Other Downtown Sights

Corrington's Museum of Alaskan History (5th Ave. and Broadway, 907/983-2637 or 800/943-2637) is a combination gift shop and free scrimshaw museum. The collection includes 40 or so exquisitely carved pieces that tell the history of Alaska on walrus ivory. It's well worth a visit. The building is flanked by a colorful flower garden.

Be sure to poke your head into **Skagway Hardware Company** (Broadway and 4th Ave., 907/983-2233, www.skagwayhardware.com), one of the few old-time hardware stores left in Alaska. The wooden floors creak, and items of all types (even washers and dryers) are crammed into the shelves. A block away is the distinctive gold-colored cupola of the **Golden North Hotel.** Built in 1898, the hotel closed in 2002.

Broadway has more than its share of soak-the-tourists gift shops staffed by folks whose only connection to Skagway is a paycheck. The most egregious examples are the Caribbean, Colombian, British, and Swiss jewelry shops that barely make an effort to sell anything remotely connected with Alaska. Despite this, do step inside the Little Switzerland Store (Broadway and 5th Ave.), where you'll discover both the world's largest and smallest gold nugget watch chains. Local people do run many of the other shops in town.

North of Town

The historic Gold Rush Cemetery sits right beside the railroad tracks two miles north of town. The largest monument is Frank Reid's, while Soapy Smith only rates a wooden plank. While you're here, be sure to follow the short trail above the cemetery to scenic **Lower Reid Falls.** City-run SMART buses will take you as far as 23rd Avenue for $2 each way; from there it's an almost-level stroll to the cemetery.

Continue out on the Klondike Highway and cross the bridge over the Skagway River. On the left is **Jewell Gardens** (907/983-2111, www.jewellgardens.com, daily 11 A.M.–3 P.M. early May–Sept., $12 adults, $6 children), with a very impressive collection of flowers and vegetables plus a garden railroad for model-train enthusiasts. Admission includes a self-guided tour of the garden and the chance to watch a glassblower at work. The café serves a fixed-menu lunch using organic ingredients from the garden.

Dyea

Located nine miles northwest of Skagway, the ghost town of Dyea is the starting point for the famed Chilkoot Trail. The old town site sits at the head of Taiya Inlet. During the Klondike gold rush of 1898, Dyea was where miners began the long trek into the Yukon Territory, and at its peak, the town provided a temporary home to some 10,000 people. Two factors caused Dyea to disappear: a devastating avalanche on Chilkoot Pass in April 1898, and the completion of the White Pass & Yukon Route Railroad in 1899. Just four years later, only six people lived in Dyea.

Little remains to be seen at Dyea except for the **Slide Cemetery,** where 45 men and women who died in the Palm Sunday avalanche of 1898 are buried. Walk through the forests that now cover old Dyea to find a few crumbling buildings and wharf pilings extending into the bay. It's hard to imagine that this was once Alaska's largest city. The town site is now part of Klondike Gold Rush National Historical Park, and not far from old Dyea is the trailhead for the Chilkoot Trail and the free **Dyea Campground.**

The Park Service leads free 1.5-hour **walking tours** (907/983-2921) of the old Dyea town site Wednesday–Sunday at 2 P.M. in the summer, but you'll need to find your own transportation from Skagway.

ENTERTAINMENT AND EVENTS

Entertainment

Skagway's best-known boozing establishment, the **Red Onion** (2nd Ave. and Broadway, 907/983-2222, www.redonion1898.com), delivers live tunes most summer afternoons courtesy of musicians off the cruise ships. The bar, mirrors, and stove are from the time it served as both a saloon and a brothel. But don't believe any tall tales about ghosts; they're all made up for the tourists. The Red Onion is now entirely nonsmoking. If you want to get down and dirty and start drinking with the locals at 10 A.M., head across the street and up the block to **Moe's Frontier Bar. Bonanza Bar & Grill** (3rd Ave. and Broadway, 907/983-6214) has pool tables, microbrews, and sports on the TVs—if you can tolerate the pall of smoke.

The most fun thing to do at night is to attend the **Days of '98 Show** (6th Ave. and Broadway, 907/983-2545, www.thedaysof98-show.com) at the Fraternal Order of Eagles building. The great-granddaddy of them all, this production is the oldest running theater in Alaska—for over 80 years! Matinees are offered most summer days at 10:30 A.M., 12:30 P.M., and 2:30 P.M., and full evening performances start at 7 P.M. Warm-up gambling with "Soapy money" comes first, then the show goes on at 8 P.M. Tickets are $18 adults, $9 for children under 16. Splurge on this one—it's worth the cash.

"Buckwheat" Donahue, a memorable local character (and head of the Skagway Convention and Visitors Bureau), occasionally recites "The Cremation of Sam McGee," "The Shooting of Dan McGrew," and other Robert Service ballads at the Park Service building on Broadway. It's a first-rate show, and Buckwheat always knows how to make people laugh; it's free and worth every penny.

Events

Skagway's first July 4th, in 1898, was celebrated with the outlaw Soapy Smith leading the parade on a white horse; he was dead four days later. **July 4th** is still a big day, with a huge parade (locals call it the best in Alaska) and other events. **Soapy Smith's Wake** on July 8 toasts the con man's life and death at the Eagles Hall. The less savory aspects of the wake have been (officially, at least) deleted from the program, but certain individuals may still join in after massive consumption of cheap champagne.

The **Klondike Road Relay** (www.klondikeroadrelay.com) takes place in early September, with more than a 150 teams composed of 10 runners each competing over a grueling 110-mile course from Skagway to Whitehorse.

The main winter event is the **Buckwheat Ski Classic,** a cross-country ski race that attracts both serious competitors and rank amateurs (including the "lazy and infirm") each March.

RECREATION

Rent a quality mountain bike from **Sockeye Cycle** (5th Ave. near Broadway, 907/983-2851, www.cyclealaska.com), which also offers a speedy ride down White Pass: Sockeye drives you up, and you roll back down on the bikes ($79). Another popular option includes a train ride up to Fraser followed by a downhill ride to town ($179). A 2.5-hour Dyea bike tour is $79. **Sourdough Car Rental** (6th Ave. and Broadway, 907/983-2523, www.geocities.com/sourdoughcarrentals) also rents bikes, including tandems.

Chilkoot Horseback Adventures (907/983-3990, www.chilkoothorseback.com) has 3.5-hour horseback rides up historic Dyea Valley, along with sled dog cart rides (www.alaskasleddog.com).

Nearby Hiking

A network of well-marked trails on the slopes just east of town makes for excellent day hikes and a place to warm up for the Chilkoot Trail. Cross the small footbridge and railroad tracks beyond the end of 3rd and 4th Avenues, then follow the pipeline up the hill. **Lower Dewey Lake** is a 20-minute climb that gains 500 feet in elevation. A trail right around the lake branches at the south end off to **Sturgill's Landing** (3.5 miles) on Taiya Inlet. **Upper Dewey Lake** and the **Devil's Punchbowl** are a steep 2.5-mile climb from the north end of the lower lake. Icy Lake is a relatively level two miles from the lower lake, but the trail to **Upper Reid Falls** is steep and hard to follow. A number of clearings with picnic tables surround the lower lake, where camping is possible; others are at the other lakes and Sturgill's Landing.

At 2nd Avenue and Alaska Street, go around the airport and take the footbridge over Skagway River. A short hike goes left to beautiful **Yakutania Point,** with views down Taiya Inlet. Go right and head steeply up to the Dyea Road; in one mile you'll see the trailhead for **A.B. Mountain,** named for the Arctic Brotherhood—the letters *AB* are supposedly visible in snow patches each spring. This five-mile hike is steep and strenuous; the summit is 5,100 feet above your starting point at sea level.

The Forest Service maintains a refurbished rail car as the **Denver Caboose Cabin** ($35). This attractive old caboose is six miles north of Skagway near where the railroad crosses the East Fork of the Skagway River. Access is by foot, or the White Pass & Yukon Route train will drop you off for $30 round-trip. Take your binoculars to scan nearby slopes for mountain goats. The **Denver Glacier Trail** begins right beside the caboose and climbs five miles and 1,200 feet to Denver Glacier. It's a beautiful hike through subalpine fir, paper birch, cottonwood, spruce, and other trees.

Another excellent hiking option begins at Glacier Station (14 miles north of Skagway). Have the White Pass & Yukon Route train drop you off ($63 round-trip), and then hike up the easy two-mile trail that leads to a Forest Service cabin ($35) near **Laughton Glacier.** Flag down the train to return. Make cabin reservations ($10 fee) for either the caboose or the cabin at 518/885-3639, 877/444-6777, or www.recreation.gov.

Located at the Mountain Shop in Skagway, **Packer Expeditions** (907/983-2544, www.packerexpeditions.com) leads guided hikes in the Skagway area, including day trips and multiday hikes over Chilkoot Pass. Its most popular trip combines a helicopter flight over the Juneau Ice Field with a four-mile hike to Laughton Glacier, followed by a train ride back to town. The cost is $340 for this 5.5-hour trip, which is mainly for cruise shippies.

On the Water

A number of companies offer charter fishing out of Skagway; get their brochures in the downtown visitors center or find them at www.skagway.com.

Skagway Float Tours (907/983-3688, www.skagwayfloat.com) has easy three-hour trips down the Taiya River ($75 adults, $55 children). A combination trip ($85 adults, $65 children) includes a one-hour hike up the first part of the Chilkoot Trail followed by a float down the river. The company also has a variety of other hiking, floating, and tour options.

Flightseeing

Temsco Helicopter (907/983-2900 or 866/683-2900, www.temscoair.com) offers 80-minute "glacier discovery" flights ($289) that include a guided 40-minute glacier hike, and a second tour with an hour on the Denver Glacier, where you get to practice dogsledding ($479).

ACCOMMODATIONS

If you're heading here in midsummer, try to make reservations at least two weeks ahead of time to be sure of a room. Visit www.skagway.com for links to local lodging places. Add an 8 percent lodging tax to the prices below.

Hostel

The delightful **Skagway Home Hostel** (3rd Ave. and Main St., 907/983-2131, www.skagwayhostel.com) is right in town. Built more than a century ago, the home was once owned by the marshal who arrested the Soapy Smith gang after the shoot-out. An 11 P.M. curfew may put a crimp in your social life, but the owners are very friendly, and the hostel is open year-round. There's only space for 12, so reserve ahead. Registration is 5–9 P.M., but late ferry arrivals are accommodated. The hostel has a kitchen, common area, showers, laundry, bag storage, and a free guest computer. Bunks are $15 in mixed dorms or $20 for gender-specific dorms. The owners also offer occasional vegetarian dinners ($5). Reservations are highly advised; you can make them on their website.

Hotels

Sgt. Preston's Lodge (6th Ave. and State St., 907/983-2521 or 866/983-2521, www.sgt-prestonslodgeskagway.com) is a tidy 35-room motel right in town, with nicely remodeled rooms and Wi-Fi. Standard units are $80–100 s or $90–110 d; families appreciate the two-bedroom units for $125 d or $145 for four.

Budget travelers can check out new but basic guest rooms at **Morning Wood Hotel** (444 4th St., 907/983-3200, www.skagwaypizzastation.com, $75 d), located over the Pizza Station Restaurant. The are no TVs or phones, and the bath is down the hall.

Skagway's largest lodging place is the seasonal **Westmark Inn** (3rd Ave. and Broadway, 907/983-2291 or 800/544-0970, www.westmarkhotels.com, $135 d), with all the charm of a retirement home. Westmark is grossly overpriced, and you'll even need to pay $10 for Wi-Fi.

Bed-and-Breakfasts

Hosted by longtime Alaskan Tara Mallory, **Mile Zero B&B** (9th Ave. at Main St., 907/983-3045, www.mile-zero.com, $135 d) is an attractive B&B with six large guest rooms, private entrances and baths, covered porches, a cozy parlor, continental breakfast, and Wi-Fi. Kids are welcome.

Housed within one of the town's oldest buildings, **Skagway Inn B&B** (7th Ave. and Broadway, 907/983-2289 or 888/752-4929, www.skagwayinn.com, mid-Mar.–Sept.) served through the years as a bordello, a residence, a boarding house, and now as a delightful inn. Six guest rooms ($149–199 d) have private baths, and the others ($119 d) share three baths. A full hot breakfast is served downstairs. The inn also has Wi-Fi and an evening guest lounge.

Built in 1902 and completely rebuilt after a fire, **The White House Inn** (8th Ave. and Main St., 907/983-9000, www.atthewhitehouse.com, $125–155 d) is a large plantation-style home with 10 guest rooms, one of which is wheelchair accessible. All rooms feature a country Victorian decor, with private baths, Wi-Fi, fridges, and continental breakfasts.

Eight miles out Dyea Road, **Chilkoot Trail Outpost** (907/983-3799, www.chilkoottrailoutpost.com) is a modern lodge with eight cabins, all containing private baths and with Wi-Fi access. Rates are $145 d in duplex cabins or $175 d for deluxe units with two queen beds, a fridge, and a microwave; add $25 for each additional guest. A full buffet breakfast is included, along with evening campfires and bikes. Guests can use the screened-in gazebo cooking area for other meals, or pay $25 for a steak-and-seafood dinner. Because of its location, this lodge is popular with hikers setting out for the Chilkoot Trail; the trailhead is just a half-mile away.

Cabins

Two miles from downtown Skagway, **Cindy's Place** (907/983-2674 or 800/831-8095, www.alaska.net/~croland, mid-May–early Sept.) includes two modern cabins with private baths, a microwave, and a mini-fridge for $125 d with a two-night minimum. Also available is a tiny cabin with twin beds and a toilet (but no shower) for $50 s or $65 d; it'll look like luxury if you just stumbled off the Chilkoot Trail. Breakfast fixins are provided (including hot baked goods for the larger cabins), along with a courtesy shuttle to town, and (sometimes) access to the hot tub.

Another place with cabins on the way to Dyea is **Skagway Bungalows** (907/983-2986, www.aptalaska.net/~saldi, Mar.–Oct., $125 d). It's a mile from town, and the two in-the-woods cabins have private baths, fridges, and microwaves.

CAMPING

The Park Service maintains a peaceful campground ($10) at **Dyea,** northeast of Skagway. It is especially popular with hikers along the Chilkoot Trail. You'll need to bring water or filter it from the river. For those without wheels, hitching is possible, or contact one of the local taxi companies for a ride. Showers are available from local RV parks or at the small boat harbor.

Skagway's three private campgrounds are all open May–September. **Skagway Mountain View RV Park** (14th Ave. and Broadway, 907/983-3333 or 888/778-7700, www.alaskarv.com, RVs $46, tents $26) is the in-town campground, with wooded sites, toilets, showers, and Wi-Fi. The narrow-gauge tracks border the grounds, making this a good place for train photo opportunities. **Pullen Creek RV Park** (907/983-2768 or 800/936-3731, www.pullencreekrv.com, RVs $36, tents $20) is next to the harbor and cruise ship dock. This is great if you like being in the heart of the action with steam engines, cruise ships, and shopping, but not so great if you're looking for a quieter, more natural setting. **Garden City RV Park** (16th Ave. and State St., 907/983-2378 or 866/983-2378) is little more than a parking lot with a bathhouse; call for current rates.

FOOD

With so many visitors flashing the cash, Skagway's high meal prices should come as no surprise. But at least the variety and quality are considerably higher than what you'll find in Wrangell!

Breakfast and Lunch

Corner Café (4th Ave. and State St., 907/983-2155, daily 8 A.M.–4 P.M.) is the local greasy spoon, with burgers and pizzas, plus reasonable breakfasts and fast service—if you don't mind all the cigarette smoke. A better (smoke-free) bet is **Sweet Tooth Café** (315 Broadway,

907/983-2405, daily 6 A.M.–3 P.M.), with all-American breakfasts and lunches. Both Corner Café and Sweet Tooth stay open year-round; most other eateries close when the cruise ships flee to the Caribbean.

Other year-round places worth a visit include **Glacial Smoothies & Espresso** (336 3rd Ave., 907/983-3223) and **Skagway Pizza Station** (444 4th Ave., 907/983-2220, www.pizzastation.eskagway.com).

Dinner

Skagway Fish Company (907/983-3474, daily May–Sept.) is the tentlike structure near the cruise ship dock and facing the small boat harbor. The menu includes T-bone steaks, pork chops, barbecue ribs, oysters, and fresh salmon or halibut, but I recommend the halibut fish-and-chips ($15). The fish is locally caught, and it comes with a pile of fries and homemade coleslaw. There is good strawberry cheesecake too.

Skagway Inn (7th Ave. at Broadway, 907/983-2289 or 888/752-4929, www.skagwayinn.com) puts on a three-hour afternoon **Alaska Garden and Gourmet Tour** for $89 where you can watch chef and owner Karl Klupar prepare a delicious three-course meal that combines fresh garden greens and seafood.

Red Onion Saloon (2nd Ave. and Broadway, 907/983-2222, www.redonion1898.com, $8–12) serves surprisingly good pizzas, chili, and sandwiches in a historic setting.

Stowaway Café (907/983-3463, http://stowaway.eskagway.com, daily 10 A.M.–10 P.M. late Apr.–late Sept.) is where locals (and tourists) go for good food in a harbor-side setting. There's even a big deck for sunny days. The café specializes in seafood of all types—bubbly button Brie is memorable—but also serves everything from smoked ribs to steaks. Be sure to ask about the daily specials. Reservations are advised for dinner. Full dinners are $16–29, with lunches around $10.

Starfire Grill (4th Ave. and Spring St., 907/983-3663, Mon.–Fri. 11 A.M.–10 P.M., Sat.–Sun. 4–10 P.M. late Apr.–mid-Oct., $12–18) serves excellent Thai lunches, chicken satay, curries, pot stickers, soups, and pad thai. The express menu is great if you're in a hurry.

Skagway Brewing Co. (7th Ave. and Broadway, 907/983-2739, www.skagwaybrewing.com, daily 10 A.M.–midnight May–Sept., daily 4 P.M.–midnight winter, $12–15) is far enough up Broadway to be missed by most cruise ship folks but close enough for locals and independent travelers. Of the 16 beers on tap, nine are made here, including a popular Spruce Tip Ale. Get a four-beer sampler for $7. The menu includes standard pub fare such as burgers, halibut fish-and-chips with hand-cut fries, and hot turkey bacon sandwiches. There is live music most Thursday nights.

Groceries

Fairway Market (4th Ave. and State St., 907/983-2220) is Skagway's grocery store. Fresh produce arrives on Tuesdays and may be wiped out by the weekend. **You Say Tomato** (2075 State St., 907/983-2784) is a spendy natural-foods market with freshly baked breads and locally grown produce.

INFORMATION AND SERVICES

Both the **National Park Service Visitors Center** (907/983-2921, www.nps.gov/klgo, daily 8 A.M.–6 P.M. early May–late Sept., closed late Sept.–early May) and the **Skagway Visitors Information Center** (907/983-2854 or 888/762-1898 message, www.skagway.com, daily 8 A.M.–6 P.M. May–Sept., Mon.–Fri. 8 A.M.–5 P.M. Oct.–Apr.) are downtown. The small **town library** (8th Ave. and State St., 907/983-2665) offers free reading material on the paperback racks inside, and you can check your email on its computers. Rent computer time at **Glacial Smoothies** (336 3rd Ave., 907/983-3223) or **Ports of Call** (363 2nd Ave., 907/983-3398). Both places also serve light meals.

Mountain Shop (4th Ave. between Broadway and State St., 907/983-2544, www.packerexpeditions.com) is the outfitter in town and also sells supplies for the trail. Books are available from **Skaguay News Depot** (Broadway, 907/983-3354, www.skagwaybooks.com).

One of Alaska's oldest bank buildings, **Wells Fargo** (6th Ave. and Broadway), changes green dollars into multicolored Canadian dollars and has an ATM.

The **Skagway Recreation Center** (13th Ave. and Main St., 907/983-2679, www.skagwayrecreation.org, $5) is a surprisingly impressive place in such a small town, with a gym, a weight room, a cardio room, a climbing wall, a skate park, and various classes.

For medical emergencies, **Skagway Medical Clinic** (11th Ave. and Broadway, 907/983-2255) has a physician's assistant on staff.

GETTING THERE

On the Water

Skagway is the northern terminus of the **Alaska Marine Highway ferry system** (907/465-3941 or 800/642-0066, www.dot.state.ak.us/amhs), and ferries arrive daily during the summer, stopping at the **ferry terminal** (907/983-2941) just a block from downtown.

Alaska Fjordlines (907/766-3395 or 800/320-0146, www.alaskafjordlines.com) operates the *Fjord Express,* a large and stable high-speed catamaran with daily summertime runs from Skagway to Haines and then on to Juneau. The boat leaves Skagway at 8 A.M., arrives in Juneau at 11 A.M., and then heads back at 5:30 P.M., returning to Skagway at 8:15 P.M. The cost is $155 adults, $125 children round-trip, including a bus to downtown Juneau. A light breakfast and dinner are included, and the boat stops for wildlife and photo opportunities. This passenger-only ferry is very popular with RVers who want to see Juneau in a day. One-way trips ($100 adults, $80 children) and overnight stays in Juneau are allowed; reservations are recommended. This is an efficiently run and friendly operation.

Haines-Skagway Fast Ferry (907/766-2100 or 888/766-2103, www.chilkatcruises.com) offers high-speed catamaran service between Haines and Skagway, with several departures a day early May–late September. The cost is $68 round- trip ($34 for children). The boat does not stop on any of these trips for wildlife-viewing or photos, but does have a few snacks on board.

Air

Wings of Alaska (907/983-2442, www.wingsofalaska.com) has daily flights connecting Skagway with Juneau and Haines. **Air Excursions** (907/697-2375 or 800/354-2479, www.airexcursions.com) lacks scheduled service but typically has daily flights connecting Skagway with Juneau, Haines, and Gustavus.

Long-Distance Buses

Yukon Alaska Tourist Tours (867/668-5947 or 866/626-7383, www.yatt.ca) has a daily bus to Whitehorse ($60), along with a mix of bus/train combo tours. In Whitehorse, catch the **Alaska Direct Bus Line** (800/770-6652, www.alaskadirectbusline.com) for service north to Anchorage or Fairbanks.

GETTING AROUND

City-run **SMART** (Skagway Municipal and Regional Transit, 907/983-2743, www.skagwaytransit.com) buses run daily, shuttling from the cruise dock into town and out to 23rd Avenue (access to the gold rush cemetery). The one-way cost is $2. Buses run continuously 7:30 A.M.–9 P.M. May–September.

Several local tour outfits offer drop-off services for hikers heading up the Chilkoot Trail and for campers staying at Dyea: **Dyea Dave's** (907/209-5031, www.dyeadavetours.com), **Frontier Excursions** (907/983-2512 or 877/983-2512, www.frontierexcursions.com), and **Klondike Taxi** (907/983-2400).

Rent new cars from **Avis** (2nd Ave. and Spring St., 907/983-2247 or 800/331-1212) or used vehicles from **Sourdough Car Rental** (6th Ave. and Broadway, 907/983-2523, www.geocities.com/sourdoughcarrentals). If you're driving to Whitehorse, stick with Avis since Sourdough slaps you with $0.25 per mile after 125 miles. **Skagway Classic Cars** (907/983-2886, www.skagwayclassiccars.com) has immaculate cars from the 1950s and 1960s, with chauffeured trips around town for $379 for a three-hour tour (maximum four people).

Tours

Given the influx of tourists to Skagway, it's no surprise to find a multitude of tour options. The most unique local tours are aboard the canary-yellow 1920s vintage White Motor Company cars run by **Skagway Street Car Company** (907/983-2908, www.skagway-streetcar.com). The complete two-hour trip costs $42 ($21 children), but most seats are pre-sold to cruise ship passengers. To be sure of a spot, book at least two days in advance. This is one of the few Alaskan guided tours that I'd actually recommend.

A number of other companies also offer van tours around the area; get their brochures at the visitors center. These typically cost $30 for a three-hour trip that includes the town of Skagway and White Pass Summit; some take an alternate route to the Chilkoot Trailhead and Dyea, or a longer trip into Yukon.

Skagway Carriage Company (907/723-3117) provides a completely different sort of tour: horse-drawn carriage rides around town. Just look for the carriages on Broadway.

CHILKOOT TRAIL

One of the best reasons for coming to Skagway is the historic and surprisingly scenic 33-mile Chilkoot Trail. During the gold rush of 1897–1898, what had once been an Indian route from the tidewater at Dyea to the headwaters of the Yukon River became a trail for thousands of men and women. Today, the trail is hiked by several thousand hardy souls each summer, along with a few insane wintertime trekkers. The western portion of this route lies within **Klondike Gold Rush National Historical Park,** while the eastern half is managed by Parks Canada as **Chilkoot Trail National Historic Park.** All hikers crossing the border must clear Canadian Customs, so a **passport is required.**

A minimum of three days and nights (but preferably 4–5) is needed to hike from Dyea to Bennett over 3,246-foot-high Chilkoot Pass.

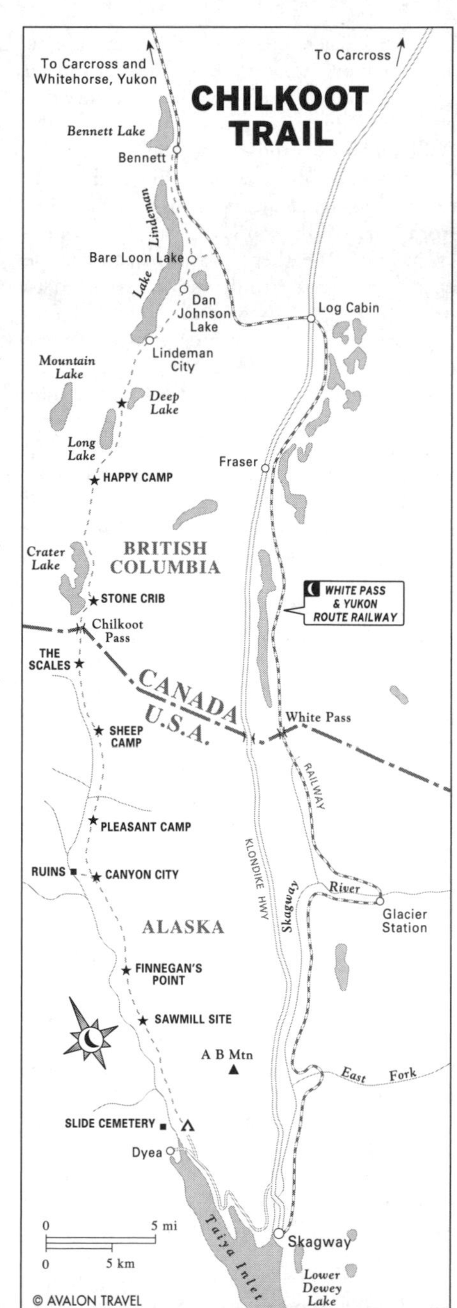

This is no easy Sunday outing: You must be fit and well prepared. It is best to hike north from Dyea rather than south from Bennett since this is the historic route, and a descent down the "Golden Stairs" can be dangerous.

You will be above the tree line and totally exposed to the elements during the 11 miles from Sheep Camp to Deep Lake (the hardest stretch). Weather conditions can change quickly along the trail, and hikers need to be prepared for strong winds, cold, low fog, rain, and snow, even in midsummer. Because of the rain-shadow effect, the Canadian side is considerably drier than the Alaskan side. Mosquitoes and other insects are an annoyance, and snowfields linger between Sheep Camp and Happy Camp well into the summer. Despite these challenges, for scenery and historical value the Chilkoot Trail is unsurpassed in Alaska and western Canada.

Flora and Fauna

The vegetation changes from coastal rain forest up the Taiya Valley to alpine tundra as you approach the pass and rise above the 2,700-foot level. On the drier Canadian side you'll find an open boreal forest of alpine fir and lodgepole pine. Although black bears are often seen along the trail, there has never been an attack on a hiker. Help keep it this way by storing food and garbage properly.

History

It took each would-be miner an average of three months and dozens of trips back and forth from cache to cache to pack his required ton of supplies into Canada. By the spring of 1898, three aerial tramways were operating on the Chilkoot. The thousands of stampeders stopped at Lindeman and Bennett, built boats and rafts, and waited for spring break-up, which would allow them to sail the 900 kilometers to Dawson City along a series of lakes and rivers. When the ice broke up in May 1898, some 7,124 boats and rafts sailed from the shores of Lakes Lindeman and Bennett. Royal Canadian Mounted Police records show 28,000 people traveling from Bennett to Dawson in 1898. Ironically, by the time they got to Dawson every claim in the Klondike was already staked. By 1900, the railway had opened from Skagway to Whitehorse, and Dyea and the Chilkoot Trail became ghost towns.

The Route

The Chilkoot Trail begins just before the bridge over the Taiya River at Dyea, nine miles northwest of Skagway. The first section of the trail traverses lush rain forests along the Taiya River. Artifacts from the gold rush litter parts of the path, including bits of clothing, rusting stoves, pulleys, cables, and old wagons. At **Canyon City,** 7.5 miles from the trailhead, a short side trail and a suspension bridge across the Taiya River provide access to the remains of one of the settlements that sprang up during the rush to the Klondike. You'll find a number of artifacts, including a boiler that powered tramways to haul supplies over the summit. Beyond this, the trail climbs steeply to another long-abandoned settlement, **Sheep Camp** (Mile 13), where a ranger is in residence nearby all summer.

Beyond Sheep Camp, the trek becomes far more challenging as the route takes hikers through a narrow valley before heading above tree line. Artifacts—including metal telegraph poles and pieces from an old tramway used to haul goods up the mountain—become more common as you climb past "The Scales" (Mile 16), where packers reweighed their loads and increased their fee for the difficult final climb. Modern-day hikers start to wonder about their sanity at this point, since the infamous "Golden Stairs" lie ahead; the name came from the steps carved in the ice and the snow by the miners. During the winter of 1897–1898 thousands of prospectors carried their heavy loads to the 3,535-foot summit of **Chilkoot Pass.** Photos of men going up here in single file are still the best-known images of the gold rush. Today, hikers struggle up this 45-degree slope with full backpacks. Snow generally covers the pass until mid-July, and can be waist-deep early in the summer. Avalanches can occur before early July, and avalanche transceivers are recommended. Ask at the Trail Center for current snow conditions and other hazards. A warming hut provides protection from the weather once you cross into British Columbia; Parks Canada wardens here check to make sure you have a permit.

After the challenging summit climb, hikers are rewarded with easier hiking and spectacular vistas (when weather permits), but it's still a long distance to the end of the trail. Many hikers camp at **Deep Lake** (Mile 23), while others continue on to **Lindeman Lake** (Mile 26) for the night. A Canada Parks warden station and warming huts are at Lindeman. During the stampede, thousands of miners halted along the shores of this lake, quickly forming the town of Lindeman City. Here they built boats for the journey down the Yukon River to the Klondike gold fields. Reminders of the gold rush can be found in the countryside here, and a small cemetery marks the final stop for those who never made it to the Klondike.

Beyond Lindeman, the trail climbs a ridge overlooking the lake and then splits, with one path turning south to meet the Klondike Highway at **Log Cabin,** where you can catch a bus back to Skagway or Whitehorse. Those who continue straight at the junction will reach a pretty place called **Bennett** on the shores of Lake Bennett. Only one family lives here today, but hikers will enjoy exploring the log church built by the miners and a grand White Pass & Yukon Route Railroad depot. Most hikers end their trip here, catching the train back to Skagway.

Hiking Permits

Backcountry permits are required of hikers on the Chilkoot, and the number of hikers is limited. The combined U.S. and Canadian permit is C$54 adults, C$27 children. For trail information, maps (including an excellent *Hiker's Guide to the Chilkoot Trail*), a listing of transportation options, and backcountry permits, contact the Park Service's **Chilkoot Trail Center** (907/983-9234, www.nps.gov/klgo, daily 8 A.M.–5 P.M. June–early Sept.) in the historic Martin Itjen house in Skagway. You can also buy trail permits through Parks Canada in Whitehorse (867/667-3910 or 800/661-0486, www.pc.gc.ca/chilkoot).

Most permits are reserved months ahead of time (C$12 extra), but eight permits are reserved for walk-ins each day at 1 P.M. In July–August, folks without permits start lining up at the Trail Center by 11 A.M. to be sure of a spot. At other times you won't have a problem getting onto the trail even at the last minute, but call the Trail Center for the latest situation.

Practicalities

Official campgrounds—most with tent platforms, outhouses, cooking shelters, and bear-proof food storage—are at nine sites along the Chilkoot Trail in addition to the one at the Dyea Trailhead; most popular are those at Canyon City (Mile 7.5), Sheep Camp (Mile 12), Happy Camp (Mile 21), Lindeman City (Mile 26), and Bennett (Mile 33). Campfires are permitted only at Canyon City and Sheep Camp. There are shelters with woodstoves at Canyon City, Sheep Camp, and Lindeman, but these are for drying out only, not overnighting. Everything along the trail dating from the gold rush—even a rusty old tin can—is protected by law, and there are severe penalties for those who damage or remove items.

Everyone entering Canada must clear Canadian Customs. If you come in along the Chilkoot Trail and do not speak to an official at either Whitehorse or Fraser, you should report at the first opportunity to either the RCMP in Carcross or the Immigration Office (open Mon.–Fri.) at the Federal Building in Whitehorse.

Getting There

Several Skagway companies offer drop-off services ($10) from town for hikers heading up the Chilkoot Trail. Best known is **Dyea Dave's** (907/209-5031, www.dyeadavetours.com), but similar services are available from **Frontier Excursions** (907/983-2512 or 877/983-2512, www.frontierexcursions.com).

The White Pass & Yukon Route Railroad's

Chilkoot Trail Hikers Service (907/983-2217 or 800/343-7373, www.whitepassrailroad.com) provides a shuttle late May–mid-September from Lake Bennett (the end of the trail) to Fraser ($50) or Skagway ($95). The schedule changes each year, so check to make sure a train will be there once you reach Lake Bennett. Make advance reservations since space is limited. Meals are available at the Bennett station.

Although most hikers choose the train, some prefer (or have no option because the rail bus is full or the timing doesn't work out) to hike out along the railroad tracks from the Lindeman area to Log Cabin, where they catch a **Yukon Alaska Tourist Tours** (867/668-5947 in Whitehorse or 866/626-7383, www.yatt.ca) bus, or get a ride with Dyea Dave or Frontier Excursions for $35; advance reservations are essential. A final option is to fly by floatplane from Lake Bennett to Whitehorse via **Alpine Aviation** (867/668-7725, www.alpineaviationyukon.com).

THE KLONDIKE HIGHWAY

This 98-mile road from Skagway to the Alaska Highway 21 miles south of Whitehorse closely follows the White Pass & Yukon Route rail line built at the turn of the 20th century. The 65-mile stretch north to Carcross was opened in 1981, completing the route started by the U.S. Army in 1942 from the Alaska Highway south to Carcross. The road ascends quickly from sea level at Skagway to White Pass at 3,290 feet in 14 miles. Many turnouts provide views across the canyon of the narrow-gauge White Pass & Yukon Route track, waterfalls, gorges, and long drop-offs—if you're lucky and the weather cooperates. At the summit, **Canadian Customs** welcomes you to British Columbia and is open 24 hours a day in the summer, 8 A.M.–midnight in other seasons; set your watch ahead an hour to Pacific time on the Canadian side. U.S. Customs is open 24 hours a day year-round.

Yakutat

The friendly village of Yakutat (pop. 600) is in a protected harbor on Yakutat Bay, halfway between Juneau and Cordova along the Gulf of Alaska. The name of this out-of-the-way settlement was derived from the Eyak name *Yak-tat* ("lagoon behind the breakers"). Behind Yakutat soars the pyramidal 18,008-foot summit of **Mt. St. Elias,** second-tallest in the United States. Across the bay is **Malaspina Glacier,** the largest piedmont glacier on the continent (it's bigger than Rhode Island). Both of these lie within mighty Wrangell–St. Elias National Park.

Yakutat is a famous fishing destination, particularly for steelhead on the Situk River, but also for king, silver, and sockeye salmon, plus halibut. But it isn't just fish that attracts visitors; in recent years Yakutat has drawn cold-water surfers who come to ride the big ones on the 70 miles of sandy beaches that stretch southeast from town. These beaches are also great places for bird-watching, beachcombing, or simply relaxing.

The weather in Yakutat can be summed up on one word: wet. Summers are rainy and winters are snowy. The town gets over 130 inches of precipitation annually, so visitors can plan on seeing their share of that. All this precipitation feeds the enormous glaciers and productive salmon and trout streams for which the area is famous.

Yakutat is home to several fishing lodges and a hodgepodge of businesses: two general stores, three places serving meals, two car rental outfits, an upscale fly-fishing shop, air-taxi operators, a little visitors center for Wrangell–St. Elias National Park, and—most surprisingly—a surf shop.

HISTORY

The area around Yakutat served for centuries as a winter village for the Eyaks, a people with links to both the Tlingits to the east and Athabascans to the north. In 1805 the Russian-American Company built a fort at Yakutat,

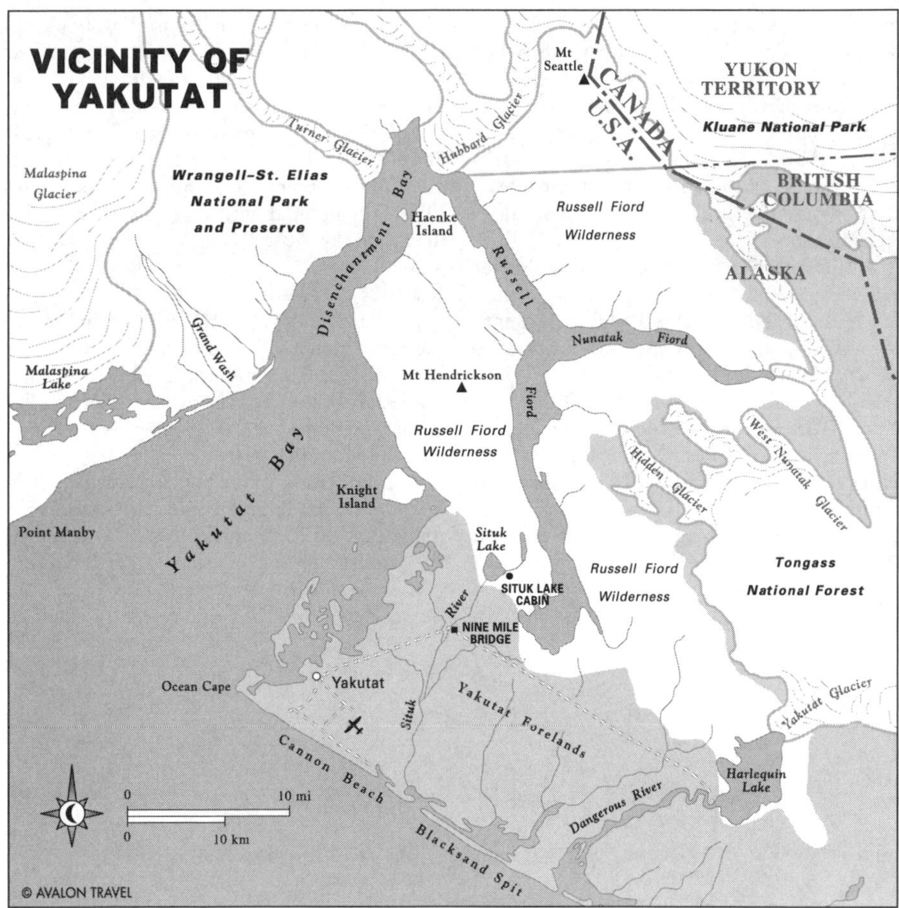

using it as a base for the harvesting of sea otters. The post was later destroyed by the Eyaks. Gold seekers came to the area in the 1860s, mining the black-sand beaches, followed by missionaries, loggers, and fishers. During World War II, Yakutat was home to an aviation base, and the long paved runway that was developed now serves as the local airport. Quite a few military bunkers, gun emplacements, and other signs of the war are still visible. Today, commercial and sportfishing provide most of the local jobs. More than half of the people who live in Yakutat are Native Alaskans.

SIGHTS

Yakutat lacks a downtown, and homes, businesses, and lodges are scattered over several miles. You'll need a rental vehicle to get around. The boat harbor is interesting, with a nice trail around the nearby lagoon. One local oddity is the old train engine and cars from the **Yakutat & Southern Railroad** at the intersection of Alsek and Airport Roads. Between 1907 and 1949 the engine was used to haul fish to a local cannery.

The typical visitor to Yakutat is a 55-year-old from Indiana who comes here with his buddies for a week of fly-fishing and beer drinking. Their main focus is the **Situk River,** where 10,000 or so steelhead return to spawn, primarily March–May. Local lodges provide boats and guides, along with ocean fishing charters for halibut and salmon. Drift boats put in at the aptly named **Nine Mile Bridge** over the Situk; it's nine miles out on Alsek Road.

A **National Park Service Visitor Center** (907/784-3295, www.nps.gov/wrst, Mon.–Sat. 8 A.M.–4:30 P.M. mid-May–mid-Sept., Mon.–Fri. 8 A.M.–4:30 P.M. mid-Sept.–mid-May) provides information on both Glacier Bay National Park and Wrangell–St. Elias National Park and Preserve. A large Tlingit house screen from 1905 is a focal point, with other exhibits on Malaspina Glacier and other sights in the area.

Stop by Tongass National Forest's **Yakutat Ranger District** (907/784-3359, www.fs.fed.us/r10/tongass) for details on the Russell Fiord Wilderness, public-use cabins, bird-watching, and other recreational opportunities. Looking for wildlife? Head out to the dump on Alsek Road, where brown bears often forage. Eleven Forest Service cabins (www.recreation.gov, $35) are scattered along the **Yakutat Forelands,** the relatively flat and forested area that stretches for 50 miles east of town. Especially popular with anglers are three cabins along the Situk River.

Country Roads

If you have a rental vehicle, take a spin out on the roads that radiate from town to Cannon Beach, Situk River mouth, Ocean Cape, and Harlequin Lake. You'll quickly learn the famous "Yakutat wave," required every time you encounter another car.

A paved road connects the airport with Yakutat harbor, but more interesting are gravel roads that lead to remote beaches and across the almost-level Yakutat Forelands. The longest is **Alsek Road** to Harlequin Lake and Dangerous River. Nine miles out of town, a

© DON PITCHER

St. Elias Mountain Range, viewed from the beach at Ocean Cape, near Yakutat bridge spans the Situk River, providing access for anglers. Alsek Road continues another 17 miles beyond the Situk, finally crossing the "bridge to nowhere" over Dangerous River where it abruptly ends. A 0.25-mile trail leads to **Harlequin Lake,** dotted with ice from the enormous Yakutat Glacier.

Cannon Beach is two miles off the main highway (unnamed; look for the binocular sign), with a picnic area and campsites amid mossy Sitka spruce forests. The cannons (disabled by cutting off the ends) are visible as you walk down this gorgeous beach, famous for its waves and endless sand. **Lost River Road** leads eight miles to the mouth of the Situk River, where you'll often see bears cruising the shore. Locals have subsistence cabins here for netting salmon when the salmon are running.

Ocean Cape sits at the end of an eight-mile drive down a narrow rutted road. Cross the one-lane wooden bridge over Ankau Lagoon and turn left past the "No Trespassing" sign (widely ignored). Go another two miles to Ocean Cape, with its remote rocky beach and full-monty views of Mt. St. Elias (when the weather cooperates) and the stormy Gulf of Alaska.

Surfing Safari

Yakutat is Alaska's surfing capital, with mile after mile of sandy beaches, virtually no competition for waves, and great swells rolling off the Gulf of Alaska. On a stormy winter day you might see as many as 15 surfers—typically a mix of locals and wandering California beach bums—riding the waves at **Cannon Beach** (named for the World War II cannons here) and other spots. Because of all the rainfall, the ocean around Yakutat is less saline than in California or Hawaii, so the boards need to be thicker and more buoyant to keep surfers from sinking. A local surfer, Jack Endicott, runs **Icy Waves Surf Shop** (907/784-3253, www.icywaves.com) from the back of his house, with a mix of surfboards (including some Cowabunga long boards), wetsuits, and boogie boards for sale or rent. Icy Wave T-shirts and hats are a great gift. Fall storms often bring the biggest waves, so the shop isn't generally open in the summer. Jack Endicott's day job as a forecaster for the National Weather Service means he has a good idea of what to expect.

Hubbard Glacier

North of Yakutat within Wrangell–St. Elias National Park, spectacular Hubbard Glacier is the largest tidewater glacier in North America. Fed by high mountains of the St. Elias Range, the glacier is six miles wide and more than 70 miles long. Many cruise ships make a stop in front of this massive glacier with an always-calving 400-foot-high wall of ice. Local air taxis offer flightseeing trips that provide an even more impressive glacier view.

Virtually all Alaskan glaciers are retreating as the global climate warms, but Hubbard Glacier is the rare exception. Not only is it advancing, but doing so in a way that threatens to block off the waters of Russell Fiord (yes, "fiord" is the official spelling). Today, just 100 yards of open water separate the ice from a rocky point of land at Point Gilbert. If the glacier continues advancing, the gap could close, creating a dam that drastically changes the surrounding landscape. This occurred in 1986 when the water rose 75 feet behind an ice dam, trapping seals, sea lions, and porpoises. The ice gave way six months later, freeing the animals and reconnecting the fiord to Disenchantment Bay. A similar situation developed in 2002, and scientists believe it is only a matter of time until ice from the surging glacier creates a relatively permanent dam. If this happens, water would eventually flood the Situk River, potentially impacting the river's acclaimed steelhead trout, not to mention the airport. Visit the U.S. Geological Survey website (http://ak.water.usgs.gov) for more on the Hubbard.

ACCOMMODATIONS

Walk out from the airport terminal and you're 100 feet from what locals call the "Airport Lodge"; the official name is **Yakutat Lodge** (907/784-3232 or 800/925-8828, www.yakutatlodge.com, Apr.–Oct.). All-inclusive fishing packages are the primary attraction, but nightly rates are available in rustic old lodge

© DON PITCHER

Hubbard Glacier flowing into Disenchantment Bay

rooms and simple cabins with a shared bathhouse. Meals are available for guests and the public, and there's Wi-Fi and sometimes a hot tub. (Note: the lodge photo on the main website page is only for high-end stays; most accommodations are much simpler.)

Leonard's Landing Lodge (907/784-3245 or 877/925-3474, www.leonardslanding.com, $75–85 s, $120–140 d) has been rebuilt following a big fire, with a rambling collection of buildings near the boat harbor. Package rates with meals and a fishing guide are available, along with boat rentals.

Glacier Bear Lodge (907/784-3202, www.glacierbearlodge.com) has a modern central lodge with a restaurant and lounge. Motel-style ($195 d) units are adjacent.

Another modern place, **Monte Bay Lodge** (425/432-0722 or 866/513-4744, www.montibaylodge.com, $100–125 pp) has a pleasant location with two upstairs suites, covered porches, and big windows fronting the bay.

The Mooring Lodge (907/784-3300 or 888/551-2836, www.mooringlodge.com, year-round, $250 d; add $75 per person for extra guests) rents out two-bedroom apartment units that can sleep six and have full kitchens, a sauna, and views across Monti Bay to the St. Elias Mountains. Other lodging options include **Red Roof B&B** (907/784-3297, www.yakutatlodging.com), **Blue Heron Inn B&B** (907/784-3287, www.johnlatham.com), and **Yakutat Bay Lodge** (907/784-3000, www.yakutatbaylodge.com).

Camping

A couple of woodsy campsites are along Cannon Beach and near the Situk River bridge. In addition, much of the land surrounding Yakutat is within Tongass National Forest and is open to camping. Above the tide line on Cannon Beach is a fun (but exposed) place to pitch a tent.

FOOD

A bit out of the way, **Glacier Bear Lodge** (907/784-3202, www.glacierbearlodge.com, daily 9 A.M.–2 P.M. and 6–10 P.M. summer; Sat.–Sun. 9 A.M.–2 P.M. and 6–10 P.M. winter) has a full-service restaurant with big breakfasts (including corned beef and hash), lunchtime burgers, wraps, salads, and halibut tacos, along with nightly specials ($19–22) and a popular Saturday-night prime rib ($29). Unfortunately, smoke from the downstairs lounge spreads into the restaurant.

For lunchtime sandwiches and soups—served from 11:30 A.M. until they run out—head to **Fat Grandma's** (907/784-3395, $5–12). The shop also has locally made Native Alaskan arts and a free book-trading library of sorts.

Next to the airport, **Yakutat Lodge** (907/784-3232 or 800/925-8828, www.yakutatlodge.com, daily 6 A.M.–3 P.M. and 5–10 P.M. Apr.–Oct.) is open for three meals a day, with the usual breakfast fare along with lunchtime sandwiches and burgers for $7–12. Steaks and seafood fill the evening menu, from $13 halibut and chips to $32 T-bone steaks. There's a bar, free Wi-Fi, and several packs' worth of cigarette smoke wafting over from the lounge.

Find groceries, supplies, espresso, and ATMs at **Mallott's General Store** (907/784-3355) and **AC Store** (907/272-4600, www.alaskacommercial.com). AC has a deli with pizzas, and Mallott's sells fresh sushi.

INFORMATION AND SERVICES

The **Yakutat Chamber of Commerce** (907/784-3933 or 888/925-8828, www.yakutatalaska.com) will send you a helpful brochure and map, or pick one up from the **City of Yakutat** (907/784-3323, www.yakutatak.govoffice2.com) office when you reach town. The best local Internet site is www.yakutat.net, with links to local businesses. **Cell phone** service is not available.

Fairweather Days each August at Cannon Beach is a good time to camp out and party with the surfers. There's live music, food, and local crafts.

Situk River Fly Shop (907/784-3087, www.situk.net) is well worth a visit even if you aren't a fly-fisher. Owner Bob Miller knows not just fly-fishing but also the area's history and attractions. The shop is housed in an aging World War II hangar. Inside is far nicer, with a good collection of outdoor and fishing gear, plus an ongoing restoration effort (detailed on his blog).

GETTING THERE AND AROUND

Yakutat is the smallest community in the world served by year-round commercial jet service. **Alaska Airlines** (800/426-0333, www.alaskaair.com) connects Yakutat to the outside world with two flights daily: a morning northbound flight to Cordova and Anchorage, and an evening southbound to Juneau.

Both **Alsek Air Service** (907/784-3231, www.alsekair.com) and **Yakutat Coastal Airlines** (907/784-3831, www.flyyca.com) provide air charters and Hubbard Glacier flightseeing trips.

Rent pickups and vans from **Situk Services** (907/784-3316, $110 per day) or **Leo's Vehicles** (907/784-3909, $85 per day). Otherwise, call for a ride from **Yakutat Taxi** (907/784-3088).

The **Alaska Marine Highway** (907/465-3941 or 800/642-0066, www.dot.state.ak.us/amhs) ferry *Kennicott* stops in Yakutat on its twice-a-month summertime sailings between Juneau and Whittier. Weather sometimes makes it impossible for the ferry to dock, so it really isn't a dependable service.

ANCHORAGE AND VICINITY

Texas always seemed so big, but you know you're in the largest State in the Union when you're anchored down in Anchorage. . . .

– From "Anchored Down in Anchorage"
by Michelle Shocked

It's hard to arrive in Anchorage (pop. 280,000) without some strong preconceived notions of what to expect—especially if you've been traveling around the state for a while. Generally, Alaskans either love or hate Anchorage, and their degree of affection or distaste is usually revealed by their chosen proximity to the city. You'll certainly have heard of Anchorage's urban sprawl, its traffic jams, sprouting apartment buildings and condos, corporate skyscrapers, mall mania, fast-food frenzy, and crime; in other words, that it's the antithesis of every virtue and value that God-fearing, law-abiding, and patriotic Alaskans hold sacred. And you've probably also heard the old joke about being "able to see Alaska from Anchorage." You might also have been told that Anchorage has nothing to offer travelers, and that if you're looking for a true *Alaskan* experience, you should avoid the city altogether. Don't believe everything you hear; Anchorage is an attraction of its own and definitely worth some time.

Anchorage can be an eminently enjoyable *and* affordable place in which to hang out. It certainly has one of the most flower-filled downtowns of any American city; visitors are always impressed with the summertime bounty

HIGHLIGHTS

Anchorage Museum: Alaska's largest and finest museum is right downtown, with fascinating exhibits, the kid-friendly Imaginarium, and a fine lunchtime café (page 178).

Alaska Native Heritage Center: Learn about the state's native peoples through exhibits, demonstrations, and cultural presentations at this large facility on the edge of town (page 182).

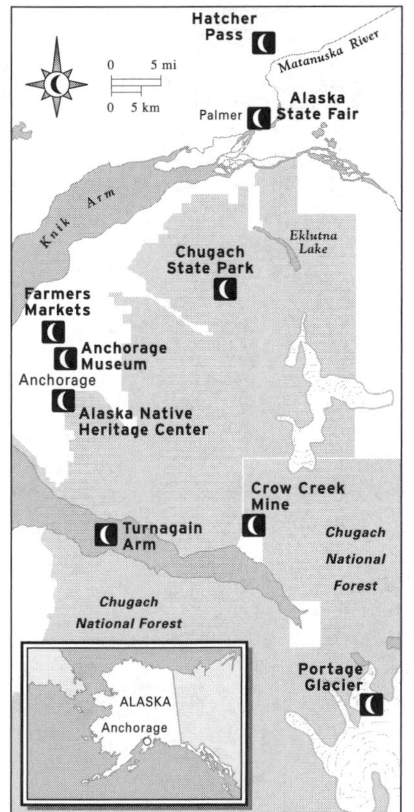

Farmers Markets: Now covering Saturdays and Sundays all summer, this downtown gathering is packed with Alaskan arts and crafts, great finger-food, and live music. Don't miss it (page 203).

Chugach State Park: Who would imagine that you could get into the wilderness so quickly from Anchorage? Lots of wonderful hiking trails are here, especially the climb up Flattop Mountain (page 209).

Turnagain Arm: South of Anchorage, the highway skirts the shore of this long inlet where you can watch for beluga whales and bore tides or turn around to see Dall sheep on the cliffs behind. Nearby Potter Marsh is great for birding (page 212).

Crow Creek Mine: Just a few miles from Alyeska Ski Resort in Girdwood are picture-perfect log cabins from this authentic old mine where you might find flakes of gold – or nuggets – in the creek (page 213).

Portage Glacier: Fifty miles south of Anchorage, this is one of the state's most-visited glaciers. A boat tour across Portage Lake leaves hourly from the visitors center (page 217).

Alaska State Fair: Where else can you find a demolition derby, supersized turkey legs, enormous peonies, and 100-pound cabbages? Take the special Alaska Railroad trains to avoid the traffic jams (page 222).

Hatcher Pass: This beautiful area of the Mat-Su Valley region is perfect for hiking in the summer or cross-country skiing when the snow flies. Take time to explore the weathered old buildings of Independence Mine State Historical Park (page 230).

LOOK FOR TO FIND RECOMMENDED SIGHTS, ACTIVITIES, DINING, AND LODGING.

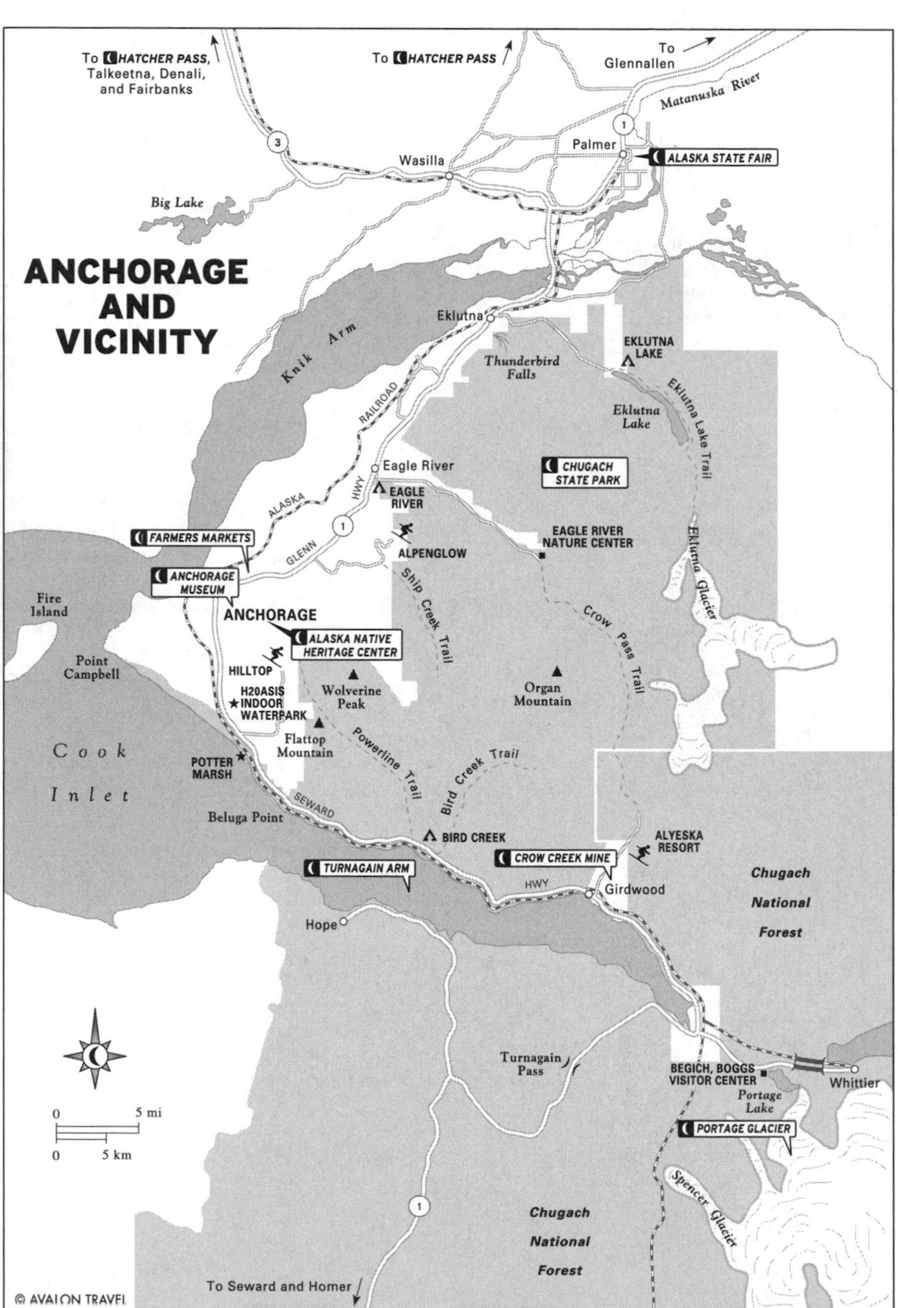
ANCHORAGE AND VICINITY
To HATCHER PASS, Talkeetna, Denali, and Fairbanks
To HATCHER PASS
To Glennallen
Matanuska River
Palmer
ALASKA STATE FAIR
Wasilla
Big Lake
Eklutna
Knik Arm
RAILROAD
Thunderbird Falls
EKLUTNA LAKE
Eklutna Lake
Eklutna Lake Trail
Eagle River
HWY
CHUGACH STATE PARK
EAGLE RIVER
ALASKA
GLENN
EAGLE RIVER NATURE CENTER
FARMERS MARKETS
ALPENGLOW
ANCHORAGE MUSEUM
Eklutna Glacier
Fire Island
ANCHORAGE
Ship Creek Trail
Crow Pass Trail
ALASKA NATIVE HERITAGE CENTER
Point Campbell
HILLTOP
Wolverine Peak
Organ Mountain
H20ASIS INDOOR WATERPARK
Flattop Mountain
Powerline Trail
Cook Inlet
POTTER MARSH
Bird Creek Trail
SEWARD
Beluga Point
BIRD CREEK
ALYESKA RESORT
CROW CREEK MINE
TURNAGAIN ARM
HWY
Girdwood
Chugach National Forest
Hope
Turnagain Pass
BEGICH, BOGGS VISITOR CENTER
Whittier
Portage Lake
0 5 mi
0 5 km
PORTAGE GLACIER
Spencer Glacier
Chugach National Forest
To Seward and Homer
© AVALON TRAVEL

of blooms. You can easily fill a whole day touring downtown, or just lying around a park for the one day in four that the sun shines. Explore Anchorage's far-flung corners such as the resort town of Girdwood south of the city (popular for winter skiing and summer hiking), rapidly growing Matanuska-Susitna Valley (home to the towns of Palmer and Wasilla), and grand mountain country at Hatcher Pass. Or spend a day researching the many places to go from Anchorage and the best ways to get there.

Of course, if you can't overcome the idea that "Alaska population center" is a contradiction in terms, you can simply breeze into town, make your connection, and quickly "get back to Alaska." But if you want a fully rounded experience of the 49th state, get to know Anchorage, *urban* Alaska, and come to your own conclusions.

CLIMATE

Two of the deciding factors in choosing Anchorage as a main construction camp for the Alaska Railroad were mild winters and comparatively low precipitation. The towering Alaska Range shelters Cook Inlet Basin from the frigid winter breath of the Arctic northerlies; the Kenai and Chugach Mountains cast a rain shadow over the basin, allowing only 15–20 percent of the annual precipitation that communities on the windward side of the ranges get. Anchorage receives around 20 inches of annual precipitation (10–12 inches of rain, 60–70 inches of snow), while Whittier, 40 miles away on the Gulf side of the Chugach, gets 175 inches. Anchorage's winter temperatures rarely drop much below 0°F, with only an occasional cold streak, compared with Fairbanks's frequent -40°F; its summer temperatures rarely rise above 65°F, compared with Fairbanks's 80s and 90s.

PLANNING YOUR TIME

Anchorage is an outstanding base for travelers to Alaska's heartland, with Denali National Park, the Kenai Peninsula, and a multitude of other attractions within a day's drive. The state's largest airport provides flights to all regions of the globe, and the Alaska Railroad has daily trains north to Denali and Fairbanks or south to Seward and Whittier. The city has long served as a hub for travelers, but it also offers many attractions not available elsewhere, and one could easily spend two or three days just exploring local museums, hiking trails, shops, and restaurants.

The city's highlights include its outstanding **Anchorage Museum** (the state's largest), the **Alaska Native Heritage Center,** the Alaska Heritage Museum, and an abundance of good restaurants, hip coffeehouses, hopping bars, **H2Oasis Indoor Water Park** for the kids, and two minor-league baseball teams—all that you might expect from the state's largest city. And don't forget the always-packed **Farmers Market** every summer weekend, with locally made crafts, tasty finger food, live music, and even a bit of fresh produce from the farmers. But with the natural beauty of Mt. McKinley and the Alaska Range visible beyond the city skyline on clear days, it's hard to forget that you're in Alaska.

And there are also attractions you would only find in an Alaskan city: a wonderful coastal trail that starts right downtown, great day-hiking in nearby **Chugach State Park,** fascinating **Turnagain Arm** with its enormous tides and beluga whales, and places to outfit yourself for any adventure in the Alaskan outdoors. Anchorage is within easy striking distance of some of the most exciting and extensive hiking, climbing, fishing, kayaking, river rafting, flightseeing, and wilderness areas. Budget travelers will enjoy reasonable food prices, inexpensive flights to the Lower 48, several hostels, and a good bus system.

Nearby to the south, the town of Girdwood is home to Alyeska Resort—Alaska's only significant ski area—and funky **Crow Creek Mine** where you still might find a gold nugget in your pan. A bit farther south is the much-photographed **Portage Glacier,** accessed by a tour boat from the Forest Service visitors center.

North of Anchorage the Glenn Highway passes a tiny Tanaina Native Alaskan village

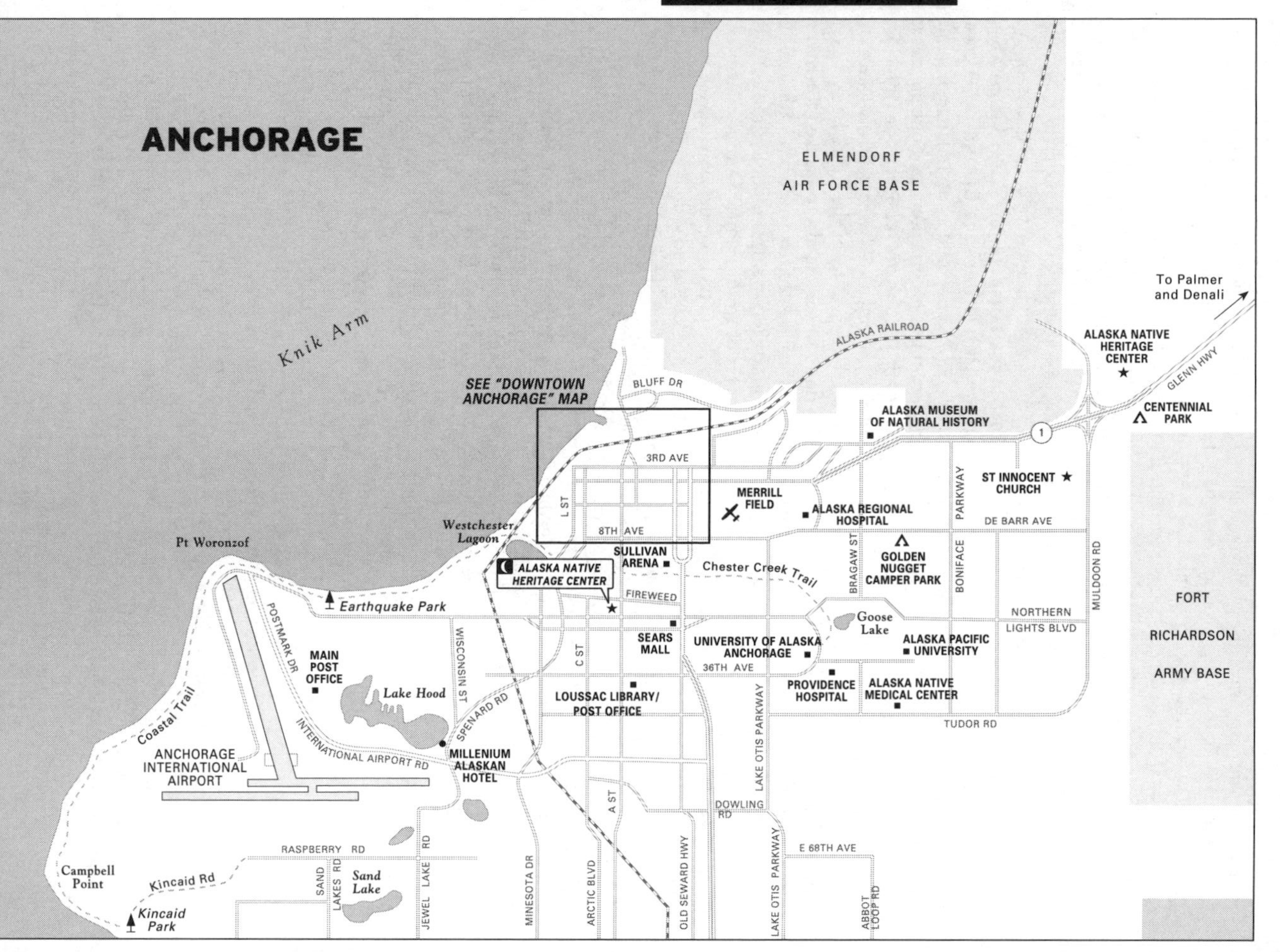
ANCHORAGE
ELMENDORF AIR FORCE BASE
Knik Arm
To Palmer and Denali
ALASKA RAILROAD
ALASKA NATIVE HERITAGE CENTER
GLENN HWY
BLUFF DR
SEE "DOWNTOWN ANCHORAGE" MAP
ALASKA MUSEUM OF NATURAL HISTORY
CENTENNIAL PARK
3RD AVE
ST INNOCENT CHURCH
MERRILL FIELD
PARKWAY
ALASKA REGIONAL HOSPITAL
L ST
8TH AVE
DE BARR AVE
Westchester Lagoon
Pt Woronzof
SULLIVAN ARENA
BRAGAW ST
GOLDEN NUGGET CAMPER PARK
BONIFACE
MULDOON RD
ALASKA NATIVE HERITAGE CENTER
Chester Creek Trail
FIREWEED
FORT RICHARDSON ARMY BASE
Earthquake Park
POSTMARK DR
Goose Lake
NORTHERN LIGHTS BLVD
WISCONSIN ST
SEARS MALL
UNIVERSITY OF ALASKA ANCHORAGE
ALASKA PACIFIC UNIVERSITY
MAIN POST OFFICE
C ST
36TH AVE
Lake Hood
PROVIDENCE HOSPITAL
ALASKA NATIVE MEDICAL CENTER
Coastal Trail
LOUSSAC LIBRARY/ POST OFFICE
SPENARD RD
TUDOR RD
INTERNATIONAL AIRPORT RD
LAKE OTIS PARKWAY
ANCHORAGE INTERNATIONAL AIRPORT
MILLENIUM ALASKAN HOTEL
A ST
DOWLING RD
RASPBERRY RD
E 68TH AVE
Campbell Point
Kincaid Rd
SAND LAKES RD
Sand Lake
JEWEL LAKE RD
MINESOTA DR
ARCTIC BLVD
OLD SEWARD HWY
ABBOT LOOP RD
Kincaid Park

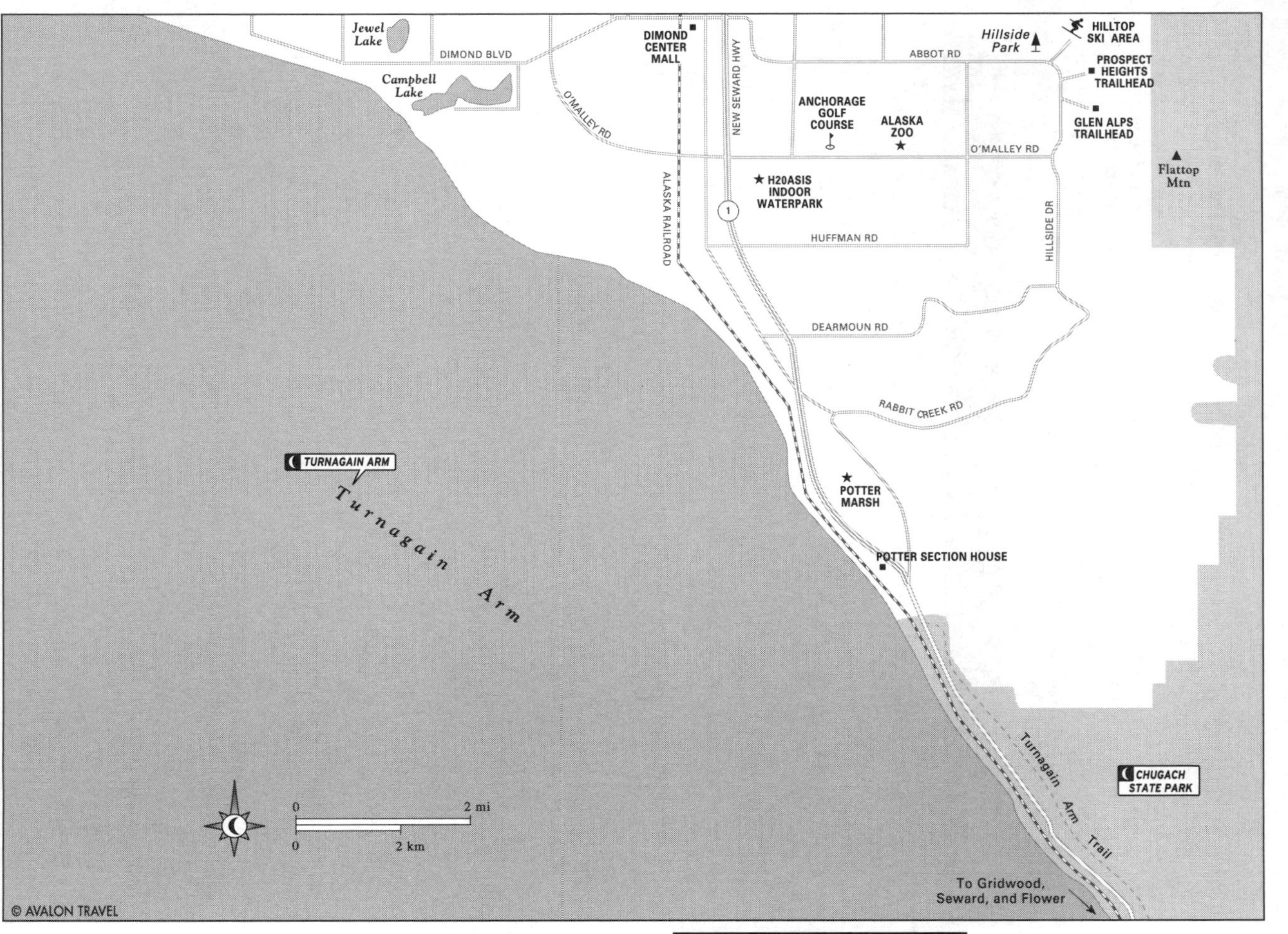

Jewel Lake
DIMOND BLVD
Campbell Lake
DIMOND CENTER MALL
O'MALLEY RD
NEW SEWARD HWY
ALASKA RAILROAD
1
Hillside Park
HILLTOP SKI AREA
ABBOT RD
PROSPECT HEIGHTS TRAILHEAD
GLEN ALPS TRAILHEAD
ANCHORAGE GOLF COURSE
ALASKA ZOO
O'MALLEY RD
Flattop Mtn
H20ASIS INDOOR WATERPARK
HUFFMAN RD
HILLSIDE DR
DEARMOUN RD
RABBIT CREEK RD
TURNAGAIN ARM
Turnagain Arm
POTTER MARSH
POTTER SECTION HOUSE
Turnagain Arm Trail
CHUGACH STATE PARK
0
2 mi
0
2 km
To Girdwood, Seward, and Flower
© AVALON TRAVEL

where Eklutna Historical Park houses a picturesque graveyard filled with spirit houses before emerging in the Matanuska-Susitna Valley (Mat-Su, for short), where the pastures and farms of the past are giving way to homes and strip malls for folks fleeing Anchorage housing prices and crowding. The valley's two main towns are booming Wasilla and semirural Palmer, home to a fun musk ox farm and the **Alaska State Fair,** a 12-day blast in late August–early September. North of the valley, the Talkeetna Mountains rise abruptly, bisected by a road over Hatcher Pass, where **Independence Mine State Historical Park** provides a base for day hikes or wintertime skis.

Sights

It doesn't take long to get the hang of downtown Anchorage. The blocks are square, with the lettered streets (A through L) going north–south and the numbered avenues (starting at 2nd Ave. just up the hill from the tracks) running east–west. Once you get east of the lettered streets they start over again using alphabetized names (Barrow, Cordova, Denali, Eagle, Fairbanks).

Beyond downtown, the city of Anchorage sprawls across the Anchorage Bowl, with hillside homes peering down on the masses below. A number of neighborhoods are scattered around Anchorage, but most travelers are likely to spend their time in downtown and **Midtown,** a nondescript Anytown, USA, collection of malls, shopping centers, supermarkets, fast-food joints, bars, movie theaters, discount stores, gas stations, and other businesses just a 20-minute walk or a 10-minute bus ride south of downtown. Midtown is encompassed by Northern Lights and Benson Boulevards between Minnesota Drive and Old Seward Highway. It isn't exactly a tourist attraction, but this, along with shopping malls on the south and east end of town, is where locals—and others looking to save money—spend their cash. Another large shopping district is along Dimond Boulevard in South Anchorage, where all the stalwarts are: Best Buy, Wal-Mart, Costco, Borders, CompUSA, and more.

DOWNTOWN

Log Cabin Visitors Center

Start your tour of downtown at the Anchorage Convention and Visitors Bureau (ACVB), a sod-roofed log cabin on the corner of 4th Avenue and F Street. The cabin isn't actually the main place for information; go out the back door to a more spacious visitors center where you'll find a plethora of brochures from around the state and helpful staff. Be sure to pick up a copy of the fat *Anchorage Big Wild Life,* which includes a downtown walking tour and an Anchorage-area driving tour, plus details on sights, attractions, activities, lodging, restaurants, and more.

The **ACVB office** (907/274-3531, www.anchorage.net) is open daily 7:30 A.M.–7 P.M. June–August, daily 8 A.M.–6 P.M. May and September, and daily 9 A.M.–4 P.M. October–April. The website is packed with information on the city and links to local businesses. Call 907/276-3200 for a recording of forthcoming events.

Free city buses (907/343-6543, www.peoplemover.org) run around downtown daily if you get tired of walking. They stop right in front of the ACVB. For a quick one-hour introduction to the city, hop on one of the red **Anchorage City Trolley Tours** (612 W. 4th Ave., 907/276-5603, $15) with daily departures on the hour 9 A.M.–6 P.M. May–mid-September.

Public Lands Center

Kitty-corner from the ACVB is the old Federal Building, which now houses the **Alaska Public Lands Information Center** (605 W. 4th Ave., 907/644-3661 or 866/869-6887, www.alaskacenters.gov, daily

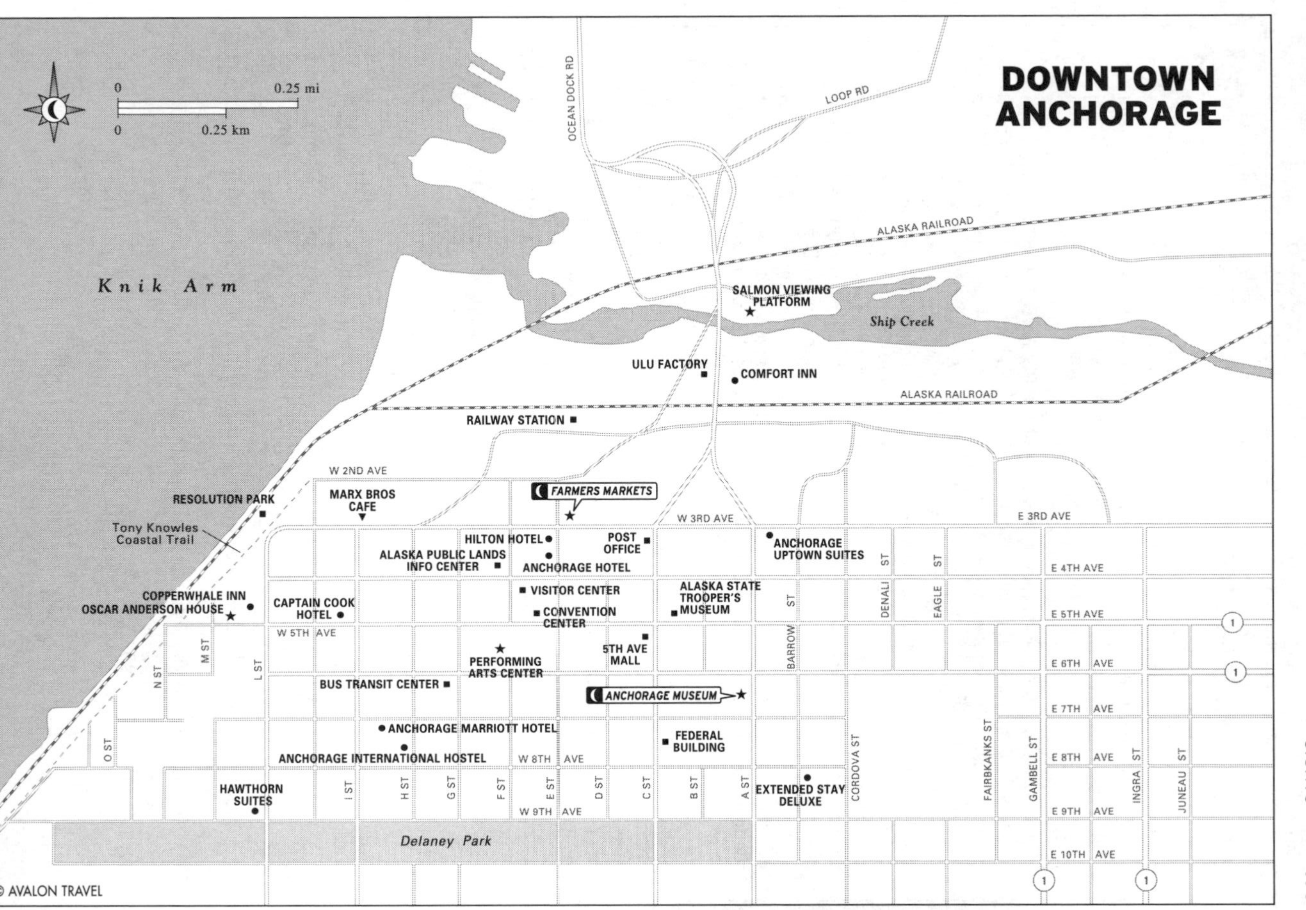
DOWNTOWN ANCHORAGE
Knik Arm
Ship Creek
Delaney Park
ALASKA RAILROAD
ALASKA RAILROAD
LOOP RD
OCEAN DOCK RD
W 2ND AVE
W 3RD AVE
E 3RD AVE
E 4TH AVE
E 5TH AVE
W 5TH AVE
E 6TH AVE
E 7TH AVE
E 8TH AVE
W 8TH AVE
E 9TH AVE
W 9TH AVE
E 10TH AVE
JUNEAU ST
INGRA ST
GAMBELL ST
FAIRBANKS ST
EAGLE ST
DENALI ST
CORDOVA ST
BARROW ST
A ST
B ST
C ST
D ST
E ST
F ST
G ST
H ST
I ST
L ST
M ST
N ST
O ST
SALMON VIEWING PLATFORM
COMFORT INN
ULU FACTORY
RAILWAY STATION
FARMERS MARKETS
ANCHORAGE UPTOWN SUITES
ALASKA STATE TROOPER'S MUSEUM
POST OFFICE
ANCHORAGE HOTEL
HILTON HOTEL
VISITOR CENTER
CONVENTION CENTER
5TH AVE MALL
ANCHORAGE MUSEUM
FEDERAL BUILDING
EXTENDED STAY DELUXE
PERFORMING ARTS CENTER
ANCHORAGE MARRIOTT HOTEL
ALASKA PUBLIC LANDS INFO CENTER
BUS TRANSIT CENTER
ANCHORAGE INTERNATIONAL HOSTEL
MARX BROS CAFE
CAPTAIN COOK HOTEL
RESOLUTION PARK
Tony Knowles Coastal Trail
COPPERWHALE INN
OSCAR ANDERSON HOUSE
HAWTHORN SUITES
0
0.25 mi
0
0.25 km
1
© AVALON TRAVEL

ANCHORAGE HISTORY

In June 1778, Captain James Cook sailed up what's now Turnagain Arm in Cook Inlet, reaching another dead end on his amazing search for the Northwest Passage. But he did dispatch William Bligh (of HMS *Bounty* fame) to explore, and he saw some Tanaina Indians in rich otter skins. George Vancouver, who'd also been on Cook's ship, returned in 1794 and noted Russian settlers in the area. A century later, prospectors began landing in the area and heading north to Southcentral Alaska's gold country, and in 1902 Alfred Brooks began mapping the Cook Inlet for the U.S. Geological Survey. In 1913, five settlers occupied Ship Creek, the point on the inlet where Anchorage now stands.

A year later, Congress passed the Alaska Railroad Act, and in April 1915 the route for the federally financed railroad from Seward to Fairbanks was made official: It would pass through Ship Creek, where a major staging area for workers and supplies would be located. This news traveled fast, and within a month a ramshackle tent city of nearly 2,000 railroad job seekers had sprung up. Things developed so quickly that in July, the U.S. Land Office auctioned off 650 parcels at the new town site. The settlement, renamed Anchorage, grew quickly, with water, telephone and power lines, sidewalks, and schools in place within a year.

SLUMPS AND SPURTS

Railroad laborers, earning 37 cents per hour (low for Alaska), went on strike in 1916, after which the minimum wage was raised to 45 cents per hour. The population continued to boom, topping out at around 7,000 in 1917. With World War I and completion of the southern portion of the railroad, the number of people dropped below 2,000 in 1920, when the town incorporated, electing its first mayor and city council. Through the 1930s, Anchorage held steady at 3,000-4,000 people, but World War II changed that in a hurry. The town's strategic location led to a huge influx of military personnel, when the Army's Fort Richardson and the Army Air Corps's Elmendorf Field were constructed outside of town. By 1950, Anchorage was a prosperous small city of over 11,000. In the following decade Anchorage also experienced the postwar boom, with the at-

9 A.M.–5 P.M. mid-May–early Sept., Mon.–Fri. 10 A.M.–5 P.M. early Sept.–mid-May). This is a great starting point to learn about federal lands in Alaska, including national parks and forests, wildlife refuges, and Bureau of Land Management areas. Displays introduce you to Alaska's wildlife and wild places, daily historical walks are offered throughout the summer, the bookstore has a good selection of Alaskan titles, and the auditorium is used for nature videos and talks.

A few blocks away is the **Department of Natural Resources Public Information Center** (550 W. 7th Ave., 907/269-8400, www.alaskastateparks.org, Mon.–Fri.). Located on the 12th floor, the information center has helpful staff and details on state parks, public-use cabins, where to pan for gold, state land sales, and much more.

Anchorage Museum

A massive $106 million expansion in 2009 transformed the Anchorage Museum (625 C St., 907/929-9200, www.anchoragemuseum.org, $10 adults, $8 seniors, $7 ages 3–12, younger children free) into the state's largest (170,000 square feet) and finest museum. One popular feature is the kid-friendly **Imaginarium Discovery Center,** with 80 hands-on science exhibits, including an amazing high-tech globe that displays today's weather patterns, an air cannon, and pulley chairs. Many exhibits focus on Alaskan science, especially earthquakes and volcanoes. Also on the first level is a planetarium and a gallery of Alaskan art, including Sydney Laurence's 6- by 10-foot oil of Mt. McKinley. The upper levels contain galleries featuring contemporary Native Alaskan art, Alaskan history, and rotating shows. Don't miss the

tendant shortages of housing and modern conveniences, which created the city's own construction mini-boom. In 1957, when Richfield Oil discovered black gold on the Kenai Peninsula, the oil companies started opening office buildings in the city, and the economy stabilized.

SINCE STATEHOOD

Much of Anchorage collapsed in the incredible **Good Friday earthquake** of March 27, 1964, which lasted an interminable five minutes, registering 9.2 on the Richter Scale. The north side of 4th Avenue wound up 8–10 feet lower than the south side of the street. A very rich residential section on the bluff overlooking Knik Arm was destroyed. Nine people were killed and upward of $300 million in damages were recorded. Anchorage was rebuilt, and because only a few large buildings survived the quake, nearly everything in the city was put up after 1964.

Though the pipeline doesn't come within 300 miles of Anchorage, oil money towers over the city in the form of tall office buildings scattered around town. The military still plays an important role in the local economy, with Elmendorf Air Force Base and Fort Richardson right on the margins of town, and military jets and surveillance planes a common presence in the sky. Tourism also affects Anchorage enormously, especially in the summer months when the city is a waypoint for many travelers. Anchorage fancies itself quite the cosmopolitan city, boasting dozens of arts organizations, a modern performing arts center, a 16-theater cinema with stadium seating, plus many fancy hotels, restaurants, cafés, and bars catering to the thousands of suits who fill the skyscrapers that gleam in the light of the midnight sun. Indeed, if Juneau is bureaucratic Alaska, and Fairbanks is rank-and-file Alaska, then Anchorage is corporate and commercial Alaska.

If you can't find it at an Anchorage store, it probably isn't sold anywhere in the state. And if you find it elsewhere, you'll probably pay more. For bush dwellers, Anchorage is a shopping trip disguised as a city. Put people from Bethel, Nome, or Homer in Anchorage for a day and they're likely to spend most of their time at Costco and Wal-Mart.

amazing second-floor collection of some 600 archaeological pieces on long-term loan from the Smithsonian Museum. In addition to exhibits, the Anchorage Museum has a fine gift shop and historical photos in the resource center. Watch Alaska films in the theater, or enjoy an upscale lunch at trendy **Muse Restaurant** (907/929-9210, www.marxcafe.com, closed Mon.). The museum is open daily 9 A.M.–5 P.M. (until 9 P.M. Thurs.) June–mid-September, and Sunday noon–6 P.M., Tuesday–Saturday 10 A.M.–6 P.M. mid-September–May. In the summer, free hour-long tours are offered, and local artists sell their crafts in the atrium. Outside is a two-acre commons, perfect for summer afternoons.

Performing Arts Center

Anchorage's central focal point is the **Alaska Center for the Performing Arts** (907/263-2900, www.myalaskacenter.com), better known as "the PAC," short for Performing Arts Center—an unusual brick-and-glass building with colorful Olympic-like rings of light around the top. Find it at 5th Avenue and G Street. Inside are three auditoriums with wonderful acoustics and horrific carpeting; wags say it looks like a pepperoni pizza. Hold the anchovies! Free tours of the center are offered Wednesdays at 1 P.M., and two IMAX films are screened throughout the summer: one on wolves, the other on the Great Land. The latter is narrated by Charlton Heston, so check your National Rifle Association pistols at the door. In addition, the center has an interesting slide show on the northern lights.

The spacious front lawn of the Performing Arts Center is **Town Square,** a fine flower-filled field of fecundity. It's a wonderful place to meet

Alaska Center for the Performing Arts

up with friends or just relax on a sunny summer day. **Egan Civic and Convention Center** is right across 5th Avenue, and the beautiful new **Dena'ina Civic and Convention Center** (www.anchorageconventiondisrict.com) at 600 W. 7th Avenue.

Museums and Historic Buildings

Anchorage is pretty short on historical buildings since much of the city was destroyed in the 1964 quake and most of the city's development and growth has taken place since the 1970s. The neighborhood around 2nd Avenue at F Street includes several of the original town-site homes constructed in the early 1900s, and historical panels describe the city's early days.

A few other structures survive from quieter times, including the **Oscar Anderson House Museum** (420 M St., 907/274-2336, $3 adults, $1 kids), open for 45-minute tours Monday–Friday noon–5 P.M. June–mid-September. This refurbished little bungalow—built in 1915 by Anchorage's first butcher—is the oldest frame residence in this young city. It reopens during the first two weekends of December, when it is festooned with traditional Swedish Christmas decorations. The Tony Knowles Coastal Trail passes right in front of the Oscar Anderson House, and adjacent is tiny **Elderberry Park,** a pleasant place to relax on a sunny afternoon, with picnic and playground facilities.

The free **Alaska State Trooper Museum** (245 W. 5th Ave., 907/279-5050 or 800/770-5050, www.alaskatroopermuseum.com, Mon.–Fri. 10 A.M.–4 P.M., Sat. noon–4 P.M.) is worth visiting to check out the gleaming 1952 Hudson Hornet patrol car.

A block from the Anchorage Museum is **Wolf Song of Alaska** (6th Ave. and C St., 907/274-9653, www.wolfsongalaska.org), a nonprofit organization dedicated to educating the public about wolves. It houses a small museum with exhibits and a gift shop.

Across the street from the old Federal Building is the **4th Avenue Theater,** built in 1947 and one of the few structures to survive the 1964 earthquake. Up the street and right next to the log cabin visitors center is **Old City Hall,** housing the offices of the ACVB. Step inside the lobby to view a few exhibits and historic photos from early Anchorage.

Ship Creek

Immediately north of downtown on West 1st Avenue is the **Alaska Railroad Depot,** where you can book train travel or check out the 1907 train engine out front. Behind it is **Ship Creek,** a favorite place to cast for king or silver salmon all summer long—it's probably the only place where you can catch kings within sight of office high-rises. But watch out for the quicksand-like mud at the mouth of the creek; it can trap unwary anglers.

Delaney Park

Enjoyable Delaney Park runs between 9th and 10th Avenues from L Street to Barrow Street. Known as the "park strip," early in Anchorage's history it marked the boundary where the town stopped and the wilderness started, and in 1923 the strip where the park is today was cleared as a firebreak. Since then it has served as a golf course, an airstrip, and now hosts half a dozen softball games every night of summer, tennis and basketball courts, and large grassy sections for Frisbee, Hacky Sack, tai chi, sunbathing, or people-watching. Right next to the park on the corner of 10th Avenue and I Street is a cage housing **Star, the pet reindeer.** The owners have had a succession of reindeer here since 1962; this is number six.

Resolution Park

A very popular stop for tour buses, visitors on foot, and the occasional (probably drunk) local is Resolution Park, on the west end of 3rd Avenue at L Street. This tiny city park consists of a viewing platform centered around a statue of Captain James Cook, who discovered what is now called Cook Inlet in 1778. The park is named for his ship, the *Resolution*. On clear days you'll delight in the mountain-scape vistas. **Mt. McKinley** (many locals call it Denali) rises 125 miles to the north, and the low mountain just northwest across Cook Inlet is aptly named **Sleeping Lady** (the maps call it Mt. Susitna). Behind it, and just a bit south, stands a chain of active volcanoes that dump ash on Anchorage every few years, including **Mt. Spurr** and **Mt. Redoubt.** If you have eagle eyes and crystalline weather, you might pick out a third volcano, **Mt. Iliamna,** far to the southwest. Out of sight is yet a fourth volcano, **Mt. Augustine,** which last spewed ash in 1986.

Tony Knowles Coastal Trail

This is one of Anchorage's highlights, a wonderful 11-mile asphalt track that wends its way along the shore from downtown past the airport to Kincaid Park at Point Campbell, where the Knik and Turnagain Arms meet. From downtown, the trail is accessible from the west ends of 2nd, 5th, and 9th Avenues, with additional access at Westchester Lagoon, Earthquake Park, Point Woronzof, and Kincaid. Stroll the trail a ways, at least through the tunnel, beyond which you leave downtown behind and emerge into a new world: the grand sweep of the Arm,

feeding ducks at Westchester Lagoon

tidal flats, railroad tracks, and a residential neighborhood. On warm summer evenings this trail is more like a freeway, with people on every kind of wheels imaginable: bike riders, inline skaters, skateboarders, and babies in carriages. In winter they trade the wheels for skis. The Coastal Trail gets especially crowded around duck-filled **Westchester Lagoon,** a mile south of downtown, which is also the city's favorite wintertime ice skating rink.

A second paved path intersects the Coastal Trail at Westchester Lagoon, the **Chester Creek Trail,** which creates another greenbelt across Anchorage. This one heads east along the creek, continuing for five miles to the University of Alaska at Anchorage campus.

BEYOND DOWNTOWN

Earthquake Park, out on West Northern Lights Boulevard near the airport, has interpretive signs about the Big One on Good Friday 1964, and a view of the skyline and the Chugach Mountains. But the views are even more dramatic from **Point Woronzof,** another mile or so out. Tony Knowles Coastal Trail parallels the coast along Earthquake Park and Point Woronzof; it continues from downtown all the way south to **Kincaid Park.** And speaking of Kincaid, the trails here are a destination for hikers and mountain bikers all summer, and cross-country skiers when the snow flies.

Covering 11 acres of land at Campbell Airstrip Road off Tudor Road, the **Alaska Botanical Garden** (907/770-3692, www.alaskabg.org, daily year-round, $5) is home to more than 1,100 varieties of plants. An information kiosk is at the entrance, and a pleasant one-mile nature trail leads through the perennial, rock, wildflower, and herb gardens. Take a guided tour of the garden daily at 1 P.M. June–August.

Alaska Native Heritage Center

Located on a 26-acre site facing the Chugach Mountains, the Alaska Native Heritage Center (907/330-8000 or 800/315-6608, www.alaskanative.net, daily 9 A.M.–5 P.M. mid-May–mid-Sept., $25 adults, $21 seniors, $17 ages 7–16, kids under 7 free) provides an excellent introduction to Native Alaskan culture in the state. A joint ticket provides access to both the Anchorage Museum and the Heritage center for $26. The central "Welcome House" has a variety of exhibits and is used for concerts and demonstrations. Outside, five traditional village settings have been recreated around a small lake, and Native Alaskan guides explain Alaska's various cultures. The Heritage Center is east of downtown near the intersection of the Glenn Highway and Muldoon Road. A free shuttle runs from the downtown Log Cabin Visitor Center and the Anchorage Museum four times daily in the summer.

Heritage Museum

Housed in the lobby of the Wells Fargo bank in Midtown, and officially called the **Alaska Heritage Museum at Wells Fargo** (Northern Lights Blvd. and C St., 907/265-2834, www.wellsfargohistory.com, Mon.–Fri. noon–4 P.M. late May–early Sept., Mon.–Fri. noon–4 P.M. early Sept.–late May, free), this is one of the state's largest privately owned collections of Alaskan artifacts and books. It will keep you spellbound for hours, if you have the time. Be sure to check out the 3.2-pound (!) gold nugget found in 1963 near Ruby, Alaska. There are only a handful of the other highlights—many Native Alaskan baskets, parkas made from bird skins and walrus intestines, Sydney Laurence's paintings, Nome and Fairbanks newspapers from the early 1900s, and bookcases filled with rare books and maps. This little gem of a museum is not to be missed.

Natural History Museum

Located off Mountain View Drive on the northeast end of town, the **Alaska Museum of Natural History** (201 N. Bragaw St., 907/274-2400, www.alaskamuseum.org, Tues.–Sat. 10 A.M.–5 P.M., $5 adults, $3 ages 6–12, younger children free, $15 families) houses exhibits on dinosaurs, wildlife, rocks, and minerals.

Up in the Air

The **Alaska Aviation Heritage Museum** (4721 Aircraft Dr., 907/248-5325, www.

alaskaairmuseum.org, daily 9 A.M.–5 P.M. mid-May–mid-Sept., Wed.–Sun. 9 A.M.–5 P.M. mid-Sept.–mid-May, $10 adults, $8 seniors, $6 ages 5–12, younger children free) is off the Lake Hood exit from International Airport Road. This unusual museum displays 25 vintage aircraft in three connected hangars—from a 1928 Stearman up to an old Alaska Airlines 737—as well as Japanese artifacts from the World War II Aleutian Island battles and historical photos. The theaters show videos on early Alaskan aviation, and the museum fronts on **Lake Hood,** the world's largest seaplane base, where floatplanes take off and land almost constantly in the summer.

One of the nation's busiest airfields is **Merrill Field,** on the east side of town along the Glenn Highway. There are more than 230,000 takeoffs and landings each year; overall, Alaska has 16 times as many aircraft per capita as the Lower 48 states (but it also has a far higher airplane accident rate).

Alaska Zoo

Located two miles east of New Seward Highway, the zoo (4731 O'Malley Rd., 907/346-2133, www.alaskazoo.org, daily 9 A.M.–6 P.M. mid-May–mid-Sept., daily 10 A.M.–5 P.M. mid-Sept.–mid-May, $12 adults, $9 seniors, $6 ages 3–17, younger children free) is connected by a special hourly shuttle bus from the Transit Center. The zoo has nice grounds, enjoyable shady paths, and all the Alaskan animals, plus a number of more exotic critters. If you have kids, they'll enjoy it, especially the star attractions: Ahpun and Louie, the polar bears. You can watch the bears' underwater antics through the glass of their swimming pool, or check out the polar bear cam on the zoo's website.

Entertainment and Events

PERFORMING ARTS

Anchorage's active cultural scene centers on the **Alaska Center for the Performing Arts** (a.k.a. PAC, 5th Ave. and G St., 907/263-2900, www.myalaskacenter.com) downtown. There are events throughout the year, including modern dance, ballet, Broadway musicals, comedy troupes, opera, and concerts by nationally known artists, along with winter performances by the **Anchorage Concert Association** (www.anchorageconcerts.org), **Anchorage Symphony Orchestra** (907/274-8668 or 800/478-7328, www.anchoragesymphony.org), the **Anchorage Concert Chorus** (907/274-7464, www.anchorageconcertchorus.org), and the **Anchorage Opera** (907/279-2557, www.anchorageopera.org).

Call 907/566-2787 for a recording of upcoming events at the PAC and elsewhere. Tickets are available at the PAC box office, in Carrs stores, and at 800/478-7328 or www.centertix.net. Check Friday's *Anchorage Daily News* (www.adn.com/play) for upcoming events.

Anchorage is a city that showers appreciation on traveling musicians who come out of their way to visit the city, particularly those with a folk-rock bent. Many of Anchorage's best performances arrive courtesy of **Whistling Swan Productions** (www.whistlingswan.net); visit their website for upcoming shows.

For plays, check out productions by **Cyrano's Off-Center Playhouse** (413 D St., 907/274-2599, www.cyranos.org), **Out North Contemporary Art House** (3800 DeBarr Rd., 907/279-3800, www.outnorth.org), and **Anchorage Community Theatre** (1133 E. 70th Ave., 907/344-4713, www.actalaska.org).

NIGHTLIFE

The best sources for Anchortown action are the Friday ***Anchorage Daily News*** (www.adn.com/play) and the ***Anchorage Press*** (www.anchoragepress.com), a free weekly newspaper available in racks all over town. Anchorage has joined many other American cities by

banning smoking in bars and virtually all other indoor places.

Bars and Clubs

Anchorage is a *Cheers*-type town, with lots of corner bars and local pubs tucked away. Downtown, a popular place is **F Street Station** (4th Ave. and F St.), which also serves good-value lunches and dinners. **Darwin's Theory** (426 G St., 907/277-5322) attracts a fun after-work crowd. There is free hot pepper schnapps—if you can stomach it—when the bartender rings the bell (quite often some evenings).

Popular Anchorage sports bars include **Peanut Farm** (5227 Old Seward Hwy., 907/563-3283, www.wemustbenuts.com), **Crossroads Lounge** (1402 Gambell St., 907/276-9014), and **Eddie's Sports Bar** (6300 Old Seward Hwy., 907/563-3970).

Anchorage's favorite downtown bar is **Humpy's Great Alaskan Alehouse** (610 W. 6th Ave., 907/276-2337, www.humpys.com). Drop by on any night of the week to rub shoulders (and arms, legs, and other body parts—it gets mighty crowded) with a hip, raucous, and youthful crowd. The bar has dozens of microbrews on tap, the kitchen cranks out pub fare, bands play nightly, and there's never a cover. Humpy's is a must-see place if you're staying downtown, especially if you're single (or pretending to be).

Chilkoot Charlie's (2435 Spenard Rd. at Fireweed Lane, 907/279-1692, www.koots.com) is a ramshackle building where you can do some serious jumping up and down to real rock and roll and generally have a night of good raunchy fun—so long as you don't ask the wrong guy's girl (or the wrong girl's guy) to dance. There are three separate dance floors and 10 (!) bars inside. It's big enough to get lost in. The main stage has loud and very live rock, while the other dance floors are filled with folks dancing to DJ Top 40 or whatever else is hot. 'Koots is a love-it-or-hate-it sort of place; if you aren't into the bar cruisin' and pickup scene, try elsewhere. The motto should give you fair warning: "We cheat the *other* guy and pass the savings on to *you!*" But you should at least go here to say you didn't miss the most famous place in town. 'Koots gets extremely crowded on weekend nights (cover charge), so you may have to wait quite a while to get in if you come after 10 P.M. You can't miss Chilkoot's: just look for the tall lighted windmill.

Chef's Inn (825 W. Northern Lights Blvd., 907/272-1341) is Anchorage's "Blues Central," with live bluesy bands nightly. The bar attracts leather-clad bikers and others. There is good food (especially the French dip) and great blues tunes.

Downtown's **Rumrunners** (415 E St., 907/278-4493, www.rumrunnersak.com) is a spacious no-cover DJ and live music club. A few blocks away is **McGinley's Irish Pub** (645 G St., 907/279-1782, www.mcginleyspub.com), with Guinness on tap, weekend bands, and no cover.

Several Anchorage bars offer a quiet and romantic atmosphere. If you luck into a clear evening, have packed something a little dressy, and don't mind blowing two days' budget on a beer, head up to the **Crow's Nest** (4th Ave. and K St., 907/276-6000) atop the Captain Cook Hotel—the view is worth the effort. The **Millennium Hotel** (4800 Spenard Rd., 907/243-2300 or 800/544-0553) has an upscale bar with outdoor seating overlooking Lake Hood.

Gay and Lesbian

If your boyfriend or girlfriend happens to be of the same sex as you, pop into **Mad Myrna's** (530 E. 5th Ave., 907/276-9762, www.alaska.net/~madmyrna) or **The Raven** (708 E. 4th Ave., 907/276-9672). Myrna's has drag shows on Fridays, karaoke Thursdays, and DJ tunes on Fridays and Saturdays; Raven is a pool-shootin' joint. **PrideFest** (www.anchoragepride.com) in mid-June is Alaska's big coming-out party, so to speak. There's also a **Gay and Lesbian Community Center** (336 E. 5th Ave., 907/929-4528, www.idntityinc.org) just up from Mad Myrna's.

MOVIES

The downtown Alaska Center for the Performing Arts (5th Ave. and G St., 907/263-2900, www.myalaskacenter.com) offers photo shows on the **northern lights,** daily on the hour 9 A.M.–9 P.M. all summer.

Bear Tooth Theatrepub (1230 W. 27th Ave., 907/276-4200, www.beartooththeatre.net) has a winning combination: inexpensive second-run and art-house movies ($3), tasty light meals (including tacos, nachos, salads, burritos, and pizzas), plus brewery-fresh draft beer. It's a great place with a family atmosphere, and it's run by the same geniuses who created Moose's Tooth Pub & Pizzeria. You can eat downstairs and drink while watching the movie; upstairs is reserved for underage kids. It also has a restaurant area (very noisy) in the lobby for those who just want a meal in a family setting, and the adjacent **Bear Tooth Grill** with a big menu of burgers, Mexican platters, pasta, and seafood. Bear Tooth is highly recommended.

See what's showing at local theaters by visiting www.anchoragemovies.com. Anchorage's main theater action is the **Century 16** (36th Ave. and A St., 907/929-3456), where all 16 theaters have stadium seating and reclining chairs. Other Anchorage multiplexes include **Totem 8** (3131 Muldoon Rd., 907/566-3329), **Fireweed 7** (Fireweed Lane and New Seward Hwy., 907/566-3328), and **Dimond Center 9** (Dimond Mall, Dimond Blvd. and Old Seward Hwy., 907/566-3327).

EVENTS

Winter is the time for Anchorage's best-known events, the Iditarod and Fur Rendezvous, but the city is certainly full of life in the summer. Check the Anchorage Convention and Visitors Bureau website (www.anchorage.net) for a complete listing of events.

Summer

Anchorage's most popular ongoing event is the **Anchorage Market & Festival** (907/272-5634, www.anchoragemarkets.com), which takes place at the parking lot on 3rd Avenue and E Street Saturday–Sunday 10 A.M.–6 P.M. mid-May–mid-September. It features over 300 vendors selling fresh produce, quality arts and crafts, and great food. Don't miss it! A smaller market takes place Wednesday afternoons at Northway Mall.

Every Wednesday and Friday at noon, head downtown to 4th Avenue and E Street for free **Music in the Park** (907/279-5650, www.anchoragedowntown.org) next to the visitors center. Other events take place here most other weekday afternoons in the summer.

Anchorage has not just one but two different semipro baseball teams—the **Anchorage Bucs** (907/561-2827, www.anchoragebucs.com) and the **Anchorage Glacier Pilots** (907/274-3627, www.glacierpilots.com)—so there's usually a game worth watching June–early August. Past players have included such pro stars as Reggie Jackson, Dave Winfield, Mark McGuire, and Randy Johnson. Games take place at Mulcahy Stadium at East 16th Avenue and Cordova Street.

The **Arctic Thunder Air Show** (907/552-7469, www.elmendorf.af.mil) at Elmendorf Air Force Base comes around each June, with a stunning performance by the Air Force's Thunderbirds.

Three Barons Renaissance Faire (907/868-8012, www.3barons.org) takes place in early June at Hilltop Ski Area, and the crowd gets into the act by pelting rotten acting with rotten tomatoes. The **Spenard Solstice Street Party** (www.spenardsolstice.com) brings an offbeat parade, live music, and food booths to Spenard, while the serious athletes race in the big **Mayor's Midnight Sun Marathon** (www.mayorsmarathon.com).

Held at Kincaid Park in June, **Blues on the Green** (907/272-1341) attracts such acclaimed artists as Otis Rush, Johnny Winter, and Bo Diddley. There's a **4th of July** parade downtown, but when the fireworks show starts at midnight the sky still isn't very dark!

Also in early July, the **Bear Paw Festival** (907/694-4702, www.cer.org) comes to nearby Eagle River, with a classic car show, races, a chili cook-off, carnival rides, and the state's biggest parade.

Several of the biggest "local" events—the State Fair in Palmer, the Girdwood Forest Fair, the Talkeetna Bluegrass Festival, the Mountain Marathon in Seward, and the KBBI Concert on the Lawn in Homer—are not in Anchorage. But if you're around when any of these are happening, get out of town to where the fun really is.

Winter

In recent years, tourism to Alaska has increased in the winter months as visitors discover what Alaskans already know—that winter opens up a panoply of outdoor options. Several companies specialize in winter tours and activities; see the visitors center for brochures.

The **Anchorage Folk Festival** (907/566-2334, www.anchoragefolkfestival.org) is a major winter diversion, with free concerts that fill two consecutive weekends in late January. Concerts take place on the campus of the University of Alaska Anchorage.

In mid-February, the **Fur Rendezvous** (907/274-1177, www.furrondy.net) is one the city's biggest annual events, with all sorts of fun activities during this 10-day-long festival. A carnival packs a downtown lot, and there are car races, fireworks, snow sculpture and ice carving contests, dress balls, concerts, ski races, dog-pulling contests, the world championship sled dog race, and a very popular run-with-the-reindeer event (slightly) modeled after the running of the bulls in Pamplona.

The one Alaskan event that always attracts national attention is the **Iditarod Trail Sled Dog Race** (907/376-5155, www.iditarod.com) from Anchorage to Nome. The start is in downtown Anchorage in early March.

Another very popular event is the **Great Alaska Shootout** (907/786-1250, www.shootout.net) basketball tournament that takes place in Sullivan Arena each November and features seven top college teams and the lowly University of Alaska Seawolves. This one gets national media attention because it's so early in the year.

The **Nordic Skiing Association of Anchorage** (907/276-7609, www.anchoragenordicski.com) keeps dozens of miles of local trails groomed, and puts on such events as the **Tour of Anchorage** (www.tourofanchorage.com) in early March. The **Ski for Women** (907/279-9581, www.alaskaskiforwomen.org) in early February is the largest North American ski event for women, attracting more than 1,500 participants.

Spring Carnival and Slush Cup, in mid-April, is a wet and wild event for skiers as they try to cross a slushy pond at Alyeska Resort (907/754-1111, www.alyeskaresort.com).

Shopping

Although big-city folks sometimes complain that Anchorage doesn't have the fancy boutiques they're accustomed to finding, it *does* have just about every other sort of place—from Sam's Club to Nordstrom. The city is a car haven, so many of these stores are scattered in the various shopping malls that help give Anchorage its "charming" urban sprawl.

Downtown Anchorage's **5th Avenue Mall** includes two big stores—JCPenny and Nordstrom—along with several dozen storefronts on four levels. The city's largest mall is **Dimond Center** (www.dimondcenter.com) on the south side at Dimond Boulevard and Old Seward Highway. Other malls include **The Mall at Sears** (Northern Lights Blvd. and Seward Hwy., www.mallatsears.com) and **Northway Mall** (Airport Heights Dr. and Glenn Hwy., www.northwaymallak.com). Anchorage has all the megastores, including Wal-Mart, Fred Meyer, Costco, Sam's Club, Lowes, Home Depot, Toys 'R' Us, Barnes & Noble, ad nauseam.

GIFTS AND NATIVE ART

Much of downtown is given over to shops selling tourist doodads, particularly along 3rd and 4th Avenues, where you'll find everything from $2 made-in-China trinkets to $20,000 sculptures.

One People (425 D St., 907/274-4063) has a fine selection of Native Alaskan art in a convenient downtown location. Also check out the nonprofit **Alaska Native Arts Foundation** (500 W. 6th Ave., 907/258-2623, www.alaskanativearts.org), which represents hundreds of artists. One of the finest places to buy Native Alaskan crafts is the out-of-the-way **Alaska Native Medical Center Gift Shop** (4315 Diplomacy Dr. off East Tudor Rd., 907/729-1122, www.anmc.org). Excellent grass baskets, dolls, masks, yo-yos, and more are sold on consignment. Another recommended place is the gift shop at the **Alaska Native Heritage Center** (Glenn Hwy. and Muldoon Rd., 907/330-8000 or 800/315-6608, www.alaskanative.net, Mon.–Fri. 10 A.M.–2 P.M.).

An unusual (and very expensive) purchase to consider is *qiviut:* caps, scarves, shawls, sweaters, or baby booties, hand-knitted by Native Alaskans from the wool of domestic musk oxen (the musk ox farm is outside of Palmer). Many times warmer and lighter than wool, these fine knits can be seen and salivated over at **Oomingmak Co-op** (604 H St., 907/272-9225 or 888/360-9665, www.qiviut.com).

GALLERIES

On the **First Friday** of each month Anchorage's art scene comes alive with openings, hors d'oeuvres, and the chance to meet regional artists at a dozen or so galleries. Check the Friday *Anchorage Daily News* or the weekly *Anchorage Press* for details.

Anchorage's premier gallery is the **International Gallery of Contemporary Art** (427 D St., 907/279-1116, www.igcaalaska.org, Tues.–Sun. noon–4 P.M.), with something new each month from top regional artists.

Three good places to buy original artwork in Anchorage are **Artique** (314 G St., 907/277-1663, www.artiqueltd.com), **Artic Rose Gallery** (420 L St., 907/279-3911, www.articrosegallery.com), and the jam-packed **Aurora Fine Arts Gallery** (737 W. 5th Ave., 907/274-0234, www.aurorafineart-alaska.com).

An outstanding option is the **Anchorage Market & Festival** (907/272-5634, www.anchoragemarkets.com) held at the parking lot on 3rd Avenue and E Street every weekend in summer. The market has works by Alaskan painters, photographers, potters, and others.

OUTDOOR OUTFITTERS

Anchorage is an excellent place to stock up on outdoor gear before heading into Alaska's bush. The biggest place to shop—and one of the best—is **REI** (907/272-4565, www.rei.com) on the corner of Northern Lights Boulevard and Spenard Road. "REI" stands for Recreation Equipment Inc. This Seattle-based cooperative, where members get an end-of-the-year dividend on their purchases, has a knowledgeable staff who offer free clinics and talks throughout the year. You can also rent canoes, kayaks, tents, backpacks, skis, snowshoes, and other outdoor equipment from REI.

Another excellent outdoor store with a technically adept staff is **Alaska Mountaineering & Hiking** (2633 Spenard Rd., 907/272-1811, www.alaskamountaineering.com)—better known as AMH—just a block from REI. Though much smaller, AMH often has equipment unavailable elsewhere. This is where the hard-core climbers and backcountry skiers go.

Check the bulletin boards at AMH and REI for used gear and travel partners. Or cross the street to **Play it Again Sports** (907/278-7529, www.playitagainsports.com), where used equipment of all sorts is available, from backpacks and tents to baseball gloves and fishing poles. They also buy used gear if you need a little cash on your way out of town.

Downtown shoppers head to the **Army/Navy Store** (320 W. 4th Ave., 907/279-2401, www.army-navy-store.com) for more traditional Alaskan outdoor clothing and boots. **B&J Commercial** (2749 C St., 907/274-6113, www.bnjsg.com) has a downstairs packed with sport and commercial fishing supplies. This is where you'll find the really heavy-duty clothing and equipment at fair prices.

BOOKS AND MUSIC

Alaska's largest independent bookstore is **Title Wave Books** (1360 W. Northern Lights Blvd., next to REI, 907/278-9283 or 888/598-9283, www.wavebooks.com). Offering a fine choice of new and used titles, this is a great hangout spot, with a literate crowd and an adjacent Kaladi Brothers shop to sip coffee and surf the Web. Also in Midtown is **Metro Music and Books** (530 E. Benson Blvd., 907/279-8622), with a big selection of CDs, any of which you can listen to before deciding to buy.

Borders Books & Music (1100 E. Dimond Blvd., 907/344-4099) features books and CDs, plus an espresso café. Even bigger (and more centrally located) is **Barnes & Noble Bookseller** (200 E. Northern Lights Blvd., 907/279-7323 or 888/279-7323). In addition to books and CDs, you'll find an impressive magazine selection, plus a Starbucks.

Recreation

SUMMER

Hiking and Horseback Rides

One of the most popular hiking trails in Alaska is the 1.5-mile path to the summit of **Flattop Mountain** within Chugach State Park. The trailhead is on the southeastern edge of Anchorage, so you'll need a car to get there.

The **Alaska Mountaineering Club** (907/272-1811, www.mcak.org) holds meetings at 7:30 P.M. on the third Wednesday of each month at the First United Methodist Church (9th Ave. and G St.). Visitors are welcome to enjoy the presentations, and it only costs $15 to join the club and go along on any of their frequent outings.

Alaska Horse Rides (907/720-7433, www.alaskahorserides.com) and **Horse Trekkin Alaska** (907/868-3728, www.horsetrekkinalaska.com) both offer horseback rides in Anchorage parks.

Biking

Anchorage has 200 miles of urban cycling and jogging trails; pick up bike trail maps at the downtown visitors center. A delightfully easy ride—it's all paved—goes 11 miles from the west end of 2nd Avenue along the Tony Knowles Coastal Trail, past Westchester Lagoon, Earthquake Park, and Point Woronzof, and then all the way to Kincaid Park at Point Campbell, out on the western tip of the city. The Chester Creek Trail meets the Coastal Trail at Westchester Lagoon and takes you almost five miles to Goose Lake, where you can take a dip if you're hot. Or just bomb around to wherever the wind blows you. Note, however, that the major Anchorage arteries are not especially bike-friendly, so you may want to stick to the side streets to avoid contending with exhaust fumes and speeding pickup trucks. Dirt biking and hiking trails abound within Kincaid Park, Hillside Park, and Far North Bicentennial Park, or you can head up Powerline Pass Trail inside Chugach State Park, Eklutna Lake (bike rentals available on-site), or out on the 40-mile Resurrection Pass from the town of Hope.

Based in Anchorage, the **Arctic Bicycle Club** (907/566-0177, www.arcticbike.org) organizes races and tours and has a very helpful website. **Alaska Backcountry Bike Tours** (907/746-5018 or 866/354-2453, www.mountainbikealaska.com) guides all-day cycling trips into backcountry areas around Anchorage.

For mountain bike rentals, head to **Downtown Bicycle Rental** (333 W. 4th Ave., 907/279-3334, www.alaska-bike-rentals.com) or **Pablo's Bicycle Rentals** (440 L St., 907/250-2871, www.pablobicyclerentals.com); both are close to the Coastal Trail. In Midtown, rent from **Coastal Trail Rentals**

(4800 Spenard Rd., 907/301-2165, www.coastaltrailrentals.com).

Glacier Tours

Several companies have downtown Anchorage offices promoting boat day-tours to glaciers in Prince William Sound (via Whittier) or Resurrection Bay (via Seward). These include Prince William Sound tours from **Phillips Tours and Cruises** (www.26glaciers.com), **Prince William Sound Cruises and Tours** (www.princewilliamsound.com), and **Major Marine Tours** (www.majormarine.com), plus Resurrection Bay trips from **Major Marine Tours** (www.majormarine.com). The companies can arrange bus transport to the starting points in Seward or Whittier, or you can ride the Alaska Railroad. Also popular are the day trips from Anchorage to Portage Glacier operated by **Gray Line of Alaska** (www.graylinealaska.com).

Flightseeing

The best way to get a bird's-eye view of the Anchorage area is from a bird's-eye vantage point: in an airplane. Anchorage has a large number of companies offering flightseeing; see the Yellow Pages under "Aircraft Charter" for the full list, or visit the flightseeing links on www.anchorage.net. Two respected Lake Hood operations have been around for many years: **Rust's Flying Service** (907/243-1595 or 800/544-2299, www.flyrusts.com) and **Regal Air** (907/243-8535, www.regal-air.com). Also check out **Spernak Airways** (907/272-9475, www.spernakair.com), located at Merrill Field.

Typical flights include a 90-minute flight over the Chugach Mountains and Knik Glacier ($200 pp); a three-hour flight over Prince William Sound and Columbia Glacier ($365, includes a remote water landing); and a three-hour flight over Mt. McKinley ($365, may include a glacier landing). The air taxis also feature fly-in fishing trips, primarily to the Susitna River area, where Rust's has rental cabins available. Charter service may be the way to go if you have a group of four or more people and a specific destination, such as a public cabin in Chugach National Forest.

Rock Climbing

Alaska Rock Gym (4840 Fairbanks St., 907/562-7265, www.alaskarockgym.com) has climbing walls, classes, a pro shop, locker rooms, and a weight room. For the real thing, most folks head south to Turnagain Arm, which is also popular with ice climbers in the winter. Talk to folks at AMH or REI for details on other climbing options.

Bird-Watching

Anchorage is home to a surprising diversity of bird species in the summer. The **Anchorage Audubon Society** (907/276-7034, www.anchorageaudubon.org) offers bird-watching field trips, sells a helpful Anchorage birding map, and maintains the **bird hotline** (907/338-2473) with the latest unusual sightings.

Fishing and Rafting

Although Anchorage sits along Cook Inlet, wild tides and strong winds create notoriously treacherous conditions. As a result, there are no charter-boat fishing operations out of Anchorage. A popular salmon-fishing stream, **Ship Creek,** flows right through downtown and has good runs of king salmon (late May–July) and silver salmon (Aug.–mid-Sept.). You can also rub shoulders with fellow anglers in mid-summer at **Bird Creek,** 25 miles south of town on the Seward Highway.

The downtown visitor center has brochures for many sportfishing options on the Kenai Peninsula, just a couple of hours by car from Anchorage. To figure out where the fish are running, or what the local regulations are, call Fish and Game (907/344-0541, recorded message 907/349-4687) or visit the Public Lands Information Center downtown for a copy of the fishing regulations. Both the *Anchorage Daily News* (www.adn.com/outdoors) and the *Anchorage Press* publish weekly fishing reports for the Anchorage area.

Increasingly popular are fly-in fishing trips. All the local air-taxi services offer guided or unguided trips to nearby rivers and lakes for world-class salmon fishing.

Two companies lead white-water trips down the wild Six Mile Creek near Hope: **Chugach Outdoor Center** (907/277-7238 or 866/277-7238, www.chugachoutdoorcenter.com) and **Nova Riverrunners** (907/745-5753 or 800/746-5753, www.novalaska.com).

H2Oasis Indoor Waterpark

If you have children, don't miss H2Oasis Indoor Waterpark (1520 O'Malley Rd., 907/522-4420 or 888/426-2747, www.h2oasiswaterpark.com, daily 10 A.M.–9 P.M. summer, reduced school-year hours), a cavernous indoor water park near the intersection of O'Malley Road and New Seward Highway on the south end of Anchorage. On busy weekends half the kids in town seem to be here, splashing in the wave pool, shooting jets of water at each other from the pirate ship, gliding down the lazy river, zipping through the body slide, and riding several fast water rides, including the roller coaster–like Master Blaster. Hot tubs are reserved for the over-16 set. Entrance is $24 ages 13 and up, $19 ages 3–12, and free for younger children with a paying adult. Towel and swimsuit rentals are available, and the food court sells greasy snacks.

Swimming

If you're lucky enough to be in Anchorage during a hot spell and want to cool off under the bright blue sky, head out to **Lake Spenard/Lake Hood** (the two are actually one connected lake). Go down Spenard Road toward the airport, then right on Lakeshore Drive. **Jewel Lake** also has swimming on Dimond Boulevard between Jewel Lake and Sand Lake Roads in the southwest corner of the city. The most developed outdoor swimming is at **Goose Lake,** near the University of Alaska Anchorage on Northern Lights Boulevard between Lake Otis Parkway and Bragaw Street, accessible on the bike trail and with basketball courts, a changing room and toilets, and a snack bar.

If you're in the mood for a swim anytime, Anchorage is a good place to experience Alaska's love affair with Olympic-size indoor pools. There are seven to choose from, including five at the various high schools; call 907/343-4474 for locations and times. Other pools are at Alaska Pacific University (APU) and the University of Alaska Anchorage (UAA). With its high ceiling, taut diving boards, and hard-bodied swimmers, the **UAA pool** (907/786-1231), is easily the finest in Alaska, and your entrance fee also provides access to the other facilities here, including a fine ice rink, a weight room, saunas, racquetball courts, and a gym.

Golf

There are four Anchorage-area public golf courses: **Anchorage Golf Course** (907/522-3363, www.anchoragegolfcourse.com, 18 holes) on lower hillside in South Anchorage, **Russian Jack Springs Course** (5200 DeBarr Rd., 907/343-6992, 9 holes), **Tanglewood Lakes Golf Club** (11701 Brayton Dr., 907/345-4600, 9 holes), and **Moose Run** (27000 Arctic Valley Rd., 907/428-0056, www.mooserungolfcourse.com, 36 holes).

WINTER

Contrary to popular belief, Alaska—and Anchorage in particular—does not go into hibernation for the long months of winter. Instead, many locals look forward to the cold and snow because of the wonderful outdoor activities they bring. Anchorage is a national center for cross-country skiing, dogsledding, skijoring (skiing behind a dog), hockey, and all sorts of other winter fun.

Visitors soon discover what the residents already know—the city is blessed with excellent facilities for all of these. There are dogsled race tracks; dozens of miles of free groomed ski trails; several excellent ice rinks; and three downhill ski areas, including the state's best resort, Alyeska. Add in such events as the Iditarod, Fur Rendezvous, and the college and semipro hockey games, and it's easy to see why more and more visitors are coming to Anchorage in the winter.

SAFETY IN AVALANCHE COUNTRY

Skiing and snowmobiling are becoming increasingly popular in Alaska's limitless backcountry. Unfortunately, many winter outdoor enthusiasts fail to take necessary precautions before heading out. Given the heavy snowfalls that occur, the steep slopes the snow piles up on, and the high winds that accompany many storms, it should come as no surprise that avalanches are a real danger in Alaska. Nearly all avalanches are triggered by the victims. This is particularly true for snowmobilers, who often attempt such dangerous practices as "high-marking" – riding as high as they can up steep slopes – and are killed in avalanches that result.

If you really want to avoid avalanches, ski only on groomed trails or "bombproof" slopes that, because of aspect, shape, and slope angle, never seem to slide. Unfortunately, this isn't always possible, so backcountry skiers and snowmobilers need to understand the conditions that lead to avalanches. The best way to learn is from a class such as the avalanche safety programs taught by the **Alaska Avalanche School** (907/345-0878, www.alaskaavalanche.com) in Anchorage, or Juneau's **Southeast Alaska Avalanche Center** (907/586-5699, www.avalanche.org/~seaac). Learn more at www.avalanche.org, including information on avalanches and course offerings around the nation.

HEADING OUT

An avalanche safety course is extremely valuable, but you can also help protect yourself by following these precautions when you head into the backcountry:

- Before leaving, get up-to-date avalanche information. The **Chugach National Forest Avalanche Information Center** (907/754-2346, www.cnfaic.org) has current snow conditions for the Kenai Peninsula; it's updated several times a week in the winter.
- Be sure to carry extra warm clothes, water, high-energy snacks, a cell phone, a dual-frequency avalanche transceiver (make sure it's turned on and that you know how to use it), a lightweight snow shovel (for digging snow pits or emergency snow shelters, or for excavating avalanche victims), first-aid supplies, a Leatherman knife, a topographic map, an extra plastic ski tip, a flashlight, matches, and a compass. Many skiers also carry that cure-all, duct tape, wrapped around a ski pole. Let someone know exactly where you are going and when you expect to return. It's also a wise idea to carry special ski poles that extend into probes in case of an avalanche.
- Check the angle of an area before you ski through it; slopes of 30-45 degrees are the most dangerous, while lesser slopes do not slide as frequently.
- Watch the weather; winds over 15 mph can pile snow much more deeply on lee slopes, causing dangerous loading on the snowpack. Especially avoid skiing on or below cornices.
- Avoid skiing on the leeward side (the side facing into the wind) of ridges, where snow loading can be greatest.
- Be aware of gullies and bowls; they're more likely to slip than flat open slopes or ridgetops. Stay out of gullies at the bottom of wide bowls; these are natural avalanche chutes.
- Look out for cracks in the snow, and listen for hollow snow underfoot. These are strong signs of dangerous conditions.
- Look at the trees. Smaller trees may indicate that avalanches rip through an area frequently, knocking over the larger trees. Avalanches can also run through forested areas, however.
- Know how much new snow has fallen recently. Heavy new snow over older, weak snow layers is a sure sign of extreme danger on potential avalanche slopes. Most avalanches slip during or immediately after a storm.
- Learn how to dig a snow pit and how to read the various snow layers. Particularly important are the very weak layers of depth hoar or surface hoar that have been buried under heavy new snow.

Downhill Skiing

Alpine skiers and snowboarders head 37 miles south of Anchorage to **Alyeska Resort** (907/754-1111 or 800/880-3880, www.alyeskaresort.com) for the finest skiing to be found, and some of the deepest snow at any American resort.

Hilltop Ski Area (907/346-1407, www.hilltopskiarea.org) is right on the edge of town at Abbott Road near Hillside Drive, and consists of a small chairlift and a rope tow. It has lights for night skiing, plus a small lodge with rentals and a snack bar, and it's a favorite place to learn skiing and boarding or to play around without having to suffer the 45-minute drive to Alyeska. Tickets cost $28 on weekends ($30 with night skiing) for adults, $26 students, free for kids under age 8 skiing with an adult. Call 907/346-2167 for the ski hotline.

A bit farther afield is **Alpenglow at Arctic Valley** (907/428-1208, www.skiarctic.net). All-day rates are $35 adults, $30 students, $25 ages 8–13 and seniors, and free for kids under age 8. There are two chairlifts and a T-bar, providing a wide range of slopes and conditions. Arctic Valley is only open weekends and holidays, generally early November–mid-April. Downhill skis and snowboards can be rented from several places in Anchorage, including REI and the ski areas. In the fall, Alpenglow is perfect for blueberries and other wild berries.

Sledders of all ages play on the steep powerline slope that cuts along the road up to Arctic Valley, with parents taking kids back uphill in their cars. Another great sledding hill, with a 600-foot run, is in Centennial Park. Popular short sledding hills are at Kincaid Park and Service High School.

Cross-Country Skiing

Any Anchorageite over the age of four seems to be involved in cross-country skiing in one form or another. The city is laced with trails that serve as summertime cycling and jogging paths and wintertime ski routes. Most of these are groomed, with set tracks for traditional cross-country skiers and a wider surface for the skate-skiing crowd. Skijorers are also often seen on the Coastal Trail in this dog-happy town (dogs aren't allowed on most ski trails).

The **Nordic Skiing Association of Anchorage** (907/276-7609, www.anchoragenordicski.com) is Alaska's largest cross-country association, and its website has all sorts of information on the sport. Pick up *The Alaska Nordic Skier* at local ski shops and newsstands; it's published October–April each year.

The best-known cross-country area is **Kincaid Park,** where a convoluted maze of paths cover the rolling terrain, offering fun for all levels of ability. One of the top three competitive ski venues in the United States, Kincaid often hosts national meets. You can warm up inside the Kincaid chalet and enjoy the vistas of Sleeping Lady and Mt. McKinley.

Russian Jack Springs Park, near Debarr Road and Boniface Parkway, has many more groomed ski trails, as well as a small rope tow and a warming house. Several more miles of groomed trails await at **Hillside Park** off Abbot Road next to Hilltop Ski Area; watch out for the moose here. All these trails are groomed for both traditional cross-country and the faster skate skis, which are becoming increasingly popular. Rent cross-country skis from REI or AMH.

Backcountry Skiing

If you're more ambitious—and have the wheels to get there—you'll find incredible backcountry skiing all around Anchorage. The Chugach Mountains offer an endless choice of skiing options that last from mid-October all the way into late June in some places. Note, however, that these areas are *not* for novices, so don't head out without knowing about and being prepared for such dangers as avalanches and hypothermia. Quite a number of skiers (and more snowmobilers) have died in mountain avalanches near Anchorage. Even such favorites as the nearby summit of Flattop Mountain have taken a high human toll over the years.

The best-known backcountry areas are in Chugach State Park and at Turnagain

Pass and Hatcher Pass. Pick up a winter routes map for **Chugach State Park** from the state park office. **Turnagain Pass** is 60 miles southwest of Anchorage on the way to Seward. The west side of the road is open to snowmobilers, but tele-skiers avoid them by heading to the east side. There's a big parking lot, and from here you can continue into the open meadows or high into the mountains for deep untracked powder.

Located 70 miles northeast of Anchorage, **Hatcher Pass** is a favorite backcountry area and serves as a training area for the U.S. National Cross-Country Ski Team. The road can sometimes be a bit treacherous if you don't have studded tires, so be sure to call the park for road conditions (907/745-2827). REI in Anchorage offers cross-country and telemark clinics.

Ice-Skating

Anchorage is wild about ice-skating and hockey. The **UAA Seawolves** (907/786-1293, www.uaa.alaska.edu) and the semi-pro **Alaska Aces** (907/258-2237, www.alaskaaces.com) attract crowds all season, and the area has five indoor rinks. All are open year-round and offer skate rentals as well as instruction: **Ben Boeke Ice Arena** (334 E. 16th Ave., 907/274-5715, www.benboeke.com) in the Sullivan Arena, **Dempsey Anderson Ice Arena** (1741 W. Northern Lights Blvd., 907/277-7571, www.sullivanarena.com), **UAA Sports Center** (2801 Providence Dr., 907/786-1233), and **Dimond Ice Chalet** (800 E. Dimond Blvd., 907/344-1212, www.dimondicechalet.com) in the Dimond Mall. Ben Boeke is an Olympic-size hockey rink.

Accommodations

As might be expected in a city of more than 250,000 people, Anchorage has a wide range of lodging options. Unfortunately, most of these also have Alaskan-sized prices. A good one-stop place to begin your search for local lodging is the Anchorage Convention and Visitors Bureau website (www.anchorage.net). Add a 12 percent lodging tax to the rates listed below. Anchorage is a spread-out city, and many of the places listed below are in Midtown rather than downtown, making a rental car a wise investment. Parking may or may not be available at downtown locations, so ask ahead to be sure.

Be sure to make Anchorage lodging reservations far ahead for July–August. If summertime prices in Anchorage seem too high, try using online resources. I recently booked a peak-season room at one of Anchorage's newer hotels for $67; the posted price was $169! Check websites such as www.biddingfortravel.yuku.com to get an idea of the deals other folks are getting.

UNDER $100

Popular with outdoors enthusiasts, **Anchorage Guesthouse** (2001 Hillcrest Dr., 907/274-0408, www.akhouse.com) is off a quiet tree-lined street above Westchester Lagoon and near the Coastal Trail. Inside are two private guest rooms ($80) for couples and families, and three bunk rooms ($30 pp). All units share three baths. Ingredients for a make-it-yourself breakfast are provided, and guests can use the living room, dining room, kitchen, and sunroom. Bike rentals and Wi-Fi are available, along with a big garage to store your kayak, camping gear, bikes, and more. Friendly owner Andy Baker is a renewable energy consultant.

Another cheap and well-run option is **Spenard Hostel International** (2845 W. 42nd Place, 907/248-5036, www.alaskahostel.org, $25 pp, $68 d), with 43 dorm spaces. There is no curfew, but alcohol is not allowed either. The hostel has three kitchens, four baths, and laundry facilities. They rent mountain bikes, have space for tents ($20 s or $35 d), and put on potluck dinners most Sunday nights. Sheets and blankets are provided. Call for reservations 2–4 weeks ahead of your visit if arriving on a midsummer weekend.

Arctic Adventure Hostel (337 W. 33rd Ave., 907/562-5700 or 888/886-9332, www.arcticadventurehostel.com, $22 pp, $46 d private room) is a clean and friendly place with a full kitchen, Wi-Fi, bike rentals, and 20 rooms housing two or three guests per room.

Other Midtown hostels are **26th Street International Hostel** (1037 W. 26th Ave., 907/274-1252, www.26streethostel.com, $25 pp with breakfast) and **Jason's International Youth Hostel** (3324 Eide St., 907/562-0263, $25 pp with breakfast). Whatever you do, avoid the **Anchorage International Hostel** (700 H St., 907/276-3635, www.anchorageinternationalhostel.org, $25 s), which leaves much to be desired in cleanliness and security. Personally, I'd sleep in my car rather than stay at this place.

Qupqugiaq Inn (640 W. 36th Ave., 907/562-5681, www.qupq.com) occupies the upstairs of a boxy Midtown building, but the interior is filled with distinctively curved walls. Accommodations are cramped but unique, with furnishings—including teak beds—from around the globe. Guests have access to the communal kitchen and computers. This is a good place for couples on a budget, but it can be noisy at times. Rooms with shared bath are $72 s or $77–90 d, while nicer downstairs units with a private bath cost $87 s or $97 d. Downstairs is Serrano's Mexican Grill. The inn also houses a hostel space (separate entrance) for $25 per person, including kitchen access.

$100-200

Creekwood Inn (2150 Gambell St., 907/258-6006 or 800/478-6008, www.creekwood-inn-alaska.com) is a no-frills Midtown place with a mix of older budget rooms ranging $110 d for standard units with microwaves and fridges to $140 for kitchen suites. There is free Wi-Fi too.

Motel 6 (5000 A St., 907/677-8640 or 800/466-8656, www.motel6.com, $104 d) is one of the newer Anchorage box hotels, with predictable Midtown accommodations, Wi-Fi, and an airport shuttle, but no microwaves or fridges in the rooms.

Lakeshore Motor Inn (3009 Lakeshore Dr., 907/248-3485 or 800/770-3000, www.lakeshoremotorinn.com) is a quiet and clean older motel close to the airport with standard guest rooms and kitchenettes for $149 d, one-bedroom suites at $189 for up to four people, and two-bedroom suites that sleep five for $199. Free airport transport, continental breakfast, in-room fridges, and Wi-Fi are included.

One of the better reasonably priced options is **Microtel Inn & Suites** (5205 Northwood Dr., 907/245-5002 or 888/680-4500, www.microtelinn.com) near the airport. Rates are $129 d in large guest rooms or $135 d in mini-suites with fridges and microwaves; continental breakfast, an airport shuttle, two hot tubs, and Wi-Fi are included.

Long House Alaskan Hotel (4335 Wisconsin St., 907/243-2133 or 888/243-2133, www.longhousehotel.com) is a large log-sided building near the airport where spacious guest rooms are $99 d, and suites go for $109–159 d. There is a free airport shuttle and continental breakfast, plus Wi-Fi in the lobby. The long and narrow configuration of the rooms is a bit odd; rumor has it the building was once an Army barracks.

It's hard to beat the location for **Copper Whale Inn** (440 L St., 907/258-7999 or 866/258-7999, www.copperwhale.com), right on the edge of downtown with a flower-packed back patio overlooking Cook Inlet. Next door is Simon and Seafort's, one of the city's finest restaurants. This attractively appointed inn has two guest rooms ($185 d) that share a bath, while the other 13 small guest rooms ($210 d) have private baths. A filling buffet breakfast is included, along with guest computers and Wi-Fi.

Right in the heart of town close to the railway depot, the 31-room **Anchorage Grand Hotel** (505 W 2nd Ave., 907/929-8888 or 888/800-0640, www.anchoragegrand.com, $169 d) is a cozy all-suites place with friendly service, continental breakfast, and a business center.

A family run hotel right downtown, **Voyager Hotel** (501 K St., 907/277-9501 or 800/247-9070, www.voyagerhotel.com, $189–209 d), offers 40 large clean guest rooms with microwaves and fridges, plus Wi-Fi in the lobby.

If you're looking for plenty of space, the 19-unit **Anchorage Uptown Suites** (234 E. 2nd Ave., 907/279-4232, www.anchorageuptownsuites.com) has one-bedroom apartments with full kitchens for $179–229 d. German is spoken, and a continental breakfast is provided in the summer.

A couple of blocks downhill from the heart of town, **Comfort Inn Ship Creek** (111 Ship Creek Ave., 907/277-6887 or 800/424-6423, www.choicehotels.com, $170–210 d) sits along this urban creek where salmon fishing draws locals and visitors alike. The railroad depot is just up the way, but that also means a fair amount of noise as the trains roll past. The hotel has decent guest rooms along with a small pool, workout machines, continental breakfast, Wi-Fi, and free shuttles.

OVER $200

Built in 1953 but remodeled, **Inlet Tower Suites** (1200 L St., 907/276-0110 or 800/544-0786, www.inlettower.com) is a 14-story tower atop a hill halfway between downtown and Midtown. Guest rooms are nicely furnished and spacious, and there are great views of the mountains or Cook Inlet from higher floors. Rooms with microwaves and fridges list at $219 d, but they're often available for $159 d. Free airport or railroad transportation is included, along with an exercise facility and Wi-Fi. The hotel's restaurant (Mixx Grill) is best known for fine dinners, or you can walk a block to the New Sagaya's gourmet market.

One of my favorite Anchorage hotels, **Dimond Center Hotel** (700 E Dimond Blvd., 907/770-5000 or 866/770-5002, www.dimondcenterhotel.com, $269–299 d), has a less-than-appealing location next to Wal-Mart and the Dimond Mall on the south side of town. But inside you'll find a gorgeous lobby, custom-designed furnishings, and luxurious rooms with plush beds and 42-inch flat-screen TVs. Even the baths are special, with soaking tubs and windows opening into the main room. A full hot breakfast is included, and the hotel has guest computers and Wi-Fi, guest passes to a nearby gym, plus free airport and train station shuttles.

Anchorage Hotel (330 E St., 907/272-4553 or 800/544-0988, www.historicanchoragehotel.com) is a classy little 26-room hotel built in 1916 and now on the National Register of Historic Places. Standard guest rooms (small in size) cost $179 d, and two-room suites are $259 d. The hotel has Wi-Fi and large TVs.

Hotel Captain Cook (5th Ave. and K St., 907/276-6000 or 800/843-1950, www.captaincook.com), occupies an entire block, with three towers and three restaurants. The hotel is owned by the family of former governor Wally Hickel, who also served as President Nixon's Secretary of the Interior in the 1970s. The hotel's 550 rooms follow a nautical theme (befitting the name), and the building has an old-money feeling with dark woods and lots of suits and power ties. Amenities include concierge service, Wi-Fi, and a full athletic club with a hot tub, a sauna, and an indoor pool. Rates start at $255 d for a standard guest room or $270 for junior suites, up to $405 d for a two-bedroom executive suite.

ALL-SUITES HOTELS

Anchorage's newest corporate boxes are geared to business travelers and families looking for more space who don't mind the inevitable this-could-be-Tacoma atmosphere. These places typically have one room with two queen beds and a separate sitting room with a pull-out sofa, plus a microwave and a fridge. All these hotels also include indoor pools, hot tubs, exercise facilities, a breakfast buffet, Wi-Fi, and shuttles to the airport and train station. Summer rates are typically $175–260 d.

One of the nicest lodging choices in Anchorage, **Embassy Suites** (600 E. Benson Blvd., 907/332-7000, www.embassysuites.com, $259 d) gets kudos for spacious upscale suites with a separate bedroom and kitchenette, friendly staff, and such amenities as a fitness center, indoor pool and hot tub, hot breakfasts, Wi-Fi, free transport, valet service, and more. It's in Midtown with a phalanx of malls in all directions.

Two recommended downtown places are **Extended Stay Deluxe** (108 E. 8th Ave., 907/868-1605 or 866/506-7848, www.extendedstaydeluxe.com) and **Hawthorn Suites** (1110 W. 8th Ave., 907/222-5005 or 888/469-6575, www.hawthorn.com).

Quite a few Midtown places have similar facilities and prices, including the following good ones: **Hilton Garden Inn** (4540 A St., 907/562-7000 or 800/445-8667, www.hiltongardeninn.com), **Fairfield Inn & Suites** (5060 A St., 907/222-9000 or 888/236-2427, www.marriott.com), **SpringHill Suites by Marriott** (3401 A St., 907/562-3247 or 888/287-9400, www.springhillsuites.com), **Hampton Inn** (4301 Credit Union Dr., 907/550-7000 or 800/426-7866, www.hamptoninn.com), and **Homewood Suites** (140 W. Tudor Rd., 907/762-7000 or 800/225-5466, www.anchorage.homewoodsuites.com).

BED-AND-BREAKFASTS AND GUEST HOUSES

Anchorage had over 175 B&Bs at last count, including luxurious hillside homes with spectacular vistas, snug downtown places, and rent-out-the-spare-room suburban houses. An excellent starting point when looking for a local B&B is the **Anchorage Alaska B&B Association** (907/272-5909 or 888/584-5147, www.anchorage-bnb.com). Its website has links to 50 or so B&Bs, with location and price details. See the *Anchorage Big Wild Life* (available from the Anchorage Convention and Visitors Bureau's Visitors Information Center downtown or on the web at www.anchorage.net) for a fairly complete listing of local B&Bs, or take a look at the blizzard of B&B brochures filling visitors center racks.

Downtown Guest House (1238 G St., 907/279-2359, www.downtownguesthouse.com, $150 for up to 4) is an immaculate and peaceful two-bedroom apartment with a full kitchen, Internet access, and laundry. It's just a block or so from New Sagaya's (gourmet food, coffees, and deli), and a short walk from downtown. Downtown Guest House is highly recommended, but with just one unit you'll need to book well ahead for the busy summer season. Tell Clark and Mitzi I sent you.

Built in 1913, **Oscar Gill House B&B** (1355 W 10th Ave., 907/279-1344, www.oscargill.com, $115–135 d) is a historic home facing the downtown Park Strip. Two attractive guest rooms share a bath, while the largest has its own. Guests appreciate the central location, full breakfasts, friendly owners, and grandma's-house atmosphere. Call well ahead since Gill House fills fast.

For top-end lodging, it's hard to compete with **Mangy Moose B&B** (5560 E. 112th Ave., 907/346-8052 or 877/777-8937, www.alaskamangymoose.com, $179–229 d). The B&B gets high marks from visitors, with three immaculate and luxurious guest rooms and suites, private entrances, Wi-Fi, a washer and dryer, and delicious breakfasts. It's on the south end of town, so you'll need a car.

The following are recommended B&Bs under $150 d: **Anchorage Downtown B&B** (907/278-9275, www.anchoragedowntown.com), **Donna's B&B** (907/522-6025 or 888/421-6025, www.anchoragedonnasbandb.com), **G Street B&B** (907/276-3284, www.gstreethouse.com), **Gallery B&B** (907/274-2567), and **Wildflower Inn** (907/274-1239, www.alaska-wildflower-inn.com).

Other recommended finer B&Bs (over $150 d) include: **Aawesome B&B Retreat** (907/338-8873 or 877/226-9645, www.aawesomeworld.com), **Anchorage Lakeside Jewel B&B** (907/242-2126 or 866/539-3555, www.anchoragelakesidejewel.com), **Alaskan Frontier Gardens B&B** (907/345-6556, www.alaskafrontiergardens.com), **Alaskan Leopard B&B** (907/868-1594 or 877/454-3046, www.alaskanleopard.com), **Arctic Fox Inn** (907/272-4818, www.arcticfoxinn.com), **Camai B&B** (907/333-2219 or 800/659-8763, www.camaibnb.com), **Highland Glenn Lodge** (907/336-2312 or 888/507-2312, www.alaskahighlandglen.com), **Lake**

Hood Inn (907/258-9321 or 866/663-9322, www.lakehoodinn.com), **Mahogany Manor** (907/278-1111 or 888/777-0346, www.mahoganymanor.com), **North County Castle B&B** (907/345-7296, www.castlealaska.com), **Parkside Guest House** (907/683-2290, www.campdenali.com), **South Bluff B&B** (907/250-9893, www.southbluffbandb.com), **Summerset B&B** (907/349-3766 or 866/349-3766, www.alaska-summersetbnb.com), and **Susitna Place B&B** (907/274-3344, www.susitnaplace.com).

CAMPING

The city-run **Centennial Park Campground** (907/343-6986, www.ci.anchorage.ak.us/parks, mid-May–Sept., $25 plus $5 for showers) has 100 spaces for tents and RVs (no hookups). Take Muldoon Road south from the Glenn, take the first left onto Boundary, then the next left onto the highway frontage road for 0.5 miles to the campground.

Other RV campgrounds include **Anchorage Ship Creek Landings RV Park** (150 N. Ingra St., 907/277-0877 or 888/778-7700, www.alaskarv.com, May–Sept., tents $26, RVs $46), **Golden Nugget Camper Park** (4100 DeBarr Rd., 907/333-5311 or 800/449-2012, www.goldennuggetcamperpark.com, year-round, RVs $45), and **Creekwood Inn** (2150 Gambell St., 907/258-6006 or 800/478-6008, www.creekwoodinn-alaska.com, year-round, RVs $41, no tents). Many travelers also park RVs for free in the Fred Meyer and Sam's Club parking lots, but check with store managers for any restrictions.

Food

If you can't find a good meal in Anchorage, you aren't trying. The city's size and diverse population are mirrored in a wide range of eating places, from grab-a-bite fast-food joints to high-class (and high-priced) gourmet restaurants. To reach many of the best places, you'll need a vehicle or knowledge of bus schedules, but there are several fine restaurants right downtown. Pick up the free ***Restaurant & Entertainment Guide*** from racks around town. Note: Smoking has been banned in Anchorage restaurants; all bars are also entirely smoke-free.

BREAKFAST

Looking for a great downtown breakfast in an unpretentious setting? Join the throngs at the spacious **Snow City Café** (1034 W. 4th Ave., 907/272-2489, www.snowcitycafe.com, Mon.–Fri. 7 A.M.–3 P.M., Sat.–Sun. 7 A.M.–4 P.M., $9–13), where meals are ample, reasonably priced, and dependably good. Breakfast is available all day; try the Mediterranean scramble, huevos rancheros, or one of the day's specials. Get here early on weekends to avoid a wait. Lunchtime sandwiches bring in the legal staff from nearby offices along "lawyer row." The café also has free Wi-Fi.

The **Middle Way Café** (1200 W. Northern Lights Blvd., 907/272-6433, $8–12) is another busy morning place, with French toast, huevos rancheros, breakfast burritos, omelets, vegan specials, and more in a noisy and colorful setting next to the REI store in Midtown. The café is also popular for lunch, lattes, and smoothies.

An old-time favorite, **Gwennie's Old Alaska Restaurant** (4333 Spenard Rd., 907/243-2090, www.gwenniesrestaurant.com) specializes in breakfast ($8–13, available all day), especially sourdough pancakes and reindeer sausage. Meals are Alaska-size, so those with small appetites may want to split an order. Memorabilia crowds the walls on this sprawling two-story place, and big tables fill with families filling up.

Two very good places for a Sunday splurge are **Sacks Café** (328 G St., 907/276-3546, www.sackscafe.com) downtown, and **Millennium Hotel** (4800 Spenard Rd., 907/243-2300, www.millennium-hotels.com). The latter has a popular Sunday brunch ($20) with crab legs, create-your-own omelets, and champagne, plus a big deck facing Lake Hood, where you can watch floatplanes take off. Sacks is à la carte.

BAKERIES AND SWEETS

Some of the best Anchorage breads and pastries come from **Europa Bakery** (601 W. 36th Ave., 907/563-5704), where the rustic thick-crusted artisan breads compare favorably to anything you might find in Europe. Similarly noteworthy breads and sweets can be found at **L'Aroma Bakeries,** inside both New Sagaya stores.

Marty's New York Bagel Deli (901 E. Dimond Blvd., 907/336-1315, www.martysnybd.com, $7–8) makes the city's most authentic bagels and bagel sandwiches. And oy vey, the owner really is from New York.

Alaska Wild Berry Products (907/562-8858 or 800/280-2927, www.alaskawildberryproducts.com) has a large chocolate factory and gift shop on Juneau Street near the corner of Old Seward Highway and International Airport Road. This is a fun place for chocoholics; there's even a 20-foot melted-chocolate waterfall, and free taste samples. Fifteen-minute tours are given throughout the day, and this is a very popular stop on the Anchorage tour-bus circuit. The big gift shop offers all the standard tourist stuff (and then some), while the theater shows a unique 30-minute film ($8) about Alaska.

COFFEE AND TEA

Anchorageites love strong coffee, and the town is packed with espresso stands and cafés—including the bland Starbucks versions. Tucked away in a Midtown shopping mall, **Café del Mundo** (341 E. Benson Blvd., 907/274-0026, www.cafedelmundo.com, $3–8) is a favorite of the lawyer and Volvo crowd, and is a relaxing place to while away a morning.

Upscale **Terra Bella** (907/562-2259, www.terrabellacoffee.com) has a good choice of sandwiches, paninis, and salads. They're in a Southside strip mall at 601 E. Dimond Avenue.

A personal favorite is the local chain of nine **Kaladi Brothers** espresso shops (www.kaladi.com), including branches inside the New Sagaya grocery stores and Titlewave Books. All have free Wi-Fi. Many other Alaskan coffee shops buy their espresso beans from Kaladi Brothers, and they've even opened a shop in downtown Seattle—the heart of enemy (Starbucks) territory.

LUNCH AND QUICK MEALS

Sacks Café (328 G St., 907/276-3546, www.sackscafe.com, Sat. brunch 11 A.M.–3 P.M., Sun. brunch 10 A.M.–2:30 P.M., dinner 5–9 P.M., Mon–Thurs. 11 A.M.–2:30 P.M. and 5–9 P.M., Fri. 11 A.M.–2:30 P.M. and 5–10:30 P.M., Sat. 5–10:30 P.M., lunch $11–13, dinner $18–34) crafts some of Anchorage's finest lunches and dinners, and is especially popular with the business crowd. Weekend brunches are also popular. You'll find an arty decor, creative cooking, and heady talk. The menu changes frequently, but typically includes fresh halibut or salmon, baked penne pasta, New Zealand rack of lamb, and Thai chicken sandwiches. The desserts are great too. Reservations are essential for dinner, though they aren't taken for the wine bar.

Just down the street is arguably Anchorage's best sandwich shop, **Urban Greens** (304 G St., 907/276-0333, www.urbangreensak.com, Mon.–Fri. 9 A.M.–5 P.M., $7–10), where the subs are made with hoagies from French Oven Bakery. Try the bootlegger club with turkey, pastrami, mortadella, and Swiss cheese.

Housed within the Anchorage Museum, the **Muse Café** (625 C St., 907/929-9210, www.marxcafe.com, Sun.–Thurs. 11 A.M.–3 P.M., Wed.–Sat. 11 A.M.–9 P.M., $7–12) is surrounded by works of art. The food is equally notable, with homemade soups, fresh salads, and creative sandwiches.

Don't miss perpetually crowded **L'Aroma Bakery and Deli** at both New Sagaya stores (3700 Old Seward Hwy. in Midtown, and 900 W. 13th Ave. close to downtown, www.laromabakery.com, $5–10) for panini sandwiches, small pizzas baked in wood-fired ovens, sushi, spring rolls, a salad bar, Chinese specials, and American "comfort food" (mac and cheese, meatloaf, lasagna, and so on), along with freshly baked breads and sweets. You're guaranteed to find something that appeals. Eat here or get it to go. Both New Sagayas also house Kaladi Brothers Coffee shops.

Middle Way Café (1200 W. Northern Lights Blvd., 907/272-6433, Mon.–Fri. 7 A.M.–6:30 P.M., Sat.–Sun. 8 A.M.–6:30 P.M., $6–10) hides out next to the REI store but always manages to fill up when lunch arrives. Check out today's specials on the board, order at the counter, and wait for your name to be called. The menu includes vegetarian sandwiches and wraps, soy burgers, salads, fruit smoothies, and daily specials. The lip-ringed barista will make a mocha while you wait or serve a big piece of carrot cake.

In the summer several vendors have downtown carts in front of the old Federal Building on 4th Avenue. The best of these—look for the queue—is the vendor of reindeer sausage and grilled onions. On weekends in the summer your best downtown bet is the weekend **Anchorage Market and Festival** (3rd Ave. and E St., 907/272-5634, www.anchoragemarkets.com, Sat.–Sun. 10 A.M.–6 P.M. mid-May–mid-Sept.). For more downtown fast food, head to the **food court** on the 4th level of the 5th Avenue Mall (5th Ave. and C St.), with fast-food eateries of all persuasions, from Thai to frozen yogurt. Another inexpensive place is **Bear Tooth Theatrepub** (1230 W. 27th Ave., 907/276-4200, www.beartooththeatre.net).

Anchorage's two top burger-and-fries joints are **Arctic Roadrunner** (2477 Arctic Blvd., 907/279-7311) and **Tommy's Burger Stop** (W. Benson Rd. at Spenard Ave., 907/561-5696).

PIZZA AND ITALIAN

Anchorage has all the national pizza chains, and the "Pizza" listing in the Yellow Pages includes some 60 different places. Among these, **Pizza Olympia** (2809 Spenard Rd., across from REI, 907/561-5264) is a personal favorite. Four generations of the Maroudas family run this place with authentic affection, rolling out such unique offerings as garlic and feta cheese pizzas and all the standard Greek specialties.

Two excellent pizza options are **Moose's Tooth Pub and Pizzeria** (3300 Old Seward Hwy., 907/258-2537, www.moosestooth.net) and **L'Aroma Bakery & Deli** (in New Segaya stores, 3700 Old Seward Hwy. in Midtown, and 900 W. 13th Ave. close to downtown, www.laromabakery.com). Other good pizza places include **Sorrento's** (610 E. Fireweed Lane, 907/278-3439), with the best southern Italian food in Anchorage, and **Fletcher's** (in Hotel Captain Cook, 5th Ave. and K St., 907/276-6000), where Anchorage waiters and cooks go after work.

For delicious northern Italian dinners with an Alaskan twist, visit the small **CampoBello Bistro** (601 W. 36th Ave., 907/563-2040, Mon.–Fri. 11 A.M.–2:30 P.M., Tues.–Sat. 5–9 P.M., $16–24). This is a relaxing and romantic spot for lunch or dinner; try the seafood crepes.

For creative Tuscany-inspired food in the heart of town, you won't go wrong at **Ristorante Orso** (737 W. 5th Ave., www.orsoalaska.com, 907/222-3232, lunch and dinner, $25–38). This popular restaurant exudes energy, and the menu includes wild mushroom ravioli, lamb osso bucco, and cashew-crusted halibut, along with a dessert selection that stars a wonderful molten chocolate cake. Reservations are recommended.

ASIAN

Chinese and Korean

Many of Anchorage's Chinese restaurants are actually run by Korean Americans, who make up a surprisingly large ethnic community in the city.

Panda Restaurant (605 E. Northern Lights Blvd., 907/272-3308, www.pandarestaurant-ak.com, Sun. noon–10 P.M., Mon.–Sat. 11 A.M.–midnight) has a big Chinese menu and gets kudos from locals. Most dinner entrées are around $13.

Twin Dragon Mongolian Bar-B-Que (612 E. 15th Ave., 907/276-7535, daily 11 A.M.–10 P.M.) is a fun place where you fill a plate with veggies and meat and watch the chefs do their show. It's reasonable too: $11 for the lunch buffet or $14 for dinner.

Yen King Restaurant (3501 Old Seward Hwy., 907/563-2627) has a big buffet and provides free delivery. **Chinese Kitchen** (2904 Spenard Rd., 907/279-2222) is a tiny family eatery with lunch specials and friendly owners. If you're adventurous, ask about the menu items listed only in Chinese.

A personal favorite is **Fu Du** (2600 E. Tudor Rd., 907/561-6610, Sun. and Tues.–Thurs. 11 A.M.–10 P.M., Fri.–Sat. 11 A.M.–11 P.M., closed Mon.), where service is efficient and friendly, the setting is cozy, and servings are enormous. Entrées ($13–21) come with soup, Chinese kimchi, rice, an egg roll, and tea. Lunch specials are an even better deal, and Fu Du offers free delivery.

Thai and South Asian

Anchorage has quite a few Thai restaurants—seven at last count. None of these measures up to what you'd find in Thailand (or Berkeley, for that matter), but several are well worth a visit. Hip locals rave about **Thai Kitchen** (3405 E. Tudor Rd., 907/561-0082, www.thaikitchenalaska.com, Sun. 5–8:30 P.M., Mon.–Fri. 11 A.M.–3 P.M. and 5–9 P.M., Sat. 5–9 P.M., entrées $8–11), tucked away in a strip mall on Tudor Road near Bragaw Street. With 120 choices on the menu, you're sure to find something to your taste, but favorites include Popeye chicken or any of the spicy soups. Get there early since it closes at 9 P.M.

Housed within an old Pizza Hut building in Midtown, **Chiang Mai Ultimate Thai** (3637 Old Seward Hwy., 907/563-8900, Mon.–Fri. 11 A.M.–9 P.M., Sat. 4–9 P.M., closed Sun.) is a family-friendly spot decorated with Thai linen and portraits of the royal family. Meals are consistently great, service is super-friendly, and the prices are fair: $12 for most items. Everything is made fresh while you wait.

Also recommended is **Thai Orchid Restaurant** (219 E. Dimond Ave., 907/868-5226, www.thaiorchidalaska.com, entrées $11–15), with the best pad thai in town and a diverse and inexpensive menu that includes many vegetarian choices.

Indian and Middle Eastern

Bombay Deluxe (555 W. Northern Lights Blvd., 907/277-1200, www.bombaydeluxe.com, Sun. noon–9 P.M., Mon.–Fri. 11 A.M.–10 P.M., Sat. 5–10 P.M., dinner $12–30) has an ample weekday lunch buffet ($12) and free delivery.

Alaska's only Tibetan restaurant, **Yak & Yeti Himalayan Restaurant** (3301 Spenard Rd., 907/743-8078, www.yakandyetialaska.com, Mon.–Fri. 11 A.M.–2:30 P.M., Thurs.–Sat. 5–8:30 P.M., entrées $9–13) is a relaxing Midtown spot with a mix of vegetarian and meaty dishes. Kids appreciate the lhasa momos (Tibetan beef dumplings), and grownups rave over the spicy chicken achari—marinated in mint and coriander, cooked in a tandoor, and served with chutney.

Aladdin's (4240 Old Seward Hwy. at Tudor Rd., 907/561-2373, www.aladdinsak.com, Wed.–Sat. 5–10 P.M., $11–19) serves traditional Mediterranean dishes from North Africa and the Middle East, including moussaka, lamb couscous, seafood kebab, and various vegetarian specialties. The restaurant has a big local following.

Japanese

Get the finest fresh sushi, tempura, and teriyaki from **Yamato Ya** (3700 Old Seward Hwy., 907/561-2128, www.yamatoyasushi.com), next to New Sagaya's.

Kumagoro (533 W. 4th Ave., 907/272-9905, www.kumagoroalaska.com) is a plant-bedecked downtown restaurant with house-made udon noodle soups and an evening-only sushi bar. The restaurant fills up for lunch with the business crowd. Local Carrs/Safeway, Fred Meyer, and New Sagaya supermarkets also have fresh sushi in their delis.

One of Anchorage's newest places is the pan-Asian **Ginger** (425 W. 5th Ave., 907/929-3680, www.gingeralaska.com, lunch Mon.–Fri. 11:30 A.M.–2:30 P.M., dinner daily 5:30–11 P.M., entrées $18–33), where the menu encompasses everything from sesame crusted ahi to duck breast chinois. Don't miss the spicy tuna tower appetizers.

MEXICAN

A longtime favorite—it's the oldest Mexican restaurant in Alaska—is **La Cabaña** (312 E. 4th Ave., 907/272-0135, www.alaskalacabana.com, $11–17). This is a good place for lunch, with tasty halibut fajitas. **La Mex** (2552 Spenard Rd., 907/274-7511, www.lamexalaska.com) is popular for evening nachos and margaritas, or for full meals. The service is fast, and the steaks aren't bad either.

In business since 1972, **Mexico in Alaska** (7305 Old Seward Hwy., 907/349-1528, www.mexicoinalaska.com, Mon.–Fri. 11 A.M.–10 P.M., Sat. noon–10 P.M.) is one of the more authentic south-of-the-border spots, but it's a long way out if you don't have a car.

If you're looking for the quick version, **Taco King** (112 W. Northern Lights Blvd., 907/276-7387, Sun. noon–10 P.M., Mon.–Sat. 10 A.M.–11 P.M.) serves fat burritos and tacos. Order at the counter and then slather it up with your choice of salsas. Burritos start at $5, up to $9 for a big dinner plate. You'll never want to go Taco Bell after this!

A great family option for nachos, burritos, and pizzas is **Bear Tooth Theatrepub** (1230 W. 27th Ave., 907/276-4200, www.beartooththeatre.net), where you can take in a $3 movie while you eat.

VEGETARIAN

Organic Oasis (2610 Spenard Rd., 907/277-7882, www.organicoasis.com, Sun. 1–6 P.M., Mon. 11 A.M.–8 P.M., Tues.–Fri. 11 A.M.–9 P.M., Sat. 11 A.M.–8 P.M., entrées $11–16), in the heart of Spenard, serves organic wraps and sandwiches (even a few with meat), fresh-squeezed juices, smoothies, and other lunch and dinner fare. The enjoyable, airy setting is right next to a yoga studio.

Natural Pantry (3801 Old Seward Hwy., 907/770-1444, www.natural-pantry.com, Mon.–Sat. 9 A.M.–9 P.M.) has groceries, organic smoothies, fresh juices, and light lunches.

All the places listed in the *Lunch* section have vegetarian specials of one sort or another; Middle Way Café is particularly notable. Also try Snow City Café, Bombay Deluxe, Yak & Yeti, and any of the listed Thai restaurants for vegetarian specialties.

SEAFOOD

Countless Anchorage restaurants serve fresh seafood in season, and some of the best are listed elsewhere in this section: Sacks Café, Ristorante Orso, Simon & Seaforts, Marx Bros. Café, Jens', and F Street Station.

They don't serve meals, but the best places to find fresh fish, clams, crab, and other Alaskan specialties are **10th & M Seafoods** (1020 M St., 907/272-3474 or 800/770-2722, www.10thandmseafoods.com) and **New Sagaya** (900 W. 13th Ave., 907/274-6173, www.newsagaya.com). For smoked salmon (and reindeer sausage), drop by **Alaska Sausage & Seafood** (2914 Arctic Blvd., 907/562-3636 or 800/798-3636, www.alaskasausage.com).

STEAK

As you might guess, Anchorage has several of the meat-lover chain restaurants, including Black Angus, Cattle Company, Lone Star Steakhouse, and Outback Steakhouse. More upscale is **Sullivan's** (5th Avenue Mall, 5th Ave. and C St., 907/258-2882, www.sullivansteakhouse.com, Mon.–Fri. 11:30 A.M.–2 P.M. and 5:30–11 P.M., Sat.–Sun. 5–10 P.M.), where two-inch-thick steaks are seared at high temperatures and cooked to perfection, and the dessert soufflés are to die for.

Just a block away is Anchorage's old-time steakhouse, **Club Paris** (417 W. 5th Ave., 907/277-6332, www.clubparisrestaurant.com, lunch Mon.–Sat. 11:30 A.M.–2:30 P.M., dinner Sun.–Thurs. 5–10 P.M., Fri.–Sat. 5–11 P.M., entrées $20–38), a plain-Jane fixture on the downtown scene since 1957. The atmosphere is dark, and one wall is lined with photos of the famous and infamous visitors who've eaten here over the decades. Super-tender filet mignon is the house specialty ($38, and worth it), but other items are somewhat cheaper, including fresh seafood, burgers, and salads.

BREWS AND PUBS

Anchorage's food-and-booze scene is thriving, with several quite different options from which to choose. Right downtown, **Glacier BrewHouse** (737 W. 5th Ave., 907/274-2739, www.glacierbrewhouse.com, Sun. noon–4 P.M., Mon.–Sat. 11 A.M.–11 P.M.) is a lively and noisy place that overflows most evenings; reservations are recommended. Chefs work furiously in the open kitchen, sending out delicious meals of salmon, steak, ribs, and thin-crusted pizzas, while the bar pours beers made in the behind-the-glass brewery. Most dinner entrées run $18–30, though you can get small pizzas for $11.

A few blocks away is **Snow Goose Restaurant** (717 W. 3rd Ave., 907/277-7727, www.alaskabeers.com, daily 11:30 A.M.–11 P.M., dinner entrées $24–29), featuring halibut, pork, steak, and more downstairs ($24–29) plus an upstairs pub ($7–20) where the outdoor patio overlooks Cook Inlet; that white triangle in the distance is Mt. McKinley. Snow Goose always has a half-dozen homebrews from its Sleeping Lady Brewery (on the premises), along with a substantial wine selection.

Moose's Tooth Pub and Pizzeria (3300 Old Seward Hwy., 907/258-2537, www.moosestooth.net, daily Mon.–Fri. 10:30 A.M.–midnight, Sat.–Sun. 10:30 A.M.–1 A.M., earlier in winter) is *the* Anchorage place for pizza and beer, hands down. The huge parking lot fills with cars most evenings, and you're likely to endure a wait for a table, but the distinctive pizzas (try the "brewhouse favorite" with chorizo sausage, sun-dried tomatoes, red onions, sauce, and cheese) are all made from scratch and baked in a stone oven. Medium pizzas cost $12–21. The 17 or so prize-winning beers are great too. The owners are the same as the equally popular Bear Tooth Theatrepub (1230 W. 27th Ave., 907/276-4200, www.beartooththeatre.net).

You won't go wrong with a meal at tiny **F Street Station** (325 F St., 907/272-5196, daily 11 A.M.–1 A.M.), where there are always reasonably priced, ultrafresh seafood specials ($17), fast service, and a convivial white-collar atmosphere. Try the perfectly cooked beer-batter halibut for $16, or the $18 New York steak and fries. Be sure to ask the bartender the story behind the huge hunk of cheddar that's always on the counter. This is a bar, so it's not for kids after 8 P.M.

They don't brew their own beers, but **Humpy's Great Alaskan Alehouse** (610 W. 6th Ave., 907/276-2337, www.humpys.com) attracts a 20-something crowd with more than 50 brews on tap and a pub menu of halibut burgers, salads, pastas, nachos, and other crunchy fare. Live bands play nightly in this perpetually packed, no-cover-charge hangout.

Midnight Sun Brewing Co. (8111 Dimond Hook Dr., 907/344-1179, www.midnightsunbrewing.com, daily 11 A.M.–8 P.M.) brews a half-dozen craft beers year-round along with seasonal specials. The brewery has an upstairs loft serving soups, salads, and sandwiches, or you can get a growler to go.

FINE DINING

Several of Anchorage's fine-dining establishments are described elsewhere, including Ristorante Orso, Sacks Café, and Club Paris. Reservations are strongly advised or required for all the following restaurants.

Simon & Seaforts (420 L St., 907/274-3502, www.simonandseaforts.com, lunch Mon.–Fri. 11 A.M.–2:30 P.M., dinner Sun. 4:30–9 P.M., Mon.–Thurs. 5–9:30 P.M., Fri. 5–10 P.M., Sat. 4:30–10 P.M.) has an eclectic menu, efficient service, and splendid views. Simon's serves daily fresh fish specials and aged prime rib; wonderful cracked wheat sourdough bread comes with each meal. Expect to pay $30 for dinner, though lunch (try the Cajun chicken fettuccine for $13) is considerably less expensive. If you don't have dinner reservations, head to the more relaxed bar, where the menu is more limited but still diverse enough to satisfy. If you're in the bar, check out the collection of single-malt Scotch whiskies, said to be one of the largest in the nation.

A much smaller and quieter place than Simon's, the elegant **Marx Bros. Café** (627 W. 3rd Ave., 907/278-2133, www.marxcafe.com, Tues.–Sat. 5:30–10 P.M.) has been in business since 1979. Hors d'oeuvres cost $13–15 and dinner entrées $34–50. The Caesar salad—made at your table—is especially memorable. The menu changes daily, but it's always innovative, and the big wine list and good dessert selection complement the meal. Reservations are essential at this dinner-only café; call well ahead of your visit to be assured of a table.

Crow's Nest (907/343-2217, www.captaincook.com, Mon.–Sat. 5–9:30 P.M., closed Sun.–Mon. winter) sits atop the Hotel Captain Cook at 4th Avenue and K Street, 20 floors above the masses, with fine dining and prices (and a view) to match. You can either order off the sky-high menu or choose a five-course tasting menu spectacular for $65, or $95 with matched wines from the 10,000-bottle wine cellar. Other entrées run $34–48. This is one of the only places in Alaska where you can't eat in Carhartt work clothes; not only would you stand out from the rest of the crowd, there's also a dress code. Reservations are strongly recommended.

Don't let the strip-mall setting for **Jens'** (701 W. 36th Ave., 907/561-5367, www.jensrestaurant.com, lunch Mon.–Fri. 11:30 A.M.–2 P.M., dinner Tues.–Sat. 6–10 P.M.) throw you off—this is a great European-style bistro with an Alaskan twist. The atmosphere is art-filled, and the food is equally beautiful, from the rockfish filets to the tenderloin of veal. Attentive service, a nice wine list, and delectable desserts complete the picture. Reservations are recommended. It's easy to spend well over $150 for two people, but you'll go away satiated and happy. You can also hang out at the wine bar, which serves appetizers until midnight (and can get noisy).

It's pretty far off the main tourist trails, but **Kincaid Grill** (6700 Jewel Lake Rd., 907/243-0507, www.kincaidgrill.com, Tues.–Sat. 5–10 P.M., entrées $26–36) is well worth the detour. Telegenic owner-chef Al Levinsohn—whom you might recognize from his Food Network appearances—has created a playful setting with a wine bar and an ever-changing menu. Alaskan seafood is always on the menu, along with rack of lamb, gumbo, and chocolate bourbon soufflé.

GROCERIES

Carrs/Safeway has 10 stores scattered around Anchorage, including one at the Sears Mall in Midtown. Grocery prices are generally a bit lower at the four big **Fred Meyer** stores, including one at Northern Lights Boulevard and New Seward Highway. Most Carrs/Safeway and Fred Meyer stores have delis, fresh sushi, salad bars, ATMs, and in-store Starbucks outlets.

A distinctive gourmet grocer is **New Sagaya** (stores at 3700 Old Seward Hwy., 907/561-5173, and 900 W. 13th Ave., 907/274-6173, www.newsagaya.com), where the featured attractions include exotic produce and Asian foods, outstanding delis, L'Aroma Bakeries, Kaladi Coffee, live crab and oysters, and fresh-from-the-sea seafood.

Many Alaskans buy groceries at the two **Costcos** (on Dimond Ave. at C St., and Muldoon at 15th Ave.), where you need to be a member and most things come in sizes meant to feed whole villages (or two rather obese Alaskans). Their pizza-by-the-slice and Polish dogs are a fattening bargain once you've finished your shopping ordeal.

FARMERS MARKETS

Anchorage's finest and freshest produce can be found at the **Anchorage Market and Festival** (907/272-5634, www.anchoragemarkets.com), held at the downtown parking lot on 3rd Avenue and E Street every Saturday and Sunday 10 A.M.–6 P.M. mid-May–mid-September. More than 300 vendors offer local arts and crafts, a diverse mix of finger food—everything from salmon quesadillas to sweet funnel cakes—and, of course, produce. Live music and entertainment add to the allure. Be sure to stop by the **Kahiltna Birchworks** (907/733-1309, www.alaskabirchsyrup.com) booth, where you'll find distinctive and flavorful birch syrups and caramels created from Michael and Dulce East's home in the Alaskan bush. A smaller **Wednesday Market** takes place at Northway Mall 9 A.M.–4 P.M. July–early October.

Information and Services

VISITORS CENTERS

One of the best things about Anchorage is how easy it is to collect all the information you could possibly need, not just for the city but also for much of the state. Two stops near the corner of 4th Avenue and F Street downtown can supply you with a ton of fliers, brochures, booklets, guides, schedules, and maps, plus the synthesizing expertise of the knowledgeable staffers who can help you make sense of it all. The **Anchorage Convention and Visitors Bureau** (ACVB) is the place to go for every possible Anchorage brochure, handout, or free newspaper. Across the intersection is the **Alaska Public Lands Information Center** where you can learn about national parks, forests, wildlife refuges, and much more.

The ACVB also maintains two **Airport Visitors Centers:** one near the baggage area in the domestic terminal (907/248-4979) and the other in the international terminal (907/266-2657). Both are staffed daily 9 A.M.–4 P.M. in the summer.

LIBRARIES

The **Z. J. Loussac Library** (36th Ave. and Denali St., 907/261-2975, http://lexicon.ci.anchorage.ak.us, Mon.–Thurs. 10 A.M.–8 P.M., Fri.–Sat. 10 A.M.–6 P.M.) is a spacious facility out in Midtown. You could easily lose an afternoon just wandering among the stacks, enjoying the cozy sitting room on Level 3, studying the huge relief map of the state, browsing among the paintings hanging on the walls, or picking a book at random from the large Alaskana collection. Getting to the Alaskana section is an adventure in its own right—the architects did everything they could to make it difficult to reach: up two flights of stairs, across a long connecting walkway, and then back down two levels. And it's back out the same way, since there is no exit here! The library has computers for free Internet access, but you may have to wait awhile.

INTERNET ACCESS

Local libraries all have computers and free Wi-Fi access. More and more Anchorage businesses—especially hotels, B&Bs, and coffee shops—now have guest computers and Wi-Fi. Visit www.free-hotspot.com or www.jiwire.com for updated listings, or try one of the following places for free Wi-Fi: Café del Mundo, Middle Way Café, Organic Oasis, Peanut Farm, and some Kaladi Brothers. The Anchorage airport has free Wi-Fi, and there is even an experimental program to add it to People Mover buses.

BANKING

As might be expected, ATMs can now be found practically anywhere, including most banks and grocery stores. Wells Fargo (907/265-2016) has a booth inside the 5th Avenue Mall to exchange traveler's checks or bills in Canadian dollars, Japanese yen, euros, and other currency for greenbacks.

MEDICAL SERVICES

Alaska's three largest hospitals are in Anchorage. Of the first two, **Alaska Regional Hospital** (2801 DeBarr Rd., 907/276-1131, www.alaskaregional.com) and **Providence Alaska Medical Center** (3200 Providence Dr., 907/562-2211, www.providence.org), Providence has a better reputation and is a nonprofit. The modern **Alaska Native Medical Center** (4315 Diplomacy Dr., 907/257-1150, www.anmc.org) is perhaps the finest facility in Alaska but is only for Native Alaskans.

To find a doctor, call the **physician referral services** offered by Providence (907/261-4900) and Alaska Regional (907/264-1722 or 800/265-8624). You'll find a 24-hour pharmacy inside the **Carrs** (907/297-0560) store at West Northern Lights Boulevard and Minnesota Drive.

Several "Doc-in-a-box" offices are scattered around Anchorage, but you're likely to see a physician's assistant rather than a doctor. Try **Alaska Health Care Clinic** (3600 Minnesota Dr., 907/279-3500) or **Urgent Care** (5437 E. Northern Lights Blvd., 907/333-8561). **Primary Care Associates** (4100 Lake Otis Pkwy., 907/562-1234) is a recommended place to find a real doctor, but you'll need an appointment.

Getting There and Around

GETTING THERE

Air

Almost everybody who flies into Alaska from the Lower 48 lands at **Anchorage International Airport** (907/266-2525, www.anchorageairport.com), even if just to connect to other carriers to travel around the state. The airport is six miles southwest of downtown, and officially it is Ted Stevens Anchorage International Airport in honor of the U.S. senator who for decades brought home the pork that funded Alaskan projects, including the airport. An information booth (907/248-0373, daily 9 A.M.–5 P.M. summer) is near the baggage area; if it's closed, check the racks for free brochures. You can store luggage (even frozen fish) nearby.

© DON PITCHER

travelers outside of Anchorage International Airport

The **People Mover** bus 7 (907/343-6543, www.peoplemover.org, $1.75) runs from the lower level into downtown Anchorage almost hourly, seven days a week. Taxi fare is $15 to downtown, and there's always a line of cabs waiting out front as you exit the baggage claim area.

The Alaska Railroad has a terminal at the airport that is used by cruise ship companies, with passengers flying into Anchorage and riding the train to Whittier or Seward, where they disembark for their cruise to Southeast Alaska (or vice versa). In addition to passengers, the airport serves as a vital link for air cargo companies. Both Federal Express and UPS have major international terminals, and hundreds of cargo flights land and refuel each week.

DOMESTIC AIRLINES

Many of the big domestic carriers fly into and out of Anchorage from the Lower 48, including **Alaska Airlines** (800/426-0333, www.alaskaair.com), **American** (800/433-7300, www.aa.com), **Continental** (800/523-3273, www.continental.com), **Delta** (800/221-1212, www.delta.com), **Frontier** (800/432-1359, www.flyfrontier.com), and **United** (800/241-6522, www.ual.com).

Most of these flights arrive via Seattle, but Alaska also has year-round nonstop flights to Chicago, Denver, Honolulu, Las Vegas, Los Angeles, and Portland, Oregon, with connecting service via Seattle to most Western cities and all the way to Boston; Denver; Washington, D.C.; Miami; Newark; Orlando; and a number of Mexican cities. Northwest has year-round nonstop service to Minneapolis–St. Paul, while Delta flies nonstop year-round to Salt Lake City, and United flies to San Francisco and Denver. In addition, **Sun Country Airlines** (800/359-6786, www.suncountry.com) has seasonal charters between Anchorage and Minneapolis. **Vladivostok Air** (www.vladivostokavia.ru/en) has flights to Vladivostok in Russia.

Summer-only nonstop Anchorage flights arrive from Chicago (American and United), Cincinnati (Delta), Dallas (American), Denver (Frontier), Detroit (Northwest), and Houston (Continental).

INTERNATIONAL FLIGHTS

Anchorage has what may be the best connections to international destinations of any city its size in the United States. The following companies offer nonstop service into Anchorage: **Air Canada** (888/247-2262, www.aircanada.com) from Vancouver, **Japan Airlines** (800/525-3663, www.jal.com) from Tokyo, **Korean Air** (800/438-5000, www.koreanair.com) from Seoul, **China Airlines** (800/227-5118, www.china-airlines.com) from Taipei, and **Condor Airlines** (800/524-6975, www.condor.com) from Frankfurt.

REGIONAL AIRLINES

Anchorage's largest regional airlines is **Frontier Alaska** (907/266-8394 or 800/866-8394, www.frontierak.com). As Frontier, the company flies from Anchorage to Fairbanks, Aniak, Dillingham, Togiak, and Galena. Their subsidiary, **Era Aviation** (907/266-8394 or 800/866-8394, www.frontierak.com) connects Anchorage with Bethel, Cordova, Homer, Kenai, Kodiak, and Valdez.

PenAir (907/243-2323 or 800/448-4226, www.penair.com) has flights to Aniak, Cold Bay, Dillingham, Dutch Harbor, Iliamna, King Salmon, McGrath, the Pribilof Islands, Sand Point, and Unalakleet, and **Arctic Circle Air** (907/842-3870 or 888/214-2364, www.arcticcircleair.com) serves Cordova, Iliamna, Unalakleet, St. Marys, and Yakutat. **Grant Aviation** (907/243-3592 or 888/359-4726, www.flygrant.com) connects with Homer and Kenai.

Alaska Railroad

Anchorage is a major stop for the Alaska Railroad, with service north all the way to Fairbanks and south to Seward and Whittier. The Alaska Railroad train depot (411 W. 1st Ave., 907/265-2494 or 800/544-0552, www.alaskarailroad.com) is just down the hill from the center of Anchorage. Its daily express to Fairbanks has prices comparable to those of the tour buses but is a much more comfortable, historical, enjoyable, and leisurely ride. The ***Denali Star*** **train** departs Anchorage daily at 8:15 A.M. mid-May–mid-September for Denali (arriving around 4 P.M., $146 one-way) and Fairbanks (arriving 8 P.M., $210 one-way). The train also stops in Wasilla and Talkeetna, where you can hop off, but you're not allowed to check any luggage—only what you can carry on.

A variety of rail-lodging and rail-lodging-boat tour options are listed in Alaska Railroad's brochure or online. Especially popular is the **Spencer Glacier float tour** ($202 round-trip from Anchorage), where the train stops in the Kenai Mountains for an easy rafting trip down the Placer River. Day-hikers and backpackers can also take advantage of special whistle-stop service at Spencer Glacier.

Take the ***Coastal Classic*** **train** (daily, $75 one-way, $119 round-trip) south to Seward for a fantastic over-the-top voyage across the Kenai Peninsula. The route diverges from the highway near Portage and then winds steeply into the Kenai Mountains past several glaciers. The Anchorage to Whittier ***Glacier Discovery*** **train** ($80 round-trip) departs at 10 A.M., arriving three hours later. Service to both Whittier and Seward is mid-May–mid-September only. Both of these trains also stop in Girdwood, but only hand-carried baggage is allowed from there.

The Alaska Railroad now offers **GoldStar** double-decker coaches with open-air viewing platforms for an old-fashioned luxury rail experience. Add $85 extra to Denali, $110 extra to Fairbanks. Both **Princess Tours** (206/336-6000 or 800/426-0500, www.princesslodges.com) and **Holland America Tours/Gray Line** (907/277-5581 or 888/452-1737, www.graylinealaska.com) hook their superdome cars to the back of the express for a similar experience. These are mostly for the cruise ship crowd, but they also sell seats to independent travelers.

Buses

A number of bus companies head out from Anchorage to other parts of the state, and most will carry bikes for an extra charge. Try a city bus for a cheaper option if you're just heading to Palmer or Wasilla from Anchorage.

Alaska/Yukon Trails (907/479-2277 or 800/770-7275, www.alaskashuttle.com) has a daily Anchorage–Talkeetna–Denali–Fairbanks run in the summer, and several times a week the rest of the year.

In the summer **Alaska Direct Bus Line** (907/277-6652 or 800/770-6652, www.alaskadirectbusline.com) has service three times a week from Anchorage to Tok, continuing to Whitehorse and Fairbanks. Winter service is twice weekly.

Denali Overland Transportation (907/733-2384 or 800/651-5221, www.denalioverland.com) offers charter service to Talkeetna and Denali and often has space for individual travelers. **Alaska Park Connection** (907/245-0200 or 800/266-8625, www.alaskacoach.com) provides summertime bus service connecting Anchorage with Seward, Talkeetna, and Denali.

Homer Stage Line (907/883-3914, www.homerstageline.com) has daily summertime service to Seward, Soldotna, Kenai, Cooper Landing, and Homer—plus all points between. Winter runs are twice a week to Homer and six days a week to Seward. **Seward Bus Lines** (907/563-0800 or 888/420-7788, www.sewardbuslines.net) provides daily year-round bus service to Seward.

Girdwood Shuttle (907/783-1900, www.girdwoodshuttle.com, May–Sept.) provides daily vans connecting Anchorage with Girdwood, Whittier, and Seward.

GETTING AROUND

City Buses

People Mover (907/343-6543 www.peoplemover.org), Anchorage's public bus system, covers the entire Anchorage Basin. Weekday service is extensive, with all routes operating 6 A.M.–10 P.M. On Saturday, most lines run 8 A.M.–8 P.M., but Sunday service is only offered on certain routes 9:30 A.M.–6:30 P.M. Visit the **Transit Center** (6th Ave. and G St., Mon.–Fri. 7 A.M.–6 P.M.), where you can pick up a *Ride Guide* timetable of all routes. Exact fare ($1.75 adults, $1 ages 5–18) is required, and transfers are valid only on a different bus traveling in the same direction within two hours of the time of receipt. People Mover buses are free all day in the downtown area; just get on board and ride. A $4 day pass—good for unlimited rides—is sold on all buses.

All People Mover buses can transport wheelchairs, or call the **Anchor Rides** program (907/562-8444) for special transportation needs. You'll need to call at least a day in advance.

Mat-Su Community Transit bus, better known as **MASCOT** (907/376-5000, www.matsutransit.com), has weekday commuter runs from Anchorage to Palmer, Wasilla, and even Big Lake for just $3.

Taxis

Taxis are expensive: Most charge $2 per flag drop plus $2.50 per mile thereafter. The companies include **Alaska Cab** (907/563-5353), **Yellow Cab** (907/222-2222, www.akyellowcab.com), and **Anchorage Checker Cab** (907/276-1234). There's always a line of waiting cabs outside the airport if you are just arriving and need a way into Anchorage; the fare is around $15 to downtown. Disabled travelers should contact Alaska Cab; it has wheelchair lifts on some vehicles.

Car Rentals

Anchorage is car-happy, so rental cars can be very hard to come by. Make car reservations as much as two months ahead to be sure of a car in the peak season. Most of the major companies (Alamo, Avis, Budget, Dollar, Enterprise, Hertz, National, and Thrifty) operate from the Anchorage airport. Don't even think of renting a car in Anchorage and leaving it elsewhere in Alaska; the charges are sky-high for this luxury.

Check www.travelocity.com to see who currently has the cheapest Anchorage rentals. The best rates are frequently through **Payless** (907/243-3616 or 800/729-5377), **Budget** (907/243-6492 or 800/248-0150), **Denali Car Rental** (907/276-1230 or 800/757-1230, www.denalicarrentalak.com), **Dollar** (907/248-5338 or 800/800-4000), or **High Country Car & Truck Rental** (a.k.a. E-Z Rent-A-Car, 907/272-0639, www.highcountryrental.net).

Most car rental companies prohibit driving on the McCarthy Road, Denali Highway, and other rough roads, but many drivers also ignore these rules. If you're traveling in the winter, ask for a car with studded tires, which are—surprisingly—not on many Anchorage rental cars; Denali Car Rental is one exception.

When making a reservation, be sure to mention if you have a AAA card; you can often save substantially on the rates. Most of the national companies have car rental desks at the airport, but if you rent one there you'll add on an extra 29 percent tax to the rate (versus 18 percent in town). Especially for long rentals, it's usually best *not* to get a rental car from the airport.

RV Rentals

Quite a few places let you rent honkin' Alaska-size RV land yachts—the ones you sit behind for miles as they waddle down the road at 30 mph and four miles to the gallon. Recreational vehicles may be of some value for groups of six or more, but are completely unnecessary for smaller groups.

The following Anchorage companies rent RVs: **Great Alaskan Holidays** (907/248-7777 or 888/225-2752, www.greatalaskanholidays.com), **Clippership Motorhome Rentals** (907/562-7051 or 800/421-3456, www.clippershiprv.com), **ABC Motorhome Rentals** (907/279-2000 or 800/421-7456, www.abcmotorhome.com), and **Alaska Motorhome Rentals** (907/258-7109 or 800/357-7368, www.bestofalaskatravel.com).

Tour Buses

At least a half-dozen tour companies are happy to sell you bus tours of Anchorage and the surrounding area; get their brochures from the visitors center. The largest companies—**Gray Line of Alaska** (907/277-5581 or 888/452-1737, www.graylinealaska.com) and **Princess Tours** (206/336-6000 or 800/426-0500, www.princess.com)—also offer a wide range of other package trips on land, sea, or air throughout Alaska.

Boat

Although there are no boat tours out of Anchorage, it *is* a good place to check out boat trips across Prince William Sound and out of Seward. Several tour companies offer trips that include a bus from Anchorage to Whittier, boat across the Sound, and flight or bus ride back to Anchorage. Or get to Whittier on your own and hop on one of these tour boats.

The **Alaska Marine Highway** (800/642-0066, www.dot.state.ak.us/amhs) does not reach Anchorage, but you can connect up with the system in Whittier via the Alaska Railroad or in Homer by bus.

Vicinity of Anchorage

CHUGACH STATE PARK

Alaska's second-largest chunk of state-owned land, Chugach State Park (907/345-5014, www.alaskastateparks.org) encompasses nearly half a million acres—half the size of Delaware. The park covers the entire Chugach Range from Eagle River, 25 miles north of Anchorage, to Girdwood, 35 miles south. It could take a committed hiker years to explore all its trails, ridges, peaks, and passes. From the short but steep 1.5-mile trail up Flattop Mountain in Anchorage to the 25-mile trek from the Eagle River Nature Center over Crow Pass down to Girdwood, there are a wide range of trails to choose from, each varying in length, elevation, difficulty, access, and congestion.

Pick up hiking brochures at the Alaska Public Lands Information Center in Anchorage, decide on a trail, then dress for rain. The clouds often sit down on these city-surrounding mountaintops, and when it's sunny and hot in Anchorage, it could be hailing only a few minutes away on the trails. But don't let that stop you. This whole park is within a few miles of where half of Alaska's population huddles, but up in these mountains it's easy to pretend you're a hundred years behind the crowds, and all the hustle and bustle on the Inlet flats is far in the future.

Jenny Zimmerman's *A Naturalist's Guide to Chugach State Park, Alaska* tells the full story on the park.

Camping and Cabins

Developed state park campgrounds are found at **Eklutna Lake** ($10) and **Eagle River** ($15) north of Anchorage, and at **Bird Creek** ($15) to the south. All three have four-day limits, outhouses, and water, and are generally open May–September. Located just off the Hiland Road exit 12 miles north of Anchorage, the often-full Eagle River Campground can be reserved (907/746-4644 or 800/952-8624, www.lifetimeadventures.net).

A wonderful cabin (www.dnr.alaska.gov/parks, $50) is available on the shore of Eklutna Lake, and three yurts and an eight-person cabin (907/694-2108, www.ernc.org, $65) are near the Eagle River Nature Center.

Hillside Trails

Two trailheads on the city's southeastern outskirts give access to a network of crisscrossing and connecting trails in the section of the range that hems in Anchorage Bowl. They're all off Hillside Drive, which skirts a suburb of sparkling glass houses and gorgeous views of the skyline, inlet, and Mt. Susitna to the west. City buses do not reach the park in this area, so you'll really need a vehicle to get to the Hillside trailheads. Day-use parking costs $5 per vehicle.

For the **Glen Alps Trailhead** drive south on New Seward Highway and turn east toward the mountains on O'Malley Road. Follow it to Hillside Drive, where you turn right, then left on Upper Huffman Road. In 0.5 miles, go right again onto aptly named Toilsome Hill Drive. Toil steeply uphill for 2.5 miles to reach the Glen Alps parking lot ($5 day-use fee). On warm summer weekends every space in the lot fills with cars, so get here early or take the **Flattop Mountain Shuttle** (907/279-3334, www.hike-anchorage-alaska.com, $22 round-trip) from downtown. Take a look from the nearby overlook, and then head up the **Flattop Mountain Trail** for even better views. This extremely popular 1.5-mile trail gains 1,500 feet and is very steep near the top as you scramble through the boulders.

Also from the Glen Alps Trailhead are several moderate and very scenic hikes: **Little O'Malley Peak,** 7.5 miles round-trip; the **Ramp and Wedge,** 11 miles round-trip; and **Williwaw Lakes,** 13 miles round-trip. A great mountain bike route is the 11-mile (one-way) **Powerline Trail** that also takes off from the Glen Alps Trailhead and goes over 3,550-foot Powerline Pass all the way to the Indian Creek Trailhead on Turnagain Arm.

Continue north on Hillside Drive past Upper Huffman Road and take a right on Upper O'Malley Road. The second left leads to **Prospect Heights Trailhead,** where the **Wolverine Peak Trail** leads to the top of this 4,455-foot mountain (11 miles round-trip). You'll discover great views of the Alaska Range and Anchorage, but go in late summer when the snow has melted.

Eagle River Area

Take the Eagle River exit 13 miles north of Anchorage on the Glenn Highway, then your first right onto Eagle River Road, a dazzling paved 11-mile ride right into the heart of Chugach State Park. Rafters and kayakers on the Class II Eagle River can put in at two access points (Miles 7.5 and 9) along this road. The road ends at the **Eagle River Nature Center** (907/694-2108, www.ernc.org, Sun.–Thurs. 10 A.M.–5 P.M., Fri.–Sat. 10 A.M.–7 P.M. June–Aug., Tues.–Sun. 10 A.M.–5 P.M. May and Sept., Fri.–Sun. 10 A.M.–5 P.M. Oct.–Apr., parking $5), which features a "close-up corner" with furs and a track book, as well as an aurora display and a gift shop. Park rangers lead daily 1.5-hour hikes at 1 P.M. June–August. The **Rodak Nature Trail** (0.5 miles round-trip) is a wide gravel route with informative signs on snow, glaciers, the forest, and the sun. It's 15 minutes well spent. For a longer walk, take the seven-mile **River Trail** along the Eagle River.

Eklutna Lake

Twenty-six miles north of Anchorage on the Glenn Highway is the exit for Eklutna Lake, a favorite weekend destination. Narrow and winding Eklutna Road follows the Eklutna River 10 miles to the lake, where you'll find a pleasant small **campground** ($10) with outhouses and a large picnic area. The 14-mile **Lakeside Trail-Eklutna Glacier Trail** starts nearby, skirting the west side of Eklutna Lake and then climbing to this very scenic glacier. Three side trails lead off the main route to Twin Peaks, Bold Ridge, and East Fork of Eklutna River. This is an outstanding mountain biking area in summer, and a popular wintertime skiing and snowmobiling trail. Most of the route is also open to ATVs Sunday–Wednesday, so you may not have peace and quiet. Experienced skiers may want to continue beyond Eklutna Glacier via a multiglacier traverse that takes them 31 miles to Crow Pass. The Alaska Mountaineering Club (907/272-1811, www.mcak.org) has three huts along the way.

Kayak and bike rentals are available near the Eklutna Campground from **Lifetime Adventures** (907/746-4644 or 800/952-8624, www.lifetimeadventures.net), along with a popular paddle-and-peddle option ($75 pp): you kayak across the lake and ride a mountain bike back.

Also from the Eklutna exit, you can follow the access road a mile south to scenic **Thunderbird Falls** (if you're heading north from Anchorage, there's a marked Thunderbird Falls exit before you reach the Eklutna exit). The trail takes you on an easy one-mile hike up Thunderbird Creek. Follow your ears to the falls.

Crow Pass

For one of the longest and most scenic hikes in the park, head out on the 25-mile **Crow Pass Trail.** This trail (also known as the Historic Iditarod Trail) provided a turn-of-the-20th-century overland route from Seward through the Chugach to the Interior gold mining town of Iditarod. The gradual climb to Crow Pass fords several streams, including Eagle River midway along the trail. It might be wise to camp overnight and cross the river in the morning, when the glacial runoff is lower. Raven Glacier and Crystal Lake are scenic highlights near Crow Pass, where you leave Chugach State Park and continue in immense Chugach National Forest. The Forest Service has a popular A-frame **cabin** (518/885-3639 or 877/444-6777, www.recreation.gov, $35) on the summit that you can rent. From the cabin it's four miles down to the trailhead on rough Crow Creek Road, then another five miles to the Alyeska Ski Resort access road. Experienced skiers sometimes use the Iditarod and Crow Pass Trails for a winter traverse of the mountains, but be aware that avalanche danger can be very high.

NORTH OF ANCHORAGE

Chugach State Park includes several popular destinations north of Anchorage around Eklutna Lake and Eagle River.

Arctic Valley

Six miles north of Anchorage along the Glenn Highway is the exit to Arctic Valley Road, which climbs seven steep miles to the parking lot at the Alpenglow ski area. A trailhead about a mile before road's end leads to long **Ship Creek Trail,** which, with a little cross-country hiking, hooks up with Bird Creek and Indian Creek Trails via the passes of the same names. It's 22 miles from Arctic Valley to Indian Creek Trailhead. Plan on 2–3 days to do this traverse. From the Alpenglow parking lot a two-mile trail goes up to **Rendezvous Peak,** an easy hike with great views of the city, the inlet, and even Mt. McKinley if you're lucky.

Eklutna Historical Park

This is one of those surprising discoveries just off the Glenn Highway. Take the Eklutna Road exit (26 miles northeast of Anchorage) and cross back over the highway to Eklutna Village. Russian Orthodoxy is strongly overlaid on Native Alaskan culture from this point, at the site of the first Tanaina (a branch of the Athabascans) settlement on the Inlet, down through the western Kenai Peninsula, Kodiak, and the Aleutians. The ancestors of most of these Indians were converted by Russian missionaries, and **St. Nicholas Russian Orthodox Church**—a miniature log chapel that dates from the 1830s and was reconstructed in the 1970s—is the oldest building in the Anchorage area. Nearby is a newer and larger church. Both are set against a backdrop of 80 or so colorful **spirit houses** that sit atop Native Alaskan graves. Informative half-hour tours (907/688-

ANCHORAGE AND VICINITY

© DON PITCHER

spirit houses (graves) at Eklutna Historical Park

6026, $5 adults, $3 seniors and children ages 10–15, children under 10 free) are offered Monday–Friday 10 A.M.–4 P.M. mid-May–mid-September, and you can stroll the grounds at other times. A small gift shop sells Native Alaskan crafts.

TURNAGAIN ARM

Cook Inlet bends east from Anchorage, becoming Turnagain Arm. The inlet was named by Captain James Cook's master, William Bligh, who later captained the ill-fated HMS *Bounty.* The Seward Highway curves around Turnagain Arm, past the town of Girdwood and the turnoff to Portage Glacier and Whittier, and finally south over the Kenai Mountains to Seward, 127 miles away. The Turnagain Arm stretch is exceptionally scenic, but traffic is often heavy, so drive carefully and keep your headlights on at all times. Many people have lost their lives in traffic accidents on this narrow highway jammed against the cliffs, so always use extreme caution. Travelers will find places to watch birds, beluga whales, Dall sheep, and rock climbers along the way, and you can stop for hikes or to fish along the way.

Potter Marsh Area

Potter Marsh is on the south edge of Anchorage, with a boardwalk extending into the marsh. This is a good spot to look for waterfowl, including Canada geese, trumpeter swans, and even the flyin'-fool Arctic terns. Bring binoculars and a light jacket for the often-breezy conditions. This marsh was created when the railroad builders installed an embankment to protect the track from Turnagain Arm's giant tides, which dammed the freshwater drainage from the mountains.

A mile south on the other side of the highway is the **Potter Section House** (907/345-5014, Mon.–Fri. 8 A.M.–4:30 P.M. year-round), a small railroad museum of interpretive displays and signs outside and inside the restored original "section" house. This is also headquarters for Chugach State Park; get brochures on local trails here. Check out the nine-foot rotary snowplow once used to clear avalanches. A small gift shop sells railroad memorabilia and books.

Turnagain Arm Trail

Across the highway from Potter Section House is the parking lot for **Potter Creek Trailhead,** the first access to the Turnagain Arm Trail, which parallels the highway for over nine miles, with good opportunities to see Dall sheep, moose, and spruce grouse. The trail began as a turn-of-the-20th-century wagon road built to transport railroad workers and supplies. This is a very popular early summer path since its south-facing slopes lose the snow early. In three miles is **McHugh Creek,** an always-crowded day-use area and trailhead for the seven-mile hike up to **Rabbit Lake.** You can continue south along the Turnagain Arm Trail past three more trailheads all the way to **Windy Corner Trailhead** nine miles from your starting point, and not far from Beluga Point.

Beluga Point

Twenty miles south of Anchorage is Beluga Point, a good place to see the small white **beluga whales** cavorting in Turnagain Arm in late May and late August; they follow salmon into these shallow waters. Unfortunately, overhunting by Native Alaskans caused the population of belugas to plummet in the 1990s, and they still have not recovered.

Look behind you for the **Dall sheep** that often wander close to the highway in this area. Or just have a picnic and wait for the Cook Inlet's famous **bore tides.** The tides here, at 30 feet, are among the world's highest, and the lead breaker can be up to eight feet high, a half-mile across, and can move at over 10 miles per hour. This is the only bore tide in the United States, created when a large body of water (Cook Inlet) is forced by strong tidal action into a narrow shallow one (Turnagain Arm). Look for a series of small swells (2–3 feet high, larger depending on the wind) that crash against the rocks and send up a mighty spray. You won't soon forget the roar of the bore, which goes by Beluga Point roughly two hours after low tide in Anchorage—check the tide tables in the daily newspapers. One warning: Never go out on the Turnagain Arm mudflats at any time. The mixture of glacial silt and mud creates quicksand; people have drowned after getting their feet stuck in the mud and being inundated by the incoming tide. Don't take a chance!

Indian and Bird Creeks

Twenty-five miles south of Anchorage, and right before Turnagain House Restaurant in Indian, take a left on the gravel road and head 1.5 miles to the **Indian Valley Trailhead.** This trail, which follows Indian Creek over Indian Pass (especially rewarding during Indian summer), is five miles of easy walking on a well-maintained path. You can then continue for several miles of undeveloped hiking until you hook up with the Ship Creek Trail, which runs 22 miles to Arctic Valley north of Anchorage. The Powerline Pass Trail goes 11 miles from the Glenn Alps trailhead to Indian Creek Trail; look for the signed turnoff 100 yards up the Indian Valley Trail. Historic **Indian Valley Mine** (907/653-1120, www.indianvalleymine.com, mid-May–mid-Sept.) has summertime gold panning, historic buildings, a little museum, and a gift shop.

Two miles down the highway from Indian is the Bird Creek area, where dozens of cars line the roadside on July–August afternoons. They're all here trying to hook a silver salmon in this very productive creek. A half-mile north of the creek is a parking area for **Bird Ridge Trail,** which climbs straight up this 3,500-foot promontory in less than two miles.

Also nearby is the **Bird Creek Campground** ($15), a surprisingly pretty place just off the busy Seward Highway. Campsites are just a few feet from Cook Inlet. This thickly forested campground is often full of anglers working Bird Creek. The **Bird to Gird Bike Trail** runs right through the middle of the campground, continuing north for three miles to Indian and south three miles to Girdwood along the old highway.

GIRDWOOD

The town of Girdwood is officially part of the hectic Anchorage municipality, but feels a world away. Located 37 miles south via the Seward Highway, the original town was leveled by the 1964 earthquake. A cluster of businesses stands along the highway, providing a rest stop for travelers, but new Girdwood and the Alyeska Resort sit at the end of a three-mile access road (Alyeska Highway). This winter resort is a favorite destination for locals, package tourists, unsuspecting travelers, and the occasional backpacker who likes a quick ride to the alpine tundra in the summer.

Girdwood doesn't have a visitors center, but you'll find information on the Web at www.girdwoodalaska.com. In addition to the resort, the town has several restaurants, a grocery store, a post office, a library, and a laundry with showers. Both the library and the coin laundry have Internet access.

Sights

The six-mile paved **Bird to Gird Bike Trail** starts from the Hotel Alyeska and continues north all the way to Bird Creek, following Turnagain Arm much of the way.

Adjacent to the Bake Shop, **Girdwood Center for Visual Arts** (907/783-3209, daily in summer) is a co-op gallery with pottery, paintings, photography, glasswork, jewelry, and other locally crafted pieces.

The Forest Service's **Glacier Ranger District office** (907/783-3242) is on the left as you drive into town from the Seward Highway and is open weekdays. It can provide details and maps for hikers, anglers, sea kayakers, and other recreation enthusiasts heading into Chugach National Forest.

Stop off at the **Alaska Candle Factory** (907/783-2354) on the access road a half-mile from Seward Highway. Their candles are not only unique and inexpensive souvenirs or gift items; they also burn until the cows come home.

Crow Creek Mine

The gravel Crow Creek Road leads from Girdwood three miles to Crow Creek Mine (907/229-3105, www.crowcreekgoldmine.com, daily 9 A.M.–6 P.M. mid-May–Sept.), one

© DON PITCHER

historic Crow Creek Mine in Girdwood

of the earliest gold strikes in Alaska (1896) and Southcentral Alaska's richest mine. The area was actively mined until World War II, producing over 45,000 ounces of gold. There's still a lot of gold to be found, and the creek attracts both casual panners looking for a flake of gold and those who come with metal detectors and large suction dredges. (When I last visited, a German tourist had just discovered a pea-sized nugget of gold.) Eight of the original mine buildings have been restored by the Toohey family and are filled with all sorts of flotsam and jetsam from the past. Entrance is $5 adults, free for kids under age 6; $15 adults or $5 kids if you want to pan for gold (a pan and instructions are provided). There's a little gift shop, panning equipment rental, and overnight campsites ($5). It's a pretty place with a rich history, and a *must* stop in the Girdwood area.

Continue another four miles out on Crow Creek Road beyond Crow Creek Mine to the **Crow Pass Trailhead.** It's an invigorating and beautiful 3.5 miles to the pass, with a 2,000-foot elevation gain. The trail is in the alpine area much of the route and passes old mining ruins and a Forest Service cabin (www.recreation.gov, $35). A half-mile beyond the pass is Raven Glacier, where you enter Chugach State Park.

Events

The big summertime event is **Girdwood Forest Fair** (www.girdwoodforestfair.com) held in early July for more than 35 years. Hundreds of folks show up to buy arts and crafts, graze through the food booths, and listen to bands cranking out the tunes from two separate stages. It's a three-day party that seems to attract every free-spirited hippie left in Alaska. No dogs, politicians, or religious orders are allowed.

Skiing and snowboarding events fill the winter calendar at Alyeska Resort (907/754-1111, www.alyeskaresort.com), but the most fun for spectators is the **Spring Carnival and Slush Cup** in late April, when costumed skiers and boarders blast downhill and attempt to make it across a slushy pond. There are lots of cold, wet folks at this one.

Summer Recreation

First, check out Alyeska Resort and the impressive lobby of the enormous Hotel Alyeska. Next, fork over $18 to catch a ride 2,300 feet up Mt. Alyeska on the **aerial tramway** (907/754-2275). On top are two restaurants. The two 60-passenger tram cars are entirely wheelchair accessible. Follow the well-marked trail to the alpine overlook onto cute Alyeska Glacier. If you have reservations to dine at Seven Glaciers restaurant, the tram ride is free. A tram-and-lunch special to Glacier Express Café costs $28; the tram office has details.

A paved path parallels the road to the Hotel Alyeska, and Crow Creek Road provides an easy dirt road for mountain bikers. Rent bikes from **Girdwood Ski & Cyclery** (907/783-2453, www.girdwood-ski-and-cyclery.com).

Guides from **The Ascending Path** (907/783-0505 or 877/783-0505, www.theascendingpath.com) lead glacier hikes ($139 for 3 hours), ice climbing classes ($220 for 5 hours), and a variety of forest hikes in the Girdwood area.

Alaska Paragliding (907/301-1215, www.alaskaparagliding.com) takes novices on exciting tandem paragliding rides from the top of the tram (tandem lesson $195).

Alpine Air (907/783-2360, www.alpineairalaska.com) has helicopter flightseeing, tours of Prince William Sound, and a very popular two-hour dog mushing adventure ($459 pp) that includes a glacier landing and the chance to drive a team of sled dogs.

Winter Recreation

Alaska's primary center for downhill skiing and boarding, **Alyeska Resort** (907/754-1111 or 800/880-3880, www.alyeskaresort.com) encompasses the ski and snowboard area, a large hotel, and several restaurants. The resort covers 500 skiable acres and has 60 trails, a 60-passenger tram, eight chairlifts, two pony lifts, and a tubing park. Most of the ski runs are at the intermediate or advanced level. In addition to abundant natural snowfall (depths generally exceed 10 feet), there is snowmaking capability on the lower slopes.

Alyeska Resort generally opens for skiing and snowboarding around Thanksgiving and closes at the end of April. Hours are daily 10:30 A.M.–5:30 P.M., with night skiing Thursday–Saturday until 9:30 P.M., and reduced hours early and late in the season. A shuttle bus connects the main ski area with the Hotel Alyeska (where the tram departs). If you're coming from Anchorage, the resort also has a wintertime ski/snowboard bus on weekends and school holidays for $16–20 round-trip. It's a good way to let someone else do the driving on this notoriously dangerous road.

Adult lift tickets cost $60 full day, $50 half-day; Thursday–Saturday there's night skiing for $10 extra. A half-day ticket plus night skiing will run you $60. There are discounts for children, students, families, and multiday passes. Skis, snowshoes, snowboards, and ice skates (for use on the skating pond) can be rented in the day lodge, where you can also get expensive cafeteria food. More cafeteria fare, along with an elaborate restaurant and lounge, is on top of the mountain. Ski and snowboarding classes at all levels are available. Traffic between Anchorage and Girdwood can back up on winter weekends, so head out early if you're driving. Call 907/754-7669 or visit www.alyeskaresort.com for the latest snow conditions.

Accommodations

Heading toward the resort on the access road, go right on Timberline, pass gorgeous ski chalets, then turn right again on Alpina. Around a couple of curves is the **Alyeska Hostel** (907/783-2222, www.alyeskahostel.com). This is a great place with a coed dorm ($20 pp in bunks; $10 ages 7–12), a private room ($50 d), a family room ($50 d), and a summer-only cabin ($65 d or $85 for 4), plus a full kitchen and two baths, free Wi-Fi, and a wood-burning sauna out back. Reservations are recommended in the summer and mid-winter, especially for the private room and cabin. There is no lockout and no curfew.

A second hostel opened in 2009—**Girdwood Alaska Backpackers Inn** (907/727-4678, www.hostelgirdwood.com)—located just off the highway behind the Tesoro station (and three miles from "downtown" Girdwood). Dorm rooms cost $25 per person, and the five private rooms are $50 s or $60 d. There's a common room, a kitchen, shared bathrooms, and decks.

Alyeska Accommodations (907/783-2000 or 888/783-2001, www.alyeskaaccommodations.com) is the best source for condo, chalet, and home rentals, representing dozens of places around Girdwood. Two organizations provide descriptions and helpful links to websites for most local B&Bs and guesthouses: **Girdwood Bed-and-Breakfast Association** (907/222-4858, www.gbba.org) and the **Alyeska/Girdwood Accommodations Association** (907/222-3226, www.agaa.biz).

The luxurious 307-room **Hotel Alyeska** (907/754-1111 or 800/880-3880, www.alyeskaresort.com) is an eight-story 304-room hotel where nicely appointed rooms include heated towel racks, fridges, ski-boot storage boxes, Wi-Fi, and safes. Other in-hotel amenities include three restaurants, a fitness center, a large indoor swimming pool, a sauna, and a hot tub. The tram to the top of Mt. Alyeska is right out the back door. Lodging rates vary, with the lowest prices ($299 d) for small rooms on levels 2 and 3, up to $339 d for an eighth-floor room. Suites start at $399 and ride the tram all the way to $2,200 per night. Be sure to ask if they have any discounted rates and packages; your savings can be substantial.

Food and Entertainment

At the intersection of the Girdwood Spur Road and Seward Highway is a little strip mall with a variety of services, including a gas station–convenience store, a coin laundry, a video store, and a restaurant. Travelers heading south to Seward or north to Anchorage stop here before pushing back out on the highway. **Alpine Diner & Bakery** (907/783-2550) serves breakfast, lunch, and dinner, but it is best known for enormous pastries. There's always a queue on winter mornings as the pre-ski gang comes in to inject sugar and caffeine into their veins.

In business since 1962, famous **Double Musky Inn** (907/783-2822, www.doublemuskyinn.com, Tues.–Thurs. 5–10 P.M., Fri.–Sun. 4:30–10 P.M. early Dec.–late Oct., entrées $22–46) is 0.25 miles up Crow Creek Road on the left. It's crowded and loud, with long waits, a tacky New Orleans–meets-Alaska decor, and brief visits from your server. They don't take reservations either. Despite these drawbacks, the food is dependably good, if not stellar. Featured attractions are Cajun shrimp, garlic seafood pasta, rack of lamb, and the house specialty, French pepper steak. Save space for the ultra-rich Double Musky pie. A close friend of former Senator Ted Stevens, the restaurant's owner figured prominently in his trial.

At the Alyeska resort is **The Bake Shop** (907/783-2831, www.thebakeshop.com, daily until 7 P.M. summer, $6–9), a fine spot for lunch or an after-ski warm-up. Homemade sourdough bread, hearty soups, sandwiches, big breakfasts, and pizza fill out the menu. The front yard is packed with flowers, including some enormous peonies. Get espresso or surf the Web on the computers at **Java Haus** (907/783-2827, www.girdwoodjava.com, daily 7 A.M.–2 P.M.), a couple of doors away.

Down the hill on Arlberg Street is **Jack Sprat Restaurant** (907/783-5225, www.jacksprat.net, Mon.–Fri. 11 A.M.–10 P.M., Sat.–Sun. 9 A.M.–10 P.M.), with "fat and lean world cuisine" in a relaxed atmosphere. Dinners include everything from halibut burritos ($18) to filet mignon ($33), plus scallop Vietnamese pho ($21) and a decadent crème brûlée for dessert. Brunches are available on weekends, featuring Alaskan Benedict, tofu scramble, and blintzes.

Located next to the post office on Hightower Road, **Chair 5 Restaurant** (907/783-2500, www.chairfive.com) is a townie spot for very good pizzas (around $20), halibut curry, rib-eye steaks, and daily specials. The bar has a great choice of single malt scotches and microbrews.

For quick burritos, tacos, quesadillas, and seviche, escape to **Casa del Sol** (907/783-0088, Sun. 2–10 P.M., Mon.–Sat. 11 A.M.–10 P.M.)

in the coin laundry building behind Chair 5—they don't call it Laundromex for nothin'. Most items run $5–10.

Après-ski partiers head to the **Sitzmark Bar & Grill** at Alyeska Resort for a pitcher of beer and the chance to dance the night away to live bands on winter weekends; Sitzmark is closed in the summer.

On top of the mountain, **Seven Glaciers Restaurant** (907/754-2237, www.alyeskaresort.com, daily 5–10 P.M. summer, variable winter hours) offers excellent food with one of the best views you're ever likely to get while dining. Sitting on a crag at 2,303 feet above sea level, you can see the valley below, across to the Crow Pass area, and up Turnagain Arm. Main courses such as ginger-citrus encrusted halibut, Alaskan king crab, or grilled elk rib eye run $34–59, or try the chef's tasting menu with six courses for $95 per person. *Très élégant,* but not at all stuffy or pretentious. The seven-minute tram ride gives you the chance to survey the area, and if you have dinner reservations (required), the tram ride is free.

Getting There and Around

The **Alaska Railroad** (907/265-2494 or 800/544-0552, www.alaskarailroad.com) connects Girdwood with Anchorage daily in the summer, but the trains stop at a small shelter out near the Seward Highway. You'll need to make advance reservations for a pickup in Girdwood, and only carry-on luggage is allowed.

Glacier Valley Transit (907/754-2547, www.glaciervalleytransit.com, $1) has daily bus service throughout Girdwood, with wintertime ski and snowboard racks.

Girdwood Shuttle (907/783-1900, www.girdwoodshuttle.com, May–Sept.) provides van connections between Girdwood and Anchorage or Whittier for $40 one-way. Both **Homer Stage Line** (907/883-3914, www.homerstageline.com) and **Seward Bus Lines** (907/563-0800 or 888/420-7788, www.sewardbuslines.net) will stop in Girdwood, but call ahead.

PORTAGE GLACIER

Fifty miles south of Anchorage on the Seward Highway is the turnoff to Portage Glacier and Whittier. A six-mile access road takes you through Portage Valley to Portage Glacier. A town that stood on this corner was destroyed when the 1964 earthquake dropped the land 6–10 feet. Saltwater from Turnagain Arm inundated the area, killing the still-standing trees; the remaining buildings are gradually disintegrating. Portage Glacier is one of the more popular tourist attractions in Southcentral Alaska, so be ready to share the ride with busloads of cruise ship travelers.

An info booth along the Seward Highway has details on Whittier, and it sells tickets for various tour options, including the Alaska Railroad's scenic trips to Grandview.

Visitors Center

The Forest Service's **Begich, Boggs Visitor Center** (907/783-2326, www.fs.fed.us/r10/chugach, daily 9 A.M.–6 P.M. late May–Sept., Sat.–Sun. 10 A.M.–5 P.M. Oct.–late May) is named after Nicholas Begich (U.S. representative from Alaska and father of current U.S. Senator Mark Begich) and Hale Boggs (majority leader of the U.S. Senate and father of journalist Cokie Roberts), whose plane disappeared in the area in 1972. They were never found. A large picture window overlooks the narrow outlet of Portage Lake. When the visitor center first opened, the glacier was readily visible, but it is now out of sight around a corner, and in recent years the number of icebergs entering the lake has decreased greatly as it continues to shrink.

The visitors center boasts an amazing array of displays, including an ice cave, a small iceberg hauled in from the lake, an engrossing relief map of local ice fields, and everything you ever wanted to know about glaciers, including displays on glacial motion and crevasses. Don't miss the vial of tiny iceworms, which inhabit the surfaces of glaciers, feeding on pollen grains and red algae and surviving within a delicate, near-freezing temperature range. There's also good footage of iceworms in the

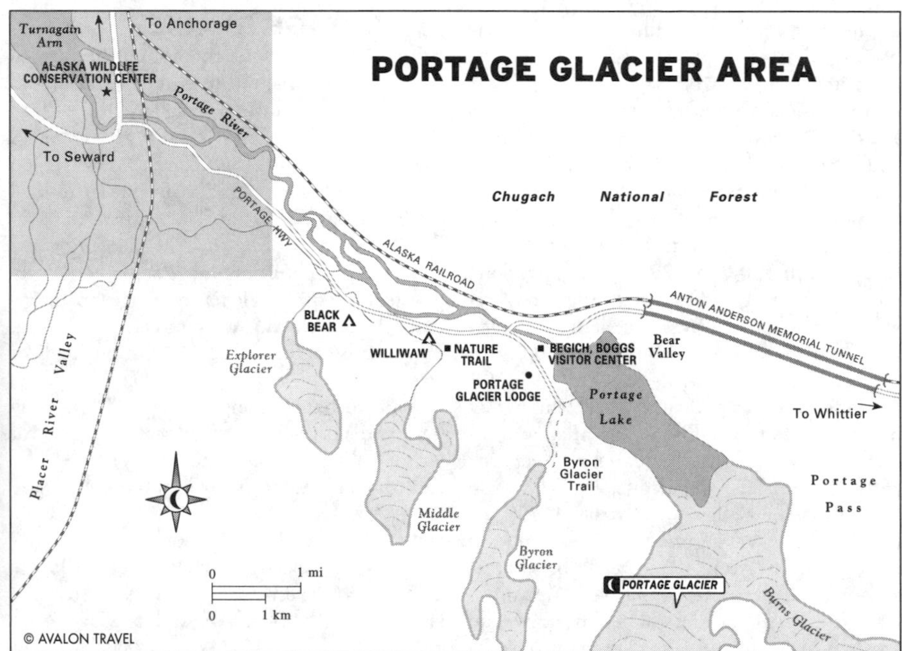

20-minute movie *Voices from the Ice* (shown every hour, $3).

During the summer, Forest Service naturalists lead half-mile nature walks. The **observation platform** near Williwaw Campground is a good place to see spawning red and chum salmon in late summer.

Seeing the Glacier

To see Portage Glacier, you'll need to hop onboard the 200-passenger ***Ptarmigan*** tour boat; catch it at the dock near the visitors center. Operated by Gray Line of Alaska (907/277-5581 or 888/452-1737, www.graylinealaska.com), these one-hour cruises across Portage Lake cost $29 and start at 10:30 A.M., with the last tour at 4:30 P.M. This boat tour, plus round-trip bus transportation from Anchorage (includes a stop at Alyeska) costs $75 on Gray Line.

Hiking

Two hikes are within walking distance of the visitors center. The **Moraine Loop Trail,** accessible from the path to the lodge, is a five-minute stroll through typical moraine vegetation; Portage Glacier occupied this ground only 100 years ago. Follow the access road past the visitors center (south) just under a mile. At the back of the parking lot starts the **Byron Glacier Trail,** an easy 0.75-mile walk along the runoff stream to below this hanging glacier.

Camping

Two Forest Service campgrounds ($14) near Portage contain woodsy sites: **Black Bear Campground** and the larger **Williwaw Campground.** The latter has summertime campfire programs on Saturday evenings and a wheelchair-accessible observation platform where spawning salmon are visible in the summer. Williwaw's sites can be reserved (518/885-3639 or 877/444-6777, www.recreation.gov).

Alaska Wildlife Conservation Center

This 140-acre game farm (907/783-2025,

www.alaskawildlife.org, $10 adults, $8 children and seniors, maximum $30 per vehicle) sits along Turnagain Arm just across the Seward Highway from the turnoff to Portage Glacier. Open daily all year, this nonprofit center for orphaned and injured Alaskan animals has grizzly and black bears, bison, moose, elk, musk oxen, deer, and caribou.

Matanuska-Susitna Valley

The Parks Highway heads north from Anchorage to Denali and Fairbanks, but before you're even close to either of these, the road takes you through the heart of the Matanuska-Susitna Valley, named for the two rivers that drain this part of Alaska. Originally established as an agricultural center, the Mat-Su is now primarily a bedroom community for Anchorage, with reasonably priced homes and fast-spreading semiurban sprawl. Two towns dominate the valley: The old farming settlement of Palmer is along the Glenn Highway 42 miles from Anchorage, while Wasilla rears its ugly face 40 miles north of Anchorage along the Parks Highway.

Visitors Center

The **Matanuska-Susitna Convention and Visitors Bureau** (907/746-5000, www.alaskavisit.com, daily 8:30 A.M.–6:30 P.M. mid-May–mid-Sept., closed mid-Sept.–mid-May) has a large visitors center just north of the junction of the Parks and Glenn Highways, and six miles south of Wasilla. Take the Trunk Road Exit and follow the CVB signs. Inside you'll find a plethora of brochures and stuffed critter heads lining the walls, Sarah Palin books (of course), plus free Wi-Fi and fishing info. When closed, check the lodging availability postings outside.

a Matanuska-Susitna Valley farm near Palmer

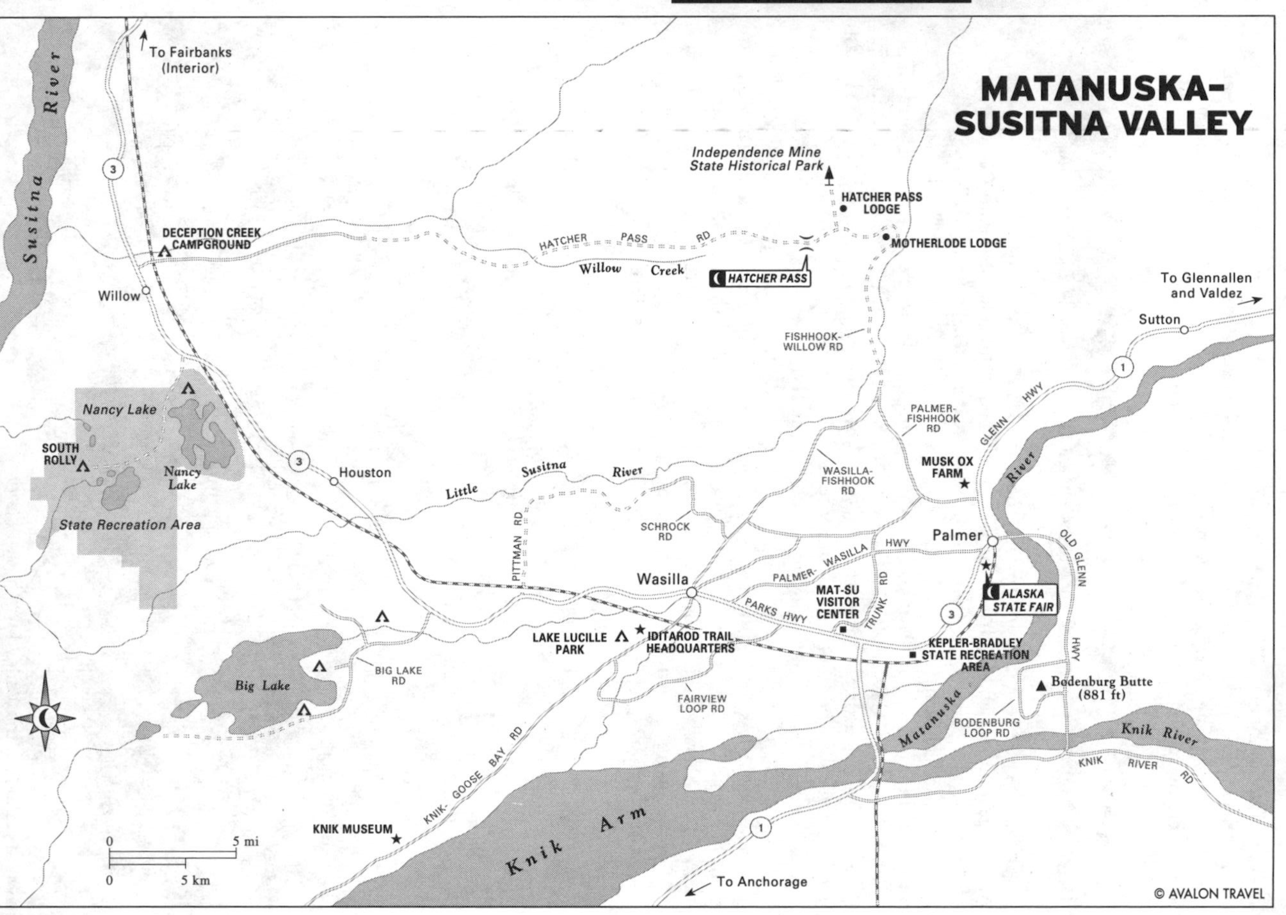
MATANUSKA-SUSITNA VALLEY
To Fairbanks (Interior)
Susitna River
3
DECEPTION CREEK CAMPGROUND
Willow
HATCHER PASS RD
Willow Creek
Independence Mine State Historical Park
HATCHER PASS LODGE
MOTHERLODE LODGE
HATCHER PASS
To Glennallen and Valdez
Sutton
FISHHOOK-WILLOW RD
1
GLENN HWY
Nancy Lake
SOUTH ROLLY
Nancy Lake
State Recreation Area
Houston
Little Susitna River
PALMER-FISHHOOK RD
WASILLA-FISHHOOK RD
MUSK OX FARM
Matanuska River
PITTMAN RD
SCHROCK RD
Palmer
OLD GLENN HWY
PALMER-WASILLA HWY
Wasilla
TRUNK RD
MAT-SU VISITOR CENTER
PARKS HWY
ALASKA STATE FAIR
LAKE LUCILLE PARK
IDITAROD TRAIL HEADQUARTERS
KEPLER-BRADLEY STATE RECREATION AREA
BIG LAKE RD
Big Lake
FAIRVIEW LOOP RD
Bodenburg Butte (881 ft)
BODENBURG LOOP RD
Knik River
KNIK RIVER RD
KNIK-GOOSE BAY RD
Knik Arm
KNIK MUSEUM
0
5 mi
0
5 km
To Anchorage
© AVALON TRAVEL

PALMER

For its first 20 years, Palmer (pop. 8,000) was little more than a railway depot for Alaska Railroad's Matanuska branch. Then in May 1935, during the height of both the Depression and a severe drought in the Midwest, the Federal Emergency Relief Administration of President Franklin D. Roosevelt's New Deal selected 200 farming families from the relief rolls of northern Michigan, Minnesota, and Wisconsin and shipped them here to colonize the Matanuska Valley. Starting out in tent cabins, the colonists cleared the dense virgin forest, built houses and barns, and planted crops pioneered at the University of Alaska's Agricultural Experimental Station. These hardy transplanted farmers endured the inevitable first-year hardships, including disease, homesickness, mismanagement, floods, and just plain bad luck. But by the fall of 1936 the misfits had been weeded out, 120 babies had been born in the colony, fertile fields and long summer days were filling barns with crops, and the colonists celebrated with a three-day harvest festival, the forerunner of the big state fair. In a few more years, Palmer had become not

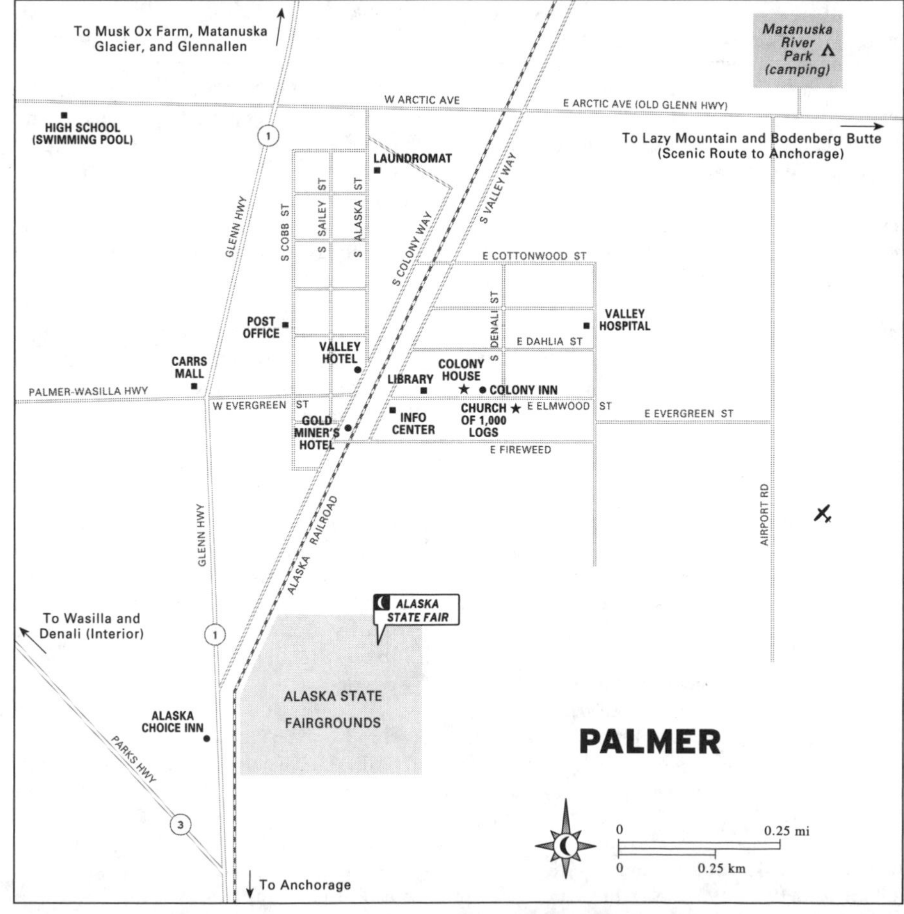

only a flourishing town but also the center of a bucolic and beautiful agricultural valley that was and still remains unique in Alaska.

Driving into Palmer from Wasilla along the Palmer-Wasilla Highway is a lot like driving into Wasilla from the bush on the Parks Highway time warp. The contrast between Palmer, an old farming community, and Wasilla, with its spontaneous combustion of helter-skelter development, is startling. Suffice it to say that Palmer is more conducive to sightseeing. I actually know people whose homes are in Wasilla but who keep a post office box in Palmer for their businesses to avoid the stigma of being labeled as from Wasilla!

Today, downtown Palmer is a blend of the old and new, with Klondike Mike's Saloon just up the street from a fine Tuscany-inspired bistro. Palmer is also home to the **National Outdoor Leadership School's** Alaska campus (907/745-4047, www.nols.edu). From this base, NOLS offers a range of courses that involve backpacking, sea kayaking, and mountaineering in remote parts of Alaska.

Sights

Start your visit at the **Palmer Visitors Information Center** (723 S. Valley Way, 907/745-2880, www.palmerchamber.org, daily 9 A.M.–6 P.M. May–Sept., Mon.–Fri. 10 A.M.–4 P.M. Oct.–Apr.). An adjacent garden features elephantine produce by late summer. Inside, load up with brochures, check out the gift shop, and wander downstairs to the little museum depicting the colonists' lives.

Colony House (316 E. Elmwood Ave., 907/745-1935, Tues.–Sat. 10 A.M.–4 P.M. summer only, $2 adults, $1 children) is just up the block from the visitors center. Built by the Beylund family, who moved here in 1935 from Wisconsin, it has been restored and filled with period furnishings to provide a window on the life of the Matanuska colonists.

Continue another block east on East Elmwood to visit the appropriately named **Church of a Thousand Logs,** built by the colonists in 1936–1937 and still in use.

Fairgrounds and Farms

Heading north through downtown, take a right on Arctic Avenue, which turns into the Old Glenn Highway. About a mile south of town on the Glenn Highway is the **Alaska State Fairgrounds.** At the fairgrounds is **Colony Village** (Mon.–Sat. 10 A.M.–4 P.M., free), which preserves some of Palmer's early buildings, including houses (one built in 1917 in Anchorage), several barns, a church, and a post office.

Five miles south of Palmer on the Old Glenn Highway, **Bodenberg Loop Road** is a five-mile drive through some of the most gorgeous valley farmland, with 6,400-foot **Pioneer Peak** towering behind. To see some of the original colony farms, head three miles north out along the Glenn Highway to **Farm Loop Road.** The valley's best-known crop isn't mentioned in any of the tourism brochures: marijuana. The local version (Matanuska Thunder) has a reputation as big as Alaska and is some of the most potent in the nation. It was formerly grown outside, but today nearly all grow-operations are indoors under lights.

Knik River Road splits off the Old Glenn Highway at Mile 9. Turn here and drive four miles to the trailhead for the **Pioneer Ridge-Knik River Trail,** which climbs a staggering 5,100 feet in less than six miles. Beyond this alpine ridge, only experienced rock climbers should consider heading to the twin summits of Pioneer Peak.

Seven miles south of Palmer on the Old Glenn Highway is the **Reindeer Farm** (907/745-4000, www.reindeerfarm.com, $6 adults, $4 children), where tours are offered daily 10 A.M.–6 P.M. in the summer. Children especially love the chance to pet a baby reindeer.

Alaska State Fair

Don't miss Alaska's biggest summertime event, a 12-day party to bring down the curtain on summer that draws 300,000 visitors annually. The state fair (907/745-4827 or 800/850-3247, www.alaskastatefair.org) cranks up the fourth Thursday of August and continues

MUSK OX FARM

While in Palmer, take the opportunity to visit the world's only domestic musk-ox farm (907/745-4151, www.muskoxfarm.org) and see 50 or so of these fascinating prehistoric Arctic creatures up close. During the half-hour tour you learn, among other things, that these exotic animals were hunted nearly to extinction in the early 1900s but have been reestablished in northwestern and arctic Alaska.

The musk ox wool is collected here, shipped back east to be spun, then distributed to Native Alaskan villages to be woven into *qiviut* wool products. *Qiviut* is eight times warmer than sheep's wool and much softer and finer even than cashmere. Scarves, stoles, caps, and tunics are sold in the showroom; don't miss the display of little squares of *qiviut*, cashmere, alpaca, and wool from sheep, camels, and llamas to compare the softness. The farm opens on Mother's Day in May (a great time to see the calves) and remains open daily 10 A.M.–6 P.M. through September; in winter admission is only for groups. Get there by taking the Glenn Highway north of town to Mile 50 and following the signs. Admission and a half-hour tour of this nonprofit facility is $8 adults, $7 seniors, $6 ages 5–12, and free for younger children.

© DON PITCHER

The musk ox farm in Palmer is a great place to view these unusual animals up close.

through Labor Day. On a weekend it may seem as though half of Anchorage has driven up to the fair. Long lines of cars wait to turn into the open field parking lots around the grounds, and crowds throng the 4-H displays, livestock auctions, horse shows, and carnival rides. There's live music daily, a rodeo, a demolition derby, three nights of fireworks, and lots of food and craft booths. Favorites always include the roasted corn on the cob, sickly sweet elephant ears, supersized turkey legs, and finger-lickin' halibut tacos. One big attraction is the gargantuan vegetables, including 125-pound pumpkins, 10-pound onions, and 2-pound radishes. The cabbage weigh-off makes front-page news in Alaska each year; a world record was set in 2009 when a Wasilla man grew a 127-pound cabbage. Entrance is $10–12 adults, $6–7 seniors and youths, and free for kids under age 5.

The **Alaska Railroad** (907/265-2494 or 800/544-0552, www.alaskarailroad.com) has direct train service from Anchorage to the fairgrounds during the state fair; it's a great way to avoid the traffic jams and parking hassles. The round-trip prices—including entrance to the fairgrounds—are just $54 adults, $47 seniors, $27 ages 6–12, $22 ages 2–5, and free for younger children.

Knik Glacier

Visible approximately seven miles up the Knik River Road, several companies offer airboat trips to the face of this unusual and impressive riverside glacier. Recommended is **Hunter Creek Adventures** (907/745-1577, www.knikglacier.com), with four-hour trips ($100) that include two hours at a camp next to the glacier, with kayaks for those who want to explore on their own. Overnight stays are possible in the fully outfitted camp for $250 per person including meals. **Mountain View Boat Tours** (907/745-5747 or 800/264-4582, www.mtviewrvpark.com) has shorter trips to the glacier.

Knik River Lodge (907/745-5002, www.knikriverlodge.com, $164 d) has 15 modern cabins 11 miles out on Knik River Road. All include private baths, decks, microwaves, fridges, Wi-Fi, and continental breakfasts. Also here is a surprisingly good restaurant (in a yurt!) with a changing menu that emphasizes locally grown produce, meats, and seafood. It's open daily for lunch and dinner with such specials as beef Wellington and rack of lamb; entrées are $21–29, and reservations are required.

Entertainment and Events

The **Palmer Open Air Market** has local produce, food, crafts, and musical entertainment. It takes place across from the downtown visitors center Fridays 11 A.M.–6 P.M. May–August.

Klondike Mike's Dance Hall & Saloon (820 S. Colony Way, 907/745-2676) has live rock and roll most nights in a rustic Alaskan setting. Also check the lineup at **Vagabond Blues** (642 S. Alaska St., 907/745-2233), which comes alive on weekends when singer-songwriter musicians pack the house.

Colony Days takes place the second weekend of June and includes a downtown parade, arts and crafts booths, bed races, foot races, and games. The main wintertime event is the **Colony Christmas Celebration,** with a lighted parade held on the second Friday and Saturday of December, along with reindeer sled rides, caroling, arts and crafts, visits with Santa, and fireworks.

Recreation

Two excellent hikes are accessible off the Old Glenn Highway east of Palmer. Heading north from downtown, go right on Arctic Avenue, which becomes the Old Glenn Highway. Just beyond the bridge across the Matanuska River, go left onto Clark-Wolverine Road, then continue about a mile until the next junction. Take a right on Huntley Road, go about a mile, bear right at the fork, and then drive 0.25 miles to the trailhead for **Lazy Mountain.** It's a two-mile hike to the summit of this 3,270-foot mountain with views of the Matanuska Valley.

A better view and a shorter hike are to the top of **Bodenberg Butte** (881 feet). Keep going south on the Old Glenn Highway, pass the first right onto the Loop Road, and take the second right. A parking lot ($3) is 0.25 miles up the road, and a 40-minute huff rewards you with a 360-degree view of the farm-filled valley, Chugach, the Talkeetnas, Knik Glacier, and some of the uncleared forest, which graphically illustrates what the colonists confronted in "clearing the land."

Swimming is available at Palmer High School's **indoor pool** (1170 W. Arctic Ave., 907/745-5091). The **Palmer Golf Course** (907/745-4653, www.cityofpalmer.org) is an 18-hole course on Lepak Avenue along the Matanuska River.

The **Mat-Su Miners** (907/745-6401, www.matsuminers.org) play semiprofessional baseball on the Alaska State Fairgrounds throughout the summer. They're part of the Alaska Baseball League.

Accommodations

Lodging is reasonable in Palmer—at least by Alaska standards. Visit the **Mat-Su Bed**

& Breakfast Association's website (www.alaskabnbhosts.com) for links to local places, including a daily vacancy listing in the summer. Located downtown, **Valley Hotel** (606 S. Alaska St., 907/745-3330 or 800/478-7666) has been here since 1948. Forty-three remodeled guest rooms go for $85 d, and a few larger ones with two queen beds are $110. Downstairs you'll find a 24-hour café plus a lounge and a liquor store.

The **Colony Inn** (325 E. Elmwood Ave., $100 d) is one of the older buildings in the valley, built in 1935 as a teachers' dormitory for the Matanuska Valley Colony. Today this historic structure has been transformed into a 12-room hotel with a central sitting room containing a fireplace and wingback chairs. Most rooms contain antiques, quilts, and jetted tubs; all are nonsmoking. It's managed by the Valley Hotel, where you register.

Located a mile west of Palmer, **River Crest Manor B&B** (907/746-6214, www.rivercrestmanor.com, $100 d) is a quiet colonial-style bed-and-breakfast with an extraordinary view of Pioneer Peak and the Chugach Mountains; private baths, Wi-Fi, and full breakfast are included.

Set on 15 acres backdropped by Pioneer Peak, **Alaska's Harvest B&B** (907/745-4263 or 877/745-4263, www.alaskasharvest.com) is an exquisite place to relax. Five guest rooms ($100 d) have private or shared baths and kitchenettes, and the 900-square-foot suite ($135 d) includes a king bed, a day bed, a kitchenette, and a private bath. All guest rooms are stocked for breakfast, and a guest computer and Wi-Fi are available.

Camping

Palmer has one of the most luxurious city campgrounds in Alaska. **Matanuska River Park** (on East Arctic Ave. about 0.5 miles east of town, 907/745-9631, www.matsugov.us, late May–early Oct., tents $10, RVs $15 without hookups) occupies a lush site full of big old cottonwoods and wild roses. There's lots of space among the 86 campsites, which are usually uncrowded except at state fair time. Surrounding the campground is a day-use area, complete with picnic tables, softball and volleyball, horseshoe pits, and a nature trail around the ponds. The park also has coin-operated showers, firewood, trails, river access, and an observation deck.

Local RV parks include **Homestead RV Park** (907/745-6005 or 800/478-3570, www.homesteadrvpark.com) and **Fox Run RV Campground** (907/745-6120 or 877/745-6120), both six miles east of Palmer; **Town & Country RV Park** (907/746-6642, www.townandcountrycampground.com), near the fairgrounds; and **Mountain View RV Park** (907/745-5747 or 800/264-4582, www.mtviewrvpark.com), three miles south of town.

Food

Palmer's **Vagabond Blues** (642 S. Alaska St., 907/745-2233, www.vagblues.com, Sun. 7 A.M.–6 P.M., Tues.–Sat. 6 A.M.–8 P.M., $5–7) is a longtime favorite, with fresh pastries, espresso, and tasty lunches. You won't go wrong ordering a big hunk of freshly baked bread and an enormous bowl of today's soup served in hand-painted pottery. There's live music on Saturday and Sunday evenings.

Turkey Red (550 S. Alaska St., 907/746-5544, www.turkeyredak.com, Mon.–Sat. 7 A.M.–9 P.M., dinner entrées $16–28) is Palmer's standout restaurant, with an open modern feel and an emphasis on fresh, local, and organic ingredients. The owner-chef hails from Tuscany, crafting a Mediterranean-Alaskan menu that includes portobello mushroom pasta, moussaka, grilled polenta, and chicken bruschetta.

If you just want a good down-home halibut sandwich or dinner of chicken, pork, steak, scallops, or pasta, head to **Round House Café** (606 S. Alaska St., 907/745-3330) at the Valley Hotel. It's open 24 hours and is nonsmoking.

Palmer has a 24-hour **Carrs** grocery store (907/745-7505) on the corner of the Glenn Highway and the Palmer–Wasilla Highway, and the **Fred Meyer** is just up the street.

Information and Services

The **Palmer Library** (655 S. Valley Way, 907/745-4690, www.cityofpalmer.org, Mon. and Wed. 10 A.M.–8 P.M., Tues., Thurs., and Fri. 10 A.M.–6 P.M., Sat. 10 A.M.–2 P.M.) has public-use computers. The large **Mat-Su Regional Medical Center** (2500 S. Woodworth Loop, 907/746-8600, www.matsuregional.com) occupies the hilltop just off the Parks Highway at Trunk Road.

Getting There

Mat-Su Community Transit, better known as **MASCOT** (907/376-5000, www.matsutransit.com), has weekday service throughout the valley ($2.50) and commuter runs to Anchorage ($3). This is half of what you'd pay for gas to drive the same distance.

WASILLA

In 2008 the town of Wasilla vaulted into the big time as the home of Alaska's then-governor (and vice presidential candidate), Sarah Palin. Her meteoric rise to fame and infamy simultaneously brought international attention to Wasilla. Although widely regarded as the hands-down ugliest town in Alaska, Wasilla does have some redeeming qualities, most notably the gorgeous mountains at nearby Hatcher Pass. You may not be able to see Russia from here, but you can see Alaska from Wasilla.

In 1977, Wasilla consisted of a landing strip and a grocery store that advertised the convenience of flying in from the bush, buying Matanuska Valley produce, and flying out again—without the hassles of Anchorage. Then, when the capital looked like it might be moved to Willow, 25 miles up the highway,

THE IDITAROD

The most Alaskan of all Alaskan events is the Iditarod Trail Sled Dog Race from Anchorage to Nome. The "Last Great Race" is run each March, attracting 60 or more of the world's best mushers, each with a team of up to 20 dogs. With a top prize of $70,000 and a $500,000 purse for the top 20 teams, the race has become an event with an international following.

Today's Iditarod Trail Sled Dog Race is run on the historic Iditarod Trail, a path that had its origins in the 1908 discovery of gold along a river the Ingalik Native Alaskans called *hidedhod,* meaning "distant place." Thousands of miners flooded into the region following the find, and trails were cut from Seward to the new boomtown of Iditarod so that mail and supplies could be brought in and gold shipped out. Once the gold ran out after a few years, the miners gradually gave up and left, and the old town began a long slow return to quietude. But other events would eventually bring Iditarod back to life in a new form.

During the winter of 1925, a diphtheria epidemic broke out in Nome, and the territorial governor hurriedly dispatched a 20-pound package of life-saving antitoxin serum to halt the disease's spread. Regular boat mail would take 25 days, and the only two airplanes in Alaska were open-cockpit biplanes. With temperatures far below zero and only a few hours of light each day (it was mid-January), that option was impossible. Instead, the package was sent by train from Seward to Nenana, where mushers and their dogs waited to carry the antitoxin on to Nome. What happened next is hard to believe: A Herculean relay effort by 20 different mushers and their dogs brought the vaccine to Nome in just six days. They somehow managed to cover the 674 miles in conditions that included whiteout blizzards, 80 mph winds, and temperatures down to -64°F. The incident gained national attention, and President Coolidge thanked the mushers, presenting each with a medal and $0.50 for each mile traveled.

Long after this heroic effort, two more people entered the picture: Dorothy Page ("Mother of the Iditarod") and Joe Redington Sr. ("Father of the Iditarod"). In 1967 the two

Anchorageites began to discover Wasilla's quiet, beauty, and affordable land, and contractors took advantage of the town's lax restrictions on development. And develop it did, with a vengeance. During 1980–1982, the town's population of 1,200 doubled, then doubled again in 1982–1984. Stores, malls, and fast-food chains popped up faster than you could say "We do chicken right." Teeland's General Store was jacked up, moved from the corner it had sat on for over 60 years, and unceremoniously dumped in a parking lot around the block to make way for a 7-Eleven. The original airstrip, which had kept Wasilla on the map for so long, was moved out from the middle of all the hustle and bustle of town.

The unbridled growth continues today, as relatively low real estate prices and good roads make the area a favorite of Anchorage commuters wanting a piece of the suburban lifestyle. In the 1990s, Wasilla's Wal-Mart proved so popular that after just a few years Wal-Mart built a new and much larger version across the highway. It's been followed by Target and Walgreens stores, plus dozens of strip-type buildings crowding the highway. Driving south into and through Wasilla on the Parks Highway is like passing through a space warp and reemerging in any Southern California suburb. It's the kind of place where locals give directions in relation to the nearest big-box store: "It's up the road a half-mile beyond Wal-Mart."

Historical Sights

Make sure to visit **Dorothy Page Museum and Historical Park** (907/373-9071, www.cityofwasilla.com/museum, Mon.–Sat. 9 A.M.–5 P.M.

organized a commemorative Iditarod race over a small portion of the trail. Six years later they set up a full-blown dogsled race from Anchorage to Nome, a distance that is officially called 1,049 miles. It took winner Dick Wilmarth 20 days, 49 minutes, and 41 seconds to make it under the Nome archway. At the finish line, Wilmarth lost his lead dog, Hot Foot. Fourteen days later the dog wandered into his master's home in Red Devil – 500 miles from Nome.

Over the years the race has become much more professional and far faster. The record run of 9 days, 58 minutes, and 6 seconds was set by Doug Swingley in 2000. And this was even with two mandatory layovers of 10 hours along the way. The Iditarod is certainly one of the most strenuous events in the world. With below-zero temperatures, fierce winds, and all the hazards that go with crossing the most remote parts of Alaska in winter, the race is certainly not for everyone. Despite this, the Iditarod has gained a measure of fame as one in which both women and men are winners. Between 1985 and 1993, five of the nine winners were women, and the late Susan Butcher won four of these races. (After Butcher won the race three consecutive years, T-shirts began appearing in local stores saying "Alaska: where men are men, and women win the Iditarod.")

The Iditarod has not one but two actual starts. The official start is from 4th Avenue in downtown Anchorage, where several thousand onlookers cheer each team that leaves the starting line. The mushers and dogs race as far as Eagle River (25 miles), where they're loaded into trucks and driven to the "restart" in Willow. (This is to avoid having to sled over the thin snow conditions around Palmer and open water on the Knik River.) At the restart, the fastest teams into Eagle River leave first, creating chaotic conditions when several 20-dog teams are pulling to the start at once. From here on, it's 1,000 miles of wilderness.

The **Iditarod Trail Committee** (907/376-5155 or 800/545-6874, www.iditarod.com) has its headquarters on Knik Road in Wasilla, where they have a museum of race memorabilia and offer wheeled dogsled rides in the summer.

Apr.–Sept., Wed.–Sat. 9 A.M.–5 P.M. Oct.–Mar., $3 adults, children under 13 free) on Main Street just off the Parks Highway. The museum houses historical photos, artifacts from early settlers and the Iditarod, plus interesting downstairs exhibits of the mining era, including a diorama of Independence Mine. The adjacent old town-site park contains a schoolhouse, a bunkhouse, a smokehouse, a steam bath, a blacksmith shop, and a cache. Just up the street is Teeland's Store (1917), one of the oldest buildings in Alaska. Today the beautifully restored structure houses a sandwich shop.

About four miles north of town at Mile 47, take a left at the sign and head 0.75 miles down to the **Museum of Alaska Transportation and Industry** (907/376-1211, www.museumofalaska.org, daily 10 A.M.–5 P.M. May–Sept., closed Oct.–Apr., $8 adults, $5 seniors and youths, children under 3 free, $18 families). This museum houses an extensive collection of antiques relating to Alaskan aviation, railroading, fishing, mining, and road transportation. Take a gander at the "Chitina auto railer," an old car built to run on rail tracks. Outside are wooden boats, farm machinery (much of it still running), ancient snowmobiles, and several rail cars.

Just beyond the museum is **Alaska Live Steamers** (907/373-6412, www.alaskalivesteam.org, $4), a scale-model railroad that takes families through the forest, over bridges, and through tunnels on summer weekends. It's a good place to meet people living out their model railroad dreams from childhood. Trains run on weekends 10 A.M.–4 P.M. June–mid-September.

Knik Museum (907/376-7755, Thurs.–Sun. 1–6 P.M. June–Aug., $2) is 14 miles from Wasilla out on Knik Road. Housed in a century-old building, it exhibits items from the Knik gold rush of 1897–1917 and the Iditarod Trail.

Other Nearby Sights

Wasilla is the headquarters for the 1,049-mile **Iditarod Trail Sled Dog Race** from Anchorage to Nome. The headquarters (907/376-5155 or 800/545-6874, www.iditarod.com, daily 8 A.M.–7 P.M. mid-May–mid-Sept., Mon.–Fri. 8 A.M.–5 P.M. mid-Sept.–mid-May) includes a log museum containing race memorabilia, Native Alaskan artifacts, videos, and dog-mushing equipment. Also here is Togo, the stuffed sled dog who led Leonhard Seppala's team during the 1925 serum delivery to Nome. Find Togo and friends two miles out on Knik Road. Admission is free, though a fee is charged to go for a ride on a wheeled dogsled.

Lakeshore Park at Wasilla Lake right off the highway has swimming (not too cold), picnic tables, and a view of the craggy Chugach Mountains—a great place to set up your tripod. A less crowded day-use lake area is at **Kepler-Bradley Lakes** just beyond the junction of the Parks and Glenn Highways, on the Glenn Highway toward Palmer.

Accommodations

Several motels are strung along the Parks Highway. On the south end of Wasilla is **Trout's Place Hotel** (907/376-4209, www.windbreakalaska.com, $70 d) with 10 budget guest rooms.

Alaskan View Motel (2650 E. Parks Hwy., 907/376-6787, www.alaskanviewmotel.com, $105–125 d) is a modern two-story log building across from Nye Ford. It's convenient for shopping and dining, and windows frame the Chugach Range.

Alaska's Select Inn (3451 Palmdale Dr., 907/357-4768 or 888/357-4768, www.alaskaselectinn.com) is a newly built place with spacious guest rooms ($116 d) and suites ($137 d), all with full kitchens and Wi-Fi.

Best Western Lake Lucille Inn (1300 W. Lake Lucille Dr., 907/373-1776 or 800/897-1776, www.bestwestern.com/lakelucilleinn, $169–199 d) has 54 roomy guest rooms ($169–199 d) and suites ($279–299 d), many with private balconies overlooking the lake. Guests will also appreciate the fitness center, sauna, hot tub, business center, Wi-Fi, and continental breakfasts.

Agate Inn (907/373-2290 or 800/770-

2290, www.agateinn.com), three miles from Wasilla on the Palmer-Wasilla Highway, has a variety of lodging options scattered over four buildings: motel-type rooms with king beds ($135–155 d), apartment suites with kitchens ($195–275), and two guest houses ($225–375 for up to 6 people). A continental breakfast is provided. The six pet reindeer on the grounds are a favorite of guests.

Mat-Su Lodge (1850 Bogard Rd., 907/376-3228, www.matsulodge.com) charges $104 d for standard guest rooms or cabins. The resort sits on the quiet north side of Lake Wasilla and has paddleboats for rent.

Lake Lucille B&B (907/357-0353 or 888/353-0352, www.alaskaslakelucillebnb.com) is a gracious home right on the shore of Lake Lucille, just a short distance from Wasilla. The four guest rooms (with shared baths) are a reasonable $79–89 d; a family suite is $99. A light breakfast starts each day.

For something more uniquely Alaskan, stay at **Pioneer Ridge B&B** (1830 E. Parks Hwy., 907/376-7472 or 800/478-7472, www.pioneerridge.com, $99–159 d). This distinctive former barn sits on a hill in the country south of Wasilla. Six guest rooms with shared or private baths are available. A buffet breakfast is served in the common room, where you can also play a game of pool, watch a video, listen to the player piano, surf the Web, or simply relax. On top of the house is a unique glass-enclosed room with a fireplace and 360-degree views.

Visit the **Mat-Su Bed & Breakfast Association**'s website (www.alaskabnbhosts.com) for links to local B&Bs, including a daily vacancy listing in the summer.

Camping

The city-run **Lake Lucille Park** (907/373-9014, www.cityofwasilla.com, $10, no RV hookups) is an 80-acre natural area with trails and campsites two miles south of Wasilla off Knik–Goose Bay Road. There's another public campground (907/746-4644 or 800/952-8624, www.lifetimeadventures.net, $15) at **Finger Lake State Recreation Site,** six miles east of Wasilla on Bogard Road.

Big Bear RV Park (2010 S. Church St., 907/745-7445, www.bigbearrv.net) has RV and tent sites, but many RVers park for free in local shopping mall lots.

Food

Perhaps because of all the early-morning commuters to Anchorage, Wasilla seems to have an espresso stand on almost every corner—along with an equal number of gun shops. It sounds like a dangerous combination, especially with all those folks listening to Rush Limbaugh each morning.

Windbreak Café (907/376-4484, daily 6 A.M.–11 P.M.) is a good choice for home-cooked meals, prime rib, and seafood. Breakfast is served all day.

International tastes include **Chepo's Fiesta** (731 W. Parks Hwy., 907/373-5656, www.cheposfiesta.com) for Mexican food in a fun setting, **Mekong Thai Cuisine** (473 W. Parks Hwy., 907/373-7690, www.mekongthaiwasilla.com), and **Bombay Valley Indian Food** (991 S. Hermon Rd., 907/376-9565, www.bombaydeluxe.com).

Near Lowe's, **Pandemonium Booksellers & Café** (907/376-3939, www.akbookstore.com) is a fine bookstore with espresso, live tunes on Saturday evenings, and free Wi-Fi.

Mat-Su Lodge (1850 Bogard Rd., 907/376-3228, daily 3–10 P.M., $18–30) has a lakeside dining room specializing in angus steaks. The lounge has live bands Monday–Saturday nights.

Across from the museum in "old town" Wasilla, **The Grape Tap** (322 N. Boundary St., 907/376-8466, www.thegrapetap.com, Tues.–Sat. 5–10 P.M., closed Sun.–Mon. tapas $12–15) is the town's fine-dining establishment, with a pleasant downstairs wine lounge and an upstairs menu featuring small tapas-style dishes of seared ahi, saffron chicken skewers, tenderloin, blue crab, and cheeses. Everything is homemade at this slow-food eatery. Sunday brunch includes apple pancakes and eggs Florentine.

Located near Settlers Bay Golf Course eight miles out Knik-Goose Bay Road, **Settlers Bay**

Lodge (907/357-5678, www.settlersbaylodge.com, daily 5–10 P.M., entrées $22–26) is a destination spot for locals who appreciate the towering windows, deck-with-a-vista dining, and menu of steaks, seafood, and pasta along with daily specials.

Wasilla's **Farmers Market** (907/376-5679, Wed. 11 A.M.–6 P.M. June–mid-Sept.) takes place at the old Wasilla town site.

Services

Adjacent to the museum, the **Wasilla Public Library** (391 N. Main St., 907/376-5913, www.cityofwasilla.com/library) is a good place to stop and check your email or play on the Web. If you don't want to wait, head to **The Digital Cup** (545 S. Knik–Goose Bay Rd., 907/373-2727, www.digitalcup.net) next to Fred Meyer. Swim at Wasilla High School's **pool** (701 W. Bogard Rd., 907/376-4222).

Mat-Su Community Transit, better known as **MASCOT** (907/376-5000, www.matsutransit.com), has weekday service throughout the valley ($2.50) and commuter runs to Anchorage ($3).

HATCHER PASS

This is one of the most beautiful parts of the Mat-Su Valley region and a wonderful side trip from either the Parks Highway north of Wasilla or the Glenn Highway at Palmer. It's a 49-mile drive, starting in Palmer and ending at Mile 71 on the Parks Highway (30 miles north of Wasilla).

Most folks get to Hatcher Pass from the Palmer end. Hatcher Pass Road (also called Fishhook-Willow Rd.) begins in rolling forest-and-farm country and then climbs along the beautiful Little Susitna River, which is popular with experienced kayakers who enjoy Class V white water. After passing Motherlode Lodge, the road climbs steeply uphill to Independence Mine State Historical Park at Mile 17, where the pavement ends, before topping out at 3,886-foot Hatcher Pass and Summit Lake in an area of vast vistas, high tundra, excellent hiking, and backcountry camping. Then it's downhill through pretty forests along Willow Creek all the way to the Parks Highway; this route was originally a wagon road built to serve the gold mines. The road is paved from Palmer all the way to Independence Mine, and for 10 miles from the Willow side; the rest is gravel. A bike path follows the road along the Little Susitna River section, and campsites can be found at Deception Creek, two miles from the Parks Highway.

Independence Mine State Historical Park

It's hard to imagine a park that better combines the elements of the Alaska experience: scenery, history and lore, and that noble yellow metal, gold. This mine is very different from the panning, sluicing, deep-placer, and dredging operations seen in Interior Alaska. This was "hard-rock" mining, with an intricate 21-mile network of tunnels under Granite Mountain. The miners drilled into the rock, inserted explosives (which they set off at the end of shifts to give the fumes time to dissipate before the next crew went in), then "mucked" the debris out by hand, to be sorted, crushed, amalgamated, and assayed.

Hard-rock or "lode" mining is often preceded by panning and placer mining. Prospectors who first took gold from Grubstake Gulch, a tributary of Willow Creek, in 1897 noticed the gold's rough unweathered nature, which indicated a possible lode of unexposed gold nearby. In 1906, Robert Lee Hatcher staked the first lode claim, and his Alaska Free Gold Mine operated until 1924. In 1908 the Independence Mine opened on the mountain's east slope, and over the next 25 years it produced several million dollars' worth of gold. In 1937 the two mines merged into the Alaska Pacific Consolidated Mining Company, which operated Independence Mine at peak production through 1942, when World War II shut it down. A series of private sales and public deals with the Alaska Division of Parks culminated in 1980, leaving the state with 271 acres, including the whole mining camp, and deeding 1,000 acres to the Coronado Mining Corporation, which has active operations in the area.

A couple of dozen camp buildings are in

various stages of ruin and refurbishing. Start at the visitors center in the rehabilitated house of the camp manager. Take some time to enjoy the excellent displays: historic charts, an overview of gold mining, a "touch tunnel" complete with sound effects, and wage summaries for workers and management. Guided tours ($5) are given daily at 1 and 3 P.M. by park personnel. At other times, just wander the site on your own; interpretive signs describe the various buildings. Independence Mine State Historical Park is a must-see on any Alaskan itinerary.

The **visitors center** (907/745-2827 summer only or 907/745-3975, www.alaskastateparks.org, parking $5) is open daily 11 A.M.–6 P.M. late May–early September, and closed the rest of the year.

Accommodations

A number of lodging options are scattered along the southern section of Hatcher Pass Road north of Palmer. **Hatcher Pass B&B** (907/745-6788, www.hatcherpassbb.com) has delightful log cabins with kitchenettes and private baths. Small "sourdough" cabins cost $109 d, and large two-bedroom chalets sleep two for $149; add $15 per person for additional guests (up to 6). Cabins are fully stocked for make-it-yourself breakfasts.

Just downhill from Independence Mine is **Hatcher Pass Lodge** (907/745-5897, www.hatcherpasslodge.com, daily 11 A.M.–7:30 P.M. summer, Fri.–Sun. 11 A.M.–6:30 P.M. Oct.–May, dinner entrées $19–33). This A-frame lodge is a great spot for sandwiches, pizza, steaks, and halibut, with a sunset view to die for. Be sure to try the house specialty, fondue made with Swiss Gruyère and Emmentaler cheeses, Kirschwasser, and French bread. Nine cozy cabins cost $100–165 d, and three tiny upstairs guest rooms are $95 d each; breakfast is available for guests. Also on the grounds is a creek-side sauna for guests. The lodge is open daily all year. Speaking from personal experience, this is the perfect place for a summer wedding. The lodge also maintains 6 miles of **groomed ski trails** in the winter, and more adventurous backcountry skiers and snowboarders head up the steep (and avalanche-prone) slopes that rise on three sides. In winter the road isn't plowed beyond Independence Mine State Park, but you can park here to play; it's a special favorite of snowmobilers.

NORTH TO DENALI

It's a long 195-mile drive from Wasilla (237 miles from Anchorage) to Denali National Park on the Parks Highway. After the first few miles, the developments peter out and roadside attractions shift from fast food, gun shops, and video stores to the real Alaska of forests and mountains. The land is a seemingly endless birch and spruce forest, with a smattering of half-finished plywood homesteads covered in blue tarps, their yards piled high with firewood. The road follows a gradual climb toward the magnificent Alaska Range that seems to grow in magnitude the farther north you get. Mile after mile of pink fireweed flowers brighten the roadside in midsummer.

Big Lake

The Big Lake area (907/892-6109, www.biglakechamber.org) is a popular recreation destination, especially on summer weekends when many Anchorageites head to summer homes here. Access is via nine-mile-long Big Lake Road, which splits off the Parks Highway at Mile 52 (10 miles north of Wasilla). Don't expect quiet along this large and scenic lake. In summer, Big Lake is Jet Ski central 24 hours a day, and when winter arrives the snowmobile crowd comes out for more motorized mayhem. Big Lake was near the center of the 1996 Miller's Reach Fire that blackened 37,500 acres and destroyed over 400 buildings.

Three state park campgrounds (www.lifetimeadventures.net, $15) are in the area: **Rocky Lake State Recreation Site, Big Lake North State Recreation Site,** and **Big Lake South State Recreation Site. Big Lake Motel** (907/892-7976) has rooms for $85 d.

Operated by four-time Iditarod champion Martin Buser, **Happy Trails Kennels** (Mile 4.5, West Lakes Blvd., 907/892-7899, www.

buserdog.com) has $35 kennel tours and demonstrations all summer.

Houston

This Podunk gathering of 900 or so souls 58 miles from Anchorage includes the usual lineup of suspects: gas, groceries, cafés, lodging, an RV park, a coin laundry, and air-taxi operators, but it is best known for its **fireworks stands.** Four of these giant eyesores—it's especially hard to miss Gorilla Fireworks—sit on the edges of town, pulling families from Anchorage looking for fun on the 4th of July. It is illegal to shoot off fireworks almost anywhere in Alaska. Of course, this is one of those legal niceties that is widely ignored. **Little Susitna River Campground** ($10) is an Alaska Department of Fish and Game facility on the south side of Houston.

Nancy Lake State Recreation Area

Access to Nancy Lake is from Mile 67 of the Parks Highway, just south of Willow and 25 miles north of Wasilla. This flat, heavily forested terrain is dotted with over 100 lakes, some interconnected by creeks. As you might imagine, the popular activities here are fishing, boating, and canoeing, plus a comfortable campground and a couple of hiking trails. As you might also suspect, the skeeters here are thick in early summer.

Follow Nancy Lake Road a little more than a mile to **Nancy Lake State Recreation Site Campground** (reservations at www.lifetimeadventures.net, $10). A half-mile past the kiosk is the trailhead to several **public-use cabins** (907/745-3975, www.alaskastateparks.org, $60). Reserve well ahead to be sure of getting one of these exceptionally popular cabins. Just under a mile beyond this trailhead is the **Tulik Nature Trail,** an easy walk that takes about an hour. Keep an eye out for loons, beavers, and terns, and watch for that prickly devil's club.

The **Tanaina Lake Canoe Route** begins at Mile 4.5 on Nancy Lakes Road. This leisurely 12-mile two-day trip hits 14 lakes, between most of which are well-marked portages, some upgraded with boardwalks over the muskeg. Hunker down for the night at any one of 10 primitive campsites (campfires allowed in fireplaces only). Another possibility, though it requires a long portage, is to put in to the Little Susitna River at Mile 57 on the Parks Highway and portage to Skeetna Lake, where you connect to the southern leg of the loop trail. **Tippecanoe** (907/495-6688, www.paddlealaska.com), at South Rolly Campground, rents canoes for the Nancy Lake canoe trails.

Willow

At Mile 69 is Willow (pop. 400), a roadside town that you'll miss if you sneeze. It has gas, groceries, hardware, a café, and air service. Back in 1980, Alaskans voted to move the state capital here. A multibillion-dollar city was planned, and real estate speculation went wild. When a second vote was held in 1982 to decide whether to actually *spend* the billions, however, the plan was soundly defeated.

Willow's big event comes in early March, as the **Iditarod Trail Sled Dog Race** slides through town. The race officially begins in Anchorage, but after a 25-mile run to Eagle River, the dogs are trucked north for the "restart" at Willow Lake. Just west of here the teams move completely away from the road system and are in wilderness all the way to Nome.

Stay at **Pioneer Lodge & RV Park** (907/495-1000), right on the creek with rustic motel units ($60 d), newer cabins ($125 d) with kitchenettes, camping (RVs $25, tents $12), plus a bar, a liquor store, and a full-service restaurant with good homemade pizzas, burgers, and smoked prime rib. Boaters launch here for trips down Willow Creek to the mouth of the Big Susitna River.

Willow Creek Resort (907/495-6343) has spaces for RVs ($30) and tents ($20) on the opposite bank, plus raft rentals and guided fishing.

Operated by Iditarod veteran Vern Halter, **Dream a Dream Dog Farm** (907/495-1197 or 866/425-6874, www.vernhalter.com) has summertime kennel tours and demonstrations in Willow.

Both **Willow Air Service** (907/495-6370 or 800/478-6370, www.willowair.com) and **Denali Flying Service** (907/495-5899) offer scenic flights over Knik Glacier, Hatcher Pass, and Mt. McKinley from Willow.

North to Talkeetna

At Mile 71 of the Parks Highway is the turnoff to **Willow Creek State Recreation Area,** four miles down the Susitna River access road. Sites are $10, but don't expect a quiet night's repose in the wilderness here if the salmon are running, which they do for most of the summer. The boat launch attracts fishing parties at all hours of the day and night, as well as lots of RVs with their inevitable generator noise. Still, it's a pretty and handy place to spend the night if it's getting late and you plan to travel over the exceptionally scenic Hatcher Pass to Independence Mine State Historical Park. Find additional camping along nearby Deception Creek, two miles up Hatcher Pass Road.

In the 45 miles from Willow to the Talkeetna cutoff are scattered lodging places, restaurants, and gas stations. The most notable place is **Sheep Creek Lodge** (Mile 89, 907/495-6227), a classic log Alaskan roadhouse rebuilt after a 1986 fire. Its restaurant serves meals (burgers, pizza, lasagna, steaks, and more) year-round. Modern rooms with private baths in the lodge are $125 d; Wi-Fi is included. Rustic cabins sleep four for $85 with a bathhouse nearby. The lodge also has tent spaces ($10) and RV sites with hookups.

Mat-Su Valley RV Park (907/495-6300, www.matsurvpark.com, RVs $35, tents $17) is at Mile 91.

Big Susitna B&B (Mile 92, 907/495-6324, www.bigsusitnabnb.com, $73 s, $93 d) has two rooms with shared baths and full breakfasts in a comfortable log home. The owners are Iditarod veterans.

The privately run **Montana Creek Campgrounds** (Mile 97, 907/566-5267 or 877/475-2267, www.montanacreekcampground.com) provides wooded sites on both sides of this popular salmon-fishing creek.

KENAI PENINSULA

The Kenai Peninsula is like a mini-Alaska, compressing all of the state's features into an area roughly 3 percent the size of the state. You'll find mountains, ice fields and glaciers, fjords and offshore islands, large fish-filled rivers and lakes, swampy plains, varied climate and precipitation, a few scattered port towns, and a sprawling population center. The Kenai is a major playground for both Anchorage residents and travelers from Outside, and it's possibly the most popular all-around destination for all Alaskans. The outdoor recreational opportunities are practically inexhaustible, with innumerable choices of every pedestrian, pedaled, paddled, piloted, portholed, piscatory, predatory, and picaresque particular you could ever ponder—just you and 300,000 other folks from the neighborhood. But don't let the possibility of crowds deter you. The resources are abundant, well developed, and often isolated. And besides, what's wrong with a little company along the trail or under sail?

At 16,056 square miles, Kenai Peninsula is a little smaller than Vermont and New Hampshire combined. The Kenai Mountains form the peninsula's backbone, with massive Harding Ice Field dominating the lower lumbar. The east side, facing Prince William Sound, hosts a spur of the Kenai Mountains, with the glimmering Sargent Ice Fields; the west side, facing Cook Inlet, is outwash plain, sparkling with low-lying swamp, lakes, and rivers. The ice fields, glaciers, and plains are all a result of ice sculpting over the million-year course of the Pleistocene, with its five major glacial periods. During the last, the Wisconsin

© DON PITCHER

HIGHLIGHTS

Hope: Now almost a ghost town, this once-booming mining town is the place that time forgot. Several fine hikes head out from here (page 238).

Alaska SeaLife Center: Touch tanks, puffins swimming underwater, and fascinating exhibits are great, but seals and sea lions steal the show at this popular Seward marine science center (page 245).

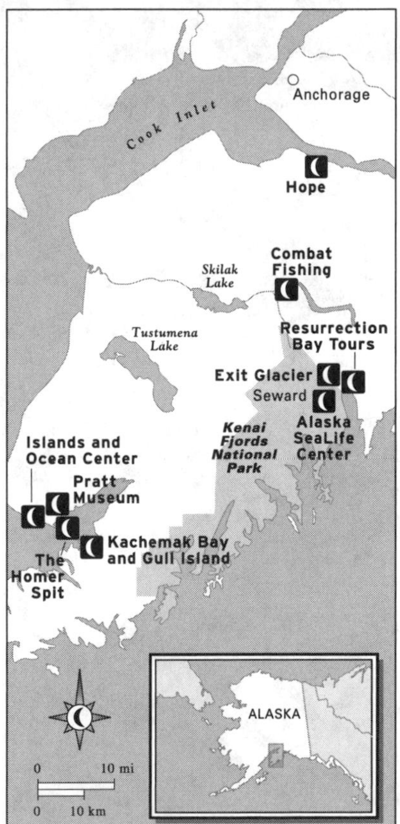

Exit Glacier: Easily accessible from Seward, this glacier is part of Kenai Fjords National Park and has camping, hiking trails (including one onto the massive Harding Ice Field), and glacier tours (page 253).

Resurrection Bay Tours: Several Seward companies offer wildlife and glacier tours by boat. Half-day excursions tour the bay; all-day versions (take your Dramamine) make it into Kenai Fjords (page 255).

Combat Fishing: The Kenai and Russian Rivers are major destinations for Anchorageites and tourists in search of their bag limit of red salmon. It's an elbow-to-elbow frenzy at the midsummer peak (page 259).

The Homer Spit: Jutting four miles into Kachemak Bay, this narrow sandy peninsula provides a great base for halibut charters, sea kayaking, bird-watching, cycling, dining, and shopping (page 270).

Islands and Ocean Center: Modern and slick, this free center houses exhibits on the Alaska Maritime National Wildlife Refuge. Don't miss the award-winning film about the refuge and its wildlife (page 270).

Pratt Museum: One of the finest small museums in Alaska, the Pratt always has something interesting, including a touch tank with tide-pool animals in the back room (page 271).

Kachemak Bay and Gull Island: Gull Island with its thousands of nesting seabirds is a favorite destination for day tours. Also popular are trips to the off-the-road-system villages of Halibut Cove and Seldovia (page 286).

LOOK FOR TO FIND RECOMMENDED SIGHTS, ACTIVITIES, DINING, AND LODGING.

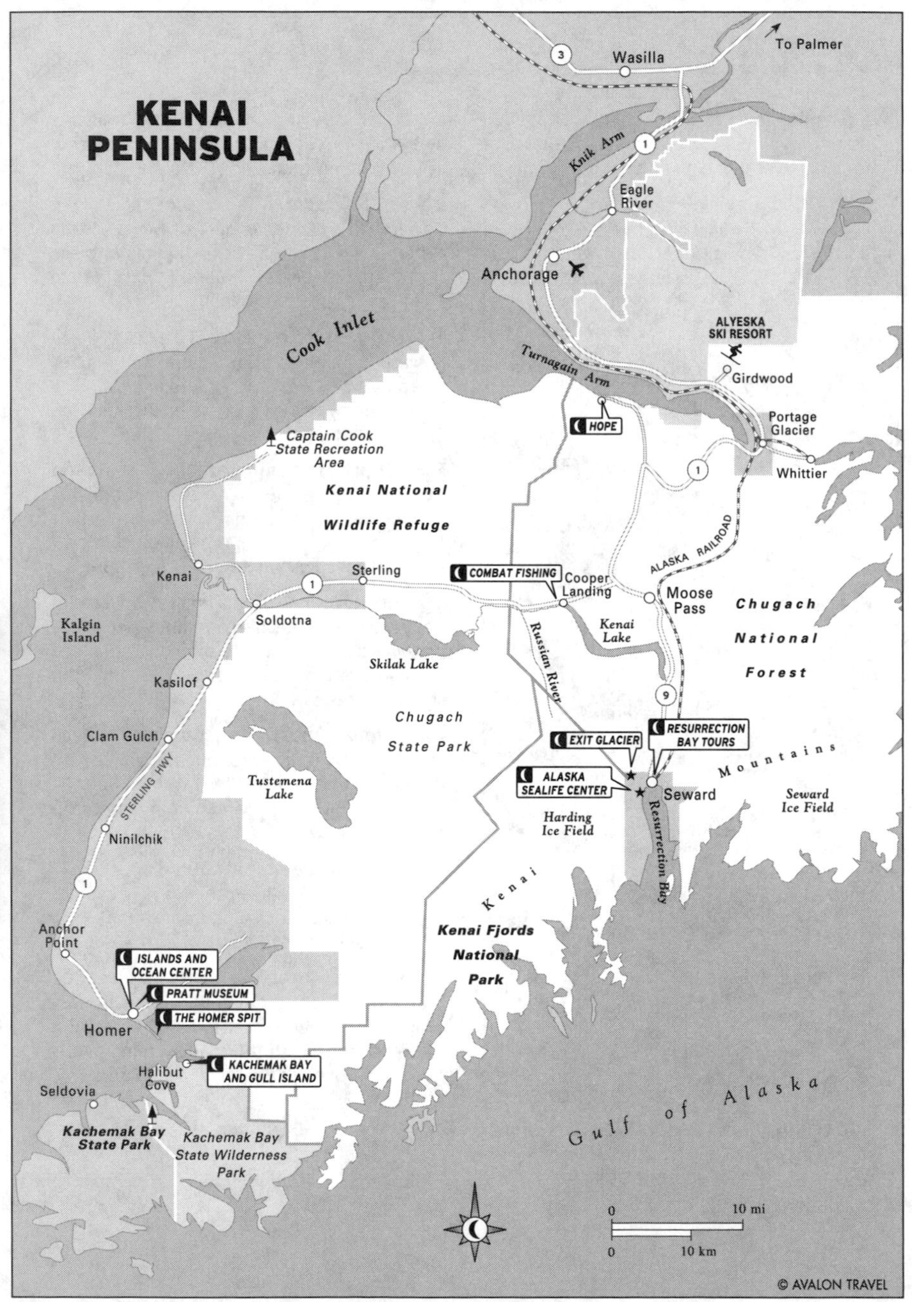
KENAI PENINSULA
To Palmer
Wasilla
3
Knik Arm
1
Eagle River
Anchorage
Cook Inlet
ALYESKA SKI RESORT
Turnagain Arm
Girdwood
HOPE
Portage Glacier
Whittier
Captain Cook State Recreation Area
Kenai National Wildlife Refuge
ALASKA RAILROAD
Kenai
Sterling
COMBAT FISHING
Cooper Landing
Moose Pass
Chugach National Forest
Soldotna
Kalgin Island
Russian River
Kenai Lake
Skilak Lake
Kasilof
9
Chugach State Park
EXIT GLACIER
RESURRECTION BAY TOURS
Clam Gulch
Mountains
ALASKA SEALIFE CENTER
Seward
Seward Ice Field
Tustemena Lake
STERLING HWY
Harding Ice Field
Resurrection Bay
Ninilchik
Kenai
Kenai Fjords National Park
Anchor Point
ISLANDS AND OCEAN CENTER
PRATT MUSEUM
THE HOMER SPIT
Homer
Halibut Cove
KACHEMAK BAY AND GULL ISLAND
Seldovia
Kachemak Bay State Park
Kachemak Bay State Wilderness Park
Gulf of Alaska
0
10 mi
0
10 km
© AVALON TRAVEL

Period, Portage Glacier filled the entire Turnagain Arm, 50 miles long and a half-mile high. Ten thousand years ago Portage stopped just short of carving a fjord between Prince William Sound and Turnagain Arm; otherwise, Kenai Peninsula would've been Kenai Island. Still, this peninsula is so digitate with peninsulettes that it has more than 1,000 miles of coastline. The land is almost completely controlled by the feds; Chugach National Forest, Kenai National Wildlife Refuge, and Kenai Fjords National Park account for nearly 85 percent of the peninsula.

Two roads provide the primary access to the Kenai. The 127-mile **Seward Highway** connects Anchorage with Seward on the southwest end of the peninsula, and the 143-mile **Sterling Highway** cuts across the Kenai, leading west and south from Tern Lake (where it meets the Seward Highway) to Soldotna and Homer.

History

You begin to feel the Russian influence strongly in this neck of the woods. Alexander Baranov's first shipyard was somewhere along Resurrection Bay down from present-day Seward. Russians built a stockade near Kasilof in 1786 and a fort at Kenai in 1791. Other than these brief incursions, the land belonged to the Kenai Natives Alaskans: part of the great Athabascan tribe on the north half of the peninsula, while the Alutiiqs occupied the southern half.

During the gold rush, color was uncovered around Hope and Sunrise on Turnagain Arm, and at Moose Creek, halfway to Seward. At first, trails ran between the mining communities, then wagon roads, and finally the railroad pushed from Seward through Anchorage to Fairbanks in the early 1920s. The Seward and Sterling Highways were completed in 1952, opening the Kenai's western frontier. When Atlantic Richfield tapped into oil (1957) and gas (1962) off the west coast, the peninsula's economic star began to twinkle. Oil and gas production has dropped steadily since the peak in the 1970s as the reserves are depleted, but new gas deposits are being developed near Ninilchik. Today, the Kenai Peninsula Borough's 50,000 residents are occupied with fishing, oil and gas, tourism, and services.

Information

Every Kenai Peninsula town of any size has its own chamber of commerce and website; they're listed under the individual towns. A good overall information source is the **Kenai Peninsula Tourism Marketing Council** (907/283-3850 or 800/535-3624, www.kenaipeninsula.org), which produces a detailed annual travel publication.

PLANNING YOUR TIME

The Kenai Peninsula is readily accessible by car, bus, plane, or train from Anchorage, making it perfect if you have a few days, but adventurers could easily spend considerably longer exploring backcountry areas or playing in the scenic towns. The off-the-beaten-path settlement of **Hope** has a picture-perfect collection of gold rush–era buildings along Turnagain Arm. A very scenic three-hour drive south from Anchorage, the town of Seward is home to the **Alaska SeaLife Center** (great for kids), along with Kenai Fjords National Park, where visitors can take guided hikes across **Exit Glacier,** join **Resurrection Bay boat tours,** or take longer day (or multiple-night) trips into the park. A second highway (the Sterling) heads west across the peninsula through Kenai National Wildlife Refuge, where the Kenai and Russian Rivers are the scene of **"combat fishing"** as hundreds of anglers crowd the banks when the salmon are running.

The Sterling Highway continues west through Soldotna before bending south to the end of the road, Homer. **The Homer Spit,** a sandy strip of land extending four miles into the bay, is the primary visitor attraction here, with charter halibut fishing, sea kayaking, **Kachemak Bay tours** to Gull Island or the remote villages of Halibut Cove and Seldovia, and some of the finest restaurants and lodging in Alaska. Inside attractions well worth a visit include the **Islands and Ocean Center** and the **Pratt Museum.**

Eastern Kenai Peninsula

THE SEWARD HIGHWAY

The 127-mile Seward Highway—a National Scenic Byway—connects Anchorage with Seward on the Kenai Peninsula. Mileposts are numbered from the Seward end; subtract these numbers from 127 for the distance to Anchorage. The Seward Highway has passing lanes, wide shoulders, and a 65 mph speed limit much of the way, but take the time to enjoy the scenery. Keep your headlights on at all times, and watch for moose.

Near Portage at Mile 48, the Seward Highway banks sharply to the west along Turnagain Arm before turning again southward as it climbs into the Kenai Mountains. At **Turnagain Pass** (Mile 69, elevation 988 feet), the west side of the road has a big pullout with portable toilets. Stop and stretch in this pretty alpine area where the snow remains until late June. In the winter the snow is often 10 feet deep. The west side is popular with snowmobilers, while the east side is reserved for those on skis or snowshoes. Turnagain Pass can be deadly at certain times of the winter, and a number of snowmobilers have died in avalanches here while riding on the dangerous upper slopes.

At Mile 64 is the northern trailhead for the **Johnson Pass Trail,** which goes 23 miles over relatively level terrain and emerges at Mile 33 of the Seward Highway. Two in-the-trees Forest Service campgrounds ($14) are nearby: **Bertha Creek Campground** (Mile 65) and **Granite Creek Campground** (Mile 63). The paved **Sixmile Bike Trail** parallels the highway from the Johnson Pass Trailhead south to the junction with the Hope Highway.

Sixmile Creek

At Mile 59 the highway crosses a staging area along Granite Creek for rafters and kayakers down Granite Creek and on to Sixmile Creek. This is one of Alaska's premier white-water areas. Check out the action from the footbridge that crosses Sixmile Creek, accessible via a short path from the parking area just east of the Canyon Creek bridge. Two companies lead white-water trips here: **Chugach Outdoor Center** (907/277-7238 or 866/277-7238, www.chugachoutdoorcenter.com) and **Nova Riverrunners** (907/745-5753 or 800/746-5753, www.novalaska.com). Three-hour trips ($99) are in Class IV water, while the five-hour trips ($149) include some intense Class V sections of the narrowly constricted lower canyon. Nova is the original company on the river, and both companies have offices near Hope (Chugach Outdoor Center has a hot tub to warm up in after your adventure). Chugach Outdoor also offers family-friendly 2.5-hour Turnagain Pass float trips ($80 pp) on the scenic East Fork of Sixmile Creek.

HOPE

Now almost a ghost town, Hope is a charming step into the past, with a quaint cluster of weathered buildings, a little museum, a couple of eateries and lodging places, quiet waterside campsites, and great hiking.

The Hope Highway begins at Mile 56 of the Seward Highway, just west of the towering bridge over Canyon Creek. This sparsely trafficked road follows Sixmile Creek north back up to Turnagain Arm; pan for gold along the first five miles of the crick. The entire 17 miles to Hope is paved.

Gold was discovered on Resurrection Creek in 1888, and by 1896 there were 3,000 people inhabiting this boom neighborhood between Hope and Sunrise on Sixmile Creek. Many came by way of the Passage Canal where Whittier now squats, portaging their watercraft over the Chugach glacial pass to Turnagain Arm, which is how Portage Glacier got its name. Large-scale mining prospered into the 1940s, but then Sunrise was abandoned and left to the ghosts. Hope (www.advenalaska.com/hope) hangs on today primarily as a place where recreation and tourism support the town's 135 people.

CHUGACH NATIONAL FOREST

Much of the eastern Kenai Peninsula lies within Chugach National Forest, the second-largest national forest in the country after the Tongass. Covering 5.5 million acres – bigger than Massachusetts – the Chugach not only encompasses this part of the Kenai but also continues eastward across all of Prince William Sound well beyond the Copper River. Developments and logging are relatively minor on the Chugach, but all this wild country provides incredible opportunities for recreation, with good fishing, hiking, mountain biking, river rafting, skiing, kayaking, wildlife-watching, glacier-gazing, and a host of other outdoor adventures. Forest headquarters is in Anchorage (3301 C. St., 907/743-9500, www.fs.fed.us/r10/chugach), with district offices in Seward (907/224-3374), Girdwood (907/783-3242), and Cordova (907/424-7661).

CABINS

The Kenai Peninsula has 18 Forest Service public-use cabins available for $45 per night. These are mostly Pan-Abode log structures that sleep four and have wood or oil stoves. Most of these are along hiking trails – including eight cabins on the Resurrection Pass Trail – but a few are accessible only by floatplane. The Chugach website has cabin details, or you can get brochures from the Alaska Public Lands Information Center in Anchorage. Because of their high popularity, it's a wise to reserve cabins well ahead of your visit at 518/885-3639, 877/444-6777, or www.recreation.gov. Additional public cabins can be found within Kenai Fjords National Park and Kachemak Bay State Park.

CAMPING AND HIKING

Six Forest Service campgrounds are located along the Seward Highway south of Portage, with another four along the Sterling Highway, and two more off the Hope Highway; all are described in this chapter. A number of very popular hiking trails cover the eastern half of the Kenai Peninsula, and it's possible to hike (or mountain bike) all the way from the town of Hope to Exit Glacier near Seward, a distance of 74 miles. Contact the Forest Service for details on various camping and hiking options within the Chugach.

Tern Lake, north of Moose Pass, Chugach National Forest

Sights

"Downtown" Hope is marked by a cluster of old buildings, some over a century old. Stop here to walk the dirt street past photogenic **Social Hall**—the original Alaska Commercial Co. store—and down to the tidal flats (caused by the earth sinking seven feet in the 1964 quake). They're dangerous; don't walk on them! Go back and turn left for new Hope, with its post office, red schoolhouse, and beautiful new and old log cabins. The old one-room school, built in 1938, now serves as a **library.**

Hope & Sunrise Historical and Mining Museum (907/782-3740, Fri.–Mon. noon–4 P.M. late May–early Sept., free) is a log museum housing historical photos and artifacts from the Turnagain Arm gold rush of 1894–1899. The grounds contain the original Canyon Creek Mining buildings.

Accommodations and Food

Seaview Café (907/782-3300, www.seaviewcafealaska.com, mid-May–mid-Sept.) has rustic cabins ($60 d) with outhouses, tent sites ($6), and RV hookups ($18) along the creek, which is a popular spot to catch pink salmon (humpies) or to pan for gold. The century-old café is open daily for lunch and dinner, but you're much better off heading to **Tito's Discovery Café** (907/782-3274, daily 7 A.M.–9 P.M., $12–15), serving three meals a day. Dinners include blackened halibut, burgers, stir-fried veggies, and daily specials, along with homemade pies and soup.

Clustered around a small pond, **Bowman's Bear Creek Lodge** (Mile 16, Hope Highway, 907/782-3141, www.bowmansbearcreeklodge.com, year-round, $150 d) has five log cabins with woodstoves and a shared bathhouse. The excellent café serves "rustic cuisine" lunches and dinners (daily 4–10 P.M. summer, Thurs.–Sun. 4–8:30 P.M. winter, $20–26), with outside dining on summer afternoons. They also operate **Sweet Mo's** (daily noon–6 P.M. summer), a seasonal ice cream shop across from the museum.

Discovery Cabins (907/782-3730 or 800/365-7057, www.adventurealaskatours.com, May–Sept., $95 d) has five modern cabins on the edge of Bear Creek in Hope. The cabins share a bathhouse and an outdoor hot tub.

You'll find a grocery, laundry, RV spaces, and motel rooms at **Alaska Dacha** (907/782-3223) along the road as you come into town.

Camping and Hiking

At the end of Hope Highway is the Forest Service's **Porcupine Campground** (www.fs.fed.us/r10/chugach, $14), featuring fine views across Turnagain Arm and red raspberries as hors d'oeuvres in late summer.

Gull Rock Trail begins from the campground and parallels the shoreline of Turnagain Arm. It's a fairly easy stroll out to Gull Rock (5 miles), making this a popular family day hike or overnight camping trip. The beautiful **Hope Point Trail** starts at the campground and climbs a steep knob into the alpine area. From here you can hike forever along the ridgeline.

Resurrection Pass Trail

A half-mile east of Hope on the Hope Highway is the junction with Palmer Creek Road. Follow it 0.75 miles to a fork. Turn left and continue seven long miles to **Coeur D'Alene Campground,** which has a couple of free spots along a noisy creek. Go right on Resurrection Pass Road four rough miles to the Resurrection Pass trailhead, with parking, an information signboard, and a fun bridge across the crick. This popular backpack or mountain bike trip leads 38 miles down to Cooper Landing on the Sterling Highway, or you can cut across on **Devil's Pass Trail** to Mile 39 on the Seward Highway.

SOUTH TO SEWARD

Beyond the Hope Highway junction, the Seward Highway climbs to scenic Summit Lake. At Mile 46 is **Tenderfoot Creek Campground** ($14) in a beautiful area on the shores of this alpine water. Next to it is **Summit Lake Lodge** (907/244-2031, www.summitlakelodge.com, May–mid-Sept.). Cozy and well placed, it has consistently recommendable food. Breakfast is served until 2 P.M., after which you have your choice of burgers, salads, and other entrées. There's also a small motel ($90 d) and a gift, ice cream, and espresso shop. The original lodge was built in 1953, but the big fireplace and chimney are the only parts of the building that survived the 1964 quake.

Perfect for a late-summer day hike or an extended backcountry trip, **Summit Creek Trail** is a hidden gem that gets you into the alpine area in less than an hour. The trailhead isn't signposted, so look for the small parking area on the west side near Mile 44; it is just above the avalanche gates. The trail gains 2,600 feet in elevation over eight beautiful miles to a junction with Resurrection Trail.

Just after Mile 40 and a mile before the Seward-Sterling junction is **Devil's Creek Trailhead;** this trail leads 10 miles to the pass, then another mile to where it joins the Resurrection Pass Trail. An alpine cabin (www.recreation.gov, $35) sits on the pass. (A great overnight hike takes Summit Creek Trail to

FOLLOWING THE RESURRECTION PASS TRAIL

The Resurrection Pass Trail covers 38 miles between the towns of Hope and Cooper Landing, with two side routes leading off to trailheads along the Seward Highway. You'll gain and lose 2,000 feet in elevation along the way. A series of Forest Service cabins make this one of the most popular hiking destinations in Southcentral Alaska. The trail winds through spruce forests and tops out in tundra, affording opportunities to see a variety of habitats. Wildlife, wildflowers, and wild fish in the lakes and streams add to the trail's appeal.

The trail begins four rough miles from Hope up Resurrection Pass Road, where a trailhead has parking, an information signboard, and a fun bridge across the creek. Eight cabins along the trail, one of which can only be reached via a floatplane, provide a welcome respite from the often inclement weather. The cabins are basic, each consisting of wooden bunks, a table and benches, a countertop for cooking, an outhouse, and a heating stove for warmth, but without running water, cooking utensils, or bedding. These very popular cabins cost $35–45 per night, and the farther in advance you can make plans, the more likely you are to secure a reservation. Make reservations through www.recreation.gov.

If you can't secure a cabin, there are plenty of spots to camp for the night. Be very careful with campfires, or better yet, use a camp stove for cooking. Also filter or boil all drinking water.

Local wildlife includes moose, black and brown bears, wolves, mountain goats, Dall sheep, and even a local caribou herd. The caribou are scattered and often hard to spot in the summer, but if you look up high in the Resurrection Pass and Devil's Pass areas, maybe you'll get lucky. They often like to bed down in snow patches during the heat of the day, so look for dark spots in the snow near ridgelines.

Loop trips are possible, and you can do the Devil's Pass trailhead–Devil's Pass cabin–Cooper Landing trip (27 miles) in three or four days, though hard-core mountain bikers often do it in one day. Hitchhiking to pick up your car is possible, but the Hope trailhead is well off the beaten path for most car traffic.

The high point of the main trail is Resurrection Pass at 2,600 feet. However, even at this comparatively low elevation, the snows of winter can linger well into June. Postholing through thigh-deep snow can dampen the enthusiasm of even the jolliest of hikers. If you're thinking of an early-season hike, check with the Forest Service office in Anchorage (907/271-2500) or the Seward Ranger District (907/224-3374, www.fs.fed.us/r10/chugach) for trail conditions.

At the southern end of the Resurrection Pass Trail at Cooper Landing, you can continue south on the 16-mile **Russian Lakes Trail,** which connects with the 16-mile **Resurrection River Trail** all the way to Exit Glacier near Seward. Together, these three trails make it possible to hike 74 miles, a 12-day trek that covers the Kenai Peninsula from head to toe.

Resurrection Pass Trail, then back down via Devils Creek Trail to the highway.)

The **Carter Lake Trail** leaves the highway at Mile 33, climbs 1,000 feet in just over two miles to Carter Lake, and continues another mile around Carter Lake to Crescent Lake. This route gets you into the alpine fast and can be used to loop back to the highway on the Crescent Lake and Crescent Creek Trails. There's a Forest Service cabin (www.recreation.gov, $45) on the south shore of Crescent Lake.

A half-mile beyond the Carter Lake Trailhead is the southern trailhead to **Johnson Pass Trail** (whose northern trailhead is at Mile 64). And just beyond that is **Trail Lakes Fish Hatchery** (daily 8 A.M.–4:30 P.M.), which has a fascinating display about spawning and stocking salmon.

Moose Pass

At Mile 30 you slow down for tiny Moose Pass (pop. 200), where the classic **Estes Brothers Grocery** (907/288-3151) has been updated with a deli and espresso; it has been here since 1928. The main event comes on the **summer solstice** in June, when the town springs to life with music, food, and games. Learn more about Moose Pass on the Web at www.moosepassalaska.com.

Trail Lake Lodge (907/288-3103 or 800/865-0201, www.traillakelodge.com) is the main place to stay at Moose Pass, with comfortable motel rooms ($109 d) and larger lodge units ($126 d); there are also a restaurant and a lounge.

An exquisite B&B, **Inn at Tern Lake** (907/288-3667, www.ternlakeinn.com, $175–200 d) sits along this picturesque lake six miles north of Moose Pass. Guests stay in five nicely appointed suites, with access to a hot tub, a sauna, a kitchen, canoes, kayaks, a golf green, and even a private airstrip. A full breakfast is included; children are not permitted. The inn is also a popular wedding spot.

Other local places well worth considering include **Alpenglow Cottage** (907/288-3142, www.alpenglowcottage.com, $135 d), **Jewel of the North B&B** (907/288-3166 or 877/317-7378, www.jewelofthenorth.net, $125 d), **Midnight Sun Log Cabins** (907/288-3627, www.midnightsunlogcabins.com, $115 d), **Spruce Moose B&B** (907/288-3667, www.sprucemoosealaska.com, $299–399, 3-night minimum stay), and **Trail River Gardens B&B** (907/288-3192, www.trailriver.com, $102–128 d).

Scenic Mountain Air (907/288-3646 or 800/478-1449, www.scenicmountainair.com) offers one-hour floatplane trips from Trail Lake for $229 per person. If it's a clear day, the views are stunning.

South from Moose Pass

Six miles south of Moose Pass is the turnoff for **Trail River Campground** ($18), a quiet wooded campground just over a mile off the highway, with some choice sites on the lakeshore loop. Next up on the left at Mile 23 is **Ptarmigan Creek Campground** ($14). Both Trail River and Ptarmigan Creek campgrounds can be reserved (518/885-3639 or 877/444-6777, www.recreation.gov). **Ptarmigan Creek Trail** climbs from the Ptarmigan Creek campground for 3.5 miles along the creek to Ptarmigan Lake, where there's good fishing for grayling.

Renfro's Lakeside Retreat (907/288-5059 or 877/288-5059, www.renfroslakesideretreat.com, Apr.–Oct.) is eight miles south of Moose Pass along the shore of Kenai Lake. Here you'll find eight cabins, all with private baths and kitchenettes. Five are right on the lake ($150) and three are back in the woods ($125); all of these sleep 4–5 people for the same price. RV hookups ($30) are also available, along with Wi-Fi, paddleboats, and a playground. There are no TVs or phones.

Magnificent **Kenai Lake** comes into view just south of here: huge, beautiful, blue-green, with snowcapped peaks all around. Three-mile **Victor Creek Trail** starts at Mile 20; in three miles is the turnoff to the small **Primrose Campground** ($14), a mile from the Seward Highway along Kenai Lake.

Primrose Trail climbs 1,500 feet in eight miles to Lost Lake, where you can hook up to **Lost Lake Trail** and come out at Mile 5 near Seward. This is one of the most popular loop trails in the area. If you planned far enough ahead and made a reservation, you can stay at the Dale Clemens cabin (www.recreation.gov, $45). On clear days, you get a magnificent view of Resurrection Bay and on out to the Gulf of Alaska.

Beautiful **Porcupine Creek Falls** is three miles in on the Primrose Trail and is a favorite day-hike destination. Above the lake are dramatic alpine views and the chance to explore this high and mighty landscape.

Seward

Seward is a pocket-size (pop. 3,000) port town on a sparkling bay surrounded by snowcapped peaks, and is the only large settlement on the east side of the Kenai Peninsula. It's connected by bus, ferry, and plane and has a maritime climate and a seafood industry, just like a half-dozen other places you've visited so far, but with a difference: Seward is right on the doorstep of Kenai Fjords National Park. This park contains some of the most inhospitable visitable country in the state. Harding Ice Field—a prehistoric frozen giant with three dozen frigid fingers—rivals Glacier Bay for scenery and wildlife but is decidedly less expensive to visit. Combine this with Seward's Alaska SeaLife Center, convenient camping, good food, and excellent access by public transportation, and you've got all the elements for a great time in this old town.

HISTORY

In 1791, Alexander Baranov, on a return voyage to Kodiak from around his Alaskan domain, waited out a storm in this bay on the Sunday of Resurrection, a Russian holiday. The sheltered waters of Resurrection Bay prompted Baranov to install a small shipyard. In 1903 surveyors for the Alaska Central Railroad laid out the town site for their port. This private enterprise, financed by Seattle businessmen, established Seward, laid 50 miles of track, and went broke. In 1911, Alaska Northern Railroad extended the track almost to present-day Girdwood. In 1912 the U.S. government began financing the completion of this line, which reached Fairbanks, 470 miles north, in 1923. From then, Seward's history parallels Valdez's as one of the two year-round ice-free ports with shipping access to Interior Alaska—Seward's is by rail, Valdez's by road. And like Valdez, Seward was almost completely destroyed by 1964's Good Friday earthquake.

Today, Seward has a diverse economy supported by tourism, commercial fishing and sportfishing, fish processing, and other activities. The Alaska SeaLife Center is the main focal point for travelers and has excellent exhibits. The Alaska Vocational Technical Center trains 1,600 students each year, and a maximum security prison on the east side of Resurrection Bay houses another 450 folks in less academic conditions.

A towering coal-shipping facility dominates the harbor; the Alaska Railroad hauls coal here from the Usibelli Coal Mine in Healy for shipment to South Korea. Some cruise ships also dock in Seward, but most companies have shifted their ships to Whittier. It's too bad for them, since they miss one of the most enjoyable towns in Southcentral Alaska.

SIGHTS

Seward's main attractions are the Alaska SeaLife Center and **boat tours** of Resurrection Bay and Kenai Fjords National Park.

The old-fashioned **Seward Museum** (336 3rd Ave., 907/224-3902, daily 10 A.M.–5 P.M. May–mid-Sept., Sat.–Sun. noon–4 P.M. mid-Sept.–Apr., $3 adults, $0.50 children) houses Native Alaskan baskets and carved ivory, equipment from the original Brown and Hawkins store, the cross-section of a 350-year-old Sitka

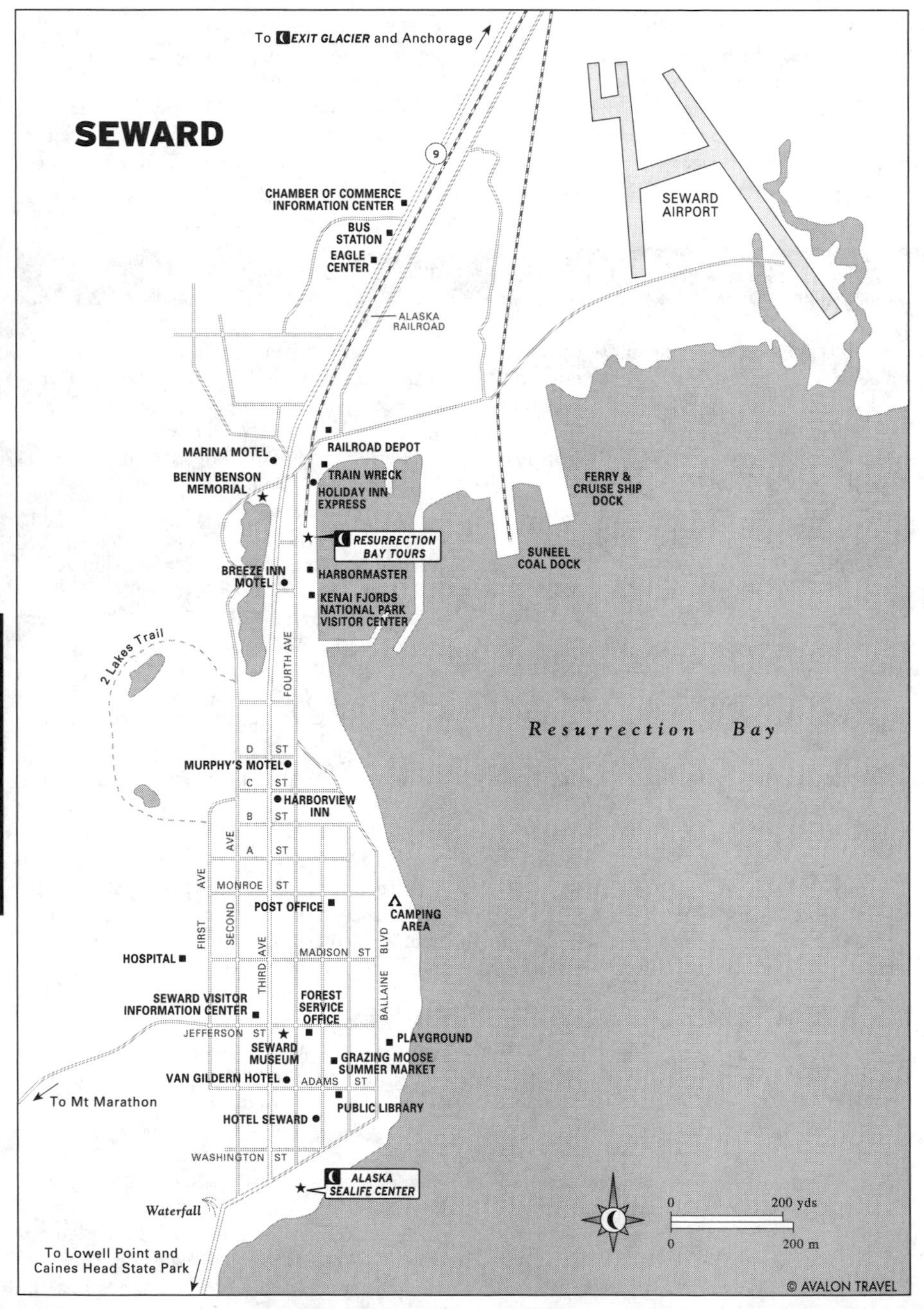
SEWARD
To EXIT GLACIER and Anchorage
9
CHAMBER OF COMMERCE INFORMATION CENTER
BUS STATION
EAGLE CENTER
ALASKA RAILROAD
SEWARD AIRPORT
RAILROAD DEPOT
MARINA MOTEL
TRAIN WRECK
BENNY BENSON MEMORIAL
HOLIDAY INN EXPRESS
FERRY & CRUISE SHIP DOCK
RESURRECTION BAY TOURS
SUNEEL COAL DOCK
BREEZE INN MOTEL
HARBORMASTER
KENAI FJORDS NATIONAL PARK VISITOR CENTER
2 Lakes Trail
FOURTH AVE
Resurrection Bay
D ST
MURPHY'S MOTEL
C ST
HARBORVIEW INN
B ST
A ST
MONROE ST
FIRST AVE
SECOND AVE
POST OFFICE
CAMPING AREA
HOSPITAL
THIRD AVE
MADISON ST
BALLAINE BLVD
SEWARD VISITOR INFORMATION CENTER
FOREST SERVICE OFFICE
JEFFERSON ST
SEWARD MUSEUM
PLAYGROUND
GRAZING MOOSE SUMMER MARKET
VAN GILDERN HOTEL
ADAMS ST
To Mt Marathon
PUBLIC LIBRARY
HOTEL SEWARD
WASHINGTON ST
ALASKA SEALIFE CENTER
Waterfall
0
200 yds
0
200 m
To Lowell Point and Caines Head State Park

spruce, and photographs from the 1964 earthquake that dropped parts of this country by six feet.

Downtown's **Brown & Hawkins Store** (205 4th Ave., 907/224-7313) is Alaska's oldest family-owned business. It's been here since 1900 and still houses the old bank vault and cash register.

If you have kids along, give everyone a break at the new **Seward Community Playground** just south of the campground at Ballaine Boulevard and Adams Street.

Parking is a challenge in Seward, particularly near the harbor, where you'll need to pay $5 per day. (Boat tour companies provide free lots with shuttle buses back to the harbor.)

Visitors Centers

For Seward maps and brochures, start out at the **Seward Chamber of Commerce** (907/224-8051, www.seward.com, Mon.–Fri. 9 A.M.–6 P.M., Sat. 9 A.M.–5 P.M., Sun. 9 A.M.–4 P.M. mid-May–mid-Sept., Mon.–Fri. 9 A.M.–5 P.M. mid-Sept.–mid-May), located two miles north of town. It's one of the first places you pass as you're driving into Seward from Anchorage.

Adjacent to the harbor, **Kenai Fjords National Park Information Center** (1212 4th Ave., 907/224-2125, www.nps.gov/kefj, daily 8:30 A.M.–7 P.M. late May–early Sept., Mon.–Fri. 9 A.M.–5 P.M. the rest of May and Sept., closed late Sept.–Apr.) has videos of the park, along with maps and publications of local interest.

The staff at **Chugach National Forest Seward Ranger District** office (334 4th Ave., 907/224-3374, www.fs.fed.us/r10/chugach, Mon.–Fri. 8 A.M.–5 P.M.) can tell you about all regional hikes, campgrounds, and cabins.

Alaska SeaLife Center

Seward's most enjoyable attraction, the SeaLife Center (907/224-6300 or 800/224-2525, www.alaskasealife.org, Mon.–Thurs. 9 A.M.–6:30 P.M., Fri.–Sun. 8 A.M.–6:30 P.M.

children at the Steller sea lion tank, Alaska SeaLife Center, Seward

May–mid- Sept., daily 10 A.M.–5 P.M. mid-Sept.– May, $20 adults, $15 ages 12–17, $10 ages 4–11, younger children free) sits on the south edge of town facing Resurrection Bay. This impressive facility provides visitors with a wonderful way to learn about marine wildlife up close. There are exhibits, aquariums filled with crabs and octopuses, tide-pool touch tanks, and a gift shop. The main attractions are three gigantic tanks, each with two-story windows where visitors can watch puffins and other seabirds, seals, and sea lions swimming. The playful 1,500-pound Steller sea lions come up to check out children next to their windows. For visitors, the SeaLife Center is a place to learn about the marine environment, but this is also an important center for marine research and the rehabilitation of wildlife, including pigeon guillemots and Steller sea lions. Behind-the-scenes tours ($15) provide an excellent hour-long look at the center's facilities. It you want a hands-on experience, take a personalized one-hour tour for $79; a maximum of four people can join this one.

ENTERTAINMENT AND EVENTS

The year kicks off in Seward with the **Polar Bear Jump-Off,** a leap of faith into the frigid 39°F water of Resurrection Bay on the third weekend in January. All sorts of goofy-costumed jumpers join the fray.

Every July 4th the **Mt. Marathon Race** attracts more than 800 runners who race up and back down the steep slopes of this 3,022-foot summit that rises behind Seward. Many do it in under an hour, but they end up with bruises and bloody knees to show for the torture—the record is 43 minutes and 23 seconds. It has been run annually since 1915. This event is a major Alaskan institution, filling the bars and campgrounds with runners and spectators.

August brings another event that draws the crowds, the **Silver Salmon Derby,** where the top prize is $10,000. This is one of Alaska's richest fishing derbies, and it's been going on for over 55 years. Entry costs $10 per day.

Liberty Theater (305 Adams St., 907/224-5418) shows movies.

RECREATION

Day Hikes

For an enjoyable one-mile walk on a winding trail through the forest and around the creatively named First Lake and Second Lake, look for the **Two Lakes Trail** behind Alaska Vocational Tech Center (2nd Ave. and C St.). There's a picnic area at the trailhead.

The high bare slope hanging over Seward is **Mt. Marathon,** featured attraction for the 4th of July Mountain Marathon Race. It generally takes nonrunners at least four hours to get up and back. Follow Jefferson Street due west up Lowell Canyon and look for the trailhead to the right just beyond a pair of large water tanks. You can run all the way back down the mountain on a steep gravel incline if your legs and nerves are good, but beware of slipping on the solid rock face near the bottom. The trail does not actually reach the summit of Mt. Marathon (4,560 feet) but rather the broad east shoulder (3,022 feet), which offers a spectacular view of Seward and the entire surrounding country.

State Parks

Two popular state parks (907/262-5581, www.alaskastateparks.org) are close to Seward on the shores of Resurrection Bay: Caines Head State Recreation Area and Thumb Cove State Marine Park.

Caines Head State Recreation Area was the site of a World War II military base, Fort McGilvray, and the old command post still stands atop a massive 650-foot headland. There are dramatic views of Resurrection Bay and the surrounding country. The 4.5-mile Coastal Trail leads to the old fort from **Lowell Point State Recreation Site,** three miles south of Seward. Parts of the trail follow the shoreline and can only be hiked at low tide; be sure to check the tide charts before heading out. Take a flashlight to explore the maze of underground passages and rooms at Fort McGilvray. Also here are ammunition magazines and firing platforms for the six-inch guns that guarded Seward. This area makes a fine overnight trip, and a walk-in campground complete with three-sided shelter is available at Tonsina Point, a mile in. Caines Head is very popular with sea kayakers who paddle here from Seward to hang out with the sea otters and seals. Also within the park are often-booked hike-in public use cabins ($65) at Derby Cove and Callisto Canyon.

Thumb Cove State Marine Park is on the east side of Resurrection Bay, seven miles from Seward, and accessibly only by boat. The park includes a long sandy beach, forested uplands, and the waters of Thumb Cove. Porcupine Glacier towers behind. Thumb Cove is a favorite stop for recreational boaters, and camping is popular along its beaches. Two cozy cabins are in the park, each sleeping up to eight people for $65 per night. Get there by water taxi from Miller's Landing.

Fishing

Fishing is one of Seward's most popular activities, and in midsummer dozens of boats dot the waters while hundreds of anglers cast from the shore. Salmon are the main attraction, made all the more enticing by a summer-long fishing derby. Your odds of catching one increase if you can get away from the shore, and many charter boats are available. Halibut fishing is another favorite, but you'll need to get quite far out—sometimes all the way to Montague Island in Prince William Sound—to catch one.

Get a complete list of charter operators from the Visitors Information Center, or contact a booking agency. Oldest and largest (it represents 30 or so boats) is **The Fish House** (907/224-3674 or 800/257-7760, www.thefishhouse.net), across from the harbormaster's office. Also try **Charter Options** (907/224-2026 or 800/224-2026, www.charteroption.com). If you aren't fishing, drop by the harbor in the late afternoon when charter operators hang today's catch up for photos. It's quite a sight. **Miller's Landing** (907/224-5739 or 866/541-5739, www.millerslandingak.com) rents 16-foot skiffs for do-it-yourselfers.

Sea Kayaking

Most Resurrection Bay sea kayaking originates from the scenic Lowell Point area, three miles south of Seward. Three companies—**Kayak Adventures Worldwide** (907/224-3960, www.kayakak.com), **Sunny Cove Sea Kayaking** (907/224-4426 or 800/770-9119, www.sunnycove.com), and **Liquid Adventures** (907/224-9225 or 888/325-2925, www.liquid-adventures.com)—offer similar paddling trips, including a half-day (or sunset) paddle for $70, and an all-day trip for $125–199. The latter typically takes you to Caines Head or up Tonsina River to watch the spawning salmon. Another choice includes a boat tour to Aialik Bay within Kenai Fjords National Park, followed by a glacier paddle and return to town for $399. In addition, all three companies offer multiday trips into Kenai Fjords National Park. Sunny Cove has day trips ($169) to Fox Island aboard a Kenai Fjords tour boat followed by a paddle, salmon bake, and wildlife cruise back to town.

Also at Lowell Point, **Miller's Landing** (907/224-5739 or 866/541-5739, www.millerslandingak.com) rents kayaks for experienced do-it-yourselfers, and provides kayaking day trips and instruction, along with water-taxi service to transport kayaks into remote parts of Kenai Fjords. Other water taxis are **Weather Permitting** (907/224-6595 or 877/907-3677, www.watertaxiak.com) and **Aquetec Water Taxi** (907/362-1291, www.sewardwatertaxi.com).

Backcountry Safaris (907/222-1632 or 877/812-2159, www.alaskakayak.com) is a long-established company with tours to Aialik Bay, kayak rentals, and an eco-adventure camp next to Bear Glacier.

Adventure 60 North (907/224-2600, www.adventure60.com) has similar services to those offered by other companies, including guided trips and kayak rentals, but also rents outdoor gear such as tents, sleeping pads, and even rubber boots. Their most unique offering combines a scenic helicopter flight to Bear Glacier followed by four hours of sea kayaking on the lake ($500).

Kayakers Cove (907/224-8662, www.

kayakerscove.com) is a unique and well-run operation a dozen miles from Seward. Reasonably priced lodging and kayak rentals are available, with access by water taxi from Millers Landing.

In the summer, **Chugach Outdoor Center** (907/277-7238 or 866/277-7238, www.chugachoutdoorcenter.com) has an easy eight-mile float down the Resurrection River from Exit Glacier. These 2.5-hour floats are $80 adults or $60 children.

Sailing

Sailors say Resurrection Bay contains some of the finest sailing waters north of San Francisco Bay, with windy conditions almost every day. Because of this, there are three local yacht clubs and dozens of sailboats berthed in the Small Boat Harbor. In business for more than 30 years, **Sailing, Inc.** (907/224-3160, www.sailinginc.com, May–mid-Sept.) has classes for both novices and experts, but the real attractions are sailing trips onboard the *Alaskan Rover,* a classic 54-foot topsail schooner ($75 adults, $65 children). Guests can help hoist sails and take a turn at the helm but won't be forced to walk the plank if they mess up.

Dogs, Horses, and Bikes

Godwin Glacier Dog Sled Tours (907/224-8239 or 888/989-8239, www.alaskadogsled.com, late May–late Aug.) has the only on-the-snow summertime dogsledding in Southcentral Alaska. The action begins from Seward Airport, where you climb aboard a helicopter for a 15-minute flight to a world of snow, ice, and rocky peaks on crevice-free Godwin Glacier. The base camp here has 90 dogs and their handlers. Guests are given a tour of the operation, an introduction to mushing, and a fun ride behind a team of 12 dogs. The entire trip lasts two hours and costs $450 adults or $429 children. Another option is a helicopter ride to the glacier with a chance to learn about the dogs (without a sled ride); it's $299 for two hours. Combine a sled dog tour with a night in a heated WeatherPort tent (sleeping bag on a cot, no showers), dinner, light breakfast, and a snowmobile ride ($520 pp). This is a first-rate operation, and definitely recommended if you have the money.

Veteran musher—and 2004 Iditarod winner—Mitch Seavey operates **IdidaRide Sled Dog Tours** (907/224-8607 or 800/478-3139, www.ididaride.com) from his home off Exit Glacier Road. Summertime visitors are pulled on a wheeled cart along a two-mile route. The cost of these 1.5-hour tours is $59 adults, $29 children, including an introduction to the Iditarod and a chance to play with husky puppies.

Bardy's Trail Rides (907/224-7863, www.sewardhorses.com) leads two-hour horseback rides ($85) twice daily throughout the summer. This is a fun way to explore the scenic country at the head of Resurrection Bay, with good chances to see bald eagles, moose, and spawning salmon.

Rent mountain bikes and baby joggers from **Seward Bike Shop** (907/224-2448, www.sewardbikeshop.com, Apr.–Oct.) in the collection of "Train Wreck" Alaska railcars (411 Port Ave.).

ACCOMMODATIONS

Seward has plenty of indoor lodging options, but be sure to book ahead in the summer, especially any weekend in August when the Silver Salmon Derby attracts throngs of visitors and fills every room for miles around. The city of Seward hits travelers with a 10 percent lodging tax.

A great first stop when looking for lodging is **Alaska's Point of View Reservation Service** (907/224-2323, www.alaskasview.com), where owner Debra Hafemeister makes bookings (no extra charge) for more than 100 local places at a wide range of prices; this service is recommended.

Hostels

Snow River Hostel (907/440-1907, www.snowriverhostel.org), 16 miles north of Seward, is a quiet place convenient to hikers coming off the Lost Lake Trail. Inside are dorm rooms with baths, a kitchen, and a common room.

Bunks are $20 per person, and a private room costs $50 d. Reservations are recommended in midsummer.

Right downtown, **Moby Dick Hostel** (432 3rd Ave., 907/224-7072, www.mobydickhostel.com, mid-Apr.–Sept.) has dorm-style rooms ($20 pp) with kitchen facilities and showers. Basic private rooms cost $59 d, while two nicer units with kitchenettes run $70–75 d.

Adventurous travelers should check out **Kayakers Cove** (907/224-8662, www.kayakerscove.com), on a small bay near Fox Island, 12 water miles from Seward. Rustic hostel-type lodging is $20 per person, or $60 d in a private cabin. There are no showers, and you'll need a sleeping bag, but a kitchen and a wood-fired sauna are on the grounds. Kayakers Cove is accessible by water taxi ($60 pp round-trip) and rents kayaks (doubles $30 per day, singles $20 per day).

Hotels and Motels

Located in the center of town and decked out with stuffed critters, the **Hotel Seward** (221 5th Ave., 907/224-2378 or 800/655-8785, www.hotelsewardalaska.com) offers economy guest rooms with a bath down the hall for $99 d, and larger guest rooms for $129 d, along with modern guest rooms for $229–279.

Just two blocks from the boat harbor, **Murphy's Motel** (909 4th Ave., 907/224-8090 or 800/686-8191, www.murphysmotel.com) provides a mix of older guest rooms ($129–149 d) and newer units ($169 d), some with balconies. All rooms contain fridges and microwaves.

Situated on the north end of town, **Marina Motel** (1603 Seward Hwy., 907/224-5518, www.sewardmotel.com, $125–150 d) is a comfortable and clean place. All rooms include fridges, and the newer and larger units have microwaves.

Opened in 1916, and now on the National Register of Historic Places, the **Van Gilder Hotel** (308 Adams St., 907/224-3079 or 800/204-6835, www.vangilderhotel.com) gets mixed reviews from guests. Some appreciate this antique-filled and immaculate blast from the past with Wi-Fi and a community kitchen, while others bemoan the lack of an elevator in a three-story structure and the small guest rooms. Rates are $99–149 d, or $189 for two-bedroom suites.

Directly across the street from the small boat harbor, clean and comfortable 100-room **Breeze Inn Motel** (1306 3rd Ave., 907/224-5237 or 888/224-5237, www.breezeinn.com) has standard rooms (no view) for $149 d, and newer units with rather limited harbor or mountain views for $229–269 d. Breeze has free Wi-Fi.

It's hard to beat the harbor-side location of **Holiday Inn Express** (907/224-2550 or 800/465-4329, www.holidayinn.com), which also offers a small indoor pool (the only one in town), a hot tub, a breakfast buffet, a business center, Wi-Fi, and balconies on some units. The predictable chain-motel guest rooms cost $179–189 d for units facing the mountains, and waterside units are $229–239 d.

Fittingly located across from the railroad station, **Whistle Stop Lodging** (411 Port Ave., 907/224-5050, www.sewardak.net/ws, open seasonally, $135–145 d) provides a fun opportunity to overnight in a vintage Alaska Railroad car.

Bed-and-Breakfasts

Seward has dozens of bed-and-breakfasts. The Visitors Information Center has rack cards from most of these, and its website (www.seward.com) provides links; or give Alaska's Point of View Reservation Service (907/224-2323, www.alaskasview.com) a call to book a good one.

Blending Asian and Scandinavian sensibilities, **Soo's B&B** (810 2nd Ave., 907/224-3207 or 888/967-7667, www.bbonline.com/ak/soos, $135 d) was designed by owner Soo Kang's architect son. Four bright guest rooms are available and include a full breakfast, private baths, and Wi-Fi.

Centrally located in a quaint 1905 home, **Ballaine House B&B** (437 3rd Ave., 907/224-2362, www.superpage.com/ballaine, mid-May–mid-Sept., $77 s, $104 d) gets raves from guests who appreciate the cozy Grandma's-house setting, reasonable rates, and Wi-Fi. Friendly owner Marilee Koszewski crafts a made-to-order breakfast each morning. Five guest rooms share two baths.

One of the finest local places, **Bear Paw Lodge** (907/224-3960, www.sewardbearpawlodge.com, Apr.–mid-Sept.) is a beautiful hand-built log home just north of town. The energetic owners are local kayak guides—they also run Kayak Adventures—who will happily provide an introduction to the area. Two downstairs guest rooms ($125 d) share a bath, and the master suite ($185 d) fills the loft. There's also a bunk room for families ($125 d, $140 for 3 people) and such amenities as a large hot tub on the deck, Wi-Fi, and filling continental breakfasts. The kitchen is stocked if you want to cook dinners on your own.

Located at Lowell Point two miles south of town, **Alaska Saltwater Lodge** (907/224-5271, www.alaskasaltwaterlodge.com, May–Sept.) is right on Resurrection Bay. There are stunning vistas from the common room, and just out the door is a quiet sandy beach. All units have private baths, and guests are served a filling breakfast. Rates run $109 d for small rooms, $189 d for larger units with windows on the bay, $249–399 d for spacious 2–3-bedroom suites with private kitchens, and $189 d for a cottage that sleeps six comfortably. Add $15 for each additional guest. The owners also operate a water taxi and a whale-watching business.

Six miles north of Seward along Bear Lake, with impressive glacier vistas, **Kim's Forest B&B** (907/224-7632 or 888/512-7632, www.sewardalaskabnb.com, $100 d shared bath, $138–175 d private bath) is a luxurious home with six guest rooms, a very friendly owner, Wi-Fi, and full breakfasts.

Three miles north of Seward, **Bell-in-the-Woods B&B** (907/224-7271 or 888/729-5655, www.bellinthewoods.net) has four guest rooms ($130–140 d), all with private baths, Wi-Fi, a guest computer, and gourmet breakfasts. A kitchenette suite (sleeps four, $160) is stocked for a continental breakfast.

Bear Lake Lodgings B&B (907/224-2288, www.bearlakelodgings.com) is six miles north of town along this quiet and pristine lake. Two guest rooms ($115 d) share a bath, and two pleasant suites ($160 d) have private baths. A "hearty continental" breakfast is included, and guests can borrow a canoe or kayak to explore the lake.

Other recommended Seward B&Bs include: **Alaska Paddle Inn** (907/362-2628, www.alaskapaddleinn.com, $199–209 d), **Sourdough Sunrise B&B** (907/224-3600, www.sourdoughsunrise.com, $139 d), and **A Swan Nest Inn** (907/224-3080 or 866/224-7461, www.aswannestinn.com, $130–150 d).

Cabins and Suites

Situated high up the hill behind Seward, the appropriately named **A Cabin on the Cliff** (907/224-2411, www.acabinonthecliff.com, $389 d) provides a unique perspective of Resurrection Bay. Originally a trapper's cabin, this beautiful log cabin has an antique brass bed, a fireplace, a kitchenette, and a large private deck with a hot tub enclosed by a gazebo.

Located on Fox Island and accessible only by boat, **Kenai Fjords Wilderness Lodge** (907/224-8068 or 877/777-4053, www.kenaifjordslodge.com) sits in the heart of Resurrection Bay. Guests stay in modern private cabins (but there is no electricity or phones) and enjoy hearty family-style meals at the lodge. Get there on board a Kenai Fjords Tours boat, and spend a night and two days on the island for $758 d, including meals, kayaking, and an all-day boat tour into Northwestern Fjord.

Angel's Rest on Resurrection Bay (907/224-7378 or 866/904-7378, www.angelsrest.com, Mar.–Sept.) encompasses a variety of lodging options in the Lowell Point area south of town. They include three waterfront cabins ($199 d) and four guest rooms ($169 d), all with private baths and kitchenettes, plus a separate home with a full kitchen ($199 d, $219 for 4 people).

Nine miles southeast of town in Humpy Cove, **Orca Island Cabins** (907/224-5846, www.orcaislandcabins.com, May–Sept.)

provides a great way to get in touch with your wild side. Three surprisingly comfortable yurts are perched along the shore of this small island, and a floating cabin is adjacent to the dock. All have decks, kitchenettes, private baths (showers and compost toilet in the yurts), and grills. The cost—including round-trip water taxi from Seward—is $310–335 d, plus $25 for each additional guest. Rates drop if you stay extra days, and kayak rentals are available.

Other recommended Seward-area suites and cabins include **Alaska's Point of View Suites** (907/224-2323 or 888/227-2424, www.alaskaspointofview.com), **River Valley Cabins** (907/224-5740, www.rivervalleycabins.com, $250 d), and **Lost Lake Trailhead Lodge** (907/224-3396 or 866/318-4315, www.lostlaketrailheadlodge.com, $150 d).

CAMPING

City officials provide a long stretch of crowded year-round camping at **Waterfront Park** (907/224-4055, www.cityofseward.net/parksrec, tents $10, RVs $15, with hookups $30) along the shore on Ballaine Boulevard, with toilets, showers, picnic shelters, beautiful views, and lots of company—there are 450 sites. You can also camp at the city's Forest Acres Campground ($10) at Mile 2 out on the Seward Highway—there are large trees, and some highway noise.

Those with wheels can head out to Exit Glacier (13 miles from town) to pitch a tent in the free **Kenai Fjords National Park Campground.** It has a dozen peaceful walk-in campsites, bear-proof storage, covered picnic tables, potable water, and outhouses. It's just a short hike to the glacier.

RVers can stay at **Bear Creek RV Park** (907/224-5725 or 877/924-5725, www.bearcreekrv.com) seven miles north of town, and **Stoney Creek RV Park** (907/224-4760 or 877/437-6366, www.stoneycreekrvpark.com, $32–37), five miles north of town. **Silver Derby Campground** (907/224-4711) is out on Lowell Point Road on the way to Miller's Landing.

FOOD

Breakfast and Lunch

On summer mornings, the fishing crowd crowds into **Bakery at the Harbor** (907/224-6091, daily 5 A.M.–7 P.M. summer, reduced winter hours) across from the Small Boat Harbor for coffee, fresh-baked pastries, and a $10 breakfast buffet. There are good lunch sandwiches and soups too, but the prices are way too high.

Housed within an old Lutheran church, **Resurrect Art Coffeehouse Gallery** (320 3rd Ave., 907/224-7161, www.resurrectart.com, daily 7 A.M.–7 P.M. summer, daily 8 A.M.–5 P.M. the rest of the year, $3–10), is a wonderful place to hang out over an espresso on a rainy day, play a game of chess, check your email (free Wi-Fi) or listen to live jazz Tuesday evenings. It's also one of the best Seward spots to buy Alaskan art, pottery, and jewelry.

Sea Bean Café (225 4th Ave., 907/224-6623, daily 7 A.M.–9 P.M.) is a pleasant downtown coffeehouse with cushy couches, street-side bay windows, computer rentals, and free Wi-Fi.

Le Barn Appetit (907/224-8706, www.myspace.com/lebarn, daily 7 A.M.–9 P.M.) is locally famous for authentic Belgian waffles and crepes from friendly chef Yvon van Driessche. It's not much from the outside, but the dinner and dessert crepes will win you over.

Housed within the Brown & Hawkins store, **Sweet Darlings** (209 4th Ave., 907/224-3011, www.sweetdarlings.com, daily 9 A.M.–9 P.M.) will be a hit with your sweet tooth, featuring homemade gelato, truffles, fudge, and other treats.

Two places serve Chinese food in town, both with $10 lunch buffets and Korean American owners: **Peking Chinese Cuisine** (338 4th Ave., 907/224-5444) and **Oriental Garden** (907/224-7677), right across the street.

Get a fast taco, burrito, or quesadilla from **Railway Cantina** (1401 4th Ave., 907/224-8226), directly across from the boat harbor; everything's under $10.

Dinner

It isn't the least bit pretentious, but you'll find

great barbecue ribs, burgers, smoked green chili burritos, creole shrimp tacos, memorable smoked Reuben sandwiches, and other "food for the soul" at **Smoke Shack** (411 Port Ave., 907/224-7427, daily 7 A.M.–8 P.M. summer, Wed.–Sun. 7 A.M.–3 P.M. winter, $9–18), located in the collection of vintage Alaska Railroad cars on Port Avenue. A few vegetarian options are also available, and everything is made from scratch. The inside tables are often full, but you can take it outside to the picnic tables.

Christo's Palace (133 4th Ave., 907/224-5255, www.christospalace.com, daily 11 A.M.–11 P.M., $13–26) offers pizzas and pasta along with Mexican dinners, charbroiled burgers, and a mean tequila honey shrimp. The 150-year-old back bar is particularly impressive, and it's noisy enough that your kids won't even be heard.

Ray's Waterfront (907/224-5632, daily 11 A.M.–10 P.M. Apr.–Sept., dinner entrées $21–29), at the Small Boat Harbor, is especially convenient for grabbing a bite while you wait for your tour boat (or for a hot toddy when you get back). The walls of Ray's are lined with all sorts of trophy fish, and picture windows look out over the harbor. It also serves big breakfasts. The main problem with Ray's is its popularity. Reservations are not taken, so you'll end up waiting an hour on summer weekends. House specialties include crab burgers, cioppino, and cedar planked salmon. Winter visitors will be disappointed: It's only open April–September.

Just up the street is **Chinooks Waterfront Grill** (907/224-2207, www.chinookswaterfront.com, daily noon–10 P.M. Apr.–mid-Oct., entrées $23–31), with two levels fronting the harbor and a menu of seafood (try the sautéed halibut cheeks) and steaks.

Out on Exit Glacier Road north of town, **Exit Glacier Salmon Bake** (907/224-2204, www.sewardalaskacabins.com, mid-May–mid-Sept., $11–34) is very popular with locals, serving good salmon, halibut, steaks, and burgers in a wooded setting. The pub specializes in Alaskan microbrews, with signs that proclaim "Cheap Beer and Lousy Food."

Markets

Downtown's **Grazing Moose Summer Market** (312 5th Ave., 907/491-1076, Thurs.–Sun. 10 A.M.–4 P.M. mid-May–mid-Oct.) has local artists, organic produce, food (tasty veggie nachos or reindeer sausages), and gifts.

Get groceries and deli sandwiches at the big **Safeway** (907/224-3698, daily 5 A.M.–1 A.M.) on the north end of town along the Seward Highway.

SHOPPING AND SERVICES

Seward has a number of interesting studios scattered around town, including the **Resurrect Art Coffeehouse Gallery** (320 3rd Ave., 907/224-7161, www.resurrectart.com, daily 7 A.M.–7 P.M. summer, daily 8 A.M.–5 P.M. the rest of the year). Also worth a look is **Ranting Raven** (224 4th Ave., 907/224-2228), with art and gifts, pastries, and light lunches.

Soap and rinse your entire naked body at the **Harbormaster Building** (907/224-3138). Additional showers are in the city campground at the foot of Madison Street. There's a **swimming pool** (907/224-3900) at the high school where they throw in a free swim with your shower. There is no laundry in town, but **Box Canyon Cabins** (907/224-5046, www.boxcanyoncabin.com), a mile out on Exit Glacier Road, has a Laundromat and Wi-Fi.

Cover to Cover (215 4th Ave., 907/224-2525) is the local bookshop. The **Seward Community Library** (238 5th Ave., 907/224-4082, www.cityofseward.net/library, Sun. 1–6 P.M., Mon.–Thurs. 10 A.M.–8 P.M., Fri.–Sat. 10 A.M.–6 P.M.) houses Alaska's original flag, designed by a local boy in 1927. The **Benny Benson Memorial** on the north end of the lagoon memorializes this bit of trivia. Also at the library are computers where you can check email.

For medical emergencies, head to **Providence Seward Medical Center** (417 1st Ave., 907/224-5205, www.providence.org).

GETTING THERE

The Alaska Marine Highway ferry doesn't stop in Seward; the closest ports are Whittier and Homer.

Train

An Alaska Railroad ***Coastal Classic* train** (907/265-2494 or 800/544-0552, www.alaskarailroad.com, $75 one-way, $119 round-trip) leaves Anchorage daily during the summer at 6:45 A.M. and arrives in Seward at 11 A.M., then returns to Anchorage at 6 P.M., arriving at 10:15 P.M. Passenger service to Seward is only available mid-May–mid-September.

Air

Located seven miles north of Seward, **Bear Lake Air** (907/224-5985 or 800/224-5985, www.bearlakeair.com) offers flightseeing trips over the Harding Ice Field. **Scenic Mountain Air** (907/224-9152 or 800/478-1449, www.scenicmountainair.com) operates out of the airport.

Bus

Seward Bus Lines (907/224-3608 or 888/420-7788, www.sewardbuslines.net) has daily year-round bus service to and from Anchorage. **Homer Stage Line** (907/362-3644, www.homerstageline.com) provides daily service all summer (and six days a week in the winter) to Anchorage, plus connections to Cooper Landing, Soldotna, Kenai, and Homer. **Alaska Park Connection** (907/245-0200 or 800/266-8625, www.alaskacoach.com) has summertime buses connecting Seward with Anchorage, Talkeetna, and Denali. **Girdwood Shuttle** (907/783-1900, www.girdwoodshuttle.com) provides daily summertime vans connecting Seward with Anchorage.

GETTING AROUND

When cruise ships are in port, the **Seward Trolley Car Company** (907/224-4378) runs from town to the harbor every half-hour; fares are $5 per ride or $15 for the tours all day.

Rent a car from **Hertz** (907/224-4378 or 800/654-3131, www.rentacaralaska.com) or catch a ride from **PJ's Taxi** (907/224-5555, www.pjstaxi.com), **Glacier Taxi** (907/224-5678, www.glaciertaxicab.com), or **Mike's Taxi** (907/224-6453, www.alaskamikestaxi.com).

Kenai Fjords National Park

Kenai Fjords National Park covers 580,000 acres of ice, rock, and rugged coastline on the southern end of the Kenai Peninsula. The centerpiece of this magnificent national park is the Harding Ice Field, a massive expanse of ice and snow broken only by "nunataks"—the peaks of high rocky mountains. The ice field pushes out in all directions in the form of more than 30 named glaciers. Along the coast, eight of these glaciers reach the sea, creating a thundering display of calving icebergs. Kenai Fjords has only been a national park since 1980, but today it is one of the most popular attractions in Alaska. Many visitors come to ride the tour boats past teeming bird colonies or up to tidewater glaciers; many others hike to scenic Exit Glacier or up a steep path to the edge of Harding Ice Field itself.

Next to the Seward harbor, **Kenai Fjords National Park Information Center** (907/224-2125, www.nps.gov/kefj) is open daily in summer. Inside are exhibits on Harding Ice Field and little-known sights within the park.

EXIT GLACIER

One of Alaska's most accessible glaciers, Exit Glacier has a pretty setting, plus a mix of hiking trails, nearby campsites, and guided glacier hikes. This is the only part of the park that is accessible by road. Get to Exit Glacier by driving four miles north from Seward and turning left at the sign. The road ends nine miles later at a big parking lot.

Exit Glacier Nature Center (daily 9 A.M.–8 P.M. late May–early Sept., daily 9 A.M.–5 P.M. the rest of May and Sept., closed Oct.–Apr.)—the only one in Alaska powered by fuel cells—houses interpretive displays and a natural history bookstore. Rangers give programs and lead one-hour nature walks several times daily, with longer all-day trips to the ice field on Saturdays in July–August.

Exit Glacier Guides (907/224-5569, www.exitglacierguides.com) leads five-hour excursions onto the glacier ($125 pp) as well as more adventurous ice-climbing trips ($185). They also provide a shuttle service ($10 round-trip) from town that runs hourly all summer. The company is located within the collection of old Alaska Railroad cars on the north end of the harbor.

Hiking

A one-mile round-trip **nature trail** provides an easy, quiet forest walk. Two paths break off from it: **Glacier's Edge Trail** climbs a steep 0.25 miles up to the 150-foot face of Exit Glacier; a second path (Toe of the Glacier Trail) crosses the rocky outwash plain where you'll probably need to wade an icy-cold creek or two (use caution) to reach the end of the glacier. Don't get too close since the glacier can calve without warning.

Harding Ice Field Trail, seven miles round-trip, forks off just after the bridge over the creek and climbs to 3,500 feet and the ice field. Plan on at least six hours for this far more difficult hike, and check at the ranger station for current trail conditions since deep snow may block this route until midsummer. In the winter, the road into Exit Glacier is not plowed but is very popular with skiers and snowmobilers.

The 16-mile **Resurrection River Trail** starts at Mile 8 of the Exit Glacier Road. This is the southern end of the 74-mile three-trail system from Kenai's top to bottom. Resurrection River Trail leads to the 16-mile Russian Lakes Trail, which hooks up near Cooper Landing to the 38-mile Resurrection Pass Trail to Hope. A Forest Service cabin (518/885-3639 or 877/444-6777, www.recreation.gov, $45) is six miles from the trailhead. Note that the Resurrection River Trail can become quite a quagmire when it rains, and it may be poorly maintained beyond the cabin; most folks simply hike to the cabin and then turn around. The trail is popular with cross-country skiers in wintertime because of its relatively low avalanche danger.

CAMPING AND CABINS

The excellent **Exit Glacier Campground** (free) has a dozen walk-in tent sites just a short distance from the glacier. There's also a bear-proof food locker and cooking shelter.

The Park Service maintains four popular public-use cabins within Kenai Fjords. Three of these are along the coast (June–early Sept., $50), and the fourth is a winter-only cabin at Exit Glacier. Each has its own treat—a pleasant beach walk at **Aialik Bay,** thunderous calving glaciers at **Holgate Arm,** and a little-used one in old-growth rain forest at **North Arm** in remote Nuka Bay. Access to the Aialik Bay and Holgate Arm cabins is primarily by charter boat from Seward, but because of the distance involved, it's cheaper to take a floatplane to North Arm from Homer (the closest town). Contact the Park Service for detailed access info. Be sure to reserve far ahead of time for these extremely popular cabins by contacting the Alaska Public Lands Information Center in Anchorage (907/644-3661 or 866/869-6887). Bookings are available in early January for the summer season, and nearly all the spaces for the Holgate and Aialik cabins fill up by the end of April.

During the winter, the park rents the **Willow Cabin** near Exit Glacier ($35). Ski to this cabin the eight easy miles from the highway along unplowed Exit Glacier Road. There is also a second enclosed winter-use structure nearby that is used as a warming shelter. Make reservations for this cabin with the Park Service in Seward (907/224-7500).

New in 2009, **Kenai Fjords Glacier Lodge** (907/283-2928 or 800/334-8730, www.kenaifjordsglacierlodge.com, June–early Sept.) is tucked into a woodsy spot near Pedersen Glacier along remote Aialik Bay. Located on Native Alaskan land, this is the only lodge inside the park. There's a main lodge, 16 cabins (two beds, private baths, and a small porch), and guided hikes and sea kayaking trips.

Round-trip boat transport from Seward and all meals are included. One night and two days costs $1,190 d.

Backcountry Safaris (907/222-1632 or 877/812-2159, www.alaskakayak.com) has a similar operation on state land next to Bear Glacier. Camp lodging (in sturdy WeatherPorts), water taxi to and from Seward, meals, kayaks, and guides cost $1,190 d for one day. Day trips are also available, but you'll probably want more time to explore this beautiful spot with towering icebergs.

RESURRECTION BAY TOURS

The most exciting thing to do in Seward is to get on a tour boat out into Resurrection Bay or into some nearby fjords. This is *the* cruise for seeing marine wildlife. On a good day, you could see three kinds of whales—including humpbacks and orcas—plus porpoises, seals, sea otters, sea lions, hundreds of puffins, kittiwakes, auklets, and the occasional bald eagle and oystercatcher. Two companies offer cruises with knowledgeable guides and onboard Park Service naturalists. Half-day trips take you around nearby Resurrection Bay and out as far as Rugged Island, while longer voyages include Aialik Bay, Holgate Glacier (with calving icebergs), and the Chiswell Islands (with a Steller sea lion rookery and nesting seabirds—most notably puffins). The latter is a far more interesting trip and actually goes inside the park rather than to its edge, but the waters are often rough, so take your seasickness pills. Hot tip: Some Seward B&Bs and hostels offer 10 percent discounts on Resurrection Bay tours; ask your lodging place if these are available before booking a tour.

Seward's largest tour company, **Kenai Fjords Tours** (907/224-8068 or 800/478-8068, www.kenaifjords.com) primarily operates big boats that hold up to 150 people. They offer a wide variety of cruises, starting with a too-quick three-hour dinner trip to Fox Island ($59). Better options are a 4.5-hour Resurrection Bay tour ($89) that includes a lunch stop on Fox Island, a six-hour trip with time in Kenai Fjords National Park and lunch ($139–149), all the way up to a nine-hour sailing to Northwestern Fjord ($169) that includes breakfast and lunch. Their most popular voyage—and my favorite—is an 8.5-hour trip ($159) to Aialik Bay that includes an hour-long stop on Fox Island for a big salmon dinner at Kenai Fjords Wilderness Lodge. Rates for children are half the adult prices. For a more intimate sailing, book a trip aboard a small 16-passenger boat of **Mariah Tours** (owned by Kenai Fjords Tours). These "Captain's choice" nine-hour tours ($189) focus on birds and wildlife, and include a light breakfast and lunch. On all Kenai Fjords Tours, rates for children under 12 are half the adult rate. The company is owned by CIRI, an Anchorage-based Native Alaskan corporation.

Major Marine Tours (907/224-8030 or 800/764-7300, www.majormarine.com) offers half-day cruises to Resurrection Bay ($69 adults, $34 children) and all-day trips to Holgate Glacier in Aialik Bay ($136 adults, $68 children). Guests are treated to an all-you-can-eat salmon and prime rib buffet for an extra $19 adults, $9 children. The boat is large and stable, which is helpful when seas are rough.

Tour boats operate mid-May–mid-September only. If you get here early or late in the season, you're likely to find lower prices and fewer people on board. Tour companies have booths on the dock behind the harbormaster's office on 4th Avenue. Binoculars and telephoto lenses are handy, and a light jacket is wise. This trip is guaranteed to be one of the highlights of your Alaskan visit, but if you get seasick easily, take along medication, especially on the all-day voyages that go into more exposed waters. You may want to wait if the marine weather report predicts rough seas.

Northwestern Kenai Peninsula

The northwestern end of the Kenai Peninsula is accessible via the **Sterling Highway,** which joins the Seward Highway 37 miles north of Seward and 90 miles south of Anchorage. The mileposts along the Sterling also start counting at 37 from this point. The Sterling Highway heads west through Cooper Landing and Soldotna, then south all the way to Homer, a total of 143 miles.

Between the junction and Cooper Landing (Mile 49) are two Forest Service campgrounds along Quartz Creek Road. **Quartz Creek Campground** (www.recreation.gov, $18–28) is in a beautiful setting right on Kenai Lake. **Crescent Creek Campground** ($14) is three miles down Quartz Creek Road. A 6.5-mile trail climbs 1,000 feet from the Crescent Creek parking lot to Crescent Lake.

COOPER LANDING

A dozen miles west of the Seward Highway junction is Cooper Landing (www.cooperlandingchamber.com), with a scattering of businesses—motels, restaurants, gas stations, and tackle shops—on both sides of the Sterling Highway. A visitors cabin (unstaffed) next to the boat launch on the south side of the Kenai River bridge is open daily in the summer. The little **Cooper Landing Museum** (907/595-3500, www.cooperlandingmuseum.com) at Mile 49 houses the articulated skeleton of a brown bear, historical items, and other items in two old cabins.

Recreation

The main attractions in Cooper Landing are Kenai River fishing and float trips. Several raft companies offer a 14-mile ride to Jim's Landing, which includes some Class II rapids at Schooner Bend. Three-hour float trips cost around $50, and all-day Kenai trips run $145 or so from **Alaska River Adventures** (907/595-2000 or 888/836-9027, www.alaskariveradventures.com), **Alaska Rivers Co.** (907/595-1226 or 888/595-1226, www.alaskariverscompany.com), and **Alaska Wildland Adventures** (907/595-1279 or 800/478-4100, www.alaskarivertrips.com). These and other companies have all-day guided fishing trips aboard drift boats ($205 pp includes lunch), or $110 for a half-day.

Kenai Lake Sea Kayak Adventures (907/595-3441, www.kenailake.com) guides sea kayaking on the lake ($73 for 3 hours). **Alaskan Horsemen Trail Adventures** (907/595-1806 or 800/595-1806, www.alaskahorsemen.com) leads trail rides into the scenic country around Resurrection Trail and Cooper Landing. Find them behind Sunrise Inn at Mile 45.

Accommodations and Food

Cooper Landing spreads out over a seven-mile stretch that centers around Mile 50 of the Sterling Highway. Lodging options are listed from east to west. On the eastern end of Cooper Landing at Mile 45, **Sunrise Inn** (907/595-1222, www.alaskasunriseinn.com, year-round) has a full-service restaurant, a bar, an RV park ($25 with electricity only), a gas station, and a motel ($134 d). The lakeside location is especially pleasant.

Primarily for cruise passengers, **Kenai Princess Lodge** (907/595-1425 or 800/426-0500, www.princesslodges.com, mid-May–mid-Sept., $249 d), near the Kenai River bridge at Mile 48, overlooks the roiling turquoise water of the river and features a restaurant, a lounge, a half-mile nature trail, and a gift shop. Bungalow-style guest rooms have a sitting area, a wood-burning stove, a TV, a phone, and a small private deck. Two large hot tubs and saunas add to the appeal.

TroutFitters Alpine Motel (907/595-1212, www.aktroutfitters.com, May–Oct., $129–149 d), at Mile 48, has a dozen kitchenette units, offers fly-fishing instruction, has a fly shop, and rents fishing gear and waders. Nearby is **Cooper Landing Grocery** (907/595-1677), and a short distance up the road is **Drifters**

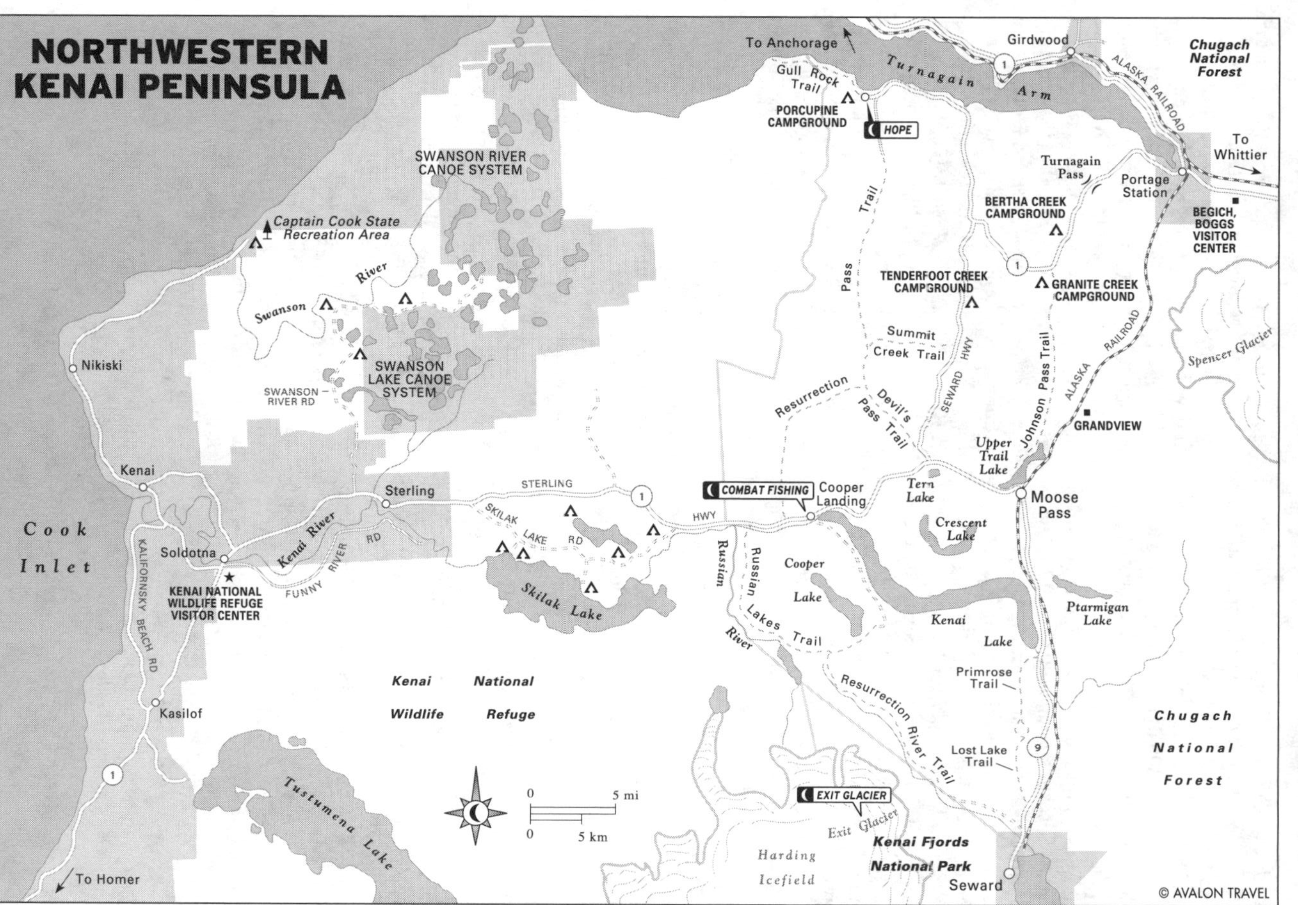
NORTHWESTERN KENAI PENINSULA
To Anchorage
Girdwood
Chugach National Forest
To Whittier
BEGICH, BOGGS VISITOR CENTER
ALASKA RAILROAD
Portage Station
Turnagain Arm
Turnagain Pass
Gull Rock Trail
PORCUPINE CAMPGROUND
HOPE
BERTHA CREEK CAMPGROUND
TENDERFOOT CREEK CAMPGROUND
GRANITE CREEK CAMPGROUND
Spencer Glacier
SWANSON RIVER CANOE SYSTEM
Captain Cook State Recreation Area
Swanson River
SWANSON LAKE CANOE SYSTEM
SWANSON RIVER RD
Nikiski
Resurrection Pass Trail
Summit Creek Trail
Devil's Pass Trail
SEWARD HWY
Johnson Pass Trail
GRANDVIEW
Upper Trail Lake
Moose Pass
Kenai
Cook Inlet
STERLING HWY
Sterling
COMBAT FISHING
Cooper Landing
Tern Lake
Crescent Lake
SKILAK LAKE RD
Skilak Lake
Soldotna
Kenai River
FUNNY RIVER RD
KENAI NATIONAL WILDLIFE REFUGE VISITOR CENTER
KALIFORNSKY BEACH RD
Russian River
Cooper Lake
Russian Lakes Trail
Kenai Lake
Ptarmigan Lake
Primrose Trail
Resurrection River Trail
Kenai National Wildlife Refuge
Kasilof
Lost Lake Trail
Chugach National Forest
EXIT GLACIER
Exit Glacier
Harding Icefield
Kenai Fjords National Park
Seward
Tustumena Lake
0 5 mi
0 5 km
To Homer
© AVALON TRAVEL

KENAI PENINSULA

Lodge (907/595-5555 or 866/595-5959, www.drifterslodge.com, Apr.–mid-Oct.), with modern chalet-cabins ($300 d) containing fridges and microwaves, along with shared-bath guest rooms ($150–200 d) in the lodge. A big breakfast, sauna access, and Wi-Fi are included in these rates.

Located on the western edge of "town" at Mile 52, **Gwin's Lodge** (907/595-1266, www.gwinslodge.com, Mon.–Fri. 6 A.M.–10 P.M., Sat.–Sun. 6 A.M.–midnight late May–early Sept., $11–19) is a classic Alaskan eatery (since 1952) and a great place to pick up tips from the anglers while enjoying down-home cooking, especially the salmon chowder, burgers, and carrot cake. Various lodging choices are available at Gwin's, but are not recommended. The store sells groceries, sodas, beer, lattes, gifts, and fishing licenses, and you can also buy or rent fishing gear, including poles and hip waders.

Upper Kenai River Inn (907/595-3333, www.upperkenairiverinn.com, $150–200 d) is a spacious and modern riverside home with four guest rooms. Breakfast is included.

Alaska Wildland Adventures (www.alaskawildland.com) operates two Kenai Peninsula lodges. Located in Cooper Landing, **Kenai River Sportfishing Lodge** (907/595-1279 or 800/478-4100) has a variety of all-inclusive fishing, food, and lodging packages; a three-night stay is $1,525 per person. More unique is **Kenai Backcountry Lodge** (907/783-2928 or 800/334-8730), hidden away on Skilak Lake and accessible only by boat. Accommodations are comfortably rustic tent cabins and log cabins, with a central bathhouse and lodge. All-inclusive stays—featuring kayaking and hiking—start at $975 per person for two nights.

Camping and Hiking

Just west of Cooper Landing is the Forest Service's **Cooper Creek Campground,** with sites on both sides of the road. The large **Russian River Campground** (tents $18, RVs $28), one of the best places in the state to catch sockeye salmon when they're running (generally mid-June and mid-July), is 1.5 miles farther. Campsites are strung along the two-mile paved road, and the sites are large and well spaced. Campground reservations (518/885-3639 or 877/444-6777, www.recreation.gov) are strongly recommended for July for Cooper Creek or Russian River. Park in the lot if you just want to hike on the 21-mile **Russian Lakes Trail** or take the "fisher's path" along the river to **Russian River Falls,** where salmon leap. The Russian River runs into the Kenai River near the entrance station.

Kenai Princess RV Park (907/595-1425, mid-May–mid-Sept., full hookups $35) is located at Kenai Princess Lodge and does not allow tents. Guests have access to hot tubs at the lodge. **Kenai Riverside Campground and RV Park** (888/536-2478, www.kenairv.com, late May–early Sept., RVs $35, tents $18) is at Mile 50.

Getting There

Homer Stage Line (907/235-2252, www.homerstageline.com) runs to Anchorage, Homer, and Seward. Service is daily to Anchorage in the summer, twice weekly in winter. Seward runs are daily in summer, three times a week the rest of the year.

At Mile 48, **Wildman's** (907/595-1456 or 866/595-1456, www.wildmans.org) has a laundry with showers, and offers a shuttle service. Gwin's Lodge also has a shuttle service for folks floating the river.

KENAI NATIONAL WILDLIFE REFUGE

This large habitat supports so many moose, Dall sheep, bears, salmon, and other wildlife that it was designated a refuge by President Roosevelt in 1941. The Alaska National Interest Lands Act of 1980 changed the name from Kenai National Moose Range and expanded the refuge to its present 2 million acres, managed by the federal Fish and Wildlife Service (907/262-7021, http://kenai.fws.gov). A visitors center is at the refuge headquarters on Ski Hill Road in Soldotna.

An information cabin is at Mile 58, right at

the junction of the Sterling Highway and the dusty 19-mile **Skilak Lake Loop Road.** Stop here to pick up a copy of the refuge's annual newspaper, with details on day hikes, wildlife viewing, fishing, canoeing, picnicking, and camping. The big action in this neck of the woods is along the Loop Road, where you'll find five different campgrounds (free–$10); **Hidden Lake Campground** features campfire programs and guided walks on summer weekends. In addition to those along Skilak Lake, three other Fish and Wildlife Service campgrounds are on the Sterling Highway between Cooper Landing and Sterling.

Oil was discovered in 1957 in the northern wilderness near the Swanson River, and an 18-mile gravel road built to the oilfields also opened up this lake-studded lowlands. Approximately 13 miles in on Swanson River Road is **Dolly Varden Lake Campground.** It is free and uncrowded, has nice views, is right on the lake, and has frequent moose visits. For additional information about the campgrounds, more than a dozen trails, and hundreds of miles of boating and fishing waterways, inquire at the Fish and Wildlife Service greeting cabin or their headquarters in Soldotna.

Combat Fishing

Alaska's most famous salmon-fishing area is near the junction of the Russian and Kenai Rivers. At Mile 55 of the Sterling Highway, the **Russian River Ferry** is a cable-guided, current-powered ferry ($8 adults, $4 children) that shuttles anglers across the Kenai River to the sockeye-rich opposite bank. Come in July to learn the true meaning of "combat fishing" as hundreds of folks fight for space, hooking both sockeye salmon and fellow anglers in the process. You'll need hip waders, and you can only use flies, not lures. Local fishing shops have the correct flies and often rent out poles and boots. Nonfishers are bemused by the oddity of such crowds, but for anglers the salmon fishing is the attraction, since many folks get their limit despite the hordes. A real fly-fishing angler wouldn't be caught dead here, but this is all about catching fish, not enjoying a wilderness or purist experience. Limited roadside parking is available around the ferry, or you can pay $9 to park in the big lot.

Hiking

The **Resurrection Pass Trail** crosses the Sterling Highway just west of Cooper Landing, and is accessible from a trailhead at Mile 53. Several short hikes take off from the Skilak Lake Loop Road, including **Bear Mountain Trail,** with panoramic views across Skilak Lake, and an easy hike along **Engineer Lake.** More challenging is the three-mile **Fuller Lakes Trail.** It takes off from a parking area at Mile 57 and climbs sharply to a pair of small lakes filled with small Dolly Varden (bring your pole).

Canoeing

Two canoe routes—the Swanson River Route and the Swan Lake Route—are accessible by Swanson River Road, a right turn off the Sterling Highway at Mile 84. Both offer a wonderful way to explore the refuge. Pick up the Fish and Wildlife Service brochure *Canoeing in the Kenai National Wildlife Refuge* for detailed information. Three companies provide canoe or kayak rentals and guided trips tailored to your interest and abilities: **Weigner's Backcountry Guiding** (907/262-7840, www.alaska.net/~weigner), **Alaska Canoe & Campground** (907/262-2331, www.alaskacanoetrips.com), and **Kenai Outdoor Canoe & Kayak** (907/394-3567, www.alaskasbackcountry.com). *Kenai Canoe Trails* by Daniel L. Quick is a useful guidebook for anyone heading out on the refuge's lakes.

Located on the northern Kenai Peninsula, **Swan Lake Canoe Route** is the most popular canoeing area within Kenai National Wildlife Refuge. This 60-mile route encompasses 30 lakes that are connected by fairly short portages (the longest is under 1 mile). The entire 60-mile route can be traversed in less than a week. In addition, the route provides access to a 17-mile float down the gentle Moose River. Canoeing on this system offers not only scenic beauty but also excellent wildlife-viewing and good rainbow trout fishing.

The **Swanson River Canoe Route** links 40 small lakes on the northern Kenai Peninsula, and also includes a 46-mile stretch of the Swanson River. The lakes are connected by portages of varying lengths and conditions, but they are more difficult than those on the nearby Swan Lake Canoe Route. Traveling from the Paddle Lake entrance (at Mile 12 on Swan Lake Rd.), trips can stretch from a long weekend to over a week. In remote lake areas of the Swanson River Route east of Pepper Lake, travel is difficult and the routes and portages are often indistinct. This is true wilderness and can be challenging. Bring a compass, an accurate map, a pair of hip waders, and a lot of patience.

STERLING TO SOLDOTNA

The unincorporated settlement of **Sterling** (pop. 6,000)—spread over a wide area around Mile 83—is mainly notable for the four-lane highway that cuts across this part of the northern Kenai Peninsula; it seems totally out of place in such a Podunk spot. The Sterling Highway crosses the Moose River in Sterling, where the Moose joins the widening Kenai River and the fishhook frenzy pervades all your senses. **Izaak Walton State Recreation Site** (907/262-5581, $10) on the east side of the river is a pretty campground with 38 sites, toilets, and water. Archaeological excavations conducted here indicate that Native Alaskans occupied this fish-rich confluence up to 2,000 years ago.

The 13-mile stretch of highway from Sterling to Soldotna bristles with guides and outfitters, fish camps, bait and tackle shops, charters, fish smokehouses, boat and canoe rentals, boat engine sales and repairs, and so forth—essential infrastructure in the eternal struggle between sport anglers and salmon.

Local lodging choices include **Angler's Lodge** (907/262-1747 or 888/262-1747, www.anglerslodge.com), **Morgan's Landing Cabin Rentals** (907/262-8343, www.mlcalaska.com), **Kenai Magic Lodge** (888/262-6644, www.kenaimagiclodge.com), and **Red Fish Lodge** (888/335-4490, www.redfish-lodge.com).

SOLDOTNA

Soldotna was established in the late 1940s, as World War II veterans filed for homestead lands along Soldotna Creek. Today this town of 4,000 is the seat of the Kenai Borough government and serves as a busy stopping point for travelers, anglers, and locals. "Slowdotna" has all the charm of Wasilla, another place disparaged by anyone not living there. Fast food joints, strip malls, fishing supply stores, shopping centers, and a jumble of signs greet your arrival in this sprawling suburban burg with no real downtown—unless you count the big Fred Meyer store. The latter's parking lot also serves as a de facto free RV campground all summer.

Sights

The **Soldotna Visitors Information Center** (907/262-9814, www.soldotnachamber.com, daily 9 A.M.–7 P.M. May–Sept., Mon.–Fri. 9 A.M.–5 P.M. Oct.–Apr.) is on Sterling Highway just south of the bridge over the Kenai River. Stop by to sift through several hundred pamphlets describing B&Bs, fishing charters, RV parks, restaurants, and other businesses. The walls are lined with photos, and be sure to see the 97-pound king salmon that was caught nearby in 1984; it's the largest ever caught by a sport angler. Just out the door, a short path leads to the Kenai River, where the **Kenai River Fish Walk** provides a spot to try your luck at catching an even bigger one.

For the **Kenai National Wildlife Refuge Visitors Center** (907/262-7021, http://kenai.fws.gov, Mon.–Fri. 8 A.M.–5 P.M., Sat.–Sun. 9 A.M.–6 P.M. June–early Sept., Mon.–Fri. 8 A.M.–4:30 P.M., Sat.–Sun. 10 A.M.–5 P.M. early Sept.–May), take a left at Kalifornsky Beach Road (named for a prominent Native Alaskan family), then an immediate right, and go a mile up Ski Hill Road. You can buy books and posters, see the free wildlife videos, stroll the mile-long nature trail, and climb the observation tower.

Soldotna Homestead Museum (Tues.–Sat. 10 A.M.–4 P.M., Sun. noon–4 P.M. mid-May–mid-Sept., free) is a collection of a half-dozen log cabins on the way into Centennial Park. Inside are the usual settlers' items, stuffed critters, and Native Alaskan artifacts. The real treat is that this surprisingly quiet spot is just a short distance from the bustling Sterling Highway.

For recreation, try the **Birch Ridge Golf Course** (907/262-5270, www.birchridgegolf.com), a nine-hole private course three miles from town.

Accommodations

More than 100 lodging options crowd the Sterling-Soldotna-Kenai area, from rustic cabins to riverside wilderness lodges. Visitors center racks are crammed with descriptive flyers, and the chamber's website (www.soldotnachamber.com) has links to most of these. Many local lodges provide freezers for your freshly caught fish.

Aspen Hotel (326 Binkley Circle, 907/260-7736 or 888/308-7848, www.aspenhotelsak.com, $179 d) is a large, well-managed, and modern place with an indoor pool, a whirlpool tub, Wi-Fi, an exercise facility, and breakfast. Rooms have fridges and microwaves, and it's right on the river.

Not far away is another sprawling motel, **Kenai River Lodge** (393 Riverside Dr., 907/262-4292 or 800/977-4292, www.kenairiverlodge.com, $105–126 d) with rooms facing the river.

Best Western King Salmon Motel (35545 Kenai Spur Hwy., 907/262-5857 or 888/262-5857, www.bestwestern.com, $189–199 d) has large rooms with fridges and Wi-Fi. A restaurant is on the property.

The website of the **Kenai Peninsula B&B Association** (866/436-2266, www.kenaipeninsulabba.com) provides links to Soldotna B&Bs. Recommended places include **Longmere Lake Lodge B&B** (907/262-9799, www.longmerelakelodge.com), **Alaskan Dream B&B** (907/260-3147 or 888/326-3147, www.alaskandream.net), and **Call of the River B&B** (907/260-6533, www.kenairiversalmon.com).

Fishing Lodges

Fishing is the main attraction for most Soldotna visitors, with many lodges catering to the hip-waders and tackle crowd. Each lodge has its own package, but most include a minimum of four nights lodging and three days of charter salmon and halibut fishing. Check out **Kenai Riverbend Resort** (907/283-9489 or 800/625-2324, www.kenairiverbend.com), **Soldotna B&B Lodge** (907/262-4779 or 877/262-4779, www.soldotnalodge.com), **King Salmondeaux Lodge** (907/360-3474 or 866/651-3474, www.kingsalmondeauxlodge.com), **Tower Rock Lodge** (907/283-3662 or 800/284-3474, www.towerrocklodge.com), and **Kenai River Raven Lodge** (907/262-5818 or 888/262-5818, www.kenairiverraven.com). **Funny Moose Lodge** (907 or 800/770-3701, www.funnymoose.com) provides the budget version.

Camping

Get to **Centennial Park City Campground** (907/262-5299, www.ci.soldotna.ak.us, $15, no reservations) by crossing the bridge on the Sterling, taking a right at the light onto Kalifornsky Beach Road, then another immediate right into the campground. This is a big city park with nice wooded sites (some right on the river), picnic tables, fire pits, water, boardwalks, fishing walkways, and a boat-launching ramp. **Swiftwater Campground** (907/262-5299, www.ci.soldotna.ak.us, $15, no reservations) is also run by the city of Soldotna, on East Redoubt Street.

Local RV parks include **River Terrace RV Park** (907/262-5593) and **Klondike RV Park & Cabins** (907/262-6035 or 800/980-6035, www.klondikecabins.com, RVs $39), the latter on Funny River Road close to the Kenai River. Free RV parking in the **Fred Meyer** parking lot (2-night limit).

Food

When I asked a longtime Soldotna resident for recommendations on local restaurants, I was told something that should perhaps come as a warning: "I'd rather eat at home." Most Soldotna dining comes courtesy of McDonald's, Subway, Dairy Queen, and Taco Bell, but the town does have a few homegrown options.

Hidden away on a side-street near the Safeway store, **Kaladi Bros. Coffee** (315 S. Kobuk St., 907/262-5890, www.kaladi.com, $4–10) serves good espresso and features art on the walls as well as occasional live music. Be sure to check out the unique ceiling tiles. There's a second (less interesting) Kaladi Bros. shop along the highway next to Subway.

Located at the Soldotna Y, **Fine Thyme Café at River City Books** (907/260-7722, Sun. 11 A.M.–4 P.M., Mon.–Sat. 9 A.M.–5 P.M.) provides a pleasant escape from the ubiquitous fast-food joints and anglers in hip waders. You'll find both a fair selection of new books and a café serving sandwiches (around $10), soups, fresh-baked breads, cookies, desserts, and espresso.

Klondike City is a little shopping center that features a bowling alley and **Sal's Klondike Diner** (907/262-2220, 24 hours), where you can get typical truck-stop food and big pieces of pie. It's *the* place in Soldotna for breakfast, served anytime.

For East Coast–style subs (at Alaska-size prices), stop by **Jersey Subs** (907/260-3343). It has the best Philly cheesesteak in these parts.

Open for lunch and dinner, **Mykel's Restaurant & Lounge** (907/262-4305 or 866/262-9169, www.mykels.com, Sun.–Thurs. 11 A.M.–9 P.M., Fri.–Sat. 11 A.M.–10 P.M., entrées $22–34) is just up Kenai Spur Highway from the Sterling Highway and features fresh salads, pasta, seafood, rack of lamb, steaks, and fine wines; there is also free Wi-Fi.

For fresh veggies and fruits, head to the **Soldotna Farmers' Market** (www.alaskaartguild.com) on Saturdays 10 A.M.–2 P.M. mid-June–mid-September; it's held at the intersection of Kenai Spur Highway and Corral Avenue.

Information and Services

Grab a shower at **Alpine Laundromat** on the highway next to Dairy Queen or **Soldotna Wash & Dry** (121 Smith Way, 907/262-8495). **Central Peninsula Hospital** (250 Hospital Place, 907/262-4404, www.cpgh.org) is especially adept at removing fish hooks from all parts of the body; in a typical year they pull out 100 of them! Be sure to wear shatterproof eyewear to protect your eyes while rubbing shoulders with the Kenai River fishing crowds.

Getting There

Air taxis offering charters and flightseeing from the Soldotna Airport include **Talon Air Service** (907/262-8899, www.talonair.com), **Natron Air** (907/262-8440 or 877/520-8440, www.natronair.com), and **High Adventure Air** (907/262-5237, www.highadventureair.com).

Get a ride from **Alaska Cab** (907/262-1555), or rent cars at **Alaska Auto Rental** (907/262-6102).

Homer Stage Line (907/235-2252, www.homerstageline.com) runs buses from Soldotna to Anchorage, Homer, and Seward. Service is daily to Anchorage, Seward, and Homer in the summer, with fewer runs in winter.

KENAI

The town of Kenai sits on a bluff above the mouth of the Kenai River overlooking Cook Inlet. With over 7,000 residents, it's the largest town on the Kenai Peninsula. Across the inlet to the southwest rise Redoubt and Iliamna, active volcanoes at the head of the Aleutian Range. The Alaska Range is visible to the northwest. Beluga whales sometimes enter the mouth of the river on the incoming tides to look for fish.

History

Kenai is the second-oldest permanent settlement in Alaska, founded by Russian fur traders who built St. Nicholas Redoubt in 1791. The U.S. Army built its own fort, Kenay, in 1869, two years after the Great Land changed hands. Oil was discovered offshore in 1957, followed by natural gas two years later, and now Kenai is the largest and most industrialized city on the peninsula. Several of the 15 Cook Inlet platforms are visible from shore. The oil and gas

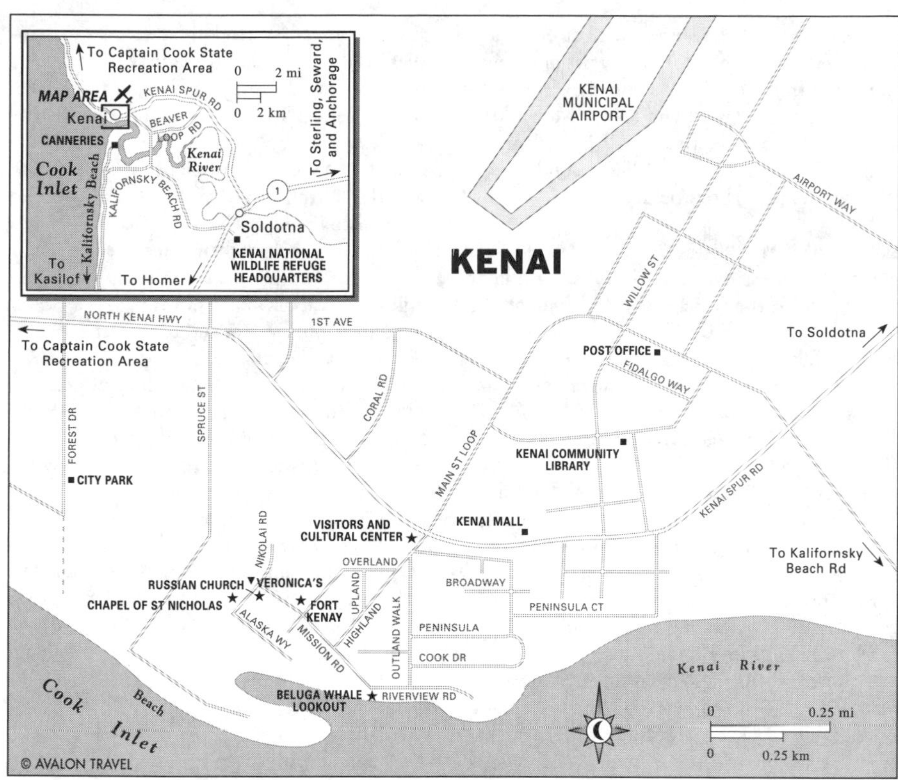

are processed at two petroleum refineries, a liquefied natural gas plant, and a fertilizer plant, all in nearby Nikiski. The rich past has been buried by a rather boring present where town isn't much more than a series of intersections and gas stations.

Sights

Most of the sights of Kenai are in one small area, which you can tour on foot in 90 minutes. Start at the **Kenai Visitors and Cultural Center** (11471 Kenai Spur Rd., 907/283-1991, www.visitkenai.com, Mon.–Fri. 9 A.M.–7 P.M., Sat.–Sun. 10 A.M.–6 P.M. late May–early Sept., Mon.–Fri. 9 A.M.–5 P.M., Sat. 11 A.M.–4 P.M. early Sept.–late May), where you'll find a complete and well-organized selection of brochures and flyers about the area. Its museum collection ($3 in the summer, free in winter and for kids) is impressive, with gorgeous cultural artifacts from Native Alaskan peoples, a permanent exhibit of local historical lore and natural history, and temporary exhibits. Various interpretive programs are taught daily in the summer.

Next, walk down toward the bluff on Overland Avenue to the replica of **Fort Kenay,** built in 1967 for the Alaska Centennial. It isn't open to the public. Next door is **Holy Assumption of the Virgin Mary Orthodox Church,** built in 1895 and the second-oldest Russian Orthodox Church in the state (the oldest is on Kodiak). It's a working church with regular services; tours are available on request, or peek through the windows at the painted altar and brass chandelier. The **Chapel of Saint Nicholas** (1906) nearby, built over the grave of Kenai's first priest, also reflects the traditional

Russian Orthodox architectural style. Walk east on Mission Road for two viewpoints over the bluff; from the first, look out over the riverside canneries, with the Kenai Mountains behind and the Aleutian and Alaska Ranges strung out across the inlet. The second has an interpretive sign about beluga whales.

Recreation

My favorite destination is **Kenai Beach** near the mouth of the Kenai River; it's one of the best and most easily accessible beaches in Alaska. Find it at the end of Spruce Street on the north side of the river. A line of low dunes backs the fine sand.

Captain Cook State Recreation Area (907/262-5581, www.alaskastateparks.org) is 25 miles from Kenai at the end of the North Kenai Road. This is a delightful place to camp, hike the rocky shoreline, look for agates, enjoy the views across Cook Inlet, or simply relax. On summer weekends locals come here to swim in the surprisingly warm waters of Stormy Lake.

Families will love spending an afternoon at the North Peninsula Recreation Area's **Nikiski Pool** (907/776-8472, www.northpenrec.com, open daily, $7 with waterslide), where the featured attractions are a corkscrew waterslide, a "rain umbrella," a hot tub, and a large pool for lap swimming.

The **Kenai Peninsula Oilers** (907/283-7133, www.oilersbaseball.com) play semiprofessional baseball at Coral Seymour Memorial Park in Kenai. The team has won several National Baseball Congress World Series championships over the years and is always fun to watch. **Kenai Golf Course** (1420 Lawton Dr., 907/283-7500, www.kenaigolfcourse.com) is an 18-hole public course. In the winter, cross-country ski trails are maintained here; call 907/283-3855 for specifics.

Accommodations

The Kenai Visitors and Cultural Center has a complete listing of local lodging places, along with their brochures. In the middle of Kenai town, **Uptown Motel** (on the Spur Rd., 907/283-3660 or 800/777-3650, www.uptownmotel.com, $169 d) has fridges, microwaves, and Wi-Fi in all the guest rooms, plus a restaurant and lounge. Check out the 100-year-old gold-plated cash register behind the front desk.

Kings Inn (907/283-6060 or 877/883-6060, www.alaskakingsinn.com, $160–170 d) is on the Soldotna side of the Spur Road near the airport. The hotel recently underwent a major renovation, with new guest rooms, microwaves, fridges, an indoor pool, a hot tub, and an exercise facility, plus Wi-Fi and breakfast.

Daniels Lake Lodge B&B (907/776-5578 or 800/774-5578, www.danielslakelodge.com) includes three rooms in the main house ($98–128 d) and three log cabins ($155–260) that are perfect for families. This is a fine get-away-from-it-all place set on 10 acres of lakeshore. Amenities include a waterside hot tub, Wi-Fi, and self-serve breakfasts.

Located in "old town" Kenai, **Harborside Cottages** (907/283-6162 or 888/283-6162, www.harborsidecottages.com, 150–195 d) are cute kitchenette units overlooking the Kenai River beach, with private baths and Wi-Fi.

Camping

The nearest public camping places are in Soldotna. Twenty-five miles north of Kenai is quiet **Captain Cook State Recreation Area** (907/262-5581, www.alaskastateparks.org), which contains **Bishop Creek Campground,** a popular tent-only area where you can see spawning salmon in late summer, and **Discovery Campground,** with fireside programs on summer weekends. Both campgrounds cost $10.

Beluga Lookout RV Park (929 Mission Ave., 907/283-5999 or 800/745-5999, www.belugalookout.com, RVs $35–60) has full hookups along Cook Inlet. **Diamond M Ranch** (907/283-9424, www.diamondmranch.com, $44) has RV sites five miles south of Kenai on Kalifornsky Beach Road.

Food

Cozy **Veronica's** (602 Petersen Way, 907/283-2725, Sun.–Thurs. 9 A.M.–8 P.M., Fri.–Sat.

9 A.M.–9:30 P.M. summer, Mon.–Thurs. 10 A.M.–3 P.M., Fri.–Sat. 10 A.M.–9:30 P.M. winter, $9–13) is *the* place in the Kenai-Soldotna area. Hidden in a historic log cabin across the street from the Russian Orthodox Church in Old Kenai, the café serves breakfast polenta-crust quiche specials, fresh salads, soups, sandwiches, espresso, and wonderful desserts. There's acoustic musical accompaniment on Friday and Saturday evenings.

A classy (and pricey) place to eat in Kenai is **Paradisos Restaurant** (907/283-2222, daily 11 A.M.–11 P.M., $14–30) on Kenai Spur Road near the visitors center. They've been serving lunch and dinner to locals and visitors since 1971. The big menu features Italian, Mexican, pizzas (free local delivery), and Greek food.

Getting There

Both **Era Aviation** (a.k.a. Frontier Alaska, 907/266-8394 or 800/866-8394, www.frontierak.com) and **Grant Aviation** (907/235-2757 or 888/359-4726, www.flygrant.com) offer daily flights between Kenai Airport and Anchorage. **Alaska West Air** (907/776-5147, www.alaskawestair.com) has flightseeing and charters. Call **Alaska Cab** (907/283-6000) or **Inlet Taxi** (907/283-4711) for rides into town.

A number of companies rent cars and vans at the Kenai Airport (www.kenaiairport.com): **Avis** (907/283-7900 or 800/331-1212), **Budget** (907/283-4506 or 800/527-0770), **Hertz** (907/283-7979 or 800/478-7980), and **Payless** (907/283-6428 or 800/729-5377).

Homer Stage Line (907/235-2252, www.homerstageline.com) runs buses to Anchorage, Homer, and Seward. Service is daily to Anchorage in the summer, and twice weekly in winter.

SOUTH TO HOMER

South of Soldotna, the Sterling Highway hugs the coastline all the way to Homer, a distance of 75 miles. The view across the Cook Inlet is of the Aleutian volcanic crown, **Mt. Redoubt** (10,197 feet) to the north and **Mt. Iliamna** (10,016 feet) to the south—both within rhyming Lake Clark National Park. On a very clear day you can also see active **Mt. Augustine,** a solitary volcanic island with a well-defined cone at the bottom of the Inlet. They're all very active; Augustine last erupted in 2006, followed by Redoubt in 2009. See www.avo.alaska.edu to check current activity levels.

Travelers will be dismayed to find that nearly all the larger spruce trees in this area have been killed by spruce bark beetles, leaving behind the brown skeletons of a once-healthy forest. Many areas of spruce have been logged, but others are simply a mass of standing dead trees. Fortunately, the youngest spruce trees have generally survived the onslaught, and other species, such as birch and alder, are unaffected. The dead spruce forests extend well south of Homer and across Kachemak Bay through Kachemak Bay State Park. It's a sad sight and one that is not likely to change for decades to come. Unfortunately, the infestation that began near here spread eastward across the Kenai Peninsula and all the way to Yukon in Canada.

Kasilof and Clam Gulch

From Kenai, backtrack on Kalifornsky Beach Road over the Kenai River and go right at the fork to the coast; this spur road joins the Sterling Highway at Mile 109 in Kasilof (ka-SEE-loff), gateway to huge Tustumena Lake, whose turnoff is at Mile 110.

At Mile 117 is the turnoff for **Clam Gulch State Recreation Area** and a two-mile gravel road down to the campground and clamming grounds. Campsites go for $10, and day use is $5 per vehicle. Make sure you have a sportfishing license (required for clam diggers over age 16), a shovel, a bucket, and gloves before you dig in the cold sand for the razor-sharp clams. Clamming is best during a low tide in early summer but is possible anytime April–September. Contact the Alaska Department of Fish and Game for regulations.

Clam Gulch Lodge (907/260-3778 or 800/700-9555, www.clamgulch.com, $105 d) is a modern place with a hearty breakfast and shared or private baths. A variety of fishing packages are available.

Several B&Bs and cabin rentals dot the Kasilof area. Especially nice are **Ingrid's Inn** (907/262-1510 or 888/422-1510, www.alaska-one.com/ingrids, $125 d) and **Gallery Lodge** (907/229-2999, www.gallerylodge.com, $110–160 d). Rent cabins from **Kasilof River Lodge and Cabins** (907/262-6348, www.kasilofriverlodge.com) or **Tustumena Ridge Cabins** (907/262-7050, www.trcabins.com).

Park RVs at **Crooked Creek RV Park** (907/262-1299, www.crookedcreekrv.com, RVs $32, others $16) or **Kasilof RV Park** (907/262-0418 summer or 785/657-1465 winter, www.kasilofrvpark.com, RVs $35).

Kasilof Mercantile (907/262-4809) has a café, groceries, and espresso.

Ninilchik

This small town of 700, located where the Ninilchik River empties into the Inlet, has a long history. Settled in the early 1800s by retired Russian-American Company workers who took Native Alaskan wives, the old village is down a short side road off Sterling Highway. In old downtown are some classic water's-edge houses, a few businesses, and some weathered structures. Follow the road that parallels the Ninilchik River around toward the "spit"; you wind up on the other side of the river and village on the hardpan inlet beach. A dozen historical buildings and signs are along the way; a short footpath leads up to the beautiful **Russian Orthodox Church,** built on an overlook in 1900. The church is also accessible by road; look for Coal Street on the left side of the highway as you head north from town. Ninilchik hosts the small-town **Kenai Peninsula Fair** the third weekend in August, with games, livestock, and craft booths.

There is no visitors center, but the **Ninilchik Chamber of Commerce** (907/567-3571, www.ninilchikchamber.com) provides links to local places. Most businesses are strung along the highway above the main town and include Ninilchik General Store (907/567-3378), restaurants, and charter fishing companies. On the shore, **Boardwalk Café** (907/567-3388, summer only) serves clam chowder, along with fresh seafood, espresso, and homemade pies.

© DON PITCHER

Russian Orthodox Church, Ninilchik

Many charter boats put in at nearby Deep Creek State Recreation Area, using large tractors to get the boat trailers out beyond the waves on the beach. It's quite the scene on a summer weekend morning, with the action generally taking place an hour or two before high tide. **Deep Creek Custom Packing** (907/567-3395 or 800/764-0078, www.deepcreekcustompacking.com) sells quality fresh and smoked fish and is open for tours.

Budget travelers should check out **Ninilchik Hostel/The Eagle Watch** (907/567-3905, http://home.gci.net/~theeaglewatch, mid-May–mid-Sept.), with dorm beds for $15 per person. A full kitchen is available, along with two private rooms for $40 d. The hostel is closed 10 A.M.–5 P.M.

Three very popular state campgrounds (907/235-7024, www.alaskastateparks.org, $10) are scattered around town: **Ninilchik River Campground** is big, woodsy, and uncrowded, **Ninilchik View Campground** is atop a high bluff, and **Ninilchik Beach Campground** has undeveloped sites. **Deep Creek State Recreation Area** is just two miles to the south, with campsites for $12. Day-use parking is $5.

Park RVs (around $35) at **Heavenly Sights Camping** (907/567-7371 or 800/479-7371, www.heavenlysights.com), **Scenic View RV Park** (907/567-3909, www.scenicviewrv.com), **Alaskan Angler RV Resort** (907/567-3393 or 800/347-4114, www.afishunt.com), and **Country Boy Campground** (907/567-3396).

Anchor Point

This small town of 2,000 people is another sportfishing destination, with the Anchor River attracting anglers in pursuit of king salmon, silver salmon, Dolly Varden, and steelhead. Anchor Point is the most westerly highway point in North America (or, more precisely, the most westerly town on a road system connected with the Lower 48).

Anchor River Inn (907/235-8531 or 800/435-8531, www.anchorriverinn.com) has aging and tiny "fishermen's special" rooms for $59 s or $64 d, and standard guest rooms with fridges and microwaves for $109 d.

Anchor River Lodge (9097/235-2130, www.anchorriverlodge.com, late May–Oct., $115–135 d) is the finest place in town, with comfortable rooms in a modern log building overlooking the bay and Mt. Iliamna. Breakfast is included.

For Alaskan-style cabins with fridges, microwaves, and private baths, try **Sleepy Bear Cabins** (907/235-5625 or 866/235-5630, www.sleepybearalaska.com, $110 d) or **Northwood Cabins** (907/235-8454, www.northwoodcabins.com, $100–150 d).

Anchor River State Recreation Area covers five campgrounds with campsites ($10) strewn along the Anchor River Beach Road just downhill from town. **Stariski State Recreation Site** ($10), four miles north of Anchor Point, has one of the best views of any state campground. Day-use parking is $5.

The Anchor Point Chamber of Commerce **Visitors Information Center** (907/235-2600, www.anchorpointchamber.org, daily 9 A.M.–5 P.M. late May–early Sept., Mon.–Fri. 10 A.M.–3 P.M. early Sept.–late May) maintains a mini-museum with historical photos and memorabilia.

Nikolaevsk

The Russian Old Believer village of Nikolaevsk is nine miles east of Anchor Point via North Fork Road and Nikolaevsk Road. This isolated community is one of several on the Kenai Peninsula where these traditional people live; nearly all speak both Russian and English. There's a picturesque church, and the women and girls wear scarves and ankle-length dresses. But they also have all the modern conveniences, including big pickup trucks, satellite dishes, and computers. Villagers are not particularly accepting of outsiders, so don't go around pointing your camera at folks.

One open local is Nina Fefelov, ultrafriendly owner of the **Samovar Café** (907/235-6867, www.russiangiftsnina.com), which serves such traditional dishes as borscht, pelmeni, piroshki, and Russian tea, and sells traditional Russian gifts. Overnight stays at her B&B are just $89 d, including a tasty Russian breakfast. Rooms have private baths, and kids are welcome. Park RVs here for $29 (no hookups, but showers are available).

Homer

Homer has a dazzling reputation for some of the finest scenery, the mildest climate, heaviest halibut, biggest bays, longest spits, coolest people, and best quality of life in the state. And the truth is, Homer is one of Alaska's peerless towns. It has an undeniably beautiful setting, with the unruly coastline, undulating fjords, and cavalcading Kenai Mountains across magnificent Kachemak Bay. The temperatures are generally mild—for Alaska. The halibut sometimes tip the scales at over 200 pounds, and you can try your luck at salmon fishing for the cost of a fishing license. An abundance of fine artists and craftspeople call Homer home, selling their wares at small galleries full of rare and tempting stuff. And some of the state's best fishing, boating, hiking, kayaking, natural history, wildlife, and photo ops revolve around Homer in Kachemak Bay. So the bottom line is: Homer distinctly deserves its reputation. Welcome to Homer, Cosmic Hamlet by the Sea.

HISTORY

The Russians knew of the limitless coal in this area in the early 1800s, and Americans were mining the seams only a decade after the Alaska Purchase. The gold rush began delivering people and supplies to the small port at the end of the sandy spit on their way to the gold fields at Hope and Sunrise up the Inlet in the mid-1890s. One of the most flamboyant prospectors to pass through, Homer Pennock left his name on the settlement. Mining the hundreds of millions of tons of accessible bituminous fuel continued until 1907, when a combination of fire in Homer, federal policy, and falling prices burned out the market. Slowly and inevitably, the fishers and homesteaders began settling in during the 1920s, and they

© DON PITCHER

the harbor in Homer

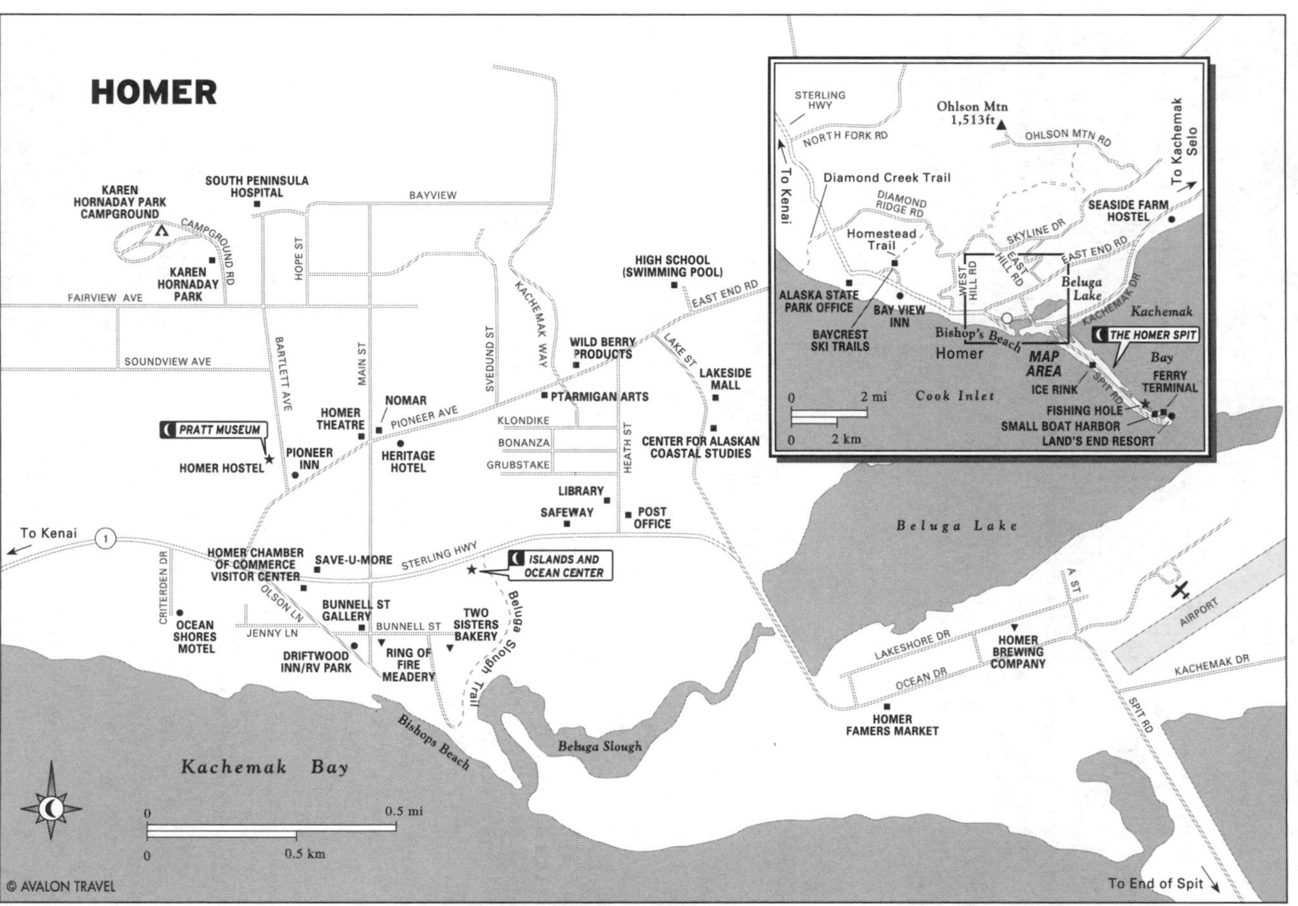
HOMER
KAREN HORNADAY PARK CAMPGROUND
SOUTH PENINSULA HOSPITAL
BAYVIEW
CAMPGROUND RD
KAREN HORNADAY PARK
HOPE ST
FAIRVIEW AVE
SOUNDVIEW AVE
BARTLETT AVE
MAIN ST
SVEDUND ST
KACHEMAK WAY
HIGH SCHOOL (SWIMMING POOL)
EAST END RD
WILD BERRY PRODUCTS
LAKE ST
LAKESIDE MALL
PTARMIGAN ARTS
NOMAR
HOMER THEATRE
PIONEER AVE
KLONDIKE
BONANZA
GRUBSTAKE
HEATH ST
CENTER FOR ALASKAN COASTAL STUDIES
PRATT MUSEUM
HOMER HOSTEL
PIONEER INN
HERITAGE HOTEL
LIBRARY
SAFEWAY
POST OFFICE
To Kenai
1
HOMER CHAMBER OF COMMERCE VISITOR CENTER
SAVE-U-MORE
STERLING HWY
ISLANDS AND OCEAN CENTER
CRITERDEN DR
OLSON LN
BUNNELL ST GALLERY
BUNNELL ST
TWO SISTERS BAKERY
Beluga Slough Trail
JENNY LN
OCEAN SHORES MOTEL
DRIFTWOOD INN/RV PARK
RING OF FIRE MEADERY
Bishops Beach
Beluga Slough
Kachemak Bay
0 0.5 mi
0 0.5 km
© AVALON TRAVEL
Beluga Lake
A ST
AIRPORT
LAKESHORE DR
HOMER BREWING COMPANY
OCEAN DR
KACHEMAK DR
SPIT RD
HOMER FAMERS MARKET
To End of Spit
STERLING HWY
Ohlson Mtn 1,513ft
OHLSON MTN RD
NORTH FORK RD
To Kachemak Selo
To Kenai
Diamond Creek Trail
DIAMOND RIDGE RD
SEASIDE FARM HOSTEL
SKYLINE DR
Homestead Trail
EAST HILL RD
EAST END RD
WEST HILL RD
Beluga Lake
KACHEMAK DR
ALASKA STATE PARK OFFICE
BAY VIEW INN
Kachemak
BAYCREST SKI TRAILS
Bishop's Beach
Homer
THE HOMER SPIT
Bay
MAP AREA
FERRY TERMINAL
SPIT RD
ICE RINK
0 2 mi
Cook Inlet
0 2 km
FISHING HOLE
SMALL BOAT HARBOR
LAND'S END RESORT

found a lifetime supply of home-heating fuel free for the taking right on the beach; it's still collected by some locals.

Homer remained a small fishing and canning port until the early 1950s, when the Sterling Highway finally connected the town with the rest of the continent. Since then, the population has grown to over 4,000 today, with commercial fishing and tourism the primary economic pillars. Homer has an interesting mix of people. Drop by the docks and you'll encounter both the long-haired Rasta crowd and Russian Old Believers whose women wear prim and proper long dresses while the men sport long beards.

SIGHTS

The Homer Spit

This four-mile finger of real estate jutting boldly into Kachemak Bay hosts the Small Boat Harbor, touristy boardwalks, a famous **Fishing Hole,** the infamous Salty Dawg Saloon, Land's End Resort, public camping, charter halibut and salmon fishing, a ferry terminal, and lazy beachcombing with an incomparable view. It is Homer's main attraction, and a wonderfully busy place in midsummer. You could easily spend several days just exploring the shops, walking the beaches, flying kites, fishing for salmon in the Hole, renting a sea kayak to paddle around, soaking up the mountain vistas, and sitting around a campfire as the midsummer sun heads down around midnight. Day breezes kick up most afternoons, making for fine sailing and ideal conditions for an increasing number of kite-surfers. And when the wind really blows the waves start rolling in, attracting surfers and kayakers. No wonder so many folks love Homer! The Pratt Museum's **Historical Harbor Walking Tours** ($5) depart from the Salty Dawg Saloon every Thursday, Friday, and Saturday at 3 P.M. in the summer.

A paved two-mile **bike path** starts at the base of the Spit and continues to the Fishing Hole; it's great for bikes and inline skates, but the traffic is constant and noisy. Come out early in the morning before the cars and wind pick up. Bike rentals are available from Hackle Shack Fly Shop (907/399-4542) on the Spit, Homer Saw and Cycle (907/235-8406), and Lands End Resort (907/235-2500).

Islands and Ocean Center

Located on the edge of Homer, this extraordinary facility provides an introduction to the 4.9-million-acre **Alaska Maritime National Wildlife Refuge,** some 2,500 islands, spires, and coastal headlands scattered from Southeast Alaska to the Arctic. These remote islands provide the largest seabird refuge in the United States, with millions of them nesting on rugged cliffs. Inside the Alaska Islands and Ocean Visitor Center (95 Sterling Hwy., 907/235-6961, www.islandsandocean.org, daily 9 A.M.–6 P.M. late May–early Sept., Tues.–Sat. noon–5 P.M. early Sept.–late May, free), a grand two-story glass lobby faces Kachemak Bay, and visitors can take a stunning voyage to the islands via a 14-minute award-winning film, step into a room that re-creates the sights, sounds, and smells of a bird rookery, and learn about the birds and marine mammals that inhabit these remote places, and the researchers that work there, through interactive exhibits. During the summer, guided bird-watching and estuary walks are offered. The building also houses **Kachemak Bay Research Reserve** (907/235-4799, www.kbayrr.org), whose hands-on Discovery Lab is open to the public several times a week.

Bishops Beach

A short trail leads from the Islands and Ocean Center past Beluga Slough to Bishops Beach, which is also accessible by car from Bunnell Avenue; turn right on Beluga Avenue and follow it to the beach. This is a delightful spot for a low-tide walk, with extraordinary views of mountains, volcanoes, and glaciers lining the bay. Intrepid hikers can follow the beach north seven miles to the Diamond Creek Trail, which heads uphill to the Sterling Highway; leave a car at the trailhead off the highway to make your return easier. You'll need to time this hike with the tides to keep from getting trapped against the cliffs.

© DON PITCHER
cow parsnip along Bishops Beach

Diamond Creek Trail is an easy and fun path, even if you don't do the long beach walk. The trailhead is directly across the Sterling Highway from Diamond Ridge Road. A narrow dirt road—small cars only—takes you a half-mile in, or you can park along the highway and walk in. The trail drops down to the gorgeous, remote beach in a fun and scenic mile.

Pratt Museum

Be sure to visit the Pratt Museum (3779 Bartlett St., 907/235-8635, www.prattmuseum.org, daily 10 A.M.–6 P.M. mid-May–mid-Sept., Tues.–Sun. noon–5 P.M. mid-Sept.–Dec. and Feb.–mid-May, closed Jan.), just up from Pioneer Avenue. This is one of the finest small museums in Alaska, with interesting historical and cultural pieces, artwork, and wildlife displays. The beaked whale skeleton extends nearly the length of one room; follow the story of how it was shot and washed up onto a Homer beach, then was taken apart and put back together piece by piece. A gift shop sells Alaskan-made crafts, and you can control the museum's webcams of McNeil River bears and Gull Island (also broadcast live on the Web). Watch them feed the sea critters Tuesdays and Fridays at 4 P.M. Entrance costs $8 adults, $6 seniors, $4 ages 6–18, free for younger children, and families are $25.

Scenic Drives and Hikes

Head back out the Sterling Highway and take a right on West Hill Road; just after the pavement ends, go right at the fork (a left puts you on Diamond Ridge Rd., which drops you back down to the Sterling) onto **Skyline Drive.** You climb along a high ridge among expensive homes and B&Bs until you see the famous view of the Spit, the bay, and the march of mountains on the southern coast, all framed by fireweed late in the summer.

Continue on Skyline Drive to the turnoff for **East Hill Road,** which takes you steeply downhill to Homer, or continue out East Skyline Drive 1.5 miles to **Carl E. Wynn Nature Center** (907/235-6667, www.akcoastalstudies.

org). Here you'll find nature trails and a learning center (Sat.–Thurs. 10 A.M.–6 P.M., Fri. 10 A.M.–8 P.M. mid-June–early Sept.). Guided walks are $7 adults, $6 seniors, $5 for youths under 18, or $20 for families.

Keep going out on East Skyline Drive and turn left on remote Ohlson Mountain Road (gravel) until it ends at **Ohlson Peak** (1,513 feet). Return to town via East Hill Road, which meets East End Road on—you guessed it—the east side of town.

Pioneer Avenue through town turns into **East End Road,** which also has beautiful homes and great views of the Spit and the bay. Nine miles out are the down-home Fritz Creek General Store (great lunches) and the Homestead Restaurant (wonderful dinners), along with increasingly jaw-dropping views of the Kachemak Bay and the glaciers. The **Kilcher Homestead Living Museum** (907/235-88713, www.kilcheronline.com) is a 600-acre homestead established by one of Homer's homesteading families. Tours are available. (Singer Jewel Kilcher is the best-known member of this talented family.)

The road ends 20 miles from town, but you can walk down a steep dirt road from here to the shore and past the Russian Old Believer village of **Kachemak Selo** along the beach at the head of Kachemak Bay. Not many folks get this far from Homer, but those who do are well rewarded for the effort. If you don't want to drive all that way, take a hard right onto Kachemak Drive three miles out of Homer, and head back down to the Spit.

ENTERTAINMENT

Homer's old favorite, **Alice's Champagne Palace** (195 E. Pioneer Ave., 907/235-6909), no longer has music on a regular basis—leaving a big hole in the town's party scene—but it is open weekends and also serves meals. Several other bars have music on a relatively regular basis, including **Fusion at Wasabi's** (five miles out on East End Rd., 907/226-3663, www.wasabisrestaurant.com),

Kilcher Homestead Living Museum

Duggan's Waterfront Pub (120 W. Bunnell Ave., 907/235-9949), and **The Alibi** (453 E. Pioneer Ave., 907/235-9199). Alice's and Fusion are both smoke-free.

The **Salty Dawg Saloon** (www.saltydawgsaloon.com) out near the end of the Spit is Homer's most famous landmark. The original building dates from 1897, the second building from 1909, and the tower from the mid-1960s. Each building housed different companies in eight different locations before settling down here on the Spit. The Salty Dawg is open from 11 A.M. until the last patron staggers out the door; have a beer for the experience (if you can stand the cigarette smoke) and leave your business card or signed bra with the thousands of others. The Dawg is closed November–February.

Homer has a high proportion of talent, and some of the performers have gotten together to do **Pier One Theater** (on the Spit, 907/235-7333, www.pieronetheatre.org). Whatever is playing, this is guaranteed to be one of the finest theater experiences in the state. It's typically open on weekends May–early September.

For a different kind of theatrical event, catch a flick at little **Homer Theatre** (Pioneer Ave. and Main St., 907/235-6728, www.homertheatre.com). Get there early to snag one of the comfy couches up front. It's Alaska's longest-running movie house.

EVENTS

The first weekend of May brings the **Kachemak Bay Shorebird Festival** (www.homeralaska.org/shorebird.htm) to Homer, with bird walks, bay tours, an arts fair, speakers, and other activities, all in celebration of the great northward migration of shorebirds. Memorial Day weekend in late May brings **K-Bay SeaFest** (907/235-7740, www.kbayseafest.com) with kayaking classes, bay excursions, Coast Guard demonstrations, and a fun wooden boat festival where kids build their own boats.

Public radio station KBBI's **Concerts on the Lawn** (907/235-7721, www.kbbi.org) is the biggest summer event, attracting musicians from around the state. It takes place the last weekend of July. This is one of Alaska's best and most eclectic radio stations; find it at 890 AM.

SHOPPING

Alaska Wild Berry Products (528 E. Pioneer Ave., 907/235-8858 or 800/280-2927, www.alaskawildberryproduct.com) specializes in Alaska-made wild berry jams, jellies, chocolates, and sauces, some of which are fashioned on the premises. The counter usually has free samples, but it's hard to resist buying some before you leave.

Downtown near the movie theater, **Nomar** (104 E. Pioneer Ave., 907/235-8363 or 800/478-8364, www.nomaralaska.com) sells high-quality handmade clothing and outdoor gear. Some of its most popular items are specifically designed for commercial fishers, but Nomar also has warm and windproof outerwear, kids' garb, hats, rain gear, purses, duffel bags, and more. Next door is **Main Street Mercantile** (907/235-9102), a beautifully restored 1936 building with gifts, home accessories, and Sweet Berries Café.

Three miles out on East End Road is **Redden Marine** (a.k.a. Kachemak Gear Shed, 907/235-8612 or 800/478-8612, www.kachemakgearshed.com), selling quality clothing and outerwear for anyone heading out on the water. It's a great place to check out the commercial fishing supplies too. The back wall has a rather unusual souvenir from the *Exxon Valdez* spill.

Homer Bookstore (332 E. Pioneer Ave., 907/235-7496, www.homerbookstore.com) has all of Tom Bodett's books, along with works of other local authors, a big Alaskana section, field guides, and lots more. (Tom Bodett is known to most Americans as the folksy "We'll leave the light on for you" voice in the Motel 6 commercials, but he is also the author of several books of humor. Like fellow Homerite celebrity Jewel, Bodett no longer lives in Homer.)

Old Inlet Bookshop (3487 Main St., 907/235-7984, www.oldinletbookshop.com) is a packed used bookstore with a café in the back and lodging upstairs. This beautifully restored (and expanded) log cabin was originally part of a 1905 fox farm on Yukon Island.

Galleries

Homer has a statewide reputation as an arts center, and a few local showcases are must-sees on any Homer itinerary. The **Homer Council on the Arts** (907/235-4288, www.homer-art.org) has a small gallery and collaborates with local art events. If you're around on the first Friday of the month, don't miss the aptly named **First Friday,** when new exhibitions open and the hors d'oeuvres come out. A number of galleries are scattered around town, most notably **Bunnell Street Arts Center** (106 W. Bunnell Ave., 907/235-2662, www.bunnell-streetgallery.org). This nonprofit gallery is in the old Inlet Trading Post, built in 1937, and just up from Bishop's Beach. Although small, Bunnell attracts nationally known artists with new exhibitions monthly.

One of Alaska's oldest cooperative galleries, **Ptarmigan Arts** (471 E. Pioneer Ave., 907/235-5345, www.ptarmiganarts.com) has a diversity of artists, all of whom also work one day a month. Here you'll find everything from handmade hats to ceramics, beaded jewelry, wildlife and landscape photos (including those of the author), and watercolors. Next door is **Fireweed Gallery** (907/235-3411, www.fireweedgallery.com), and **Picture Alaska** (907/235-2300 or 800/770-2300, www.picturealaska.com) is across the street. **Art Shop Gallery** (907/235-7076 or 800/478-7076, www.artshopgallery.com) is a block or so away.

Spit Shops

Gift shops, restaurants, art galleries, and other businesses are located in several clusters near the end of the Spit. Nearly all of these are open late May–early September, though a few places such as Coal Point Seafood remain open year-round. Art galleries on the Spit include **Sea Lion Gallery** (907/235-3400, www.sealiongallery.com), **High Tide Arts** (907/226-2600, www.leslieklaar.com), **Local Showcase** (907/235-8415, www.local-showcase.com), and **Homer Clay Works** (907/235-6118).

The most distinctive shop is **Time Bandit** (907/226-2722, www.timebandit.tv), with sweatshirts, hats, flags, books, and kid stuff emblazoned with the boat's distinctive pirate emblem. If you've been living under a rock, the crab boat *Time Bandit* is a fixture on the popular Discovery Channel show *Deadliest Catch,* and the crew have become minor celebrities wherever they go. Captains Andy and John Hillstrand make occasional appearances to sign autographs and pose for photos, and the boat is in the Homer harbor at various times throughout the year.

RECREATION

Homer High School houses the local **swimming pool** (907/235-7416), open daily for lap swimming. The **Bay Club** (2395 Kachemak Dr., 907/235-2582) is a fine private facility with a small pool, a racquetball court, workout equipment, yoga classes, and a climbing wall. Entrance costs $15 for visitors, with child care available while you work out.

Seven miles out on East End Road, **Kachemak Bay Lynx Golf Course** (907/235-0606 or 800/295-5969, www.lynxgolfbnb.com, daily mid-Apr.–Oct.) is a par-three course with great views of the bay. The little clubhouse rents clubs.

Kachemak Bay is a great place for sailing, and the **Homer Yacht Club** (907/235-8503, www.homeryachtclub.org) holds semicompetitive races on weekends all summer, with the Land's End Regatta the last weekend of June. Crewmembers are often needed; contact the club if you're interested in joining the fun—no experience necessary.

Located three miles out on East End Road, **Cycle Logical** (907/226-2925, www.cycle-logicalhomer.com) is the local bike shop. Owner Derek Reynolds also rents cruiser bikes through **Hackle Shack Fly Shop** (907/399-4542, www.kgbalaska.com) on the Spit. Both **Homer Saw and Cycle** (1532 Ocean Dr., 907/235-8406) and **Lands End Resort** (907/235-2500) rent mountain bikes. Local water taxis will transport your bikes across the bay at no extra charge; Red Mountain is an especially enjoyable backcountry ride.

Mark Marette of **Trails End Horse Adventures** (907/235-6393) leads horseback rides in the beautiful Fox River area at the head of Kachemak Bay ($85 for 4 hours).

If you have kids in tow, drive uphill on Bartlett Street, then left on Fairview Avenue to **Karen Hornaday Park,** where the playground has all sorts of fun adventures.

Sea Kayaking

A number of local companies lead seasonal guided sea kayak trips within Kachemak Bay, or rent kayaks to do it on your own. Based on protected Yukon Island near Kachemak Bay State Park, **True North Kayak Adventures** (907/235-0708, www.truenorthkayak.com) offers a range of guided trips, from half-day paddles ($105) to multiple-night packages. The all-day trip ($150 with lunch) is especially popular. All trips include a round-trip water-taxi ride to Yukon Island, sea kayaks, and a guide. Kayak rentals ($195 for 2 people with water taxi) are available for experienced paddlers.

St. Augustine's Kayak & Tours (907/299-1894 or 800/770-6126, www.homerkayaking.com) has a base in Peterson Bay, adjacent to the Center for Alaskan Coastal Studies field station, with half-day ($95) and full-day ($135) trips, plus a combination version that includes a morning with naturalists at CACS and an afternoon of paddling for $155. Many people book through the Inlet Charters office on the Spit. All trips include round-trip transportation by water taxi from Homer.

Kachemak Guide Bureau (907/399-4542, www.kgbalaska.com) sets up custom kayak trips of all sorts, including ones that include fly fishing, hiking, of flightseeing. Local water taxis have complete details on their various adventure trips.

Across the Bay Tent & Breakfast Adventure Company (907/235-3633 summer or 907/345-2571 winter, www.tentandbreakfastalaska.com, late May–early Sept.) has a distinctive operation that's perfect for adventurous travelers on a budget. Guests stay in furnished canvas wall-tents set atop wooden platforms along Kasitsna Bay (8 miles out of Seldovia), with showers, a sauna, and "two of the most beautiful outhouses in Alaska." Tent and all meals are $110 per day per person; tent and breakfast only are $75 per day. You can rent a mountain bike, take a sea kayak tour, or join a Kachemak Bay tour.

Seaside Adventures (907/235-6672, www.seasideadventure.com, May–mid-Oct.) operates out of Little Tutka Bay, a lovely wooded spot surrounded by Kachemak Bay State Park. Tours ($150 all day or $110 half-day) include a water-taxi ride from the Spit, knowledgeable guides, and a distinctive lunch that includes "beach soup" made from mussels and clams found along the way.

Local water-taxi companies (including Mako's, Smoke Wagon, and Triton) will also book kayak trips through the above companies, and offer rental kayaks. A package for two people that includes round-trip water taxi to the park and a double kayak is $190 d.

Alaska Kayak School (907/235-2090, www.alaskakayakschool.com) offers kayaking lessons year-round from experienced professionals.

Charter Fishing

Homer calls itself the halibut fishing capital of the world, with commercial fishers often landing more halibut here than at any other port. Sportfishing attracts droves of enthusiasts every day of the summer, not only for halibut but also for king and silver salmon. Wear warm, layered clothing topped by rain gear, and soft-soled shoes. Binoculars are a definite plus, since seabirds and marine mammals are usually viewable. You can have your catch vacuum-packed, frozen, and shipped home for additional fees, but they add up quickly. Half-day fishing charters typically cost $105 per person, with all-day charters for $225–260. Rates are a bit lower on the larger boats that carry up to 18 people (versus 6 on most boats), and during the shoulder seasons. Add $50 or so for a trip that combines halibut and salmon fishing.

Whatever you do, don't forget to enter the

summerlong **Homer Jackpot Halibut Derby** (www.homerhalibutderby.com) if you go fishing. First prize tops $45,000, with additional monthly prizes. Sob stories abound of people who saved $10 by not entering, then caught potential prizewinning sea monsters. Don't let this happen to you!

Homer has dozens of fishing charter boats to help you go out and bag a big halibut. An easy way to find one is through **Central Charter Booking Agency** (907/235-7847 or 800/478-7847, www.centralcharter.com), **Homer Ocean Charters** (907/235-6212 or 800/426-6212, www.homerocean.com), **Inlet Charters** (907/235-6126 or 800/770-6126, www.halibutcharters.com), **Tacklebuster Charters** (800/789-5155, www.tacklebuster.com), or **North Country Charters** (907/235-7620 or 800/770-7620, www.northcountrycharters.com). In addition to charter fishing, all of these can set up sea kayaking, water-taxi service, flightseeing, bear-viewing, and lodging for the area.

Once you do catch a big halibut or salmon, how do you get it back home? **Coal Point Seafood** (907/235-3877 or 800/325-3877, www.welovefish.com) offers processing and flash-freezing, and will FedEx the fish to your home. If you're going to be flying out and can take the fish with you, be sure to get the specially coated cardboard box (sold in grocery stores and at Redden Marine) and pack it with blue ice. Freezers are available at the Anchorage airport (fee charged).

The Fishing Hole

If you simply want to drive into town and cast a line in the water, head out to the famous Fishing Hole on the Spit, across from Glacier Drive-In and Sportsman's Supply. The Alaska Department of Fish and Game stocks this little bight with king and silver salmon smolt, and their return draws crowds of anglers all summer long. It's a classic roadside fishing stop for RVers, kids, lazy locals, and the like. On a busy weekend, you might be able to squeeze in at water's edge.

Get fishing licenses or rent a pole from **Sport Shed** (907/235-5562) across from the Hole or **Sportsman's Supply** (907/235-2617) near the boat launch.

Bear-Viewing and Flightseeing

Homer is a popular base for flightseeing trips and bear-viewing flights to coastal Katmai National Park in the summer, primarily the stretch between Geographic Harbor and Swikshak Lagoon (some trips go to Lake Clark National Park). All-day trips cost around $550–625 per person and are offered late May–mid-September. Call ahead for reservations during July-August, but walk-ins may be available one day before.

Operated by lifelong Alaskans Gary and Jeanne Porter, **Bald Mountain Air Service** (907/235-7969 or 800/478-7969, www.baldmountainair.com) is a long-established company with a fine reputation. Another company, **Emerald Air Service,** (www.emeraldairservice.com), may also be offering bear viewing trips. Book your midsummer trip in January or February to be assured of a space.

Jose de Creeft of **Northwind Aviation** (907/235-7482, www.northwindak.com)—one of the best bush pilots around—offers flightseeing and trips to Brooks River or McNeil.

Hallo Bay Bear Lodge (907/235-2237, www.hallobay.com) is a unique camp setting in the heart of Katmai National Park, described in the *Southwest Alaska* chapter but accessed by Homer air taxis.

Smokey Bay Air (907/235-1511 or 888/482-1511, www.smokeybayair.com) takes guests bear-viewing at Hallo Bay in Katmai or Homestead Lodge in Lake Clark National Park.

Maritime Helicopters (907/235-7771, www.maritimehelicopters.com) guides eagle-eye tours of the region's glaciers, islands, and mountains on a charter basis.

Birding

Kachemak Bay provides a fine opportunity for birders, especially during the spring migration when thousands of sandpipers and other species fill the tide flats. Call

© DON PITCHER

bald eagles in Homer

the **Kachemak Bay Bird Alert** (907/235-7337) for a recording of recent bird sightings, or head to www.birdinghomeralaska.org for more information and a link to the Islands and Ocean Center's bird sightings. The Chamber of Commerce has a weekly sheet listing unusual birds. In early May, the Kachemak Bay Shorebird Festival brings guest speakers and bird experts.

Winter Sports

Homer is just above sea level, and it might even rain in January, but surrounding hills often pile high with snow. **Kachemak Nordic Ski Club** (907/235-6018, www.kachemaknordicskiclub.org) maintains 22 miles of groomed cross-country trails near McNeil Canyon (13 miles east of town), at Baycrest (just west of town off Sterling Hwy.), and at Lookout Mountain (out on Ohlson Mountain Rd.). The last of these has the best snow and most adventurous trails. Check the website for current conditions and the grooming status. Also popular in the winter are snowmobiling and ice skating on Beluga Lake. Located halfway out on the Spit, the **Homer Ice Arena** (907/235-2647, www.homericerink.com) is open for skaters and hockey players throughout the fall and winter.

ACCOMMODATIONS

The Homer Chamber of Commerce website (www.homeralaska.org) has links to most local lodging places. Many people come to Homer to fish, and this typically means very early departures. Because of this you may be subjected to noise at 5 A.M. as folks head out for the one day when you just wanted to sleep in.

Hostels

Homer's old-time favorite is **Seaside Farm Hostel** (907/235-7850, www.seasidealaska.com, May–Sept.), five miles out on East End Road. It's a great rural location with horses in the pasture below, an organic garden, beach access, campfire cookouts, and killer views across Kachemak Bay. Beds in the coed dorm cost $15 per person if you have a sleeping bag or $20 with bedding, including cooking facilities and showers. Private rooms in the lodge and simple cabins are $65–85 d; showers are in the lodge. Scenic tent spaces cost $10 d. (Seaside Farm is owned by Mossy Kilcher, whose internationally known niece is the singer Jewel Kilcher, better known as simply Jewel. Homer's most famous former resident now lives in Texas.)

Housed within the historic Pratt House (built in 1939), the **Homer Hostel** (304 W. Pioneer Ave., 907/235-1463, www.homerhostel.com, late Apr.–Sept.) is a pleasant spot to bed down in the heart of town. Bunks are $25 per person, and three simple private rooms cost $54 s or $65 d. The hostel has a full kitchen, laundry, showers, bike rentals, a guest computer, Wi-Fi, an outdoor grill, a convenient downtown location, a friendly owner, and no curfew.

Motels and Hotels

Driftwood Inn (907/235-8019 or 800/478-8019, www.thedriftwoodinn.com) is an unexpected gem in the rough. The historic main building has a wonderful common room with a stone fireplace, comfortable chairs for relaxing, Wi-Fi, and inexpensive breakfast and snack items. Several budget guest rooms ($70–75 d)—cute but basic—have shared baths, and a half-dozen "ships quarters rooms" ($80–85 d) provide only slightly more space than a ship's bunk but come with private baths and a charming nautical interior; they're not for anyone with claustrophobia. More standard units with private baths are $119–139 d. Across the street is Seaside Lodge (owned by Driftwood Inn), a modern home overlooking Bishops Beach and Kachemak Bay with five guest rooms ($159–169 d), private baths, and a full kitchen. A separate two-bedroom cottage ($250 for up to 4 people) next door is also available. The latter two places are especially popular for weddings.

It's hard to miss the **Heritage Hotel** (147 E. Pioneer Ave., 907/235-7787 or 800/380-7787, www.alaskaheritagehotel.com). Built in 1948, this rambling log building has heart-of-town rooms for $119–129 d, and large apartment-style suites for $165 d. This is a love-it-or-hate-it place; some folks rave about the classic guest rooms, while others prefer something more modern and complain of thin walls and the older furnishings. There is free Wi-Fi.

Pioneer Inn (244 W. Pioneer Ave., 907/235-5670 or 800/782-9655, www.pioneerinnhomerak.com) is an unpretentious downtown motel with standard guest rooms for $109 d and five large apartment-style units with full kitchens for $119 d. The TVs are miniscule, but the rooms are very clean and the owner makes you feel at home.

Popular with fishers are three units over the **Sport Shed** (907/235-5562, Apr.–Sept.), a fishing shop. These studio units—all with full kitchens and water views—are $95 d plus $5 for each extra guest.

Ocean House Inn (1065 Krueth Way, 907/235-3294 or 888/353-3294, www.homeroceanhouse.com) sits atop a low cliff facing the Homer Spit, with beach access, private entrances, a large hot tub, Wi-Fi, and a guest computer. Accommodations encompass rooms and suites ($139–159 d) with microwaves and fridges, along with condos ($209–259 d) containing full kitchens.

Spread across four buildings on a gentle slope, **Ocean Shores Motel** (451 Sterling Hwy., 907/235-7775 or 800/770-7775, www.akoceanshores.com) is an old-fashioned plain-vanilla place, with prices matching your proximity to the water: $149–179 d. A few $99 rooms are popular with fishers who don't care much about where they sleep.

Located on the hillside as you drive into Homer, **Bay View Inn** (907/235-8485 or 800/478-8485, www.bayviewalaska.com) has older rooms and kitchenettes ($119–129 d), plus a suite and a cottage ($179 d) with full kitchens. The incredible panoramic K-Bay vistas are the real attraction, and the picnic tables out front are perfect for a summer evening.

Advertised as Alaska's only beachfront hotel, **Land's End Resort** (907/235-0400 or 800/478-0400, www.lands-end-resort.com) occupies the very tip of Homer Spit, with bay-and-mountain views from some rooms, a waterside hot tub, a little exercise pool, and Wi-Fi in the lobby. The 84 rooms range greatly in price and quality, from $126 d for an economy unit facing the parking lot to $221 d for luxurious two-room suites in the new building. The in-house restaurant features a big back deck on the water and an upstairs reception hall that's popular for summer weddings. Also available are a number of elaborate condos (Land's End Lodges) that line the beach. Downstairs studio apartments are $325 d, and more impressive upstairs two-bedroom apartments cost $450 d.

Alaskan Suites (907/235-1972 or 888/239-1972, www.alaskansuites.com, $265 for up to 5 people) consists of five modern cabins on the west side of Homer, each containing two queen beds, a fridge and a microwave, a private bath, and Wi-Fi. The panoramic views include Kachemak Bay and several volcanoes.

Bed-and-Breakfasts

More than 100 (!) Homer bed-and-breakfasts await your visit. A pair of bed-and-breakfast organizations provide one-stop shopping: **Homer's Finest B&B Network** (907/235-4983 or 800/764-3211, www.homeraccommodations.com) and **Homer B&B Association** (907/226-1114 or 877/296-1114, www.homerbedbreakfast.com).

Old Town B&B (106 W. Bunnell St., 907/235-7558, www.oldtownbedandbreakfast.com) is owned by artist Asia Freeman, who also manages Bunnell Street Arts Center downstairs. The three immaculate rooms have period pieces in this renovated 1936 building with a false-front exterior, and they are priced at a remarkable $95 d with a shared bath or $115 with a private bath. A full breakfast is served in the parlor.

A block up the hill is **Mermaid B&B** (3487 Main St., 907/235-7984, www.mermaidcafe.net, $185 d), a gorgeous little apartment over Old Inlet Bookshop. It has a hot tub on the deck along with a full kitchen and private bath, and includes $10 off breakfast at the cozy downstairs café. The craftsmanship of builder and bookstore-owner Andy Wills shows in all the little details.

One of Homer's oldest—and finest—B&Bs, **Halcyon Heights B&B** (100 Mission Rd., 907/235-2148, www.homerbb.com) has a beautiful East Hill location with panoramic views of Kachemak Bay from the deck. Amenities include an outdoor hot tub, private entrances and baths, full breakfasts, and Wi-Fi. Three upstairs rooms ($155–195 d) open onto the deck, and families appreciate the garden-level suites ($195–295). Halcyon has a two-night minimum stay.

Beach House B&B (1121 Seabreeze Ct., 907/235-3232 or 800/936-7571, www.alaskabeachhouse.com) is a favorite of travelers, with four guest rooms ($99–209 d) and a modern cottage ($249 d), private entrances and baths, a beach-side hot tub, Wi-Fi, microwaves, fridges, and continental breakfasts brought to your room the evening before.

Whalesong B&B (4002 Kachemak Way, 907/235-7628, www.thewhalesong.com, $125 d) is a reasonably priced option just a block from downtown galleries and restaurants. Two rooms have private entrances and guests are served a continental breakfast.

A fine option is **Bay Avenue B&B** (907/235-3757 or 800/371-2095, www.bayavebb.com), with seven rooms ($145 d) in the main house and two apartment-style units ($150 d) that are a deal for anglers and families. The big breakfast features local items, and guests love the hot tub, where you can watch the sunset over Kachemak Bay. The marsh below is a good place to spot shorebirds and bald eagles; there is also free Wi-Fi.

A Room with a View (840 Rosebud Court, 907/235-3706, www.aroomwithaviewhomer.com, $125 d) is a large hillside home off West Hill Road with two guest rooms, private baths, and filling breakfasts. The owners speak German, and their decades as florists show in the immaculately landscaped grounds. No children under age 8 are allowed.

Victorian Heights B&B (61495 Race Rd., 907/235-6357, www.victorianheightsbedandbreakfast.com, $135–165 d) is a hilltop mansion off East Hill Road with four spacious guest rooms, all with private baths. A full breakfast and Wi-Fi are included, and guests love the big deck overlooking the bay. There is a two-night minimum stay.

Just up the road, the aptly named **Majestic View B&B** (907/235-6413 or 888/246-6413, www.majesticviewbb.com) is another very comfortable home with five guest rooms, three with private baths ($125 d), and two that share a bath ($150 d). Families are welcome—all rooms contain queen and twin beds—and kids like the downstairs rec room, while adults appreciate the big deck with unobstructed bay vistas, an outdoor hot tub, and Wi-Fi. The deluxe room has a whirlpool tub, a private balcony, and tall windows. A homemade breakfast is served family style.

Aloha B&B (62209 Glacier View Court, 907/235-0607 or 877/355-0607, www.alohabb.com, May–Oct., $114–129 d) has one of Homer's famous "million-dollar" views—a 180-degree panorama of bay, mountains, and glacier. The owners are natives of Hawaii, and a Hawaiian theme carries through all four guest rooms (two of which share a bath). A continental breakfast and Wi-Fi are included.

Seven miles out on East End Road, **A B&B on the Green** (907/235-0606 or 800/295-5969, www.lynxgolfbnb.com, May–Sept.) sits alongside a par-3 golf course. Two rooms over the clubhouse are $115 s or $125 d, or you can rent the adjacent three-bedroom home for $150 d. Rates include private baths, a continental breakfast, and unlimited golf.

A delightful log home six miles out on East End Road, **Good Karma Inn** (907/235-4728 or 866/435-2762, www.goodkarmainn.com, $155 d) fits Homer to a T, mixing functionality and comfort with a fine bay and mountain view, plus distinctive local artwork on the walls. Kindly owner Michael LeMay will fill you in on local attractions, and he stocks the kitchen with breakfast ingredients. Three guest rooms (with private baths and Wi-Fi) are available; one is completely accessible for disabled travelers.

Three miles east of town, **Bear Creek Winery and Lodging** (907/235-8484 or 888/649-2176, www.bearcreekwinery.com, $225 d) has two lovely log cottages with kitchenettes. Guests are provided a continental breakfast and can unwind in the cedar hot tub or steam bath. A surprisingly good winery here crafts distinctive fruit wines, and the unique four-person swing out front is guaranteed to please kids.

Cabins and Guest Houses

Cabins and guest houses provide the perfect option for families looking for a place to call their own, and Homer has a multitude of choices; find them on the chamber website, www.homeralaska.org, or visit **Homer Cabins & Cottages Network** (907/235-0191 or 888/364-0191, www.cabinsinhomer.com), with two-dozen rental cabins in the Homer area.

Near the end of Homer Spit, **Sea Lion Cove** (907/235-3400 summer or 907/235-8767, www.sealiongallery.com, mid-May–mid-Sept., $135–145 d) is operated by artist Gary Lion, whose gallery is downstairs. The two rooms are right in the heart of the summertime fishing action. Each has a kitchenette, a TV, a phone, and a shared deck delivering full-on bay vistas.

Alaska by the Sea (907/235-2716 or 877/374-2716, www.alaskabythesea.com) rents seven cottages, cabins, and homes, including several near Bishops Beach ($150–200 d), a small in-town cabin ($120 d), and a large house that sleeps 12 ($400).

A fine shore-side place, **Homer Inn & Spa** (907/235-2501 or 800/294-7823, www.homerinn.com), has a beachside hot tub, day spa facilities (including side-by-side massage), and plush king-size beds. Three mini-suites are $159–199 d, and a separate villa ($229 d) is perfect for families. A hot breakfast is brought to your room each morning.

Situated atop a high bluff on the west side as the highway drops into Homer, **Alaska Adventure Cabins** (907/223-6681, www.alaskaadventurecabins.com, $245–345 for up to 4 people) has a fun mélange of lodging: three gorgeous cabins, a large guesthouse, a restored Alaska Railroad caboose, and a landlocked boat called the *Double Eagle* that began life as a Gulf Coast shrimper. Each unit contains a full kitchen, a private bath, Wi-Fi, and a large deck with all-encompassing views of volcanoes, glaciers, Kachemak Bay, and the Spit.

CAMPING

Camping on the Spit is what most budget travelers, RVers, and backpackers do, although it's no picnic. It's within spitting distance of the noisy road, and it's barren and often windy. City-maintained camping areas on the Spit cost $8 for tents and $15 for RVs (no hookups), with bathrooms or portable toilets close by. Self-register at the sites or pay at the camping-fee office (907/235-1583) near the Fishing Hole. Campsites are open April–October, though a few hardy folks try their luck in winter when the Spit is officially closed to camping. A quieter and more protected (but less scenic) seasonal campground is at **Karen Hornaday Park** (907/235-3170, www.ci.homer.ak.us, tents $8, RVs $15) near the hospital on Fairview Avenue.

In addition to the city campsites, the Spit is home to three RV parks with full hookups. Close to the tip of the Spit, the privately run **Homer Spit Campground** (907/235-8206, May–mid-Sept., tents $22, RVs $30) has rustic and crowded sites (electricity only, showers available), some right along the beach. **Sportsman's Supply** (907/235-2617, RVs $30) has a few spots right across from the boat launch.

With a prime spot next to the Fishing Hole, plus all the latest amenities—including satellite TV and Wi-Fi—**Heritage RV Park** (907/226-4500 or 800/380-7787, www.alaskaheritagervpark.com, May–early Sept., RVs $78) commands top dollar; it's easily Alaska's priciest RV park.

Driftwood Inn RV Park (907/235-8019 or 800/478-8019, www.thedriftwoodinn.com, $49) is close to Bishops Beach, and **Oceanview RV Park** (907/235-3951, www.oceanview-rv.com, May–Sept., RVs $45, tents $22) is a crowded RV lot on the west edge of town.

If you're staying in the city campgrounds, showers ($4) are available at Sportsman's Supply or the Homer Spit Campground. Local coin laundries also have shower facilities; a good bet is **The Washboard** (1204 Ocean Dr., 907/235-6781), where you can even surf the Web for free or get an espresso while watching the clothes spin or after showering. An even better deal is the high school pool, where they throw in a free swim for the cost of a shower.

FOOD

Homer's dining-out options are varied, with several excellent choices. Many of the town's second- or third-tier eateries would be standouts almost anywhere else in Alaska, and the town's best restaurants are truly memorable.

Breakfast and Lunch

Mermaid Café (907/235-7649, www.mermaidcafe.net, Wed.–Sun. 9 A.M.–2 P.M., Fri.–Sat. 5–9 P.M., closed Mon., dinner entrées $18–24) fills the back of Old Inlet Bookshop, with delicious breakfasts and lunches, plus weekend dinners in a cheery setting. A couple of tables on the deck are popular on a summer day.

Sweet Berries Café (104 E. Pioneer Ave., 907/226-1118, www.sweetberriescafe.com, daily 6:30 A.M.–3 P.M.) has a few tables in the back of the historic Main Street Mercantile building. Try the eggs Benedict or a "one-eyed sailor" for breakfast. Lunch faves include barbecue pulled pork and chicken tarragon sandwiches, plus a blue cheese salad. There are good desserts too.

Duncan House Diner (125 E. Pioneer Ave., 907/235-5344, daily 7 A.M.–2 P.M., $6–10) is a family place with substantial all-American meals for breakfast and lunch; it's often crowded on weekend mornings. Daily specials are often your best bet.

Open seasonally since 1982 and a real favorite with travelers, **Fresh Sourdough Express Bakery & Café** (1316 Ocean Dr., 907/235-7571, www.freshsourdoughexpress.com, daily 7 A.M.–9 P.M. May–Sept., dinner $22–38) is a homey Homer spot serving sourdough hotcakes, scrambles, granola, muffins, and monster pastries for breakfast. Lunch includes sandwiches, buffalo burgers, homemade soups, and salads, while dinners cover the salmon, chicken, and steak terrain. The menu includes vegetarian meals, but also plenty of carnivorous protein.

Inside the historic Old Town B&B building a block away is tiny **Maura's Café** (907/235-

1555, Mon.–Sat. 11 A.M.–4 P.M., $11–13), where the chalkboard lists today's always-delicious sandwiches, soups, and salads.

Far from the hubbub on the Spit is **Fritz Creek General Store** (907/235-6753, Sun. 10 A.M.–8 P.M., Mon.–Sat. 7 A.M.–9 P.M., $5–10), eight miles out on East End Road. The store has a small selection of groceries, a little post office, booze, and an eclectic video selection. The real attraction here is the deli, featuring freshly baked bread, hot sandwiches, unusual burritos, pizza by the pie or slice, ribs, sweets, and coffee. Fritz Creek is a delightful place to hang out in an old-time country setting. Fine dining at Homestead Restaurant is right across the road.

Coffee

Homer is a coffee drinker's paradise, with two roasters and several excellent espresso joints. **Captain's Coffee Roasting Co.** (528 E. Pioneer Ave., 907/235-4970, www.captainscoffee.com) has a downtown location and a bright airy space to relax. Ask owner Ty Gates for tips on surfing in Homer.

A real surprise is **K Bay Caffé** (907/235-1551, www.kbaycaffe.com), three miles out East End Road next to Redden Marine. This one is actually little more than a drive-up window and outside deck, with enough space inside for a few people to read the newspaper and talk politics. Owner Michael McGuire really knows his (all-organic) coffee—he won top prize at a national barista contest a while back—-and is a connoisseur when it comes to creating the perfect roast.

Just a block from Bishops Beach, **Two Sisters Bakery** (233 E. Bunnell St., 907/235-2280, www.twosistersbakery.net, Sun. 9 A.M.–2 P.M., Mon.–Fri. 7 A.M.–6 P.M., Sat. 7 A.M.–4 P.M. summer, reduced winter hours, $5–10) is a great place to meet the locals any time of year. It's always warm and fragrant with the smell of fresh-baked pastries, breads, and savories from the brick oven, along with sandwiches, focaccia, and deep-dish pizza by the slice. It's pricey, but highly recommended. A covered deck wraps around the back.

Housed within Lake Street Mall, **Latitude 59°** (3858 Lake St., 907/235-5574) is a friendly spot for wraps, sandwiches, bagels, salads, and mochas, along with a free computer and Wi-Fi. On the Spit, stop by the seasonal **Coal Town Coffee** (907/235-9463, www.coaltowncoffee.com, daily 5 A.M.–8 P.M. early May–mid-Sept.).

Meals on the Spit

Yes, Homer does have McDonald's and Subway, but you're much better off heading out on the Spit, where two summer-only places fish for your attention. Best-known is the perpetually crowded **Boardwalk Fish and Chips** (907/235-7749, daily 11 A.M.–9 P.M. early May–mid-Sept., but hours vary, $9–15) across from the harbormaster and Salty Dawg, with crunchy halibut fish-on-a-stick and chips that will have you smackin' your chops.

On the same side, but not as far out on the Spit, **Fresh Catch Café** (907/235-2289, $19–27) has lightly breaded fish-and-chips that are not as greasy. They also serve a tasty halibut curry, plus scallop fettuccini and steaks.

A few doors from Boardwalk is **Finn's Pizza** (907/235-2878, daily noon–9 P.M. early May–early Sept., pizzas $12–28, slices $4–5), with hot-from-the-oven wood-fired pizzas and daily soups, along with local beers on tap. Be sure to try the blue pear version, made with D'Anjou pears, Gorgonzola cheese, and roasted pine nuts. Climb the side stairs for rustic dining with a beach vista.

Open seasonally, **Spit-Fire Grille** (907/235-9379, daily 10 A.M.–7 P.M., but hours can be sporadic, $10–15) occupies a tiny shop just down from El Pescadero Restaurant. Eat inside on stools along the windows or at the picnic table on the deck. The food is amazingly good and reasonable, with daily fish specials, ribs, pulled pork sandwiches, salads, and buffalo burgers. The emphasis is local and organic, but be sure to sample the homemade ice cream and fresh lemonade. Walls are decorated with paintings by chef Mike's wife, Margorie Scholl (www.margiescholl.com).

Directly across the boardwalk is **Spit**

Sisters Café (907/235-4921, www.spitsistercafe.com, mid-May–early Sept., $8–10), serving pastries from Two Sisters, light breakfasts, grilled panini sandwiches, and espresso. They open daily at 5 A.M. to provide box lunches for folks heading out on fishing charters, closing at 4 P.M.

International

Downtown's **Cosmic Kitchen** (510 E. Pioneer Ave., 907/235-6355, www.cosmickitchenalaska.com, Mon.–Sat. 9 A.M.–8 P.M., $7–11) serves quick Mexican food such as cosmic burritos, soft tacos, and steak enchiladas, plus avocado-bacon burgers, chicken tikka with chutney sandwiches, and homemade soups. It's all good and tasty, with a big choice of homemade salsas to spice things up. Cosmic is popular for lunch, but also serves dinner specials ($13–15) such as a fajita steak and shrimp platter and Greek gyros; *delicioso*. There's a second Cosmic Kitchen near the end of the Spit.

Another local standout is **Wasabi's** (907/226-3663, www.wasabisrestaurant.com, daily 5–10 P.M. May–Aug., Wed.–Thurs. 5–9 P.M., Fri.–Sat. 5–10 P.M., closed Sun.–Tues. winter, dinner entrées $18–36), located five miles out East End Road. Asian fusion specialties populate the menu, including a good choice of fresh sushi (try the Tutka Bay roll with shrimp, avocado, and masago for $11) along with alderwood grilled tuna, baby back ribs, and tempura prawns. Get a window seat for bay vistas. Singles can sit at the wraparound bar for meals, and Wasabi's has a great selection of infused vodkas. The bar downstairs (Fusion) has occasional live music or a DJ.

Fine Dining

You can't miss **Café Cups** (162 W. Pioneer Dr., 907/235-8330, www.cafecupsofhomer.com, Tues.–Sat. 4:30–9:30 P.M., entrées $22–30)—four Alaska-size teacups hang from the front of the converted house. Lunches feature creative sandwiches, salads, and savories, and dinners encompass everything from Kachemak Bay oysters and chicken coconut curry to baby back ribs and "Dave's twisted fettuccine." I usually opt for the daily specials, especially the fresh seafood. Cups gets crowded and noisy, so call ahead for reservations. A small side patio is fun on warm afternoons.

Homer's fine-dining place, **The Homestead Restaurant** (907/235-8723, www.homesteadrestaurant.net, daily 5–10 P.M. late Mar.–Sept., Wed.–Sat. 5–9 P.M. Oct.–Dec., closed Jan.–late Mar., entrées $22–34) is eight miles out on East End Road. The ever-changing menu specializes—not surprisingly—in fresh Alaskan seafood, but also features made-at-your-table Caesar salads and melt-in-your-mouth prime rib (just $19 if you get there at 5 P.M.). Homestead is open for dinner only, and it is where locals go for a special-event meal. Reservations are strongly advised, especially for the window seats. Also be sure to check out Fritz Creek Store, directly across the road.

Another place that gets high marks is **Fat Olives Restaurant** (276 Olson Lane, 907/235-8488, daily 11 A.M.–9:30 P.M. summer, 11 A.M.–8:30 P.M. winter, $16–29). The setting evokes a trendy Italian bistro, and the menu stars wood-fired pizzas, calzones, fresh salmon, Kachemak Bay oysters, seafood pasta, and delicious appetizers (including a champagne three-cheese fondue). It's noisy and fun, perfect for kids and adults. Fat Olives is just off the Homer Bypass as you enter town. In a hurry? Get a giant thin-crust pizza slice to go for $5.

At the very tip of the Spit is Land's End Resort, where panoramic views and a big beachside deck are the main attractions. The **Chart Room Restaurant** (907/235-0400 or 800/478-0400, www.lands-end-resort.com) at Lands End is open for three meals a day, serving seafood, steaks, prime rib, and daily dinner specials.

Groceries and Markets

Open 24 hours, **Safeway** (on Homer Bypass, 907/235-2408) is the main grocery store in town, but locals shop at the warehouse-style **Save-U-More** (907/235-8661), also on Homer Bypass.

In addition to its reputation as a halibut fishing center, Homer is famous for oysters, and you'll find acclaimed **Kachemak Bay oysters** in local restaurants and from the Kachemak Shellfish Growers Co-op building (907/235-1935, www.alaskaoyster.com, $13–15 per dozen) across from the Fishing Hole on the Spit.

Get frozen local seafood on the Spit at **Coal Point Trading Company** (907/235-3877, www.welovefish.com, daily 8 A.M.–8 P.M. summer, daily 9 A.M.–5 P.M. winter), or sidle up to the bar for seafood chowder, steamed crab, and K-Bay oysters on the half shell.

The **Homer Farmers Market** (www.homerfarmersmarket.org) takes place along Ocean Drive on Saturdays 10 A.M.–2 P.M. and Wednesdays 4–6 P.M. mid-June–late September. Booths carry local produce, arts and crafts, food, and games for kids. It's a great way to find a sampling of work by local artists.

Alcohol

Homer has a diversity of locally made spirits. A must-see is **Homer Brewing Company** (1411 Lakeshore Dr., 907/235-3626, www.homerbrew.com, daily noon–5 P.M. or later), where you can sample the China Poot Porter, Old Inlet Pale Ale, Red Knot Scottish, and other specialties before buying a half-gallon growler to go. The brewery also crafts Zen Chai and Alaska Chai teas.

A surprise is **Bear Creek Winery** (907/235-8484 or 888/649-2176, www.bearcreekwinery.com), producing notable wines from local fruits. If chocolate raspberry wine is in stock, you'll want buy several bottles of this decadent dessert wine.

Even more unexpected is **Ring of Fire Meadery** (178 E. Bunnell Ave., 907/235-2656, www.ringoffiremeadery.com), where you can sample eight different meads crafted from local fruits. The black current and apple cyser meads are especially popular. Both Bear Creek and the Meadery are open daily in the summer.

INFORMATION AND SERVICES

Stop by the Homer Chamber of Commerce **Visitors Information Center** (on the Homer Bypass at Main St., 907/235-7740, www.homeralaska.org, Mon.–Fri. 9 A.M.–7 P.M., Sat.–Sun. 10 A.M.–6 P.M. late May–early Sept., Mon.–Fri. 9 A.M.–5 P.M. early Sept.–late May), for local details and a plethora of brochures.

Homer's gorgeous library has an atrium fireplace for relaxing, tall windows facing Kachemak Bay, a large kids room, and plenty of computers and free Wi-Fi for Internet users. Find the **Homer Public Library** (500 Hazel Ave., 907/235-3180, http://library.ci.homer.ak.us, Mon., Wed., and Fri.–Sat. 10 A.M.–6 P.M., Tues. and Thurs. 10 A.M.–8 P.M. , closed Sun.) a block up Heath Street from the post office. A number of businesses—even a Laundromat—provide free Wi-Fi hotspots, and one local company (www.spitwspots.com) has antennas on the Spit and around town providing free Wi-Fi; pop open you laptop to see if it's working.

The **post office** (907/235-6129) is nearby on the Homer Bypass, and **South Peninsula Hospital** (4300 Bartlett St., 907/235-8101, www.sphosp.com) is a modern, fully staffed facility.

GETTING THERE

Air

Homer Airport is out on East Kachemak Road, which forks off from the Spit Road. **Era Aviation** (907/266-8394 or 800/866-8394, www.frontierak.com) and **Grant Aviation** (907/235-2757 or 888/359-4726, www.flygrant.com) both fly between Homer and Anchorage several times a day.

Two local companies have daily flights from the airport to Seldovia ($96 round-trip) and the Native Alaskan villages of Nanwalek and Port Graham: **Homer Air** (907/235-8591 or 800/478-8591, www.homerair.com) and **Smokey Bay Air** (907/235-1511 or 888/482-1511, www.smokeybayair.com).

Homer Stage Line (907/235-2252, www.homerstageline.com) runs buses to Anchorage, Soldotna, Seward, and all points in between. Service is daily in summer, and twice a week in winter.

© DON PITCHER
sea otter in Kachemak Bay, near Homer

Ferry

The **Alaska Marine Highway** ferry terminal (907/235-8449, www.dot.state.ak.us/amhs) is out near the end of the Homer Spit. From here, you can catch the *Tustumena* to Seldovia three times a week and to Kodiak four times weekly. Once a month it runs all the way out to Dutch Harbor in the Aleutians.

GETTING AROUND

Rent cars at the airport from **Hertz** (907/235-0734 or 800/654-3131, www.rentalcarhomeralaska.com) or **Polar Car Rental** (907/235-5998 or 800/876-6417, www.polarcarrental.com). **Adventure Alaska Car Rental** (907/235-4022 or 800/882-2808, www.adventurealaskacars.com) has somewhat lower rates for used cars (starting at $30), and will pick you up anywhere in town.

Call **Kache Cab** (907/235-1950, www.kachecab.com), **Chux Cab** (907/235-2489), or **Kosta's Taxi** (907/399-8008) for a taxi ride; $5 gets you around town.

Water Taxis

A small fleet of boats plies the waters of Kachemak Bay all summer, offering wildlife-viewing trips to Gull Island, transport for kayakers and hikers heading into the state park, and access to lodges across the bay. You'll find their offices on the Spit; fares are $75 per person round-trip to most places. The following are all good operators: **Bay Excursions** (907/235-7525, www.bayexcursions.com), **Bay Roamers Water Taxi** (907/399-6200, www.halibutcovealaska.com), **Mako's Water Taxi** (907/235-9055, www.makoswatertaxi.com), **Smoke Wagon Water Taxi** (907/235-2947 or 888/205-2947, www.homerwatertaxi.com), **Ashore Water Taxi** (907/399-2340), **Red Mountain Marine** (907/235-6384), and **Tutka Bay Taxi** (907/399-1723, www.tutkabaytaxi.com). Most of these are seasonal, but Mako's operates year-round.

Tours

The Pratt Museum operates excellent 1.5-hour **walking tours of Homer Spit** and the harbor for $5. These depart Friday and Saturday at 3 P.M. throughout the summer, and include local history and lots of detail on commercial fishing and sportfishing. Get tickets at the Pratt (3779 Bartlett St., 907/235-8635) or in the little booth next to the Salty Dawg Saloon on the Spit.

Shelly Erickson of **Homer Tours** (907/235-6200, www.ptialaska.net/~ericson) leads custom van tours of the Homer area.

Across Kachemak Bay

KACHEMAK BAY AND GULL ISLAND

If you have three days in Homer, spend one of them on beautiful Kachemak Bay. A great way to do this is through a **Natural History Tour** (907/235-6667, www.akcoastalstudies.org, late May–early Sept.) with professional naturalists from the nonprofit Center for Alaskan Coastal Studies. You'll spend time at bird rookeries, tide pools, rain forest trails, and prehistoric sites, and will gain a lifetime appreciation for the marine world. These eight-hour experiences cost $105 ($73 for children under 12)—a bargain—and includes a visit to Gull Island during your ride across to Peterson Bay. Bring your own lunch, rubber boots, binoculars, and camera. Overnight stays (just $25 pp in a yurt) and kayak trips are also available at the Peterson Bay field station. Their office is in a yurt behind Mako's Water Taxi on the Spit; they are highly recommended.

Local water taxis lead two-hour Gull Island and 60-Foot Rock tours ($60 pp); Karl Stolzfus of **Bay Excursions** (907/235-7525, www.bayexcursions.com) is especially good. He also guides three hour K-Bay birding trips

Halibut Cove

for $70. **Central Charters** (907/235-7847 or 800/478-7847, www.centralcharter.com) books two other boats that spend time at Gull Island: the *Danny J* on its runs to Halibut Cove, and the *Discovery* as it heads to Seldovia. Watch the Gull Island action in real time through the "birdcam" on the Web at www.prattmuseum.org.

Biologist Glenn Seaman operates **Seaman's Adventures** (907/235-2157, www.seamansadventures.com), providing a variety of boat-based environmental tours around Kachemak Bay, from tide-pooling to wilderness hikes. Half-day trips are $150 per person for three guests. The former head of Kachemak Bay Research Reserve, Glenn has a deep knowledge of the region.

HALIBUT COVE

Even if you only have two days in Homer, spend half of one visiting this enchanted village (pop. 75) across Kachemak Bay on Ismailof Island. At one time Halibut Cove was the center for a thriving herring fishery, with 36 saltries operating. The fishery collapsed in 1928, and today the town is a small center for artists and fishers. Halibut Cove has long been known for its picturesque harbor ringed by dense green forests; unfortunately, most of the trees were killed by a devastating spruce bark beetle infestation in the 1990s, so the land is in recovery mode now. The town consists of a long boardwalk that connects shorefront businesses and homes. Learn more about the area at www.halibutcove.com.

Sights

The boat docks in front of the Saltry Restaurant. Follow the boardwalk through an old boat barn, past the horses, and on to **Halibut Cove Experience Gallery** (907/296-2215, www.halibutcoveexperience.com), an excellent cooperative. A short distance down the boardwalk are side stairs climbing steeply to the studio of the late **Diana Tillion** (907/296-2207), known for her subtle octopus-ink watercolors. The boardwalk passes Clem and Diana Tillion's classic Alaskan home (a resident for over 70 years, Clem is jokingly called "the king of Halibut Cove") before ending at a sandy beach.

If you're looking for a little hike, walk along the boardwalk from the Saltry Restaurant till you see a gate on the left. Go through the gate and follow the trail up the hill for all-encompassing views of Halibut Cove, Kachemak Bay, eagles, and a rocky arch along the shore below.

Accommodations

At **Cove Country Cabins** (907/235-6374 or 888/353-2683, www.halibutcovealaska.com) stay in three attractive timber-frame cabins, each with a kitchenette, running water, and an outhouse, plus a central shower house. These range from a little unit ($150 d) to a two-story house ($200 d) with a fine view. The owners also operate Bay Roamers Water Taxi.

Quiet Place Lodge (907/296-2212, www.quietplace.com) features three romantic cabins and all-inclusive packages: $3,360 d for three nights.

Alaska's Ridgewood Lodge (907/296-2217, www.ridgewoodlodge.com, $450 pp per day) is a large and modern place in Halibut Cove.

Stillpoint in Halibut Cove (907/296-2283, www.stillpointlodge.com) hosts workshops, retreats, and weddings in an architecturally stunning setting.

Food

Halibut Cove's acclaimed **Saltry Restaurant** (907/296-2223, www.thesaltry.com, lunch and dinner, entrées $16–35, mid-May–early Sept.) serves daily pasta specials, a wonderful seafood chowder ($8 with bread), Kachemak Bay oysters, and buffalo steaks. Everything is homemade, from the decorated plates to the fresh breads, pies, and chocolate cheesecake. There's a waterfront deck for alfresco dining on a sunny afternoon, a full bar, a clamshell-shaped aquarium filled with tidepool creatures (free talks are at 3:30 P.M.), and a blazing fire in the outdoor pit. The Saltry is open for lunch and dinner; dinner reservations are required.

© DON PITCHER

arch near Halibut Cove

Getting There

Most visitors arrive on board the ***Danny J,*** a classic wooden boat that has been transporting passengers from Homer Spit to Halibut Cove for decades. It does the run twice daily Memorial Day–Labor Day. The noon sailing costs $49 adults, $45 seniors, $30 kids and includes a tour of the Gull Island bird sanctuary, which Alfred Hitchcock should've known about; wear a hat and breathe through your mouth! After three hours onshore in Halibut Cove, the boat returns to Homer. Its second trip ($30) leaves Homer at 5 P.M., and is only for visitors with dinner or lodging reservations. For details and reservations, contact **Central Charters** (907/235-7847 or 800/478-7847, www.centralcharter.com).

As an alternative, **Bay Roamers Water Taxi** (907/399-6200, www.halibutcovealaska.com) has a combination trip ($105) that includes transport from Homer to Kachemak Bay State Park (typically Grewingk Glacier trails), an evening water taxi to the Saltry in Halibut Cove, and return on board the *Danny J.*

SELDOVIA

A sleepy fishing village (pop. 300), Seldovia (from the Russian for "herring") was once the bustling metropolis that Homer is now. The road, the earthquake, and fate exchanged their roles. On the same latitude as Oslo, Norway, Seldovia was first settled by Russians in the early 1800s and became an active fur-trading post. Through the years, Seldovia has had many ocean-oriented industries, from the short-lived herring boom to salmon, king crab, and tanner.

Seldovia is a convenient place for really getting away from it all. Catch a ride over from Homer on the new fast ferry, with its twice-daily service, or on one of the tour boats.

Find more about Seldovia from the Seldovia Chamber of Commerce's website (www.seldoviachamber.org). The free ***Seldovia Visitor*** newspaper (www.seldoviagazette.com) is available in visitors centers around Alaska.

Sights

Start out by strolling along Main Street. Interpretive signs describe Alaska's Russian

history, commercial fishing, the earthquake, and more. The picturesque **Russian Orthodox Church** sits atop a small hill overlooking the town like a proud parent.

The Seldovia Tribe's interesting **Museum and Visitors Center** (907/234-7898, www.svt.org, daily 10 A.M.–5 P.M. summer, $3) is across from the boat harbor, with exhibits on Native Alaskan culture and the town. Just up the road is Seldovia Slough, where you can walk the last remaining section of original **boardwalk**—the rest was wiped out in the 1964 earthquake. Up the road in the other direction is **Alaska Tribal Cache** (907/234-7875 or 800/270-7810, www.alaskatribalcache.com) selling Native Alaskan–made jams, jellies, and syrups made from local berries.

Recreation and Events

One of the most fun things to do in Seldovia is to pedal out on the road to beautiful Outside Beach and Jakolof Bay, where you can savor the great views across Kachemak Bay; **Herring Bay Mercantile** (907/234-5500) rents mountain

© DON PITCHER

Seldovia Slough

bikes. The **Rocky River Road Trail** at the end of Jakolof Bay Road is a locals' favorite. Well-marked **Otterbahn Trail** leads 1.5 miles from the school grounds around the headland to Outside Beach.

For on-the-water fun, rent a kayak or take a guided tour from **Kayak'Atak** (907/234-7425, www.alaska.net/~kayaks); five-hour tours are $120 per person, including a delicious gourmet lunch.

Seldovia's big party is **4th of July,** which kicks this sleepy town into action with a parade, canoe jousting, log rolling, an egg toss, and other events.

Accommodations

Dancing Eagles Cabin Rental (907/234-7627 summer or 907/360-6363 winter, www.dancingeagles.com, late May–early Sept.) has perhaps the finest location in Seldovia, with a big deck perched on the water at the entrance to Seldovia Slough. A cabin ($210 d, $40 for each extra guest) sleeps six and includes a kitchen and bath.

Seldovia Seaport Cottages (907/234-7483, www.acsalaska.net/~seaportcottages) has two homey cottages ($125 d) along Seldovia Slough, with kitchens and baths, plus free bikes to tool around town and Wi-Fi to roam the Web. Also available is a spacious three-bedroom home that sleeps four for $150.

Seldovia Rowing Club B&B (907/234-7614, www.seldoviarowingclub.net, $135 d) is another fun over-the-water place where the two suites feature a "nautical Victorian" decor, along with private baths and decks. A big breakfast is served.

Seldovia Bayview Suites (907/234-7631 or 800/478-7898, www.alaskaadventurelodge.com) has spacious three-bed suites that sleep six for $159–179, and a four-room apartment with a full kitchen and a living room that sleeps up to 10 for $299. There's a hot tub on the deck facing the harbor, and the rooms are upstairs over Main Street Market; there is also free Wi-Fi.

Boardwalk Hotel (907/234-7816, www.theseldoviaboardwalkhotel.com) is right on the boat harbor; the back patio is a great place to hang out. Small rooms with double beds cost $144 d, but a better bet are the larger waterside rooms for $154–164 d.

Just down the street is **Seldovia Harbor Inn** (907/234-1414, www.seldoviaharborinn.com, $155–165 d), with three comfy units, each with a kitchen. Two of these open onto a deck with a great harbor view.

Open seasonally, **Bridgekeeper's Inn** (907/234-7535, www.thebridgekeepers-inn.com, $125–135 d) overlooks the bridge across Seldovia Slough. Two nicely furnished guest rooms have queen beds, private baths, and full breakfasts.

Alaska TreeTops Lodge (907/234-6200 summer or 480/767-3535 winter, www.alaskatreetops.com) is a luxurious hilltop lodge with a mix of activities for guests, from kayaking and fishing to bear-viewing. TreeTops is open seasonally and can accommodate a maximum of 10 guests; most guests stay five days or longer.

Camping

Pitch a tent for $5 or park RVs for $8 (no hookups) at **Wilderness RV Park** (907/234-7643) along Outside Beach. It's 1.5 miles out on Jakolof Bay Road, and there are a water pump and outhouses. Showers are available in town across from the boat harbor.

Food

Open daily, **Tide Pool Café** (907/234-7502, Mon.–Tues. 7 A.M.–3 P.M., Wed.–Sun. 7 A.M.–8 P.M. summer, daily 8 A.M.–3 P.M. winter, $10–16) is a great lunch spot, with sandwiches, wraps, salads, burgers, and fish-and-chips. Their deck faces the boat harbor, and the glass-top tables are inset with playful beach scenes.

For the best local meal, head to **Mad Fish Restaurant** (907/234-7676, www.seldovia.com/madfishrestaurant, daily noon–4 P.M. and 6–9 P.M. late May–early Sept., dinner $28–34), with a menu of local seafood (including halibut seviche), steaks, and Caesar salads for dinner, plus lunchtime burgers, fish-and-chips, and sandwiches.

Fenske's High Tide Originals (907/234-7850, late May–early Sept.) sells new and used books—along with coffee—from a tiny building on pilings just up from the bridge. The covered deck is a good spot to watch the tide come in.

Get groceries and supplies from **Main Street Market** (907/234-7633).

Getting There

The **State Ferry** (907/235-8449, www.dot.state.ak.us/amhs) *Tustumena* sails over to Seldovia from Homer four times a week, taking 90 minutes and laying over for several hours before returning to Homer. **Seldovia Cab** (907/234-7830) will haul you around town and out to Jakolof Bay.

A new fast ferry debuted twice-daily summertime service between Homer and Seldovia in 2010. The 150-passenger high-speed catamaran—operated by the Seldovia Village Tribe (907/234-7898, www.kachemakvoyager.com)—makes the run in 35 minutes.

In the past, two other companies have offered summertime trips between the Spit and Seldovia. The future of these two is unclear, so call to see who is running. The 75-foot ***Discovery*** departs Homer at 11 A.M., stopping to watch the puffins and gulls at Gull Island and the sea otters near Sixty Foot Rock. They dock in Seldovia for three hours—perfect for lunch and a walk around town—before heading back across Kachemak Bay, arriving at 5:15 P.M. These very informative tours are $45 adults, $40 seniors, $25 children. Make reservations at **Central Charters** (907/235-7847 or 800/478-7847, www.centralcharter.com).

The **Rainbow Tours** (907/235-7272, www.rainbowtours.net) shuttle boat leaves Homer at 10 A.M., returning at 5 P.M. with no stops along the way, but the round-trip fare is just $45 adults, $40 seniors, $35 children. They also have a second trip that includes three hours in Seldovia and a tour of Gull Island and Eldridge Passage for $50 adults, $45 seniors, $40 children.

Two Homer **water taxis**—Mako's (907/235-9055, www.makoswatertaxi.com) and Smoke

Wagon (907/235-2947 or 888/205-2947, www.homerwatertaxi.com)—will set up combo trips that include a water taxi to Jakolof Bay, a taxi ride into Seldovia, and a return flight back to Homer for $135. You can also do this as part of an overnight (or multiple-night) trip. There's a wonderful seven-mile mountain bike ride up Red Mountain from Jakolof Bay if you're ambitious.

Both **Homer Air** (907/235-8591 or 800/478-8591, www.homerair.com) and **Smokey Bay Air** (907/235-1511 or 888/482-1511, www.smokeybayair.com) fly the 15 minutes from Homer ($96 round-trip) on a daily basis.

KACHEMAK BAY STATE PARK

One of the largest coastal parks in the nation, Kachemak Bay State Park spreads for 200 miles along the southwestern edge of the Kenai Peninsula. Within the park's 400,000 acres are glaciers, high mountains, lakes, islands, beaches, and a scenic rocky shoreline. Highlighted by constantly changing weather patterns, the park's outstanding scenery is a backdrop for high-quality recreation. Hiking and camping along the shoreline and in the surrounding forests and mountains are excellent. Above tree line, skiers and hikers will find glaciers and snow fields stretching for miles.

Almost three-quarters of the land is wilderness; it's officially called Kachemak Bay Wilderness State Park. Land mammals include moose, black bears, mountain goats, coyotes, and wolves. Kachemak Bay supports a rich diversity of marine life and is famous for its halibut and salmon fishing, plus the chance to view sea otters, seals, porpoises, and whales. Five very popular public-use cabins are available ($65), along with over 80 miles of hiking trails. Unfortunately, a major spruce bark beetle outbreak in the 1990s left massive stretches of dead trees within Kachemak Bay State Park (and in many other parts of Alaska). New trees are gradually moving into these areas.

The Kachemak Bay State Park office (907/235-7024, www.alaskastateparks.org) is four miles northwest of Homer along the Sterling Highway.

For something different, **Alaskan Yurt Rentals** (907/235-0132, www.alaskanyurtrentals.com, May–Sept.) maintains nine cozy yurts ($65) located at trailheads around the park, including China Poot Bay, Glacier Spit Beach, Haystack Beach, and Tutka Bay. Each includes a woodstove, sleeping space for six, foam mattresses, and a camp stove. These can also be booked through local water taxis. The yurts are made in Homer, and you can visit the Nomad Shelter (www.nomadshelter.com) facility at Sterling Highway and Olson Lane.

Grewingk Glacier

For an outstanding day (or multiple-night) hike, have the water taxi drop you at the Glacier Spit Trailhead, where an easy and very scenic two-mile hike leads to a lake in front of picture-perfect **Grewingk Glacier.** You can camp nearby, and return via the one-mile **Saddle Trail,** which takes you over a small ridge to Halibut Cove, where you can get a ride back to Homer. Water taxis cost $75 per person round-trip. A multitude of side trips are available along this route, including ones that take you high into the alpine area over the glacier, and a delightful beach walk. Contact the park for many other hiking options.

Guided sea kayak tours to Grewingk are available through **Three Moose Meadow Guide Service** (907/235-0755 or 888/777-0930, www.threemoose.com). These cost $175 per person, including a water taxi from Homer, a hike to the lake, and inflatable kayaks to paddle up to the glacier. Fly-in trips are $295.

Access

In addition to the daily summertime boat tours of Kachemak Bay, local water taxis provide hiker or sea kayaker drop-offs within park waters, for around $75 per person round-trip, or $190 for a double sea kayak and transport of two people, no extra charge for kayaks or bikes.

Remote Cabins and Lodges

A number of delightful lodges fill coves surrounding Kachemak Bay State Park. Note,

© DON PITCHER

Grewingk Glacier in Kachemak Bay State Park

however, that spruce bark beetles have killed the forest in much of this area, so it may not look quite as nice as the Web photos. One exception is Tutka Bay Wilderness Lodge, where the beetles have not wreaked havoc.

For a wonderful escape, **Porter's Alaskan Adventures** (907/235-8060, www.portersak.com) rents three modern cabins on the shore of Hesketh Island near the mouth of Tutka Bay, seven miles from Homer. All cabins contain full kitchens, decks, and waterfront views, but you'll need to bring sleeping bags. There's a sauna on the beach for bathing, and an outhouse in the back. Four people can stay here for $150 on weekdays or $165 on weekends; add $70 per person round-trip for the water taxi from Homer. Sea kayak rentals are available through True North Kayak Adventures (907/235-0708, www.truenorthkayak.com).

Sadie Cove Wilderness Lodge (907/235-2350 or 888/283-7234, www.sadiecove.com) is an off-the-grid wilderness retreat in the heart of Kachemak Bay State Park. Guests stay in quaint cabins built by Keith and Randi Iverson, who have lived here since the 1970s. This is a place to escape to a quieter time, so you won't find in room phones or TVs, though they do have a sauna and creek-side bathhouse, communal lounge, and professional chef. Lodging, three meals, and kayaks cost $450–550 per person per day, plus $150 for the water taxi from Homer. A two-night minimum is required, but most guests book for five nights.

Tutka Bay Wilderness Lodge (907/235-3905 or 800/606-3909, www.withinthewild.com, mid-May–mid-Sept.) occupies the south shore of Kachemak Bay between Halibut Cove and Seldovia, nine water miles from the Spit. The lodge caters to nature lovers, photographers, bird-watchers, and anglers with an appreciation for the finer things in life and a willingness to pay dearly; two people pay $2,740 for one day, up to $6,730 for four days. This includes round-trip transportation from Anchorage, delicious family-style meals, boat tours, sea kayaking, guided walks, beachcombing, clam digging, wildlife viewing, yoga, or just soaking in the hot tub. Also available for an extra fee are deep-sea fishing, flightseeing, and bear-viewing. Accommodations are luxurious; there is no roughing it here, and it's where you might run into the likes of Jim Carey and other celebrities.

Peterson Bay Lodge & Oyster Camp (907/235-7156 or 866/899-7156, www.petersonbaylodge.com) occupies the head of this remote bay, where the owners raise famous Kachemak Bay oysters. Guests stay in four surprisingly comfortable canvas-walled cabins with screened porches, a sauna, and access to the lodge kitchen to cook meals. Upon arrival, they are given a tour of the oyster farm, along with the chance to sample fresh oysters and mussels. Lodging, kayaks, and a continental breakfast costs $145 per person; a water taxi from Homer is $65 round-trip.

A classic Alaskan lodge, gorgeous **Kachemak Bay Wilderness Lodge** (907/235-8910, www.alaskawildernesslodge.com) lies within China Poot Bay in the heart of the state park, with trails to nearby Peterson Bay. Guests stay in cozy artistic cabins, each with a cedar bath, a picture window, and homemade quilts, and are served gourmet organic meals. All-inclusive rates are $3,750 per person for five days or $1,750 for two nights.

THE WRANGELLS AND PRINCE WILLIAM SOUND

This sprawling region includes several mountain ranges and gorgeous Prince William Sound. The Wrangell Mountains and St. Elias Mountains form the backbone of massive Wrangell–St. Elias National Park and Preserve, home to the second highest peak in the United States (18,008-foot Mt. St. Elias), a glacier larger than Rhode Island, towering volcanoes, and country that seems to define the word *spectacular.* The park is located on the eastern margin of Alaska and is bordered by Canada's Kluane National Park and Tatshenshini-Alsek Park, and Southeast Alaska's Glacier Bay National Park. Together they include more than 24 million acres—the largest protected area on planet earth. The equally impressive Copper River drains much of the Wrangells, reaching the Gulf of Alaska east of Cordova. Given the grandeur of this country, the settlements seem minor in this part of Alaska; the largest are Glennallen, Copper Center, and Chitina. Two primary roads cut through this country: the east-west Glenn Highway and the north-south Richardson Highway.

Prince William Sound arcs around the Gulf of Alaska, encompassing a multitude of densely forested islands, dissected bays, and rugged coastlines, with the Chugach Mountains forming a glacier-topped northern border. Virtually all of this wild country lies within Chugach National Forest, the nation's second largest national forest. Within the Sound are three towns: Whittier on the west is connected by tunnel and road to Anchorage, Valdez on the north serves as

© DON PITCHER

HIGHLIGHTS

Matanuska Glacier: One hundred miles from Anchorage on the Glenn Highway, this is a good place to get out on the ice – and under it in ice caves (page 298).

McCarthy Road: This 60-mile gravel road cuts into the heart of magnificent Wrangell-St. Elias National Park along an old railroad bed. The Kuskulana River bridge is a high point (literally) with the river 400 heart-stopping feet below (page 305).

McCarthy: Think *Northern Exposure* with fewer residents and older buildings; this is a wonderful end-of-the-road settlement from another era. Park your car on the other side of the river and walk the footbridge into town (page 306).

Kennicott: Just five miles up the road from McCarthy are the enormous red buildings from the heyday of copper mining a century ago. The Park Service offers historical tours, and concessionaires guide hikes onto Root Glacier (page 306).

Thompson Pass: North of Valdez, the Edgerton Highway climbs over this scenic alpine pass. Stop at Worthington Glacier for a hike, and come back in winter for world-class heli-skiing (page 313).

Keystone Canyon: The Lowe River drops through this narrow canyon where high waterfalls plunge from the cliffs. Located just north of Valdez, this is a popular spot for summertime rafting and winter ice climbing (page 313).

Prince William Sound Boat Tours: Several companies operate day trips from Valdez or Whittier, offering the chance to see glaciers (especially massive Columbia Glacier), sea lions, otters, and the occasional killer whale (page 319).

Copper River Highway: One of Alaska's finest back roads, this 50-mile gravel road leads from Cordova to the Million Dollar Bridge over the Copper River, with opportunities for hiking and wildlife viewing along the way (page 327).

Childs Glacier: Located near the end of the Copper River Highway, this very active glacier dumps enormous chunks of ice into the river on a regular basis. There's nothing like it anywhere in Alaska (page 327).

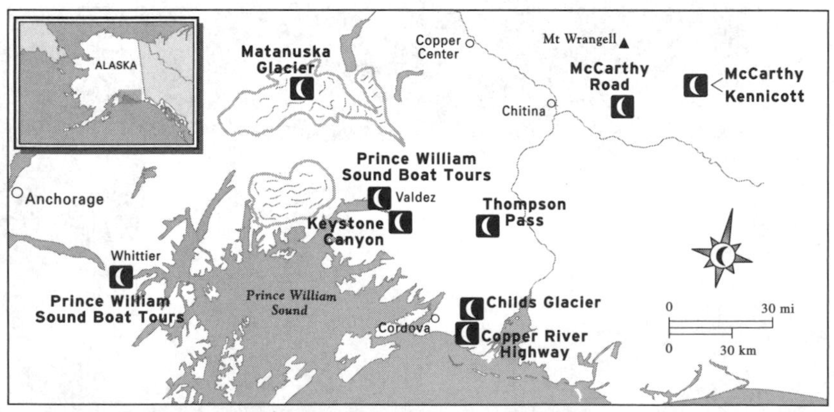

LOOK FOR TO FIND RECOMMENDED SIGHTS, ACTIVITIES, DINING, AND LODGING.

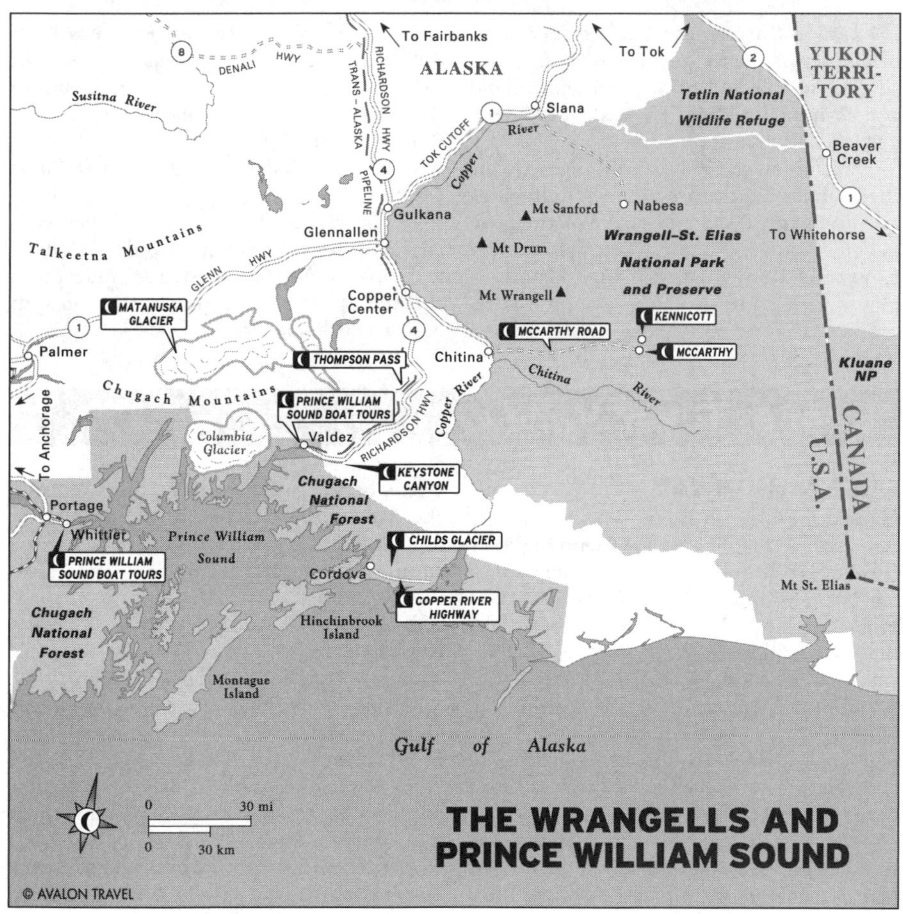

the terminus of the Alyeska Pipeline, and the fishing town of Cordova on the east provides a gateway to the Copper River.

PLANNING YOUR TIME

From Anchorage, it is an easy day trip by car or train to the town of Whittier, where state ferries provide connections to the remote town of Cordova as well as Valdez, which is on the road system. A fun one-week loop (it could be done in three days if you saw everything in a blur) would allow time to see Cordova, Valdez, and Wrangell–St. Elias National Park before circling back to Anchorage.

The Glenn Highway connects Anchorage with the town of Glennallen, passing **Matanuska Glacier** (a fun spot for guided glacier hikes) at Mile 102. The mighty Copper River and 13-million-acre Wrangell–St. Elias National Park lie just east of Glennallen. For a wonderful taste of this country, turn east on the Edgerton Highway to the dusty and rusty collection of old buildings called Chitina, then out the gravel **McCarthy Road** for 60 miles to the heart of the Wrangells. The route follows an old railroad bed, with an amazing high bridge and fine vistas en route to the tiny town of **McCarthy,** accessible from a footbridge across the Kennicott River. Vans will shuttle you to **Kennicott,** where colorful old copper-mine buildings are wedged between glaciers and mountain peaks.

Back out on the Richardson Highway, the road climbs south through the alpine area at **Thompson Pass** and past Worthington Glacier before dropping through narrow **Keystone Canyon,** where high waterfalls plummet off cliffs. The road ends at Valdez, terminus of the Trans-Alaska Pipeline, and a jumping-off point for **touring Prince William Sound.** The ferry system provides access to the fishing town of Cordova near the mouth of the Copper River. A 50-mile gravel road, the **Copper River Highway** ends near the Million Dollar Bridge. A short distance away is **Childs Glacier,** where icebergs thunder into the river; this may be the most dramatic glacier in Alaska. Ferries also connect Cordova with the little town of Whittier, where a 2.5-mile tunnel cuts through the mountains and the road leads back to Anchorage.

Copper River Valley

GLENN HIGHWAY

Named for Captain Edwin Glenn, an early Army explorer of the area, the **Glenn Highway** (Route 1) stretches 328 miles from downtown Anchorage to Tok, where it joins the Alaska Highway. Most of the Glenn was built during the corridor-construction craze of 1942, first from Tok to Gulkana, where it joins the Richardson Highway, then from Glennallen, where it leaves the Richardson, and finally to Palmer. Palmer was already connected to Anchorage by rail; the final 42 miles of road were completed a few years later.

Twenty miles east of Palmer is the tiny settlement of **Sutton** (pop. 470). Of interest here is the nonprofit **Alpine Historical Park** (907/745-7000, www.alpinehistoricalpark.org, daily 9 A.M.–7 P.M. late May–early Sept.), with its collection of historical buildings, coal-mining relics, and Athabascan Indian artifacts.

At Mile 72 (30 miles from Palmer), **Castle Mountain B&B** (907/745-7818, www.castlemountainb-b.com, $110–140 d) is a bright modern log home with a large deck facing King Mountain, three guest rooms with shared or private baths, Wi-Fi, and big breakfasts. The owners are friendly too.

Four miles up the road is **King Mountain State Recreation Area** (907/746-4644 or 800/952-8624, www.lifetimeadventures.net, $15), a large beautiful campground with water, outhouses, and choice spots right on the Matanuska River (though the interior loop might be less windy). The site faces King Mountain, a perfect triangular peak, across the river.

Based in Chickaloon at Mile 77, **Nova Riverrunners** (907/745-5753 or 800/746-5753, www.novalaska.com) guides daily summertime raft trips. Two options are a white-water ride along the Matanuska River past dramatic Lion Head (Class IV) for $110 or an easy float trip along lower reaches of the river for $90. The company also does a variety of multiple-night trips around Alaska.

A few miles up is **Long Lake State Recreation Area,** at Mile 85, where you can stretch your legs. A handful of free campsites (no water) are available.

At Mile 98, pull out your binoculars and look to the north for scattered bunches of white dots—Dall sheep like to congregate here, apparently for a mineral lick on the hillside.

Matanuska Glacier

Located at Mile 102 of the Glenn Highway, Matanuska Glacier is a don't-miss highlight. Today, this glacier is 27 miles long and four miles wide; 18,000 years ago it occupied Palmer, but it hasn't done much in the last 400 years. Much of the land in front of the glacier is owned by Jack Kimball, who spent decades developing a road and bridges to a bluff overlooking the ice. Access to **Glacier Park** (907/745-2534 or 888/253-4480, www.matanuskaglacier.com, May–mid-Oct.) costs $15 adults, $13 seniors, $10 students, $5 ages 6–12, and free for younger children. You can hike on the easier sections with tennis shoes, but will need a guide for the steeper parts of the glacier. Glacier Park also has a snack bar and campsites (no hookups) close to the glacier for $15 (plus your admission), but no water. Based just up the road, **MICA Guides** (907/351-7587 or 800/956-6422, www.micaguides.com) leads glacier hikes ($45) that often include the chance to explore an ice cave, three-hour ice fall treks ($100), and all-day ice climbing adventures ($130); entrance to Glacier Park is not included in the prices.

Out along the highway is **Matanuska Glacier State Recreation Site** ($15), on a hillside overlooking the ice giant. Nearby is **Long Rifle Lodge** (907/745-5151 or 800/770-5151, www.longriflelodge.com), with homemade meals, a lounge, and motel rooms ($80 d with private bath). However, the real reason to stop here is the view from the dining room of the nearby glacier and valleys—it's hard to keep your eyes on your plate with this mountain panorama in front of you.

Over Eureka Summit

After Long Rifle, it's another 85 miles east to Glennallen and the intersection of the Glenn and Richardson Highways. If you have a chance to make this drive in September, by all means, do it. The acres of aspen trees along this route turn a brilliant gold, and the contrasting dark green spruce, combined with the backdrop of glaciers and snowcapped peaks, make for some extraordinary photo ops. **Grand View RV Park** (Mile 110, 907/746-4480, www.grandviewrv.com) has RV sites ($28–33), cottages, and a café.

Sheep Mountain Lodge (907/745-5121 or 877/645-5121, www.sheepmountain.com) at Mile 113 is a rustic summer and winter destination. Its greenhouses and flower gardens add to the gorgeous mountain-backed setting in the summer, and the lodge serves home-cooked meals (summer only). Eleven cabins all have private baths and wonderful views; prices are $159 d for standard units or $189 d with kitchens. Basic hostel-style dorm rooms with a shared bath are a great bargain in the summer at $60 for up to four people. The wood-fired sauna and glassed-in hot tub are great places to relax after a winter day of skiing on the 10 miles of groomed trails.

Two miles away is **Majestic Valley Wilderness Lodge** (907/746-2930, www.majesticvalleylodge.com), another place with a country setting and grand vistas. Guests stay in lodge rooms ($120 d), motel units ($165 d), or cabins ($155 d) and have access to a wood-heated sauna.

Slide Mountain Cabins (Mile 135, 907/822-5864, www.rvparkalaska.com) has modern log cabins for $99 d with private baths, or $75 d with a shared shower house. RV spaces are $20, tent sites $7.

When you get past **Eureka Summit** (Mile 130), you're in caribou country, so scan the open ground everywhere for members of the Nelchina herd. From Eureka to Glennallen, and then north on the Richardson Highway toward Tok, it's possible to spot caribou almost anywhere. Slow down and keep your eyes open to avoid colliding with one. Lodging, RV spots, and meals (breakfast, burgers, and pies) are available near the summit at **Eureka Lodge** (907/822-3808, www.eurekalodge.com). Lodging is $115–125 d in motel rooms with private baths and Wi-Fi, or $85 d for simple cabins (2-night minimum stay) with a shower house. In the winter, this is a very popular snowmobiling destination.

Pitch a tent at the free **Little Nelchina State Recreation Site** at Mile 138.

Located 17 miles west of Glennallen at Mile 170, **Tolsona Lake Resort** (907/822-3433 or 800/245-3342, www.tolsonalakeresort.com) is off the Glenn Highway, with a motel ($125 d), suites ($145 for 4 people), plus a full-service restaurant and bar. All rooms contain fridges, microwaves, and Wi-Fi, plus access to the sauna and laundry.

Three miles up the road toward Glennallen is **Tolsona Wilderness Campground** (907/822-3865, www.tolsona.com, mid-May–mid-Sept., RVs $35, tents $25). A collection of 1920s logging-camp artifacts fills the little museum here.

Lake Louise

At Mile 160 on the Glenn Highway (27 miles west of Glennallen), the Lake Louise Road turns north, continuing 19 miles to this popular summer fishing and winter snowmobiling destination. The **Lake Louise State Recreation Area** has campsites ($15) and a swimming area for those who can brave the water.

Stay at **Lake Louise Lodge** (907/822-3311 or 877/878-3311, www.lakelouiselodge.com, year-round), where the log building overlooks the lake. Modern guest rooms ($115–150 d) include private baths, breakfast, and the use of canoes. Simple cabins ($70–80 d) share a bath in the lodge. There are a restaurant and bar, and you can also rent motorboats.

The Point Lodge at Lake Louise (907/822-5566 or 800/808-2018, www.thepointlodge.com) has comfortable rooms with panoramic views from a wraparound deck. Rates are $90 s or $110 d in the lodge (shared bath) or $80 d in cabins (baths in the lodge). Guests in all units get a full breakfast and can use the sauna, canoe, and paddleboat. Family-style dinners are available.

GLENNALLEN AND VICINITY

At Mile 187 of the Glenn Highway, just before the junction with the Richardson Highway, is the small service town Glennallen, named for both Edwin Glenn and Henry Allen, leader of the first expedition up the Copper River. Strung along both sides of the road, Glennallen (pop. 1,000) is the gateway to the big Copper River Valley country and Wrangell–St. Elias National Park.

Glennallen is an odd amalgamation of businesses, including the standard gas stations, motels, and food stops along with seven churches and three liquor stores. This is the heart of right-wing Christian Alaska, as you will quickly discover with a spin of the radio dial; KCAM 790 AM dominates the air waves with stirring messages of conversion along with its "Caribou Clatters" for those without phone service. The station beams out from the small campus of the Alaska Bible College in Glennallen (www.akbible.edu). Fortunately, the area also has a repeater for the public radio station at Valdez, KCHU.

The best thing about Glennallen is its setting. As you approach the town from the west—if the weather's clear—there's a dramatic view of the Wrangell Mountains: Mt. Drum is the beautiful snowcapped peak right in the middle at 12,010 feet in elevation, Mt. Sanford is just to the north (left) at 16,237 feet, and Mt. Wrangell is to the south at 14,163 feet. It's an incredible backdrop for a very ordinary junction town.

The **Greater Copper River Valley Visitor Center** (907/822-5555, www.traveltoalaska.com, daily 9 A.M.–6 P.M. mid-May–mid-Sept., closed winter) occupies the highway junction at the Hub gas station. You'll find exhibits on local attractions and details about every place between Tok and Cordova. Both Wells Fargo Bank and First National Bank have ATMs. Warning: Alaska State Troopers have a base in Glennallen, so don't even think about exceeding the speed limit for 50 miles in any direction.

Accommodations

Caribou Hotel (907/822-3302 or 800/478-3302, www.caribouhotel.com) is the largest place in town, but it gets negative reviews from many travelers. Choose from overpriced guest rooms ($143 d) and suites ($168 for up to 6 people) in the main building, or very basic tiny guest rooms with twin beds and communal baths ($69 s, $79 d) in an ancient ATCO unit. Apartments and cabins are also available, and the hotel has a guest computer, Wi-Fi, and a so-so restaurant. Anywhere but Glennallen, and this hotel wouldn't survive.

Located 11 miles north of Glennallen, **Bear Creek Cabin** (907/822-5852, $100 d) is a clean and nicely appointed cabin with a full kitchen, continental breakfast, and a spectacular view of the Wrangells.

Historic **Gakona Lodge** (907/822-3482, www.gakonalodge.com) sits along the Gakona and Copper Rivers 18 miles north of Glennallen. Built in the 1920s, the picturesque log building includes a bar and a gift shop with locally made Native Alaskan crafts. Carriage House Restaurant is open mid-May–mid-September with steaks, seafood, burgers, and chicken for $11–28. Remodeled century-old cabins with private baths are $115–150 d, and old-fashioned guest rooms inside the lodge cost $95 d with shared baths. Continental breakfast is included, along with a guest computer, Wi-Fi, raft rentals, and guided fishing.

Three miles up the Tok Cutoff from Gakona Lodge (17 miles north of Glennallen) is **Riverview B&B** (907/822-3321, www.cvalaska.net/~riverv, $100–110 d), with great views across the Copper River to the Wrangell Mountains. Ten guest rooms (seven with private baths and entrances) are available with decks, king or twin beds, a full breakfast, and Wi-Fi. Next door is **River Wrangellers** (907/822-3967 or 888/822-3967, www.riverwrangellers.com), offering rafting and fishing trips down nearby rivers.

Other local lodging options include **Fireweed Hill B&B** (907/822-3627, www.fireweedhill.com, $80 d).

Camping

The state's **Dry Creek Campground** ($12) is five miles north of the Glenn-Richardson junction and has pit toilets and too-friendly mosquitoes. **Northern Nights Campground & RV Park** (907/822-3199, www.northernightscampground.com, May–Sept., RVs $30, tents $15, showers $3) is the nicest local RV park, with a wooded setting, Wi-Fi, room for big rigs, and free desserts on Monday and Friday nights.

Food

Particularly popular with locals is **The Freeze** (907/822-3923, daily 10:30 A.M.–8 P.M. May–Sept.), serving fried chicken, burgers, hot dogs, halibut fish-and-chips, shakes, malts, and ice cream for under $12. There is nothing low-calorie about this place!

Brown Bear Rhodehouse (907/822-3663, Mon.–Sat. 11:30 A.M.–9 P.M., closed Sun.), three miles west of the junction at Mile 184 on the Glenn Highway, is famous for its hunting lodge atmosphere where dead critters stare from the walls. The filet mignon is great, and they also serve sandwiches, seafood, and broasted chicken; entrées run $18–39. Even if you aren't hungry, stop by to take a gander at the photos or to talk with the locals about those "damn Outside environmeddlers" (unless you are one).

Omni Parks Place (907/822-3334, www.omnialaska.com, daily 7 A.M.–10 P.M., reduced winter hours) is a surprisingly large and modern grocery store with a deli, bakery, fresh produce, and even espresso.

Getting There

Alaska Direct Bus Line (907/277-6652 or 800/770-6652, www.alaskadirectbusline.com) has service to Glennallen, continuing on to Whitehorse, Fairbanks, or Anchorage. Buses run three times a week in the summer, twice weekly in winter.

Glennallen's airport is just north of town, but for some reason it's officially called the Gakona Airport. **Ellis Air Taxi** (907/822-3368 or 800/478-3368, www.ellisair.com) will fly you from Glennallen to McCarthy for $118, or from Anchorage to McCarthy for $300. **Copper Valley Air Service** (907/822-4200 or 866/570-4200, www.coppervalleyair.com) also provides air-taxi service and flightseeing.

Wrangell-St. Elias National Park and Preserve

Though somewhat less accessible than Denali, this park is an excellent alternative to the crowds, clouds, wows, and crying-out-louds. The mountains (Chugach, Wrangells, and St. Elias) are incredible, and Mt. Wrangell—the highest volcano in Alaska at 14,163 feet—sometimes puffs away on earth's crustal cigar. In fact, of the 16 tallest mountains in North America, nine are in this park. The ice fields are world class, and their glacial tentacles rival any in the state. The Copper River can provide weeks-long raft or canoe rides, with all the fish you can stand. The wildlife is abundant, and this park even has beaches on the Gulf of Alaska. Two roads plunge deep into the park's wildland, and bus and plane service are available.

This is the largest national park in the country (and larger than southern New England), with over 12 million acres; along with Kluane National Park across the Canadian border, the whole area was the first designated UN World Heritage Site. Finally, you don't need backcountry permits to traipse around or camp on this federal land—just pick a direction and backpack until you crack. But you will certainly need mosquito repellent and a head net; the bugs can get downright vicious.

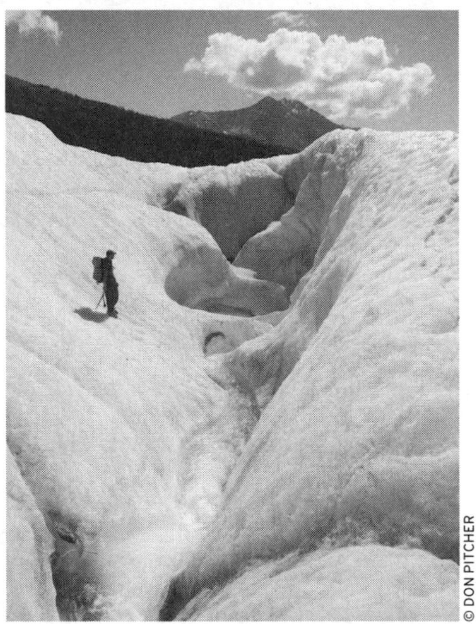
© DON PITCHER

on the surface of Root Glacier, in Wrangell-St. Elias National Park and Preserve

Air taxis and charter services can drop you off anywhere inside the park, with flights departing from Glennallen-Gulkana, Cordova, Chitina, or McCarthy.

ORIENTATION

The large **Wrangell-St. Elias National Park and Preserve Visitors Center** (907/822-7440, www.nps.gov/wrst, daily 8 A.M.–6 P.M. summer, Mon.–Fri. 8 A.M.–4:30 P.M. the rest of the year) is at Mile 107 on the Richardson Highway, seven miles south of Glennallen. Rangers can help with trip planning or sell you books and topographic maps. Talks and guided walks are offered daily, and an acclaimed 20-minute film about the park shows hourly. Outside, an easy trail leads through the forest to a vista point overlooking the Copper River and three of the park's most prominent peaks: Mt. Drum, Mt. Wrangell, and Mt. Blackburn. Seasonal ranger stations are in McCarthy, Kennicott, Chitina, and Yakutat.

Nabesna Road

Ground access to the park is via the Edgerton Highway and McCarthy Road in the center, and the Nabesna Road on the north side. The 42-mile Nabesna Road turns off at Mile 65 of the Tok Cutoff and leads to the abandoned gold mining town of Nabesna. The Park Service maintains the **Slana Ranger Station** (907/822-5238, daily 8 A.M.–5 P.M. summer, Mon.–Fri. 8 A.M.–4:30 P.M. the rest of the year), just up Nabesna Road from the junction.

Located at Mile 4 on the Nabesna Road, **Huck Hobbit's Homestead** (907/822-3196) has three cabins on a lovely 87-acre spread. Hostel-type accommodations are available at a budget price, just $20 per person. One larger cabin sleeps up to six and has its own kitchen. The setting is quiet, and the owners also offer the full-service version with meals, guided fishing, and entertainment for $100 per person. This is the real deal in a picturesque setting adjacent to Wrangell–St. Elias National Park. Canoe rentals ($50) are available for trips down the Slana River.

RIVER RUNNING

Cordova-based **Alaska River Expeditions** (907/424-7238 or 800/776-1864, www.alaskarafters.com) leads a variety of rafting trips inside the park, including a five-day float ($1,850) on the powerful Copper River, and 10-day trips ($2,500) that begin in McCarthy and continue all the way to the Million Dollar Bridge near Cordova.

Operating from McCarthy, in the heart of the park, **Copper Oar** (907/554-4453 or 800/523-4453, www.copperoar.com) offers a float-and-fly day trip that includes a float down the Kennicott and Nizina Rivers followed by a flight back to McCarthy for $275. The company also runs a wide variety of longer floats.

Gakona-based **River Wrangellers** (907/822-3967 or 888/822-3967, www.riverwrangellers.com) has Class III trips down the Klutina River ($99 for 4 hours), and the accessible Tonsina River ($199 for 8 hours). They also rent out rafts and other river gear, and provide shuttles for do-it-yourselfers.

St. Elias Guides (907/554-4445 or 888/933-5427, www.steliasguides.com) has multiday raft trips in the Wrangells, starting with a three-day trip down the Chitina River for $990.

McCARTHY AND KENNICOTT

The McCarthy-Kennicott area is a mostly private island surrounded by the vast Wrangell–St. Elias National Park. This was once an incredibly important copper mining area, but today it contains Alaska's most famous almost-ghost towns. Access to the area is via the McCarthy Road, which leads from the town of Chitina to the Kennicott River. Located within

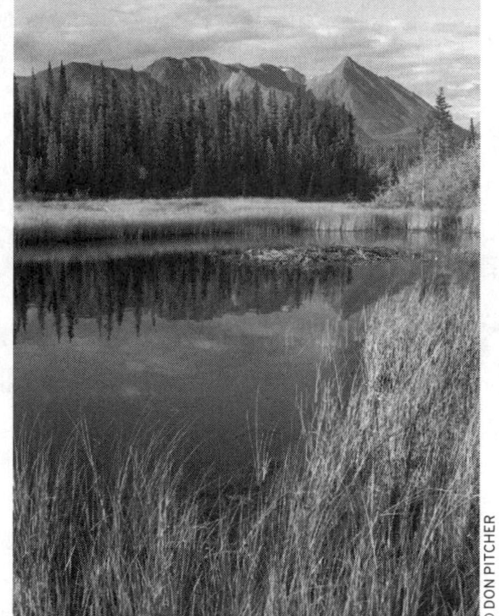

© DON PITCHER

pond with beaver lodge at Mile 20, McCarthy Road

Wrangell–St. Elias National Park and Preserve, the historic Kennecott Mine contains picturesque old buildings right alongside Kennicott Glacier, with the pinnacles of snowcapped mountains ringing the horizon.

History

Prospectors discovered rich copper deposits at Kennecott Mine in 1900, and at its peak the mine employed some 600 workers. (Note: Because of a typographic error when the mine was established, the mine, town, and company names are spelled Kennecott, while the glacier, river, and valley are generally spelled Kennicott.) The mines, in their nearly 30 years of operation, extracted $220 million in rich ore, nearly 70 percent copper, with a little silver and gold on the side. The Alaska Syndicate—owned by J. P. Morgan and Daniel Guggenheim—held the controlling interest. They also owned the Copper River and Northwestern Railway, which freighted the ore to tidewater, plus the Alaska Steamship Co., which shipped the ore to Tacoma, Washington.

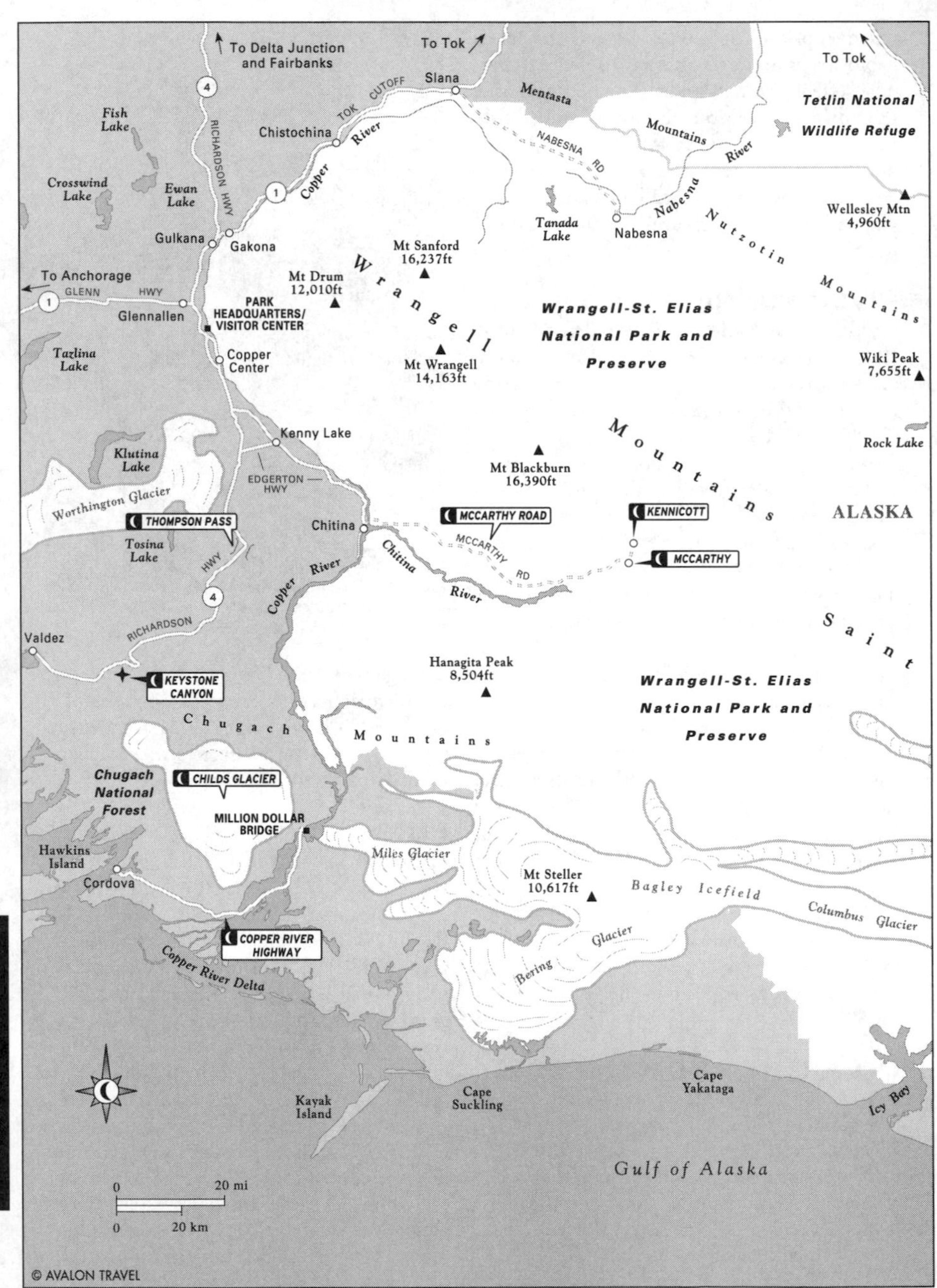
To Delta Junction and Fairbanks
To Tok
To Tok
Slana
Mentasta
Tetlin National Wildlife Refuge
Mountains
Fish Lake
Chistochina
Copper River
NABESNA RD
River
TOK CUTOFF
RICHARDSON HWY
Crosswind Lake
Ewan Lake
Nabesna
Wellesley Mtn 4,960ft
Tanada Lake
Nabesna
Nutzotin Mountains
Gulkana
Gakona
Mt Sanford 16,237ft
To Anchorage
GLENN HWY
Mt Drum 12,010ft
Wrangell
Glennallen
PARK HEADQUARTERS/ VISITOR CENTER
Wrangell-St. Elias National Park and Preserve
Tazlina Lake
Copper Center
Mt Wrangell 14,163ft
Wiki Peak 7,655ft
Kenny Lake
Mountains
Klutina Lake
Mt Blackburn 16,390ft
Rock Lake
EDGERTON HWY
Worthington Glacier
THOMPSON PASS
MCCARTHY ROAD
KENNICOTT
ALASKA
Chitina
Tosina Lake
MCCARTHY RD
MCCARTHY
Chitina River
Copper River
Saint
Valdez
RICHARDSON
Hanagita Peak 8,504ft
KEYSTONE CANYON
Wrangell-St. Elias National Park and Preserve
Chugach Mountains
Chugach National Forest
CHILDS GLACIER
MILLION DOLLAR BRIDGE
Hawkins Island
Miles Glacier
Cordova
Mt Steller 10,617ft
Bagley Icefield
Columbus Glacier
COPPER RIVER HIGHWAY
Bering Glacier
Copper River Delta
Kayak Island
Cape Suckling
Cape Yakataga
Icy Bay
Gulf of Alaska
0 20 mi
0 20 km
© AVALON TRAVEL

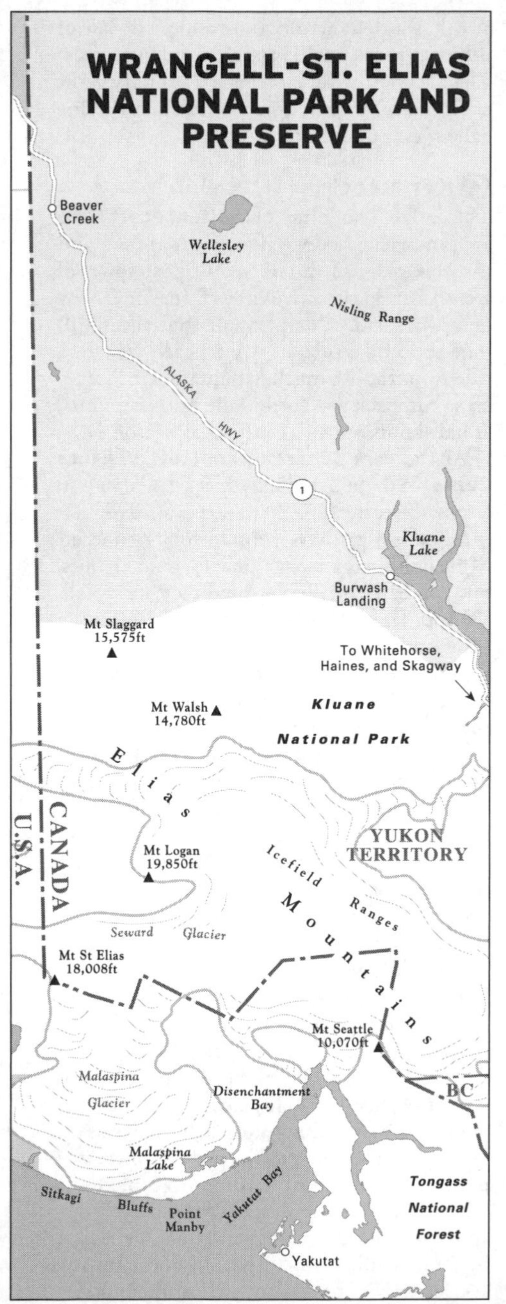

The mines shut down in 1938 when world copper prices dropped and the cost of production became prohibitive. After the mine's closure, the buildings were abandoned and gradually deteriorated. Today, these dark red buildings are in varying states of disrepair. Along with 3,000 acres of surrounding land, they were purchased by the Park Service in 1998, and the agency is spending millions of dollars to stabilize and rebuild the buildings. You can walk through the beautifully restored structures, or take a guided tour through ones still being worked on.

McCarthy Road

Cutting into the heart of the Wrangells, this challenging road follows an old railroad route past ragged mountain peaks, picturesque ponds where you'll hear loons (and buzzing mosquitoes), and sweeping vistas of the mighty Copper River. This could be the longest 60-mile road in Alaska—plan on three hours from Chitina, several more if it's clear and you stop for views of the Wrangells. The road has been substantially improved in the last few years and is in fairly good shape, but you may have to contend with choking dust if it hasn't rained recently. There are tire repair and towing services in Chitina and McCarthy, along with various lodging options as you approach McCarthy. You may be tempted to speed on the road at times, but try to keep around 30 mph since you never know what's around the next bend. It's also a good idea to have a full-size spare tire.

Note that many car rental and RV companies will not allow their vehicles on the McCarthy Road. Of course, this doesn't stop folks from driving the road. As one lodge owner told me, "If everyone obeyed that rule, I wouldn't have any guests."

At Mile 16, get ready for an adrenaline-pumping drive across the **Kuskulana River** on a narrow three-span bridge built in 1910 by the railroad and improved in 1988 (when guardrails were added). The bridge is nearly 600 feet long and sits almost 400 feet above the water—perfect, in other words, for bungee jumping, which does occasionally take place here. Another attraction is the abandoned railroad trestle across the Gilahina River at Mile 28. Just before the end of the road is a spectacular overlook of the town of McCarthy, the surrounding mountains, and the Kennicott and Root Glaciers.

The road ends on the west side of the Kennicott River, and parking is available ($5 per day) on nearby private land. The general public is not allowed to drive vehicles beyond this point, and two **footbridges** cross the river and a smaller tributary. Once across, walk up the road; the right fork takes you a mile to McCarthy, the left fork nearly five miles to Kennicott. **Shuttle buses** ($5 one way, through Wrangell Mountain Air) transport visitors from McCarthy to Kennicott, and mountain bikes are available to rent from Glacier View Campground. **Backcountry Connection** (907/822-5292, www.kennicottshuttle.com) provides van service to McCarthy from Glennallen or Chitina.

McCarthy

The quaint little settlement of McCarthy (pop. 25) was a boomtown from the early 1900s to 1939, serving the copper workers at Kennecott mines and the railroad workers on the Copper River and Northwestern Railway. At its peak, the town was full of hotels, restaurants, bars, and pool halls, along with the obligatory red-light district. Today it's a busy base from which outdoor enthusiasts explore spectacular mountain country and the nearby mine buildings in Kennicott. Tiny **McCarthy-Kennicott Museum** is open daily in the summertime; find it just as you arrive in McCarthy from the footbridge. Inside are interesting photos, maps, and artifacts. A model of the Bonanza mine occupies the adjacent boxcar.

Downtown McCarthy is a fun place to wander about, with dogs lazing on the dirt streets, lots of interesting buildings to explore, and a mix of businesses offering lodging, food, and various adventures. You'll hear the hum of generators behind the log buildings, and the buzz of mosquitoes around your head. McCarthy also has a delightfully old-fashioned **4th of July** celebration with a parade and live music. The old McCarthy Hotel is the primary gathering place, with lodging, meals, and a fine gallery called **Mountain Arts.**

Kennicott

The dark red buildings of the **Kennecott Mine** are sandwiched between steep mountains and massive glaciers in the semi-ghost town of Kennicott, located five miles from McCarthy on a dirt road. It's a pleasant (but all uphill) mountain bike ride, or pay $5 each way for a ride from the Wrangell Mountain Air shuttle. Vans run back and forth daily in the summer, at half-hour intervals in the peak season.

At the Park Service's **Kennicott Visitors Center** (907/960-1105, daily 9 A.M.–5:30 P.M. late May–early Sept.), rangers offer daily nature and history hikes. Most historic Kennecott Mine buildings are open only for guided tours, but you can visit the restored recreation hall. Visitors are welcome to explore the building exteriors, but watch for nails, glass, and metal scraps underfoot, and don't try to walk on decks or stairs alongside the buildings since the boards may be unsafe.

St. Elias Guides (907/554-4445 or 888/933-5427, www.steliasguides.com) leads educational 3.5-hour historic tours ($25 pp) of Kennecott Mine buildings. The company's specialty is 4–12-day mountaineering expeditions and backcountry hikes in the St. Elias Range, but it also offers glacier day hikes and ice climbing, along with all-day trips to Jumbo Mine or Erie Mine ($95) and various fly-in and rafting adventures.

For a taste of this magnificent place, join **Kennicott Wilderness Guides** (907/554-4444 or 800/664-4537, www.kennicottguides.com) on one of their half-day glacier hikes ($60 pp) or all-day ice-climbing treks ($120). These require a 1.5-mile hike to the glacier, where you put on crampons and head out to explore the otherworldly terrain of creeks that abruptly disappear and deep aquamarine pools, all backed by an incredible ring of peaks. The company also leads fly-in backcountry trips and multiday

© DON PITCHER
historic Kennecott Mine buildings

mountaineering and glacier skills courses; these adventures are highly recommended.

An easy and popular hike or mountain bike ride follows the east side of Kennicott Glacier and Root Glacier. When the weather cooperates, hikers are treated to striking views of Mt. Blackburn, Regal Mountain, and Donaho Peak. Take the old road north from Kennecott Mine for 0.5 miles, turning left when it diverges. The trail follows the Root Glacier, crossing bridges over Bonanza Creek and Jumbo Creek along the way. At approximately 1.25 miles, a side trail leads to primitive campsites near the glacier. An outhouse is nearby, and storage lockers are available to keep food away from the bears that sometimes roam through. The Kennicott Visitors Center has additional details on this and other local hikes.

Fireweed Mountain Arts and Crafts (907/554-4500, late May–mid-Sept.) sells quality works by Alaskan artists and has a wonderful back deck overlooking Kennicott Glacier. They're just downhill from Kennicott Glacier Lodge.

Accommodations

In McCarthy, stay at the historic—built in 1916—☾ **McCarthy Lodge** (907/554-4402, www.mccarthylodge.com), the true heart and soul of the area. Friendly owner Neil Darish offers two divergent lodging choices. **Lancaster's Backpacking Hotel** (June–early Sept., $48 s, $68 d) has no-frills private rooms with twin beds (bedding included), shared baths, and a common area, but no kitchen. Considerably more upscale is **Ma Johnson's Hotel** (mid-May–mid-Sept., $129 s, $169 d), where the six bedrooms are furnished in period antiques and share three baths. There's even an ATM in the bar.

Located near the end of the McCarthy Road, **Kennicott River Lodge & Hostel** (907/554-4441 summer or 941/447-4252 winter, www.kennicottriverlodge.com, mid-May–mid-Sept.) has a variety of pleasant lodging choices, all with access to a full kitchen, a common area with satellite TV, a shower house, and a large sauna. Coed hostel bunks cost $28 per person (includes bedding). Also available are lodge rooms ($70–90 d) and private cabins ($100 d plus $25 each extra guest).

Aspen Meadows of McCarthy B&B (907/554-4454, www.wsen.net/aspenmeadows) is two miles before the end of the McCarthy Road. Three basic cabins (one is an old trailer) share a bathhouse ($85–110 d) and are stocked with breakfast fixings.

Kennicott Glacier Lodge (907/258-2350 or 800/582-5128, www.kennicottlodge.com, mid-May–mid-Sept.) is a sprawling and spotlessly clean modern lodge five miles from McCarthy. The setting is graceful, with a long covered porch facing Root Glacier and the colorful mine buildings. Vacation package rates for guest rooms—which include three meals, transportation to and from McCarthy, and a tour of the ghost town—are $285–315 d per day in the main lodge (with shared baths) or $750 d per day in the newer south wing (with private baths). The à la carte rate (lodging and transportation only) is $169–199 d in the main lodge or $259 in the south wing. Be sure to request a room facing the glacier.

A half-mile from the end of the McCarthy Road, **McCarthy B&B** (907/554-4433, www.mccarthy-kennicott.com/mccarthybb, May–Sept., $110 d, $170 for 4 people) includes five small cabins with private baths, and a guest house ($200) with space for five. The rustic screened gazebo is stocked with breakfast items, and guests can also cook meals here.

Currant Ridge (907/554-4424 or 877/647-2442, www.currantridgecabins.com, mid-May–mid-Sept., $189 d plus $20 each additional guest), at Mile 56 on the McCarthy Road (2.5 miles from McCarthy), serves up six deluxe log guest houses with queen beds, full kitchens, and private baths.

Accessible only by air, remote **Ultima Thule Lodge** (907/688-1200, www.ultimathulelodge.com) sits along the Chitina River 50 miles southeast of McCarthy, with seven-day package trips that include a different adventure each day.

For the real Alaskan bush experience, the Park Service (www.nps.gov/wrst) maintains 13 free public-use **cabins** within Wrangell–St. Elias, most of which are accessible only by air.

Camping

There are no Park Service campsites in McCarthy or Kennicott, but hike-in campsites are located at Root Glacier two miles north of Kennicott. A half-mile from the end of the McCarthy Road, **Glacier View Campground** (907/554-4490, www.glacierviewcampground.com, May–mid-Sept.) has tent and RV spaces for $20 and parking for $5. **Base Camp Root Glacier** (907/746-0606, May–mid-Sept.) occupies the end of the road next to the McCarthy footbridge and has campsites for $20 (running water, vault toilets), showers for $7, and parking for $5 per day. Kennicott River Lodge & Hostel provides showers and a sauna for $10.

Food

The restaurant at **Kennicott Glacier Lodge** (907/258-2350 or 800/582-5128, www.kennicottlodge.com) serves excellent "wilderness gourmet" meals three times a day, including a breakfast buffet (7–10 A.M., $10–16), lunch specials (noon–3 P.M.), and filling family-style dinners (7 P.M. seating, $35–45). It's open to both lodge guests and the general public, but dinner reservations are required if you aren't staying here.

McCarthy Lodge (907/554-4402, www.mccarthylodge.com) is open for breakfast (7–10 A.M.) and dinner (5:30–10 P.M.) mid-May–mid-September. Dinners typically feature Copper River red salmon, New York steaks, and elk; entrées are $14–45. There's an extensive wine list. Adjacent is New Golden Saloon, with a lighter bar menu of buffalo burgers, pizzas, fish-and-chips, salads, and similar fare for $10–15. You'll find occasional bands at the saloon in the summer. In 2010 the hotel also opened a new gourmet restaurant with multicourse offerings. If you're staying at Kennicott, the lodge provides a free evening shuttle to McCarthy.

Glacier View Campground (907/554-4490, www.glacierviewcampground.com, daily noon–9 P.M. late May–early Sept., $10–15), near the end of the McCarthy Road, has a barbecue menu for lunch and dinner, plus their famous half-pound Glacier Burgers, and even barbecue-grilled pizzas.

For tasty and inexpensive meals in downtown McCarthy, head to **The Potato** (907/554-1100, Mon.–Wed. 10 A.M.–7 P.M., Fri.–Sun. 9 A.M.–7 P.M. late May–mid-Sept.). It's locally famous for potato and egg burritos, Philly cheese sandwiches, and fresh-cut curly fries, but also serves healthier fare such as falafels, wraps, and salmon burgers, plus the only espresso in McCarthy. Most items run around $9–10.

The **McCarthy Mercantile** (907/554-4506, daily 9 A.M.–7 P.M. late May–early Sept.) has a fair selection of groceries and meats, plus homemade bread (they mill their own wheat), a deli, fresh pastries, soups, chili, and ice cream. Get a picnic lunch for $12. Fresh produce arrives Thursday evenings.

Information and Services

The Park Service maintains a small **visitors kiosk** (daily 9:30 A.M.–5:30 P.M. Memorial Day–Labor Day) 0.75 miles from the McCarthy bridge, plus a seasonal visitors center in Kennicott.

Regional visitors centers have a useful free visitors guide to the area, or find the same information online (www.mccarthy-kennicott.com/vg). Also check out the **Wrangell Mountains Center** (www.wrangells.org), a McCarthy-based organization dedicated to environmental education and research.

McCarthy Lodge has computers and Wi-Fi for **Internet access** (for a fee). Pay phones are located at the bridge and next to the McCarthy Lodge. Cell phones sometimes work in the McCarthy area, but it depends on your service provider.

For artwork, visit **Mountain Arts** at McCarthy Lodge or **Fireweed Mountain Arts and Crafts** in Kennicott.

Getting There and Around

It's a rough ride to McCarthy, but you can save wear and tear on your car with a van ride from **Backcountry Connection** (907/822-5292, www.kennicottshuttle.com, daily mid-May–mid-Sept.). The round-trip cost is $139 from Glennallen or Chitina if you come in and go out on different days, and $99 round-trip if you're crazy enough to try this in one day. Call at least two months ahead for reservations in July since the vans are often full. They also have a fly-drive option for $200 round-trip that includes a flight from Glennallen to McCarthy combined with a van ride in the other direction.

Wrangell Mountain Air (907/554-4411 or 800/478-1160, www.wrangellmountainair.com) has scheduled service several times a day connecting Chitina with McCarthy ($115 one way), plus a variety of flightseeing trips from McCarthy, starting with a $95 half-hour glacier tour. They also operate a shuttle bus ($5 one way) between the footbridge, McCarthy, and Kennicott on an hourly basis all summer.

Ellis Air Taxi (907/822-3368 or 800/478-3368, www.ellisair.com) will fly you from Gulkana to McCarthy on Wednesdays and Fridays for $222 one way, or from Anchorage to McCarthy for $300 one way.

A one-man operation run by the affable Gary Green since 1988, **McCarthy Air** (907/554-4440 or 800/245-6909, www.mccarthyair2.com) does flightseeing and backcountry drop-offs; Green is one of the most experienced pilots in the region.

Glacier View Campground (907/554-4490, www.glacierviewcampground.com), near the end of the road, has several beat-up mountain bikes for rent for $25 per day.

CHITINA AND VICINITY

The turnoff for the **Edgerton Highway** is at Mile 82 of the Richardson Highway (18 miles south of Copper Center). This paved 34-mile road leads past the dispersed farming community of Kenny Lake and on to the town of Chitina (CHIT-nuh, from the Athabascan *chiti,* "copper," and *na,* "river"). The Chitina Indians used copper tools to hammer copper nuggets into plates, which they traded with the Tlingits; someone who owned five or six plates was considered very rich. Chitina became an important junction in 1909 when the Copper River and Northwestern Railway arrived; a spur road connected the track to the

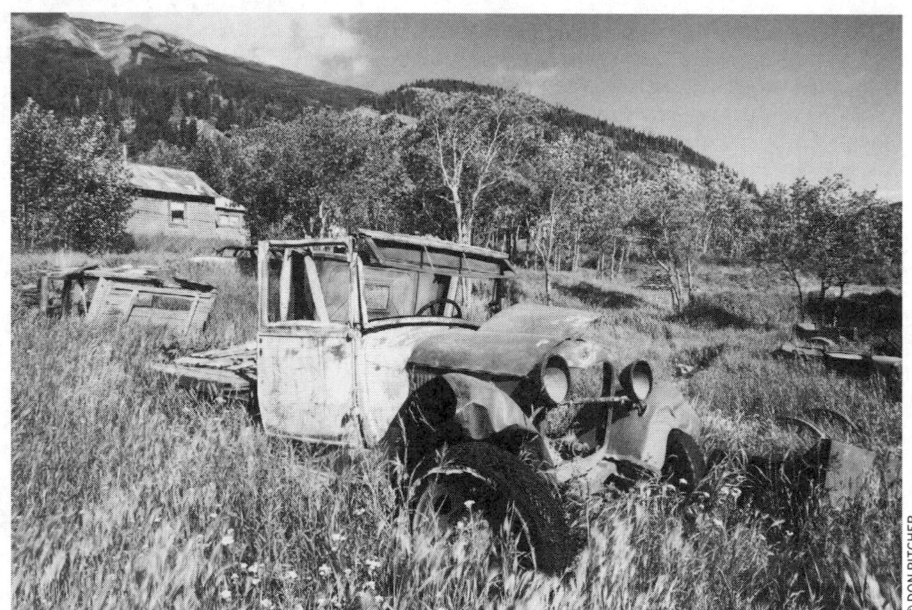
rusty old Model A truck, Chitina

© DON PITCHER

original Richardson wagon trail to Fairbanks. The town began its decline in 1938 when the railroad shut down, and its future was further eroded by the Good Friday earthquake of 1964, which knocked out several bridges on the Copper River Highway. The highway project to link Cordova and Chitina was abandoned at that time.

Home to less than 100 people, Chitina is famous for its dip-netting season in June, when Alaskan residents converge on the confluence of the Copper and Chitina Rivers, "dip" 35-gallon nets on 15-foot-long aluminum poles into the water, and lift out 8-pound reds and 25-pound kings by the score. The dip-net fishery is only open to Alaskans. In addition, a number of **fish wheels** can be seen above the bridge throughout the summer. Chitina also serves as a way station for folks heading out on the McCarthy Road.

Chitina is decidedly rustic, with aging log cabins in various stages of collapse lining the dusty dirt roads. Poke around a bit more to find antique vehicles, an abandoned railcar, and even an old-fashioned gas pump. The town is also an unbelievably windy spot, with winds funneling through the narrow mountains along the Copper River. Because of the in-the-mountains location, none of the local businesses have TV or radio reception.

Accommodations and Food

Built in 1914, **Hotel Chitina** (907/823-2244, www.hotelchitina.com, May–Sept., $165 d) occupies a corner lot as you come into town. This two-story frontier building was restored 90 years later with an arts and crafts decor in the downstairs restaurant and rustic bar. Guests stay in small guest rooms with modern furnishings, queen beds, private baths, and limited Wi-Fi, but no TVs or phones. The restaurant (daily 7:30 A.M.–10 P.M. late May–early Sept., dinner entrées $17–29) serves three meals a day; try the specials such as rockfish St. Elias, blackened Copper River reds, and steaks. Save room for house-made desserts, especially the cheesecakes.

Get groceries, gas, and supplies at **Hem's**

Chitina 1 Stop (907/823-2288). **Uncle Tom's Tavern** (907/823-2253) is the local drinking establishment for the "nip and dip" crowd.

Built in 1910 and on the National Register of Historical Places, **Chitina House B&B** (907/823-2298, www.chitinahouse.com, May–Sept., $150 d) is a cute red home that once served as a railroad bunkhouse. Two rooms share a bath, and a continental breakfast is included.

Located in a quiet spot a mile out of town, **Chitina Guest Cabins** (907/823-2266, www.pawandfeathers.com, May–Oct.) rents two recently constructed cabins ($150 d with breakfast) that provide an authentic taste of the real Alaska. The cabins are quaint, with outhouses and a washbasin. Hostel-type bunkrooms are $35 per person with your own sleeping bag, or $45 per person with sheets, blankets, and towel provided. A private room here is $60 d, and bunkroom guests have kitchen access.

Camp for free along the Copper River just across the bridge a mile east of Chitina at **Copper River State Campground,** with no facilities but lots of sandy land to pitch a tent or park an RV for free. The constant wind keeps mosquitoes away, but it can make tenting virtually impossible. **Liberty Falls State Recreation Site** has several campsites ($10) along the Edgerton Highway 10 miles west of Chitina. It's a beautiful spot.

Practicalities

Housed within a historic cabin, the National Park Service's **Chitina Ranger Station** (907/823-2205, Fri.–Mon. 2–6 P.M. late May–early Sept.) has information and videos on the park and the McCarthy Road.

Spirit Mountain Artworks (907/823-2222, www.spiritmountainalaska.com, open seasonally) sells quality Alaskan art from a classic false-front building in the heart of town.

Local events include a country 4th of July parade and the **Labor Day Cabbage Festival** with giant cabbages, a pig roast, races, and smoked salmon. Learn more about the town from the **Chitina Chamber of Commerce** website (www.chitinachamber.org).

Wrangell Mountain Air (907/554-4411 or 800/478-1160, www.wrangellmountainair.com) provides scheduled flights between Chitina and McCarthy.

Kenny Lake

Kenny Lake Mercantile (907/822-3313, www.kennylake.com) has groceries and gas, a diner with three meals a day, austere lodging, a wooded RV park ($24), a coin laundry, and showers. It's at Mile 7 on the Edgerton Highway, 26 miles west of Chitina.

Find considerably nicer accommodations at **Wellwood Center B&B** (Mile 6, 907/822-3418, www.wellwoodcenter.com, $114–135 d) with three guest rooms and private or shared baths. Make your own breakfast in the stocked kitchen. The home occupies a 95-acre spread with hiking trails leading to mountain vistas.

Golden Spruce Cabins (Mile 10, 907/822-5556, www.goldensprucecabins.com, $75 d) has five comfy year-round cabins with a shared bathhouse, plus an espresso stand and a convenience store.

Pippin Lake B&B (907/822-3046, www.pippinlakebnb.com, $150 d plus $10 per additional guest), at Mile 82 on the Richardson Highway near the Edgerton turnoff, has a cozy lakeside cabin that sleeps five. The kitchen is stocked for a make-it-yourself breakfast, and a canoe, kayak, and paddleboat add to the allure.

At **Copper Moose B&B** (Edgerton Hwy. Mile 5.8, 907/822-9244 or 866/922-4244, www.coppermoosebb.com, $135 d), four guest rooms share three baths in a large log home. Full breakfasts are included, and you can take in the Wrangell Mountains from the deck while surfing the Web with free Wi-Fi.

Richardson Highway South

The 366-mile Richardson Highway provides a north–south connection between Fairbanks and Valdez, passing through the towns of North Pole, Delta Junction, Glennallen, and Copper Center along the way. The 115-mile stretch between Glennallen and Valdez cuts between the rugged Chugach Mountains to the west and the massive Wrangell Mountains to the east. This route—the oldest road in Alaska—was blazed during the stampede of 1898 and has since been used as a footpath, a telegraph right-of-way, a wagon trail, and an auto thoroughfare. The last 25 miles to Valdez is one of the most spectacular drives in Alaska.

COPPER CENTER

Copper Center (pop. 500) is 15 miles south of Glennallen on a side road (the Old Richardson Highway) that splits off at Mile 106 on the Richardson Highway. Settled in 1896, this was the first non–Native Alaskan town in the interior of Southcentral Alaska, opened up by all the exploration on the mighty Copper River. This was also the point where the perilous trail over Valdez Glacier came down from the mountains. When the stampeders arrived, they found a score of tents, several log cabins, a post office, and the Blix Roadhouse, which opened in 1898 for $15,000 and featured spring beds and a modern bath. Today the settlement has a handful of businesses and a mixed population, including Athabascans in the neighboring village of Kluti Kaah.

Just north of town at Mile 107 is the **Wrangell-St. Elias National Park and Preserve Visitor Center** (907/822-7250, www.nps.gov/wrst, daily 9 A.M.–7 P.M. late May–mid-Sept., Mon.–Fri. 8 A.M.–4:30 P.M. mid-Sept.–late May). Rangers can help with trip planning, sell you books and topographic maps, or show an acclaimed film about the park.

Practicalities

The old Blix Roadhouse was replaced in 1932 by **Copper Center Lodge** (907/822-3245 or 866/330-3245, www.coppercenterlodge.com), a charming two-story log building. Comfortable rooms cost $125 d; request one with a private bath. The restaurant (daily 5 A.M.–9:30 P.M. summer, daily 7 A.M.–8:30 P.M. winter, dinner entrées $17–30) serves sourdough pancakes—using a century-old sourdough starter—along with burgers, sandwiches, shrimp, halibut, and steaks. There are great homemade blueberry and rhubarb pies too.

Next door are two small cabins that form the **George Ashby Museum** (907/822-5285, daily 11 A.M.–5 P.M. mid-May–mid-Sept.). Exhibits trace the history of the Copper River Valley, including Athabascan Indian and early-settler artifacts. Gold rush and pioneer days are remembered with photographs, tools used to develop the area, and old Sears catalogs, the only way the local inhabitants could procure many necessary supplies from Outside.

Out on the loop road, **Chapel on the Hill,** the oldest log chapel in the Copper River Basin, was built by Army volunteers in 1943.

Enjoy a comfortable night at **Sawing Logzz B&B** (907/822-3242, www.sawinglogzz.com, $125 d) where the private suite includes a queen log bed, a futon couch, a stocked kitchenette for a self-serve breakfast, and a private bath.

Set on a hilltop, the modern 85-room **Copper River Princess Lodge** (907/822-4000 or 800/426-0500, www.princesslodges.com, $179 d) is at Mile 102 on the Richardson Highway. Upscale guest rooms are large and comfortable, but the view is the real feature, with vistas over the Copper River Valley to Mt. Drum and the Wrangells. Most guests are cruise ship passengers, but independent travelers are welcome, and discounted rates are often available. A restaurant and lounge are on the premises.

Park RVs at two seasonal campgrounds on opposite sides of the Klutina River: **Klutina Salmon Charters** (907/822-3991, www.klutinasalmoncharters.com) and **Grove's Klutina Charters** (907/822-5822 or 800/770-5822, www.groveklutina.com).

THOMPSON PASS

From the Edgerton Highway junction to Valdez is 82 beautiful miles through green forested hillsides along surging creeks with countless waterfalls emanating from ice patches and small glaciers atop the jagged Chugach. If you're terminally enchanted by this stretch of road and want to linger, two state recreation sites offer camping ($12): **Squirrel Creek** at Mile 79 and **Little Tonsina** at Mile 65. The Tonsina site is a bit noisy, located a half-mile from pipeline pump station number 12, which is run by jet aircraft turbines and sounds like a plane perpetually taking off. Signboards across the highway from the pump station (Mile 65) describe pipeline history, oil spills, communications, the turbines, and the pump station. At Mile 56, the **Tiekel River Lodge** (907/822-3259) has food, gas, rooms, campsites, and a gift shop.

Worthington Glacier

Near Mile 33 of the Edgerton Highway, you come around a bend, unsuspecting, and the Worthington Glacier looms into view, its three fingers creeping out of Girls Mountain like a grotesque hand in a horror movie. In another few miles is the turnoff to this state recreation site, on a short road that leads to the overlook parking lot. There's no established campground here, but a small visitors center is staffed by State Parks folks in the summer. Trails cover the short distance to the glacier, and a one-mile path climbs the lateral moraine for even more dramatic vistas.

Topping Out

A mere three miles down (or more accurately, *up*) the road from Worthington Glacier is **Thompson Pass** (2,771 feet). A long row of serrated peaks, like a cosmic crosscut saw with only a few dull or missing teeth, lines the high horizon. Blueberry and Summit Lakes are accessible by a loop road about a mile on the Valdez side of the pass; the small campground at Blueberry is beautiful, but it's exposed, especially if Thompson Pass is in the process of maintaining its record-setting precipitation levels. Confirming that this is one of the snowiest spots on earth are 15-foot-tall right-angle orange poles that show snowplow drivers the edge of the road.

Thompson Pass Mountain Chalet (907/835-4817, www.thompsonpass.com, $140 d, $10 for each additional guest) is a rustic cabin at Mile 19 with space for four people, a private bath, a kitchenette, and a continental breakfast basket. The owners live in a nearby cabin and guide summertime hikes and wintertime backcountry ski adventures.

KEYSTONE CANYON

About seven miles south of Thompson Pass you drop to Keystone Canyon, one of the most gorgeous sights in Alaska, even in the rain. This four-mile section is steeped in gold rush and copper-frenzy history. At the height of Klondicitis, accounts of the heavy tax and strict regulations that Canadian authorities imposed on the stampeders (which saved countless lives) were passed down the coast, and rumors of an old Indian-Russian trail from Valdez to the Yukon circulated simultaneously. The vague story of an "all-American route" to the gold sent 4,000 would-be prospectors headlong to Valdez—a measure of the madness that gripped the land. Suicidally unprepared, like lemmings they attempted to cross the brutal Valdez Glacier. Also responding to the rumors, the U.S. Army dispatched Captain William Abercrombie in 1898 to find or blaze a route from Valdez to the Interior. Abercrombie had been on the original American expedition to Copper River country in 1884. He *knew* the land and the conditions; when he crossed Valdez Glacier in 1898, he postponed his trail-blazing assignment in order to deal with the horror that he found. Abercrombie returned in 1899 and thoroughly explored and mapped the whole area, locating and naming the Lowe River, Keystone Canyon, and the Thompson Pass route to the Interior.

Then in 1906, during the often-violent race to build a railroad from tidewater to the Kennecott copper mines, two of the competing construction companies clashed over the right-of-way through Keystone Canyon; one man was killed. The ensuing murder trial further fanned the flames, and the "Shoot-out at Keystone Canyon" became a great issue between the opposing sides. All this is highly dramatized in Rex Beach's novel *The Iron Trail.*

Today, you drive along the raging Lowe River, at the bottom of nearly perpendicular 300-foot cliffs. The entire canyon is a psychedelic green; every crack and crevice in the sheer walls is overgrown with bright lime moss. Waterfalls tumble over the walls to the river below, spraying the road with a fine mist. **Bridal Veil Falls** and **Horsetail Falls** live up to their names. And now you're ready to enter Valdez.

Valdez

At the end of Valdez Arm and completely surrounded by snowcapped peaks, Valdez (val-DEEZ, *never* val-DEZ, pop. 4,000) occupies one of the most picturesque settings in Southcentral Alaska. The prosperous town has wide streets and year-round access by land and sea; it's the northernmost ice-free port in the United States. Because of that, Valdez was chosen as the terminus for the 800-mile Trans-Alaska Pipeline. And because of it, the town always seems to prosper.

HISTORY

Captain James Cook sailed into and named Prince William Sound in 1778; Spanish explorer Don Salvador Fidalgo entered "Puerto de Valdez" in 1790, naming it after Spain's Marine Minister. In 1898, Valdez was a tent

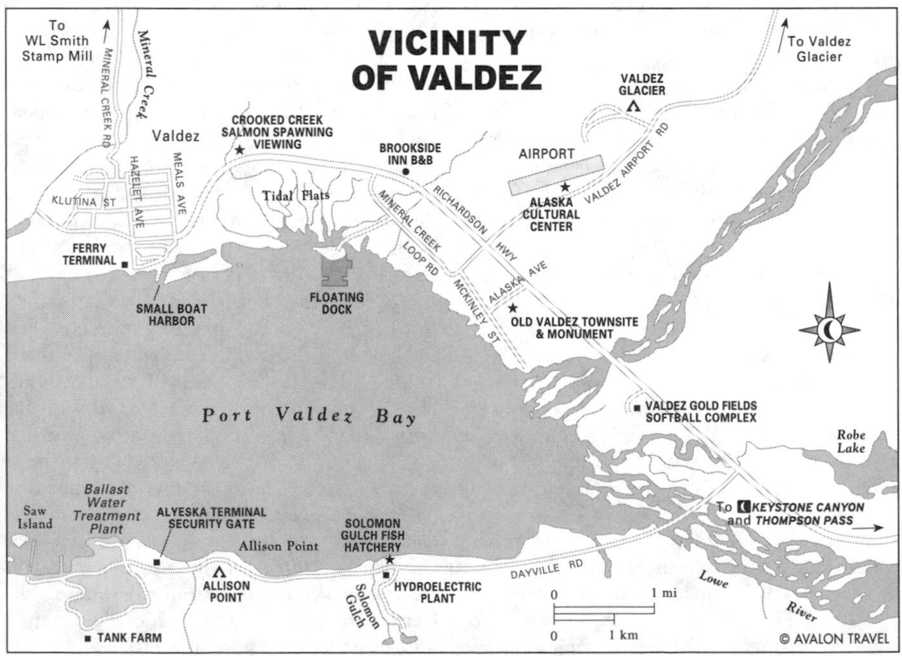

city of stampeders similar to Skagway, except for one critical detail: There was no trail to the Interior. Still, 4,000–6,000 death-defying cheechakos crossed the Valdez Glacier that year. Army Captain William Abercrombie described the foolhardy newcomers as "terrifyingly incompetent...wholly unprepared physically and morally for what they would face." They barely knew how to strap packs on their backs, and few thought to carry the two basic necessities: water and wood. Many were blinded by the sun's reflection off the ice. Many got lost in howling storms, in which it was impossible to see or hear the person ahead. Of those who managed to reach the summit, many lost their loads and lives on slick downhill slides into oblivion. Those who actually got off the glacier intact had to contend with the fast cold waters of the runoff. Many men with heavy packs lost their footing and drowned in knee-deep water. Some attempted to build boats and float down the Klutina River to Copper Center; few made it. And those stuck between the glacier and the river had nothing.

In the final count, by fall all but 300 (and the countless dead) of those who'd set out from Valdez during the spring and summer of 1898 returned to Valdez the way they came. Abercrombie found them destitute and broken. Many had gone mad, most had scurvy and frostbitten hands, feet, and faces. Facilities were squalid, and there was no food. Abercrombie postponed his orders to blaze a trail into the Interior for six months to feed, clothe, house, and arrange transportation home for the survivors. Eventually, the army built a road through Keystone Canyon—providing access to the Interior—as well as a military base across the bay from Valdez called Fort Liscum; it lasted until 1923.

The 20th Century

In the early 1900s a corporate copper rush kicked off a fierce competition among Valdez, Cordova, and a town called Katalla, all vying to be selected as the tidewater terminus of the proposed railway to the copper mines of what's now Kennecott. A dozen projects were conceived, and one was even begun out of Valdez, but Cordova won out in the end. For the next 60 years, Valdez was a sleepy fishing and shipping port, competing with Seward, and later Whittier, to provide access for freight to the Interior. Then in 1964 the Good Friday earthquake struck, wiping out the entire town, which was rebuilt four miles inland on property donated by a local. Finally, in 1974, civic leaders sold the virtues of Valdez—its ice-free port, 800-foot-deep harbor, and proximity to the Interior—to the pipeline planners, who chose the town as their terminus.

Everything went along without serious incident until March 29, 1989 (Good Friday once again), when the *Exxon Valdez* ran aground on Bligh Reef a few hours after leaving the pipeline terminal in Valdez, dumping 11 million gallons of North Slope crude into Prince William Sound. The unthinkable had happened. In the mad summer of 1989, Valdez was turned on its head by the "Exxon Economy." The waters of Port Valdez escaped the spill, but Prince William Sound is still a long way from returning to the way it was before the spill.

SIGHTS

Museums

For its size, **Valdez Museum** (217 Egan Dr., 907/835-2764, www.valdezmuseum.org, daily 9 A.M.–5 P.M. May–mid-Sept., Mon.–Sat. 1–5 P.M. mid-Sept.–Apr.), right in the middle of town, has an extraordinary number of comprehensive displays. Check out the fascinating photo display on the pipeline's impact, and the early black-and-whites. Some rare early maps and charts include a Russian one from 1737; look for the beautiful engraving by Webber, Captain Cook's prolific ship's artist. Informative displays illustrate Native Alaskan, mining, and military history, but two beautifully restored fire pumpers—one from 1886—are the striking centerpieces, along with the lens from Cape Hinchinbrook Lighthouse. There's a small section from the hull of the *Exxon Valdez,* but surprisingly little information on that disaster.

Close to the ferry terminal, the

THE *EXXON VALDEZ* OIL SPILL

On March 23, 1989, Good Friday, at 11 P.M., just a few hours after leaving the pipeline terminal loaded with over 20 million barrels of Prudhoe Bay crude, Captain Joseph Hazelwood turned the 987-foot *Exxon Valdez* supertanker out of the normal shipping lanes of Prince William Sound to avoid icebergs from Columbia Glacier. Through a series of mistakes and misunderstandings, and ignoring standard procedure, at 12:01 A.M. on March 24 the *Valdez* ran up hard aground on Bligh Reef, opening a tractor trailer-size hole in the ship, which began to leak oil at a rapid rate. It took 3 hours for the Coast Guard to be notified, and 12 hours for the spill-response team to arrive at the scene. It was a full 72 hours after the oil began to spill before a containment boom was installed to surround the tanker. But as the rest of the oil was off-loaded onto the *Exxon Baton Rouge,* the fate of more than 1,000 miles of Southcentral Alaska coastline had already been sealed: The oil began its inexorable spread.

THE CLEANUP

In the following weeks, the technology available to clean up an environmental disaster of such magnitude proved grossly inadequate. To begin with, Alyeska Pipeline Company's emergency procedures and equipment had atrophied over the years. The use of chemical dispersants, a major part of the plan, was not only ineffective but controversial as well: Later in the summer workers who'd handled them began to show symptoms of toxic poisoning. Of the few skimmers that could be deployed (a dozen after a week), those that worked were able to clean up 500 gallons of oil an hour – in the face of millions. And then there were no support facilities for unloading the skimmed crude.

Local fishers mobilized to try to contain the oil with booms, keeping it away from some of the most bountiful fisheries on earth at the peak of their seasons. As the oil washed up on the wildlife-rich shorelines of Prince William Sound, crews were sent to attack the thickening, hardening sludge with shovels, buckets, and plastic bags. As early as the first week in June, 24,000 birds and 1,000 sea otters, killed by the oil, had been counted – some so covered with crude that they were impossible to identify. At the height of the summer cleanup, 10,000 workers were engaged in a somewhat futile effort to return the beaches of Prince William Sound, the Kenai and Alaska Peninsulas, Kodiak Island, and all the way down to the Shumagin Islands in the Aleutians to their previously pristine state. Garbage cleanup crews were cleaning up after the oil cleanup crews. It's estimated that Exxon spent $1.25 billion on the effort.

THE AFTERMATH

Well over a decade after the spill, oil can still be found on some Prince William Sound beaches, particularly under rocks on the worst-hit beaches. Many species of birds and mammals are far below their pre-spill populations, including killer whales, sea otters, loons, cormorants, harbor seals, pigeon guillemots, and harlequin ducks. In addition, research shows that even tiny concentrations of crude oil can harm the eggs of pink salmon and herring. Herring fishers have been especially hard-hit, and the value of commercial salmon fishing permits has plummeted.

Shortly after the spill, Exxon renamed all its ships, replacing the "Exxon" with "Sea River"; if there's ever another Exxon-caused spill, its name won't be so indelibly etched into the news accounts. The 1989 spill led to enactment the following year of the Oil Pollution Act, which requires double-hulled tankers in Prince William Sound by 2015. Unfortunately, the aging single-hulled tankers are still used today. Many other measures have been taken to prevent a repeat, however, including the addition of large oceangoing tugs and response vessels (containing spill equipment) to escort all tankers.

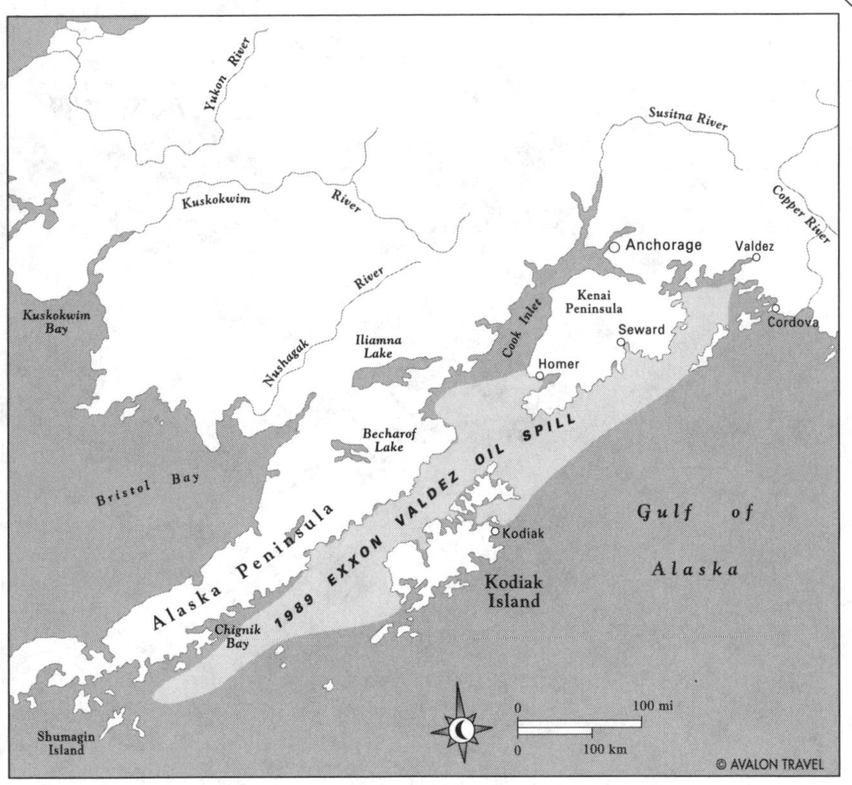

In a 1991 out-of-court settlement, Exxon agreed to a $900 million payout that has been used to buy land, reimburse cleanup expenses, and fund environmental research and restoration. More contentious was a 1994 case in which a jury awarded 40,000 commercial fishers and others damaged by the spill $5 billion in punitive damages. It was one of the biggest damage awards ever. Exxon dragged out the appeals process until 2008, when a Supreme Court packed with conservative justices ruled that Exxon's actions were "worse than negligent but less than malicious." The fishers ended up with $507 million instead of the original $5 billion the jury had awarded.

And what of Captain Hazelwood? He was convicted in 1990 of a misdemeanor charge of negligent discharge of oil. After nine years of appeals, Hazelwood was finally sentenced to 1,000 hours of community service, including working in an Anchorage soup kitchen.

For the latest on the spill, visit the *Exxon Valdez* Oil Spill Trustee Council website (www.evostc.state.ak.us).

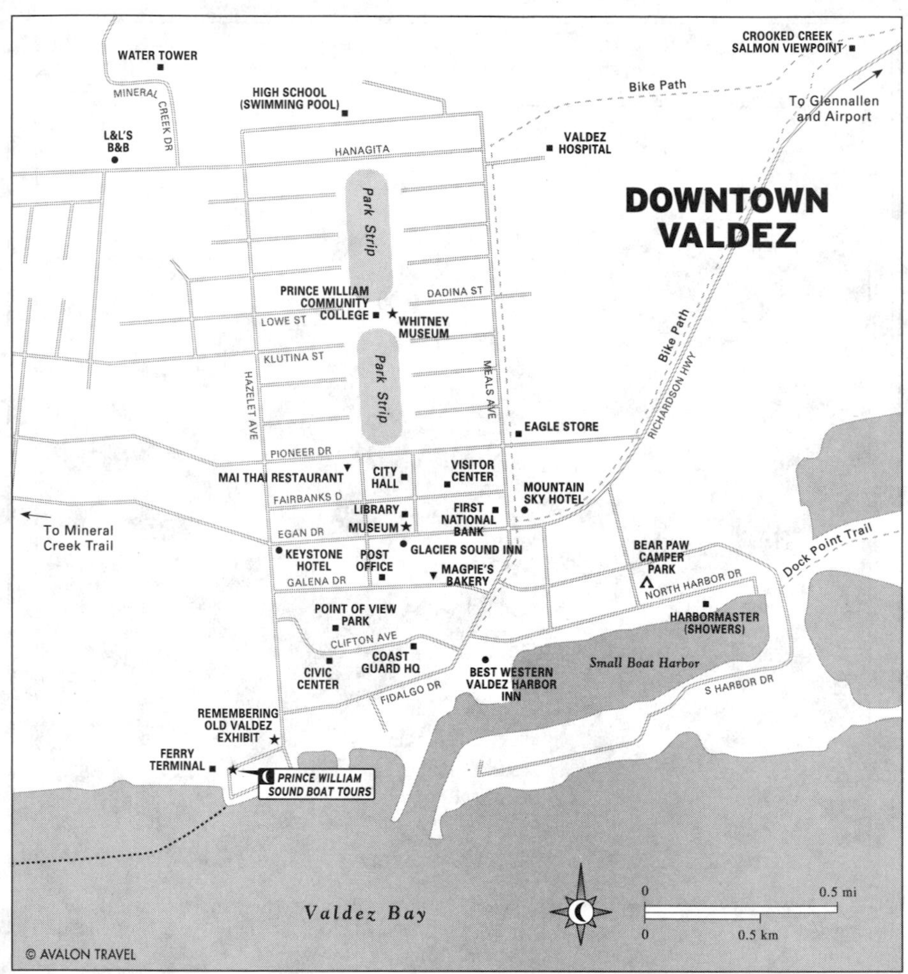

Remembering Old Valdez Exhibit (436 S. Hazelet St., 907/835-5407, daily 9 A.M.–5 P.M. mid-May–early Sept.) is a warehouse full of earthquake exhibits, including a sprawling 1:20 scale replica of Valdez as it appeared before the big one hit in 1964. You can also watch a video on the quake, check out the 1950 Wurlitzer, and watch the seismograph for more activity. There's even a 1950s Civil Defense Jeep on display. One entrance fee ($5 adults, $4.50 seniors, $4 ages 14–18, younger children free) gets you into both the Valdez Museum and the Remembering Old Valdez Exhibit.

The **Whitney Museum** (303 Lowe St., 907/834-1690, www.pwscc.edu, daily 9 A.M.–7 P.M. May–mid-Sept., $5 adults, $4 seniors, $3 kids) is a brand-new facility adjacent to Prince William Sound Community College. Housed here are items collected over several decades by Jeese and Maxine Whitney, including trophy big-game mounts, an Eskimo kayak and umiak, and a wide range of elaborate Native

Alaskan fur parkas, baskets, masks, dolls, and beautifully carved ivory pieces. Of particular interest is a large and elaborate model ship built of ivory and baleen; the Smithsonian Museum once attempted to purchase the piece. All told, Whitney Museum houses one of the largest collections of Native Alaskan art and artifacts anywhere. The museum also shows several videos, including one on the building of the Trans-Alaska Pipeline.

Down Meals Avenue by the harbor, bear left onto Clifton Drive and go up past Coast Guard Headquarters to the **Civic Center,** where a viewing pavilion has an interpretive signboard describing the pipeline terminal across the bay. Climb the steep stairs up to **Point of View Park** for the panorama of town.

Out of Town

The Forest Service's **Crooked Creek Information Site** (907/835-4680, daily 9 A.M.–6 P.M. late May–early Sept.) is out on the Richardson Highway about a mile from town. In late summer, walk out on the boardwalk to see salmon go through the final act of their incredible life cycle. The TV inside the information center provides a live underwater view of the spawning action for salmon voyeurs. A four-mile paved **bike path** leads north from town past Crooked Creek.

Continue out on the Richardson about 3.5 miles to where a historical sign points to **Old Valdez.** The only thing left of the old town site besides the post office foundation and memorial plaque are the mileposts on the Richardson: Mile 0 still starts here. In another three miles, turn right onto Dayville Road. In several miles you come to the hydroelectric plant and **Solomon Gulch Hatchery** (907/835-4874). Pause here to see the powerful small falls and to take a self-guided tour around this private pink and coho salmon hatchery. The staff is generally around to answer questions. Black bears sometimes emerge from the nearby forest to catch salmon in late summer. The **Alyeska Pipeline Terminal** is farther out on Dayville Road, but it's no longer open to the public due to security concerns.

TOURING PRINCE WILLIAM SOUND

Columbia Glacier

Prince William Sound has the greatest concentration of tidewater glaciers in Alaska, including Columbia Glacier, the stunning grandfather of glaciers in the Sound. Covering about 440 square miles, Columbia Glacier is 40 miles long and more than three miles wide at its face, which rises up to 250 feet above the water and plunges an incredible 2,000 feet below. Although it's the second largest of its kind in Alaska and still extends 15 miles out into its ancestral fjord, Columbia Glacier is but a minor remnant of the vast glacier that only a few thousand years ago filled Prince William Sound; its face reached a height of 4,000 feet.

Since 1982 the glacier has been in rapid retreat, at a rate averaging a half-mile per year. This retreat has filled Columbia Bay with icebergs, and tour boats can no longer get within six miles of the face. Ice in the bay has also caused navigational hazards in Prince William Sound, and it was to avoid ice that the *Exxon Valdez* took its fateful shortcut near, and onto, Bligh Reef. Scientists speculate that by the time the glacier stops its current rate of backward movement, a new fjord 25 miles long will be exposed, into which several calving glaciers will flow.

Prince William Sound Boat Tours

The state ferry pauses on its trip between Valdez and Whittier to view the Columbia Glacier, or you can join a private tour. Because of the glacier's recent movement back up the bay, boats can only get to within about six miles of the face. This changes, but does not diminish, the experience, as the boats cruise through and over the fields of drifting ice towering above the deck to see the glacier as more huge chunks shear off and drop into the bay. Beyond the glaciers, the main attraction of Prince William Sound is wildlife, including the chance to see humpback and killer (orca) whales, Dall's porpoises, sea otters, Steller sea lions, and other marine mammals. These

© DON PITCHER

Columbia Glacier

animals are most often seen on the southern end of the Sound, an all-day boat ride from Whittier or Valdez.

The ***Lu-Lu Belle*** (907/835-5141 or 800/411-0090, www.lulubelletours.com) is a comfortable 60-passenger boat with daily Columbia Glacier and wildlife tours ($100 for 5 hours or longer) in the summer. A snack bar is on board. This is a fun and personalized tour by owner-operator Fred Rodolf.

A larger company, **Stan Stephens Glacier & Wildlife Cruises** (907/835-4731 or 866/867-1297, www.stanstephenscruises.com, mid-May–mid-Sept.), has a seven-hour Columbia Glacier tour ($115 adults, $57 children) and a nine-hour trip ($150 adults, $75 children) that encompasses Columbia and Meares Glaciers, plus the sea lions of Glacier Island, and includes a big lunch.

State Parks

Three state marine parks (www.alaskastateparks.org) offer a variety of recreational opportunities within an hour's boat ride of Valdez. The serene forest-ringed **Sawmill Bay State Marine Park** has protected anchorage and good camping. For island camping and a fair-weather anchorage, visit **Jack Bay State Marine Park** on the east side of Valdez Narrows. At **Shoup Bay Marine Park** the Shoup Glacier spills into an iceberg-filled saltwater lagoon accessible on most high tides by sea kayaks and small boats. Visitors will enjoy this pretty bay with lots of icebergs and thousands of nesting kittiwakes.

EVENTS

Each June, the acclaimed **Last Frontier Theatre Conference** (www.pwscc.edu) takes place at the Civic Center. It's a weeklong theatrical event with performances and seminars by nationally known playwrights and actors.

Valdez has two popular summertime fishing derbies (907/835-5680, www.valdezfishderbies.com): the **Halibut Derby** all summer and **Silver Salmon Derby** in August. Each has a $15,000 top prize. Other popular summer events are the **4th of July** celebration as well as **Valdez Gold Rush Days** (www.valdezgoldrushdays.org) in early August, a week-long celebration complete with cancan girls, a hoosegow, a parade, and a fish fry.

RECREATION

Hiking

Get complete details on local hikes from the Forest Service's Crooked Creek visitors center. The easiest local path, the **Dock Point Trail,** starts from Kobuk Drive across from the boat ramp. This 0.75-mile trail (partially a boardwalk) has a grassy meadow and good viewpoints across Valdez Bay. **Mineral Creek Valley** is a beautiful canyon accessible from the north end of town via Mineral Creek Drive. A bumpy gravel road—great for mountain bikes—crosses the creek and then parallels it for the next 5.5 miles, ending at a locked gate. From here it's a one-mile walk to the abandoned W. L. Smith Stamp Mill (1913), which crushed ore from mines up the mountain. A number of beautiful waterfalls crowd the slopes of Mineral Creek Valley, so be sure to bring your camera.

The **Keystone Canyon Pack Trail** (a.k.a. Goat Trail or Trans-Alaska Military Trail) begins from a trailhead at Mile 14 on the Richardson Highway, climbing gradually 2.5 miles. The trail was built in 1899 by the Army to provide an "All-American" route to the gold fields, and this short portion was restored almost a century later.

For an excellent overnight trip, hike the **Shoup Bay Trail,** which begins from the west end of Egan Street. This trail affords views of Valdez and Valdez Bay, and passes a fine camping area along Gold Creek at three miles. It ends at Shoup Bay (across from majestic Shoup Glacier), 10 miles from town.

Sea Kayaking

If you've always wanted to learn how to kayak, or if you know how and want to explore Prince William Sound around Valdez in style, contact Hedy Sarney of **Anadyr Adventures** (225 N. Harbor Dr., 907/835-2814 or 800/865-2925, www.anadyradventures.com). Trips range from a kid-friendly three-hour natural history tour ($75) to customized mother-ship multiple-night tours. Especially popular are eight-hour Shoup Glacier trips ($189) and 10-hour Columbia Glacier paddles ($229), both of which include an open-water crossing by charter boat. Anadyr's most popular multiple-night trip is a five-day paddle that encompasses Columbia Glacier, Sawmill Bay, and Shoup Glacier ($965 or $1,225 with meals). Anadyr conducts other excursions of varying lengths, including boat-based and lodge-based trips, along with a remote drop-off and pickup service. They also rent kayaks, bikes, and camping gear, and the Alaskan arts and crafts sold here make it worth a visit even if you aren't planning to paddle.

Pangaea Adventures (101 N. Harbor Dr., 907/835-8442 or 800/660-9637, www.alaskasummer.com) also leads a wide range of sea kayaking trips. Least expensive is a two-hour paddle around the duck flats ($59), but more challenging are day trips to Gold Creek ($99), Shoup Glacier ($179), and Columbia Glacier ($229). The Columbia Glacier trip lasts 10 hours and includes a water-taxi ride to and from the glacier, along with time to explore this magnificent place. Longer trips are available, along with kayak rentals if you just want to head out on your own. Pangaea also leads ice-climbing trips to Worthington Glacier.

Rafting

Keystone Raft and Kayak Adventures (907/835-2606 or 800/328-8460, www.alaskawhitewater.com) offers an exciting two-hour raft trip down the Class III Lowe River through Keystone Canyon for $55. Other choices include a half-day trip on the Tsaina River (Class IV, $105) near Thompson Pass and all-day Tonsina River trips (Class III–IV, $165), 80 miles from town. Trips depart from their office at Mile 17 on the Richardson Highway; transport from Valdez is extra. Also ask about longer trips throughout the Copper River Valley.

Fishing and Biking

Valdez has three dozen charter fishing and cruising boats. Contact the visitors center for a listing, or visit their website (www.valdezalaska.org). **Fish Central** (907/835-5090 or 888/835-5002, www.fishcentral.net) books fishing charters, boat rentals, and sightseeing trips. Find them next to the boat harbor. Rent mountain bikes from Anadyr Adventures.

Winter Sports

When winter comes, Keystone Canyon's waterfalls freeze, making them destinations for ice climbers, particularly during the Ice Climbing Festival in February. Valdez itself gets some of the heaviest snowfalls anywhere in Alaska, averaging 25 feet per year; the record came in the winter of 1989–1990 with 47 feet! It isn't uncommon to arrive in March to find the town buried to the rooftops in snow. More snow falls here than at any other sea-level location in North America. Because of all this snow, the area can be a winter-lovers' paradise, especially since the temperature rarely drops below 20°F. Groomed cross-country ski trails are maintained in Mineral Creek Valley.

Several companies offer heli-skiing at Thompson Pass for the ultimate mountain skiing adventure: **Valdez Heli-Ski Guides** (907/835-4528, www.valdezheliskiguides.com), **Valdez Heli-Camps** (907/783-3243, www.valdezhelicamps.com), **Alaska Backcountry Adventures** (530/581-1767 or 888/729-9222, www.swayback.com), and **H2O Guides** (907/835-8418 or 800/578-4354, www.alaskahelicopterskiing.com).

ACCOMMODATIONS

Valdez has a good selection of lodging places, but book a room well ahead for July–August, when most rooms get taken early. Visit the Valdez Convention and Visitors Bureau website (www.valdezalaska.org) for links to most local lodging places; their office keeps a list of who has rooms available.

Hotels and Motels

Keystone Hotel (Hazelet Ave. and Egan Ave., 907/835-3851 or 888/835-0665, www.keystonehotel.com, late May–early Sept.) has cramped little guest rooms ($85 s, $95 d) with thin walls and older furnishings. Larger guest rooms with two double beds are $105 d, and units with space for four and two baths are $115. The hotel is clean and a continental breakfast is included, as well as limited Wi-Fi. Hurriedly built from ATCO trailers in 1989, the building was originally constructed as headquarters for the oil spill cleanup, so it may not appeal to everyone.

The **Best Western Valdez Harbor Inn** (100 Fidalgo Dr., 907/835-3434 or 888/222-3440, www.valdezharborinn.com, $170 d) faces the small boat harbor, and is generally considered the best lodging option in town. Amenities include a hot buffet breakfast, free airport shuttle, a workout room, and Wi-Fi, plus a decent restaurant (Alaskan Bistro) on the premises.

Totem Inn (144 E. Egan Dr., 907/835-4443 or 888/808-4431, www.toteminn.com) has a variety of lodging options, including standard guest rooms with fridges and microwaves ($179 d), cabins ($199 d) with kitchenettes, and apartment suites ($219 d) with full kitchens, washers, and dryers. There is also free Wi-Fi.

Mountain Sky Hotel (100 Meals Ave., 907/835-4445 or 800/478-4445, www.mountainskyhotelsuite.com) features an indoor pool, a hot tub, an exercise room, microwaves, small fridges, Wi-Fi, and continental breakfast. Standard rooms are $179 d, and a variety of two-room suites ($199 d) with full kitchens are also available, including ones with king beds and jetted tubs, as well as others for families.

Bed-and-Breakfasts

Brookside Inn B&B (907/835-9130 or 866/316-9130, www.brooksideinnbb.com) is a quaint home with a long history. Constructed in 1898, it survived the earthquake and was moved to new Valdez. The five guest rooms are $135 d, and the private suite costs $160 d; all have private baths. A full breakfast is served, kids are welcome, and Wi-Fi is available. The front porch and the hot tub on the back deck are good places to relax.

Located 1.5 miles from town, **Wild Roses by the Sea B&B** (907/835-2930, www.alaskabytheseabnb.com) sits atop a bluff with an incredible view across Port Valdez. The home features a mix of Chinese and Alaskan decor, plus a delicious full breakfast. Two guest rooms ($134–155 d) and a separate apartment ($173 d) are available, all with private baths.

L&L's B&B (533 W. Hanagita St., 907/835-4447, www.lnlalaska.com, $75–85 d) is a large and modern home with five immaculate guest rooms sharing three baths, continental breakfasts, and Wi-Fi.

CAMPING

The closest public campground is five miles away. Go back out on the Richardson Highway, turn left toward the airport, and continue another mile past it to the **Valdez Glacier Campground** (907/873-4058, $15). This large and scenic campground has picnic and barbecue areas, outhouses, and water, plus a nearby waterfall and nesting eagles. It's operated by the Army's Fort Greely, but is open to the public with equipment rentals available (including tents, sleeping bags, mountain bikes, and fishing gear).

Allison Point Campground (907/835-2282, $10–12) is on Dayville Road near the Alyeska oil terminal, with toilets and water but no electricity. There's good fishing from shore nearby.

Find **public showers** at the harbormaster's office (corner of Meals Ave. and Harbor Dr.) across from the chamber of commerce. Showers are also available from **Like Home Laundromat** (Egan Dr. near Meals Ave., 907/835-2913). A better deal is the **swimming pool** at Valdez High School (907/835-3200), where the showers are free with a swim.

Large RV parks abound right in Valdez: **Bear Paw Camper Park** (907/835-2530, www.bearpawrvpark.com), **Bayside RV Park** (907/835-4425 or 888/835-4425, www.baysiderv.com), **Sea Otter RV Park** (907/835-2787 or 800/831-2787), and **Eagle's Rest RV Park** (907/835-2373 or 800/553-7275, www.eaglesrestrv.com). Open May–September, these are primarily for RVs ($35–45), but tent spaces ($20–25) may be available. Bear Paw and Sea Otter are right along the waterfront.

FOOD

Magpies Bakery (224 Galena St., 907/461-3092, www.magpiesbakery.com, Tues.–Fri. 7 A.M.–5 P.M., Sat. 7 A.M.–3 P.M., closed Sun., Mon., and winter Sat.) has daily breads, fresh-baked cinnamon rolls, bear claws, breakfast sandwiches, and lunchtime soups, plus pies, cookies, and other treats—not to mention the best local espresso. It's a great place to relax with friends.

Located right along the water, **Harbor Café** (255 N. Harbor Dr., 907/835-4776) serves upscale fast-food: burgers, crunchy halibut burritos, sandwiches, and salads. Also of note for lunch is the local health food store, **Rogue's Garden** (354 Fairbanks Dr., 907/835-5880), with bagels, sandwiches, organic espresso, and smoothies.

Ernesto's Taqueria (326 Egan St., 907/835-2519) serves authentic, reasonable, and tasty Mexican meals, including $10 lunch specials. They open early (7 A.M.) in summer but serve lunch and dinner only in winter.

Fu Kung (207 Kobuk Dr., 907/835-5255, daily 11 A.M.–11 P.M.) occupies a Quonset hut and, in addition to the expected Chinese favorites, also has seafood (try the mu shu shrimp), sushi, and lunch specials. Find Thai meals at **Mai Thai** (310 Pioneer Dr., 907/835-5606). Best pizzas around? Cruise over to **No Name Pizza** (121 Egan St., 907/835-4419).

Get groceries at **Eagle** (907/835-2100), the Safeway-owned market near Egan Avenue.

INFORMATION AND SERVICES

The **Valdez Visitors Information Center** (200 Fairbanks St., 907/835-4636, www.valdezalaska.org, Mon.–Fri. 8 A.M.–7 P.M., Sun. 8 A.M.–6 P.M. Apr.–Sept., Mon.–Fri. 8 A.M.–5 P.M. Oct.–Mar.) is across from city hall. Out front are phones with direct lines to local businesses, including several B&Bs.

The **Valdez Consortium Library** (Fairbanks St., 907/835-4632, www.ci.valdez.ak.us/library, Sun. 1–5 P.M., Mon. and Fri. 10 A.M.–6 P.M., Tues.–Thurs. 10 A.M.–8 P.M., Sat. noon–5 P.M.) has computers for checking your email and shows a 30-minute video on Valdez on request. **Anadyr Adventures** (225 N. Harbor Dr., 907/835-2814 or 800/865-2925) also has Web access (as do RV parks and hotels), and their gift shop sells quality Alaskan arts and crafts.

GETTING THERE

Valdez is 366 miles from Fairbanks on the Richardson Highway; from Anchorage it's 189 miles on the Glenn Highway to Glennallen, then another 115 on the Richardson Highway. **Valdez U-Drive** (907/835-4402 or 800/478-4402, www.valdezudrive.com) has rental cars at the airport.

Era Aviation (907/266-8394 or 800/866-8394, www.frontierak.com) flies between Valdez and Anchorage several times a day. The airport is four miles outside town; call a **Yellow Cab** (907/835-2500) to get a ride into town.

Ferry

The **Alaska Marine Highway** (907/465-3941 or 800/642-0066, www.dot.state.ak.us/amhs) has daily ferry service connecting Valdez with Whittier and Cordova on both the high-speed *Chenega* and the older (and much slower) *Aurora*. A Forest Service naturalist is on board for summer sailings, and the trip to Whittier includes time among the icebergs near Columbia Glacier.

Cordova

Cordova (pop. 2,200) is noticeably less populated, less prosperous, and less accessible than its big-sister city Valdez—and most people like it that way. Though only a ferry ride away, its setting is its own, its climate is milder and wetter, and its vibration is nothing like Valdez's. Cordova might feel more at home somewhere between Petersburg and Juneau: connected only by boat and plane, with a large commercial fishing fleet, lush forests, small islands, and snowcapped peaks.

But Cordova is more than just the coast; it's also Chugach National Forest, Prince William Sound, and their abundant outdoor recreation; the Copper River and its wild rides and massive delta; spectacular Childs Glacier; railroad history and the Million Dollar Bridge. Amid all of this is a bustling little community bursting at its seams during the summer fishing season, but also glued together by the magic of the fishing lifestyle. Drift over to Cordova and spend a couple of days exploring this special corner of Alaska—you'll be glad you did.

HISTORY

In 1884, Army Captain William Abercrombie surveyed the Copper River delta, which made the area known to a few hardy prospectors. The crazed stampede of 1897–1898 opened up the area to settlement. Still, in 1905, Cordova was little more than a couple of canneries processing the pinks and silvers from the Sound. Then Michael J. Heney showed up.

After years of surveying rights-of-way, watching railroad ventures to the rich coal and copper mines nearby start and fold, and failing to convince the Morgan-Guggenheim Alaska Syndicate not to start its road from Katalla, Heney invested his entire savings and in 1907 began laying track from Cordova toward Kennecott Mines. After the Katalla facilities were destroyed by a storm, the syndicate bought the Copper River and Northwestern line from Heney and completed it in 1911 at a total cost of $23 million; by 1917 it had hauled over $100 million in ore to Cordova for transshipment to smelters. Cordova was a boomtown until the Kennecott Mines closed in 1938.

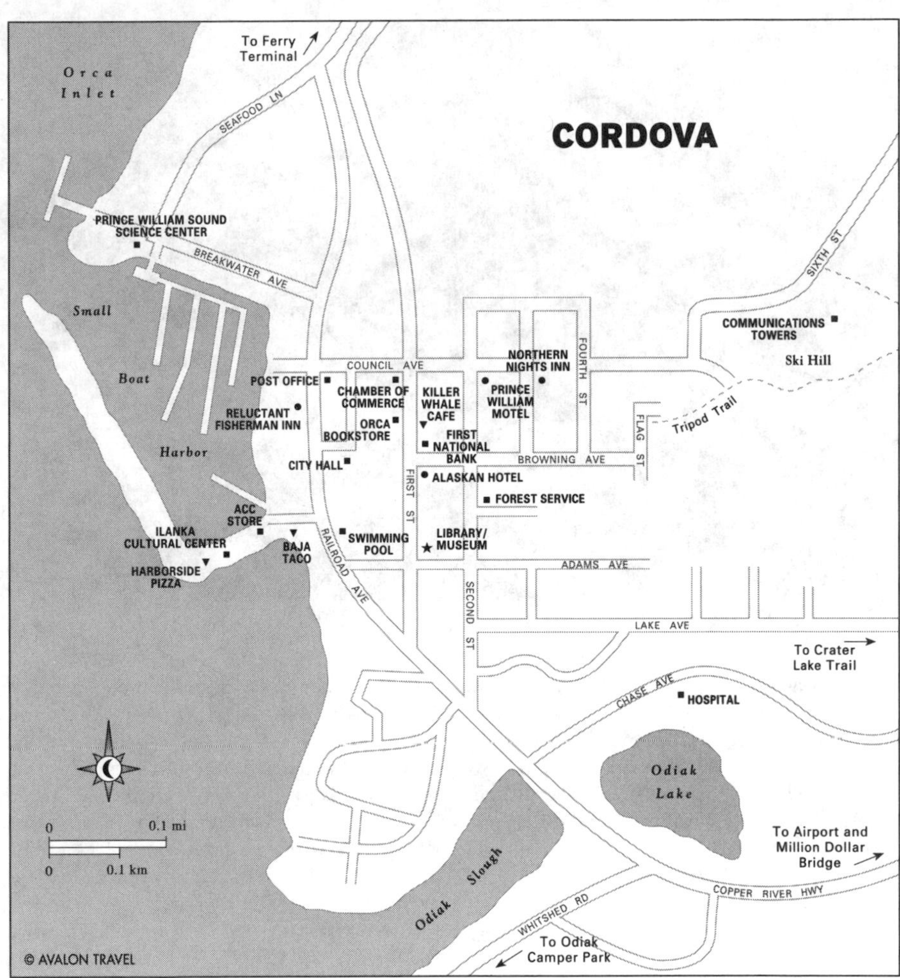

The 1964 earthquake caused extensive damage to the town, and uplifted the sea floor six feet. Since then the town's economy has reverted to fishing and canning. The year-round population doubles in the summer, and in good years there's plenty of work. The town's fishing fleet tops 800 vessels at the peak of the sockeye salmon season.

Copper River red and king salmon have attained an almost mythical status. The first major run of Alaska salmon each summer, they're prized for their rich flavor and deep red color, and always garner a high price. Anchorage restaurants often compete to get the first shipment of these salmon, and others are shipped by air directly to markets and restaurants throughout the United States. Find out more at www.copperriversalmon.org.

SIGHTS

Anything you want to know about Cordova you can find out at the **Cordova Chamber of**

© DON PITCHER

seafarer's memorial, Cordova

Commerce (404 1st St., 907/424-7260, www.cordovachamber.com, Mon.–Fri. 9 A.M.–5 P.M. year-round). Also stop by the Chugach National Forest **Cordova Ranger District office** (2nd Ave., 907/424-7661, www.fs.fed.us/r10/chugach) for local maps, handouts, and info on cabins and trails.

The **Cordova Historical Museum** (622 1st St., 907/424-6665, www.cordovamuseum.org, Thurs.–Fri. 10 A.M.–5 P.M., Sat. 1–5 P.M. summer, Tues.–Sat. 1–5 P.M. the rest of the year, $1) is in the Centennial Building. This museum is small but packed with artifacts, including an old Linotype, an ancient slot machine, a three-seat *baidarka,* and an amusing exhibit on Cordova's famous Iceworm Festival. Look for the aerial views of earthquake damage to the Million Dollar Bridge. The 30-minute *Cordova Story* is shown daily. Next door is the **Cordova Library** (907/424-6667, www.cordovalibrary.org, Tues.–Fri. 10 A.M.–8 P.M., Sat. 1–5 P.M.), a good place to read, rest, check your email (free Wi-Fi), and meet fellow travelers.

Many buildings around town were built during Cordova's original construction in 1908, including, on 1st Street, the Alaskan Hotel and Cordova House, as well as the Red Dragon, the oldest building in town, which served weekdays as a rowdy clubhouse but on Sundays became a church when the altar was let down by ropes from the beams. Pick up the historic walking-tour map at the museum for a complete list of the old buildings.

Adjacent to the harbor, the **Ilanka Cultural Center** (110 Nicholoff Way, 907/424-7903, www.ilankacenter.org, Mon.–Fri. 10 A.M.–5 P.M. summer, Tues.–Fri. 10 A.M.–5 P.M. winter, donation) houses a small collection of Eyak Native pieces—both prehistoric and modern—as well as a fine gift shop and a workshop space; but the real attraction is the killer whale skeleton that hangs along the entryway, one of just five in the world.

Located at the harbor entrance, the **Prince William Sound Science Center** (907/424-5800, www.pwssc.org, Mon.–Fri. 9 A.M.–5 P.M.) is a scientific facility for research and education on the regional ecosystem. There are no exhibits to speak of, but you may want to stop by with questions about the *Exxon Valdez* spill and how it has affected Prince William Sound, or just to enjoy the view from the waterfront deck.

COPPER RIVER HIGHWAY

There aren't enough superlatives in the English language to describe adequately the 50-mile ride out on the Copper River Highway from Cordova to the famous Million Dollar Bridge. The scenery—mountains, glaciers, the river, and the delta—rivals any 50 miles of road on the continent, never mind the state. The wildlife—thousands of shorebirds and ducks, Canada geese, trumpeter swans, bald eagles, moose, bears, and spawning salmon—gives Denali a run for its money. The history encompasses punching an early-20th-century railroad 200 miles into the Interior and starting a road in the 1960s on its right-of-way, only to be destroyed by the largest earthquake ever recorded in North America. The crowning glory of the trip, as visible in rain or fog as in bright sunshine, built at great expense and great danger in 1910 between the faces of two moving glaciers and left mostly standing by the earthquake, is the Million Dollar Bridge, the vista from which is unsurpassed in a land of unsurpassed vistas.

Just outside of town, the Copper River Highway passes beautiful **Eyak Lake** at the base of Eyak Mountain. Notice how the lake is two colors, deep blue and light green, which don't merge. From around Mile 6 at the bridge over Eyak River to Mile 12 where the pavement ends, keep a sharp eye out for waterfowl and wildlife in the runoff sloughs from nearby Scott Glacier. Take a left at Mile 13 (across from the airport road) and follow a two-mile gravel road up to **Cabin Lake,** with trout fishing, picnic tables, and trails to three other lakes.

At Mile 14, another left and another four miles of gravel bring you to the **Mt. Sheridan** trailhead; hike a mile on the 4WD extension spur and scramble up on the ridge to look out over the two-finger **Sheridan Glacier** flowing down either side of the mountain, and the iceberg-clogged lake at its face. A side road to the right at Mile 17 goes off to **Alaganik Slough;** the three rough miles are excellent for viewing shorebirds. Picnic tables and an information plaque occupy the end of the road, and you can pitch a tent anywhere along here.

The **Haystack Trail** at Mile 19 is a little under a mile, mostly uphill over boardwalks and through second-growth forest. It terminates at a wonderful overlook spot, affording sweeping views of the delta, well worth the short trek. This is a good place to find moose and bears. At Mile 21, the **Pipeline Lakes Trail** leads to the south on a marshy two-mile path. The Forest Service's **McKinley Trail Cabin** is just off the highway at Mile 22. From here, it's an easy two-mile saunter along **McKinley Lake Trail** to McKinley Lake where you can fish for trout or stay in a second cabin.

Across the River

At Mile 27, you cross the first of nearly a dozen bridges and causeways to the other "side" of the Copper River, more than 10 miles distant—it might remind you of the Florida Keys. Long Island, from Mile 28 to Mile 34, sits smack in the middle of the mighty river delta. Out here you can understand why, out of 196 miles of track from Cordova to Kennicott, 96 miles were built over bridges or trestles.

Finally, at Mile 48, you arrive at **Million Dollar Bridge.** This bridge, which cost a little over $1 million to build in 1910, was the culmination of Michael Heney's vision, faith, and employee loyalty—not to mention the uncanny abilities of his civil engineers. It had to be built entirely in winter, when the Childs Glacier was dormant. The working conditions were unbearable at best, and the danger was extreme, especially as the builders raced to finish the final span even as its supports were being washed away by breakup. The north span collapsed in the 1964 earthquake, but the state eventually repaired the structure.

Childs Glacier

On the Million Dollar Bridge, look to your left at the massive face of the Childs Glacier;

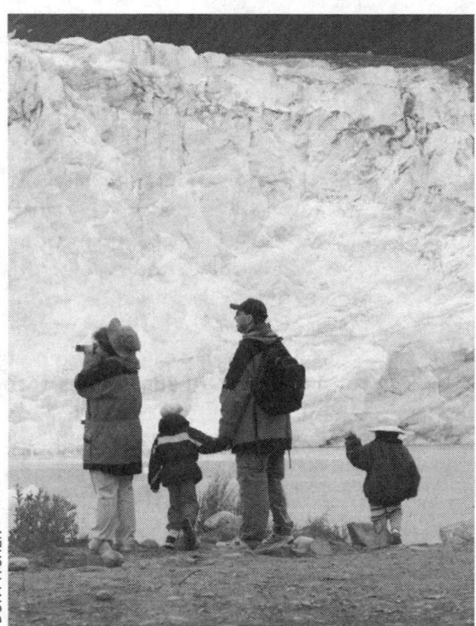
© DON PITCHER
Childs Glacier

look right about three miles across Miles Lake to the **Miles Glacier,** which has receded more than two miles since 1910. A short side road on the left just before the bridge leads to a viewing pavilion set up on a small bluff over the river. From here you can safely view the face of Childs Glacier, under cover from the often inclement weather. Informative displays give you something to read while you wait for huge chunks of ice to fall into the river. Plan to spend all afternoon here as the glacier creaks, groans, and cracks, dropping calves into the river. Be careful of particularly big calves, whose waves can roll across the river in a few seconds and splash high up the embankment. This is the only road-accessible glacier in Alaska where you will see so much calving action. Don't miss it!

ENTERTAINMENT AND EVENTS

Cordova's **Iceworm Festival** (www.iceworm.org) comes to town the first full week of February. A 140-foot "iceworm" parades through the streets during this offbeat festival. Other events include a fun fair, a talent show, the crowning of Miss Iceworm, fireworks, and various wacky contests.

The big springtime event is the **Copper River Delta Shorebird Festival** in early May. Held as the first shorebirds appear, it includes workshops, educational seminars, a seafood dinner, and guided field trips to witness the migration of millions of shorebirds.

The arrival of the justly famous Copper River reds (sockeye salmon) is cause for celebration in this fishing town. The **Copper River Wild Salmon Festival** (www.copperriverwild.org) in early June includes a community salmon feed, street dance, and marathon race up the Copper River Highway. One of the more unique annual events is the **Cordova Fungus Festival** in early September, with workshops, gourmet dining, and experts from the world of mushrooms. The **Eyak Sobriety Celebration** in mid-November attracts Native Alaskan dancers from across the state.

Don't come to Cordova for the night life; other than drinking with the fishers, it's strictly make-your-own. The **Alaskan** and **Cordova** bars, next to each other on 1st Avenue, and the **Anchor Bar** on Breakwater Avenue, are all hardcore. The Alaskan sometimes has live bands on summer weekends. At the **Powder House** a mile out the Copper River Highway, you can have a drink on the deck along Eyak Lake.

RECREATION

Hiking

Two trails climb **Mt. Eyak**—one through the forest, the other up the ski slope. The unmarked **Tripod Trail** is a little hard to find, but if you cut to the right between a cabin and a driveway near the end of 5th Street, you'll see the trailhead. This is a pretty hike through forest primeval, with salmonberries ripe for the picking in August. Otherwise, head straight up Council Avenue, bear left onto 6th Street, and follow it around the communications apparatus. You can start right up the mountain from there, and you don't have to go far to get a great view of the town and harbor.

The excellent **Crater Lake Trail** begins opposite Skaters Cabin on Eyak Lake, two miles from town beyond the old cemetery, the seaplane base, and the municipal airstrip. The trail climbs 1,500 feet in two miles through a beautiful forest, with panoramic views near the top of Eyak Lake and the Heney Range. The terrain around Crater Lake is fairly open, and it would be easy to scale the surrounding summits if you have the time and energy. Allow a minimum of two hours round-trip from the road to the lake. The trail is solid and very easy to follow; even if a wet wind is blowing, it will be relatively still in the forest, but be careful not to slip. Don't miss this one.

At the end of Power Creek Road, six miles from town, a trail leads about a mile up to Ohman Falls—and when you see it you'll definitely say, "Oh, man!" Continue another three miles on **Power Creek Trail** to the Power Creek Cabin.

The Forest Service maintains a number of trails along the Copper River Highway. Pick up a handout on these hikes at the Forest Service office in Cordova (907/424-7661).

Cabins

Ten **Forest Service cabins** are available for rent (518/885-3639 or 877/444-6777, www.recreation.gov, $35) in the Cordova area; all but three are accessible only by plane or boat. There are cabins at both ends of the McKinley Lake Trail. If you've never seen one, hike for 75 yards up the McKinley Lake Trail (Mile 20) and peer in the windows. Staying here is quiet (except for the spawning salmon), secluded, and beautiful. The other foot-accessible cabin (Power Creek Cabin) is four miles north of Cordova via the Power Creek Trail.

On the Water

Alaska River Expeditions (907/424-7238 or 800/776-1864, www.alaskarafters.com) guides fun half-day adventures, including hiking and rafting trips on the Sheridan River ($95), Sheridan Glacier trekking ($95), and ice-climbing classes ($125). Multiday trips go all the way up to 10-day raft trips ($2,500) from headwaters of the Copper River to the Million Dollar Bridge. These are good folks.

The MV ***Auklet*** (907/424-3428, www.auklet.com) is a classic wooden boat that has been used as a fisheries research vessel. Captain Dave Janka leads overnight or multiple-night adventure cruises around Prince William Sound.

Cordova Coastal Outfitters (907/424-7424 or 800/357-5145, www.cdvcoastal.com) is a one-stop operation with sea kayak day trips and overnight tours, wildlife cruises in Orca Inlet, and shorebird jet-boat trips on the Copper River Delta. In addition they rent gear, including kayaks, canoes, small boats, inflatables, mountain bikes, fishing poles, and camping supplies. They even provide drop-offs and pickups by van or boat.

Cordova's Olympic-size **swimming pool** (907/424-7282) is on Railroad Avenue.

ACCOMMODATIONS

The Cordova Chamber's website (www.cordovachamber.com) has links to most local lodging places. Add a 12 percent lodging tax to the rates below.

In the heart of town on 1st Street, the **Alaskan Hotel** (907/424-3299) is an old-time place with eight clean and well-maintained guest rooms over the Alaska Bar. Noise and smoke carry up from below on weekends, but it's inexpensive and authentic. Six simple rooms with no phones or TVs and a bath down the hall are only $50 d; larger rooms with private baths cost $74 d.

Operated by the Salvation Army, **Red Shield Inn** (514 1st St., 907/424-3134, $90 d) is certainly Cordova's most unique lodging choice. Two furnished studio apartments are available with full kitchens (including dishes and pans) and two double beds; book a month or more ahead for the peak of summer.

The Reluctant Fisherman (407 Railroad Ave., 907/424-3272, www.reluctantfisherman.com, $150–170 d) provides pleasant accommodations, plus a popular restaurant and lounge. Rooms are large, but request a remodeled unit facing the harbor. A continental breakfast is included, along with Wi-Fi and guest computers.

Built in 1910, **Northern Nights Inn** (500 3rd St., 907/424-5356, www.northernnightsinn.com, $75–115 d) has four newly renovated rooms with private baths and entrances, kitchenettes, and Wi-Fi in a lovely downtown home above the harbor.

The **Prince William Motel** (501 2nd St., 907/424-3201 or 888/796-6835, www.pwmotel.com, $120 d) has 16 attractive rooms. All include fridges, microwaves, and Wi-Fi; kitchenettes are $20 extra.

An old cannery just north of Cordova has been transformed into **Orca Adventure Lodge** (907/424-7249 or 866/424-6722, www.orcaadventurelodge.com, Mar.–Sept., $155 d). The rambling buildings sit right on the water. The old bunkhouse rooms are very plain but include private baths and ocean vistas. Meals are available (good breakfasts) along with kayak rentals. You can also book a wide range of activities, from white-water rafting and flightseeing in summer to wintertime heli-skiing.

Bayside B&B (907/424-3675, www.cordovabayside.com, $85 d) is a comfortable home two miles out of town along Orca Inlet. The unit includes two beds, a private bath, and a stocked kitchenette to create your own breakfast.

Bear's Den Cabins (a.k.a. Eyak River Lodge, 907/424-7168, www.alaskaeyakriverlodge.com, May–mid-Oct., $150–200 d) consists of five delightful cabins (with kitchens, private baths, and a canoe) situated along the Eyak River six miles from town. The largest cabin sleeps eight. During the silver salmon season in August–September the rate is $200 per day per person, including a skiff and motor.

For something unique, **Cordova Rose Lodge** (1315 Whitshed Rd., 907/424-7673, www.cordovarose.com, Apr.–mid-Oct., $135 d) has rooms in a converted landlocked barge filled with nautical antiques and photos. The private lighthouse actually acts as a navigation aid for ships. Rates include a full sourdough pancake breakfast and a sauna.

Cordova Lighthouse Inn (907/424-7673, www.cordovalighthouseinn.com) has the same owners and a great location right next to the small boat harbor. Six guest rooms ($135 d) and two suites ($199 d) all include private baths, fridges, Wi-Fi, and access to a big kitchen. Request a harbor-side room.

Two comfy places provide private apartments or homes three miles out of town near Eyak Lake: **Bear Country Lodge** (907/424-5901, www.bearcountrylodge.net, $100–125 d) and **Eyak River Hideaway** (907/424-3922, www.eyakriverhideaway.com, $125 d, $225 for up to 4 people).

Lighthouse

For something totally out of the ordinary, spend time at **Cape St. Elias Lighthouse** on Kayak Island in the wild Gulf of Alaska 60 air miles southeast of Cordova. This 22-mile-long and 2-mile-wide island was the first place that Europeans landed on the northwest coast of North America. Captain Vitus Bering set foot here in 1741, and the island remains virtually unchanged more than two and a half centuries later.

The nonprofit **Cape St. Elias Lightkeepers Association** (907/424-5182, www.kayakisland.org) works with the Coast Guard to preserve the lighthouse at the southern end of the island. The old lightkeeper's house still needs work, but you can stay in a comfortable cabin with a kitchen, a woodstove, and space for 10 people for $70 d. There is no electricity or running water, and you'll need to hike 1.5 hours from where the plane lands on the beach. It costs around $700 round-trip to fly three people from Cordova to Kayak Island. The lighthouse (built in 1916) is of interest, a Steller sea lion haul-out and seabird rookery are nearby, and the beachcombing is some of the best in Alaska, with lots of glass balls.

CAMPING

City-run **Odiak Camper Park** (907/424-7282, mid-Apr.–Sept.) is a half-mile out on Whitshed Road. Camping on this gravel-surfaced area overlooking Orca Inlet is $5 for tents (with showers) and RV sites with electricity are $20 (reservations required). Showers are also available at the harbormaster's office.

If you've got wheels, head out of town toward the Million Dollar Bridge, and as soon as you pass Mile 17, you're on Forest Service land. You can theoretically camp anywhere after this point, but the most comfortable places are at the roadside picnic area at Mile 22, or at the parking area of Alaganik Slough.

Out near the airport at Mile 13, **Alaska River Expeditions** (907/424-7238 or 800/776-1864, www.alaskarafters.com, June–mid-Oct., $15) provides a dozen forested campsites.

FOOD

Killer Whale Cafe (507 1st Ave., 907/424-7733) is a fine brunch spot. The big breakfast menu includes omelets, biscuits and gravy, and waffles, while lunchtime (around $10) features sandwiches, homemade soups, burgers, and salads, along with baked goods and espresso.

The wood-fired oven at **Harborside Pizza** (Nicholoff Way, 907/424-3730, closed Sun.) is put to great use baking creative pizzas, available by the pie or slice to go. They'll deliver to your hotel for $2 extra.

Head two miles out on the Copper River Highway to **Powder House Bar and Restaurant** (907/424-3529, daily 11 A.M.–9:30 P.M., dinner $17–28), where a deck overlooks pretty Lake Eyak. (Their motto: "I got blasted at the Powder House.") Sandwiches, burgers, and soups are featured, but there are also daily lunch specials along with steak, halibut, clams, and salmon dinners. Powder House is now smoke-free.

OK Restaurant (616 1st St., 907/424-3433), serves better-than-OK Chinese, Korean, and American dishes, plus fresh sushi.

Alaska Commercial Co. (Nickoloff Rd., 907/424-7141, www.alaskacommercial.com, daily 8 A.M.–9 P.M. Apr.–Sept.) is Cordova's supermarket. Nearby is **Baja Taco** (907/424-5599, www.bajatacoak.com, $11 or less), where the friendly staff serves fish tacos, veggie burritos, chicken mole, breakfast burritos, espresso, and other fast food. Order from the kitchen in the funky old red bus and enjoy your meal in the adjacent building with a wraparound deck. Baja has free Wi-Fi.

The Reluctant Fisherman (407 Railroad Ave., 907/424-7445, www.reluctantfisherman.com, daily 11:30 A.M.–10 P.M., dinner entrées $17–24) is a surf-and-turf restaurant and lounge with a big back deck to take in the harbor action; free Wi-Fi is available.

SERVICES

Orca Book and Sound (501 1st St., 907/424-5305) is a longtime fixture, with a good choice of regional titles, big art lining the walls, computer rentals upstairs, and free Wi-Fi.

Jenny Parks of **Copper River Fleece** (504 1st St., 907/424-4304 or 800/882-1707, www.copperriverfleece.com) crafts handsewn outerwear using wind-stop material and displays them in her downtown shop. The designs are beautiful, warm, and durable. These garments are recommended, but be sure to bring your wallet.

Cordova Community Medical Center (Chase Ave., 907/424-8000, www.cdvcmc.com) is the local hospital.

GETTING THERE

Ferry

The **Alaska Marine Highway** (907/465-3941 or 800/642-0066, www.dot.state.ak.us/amhs) has daily ferry service connecting Cordova with Whittier and Valdez on both the high-speed *Chenega* and the older (and much slower) *Aurora;* a Forest Service naturalist is on board. It's a 20-minute walk from the Cordova ferry terminal to town; take a right at the fork onto Railroad Avenue to avoid the 1st Avenue hill, then walk up Council Avenue.

Air

The airport is 13 miles from town out on the Copper River Highway. **Alaska Airlines** (800/426-0333, www.alaskaair.com) provides daily connections to Anchorage, Yakutat, and Juneau. **Era Aviation** (907/266-8394 or 800/866-8394, www.frontierak.com) flies turboprops two or three times a day between

Cordova and Anchorage. **Cordova Air Service** (907/424-3289) has flightseeing and charter flights throughout Prince William Sound.

GETTING AROUND

If you want to get out to the glaciers or Million Dollar Bridge, you have two options. You can ferry your own car across from Valdez, but advance reservations are required. **Chinook Auto Rentals** (907/424-5279 or 877/424-5279, www.chinookautorentals.com) has a variety of cars, SUVs, and vans for $55–85 per day.

Catch a cab to town from the airport ($25) or within the downtown area ($8) from **Cordova Taxicab** (907/424-5151). Half-hour town tours are $30.

Whittier

Named for poet John Greenleaf Whittier, this town of 300 friendly people has a picturesque mountains-and-bay setting. Unfortunately, the town itself is anything but poetic, and several other less flattering words come more quickly to mind. Thousands of tourists pass through this settlement every week, but very few choose to spend much time in this strange place where the entire population lives in concrete high-rises and the wind never seems to stop. Ask an Alaskan about Whittier and you're likely to hear the little ditty, "Nothing could be shittier than a day in Whittier." OK, perhaps I'm too harsh, since Whittier *does* have a gorgeous setting and lots of great outdoorsy things to do on nearby Prince William Sound. So come here for the surrounding land, but don't expect to fall in love with the town, no matter how poetic the name.

HISTORY

While less well known than the Alaska Highway, the construction of the railway to Whittier was one of the great engineering feats of World War II. Two tunnels, 1 mile and 2.5 miles long, were carved through the Chugach Mountains to link the military bases in Anchorage and Fairbanks to a secret saltwater port. Seward, the main ice-free port in Southcentral Alaska at that time, was considered too vulnerable to Japanese attack, so in 1941–1943 the Army blasted through the mountains and laid the tracks that would ensure the flow of supplies for the defense of Alaska. After the defeat of Japan, the military pulled out of Whittier, but a year later they were back as the Cold War began with the Soviet Union. Whittier became a permanent base, and large concrete buildings were built at that time. The 14-story Begich Tower (completed in 1954), an unlikely skyscraper in this small village, is near another anomaly, the "City under One Roof," which once housed 1,000 personnel and was the largest building in Alaska. Why did they build high-rises? To lessen the need for snow removal in a place where the snow sometimes tops 14 feet.

The base was deactivated in 1960, and the buildings were heavily damaged in the 1964 earthquake. One of them is still vacant, but Begich Tower has been restored and converted into condos. A third high-rise, Whittier Manor, was privately built in the 1950s and later turned into more condos. The military presence today is limited to an oil pipeline that supplies military installations in Anchorage. Ships from Princess Cruises and Carnival Cruise Line stop in Whittier, but most of their passengers quickly depart the town.

For nearly half a century the town of Whittier was connected to the road system only via the Alaska Railroad. This changed in 2000, when an $80 million project made it possible for cars to drive in directly from the Seward Highway through two tunnels, one of which is shared with the railroad.

SIGHTS

Get local info from the chamber website (www.whittieralaskachamber.org). Most travelers never get farther than the tourist action on the waterfront, where boats of all sizes bob in the picturesque harbor.

Follow the signs for Whittier down past the dry dock, then go left across the tracks onto Whittier Street. Take a right on Glacier Avenue to the **Begich Tower.** In its 198 condos live most of the town's population; the rest reside in the 70 condos at **Whittier Manor.** Many are owned by Anchorageites who use them for weekend and summer getaways, boosting Whittier's summer population to nearly 1,000.

Continue a quarter-mile out on Eastern Avenue to quiet and scenic **Smitty's Cove,** where one of Whittier's few freestanding residences sits. You'll get a great view across Passage Canal of waterfalls, a kittiwake rookery, and Billing's Glacier.

BOAT TOURS

Whittier is a popular departure point for day trips to the glaciers of Prince William Sound mid-May–late September. **Phillips Tours and Cruises** (907/276-8023 or 800/544-0529, www.26glaciers.com) operates the 4.5-hour 26-Glacier Cruise for $139 ($79 children). The trip aboard its 340-passenger *Klondike Express*—a high-speed three-deck catamaran—covers a lot of ground but still allows plenty of time to linger at the faces of several glaciers. A hot lunch is included, there's a bar on board, and the lounges provide plenty of room inside should the weather be less than perfect. The schedule is timed so that you can ride the train from Anchorage and back (an additional $80) or take a bus (an additional $50).

Prince William Sound Cruises and Tours (907/835-4731 or 800/992-1297, www.princewilliamsound.com) runs a six-hour "Wilderness Explorer" tour ($139 adults, $70 children under 12) that includes Barry Arm (Barry and Cox Glaciers) and Esther Passage. Their four-hour trip to Blackstone Glacier is $109 adults, $55 kids. Lunch is included on both of these tours.

© DON PITCHER

Blackstone Glacier, Prince William Sound, near Whittier

Major Marine Tours (907/274-7300 or 800/764-7300, www.majormarine.com, $118 adults, $64 ages 2–11, younger children free) takes visitors on a leisurely five-hour voyage into stunning Blackstone Bay daily. If you want to include the filling salmon and prime rib buffet, the cruise price is $137 adults, $73 children.

In addition to these large operators, a number of locals offer small-boat trips into Prince William Sound. The prices may be a bit higher, but you get a more personal journey. Recommended companies for sightseeing, fishing, water taxis, and kayak drop-offs are **Honey Charters** (907/472-2493 or 888/477-2493, www.honeycharters.com), **Lazy Otter Charters** (907/345-1175 or 800/587-6887, www.lazyotter.com), and **Sound Eco Adventures** (907/472-2312 or 888/471-2312, www.soundecoadventure.com).

RECREATION

Up Portage Pass

The most popular Whittier trail is up to Portage Pass. In the early days when gold was discovered around Hope on the Kenai Peninsula, Hope-bound hopefuls would boat to this harbor, portage their supplies over the glacier pass, and float down Turnagain Arm to their destination. This highly recommended day hike from Whittier affords splendid views of Passage Canal, Portage Glacier, and the Chugach Mountains. On a clear day, the views of the glacier from the Portage Pass area are far superior to those from the Portage Visitors Center.

This trail starts near the oil tanks and tunnel entrance at the foot of Maynard Mountain. Cross the tracks on the dirt road to the left. Take the road to the right and climb southwest along the flank of the mountain up a wide easy track. If you walk briskly, you can be at Portage Pass (700 feet) in less than an hour. There are places to camp or picnic beside Divide Lake, but beware of strong winds at the pass. From the lake follow the stream down toward the glacier, then find a way via a tributary on the right up onto one of the bluffs for a view of Portage Lake. Deep crevasses in the blue glacial ice are clearly visible from here. **Portage Glacier** has receded far enough that the gold-rush route is no longer traversable because of the lake; you must go back the way you came. This hike is highly recommended; allow a minimum of three hours round-trip. Note that there is no clear trail beyond Divide Lake, so you must find your own way. Do not attempt to walk on the glacier itself, as the crevasses can be deadly.

Sea Kayaking

A seasonal **Forest Service information station** is usually housed in the yurt next to the boat harbor; stop by for details on sea kayaking and other outdoor options. If it isn't here, get kayaking information from the Ranger Station in Girdwood (907/783-3242). Although it is possible to paddle from Whittier to the heart of Prince William Sound, most people prefer to get a boat ride out so they can spend more time near the glaciers and wild country that make this such a special place. A number of local water taxis provide these services, transporting sea kayaks, paddlers, and their gear, then picking them up several days later.

Two companies offer kayak rentals and guided day trips: **Alaska Sea Kayakers** (907/472-2534 or 877/472-2534, www.alaskaseakayakers.com) and **Prince William Sound Kayak Center** (907/472-2452 or 877/472-2452, www.pwskayakcenter.com). An easy three-hour paddle to the kittiwake rookery runs around $79, or take an all-day Blackstone Glacier trip for $300. Multiple-night trips are also available.

ACCOMMODATIONS AND CAMPING

June's Whittier B&B (907/472-6000 or 888/472-2396, www.breadnbuttercharters.com) consists of 12 condo suites on the 14th and 15th floors of Begich Tower, starting for $155 d in a one-bedroom apartment, up to $245 for a three-bedroom unit that sleeps six. A continental breakfast is included.

Housed within Whittier Manor, **Soundview Getaway B&B** (907/472-2358 or 800/515-

2358, www.soundviewalaska.com, $120–145 d) features four condo units with full kitchens and Wi-Fi.

It's hard to miss the **Inn at Whittier** (907/472-3200, www.innatwhittier.com), an elaborate New England–style building right on the harbor. Now owned by Hooper Bay Native Corporation, the hotel has 23 standard rooms ($169–189 d) and a pair of two-story townhouse suites ($249 for 4 guests).

Camping (907/472-2670, $10) next to Begich Tower is plentiful, with secluded spots for tents and RVs, and a shelter for cooking and socializing in the rain. There are no hookups or running water, but you can use bathrooms on the first floor of Begich Tower, and showers are available at the harbormaster's office.

FOOD

In addition to grilled halibut, glacier burgers, sandwiches, salads, and espresso, **Café Orca** (907/472-2549, www.cafeorca.com) has a pleasant waterside deck with picnic tables for sunny mornings.

Inn at Whittier (907/472-3200, www.innatwhittier.com, daily 6 A.M.–10 P.M. Apr.–Sept., Fri.–Sun. 8 A.M.–9 P.M. Oct.–Mar., entrées $15–29) has a fantastic location, with tall windows fronting on the boat harbor. The breakfast buffet ($10) is popular in the summer, and dinners include everything from burgers to steak and seafood.

Swiftwater Seafood Cafe (907/472-2550, www.swiftwaterseafoodcafe.com, Sun.–Thurs. 11:30 A.M.–9 P.M., Fri.–Sat. 11:30 A.M.–10 P.M.) is popular for fish-and-chips, halibut burgers, and seafood chowder, with smoked prime rib dinners on Friday and Saturday nights.

China Sea Restaurant (907/472-2222) has an all-you-can-eat $11 lunch buffet with soup and salad bar. **Quigley's Ice Cream Parlor** (907/472-2459) gets crowded on those rare sunny days in summer.

SERVICES

Anchor Inn has a small grocery store, but don't miss the **Harbor Store** (907/244-1996), a combination grocery, dry goods, clothing, sporting goods, Laundromat, hardware, bait-and-tackle, supermarket, and department store—all in an ATCO trailer. The post office is on the first floor of Begich Tower; the library is in the fire hall. Get showered at the Harbor Office, next to Hobo Bay.

With an exterior in all sorts of Alaskan memorabilia, **Log Cabin Gifts** (907/472-2501) features arts and crafts items, ivory, and watercolors by the owner, Wilma Buethe Wilcox. You can pet, photograph, and even feed the two pet **reindeer** next door. Also check out at **Sound Ideas** (907/472-2535) for gifts and homemade fudge.

The main Whittier event—other than the rain in summer, snow in winter, and year-round wind—is the **4th of July** celebration featuring a parade, a picnic, kid's games, and fireworks.

GETTING THERE

Whittier is accessible by boat, ferry, train, or car. Drivers get here by turning from Seward Highway at Mile 79 (50 miles south of Anchorage) onto Portage Glacier Highway. The road to Whittier splits off near the Begich, Boggs Visitors Center and heads through a 400-foot tunnel before emerging into Bear Valley. Here you'll find a staging area for access to the 2.5-mile **Anton Anderson Memorial Tunnel** that is shared by both trains and cars. It's the longest auto tunnel in North America, and one of the only tunnels in the world where the same roadbed is used by both rail and auto traffic. The tunnel is open to one-way travel throughout the day, but only for 15 minutes out of each hour in each direction (and not at all when trains are transiting the tunnel). Ferry travelers and anyone else on a tight schedule should check the tunnel times in advance to make sure they don't miss their connections. Get a schedule at 907/472-2584 or 877/611-2586, or online at www.tunnel.alaska.gov. The eastbound toll is $12 for autos; no charge heading west.

The tunnel is not recommended for anyone with claustrophobia, and you will be driving on an odd roadbed over the railroad tracks. There are pullouts for emergency use, and enormous fans to clean the air after trains pass through. Once you reach Whittier, parking costs $10 per day, or $5 if you're on one of the glacier cruises.

Girdwood Shuttle (907/783-1900, www.girdwoodshuttle.com, May–Sept.) provides daily vans connecting Whittier with Anchorage and Girdwood ($40 one way).

Train

The **Alaska Railroad** (907/265-2494 or 800/544-0552, www.akrr.com, $74 round-trip) train connects Whittier with Anchorage daily in the summer, departing Anchorage at 10 A.M. and arriving in Whittier at 12:20 P.M. The northbound train leaves Whittier at 6:45 P.M. and arrives in Anchorage at 9:15 P.M. This makes an excellent day trip from the city. A trivia note: The route to Whittier was used in scenes from the 1986 film *Runaway Train*.

Ferry

The **Alaska Marine Highway** (907/465-3941 or 800/642-0066, www.dot.state.ak.us/amhs) has daily ferry service connecting Whittier with Valdez and Cordova on both the high-speed *Chenega* and the older (and much slower) *Aurora;* a Forest Service naturalist is on board. In addition, the *Kennicott* has a once-a-month summer sailing across the Gulf of Alaska from Whittier to Yakutat, continuing south to Juneau and then all the way to Prince Rupert, British Columbia.

THE INTERIOR

Interior Alaska is a great tilted plateau between the crests of two long mountain ranges, the Alaska Range and the Brooks Range. The mighty Yukon and Tanana Rivers are the main features of this region, but vast expanses of rolling hills are usually in view. Interior Alaska has one fair-sized city, Fairbanks, several small towns, and a number of bush villages, the most interesting along the rivers but some beside the highways. Much of the region is expensive or inaccessible to visit without your own vehicle, but great adventures await on the many wild and scenic rivers, in the wildlife refuges, and in the national parks, especially spectacular Denali National Park.

One of the wonderful aspects of Alaska's Interior is its vastness. A few places—Talkeetna, Fairbanks, and most notably the entrance to Denali National Park—are packed with travelers all summer long, but it's amazingly easy to escape the crowds and find yourself in a land that seems unchanged from time immemorial. Take the time to pull off the highway and fish a bit on one of the creeks or climb a hill for the view. You won't regret it!

This is a place of exceptionally harsh winters, but those long winter nights bring something else, the mysterious northern lights. Winter weather is often clear over Interior Alaska, and scientists can now predict the aurora activity level with relative accuracy up to a month in advance. Some lodges around Fairbanks make a special effort to accommodate aurora lovers, and so many Japanese people visit that Japan Airlines even has nonstop flights from Tokyo all winter.

HIGHLIGHTS

Mt. McKinley Flightseeing: Talkeetna is the base for several air charter operators with flights over McKinley that include a bush plane landing on Ruth Glacier (page 342).

Denali Highway: This 136-mile mostly gravel road provides dramatic views of the Alaska Range and access to vast stretches of wild country (page 349).

Denali Shuttle Bus Tours: This is the only way to reach the heart of Alaska's most famous park. Tours last all day and can be grueling, but grizzlies, moose, wolves, and Dall sheep are commonly seen and you may even get lucky enough to see Mt. McKinley in all its glory (page 360).

University of Alaska Museum of the North: This Fairbanks museum is notable not just for its natural history, art, and cultural collections, but also for the monumental building with its high glacier-like entrance (page 382).

Pioneer Park: Combining a low-key theme park with a multitude of historical attractions, this city-run facility has everything from an old paddlewheel boat to theatrical productions and carousel rides. Pig out at the salmon bake; it's the best in Alaska (page 383).

Riverboat Tours: Hop on board a modern-day paddle-wheeler to cruise the Chena and Tanana Rivers. Although primarily for the package-tour crowd, this is a great way to see the country around Fairbanks (page 384).

Santa Claus House: The town of North Pole is home to this kitschy spot with the 40-foot waving Santa out front and all sorts of Christmas paraphernalia inside (page 397).

Gold Dredge No. 8: A few miles north of Fairbanks this mechanical monster operated until 1959. It's now open for tours and the chance to practice your gold panning (page 400).

Chena Hot Springs Resort: Indoor and outdoor pools are fed by geothermally heated water, and winter guests come to view the northern lights, but the most unusual feature here is the year-round ice museum filled with intricately carved works of ice art. Chena is an hour's drive east of Fairbanks (page 402).

Eagle: Accessible via an arduous 160-mile dead-end road off the Alaska Highway or a fast catamaran from Dawson City, this tiny town displays a multitude of artifacts and historic buildings from the 1890s gold rush (page 419).

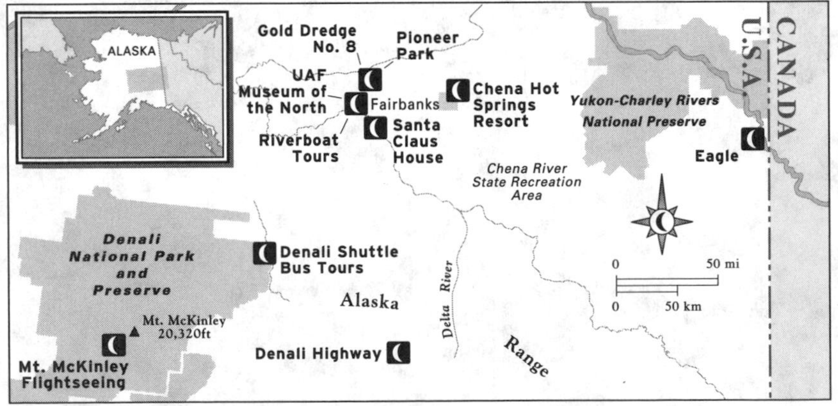

LOOK FOR TO FIND RECOMMENDED SIGHTS, ACTIVITIES, DINING, AND LODGING.

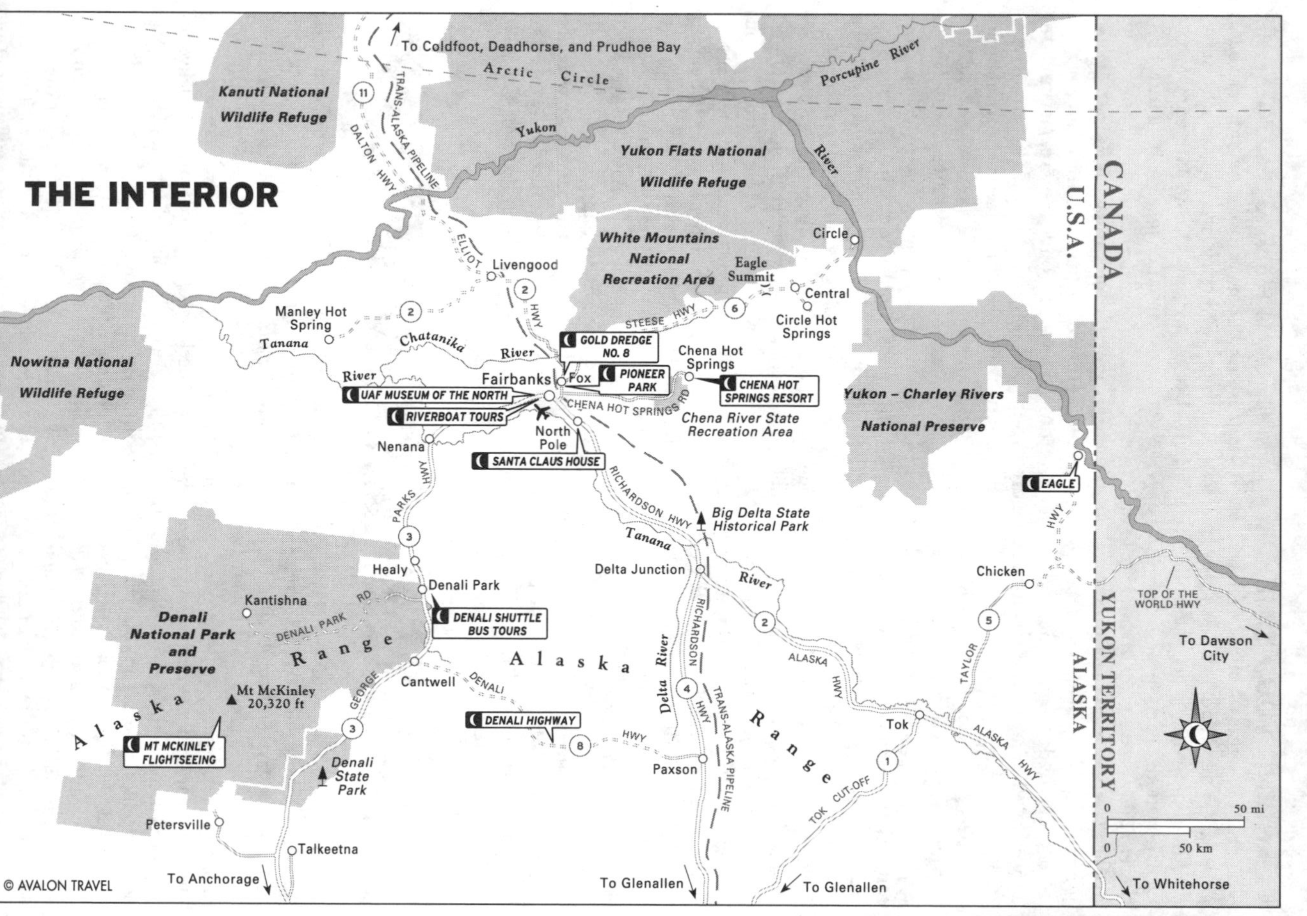
THE INTERIOR
To Coldfoot, Deadhorse, and Prudhoe Bay
Arctic Circle
Kanuti National Wildlife Refuge
TRANS-ALASKA PIPELINE
DALTON HWY
Yukon
Porcupine River
Yukon Flats National Wildlife Refuge
River
CANADA
U.S.A.
White Mountains National Recreation Area
Circle
ELLIOT
Livengood
Eagle Summit
Central
Circle Hot Springs
Manley Hot Spring
Tanana
Chatanika
River
STEESE HWY
HWY
GOLD DREDGE NO. 8
Nowitna National Wildlife Refuge
Chena Hot Springs
Fairbanks
Fox
PIONEER PARK
CHENA HOT SPRINGS RESORT
UAF MUSEUM OF THE NORTH
CHENA HOT SPRINGS RD
Yukon – Charley Rivers National Preserve
RIVERBOAT TOURS
Chena River State Recreation Area
North Pole
Nenana
SANTA CLAUS HOUSE
EAGLE
PARKS HWY
RICHARDSON HWY
Big Delta State Historical Park
Tanana
HWY
Healy
Delta Junction
River
Chicken
Denali Park
Kantishna
DENALI PARK RD
DENALI SHUTTLE BUS TOURS
TOP OF THE WORLD HWY
Denali National Park and Preserve
Range
YUKON TERRITORY
ALASKA
To Dawson City
Alaska
Delta River
RICHARDSON
ALASKA HWY
TAYLOR
Cantwell
DENALI
GEORGE
Mt McKinley 20,320 ft
HWY
TRANS-ALASKA PIPELINE
Tok
DENALI HIGHWAY
Alaska
Range
MT MCKINLEY FLIGHTSEEING
Denali State Park
Paxson
Range
ALASKA HWY
TOK CUT-OFF
0
50 mi
0
50 km
Petersville
Talkeetna
© AVALON TRAVEL
To Anchorage
To Glenallen
To Glenallen
To Whitehorse

PLANNING YOUR TIME

The primary sights of Interior Alaska are on the road system and provide ready access. Starting from Anchorage, one could drive to Denali National Park, spend two or three days there, and then on to Fairbanks for another day or two, followed by a return through Delta Junction and Glennallen in another two days. That is a lot of driving for one week, however, at over 1,000 miles, so you might be better off sticking to a few select areas.

Talkeetna is a delightful destination, with outstanding vistas across to Mt. McKinley and a quaint historic downtown filled with mountaineers and outdoor enthusiasts. Several air-taxi operators offer **Mt. McKinley flightseeing** trips that often include a glacier landing. Farther north is the **Denali Highway,** a partly paved, mostly gravel 126-mile route that cuts east to west along the magnificent Alaska Range. **Denali National Park** is always a favorite of travelers and Alaskans. The big draws are 20,320-foot Mt. McKinley (often obscured by clouds), a grand landscape of open tundra and boreal forests, and the chance to watch grizzly bears, moose, wolves, Dall sheep, and caribou. Private cars are not allowed on the road, but **shuttle buses into the park** provide a wonderful way to see the land or to access remote areas for hiking and camping.

The city of Fairbanks is Alaska's second largest, and home to two large military bases and the University of Alaska. The striking **University of Alaska Museum of the North** is notable not just for its natural history, art, and cultural collections but also for the memorable building with its high glacier-like entrance. Other local attractions include tourist-friendly paddle-wheel **riverboat tours** down the Chena and Tanana Rivers; **Pioneer Park** with its mix of historical buildings, fun-rides, and a great salmon bake; and a visit with St. Nick at **Santa Claus House** in nearby North Pole. A few miles north of Fairbanks is **Gold Dredge No. 8,** which operated until 1959 and is now open for fascinating tours. **Chena Hot Springs Resort** is an hour's drive east of town, with outdoor and indoor pools, wonderful northern lights viewing all winter, and a year-round ice museum filled with intricately carved works of ice art. North of Fairbanks, the challenging Dalton Highway crosses the Arctic Circle and parallels the Trans-Alaska Pipeline all the way to Prudhoe Bay. The town of **Eagle** is accessible via an arduous 160-mile dead-end road off the Alaska Highway, and because of its remoteness it still has many artifacts and historic buildings from the 1890s gold rush.

Talkeetna

The outdoorsy and youthful town of Talkeetna (pop. 360) lies at the end of a 14-mile side road that splits away from the Parks Highway 98 miles north of Anchorage. Two closely related phenomena dominate this small bush community: The Mountain, and flying to and climbing on The Mountain. On a clear day, from the overlook a mile out on the Spur Road, Mt. McKinley and the accompanying Alaska Range scrape the sky like a jagged white wall.

All summer, local flightseeing and air-taxi companies take off in a continuous parade to circle Mt. McKinley, buzz up long glaciers or even land on them, then return to Talkeetna's busy airport to drop off passengers whose wide eyes, broad smiles, and shaky knees attest to the excitement of this once-in-a-lifetime thrill. Late April–early July, these same special "wheel-and-ski" planes might be delivering an American, European, Japanese, or Korean climbing expedition to the Kahiltna Glacier (elevation 7,000 feet), from which—if they're lucky—they inch their way up the popular West Buttress route 13,000 feet to the peak. On a clear day, if you're anywhere within striking distance, make a beeline for Talkeetna and be whisked away to some of the most stunning and alien scenery you'll ever see.

If you visit Talkeetna early in the summer, you'll find a peculiar mixing of people: the earthy locals with their beards and rusty pickups, the mountaineers—mostly male—decked in color-coordinated Gore-Tex, and the busloads of cruise ship passengers who unload on the south side of town and wander through in a dazed blur of gawks and photo-ops.

Talkeetna ("where the rivers meet"), nesting at the confluence of the Talkeetna, Chulitna, and Susitna Rivers, was originally settled by trappers and prospectors who paddled up the Susitna River to gain access to rich silver, coal, and fur country around the Talkeetna Mountains. The settlement got a boost when the railroad was pushed through in the early 1920s, and it still remains a popular stop on the route. In 1965 the Spur Road from the Parks Highway to Talkeetna was completed, providing further access to the town.

Information

At the intersection of the Parks Highway and Talkeetna Spur Road is **Talkeetna/Denali Visitors Center** (907/733-2688 or 800/660-2688, www.talkeetnadenali.com, daily 9 A.M.–7 P.M. mid-May–mid-Sept.), covering the area from Willow (south) to Healy (north); look for the giant bear out front. The visitors center is owned by Talkeetna Aero Services, but the always-helpful staff will book flights with any local air taxi, provide current weather conditions on Denali, set up fishing expeditions or guided hikes, book rooms at hotels and B&Bs, or just supply brochures and information on the area. They also have a tiny downtown visitors center (daily 9 A.M.–8 P.M. May–Sept.) next to Nagley's Store. The Talkeetna Chamber of Commerce (907/733-2330, www.talkeetnachamber.org) has a useful website, and can send out brochures.

SIGHTS

Talkeetna is a wonderful walk-around town, with most of the action within a couple of blocks of Nagley's Store and the Fairview Inn. This is one of the few Alaskan towns that still looks the way people imagine Alaskan towns should look, with rustic log buildings lining Main Street and a local population that encompasses grizzled redneck miners and back-to-the-earth tree huggers. Local bumper stickers proclaim "Talkeetna, where the road ends and life begins." If you ever saw *Northern Exposure* on TV, this is the place it must have been modeled on.

For a graphic and detailed look at the history of the town and its connection to The Mountain, check out the excellent **Talkeetna Historical Museum** (907/733-2487, www.talkeetnahistoricalsociety.org, daily 10 A.M.–6 P.M. mid-May–Sept., or by appointment the rest of the year, $3 adults, children under 16 free). Take a left after Nagley's Store, which you can read all about in the museum; the museum is a half-block down the side street on the right in a red schoolhouse built in 1936. Inside are all sorts of local artifacts—including a horsehide coat from the 1890s—but more interesting is the old railroad section house out back, which now houses an enormous relief map of Denali surrounded by photos and the stories of climbers, including several famous adventurers who lost their lives on this treacherous peak. Other exhibits show the gear climbers use, such as the required "clean mountain cans" for transporting human waste. Return at 1 P.M. for a Park Service ranger talk on climbing Mt. McKinley.

The Park Service's log **Talkeetna Ranger Station** (B St., 907/733-2231, www.nps.gov/dena, daily 8 A.M.–6 P.M. mid-Apr.–early Sept., Mon.–Fri. 8 A.M.–4:30 P.M. early Sept.–mid-Apr.) is a pleasant place to watch a video or look over the mountaineering books. Park rangers give natural history talks daily in the summer at 7 P.M.

You might also glance inside the **Museum of Northern Adventure** (Main St., 907/733-3999, $2 adults, $1 seniors and children), a combination gift shop and private collection with 24 north country dioramas.

The **Sheldon Community Arts Hangar**

(downtown behind the post office, $8 adults, $6 children) hosts plays and other events throughout the summer, including showings of a video on the life of legendary bush pilot Don Sheldon, who used this building as his airplane hangar.

ENTERTAINMENT AND EVENTS

Talkeetna loves to party. The **Talkeetna Moose Dropping Festival** drops into town the second weekend of July, with a big parade, a "mountain mother" contest, foot races, dozens of food and craft booths, and the infamous moose-nugget toss and moose-nugget dropping contests. If you don't know what moose nuggets are, just ask any Alaskan. The 2009 festival brought more than 5,000 people to the town, along with a host of problems, including lots of rowdy behavior and even a death when a drunken partier drowned in the river. Future festivals—if they continue—will be better policed to tame things down.

The other big event in these parts is the **Talkeetna Bluegrass Festival** (907/495-6718, www.talkeetnabluegrass.com), held the first weekend of August at Mile 102 on the Parks Highway. Called "Alaska's greatest campout" or "Woodstock Mudhole," this is a great chance to get in touch with your earthy side, hang out with the freaks, and see what mind-altering substances are in fashion. The music rarely strays to bluegrass; more often it's rock, folk, or blues. It is great fun, even if it rains.

When winter arrives with a vengeance, **Talkeetna Winterfest** brightens December spirits, especially those of the many local bachelors. The main events are a Wilderness Woman Contest that includes all sorts of wacky activities, followed later that evening by a Bachelor Society Ball during which local bachelors are bid on by single women, many of whom drive up from Anchorage for the chance. It has all the sexual energy of a male-stripper night, except that some of the men are considerably less fit and keep their clothes on (at least during the bidding). This is one of Alaska's most authentic winter events.

The classic **Fairview Inn** (907/733-2423, www.denali-fairview.com) has live bands nightly in the summer, and is a great place to soak up the old-time atmosphere.

RECREATION

Mt. McKinley Flightseeing

Talkeetna is famous as a launching point for flights over Mt. McKinley, and on a clear summer day a constant parade of planes takes off from the airport on the edge of town. The flight services in town offer a bewildering array of possibilities, including short scenic flights, glacier landings, drop-off hiking or fishing, wildlife-viewing, overnight trips, and flights to, around, or over the top of The Mountain. Rates vary according to the type of airplane, length of the flight, and how many people there are in your group. Most outfits will try to match you up with other folks to maximize your flightseeing dollar. Be flexible in your plans, since weather is infinitely variable and is always the most important consideration when it comes to flying you safely. A one-hour flight typically costs $250 per person, or $325 with a glacier landing. A flight to the summit of Mt. McKinley (a good chance to see the climbers) is $295.

Reservations are recommended, but not always necessary. Note that the climbing season on Mt. McKinley runs from early spring until mid or late June, and the flight services are busiest then. As always with bush flying, risks are involved, and fatalities have taken the lives of some of the best local pilots and climbers over the years. Your odds (not to mention the vistas) are probably better if you wait until a clear day to fly.

A number of charter companies provide service to Mt. McKinley. The very knowledgeable staff at the visitors center can set up any of these, or you can contact them directly: **Hudson Air Service** (907/733-2321 or 800/478-2321, www.hudsonair.com), **K2 Aviation** (907/733-2291 or 800/764-2291, www.flyk2.com), and **Talkeetna Air Taxi** (907/733-2218 or 800/533-2219, www.talkeetnaair.com). The largest operators are K2

Aviation (especially popular with tourists) and Talkeetna Air Taxi (a favorite of climbers). **McKinley Flight Tours** (a.k.a. Talkeetna Aero Services, 907/683-2899 or 888/733-2899, www.mckinleyflighttours.com) has limited flightseeing from Talkeetna, with a much larger operation out of Healy.

On the Water

Denali View Raft Adventures (907/733-2778 or 877/533-2778, www.denaliviewraft.com) has three-hour Susitna River trips ($105 adults, $65 children), two-hour Talkeetna River floats ($69 adults, $49 children), and a unique 4.5-hour trip that starts with a train ride upriver followed by a float and lunch on the Susitna River ($169 adults, $110 children).

Talkeetna River Guides (907/733-2677 or 800/353-2677, www.talkeetnariverguides.com) offers two-hour Talkeetna River floats for $79, and four-hour Chulitna River trips for $129. They primarily book customers from the large hotels.

Mahay's Riverboat Service (907/733-2223 or 800/736-2210, www.mahaysriverboat.com, $65 adults, $33 children) has a popular two-hour jet-boat tour up the Susitna River. Longer trips are also offered, including a five-hour run into Devil's Canyon ($155 adults, $78 children).

The fishing in Talkeetna is excellent all summer long; rainbow trout, grayling, Dolly Varden, and all five species of Pacific salmon are there for the catching. Local riverboat services can supply you with a fishing guide or drop you off along the river for the day or overnight. The visitors center has rack cards from most local guides.

Biking and Horseback Riding

A paved bike path parallels the Spur Road all the way to Talkeetna. Turn off onto gravel roads at Miles 3 and 12 for out-of-the-way lakes and camping spots. At Mile 13 is the big turnout with an interpretive sign on the Alaska Range and heart-stopping views—if the clouds are cooperating. **Talkeetna Alaskan Lodge** is on the opposite side of the road; stop in for the Mt. McKinley view from its Great Room even if you aren't overnighting here.

D&S Alaskan Trail Rides (907/733-2205, www.alaskantrailrides.com) has wagon rides and guided horseback rides into the country around Talkeetna. Tour the kennels of Iditarod musher Jerry Sousa and take a cart ride behind a team of sled dogs at **Sundog Racing Kennel** (907/733-3355 or 800/318-2534, www.sundogkennel.com). Another Iditarod veteran, Randy Cummins of **Huskytown Kennel** (907/733-4759, www.huskytown.com), has similar summertime tours.

ACCOMMODATIONS

Add a 5 percent lodging tax to the rates listed below.

Hostels

Talkeetna Hostel International (907/733-4678, www.talkeetnahostel.com, mid-Apr.–Sept.) is a fine option for budget travelers. The bunks are comfortable enough, the location—a few blocks east of downtown on I Street—is quiet, and the rate is just $22 per person in a dorm room and $50 s or $55 d for a private room. There are three baths, a full kitchen and laundry, free mountain bikes, a guest computer, Wi-Fi, a TV, and no curfew.

Located right in the center of town on Main Street, **House of 7 Trees** (907/733-7733, late Apr.–early Sept.) is a cozy little place with hostel bunks ($25 pp) and four private rooms ($75–90 d) upstairs. Guests have access to the common room with a commercial kitchen, a grand piano, and Wi-Fi. Talkeetna Roadhouse also has bunks.

Hotels

Talkeetna Roadhouse (907/733-1351, www.talkeetnaroadhouse.com, $55–75 s, $65–85 d) has simple but clean guest rooms with period antiques, two cozy cabins ($95 and $110), and a four-bed coed hostel ($20 pp). All rooms have baths down the hall in this classic Alaskan lodge, constructed in 1917 and in business since 1944.

Latitude 62 Motel (907/733-2262, www.

latitude62.com, $65 s, $75 d) is a two-story log building on the south end of town with 10 budget rooms. The furnishings are older, and there are no phones or TVs, but Latitude does have Wi-Fi.

Downtown above Wildflower Café, **Main St. Suites** (907/733-2694, www.talkeetna-suites.com, summer only) consists of a one-bedroom studio ($140 d) and a two-bedroom suite ($160 d), both with private baths and kitchenettes.

Head across the railroad tracks to **Swiss-Alaska Inn** (907/733-2424, www.swissalaska.com, $89 s, $119 d), with 20 motel rooms, homemade quilts, private baths, and bathtubs. There is no TV reception, but videos are available along with Wi-Fi in the adjacent restaurant. German is spoken.

Talkeetna Alaskan Lodge (907/733-9500 or 888/959-9590, www.talkeetnalodge.com, mid-May–Sept.) sits atop a hill a mile south of Talkeetna, with spacious, modern rooms for $309 d ($409 d for those that face Mt. McKinley). Luxury suites—most with gas fireplaces and jetted tubs—are $479–569 d. The grand lobby includes a stone fireplace and towering windows framing The Mountain, and a fine-dining restaurant is on the premises. There's a free shuttle to town and the train depot. This 200-room Native Alaskan–owned lodge serves up million-dollar views for an upscale clientele, pretty much the opposite of most Talkeetna lodging places.

Cabins

Paradise Lodge & Cabins (907/733-1471 or 888/205-3553, www.paradiselodge.net, year-round, $115 d) is aptly named, with a delightful location along Fish Lake five miles south of Talkeetna. Four rustic cabins share a bathhouse, or you can stay in the main lodge where two rooms share a bath. Also available is a spacious three-bedroom home ($500 for up to 8 guests).

Right in town, **Talkeetna Cabins** (907/733-2227 or 888/733-9933, www.talkeetnacabins.org) consists of duplex log cabins ($175 d) and a large three-bedroom cabin ($350 for 4 people), all with full kitchens, private baths, and Wi-Fi.

Susitna River Lodging (907/733-1505 or 866/733-1505, www.susitna-river-lodging.com) has four modern cedar cabins ($229 d) and lodge rooms ($159–179 d) a half-mile south of Talkeetna. All guest rooms and cabins have private baths, kitchenettes, and Wi-Fi.

Bed-and-Breakfasts

When it comes to Talkeetna B&Bs the old "location, location, location" saying applies, with several places providing Denali vistas to die for.

Five miles east of town, **Traleika B&B** (907/733-2711, www.traleika.com) has a mountaintop location facing Denali. The guesthouse rents for $205 d, and two smaller cabins are $165–185 d; add $20 for each extra guest. All three places include full baths and kitchens with breakfast supplies.

Not far away—with an equally fine vista—is the reasonably priced **Freedom Hills B&B** (907/733-2455 or 888/703-2455, www.gbfreedomhillsbb.com, $120 d shared bath, $140 d private bath) where five guest rooms are in two adjacent homes. Co-owner and chef Bill Germain creates a delicious breakfast each morning, and there is free Wi-Fi too.

Built in 1946 and beautifully maintained, **Fireweed Station** (907/733-1457 or 888/647-1457, www.fireweedstation.com) is a gorgeous log home off Mile 2 of the Talkeetna Spur Road. A spacious suite ($205 d) occupies the entire upstairs, and downstairs are two guest rooms ($175–185 d) with private baths. All rates include a full breakfast, Wi-Fi, and access to the big deck. Dinners are available on request.

CAMPING

Find free camping at shady **River Park** at the end of Main Street, but it has no running water. Also on the river, but a bit farther from town, is **Talkeetna Alaska RV** (907/733-2604), with in-the-trees tent and RV sites for $20. There are no hookups, but showers ($2) are available. **Talkeetna Camper Park** (907/733-2693, www.talkeetnacamper.com, Apr.–Oct.,

RVs $36) has wooded RV sites; it's on the right just before you enter town.

Take **showers** and wash your clothes at Washi-Washi on the south end of town, or at Suds, the coin laundry behind Twister Creek Restaurant.

FOOD

Talkeetna has turned into quite the spot for good inexpensive food, a definite rarity on the Alaska road system. Most places are downtown, so you can just walk a block or so to see what appeals.

At **Talkeetna Roadhouse** (907/733-1351, www.talkeetnaroadhouse.com, $8–12) excellent breakfasts start at 7 A.M., and late risers can still get breakfast until 3 P.M. when the restaurant closes. The chalkboard menu lists lasagna, sandwiches on homemade bread, salads, and soups, or choose one of their Paul Bunyan–size cinnamon rolls. Long tables make for fun family-style dining with crowds of locals and visitors.

New, and already gaining a big reputation, **Twister Creek Restaurant** (907/733-2537, www.denalibrewingcompany.com, daily 7 A.M.–midnight summer, reduced winter hours, entrées $14–22) has a big front deck in the heart of town, Talkeetna's best espresso, plus a dinner menu ranging from flatiron steaks and seared ahi tuna to vegetarian Thai coconut curry. The restaurant is also open for breakfast and lunch, and several beers are brewed on the premises, including a "Big Mama" black and tan; there is also free Wi-Fi.

Nagley's Store (907/733-3663, www.nagleysstore.com) opened in the 1920s and is still the main place for (limited) groceries in town, but it has also added such staples of 21st-century life as an ATM and lattes. A newer and larger grocery store, **Cubby's Marketplace** (907/733-5050, Mon.–Sat. 8 A.M.–8 P.M., Sun. 8 A.M.–10 P.M.) is 14 miles south of town at the junction with the Parks Highway.

Behind Nagley's is **West Rib Deli and Pub** (907/733-3663, www.westribpub.info, daily

© DON PITCHER

Nagley's Store, Talkeetna

11:30 A.M.–11 P.M., $9–28), with seafood, sandwiches, salads, burgers, and Alaskan brews on tap. Everyone raves about the caribou chiliburger. Best deal? Meet the locals at the Friday-night burger-and-beer for just $7. There's an outside deck for sunny days.

Housed in a modern log building, **Wildflower Café** (907/733-1275, www.talkeetnasuites.com, daily 11:30 A.M.–9 P.M. May–Sept., $13–30) is popular for a cheeseburger and fries, Philly steak sandwich, tenderloin Madeira, or veggie stir-fry wrap, but don't miss the Caesar salads. Wildflower also has nightly dinner specials.

Mt. High Pizza Pie (907/733-1234, www.mhpp.biz, daily 11 A.M.–10 P.M., most pizzas $14–23), in the purple log cabin, is a busy spot for pizzas, calzones, flatbreads, salads, and subs. They have all the standard pizzas plus a "mountain high" version ($32), piled with all the ingredients. In summer, the side deck is a great spot to enjoy your pizza with a beer (there are eight Alaskan brews on tap); it erupts with live music six nights a week.

One place really stands out in Talkeetna, **Café Michele** (907/733-5300, www.cafemichele.com, daily 11 A.M.–3 P.M. and 5:30–10 P.M. May–Sept., dinner entrées $26–34), where the bistro atmosphere is decidedly classy. Chef Michele Camera-Faurot's menu includes such treats as Thai-style flank steak, soy-ginger king salmon, and substantial salads. Open for lunch (try the Philly cheesesteak) and dinner, with wonderful desserts, including the Madagascar bourbon vanilla cheesecake.

SERVICES

Keep in touch with the outside world via the Internet at the **Talkeetna Public Library** (907/733-23559, www.matsulibraries.org/talkeetna, Mon.–Sat. 11 A.M.–6 P.M., closed Sun.) on the south side of town.

Shopping

Talkeetna's **Open Air Market** takes place all summer Saturday–Monday 10 A.M.–6 P.M., with jewelry, clothing, and local crafts. It's in front of the Sheldon Community Arts Hangar.

Several local shops are worth a visit, including the downtown **Denali Images Art Gallery** (907/733-2026), which displays wildlife and nature images from a half-dozen local photographers. More art, plus a good selection of beads and jewelry, are at **Beadberry Patch** (907/733-5678, www.beadberrypatch.com) on the south side of town. Find paintings by David Totten at **Wildlife North Art Gallery** (907/733-5811, www.davidtotten.com) four miles south of Talkeetna.

GETTING THERE

The turnoff to Talkeetna is 100 miles north of Anchorage on the George Parks Highway, and the town is another 14 miles out on Talkeetna Spur Road.

Buses

Several companies provide van transportation to Talkeetna; one-way rates are around $65 to Anchorage, $75 to Denali, or $99 to Fairbanks. **Alaska/Yukon Trails** (907/479-2277 or 800/770-7275, www.alaskashuttle.com) has a daily run from Anchorage to Talkeetna, Denali, and Fairbanks in the summer. **Denali Overland Transportation** (907/733-2384 or 800/651-5221, www.denalioverland.com) has charter service connecting Anchorage, Talkeetna, and Denali, and often has space for individual travelers. **Alaska Park Connection** (907/245-0200 or 800/266-8625, www.alaskacoach.com) provides summertime service connecting Talkeetna with Seward, Anchorage, and Denali.

Train

The **Alaska Railroad** (907/265-2494 or 800/544-0552, www.alaskarailroad.com) *Denali Star* costs $146 one-way from Anchorage to Talkeetna. The train leaves Anchorage every morning at 8:15 A.M. and arrives in Talkeetna at 11:05 A.M., and a second train leaves Talkeetna for the return trip at 4:40 P.M. A local flag-stop train, the *Hurricane Turn,* runs the 50 miles from Talkeetna north to Hurricane and back Thursday–Sunday in the summer. It's a great way to see the countryside with locals for $96 round-trip.

North from Talkeetna

TRAPPER CREEK AND PETERSVILLE ROAD

The minuscule settlement of Trapper Creek (pop. 350) is at Mile 115 of the Parks Highway, and 16 miles north of the junction with Talkeetna Spur Road. Petersville Road splits off at Trapper Creek, providing access to the western end of Denali State Park, and offering some of the finest views of Mt. McKinley. A half-mile out on Petersville Road is **Trapper Creek Museum** (907/733-2555), a collection of local historical items and local crafts in a log cabin built in 1959. The museum is on Spruce Lane Farms, which raises miniature horses.

A number of rural subdivisions and homesteads are found along Petersville Road, and this is a popular winter destination for dog mushers and hordes of snowmobilers. The road continues all the way to old mining developments in the Petersville mining camp, 30 miles in, although the last section may not be passable without a high-clearance vehicle.

Accommodations

Located at Mile 114 of the Parks Highway, **Trapper Creek Inn & General Store** (907/733-2302, www.trappercreekinn.net) has guest rooms ($99–139 d), camping sites (RVs $27, tents $10), groceries, a deli, and a coin laundry with showers.

Alaska's Northland Inn (907/733-7377, www.alaskasnorthlandinn.com, $120 d) has a pair of two-level apartments with private baths and full kitchens. Relax in the great room with a pool table and satellite TV.

Set along two ponds, **Gate Creek Cabins** (907/733-1393, www.gatecreekcabins.com, $145 d plus $45 for each additional guest) is 11 miles out on Petersville Road, and the 10 modern log cabins (the largest has four bedrooms) contain kitchens, private baths, and a community sauna. Guests can borrow a canoe or paddleboat to cruise the ponds or try a bit of fishing. Be sure to ask about the mid-July bear-viewing opportunities. The cabins provide an extremely popular winter base for snowmobilers.

Forks Roadhouse (907/733-1851, www.forksroadhouse.com), 19 miles out, is a classic Alaskan bush roadhouse with a genuine sense of history. Rooms upstairs above the bar are $69 d (bath down the hall), a four-bed hostel room is $30 per person, and basic cabins cost $80 for four people (bath inside the lodge). Breakfast, burgers, and sandwiches ($8–13) are served in the roadhouse, or you can shoot a game of pool and tip a brew in the bar. There's live music most weekends, and campers can take a shower for $5.

If you want remote, check out **Cache Creek Cabins** (907/733-5200 summer or 907/776-5173 winter, www.cachecreekcabins.com, mid-June–Sept.), 39 rugged miles out on the Petersville Road. Six little cabins ($50 d) share a common bathhouse, and a nicer two-story cabin sleeps eight for $150; it has a private bath. The friendly owners can provide home-cooked meals ($50 pp per day) and gold panning in the creek ($25). It's a pretty setting with wonderful views of Denali on the drive in. High-clearance vehicles are best on this potholed road, but many folks make it here in rental cars. It is, however, a long and rough ride.

DENALI STATE PARK

This 325,240-acre state park (907/745-3975, www.alaskastateparks.org) lies just southeast of Denali National Park and Preserve and is bisected by the Parks Highway from Mile 132 to Mile 169. Situated between the Talkeetna Mountains to the east and the Alaska Range to the west, the landscape of Denali State Park varies from wide glaciated valleys to alpine tundra. The Chulitna and Tokositna Rivers flow through western sections of the park, while the eastern half is dominated by Curry Ridge and Kesugi Ridge, a 35-mile-long section of alpine country.

Denali State Park provides an excellent alternative wilderness experience to the crowds and hassles of its federal next-door neighbor. The Mountain is visible from all over the park, bears are abundant, and you won't need to stand in line for a permit to hike or camp while you wait for Mt. McKinley's mighty south face to show itself. Several trails offer a variety of hiking experiences and spectacular views. Trailhead parking is $5 per day.

Sights

Denali State Park is best known for its breathtaking **views of Mt. McKinley** and the Alaska Range from pullouts along the Parks Highway. If The Mountain or even "just" some of the lower peaks of the Alaska Range are out, you won't need to read the next sentence to know what or where the sights are. The best viewpoint along the highway in the park, and the most popular, is at Mile 135, where on a clear day you will find an interpretive signboard and crowds of fellow travelers. Set up your tripod and shoot, shoot, shoot. Other unforgettable viewpoints are at Miles 147, 158, and 162.

The **Alaska Veterans Memorial** at Mile 147 (within walking distance of Byers Lake Campground) consists of five monumental concrete blocks with stars carved out of them. Turn your back to the monument, and if you're lucky, there's blue-white McKinley, perfectly framed by tall spruce trees.

The western section of Denali State Park lies within the remote Peters Hills, an area known for its pristine Mt. McKinley vistas and open country. This section is accessed via the Petersville Road.

Recreation

Little Coal Creek trailhead is at Mile 164, five miles south of the park's northern boundary. This is the park's gentlest climb to the alpine tundra—five miles east up the trail by Little Coal Creek, then you cut southwest along Kesugi Ridge, with amazing views of the Range and glaciers; flags and cairns delineate the trail. Watch for bears! The trail goes 27 miles until it hooks up with Troublesome Creek Trail just up from Byers Lake Campground. About halfway there, **Ermine Lake Trail** cuts back down to the highway, an escape route in case of really foul weather.

Troublesome Creek Trail is so named because of frequent bear encounters; in fact, Troublesome Creek Trail is frequently closed in late summer and early fall because of the abundance of bears. It has two trailheads, one at the northeast tip of Byers Lake (Mile 147), the other at Mile 138. The park brochure describes this 15-mile hike along Troublesome Creek as moderate. It connects with Kesugi Ridge Trail just up from Byers Lake or descends to the easy five-mile **Byers Lake Loop Trail,** which brings you around to both campgrounds. Just down and across the road from the Byers Lake turnoff is a family day-hike along Lower Troublesome Creek—a gentle mile.

Based at Byers Lake, **Alaska Nature Guides** (907/733-1237, www.alaskanatureguides.com) guides easy 2.5-hour nature walks ($59 adults, $39 children), and more interesting 5.5-hour hikes up Kesugi Ridge ($94 adults, $39 children, including lunch and gear). The guides are former national park rangers with years of local experience; the company also provides custom trips for birders.

Denali Southside River Guides (907/733-7238, www.denaliriverguides.com) rents canoes and sit-on-top kayaks at Byers Lake; they're located at the day-use parking lot.

Accommodations

Turn off the highway at Mile 133 for a one-mile side road into **Mt. McKinley Princess Lodge** (907/733-2900 or 800/426-0500, www.princesslodges.com, mid-May–mid-Sept., $189 d). This stylish 334-room retreat is famous for its riverside location and picture-perfect vistas of the Alaska Range and Mt. McKinley. Most rooms are filled with Princess cruise passengers, but anyone can stay or eat here. The lodge itself centers around a "great room" with a stone fireplace, a pianist at the grand piano most evenings, and enormous windows fronting the mountain. Lodging is in smaller buildings scattered around the grounds; ask for one of the new rooms with a king bed. There's also a small fitness center, two outdoor hot tubs, a restaurant, and a café.

Located at the southern edge of Denali State Park near Mile 134, **Mary's McKinley View Lodge** (907/733-1555, www.mckinleyviewlodge.com) has a restaurant, great views of The Mountain out the big picture windows, and eight guest rooms ($100 d) with private baths. You can buy autographed copies of the many books authored by owner Jean Carey Richardson and her late mother, Mary Carey.

Cabins and Camping

Byers Lake Campground ($10) has large and uncrowded sites, water, outhouses, interpretive signs, and beautiful Byers Lake a stone's throw down the road. Also at Byers Lake are two popular **public-use cabins** (907/745-3975, www.alaskastateparks.org, $60). Just under two miles along the Loop Trail from the campground or across the lake by boat is **Lakeshore Campground,** with six primitive sites, outhouses, no running water, but unimpeded views of The Mountain and Range from your tent flap. Across the road and a quarter-mile south, **Lower Troublesome Creek Campground** ($10) has 20 sites and all the amenities of Byers Lake.

DENALI HIGHWAY

The Denali Highway, which stretches 136 miles east–west across the waist of mainland Alaska from Cantwell, from 30 miles south of Denali Park to Paxson at Mile 122 on the Richardson Highway, may be the best-kept secret in Alaska. Originally the Denali Highway was the only road into Denali National Park, and this beautiful side trip has been largely ignored by visitors since the opening of the George Parks Highway in 1971. Denali Highway is paved for 21 miles on the east end of the road (from Paxson to Tangle Lakes), and for three miles on the western end, but the rest is well-maintained gravel, which has received an undeserved bad rap—usually from folks hoping to set world land-speed records on their Alaska vacation.

The Denali Highway offers a varied selection of outstanding scenery and wildlife-viewing opportunities. Much of the route punches through the foothills of the magnificent Alaska Range. This area is part of the home range of the huge 30,000-strong Nelchina caribou herd. In the fall they begin to group in the greatest numbers—sightings of several hundred caribou arc not unusual.

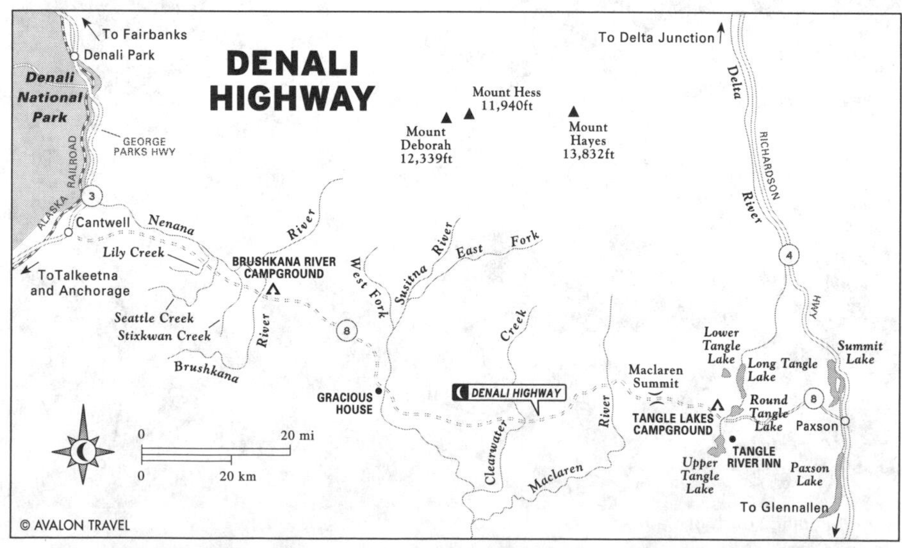

The Denali Highway is closed October–mid-May, but in the winter it becomes a popular trail for snowmobilers, dog mushers, and cross-country skiers. Die-hard Alaskans also use this trail in the winter for access to unparalleled ice fishing and caribou and ptarmigan hunting.

As always, travelers on the Denali Highway should be prepared for emergencies. Always carry a spare tire and tire-changing tools, water, some snacks, and warm clothing. Towing is available from Paxson, Gracious House, and Cantwell, but it ain't cheap, so take your time and be safe.

History

The Denali Highway began as a "cat" track in the early 1950s when a man named Earl Butcher first established a hunting camp at Tangle Lakes. Known for years as Butcher's Camp, it's now the site of Tangle Lakes Lodge. About the same time, Chalmer Johnson established a camp at Round Tangle Lake. Now known as the Tangle River Inn, this lodge is still operated by the Johnson family.

Cantwell

A minuscule settlement (pop. 160) at the junction of the Parks Highway and Denali Highway, Cantwell began as a railroad settlement, and a cluster of decrepit buildings are strewn along the tracks two miles west of the highway. Cantwell is less than 30 miles south of Denali National Park, and a couple of businesses provide the staples: fuel, food, lodging, and booze. Most folks stop to fill up on the expensive gas, get a soda, and tool on up the highway. There aren't a lot of reasons to stay in Cantwell itself, though the surrounding country is grand.

Two miles off the main highway, **Cantwell Lodge** (907/768-2300, www.cantwellodgeak.com) houses a café, a bar, a liquor store, a laundry, showers, and Wi-Fi. Just a quarter-mile up Denali Highway, **Backwoods Lodge** (907/768-2232 or 800/292-2232, www.backwoodslodge.

igloo building south of Cantwell

com, $140–170 d) has modern motel rooms with fridges and microwaves.

Blue Home B&B (907/768-2020, www.cantwell-bluehome.de, $120 d) is two miles off the highway, with two guest rooms that share a bath, full breakfasts, and Wi-Fi. The owners also speak German.

Park RVs at **Cantwell RV Park** (907/768-2210 or 800/940-2210, www.alaskaone.com/cantwellrv, mid-May–mid-Sept., tents $18, RVs $30), an open lot near the junction with the Parks Highway. Services include Wi-Fi, showers, and a dump station.

Denali Sightseeing Safaris (907/240-0357, www.denalisights.com, June–mid-Sept.) operates from the igloo on steroids at Mile 188 of the Parks Highway (22 miles south of Cantwell). These unique tours are in customized big-tired trucks to allow them to cross glacial rivers and take you up old mining roads into the spectacular alpine area. Seven-hour treks are $160 adults, $80 children under 13.

EAST ON THE DENALI HIGHWAY

About three miles east of the Denali Highway–Parks Highway junction is a turnout with a view of Cantwell and Mt. McKinley, if it's out. There's another potential view of the mountain at Mile 13, then in another five miles the highway runs parallel to the Nenana River. The headwaters of the Nenana emanate from a western digit of the ice fields atop the Alaska Range trio of peaks: **Mt. Deborah** on the left at 12,339 feet, **Mt. Hess** in the middle at 11,940 feet, and **Mt. Hayes** on the right at 13,832 feet.

Over the next 10 miles the road crosses Lily Creek, Seattle Creek, and Stixkwan Creek; throw in a line and pull up some grayling or Dolly Varden. At Mile 31 you come to the **Brushkana River,** where the Bureau of Land Management (BLM) has a good campground ($8) right on the river, and over the next 10 miles you get some great views of the three prominent peaks, along with the West Fork Glacier. The southern glaciers off Deborah, Hess, and Hayes feed the Susitna River, which flows west to the Parks Highway, and then south to empty into Cook Inlet across from Anchorage.

Gracious House Lodge and Beyond

Fifty-four miles east of the junction of the Parks and Denali Highways is Gracious House Lodge (907/259-1111 summer or 907/333-3148 winter, www.alaskaone.com/gracious, June–mid-Sept.), with motel rooms ($130 d with private bath and continental breakfast, $80 s, $100 d with shower house). RV and tent spaces are also available, along with minor tire and mechanical repairs and towing. The owners can set up air-taxi and guide services.

Five miles farther, you cross the single-lane 1,000-foot-long Susitna River bridge. Farther south, the Susitna is a popular river to float, but passage between here and there is considered impossible because of the impassable Devil's Canyon just downriver from the bridge.

At Mile 79, the highway crosses Clearwater Creek; there are pit toilets at a rest stop and camping area here. In six miles is a turnout with a view of numerous lakes and ponds that provide a staging area for waterfowl; look for ducks, cranes, geese, trumpeter swans, and migrating shorebirds.

Maclaren

At Mile 93 out of Cantwell, the road crosses the Maclaren River, a tributary of the Susitna, flowing from the southern ice fields of mighty Mt. Hayes. From here to the other end of the Denali Highway, you get occasional views of the three Alaska Range peaks. A mile west of the bridge is Maclaren River Road, which leads 12 miles north to Maclaren Glacier.

Just before the bridge crossing is **Maclaren River Lodge** (907/822-5444, www.maclarenlodge.com). This year-round facility caters to hikers, hunters, anglers, and sightseers in the summer, and snowmobilers, skiers, and dog mushers all winter. You can stay overnight in a recently built duplex lodge ($60 d or $120 for up to 5 people) with shared baths, or in a separate lakeside cabin ($90 d) with a bathhouse.

The lodge has a restaurant (daily 7 A.M.–9 P.M., dinner $20–25) serving burgers, steaks, seafood, and vegetarian specials. The small bar has beer and wine, and all sorts of day trips into the backcountry are offered, including a river trip to Maclaren Glacier for $175 d.

In another seven miles is Maclaren Summit, at 4,080 feet the second-highest road pass in Alaska. It provides breathtaking views of Mt. Hayes and the Maclaren Glacier. Peer through binoculars at the plains below to spot wildlife. Up at the summit you might see rock ptarmigan.

East End

The BLM's **Tangle Lakes Campground** (907/822-3217, www.blm.gov/ak, free) at Mile 113, has water pumps, pit toilets, blueberries in season, and a boat launch for extended canoe trips into the "tangle" (or maze) of lakes and ponds and creeks in the neighborhood.

Two miles east of the campground is **Tangle River Inn** (907/822-3970 summer or 907/895-4022 winter, www.tangleriverinn.com, late May–Sept.). Jack and Naidine Johnson have owned this classic Alaskan lodge since 1970. The Johnsons sell gas, liquor, and gifts, and they offer good home cooking, a lively bar, lodging ($40 s in the bunkhouse, $74 d with shared bath, or $100 d for units with full baths), canoe rentals, and fishing gear.

The **Tangle Lakes Archaeological District** begins at Mile 119 and extends back to Crazy Notch at Mile 90. A short hike from the highway to any given promontory along this 30-mile stretch could have you standing at an ancient Athabascan hunting camp where no human footprints have been made for hundreds of years.

At Mile 122, there's a viewpoint from the summit that looks south over a great tundra plain. The three most prominent peaks of the Wrangell Mountains are visible from here: Mt. Sanford on the left, Mt. Drum on the right, and Mt. Wrangell in the middle.

At Mile 125 is a paved turnout with a view of **Ten Mile Lake.** A short trail leads down to the lake, where you can catch grayling and trout. A turnout at Mile 129 affords a spectacular view of the Alaska Range to the north. The Gulkana and Gakona Glaciers can be seen from this point. The Denali Highway joins the Richardson Highway at Paxson.

Paxson and Points North

This tiny settlement at Mile 186 of the Richardson Highway and Mile 136 (from Cantwell) of the Denali Highway has two lodging options. **Paxson Lodge** (907/822-3330, www.paxson-lodge.com) offers gas, meals, lodging ($80 s, $90 d), and free Wi-Fi. There's a big deck for summertime dining three meals a day.

Located just north of the highway junction,**Paxson Alpine Tours** (907/822-5972, www.denalihwy.com), guides wildlife float trips on the Gulkana and Delta Rivers, birding hikes, and other adventures. Owners Audie Bakewell and Denali Jenny also operate **Denali Highway Cabins,** with peaceful riverside cabins containing private baths for $100–150 d, including a communal kitchen. A large guesthouse with a full kitchen is available for $175 d plus $25 per additional guest. There's a two-night minimum stay. Rent a mountain bike or one of their canoes to paddle the Tangle Lakes.

One of Alaska's top spring events, **Arctic Man Ski and Sno-Glo Classic** (www.arcticman.com) takes place in early April at Summit Lake, on the Richardson Highway 10 miles north of the Denali Highway junction. This four-day event attracts thousands of spectators and motorheads with a combination of downhill skiing and snowmobiling. Skiers first descend 1,700 feet in elevation in less than two miles, ending in a narrow canyon where they meet up with a snowmobiler who tows them up another steep hill at speeds topping 85 mph. From here, the skier drops another 1,200 feet to the finish line. Its an adrenaline rush for all involved.

For one of Alaska's most memorable drives, head north from Paxson along the Richardson Highway. The pipeline parallels the route as it climbs through a grand landscape of tundra, mountains, and rivers. Another 30 miles north is the century-old **Black Rapids Roadhouse,** slowly being restored after years of neglect. Behind this and up the hill is **Black Rapids Lodge** (907/455-6158 or 877/825-9413, www.lodgeatblackrapids.com), a beautiful timber-frame structure with lodging ($175–260 d) in 10 spacious guest rooms with private or shared baths and Wi-Fi. Meals are $10 for breakfast, $15 for lunch, or $25 for dinner; reservations are preferred.

The BLM's **Paxson Lake campgrounds** ($8) is at Mile 175 of the Richardson, 10 miles south of the junction with the Denali Highway.

Denali National Park and Preserve

Alaska's most famous tourist attraction, Denali National Park (907/683-2294, www.nps.gov/dena) draws over 400,000 visitors during its brief summer season. Most travelers come to see Mt. McKinley, highest peak in North America (20,320 feet), which towers above the surrounding lowlands and 14,000–17,000-foot peaks. Although it's visible only one day in three, and often shrouded for a week or more at a time, those who get lucky and see the mountain experience a thrill equivalent to its majesty and grandeur. Those who don't are usually consoled by lower snowcapped mountains and attending glaciers, high passes and adrenaline-pumping drops off the road, tundra vistas and "drunken forests," and an incredible abundance of wildlife, including caribou, moose, sheep, and bears. But even if the mountain is socked in, the grizzlies are hiding, and the shuttle-bus windows are fogged up, you're still smack in the middle of some of the most spectacular and accessible wilderness in the

Flightseeing trips from Talkeetna often land in Denali National Park.

world. It was the call of the wild that brought you out here in the first place; all you have to do is step outside and answer.

THE LAND

The Alaska Range is a U-shaped chain that extends roughly 600 miles from the top of the Alaska Peninsula (at the head of the Aleutians) up through the park and down below Tok. It's only a small part, however, of the coastal mountains that include California's Sierra Nevada, the Northwest's Cascades, the Coast Mountains of British Columbia, Yukon's St. Elias Range, and eastern Alaska's Wrangell Range. The Park Road starts out a bit north of the Alaska Range and follows the U 90 miles southwest toward its heart—Mt. McKinley. One thing that makes the mountain so spectacular is that the surrounding lowlands are so low: The entrance is at 1,700 feet, and the highest point on the road, Thoroughfare Pass, is just under 4,000 feet. The base of Mt. McKinley is at 2,000 feet, and the north face rises at a 60-degree angle straight up to 20,000 feet—the highest vertical rise in the world.

Weather patterns here differ between the south side of the range (wetter and cooler) and the north. During the summer, the prevailing winds come from the south, carrying warm moisture from the Pacific. When they run smack into the icy rock wall of the Alaska Range, they climb, the moisture condenses, and depending on the amount of moisture and altitude, it either rains or snows—a lot. On top of that whole system sits mighty Mt. McKinley, high, cold, and alone; it's so alone that the mountain has its own relationship to the weather. The combination of wind, wet, cold, and height creates extremely localized—and often violent—weather around Mt. McKinley. Storms can blow in within an hour and last a week or more, dumping 10 feet of snow. Winds scream in at up to 80 mph. The mercury drops below zero in mid-July. Some of the worst weather in the world swirls around up there. But when the mountain emerges bright white against bright blue, and you're craning your neck to see the

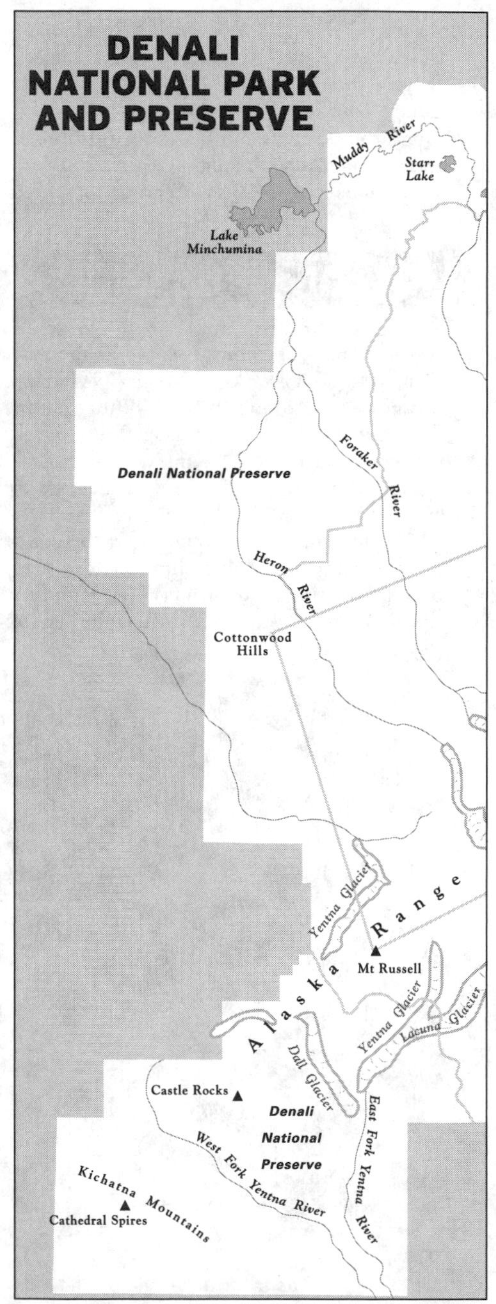

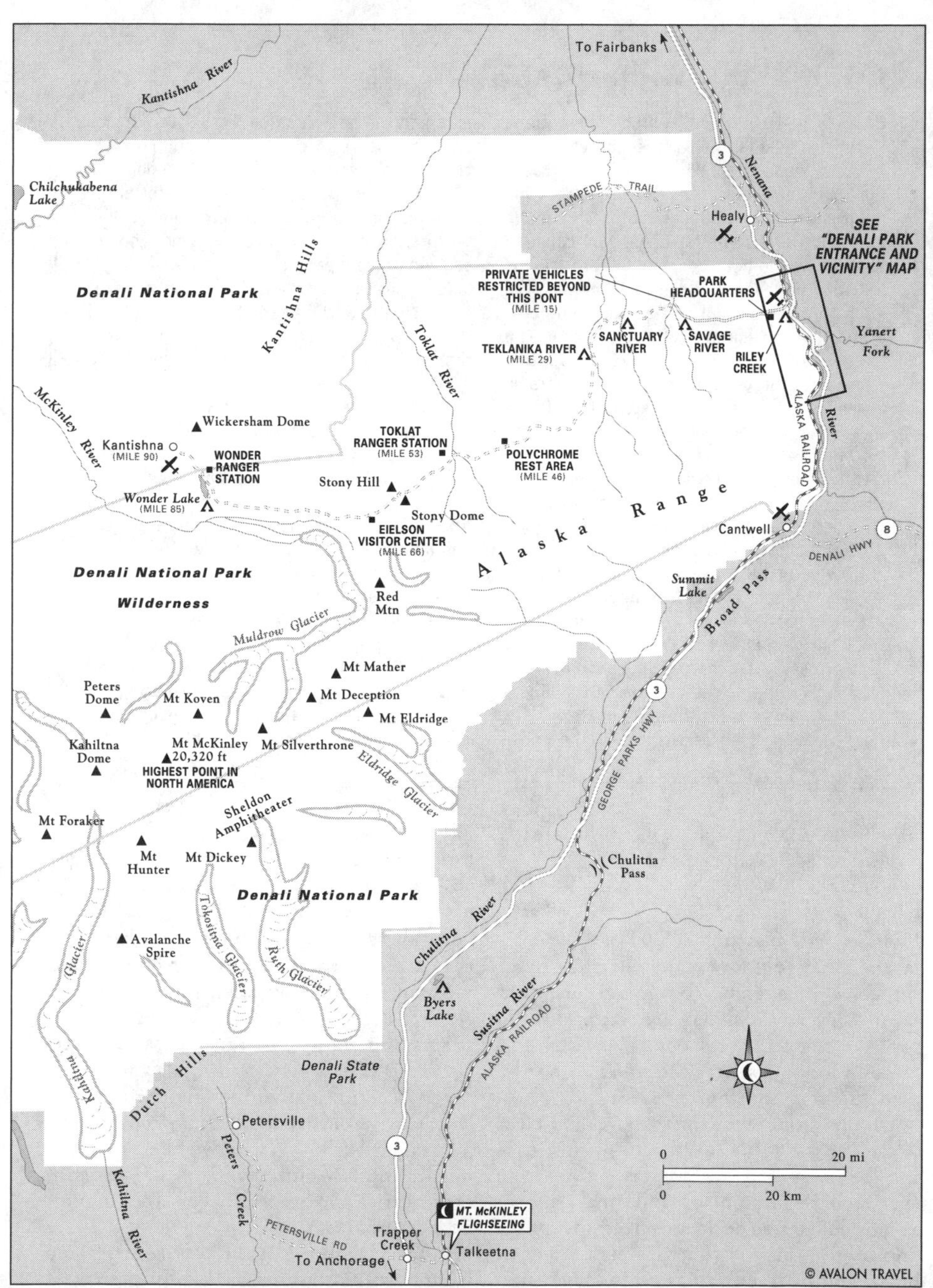
To Fairbanks
Kantishna River
Chilchukabena Lake
STAMPEDE TRAIL
Nenana
Healy
SEE "DENALI PARK ENTRANCE AND VICINITY" MAP
Denali National Park
Kantishna Hills
PRIVATE VEHICLES RESTRICTED BEYOND THIS PONT (MILE 15)
PARK HEADQUARTERS
Toklat River
SANCTUARY RIVER
SAVAGE RIVER
TEKLANIKA RIVER (MILE 29)
RILEY CREEK
Yanert Fork
McKinley River
Wickersham Dome
Kantishna (MILE 90)
WONDER RANGER STATION
TOKLAT RANGER STATION (MILE 53)
POLYCHROME REST AREA (MILE 46)
ALASKA RAILROAD
River
Stony Hill
Wonder Lake (MILE 85)
Stony Dome
Alaska Range
EIELSON VISITOR CENTER (MILE 66)
Cantwell
8
DENALI HWY
Denali National Park Wilderness
Red Mtn
Summit Lake
Broad Pass
Muldrow Glacier
Mt Mather
Mt Deception
3
Peters Dome
Mt Koven
Mt Eldridge
GEORGE PARKS HWY
Kahiltna Dome
Mt McKinley 20,320 ft
HIGHEST POINT IN NORTH AMERICA
Mt Silverthrone
Eldridge Glacier
Sheldon Amphitheater
Mt Foraker
Mt Hunter
Mt Dickey
Chulitna Pass
Denali National Park
Chulitna River
Avalanche Spire
Glacier
Tokositna Glacier
Ruth Glacier
Byers Lake
Susitna River
ALASKA RAILROAD
Kahiltna
Dutch Hills
Denali State Park
Petersville
Peters Creek
3
0
20 mi
0
20 km
Kahiltna River
PETERSVILLE RD
MT. McKINLEY FLIGHSEEING
Trapper Creek
Talkeetna
To Anchorage
© AVALON TRAVEL

COEXISTING WITH BEARS

Bears seem to bring out conflicting emotions in people. The first is an almost gut reaction of fear and trepidation: What if the bear attacks me? But then comes that other urge: What will my friends say when they see these *incredible* bear photos? Both of these reactions can lead to problems in bear country. "Bearanoia" is a justifiable fear, but it can easily be taken to such an extreme that one avoids going outdoors at all for fear of running into a bear. The "I want to get close-up shots of that bear and her cubs" attitude can provoke a bear attack. The middle ground incorporates a knowledge of and respect for bears with a sense of caution that keeps you alert for danger without letting fear rule your wilderness travels. Nothing is ever completely safe in this world, but with care you can avoid most of the common pitfalls that lead to bear encounters.

Brown (grizzly) bears occur throughout Alaska, except on islands in southern Southeast Alaska, in the Bering Sea, and out on most of the Aleutian Chain. Black bears are found in forested area across most of the state, but not on several islands in northern Southeast Alaska. Old-timers joke that bears are easy to differentiate: A black bear climbs up the tree after you, while a grizzly snaps the tree off at the base. Both grizzlies and black bears pose potential threats to backcountry travelers; polar bears are potentially the most dangerous of the three species, but they are almost never encountered by summertime visitors, since they only occur in remote northern and western parts of the state.

Enter bear country with respect but not fear. Bears rarely attack humans; you're a thousand times more likely to be injured in a highway accident than by a bear. In fact, more people in Alaska are hurt each year by moose or dogs than by bears. Contrary to the stories you often hear, bears have good eyesight, but they depend more upon their excellent senses of smell and hearing. A bear can tell who has walked through an area, and how recently, with just a quick sniff of the air. Most bears hear or smell you long before you realize their presence, and they hightail it away.

Bears are beautiful, eminently fascinating, and surprisingly intelligent animals. They can be funny, playful and inquisitive, vicious or protective, and unpredictable. The more you watch bears in the wild, the more complex their lives seem, and the more they become individual animals, not simply the big and bad.

top, it's an unforgettable sight worth waiting around for—even in the rain.

Flora and Fauna

From sea level to around 2,300 feet is the habitat for the **boreal forest,** in which the black spruce, with its somber foliage and clusters of tawny cones, is the climax tree. Younger white spruce, along with deciduous aspen, birch, and cottonwood, grow near the streams and the road and in recently burned areas.

Climbing out of the forest above 2,300 feet you enter the **taiga,** a Russian word meaning "land of twigs." This transition zone (between the forest below and tundra above) accommodates no deciduous trees; the spruce are thinned out and runty (though they can be over 60 years old), and a green shag carpet of bush, mostly dwarf willow, layers the floor. Sitka spruce is the state tree because of its size, grandeur, and commercial value, but it's the willow that vegetates Alaska. And it has endless uses: Before synthetics like nylon, the bark was stripped, split, and braided and made into rope, bows, wicker baskets, snowshoes, fishnets, and small game and bird snares and traps. The inner bark is sweet; the sap is very sweet. Young buds and shoots are edible and nourishing, and willows are the nearly exclusive staple of the moose diet. The taiga also hosts a variety of berries: blueberries and low-bush cranberries by the ton, crowberries, bearberries, soap and salmon berries, and raspberries.

Above 2,500 feet is the **tundra,** its name a Lapp word meaning "vast, rolling, treeless

© DON PITCHER
caribou in Denali National Park

plain." There are two types of tundra: The moist, or Alaskan, tundra is characterized by the taiga's dwarf shrubbery, high grasses, and berries, but no trees; the alpine tundra, the highest zone, has grasses, moss, lichens, and small hardy wildflowers, including the stunning forget-me-not, Alaska's state flower.

The animal life varies with the vegetation. In the forest, look for moose, porcupine, snowshoe hare, marten, lynx, two kinds of weasels, red or tree squirrels, and several varieties of small rodents. On the taiga—or in both the forest and the tundra—you might see coyotes, wolves, foxes, grizzlies, and ground squirrels. In the tundra, keep an eye out for caribou, wolverines, Dall sheep, marmots, voles, lemmings, and shrews.

HISTORY

In 1896 a prospector named Bill Dickey was tramping around Interior Alaska looking for gold. Like everyone who sees it, Dickey was captivated by the size and magnificence of the mountain that was then variously known as Tenada, Denali, Densmore's Mountain, Traleika, and Bulshaia. Dickey was from Ohio, William McKinley's home state, and a Princeton graduate in economics. When he came out of the bush and heard that McKinley had been nominated for president, he promptly renamed the mountain "McKinley," wrote numerous articles for stateside magazines, and lobbied in Washington, D.C., in support of adoption of the name, which finally caught on after President McKinley was assassinated in 1901. The name has been something of a sore point with Alaskans ever since, for McKinley had absolutely nothing to do with the mountain, and the more lyrical Native Alaskan names were completely ignored. Many in Alaska support renaming the peak Denali ("the high one"), a term used by Native Alaskans of the lower Yukon and Kuskokwim Rivers. Unfortunately, any move to eliminate "McKinley" from maps is inevitably met by howls of protest from Ohio's congressional delegation.

Creating a Park

Harry Karstens reached the Klondike in 1898 when he was 19, bored by Chicago and attracted by adventure and gold. Within a year he'd crossed over into U.S. territory and wound up at Seventymile, 20 miles south of Eagle. When the local mail carrier lost everything one night in a card game and committed suicide, Karstens took his place. He became proficient at dog mushing and trailblazing and within a few years was delivering mail on a primitive trail between Eagle and Valdez, a 900-mile round-trip every month (the Richardson Highway follows the same route). Later he moved on to Fairbanks and began delivering mail to Kantishna, the mining town on what is now the west end of the park, growing very fond of and familiar with the north side of the Alaska Range. So when a naturalist from the East Coast, Charles Sheldon, arrived in 1906 to study Dall sheep in the area, Karstens guided him around Mt. McKinley's northern foothills, delineating the habitat of the sheep. Karstens was also the coleader of the four-man expedition that was the first party to successfully climb the true peak of Mt. McKinley, the south summit, in 1913.

Meanwhile, Charles Sheldon was back in Washington, lobbying for national-park status for the Dall sheep habitat, and when Mt. McKinley National Park was created in 1917, Karstens was the obvious choice to become the first park superintendent. He held that post 1921–1928, patrolling the park boundaries by dogsled.

Woodrow Wilson signed the bill that created Mt. McKinley National Park, Alaska's first, in 1917. The Park Road, begun five years later, was completed to Kantishna in 1940. In 1980, with the passage of the Alaska National Interest Lands Conservation Act, McKinley Park was renamed Denali National Park and Preserve and expanded to nearly 6 million acres, roughly the size of Vermont.

Pioneer Climbs

Many pioneers and prospectors had seen the mountain and approached it, but Alfred Brooks, a member of the first U.S. Geological Survey expedition in Alaska in 1902, was the first to set foot on it. He approached it from the south and reached an elevation of 7,500 feet before running out of time. He published an article in the January 1903 issue of *National Geographic* in which he recommended approaching the mountain from the north. Following that suggestion, the next attempt was from the north, led by James Wickersham, U.S. district judge for Alaska. Judge Wickersham was sent from Seattle to bring law and order to Eagle in 1900; he moved to Fairbanks in 1903. That summer, he had a spare couple of months and set out to climb the mountain, traveling more than 100 miles overland and reaching the 7,000-foot level of the north face, later named Wickersham Wall in honor of His Honor.

That same summer, Dr. Frederick Cook, who'd been with Peary's first party to attempt to reach the north pole in 1891 and Amundsen's Antarctic expedition of 1897, also attempted to climb the mountain from the north and reached 11,300 feet. In 1906, Cook returned to attempt Mt. McKinley from the south, but he failed to get near it. His party broke up and went their separate directions, and a month later, Cook sent a telegram to New York claiming he'd reached the peak. This was immediately doubted by the members of his party, who challenged his photographic and cartographic "evidence." But through public lectures and articles, Cook's reputation as the first man to reach the peak grew. Two years later, he claimed to have reached the North Pole several months ahead of another Peary expedition, and Cook began to enjoy a cult status in the public consciousness. Simultaneously, however, his credibility among fellow explorers rapidly declined, and Cook vanished from sight. This further fueled the controversy and led to the Sourdough Expedition of 1910.

Four sourdoughs in Fairbanks simply decided to climb the mountain to validate or eviscerate Cook's published description of his route. They left town in December and climbed to the north peak in early April. The three members who'd actually reached the peak stayed in Kantishna to take care of business, while the fourth member, Tom Lloyd, who hadn't reached the peak, returned to Fairbanks and lied that he had. By the time the other three returned to town in June, Lloyd's story had already been published and widely discredited. So nobody believed the other three—*especially* when they claimed they'd climbed up to the north peak and down to their base camp at 11,000 feet in 18 hours, with a thermos of hot chocolate, four doughnuts, and dragging a 14-foot spruce log that they planted up top and claimed was still there. Finally, in 1913, the Hudson Stuck–Harry Karstens expedition reached the true summit, the south peak, and could prove that they'd done so beyond a shadow of a doubt. Only then was the Sourdough Expedition vindicated: All four members of the Stuck party saw the spruce pole still standing on the north peak!

Today more than 1,000 mountaineers attempt the summit of Mt. McKinley each year, and approximately half of them actually reach the top. The youngest climbers ever to summit, a girl and a boy, were 12; the oldest man was 71, and the oldest woman 62.

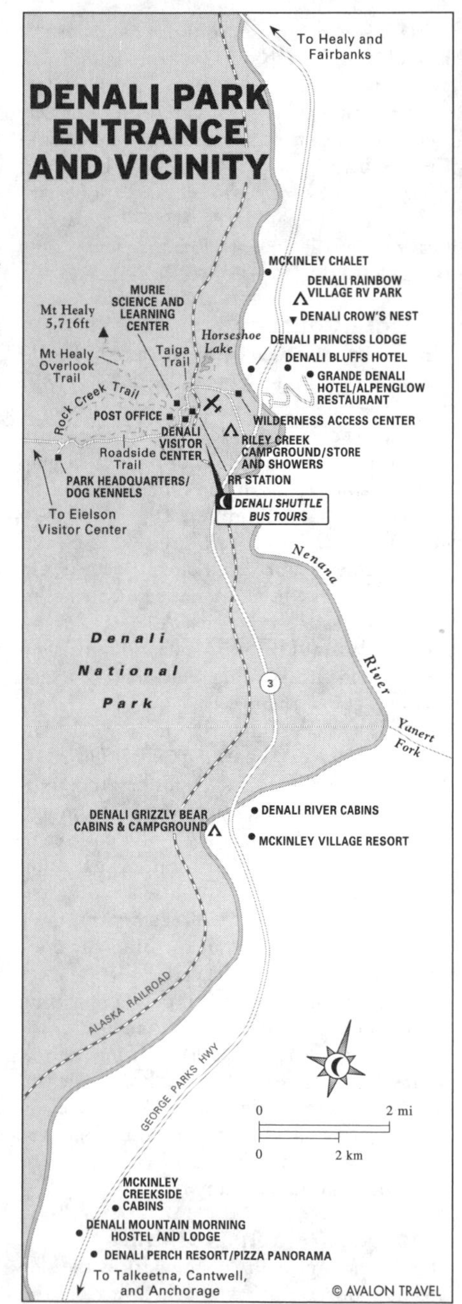

PARK ENTRANCE

Park admission is $10 per person or $20 per vehicle, or buy a National Park Pass—good for all national parks—for $80 per year. A Senior Pass for all national parks is available to anyone over age 62 for a one-time fee of $10, and people with disabilities can get a free Access Pass that covers all the parks. Get additional park information at 907/683-2294, www.nps.gov/dena.

Planning Your Time

Denali National Park is open year-round, though most facilities only operate mid-May–mid-September. Plowing of the Park Road generally starts in early May, but only the first 30 miles are open before late May, when the shuttle buses begin running. Those who arrive before this date will not be able to reach the best vantage points for Mt. McKinley.

The wildflowers peak around summer

solstice—as do the mosquitoes. The berries, rose hips, and mushrooms are best in mid-August—as are the no-see-ums. The fall colors on the tundra are gorgeous around Labor Day weekend, when the crowds start to thin out and the northern lights start to appear, but it can get very cold. A skeleton winter Park Service crew patrols the park by dogsled. After the first heavy snowfall, the Park Road is plowed only to headquarters.

Visitors Centers

The **Denali Visitors Center** (daily 8 A.M.–6 P.M. mid-May–mid-Sept.) is at Mile 1.2 of the Park Road and right across from the railroad depot. Step inside to explore the exhibits, get oriented from the enormous relief map of the park, talk with the rangers, and view an extraordinary 20-minute film, *Heartbeats of Denali*. Pick up a copy of *Denali Alpenglow,* the park newspaper, and check the bulletin board for a schedule of today's guided walks, talks, and kids' programs. Adjacent are an Alaska Natural History Association gift shop and Morino Grill, serving sandwiches, burgers, fish-and-chips, and pizzas.

On the other side of the traffic circle, the **Murie Science and Learning Center** (907/683-1269 or 888/688-1269, www.murieslc.org) promotes scientific research and education through youth camps, field seminars, and courses in the summer. In the off-season—when other facilities are closed—the Murie building becomes the **winter park visitors center** (daily 9 A.M.–4 P.M.). Check out the dinosaur track here that was found in the park.

Get park shuttle bus tickets and campground information at the **Wilderness Access Center** (daily 5 A.M.–8 P.M. mid-May to mid-Sept.), located a half-mile up the Park Road. The reservations desk opens at 7 A.M. While here you could also watch an 18-minute film about the park or buy snacks. This facility is run by the park concessionaire, Aramark.

Sled Dog Demonstrations

One of the highlights of the park is the sled dog demonstration at the kennels behind headquarters. The dogs are beautiful and accessible (the ones not behind fences are chosen for friendliness and patience with people), and the anxious collective howl they orchestrate when the lucky six dogs are selected to run is something to hear. Naturalists give a talk about the current and historical uses of dogs in the park, their breeding and training, different commands for controlling them, and the challenge of maintaining a working kennel in a national park. Then dogs are hitched up to a wheel sled and run around a gravel track. The enthusiasm of the dogs to get off the chain and into the harness is an eyebrow-raising glimpse into the consciousness of Alaskan sled dogs—they live to run.

Demonstrations are given daily at 10 A.M., 2 P.M., and 4 P.M. A free shuttle bus leaves the Denali Visitors Center and the Riley Creek bus shelter 30 minutes before the demos. Don't miss this one!

GETTING AROUND DENALI

In 1971, before the George Parks Highway connected McKinley National Park to Fairbanks (125 miles) and Anchorage (245 miles), you had to take the train, or from Fairbanks you had to drive down to Delta Junction, take the Richardson Highway to Paxson, the Denali Highway to Cantwell, then the Parks Highway up to the park entrance, for a grand total of 340 miles. From Anchorage you had to drive to Glennallen, then up the Richardson to Paxson, over to Cantwell and beyond, for 440 miles. That year, nearly 45,000 visitors passed through the park. In 1972, when the George Parks Highway radically reduced driving times from both main urban centers, almost 90,000 visitors came. In anticipation of the huge jump in tourism, the Park Service initiated the shuttle system of school buses running a regularly scheduled service along the Park Road. Today, the park sees 400,000 visitors annually.

Denali Shuttle Bus Tours

There's no question that the shuttle system is highly beneficial to the park experience: The road is tricky and dangerous, crowds are much more easily controlled, there's much less impact on the wildlife (which take the buses for granted), and it's much easier to see wildlife when 40 passengers have eyeballs, binoculars, spotting scopes, and telephotos trained on the tundra. The excellent *Denali Road Guide,* available in park bookstores, has detailed information on sights along the road.

Green buses depart from the Wilderness Access Center daily mid-May–mid-September, with some continuing all the way to the Kantishna, an exhausting 89-mile 13-hour round-trip ride. Most visitors don't go that far (or certainly not in one day), turning around instead at Polychrome Pass, Eielson, Wonder Lake, or other places along the way. Buses for Eielson begin departing from the Wilderness Access Center at 5 A.M. and continue roughly every 30 minutes through 3:30 P.M. Other buses depart during the day for Polychrome/Toklat and Wonder Lake.

You can reserve tickets in advance (907/272-7275 or 800/622-7275, **www.reservedenali.com**), starting in mid-February over the phone or on December 1 via the Web, and up to the day before you travel. Sixty-five percent of the available tickets go on sale December 1; the other 35 percent are made available just two days ahead of the travel date. Adults pay $25 to Polychrome/Toklat (6 hours round-trip), $32 to Eielson (8 hours round-trip), $43 to Wonder Lake (11 hours round-trip), and $47 to Kantishna (12 hours round-trip). Kids under 15 ride free, and fares are half the adult price for children ages 15–17. Fares do not include park entrance fees ($10). Wheelchair-accessible shuttle buses are available. Backpackers pay $31 round-trip to anywhere in the park on the special **camper bus.**

It's recommended that you try to get on an early-morning bus into the park: There is a better chance to see wildlife and the mountain in the cool of the morning, and more time to get off the bus and fool around in the backcountry.

Schedules are readily available at the visitors centers and hotels. Take everything you need, as nothing (except books and postcards) is for sale once you get into the park. You can get off the bus and flag it down to get back on (if there's room; the buses leave with a few seats empty to pick up day-hikers in the park) anywhere along the road. Many riders never get off the bus at all and just stay on it for the entire exhausting round-trip.

Local Shuttles

A free **Riley Creek Loop Bus** provides service connecting the Riley Creek Campground, Wilderness Access Center, and train depot every half hour 5:30 A.M.–9:30 P.M. In addition, a free bus connects the Wilderness Access Center with the dogsled demonstrations at park headquarters. The **Savage River Shuttle** also provides a free shuttle service from the visitors center to Savage River Bridge. Private shuttle buses run between the visitors center and Denali Bluffs Hotel, Princess Lodge, and McKinley Village.

Tour Buses

The park's **tan nature tour buses** leave from the Wilderness Access Center throughout the day. For a good introduction, take a five-hour **Denali natural history tour** ($62 adults, $32 children) to Primrose Ridge (17 miles each way), or for a better look, join the seven-hour **tundra wilderness tour** ($104 adults, $53 children, includes a box lunch) to Toklat (53 miles each way). **Kantishna Experience** is a 12-hour tour ($155 adults, $78 children, includes lunch) that focuses both on wildlife and the history of this old gold mining town. These tours are extremely popular, and they fill up fast, so you need to make your reservations (907/272-7275 or 800/622-7275, www.reservedenali.com) as far in advance as possible.

Katnishna Wilderness Trails (907/683-8002 or 800/230-7275, www.denaliwildlifetour.com, $145) provides private all-day bus tours that leave Denali Park hotels at 6:30 A.M. These take you to Kantishna Roadhouse near the end of the road for a lunch, gold panning, and sled dog demonstration before heading back out, arriving at the hotels by 7 P.M.

Driving

For most of the summer, *only the first 15 miles (to Savage River) of the Park Road are open to private vehicles.* This portion is paved and makes for an excellent day trip. From early May, when the road is plowed, to late May, when the shuttle buses start running, it is possible to drive as far as the Teklanika River rest area at Mile 30. The road beyond this doesn't open until late May, so early park arrivals will not be able to see many of the sights for which it is famous.

At the end of summer, the Park Road is opened to auto traffic for four days in mid-September. Only 400 vehicles are allowed per day, and passes are selected by a lottery. In a typical year, you may be competing with 10,000 other entries for these passes! You'll need to apply during July, but contact the Park Service (907/683-2294, www.nps.gov/dena) for details. A handful of professional photographers are allowed vehicular access to the park during the summer, but these slots are highly sought after, and may involve giving up your first-born child and opening your home as a lodging place for all Park Service employees who might be passing through.

HEADING OUT ON THE PARK ROAD

A few miles beyond headquarters the road climbs out of the boreal forest, levels off, and travels due west through a good example of taiga. The ridgeline to the north (right) of the road is known as the **Outer Range,** foothills of the massive Alaska Range to the south (left). The Outer Range is much older, of different geological origins, and much more rounded and eroded than the jagged Alaska Range. The first view of the mountain comes up at Mile 9; look southwest. The day has to be nearly perfectly clear to see Mt. McKinley from here: You're at around 2,400 feet, and the mountain is at 20,000 feet, which leaves nearly an 18-grand spread over 70-odd miles of potential cloud cover. That's a lot of potential.

Next you pass the **Savage River Campground,** then wind down to the river valley and cross the bridge that marks the end of road access for those in private vehicles. The "Checkpoint Charlie" kiosk at Mile 15 has a park employee to turn back private vehicles; they're prohibited beyond this point. From the bridge, look upriver (left) and notice the broad, U-shaped, glacial valley with large gravel deposits forming braids or channels, then look right to compare the V-shaped valley obviously cut by running water. The Savage Glacier petered out right where the bridge is now around 15,000 years ago during the last ice age. Here you also kiss the pavement good-bye, then start climbing Primrose Ridge, which offers excellent hiking, especially in June–early July when the wildflowers are in full bloom. Turn around and look back at the Savage Bridge; the stark rock outcropping just up from it has a distinct resemblance to an Indian's facial bone structure, which is how the Savage got its politically incorrect name. Just up the road is a pullout—if the mountain's out, the driver should stop for the clear shot.

Savage River to Igloo Canyon

Mt. McKinley disappears behind jagged lower peaks as the road descends into the broad, glacial **Sanctuary River** valley at Mile 23. Watch for moose, caribou, foxes, lynx, waterfowl, and eagles along here. Right on the other side of the Sanctuary is a good view down at a "drunken forest," one effect that permafrost has on the vegetation. Notice how many of the trees are leaning at bizarre and precarious angles, with some of them down entirely. As an adaptation to the permafrost, these spruce trees have evolved a root system that spreads horizontally across the surface soil; there's no tap root to speak of. So the taller a tree grows around here, the less support it maintains, and the more susceptible it is to falling over. When the surface soil becomes saturated (because of lack of absorption over the permafrost), it sometimes shifts, either spontaneously or because of slight tremors (a major fault runs through here), taking the trees with it.

Next you descend into the broad **Teklanika River** valley, with a good view across the river

© DON PITCHER

Mt. McKinley, Denali National Park

of the three vegetation zones on the mountain slopes: forest, taiga, and tundra. You pass a number of small ponds in this area, known as "kettles," usually formed when a retreating glacier drops off a large block of ice, which melts, leaves a depression, which fills with rainwater. The stagnant water is rich in nutrients and provides excellent hatching grounds for Alaska's famous mosquitoes, and as such the ponds are good feeding spots for ducks and shorebirds. Look for mergansers, goldeneyes, sandpipers, buffleheads, and phalaropes in these ponds. And in some of the higher, smaller, more private kettles, look for hikers and park employees with no clothes on...maybe even join them, if you care to brave the skeeters, which have been known to show up on Park Service radar screens.

Cross the river and enter **Igloo Canyon,** where you turn almost due south. The mountain on the right is Igloo (4,800 feet); the one on the left is Cathedral (4,905 feet). Igloo is in the Outer Range, Cathedral in the Alaska Range. At the closest distance between the two ranges, the canyon is right on the migration route of the Dall sheep and a great place to view them as white dots on the slopes; or climb either mountain to get closer.

Sable Pass is next at Mile 38, at 3,900 feet the second-highest point on the road. This area is closed to hiking and photography because of the large grizzly population. Keep your eyes peeled. The next good views of the mountain are from these highlands.

Over Polychrome Pass to Eielson

Once you cross the **East Fork River** at Mile 44 (there is great hiking out onto the flats from here), you begin your ascent of Polychrome Pass, one of the most spectacular and sphincter-clamping sections of the road. If you're scared of heights or become frightened at the 1,000-foot drop-offs, just do what the driver does—close your eyes. These rocks have a high iron content; the rate of oxidation and the combination of the iron with other minerals determine the different shades of rust, orange, red, and purple. Look and listen for hoary marmots in the nearby rocks, and from here almost the rest of the way to Eielson Visitors Center, watch for caribou and wolves; these are the Murie flats, where wildlife biologist Adolph Murie studied the lifestyle of *Canis lupus.*

Descend to the **Toklat River** at Mile 53, the last and largest you cross before Eielson. This is the terminus of the wildlife tour, but the shuttle buses continue on to Eielson and Wonder Lake. The Toklat's source is the Sunrise Glacier, just around the bend upriver (left). You can see from the size of the river how big the glacier was 20,000 years ago. There is great hiking up into the Alaska Range from here. Next you climb up **Stony Hill** and, if the weather is cooperating, when you crest the ridge you're in for the thrill of a lifetime: Denali, The Great One, in all its immense majestic glory. It's hard to believe that the mountain is still 40 miles away! But wait, you get another five miles closer, crossing **Thorofare Pass,** the highest elevation (3,950 feet) on the road, at Mile 62.

Eielson Visitors Center

Open daily 9 A.M.–7 P.M. June–mid-September, Eielson is four hours and 66 miles from the park entrance. The view from here—weather cooperating—is unforgettable. Even if you can only see the bottom 12,000–14,000 feet, have a naturalist or your driver point to where the top of Mt. McKinley is, and visualize it in your mind's eye. Also, things change fast around here, so keep an eye out for the peak popping out of the clouds as a surprise just for you.

A spectacular new visitors center opened at Eielson in 2008, featuring exhibits, tall windows facing McKinley, a gift shop, an outdoor deck, 24-hour bathrooms, and space to enjoy your lunch or relax. No food is available at Eielson. Naturalists lead 45-minute walks daily at 1 P.M. The excellent backpacking zones in this area are usually the first to fill up.

To Wonder Lake

Beyond Eielson, the road comes within 25 miles of the mountain, passing **Muldrow Glacier,** which is covered by a thick black layer of glacial till and vegetation. From Wonder Lake, the **Wickersham Wall** rises magnificently above the intervening plains, with the whole Alaska Range stretching out on each side. In addition, the reflection from the lake doubles your pleasure and doubles your fun, from which even the mosquitoes here, some of the most savage, bloodthirsty, insatiable beasts of the realm, cannot detract.

HIKING

Note: Guns are not permitted within Denali National Park (this may change if the NRA has its way), but many hikers carry Counter Assault or other pepper-based sprays for protection. There has never been a fatal bear attack in the park, but bears certainly are a potential hazard. Obey all park regulations and follow safety tips from the rangers.

Ranger-led walks are available daily all summer at both the Denali Visitors Center and Eielson Visitors Center. More ambitious are the half-day **Discovery Hikes** led by rangers to more remote areas. These cost $31–45 and include several hours on the bus; reserve a day or two in advance.

Entrance Area Day Hikes

Several paths take off from the Denali Visitors Center, including two easy ones: the **Spruce Forest Trail** (15 minutes) and a longer **Murie Science and Learning Center Trail** (20 minutes). **Horseshoe Lake Trail** (3 miles round-trip) starts at the shuttle bus stop and then descends to the lake, where you might see waterfowl and beavers.

Hiking the five-mile round-trip **Mt. Healy Overlook Trail** is a great way to get the lay of the land, see the mountain if it's out, quickly leave the crowds behind, and get your heart pumping. Once at the overlook (1 mile in), keep climbing the ridges for another several hours to get to the peak of Mt. Healy (5,200 feet).

The 2.3-mile **Rock Creek Trail** starts near the post office and climbs to park headquarters, gaining 400 feet along the way. You can then loop back along the road via the 1.8-mile **Roadside Trail. Taiga Trail** is an easy 1.3-mile loop that also begins near the post office.

Backpacking Trips

For details on backcountry hikes and camping, head to the **Backcountry Information Center** (907/683-9510, daily 9 A.M.–6 P.M. May 20–Sept. 20); the office is just across the parking lot from the Wilderness Access Center.

Popular backpacking areas include up the Savage River toward Fang Mountain; down the far side of Cathedral Mountain toward Calico Creek (get off the bus just before the Sable Pass closure); up Tatler Creek a little past Igloo Mountain; anywhere on the East Fork flats below Polychrome toward the Alaska Range; anywhere around Stony Hill; and the circumnavigation of Mt. Eielson (get off 5–6 miles past the visitors center, cross the 100 braids of the Thorofare River, and walk around the mountain, coming back up to the visitors center). There are backcountry description guides at the backcountry desk, or you can find the same info online, with photos. For additional details and hiking tips, get a copy of *Backcountry Companion* ($9).

On all these hikes, you can get off the outbound bus, explore to your heart's content, then get back on an inbound bus, if space is available. Consult with the driver and study the bus schedule closely; the camper buses usually have space coming back.

Large as it is, it's hard to get lost in Denali—you're either north or south of the road. And since the road travels mostly through open alpine tundra, there aren't any artificial trails to follow—just pick a direction and book. Usually you'll want to make for higher ground in order to: (a) get out of the knee- to hip-high dwarf shrubbery of the moist tundra and onto the easy hiking of the alpine area, (b) get to where the breeze will keep the skeeters at bay, and (c) see more. Or walk along the river gravel bars into the mountains, although depending on the size of the gravel, it can be ankle-twisting. Hiking boots are a must, and carry food, water, a compass, binoculars, maps, rain gear, and a bear-proof food canister. Keep your eyes and ears wide open for wildlife that you don't want to get close to, sneak up on, or be surprised by.

Backcountry Permits

You need a free permit to spend the night in the backcountry. Permits are issued 24 hours in advance from the Backcountry Information Center, and reservations are not accepted. Check the big maps and look over descriptions of the 43 units, where a limited number of backpackers are allowed. (The same info can be found online at www.nps.gov/dena to help you plan prior to your trip.) Now check the board to find the vacancies in the units. Make sure the unit is open (some are always closed; others periodically close because of overcrowding or bears) and that there are enough vacancies to accommodate your whole party. Watch the 30-minute backcountry video that describes bear safety, river crossings, minimum-impact camping, emergencies, and other topics; listen to a 10-minute safety talk; and finally get a permit from the ranger. You might have to wait a few days for openings in your chosen area, or have a plan B or C in mind. The park loans out free bear-proof food storage containers; be sure to get one for your hike. Finally, reserve a seat on one of the camper buses ($31) to get you and your gear into the park.

OTHER RECREATION

Mountain Biking

An excellent way to explore Denali at your own pace is by mountain bike. Bikes are allowed on the Park Road, and can be transported aboard the camper shuttle bus, but be sure to mention the bike when you make a reservation. Note that only the camper buses carry bikes and that they only carry two at a time, so it is possible to get far out on the Park Road and then find yourself unable to catch a bus back. Be sure to pick up a "rules of the road" handout at the visitors center before heading out.

Denali Outdoor Center (907/683-1925 or

PROTECTING YOURSELF DURING A BEAR ENCOUNTER

If you do happen to encounter a bear suddenly and it sees you, try to stay calm and not make any sudden moves. Do not run, since you could not possibly outrun a bear; they can exceed 40 mph for short distances. Bear researchers now suggest that quickly climbing a tree is also not a wise way to escape bears, and it may actually incite an attack. Instead, make yourself visible by moving into the open so the bear will (hopefully) identify you as a human and not something to eat. Never stare directly at a bear. Sometimes dropping an item such as a hat or jacket will distract the bear, and talking calmly (easier said than done) also seems to have some value in convincing bears that you're a human. If the bear sniffs the air or stands on its hind legs, it is probably trying to identify you. When it does, it will usually run away. If a bear woofs and postures, don't imitate – this is a challenge. Keep retreating. Most bear charges are also bluffs, and the bear will often stop short and amble off.

If a **brown (grizzly) bear** actually attacks, hold your ground and freeze. It may well be a bluff charge, with the bear halting at the last second. If the bear does not stop its attack, curl up facedown on the ground in a fetal position with your hands wrapped behind your neck and your elbows tucked over your face. Your backpack may help protect you somewhat. Remain as still as possible even if you are attacked, since sudden movements may incite further attacks. It takes an enormous amount of courage to do this, but often a bear will only sniff or nip you and leave. The injury you might sustain would be far less than if you tried to resist. After the attack, prevent further attacks by staying down on the ground until the grizzly has left the area.

Bear authorities recommend against dropping to the ground if you are attacked by a **black bear,** since they tend to be more aggressive in such situations and are more likely to prey on humans. If a black bear attacks, fight back with whatever weapons are at hand; large rocks and branches can be surprisingly effective deterrents, as can yelling and shouting. (This assumes, of course, that you can tell black bears from brown bears. If you can't, have someone who knows – such as a park ranger – explain the differences *before* you head into the backcountry.)

Nighttime bear attacks are perhaps the most frightening, and could happen to even the most seasoned adventurer. In 1996, one of Alaska's best-known wildlife photographers, Michio Hoshino, was sleeping in his tent on Russia's Kamchatka Peninsula when a brown bear attacked and killed him. In the rare event of a night attack in your tent, defend yourself *very* aggressively. Never play dead under such circumstances, since the bear probably views you as prey, and may give up if you make it a fight. Before you go to bed, try to plan escape routes should you be attacked in the night, and

888/303-1925, www.denalioutdoorcenter.com) has mountain bike rentals and tours from its office next to the Denali Riverside RV Park.

Rafting

Three raft companies run the Nenana River along the eastern margin of the park, including two-hour Class II–IV white-water trips or Class II–III float trips ($85): **Denali Outdoor Center** (907/683-1925 or 888/303-1925, www.denalioutdoorcenter.com), **Denali Raft Adventures** (907/683-2234 or 888/683-2234, www.denaliraft.com), and **Nenana Raft Adventures** (907/683-7238 or 800/789-7238, www.raftdenali.com). All provide rain gear, boots, and life jackets, plus transportation to and from local hotels. Denali Raft Adventures and Denali Outdoor Center also offer trips that combine both segments for a four-hour trip that includes both the rapids and easy sections of the river ($115–120). Float trips are OK for children, but only adults can do the white-water runs. Denali Outdoor Center would be my first choice, and they also

be sure to have a flashlight and pepper spray handy. Keeping your sleeping bag partly unzipped also allows the chance to escape should a bear attempt to drag you away. There are advantages to having multiple tents in case one person is attacked, and if someone is attacked in a tent near you, yelling and throwing rocks or sticks may drive the bear away.

The latest development for campers in bear country is the use of portable **electric fences** made by Electro Bear Guard (907/232-9758, www.electrobearguard.com) to surround your campsite; a backpacker unit runs on two AA batteries, weighs just two pounds, and costs $280.

Many Alaskan guides, government employees, and others working in wild places carry weapons of some sort; 12-gauge shotguns are a common choice. Visitors to Alaska are unlikely to carry such weapons, and even less likely to know when to use them. Don't endanger the lives of bears by heading out into the wilderness with a gun but without an understanding of bear behavior. You have plenty of alternate places to go; the bears do not. Far too many bears die unnecessarily in Alaska following encounters with humans. Guns are not allowed in several Alaskan national parks, including Denali, Katmai, Glacier Bay, Sitka, and Klondike Gold Rush.

Cayenne pepper sprays such as Counter Assault (800/695-3394, www.counterassault.com) have proven useful in fending off bear attacks in some situations; they're sold in most Alaskan camping supply stores. These "bear mace" sprays are effective only at close range, particularly in tundra areas, where winds quickly disperse the spray or may blow it back in your own face. Another real problem with bear mace is that you cannot carry it aboard commercial jets, and most air taxis do not allow it inside an aircraft, because of the obvious dangers should a canister explode. Many floatplane pilots will, however, carry it in the storage compartments of the floats. But be sure to let the pilot know that you have it with you on the flight.

If you do carry a pepper spray on a hike, make sure it is readily available by carrying it in a holster on your belt or across your chest. Also be sure to test-fire it to see how the spray carries. Though they *are* better than nothing, pepper sprays are certainly not a cure-all or a replacement for caution in bear country. It's far better to avoid bear confrontations in the first place.

Detailed bear safety brochures are available at Alaska Public Lands Information Centers (www.alaskacenters.gov) in Ketchikan, Tok, Anchorage, and Fairbanks, or on the Alaska Department of Fish and Game's website (www.adfg.state.ak.us). Two good bear safety books are *Bear Attacks: Their Causes and Avoidance* by Stephen Herrero and *Bear Aware: Hiking and Camping in Bear Country* by Bill Schneider.

provide inflatable kayak tours for those who want to paddle on their own.

Flightseeing

If the mountain is out and there's room on the plane, this is the time to pull out the credit card. These one-hour flights around Mt. McKinley will leave you flying high for days.

Denali Air (907/683-2261, www.denaliair.com) operates from a private airstrip at Mile 229 of the Parks Highway (eight miles south of the park entrance). Their one-hour trip over the mountain is $350 in a twin-engine plane. **McKinley Flight Tours** (907/683-2899 or 888/733-2899, www.mckinleyflighttours.com) is based in Healy (12 miles north of the park entrance) and has 2.5-hour flights that include a glacier landing for $450.

Based in Kantishna at the center of the park, **Kantishna Air Taxi** (907/683-1223, www.katair.com) provides charter air service to end-of-the-road Kantishna lodges, and flightseeing trips within the park. Quite a few other flightseeing companies operate out of Talkeetna and Anchorage.

You can go for a helicopter ride on **Era Helicopters** (907/683-2574 or 800/843-1947, www.eraflightseeing.com), based along the river in Denali Park. Tour options include a 50-minute flight over the park ($335), or a 75-minute trip that includes a glacier landing ($435).

Mountaineering

Mt. McKinley—the tallest peak in North America—is a major destination for mountaineers from around the globe. Over 1,000 climbers attempt to summit Mt. McKinley each year, with three-quarters of these attempts via the West Buttress. The primary climbing season is May–July. From the south side of Mt. McKinley, the usual approach is by ski plane from Talkeetna to the Southeast Fork of the Kahiltna Glacier or to the Ruth Glacier in the Don Sheldon Amphitheater. From the north, the approach for Denali and other peaks is by foot, ski, or dogsled. Specific route information can be obtained from the Talkeetna Ranger Station. Climbers on Mt. McKinley and Mt. Foraker are charged a special use fee of $200 per climber. Call the ranger in Talkeetna (907/733-2231), or visit the Park Service website (www.nps.gov/dena) for additional mountaineering information.

Six companies are authorized to lead guided mountaineering climbs of Mt. McKinley and other peaks in the Alaska Range; contact the Park Service for specifics. Two of the best are **Alaska Mountaineering School** (907/733-1016, www.climbalaska.org) in Talkeetna and **NOLS** (907/745-4047, www.nols.edu) in Palmer.

Dog Mushing

Visitors whose appetite is whetted by the daily dogsledding demonstrations at park headquarters may want to return when the snow flies for the real thing. **Earth Song Lodge** (907/683-2863, www.earthsonglodge.com) offers wintertime dogsled adventure tours into Denali National Park. These range from an easy overnight trip to ones lasting 10 days.

Four-time Iditarod winner Jeff King lives with his family at Goose Lake near Denali, and his staff offers summertime tours of his state-of-the-art **Husky Homestead** (907/683-2904, www.huskyhomestead.com) kennels and training area. Two-hour tours and demonstrations ($49 adults, $29 children) depart from local hotels.

ENTERTAINMENT

All the Denali Park hotels have lounges, but if you want to hang out with the young worker-bee crowd, head to Denali Salmon Bake. For frivolity, check out **Alaska Cabin Nite Dinner Theater** at the McKinley Chalet Resort or the **Music of Denali Dinner Theater** at Denali Princess Lodge.

Park Service rangers give talks, walks, and kid programs. For specifics, check the bulletin boards at the Denali Visitors Center or the free park newspaper, *Denali Alpenglow*.

ACCOMMODATIONS

Most of the local lodging action centers around busy Denali Park, though other lodges and B&Bs are a few miles south of the park entrance, or 10 miles north in the town of Healy. Denali area lodging options are expensive, so those on a tight budget will either need to camp or head to the hostel 13 miles south at Carlo Creek.

Denali Park Lodging

If you've been driving the Parks Highway north from Anchorage, soaking up the wild Alaskan wilderness, you're in for a rude awakening when you reach the unincorporated settlement called Denali Park, a.k.a. "Glitter Gulch." Just a mile north of the Denali National Park turnoff, it's impossible to miss: an ugly hodgepodge of giant hotels, restaurants, RV parks, rafting companies, and gift shops crammed between the highway and the Nenana River to the west, and climbing the steep hillside to the east. The area is packed with tour buses, tottering tourists, and rumbling RVs. It's enough to make Wasilla look good.

Most lodging choices start well over $150 per

night, but one place offers a less-expensive option: **Denali Salmon Bake Cabins** (907/683-2733, www.denaliparksalmonbake.com, early May–mid-Sept.). For the full-on Alaskan experience, stay in an "economy cabin" ($74 s, $79 d) consisting of insulated tent-like structures with two double beds and a shared bath. Standard cabins with private baths, TVs, and air-conditioning are $135 s or $145 d. It's not for everyone, but the "Bake" is right there in the thick of things near the park entrance. Reservations are advised.

Denali Crow's Nest (907/683-2723 or 888/917-8130, www.denalicrowsnest.com, $159 d) has 39 cabins perched on a very steep hill. The outdoor hot tub is relaxing after a day of exploring, and they provide a free shuttle for the railroad depot and park visitors center. Parking is limited.

Denali Bluffs Hotel ($256–301 d) is a pleasant hillside place where 111 rooms all contain two double beds (or one king) and fridges. Request one with a private balcony. High atop the bluff is **Grande Denali Lodge,** a modern 154-room hotel accessed by a very steep switchbacking road. Guests stay in spacious rooms ($299 d) or family style cabins ($459 d). Both Denali Bluffs and Grande Denali have the same Denali Park Resorts (Aramark) management: 907/683-8500 or 866/683-8500, www.denalialaska.com. They provide free shuttles from the rail depot and park visitors center.

Also managed by Aramark, **McKinley Chalet Resort** (907/276-7234 or 800/276-7234, www.denaliparkresorts.com, mid-May–mid-Sept., $299–329 d) is a 345-room hotel along the Nenana River. Most rooms are set aside for Holland America passengers, so call well ahead of your visit.

Though primarily for cruise ship passengers, the sprawling **Denali Princess Lodge** (907/683-2282 or 800/426-0500, www.princesslodges.com, mid-May–mid-Sept., $199 d) is also open to independent travelers if they don't mind the corporate feeling and constant parade of tour buses. There are so many buildings here that you'll need a map to find your way around. Amenities include outdoor hot tubs overlooking the Nenana River, a fitness center, restaurants and cafés, a dinner theater, and a bar.

Carlo Creek Area Lodging

A number of lodging places are in the Carlo Creek area near Mile 224 of the Parks Highway, 14 miles south of the park entrance. The least expensive is the friendly **Denali Mountain Morning Hostel and Lodge** (907/683-7503, www.hostelalaska.com, mid-May–late Sept.), with earthy creek-side accommodations: Bunk cabins ($32 pp), private rooms and cabins ($80–95 d), and family cabins ($128 for 4 people). There is a two-night minimum stay in the private accommodations. A shower house is separate, and guests can use the central kitchen, computers, free Wi-Fi, and lounge. Gear rentals and storage are available, and two good restaurants (Pizza Panorama and McKinley Creekside Café) are right across the highway. The hostel provides a free twice-a-day shuttle to the park visitors center and rail station that's available to anyone.

Denali Perch Resort (907/683-2523 or 888/322-2523, www.denaliperchresort.com, year-round) has 20 very small cabins for $85 d with a shared bathhouse, or $125 d with Lilliputian private baths. Nearby is **Carlo Creek Lodge** (907/683-2576, www.ccldenaliparkalaska.com, late May–early Sept., $85–90 d with shared bath or $120–145 d with private bath), which has a variety of attractive cabins near the creek. Guest computers are available, along with Wi-Fi. **McKinley Creekside Cabins & Café** (907/683-2277 or 888/533-6254, www.mckinleycabins.com, $139–199 d) has cabins, a fine café, and Wi-Fi.

At Mile 231 (8 miles south of the park turnoff), you'll find **Denali River Cabins** (907/683-8002 or 800/230-7275, www.denalirivercabins.com), in a pleasant location right on the Nenana River. These Pan-Abode units include private baths, continental breakfast, and access to a large riverfront deck with a hot tub and sauna. Cabins on the river are $209 d, while those back from the water cost $150 d. Rooms in the recently built lodge cost $194 d.

Across the highway is **Denali Grizzly Bear Cabins & Campground** (907/683-2696, www.denaligrizzlybear.com, mid-May–mid-Sept.), with a range of lodging choices sprawling up the hillside. These include simple little cabins ($65–92 d), some of which use a central shower house, and attractive log cabins with private baths and kitchens ($192–260 for up to 6 people). Traffic noise can be an annoyance. Recently added hotel rooms ($192 d) overlook the Nenana River.

McKinley Village Lodge (907/276-7234 or 800/276-7234, www.denaliparkresorts.com, $275–315 d) is along the Nenana River at Mile 231. Here you'll find 150 comfortable hotel rooms, a café, and a lounge. It's run by Denali Park Resorts (Aramark), the park concessionaire.

Kantishna Lodges

The town of Kantishna, 91 miles from the park entrance at the western end of the Park Road, has four roadhouses. The area was first settled in 1905, when several thousand miners rushed to the foothills just north of Mt. McKinley to mine gold, silver, lead, zinc, and antimony. After 1980 and the Alaska National Interest Lands Conservation Act, which expanded Denali National Park's boundaries, Kantishna found itself inside the park, and in 1985 mining was halted by court order. A number of the property owners have moved into the tourism business, and the area is a popular destination for people wanting to escape to the heart of the park. These upscale lodges are definitely not for budget travelers, and it's a long bus ride to Kantishna, so most guests stay at least three nights in this very scenic area. All four of the lodges are open only early June–mid-September. Private buses transport visitors to the lodges at Kantishna, or you can fly out on Kantishna Air Taxi (907/683-1223, www.katair.com).

At **Kantishna Roadhouse** (907/683-8003 summer or 800/942-7420, www.kantishnaroadhouse.com, June–mid-Sept.) the all-inclusive rate of $810 d per day includes lodging in cabins or duplex rooms, meals, bus transportation from the park entrance, dogsled demonstrations, mountain bikes, gold panning, guided hikes, and interpretive programs. A bar and restaurant are on the premises. A two-night minimum stay is required.

Two wonderful Kantishna lodges—Camp Denali and North Face Lodge—have the same management and contacts (907/683-2290, www.campdenali.com, June–mid-Sept.). At both places, the emphasis is on the natural world, with guided hikes, mountain biking, canoeing, fishing, evening programs, and delicious meals. **Camp Denali** has spectacular views of Mt. McKinley, and is operated as a low-key wilderness retreat for a maximum of 40 guests. Special programs are offered throughout the summer, focusing on such topics as bird conservation, nature photography, northern lights, and environmental issues. Lodging is in 18 cozy cabins with woodstoves, propane lights, an outhouse, and a shower building. If you can't handle an outhouse, book a room at North Face Lodge instead.

One mile from Camp Denali is **North Face Lodge,** which is operated more like a country inn, with 15 guest rooms, all containing private baths. All-inclusive rates at either Camp Denali or North Face Lodge cost $1,425 adults for three nights ($1,069 for children under 12), or $1,900 for four nights ($1,425 children). The price includes lodging, food, bus transportation to and from Kantishna, lectures, guided hikes, and other activities. Guests must stay at least three nights, with fixed arrival and departure dates.

Denali Backcountry Lodge (907/644-9980 or 877/233-6254, www.denalilodge.com) has crowded and overpriced log units ($860 d all-inclusive) with private baths. The food is nothing special either; add $120 extra for riverside cabins.

CAMPING

Park Campgrounds

Inside Denali National Park are seven campgrounds, four of which have evening nature programs throughout the summer.

Riley Creek Campground ($22–28 for

pull-in sites, $14 for walk-in sites) is the largest and most accessible campground, located just a quarter-mile off the Parks Highway. It's open year-round, but with limited facilities September–May. This campground is very popular with RVers and car campers, but suffers somewhat from highway noise. Adjacent is **Riley Creek Mercantile** with a few supplies (including firewood), a dump station, and $5 showers.

Savage River, Teklanika River, and **Wonder Lake campgrounds** all have water and flush toilets, and go for $16–22 per night. **Sanctuary River Campground** has chemical toilets and costs $9. Savage River, Sanctuary River, and Teklanika River campgrounds are open May–September, but Wonder Lake Campground doesn't open until June, and may close early because of snow.

All but the Sanctuary River Campground can be reserved in advance (907/272-7275 or 800/622-7275, www.reservedenali.com, $5 fee) starting in mid-February. You can also reserve campsites at any of these at the visitors center if they aren't already full.

You can drive to Riley Creek, Savage River, and Teklanika River campgrounds, so they fill up fast. There's a three-night minimum stay for vehicular campers at Teklanika River, and only hard-sided campers are allowed. Otherwise, campground access is via the camper buses ($31 pp). The Wonder Lake Campground is also extremely popular for hiking and the potential to see the mountain in all its glory. Reserve well ahead of your trip for campsites there.

RV Parks

Denali Rainbow Village (907/683-7777, www.denalirv.com, mid-May–mid-Sept., $41 RVs, $30 tents) is in the heart of the Denali Park action, with a big lot behind the row of buildings on the east side of the road. It has free Wi-Fi and cable TV. Showers are $5 if you aren't camping here.

Denali Riverside RV Park (907/388-1748 or 866/583-2696, www.denaliriversiderv.com, May–Sept., RVs $38, tents $16) is a gravel lot two miles north of the park entrance.

Eight miles south of the park entrance is **Denali Grizzly Bear Resort** (907/683-2696 or 866/583-2696, www.denaligrizzlybear.com, RVs $36, tents $24). Showers and laundry are available. Nearby is **Carlo Creek Lodge** (907/683-2576, www.ccldenaliparkalaska.com, late May–early Sept., RVs $17 with electricity only, tents $15), with wooded campsites near the creek. Additional RV parks are in Healy.

FOOD

A number of places offer pricey summertime eats just north of the park entrance at the development called Denali Park; most are shuttered when the tourists flee south. Start your day at **Black Bear Coffee House** (907/683-1656, daily 6:30 A.M.–10 P.M. mid-May–mid-Sept., $5–10) with eggy breakfasts, bagels, espresso, sandwiches, and muffins, along with Wi-Fi and a couple of computers to check email ($5).

Located high atop the bluff at Denali Park, **Alpenglow Restaurant** (907/683-8500 or 866/683-8500, www.denalialaska.com, daily 5 A.M.–midnight mid-May–mid-Sept., entrées $29–35) has the most impressive vistas in the area. Wraparound windows face Denali National Park, and the high ceilings are accented by a beautiful timber-frame design. In addition to a good steak and seafood selection, there's a lighter bar menu with burgers, salads, and a tasty Alaskan coconut shrimp appetizer.

In business for more than 25 years, **Denali Salmon Bake** (907/683-2733, www.denaliparksalmonbake.com, daily 7 A.M.–midnight early May–mid-Sept., dinner entrées $20–37) is extremely popular and quite reasonable for breakfast, lunch, and dinner. This rustic old building with slanting floors is open for three meals a day, with a menu that stars halibut tacos, king crab, and cedar plank salmon, along with Wi-Fi and a free shuttle to local hotels and campgrounds. At night it turns into a hopping no-smoking bar with live bands, karaoke, or DJs nightly, plus 21 beers on tap and an enormous frozen blue concoction called the McKinley margarita. Join all the Ukrainian, Russian, and Slavic seasonal workers for Tuesday-night dance parties.

Heading into the park? Have the "Bake" make a big box lunch for $12. Hungry late? Halibut tacos are available till 4 A.M.

If you're just hankering for that old standby, head over to **Great Alaska Fish & Chips Co.** (907/683-3474, www.alaskafishandchip.com, daily 10:30 A.M.–10 P.M. summer) for a big serving of halibut or cod fish-and-chips. There's a salad bar and a handful of other choices too, including buffalo burgers and cold pitchers of Alaskan Amber.

One of the better restaurants in the Denali area is 11 miles south of the park entrance at Mile 224: **McKinley Creekside Café** (907/683-2277 or 888/533-6254, www.mckinleycabins.com, daily 6 A.M.–10 P.M. May–Sept., entrées $14–25). You'll find great breakfasts (including gigantic half-pound cinnamon rolls), homemade soups, sandwiches, and tacos for lunch, plus meatloaf, pasta specials, and fresh Alaskan halibut in the evening. The little deck is perfect for mid-summer dining. Pop open your laptop for free Wi-Fi. Right across the creek is **Panorama Pizza Pub** (907/683-2623, www.panoramapizzapub.com), with excellent pizzas and live music some nights. They provide a free shuttle from Denali Park.

At **229 Parks Restaurant** (907/683-2567, www.229parks.com, Tues.–Sun. 8–11 A.M. and 5–10 P.M., closed Mon. and in Nov. and Dec.) the name is also the location: Mile 229 on the Parks Highway. Housed within a bright timber-frame building nine miles south of Denali Park, the restaurant serves a bistro-style menu that changes frequently. Organic locally grown vegetables and free-range meats are used whenever possible. Dinner entrées are $24–36, but "tavern fare" options such as salads, tomato flatbread, or king crab cakes offer a less expensive option. Save room for their ice cream sandwich with homemade ice cream between dark chocolate cookies. In addition to dinner, the restaurant serves pastries and espresso for brunch. Don't come here in a hurry; service can be slow since everything is made fresh. There's a seasonal **Farmer's Market** in the parking lot Saturday 10 A.M.–2 P.M. with local crafts and produce.

PRACTICALITIES

Services

The Denali Park "Glitter Gulch" area is filled with gift shops. Two good seasonal places for Alaskan art are **Denali Glass Studio** (907/683-4527) behind Princess Lodge, and **Three Bears Gallery** (907/683-3343) on the boardwalk.

The large Denali Park hotels all have ATMs, as does the Lynx Creek Store. A **post office** is adjacent to the Riley Creek Campground.

For medical help at Denali Park, head to **Canyon Clinic at Denali** (907/683-4433), open daily in the summer; it's close to Denali Princess Lodge. The nearest hospital is in Fairbanks.

Getting There

The Alaska Railroad's (907/265-2494 or 800/544-0552, www.alaskarailroad.com) *Denali Star* train leaves Fairbanks at 8:15 A.M. and arrives at Denali at noon ($64 each way); it departs Anchorage at 8:15 A.M., arriving at Denali at 3:45 P.M. ($146).

Several companies have van transportation to Denali, with one-way rates to the park at around $75 from Anchorage, $60 from Talkeetna, and $60 from Fairbanks. **Alaska Park Connection** (907/245-0200 or 800/266-8625, www.alaskacoach.com) provides summertime service connecting Denali with Talkeetna, Anchorage, and Seward. **Denali Overland Transportation** (907/733-2384 or 800/651-5221, www.denalioverland.com) has charter service from Anchorage to Talkeetna and Denali, and often has space for individual travelers. **Alaska/Yukon Trails** (907/479-2277 or 888/770-7275, www.alaskashuttle.com) connects Denali with Anchorage or Fairbanks. Van service is daily in the summer only; for $99 one-way you can stop anytime and get a later bus.

Local air taxis include **Denali Air** (907/683-2261, www.denaliair.com), which operates from Mile 229 of the Parks Highway, and **Kantishna Air Taxi** (907/683-1223, www.katair.com) from Kantishna. **Era Helicopters** (907/683-2574 or 800/843-1947, www.eraflightseeing.com) is based next to the river in Denali Park.

North to Fairbanks

HEALY AND VICINITY

Located 11 miles north of the turnoff to Denali National Park at Mile 249 of the Parks Highway, the town of Healy (pop. 640) has most of the necessities of life, including gas stations (considerably cheaper than at Denali Park), convenience stores, restaurants, a coin laundry, and a medical clinic. Healy has grown up around the coal mining that has operated here since the 1930s. **Usibelli Coal Mine** (907/683-2226, www.usibelli.com) is the largest in Alaska, which isn't saying much, since it's Alaska's *only* commercial coal mine. However, its 1.5 million tons of subbituminous coal mined a year does say something: a 4-million-pound "walking dragline" digs 1,000 cubic yards of overburden every hour, exposing the seams. The coal is shipped to Korea or used at an adjacent power plant that supplies the Tanana Valley and Fairbanks. Healy also benefits greatly from tourism to nearby Denali National Park.

Into the Wild

A few miles north of Healy is the turnoff for the Stampede Road, made famous in the book and movie *Into the Wild*. Access to the old bus where Chris McCandless died is very difficult. Here's what the locals tell folks trying to get there: "This is where you turn off the highway; this is where you park the car; this is where you get eaten to death by mosquitoes; this is where you might drown; this is where the bear mauls you; and this is where you starve to death and die."

Accommodations

Three miles south of Healy is **Denali RV Park and Motel** (907/683-1500 or 800/478-1501, www.denalirvpark.com, late May–early Sept.), where motel rooms with private baths are $94 d. Family units with kitchens run $149 for four people. Units have cable TV, and there is Wi-Fi in the office.

Earth Song Lodge (907/683-2863, www.earthsonglodge.com, year-round, $155 d, plus $10 for each additional guest) rents 12 cozy cabins, all with private baths. It's four miles down Stampede Road off the Parks Highway at Mile 251. Earth Song is open all year, with a nightly slide show at the coffeehouse, Wi-Fi in the lodge, and winter dogsledding into Denali National Park.

White Moose Lodge (907/683-1231 or 800/481-1232, www.whitemooselodge.com, early May–late Sept., $105 d) has 15 reasonably priced no-frills motel rooms with continental breakfast and Wi-Fi.

Park's Edge Log Cabin Accommodations (907/683-4343, www.parks-edge.com, late May–early Sept.) has simple cabins for $100 d, and a larger one for $125 d or $145 for four people. All include private baths and Wi-Fi.

Open all year, **Motel Nord Haven** (907/683-4500 or 800/683-4501, www.motelnordhaven.com, year-round, $135 s, $147–165 d) is a fine lodging choice with nicely appointed rooms, continental breakfasts, a guest computer, and Wi-Fi. Kitchenettes ($175 d) are also available.

It's hard to miss the geodesic-shaped **Denali Dome Home B&B** (907/683-1239 or 800/683-1239, www.denalidomehome.com, year-round, $190 d), where lodging is available in a unique 7,000-square-foot house with rock fireplaces and seven guest rooms, all with private baths. Guests appreciate the sauna, five acres of park-like grounds and flower gardens, Wi-Fi, extensive art collection, and traditional family-style breakfasts.

Touch of Wilderness B&B (907/683-2459 or 800/683-2459, www.touchofwildernessbb.com, $160–195 d) is another large home in a quiet location five miles north of Healy along Stampede Road. Nine guest rooms have private baths, full breakfasts, and Wi-Fi.

Denali Lakeview Inn (907/683-4035, www.denalilakeviewinn.com, $170–195 d) is a large place right on Otto Lake with 20 bright guest rooms and suites, plus in-room continental breakfast and Wi-Fi.

Aspen Haus B&B (907/683-2004, www.aspenhaus.com, May–Aug.) has a quiet in-the-trees setting and four spacious cabins ($129–179 d), the largest with room for six people—plus two upstairs suites ($145 d). Each unit includes private baths, queen beds, a fridge, a microwave, and breakfast ingredients.

Camping

Three miles south of Healy, **Denali RV Park and Motel** (907/683-1500 or 800/478-1501, www.denalirvpark.com, late May–early Sept.) has RV spaces for $33; showers cost $2 extra.

McKinley RV and Chevron (907/683-1418 or 800/478-2562, www.mckinleyrv.com, May–Sept., RVs $32, tents $15) occupies a somewhat wooded area right next to the gas station. There is free Wi-Fi as well as a 24-hour convenience store, a deli, an espresso bar, and a laundry.

Food

There is nothing great on the Healy food scene, but you'll find a lounge and a 24-hour restaurant with family fare and pizzas at **Totem Inn** (907/683-6500, www.thetoteminn.com). Try the bacon cheeseburgers ($11) and other home-cooked food at friendly **Rose's Café** (907/683-7673, www.rosescafealaska.com, Mar.–Oct.), open for three meals a day.

Henry's Coffeehouse at Earth Song Lodge (907/683-2863, www.earthsonglodge.com) has bagels, baked goods, soups, sandwiches, salads, pizzas, and espresso. They're open for breakfast and dinner in the summer.

Play a round of golf at the nine-hole **Black Diamond Golf Course** (907/683-4653, www.denalihorsetours.com) or take a covered wagon ride two miles south of town on Otto Lake Road. For food, the **Black Diamond Grill** (daily 11 A.M.–11 P.M., entrées $18–36) serves a menu of prime rib sandwiches, steaks, and halibut. The restaurant has a free shuttle bus if you're staying in Healy or Denali Park hotels.

Information and Services

The **Greater Healy/Denali Chamber of Commerce** (907/683-4636, www.denalichamber.com) will send you local brochures. For medical care, head to **Interior Community Health Center** (907/683-2211, www.myhealthclinic.org, Mon.–Fri. 9 A.M.–5 P.M.); a physician's assistant and nurse are on call.

Transportation

Call **Denali Transportation** (907/683-4765) for taxi service in the Healy/Denali Park area. The owners of Denali Dome Home B&B provide rental cars ($110–130) through **Keys to Denali** (907/683-5397), and can pick you up at the Denali train station. This is a great way to explore the area without having to drive all the way from Anchorage.

Clear and Anderson

At Mile 283 of the Parks Highway—45 miles north of Healy and 21 miles south of Nenana—is the turnoff to Clear and Anderson. Clear is a military early-warning station for ballistic missiles, and not surprisingly, entry is prohibited. Six miles down the Clear road is the little settlement of Anderson, along the Tanana River. The town is best known for the popular **Anderson Bluegrass Festival,** held the last weekend of July. You'll hear country and bluegrass tunes by musicians from all over Alaska.

Run by the town of Anderson, 600-acre **Riverside Park** (907/582-2500) has tent and RV sites ($15), toilets, and showers along the Nenana River. Gas, groceries, and food are also available in town.

At Mile 280 is **Clear Sky Lodge** (907/582-2251), with gas, a steakhouse, a lounge, and Wi-Fi. Four miles south of there is the popular **Tatlanika Trading Company and RV Park** (Mile 276, 907/582-2341), with a major selection of Alaskan-made arts and crafts. It's worth a stop to browse. They also have RV and tent sites along the Nenana River.

NENANA

Nenana (nee-NA-na; pop. 370) sits at the junction of the Nenana River and Tanana (TAN-na-naw) River; a large steel bridge crosses the Tanana here. Nenana was an Athabascan village at the confluence of the two rivers (*na* in Athabascan means "river"; *Nenana* means "camping spot at two rivers") until it mushroomed into a town of 5,000 in 1916 as a base for construction on the northern leg of the Alaska Railroad. The town is 300 miles north of Anchorage, 67 miles north of the entrance to Denali National Park, and 57 miles south of Fairbanks.

At the north end of the 700-foot railroad bridge spanning the Tanana, Warren G. Harding, the first president to visit Alaska, drove in the golden spike, marking the completion of the line on July 15, 1923. Harding's visit was the culmination of a long train tour across the country, on which he attempted to rally support for his flagging administration, which was dogged by suspicions of high-level corruption. Before his trip, Harding had supported exploitation of Alaska's resources, but the firsthand experience changed his mind. Returning from Alaska to Seattle, he made a speech calling for more roads and agriculture, and conservation of lumber, fish, and mineral resources. "We must regard life in lovely, wonderful Alaska as an end and not a means, and reject the policy of turning Alaska over to the exploiters." Unfortunately, Harding died a week later under extremely mysterious circumstances; his new vision was buried with him. Today, the Alaska Railroad still passes through, but it's not a scheduled stop. You can get off there if you want to, but you can't check any baggage.

Ice Classic

Nenana is famous for its yearly Ice Classic, "Alaska's Biggest Guessing Game" (907/832-5446, www.nenanaakiceclassic.com). It all began in 1917, when Alaska Railroad workers started a pool for the exact time the ice on the Tanana River would break up; the payoff was $800. Today, the prize has grown to over $280,000, which is 50 percent of the gross. The rest goes to taxes, salaries, promotion, and the town till. Tens of thousands of Alaskans and Outsiders place $2.50 bets on the day, hour, and minute of the break-up. A four-legged tripod (the town's symbol) is set up on the river ice in February, with a cable running to a clock tower on the riverbank. When the ice moves, the cable stops the clock, recording the official time. The earliest break-up was April 20, in 1940; the latest was May 20, in 1964. Pick up entry forms at the visitors center or the Tripod Gift Shop and enter before the April 1 deadline. They're also available at many locations around Alaska.

© DON PITCHER

Nenana Ice Classic

The Ice Classic and the town's active waterfront, where freight and supplies are loaded onto barges for bush towns strung along the Tanana and Yukon Rivers, make Nenana a prosperous, photogenic, and friendly little place—great for a leisurely stroll to break up (sorry) the trip from Fairbanks to Denali.

Sights

Stop off at the log-and-sod **visitors center** at the bottom of the bridge (Parks Highway and A St., 907/832-5435, daily 8 A.M.–6 P.M. late May–early Sept.). Behind the cabin is the *Taku Chief,* the last commercial wooden tugboat to ply the Yukon and Tanana Rivers, until it was condemned in 1978 in Nenana, where it still sits. Unfortunately, you can't climb on it.

Walk up A Street toward the river. Go right on Front Street and enter the old depot. Inside is the **Alaska State Railroad Museum** (907/832-5556, daily 9:30 A.M.–6 P.M. mid-May–Sept., free). Built in 1922 as a depot, this is a wonderful little museum, full of information, photographs, and artifacts from planning, construction, and maintenance of the Alaska Railroad. Be sure to read the railroad bridge-building history, and flip through the logbooks on the stationmaster's counter. The gift shop inside is worth a few minutes, and sells the fine historical video on the railroad.

Outside there's a monument with a memorial plaque and the once-golden spike. A block over at Front Street and B is **St. Mark's Mission Church,** established in 1904 to educate Native Alaskan children from around the Interior. The inside of this beautiful log building is equally impressive, with a big stained glass window, hand-hewn pews, and an altar covered with Athabascan moosehide beadwork. Keep heading down toward the big single-span bridge, then go left into the heavy-equipment parking lot on the waterfront. Here is the **Ice Classic tower;** next to it is a building with the clock. Information signs about riverboats and railroads stand in the center of the parking lot.

The **Alfred Starr Cultural Center** (907/832-5520, daily 9 A.M.–7 P.M. summer only) houses displays on the Yukon 800 boat race, fish wheels, the Episcopal mission, and dog mushing. Also here is a gift shop with Native Alaskan crafts. Out front are two old railcars. The **Nenana Public Library** (907/832-5812) has computers you can use to check your email.

The white markers across the river on the hillside are Native Alaskan headstones in a hillside cemetery. A second graveyard just south of town contains the bodies of those who died during the railroad's construction and in a deadly influenza epidemic in 1920. And on the way out of town, don't miss the oft-photographed log-cabin bank on the left. Fish wheels are visible on both sides of the river.

Accommodations and Food

Bed and Maybe Breakfast (907/832-5272, mid-May–mid-Sept., $89 d) is upstairs from the Railroad Museum at the depot; this could be the most historic B&B in the state, with hardwood floors, braided rugs, brass beds, and a railroad theme. Four simple rooms share one bath. Request the engineer's room. Breakfast ($10 extra) is served across the street, hence the "maybe breakfast" part of the name.

Rough Woods Inn (2nd St. and A St., 907/832-5299, www.roughwoodsinn.biz) has motel rooms ($105–140 d) with kitchenettes and Wi-Fi, plus a café serving three meals daily 8 A.M.–8 P.M. Dinners run around $15–25, with homemade soups, steaks, and "world-class pies" including the locals' favorite, strawberry rhubarb.

Five miles north of town is **Monderosa Bar & Grill** (907/832-5243), whose "best burger in Alaska" is in fact a great deal—one fills up two. Great fries too.

Nenana Valley RV Park & Campground (4th St. and B St., 907/832-5230, tents $8, RVs $16) has campsites and a laundry.

Coghill's General Store (907/832-5422, Mon.–Sat. 9 A.M.–6 P.M.) has been selling groceries, fresh meat and produce, hardware, guns, and fishing and hunting licenses to Nenanans and travelers since 1917. The building is starting to show its age, as evidenced by the slanting wooden floors. The Coghills are a sixth-generation Alaskan family, known throughout the state for their right-wing politics.

North to Fairbanks

North of Nenana, the highway begins a gradual climb into the wooded Tanana Hills, with a multitude of vista points featuring the Alaska Range to the east. Much of this country lies within **Tanana Valley State Forest.**

At Mile 328 you pass the infamous **Skinny Dick's Halfway Inn** (907/388-5770, www.skinnydicksak.com); it *is* halfway between Fairbanks and Nenana, which makes it an even better pun. If it's tasteless, Skinny Dick's has it, including a chef's apron complete with a small towel covering the "skinny dick."

Fairbanks

Just 150 air miles from the Arctic Circle, Fairbanks sits at 64 degrees 49 minutes north latitude, on par with Reykjavik, Iceland, and considerably north of Helsinki, Stockholm, and St. Petersburg—not to mention Honolulu. The second-largest city in the state (pop. 31,000) and one of the largest population centers on earth this far north, it's still just one-ninth the size of Anchorage, but with a hospitable hominess its big sister has long since forgotten.

Fairbanks has much to offer summer visitors, including a classy new museum, flower-filled downtown, creative restaurants, and an abundance of wild adventures in all directions. Occupying a broad valley surrounded by rounded hills, the city straddles both sides of the Chena River—a major boating playground all summer—with the much larger Tanana River just south of Fairbanks. City streets are convoluted and confusing, partly because of the winding river, so get a map and follow it closely when driving around town.

Fairbanksians take extrovert pride in their toughness surviving the cold dark winters, but also love to play in the lazy days of summer when the sun is almost always visible. Today, Fairbanks is transitioning from the hard-edged frontier days exemplified by the log cabins that still fill residential neighborhoods to a present that also mixes in Wal-Marts, in-floor heating, and Wi-Fi.

Climate

Fairbanks has one of the widest temperature ranges of any city in the world. The mercury can plummet to -66°F in January and soar to 99°F in July, a whopping 165-degree differential. In addition, one day in July could be 90°F and cloudless, while the next day could be 40°F and rainy. But it isn't just the temperatures that change so much. On the summer solstice, Fairbanks days last 21 hours and 50 minutes of glorious daylight, but winter nights get longer and longer. At the winter solstice low point (Dec. 21) the sun creeps above the horizon for just three hours and 42 minutes.

Fairbanks winters are notoriously cold, with temperatures often dropping below zero (though you might also see some times when it's a balmy 20°F). By 40 or 50 degrees below zero, car tires go hard as a rock and can explode if you drive too fast before they warm up. Fan belts snap in the cold, and vehicles need block heaters or they will never start (electrical outlets are in front of many businesses). Fairbanks folks adapt to the harsh winters, and you'll even find them out skiing, dogsledding, or snowmobiling when the mercury hides out at the bottom of the thermometer. But they also have a comfortable central library with indoor trees where they can pretend it's spring even when it's months away.

HISTORY

E. T. Barnette

In August 1901, E. T. Barnette was traveling up the Tanana River on the *Lavelle Young* with a boatload of supplies bound for Tanacross to set up a trading center on a well-used gold-rush trail. Unable to negotiate some rapids, Captain Charles Adams turned into the Chena River to try to bypass them but got stuck on the Chena's silt-laden sandbars. Adams refused to go any farther, and Barnette refused to turn back, leaving the two men as stuck as the boat.

Peering through field glasses from a distant hill, Felice Pedroni (Felix Pedro, as he's remembered) watched the boat's progress—or lack thereof—by the smoke from its stacks. A mountain man and prospector, Pedro had been looking for gold in the huge wilderness north of the Tanana and Chena Rivers for several years and had found signs of color on some creeks near where he stood watching the steamer. However, running low on provisions, he was facing a several-hundred-mile round-trip to Circle to restock, unless . . .

Meanwhile, Captain Adams was unceremoniously dumping Barnette, his wife, and their

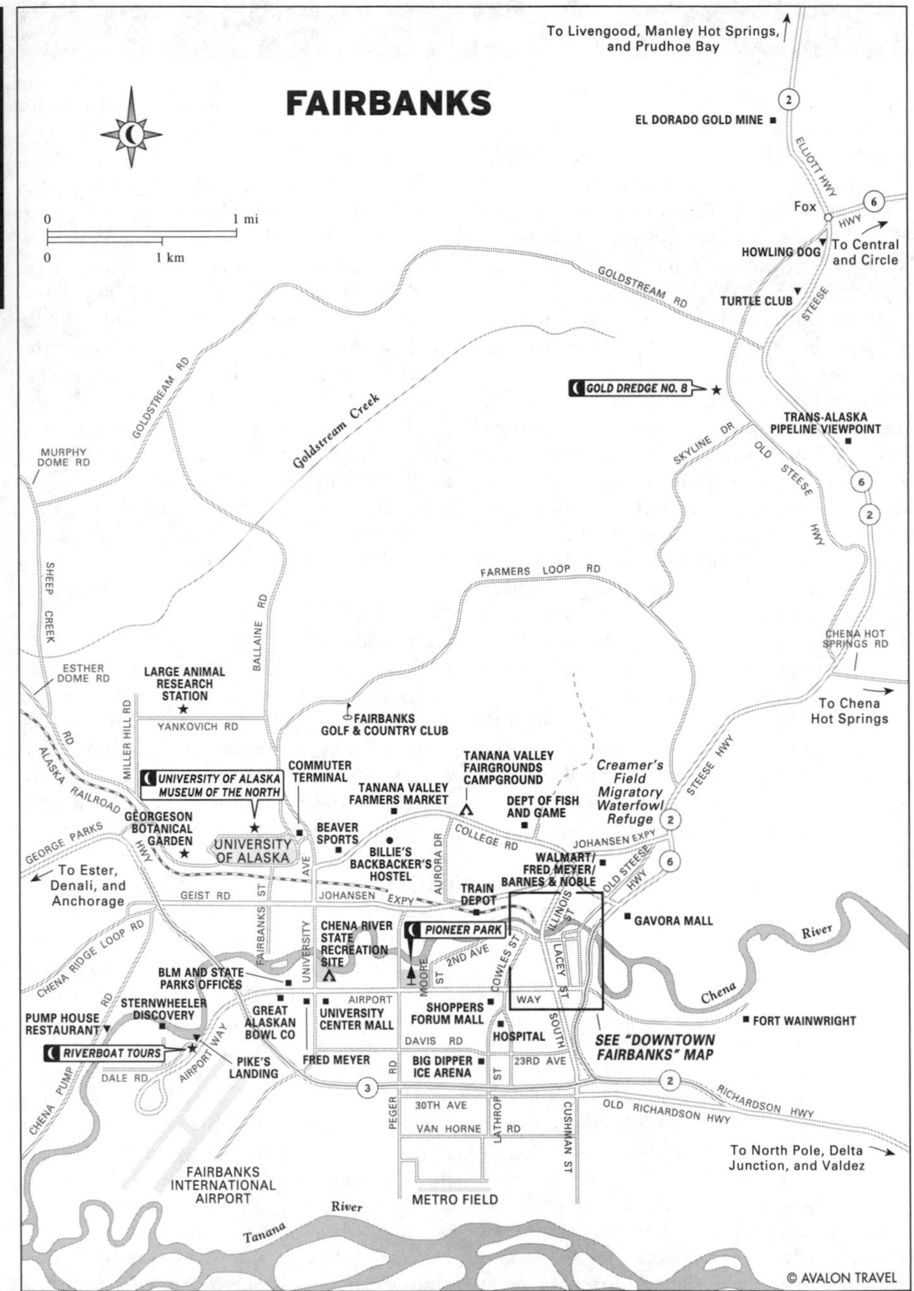
FAIRBANKS
To Livengood, Manley Hot Springs, and Prudhoe Bay
EL DORADO GOLD MINE
ELLIOTT HWY
Fox
HWY
To Central and Circle
HOWLING DOG
TURTLE CLUB
STEESE
GOLDSTREAM RD
GOLD DREDGE NO. 8
TRANS-ALASKA PIPELINE VIEWPOINT
SKYLINE DR
OLD STEESE HWY
GOLDSTREAM RD
Goldstream Creek
MURPHY DOME RD
SHEEP CREEK
BALLAINE RD
FARMERS LOOP RD
CHENA HOT SPRINGS RD
To Chena Hot Springs
ESTHER DOME RD
LARGE ANIMAL RESEARCH STATION
MILLER HILL RD
YANKOVICH RD
FAIRBANKS GOLF & COUNTRY CLUB
ALASKA RAILROAD
UNIVERSITY OF ALASKA MUSEUM OF THE NORTH
COMMUTER TERMINAL
TANANA VALLEY FARMERS MARKET
TANANA VALLEY FAIRGROUNDS CAMPGROUND
Creamer's Field Migratory Waterfowl Refuge
DEPT OF FISH AND GAME
STEESE HWY
GEORGESON BOTANICAL GARDEN
UNIVERSITY OF ALASKA
BEAVER SPORTS
BILLIE'S BACKBACKER'S HOSTEL
AURORA DR
COLLEGE RD
JOHANSEN EXPY
GEORGE PARKS HWY
To Ester, Denali, and Anchorage
WALMART/ FRED MEYER/ BARNES & NOBLE
OLD STEESE HWY
GEIST RD
JOHANSEN EXPY
TRAIN DEPOT
ILLINOIS ST
GAVORA MALL
FAIRBANKS ST
UNIVERSITY AVE
CHENA RIVER STATE RECREATION SITE
PIONEER PARK
2ND AVE
COWLES ST
LACEY ST
Chena River
CHENA RIDGE LOOP RD
BLM AND STATE PARKS OFFICES
MOORE ST
AIRPORT WAY
SHOPPERS FORUM MALL
STERNWHEELER DISCOVERY
PUMP HOUSE RESTAURANT
GREAT ALASKAN BOWL CO
UNIVERSITY CENTER MALL
HOSPITAL
SOUTH
FORT WAINWRIGHT
DAVIS RD
SEE "DOWNTOWN FAIRBANKS" MAP
RIVERBOAT TOURS
PIKE'S LANDING
FRED MEYER
BIG DIPPER ICE ARENA
23RD AVE
DALE RD
AIRPORT WAY
CHENA PUMP RD
RICHARDSON HWY
OLD RICHARDSON HWY
PEGER RD
30TH AVE
VAN HORNE RD
LATHROP ST
CUSHMAN ST
To North Pole, Delta Junction, and Valdez
FAIRBANKS INTERNATIONAL AIRPORT
METRO FIELD
Tanana River
0
1 mi
1 km
© AVALON TRAVEL

goods on the shore. "We cut some spruce and helped him get his freight off," Adams recalled 30 years later. "We left Barnette furious. His wife was weeping on the bank." They were standing directly in front of the present site of downtown Fairbanks. That's when Pedro showed up, quietly informed Barnette of his prospect, and bought a winter's worth of supplies. Back at his promising creek, Pedro finally hit pay dirt.

News of the strike traveled far and fast. Miners abandoned the played-out Klondike and Nome and headed for the tiny outpost on the Chena River, named after Illinois Senator Charles Fairbanks, who soon became vice president under Teddy Roosevelt. Unfortunately, Barnette wasn't content with his good fortune of owning most of the town site of rich little Fairbanks. In 1911, he was tried for embezzling funds from his own Washington-Alaska Bank. Though he was acquitted, he left town with his family, never to return. His wife divorced him in 1920 in San Francisco; where he went from there, and when or how he died, are complete mysteries. Only one clear photograph of his face survives today: Barnette standing in a line with several other early Fairbanks bankers. But when the photo was found, old-timers were hard-pressed to identify which one was the town father. In fact, a discrepancy even exists over his first name. In *E. T. Barnette,* Terrence Cole calls him "Elbridge," while *The $200 Million Gold Rush Town,* by Jo Anne Wold, remembers him as "Eldridge," and the city fathers commemorated him by naming an elementary school Ebenezer T. Barnette. Whatever his name, possibly no man embodies the boom-bust character of Fairbanks better than its founder, E. T. Barnette.

Gold and Oil Fever

The Fairbanks strike differed markedly from the shiny shores of the Klondike and the golden sands of Nome—this gold was buried under frozen muck anywhere from 8 to 200 feet deep. Fortune hunters quickly became discouraged and left, which rendered Fairbanks' boom much less explosive than Dawson's or Nome's. Even determined miners eventually reached the limits of both their endurance and the primitive placer-mining technology. After fires and floods, by 1913, when the road from Valdez to Fairbanks was completed, the town was in the midst of a serious bust cycle. But in 1923 the Alaska Railroad reached Fairbanks from Seward and Anchorage, which inaugurated the real Golden Age. Major mining corporations freighted up and installed large dredges to uncover the gold, and eventually $200 million worth was pulled from the surrounding area. When the Alaska Highway was pushed through to Delta from Canada in 1942, connecting the Richardson Highway to the outside world, the city's future was assured.

Only one word can really be applied to Fairbanks in the 1970s: *boomtown.* The Prudhoe Bay oil discovery of 1968 led to a massive influx of pipeline workers and hangers-on. Suddenly demand far exceeded supply, making it a seller's market for everything from canned food to cocaine, from housing to hookers. So many people poured in with dreams of big bucks that officials took out ads in Lower 48 newspapers telling everyone to stay away. Only half the job-seekers ever got hired, and the lines at the bank were only exceeded in length by those at the unemployment office.

Fairbanks today is a vastly different place from the pipeline era, with an economy that prospers on the university and military payroll, on the summer tourist season, as a supply center for the bush, on construction, and on the nearby Fort Knox gold mine.

DOWNTOWN SIGHTS

Visitors Center

Start out at the gleaming new **Morris Thompson Cultural & Visitors Center** (907/459-3701, www.morristhompsoncenter.org, daily 8 A.M.–9 P.M. mid-May–mid-Sept., daily 8 A.M.–5 P.M. mid-Sept.–mid-May) along the Chena River at the intersection of Wendell Avenue and Dunkel Street. In addition to brochure racks packed with local info from the Fairbanks Convention and Visitors Bureau (907/456-5774 or 800/327-5774 recording,

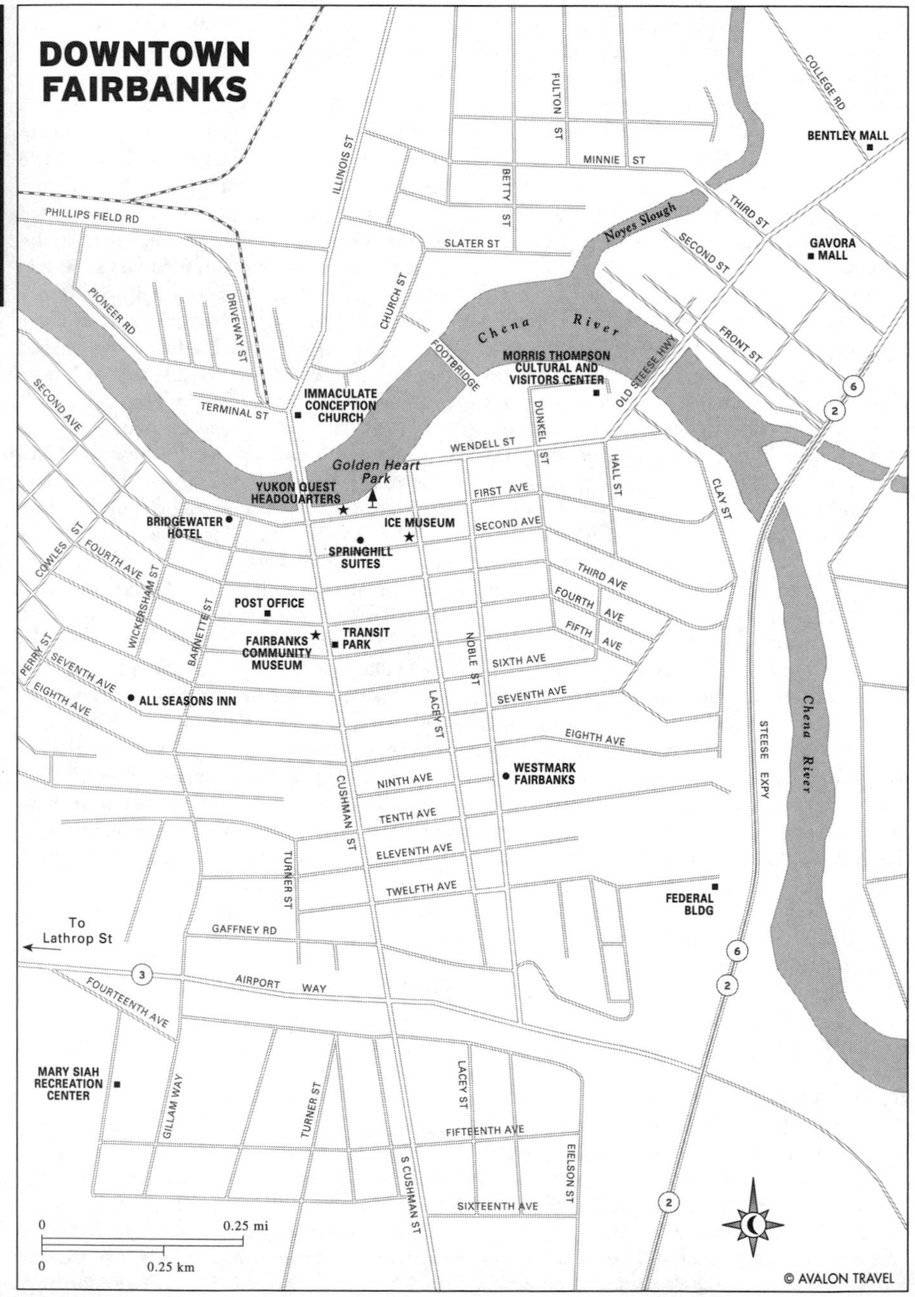
DOWNTOWN FAIRBANKS
BENTLEY MALL
GAVORA MALL
Noyes Slough
Chena River
MORRIS THOMPSON CULTURAL AND VISITORS CENTER
IMMACULATE CONCEPTION CHURCH
Golden Heart Park
YUKON QUEST HEADQUARTERS
ICE MUSEUM
BRIDGEWATER HOTEL
SPRINGHILL SUITES
POST OFFICE
TRANSIT PARK
FAIRBANKS COMMUNITY MUSEUM
ALL SEASONS INN
WESTMARK FAIRBANKS
FEDERAL BLDG
To Lathrop St
MARY SIAH RECREATION CENTER
FULTON ST
COLLEGE RD
MINNIE ST
THIRD ST
SECOND ST
FRONT ST
BETTY ST
ILLINOIS ST
PHILLIPS FIELD RD
SLATER ST
CHURCH ST
PIONEER RD
DRIVEWAY ST
FOOTBRIDGE
OLD STEESE HWY
DUNKEL ST
TERMINAL ST
SECOND AVE
WENDELL ST
HALL ST
FIRST AVE
CLAY ST
COWLES ST
FOURTH AVE
WICKERSHAM ST
BARNETTE ST
THIRD AVE
FOURTH AVE
FIFTH AVE
PERRY ST
SEVENTH AVE
EIGHTH AVE
SIXTH AVE
NOBLE ST
LACEY ST
STEESE EXPY
NINTH AVE
TENTH AVE
CUSHMAN ST
ELEVENTH AVE
TWELFTH AVE
TURNER ST
GAFFNEY RD
AIRPORT WAY
FOURTEENTH AVE
GILLAM WAY
FIFTEENTH AVE
EIELSON ST
S CUSHMAN ST
SIXTEENTH AVE
0 0.25 mi
0 0.25 km
© AVALON TRAVEL

www.explorefairbanks.com), the center houses fascinating life-size dioramas on the region and it's people. There are free nature films daily in the theater, evening Native Alaskan cultural programs ($12 adults, $10 children), an artisans' workshop, and an Alaska Geographic gift store. Tall windows let in light on those brief winter days, computers are available to check your email, and the staff is fluent in German and Japanese. Out back, a bike path follows the river in either direction.

The old visitors center—a sod-roofed log cabin downtown at 1st Avenue and Cushman Street—is now headquarters for the **Yukon Quest International Sled Dog Race** (907/452-7954, www.yukonquest.com, daily 11 A.M.–8 P.M.). Adjacent is **Golden Heart Park,** a flower-packed plaza centered around a large heroic sculpture of *The First Unknown Family,* representing those who first crossed into Alaska over the Bering Land Bridge. Cushman Street Bridge crosses Chena River here, with flags of all 50 states lining the bridge. Visit the **Immaculate Conception Church** (1904), just over the river, for its beautiful stained-glass windows.

© DON PITCHER

Morris Thompson Cultural & Visitors Center

Ice Museum

At the corner of 2nd Avenue and Lacey Street in the historic Lacey Street Theatre is the Fairbanks Ice Museum (907/451-8222, www.icemuseum.com, daily 10 A.M.–8 P.M. May–Sept., $12 adults, $6 ages 6–12, younger children free). This is the "coolest show in town," with a 25-minute film about the process of creating ice art at the World Ice Art Championships in Fairbanks each March. There's also a glass-walled walk-in freezer that displays intricate pieces of sculpted ice, and you can often watch artisans demonstrate their craft.

Community Museum

The Fairbanks Community Museum (410 Cushman St., 907/457-3669, www.fairbankshistorymuseum.com, Mon.–Fri. 10 A.M.–4 P.M. mid-May–mid-Sept., Mon.–Fri. 11 A.M.–3 P.M. mid-Sept.–mid-May, free) is housed within historic City Hall. Inside are displays and photos on dog mushing, the gold rush, and the growth of Fairbanks.

CREAMER'S FIELD

Head north about a mile on Illinois Street and take a left at College Road. In another mile is the 2,000-acre **Creamer's Field Migratory Waterfowl Refuge** (907/459-7307, www.creamersfield.org) where you might observe migratory birds. Early in the year, the field is plowed and tons of barley is spread around. Sandhill cranes, Canada geese, and many species of ducks stop off at the field in April–May on their migratory route north—a local herald for the arrival of spring.

Follow the driveway to the old dairy barn, where you can pick up a free trail guide. The dairy was the first in Alaska (1904) and the northernmost in the western hemisphere. Charles Creamer owned it from 1928 to 1966, when he sold it to Fish and Game for use as a migratory-waterfowl refuge. Volunteer-led nature walks (free) depart on weekdays from the **Farmhouse Visitors Center** (Mon.–Fri. 10 A.M.–5 P.M., Sat.–Sun. 10 A.M.–6 P.M. mid-May–mid-Sept., Sat. noon–4 P.M. mid-Sept.–mid-May). Guided birding hikes are offered Monday–Friday at 10 A.M. , plus Wednesday at 7 P.M. June–August. The **Tanana Valley Sandhill Crane Festival** at Creamer's Field brings nature walks, photography and drawing workshops, music, and talks the last week of August.

At other times, you can head out on the five miles of nature paths to explore forest, shrub, muskeg, and riparian areas. The trail is mostly boardwalk over swamp, with the predictable insectoid results, so bring your bug dope.

WEDGEWOOD RESORT

Trails connect Creamer's Field with nearby Wedgewood Resort, home to the 75-acre **Wedgewood Wildlife Sanctuary,** with accessible trails and a small lake. The **Alaska Bird Observatory** (414 Wedgewood Dr., 907/7159, www.alaskabird.org) is the only organization of its kind in the state, conducting long-term research on Interior Alaska birds and working to protect their habitat. Visitors can watch bird banding most mornings June–mid-July and mid-Aug.–Sept., but call ahead for specifics. Their website lists unusual bird sightings in the Fairbanks area, or call the **Arctic Audubon Birding Hotline** (907/451-9213, www.arcticaudubon.org).

Also located at Wedgewood Resort, **Fountainhead Auto Museum** (212 Wedgewood Dr., 907/450-2100, www.fountainheadhotels.com, Sun.–Thurs. 11 A.M.–10 P.M., Fri.–Sat. 11 A.M.–6 P.M. mid-May–mid-Sept., Sun. noon–6 P.M. in winter, $8 adults, $6 children, under age 6 free) encompasses over 60 rare and historic automobiles from 1898 to 1938. All of these still run, and you'll see folks driving several of them around the resort most summer evenings.

UNIVERSITY OF ALASKA

Continue west on College Road to the University of Alaska Fairbanks (UAF), Alaska's primary educational facility (Admissions Office 907/474-7500 or 800/478-1823, www.uaf.edu). When it opened in 1922 as Alaska Agricultural College and School of Mines, there were six students and as many faculty; today 9,000 students attend the 2,500-acre campus. This facility is highly regarded for its Arctic research and Native Alaskan studies. Smaller University of Alaska campuses are in Anchorage and Juneau. Ask any student to direct you to the **Wood Campus Center,** where you can pick up a free map of the grounds, check the ride board, and grab a cheap breakfast, a slice of pizza, an espresso, a cafeteria lunch, or a beer in the pub. A free shuttle bus runs every 15 minutes around campus.

Free two-hour **walking tours** (907/474-7021) of the campus take place Monday–Friday at 10 A.M. June–August. Led by UAF students, these start and end at the admissions office. No reservations are needed, but the tours may be canceled if it is raining; call to confirm.

University of Alaska Museum of the North

One of Alaska's finest collections on art, human history, and natural history, the University of Alaska Museum of the North (907/474-7505, www.uaf.edu/museum) is housed within the state's most distinctive building. A new wing designed by renowned architect Joan Soranno opened in 2005, with a gleaming white exterior that curves and swoops like an enormous chunk of glacial ice. The interior is equally interesting, both as a structure and for the contemporary and ancient Alaskan art. There's even a "Great Alaska Outhouse Experience" that's bound to amuse. Don't miss the door marked "The Place Where You Go to Listen," where the lights and sounds give voice to real-time data from movements of the sun, moon, seismic activity, and auroras.

The second (older) half of the museum houses collections divided according to the state's five geographical areas, and includes hands-on objects, dioramas, and videos. The wildlife and gold exhibits are mind-boggling; the Russian artifacts and the permafrost display are exceptional. So is an exhibit dealing with the incarceration of Japanese Americans during World War II; read the heartbreaking personal letters from the families pleading for compassion. Other highlights include Blue Babe, a mummified 36,000-year-old steppe bison discovered in 1979 at a placer mine, a 1,250-pound brown bear, a video on whaling, fist-sized gold nuggets, ancient ivory carvings, dinosaur bones from the North Slope, and lots more.

Back in the new wing you'll find a fine gift shop, a café, and an auditorium with daily demonstrations by World Eskimo-Indian Olympic athletes. On a clear day, Mt. McKinley—across the broad Tanana Valley—can be seen in all its awesome eminence from the museum's tall windows.

The museum is open daily 9 A.M.–9 P.M. mid-May–mid-September, and Monday–Saturday 9 A.M.–5 P.M. the rest of the year. Admission costs $12 adults, $11 seniors, $6 ages 7–17, and free for younger children. Add $5 for admission to the 30-minute auditorium shows, offered hourly in the summer.

Large Animal Research Station

This Arctic biology research center (907/474-7207, www.uaf.edu/lars, late May–early Sept.) houses more than 100 relatively tame animals, including musk oxen, caribou, and reindeer used for nutritional, physiological, and behavioral studies. Find the 150-acre research station north of the campus on Yankovich Road, 1.5 miles off Ballaine Road. This unique facility is open for guided 45-minute tours ($10 adults, $9 seniors, $6 students, children under 7 free) seven times a day in the summer. A free viewing-stand area is open at any time.

Georgeson Botanical Garden

This five-acre garden (907/470-1944, www.uaf.edu/salrm/gbg, daily 8 A.M.–8 P.M. May–Sept., $2) is on the grounds of the Agricultural and Forestry Experimental Station downhill from the museum on the west end of campus. It's the northernmost botanical garden in the western hemisphere, and contains flowers, vegetables, fruits, herbs, and perennials that can withstand the northern rigors. Giant cabbages and other veggies are the star attractions, and the gazebo is perfect for a picnic lunch.

Other University Sights

Learn about the northern lights, earthquakes, and more in a tour of the **Geophysical Institute** (www.gi.alaska.edu) on Wednesdays at 2:30 P.M. June–August. This building (the tall one with the satellite dishes on top) also houses a Map Office, where you can buy topographic maps. The **International Arctic Research Center** (www.iarc.uaf.edu) is open for tours on Wednesdays at 4 P.M. June–August; it's adjacent to the Geophysical Institute. Call 907/474-7558 for details on either of these tours. Take a virtual visit to one of the world's fastest supercomputers at the Rasmuson Library on the east side of the campus. Tours (907/474-6935) are given on Wednesdays at 1 P.M. June–August.

Poker Flat Research Range (907/474-7558, www.pfrr.alaska.edu)—the only university-operated sounding rocket range anywhere—is 33 miles north of Fairbanks on the Steese Highway. Tours are offered some Thursdays in the summer.

PIONEER PARK

This delightful 44-acre theme park (907/459-1087, www.co.fairbanks.ak.us, daily noon–8 P.M., grounds year-round, shops and rides late May–early Sept., free)—the only one of its kind in the state—occupies the site of the 1967 state centennial celebration. Many of the original buildings from the early days of Fairbanks and various locations around Alaska have been moved here and assembled into a gold rush–era town. Park headquarters is in one such restored building just inside the entrance off Airport Way between Nome and Peger Roads. Pick up a map of the park and spend a few hours exploring the grounds of this free open-air museum.

The big 1933 stern-wheeler riverboat ***Nenana*** sits just inside the entrance. The second-largest wooden-hulled vessel in existence at 227 feet long, it houses an amazingly detailed diorama of towns along the Yukon and Tanana Rivers.

To your right inside the entrance is the **Harding Car,** a railcar used by Warren G. Harding when he came to Alaska on his ill-fated trip in 1923, just before his death under suspicious circumstances.

Continue to **Gold Rush Town,** a collection of 29 colorful and historic buildings that includes the interesting home of Alaska's first Territorial Governor, James Wickersham. The **Palace Theatre** has a musical-comedy revue nightly ($18 adults, $9 children), while the **Pioneer Museum** is a free collection of mining and other memorabilia, including a large 1912 map of Alaska. The same building houses **The Big Stampede Show** ($4 adults, $2 ages 6–16), a 50-minute look at the lives of early pioneers.

Pioneer Air Museum (907/451-0037, daily noon–8 P.M. summer, $2) is housed in a dome-shaped *Jetsons*-esque building near the center of Pioneer Park. Inside are a number of historic and modern aircraft, including a 1933 Stinson SR-5 and a 1966 Bell UH1 helicopter.

The narrow-gauge **Crooked Creek and Whiskey Island Railroad** ($2 adults, $1 children) circles Pioneer Park throughout the day, and the depot doubles as a little museum that houses the oldest operating steam locomotive in Alaska, built in 1899. Families also love the vintage 1915 carousel, dogsled rides, and miniature golf. Browse around the replica mining valley with its antique mining equipment, and the Native Alaskan village where you will find historic artifacts. For dinner, visit Pioneer Park's excellent **salmon bake.**

RIVERBOAT TOURS

The Binkley family, now in its fourth generation of riverboat pilots, runs **Riverboat Discovery Cruises** (907/479-6673 or 866/479-6673, www.riverboatdiscovery.com, $54 adults, $38 ages 3–12, younger children free). This 3.5-hour 20-mile cruise on the Chena and Tanana Rivers—a bargain—includes the chance to view an Athabascan-style camp, to watch a floatplane take off, and to

steamboat *Nenana* in Pioneer Park

see dogs from the late Susan Butcher's team in action (from the boat). Reservations are necessary. Cruises depart from the dock at the end of Dale Road near the airport at 8:45 A.M. and 2 P.M. mid-May–mid-September. A large gift shop awaits if you get there early.

The ***Tanana Chief*** (907/452-8687 or 866/452-8687, www.greatlandrivertours.com), is a smaller paddle-wheel boat with two-hour summertime sightseeing trips ($25), along with prime rib dinner cruises ($50), and Sunday brunch cruises ($37).

RECREATION

Midnight Sun Balloon Tours (907/456-3028, www.alaskaballoontours.com, $200 adults, $150 children) has one-hour flights over the Tanana Valley, with departures scheduled when wind conditions are mild.

Play a midnight round of summertime golf at **Fairbanks Golf & Country Club** (1735 Farmers Loop Rd., 907/479-6555), where 24-hour tee times are available on the nine-hole course in June and July! **North Star Golf Club** (330 Golf Club Dr., 907/457-4653, www.northstargolf.com), "America's northernmost," is the other local nine-hole club.

Hiking and Biking

For local trails, try Creamer's Field and Chena River Wayside. Farther afield, find hiking and backpacking opportunities in the White Mountains and in the Pinnell Mountains.

Fairbanks has an excellent series of connecting walking or biking paths: from downtown along the river to Pioneer Park; from University Avenue and Airport Way out on Chena Pump Road; and a great up-and-down route on Farmers Loop Road from the Steese Highway to the university. These paved trails connect to all sorts of other paths for more adventurous cyclists. Before heading out, pick up a free bikeways map at the downtown visitors center.

Alaska Outdoor Rentals & Guides (907/457-2453, www.akbike.com, $27–49 for all day) has mountain bike rentals along the river behind Pioneer Park. You can also rent bikes from **GoNorth Adventure Travel Center** (3500 Davis Rd., 907/479-7272 or 866/236-7272, www.gonorthalaska.net).

Bradley Hodges of **Fairbanks Paddle & Pedal** (907/388-4480, www.fbxpp.com) leads a unique trip that combines a morning canoe paddle down the Chena River, followed by lunch at Pikes Landing, and an afternoon bike ride for $80. He also puts together custom trips if you have your own ideas.

Swimming

Three indoor pools are open to the public: **Hamme Pool** (Airport Way and Cowles St., 907/456-2969) at Lathrop High School, **Mary Siah Recreation Center** (1025 14th Ave., 907/456-6119), and **Patty Gym Pool** (at UAF, 907/474-7205).

Floating the River

The peaceful Chena River is a favorite destination for canoeists. **Alaska Outdoor Rentals & Guides** (907/457-2453, www.2paddle1.com, late May–mid-Sept.) runs a popular canoe and kayak rental business along the river at Pioneer Park. Put in here and paddle two hours to the Pump House—a great place for a drink or meal while you wait for the van ride back. Half-day rentals cost $52–71. The company can also provide canoes and transport for longer trips, including overnighters. **GoNorth Adventure Travel Center** (3500 Davis Rd., 907/479-7272 or 866/236-7272, www.paratours.net) has a similar service, with canoe rentals and transportation. **Northern Alaska Tour Company** (907/474-8600 or 800/474-1986, www.northernalaska.com) combines dinner (prime rib, steak, chicken, or salmon) at Two Rivers Lodge with a leisurely evening float down the Chena River for $169.

Fishing

A number of local companies offer Chena River fishing trips; get their brochures at the visitors center. Fishing in the Chena for grayling is fair, but better grayling fishing is found in the Chatanika River, between miles 30 and 40 on the Steese Highway toward Circle. Chum, silver, and a few kings run up here from mid-

July. Chena Lakes Recreation Area has good rainbow-trout fishing. Fish and Game provides a recorded hot line (907/459-7385) of fishing tips. The *Fairbanks Daily News-Miner* carries fishing updates every Friday.

Dog Mushing

Fairbanks is a major center for dog mushing. Well-known musher and author **Mary Shields** was the first woman to finish the Iditarod. She offers two-hour summer visits (907/457-1117, www.maryshields.com, $28 adults, $20 children) that include time with the dogs at her home.

Other dogsledding tours or rides (depending on the season) are available from **Paws for Adventure** (907/378-3630, www.pawsforadventure.com), **Chena Hot Springs Resort** (907/452-7867 or 800/478-4681, www.chenahotsprings.com), **Sled Dog Adventures** (907/479-5090, www.sleddogadventures.com), and **Sun Dog Express** (907/479-6983, www.mosquitonet.com/~sleddog).

Skiing

Moose Mountain (907/479-4732, www.shredthemoose.com, Sat.–Sun. 10 A.M.–5 P.M. winter, $35 adults, $30 students, $20 ages 7–12) is 20 minutes north of Fairbanks near Murphy Dome. It has 1,250 feet of vertical drop, and an unusual lift system: a "variable capacity terrestrial tram," more commonly called a bus with ski racks. Get the snow report at 907/459-8132. Fortunately, temperatures are typically 20–30 degrees warmer here than in Fairbanks (because of an inversion).

Mt. Aurora Skiland (907/389-2314, Thanksgiving–mid-Apr., $30 adults, $23 students, children under 7 free) is 21 miles north of town off the Steese Highway, and features downhill skiing and snowboarding. The area has a double chairlift, a day lodge, and a snack bar, plus ski and snowboard rentals. Call 907/456-7669 for the snow report.

Cross-country skiing is very popular around Fairbanks; the nicest place is **Birch Hill Ski Area,** with a modern Nordic center and 20 miles of groomed trails, 4 miles of which are lighted. Contact the **Nordic Ski Club of Fairbanks** (907/474-4242, www.nscfairbanks.org) for details and online maps for these and others, including 9 miles next to the university.

Northern Lights Viewing

The Fairbanks area has some of the finest aurora displays anywhere on the planet. The clear winter nights and proximity to the north pole create ideal viewing conditions (once you get away from the city lights). For predictions of upcoming activity, visit the website for UAF's Geophysical Institute (www.gedds.alaska.edu/auroraforecast). A number of lodges in the Fairbanks area have geared their winter season for people who come to view and photograph the northern lights—notably Chena Hot Springs Resort and Mt. Aurora/Skiland—and many Fairbanks hotels provide aurora wake-up calls upon request.

ENTERTAINMENT

Drinking and Dancing

Visit www.fbxsquare.com for tips and blogs on the Fairbanks bar and music scene. Three miles south on the Parks Highway is **Blue Loon** (907/457-5666, www.theblueloon.com), Fairbanks' party place with hot bands, arthouse movies, dancing, 15 beers on tap, and good pub meals. Don't miss their Jerry Garcia pig roast each August.

Other dance-till-2 places are **The Marlin** (3412 College Rd., 907/479-4646, www.themarlin.alaskansavvy.com), and **Silverspur Nightclub** (285 Old Richardson Hwy., 907/456-6300).

For a nice riverside drink and hors d'oeuvres in a historic setting, head out to the **Pump House** (Mile 1.3, Chena Pump Rd., 907/479-8452, www.pumphouse.com). **College Coffeehouse** (3677 College Rd., 907/374-0468, www.collegecoffeehousefairbanks.com) has folksy music.

Out in Fox, **Silver Gulch Brewery** (907/452-2739, www.silvergulch.com) has a popular restaurant and pub. Across the road is the infamous **Howling Dog Saloon** (907/456-4695), a great spot for dancing and midnight volleyball.

The **Palace Theatre** (at Pioneer Park, 907/456-5960 or 800/354-7274, www.akvisit.com) offers a musical-comedy revue nightly mid-May–mid-September. The show, *Golden Heart Revue,* goes on at 8:15 P.M. It's professionally produced, and worth the admission ($18 adults, $9 children).

Movies and Plays

Out on Airport Way at Lathrop Street, **Regal Cinema** (907/456-5113, www.regmovies.com) has comfortable seating and 16 movie screens. The Blue Loon sometimes shows films too. **Fairbanks Shakespeare Theatre** (907/457-7638, www.fstalaska.org) performs plays behind the University Museum in July and August.

Baseball

Composed of top college players, the **Alaska Goldpanners of Fairbanks** (907/451-0095, www.goldpanners.com) plays against teams in the Alaska Baseball League. The games are played at Growden Field (2nd Ave. and Wilbur St., behind Pioneer Park), starting at 7 P.M. The famous Midnight Sun game, played around the summer solstice, starts at 10:30 P.M. and goes nine innings without using the field's artificial lights. The Goldpanners are composed of college players, dozens of whom have gone on to play in the major leagues, including Dave Winfield, Graig Nettles, and Tom Seaver.

EVENTS

Summer

Locals have roughly 90 days per year to get their fill of outdoor extravaganzas, and they go at it with a vengeance. The first big event of the season is the **Midnight Sun Festival,** held on summer solstice (June 21), with 30 live bands, food, a car show, and the famous Alaska Goldpanners **Midnight Sun baseball game** that continues past midnight without lights. For details, visit www.downtownfairbanks.com.

Next comes **Golden Days,** between the second and third weekends in July—a week-long party culminating in a fun parade. The whole town turns out, and if you happen to be there, even without your camera, you won't forget it.

After that comes the **World Eskimo-Indian Olympics** (907/452-6646, www.weio.org), featuring Native Alaskan athletic games, dance, and art. This three-day mid-July event includes such unusual competitions as the Ear Pull, Greased Pole Walk, Kneel Jump, Knuckle Hop, Seal Skin, Toe Kick, and Blanket Toss. There's even a Native Alaskan baby contest. It could be one of the most exotic and memorable events in Alaska.

The **Fairbanks Summer Arts Festival** (907/474-8869, www.fsaf.org) is a two-week-long series of workshops, performances, and concerts encompassing classical music, opera, dance, theater, figure skating, and visual arts. It takes place late July–early August and attracts hundreds of students and instructors.

The big **Tanana Valley State Fair** (907/452-3750, www.tananavalleyfair.org) is at the Fairgrounds on College Road during the second and third weeks of August, with rides, music, food booths, craft booths, and those famous giant cabbages.

In late August, the **Sandhill Crane Festival** (www.arcticaudubon.org) celebrates these majestic birds as they begin their journey south. Bird watching, talks, and workshops are the main attractions.

Winter

The biggest winter event is the **Yukon Quest International Sled Dog Race** (907/452-7954, www.yukonquest.com), held in February. Other sled dog races include the **Limited North American Sled Dog Championships** in early March followed by the **Open North American Championship Sled Dog Races** in mid-March. Details on both are available from the Alaska Dog Mushers Association (907/457-6874, www.sleddog.org).

The **World Ice Art Championships** (907/451-8250, www.icealaska.com) is an early March event that attracts international sculptors who create truly amazing works of art with dramatic and colorful lighting. This isn't your standard fancy restaurant art; some of these

YUKON QUEST

The **Yukon Quest International Sled Dog Race** began in February 1984 with 26 teams in competition. The race has close ties to the past of Yukon and Interior Alaska, taking place along trails that once carried fur traders and missionaries, gold-hungry pilgrims, and determined mail carriers. In the days before airplanes and automobiles, the dog team was often the only method of transportation in the great North. The Yukon Quest has been called the "toughest race on earth," and for good reason.

The race, which takes place in early February, runs from Fairbanks to Whitehorse in even-numbered years and from Whitehorse to Fairbanks in odd-numbered years. It is named for the mighty Yukon River, "the Highway of the North," and travels across some of the wildest and most sparsely populated country in the world. Terrain, trail conditions, and temperatures vary wildly along the trail, from steep hills to miles of flat frozen lake, from hard-packed snow and frozen rivers to rough gravel, from -60°F to 30°F.

Although most of the media focus is on the mushers, the real stars of this or any sled dog race are the canine athletes. Since the teams are limited to 14 dogs, the Quest is musher-friendly to those with smaller kennels. And a smaller team ensures better care for individual dogs.

Depending on weather and trail conditions, the race takes 10-14 days. There is a mandatory 36-hour layover in Dawson City, Yukon. This is the only stop where dog handlers can feed and care for the teams while the mushers get some much-needed rest. A large veterinary tent is set up in the dog camp, which lies across the frozen Yukon River from Dawson.

If a dog exhibits signs of fatigue or illness at a checkpoint, the animal is dropped from the race and turned over to the handlers. If dropped at a remote spot, the dog is transported by one of the many volunteer pilots to a point where it can be met by the handlers.

Unlike other long-distance races, the Quest is easily accessible to onlookers. Race fans may follow the mushers' progress by driving to many of the checkpoints along the way. Photo opportunities are plentiful from start to finish. For further information, visit the Quest headquarters in downtown Fairbanks (907/452-7954, www.yukonquest.com).

pieces may stand 20 feet tall and contain incredibly intricate work. Just getting the 1,500 tons of clear ice is a challenge. The children's ice park here has a superfast luge for adrenaline junkies.

SHOPPING

On Wednesdays and Saturdays in the summer, the **Tanana Valley Farmers Market** (College Rd., 907/456-3276, www.tvfmarket.com) is *the* place to find locally grown or crafted items, from asparagus and berry pies to Native Alaskan beadwork and polar-fleece booties.

Great Alaskan Bowl Company (4630 Old Airport Rd., 907/474-9663 or 800/770-4222, www.woodbowl.com) sells nesting birch hardwood bowls, all fashioned from a single split log. This is a good made-in-Alaska product to take home with you. A window overlooks the wood shop; the wood shavings are used for packing material and decoration in the showroom.

Galleries and Gifts

Local galleries of note include **Alaska House Art Gallery** (10th Ave. and Cushman St., 907/456-6449, www.thealaskahouse.com), **Expressions in Glass** (1922 Peger Rd., 907/474-3923 or 888/574-3923, www.expressionsinglass.net), and **The Artworks** (3677 College Rd., 907/479-2563).

Gift shops abound downtown; **Arctic Traveler's** (201 Cushman St., 907/456-7080, www.arctictravelersgiftshop.com) is the biggest. **The Craft Market** (5th Ave. and Noble St., 907/452-5495) has a good collection of carved ivory, woven baskets, masks, dolls, and other Native Alaskan arts and crafts.

Alaska Rag Co. (603 Lacey St., 907/451-4401, www.alaskaragco.com) is a unique shop with hand-woven rag rugs made on the premises, plus jewelry, stained glass, and other gifts. (The rugs are woven from locally recycled cloth, and many of the workers are developmentally disabled individuals who could not otherwise find work.) **The Spinning Room** (516 2nd Ave., 907/458-7610, www.spinning-room.com) sells handspun fabrics, including those made from musk ox wool.

Outdoor Gear

Beaver Sports (3480 College Rd., 907/479-2494, www.beaversports.com) is *the* place for outdoor gear of all types in Fairbanks, and has the largest selection of canoes in Alaska. They also rent canoes, mountain bikes, skis, and snowshoes.

Go North (3820 University Ave., 907/479-7272 or 866/236-7272, www.paratours.net) has rental canoes, mountain bikes, tents, sleeping bags, cooking utensils, and all sorts of other gear, including satellite phones! Also check out **Big Rays** (507 2nd St., 907/452-3458 or 800/478-3458, www.bigrays.com) and **The Prospector** (1512 S. Cushman St., 907/457-7372 or 800/495-7372, www.prospectoroutfitters.com) for rugged Alaskan wear. Get hand-sewn outdoor creations along with fast repairs from **Apocalypse Design** (201 Minnie St., 907/451-7555 or 866/451-7555, www.akgear.com).

ACCOMMODATIONS

Fairbanks has the complete lodging spectrum, from backpacker hostel beds to modern hotels with top-end features and amenities. Start your exploration by looking over the descriptions in the *Fairbanks Visitors Guide* from the Convention and Visitors Bureau, or their online version (www.explorefairbanks.com). The visitors center keeps track of daily room availability.

Under $100

Billie's Backpackers Hostel (2895 Mack Rd., 907/479-2034, www.alaskahostel.com, year-round) has four-person dorms for $30 per person, or pay $15 per person for a tent space. Private rooms are $80 d, but these go fast. The hostel provides a kitchen, showers, computers, Wi-Fi, and travel information, and has the added bonus of a sundeck, a barbecue, and free bikes. The friendly owner, Billie Maire Cook, bakes bread and cinnamon rolls daily for guests. You can call any time if you're coming in late at night.

GoNorth Base Camp Hostel (3500 Davis Rd., near the airport, 907/479-7272 or 866/236-7272, www.paratours.net, mid-May–mid-Sept.) has beds in cozy tent cabins ($25 pp), along with tent spaces ($12 s, $18 d). Kids love the tepee, and other facilities include a kitchen, a barbecue, coin-op showers, guest computers, Wi-Fi, outdoor equipment rentals (from canoes to satellite phones), and trip planning. Staff members are fluent in German and French.

Close to the airport, **Golden North Motel** (4888 Airport Way, 907/479-6201 or 800/447-1910, www.goldennorthmotel.com, $79–99 s, $89–109 d) has clean and quiet (but small) rooms at reasonable prices. Don't come here expecting the Ritz Carleton, but guests appreciate the continental breakfast, computer, free Wi-Fi, and 24-hour courtesy van.

$100-200

Fountainhead Development (907/452-6661 or 800/528-4916, www.fountainheadhotels.com) owns three Fairbanks lodging places: Bridgewater Hotel, Sophie Station Hotel, and Wedgewood Resort. All three include free airport and train depot shuttles, along with guest computers. There is free Wi-Fi throughout Sophie Station, plus in the lobby area and some rooms at Wedgewood and Bridgewater.

Conveniently located downtown, **Bridgewater Hotel** (723 1st Ave., mid-May–mid-Sept., $145 d) has attractive rooms; ask for a corner unit overlooking the river.

Sophie Station Hotel (1717 University Ave., 907/479-3650, $185 d) provides large and attractive suites—all with full kitchens. It's also smoke-free, with a fitness center, a restaurant, and a lounge on the premises.

On the north side of town, **Wedgewood Resort** (212 Wedgewood Dr.) offers homey apartment-style units, all with full kitchens, living rooms, and dining rooms. One-bedroom units are $170 d or $190 for four people, and two-bedroom units run $220 d or $260 for six people. Also on the resort grounds is the seasonal **Bear Lodge,** with standard hotel rooms for $170 d, along with the Alaska Bird Observatory.

Regency Fairbanks (95 10th Ave., 907/452-3200 or 800/478-1320, www.regencyfairbankshotel.com, standard rooms $162–172 d, suites $210 d) is a large, centrally located hotel where the well-kept guest rooms all have full kitchens. The Regency provides a free airport and railroad shuttle, plus a business center, a workout room, and Wi-Fi.

Extended Stay Deluxe (4580 Old Airport Rd., 907/457-2288 or 888/595-2151, www.extendedstaydeluxe.com, $125–135 d) has all the amenities travelers have come to expect: an indoor pool, a hot tub, an exercise room, a business center, in-room fridges, microwaves, Wi-Fi, free airport and train shuttles, and a continental breakfast. Standard rooms, family suites, Jacuzzi suites, and suites with full kitchens and king beds are all the same price.

Similarly set up, and brand-new in 2009, the 101-room **Hampton Inn & Suites** (433 Harold Bentley Ave., 907/451-1502 or 800/426-7866, www.hamptoninn.com, $189 d) has an indoor pool, a hot tub, an exercise facility, a hot breakfast, big TVs, microwaves, fridges, Wi-Fi, and a business center. It's located across from Wal-Mart off Johansen Expressway.

Over $200

River's Edge Resort (4200 Boat St., 907/474-0286 or 800/770-3343, www.riversedge.net) consists of 90 modern cottages crowded together along the Chena River. Each is charmingly decorated and includes two queen beds; rates are $189 d or $209 d for riverside units. A restaurant and pub are on the premises.

A modern six-story hotel in the center of Fairbanks, **SpringHill Suites by Marriott** (575 1st Ave., 907/451-6552 or 877/729-0197, www.springhillsuites.com, $189 for up to 5 people) is just across the street from the Chena River. Spacious suites contain two queens or one king bed, and guests appreciate the excellent restaurant (Lavelle's Bistro), indoor pool, exercise room, Jacuzzi, sauna, mini-fridges, microwaves, flat screen TVs, Wi-Fi, buffet breakfast, and free airport shuttle.

The 180-room **Pike's Waterfront Lodge** (907/456-4500 or 877/774-2400, www.pikeslodge.com) is on Airport Way next to Pike's Landing Restaurant. Rooms and suites are attractively furnished, sleeping four people for $220 d, but the cozy modern cabins are more private at $235 d. All guests have access to the fitness center, sauna, steam room, Wi-Fi, and courtesy airport and train station shuttle. More unique is the hydroponic greenhouse next to the lodge, which grows tomatoes, lettuce, and strawberries for their restaurant (Pike's Landing). Owner Jay Ramras is a well-known Republican state representative.

Bed-and-Breakfasts

For many travelers, B&Bs are the best deal in Fairbanks, with reasonable prices, friendly hosts, and a free breakfast to boot. The downtown visitors center has racks of cards from local B&Bs, or find links on their website (www.explorefairbanks.com) or that of the **Fairbanks Association of B&Bs** (www.ptialaska.net/~fabb).

A fine bargain choice, **Ah, Rose Marie B&B** (302 Cowles St., 907/456-2040, www.akpub.com/akbbrv/ahrose.html, $65 s, $90 d) is a small historic home a few blocks from downtown. The four guest rooms have shared or private baths, and the big hot breakfast is always a hit.

Another good budget option is **Downtown Log Cabin Hideaway** (304 Badger St., 907/452-1100 summer or 520/841-2913 winter, www.mosquitonet.com/~apfvrf, mid-May–mid-Sept.), where the five rooms are just $75–85 d, including a full breakfast. They also provide free train or airport pickups and Wi-Fi.

Conveniently located in the heart of town, **All Seasons B&B Inn** (763 7th Ave., 907/451-6649 or 888/451-6649, www.allseasonsinn.

com, $165–215 d) features eight elegant rooms, delicious full breakfasts, friendly owners, Wi-Fi, a guest computer, private baths, and air-conditioning for those hot summer days.

Minnie Street B&B Inn (345 Minnie St., 907/456-1802 or 888/456-1849, www.minniestreetbandb.com) is a large and modern downtown place with 13 rooms ($119–159 d), deluxe suites ($179–219 d) with jetted tubs and full kitchens, and a small private house ($189 d, summer only). All include a big breakfast, an outdoor hot tub, a guest computer, Wi-Fi, and a surprisingly quiet setting. Check out unusual breakfast recipes on their website.

A Taste of Alaska Lodge (907/488-7855, www.atasteofalaska.com) is a 7,000-square-foot log home five miles out Chena Hot Springs Road. Located on a 280-acre homestead, the hilltop location faces south toward the Alaska Range, making for dramatic wintertime aurora displays. Eight rooms are available in the antique-filled main lodge ($185–195 d). Also available is a two-bedroom log home ($235 d) with its own hot tub, and a one-bedroom house ($205 d); add $35 for each additional guest. Amenities for all accommodations include private baths, an indoor hot tub, a guest computer, Wi-Fi, and full breakfasts.

On a hill a dozen miles southwest of Fairbanks near the town of Ester, **A Moose in the Garden B&B** (1691 Flat Pick Rd., 907/479-2767, www.amooseinthegarden.com) is another real-Alaskan treat. One room ($129 s, $149 d) features views of wintertime northern lights, plus a corner hot tub and a separate loft with twin beds for the kids. Two downstairs rooms ($89 s, $109 d) share a bath, and all guests have access to the sauna, the large deck facing Denali, Wi-Fi, and full breakfasts.

Fairbanks's most unique lodging is—without a doubt—**Aurora Express** (907/474-0949 or 800/221-0073, www.aurora-express.com, late May–early Sept., $145–160 d). Susan and Mike Wilson have assembled a nostalgic collection of seven Alaska Railroad cars (the oldest dates from 1924) and decorated the interiors with playful themes, including a 19th-century bordello with antiques and crystal chandeliers! Families will love the restored Pullman sleeper with two baths; it sleeps four for $225 (but kids must be over age 12). A big breakfast is served in the dining car each morning. Be sure to ask Susan about her time as the only woman on a pipeline construction crew in the 1970s. Aurora Express is definitely recommended, especially if you're a train enthusiast.

A gorgeous log home along Chena Ridge west of town, the appropriately named **Grand View B&B** (907/479-3388, www.grandview-bb.com, $135 d) overlooks the Tanana River and the Alaska Range. Guests can relax in the big hot tub, warm up in the sauna, or just enjoy the vistas from the back deck. Four guest rooms all have private baths and Wi-Fi. A filling breakfast is included.

Constructed from massive logs in 1976, **Anschen Log House** (1260 Heldiver St., 907/452-6336, www.anschenloghouse.com) is everything you might imagine in an Alaskan lodge. A rugged stone fireplace dominates the living room, and you'll enjoy a delicious breakfast with picture-window views across the Chena River. The B&B contains two large guest rooms ($100 d) that share a bath. The suite ($125 d; named for Sarah Palin "because it is just as pretty") has a king bed, a private entrance, and a sun porch. Children are not allowed; this is a romantic adults-only place.

Located on Chena Ridge with sweeping views—sometimes all the way to Mt. McKinley—**Dale & Jo View Suites** (3260 Craft Rd., 907/378-0186, www.daleandjo.com) consists of two rooms on the third floor ($175–198 d) and two on the first floor ($137–160 d), all with private baths, Wi-Fi, and a full breakfast. Winter guests come for the spectacular northern lights viewing from this ridgetop location.

CAMPING

Public Campgrounds

The **Pioneer Park** parking lot is open to motor homes for $12. It has no hookups or showers but has potable water, restrooms, and a disposal station. Register in the cabin just inside the entrance.

Located within the fairgrounds, **Tanana Valley Campground** (College Rd., 907/456-7956, www.tananavalleyfair.org, mid-May–Aug., RVs $20, tents $16) is close to hiking and biking trails, and not far from Creamer's Field. The setting is woodsy and quiet.

Chena River Wayside (907/452-7275, www.chenawayside.com, RVs $25, tents $10–17) is a state campground on University Avenue just north of Airport Way. It has running water, flush toilets, fireplaces, a boat launch, and fishing—a bit high density, but not bad for city camping, if you arrive early enough to get a site; the 11 RV hookup sites go quickly. There are no showers here, so you'll need to find one at a local coin laundry. Another fine public campground ($10–12) is **Chena Lakes Recreation Area,** near North Pole.

Private Campgrounds and RV Parks

RVers often park for free at the Wal-Mart parking lot, but check with store personnel first. **River's Edge RV Park** (on Boat St. off Airport Way near University Ave., 907/474-0286 or 800/770-3343, www.riversedge.net, mid-May–mid-Sept., RVs $38, tents $21) is a large handy campground on the banks of the Chena River.

Riverview RV Park (1316 Badger Rd., 907/488-6281 or 888/488-6392, www.riverviewrvpark.net, mid-May–mid-Sept., RVs $41, tents $20) is three miles east of town near North Pole and right along the Chena River. Sites include Wi-Fi and cable TV, and they throw in a free car wash.

FOOD

Fairbanks has a fine diversity of food choices, including not just places with down-home meals (and prices), but also those offering gourmet meals (and prices).

Breakfast and Coffee

The Diner (244 Illinois St., 907/451-0613) serves breakfast anytime—with gigantic portions, efficient service, and reasonable prices. It opens daily at 6:30 A.M.

Popular with families, **The Cookie Jar** (1006 Cadillac Court, 907/479-8319, www.cookiejarfairbanks.com, Sun. 8 A.M.–4 P.M., Mon.–Thurs. 6:30 A.M.–8 P.M., Fri.–Sat. 6:30 A.M.–9 P.M.) offers a full breakfast selection (available all day, $6–18), giant cinnamon rolls, and espresso. Lunch and dinner are also available.

Alaska Coffee Roasting Company (4001 Geist Rd., 907/457-5282, www.alaskacoffeeroasting.com) serves the best espresso drinks in town, but their fresh-baked breads and pastries (from a wood-fired oven), sandwiches, mini-pizzas, free Wi-Fi, and friendly setting are the real attractions.

Inside the Coop Mall, **River City Café & Espresso** (523 2nd Ave., 907/456-6242, Mon.–Sat., $4–7) is a popular heart-of-town coffee fix with sandwiches and ice cream. **College Coffeehouse** (3677 College Rd., 907/374-0468, www.collegecoffeehousefairbanks.com, daily, $4–10) is out by the university. Both of these have computers (for a fee) and Wi-Fi (free).

Lunch and Quick Meals

Looking for lunch in a hurry? You certainly won't go wrong at **Bun on the Run,** a little trailer parked out in front of Beaver Sports (3480 College Rd.) near the university. Sandwiches are made to order; check the board for today's specials ($9) and then wait at one of the cable-spool tables in the parking lot. The Bun is open for lunch Monday–Saturday May–September.

L'Assiette de Pomegranate (414 2nd Ave., 907/451-7505, Mon.–Fri. 10:30 A.M.–5 P.M., Sat.–Sun. 11 A.M.–2 P.M. summer, Mon.–Sat. winter, $8–12) is a downtown lunch spot with creative sandwiches, salads, and daily soups, as well as outstanding desserts.

Second Story Café (College Rd. at University Ave., 907/474-9574, www.gullivers-books.com, Sun. 11 A.M.–5 P.M., Mon.–Fri. 9 A.M.–7 P.M., Sat. 9 A.M.–6 P.M., $6–8) is upstairs inside Gulliver's Books. The menu covers the latest trends in wraps, espresso, homemade soups, salads, and other light fare. There is free Internet access, and plenty of books to read.

Satisfy your sweet tooth at **Hot Licks** (3453 College Rd., 907/479-7813, www.hotlicks.net, $3–7). There's often a line out front on a summer afternoon as folks wait for a scoop of the 20-plus flavors of homemade ice cream, including wild cranberry and Alaska blueberry. Also on the menu are banana splits, Hawaiian shaved ice, and blended coffee drinks.

Long a favorite of locals, **Geraldo's Restaurant** (701 College Rd., 907/452-2299, Sun. 3–10 P.M., Mon.–Fri. 11:30 A.M.–11 P.M., Sat. noon–11 P.M., around $20) gets packed on weekends. Although best known for pizzas—including a garlic-packed version—the restaurant also serves everything from calamari and veal to cheesesteak sandwiches.

College Town Pizzeria (3549 College Rd., 907/457-2200, Mon.–Sat. 11:30 A.M.–9 P.M.) serves very good pizza by the slice or pie, eggplant parmesan calzones, and "heart attack in a tube" strombolis.

Tourists love **Fudge Pot** (515 1st Ave., 907/456-3834, www.thefudgepot.com, daily 9 A.M.–7 P.M. summer, Mon.–Sat. winter), downtown across from Golden Heart Park, where you'll find 30 types of fudge, plus soups, sandwiches, and espresso.

International

If you like Thai food, you could eat in a different place every night for a week. Best known and always great is **Thai House Restaurant** (412 5th Ave., 907/452-6123, Mon.–Sat. 11 A.M.–9:30 P.M., entrées $13–15) with big portions spiced to your taste and a casual downtown setting. Try the chicken satay appetizer or the chef's choice: pad-ped sam-sahai (sautéed prawns, squid, and fish with chili sauce, lemon grass, ginger, and crispy basil leaves). There are vegetarian specials too.

Located near Chena Pumphouse, **Lemongrass Thai Cuisine** (388 Old Chena Pump Rd., 907/456-2200, Mon.–Sat. 11 A.M.–10 P.M., closed Sun., dinner $13–18) is another family-run Thai restaurant with gracious service and wonderful food, especially the halibut red curry. The extensive menu features produce from Fairbanks whenever possible, and it's perfect for kids.

Try **Ichiban Noodle Restaurant** (400 College Rd., 900/479-1251, www.ichibanalaska.com) for a fast lunch at a good value; combo plates and noodle dishes are $9–11. There is free Wi-Fi, and it's open till midnight most days. For Chinese meals, head to Pagoda Restaurant in North Pole.

A number of Mexican-style places are found around Fairbanks, but more interesting is **Azucar Fina** (3677 College Rd., 907/456-2822, Sun. 5–9:30 P.M., Mon.–Thurs. 11:30 A.M.–10:30 P.M., Fri.–Sat. 11:30 A.M.–11:30 P.M., $15–24), with Cuban-style meals in the Campus Corner Mall, plus live Latin tunes on Friday and Saturday nights. Try the mofongo, made from fresh shrimp and plantains.

Gambardella's Pasta Bella has outstanding Italian meals, but an out-of-town spot, **The Vallata** (2190 Goldstream Rd., 907/455-6600, Tues.–Sun. 6–10 P.M., $20–30) has many local fans as well, with pasta, pizzas, veal, chicken, steaks, and lobster on the menu.

For a hint of what's inside, check out the Greek columns guarding the entrance to **Bobby's Downtown** (907/456-3222, Mon.–Fri. 11 A.M.–10 P.M., Sat. 5–10 P.M., dinner entrées $17–33). In addition to spanakopita, dolmades, moussaka, and other Greek fare, you'll find rack of lamb and a good choice of pizzas. The setting is quiet and upscale; even the restrooms are worth a gander.

Salmon Bake

Don't miss the **Alaska Salmon Bake** (907/452-7274 or 800/354-7274, www.akvisit.com) at Pioneer Park. For $31 adults or $15 children, you get all-you-can-eat salmon (flown in fresh daily), halibut, and prime rib, plus a big salad bar and desserts. The owner grew up in Juneau, where his father was a commercial fisherman, so he knows his fish. This is the best salmon bake in Alaska. It's open daily 5–9 P.M. mid-May–mid-September, and a salmon-bake shuttle bus runs 6–9:30 P.M., stopping at the major hotels and RV parks around town.

Riverfront Dining

A longtime Fairbanks establishment, **Pike's Landing** (out on Airport Rd., 907/479-6500, www.pikeslodge.com, entrées $20–28) is known for its huge wooden deck that accommodates hundreds of diners, and for the dock where boaters and Jet Skiers pull up for a meal. The seafood and burger menu isn't especially notable, but Pike's is all about location, location, location. Inside dining and a sports bar are also available if the engine noise gets too deafening.

For a more old-time atmosphere on the river, head out to the **Pump House Restaurant & Saloon** (Mile 1.3, Chena Pump Rd., 907/479-8452, www.pumphouse.com, daily 11:30 A.M.–11 P.M. summer, dinner only and closed Mon. winter). On the National Register of Historic Places, the Pump House was built in 1933 to pump water up Chena Ridge to provide pressure for the hydraulic "giants" used in gold dredging. The restaurant-bar has a fascinating interior of mining and pumping artifacts, along with antique Brunswick pool tables, one of which was in Dawson City during the gold rush. Waterside dining (or drinks) on the big riverside deck is a draw for locals. The food is quite good too, especially the big lunch buffet (summer only, $14). Dinner entrées cost $16–36 and include the usual Alaskan favorites: steak, chicken, burgers, salmon, pepper steak, and king crab. The Sunday brunch (10 A.M.–2 P.M., $21) is justifiably popular.

Downtown Dinners

In the heart of downtown, **Gambardella's Pasta Bella** (706 2nd Ave., 907/457-2992, www.gambardellas.com, Sun. 4–10 P.M., Mon.–Sat. 11 A.M.–10 P.M., entrées $12–24) is justifiably popular for pasta, homemade Italian bread, the "mother of all lasagnas," gourmet pizzas, calzones, and double fudge cheesecake. The atmosphere is warm and inviting, service is accommodating, and there's a small upstairs deck. Dinner prices are reasonable.

A modern and trendy downtown eatery inside Springhill Suites, **Lavelle's Bistro** (575 1st Ave., 907/450-0555, www.lavellesbistro.com, lunch daily 11 A.M.–2 P.M. summer, dinner daily 4:30–10 P.M. year-round, entrées $17–30) has a 3,000-bottle wall of wine, an open kitchen where you can watch the chefs at work, and outside dining in the summer. The upscale menu encompasses seafood risotto, rack of lamb, oven-roasted duck, French onion soup, and great salads (try the salad Teresa), but locals also rave about the desserts, especially the warm banana wontons with roasted pecans and Meyer's rum.

Groceries and Farmers Market

Fairbanks lacks a downtown grocery store, but you'll find **Safeways** at University Center on Airport Way and in the Bentley Mall on College Road, **Fred Meyer** shopping centers at 3755 Airport Way and on the corner of Johansen Expressway and Old Steese Highway, plus a **Wal-Mart Supercenter** on Johansen Expressway.

Out on College Road at Caribou Way, the **Tanana Valley Farmers Market** (907/456-3276, www.tvfmarket.com) is *the* place to buy locally grown produce, flowers, baked goods, arts, and crafts. The market is open Wednesday 11 A.M.–4 P.M. and Saturday 9 A.M.–4 P.M. mid-May–late September. This is a wonderful place to get a taste of Alaska (literally).

INFORMATION AND SERVICES

In addition to the new downtown visitors center, go to the State of Alaska's **Department of Natural Resources Public Information Center** (3700 Airport Way, 907/451-2705, www.alaskastateparks.org, Mon.–Fri. 9 A.M.–5 P.M.) across the street from Fred Meyer on the west side of town. Stop in to get brochures on state parks and trails, reserve a state park cabin, or learn about mining claims and state land sales.

Useful **Fairbanks websites** include the Fairbanks Visitors and Convention Bureau (www.explorefairbanks.com), the *Fairbanks News-Miner* (www.newsminer.com), and the aurora forecast at the Geophysical Institute (www.

gedds.alaska.edu/auroraforecast). How cold (or hot) is it in Fairbanks? Visit the National Weather Service (www.arh.noaa.gov).

Books and Internet Access

The **Noel Wien Library** (corner of Airport Way and Cowles, 907/452-5177, http://library.fnsb.lib.ak.us, Mon.–Thurs. 10 A.M.–9 P.M., Fri. 10 A.M.–6 P.M., Sat. 10 A.M.–5 P.M. year-round, plus Sun. 1–5 P.M. winter) is a comfortable and complete facility (with indoor trees, even). One look inside tells you a lot about Fairbanks's long winters and why the library is such a wonderful escape. You can surf the Web for free in the library, and several local coffee shops have free Wi-Fi and rental computers.

Gulliver's Books (College Rd. and University Ave., 907/474-9574 or 800/390-8999, www.gullivers-books.com) is a great little two-story place with both new and used titles. A large **Barnes and Noble Booksellers** (421 Mehar Ave., 907/452-6400, www.bn.com) is on the north end of town.

Services

B&C Laundromat (College Rd. and University Ave., 907/479-2696) has showers, or shower and then swim at **Mary Siah Recreation Center** (1025 14th Ave., 907/459-1082). The post office is downtown between 3rd and 4th Avenues.

If you need a doctor, walk in to **Fairbanks Urgent Care** (1867 Airport Way, 907/452-2178) or **1st Care Center** (1101 Noble St., 907/458-2682), and for emergencies, drag yourself to **Fairbanks Memorial Hospital** (1650 Cowles St., 907/452-8181, www.fairbanksmemorial.com).

GETTING THERE

Air

Beautifully remodeled in 2009, **Fairbanks International Airport** (www.dot.state.ak.us/faiiap) is six miles southwest of downtown. The main level includes an information booth with brochures. **Alaska Airlines** (907/452-1661 or 800/426-0333, www.alaskaair.com) has multiple daily flights between Fairbanks and Anchorage, plus once-a-day nonstop service to Seattle. Both options are available year-round.

Seasonal service includes nonstop flights to Fairbanks from Minneapolis–St. Paul on **Northwest Airlines** (800/225-2525, www.nwa.com), from Salt Lake City on **Delta Airlines** (800/221-1212, www.delta.com), and from Frankfurt (with a stop in Whitehorse, Yukon) aboard **Condor Air** (800/524-6975, www.condor.com). **Japan Airlines** (800/525-3663, www.japanair.com) has winter-only flights between Tokyo and Fairbanks for the legions of Japanese aurora fans. **Air North** (867/668-2228 or 800/661-0407, www.flyairnorth.com) has summertime flights connecting Fairbanks with Dawson City and Whitehorse in Yukon.

In business since 1950, **Frontier Alaska** (907/266-8394 or 800/866-8394, www.frontierak.com) is the largest regional carrier, with daily flights between Fairbanks and Anchorage, plus scheduled service across most of Interior Alaska. They're also the parent company for Era Aviation and Hageland Aviation. **Warbelow's Air Ventures** (907/474-0518 or 800/478-0812, www.warbelows.com) is another long-established air taxi with extensive connections throughout the Interior. **Larry's Flying Service** (907/474-9169, www.larrysflying.com), **Arctic Circle Air** (907/474-0112, www.arcticcircleair.com), **Everts Air Alaska** (907/450-2350, www.evertsair.com), and **Wright Air Service** 9907/474-0502, www.wrightair.net) also have scheduled regional flights.

Train

The **Alaska Railroad** (907/265-2494 or 800/544-0552, www.alaskarailroad.com) chugs out of Fairbanks from a modern depot at 1745 Johansen Expressway. Mid-May–mid-September there are daily departures at 8:15 A.M. arriving in Denali National Park at noon ($64) and in Anchorage at 8:15 P.M. ($210). Tour-bus fares to Denali and Anchorage are cheaper, but the train is a more comfortable, enjoyable, and historical way to see this part of Alaska. If you want to go in luxury, however, buy a ticket ($85 extra to Denali, $110 extra to Anchorage) on the elaborate double-decker GoldStar coaches, where open-air viewing decks are the main attraction.

Buses

Alaska Direct Bus Line (907/277-6652 or 800/770-6652, www.alaskadirectbusline.com) has service to Tok, continuing on to Whitehorse and Anchorage. Buses run three times a week in the summer, twice weekly in winter. **Alaska/Yukon Trails** (907/479-2277 or 888/770-7275, www.alaskashuttle.com) runs a daily summer-only service connecting Fairbanks with Denali, Talkeetna, and Anchorage, plus three-times-a-week runs to Delta Junction, Tok, Chicken, Dawson City, and Whitehorse.

GETTING AROUND

City Buses

Fairbanks's public bus system, **Metropolitan Area Commuter Service** (907/459-1011, www.co.fairbanks.ak.us/transportation), known as "MACS," operates Monday–Saturday; pick up timetables at the information center. All routes stop at **Transit Park** on Cushman Street and Fifth Avenue. The fare is $1.50, or $3 for an all-day pass.

Taxis and Shuttles

There are 20 or so local cab companies; find them in the Yellow Pages. Taxis charge $20 or so to get downtown from the airport. **Airlink Shuttle & Tours** (907/452-3337) has flat-rate shared ride service: $11 for up to three people heading to the airport or train station.

Car and RV Rentals

The following companies all have airport counters: **Avis** (907/474-0900 or 800/831-8000), **Budget** (907/474-0855 or 800/474-0855), **Dollar** (907/451-4360 or 800/800-4000), **Hertz** (907/452-4444 or 800/654-3131), **National** (907/451-8234 or 800/227-7368), and **Payless** (907/474-0177 or 800/729-5377).

Both **Rent A Wreck** (907/452-1606, www.rentawreck.com) and **Arctic Rent-A-Car** (907/479-8044 or 800/478-8696, www.arcticrentacar.com) are located away from the airport, so you'll need a cab ride (but rates are lower).

Most rental car companies do not allow their vehicles north of the Arctic Circle, and other road restrictions are often imposed, but **Arctic Outfitters** (907/474-3530, www.arctic-outfitters.com) rents cars with extra gear such as CB radios and two spare tires for travel on the Dalton Highway.

Rent pickup-truck-based campers from **GoNorth RV Camper Rental** (907/479-7272 or 866/236-7272, www.paratours.net) and gas-guzzling RVs from **Adventures in Alaska RV Rentals** 907/458-7368, www.adventuresakrv.com).

Bus Tours

Gray Line of Alaska (907/451-6835 or 888/452-1737, www.graylinealaska.com) leads regional bus tours, but you can do these on your own for less if you have a vehicle. Several other companies offer less corporate versions: try **River's Edge Resort** (907/474-0286 or 800/770-3343, www.riversedge.net) for historical city tours.

Vicinity of Fairbanks

NORTH POLE

In 1949, Con Miller was cleaning out the Fairbanks trading post he'd just bought and found a Santa Claus suit. He liked it so much that he took to wearing it during his trips to the Interior to buy furs and sell supplies. The costume made a big impression on the Native Alaskan children. A few years later, when he moved 12 miles southeast of Fairbanks near Eielson Air Force Base, he built a new trading post and called it Santa Claus House. Miller and his neighbors chose the name North Pole for their new town, reportedly to attract a toy manufacturer to the area. It never arrived, but the name stuck.

Today, North Pole (pop. 1,600) is a suburb of Fairbanks, but the business he established has become the town's primary attraction. The town is dotted with more Xmas fever: street names like St. Nicholas and Kris Kringle Drives and Santa Claus and Mistletoe Lanes, business names such as Santaland RV Park, Santa's Pull Tabs, and Elf's Den Diner, along with a 50,000-watt Christian radio station, KJNP (King Jesus of North Pole). There are almost two dozen churches in the area, including, of course, St. Nicholas Church. But, as if to counteract all the religion, there's also Fantasy Video just north of town, where the fantasies certainly aren't about sugarplums.

© DON PITCHER

It's Christmas 365 days a year in North Pole.

Santa Claus House

Santa Claus House (907/488-2200 or 800/588-4078, www.santaclaushouse.com) right along the Richardson Highway, is the largest and tackiest gift shop in the state, and probably the biggest one this side of Las Vegas. Out front stands a 40-foot Santa figure ("the world's tallest"), and inside you'll find Santa in the flesh Wednesday–Sunday 10 A.M.–7 P.M., any day of the year. Outside, two of Santa's reindeer are housed in a pen.

Santa Claus House is open daily 8 A.M.–8 P.M. in the summer, with variable hours the rest of the year. Buy a "holiday message from Santa," mailed in December from North Pole to anyone in the world for $8. For an extra $10 they'll send you a deed to one square inch of the Santa Claus subdivision in town. There's even a free summertime shuttle bus to Santa Claus House from hotels and RV parks in Fairbanks.

One of the attractions in town is getting your letters postmarked from "North Pole, Alaska." Mail them at the Santa Claus House or the post office on 5th Avenue. Throughout December, this post office is deluged with letters and cards from people wanting a North Pole postmark—the stacks can be piled 10 feet high. And that's *not* including the estimated 10,000 letters to Santa Claus himself, which are all answered by students at North Pole Middle School.

Not everything is about Christmas here. North Pole is also home to Flint Hills Refinery

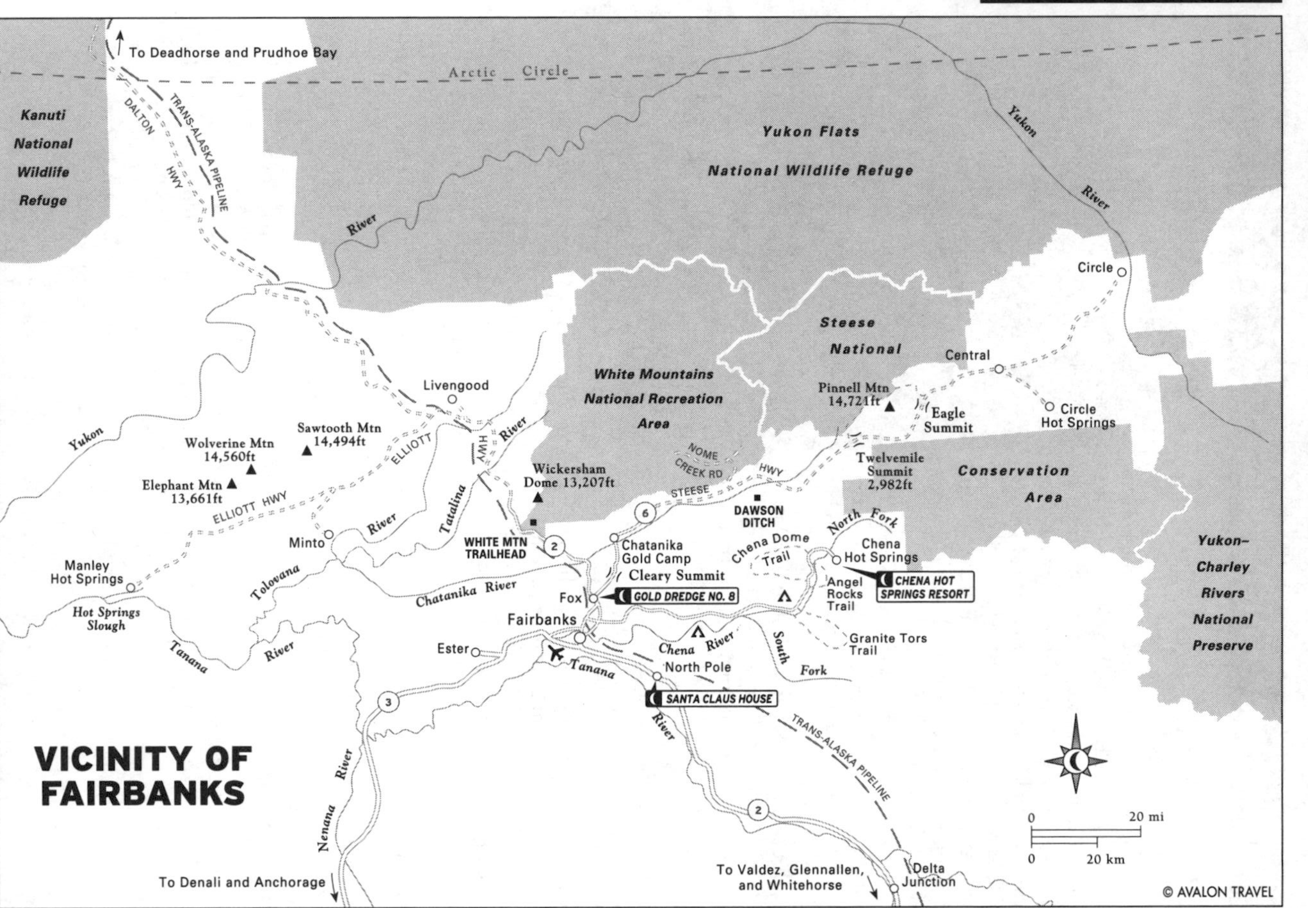
VICINITY OF FAIRBANKS
© AVALON TRAVEL
To Deadhorse and Prudhoe Bay
Arctic Circle
Kanuti National Wildlife Refuge
Yukon Flats National Wildlife Refuge
DALTON HWY
TRANS-ALASKA PIPELINE
Yukon River
Circle
Central
Circle Hot Springs
Eagle Summit
Steese National Conservation Area
Yukon–Charley Rivers National Preserve
Pinnell Mtn 14,721ft
Twelvemile Summit 2,982ft
White Mountains National Recreation Area
NOME CREEK RD
STEESE HWY
DAWSON DITCH
Livengood
HWY
Tatalina River
Yukon
Wolverine Mtn 14,560ft
Sawtooth Mtn 14,494ft
Elephant Mtn 13,661ft
ELLIOTT HWY
Wickersham Dome 13,207ft
WHITE MTN TRAILHEAD
Minto
Manley Hot Springs
Hot Springs Slough
Tolovana River
Tanana River
Chatanika River
Chatanika Gold Camp
Cleary Summit
Fox
GOLD DREDGE NO. 8
Fairbanks
Ester
Chena Dome Trail
North Fork
Chena Hot Springs
CHENA HOT SPRINGS RESORT
Angel Rocks Trail
Granite Tors Trail
Chena River
South Fork
North Pole
SANTA CLAUS HOUSE
Tanana River
Nenana River
To Denali and Anchorage
To Valdez, Glennallen, and Whitehorse
Delta Junction
0 20 mi
0 20 km

(it taps into the Trans-Alaska Pipeline), along with **Eielson Air Force Base** (12 miles south of town, 907/377-2116, www.eielson.af.mil).

On the Richardson Highway at Mission Road, the North Pole **Visitors Log Cabin** (907/488-22842, www.northpolechamber.us) is open daily 10 A.M.–6 P.M. late May–early September.

Accommodations and Food

Located on a small private lake, **Beaver Lake Resort Motel** (2555 Mission Rd., 907/488-9600, www.beaverlakeresort.net) has rooms for $139 d, and two-bedroom apartments that sleep six for $179. All units include full kitchens, access to the sauna, and Wi-Fi.

New in 2009, **Hotel North Pole** (449 Santa Claus Lane, 907/488-4800 or 877/488-4801, www.hotelnorthpole.com) has spacious guest rooms ($146–166 d) and apartment-style suites ($193–211 d), flat screen TVs, Wi-Fi, and continental breakfast.

North Pole Cabins (907/490-6400, www.northpolecabins.com, $139–209 d) rents modern cabins with baths. A continental breakfast is provided.

Santaland RV Park (907/488-9123 or 888/488-9123, www.santalandrv.com, Apr.–Oct., RVs $35, no tents) is right next to Santa Claus House. Amenities include cable TV and Wi-Fi.

North Pole is home to the best Chinese restaurant in the Fairbanks area, **Pagoda Restaurant** (North Pole Plaza, 907/488-3338, www.pagodanorthpole.com, daily 11:30 A.M.–9:30 P.M.). The setting is colorful, and the Mandarin, Szechuan, and Cantonese food is always good. Lunch specials are $11, with full dinners for $17–20.

Chena Lakes Recreation Area

In August 1967 it rained seven inches in seven days, and the Chena River overflowed, inundating low-lying Fairbanks under five feet of floodwater. Half the town's residents were evacuated, and damage neared $200 million. The task of preventing a similar disaster in the future fell to the Army Corps of Engineers, which mucked around for 15 years, building a dam at Moose Creek, a levee and spillway into the Tanana River, and this 2,000-acre park of artificial lakes and recreational facilities. The recreation area contains the nearest beach to Fairbanks, and on hot weekends the exodus is not unlike that of Bostonians fleeing to Cape Cod—you might be able to wedge a dishtowel onto some sand and swim in place.

Most of the season, though, Chena Lakes (907/488-1655, www.co.fairbanks.ak.us) is a delightful place to picnic, stroll the self-guided nature trail, bike the seven-mile cycling trail, play volleyball and horseshoes, pick berries, camp, fish, and rent canoes, paddleboats, and sailboats. In the winter, the trails are groomed for cross-country skiing. Camp at either the Lakes campground or the river park. From Fairbanks, go five miles south of North Pole on the Richardson Highway (Mile 347), take a left on Laurance Road, and follow the signs. Fees are $4 for day use, $10–12 for camping. Canoes, kayaks, and pedal boats are available for rent.

FOX

In 1901, Felice Pedroni (a.k.a. Felix Pedro) found color on what is now Pedro Creek and was credited with the discovery of the Cleary and Goldstream veins, which touched off the rush from the Klondike and Nome to the Fairbanks area. However, the gold here was anything but easy for the taking: This gold-laden bedrock was normally 80–100 feet under gravel, muck, and permafrost. Within 20 years of the find, the rich creeks were worked out, the shallow low-grade ground was exhausted, and most miners couldn't afford the expense of working the deep claims. In 1923, however, the railroad was finished from Seward to Fairbanks and brought with it the feasibility of large-scale gold production. Hydraulic giants, monster dredges, miles of tailings, and businessmen in three-piece suits replaced the lone prospector with a hammer and bucket. This second gold rush to Fairbanks—a corporate gold rush—eventually produced almost $200 million worth of the precious heavy metal.

A ride 10 miles up the Steese Highway from Fairbanks to and around Fox clearly reveals the impact of this second boom. Huge cleared fields and stripped hillsides trace the progress of the giants and dredges, and the tailings lie in the snaking mounds they were spit into 50 years ago. Marble, gravel, and sand are for sale along the roadside. Heavy machinery dots the land with the bovine patience of metal and rubber.

Housed within a large warehouse-type metal building, **Silver Gulch Brewery** (907/452-2739, www.silvergulch.com) is a locals' favorite, crafting Copper Creek Amber Ale, Fairbanks Lager, Pick Axe Porter, Coldfoot Pilsner, Old 55, and other specialty beers. Free tours are generally offered Monday, Wednesday, and Friday at 3 P.M., but call ahead to be sure. A popular restaurant (Mon.–Fri. 4–10 P.M., Sat.–Sun. 11 A.M.–10 P.M., $13–30) is on the premises, serving upscale pub fare that encompasses fish-and-chips, brick-oven pizzas, burgers, sandwiches, and steaks.

A rowdy and popular roadhouse bar, **Howling Dog Saloon** (907/456-4695) is right across the road, with live music Wednesday–Saturday nights.

Up the Old Steese a hair (or is it *hare*?) is the **Turtle Club** (907/457-3883, www.alaskanturtle.com, $20–34), with prime rib (the house specialty), halibut, prawns, lobster, and king crab. It can get somewhat smoky at times. Check out the turtle collection scattered around the restaurant. Seatings are nightly at 6, 7:30, and 9 P.M.; reservations are recommended.

Continue another five miles past Fox on the Steese Highway for the monument to **Felice Pedroni,** who started it all rolling in 1902. Across the road is Pedro Creek; try your hand at panning for a little dust, and note the unnatural look of a creek played for gold for most of a century.

Pipe Dreams

Eight miles out the Steese Highway on the way to Fox is a **Trans-Alaska Pipeline Viewpoint,** a favorite pose-for-a-photo stop. Interpretive displays describe the site, and Alyeska Pipeline Services runs a little visitors center here (907/456-9391, daily mid-May–mid-Sept.). The viewing area itself is open year-round.

Gold Dredge No. 8

Local placer gold derives from ancient quartz veins once exposed in creek beds, now buried up to 100 feet below the surface. To get to it, first you hose off the surface layer down to two feet with hydraulic cannons or "giants," then down another few feet as the exposed frozen gravel thaws on its own. The deeper frozen muck and rock is thawed over a year or so by water pumped through pipes from the surface to bedrock, supplied by monumental aqueducts such as the Davidson Ditch. Once the earth down to bedrock is diggable, a gold dredge is brought in.

The dredge dwarfs even the largest machines in this land of giant machines. It's a true Alaska-size contraption that looks like a cartoon cross between a houseboat and a crane. An endless circular conveyor of up to 100 steel buckets scoops up the gravel, conveys it to the top end of a revolving screen, and dumps it. The screen separates the larger rocks, shunting them off to the tailing piles, from the golden gravel, which is sifted from the screen to riffles, where quicksilver (mercury) gleans the gold, forming an amalgam. The riffles are cleaned every couple of weeks, then the gold is further processed and assayed. In the old days during the height of production, the gold would next be shipped to the mint, where it earned $35 per troy ounce.

Gold Dredge No. 8 (907/479-6673 or 866/479-6673, www.golddredgeno8.com, daily mid-May–mid-Sept.), the only National Historic Mechanical Engineering Landmark in Alaska, is just a little larger than its official designation. One of Alaska's first steel-hulled bucket-line dredges, it was installed in 1928—five stories tall, 250 feet long, weighing over 1,000 tons. The dredge stopped operating in 1959, but it has been completely restored with fascinating exhibits and guides stationed around the dredge. The $15 admission also includes a hearty lunch. To get there, drive eight miles up the Steese Highway toward Fox, take a left on Goldstream Road, and another left on the Old Steese Highway. Riverboat Discovery and El Dorado Gold Mine have the same owners, so package tours are available.

El Dorado Gold Mine

Located a mile north of Fox on the Elliott Highway, this active placer mine (907/479-6673 or 866/479-6673, www.eldoradogoldmine.com) is a made-for-tourists attraction. Here, you climb onboard a small-scale railroad to view the mine, walk into a tunnel in the permafrost, and get a chance to try your hand at panning for a flake or two. Two-hour tours take place mid-May–mid-September and cost $35 adults or $22 children. A $5 shuttle is provided from Fairbanks; reservations are recommended. As an aside, the Fort Knox Gold Mine—Alaska's largest active mine—is 25 miles northeast of Fairbanks. It is not open to the public.

Heading out from Fairbanks

The country around Fairbanks offers outstanding opportunities to explore and experience the land and waterways, and then to luxuriate in hot springs that have soothed and refreshed travelers for well over a century. With the Interior's predictable good weather, the long days and low lighting, and the humbling power of this vast humanless wilderness, you'll return from any of these trips knowing a lot more about Alaska, and yourself.

Chena Hot Springs Road boasts three exciting hiking trails, two campgrounds, a cozy public cabin, a choice of canoe routes and fishing spots, and a large pool resort, all within an hour's drive of town on a good paved road. The **Steese Highway** has five campgrounds, abundant canoeing and fishing, a high-country backpack that rivals much of Denali National Park, and the fascinating evidence of gold fever—past and present. The **Elliott Highway** is the longest, roughest, and most primitive ride of the three. Along it is one long trail close to Fairbanks, no campgrounds to speak of, and no facilities of any kind, all of which make the small pool and hot tubs at the road's end in friendly Manley all the more rewarding.

And for a real road adventure, you can head up the **Dalton Highway,** which begins at Mile 73 on the Elliott Highway and continues 414 miles all the way to Deadhorse, a few miles south of Prudhoe Bay.

CHENA HOT SPRINGS ROAD

Depending on whom you believe, either Felix Pedro (1903) or the U.S. Geological Survey (1907) discovered the hot springs off the north fork of the Chena River. Shortly after, the land was homesteaded by George Wilson, who built a lodge and cabins and enclosed the springs in a pool. The site has been considerably improved over the years, and today Chena Hot Springs Resort is one of the most popular regional destinations, with access via a 55-mile paved road. Take the Steese Highway just north of town to the Chena Hot Springs Road exit. The road starts out somewhat roller-coasterish from frost heaves, but the scenery is pleasing—rolling green hills dotted by small verdant farms. From Mile 26 to Mile 51 is **Chena River Wayside,** a well-developed and beautiful playground in Fairbanks' backyard, where numerous trails, river access, picnic areas, and two campgrounds are within an easy hour's drive from town. You could easily fill up three or four days camping, hiking, backpacking, and canoeing (all free), and then satisfy the creature-comfort yearnings you accumulated in the backcountry with a soak in the pool and a drink at the resort at the end of the road. (Note: Don't mix up three confusingly named recreation areas around Fairbanks—the Chena River Wayside along Chena Hot Springs Road, the Chena Lakes Recreation Area near North

Pole, and the Chena River State Recreation Site in Fairbanks!)

Nestled along a small lake at Mile 16, **Two Rivers Lodge** (907/488-6815, www.tworiverslodge.com, daily 5–10 P.M., entrées $20–36) serves gourmet seafood, pasta, and chicken, but their specialty is all-you-can-eat Dungeness crab prepared in a spicy brine. The lounge serves a simpler menu of wood-fired pizzas, fish-and-chips, and burgers. There's a rustically Alaskan decor, with a big summertime deck, along with a rather un-Alaskan boccie court outside.

Just up the road a mile, **Earthtone Huskies B&B** (907/488-8074, www.earthtonehuskies.com/bb/bb.htm) has comfortable log cabins (no running water) for just $40 s or $50 d, including a continental breakfast. Owner Judy Cooper leads dogsled rides in the winter.

Chena River Wayside

Covering 254,000 acres, Chena River Wayside boasts luxurious campgrounds, excellent outdoor recreational opportunities, lush greenery, towering trees (for Interior Alaska), rolling hills, the curvy Chena River, and best of all, no crowds. When town becomes oppressive, head a half-hour east to some of the best that the Interior has to offer. For the complete story, contact the Alaska Department of Natural Resources in Fairbanks (907/451-2700, www.alaskastateparks.org).

Numerous well-marked pullouts give easy river access and your choice of the length of a canoe trip. A good place to put in is at the Mile 44 bridge—it's a little faster and more fun than downriver. Watch for sweepers, deadheads, shallows, and especially the many impassable sloughs—they are stagnant, stinking, and mosquito-ridden. Get details from local canoe rental companies or state park folks before heading out.

Rosehip Campground (Mile 27, $10) right at the entrance to the recreation area, is as big and lush a campground as you could ever want, only a half-hour from town. The river is never more than a two-minute walk away. There are 25 sites, pit toilets, water pumps, and numerous signboards with information about trails, wildlife, and canoe routes.

The road parallels the river all the way to the hot springs and crosses it four times, at Miles 37, 40, 44, and 49. After heavy rains, the road often floods, especially around Mile 37.

The **Chena River Cabin** ($50) is an easily accessed and attractive log cabin right on the river at Mile 32, with a porch and space for nine people. Make reservations in the Department of Natural Resources Information Center (3700 Airport Way, Fairbanks, 907/451-2705, www.alaskastateparks.org). **Granite Tors** loop trail starts across the road from the campground, and just before the bridge. This well-maintained path is a 15-mile six-hour round trip. The first mile or so is on boardwalk over muskeg; the first tors (strange granite sculptures thrust near the surface, then exposed when the surrounding earth eroded away) are around six miles from the trailhead on both the north and south forks of the trail.

Angel Rocks trail begins at Mile 49 just beyond a pullout and right before the fourth bridge over the Chena River. It's only three miles or so, though the first few miles are uphill. The rock outcroppings in the high country are worth the huff. Allow three to four hours.

For the **Chena Dome Trail,** take the northern trailhead, which starts at Mile 51, a half-mile past Angel Creek on the left side of the road; it's a three-day, 29-mile loop trail mostly along ridgetops marked by cairns, and has great views. A quarter-mile up the trail is the sign for Chena Dome (9 miles); after a short boardwalk you start to climb and leave the mosquitoes and heat behind. One mile up the trail is a good viewpoint.

Chena Hot Springs Resort

At Mile 57, the road ends at a sprawling resort (907/451-8104, www.chenahotsprings.com) that always seems to be adding something new. Owner Bernie Karl is working to create a completely off-the-grid settlement where everything runs on geothermal energy, from the refrigeration system that cools an ice museum

© DON PITCHER

Chena Hot Springs Resort

all summer to the greenhouses filled with year-round tomatoes.

Chena's featured attraction is, of course, the hot springs, discovered by Anglos in 1905. The water comes out of the spring at nearly 160°F, and is a little under 110°F in the pools. There's an indoor pool and hot tub, plus a second outdoor hot tub, a redwood deck, and a large sandy-bottom pond that is best experienced when the stars are obscured by the aurora borealis. It's all first-rate, but only adults (over age 18) are allowed in the outdoor pond. Resort guests (except campers and RVers) get free access to the springs, but if you aren't staying here a day pass costs $10 adults, $8 seniors and children ages 6–17, free for younger children. Towels are $5 extra. The pools are open daily 7 A.M.–midnight.

A unique feature at Chena is the **Aurora Ice Museum,** the largest year-round ice environment in the world. Step inside the 30-foot-high arched structure to view intricately carved pieces crafted by famed ice artist Steve Brice, including chandeliers, a giant chess set, life-size jousting knights on horses, and a bar made entirely from ice. Tours of the ice museum are $15 adults, $8 children. Add $15 to enjoy a Stoli apple martini in a goblet carved from ice; you keep the "glass." For the complete experience, spend a night snuggled beneath reindeer hides atop ice beds. The cost is an icy $600 d, but this also includes a room in the main lodge when you get too chilly.

All sorts of activities are available at the 440-acre resort (for an extra fee), including rafting, canoe rentals, fishing, mountain bike rentals, and horseback rides in the summer, along with dogsled rides, a dog mushing school, snowmobiling, horse-drawn sleigh rides, cross-country skiing (8 miles of groomed trails), and ice skating in the winter. And if that isn't enough, the resort has free activities such as volleyball, badminton, hiking, horseshoes, and basketball. In the summer months Chena Hot Springs attracts a mixed American and European crowd, but in winter it's even busier with Japanese travelers who come to experience the spectacular northern lights shows. You'll see aurora displays 90 percent of the winter nights here, and you can even watch in heated comfort at the glass-enclosed aurorium. If you visit in winter, don't miss the nightly snow coach tours to a heated mountaintop yurt with panoramic vistas ($70 for a 4-hour adventure). These depart at 10 P.M., returning at 2 A.M.

Along with the hot springs and ice museum, the resort offers hotel rooms and suites ($189–289 d), bring-your-sleeping-bag yurts ($65 d), plus summer-only tent and RV sites ($20 with showers). The Victorian-style dining room specializes in steaks, prime rib, chicken, pasta, and seafood, but is also open daily for breakfast and lunch. If you don't have wheels, the resort provides a shuttle van from Fairbanks for $75–115 per person roundtrip.

STEESE HIGHWAY

Gold is the color of this country: The precious metal wrested with brute force from the reluctant earth, the golden-green panoramas of the alpine tundra, and the golden light sparkling through the plumes of dust-fog along the road.

Other than the drive itself and the unlimited fishing and canoeing on the Chatanika River and Birch Creek, the excitement on the Steese can be found at the **Davidson Ditch** and on the challenging **Pinnell Mountain Trail.** The Davidson Ditch was one of the first miracle-of-engineering pipelines in this country, and unlike the oil pipeline, you can play on it! The Pinnell Trail is a three-day stroll along the windswept ridges of the White Mountains, with distant jagged horizons for the farsighted, and stunning alpine wildflowers for the nearsighted.

The Road

Named for Army general James G. Steese, president of the Alaska Road Commission 1920–1927 who oversaw its entire construction, the Steese Highway parallels the original Fairbanks–Circle Trail. Thousands of fortune seekers floated up and down the Yukon to Circle, hit the trail after news of Felix Pedro's strike spread, and helped open up the Interior in the early 20th century. The road was completed in 1928, and is paved for the first 44 miles.

Starting from Fairbanks, the highway immediately climbs into the gold-bearing hills, with a great viewpoint overlooking the Tanana Valley on the left at Hagelbarger Road. On a clear day, turn around to see if the Alaska Range is "out"—a stunning panorama from Mt. McKinley to the eastern peaks of Deborah, Hess, and Hayes. Just up the road is a pullout to view the **Trans-Alaska Pipeline**—which runs aboveground here—and an informative sign. In a few miles you come to the town of Fox, where you'll note the extensive placer mine tailings from **Gold Dredge No. 8,** which operated from 1927 to 1959.

At the junction with the Elliott Highway (Rte. 2), take a right for the Steese (Rte. 6). At Mile 16 is a turnout with a plaque mounted on a stone monument to Felix Pedro; walk across the road to Pedro Creek, whose golden sands infected the stampeders with Fairbanks fever.

Cleary Summit

From Pedro Creek the frost-heaved pavement climbs quickly to 2,233-foot Cleary Summit, home to **Mt. Aurora Skiland** (907/389-2314). Nearby is **Mt. Aurora Fairbanks Creek Lodge** (907/389-2000, www.mt-aurora.com), a 12-room lodge (shared baths) that was once a bunkhouse for miners. Lodging is $118 d including a continental breakfast; lunch and dinner are available by request. Most visitation takes place in the winter when this is a prime spot to view and photograph the northern lights.

Fairbanks Exploration Company

Beyond the summit, the road twists and turns down to **Chatanika;** at Mile 28, take a hard right and climb to the site of the Fairbanks Exploration Company Gold Camp. After the completion of the Alaska Railroad in 1923, the U.S. Smelting, Refining, and Mining Co. began acquiring and consolidating many of the placer properties around Fairbanks. By 1938, the subsidiary F. E. Co. had three dredges operating between Chatanika and Ester, had installed the Davidson Ditch, and was fueling the entire operation with its own power plant in Fairbanks. In its 30 years of production, F. E. Co. took out nearly $100 million in gold—and that was at no more than $35 per troy ounce. The grounds are covered with vintage equipment and 15 restored buildings that are still maintained by machinery used during the 1940s. Gold Dredge No. 3 is visible near Mile 29 amid tailings on the north side of the road.

Now on the National Register of Historic Places, the **Chatanika Old F. E. Gold Camp** resort (907/389-2414, is chock-full of early Alaska memorabilia and mining artifacts. Rooms in the old lodge are $69 d with shared baths, or $85 d for two cabins that share a bath containing a Jacuzzi tub. Tent spaces cost $15. The restaurant (Tues.–Sun. 11 A.M.–9 P.M., entrées $19–30) is particularly notable, with dinner steaks and seafood, lunchtime burgers, Reubens, and salads, plus a great Sunday champagne brunch ($19). A pleasant deck overlooks the mining valley. The lodge, restaurant, and saloon are open March–October.

A mile up the road is the **Chatanika Lodge** (907/389-2164, $65 s, $75 d), with a bar (live music Sunday nights), hearty meals, and basic bath-down-the-hall rooms. They host **Chatanika Days Outhouse Races** on the second weekend of March. Five-person outhouse teams race a one-mile course, with four pushing and one riding in the specially built "racing outhouses."

1st Alaska Outdoor School (907/590-5900, www.1stalaskaoutdoorschool.com) is located along the Chatanika River north of Fairbanks. Popular with travelers on a budget, the school has canoeing, kayaking, camping ($15), and hostel accommodations ($25), along with wintertime ski touring, dog mushing, and aurora viewing. The owners are from Germany and Japan, and so are many of the visitors. Access is by a seven-mile hike from Murphy Dome, so this isn't for everyone. Meals are available.

Poker Flat

At **Poker Flat Research Range** (907/474-7558 for times, www.pfrr.alaska.edu), two miles up the Steese from Chatanika, the Geophysical Institute of the University of Alaska Fairbanks studies the aurora and upper atmosphere. When it was constructed in the late 1960s, Poker Flat took its name from a Bret Harte short story, "The Outcasts of Poker Flat," about a gambler and a prostitute who were banished from a mythical California goldrush town in the winter and eventually froze to death. The construction crew building the rocket range for the Geophysical Institute considered themselves similarly outcast. This is the only rocket range owned by a university in the world, and it is used for launching suborbital rockets. Poker Flats is open some Thursdays in the summer for tours.

Upper Chatanika River Recreation Site

Located at Mile 39, this excellent state campground ($10) has pit toilets, a water pump, and plentiful river access for fishing (grayling) and boating. Head around to the back of the grounds and try for a campsite right on the river. Bring an inner tube and ride from the bridge down to your tent.

Davidson Ditch

The pavement ends at Mile 44; at Mile 57, the U.S. Creek Road leads seven miles to two Bureau of Land Management (BLM) campgrounds, a recreational gold panning area along Nome Creek, and a put-in point for floating Beaver Creek, all within the White Mountains Recreation Area.

Also at Mile 57 is a highway pullout for a long stretch of pipe, a remnant of the Davidson Ditch, the amazing engineering feat (1925) that slaked the F. E. Co. dredges' enormous thirst for water; the dredges floated on artificial ponds so they could be moved. Starting at a dam on the upper Chatanika River, the 12-foot-wide, 4-foot-deep, 83-mile-long ditch, along with nearly seven miles of 48-inch pipe and a combined mile of tunnels, crossed 90 miles of hilly wilderness, directing 56,000 gallons of water per minute to the gold fields. Notice the expansion or "slip" joint in the middle of the level section of the pipe here, and the wooden saddle below it. The pipe was drained in the winter but the cold still took its toll: Note the bulge in the pipe where it cuts uphill, and the repair job on the joint.

This is one of several views of the ditch in the next 10 miles, standing in mute testimony to the struggle of rugged miners against rugged terrain and harsh elements in the quest for gold. You can't help but be amazed by this project, especially when you consider that the road was barely built, the machinery was primitive, and the land unyielding. F. E. Co.'s contract did not require the removal of the pipe when gold production ceased, so here it still sits—either a blight on the landscape or evidence of the colorful history of this land, depending on your perspective. Whichever it is, watch your footing if you monkey around on the pipe.

Cripple Creek Campground and Beyond

This BLM facility (Mile 60, 907/474-2200, www.blm.gov/ak, $6) consists of an inner loop for cars and RVs and a walk-in section. Either take a site with the RV crowd or park in the walk-in lot by the toilets, head to the back of the campground, and pitch your tent right by the river. The mosquitoes are fierce in mosquito season. A public-use cabin is also nearby.

The road out here gets smoother, wider, and less slippery. From the back of a large pullout at Mile 62 is another view of the pipe disappearing into a tunnel. At Mile 81, natural spring water gushes cold and delicious from an open spigot, about five gallons per minute. While you've got the Davidson Ditch on your mind, multiply the pressure of the water from the spigot by a factor of 10,000 for an idea of the force with which the ditch moved its water.

Steese National Conservation Area

The BLM's Steese National Conservation Area encompasses 1.2 million acres of land just north of the Steese Highway. This area protects important caribou calving grounds and Dall sheep habitat, and includes the 23-mile **Pinnell Mountain National Recreation Trail.** This trail provides access to alpine tundra, with excellent views of nearby mountain ranges.

The first trailhead for Pinnell Mountain leaves the Steese near Mile 85 at **Twelvemile Summit** (elevation 2,982 feet); the second rejoins the highway near Eagle Summit (Mile 107). A short access road (right) at the first trailhead leads past a signposted section of the Fairbanks–Circle Trail to a small mountain pond—a nice spot for a picnic. The Pinnell Mountain Trail follows a boardwalk for the first quarter-mile, then climbs steadily for a long time. Most hikers prefer to start at the second trailhead, 700 feet higher, which has a great signboard full of fascinating information. This beautiful 27-mile three-day trail through alpine tundra along White Mountain ridgelines is famous for its views of the Alaska and Brooks Ranges and the midnight sun on solstice, plus the incomparable wildflowers (especially the state flower, forget-me-not, with its striking blue dots on the tundra), which also peak in mid-June. Small emergency shelters are at Miles 10 and 18 along the trail. This rolling, treeless high country, with long-distance views in all directions, makes you want to stop, get out, and book all the way to the Edge. But be prepared for wind! Get information and a trail map at the Public Lands Information Center in Fairbanks or the BLM website (www.blm.gov/ak).

Eagle Summit and Beyond

At Mile 94 a road to the right leads to undeveloped camping and the launching point for the popular **Birchcreek Canoe Trail.** Eagle Summit, 13 miles farther out on the Steese Highway, is the third of three summits that the highway tops (the others are at Cleary and Twelvemile). At 3,624 feet, Eagle Summit is the highest point on the road, and a popular destination for locals and travelers around solstice time to watch the sun skirt the horizon, never setting. If the sun is *shining,* that is. It's been known to snow up here on solstice, or you could be socked in by clouds or fog. In fact, you might wish for a nice blizzard to hold down the skeeters, so thick and ferocious that they've been rumored to pick up people—large people—and carry them off. A mile-long trail leads to the summit, which is carpeted with wildflowers in midsummer.

Coming down from the summit, there are gorgeous views of the current gold-mining activities on the valley floor, along Mammoth and Mastodon Creeks, so named for the frozen remains of large Alaskan mammals uncovered by strip mining. The tusks on display at the University of Alaska Fairbanks Museum came from here. Make sure to stop at 101 Gas to check out the ancient gas pump, which pumped its last gas(p) in the past. Take a left at Mile 119 and go straight at the fork for Bedrock Creek, a good spot to camp if you can handle the skeeters.

Central

Nine miles farther is Central, whose year-round population of 60 souls triples in the summer because of the influx of miners. **The Circle District Museum** (907/520-1893, daily noon–5 P.M. May–Sept., $1) in the log cabin in town has mining and mushing artifacts from the early days and a good wildflower photo display. Walk around back to see the wagon-wheel camper. Eight miles out on Hot Springs Road is historic Circle Hot Springs Resort, with its buildings from 1905. Unfortunately, it has been closed since 2002.

Circle

Erroneously named by miners who thought the town site was close to the Arctic Circle—it's actually 50 miles north—Circle is a long 34 miles beyond Central. The road is in good condition, but it is quite winding, particularly the last 11 miles. Gold was discovered on nearby Birch Creek in 1893, and Circle was a boomtown with two-dozen saloons, a library, a hospital, and even an opera house long before anyone had heard of the Klondike. When the miners did hear of the Klondike a few weeks after the strike, Circle immediately lost half its population. The town gradually declined as a supply center for the big Circle Mining District, the largest in Alaska, after the Steese Highway hooked up to Fairbanks.

Today, with a population of 75 or so, Circle is typical of end-of-the-road Alaska—a couple of streets, lots of cars (mostly junked). The main attraction is the mighty Yukon River. Pitch your tent at the denuded campground (free) on the banks and watch the river flow. **H. C. Company Store** (907/773-1222) sells gas, repairs tires, and has groceries, gold pans, and gifts. Get directions here to the Pioneer Cemetery.

Warbelow's Air Ventures (907/474-0518 or 800/478-0812, www.warbelows.com) flies to Central and Circle. **Circle Air** (907/520-5223 or 866/520-5223, www.circleair.com) has air charters out of Central, and rents rafting equipment.

THE ELLIOTT HIGHWAY

The Elliott Highway, named after Major Malcolm Elliott, president of the Alaska Railroad Commission 1927–1932 (following George Steese), begins at the junction with the Steese Highway in Fox, 11 miles north of Fairbanks. The road is paved to Mile 28 (but watch for frost heaves), then turns into a very wide, occasionally smooth, two-lane gravel road until the junction with the Dalton, where it narrows to a 1.5-lane rough hard-dirt ribbon through total wilderness.

Other than the Bureau of Land Management (BLM) White Mountain Trail at Mile 28, and gorgeous views in several spots on the road (especially Miles 95–96), there's little on the way to Manley Hot Springs, a small town at the end of the highway, 152 long miles from Fox. In fact, there's only one facility between the **Hilltop Truck Stop** (surprisingly good food just outside Fox, 907/389-7600, daily 5 A.M.–11 P.M.) and Manley: It's the **Arctic Circle Trading Post** (907/474-3507) at Mile 49. Most of the road is in the 40–50 mph range, with a few 20–30 mph stretches, totaling 4–5 hours one-way from Fairbanks.

Between Fox and the Dalton Highway junction, huge supply trucks to and from Prudhoe Bay barrel along, raising blinding clouds of dust; by the time you get back to Fairbanks from Manley, a fine layer of dust will have settled over everything you've got, including your entire respiratory tract. It's essential to have *plenty* of water along for this ride. Also take food, as there's no Denny's at the next exit, since there aren't any exits. And don't forget your bathing suit.

The road climbs quickly out of Fox, with good views of the Interior's rolling hills. One mile north of the abandoned railroad and mining town of **Olnes,** just before the Mile 11 bridge over the Chatanika River, a large gravel road on the left goes a mile in to Chatanika Pond, part of the **Lower Chatanika River State Recreation Site:** There are no facilities, but fishing is fair and there is primitive camping. On the other side of the Mile 11 bridge is the rest of the recreation site: free camping, picnicking, pit toilets, and fishing for grayling in the summer and for whitefish in the fall.

White Mountains National Recreation Area

The BLM's White Mountains National Recreation Area covers 1 million acres of forests, rivers, and mountains approximately 30 miles north of Fairbanks. It is the largest national recreation area in the country, and a favorite weekend escape for locals who enjoy the 200 miles of backcountry trails.

At Mile 28 of the Elliott Highway are trailheads for myriad paths through the White Mountains. Read the information board carefully. Most trails are for winter use and are not maintained during the summer for hiking. The **Summit Trail** starts from the trailhead on the left and is designated for summer use. This 21-mile trail (one-way), mostly along alpine ridgetops through the foothills of the White Mountains, ends at Beaver Creek. This trail starts out high up to begin with, and the first mile or so of the Wickersham Creek Trail takes you out of the taiga and onto a ridgetop, with a beautiful 300-degree view of the Tanana Valley, Alaska Range, and gigantic sky. Even if you're not hiking all the way, it's worth it to day-hike this mile for the view.

During the winter, 12 public-use cabins—each a day's ski apart—are available to rent in the White Mountains. Each cabin has a cookstove and lantern, a woodstove, a table and benches, bunk beds, and an outhouse. In the summer only two of these cabins are readily accessible; the others are difficult to reach because of wet and muddy trail conditions. Cabins rent for $25. Contact the BLM (907/474-2251 or 800/437-7021, www.blm.gov/ak) for details. Also check out **Trailhead Cabins** (907/374-0717, www.trailheadcabins.com, $65), road-accessible three-person cabins on the south side of the mountains.

Bye Bye Pavement

The pavement ends 100 yards north of the White Mountains trailhead. Enjoy this wide gravel stretch while you've got it! There are nice views of the oil pipeline here—shining in the sunlight, twisting through the tundra, suddenly disappearing underground and surfacing again. At Mile 49 is **Arctic Circle Trading Post** (907/474-4565)—a.k.a. Wildwood General Store—where you can get snacks, drinks, fresh sandwiches, and Arctic Circle gifts. There is no gas or lodging, and it's only open mid-May–mid-September.

At Mile 71 is the two-mile access road to **Livengood,** a tiny mining center that flourished briefly as a pipeline construction camp. It now has a population of 30. Two miles farther is Mile 0 of the Dalton Highway. Take a left to stay on the Elliott Highway.

To Manley

A bit past the junction with the Dalton, and right after the bridge over the Tolovana River, is a little pullout (left), a nice spot for a picnic, camping, fishing, or even swimming (no facilities). Here the road narrows considerably, and you follow the two tire-packed stripes down the middle of it, hoping nobody is coming in the other direction. At Mile 96 is a fantastic view overlooking the Minto Flats, the Tanana

River, and the foothills of the Alaska Range. If you're very lucky and have charmed cloud karma, you'll get a breathtaking view of Mt. McKinley and the accompanying snowcapped peaks to its right and left, jutting straight up like a big militant fist from the lowlands. Even though the range is more than 100 miles due south, the possibility of seeing it is worth the whole ride—even the dust. From here to Manley are some fun roller-coaster humps and curves; watch for porcupines, foxes, snowshoe hares, squirrels, hawks, and other cars.

Manley Hot Springs

This relaxing and friendly town (pop. 70) is a couple of miles this side of the end of the Elliott at the Tanana River. Like many Interior villages, Manley Hot Springs had its heyday in the early 1900s during the peak activity of nearby mines. The U.S. Army Signal Corps set up a telegraph station here in 1903, and Frank Manley built the town's first resort in 1907. Because of the geothermal activity, Manley boasts agricultural features uncommon for the Interior—rich warm soil, a long growing season, even earthworms—and is known for its abundant produce. Manley also has a roadhouse, a popular landing strip, and more ATVs than cars—a lot more. Best of all, the hot springs have no sulfur, so you can enjoy the soak without the stench.

Open since 1906, the **Manley Roadhouse** (907/672-3161, www.manleyroadhouse.com, May–Sept.) is a popular meeting place for local miners, trappers, and dog mushers. It has many prehistoric and historic artifacts on display that were collected from around the area, along with the usual bar, restaurant with down-home food three meals a day, friendly atmosphere, and rooms with a bath down the hall for $70 d. Modern motel-type rooms are $120 d, and cute cabins with outhouses cost $135 (shower in the lodge).

Right on the edge of town are the **Manley Hot Springs** (907/672-3171), on private property belonging to Chuck and Gladys Dart. These longtime Manley residents—the school is named after Gladys—are friendly Alaskan farmers who use the hot springs bubbling up on their property to grow flowers and grapes in greenhouses. Inside the first greenhouse are three concrete soaking tubs ($5) with 108°F spring water.

Keep going toward town and park by the bridge over Hot Springs Slough. Go right just before the bridge and walk a half-mile to the first road to the right. The first part of the trail past the cabins is private property. Then it's three miles to the tower, and two more up to Bean Ridge. There are great views and camping up here.

The public campground ($5) below the bridge on the other side of **Hot Springs Slough** in the middle of town has toilets, picnic tables, and barbecues.

The Elliott Highway continues past the landing strip and trading post 2.5 miles to the end of the road at the mighty Tanana River. It's scenic and breezy, and you could camp here in a pinch.

DALTON HIGHWAY TO DEADHORSE

Before the pipeline days, the Elliott Highway ran from just outside Fairbanks to Livengood, where a 56-mile spur road cut north to the Yukon River. The Dalton Highway began as the "Haul Road" in 1974, constructed to run parallel to the **Trans-Alaska Pipeline** from the Yukon River to Deadhorse, a small oil settlement on Prudhoe Bay. In 1981 the spur road and the Haul Road, a total of 414 miles, were renamed the Dalton Highway after James Dalton, who pioneered early oil exploration efforts on the North Slope. This long road traverses some of the most spectacular and remote land accessible by road in Alaska (and therefore in the country), through taiga and tundra, over the Arctic Circle, past towering snowcapped peaks, through the Brooks Range, and within a mile of Gates of the Arctic National Park. Wildlife is abundant: Caribou, Dall sheep, and wolves can be seen if you look closely. For additional information on the Dalton Highway, contact the Bureau of Land Management (907/474-2200 or 800/437-7021, www.blm.

gov/ak/dalton) to request—or download—their very helpful publication.

Driving

The Dalton Highway is still primarily a truck-supply route and is fairly wide, but it can become very dusty or slippery depending on recent weather. The road is open all the way to Deadhorse, but make no mistake: this is a somewhat excruciating 7–11 hours on a tire-eating, bone-jarring, teeth-grinding, anus-clenching "highway." A trip up the Dalton is not to be taken lightly!

There are only a few service stations/supply stops along the way: at Yukon River crossing (Mile 56), Coldfoot (Mile 175), Wiseman (Mile 189), and the end of the line in Deadhorse (Mile 414). You'll be maxing out your Visa card if you get towed very far, so extended towing coverage (such as AAA's Plus policy) is strongly recommended. Always travel with plenty of water, keep your headlights on, carry two spare tires, and ***watch for trucks.*** The trucks do not slow down for oncoming traffic, but in most cases you can see them coming thanks to the dust trails they raise. Be prepared for all that dust to come your way, along with a hail of flying gravel that sometimes shatters windshields.

Once you reach Deadhorse, don't expect to simply drive around the oilfields; all access is tightly controlled, and only authorized tour operators can pass through the checkpoints.

Arctic Outfitters (907/474-3530, www.arctic-outfitters.com) in Fairbanks rents cars for travel on the Dalton with two full-size spare tires, a CB radio, first aid kit, and other useful items.

Getting There and Around

Alaska Airlines (800/426-0333, www.alaskaair.com) has daily flights from Anchorage to Prudhoe Bay/Deadhorse or from Fairbanks to Barrow and on to Prudhoe. Two companies offer tours up the Dalton Highway to the Arctic Circle and beyond if you want to save the wear and tear on yourself and your vehicle: **Northern Alaska Tour Company** (907/474-8600 or 800/474-1986, www.northernalaska.com) and **Alaskan Arctic Turtle Tours** (907/457-1798 or 888/456-1798, www.wildalaska.info). Northern Alaska is considerably larger, and the company also owns several businesses along the way, including Coldfoot Camp and Yukon Crossing.

The 12-hour tours from Fairbanks to the Circle and back in a day cost $169 per person. Arctic Turtle has a two-day butt-bustin' bus tour to Prudhoe Bay and back to Fairbanks for $989 including meals; lodging (another $220 d) and an oilfield tour ($40 pp) are extra. Northern Alaska offers many other options, including multiple-night trips to Prudhoe Bay or the Brooks Range. One popular choice ($1,169 s or $1,978 d) includes a flight from Fairbanks to Prudhoe where you tour the oilfield and stay overnight before taking a bus excursion down the Dalton Highway, stopping in Coldfoot for a night, reaching Fairbanks the third evening.

Dalton Highway Express (907/474-3555, www.daltonhighwayexpress.com) has scheduled summertime bus service up the Dalton Highway; reservations are required. Round-trip fares are $168 to the Arctic Circle, $260 to Coldfoot, and $500 to Deadhorse/Prudhoe Bay.

To the Arctic Circle

Mile 0 of the Dalton Highway is 73 miles north of Fairbanks, accessed by the Elliott Highway. From here it's 56 miles to the Yukon River, with sweeping views of the undulating landscape and good glimpses of the pipeline. Only one developed campground is maintained along the Dalton, but the first of many undeveloped areas is at **Hess Creek,** at Mile 24.

A 2,290-foot **wooden-deck bridge** crosses the mighty Yukon at Mile 56. On the north side is **Yukon River Camp** (907/474-3557, www.yukonrivercamp.com, May–Sept.), with a mercantile store, gas, tire and minor auto repairs, motel rooms ($199 d with shared bath) and a restaurant (daily 9 A.M.–9 P.M.).

Five miles north is the unpretentious **Hot Spot Café** (907/451-7543) serving surprisingly good meals 10 A.M.–midnight, a fun gift shop, gas and flat-fixin', and simple guest rooms.

An interesting pipeline interpretive display is near the bridge, and the Bureau of Land Management's **Yukon Crossing Visitors Station** is open daily 9 A.M.–6 P.M. June–August. Cross the road and drive under the pipeline for an undeveloped camping area.

Isolated granite tors are visible to the northeast at Mile 86, and at Mile 98 are excellent views of the mountains across the tundra before the road descends again to travel along the valley floor. At Mile 115 is the **Arctic Circle:** latitude 66 degrees, 33 minutes. A huge sign proclaims the location, and nearly everyone stops to pose for a photo. A road behind the sign leads a half-mile to camping.

Coldfoot

At Mile 132 are **Gobbler's Knob** and the first views of the Brooks Range on the distant northern horizon. The road winds past Pump Station 5, over numerous rivers and creeks, and by great fishing; at Mile 175 it rolls into Coldfoot. Gold was discovered at Tramway Bar in the upper reaches of the Koyukuk River in 1893, attracting enough prospectors and miners to found the town of Coldfoot. Still, the town reportedly received its sobriquet when most of them got cold feet at the onset of the first winter and left the country. Two of the original mining cabins are still in the bush at the northern end of the airstrip.

It's no wonder the old miners' feet became frosty. In January 1989, Coldfoot recorded a temperature of -82°F, and for 17 days the mercury refused to rise above 62° below. Then, that summer, it got up to 97° above—the 179-degree differential broke all North American records.

The spacious **Arctic Interagency Visitors Center** (907/678-5209, www.blm.gov/ak, daily 10 A.M.–10 P.M. late May–early Sept.) is staffed by Bureau of Land Management, Park Service, and Fish and Wildlife personnel. Stop here for travel information, wildlife films, natural history publications, and nightly natural history programs.

Coldfoot Camp (907/474-3500 or 866/474-3400, www.coldfootcamp.com, $199 s or d) has gas, repairs, and lodging in pipeline-era ATCO trailers with two twin beds and private baths. There are no TVs or phones in the rooms, and there is no cell service or Wi-Fi. Trucker's Café is always open, serving buffet breakfasts ($13) and dinners ($19) in the summer, plus a la carte menu items year-round. Top off your tank; the next gas is 239 miles away at Deadhorse. The Coldfoot post office and a gift shop are also here.

For flights into the Brooks Range or Arctic National Wildlife Refuge, contact **Coyote Air Service** (907/678-5995 or 800/252-0603, www.flycoyote.com).

Camp at the BLM's beautifully situated **Marion Creek Campground** (5 miles north of Coldfoot, June–mid-Sept., $8).

Wiseman

A mining village that dates back to 1910, Wiseman is home to 20 or so folks. The settlement is three miles out on a spur road off the Dalton Highway at Mile 185, and 12 miles north of Coldfoot. A number of picturesque log cabins are scattered around beneath a fantastic mountain setting, including the little Wiseman Museum (open for Northern Alaska Tour Company buses). Wiseman Trading Company is open sporadically in the summer with a few snacks and some interesting artifacts from the Koyukuk River gold rush.

Arctic Getaway B&B (907/678-4456, www.arcticgetaway.com, $95 d, $175–195 for 4 people) rents out three comfortable log cabins. Two connected cabins ($95 d and $175 for 4 people) share a bath, and a two-story cabin ($195) sleeps four and has its own bath. The cabins have stoves and sinks, and guests can use the traditional root cellar to keep things cold. A big Alaskan breakfast is served at the main house.

At the seasonal **Boreal Lodge** (907/678-4566, www.boreallodge.com) guests stay in a four-room lodge ($70 s, $90 d) or a private cabin ($140 for up to 4 people); all include kitchens, phones, TVs, and baths.

JURASSIC PARK ALASKA

Dinosaurs in Alaska? Unlikely as it may sound, dinosaurs did live here during the Triassic, Jurassic, and Cretaceous Periods (66 million-248 million years ago). The first discovery of dinosaur bones came in 1961 when a Shell Oil geologist happened upon strange bones along the Colville River. Thinking they were just mammoth bones from the last ice age, the company shelved them for two decades. When government scientists finally took a look, they were stunned to discover that these were instead the bones of dinosaurs. This discovery is now regarded as one of the most important dinosaur finds of the last several decades, and one of the greatest Cretaceous vertebrate deposits anywhere on earth.

Over the last two decades, scientists have come to the Colville site – right along the Arctic Ocean – to discover how the supposedly cold-blooded dinosaurs could survive such a harsh northern climate. Their findings threw several scientific theories into question, and most paleontologists now believe the dinosaurs were warm-blooded and could move fast enough to migrate long distances, much as the caribou do on today's North Slope. In 1998, dinosaur tracks were discovered at more than a dozen sites along the Colville River, providing evidence that these animals were not only present but actually common 100 million years ago.

TEMPERATE TIMES

The world the dinosaurs inhabited was vastly different from that of northern Alaska today. A warm inland sea ran from the tropics to the polar regions east of Alaska. The Arctic land was covered with dense fern-filled redwood forests, and winter temperatures rarely dropped below freezing. This moderate climate and abundant food source allowed the dinosaurs to survive for millions of years. The largest animals were the four-ton horned pachyrhinosaurs and the three-ton duck-billed hadrosaurs, both of which were vegetarians. They were preyed upon by such meat-eaters as the tyrannosaurs. Why the dinosaurs disappeared is one of the ongoing mysteries in science, although the prevailing theory is that a giant comet slammed into the earth some 65 million years ago, causing the planet to cool so rapidly that the dinosaurs could not survive.

And what of the possibility of a "Jurassic Park" in Alaska? The dinosaur discoveries along the Colville River are unique in that some of the bones were never mineralized (turned into stone). Some of these are still the original bones, and it is even possible that a bit of the original DNA is present. Don't expect to see mutant dinosaurs roaming around Alaska anytime soon, but the bones could potentially provide information on what the dinosaurs ate and whether or not they were cold-blooded.

To the Slope

North of Wiseman the Dalton Highway parallels the Koyukuk River for 20 miles or so. The edge of Gates of the Arctic National Park is high up on the slopes west of Wiseman. At Mile 194 are the first views of 4,000-foot **Sukakpak Mountain.** The road passes along the base of this rugged peak, and a trail at Mile 203 leads a half-mile right to the base. The strange-looking mounds between the road and the mountain are "palsas" formed by ice beneath the soil pushing upward.

Above Disaster Creek at Mile 211, the road climbs quickly to Chandalar Shelf, a huge basin with a healthy population of grizzlies, then over **Atigun Pass** at Mile 244, the highest highway pass in Alaska (4,800 feet). The road winds quickly down through the Atigun Valley and onto the North Slope. At Mile 414 is the town of Deadhorse.

Prudhoe Bay/Deadhorse

This is the place that makes Alaska run, home to the massive Prudhoe Bay Oilfield (the largest in North America and 18th largest in the world), and starting point for the Trans-Alaska Pipeline that carries oil to Valdez, 800 miles to the south. The oilfield encompasses a 250-square-mile area, though the wells, roads, and facilities actually cover just 2 percent of this land. Keep your eyes open for the caribou that graze amid the small city of buildings, pump stations, and other equipment. Some 3,500 well-paid oilfield and related workers stay around Deadhorse, working on a rotating basis that is typically two weeks on followed by two weeks off. The oil companies fly them home for their days off.

The developed areas are called Deadhorse, but the entire area is commonly called Prudhoe Bay, or even more generically the North Slope, or in local parlance simply the Slope. It is just a few miles from Deadhorse to Prudhoe Bay on the Beaufort Sea (Arctic Ocean). Are you confused yet? If so, try the Prudhoe website (www.prudhoebay.com). Alaska Airlines has flights to Deadhorse, but the only way to get to the Arctic Ocean or into the oilfields is on a tour. Cell phone coverage is generally good around Deadhorse, but nonexistent as you head south down the Dalton Highway.

Artic Caribou Inn (907/659-2368, www.arcticcaribouinn.com, late May–early Sept.) has rooms with two single beds for $190 d. All-you-can-eat buffet meals cost $15 for breakfast, $18 for lunch, and $20 for dinner. They also lead two-hour **Prudhoe Bay tours** ($40 pp) that include the Oilfield Visitors Center and a stop at the Arctic Ocean, but reservations are required if you aren't staying at the hotel.

Although primarily for oilfield workers, **Prudhoe Bay Hotel** (907/659-2449, www.prudhoebayhotel.com) is open to the public year-round. Lodging and three meals a day cost a very reasonable $125 s or $220 d for simple guest rooms with twin beds and a bath down the hall (but no TV or phone), or $150 s or $250 d for nicer units with double beds, private baths, phones, and TVs. If you aren't staying here, meals cost $12 for breakfast, $15 for lunch, and $20 for dinner.

The newest year-round lodging option is **Deadhorse Camp** (907/474-3565 or 877/474-3565, www.deadhorsecamp.com, $199 s or d), with small rooms containing two twin beds. Guests have access to a lounge with a TV, plus buffet-style meals.

Prudhoe Bay General Store (907/659-2412, www.brooksrangesupply.com) has supplies, a post office, and the Deadhorse Museum (of sorts). Auto and RV parts and repairs are available, and the Tesoro gas station provides free RV parking (but no hookups).

Eastern Interior Alaska

DELTA JUNCTION

This town of 900 people is 100 miles south of Fairbanks on the Richardson Highway at its junction with the Alaska Highway. Delta Junction marks the official ending point for the Alaska Highway, and Milepost 1,422 stands in front of the visitors center. The World War II road designers specifically aimed the Alcan to join at Delta, connecting it to both Interior Alaska and tidewater at Valdez (266 miles to the south).

History

Alaska's first road, the **Richardson Highway** was originally envisioned as an "all-American route" to the Yukon gold fields in the late 1890s, and a trail was constructed in conjunction with the WAMCATS telegraph cable all the way to Eagle. But with the shift of attention to the Fairbanks area in the early 1900s, the trail was redirected there and upgraded to a wagon road in 1907 under the auspices of Wilds P. Richardson, first president of the Alaska Road Commission.

Delta began as one of the numerous roadhouses along the trail, which were spaced a day's journey apart (roughly 30 miles). Bate's Landing was opened in 1906 at the confluence of the Delta and Tanana Rivers, where travelers crossed the Tanana on a government-operated ferry that utilized the current for propulsion.

Delta hit the big time, however, with the construction of the Alcan, and when Allen Army Airbase (later Fort Greely) was established nearby as one of the many military installations along the highway. Delta received another boost when a pipeline-construction camp was located here; the pipe crosses the Tanana right next to the highway—a spectacular first view of it for overland travelers. Today, Fort Greely is a major center for the Missile Defense System, a questionably effective system pushed into deployment in 2004.

Delta serves the largest agricultural area in the state, including thousands of acres of grain and potato farms and smaller farms. Delta is also home to a herd of nearly 500 bison, a species that once outnumbered caribou in Alaska before being driven into extinction. In 1920 the Delta area was stocked with 23 bison from Montana, and the 70,000-acre Delta Bison Range was created in 1980. Ask locally to find the bison since they are often not visible from the highway. In addition to wild bison, local ranchers raise other bison for meat, along with such exotics as reindeer, elk, and even yaks.

Sights

The **Delta Junction Visitors Center** (907/895-5068 or 877/895-5068, www.deltachamber.org, daily 8 A.M.–7 P.M. late May–early Sept., daily 8 A.M.–4 P.M. the rest of May and through mid-Sept., closed the rest of the year) is right at the junction of the Alaska Highway and the Richardson Highway.

Next door is the **Sullivan Roadhouse Historical Museum** (907/895-5068, daily 9 A.M.–4:30 P.M. late May–mid-Sept., free). The oldest roadhouse in Interior Alaska, built in 1905, this log building is packed with memorabilia and old photos from the Valdez–Fairbanks Trail and the roadhouses that operated along its route.

You can take a short loop through Delta's rich **agricultural area** by heading eight miles east down the Alaska Highway; take a left at Sawmill Creek Road, another left on Bailey Way, again a left on Hansen Road, and one more left on Clearwater, which delivers you back to the highway. There are good views of the eastern peaks of the Alaska Range from the Clearwater area, if it's clear.

To get the total 360 degrees, though, head to **Donnelly Dome,** 23 miles south of town on the Richardson Highway. Go right on the gravel road at Mile 248, continue for a quarter-mile past the second sharp bend; there is an obvious though unmarked trailhead at the parking lot here. Allow a half-day to hike to the dome and back.

A dozen miles north of town at Mile 278 is **Quartz Lake State Recreation Area,** known for excellent rainbow trout and silver salmon fishing. Several day-hiking trails head out from the campgrounds, past a homestead cabin from the 1950s and archaeological sites to hilltop vistas.

Delta's big annual event is **Deltana Fair** (907/895-3247, www.deltanafair.com), a three-day festival of farming exhibits, a rodeo, a carnival, a parade, mud bog races, and outhouse races. It takes place the last weekend of July.

Big Delta State Historical Park

If you only do one thing in Delta, take an enjoyable and educational stroll through history at Big Delta State Historical Park (8 miles north of town, daily 8 A.M.–8 P.M.). Set in a scenic spot along the banks of the Tanana just below the pipeline crossing, this lush 10-acre piece of property centers around **Rika's Roadhouse** (www.rikas.com), a longtime travelers' stop on the Richardson Road between Valdez and Fairbanks. The park features a museum, barns, poultry pens, flourishing gardens, cabins, signboards, outhouses new and old, and displays on mining, trapping, clothing, and more. Guided tours are given several times a day. The Roadhouse itself now houses a fine gift shop with Alaskan-made items, and you can grab a bite at the **Packhouse Pavilion Restaurant** (907/895-4201), known for dependably good breakfasts, along with lunchtime sandwiches, homemade soups, salads, and delicious pies and bear claws. Get here early since the restaurant closes at 5 P.M.

Accommodations

Right in the center of town, **Kelly's Alaska Country Inn** (907/895-4667, www.kellysalaskacountryinn.com, $109 s, $119 d) is

© DON PITCHER

Rika's Roadhouse at Big Delta State Historical Park

probably your best lodging option in Delta Junction. It's nothing special, but has clean rooms, friendly owners, and some unusual units with curved wooden ceilings. Another fair-priced option is **Alaska 7 Motel** (907/895-4848, www.alaska7motel.com, $99 d), with fridges, microwaves, and Wi-Fi.

The Garden B&B (907/895-4633, www.alaskagardenbandb.com, $89–109 d) is a large country home surrounded by flower gardens. Four guest rooms have private or shared baths, Wi-Fi, and fridges. A full breakfast is included.

Located six miles north of town, **Bald Eagle Ranch B&B** (907/895-5270 or 877/895-5270, www.baldeagleranchbb.com) has a wide range of lodging, from campsites for cyclists to fully furnished homes. The options are too complex to describe here, but B&B rooms start around $100 d.

Camping

You'll find many camping options in the Delta Junction area. Pitch your tent at **Delta State Recreation Site** ($10), just a half-mile west of town near the airport. There's a good view across the flats of the eastern Alaska Range. In the morning, grab a shower at the **Delta Laundry** (907/895-4561), another half-mile west. **Clearwater State Recreation Site** is 11 miles from town on Jack Warren Road, with 16 campsites ($10) and a picnic area along Clearwater Lake. **Big Delta State Historical Park,** eight miles north of town, has parking for RVs ($5; no tents) in its lot. **Quartz Lake State Recreation Area,** 12 miles north of town, has campsites for $10.

Right in town, **Green Acres RV Park** (907/895-4369 or 800/895-4369, www.smithsgreenacres.com, RVs $36, tents $16) has attractive spaces.

Food

Serving a big menu three meals a day, **Buffalo Center Drive In** (907/895-5089, daily 7 A.M.–9 P.M.) gets thumbs up from locals and travelers. Top picks are tasty $8 buffalo burgers made from locally raised bison and crunchy corn fritters. There's a screened gazebo for outside dining.

Across from the visitors center on the Richardson is **Pizza Bella** (907/895-4841, www.pizzabellarestaurant.com), where pizzas, pastas, seafood, steaks, and sandwiches fill the menu. Get steaks and other meaty fare at **Alaskan Steakhouse & Motel** (907/895-5175). **IGA Food Cache** (907/895-4653) has a deli and decent bakery, or head to the Wednesday and Saturday **Highway's End Farmers Market** all summer long next to the visitors center.

Getting There

Alaska Direct Bus Line (907/277-6652 or 800/770-6652, www.alaskadirectbusline.com) stops in Delta Junction en route to Fairbanks, Tok, Anchorage, and Whitehorse. Buses run three times a week in the summer, twice weekly in winter.

TOK

The Alaska Highway leads east from Delta Junction toward the border with Canada and then continues south all the way to Dawson Creek, British Columbia. One hundred and eight miles east of Delta Junction—and 96 miles from the border—is the town of Tok (rhymes with "joke"). Tok (pop. 1,200) considers itself the "gateway to Alaska" and acts as the service center for several Native Alaskan villages in the upper Tanana Valley. The Tok Cutoff of the Glenn Highway heads south from Tok, providing connections to Anchorage, 326 miles away.

The town of Tok grew from a mid-1940s highway-construction camp, and it is still unincorporated. Where the Tok River empties into the Tanana, the Athabascan tribes once gathered to affirm peace, and Tok is usually translated to mean "peace crossing." (Other folks say the name came from "Tokyo Camp"—a term used during construction of the Alcan Highway in 1942. There is, however, no evidence that the town was named by potheads, though more than a few folks have posed next to the town's entrance sign with a joint in hand.)

Much of the land around Tok was burned in a massive 100,000-acre fire in 1990, but the winds abruptly shifted, sparing the town itself.

Sights

The main Tok attractions are restaurants, motels, gas stations, and information centers. The Civic Center houses **Tok Mainstreet Visitors Center** (907/883-5775, www.tokalaskainfo.com, daily 8 A.M.–7 P.M. May–mid-Sept., closed mid-Sept.–Apr.). Next door in the State of Alaska building is a tiny **Alaska Public Lands Information Center** (907/883-5667, www.alaskacenters.gov, 8 A.M.–7 P.M. June–Aug.).

Mukluk Land (907/883-2571, www.mukluk-land.net, June–Aug.) is a little amusement park with a kids' igloo for bouncing, skee-ball machines, minigolf, Alaska's largest "mosquito," gold panning, gardens, videos, and a museum of sorts. This peculiar collection of bush Alaska humor costs $5 adults, $2 children.

Tetlin National Wildlife Refuge

This 730,000-acre refuge occupies much of the land east of Tok and south of the Alaska Highway. It borders on Wrangell–St. Elias National Park and Canada's Kluane National Park. The refuge gets very little use by travelers, but it is an important home for trumpeter swans, moose, black and grizzly bears, caribou, wolves, and other animals. Marshes here contain some of the highest densities of waterfowl in Alaska, not to mention mosquitoes. Two free refuge campgrounds are accessible from the Alaska Highway. The Tetlin National Wildlife Refuge Visitors Center (907/774-2245, http://tetlin.fws.gov, daily 8 A.M.–4:30 P.M. mid-May–mid-Sept.) is 85 miles east of Tok. The staff offers nature talks here daily in the summer, plus evening programs at Deadman Lake Campground (Mile 1,249). A 0.75-mile nature trail is at the campground.

Accommodations

Tok has a number of reasonably priced places to spend the night, including **Young's Motel** (907/883-4411, $89 s, $94 d), right next to

Fast Eddy's Restaurant, with clean guest rooms containing two beds and updated furnishings. Wi-Fi is available.

Snowshoe Motel (907/883-4511 or 800/478-4511, www.alaskasnowshoemotel.homestead.com, $90 s, $95 d) has simple two-room units with fridges, microwaves, and Wi-Fi.

Golden Bear Motel (907/883-2561 or 866/883-2561, www.alaskagoldenbear.com, $99–120 d) is an inexpensive but surprisingly nice motel, with large clean guest rooms and Wi-Fi, while **Tok Motels** (907/883-2852 or 800/883-3007, www.tokmotels.com) charges $95 s or $99 d.

Burnt Paw Cabins (907/883-4121, www.burntpawcabins.com, $129–139 d) has seven modern log cabins with private baths, full breakfasts, a guest computer, and Wi-Fi. They're next to the post office and open all year. Kids will love a visit with the husky puppies.

Cleft of the Rock B&B (907/883-4219 or 800/478-5646, www.cleftoftherock.net, $130–160 d) has cabins and guest rooms with private baths and a full breakfast.

Camping

Pitch your tent at the pleasant **Tok River State Recreation Site** ($15), five miles east of Tok on the Alaska Highway. The site is too close to the highway for a quiet night, but a short trail follows the river and climbs stairs up the hillside.

Tok offers plenty of summertime parking choices for RVers: **Golden Bear Motel and RV Park** (907/883-2561 or 866/883-2561, www.alaskagoldenbear.com, RVs $35, tents $20), **Sourdough Campground** (907/883-5543, www.sourdoughcampground.com, RVs $40, tents $22), **Tok RV Village** (907/883-5877 or 800/478-5878, www.tokrv.net, RVs $40–46, tents $26), and **Tundra Lodge & RV Park** (907/883-7875, RVs $32, tents $20).

Food

Although a number of places serve food in Tok, you only need to know one: **Fast Eddy's** (907/883-4411, daily 6 A.M.–11 P.M. summer, 6 A.M.–10 P.M. winter, dinner $13–23). Tok's main restaurant action, it's a clean and classy family place with good food and fair prices. The menu covers most standards: pizzas, halibut burgers, salad bar, sandwiches, ribs, and steaks.

Getting There

Alaska Direct Bus Line (907/277-6652 or 800/770-6652, www.alaskadirectbusline.com) provides year-round service connecting Tok with Whitehorse, Anchorage, and Fairbanks. Service is three times a week in the summer, and twice weekly the rest of the year. Reservations are recommended. **Alaska/Yukon Trails** (907/479-2277 or 888/770-7275, www.alaskashuttle.com) has three-times-a-week summertime vans connecting Tok with Fairbanks, Dawson City, and Whitehorse.

The Alaska Highway crosses into Yukon 124 miles east of Tok. Both U.S. and Canadian customs are open 24 hours a day year-round. Be sure to reset your watches since the time is an hour earlier in Alaska.

TAYLOR HIGHWAY

This is the scenic shortcut to Dawson City from Alaska, a 160-mile gravel-and-pavement road through wild and undeveloped country. The road starts at Tetlin Junction (Mile 1,302 on the Alaska Highway), 11 miles east of Tok, and is paved for the first 50 miles. The road is typically open to traffic May–mid-October, but closed the rest of the year by heavy snows. The first portion of the Taylor Highway cuts through the 1.8-million-acre **Tanana Valley State Forest,** with periodic hilltop vistas over the rolling green countryside, particularly near the road summit on the slopes of 5,541-foot **Mt. Fairplay.** Keep your eyes open for the Fortymile caribou herd along the highway. Beyond Mt. Fairplay the road descends to the Fortymile River country, reaching the little settlement of Chicken at Mile 66.

Chicken

With just six year-round residents (50 or so in summer), you wouldn't think this wide spot in the road would be worthy of mention, but it is actually a favorite stopping point for travelers. The town was originally named "Ptarmigan," for the chicken-like bird that inhabits the country. The spelling of *Ptarmigan* proved problematic for the miners who were mucking for gold around here in 1895, so the name was switched to something they could handle: "Chicken." Anyone who's read *Tisha* by Ann Purdy, the story of a young teacher who overcame enormous local resistance to teach in this neck of the tundra, will be interested to know that the author made her home here.

High gold prices in the last few years have brought a flock (pun intended) of miners and wannabes to Chicken. There's still a lot of gold in the surrounding country, as evidenced by all the suction dredges and Caterpillar tractors working through the creek beds. One of Alaska's largest nuggets, a 57-ounce piece, was found on Jack Wade Creek in 1983.

Be sure to stop at **Chicken Mercantile** (www.chickenalaska.com) in "downtown Chicken" for copies of *Tisha,* funny T-shirts, and a taste of Sue Wiren's enormous cinnamon rolls and great pies, along with homemade chicken soup (of course), reindeer bratwurst, sandwiches, a daily salmon bake on summer afternoons, plus a computer and free Wi-Fi. Tenters and RVs can park for free at the Mercantile.

Just up the road is **The Goldpanner** (907/883-5081, www.chickenak.com), where you can also buy groceries and gas, or try your luck at panning for the yellow stuff. The Goldpanner has cabins ($120 for up to 4 people) and hotel rooms ($75 s, $85 d, or $45 s in hostel rooms), along with RV hookups ($30) and tent spaces ($10). Showers are $8, and as a bonus, they feature the only flush toilets in the area. Not far from the Goldpanner is **Gold Dredge No. 4,** in use 1959–1967 and moved here from Pedro Creek. The original town of Chicken, an abandoned mining camp, is now on private property. Hour-long tours are given twice daily in the summer; ask at the Goldpanner.

Over on Airport Road, **Chicken Gold Camp & Outpost** (907/235-6396, www.chickengold.com) has a campground (tents $10, RVs $18), cabins and apartment units ($90–105 d), gifts, Wi-Fi, a fine little café (paninis and homemade soups), and espresso, plus tours of the 1930s Pedro dredge (on the National Register of Historic Places), kayak rentals, and gold panning.

During the summer, **Alaska/Yukon Trails** (907/479-2277 or 888/770-7275, www.alaskashuttle.com) has vans connecting Chicken with Fairbanks and Dawson City three times per week.

To Jack Wade Junction

It's another 30 miles from Chicken to Jack Wade Junction on the Taylor Highway. This section is the most challenging part of the drive: narrow, winding, and often rough as it passes through the forested **Fortymile Country** with its dramatic vistas and tailings from past and present mining operations. Stop for a break at the Bureau of Land Management's **Walker Fork Campground** (Mile 82, $8) to stretch your legs—and maybe soak your feet if it's really hot. The campground is on a beautiful site where the South and Walker Forks of the Fortymile meet. A footbridge across the creek leads to a three-minute trail to the top of the limestone wall—it has a nice view of the valley, one of innumerable similar valleys in the immense Interior of Alaska. Four miles ahead is the gotta-take-a-photo **Jack Wade Dredge No. 1,** abandoned in 1942, and a few miles beyond this are active placer mining operations and the old **Jack Wade** mining camp—take care not to trespass.

To Dawson City

From Jack Wade Junction (Mile 96) the Taylor Highway heads north to Eagle, while the **Top of the World Highway** (the main road) continues east to Dawson, Yukon, 79 miles away. From the junction it is only 13 miles to the U.S.-Canada border, the northernmost border crossing on the continent. The road is wide and well-maintained gravel on the U.S. side, and paved on the Canadian side. The name Top of the World says it all; this is a grand exit from (or entrance into) Alaska, with vistas in all directions on a clear day. The border crossing is at **Poker Creek** on the U.S. side, and Canadian Customs are at **Little Gold Creek.** Both American and Canadian Customs operate 8 A.M.–7 P.M. Alaska time (9 A.M.–8 P.M. Pacific time) mid-May–mid-September. **Boundary Lodge** on the U.S. side has gas and other emergency supplies—for a price.

To Eagle

From Jack Wade Junction, the Taylor Highway continues north to Eagle, 65 miles away. This stretch is almost more trail than road: it is very narrow and winding, with steep grades, a rough surface, endless hairpin turns, and little traffic—you can travel at a maximum of 30 mph. For the same reasons, it's one of the most fun roads in the state: lots of twists and turns, ups and downs, and not many cars. The scenery is the same Interior hills and spruce trees you've been accustomed to, so it's not a loss to keep your eyes glued to this road at all times; one glance away and you're driving into a ditch or off a 300-foot cliff. Expect to spend at least two hours on these 65 miles—two hours of white-knuckled, bug-eyed, teeth-chattering thrills and chills, hopefully without the spills.

EAGLE

It takes a strong desire and a serious commitment to get to Eagle, more than 160 miles from Tetlin Junction and 145 miles from Dawson. Even if you're on the way from Dawson into Alaska, it's 130 miles, at least five hard hours of driving, from the junction of Top of the World and Taylor Highways to Eagle and back. Is it worth it? Consider this: Eagle is a total history lesson. The small photogenic town of 150 may have more square feet of museum space than anywhere else in the state, and the moving-right-along walking tour can take up to three hours. Add to that a beautiful free campground, great showers, good food, friendly people, and Yukon River scenery, and Eagle

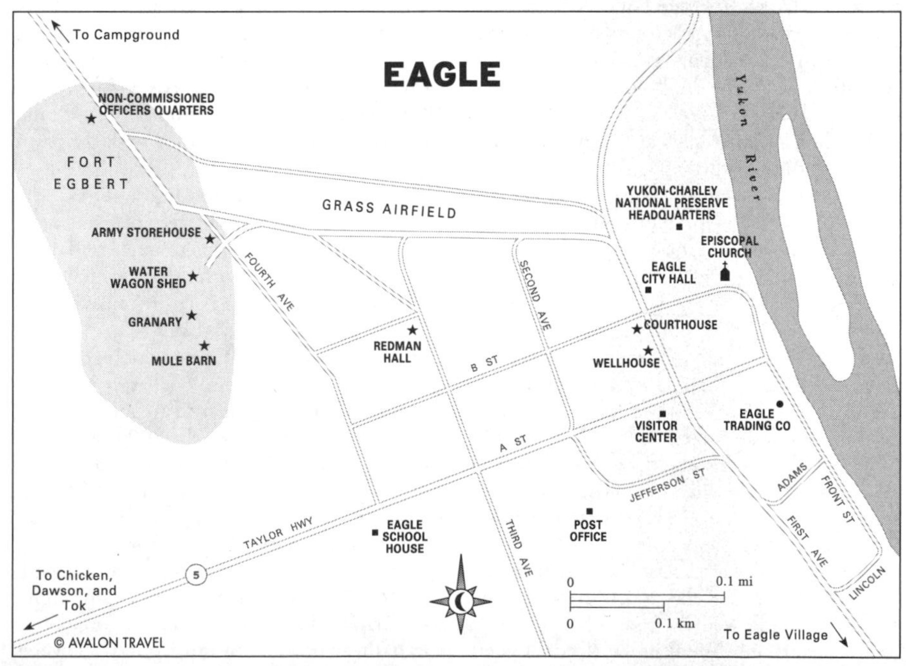

is, without hesitation, worth the extra time, effort, and expense. This is one friendly, peaceful, close-knit community.

History

In 1881, Francis Mercier, a French Canadian trader, established a trading post at the site of Eagle to compete with Fort Yukon and Fort Reliance, two Hudson's Bay Company posts along this eastern stretch of the Yukon River. It was a shrewd choice of location. Just inside the U.S. border, stampeders fed up with Canada's heavy-handed laws and taxes organized a supply town here in spring 1898, naming it Eagle for the profusion of the majestic birds in the area. Also, sitting at the southernmost point on the Yukon River in eastern Alaska, Eagle occupied a strategic spot for transportation, communication, and supply routes to the Interior from tidewater at Valdez. Within six months, three large trading companies had developed Eagle into a major Yukon port. In 1899, the Army began building Fort Egbert next to the town site. In 1900, Judge James Wickersham arrived to install the Interior's first federal court, with jurisdiction over half the state. And by 1902, the WAMCATS telegraph line was completed between Eagle and Valdez, inaugurating the first "all-American" communication system to the Lower 48.

The biggest event in Eagle's history happened in 1905, when a Norwegian Arctic explorer appeared out of the icy fog and somehow communicated to the townspeople (he spoke no English) who he was and what he'd done. The man was Roald Amundsen, and he had just navigated the Northwest Passage, the first time in more than 350 years of attempts, and had crossed over 500 miles of uncharted country by dogsled in the deepest Arctic winter from his ice-locked ship off the north coast of Alaska to announce his feat to the world. The message, going out over the telegraph line, was the news story of the decade.

By then, however, Eagle's star had faded. The stampeders had moved on to Nome and Fairbanks, followed by Judge Wickersham and his court. The importance of Fort Egbert declined until it was abandoned in 1911. WAMCATS was replaced, seven years after it was installed, by wireless communication. Eagle's population continually dwindled to a low of 13 in 1959. Fortunately, the remoteness of the town made it almost impossible to haul out the antiques that had accumulated over the decades, so they stayed in Eagle, where they remain today.

In May 2009 the Yukon River backed up behind an ice dam, causing massive flooding in Eagle. Thirteen homes were destroyed in Eagle itself, and Eagle Village, the Native Alaskan town, was severely damaged, forcing residents to rebuild in a new location upriver. With help from many volunteers, locals rebuilt many of Eagle's homes, finishing before the snow came in the fall. Fortunately, most of the town's historic buildings were spared.

Sights

In Eagle (907/547-2325, www.eagleak.org), it's almost impossible to find a resident who isn't something of a historian (and a cheerleader) for the area. The Eagle Historical Society is one of, if not the, most successful and well-organized groups in the state. It was founded in 1961 after someone showed up at the old mule barn with a truck and made off with the entire collection of saddles.

The care, devotion, and thoroughness with which they display Eagle's awe-inspiring array of artifacts is something to see. And their guided summertime tours ($7), which leave from Judge Wickersham's courthouse steps at 9 A.M., is really the only way to see it; it's a fun hands-on outing, during which you're encouraged to operate an old peanut-warming machine or tickle the keys of an ancient pump organ. One casualty from the 2009 floods was the **well house** next door to the court. The well, dug 60 feet deep by hand in 1910, still has water, but it's no longer potable due to contamination from diesel and sewage.

The tour begins appropriately inside the **courthouse,** built in 1901 by Judge Wickersham for $5,000. All four rooms plus the hallway on the ground floor are covered with displays of the Han Native Alaskans, geology and archaeology, early pioneers, the telegraph story, and more. Be sure to check out the front page of the December 7, 1905, issue of the *New York Times* with Amundsen's story, plus the map of the Northwest Passage in the hallway. (A romantic footnote: The intrepid Suzan Amundsen, Roald's great-granddaughter, continues a family tradition by taking a rest at the popular Eagle checkpoint during the Yukon Quest Sled Dog Race.) Don't miss the amazing Nimrod's false teeth (homemade from caribou and bear teeth) and his remarkably accurate relief map of the vicinity—newspaper papier-mâché printed with moose blood. Upstairs in Wickersham's courtroom is a small gift shop run by the Historical Society.

Then you mosey down to the **Customs House** on the Yukon waterfront, another two-story museum brimming with history. Study the six dated shots of the freezing of the Yukon River from October 13, 1899, to January 12, 1900, plus the photos upstairs of "wild" animals—Fred Ferwilliger's wolf pups, Mae Collins's pet black bear, and some bewildered-looking moose hitched to wagons and carriages. Sign the original U.S. Customs entry book. The building barely survived the 2009 flood.

A walk along the town's grassy airstrip leads to **Fort Egbert.** The huge old mule barn, at 150 feet long and 30 feet wide one of the largest restored buildings in Alaska, is full of relics from Eagle's past: tools, weapons, uniforms, wagons and tack, dogsleds, boats, a prototype Sears chain saw, an old outboard motor that looks like a cross between an early sewing machine and a Weedwhacker, and much more. Upstairs is the gold-mining exhibit with its own collection of Rube Goldberg equipment. The water-wagon shed houses historic vehicles, including a Model A pickup and a Model B dump truck.

The **Improved Order of Redmen Building,** a wilderness version of a lodge or benevolent society, was ostensibly dedicated to the preservation of the ways and traditions of the area's Native Alaskan people. Of course, only white guys were allowed to be members.

For more on the town and its rich history, pick up a copy of *Jewel on the Yukon: Eagle City* by Elva Scott; it's sold in the courthouse.

Services

Follow the signs from town left to the free Bureau of Land Management **campground** just beyond the cemetery, where there are a few old markers, including Nimrod's grave. The campground is big and uncrowded with nice wooded sites, firewood, and vault toilets. There's an easy nature walk between the campground and the airstrip.

Eagle Trading Co. (907/547-2220) on the riverfront has groceries, a Laundromat, gas, and tire repairs. **Falcon Inn B&B** (907/547-2254, http://falconinn.mystarband.net, open May–Sept.) is an attractive three-story log structure with dormers, three big decks, and a lookout tower right on the Yukon. Rooms are $125 d with a full breakfast. This was one of many buildings destroyed in the 2009 floods, and is the only Front Street building that was rebuilt (on a much higher foundation).

Getting There

The ***Yukon Queen II*** (206/281-3535 or 888/452-1737 Gray Line of Alaska, 867/993-5599 in Dawson City, www.graylinealaska.com) is a high-speed 120-passenger vessel with daily summertime runs between Eagle and Dawson City in Yukon. Most passengers are part of a Holland America/Gray Line of Alaska trek, but independent travelers can ride for $90 each way, including a meal. No buses run to Eagle, and it's a good four hours by car from Dawson and at least another five hours down to Tetlin Junction.

Everts Air Alaska (907/450-2350, www.evertsair.com) and **Arctic Circle Air** (907/474-0112, www.arcticcircleair.com) offer flights from Fairbanks. This is a real bush-pilot trip, a daily mail and supply run.

YUKON-CHARLEY RIVERS NATIONAL PRESERVE

Eagle itself is pretty far out there, but if you really want to disappear, you can explore Yukon-

Charley Rivers National Preserve. This huge 2.5-million-acre park is primitive, with virtually no facilities or established transportation and only a skeleton Park Service staff. The park protects 115 miles of the Yukon River and the entire Charley River basin.

The park's **Visitors Center** (1st Ave. and Fort Egbert Ave., Eagle, 907/547-2233, www.nps.gov/yuch, daily 8 A.M.–5 P.M. mid-May–early Sept.) has a selection of books and maps on the preserve, and the staff will plug in a video on request and can provide advice for those contemplating a trip.

Most park visitors float the Yukon by raft, kayak, or canoe, starting in Eagle (on the eastern margin) and taking out in Circle (on the western edge of the park). The float takes 5–10 days. Within the park are four public-use cabins available on a first-come, no-cost basis.

You can also charter a bush plane to drop you and a kayak or raft way up around the Charley headwaters and float down to the Yukon. You must be highly experienced, entirely self-sufficient, and have at least a tolerance for, if not a love of, mosquitoes. Check in at headquarters for advice and conditions, and to leave your intended itinerary.

Eagle Canoe Rentals (907/547-2203, www.eaglecanoerentals.com) rents canoes to paddle the Yukon from Eagle to Circle City, for experienced paddlers only.

SOUTHWEST ALASKA

Southwest Alaska includes Kodiak Island, the Alaska Peninsula, and the barren windswept Aleutian and Pribilof Islands—all told, an incredible sweep of wild and stormy coastline. This part of the state contains world-famous brown bear–viewing opportunities in Kodiak Island National Wildlife Refuge, Katmai National Park, and McNeil River State Game Sanctuary. In addition, it encompasses less-visited Lake Clark National Park, the remote Aniakchak National Monument, and four national wildlife refuges, one of which reaches all the way out the Aleutian chain. Fur seals, sea otters, walrus, and other marine animals are common around the Aleutians and Pribilofs, and the islands are also a bird-watcher's paradise. Because of climatic conditions there are no forests west of northern Kodiak Island and the adjacent mainland; most of the Alaska Peninsula and all the Aleutians are open tundra.

The largest settlements in Southwest Alaska are Kodiak and Unalaska/Dutch Harbor, but many smaller fishing towns and Native Alaskan villages are sprinkled over this remote landscape. Only Kodiak is fairly reasonable to visit; other places will require considerable outlays of cash. A useful regional website is run by the Southwest Alaska Municipal Conference (www.southwestalaska.com).

From Denali National Park the Alaska Range swings southwest to become the Aleutian Range, marching right into the North Pacific as the Alaska Peninsula and Aleutian Islands. This 1,100-mile arc from the northern end of the Alaska Peninsula to

HIGHLIGHTS

Baranov Museum: Occupying the oldest Russian building in North America, this Kodiak museum has an interesting collection of artifacts. The gift shop sells rare samovars, Russian porcelain, and Ukrainian Easter eggs (page 430).

Fort Abercrombie State Park: Remains of the old World War II fort are still visible, but visitors appreciate the lush rain forest, fun hiking paths, and high cliffs with nesting puffins (page 431).

Exploring Kodiak Roads: Nearly 100 miles of roads fan out from the town of Kodiak. The most interesting one leads south to remote beaches where you'll find fossils, perfect surfing waves, wandering bison, and even a rocket launching complex (page 432).

Kodiak Brown Bears: Floatplanes depart Kodiak for inland parts of the island or the shores of Katmai National Park. These trips are expensive but provide an unforgettable opportunity to view these powerful animals (page 440).

Valley of Ten Thousand Smokes: Located within Katmai National Park, this remote valley reveals the devastation wrought by the enormous eruption of Novarupta volcano in 1912. A bus takes visitors there from Brooks Camp (page 445).

Brooks Camp: Located along the shore of Naknek Lake, this lodge and campground provide a fine base for exploring Katmai National Park, with bear-viewing and fishing a short hike away. Access is primarily by floatplane from the town of King Salmon (page 446).

Unalaska/Dutch Harbor Historical Sights: Primarily a commercial fishing center, this Aleutian town also has a Russian Orthodox church from the 1820s, an outstanding museum, gorgeous tundra, plus aging bunkers and gun emplacements from World War II (page 456).

St. Paul Island: It's a long flight to this tiny outpost in the middle of the Bering Sea where the weather is almost always wet and chilly, but visitors are rewarded with the chance to find colonies of fur seals and cliffs crowded with puffins, murres, kittiwakes, and other seabirds (page 461).

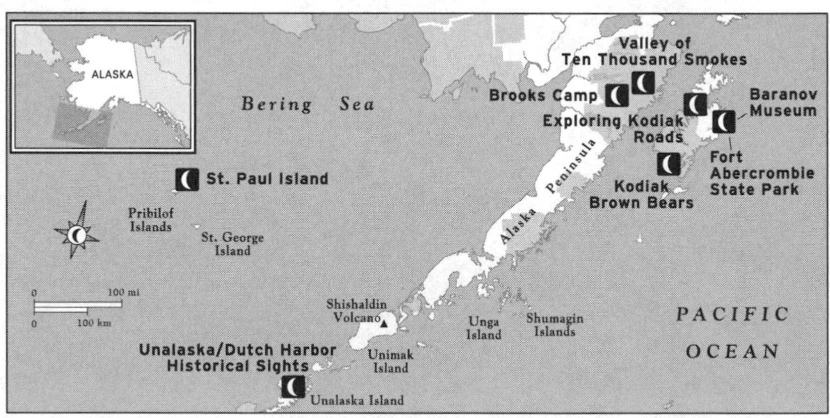

LOOK FOR TO FIND RECOMMENDED SIGHTS, ACTIVITIES, DINING, AND LODGING.

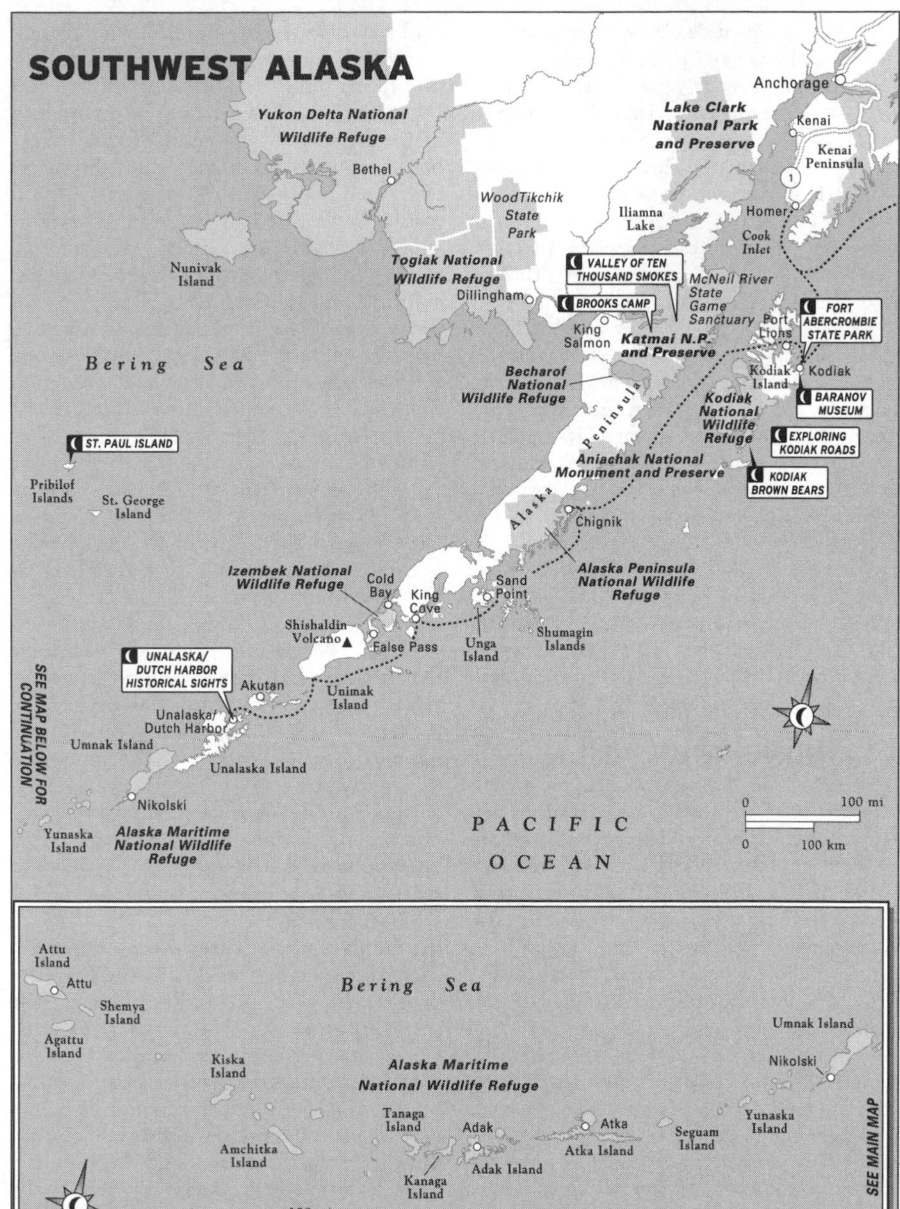

SOUTHWEST ALASKA
Yukon Delta National Wildlife Refuge
Bethel
Anchorage
Lake Clark National Park and Preserve
Kenai
Kenai Peninsula
WoodTikchik State Park
Iliamna Lake
Homer
Cook Inlet
Nunivak Island
Togiak National Wildlife Refuge
Dillingham
VALLEY OF TEN THOUSAND SMOKES
BROOKS CAMP
McNeil River State Game Sanctuary
King Salmon
Katmai N.P. and Preserve
Port Lions
FORT ABERCROMBIE STATE PARK
Bering Sea
Becharof National Wildlife Refuge
Kodiak Island
Kodiak
Kodiak National Wildlife Refuge
BARANOV MUSEUM
Alaska Peninsula
ST. PAUL ISLAND
EXPLORING KODIAK ROADS
Aniachak National Monument and Preserve
KODIAK BROWN BEARS
Pribilof Islands
St. George Island
Chignik
Alaska Peninsula National Wildlife Refuge
Izembek National Wildlife Refuge
Cold Bay
King Cove
Sand Point
Shishaldin Volcano
False Pass
Unga Island
Shumagin Islands
UNALASKA/ DUTCH HARBOR HISTORICAL SIGHTS
Akutan
Unimak Island
SEE MAP BELOW FOR CONTINUATION
Unalaska/ Dutch Harbor
Umnak Island
Unalaska Island
Nikolski
Yunaska Island
Alaska Maritime National Wildlife Refuge
PACIFIC OCEAN
0 100 mi
0 100 km
Attu Island
Attu
Shemya Island
Agattu Island
Bering Sea
Umnak Island
Kiska Island
Alaska Maritime National Wildlife Refuge
Nikolski
Tanaga Island
Adak
Atka
Seguam Island
Yunaska Island
Amchitka Island
Atka Island
Adak Island
Kanaga Island
SEE MAIN MAP
0 100 mi
0 100 km
PACIFIC OCEAN

SOUTHWEST ALASKA

the western tip of the Aleutians is an area of extraordinary volcanic and seismic activity, accounting for an amazing 10 percent of the world's recorded earthquakes. Tremors of all sizes—some too small to feel—are a daily occurrence, and three of the four largest earthquakes ever recorded in the United States occurred in the Aleutians; all three had a magnitude of 8.2 or greater. Only the massive Good Friday quake of 1964 that hit Southcentral Alaska was larger.

Kodiak Island sits uneasily on the edge of the Aleutian Trench; Kodiak is nonvolcanic but bears the brunt of its fiery neighbors. Great collapsed craters at Katmai and Aniakchak are now administered by the National Park Service, and the 50–60 volcanoes along the archipelago are the longest and straightest line of smoke-belchers and ash-spewers anywhere on earth.

The vegetation of Southwest Alaska is a thick, luxurious shag carpet of grass and brush; you can travel for hundreds of miles here without seeing a single tree. The climate, however, is particularly disagreeable—fog, rain, snow, and wind.

PLANNING YOUR TIME

Getting to Southwest Alaska can be a challenge due to both the remoteness of the setting and weather conditions that can shut down flights for days at a stretch. Access is primarily by air, but the state ferry system serves Kodiak several times a week, continuing out along the Aleutian Islands twice a month. The second-largest island in the United States, Kodiak is a fascinating and lush place with forests on the northeast end that give way to tundra across the rest of the island. The small city of Kodiak is home to a big fleet of commercial fishing vessels and a large Coast Guard base, but also has a rich Russian heritage, as evidenced by the **Baranov Museum.** A few miles north is **Fort Abercrombie State Park** with rain forests and dramatic rocky cliffs. **Kodiak roads** also lead south to remote beaches where you'll find fossils, perfect surfing waves, a winery, wandering bison, and even a rocket-launching complex. Kodiak **bear-viewing** is a major attraction, but many of these floatplane day-trips actually land on the shores of Katmai National Park. The park itself is primarily accessed by jet from Anchorage to the town of King Salmon, followed by a floatplane flight to **Brooks Camp,** home to a comfortable lodge and outstanding opportunities to watch bears or fish. Another favorite park feature is the **Valley of Ten Thousand Smokes,** the remnants from a massive eruption by the Novarupta volcano in 1912.

The Aleutians are a volcanic chain of islands that arc west for 1,000 miles from the tip of the Alaska Peninsula. Only one of these is readily accessible by air and ferry: Unalaska Island, home to the major fishing town of Unalaska (also called Dutch Harbor). Local **historical sights** include a fine museum, a historic Russian Orthodox church, and various World War II sites. Even more remote are the Pribilof Islands, consisting primarily of St. George Island and **St. Paul Island.** The latter is a very long flight from Anchorage over open water to a dot of a place in the Bering Sea, but the trip is worthwhile for the chance to see colonies of fur seals and cliffs packed with massive numbers of puffins, murres, kittiwakes, and other seabirds.

Getting There

With ferry service from Homer and Seward three times a week, Kodiak is the only easily accessible place in Southwest Alaska. The trusty *Tustumena* sails out as far as Dutch Harbor once a month, but only in summer. Alaska Air flies from Anchorage to Kodiak, Dutch Harbor/Unalaska, and Adak, and PenAir serves King Salmon, Sand Point, Dutch Harbor/Unalaska, and the Pribilofs. Access to remote backcountry areas is by small floatplanes that land on the myriad lakes and ponds.

Kodiak Island

Kodiak Island is an unlikely land of superlatives. At 60 by 100 miles, it is the largest island in Alaska, and the second largest in the United States (after Hawaii's Big Island). Kodiak has the world's biggest brown bears, Alaska's longest history, and one of the largest fishing fleets, along with the country's largest Coast Guard station and weirdest golf tournament. Besides, what other town has chewing tobacco named for it, and a dump once voted the nation's "most scenic?"

Kodiak Island is home to nearly 14,000 people, 9,000 of whom live in and around the city of Kodiak. Only 250 air miles from Anchorage or 84 nautical miles from Homer, Kodiak is a highly accessible and pleasurable place to visit. The city of Kodiak sits on the island's northeast side along St. Paul Harbor, protected from

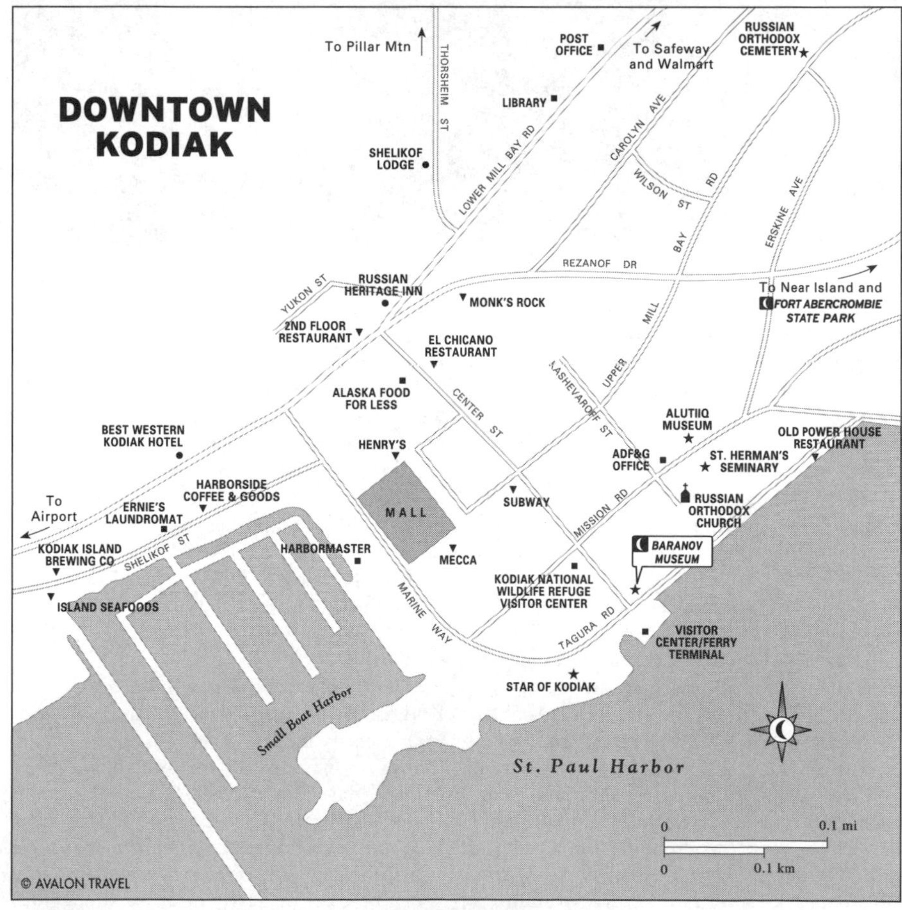

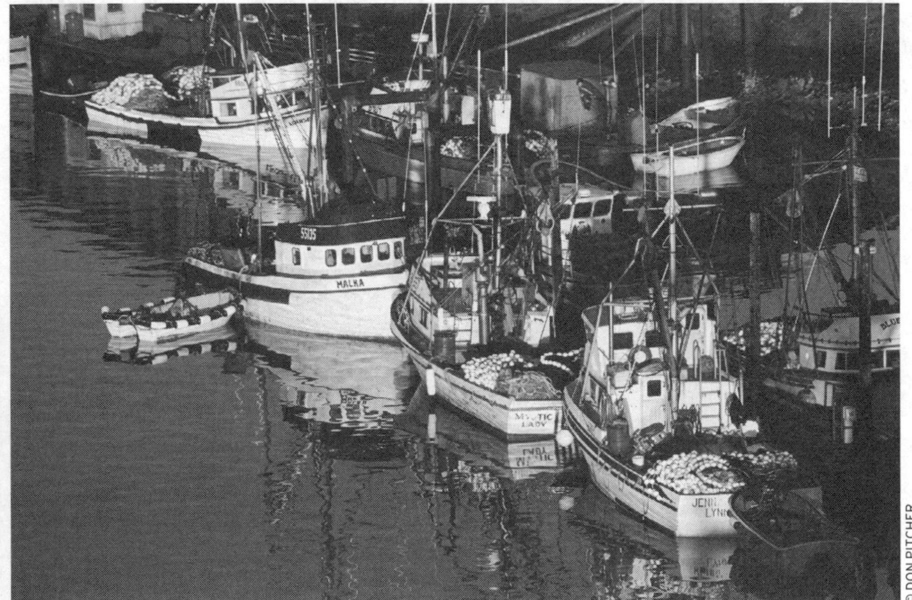

© DON PITCHER

Kodiak boat harbor

the wild Gulf of Alaska by wooded islands in Chiniak Bay. Visitors will quickly learn that the town runs on commercial fishing; it's hard to escape not only the sights but also the smell of fish.

THE LAND

The Kodiak Island group, an extension of the Chugach-Kenai Ranges, was once possibly connected to the mainland but is now separated by the "entrances" to Cook Inlet and Shelikof Strait. The group perches on the continental shelf, right on the edge of the Aleutian Trench. This makes it highly susceptible to the aftereffects of volcanic and seismic activity, such as the ash of Novarupta and the tsunamis of the 1964 earthquake. However, glaciation, not volcanism, has been the primary agent in shaping Kodiak's geological features. Snow and ice almost completely covered the group during the last ice age, and the alpine region consists of chiseled roughly steep slopes, short fast runoff streams, and rounded kettles. In addition, Kodiak's coastline is so characterized by long fjords that even with a maximum width of 60 miles, no point on the island is more than 20 miles from tidewater.

Dense Sitka spruce forests cover the northwest corner of Kodiak Island, along with nearby Afognak and Shuyak islands. The trees are slowly spreading southward, but most of Kodiak is an open mix of tundra, tall grass, bushes, alders, and other plants that turn florescent green in the too-brief peak of summer. Visit in July to see why they call this "The Emerald Isle."

Climate

Expect cool, wet, and windy weather on Kodiak. The average temperature in August, the "hottest" month, is 54°F. Kodiak's record high is 86°F, but most years only half a dozen summer days even exceed 70. Kodiak receives 75 inches of rain per year, of which 12 inches fall June–September. Locals claim that some sun shines one out of every three days—but it can be clear or partly clear for three glorious days, then soupy for nine in a row. Dress warmly, and if you intend to explore the back-country, bring rain gear and rubber boots.

HISTORY

Russian America

Russian fur trader Glotoff "discovered" Kodiak in 1763 and told Grigorii Shelikov (also spelled Shelikof) about the abundant sea otters there. The island's second-highest peak (4,450 ft.) was named for Glotoff. Shelikov is remembered as the founder of the Russian-America Company and the first European settlement in Alaska, at Three Saints Bay, Kodiak, in 1784. This is the site of present-day Old Harbor and had long been an important Alutiiq (also called Koniag) village. To gain the site, Shelikov ordered his men to massacre hundreds of the Alutiiq on the rock where they had taken refuge. Native leaders refer to the battle as the "Wounded Knee of Alaska." This slaughter broke the back of Native Alaskan resistance to Russian rule.

Alexander Baranov (often spelled Baranof) arrived in 1791 to manage the company and colony; he promptly relocated the whole settlement to St. Paul's Harbor (present-day Kodiak town) after a tsunami nearly wiped out the previous town. The Eskimo-related Alutiiq population wasn't sorry to see the Russians and their Aleut slaves move again, in 1800, to New Archangel (Sitka)—except that the sea otters in the vicinity had been almost completely eradicated, and as happened in the Queen Charlottes, the 20,000 Native Alaskan inhabitants were decimated to 1,500 in a couple of decades because of war and introduced diseases such as smallpox.

Later Years

Kodiak survived the 19th century by fur trading, whaling, fishing, and even ice-making (Russian diehards began producing ice in the 1850s to supply California gold-rush boom towns; they introduced the first horses and built the first roads in Alaska). Salmon fishing really caught on in the early 1900s, and the living was easy until the awesome explosion of Novarupta on Katmai across the strait in 1912. It showered ash down on the town, blanketing fields and villages, crushing roofs, and changing the green island into a gray-brown desert overnight. After 48 hours of total blackness and gasping for air, 450 residents were evacuated by a U.S. revenue cutter in a daring rescue. It took over two years for life to return to normal, and the deep ash layer can still be seen on stream-cut banks around the island.

Kodiak, like the rest of Alaska, was mobilized during World War II, but the fortifications here had a more urgent quality: Forts, gun emplacements, submarine bases, and command centers were installed to protect the island from Japanese invasion and to manage the Aleutian campaign. Thousands of service members left a large economic legacy as well. The major economic boom for the island came later, in the form of the famous Kodiak king crab, harvested by the hundreds of millions of pounds in the early 1960s. Then the Good Friday earthquake struck in 1964, quaking the earth for over five minutes, then flooding the town for the next 12 hours with several "waves" that first sucked the tidewater out, exposing the harbor bottom, then swept half the town from its moorings with swells up to 35 feet high. For a gripping description of that terrible night—and a fascinating firsthand look at Kodiak fishing life—read *Highliners* by William B. McKloskey.

Kodiak Today

Since the earthquake, Kodiak has rebuilt and retooled for the harvesting of salmon, halibut, shrimp, herring, and bottom fish (king crab were nearly fished out by 1983). The bottom-fishing industry—especially for pollock—grew dramatically in the 1990s; these "junk fish" are processed into surimi, imitation crab and shrimp meat. Today, Kodiak consistently ranks near the top of U.S. ports in value of fish landed, and there are eight different canneries around the city.

A 1993 *National Geographic* article noted that "Kodiak's the kind of town where you think the municipal emblem ought to be a red pickup hauling a golden retriever, with the truck shaking to a country tune like 'Achy

Breaky Heart.'" Despite this impression, visitors to modern-day Kodiak may be surprised to see how diverse the population actually is. Many of the taxi drivers, cannery workers, and other blue-collar employees are of Filipino, Mexican, or Latin American heritage. You'll hear more Spanish spoken here than almost anywhere else in Alaska. A controversial Korean church has a significant presence in the local economy, and the island even has the only state-owned missile spaceport anywhere.

SIGHTS

Wander along the shore to Kodiak's **Small Boat Harbor,** one of the state's most crowded. When the fleet is in, all the masts, rigging, and fishing equipment make the harbor an almost impenetrable thicket. The danger in a seafarer's life is revealed by the monument in front of the harbormaster's office. The plaque lists the names of more than 150 men and women lost at sea.

A high bridge links Kodiak with nearby Near Island, home to a second boat harbor and floatplane dock. This harbor has one of the largest travel lifts in the world; it can hoist boats up to 600 tons (including the crabbers from *Deadliest Catch*). **North End Park** is on your left side just after crossing the bridge. An easy 0.5-mile path leads through the woods to a rocky beach where you're rewarded with a good view of town. Near Island is also home to the **Kodiak Fisheries Research Center** (907/481-1800, www.afsc.noaa.gov/kodiak, open weekdays), which houses a small interpretive center along with a fascinating large aquarium and touch tank. Most of the facility, of course, is devoted to research.

Continue left down Shelikof Street to "cannery row," where **Steller sea lions** are often just off the docks. Additional canneries line the shore on either side of the ferry terminal. Certainly the hardest cannery to miss is the ship-ashore ***Star of Kodiak.*** Originally christened the *Albert M. Boe,* this was the last Liberty Ship built. It was launched in 1945 as a troop ship, but was towed up from the "mothball" fleet after the 1964 tsunami wiped out other canneries in Kodiak. Today, it's owned by Trident Seafoods. One of the other plants—International Seafoods—is owned by the controversial Unification Church (otherwise known as the Moonies). They also own several commercial fishing boats, a group house/day care center in town, and a lodge along the Ayakulik River. Reverend Moon himself has come here several summers—along with hundreds of followers—to sport-fish for salmon.

Join a van tour of town from **Kodiak Tour Company** (907/486-3920, www.kodiaktours.com) for an introduction to Kodiak sights and history.

Visitors Centers

The **Kodiak Visitors Information Center** (907/486-4782 or 800/789-4782, www.kodiak.org, Mon.–Fri. 8 A.M.–5 P.M. year-round, longer hours summer) shares the same building with the ferry office (Marine Way and Center St.). Pick up the Kodiak Island map and the excellent visitors' guide.

Nearby is the recently opened **Kodiak National Wildlife Refuge Visitor Center** (420 Center St., 907/487-2626 or 888/592-6940, www.kodiakwildliferefuge.org, daily 9 A.M.–5 P.M. summer), with exhibits detailing the refuge and its wildlife, a model of the Karluk River ecosystem, a fine orientation video, and the only intact gray whale skeleton in the nation. Various interpretive programs are offered.

Baranov Museum

Several downtown buildings are reminders of Kodiak's deep Russian heritage. The Baranov Museum (907/486-5920, www.baranovmuseum.org, Sun. noon–4 P.M., Mon.–Sat. 10 A.M.–4 P.M. summer, Tues.–Sat. 10 A.M.–3 P.M. the rest of the year, $3, children under age 13 free), housed in the oldest Russian building in North America, was built around 1808 as a storehouse for sea otter pelts.

Displays include an impressive Russian samovar and china collection, along with other artifacts such as a 10-kopek note printed on sealskin; it's from Alexander Baranov's time.

Also here are Alutiiq and Aleut items, including a remarkable three-person kayak, an impressive collection of historic grass baskets, and a bear-muzzle carving found in 1956 on Cape Douglas. The photos from the 1964 tsunami are hard to believe: Boats were strewn throughout downtown. The **gift shop**—one of the most unusual in Alaska—sells Lomonosov porcelain china, painted Ukrainian Easter eggs, lacquered boxes, Father Frost carvings, and Russian nesting dolls ($6–800). If you have the money, take a look at the gorgeous antique Russian samovars that start around $600; this is the only place in Alaska where you can buy them. Out front are several large whalebones.

Orthodox Church and Seminary

Just across the green is **Holy Resurrection Orthodox Church** (Mission Rd. and Kashevaroff Ave.), under the distinctive blue onion domes. This is the third church in which Kodiak's Orthodox faithful have worshipped since the parish was founded in 1794. It shelters the earthly remains of St. Herman of Spruce Island, the only Russian Orthodox saint in the western hemisphere; he was canonized in 1970. The interior contains colorful icons and religious paraphernalia, with a good view of the room from the balcony. To get inside, either put on clean clothes and attend a service (Thurs. 7:30 P.M., Sat. 6:30 P.M., Sun. 9:30 A.M.) or take a tour (Mon.–Fri. 1 P.M. summer). Call the parish priest (907/486-3854) for details. A small gift shop is adjacent.

Walk up toward the bridge overpass to the **St. Herman's Theological Seminary** (www.sthermansseminary.org), one of three Orthodox seminaries in the United States. The beautiful seminary chapel is open all the time, and it is worth a visit.

Alutiiq Museum

The Alutiiq Museum (215 Mission Rd., 907/486-7004, www.alutiiqmuseum.org, Mon.–Fri. 9 A.M.–5 P.M., Sat. 10 A.M.–5 P.M. June–Aug., Tues.–Fri. 9 A.M.–5 P.M., Sat. 10:30 A.M.–4:30 P.M. Sept.–May, $5, children under age 13 free) has a collection featuring a tiny sampling of the thousands of artifacts found during archaeological digs at the village of Karluk—masks, wooden spoons, stone oil lamps, knives, *ulus,* and more—along with a diorama of a prehistoric village, kayak replicas, and other items such as spruce baskets and seal pokes. The museum store sells Native Alaskan crafts, or you can watch a video on local archaeology. A summertime archaeological dig at Women's Bay is open to the public.

OUT-OF-TOWN SIGHTS

Fort Abercrombie State Park

This evocative historical and recreational site (907/486-6339, www.alaskastateparks.org) is five miles northeast of town on East Rezanof Drive. The peninsula supports a lush rain forest of huge Sitka spruce thriving on the volcanic ash from Novarupta. Thick chartreuse moss clings to these stately trees. Check out the gun emplacements on the cliff above the bay—ancient cannons that could never have hit the broad side of any Japanese (floating) barn. From this overlook, watch for whales, puffins (one of the few places in Alaska where they can readily be seen from the shore), sea otters, sea lions, and cormorants. The trails are all well maintained, and one takes you past Lake Gertrude to a beautiful beach. The park also has a campground and some fascinating tide pools. Rangers guide summertime hikes and provide Saturday evening lectures.

The **Kodiak Military History Museum** (907/486-7015, www.kadiak.org, Fri.–Mon. 1–4 P.M. summer, $3 adults, children under age 12 free) is within a World War II ammunition bunker at Miller Point. Inside is a 1944 Ford jeep and other items from that era. A self-guided tour takes you past other structures from the war; pick up a free brochure at the museum.

Monashka Bay

Monashka Bay Road begins at Fort Abercrombie State Park and skirts around this bay north of town, passing the Pillar Creek Hatchery, and a black sand beach at the mouth of Pillar Creek, before terminating 11 miles

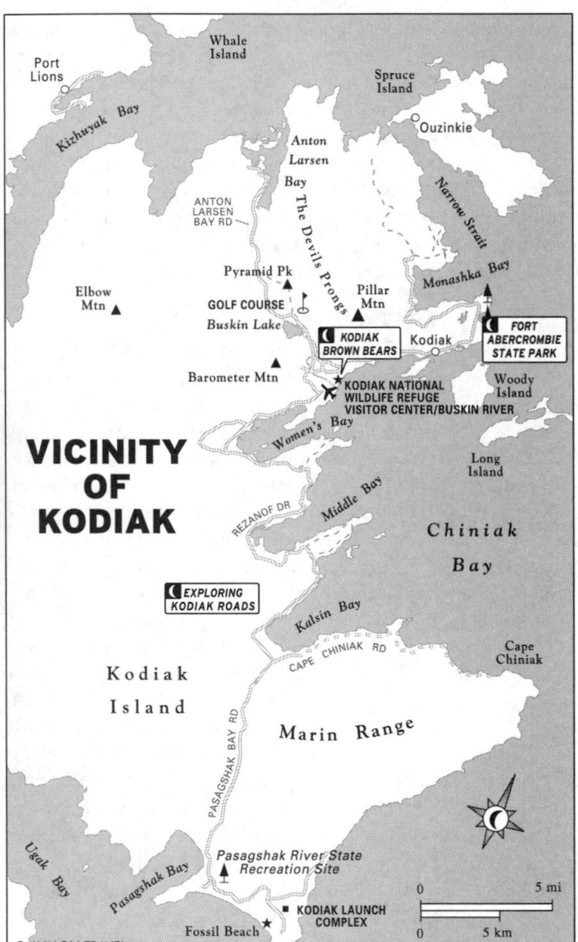

from Kodiak at Monashka Bay, with its shallow bay and delightful sandy beach. Follow the coast north along the beach, and head into the trees to find a trail that continues three miles to a scenic bluff called **Termination Point.**

Pillar Mountain

A good road climbs right up to the top of Pillar Mountain, from which all the overviews of Kodiak town are photographed. Start out at Thorsheim Street and go as far as Maple Avenue, where you turn left and go up Pillar Mountain Road. Hikers can scramble up the front of the mountain from Rezanof Drive (west of town)—it is steep but much faster than walking up the road. Three tall wind turbines atop the peak provide electricity for Kodiak.

Exploring Kodiak Roads

All told, Kodiak Island has nearly 100 miles of fun-to-explore roads, making a rental car a wise investment for visitors. A detailed mileage guide for all the roads is found in the *Kodiak Island Visitors Guide,* but even better is the outstanding *Kodiak Audubon's Hiking & Birding Guide,* a very detailed waterproof map and guide to wild places on the road system. It's available at the visitors center for $10.

The longest road—**Chiniak Road**—heads south from town all the way to Cape Chiniak (43 miles). The drive is worth the time, even if it's foggy or raining, to see this part of the Emerald Isle. The first 12 miles are paved. Four miles out is the **Kodiak National Wildlife Refuge** visitors center, and **Buskin River State Recreation Site,** with campsites and great fishing in late summer for Dolly Varden and coho.

Another mile down Chiniak Road is the unmarked turnoff to **Anton Larsen Bay,** on the island's northwest tip. This winding, 12-mile, mostly gravel road goes by Coast Guard communications towers, a golf course, trailheads to pointy Pyramid Peak and Cascade Lake, and finally the boat launching area on this scenic and protected fjord.

Back on Chiniak Road, cruise by the airport

(Mile 5) and the trail to Barometer Mountain to the overlook of the **U.S. Coast Guard Station** at Mile 6. At 21,000 acres the largest in the nation, this support center is home to four large cutters and more than 1,100 personnel. Their main activities include patrolling the 200-mile fishing zone for illegal fishing (offenders are mostly Japanese and Russian trawlers), as well as search and rescue for commercial fishing boats.

Beyond the Coast Guard Station, the road continues around scenic Women's Bay and on to Kalsin Bay (Mile 30), where you'll find the aging Kalsin Bay Inn—best known for its hat collection. Scan nearby slopes for mountain goats, especially in the spring or fall.

Several pretty beaches are located over the next 10 miles, including **Roslyn Bay Beach** at Mile 37. The road ends at Mile 43 near Chiniak Point on the island's eastern tip, and a trail leads to the point itself.

A side route, **Pasagshak Bay Road,** turns south off Chiniak Road in Kalsin Bay and leads nine miles to **Pasagshak River State Recreation Site** with free camping and a great beach. Beyond this, the road continues to Narrow Cape (16 miles from Kalsin Bay) where you're treated to all-encompassing views. Be sure to take the rather steep side road (not for RVs) to **Fossil Beach,** a fascinating and remote place to look for rocks containing fossilized shells. The beach is also a favorite of local surfers. Several of Kodiak's large cattle ranches are visible along the Chiniak and Pasagshak Bay roads, and near Narrow Cape you're likely to see grazing buffalo—part of a herd of 400 that wander freely here. It's a 47-mile drive from Kodiak to the end of the road.

Kodiak Island's unlikeliest surprise is also at Narrow Cape, the **Kodiak Launch Complex** (907/273-1582). The first rocket launch here took place in 1998, and the site will continue to be used to blast military satellites into low polar orbits and as a base for testing "Star Wars" interceptor missiles. See www.akaerospace.com for information on upcoming launches.

Shuyak Island State Park

Shuyak Island is 50 miles and a 40-minute floatplane trip north from Kodiak (or south from Homer); it is a flight that takes you to another world. This 47,000-acre park contains virgin Sitka spruce forests and a gorgeous coastline pockmarked with small islands and protected waterways. It's perfect for sea kayaking and wildlife watching.

The state maintains four excellent public-use cabins ($60) at Shuyak. Each can sleep up to eight people and includes a propane cookstove, a woodstove, a water system, an outhouse, and a shower. Two of these—**Eagle's Nest Cabin** and **Salmon Cove Cabin**—are within Big Bay, and the other two are **Deer Haven Cabin** in Carry Inlet and **Mulcahy View Cabin** in Neketa Bay. There are only a few hiking trails on Shuyak, and the dense devil's club makes bushwhacking very difficult; it is possible to hike along the shore at low tide if you don't have a kayak.

Request a brochure on Shuyak sea kayaking or make cabin reservations by contacting Alaska State Parks (907/486-6339, www.alaskastateparks.org). The cabins are generally available, but reserve well ahead for the silver salmon run in September.

Afognak Island

This large island lies 30 miles north of Kodiak Island, but it is vastly different from its neighbor. Afognak is—or rather was—covered with a luxuriant dense spruce forest. Unfortunately, much of this spectacular country was logged in the 1990s by the local Native Corporation. Much of what remains is within the 49,000-acre **Afognak Island State Park** on the east side of the island, where the land is covered with a mix of forested areas and alpine country. A public use cabin at **Pillar Lake** (907/486-6339, www.alaskastateparks.org, $35) has space for up to six people. The cabin is used as a base for backcountry hiking, fishing, and hunting. A raft or kayak is useful for getting around on Pillar Lake, and you can reach the alpine country in approximately one hour of hiking. When making flight arrangements for the Pillar Lake Cabin, make sure the air-taxi service can land on wheels at Izhut Bay beach near the cabin. In addition, the U.S. Fish and Wildlife Service has a wheelchair-accessible cabin (907/487-2600 or 888/408-3514, http://kodiak.fws.gov, $45) in remote **Blue Fox Bay** on Afognak Island.

Another area that managed to escape the chainsaw is the property that surrounds **Afognak Wilderness Lodge** (907/486-6442 or 800/478-6442, www.afognaklodge.com). Anyone willing to part with $750 per person per day (including three meals, guides, and accommodations) will find some of the finest old-time accommodations in Alaska.

Afognak Native Corporation are the folks behind the wholesale clear-cutting of Afognak's forests, but they have four rental cabins ($300) in unlogged sections. Reservations are through **Andrew Airways** (907/487-2566, www.andrewairways.com).

Port Lions

This community of 250 people came into existence after the 1964 earthquake and tsunami destroyed the nearby village of Afognak. It was named to honor the funding and support from the Lions International Club that led to its establishment. The town has a commercial fishing base and also has a handful of lodges, eating places, and stores. The state ferry stops here, and there is air-taxi service to the surrounding country.

Contact **Whale Pass Lodge** (907/454-2500 or 800/456-3425, www.whalepasslodge.com) or **Port Lions Lodge** (907/454-2264 or 800/808-8447, www.portlionslodge.com) for fishing packages and whale-watching.

Old Harbor

Located along protected Sitkalidak Straits near the center of Kodiak Island, this village of 250 people has a mixed Native Alaskan and Russian heritage and is home to a lovely Russian Orthodox church and an active fishing fleet. Ongoing archaeological digs continue each summer on 8,500-year-old sites.

Find accommodations and meals at **Mountain View Guest House** (907/286-2214) or multiple-night stays at the fishing lodges: **Kodiak Sportsman's Lodge** (801/475-0718 or 866/744-8777, www.kodiaksportsmanslodge.com) or **Ocean View Lodge** (907/286-2381, www.oceanviewlodge.com). There are no cafés, but limited groceries are available. **Servant Air** (907/487-4444 or 877/487-4400, www.servantair.com) and **Island Air** (907/487-4596 or 800/478-6196, www.kodiakislandair.com) have daily flights from Kodiak.

ENTERTAINMENT AND EVENTS

You'd expect a town whose inhabitants live close to the "Edge" to party hearty, and Kodiak definitely won't disappoint. You don't even have to venture any farther than downtown, where many storefronts are occupied by bars—big bars. After a big salmon opener, a beer can thrown in any direction would hit a drunk fisher.

The **Mecca** (907/486-3364) has a popular dance floor; this place competes with the ocean for rockin' and rollin'. For hard drinking with the highliners, sit down at **The Village** or **Tony's.** Tony's advertises itself as the "biggest navigational hazard on Kodiak" and simultaneously "a friendly neighborhood bar with over 3 million drinks spilled." **Tropic Lounge** is a huge bar where some people go bowling. For TV sports, a big choice of draft beers, and good pub grub, head to **Henry's** (512 Marine Way, 907/486-3313), where the decor includes a gorgeous Chilkat robe and other Alaskan pieces of the past. Otherwise, take in a flick at **Orpheum Theater** (Center St., 907/486-5449).

If you're heading out to Pasagshak Bay, you may want to stop at **Kalsin Bay Inn** (907/486-2659, www.chiniak.net/kalsin), an old place with an impressive collection of military caps from Navy and Coast Guard ships, signed dollar bills, and big bear photos. It's 30 miles south of Kodiak.

Events

The new year begins with a masquerade ball and celebration of **Russian New Year** in mid-January. Shortly before this is the starring ceremony, during which a choir follows a twirling star to the home of the Russian Orthodox faithful.

The infamous **Pillar Mountain Golf Classic,** at the end of March, is a deranged, par-70, one-hole tournament up the side of the 1,400-foot mountain behind town. The course, cleared by spotters with machetes, runs all the way to the peak, where a bucket in the snow serves as the hole and lime Jell-O as the green. No power tools are allowed, so leave your chainsaw at home.

In mid-April, **Whalefest** (www.whalefest-kodiak.com) celebrates the return of migrating whales with tours, performances, and other productions. The big summertime event on Kodiak is the **Crab Festival,** held on Memorial Day weekend. There's a parade, survival-suit races, a foot race, the blessing of the fleet, and various concerts. It is lots of fun.

The **Kodiak State Fair and Rodeo** (www.kodiakrodeoandstatefair.com) comes around on Labor Day weekend and features everything from craft demonstrations and live music to stock car races and a small-town rodeo with bull riders.

RECREATION

Rent a mountain bike from **58° North** (1231 Mill Bay Rd., 907/486-6249). This is also a good place to buy outdoor gear, snowboards, clothes, and even sea kayaks. Just up the street is **Orion's Mountain Sports** (907/486-8380), with more backcountry supplies, including surfboards and wetsuits.

The nine-hole **Bear Valley Golf Course** (907/486-5323) is out Anton Larson Bay Road.

Hiking

Many hikes are available around Kodiak in addition to those at Pillar Mountain, Fort Abercrombie, and the Termination Point Trail; drop by the visitors center (next to the ferry) for a helpful waterproof hiking and birding map ($12) that details 40 popular routes. On summer weekends **Kodiak Audubon** (907/486-8148, www.kodiakaudubon.blogspot.com) leads free hikes from this office at 9:30 A.M.

Pyramid Peak has two trailheads off Anton Larsen Bay Road that climb this precipitous 2,400-foot mountain just west of town. Start near the ski lift 1.5 miles past the golf course. There are great vistas from the summit of Kodiak's mountainous interior. **Barometer Mountain Trail** is a steep five-mile hike to the 2,500-foot peak. It starts at an unmarked (but recognizable) trailhead on the first road to the right past the airport runway out on Rezanof Drive West. This is one of the most popular local hikes.

Sea Kayaking

Wendy Eskew of **Alaskan Wilderness Adventures** (907/487-2397, www.akwildadventures.com) has half-day kayak trips ($110 pp) and 2.5-hour trips ($85) from Kodiak town.

Orcas Unlimited (907/539-1979, www.orcasunlimited.com) guides all-day trips from Anton Larson Bay, plus a variety of longer trips, up to a five-day circumnavigation of Raspberry Island. Rates depend on group size.

Fishing and Boating

Kodiak is world-famous as a fishing destination, with remote fishing lodges, charter halibut and salmon fishing boats, and surprisingly good road-accessible fishing. Pick up the informative sportfishing brochure from the visitors information center, which also has a listing of more than 30 charter operators; find them online at www.kodiak.org.

ACCOMMODATIONS

The Visitors Bureau website (www.kodiak.org) has links to many local lodging places, and is a good place to start when looking over the lodging options.

Hostel

Newly opened in 2010, the downtown **Kodiak Island Hostel** (508 W. Marine Way, 907/486-0373, www.kodiakislandhostel.com, $34 pp) is upstairs over The Treasury gift shop. The main bunk room has a dozen bunks, and there's also a kitchen with a fridge and a microwave (but no stove), plus showers and laundry facilities.

Motels

Two modest motels are right in the heart of town. **Shelikof Lodge** (211 Thorsheim Ave., 907/486-4141, www.shelikoflodgealaska.com, $90 s, $100 d) offers well-maintained guest rooms (many with fridges and microwaves), Wi-Fi, and a courtesy van to the airport. Nearby is **Russian Heritage Inn** (119 Yukon St., 907/486-5657, www.russianheritageinn.com, $90 d, kitchenettes $100 d, 2-room suites $140 d), with a mix of rooms, all with fridges, microwaves, and Wi-Fi.

It's overpriced, but **Best Western Kodiak Inn** (236 Rezanof Dr. W., 907/486-5712 or 888/563-4254, www.kodiakinn.com, $179 d, suites $259 d) has microwaves and fridges in all guest rooms, plus a hot tub, a fitness center, Wi-Fi, continental breakfast, and an airport shuttle.

Recently remodeled, **Comfort Inn** (1395 Airport Way, 907/487-2700 or 800/544-2202, www.choicehotels.com, $170–180 d, suites $200–250 d) is a well-managed 50-room motel close to the airport. The guest rooms have fridges and microwaves, free Wi-Fi, and there is a filling breakfast, but you're five miles from town, so a rental car comes in handy. Eagle's Landing Restaurant is also on the premises, serving brunch and dinner.

Bed-and-Breakfasts and Guest Houses

The Visitors Bureau website (www.kodiak.org) provides links to more than 50 local B&Bs and vacation rentals.

Beaver Creek Lodge B&B (907/487-4433, www.bclodgekodiak.com, $110–155 d) is 11 miles south along the Russian River. This spacious home has a stone hearth, six guest rooms, big home-cooked breakfasts, Wi-Fi, and friendly owners. Anglers appreciate such services as fish processing and rental gear, while honeymooners love the quiet setting and outdoor hot tub.

Kodiak's newest place—built in 2008—is **Cliff House B&B** (907/486-5079 or 800/253-6331, www.galleygourmet.biz). It's a short walk from downtown, with a big deck and "million-dollar views" from each room. A deluxe room ($190 d) in the main house includes a big breakfast. Three guest rooms ($125–150 d) in the adjacent suite have access to a fully stocked kitchen where owner Marion Owen provides homemade granola and pastries each morning. There's a bottomless cookie jar, Wi-Fi, and beautiful artwork throughout.

Right in town, **Kodiak B&B** (308 Cope St., 907/486-5367, www.kodiakbedandbreakfast.com, $98 s, $148 d) has two guest rooms sharing a bath, full breakfasts, Wi-Fi, and a fine harbor view from the deck. In business since 1986, this is the oldest B&B on Kodiak Island.

Emerald Isle B&B (1214 Madsen Ave., 907/486-4427 or 866/399-4427, www.kodiaklodging.com, $120 d) has three bedrooms with private or shared baths, a patio, Wi-Fi, and a self-serve breakfast.

You'll need a rental car for **Lagoonside B&B** (907/486-5445, www.chiniak.net/lagoonside), located in a serene spot 35 miles south of Kodiak at Chiniak. The five bedrooms share two baths, and guests have access to a pleasant deck, kayaks, and a canoe. Lodging plus three meals a day is $150 per person.

Other recommended Kodiak B&Bs include **Beachside B&B** (907/486-4941, www.beachsidebandb.com, $95 s, $105 d), a waterside apartment unit just north of town, and **A Smiling Bear B&B** (907/481-6390, www.asmilingbear.com, $125–150 s, $150–175 d), with two suites north of town along Monashka Bay.

Several guesthouses are available for families or couples looking for their own place to settle into the Kodiak scene. **Parkside Guesthouse** (907/486-9446, www.parksideguesthouse.com, $160 d, add $20 for each extra guest up to 6) is an attractively furnished modern home with one bedroom, a loft with twin beds, a kitchen, and laundry. It's next to Fort Abercrombie State Park. **AAA Bayview Inn** (907/481-2882 or 888/568-2882, www.aaabayview.com, $165

d) has two suites, each with a private entrance, a bath, and a kitchenette. It's four miles out of town and right on the shore of beautiful Monashka Bay.

Also check out two places in the rain forest near Chiniak 37 miles south of town: **Distant Loon Cabin** (907/486-1789, www.chiniak.net/distantloon, $150 d), a nicely appointed small house, and **Roslyn Ridge Retreat** (907/486-5972, http://home.gci.net/~roslyn, $250 d), a gorgeous two-bedroom home with a hot tub.

Wilderness Lodges

Kodiak is home to more than 30 remote lodges, most focused on fishing, bear-viewing, and hunting, with all-inclusive rates and access by floatplane. Visit www.kodiak.org for links to most of these. A few of the more established lodges are **Kodiak Lodge** (206/368-8338 or 888/556-3425, www.kodiaklodge.com), **Larsen Bay Lodge** (907/847-2238 or 800/748-2238, www.larsenbaylodge.com), **Munsey's Bear Camp** (907/847-2203, www.munseysbearcamp.com), **Raspberry Island Remote Lodge** (701/526-1677, www.raspberryisland.com), **Spirit of Alaska Wilderness Adventures** (866/910-2327, www.spiritofalaska.com), **Uyak Bay Lodge** (907/847-2350 or 877/263-8833, www.uyakbaylodge.com), and **Zachar Bay Lodge** (907/486-4120 or 800/693-2333, www.zacharbay.com).

Kodiak Treks (907/487-2122, www.kodiaktreks.com) offers overnight lodging and meals, bear-viewing hikes, and multiday hiking trips from the lodge at Uyak Bay on the west side of Kodiak Island.

CAMPING

The closest official campground, **Buskin River State Recreation Site** ($10), is four miles south of town on Buskin Beach Road next to the airport. This is an OK site on the water, with shelters, pit toilets, trails, and runways in your ear. RVers appreciate the flat sites with plenty or room, and fishers will find plenty of salmon to catch.

A quieter option is **Fort Abercrombie State Park** ($10) on the eastern tip of town, five miles away. It's worth the hitch, bike ride, or extra miles on the rental car—this is a magical place to pass your nights on Kodiak. The sites are beneath tall spruce trees and out of the weather.

Pasagshak River State Recreation Site, 40 miles south of town, also has camping (no charge) at the mouth of this popular salmon-fishing river.

Park RVs year-round at **VFW RV Park** (907/486-5816, $30 with hookups) seven miles north of town on Monashka Bay Road. You may also be able to use the Wal-Mart parking lot.

FOOD

Coffeehouses

Kodiak's favorite hangout is **Harborside Coffee & Goods** (216 Shelikof St., 907/486-5862, Sun. 7 A.M.–6 P.M., Mon.–Sat. 6 A.M.–7 P.M.), with lattes, pastries, fresh soups, bagels, and rich espresso shakes. It's a wonderful place to relax on a rainy day.

Run by a splinter group of the Russian Orthodox Church, **Monk's Rock Coffee House** (202 E. Rezanof Dr., 907/486-0905) is undoubtedly Kodiak's most distinctive gathering place. Icons line the walls, and you can check out the books, samovars, and handmade prayer ropes, buy some freshly baked bread, and enjoy a sandwich, smoothie, or ice cream. Pick up the brochure about nearby Spruce Island, a fascinating place where you can learn Russian Orthodox history and meet monks at St. Michael's Skete.

Don't miss Kodiak's legendary **Mill Bay Coffee & Pastry** (3833 E. Rezanof Dr., 907/486-4411, www.millbaycoffee.com, Sun. 8 A.M.–5 P.M., Mon.–Thurs. 7 A.M.–6 P.M., Fri.–Sat. 7 A.M.–7 P.M.), where baker Joel Chenet once served as head chef for the president of France! When you sample the chocolate éclairs you'll know why; I've never tasted better anywhere. Delectable pastries and cakes fill the cases, but the café also serves waffles and light breakfasts, quiche, French onion soup, salads, sandwiches, and a locally famous Kodiak salmon burger. The shop is out near

Fort Abercrombie, making this a fine lunch stop. Most lunch items are around $11, with breakfast waffles for $6 and up. There is free Wi-Fi too.

All-American

Locals looking for the best burgers and other dense American grub head to **King's Diner** (1941 Mill Bay Rd., beside Lilly Lake, 907/486-4100, Sun. 6:30 A.M.–3 P.M., Mon.–Sat. 5:30 A.M.–3 P.M.). It's open for breakfast and lunch daily, with lots of food for the money: $7 for biscuits, gravy, eggs, and hash browns. King's is noisy, family-friendly, and recommended.

Get good pub grub at **Henry's Great Alaskan Restaurant** (512 Marine Way, 907/486-8844, www.henryskodiak.com, dinner entrées $16–30), where the menu covers the spectrum of pasta, burgers, seafood, and fish-and-chips, along with nightly specials—including a Wednesday crawfish pie. This lively no-smoking sports bar is right downtown across from the harbor.

Subway (326 Center St., 907/486-7676) is open until 11 P.M. in the summer, and the downtown McDonald's has an indoor playground for kids in need of a rainy-day break.

Big Al's Pizzeria (2161 Mill Bay Rd., 907/486-0044), inside Cost-Savers, makes the best local pizzas, and also sells them by the slice.

International

El Chicano (103 Center St., 907/486-6116, Sun. 4:30–9 P.M., Mon.–Fri. 11 A.M.–9:30 P.M., Sat. noon–9:30 P.M., $11–20) serves Mexican food in a party atmosphere, with chiles rellenos, homemade tamales, *chorizo con huevos,* and even a little *menudo* for your hangover. But you might as well start another one; their margaritas go down easy, and the bar stays open late. For the fast version, look for **Martha's Place** (907/496-0752), a taco truck that can be spotted in various parts of town. This is authentic and tasty.

Several places serve Chinese meals, including **Kodiak Mongolian Barbecue** (1247 Mill Bay Rd., 907/486-2900), an all-you-can-stuff-in place where the chef cooks your spicy meal while you watch.

2nd Floor Restaurant (116 W. Rezanof Dr., 907/486-8555) serves good—but expensive—Japanese food, including tempura and sushi.

Fine Dining

Just up the street from the ferry terminal, **The Old Power House Restaurant** (516 E. Marine Way, 907/481-1088, Sun. 5–9 P.M., Tues.–Sat. 11:30 A.M.–2 P.M. and 5–9 P.M., closed Mon., dinner entrées $18–25) is Kodiak's classiest restaurant. Seafood and steaks occupy important places on the menu, but sushi and sashimi are the real standouts, especially the spicy tuna rolls.

Operated by chef–master gardener–author Marion Owen and her harbormaster husband Marty Owen, **Galley Gourmet** (907/486-5079 or 800/253-6331, www.galleygourmet.biz, $135 pp) is the perfect way to spend a relaxing evening. Three-hour cruises take place onboard their immaculate 42-foot motor yacht, with time to watch for sea lions, otters, puffins, and whales. The boat anchors in a quiet bay off Long Island for a sit-down meal of creative appetizers, seafood entrées, organic salads, and desserts. Various other custom trips are also available, including all-day hiking adventures, photo trips, or whale-watching. The Owens also own Cliff House B&B.

Groceries and Brews

Many visitors to Kodiak buy their groceries at the downtown **Alaska Food for Less** (111 W. Rezanof Dr., 907/486-5761), but the best selections are at **Safeway** (2 miles out on Mill Bay Rd., 907/486-6811) or **WalMart** (3 miles out on Mill Bay Rd., 907/486-1670).

Island Seafoods (330 Shelikof Ave., 907/486-8575 or 888/355-8575, www.islandseafoods.com), next to the harbor, has a retail shop with salmon, scallops, halibut, shrimp, and king crab; they will process and ship your sport-caught fish.

Kodiak Island Brewing Co. (338

Shelikof Ave., 907/486-2537, www.kodiakbrewery.com, daily 2–7 P.M.) is opposite the harbor. Owner-brewer Ben Millstein typically has a half-dozen brews, most notably Wing-Nut Brown Ale and Liquid Sunshine Pale Ale. They're available to go in growlers and pigs.

Alaskan Wilderness Wines (907/486-1420, www.alaskawildwine.com) is based in the little settlement of Port Lions, and their wines are available in local shops.

SHOPPING AND SERVICES

Budget shoppers head to Kodiak's **Wal-Mart** (907/486-1670); it's three miles north of town on Mill Bay Road.

The too-small **library** (319 Lower Mill Bay Rd., 907/486-8680, www.city.kodiak.ak.us) downtown has books on Alaskan history, plus computers for surfing the Web.

The Next Page (3833 E. Rezanof Dr., 907/481-7243) has a good selection of works by local artisans. Mill Bay Coffee & Pastry is adjacent. Also check out **The Treasury** (104 Center St., 907/486-0373) for gifts and Internet access, and **Northern Exposure Gallery** (1314 Mill Bay Rd., 907/486-4956, www.northernexposuregallery.com) for prints.

For an indoor shower, head straight to **Dillard's Stop or Drop Laundromat** (907/486-2345), across the street from the Small Boat Harbor on Shelikof Street.

Providence Kodiak Island Medical Center (1915 E. Rezanof Dr., 907/486-3281, www.providence.org/alaska/kodiak) is the local hospital.

GETTING THERE

On the Water

If you have time and want to save a bundle on transportation, catch the **Alaska Marine Highway**'s (800/642-0066, www.dot.state.ak.us/amhs) trusty *Tustumena* in Homer, arriving in Kodiak 12 hours later (some runs include a stop in Port Lions). This is a great relaxing way to reach Kodiak, but take seasickness pills upon boarding—you'll need them. A Fish and Wildlife Service naturalist is onboard to help identify whales and birds along the way, especially around the Barren Islands. Twice a month in the summer the *"Tusty"* also heads west out along the Aleutians all the way to Dutch Harbor. The downtown Kodiak ferry terminal (907/486-3800) is open Monday–Friday 8 A.M.–5 P.M.

Air

Era Aviation (907/266-8394 or 800/866-8394, www.frontierak.com) and **Alaska Airlines** (800/426-0333, www.alaskaair.com) both have daily flights from Anchorage. If you're a little short on time and don't want to ride the ferry, this is the way to experience Kodiak. (This assumes, of course, that the plane can land. It isn't uncommon to have flights unable to land for days.) On the way down, if you're very lucky and it's clear, sit on the right side of the plane for a view of Mounts McKinley and Foraker, down to Mounts Spurr, Redoubt, Illiamna, and even Augustine—nearly 500 miles of spectacular peaks with just a slight twist of your head. You'll also see enormous swaths of clear-cut Native Alaskan land on Afognak Island. On the way back, also sit on the right to see the vast Harding Icefield and Kenai Mountains. The airport is five miles from Kodiak town; a cab ride there costs $20.

Air Taxis

A number of companies offer flightseeing and floatplane flights to various parts of Kodiak from the dock on Near Island (across the bridge). They include **Sea Hawk Air** (907/486-8282 or 800/770-4295, www.seahawkair.com), **Island Air** (907/487-4596 or 800/478-6196, www.kodiakislandair.com), **Andrew Airways** (907/487-2566, www.andrewairways.com), **Harvey Flying Service** (907/487-2621, www.harveyflyingservice.com), and **Kingfisher Aviation** (907/486-5155 or 866/486-5155, www.kingfisheraviation.com). Harvey Flying Service uses a classic Grumman Widgeon built in 1943—one of the few still flying in Alaska. If you want to fly with one of the finest pilots in Alaska, ask for Rolan Ruoss at Sea Hawk Air. Most air taxis offer **bear-viewing** flights around Kodiak or to the Alaska Peninsula.

Operating from the airport, **Servant Air** (907/487-4444 or 866/487-9001, www.servantair.com) provides daily wheeled-plane flights to Old Harbor, Ouzinkie, Port Lions, Karluk, Larson Bay, and Akhiok. Island Air has scheduled floatplane service to the same villages.

GETTING AROUND

Car Rentals and Taxis

Avis (907/487-2264 or 800/331-1212) and **Budget** (907/487-2220 or 800/527-0700) both have cars at the airport. The Budget folks also run **Rent-A-Heap** (907/486-8550), located downtown, where rates are $37 per day plus 37 cents per mile—good for short jaunts, but not if you really plan to explore Kodiak's wonderful back roads. **A&B Taxicabs** (907/486-4343) charges $12 north to Fort Abercrombie or $20 south to the airport.

KODIAK NATIONAL WILDLIFE REFUGE

Established in 1941 to preserve brown bear habitat on Kodiak, this 1.9-million-acre refuge covers the southwestern two-thirds of the island, along with Uganik Island, Ban Island, and a small portion of Afognak Island. The fascinating **Kodiak National Wildlife Refuge Visitors Center** (420 Center St., 907/487-2626 or 888/592-6940, www.kodiakwildliferefuge.org) is downtown.

Kodiak National Wildlife Refuge itself begins 25 miles southwest of the headquarters and is accessible only by floatplane (unless you have a boat or are willing to do some Olympic-class hiking). Most visitors to the refuge fly to one of the lakes and camp or stay in a Fish and Wildlife Service cabin. Many others stay at one of the expensive wilderness fishing lodges around the island.

Kodiak Brown Bears

Kodiak is world-renowned for its enormous brown bears. The largest reach 10 feet tall when standing and approach 1,500 pounds, and most adult males (boars) average 800 pounds, with adult females (sows) averaging 550 pounds. Of the 10 largest brown bears ever killed, eight were taken on Kodiak Island. There are some 2,500 bears on the island, or an average of 1 for every 1.5 square miles. Visitors often come to watch or photograph these magnificent animals. Unfortunately, quite a few hunters come to kill them as well. Anyone who has spent time around Kodiak bears quickly gains an appreciation for their beauty and a respect for their intelligence. Hunting for food is justifiable; how someone could kill such an animal just to mount it as a trophy—often in a ludicrously menacing position—is beyond me.

Assuming that you're on Kodiak to see, rather than kill, the bears, several local air-taxi operators will fly you on 4–5-hour bear-viewing trips. The price varies depending on the number of passengers, from around $500–600 per person with a two-person minimum. This includes at least an hour on the ground watching the bears. Depending on the weather and what the bears are doing, these floatplanes land either within Kodiak National Wildlife Refuge (the Frazer Lake fishpass is a popular destination) or to the west on the coast of Katmai National Park and Preserve. The companies include my favorite by far **Sea Hawk Air** (907/486-8282 or 800/770-4295, www.seahawkair.com), along with **Andrew Airways** (907/487-2566, www.andrewairways.com) and **Kingfisher Aviation** (907/486-5155 or 866/486-5155, www.kingfisheraviation.com).

Kodiak Island lodges specializing in bear-viewing include **Kodiak Treks** (907/487-2122, www.kodiaktreks.com), **Munsey's Bear Camp** (907/847-2203, www.munseysbearcamp.com), **Rohrer Bear Camp** (907/486-5835, www.kodiakbearcamp.com), and **Zachar Bay Lodge** (907/486-4120 or 800/693-2333, www.zacharbay.com).

These bear-viewing flights and lodges are not, of course, the only way to see brown bears. They are present along all of Kodiak's salmon streams in midsummer (the best time is July), especially where there are major runs of sockeye or king salmon. Ask at the visitors center for your best viewing opportunities. In late summer the bears tend to move up to the smaller spawning streams and into berry patches where

© DON PITCHER
Kodiak brown bears

they are less visible. You aren't likely to see a brown bear from the Kodiak road system; most of those bears were shot long ago, and the rest tend to stay out of sight during the day.

Hiking

The vast Kodiak National Wildlife Refuge is undeveloped country with few trails (other than those created by bears and deer). Despite this, backcountry hiking can be relatively easy since there are almost no trees on the southern three-fourths of the island. The best time is early in summer after the snow is gone and before the grass and brush get too dense; by mid-August hiking can be a real struggle. Besides, it's a bit more risky crawling through bear country when the willow thickets are too dense to see the bears! Be sure to make noise while hiking to alert bears to your presence. Once you get above the brush line (approximately 2,000 feet in elevation) the hiking gets very easy even in late summer. Much of Kodiak Island is marshy, so rubber boots are strongly advised.

Floating Karluk River

The Karluk and Ayakulik Rivers are world-famous for their king, sockeye, and silver salmon runs, but they also have impressive runs of pink and chum salmon, along with Dolly Varden, steelhead, and rainbow trout. At the turn of the century—before seven local canneries wiped the salmon out and then went out of business—the Karluk River had runs of up to 10 million red salmon. It has taken decades of careful Fish and Game management for the populations to recover, and today this is some of the finest fishing anywhere on the planet.

The most popular time to float the 25-mile-long Karluk River is at the peak of the king salmon run in July. Kodiak air taxis can drop you off either at the Karluk Lake outlet or Portage, halfway downriver. Most of these companies also rent rafts. A free **public-use permit** from the Fish and Wildlife Service (907/487-2600 or 888/408-3514, http://kodiak.fws.gov) is required for the Karluk River, and just 28 permits are allowed per day during the king salmon season (June 10–July 15).

Because of their popularity, these are distributed on a lottery system.

The Karluk River enters the waters of Shelikof Straits near the tiny village of **Karluk** (pop. 30), where you'll find a picturesque old Russian Orthodox church, built in 1888, along with a pretty cliff-and-ocean backdrop. There is also a small store and a couple of fishing lodges. Daily plane service takes you back to Kodiak.

Cabins

The wildlife refuge maintains rustic public-use cabins (www.recreation.gov, $45) at seven different locations around Kodiak and Afognak islands. These provide a wonderful way to see the wilderness up-close and personal. You will need to bring fuel oil for the heater, plus all the standard camping supplies. And don't forget insect repellent and head nets for the abundant and pesky no-see-ums. Because of their popularity, mail-in lotteries are held for the cabins on the first days of January, April, July, and October. Apply before January for the months of April–June and before April for the months of July–September. The most popular time is July. Because of cancellations, the cabins sometimes become open; call the refuge at 907/487-2600 or 888/408-3514 if you decide to go at the last minute.

Anyone interested in bear-viewing may want to check out the cabins at **South Frazer Lake** or **Uganik Lake.** It's very helpful to have an inflatable boat or folding kayak to get around these lakes; air-taxi operators have them for rent. It is also possible to camp out anywhere on the refuge without a permit. The abundance of both bears and rain can make this a less enjoyable experience, but experienced backcountry travelers will enjoy the chance to savor an untouched landscape.

Alaska Peninsula

LAKE CLARK NATIONAL PARK

This 3.6 million-acre national park reaches from the western shore of Cook Inlet and across the Chigmit Mountains to enclose 50-mile-long Lake Clark. The park was established in 1980. Although there are a few lodges and cabins, the only developed site within the park is **Port Alsworth** (pop. 60) on the east side Lake Clark. Despite its name, Port Alsworth is not a port, since the ocean is 50 miles away.

Because of the park's ocean-to-mountaintop coverage, it includes a diversity of ecosystems, from dense spruce forests along the coast to active volcanoes (Iliamna and Redoubt). The western flank of the Chigmit Mountains is covered with tundra and boreal forests. Just south of the park is huge Iliamna Lake, Alaska's largest. The settlement of **Iliamna** (pop. 100) sits on the shore of this lake and has a store selling limited supplies.

Once you get away from the scattering of lodges, Lake Clark National Park is a vast, undeveloped wilderness without roads, trails, or other facilities. Those not staying in the lodges come here to boat and fish on the lake, or to backpack in the mountains. The western foothills have open dry tundra that's perfect for hiking. Floating down the various rivers that lead westward from the park is another popular activity. Wildlife viewing can be impressive, since you can find caribou, moose, wolves, brown and black bears, and Dall sheep, among other mammals.

Practicalities

Lake Clark National Park headquarters is in Anchorage (907/644-3626, www.nps.gov/lacl). The **Port Alsworth Visitor Center** (907/781-2106, Mon.–Fri. 8 A.M.–5 P.M. year-round, also Sat. in summer) offers short hikes, slide shows, and videos. There are no stores in Port Alsworth, but local lodges rent boats. There's a pretty waterfall on the Tanalian River near town.

Expensive accommodations and bear-viewing are available from more than a dozen fishing lodges on Lake Clark or within the park boundaries along Cook Inlet. These include **Silver Salmon Creek Lodge** (907/252-5504 or 888/872-5666, www.silversalmoncreek.com), **Homestead Lodge** (907/262-1960 or 888/677-9383, www.alaskawildlife.com), **Redoubt Bay Lodge** (907/274-2710, www.withinthewild.com), and **The Farm Lodge** (907/781-2208 or 888/440-2281, www.thefarmlodge.com).

Located along Cook Inlet and surrounded by the park, **Lake Clark Bear Camp** (800/544-2261, www.greatalaska.com) is a unique operation with a comfortable cabin-like WeatherPort base camp and lots of nearby bear activity. Guests come on quick day-trips ($550) or multiple-night stays ($1,095 pp for one night, 2 days) from Anchorage.

Lake Clark Air (907/278-2054 or 888/440-2281, www.lakeclarkair.com) has daily service between Anchorage and Port Alsworth, plus flightseeing trips. Several Kenai and Homer air taxis fly to the Lake Clark shoreline for bear-viewing; contact the Park Service for specifics.

KATMAI NATIONAL PARK

Katmai National Park occupies a large chunk of the northern Alaska Peninsula, over 4 million acres (roughly the size of Connecticut and Rhode Island) just northwest of Kodiak Island across Shelikof Strait. Several features attract visitors to Katmai: its wild volcanic landscape, outstanding salmon fishing in a world-class setting, and the opportunity to see brown bears up close. The bears are the big attraction nowadays; they're big, they're bad, and they're ubiquitous, thanks to the 1 million or so salmon that run up the Naknek River drainage system from Bristol Bay each year. Dozens of other mammal, bird, and fish species thrive in the park.

The primary starting point for trips into Katmai is the town of King Salmon, which is accessible by jet from Anchorage. From King Salmon, most visitors fly into Naknek Lake to either stay at Brooks Lodge or camp at the nearby park campground. The Valley of Ten Thousand Smokes is accessible by a park bus from Brooks Lodge.

brown bear chasing salmon in Katmai National Park

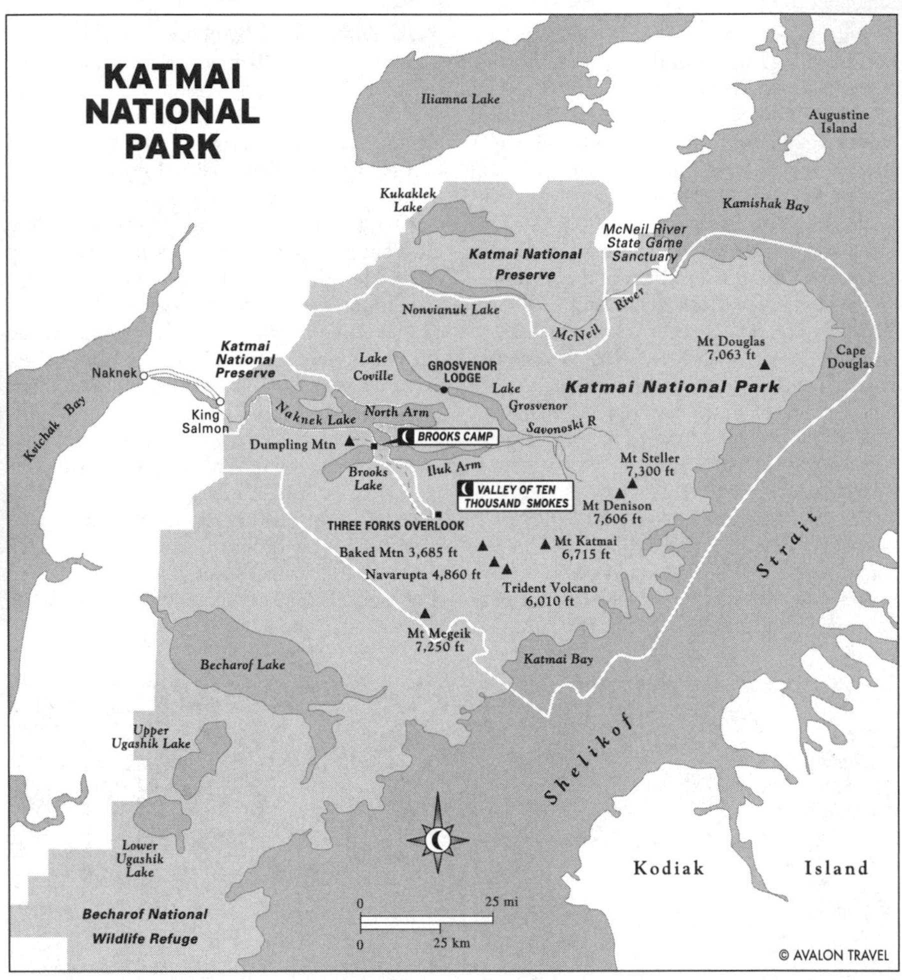

Novarupta Erupts

In June 1912, one of the great cataclysms of modern history took place here as Mt. Novarupta blew its top, violently spewing volcanic glass, ash, and sulfurous fumes for three days. One of the explosions was heard in Ketchikan, 860 miles away. The fallout choked Kodiak, whose 450 inhabitants were evacuated in a daring marine rescue, but nobody is known to have been killed. Hot ash and pumice piled up 700 feet deep over a 40-square-mile area, and acid rain destroyed clothing hanging on clotheslines in Vancouver, B.C. Massive amounts of dust cloaked the vicinity in pitch darkness for 60 hours and circulated in the upper atmosphere for two years, changing weather patterns worldwide. Scientists say this was the second largest blast in recorded history, exceeded only by the eruption of Greece's Santorini in 1650 B.C. By way of comparison, the 1883 eruption of Krakatoa in Indonesia was only half as large (though it killed 35,000 people).

It's been almost a century since the "Noveruption," but volcanologists are still studying this unique phenomenon—a young intact volcano created by a single event—to determine the hazards from future eruptions. Novarupta, however, is only one of 15 active volcanoes monitored within Katmai National Park. The last to spew was Trident Volcano in 1968, but steam plumes occasionally rise from Megeik and Martin Volcanoes as well.

Information and Services

The helpful **King Salmon Visitors Center** (907/246-4250, daily 8 A.M.–5 P.M. June–Sept., Mon.–Sat. 8 A.M.–5 P.M. Oct.–May) is at King Salmon airport. Stop here for details on Katmai National Park, Aniakchak National Monument, Alaska Peninsula National Wildlife Refuge, and Bacherof National Wildlife Refuge. There's a big selection of books and cards too. Need cash? The Wells Fargo in King Salmon has an ATM.

The Park Service's **Brooks Camp Visitors Center** inside the park is open daily June–mid-September. All visitors must check in here on arrival to watch a video about bear safety and to get a park orientation. Rangers lead free afternoon **cultural and nature walks,** evening slide shows at Brooks Camp daily throughout the summer, and guided hikes up Dumpling Mountain. Check the bulletin boards at the visitors center, campground, and lodge for today's events.

For more on Katmai, contact the National Park Service in King Salmon (907/246-3305, www.nps.gov/katm). You can also pick up a map of the park and a copy of the informative park paper, ***The Novarupta,*** at the Alaska Public Lands Information Center in Anchorage (605 W. 4th Ave., 907/271-2737 or 866/869-6887, www.alaskacenters.gov).

Valley of Ten Thousand Smokes

Robert Griggs, a botanist sent by the National Geographic Society, discovered in 1916 the nearby Valley of Ten Thousand Smokes, where hot gases surfaced through tens of thousands of holes and cracks when the hot ash contacted buried rivers and springs. He reported, "The whole valley as far as the eye could reach was full of hundreds, no thousands—literally, tens of thousands—of smokes curling up from its fissured floor." The area has gradually cooled, and only a few small fumaroles remain today. A national monument was created here in 1918; it has since been expanded five times to encompass the large brown bear and salmon habitat. In 1980, under the Alaska National Interest Lands Conservation Act (ANILCA), it was declared a national park.

Be sure to take the guided, eight-hour, 46-mile (round-trip) bus tour from Brooks Camp to a viewpoint over the Valley of Ten Thousand Smokes. From Three Forks Overlook, you can join a three-mile hike (round-trip) to the valley floor and back. The bus leaves Brooks Lodge daily at 9 A.M. June–mid-September and costs $96 round-trip, including a sack lunch. Take warm clothing and rain gear, along with your binoculars and camera. Advance reservations for the bus are strongly recommended in July–August; contact Katmailand (907/243-5448 or 800/544-0551, www.katmailand.com) a few days in advance of your trip.

Hikers use this bus to access the valley, catching a later bus for the return trip ($51 each way). Two of the most popular hiking destinations are **Megeik Lake** (15 miles away) and **Baked Mountain** (12 miles away). There are no trails across the valley, and the rivers make for hazardous crossings, but the barren country is relatively easy to hike through. A U.S. Geological Survey research cabin at Baked Mountain offers protection from the sometimes harrowing wind conditions that can create fierce dust storms, but check at the visitors center to be sure it is available. Bring ski goggles for your eyes and a bandanna to protect your mouth and nose from the flying ash. Don't let this dissuade you from hiking here, however. This is spectacular country, with a lunar landscape cut through by deep and colorful canyons. Before heading out, stop by the Park Service visitors center in Brooks Camp for a map, a backcountry permit, and more information. Jean Bodeau's *Katmai National Park and Preserve* (available at the visitors centers) provides detailed hiking information.

If you can get a bike to Brooks Camp, the 23-mile dirt road to the Valley of Ten Thousand Smokes is a fine place to cycle; the views get more dramatic as you go. **Lifetime Adventures** (907/746-4644 or 800/952-8624, www.lifetimeadventures.net) guides seven-day hike-bike-kayak trips in the park for $4,600 for two people.

Brooks Camp

Katmai has gained worldwide fame for its brown bears, and it is one of the few places where large numbers of visitors can see wild bears throughout the summer. Bear activity centers on the Brooks River, which flows into Naknek Lake just a half-mile from the campground. A floating bridge crosses the river to an elevated viewing platform where you can watch the bears. Rangers close bridge access when bears are near (and this is frequent), so it's easy to get stuck on one side of the bridge for hours at a time. If you're visiting on a day trip, be sure to get back across the bridge well before your departure flight.

It's an easy 1.2-mile hike beyond the bridge to **Brooks Falls,** where all those famous bear-with-jumping-salmon photos are taken. The last portion of the trail is on an elevated footbridge that leads to a big covered area with displays on bears and salmon. Two footbridges continue beyond this, one to the lower riffles for a good perspective across the area, and the second to a small viewing platform that gets crowded during the peak of the season (July). You may need to wait a bit to access the latter platform. It is OK to go off the platforms, but you may encounter bears in the tall grass and thick brush.

Brooks River is open to sportfishing—mainly for sockeye salmon—and is often lined with anglers in mid-summer. When bears wander by, and this is often, anglers are required to release any fish immediately. Park rangers

brown bear cubs at Brooks Camp

will even cut your line if you don't act quickly enough. Unfortunately, some bears are starting to equate anglers with free fish; sometimes the park has been forced to close the river to fishing to keep the bears from becoming more aggressive toward humans.

The **Dumpling Mountain Trail** leaves from Brooks Camp and climbs four miles to the top of this 2,440-foot peak. You'll discover outstanding panoramic vistas from the summit across the surrounding lake-filled, volcano-crowned country.

Coastal Bear-Viewing

Bear-viewing is becoming increasingly popular on the eastern side of Katmai along Shelikof Strait, where brown bears dig for clams, eat grass and sedges, catch salmon, and scavenge for carcasses that wash ashore. A number of air-taxi operators out of Homer, Kodiak, Soldotna, and Anchorage take clients on day trips ($550–625 pp). Note that many of these fly-in trips have big groups, and a number of planes can be in one area at once, reducing your wilderness experience. In addition, the day trips are literally that, while bears are generally more active in the early morning or late in the day, when most bear-viewing flights have already headed back home. Although they primarily go to coastal Katmai, the companies sometimes fly to Brooks Camp late in the season.

Hallo Bay Bear Lodge (907/235-2237, www.hallobay.com, late May–early Oct.) is a unique wilderness camp on a wild and beautiful stretch of the Katmai coast. Access is by air from Homer, a one-hour flight with a beach landing. The camp is entirely surrounded by national park land and includes a half-dozen cabin-like structures (WeatherPorts) with a central building for dining and relaxing. Experienced bear guides lead hikes to viewing areas around the camp with a maximum of five guests per guide. Extended backpacking trips and professional photography workshops are also offered. Meals are filling and delicious, and other amenities include hot showers, heated cabins, satellite phones, and wind-powered electricity. You might even see a wolf or two close to camp. An all-inclusive three-day, two-night trip is $1,200 per person, and a five-day trip costs $3,000. Bear-viewing day trips from Homer cost $550 for five hours. Hallo Bay is highly recommended.

Located on a private inholding on Kukak Bay, **Katmai Wilderness Lodge** (907/486-8767 or 800/488-8767, www.katmai-wilderness.com) is a modern log cabin–style lodge on Kukak Bay. The rooms have private baths and hot showers. Guests come here to fish, hike, or watch bears. It's a beautiful spot, but the weather can make it difficult for flights to get in or out. A variety of package trips are offered, starting at three nights for $3,000 d; this includes floatplane travel from Kodiak, lodging, guided bear-viewing, home-style meals, kayaking, and fishing.

Katmai Coastal Bear Tours (907/235-8337 or 800/532-8338, www.katmaibears.com) operates from two boats, the 73-foot wooden tug *The Waters* and the 100-foot *Kittiwake*. The boats serve as floating lodges for photographers, cinematographers, and others who use skiffs to go ashore along the Katmai coast. Meals are great, and the guides are highly knowledgeable naturalists. The boats go where the bears are, providing a mobility lacking in shore-based operations. Most visitors choose a four-day, three-night package for $3,750 per person, including access by floatplane from Kodiak. Skipper-owner John Waters is a respected advocate for bear conservation; the IMAX film *Bears* and many others were filmed from his boats.

Many companies offer bear-viewing day trips ($550–625 pp) to the Katmai coast from Homer, Kodiak, or Anchorage.

Recreation

Savonoski Loop is a favorite backcountry canoe or kayak trip. Boaters start in Brooks Camp, head up the north arm of Naknek Lake, portage a mile to Lake Grosvenor, float down the Grosvenor and Savonoski Rivers, and paddle across the Iluk Arm of Naknek Lake back to Brooks Camp. Be ready for a 4–10-day trip, and be sure to talk with Park Service rangers for precautions and backcountry permits before

McNEIL RIVER STATE GAME SANCTUARY

Wedged above the northeast corner of Katmai and 100 air miles west of Homer, this state sanctuary is where many of the famous photographs of brown bears were taken. At the peak of the season (late July-early Aug.), visitors may see 40 or more bruins as they catch chum salmon at McNeil River falls. More brown bears congregate here than in any other single site on earth; up to 130 have been counted in a single day. The sanctuary is managed by the Alaska Department of Fish and Game (ADFG), which allows only 10 people per day into the viewing area. Because of all these bears, the department has stringent rules, and visitors must remain within small viewing areas throughout the 6-8 hour day. A permit and user fees are required of all visitors.

National Geographic photographer Cecil Rhode first published frames of McNeil River – without identifying it – in 1954, after which the federal government closed the area to hunters. It became a state game sanctuary in 1967, and the limited permit system was installed in 1973. In 1979 the river was completely closed to sportfishing. Since ADFG instituted these restrictive usage policies, there have been no casualties to either humans or bears. This is particularly amazing given how close the bears often come.

GETTING IN

Each year more than 2,500 people apply to visit McNeil River and nearby Mikfik Creek; only 250 or so permits are granted (including standby permits). **Nontransferable permits** are required for all visitors June 7-August 25. Only 10 of these are available per day, and a $25 per person nonrefundable application fee is required. The ADFG (907/267-2182, www.wildlife.alaska.gov) can provide you with details and an application. Forms must be postmarked or emailed no later than March 1. The best time to find bears at McNeil is mid-July-early August, when the chum salmon are running, but it's also the time that most people apply to visit. Second choice is as close to peak as possible on the earlier side; later the excitement tapers off.

Because of McNeil's immense popularity, a lottery system is used to decide who gets the available time slots. Winners are given a four-day period at McNeil, and in addition to the application fee they pay $350 per person ($150 for Alaskan residents) to visit the sanctuary. As a backup, many people also apply for a **standby permit** to get into McNeil in case they're not among the lucky applicants for the regular permits. Only three of these are available each day. A separate standby lottery is held, and those chosen pay $175 ($75 for Alaskan residents) and wait for slots to open up when regular per-

heading out. Canoes and kayaks can be rented from Brooks Lake Lodge.

Lifetime Adventures (907/746-4644 or 800/952-8624, www.lifetimeadventures.net) sets up do-it-yourself folding kayak trips around the Savonoski Loop; for $1,900 d, you get airfare from Anchorage to King Salmon, charter flights to and from the park, and folding kayaks. They can also provide camping equipment or food for an extra charge, and offer guided kayak trips on the Savonoski Loop (7 days for $4,600 d). Folding mountain bikes—great for a ride back from Valley of Ten Thousand Smokes—are also available.

Several companies offer guided sportfishing, boat tours, and skiff rentals on Naknek Lake; see the King Salmon Visitors Center (907/246-4250) for details.

Park Accommodations

If you want to stay the night at famous **Brooks Lodge** (907/243-5448 or 800/544-0551, www.katmailand.com, June–late Sept.), be prepared to shell out wads of cash. During the peak season (June 20–Aug. 10), a package trip that includes round-trip airfare from Anchorage to Brooks Lodge and one night's lodging (far too brief) costs $1,860 d, and a two-night package is $2,500 d. Stuff-yourself buffet meals are extra. If you're willing to arrive

mit holders decide to stay in camp rather than going out that day (typically when the weather is bad). People who visit on a standby basis usually get to spend at least one day at the falls, but bears are also visible around the campground and along the nearby beach.

SEEING THE BEARS

People come from around the world to see and photograph bears within McNeil River State Game Sanctuary. Visitors actually have the chance to view bears at two seasonal locations. In June, several dozen bears (primarily females with cubs) can be found feeding on a small run of sockeye salmon in **Mikfik Creek.** This area provides a great opportunity to see bears in a lush and intimate setting – they're all around you. Also, the weather is generally better than later in the summer.

The big show takes place on the nearby **McNeil River** early July–mid-August, when a major run of chum salmon heads up this much larger river. The activity peaks around July 15, when dozens of bears, including many large males, come to a low waterfall – McNeil Falls – where the fish are easier to catch. Visitors have opportunities to see and photograph bears 75–200 feet away, though the bears may occasionally come within 30 feet. Be sure to bring plenty of digital storage cards and batteries! A note to professional photographers: Because so many people have photographed bears at McNeil for so long, the market for bear pics from here is flooded. Try somewhere else if you want a shot that stands out from the crowd.

PRACTICALITIES

Visitors to McNeil overnight in a camping area and hike two miles to the viewing areas overlooking McNeil Falls (in June they head to areas along Mikfik Creek, where you're more likely to see females with cubs than at McNeil). The campground has a cabin for food storage and cooking, a sauna, outhouses, and staff cabins, but no other developments or services.

ADFG employees carry shotguns and stay with the visitors at all times when they are away from the campground. Visitors need to be in good physical condition for the hike to the falls, and if the weather is bad (a common situation) it's easy to get cold while sitting for hours in the rain and wind. Hip boots are essential, along with heavy-duty rain gear, wind-resistant clothes, and gloves. People typically remain at McNeil Falls for a 6–8 hour period.

Quite a few air taxis provide transport to McNeil from Homer (the primary departure point), King Salmon, Kodiak, or Anchorage.

sometime other than July, your overall cost will be somewhat lower. Brooks Lodge fills up quickly, so *make reservations a full year ahead* to be assured of a place in July.

A tiny gift shop at the lodge sells snacks, T-shirts, hats, and tourist trinkets, and rents canoes, kayaks, fishing poles, hip waders, and even bear-resistant containers. Two other fishing lodges are on other lakes within the park. They're even more expensive than Brooks Lodge but are far from the hubbub. With space for just six people, **Grosvenor Lodge** charges $5,250 d for three nights' lodging, meals, a fishing guide, and airfare; **Kulik Lodge** charges $5,450 d for the same. Brooks, Kulik, and Grosvenor lodges are all owned by Katmailand (907/243-5448 or 800/544-0551, www.katmailand.com). Note that the three lodges, along with services such as the bus tours, operate only June–late September. Before or after that, you're on your own.

King Salmon Accommodations

The town of King Salmon is the main gateway to Katmai National Park. Travelers who are unable to get a lodge or campground space at Brooks Camp often stay here and make day trips by floatplane into the park. The village of Naknek, 15 miles west of King Salmon by road, is an important commercial fishing port.

Both towns have food and lodging, and taxi service connects the two. The towns represent an odd clash between the upscale tourists out to see Katmai bears and grubby commercial fishers out to make a buck (or several thousand bucks). Add a 10 percent lodging tax to the rates quoted.

Several places in King Salmon offer lodging, including **King Ko Inn** (907/246-3377 or 866/234-3474, www.kingko.com, summer only, $195 s, $215 d) with comfortable modern cabins (some with kitchenettes). **Antlers Inn** (907/246-8525 or 888/735-8525) has two guest rooms for $170 s or $190 d, and five suites with full kitchens for $240 s or $260 d. The in-town location can be a bit noisy, but it's open all year.

A mile out of town is **King Salmon Inn** (907/246-3444, www.kingsalmoninn.com, $155 s, $210 d). The guest rooms are simple but clean and have two twin beds; rates include transport from King Salmon. Most clients are fishers who get multiple-night packages that include a room, meals, and a boat rental.

Visit www.southwestalaska.com for links to a multitude of fishing lodges in the region, including two near King Salmon: **Bear Trail Lodge** (907/246-2327, www.beartraillodge.com) and **Rainbow Bend Charter Adventures** (907/246-3750 or 888/575-4249, www.bristolbayfishing.com).

Camping

A short distance from the Brooks Lodge, the 60-person campground at **Brooks Camp** (June–mid-Sept., $8 pp) has potable water. It's extremely popular, and the spaces fill fast. Reservations are required far ahead of your visit; reserve at 877/444-6777 or www.recreation.gov. The campground often gets booked for the month of July within a few hours of when reservations open in early January.

Leave your kitchen sink at home for this trip; you'll have to carry it 0.25 miles from the floatplane dock to the campground, and the bear-proof caches don't have room for a sink anyway. (The Park Service provides carts to make transportation easier.) This is the only developed campground in Katmai, and backcountry camping is not allowed within five miles of Brooks Camp, so don't come here without a reservation unless you're willing to hike. No-shows sometimes create openings at the campground even when it is officially full, but it's pretty risky to arrive in Brooks Camp without a place reserved. Campers can buy meals at Brooks Lodge or take showers there for $5. Katmai experiences weather similar to that of the rest of the Aleutian arc—cool, wet, and wildly windy; so come prepared to get wet.

Food

Brooks Lodge (907/243-5448 or 800/544-0551, www.katmailand.com, daily 7:30–8:30 A.M., 11:30 A.M.–1:30 P.M., 5:30–7:30 P.M. June–mid-Sept., breakfast $15, lunch $20, dinner $35) serves filling buffet meals and is open to both guests and the general public. The bar serves mixed drinks.

King Ko Inn (907/246-3377 or 866/234-3474, www.kingko.com, daily 7 A.M.–10 P.M. mid-Apr.–mid-Oct., entrées $15–35) in King Salmon has dependably good food three times a day in the summer, with fresh seafood, pizzas, burgers, steaks, pasta, and other faves. The big bar has live music some summer weekends.

Also in King Salmon, **Eddie's Fireplace Inn** (907/246-3435, daily 8 A.M.–9 P.M.) has lower prices and great burgers ($12) or steaks ($30). They're open for three meals a day year-round. Get groceries, sporting goods, and even espresso at **Alaska Commercial Company** (907/246-6109, www.alaskacommercial.com) in King Salmon.

Getting There

Getting to Katmai isn't cheap. First, fly from Anchorage to King Salmon on **Alaska Airlines** (800/426-0333, www.alaskaair.com) by jet or by turboprop on **PenAir** (907/246-3373 or 800/448-4226, www.penair.com). From King Salmon it will cost another $200 round-trip to get out to Brooks Camp. **Katmai Air**

(907/246-3079 or 800/544-0551, www.katmailand.com) has scheduled service. **Branch River Air Service** (907/248-3539, www.branchriverair.com) has daily flights, along with flightseeing and trips to nearby McNeil River. One warning: The weather in King Salmon is often bad, so flight cancellations are not uncommon, and it's easy to get stuck here.

ANIAKCHAK NATIONAL MONUMENT

This remote and rarely visited park covers over 600,000 acres approximately 400 miles southwest of Anchorage on the Alaska Peninsula. The park centers around the six-mile-wide **Aniakchak Caldera,** which last erupted in 1931. Located in the volcanically active Aleutian Range, the crater contains lava flows, cinder cones, and explosion pits. Dominating the crater is 3,350-foot-high Vent Mountain, with a volcanic cone that occasionally sends up plumes of smoke. On the northwest inner edge is a large eruption crater covered with patterned lava that presents an otherworldly appearance from the air. **Surprise Lake,** on the northeast side of the caldera, is the source of the Aniakchak River, which cascades through a 1,500-foot gorge cut in the caldera wall. The river is a wild white-water trip for the experienced.

Getting There

Aniakchak Monument is infamous for bad weather, and it's an expensive flight from Homer, King Salmon, or Kodiak (the closest towns of any size). There are no developed facilities, but floatplanes can land in Surprise Lake, and the northern portion of the park is smooth enough for wheeled landings. For additional information, contact the Aniakchak National Monument office in King Salmon (907/246-3305, www.nps.gov/ania).

NATIONAL WILDLIFE REFUGES

Much of the land on the lower Alaska Peninsula and out along the Aleutian Island chain lies within four national wildlife refuges. These are rarely visited by human travelers but provide vital habitat for many species of animals.

The **Alaska Maritime National Wildlife Refuge** covers 3.5 million acres, encompassing 2,500 islands that stretch from Forrester Island in southern Southeast Alaska all the way out the Aleutians as well as in scattered places up the mainland to Barrow. The refuge headquarters is in Homer (907/235-6961, http://alaskamaritime.fws.gov).

The **Alaska Peninsula National Wildlife Refuge** covers 3.5 million acres on the peninsula and includes a chain of volcanoes dominated by 8,400-foot Mt. Veniaminof. This massive volcano has a base almost 30 miles across, larger than any active volcano on record. The summit crater contains the most extensive crater glacier in North America. The refuge is based in King Salmon (907/246-3339, http://alaskapeninsula.fws.gov).

Also based in King Salmon is **Becharof National Wildlife Refuge** (907/246-3339, http://becharof.fws.gov), sandwiched between Katmai National Park and Preserve and Alaska Peninsula National Wildlife Refuge. The refuge is dominated by Becharof Lake, the second largest lake in Alaska. The lake is surrounded by low rolling hills, tundra wetlands, volcanic peaks, and to the east the 477,000 acre Becharof Wilderness. Some 10,000 caribou migrate through the refuge each spring and fall, and other wildlife—from seabirds to salmon—abound.

Izembek National Wildlife Refuge spans the tip of the Alaska Peninsula and protects the watershed of Izembek Lagoon, a State Game Refuge containing one of the largest eelgrass beds in the world. The state and federal refuges act as an international crossroads to many thousands of migrating waterfowl and shorebirds, including the world's entire population of Pacific brant and emperor geese. For migrating shorebirds, this is the last stop before their unbelievable flights over water to wintering areas as far away as South America, Polynesia, and New Zealand. The refuge is based in Cold Bay (907/532-2445, http://izembek.fws.gov).

The Aleutian Islands

From the tip of the Alaska Peninsula, an arc of 200 islands curves more than 1,000 miles southwest to Attu Island, separating the North Pacific Ocean from the Bering Sea. The Aleutian Islands are part of the circum-Pacific "Ring of Fire," one of the most geologically unsettled regions on earth. The titanic tectonic forces clash as the Pacific plate pushes under the North American plate at the deep Aleutian Trench, making the earth rumble, quake, and spew. Of the 79 named Aleutian Islands, only 8 are occupied by humans. The 14 large and 65 smaller islands (plus countless tiny islets) are all windswept northern Pacific outposts. The meeting of the mild Japanese Current with the icy Bering Sea causes a climate of much fog, rain, and wind, but little sun. Compounding this is a meteorological phenomenon known as the "Aleutian low," a low-pressure atmospheric valley that funnels a number of intense storms east into North America. In short, it's not the greatest place to get a tan.

High peaks drop abruptly to the sea. There is no permafrost, but the constant strong winds inhibit tree growth; only tundra and brushy vegetation survive. Frequent storms blow through (Unalaska experiences almost 250 rainy days per year), but because of the warm currents the sea never freezes. Given these harsh climatic conditions, it's perhaps surprising that, before the arrival of the Russians, every island was inhabited by Aleut peoples. On the other hand, given the bounty of the ocean, the Aleut were skillful hunters who lived in balance with the fish, marine mammals, and birds of their islands. The Russians enslaved and slaughtered the Aleut, and their numbers plummeted from around 25,000 in 1741 to 2,000 a century later. The Russians also hunted the sea otters and fur seals of the islands to near extinction, and the single-minded exploitation of the islands' resources continues even today. Get the latest on the status of sea lions at www.stellersealions.noaa.gov and on sea otters at www.ry.fws.gov/fisheries/mmm.

Getting There

PenAir (907/243-2323 or 800/448-4226, www.penair.com) provides daily nonstop flights connecting Anchorage with Aniak, Cold Bay, Dillingham, King Salmon, McGrath, Sand Point, Unalakleet, and Unalaska/Dutch Harbor, plus service several times a week to St. George and St. Paul Islands. The airline also has connecting flights to smaller villages, including Atka, Akutan, Chignik Lagoon, Cold Bay, Egegik, False Pass, King Cove, Nelson Lagoon, Nikolski, and Port Moller. (Alaska Airlines no longer flies its jets to Unalaska, but the PenAir flights may be labeled "Alaska Air" on your ticket.) Try to get a seat on the right side of the plane when you fly out of Anchorage; the flight passes near the dramatic volcanic summits of Mt. Iliamna and Mt. Redoubt.

The state ferry ***Tustumena*** (907/465-3941 or 800/642-0066, www.dot.state.ak.us/amhs) heads out twice a month (Apr.–Oct.) to Dutch Harbor by way of Homer, Kodiak, Chignik, Sand Point, King Cove, Cold Bay, and Akutan. The trip takes 3.5 days one-way and can be very rough, so bring lots of Dramamine and an iron stomach.

HISTORY

The Japanese Challenge

During the spring of 1942, Japan was sweeping triumphantly across the Pacific to the gates of Australia and Hawaii. However, the strength of the U.S. aircraft carriers—none of which had been lost at Pearl Harbor—worried Fleet Admiral Isoroku Yamamoto, commander in chief of the Japanese navy. He knew that time was on the side of the United States. To win, he would have to draw the American carriers into a great naval battle where his superior forces could crush them and end the war. His target was Midway, a tiny island west of the Hawaiian chain, where the United States had recently built a base. But to first split the American forces, Yamamoto ordered a diversionary thrust at the Aleutians. In June 1942, Japanese carrier-based planes struck twice at Dutch Harbor, a large new U.S. naval base in Unalaska Bay, but inflicted only slight damage; the base continued to function. Meanwhile, at Midway, the United States had broken the Japanese naval code, and Yamamoto's plans were falling apart. Their own strength divided, one Japanese carrier after another sank in the face of American momentum. As a face-saving move, the retiring Japanese occupied undefended Attu and Kiska at the west end of the Aleutians in the hope that bases on these islands would shield northern Japan and drive a wedge between the United States and Russia.

The Struggle for the Islands

In August 1942 the U.S. Navy occupied Adak Island and built an airfield from which to attack nearby Attu and Kiska. In January 1943 the Navy leapfrogged to Amchitka Island, right next door to Kiska, to provide an advance base. Continuous bombing and a naval blockade weakened Japanese resistance, and 16,000 U.S. troops landed on Attu on May 11, 1943. Of these, 549 Americans were killed before the 2,650 Japanese troops entrenched in the mountains were overcome. On May 29 about 800 remaining Japanese staged a banzai charge. At first they overran the American lines, but their thrust was finally quelled by reserve forces. Only 28 Japanese prisoners were taken, and the 6,000 Japanese on Kiska seemed to face a similar fate.

Late in July, however, Japanese destroyers slipped through the U.S. blockade in dense fog and evacuated their soldiers. On August 15 some 34,000 U.S. and Canadian troops landed, unopposed, on Kiska. Although there was no one to attack and rout, incredibly, they suffered a shocking 99 dead and 74 wounded through landing mishaps, "friendly fire," and other accidents. The Japanese had also booby-trapped all the structures. With their masterful evacuation, the Japanese had ended the Aleutian campaign.

UNALASKA/DUTCH HARBOR

Located about 800 miles southwest of Anchorage, Unalaska Bay cuts into the north side of mountainous Unalaska Island, creating the finest and most sheltered ice-free harbor in the Aleutians. On a clear day you can see the sometimes-smoking 6,680-foot cone of **Makushin Volcano** rising to the west. The city of Unalaska spreads across both Unalaska Island and the much smaller Amaknak Island. A 500-foot bridge officially named *Bridge from the Other Side* links the two islands.

Although often called Dutch Harbor, this name actually refers to the protected harbor rather than the town itself. Longtime Unalaskans take umbrage at the suggestion that they live in Dutch Harbor; to them it's sort of like saying "Frisco" instead of San Francisco. That doesn't stop most folks—especially the transient fishers and cannery workers—from calling it Dutch Harbor, or simply Dutch. The folks who live in Unalaska take pride in their small city, but many others just view it as a place to get rich quick and get out.

Dutch Harbor today is an extremely busy place, consistently ranking as the nation's number-one port in both pounds of seafood caught and total dollar value. At any given time you're likely to see a dozen or more cargo ships waiting to load fish, surimi, or crab destined for Japan, Korea, the Lower 48, or elsewhere. This is industrial fishing on a grand scale. Although the island itself remains wild, Dutch Harbor is wild in its own ways. It's Alaska's melting-pot city, a place where people from the Philippines, Japan, Samoa, Sudan, the U.S., and many other countries are working, working, working (with some hard-core partying as well). And when the fisheries close and work stops, many of them head home for a month off before heading back to the moneymaking grind.

It's hard to imagine the industrial character of Dutch until you see it firsthand. Most impressive of all is the huge container crane that drops truck-size loads onto ships. Crab pots and nets line the roads, and seven different seafood processing plants are scattered around the harbors, processing pollock, crab, salmon, halibut,

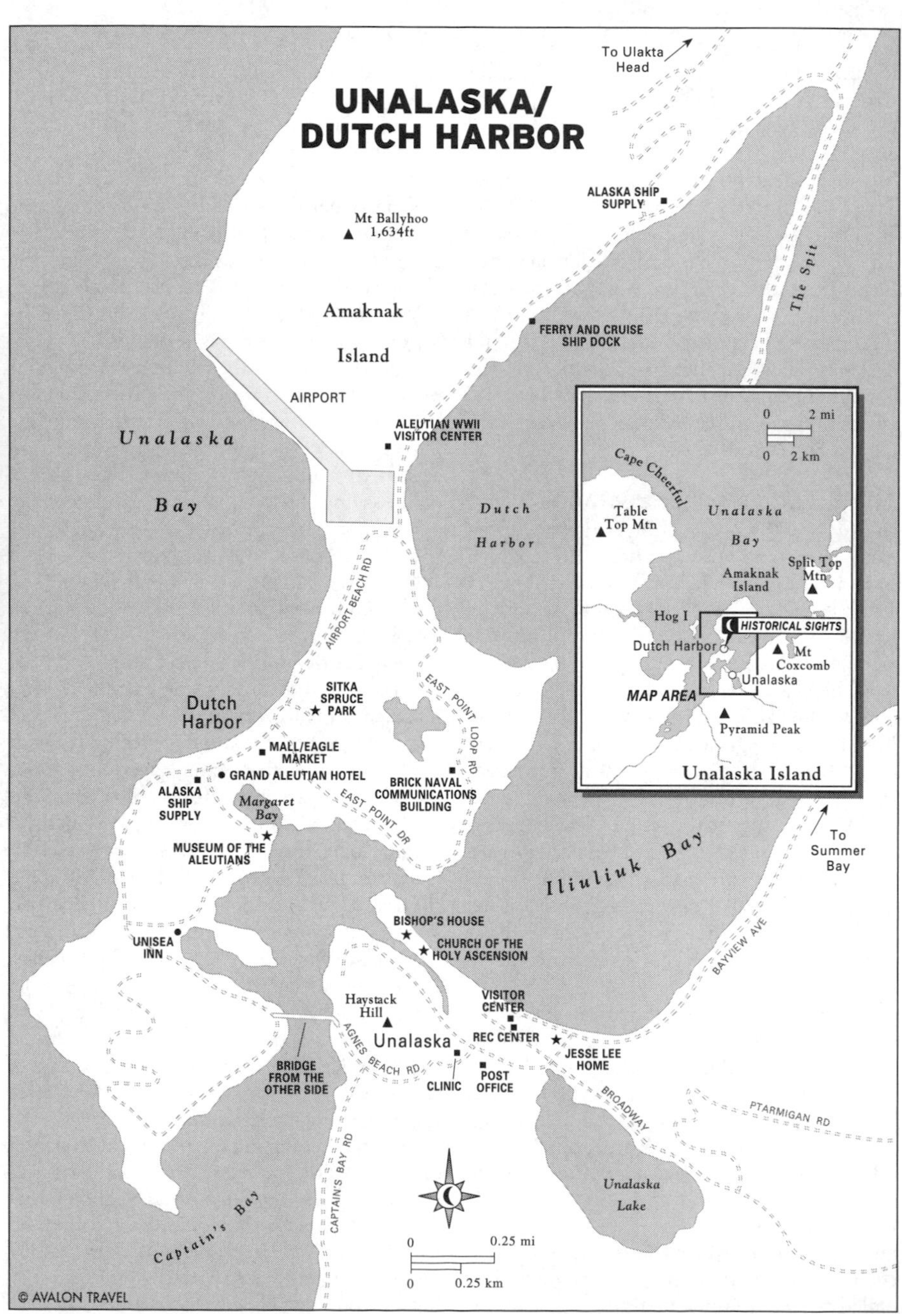
UNALASKA/
DUTCH HARBOR
To Ulakta Head
ALASKA SHIP SUPPLY
Mt Ballyhoo 1,634ft
Amaknak Island
FERRY AND CRUISE SHIP DOCK
The Spit
AIRPORT
ALEUTIAN WWII VISITOR CENTER
Unalaska Bay
Dutch Harbor
AIRPORT BEACH RD
EAST POINT LOOP RD
SITKA SPRUCE PARK
Dutch Harbor
MALL/EAGLE MARKET
GRAND ALEUTIAN HOTEL
ALASKA SHIP SUPPLY
Margaret Bay
BRICK NAVAL COMMUNICATIONS BUILDING
EAST POINT DR
MUSEUM OF THE ALEUTIANS
Iliuliuk Bay
To Summer Bay
BISHOP'S HOUSE
CHURCH OF THE HOLY ASCENSION
UNISEA INN
BAYVIEW AVE
Haystack Hill
VISITOR CENTER
REC CENTER
Unalaska
JESSE LEE HOME
AGNES BEACH RD
BRIDGE FROM THE OTHER SIDE
CLINIC
POST OFFICE
BROADWAY
PTARMIGAN RD
CAPTAIN'S BAY RD
Captain's Bay
Unalaska Lake
0 0.25 mi
0 0.25 km
0 2 mi
0 2 km
Cape Cheerful
Table Top Mtn
Unalaska Bay
Split Top Mtn
Amaknak Island
Hog I
HISTORICAL SIGHTS
Dutch Harbor
Mt Coxcomb
Unalaska
MAP AREA
Pyramid Peak
Unalaska Island

© DON PITCHER

Russian Orthodox Church of the Holy Ascension, in Unalaska/Dutch Harbor

cod, herring roe, and other seafood. Most of the catch is processed during the hectic winter fishing season, November–April. Despite this rowdy "make a million bucks" present, Unalaska/Dutch Harbor is filled with history, and visitors will find a number of places worth exploring. But do hope the weather cooperates and the ever-present windblown rain lets up for an hour or so during your visit.

History

When the first Russians "discovered" Unalaska in 1759, it was already home to more than 1,000 Aleut people scattered in 24 settlements. Over the next century the Russians decimated the Aleut, enslaving many of them to harvest fur seals and sea otters. The first permanent Russian settlement of Unalaska began in 1772, and six years later Captain Cook spent three weeks here. Under the Russians, Unalaska quickly became the main trading center in the Aleutians. After the United States took over in 1867, the focus gradually shifted, and it became an important coal and supply station for the Nome gold rush.

In the 1940s the U.S. Navy appropriated Dutch Harbor. After the city was bombed by the Japanese in June 1942, all the Aleuts were shipped off to relocation camps in Southeast Alaska. Ten percent of them died in these refugee camps (generally abandoned canneries) in part due to unsanitary conditions and overcrowding. Once World War II ended, they returned to a vastly different place filled with military facilities. Many of their homes had been ransacked.

The boom in bottom-fishing for pollock led to rapid growth in Unalaska/Dutch Harbor, and the population now tops 4,200—plus another 2,500 transient workers. Boom times continue in the Aleutians, with lots of blue-collar jobs paying relatively high wages. The island also sees a handful of cruise ships each summer, but this is a long way from anywhere else, and the Gulf of Alaska can get mighty rough.

Information

The little **Unalaska/Port of Dutch Harbor**

Convention and Visitors Bureau (Broadway and 5th St., 907/581-2612 or 877/581-2612, www.unalaska.info) is in downtown Unalaska at the old World War II Army chapel. Hours are Monday–Friday 9 A.M.–5 P.M., plus when cruise ships or ferries are in port.

Historical Sights

The most distinctive attraction in Unalaska is the beautiful **Russian Orthodox Church of the Holy Ascension** (907/581-3790). Built 1824–1827 and restored in the 1990s, this is the oldest Russian church still standing in Alaska, and a National Historic Landmark. Inside are priceless icons from Catherine the Great. The church is only open for services and group tours. Out front is a small graveyard, and not far away is the **Bishop's House,** built in 1882. Another historic site is the **Jesse Lee Home** near the cemetery. It was constructed by Methodist missionaries in 1890.

Another reminder of the Russian era is **Sitka Spruce Park** (behind Eagle grocery store) where you'll find several scraggly stolid spruce trees planted by Russian settlers in 1805. At their base lies a plethora of stunted and struggling younger spruce. These, plus a couple of other clusters of trees around town, make up the only "forest" in this otherwise treeless country. The park is a National Historic Landmark.

The **Museum of the Aleutians** (314 Salmon Way, 907/581-5150, www.aleutians.org, Tues.–Sun. 11 A.M.–5 P.M. June–Aug., Tues.–Sat. 11 A.M.–5 P.M. Sept.–May, $5) is a spacious modern facility with the only archaeological collection in the Aleutians. On exhibit are artifacts from original Native Alaskan cultures, including some amazing finds from a 2003 archaeological excavation next to the bridge. Also here are items from the Russian era and World War II, plus changing exhibits.

Adjacent to the airport, the fascinating **Aleutian World War II Visitors Center** (907/581-9944, www.nps.gov/aleu, daily 11 A.M.–8 P.M. summer, Tues.–Sat.

World War II gun emplacement center near Unalaska/Dutch Harbor

11 A.M.–6 P.M. other seasons, $4 adults, $2 seniors) is housed in the aerology building, constructed in 1943 as a weather-monitoring station for pilots defending the islands from the Japanese. Inside are historical photos and artifacts from the war, a World War II–era radio room, and exhibits on the Aleutian campaign and the evacuation and internment of the Aleut people. Step into the old-fashioned theater to watch documentaries and old newsreels from the war in the Aleutians, or make faux dog tags for yourself. The facility is a partnership between the National Park Service and the Ounalashka Corporation, which operates it.

Other reminders of the war are scattered around town, including numerous concrete pillboxes, the old hangar (fenced off), and a Tudor-style redbrick building that housed a Naval communications center. It's the only brick building in the Aleutians.

Exploring the Country

The countryside around Unalaska is pockmarked with all sorts of evidence from World War II, including underground bunkers, gun emplacements, buildings of all types, and various flotsam and jetsam from the military. The best places to find these are on the northeast end of Amaknak Island near Ulakta Head and in the Summer Bay area on Unalaska Island.

A popular hiking place is 1,634-foot-tall **Mt. Ballyhoo,** northeast of the airport on Amaknak Island. The easiest way to the top is to drive or mountain bike up the steep road that ends at Ulakta Head. The first portion is paved, but the road deteriorates into a rough track near the end (usually passable in a rental car). The open country is very pretty in late summer, with flowers galore, plus Arctic ground squirrels, ptarmigan, and bald eagles. (Red foxes are the only other wild mammal found on these islands, though some of the fishers could fall into the "wild mammal" category.) Climb up the ridge from the end of the road for more dramatic vistas out to sea and back to the mountain-rimmed harbors. The west side of Amaknak Island consists of a harrowing series of cliffs that plummet to the sea 1,500 feet below, so stay away from the edge.

The area around Ulakta Head is packed with decaying military structures from **Fort Schwatka,** including ammunition magazines, a wooden gun sled, observation posts, an underground command post, and a battery that held two eight-inch guns linked by a sod-covered roadway. These guns could launch a 240-pound shell at Japanese ships 22 miles away (in theory). Today the war is a distant memory, but it's easy to imagine the hard lives of the soldiers stationed at this bleak, cold, wet, and windy place.

For a good view of town, climb **Haystack Hill** on the south side of the Iliuliuk River (filled with spawning pink salmon in late summer). More panoramic vistas (and military bunkers) are atop the 421-foot Bunker Hill. A road up this hill veers west of the bridge.

Get to **Summer Bay** by heading northeast out of town on Summer Bay Road past the dump, a good place to see eagles. Five miles out is a lagoon where you can swim on a sunny day or practice your long-jumping form on the tall **sand dunes.** Continue out on the progressively rougher road past bunkers, Quonset huts, and a gun emplacement that guarded Iliuliuk Bay. Keep your eyes open for the two horses—the only ones on Unalaska—that graze here. If you're driving a low-slung rental car, park at the second bridge and walk in the last mile or so.

Because of its location on the Aleutian chain, pelagic and Asian birds can be seen around Unalaska Island. Some of the more unusual finds have included oriental cuckoos, Baikal teal, and Cook's petrels. Pick up a checklist of birds from the visitors center.

Tours and Fishing

Bobbie Lekanoff of **The Extra Mile Tours** (907/581-6171, www.unalaskadutchharbortour.com) leads excellent tours of the area's historical sites, natural areas, and industrial fishing. She also has a good knowledge of local birds and plants.

Several charter fishing operators take sportfishers out in search of the monster halibut;

contact the information center for a list of charter boats. The world's largest sport-caught halibut—a 459-pound fish—was caught nearby in 1996.

Accommodations

Owned by UniSea, one of the country's largest seafood processors, the upscale 112-room **Grand Aleutian Hotel** (907/581-1325 or 866/581-3844, www.grandaleutian.com, standard rooms $164 d, suites $254 d) is *the* place to stay if you've got the bucks to go in style. Two restaurants and a lounge are on the premises, and Wi-Fi is available in the lobby (with limited connectivity in the rooms). The **UniSea Inn** (907/581-1325 or 866/581-3844, www.grandaleutian.com, $99 d) has the same owners and 42 clean but simple guest rooms that include TVs, phones, and private baths. The UniSea Inn building also houses the Harbor View Bar & Grill.

Food and Entertainment

Given the tradition of smoking among fishers, you certainly would not expect to find smoke-free places in Unalaska, but times have changed. In 2009 the city banned smoking in all restaurants, bars, businesses, and public buildings. Even more amazingly, the city council's vote on the issue was 7 to 0.

Amelia's Restaurant (907/581-2800, daily 6 A.M.–10 P.M., dinner $19–30) serves hearty breakfast all day and features a diverse menu of Mexican food, steaks, seafood, chicken, and more. It's close to the Eagle grocery store.

Alcohol and fishing have probably gone hand in hand since the first fisher discovered beer, and that tradition continues in Unalaska. The main drinking establishment is the **Harbor View Bar & Grill** (907/581-7246, Sun. noon–9:30 P.M., Mon.–Thurs. 8:30 A.M.–10 P.M., Fri.–Sat. 8:30 A.M.–2 A.M., $12–27), with pizzas, burgers, baskets, halibut sandwiches, soups, and salads. There's a pool table, horseshoes out back, and live bands most weekends. It attracts a young 20-something crowd of guys and a few gals.

Occupying the back of the same building, **Harbor Sushi** (907/581-7190, Thurs.–Tues. 5–10 P.M., closed Wed.) serves surprisingly good sushi (it has a Japanese chef) and miso, starting at $8 for a California roll up to $15 for the "bitchin" king crab roll. It's a bright setting with big windows facing the old small-boat harbor.

Planet Dutch (907/581-3809, Tues.–Sun. 9 A.M.–9 P.M.) is just up the street, with filling Filipino lunch and dinner specials for around $12. Everything is takeout.

The only eatery in Unalaska itself is **Dutch Harbor Fast Food 2** (2nd St. and Broadway, 907/581-5966, Sun. 11 A.M.–6 P.M., Mon.–Sat. 11 A.M.–10 P.M., $10–20), serving Chinese food, burgers, and even pizzas.

By far the fanciest local eating places—and the best spots for fresh fish—are inside the Grand Aleutian Hotel. Downstairs find **Margaret Bay Café** (907/581-7122, Mon.–Sat. 7 A.M.–3 P.M., closed Sun.), with filling breakfasts (including crab Benedict), along with an all-you-can-eat soup, salad, and dessert bar for lunch ($13). Upstairs is the fine-dining **Chart Room** (907/581-7120), with a reasonable lunch buffet on weekdays, a Wednesday-night seafood buffet ($35), and a $27 Sunday brunch. There's an impressive wine selection and live music on Friday and Saturday nights, not at all what you might expect in this blue-collar fishing town. Both Margaret Bay Café and the Chart Room have big windows facing the water.

Get groceries at **Alaska Ship Supply** (907/581-3032, www.westernpioneer.com) or **Eagle Quality Centers/Safeway** (907/581-4040), located on either side of the Grand Aleutian Hotel. Both have in-store delis and bakeries, and the Eagle store serves **espresso,** as does Amelia's.

Services

Unalaska Public Library (907/581-5060, www.ci.unalaska.ak.us, Mon.–Fri. 10 A.M.–9 P.M., Sat.–Sun. noon–6 P.M.) is downtown and has computers but no Wi-Fi. Find free Wi-Fi in the lobby of the Grand Aleutian Hotel.

The **Community Aquatics Center** (907/581-1649, $5) in downtown Unalaska has a lap pool, a water slide, and a sauna. The building also houses an indoor track, a weight room, and a basketball court. Get fast cash from **ATMs** inside the Eagle store and Key Bank.

Cell phone users will need to purchase minutes from the local monopoly, **Alaska Wireless** (www.alaska-wireless.com).

Getting There

Unalaska has not traditionally been a place for tourists, and most everyone comes here to make money, not to vacation. The high costs of transportation and accommodations will continue to keep most tourists away, though a few cruise ships visit during the summer. If you decide on a quick visit by air, try to schedule it around a period of good weather. On a clear day the countryside is stunning, but much more common are the rainy and windy periods when the place doesn't look so great, and you start to wonder why you spent so much cash to get here. Besides, you may find yourself stuck for days waiting for the weather to lift enough for planes to land.

The state ferry ***Tustumena*** (907/465-3941 or 800/642-0066, www.dot.state.ak.us/amhs) heads out once a month (Apr.–Oct.) from Homer to Dutch Harbor. The trip takes 3.5 days one-way and can be somewhat rough, so bring lots of Dramamine. The ferry docks near the airport on Amaknak Island.

The other way to reach Unalaska is by air from Anchorage on **PenAir** (907/243-2323 or 800/448-4226, www.penair.com). These three-hour flights are in a 30-passenger turboprop plane. Alaska Airlines no longer flies their jets to Unalaska, but there is daily service on chartered PenAir planes. PenAir flights are labeled "Alaska Air" on your ticket (the companies code-share). Book your flight through Alaska Air since their agents are better able to handle complex bookings involving other airlines or mileage tickets. Because of the limited service and high demand from workers, flights to Unalaska often fill up far in advance, and mileage ticket seats are almost impossible to obtain. Call at least two months ahead to reserve your flight. The tickets are expensive—said to be the world's most expensive one-way flight—with fares sometimes topping $1,200 one-way. PenAir also offers frequent service between Unalaska and the villages of Atka, Akutan, and Nikolski.

Getting Around

The settlements of Dutch Harbor and Unalaska are spread over two islands, and the distances mean some sort of transport is needed. Mountain bikes offer the most enjoyable way to explore the many dirt roads leading into the hills. They are not nearly as much fun, however, in the wind and rain.

Most folks don't have cars in Unalaska, so there's a thriving **taxi** business. The companies—eight of them at last count—all cruise around town, so it's very easy to get a ride to the airport or other places. Expect to pay $6–10 to most points.

Car rentals are expensive (starting around $85 per day with taxes) and so is gas; get the specifics at **BC Vehicle Rental** (907/581-6777, www.bcvehiclerental.com), which has a booth in the airport, or **North Port Rentals** (907/581-3880, www.northportrentals.net). Both companies offer unlimited mileage, but there are only 38 miles of roads to drive on.

OTHER ALEUTIAN ISLANDS

The main tourist attraction for Alaska's far-flung Aleutians is probably birds; the islands get quite a few Asian species.

Akutan (pop. 400), a small island 35 miles northeast of Dutch Harbor, is a minor fishing center, with a general store, a restaurant, and a hotel, but not much else.

Tiny Aleut villages exist at **Atka** (pop. 100) on Atka Island and **Nikolski** (pop. 35) on Umnak Island. Despite its fragile geological situation and frequent earthquakes, the remote volcanic island of Atka was used by the United States for underground nuclear testing as late as 1971. In its first public action, Greenpeace sent a protest vessel into the area, and the resulting controversy led to cancellation of the tests.

Adak

This 28-mile-long island is midway out along the Aleutian chain, 500 miles west of Dutch Harbor. **Alaska Air** (800/426-0333, www.alaskaair.com) provides Sunday and Thursday service to the island from Anchorage, and cruise ships visit once or twice each summer. There's a general store with expensive supplies, while **Adak Island Inn** (907/592-2325, $225 d) has townhouse lodging.

Anyone planning on exploring the island should drop by the Alaska Maritime National Wildlife Refuge's summer office to see a video on avoiding the unexploded ordinance on parts of the Adak. Get details from the U.S. Fish and Wildlife Service (year-round 907/235-6961, summer 907/592-2406, http://alaskamaritime.fws.gov).

The Navy had a major base on Adak from 1943 until 2000, when they left following the end of the Cold War. Suddenly Alaska's sixth-largest city became a virtual ghost town, with 300 or so year-round residents. The population jumps in summer due to an influx of contractors cleaning up unexploded ordinance and other hazards on the island. The now-abandoned city would make a great setting for a postapocalyptic movie, with the incessant wind blowing through empty houses, schools, and businesses. The island is also home to some 3,000 caribou, an introduced species that is popular with hunters.

Attu and Shemya

At the far western end of the Aleutians lies the surprisingly beautiful island of Attu, less than 200 miles from Siberia. The Aleut villagers of Attu were deported to Japan in 1942 by the Japanese, and more than 2,500 Japanese and Americans died in battles here. After the war, the U.S. government refused to allow the Aleuts to resettle on their island, and today the only inhabitants are the staff of the Coast Guard loran station. Birdwatchers visit Attu to look for Asian species that have strayed into the Aleutians, and this is also the only place in the United States where the white-tailed eagle breeds. Access is by charter flight only.

Minuscule Shemya Island—so small that the airport covers half of its four-mile length—is 40 miles east of Attu, near the end of the Aleutians. The Missile Defense Agency is upgrading an early-warning radar base here, and a security clearance is required to visit.

Pribilof Islands

The remote volcanic Pribilofs sit in the middle of the Bering Sea 250 miles north of the Aleutians, 300 miles west of the mainland, and 1,000 miles from Anchorage. The two main islands—**St. Paul** (pop. 760), with the world's largest Aleut community, and **St. George** (pop. 150)—host what may be the largest concentration of mammals and seabirds anywhere on earth. Although both islands have abundant wildlife of all sorts, St. Paul is best known for its fur seal colonies, and St. George for its seabird rookeries. Tiny Walrus and Otter Islands also support thousands of seals and birds.

St. Paul is the largest of the islands, 14 miles long and 8 miles wide, with hills reaching 500 feet in elevation. St. George has a sheer wall rising from the sea to almost 1,000 feet, with millions of waterfowl breeding in its nooks and crannies. There are no trees on either island, but the rolling tundra becomes a dense rainbow of flowers in mid-July. The weather is similar to that of the Aleutians—cool, damp, foggy, and windy; summer temperatures average 47°F, with an occasional 60°F day in July. A useful regional website is run by the Southwest Alaska Municipal Conference (www.southwestalaska.com) and has details on the Pribilofs.

HISTORY

Soon after Russian fur finder Gerassim Pribylov discovered the uninhabited islands in June 1786—and named them for himself—his fur company brought Aleut slaves to harvest the seals. Conflicting accounts claim that the Russians slaughtered the seals here nearly to extinction, or that in 1867 the population had regenerated to record numbers and that it was the Americans who trimmed their skins by the millions (these fur seal rookeries were a prime reason the U.S. government bought Alaska from the Russians). In either case, by 1911 the seal population had dwindled to fewer than 150,000 animals, 10 percent of what it had been. That same year, the United States, Russia, Britain, and Japan signed a treaty banning ocean hunting and limiting the number allowed to be taken on land. It wasn't until 1985 that commercial seal harvesting was finally halted, in large part because of pressure from environmental groups. The Aleut people were not given full control of their islands until 1983.

horned puffin on St. Paul Island

Today, the economy of St. Paul struggles along with limited seafood processing and tourism. Steller sea lions and fur seals have declined in recent years, and there is growing concern among biologists over the health of the Bering Sea ecosystem. This is still a remarkable place for anyone who loves wildlife, with outstanding birding opportunities throughout the summer and many unusual species. A large herd of reindeer live on St. Paul Island.

Wildlife

Each summer thousands of northern fur seals return to the Pribilofs (the majority to St. Paul) to breed and give birth. The "beachmasters" are first to arrive at the haul-out sites and rookeries (late May), with the females coming ashore in June to give birth. At 90–130 pounds, the females are far smaller than the largest males, which can reach 600 pounds. Harbor seals, sea otters, Steller sea lions, and long-tusked walrus round out this brawling, bawling, and caterwauling marine mammalian gumbo. Nowhere else in North America, and arguably the world, is wildlife so easily seen in such numbers. If you're set on doing something really wild (and expensive) during your trip North, this would be it.

In addition to the sea mammals, over 220 species of birds have been identified on the Pribilofs, including millions of murres and thousands of puffins, cormorants, kittiwakes, and fulmars. The late birder and artist Rodger Tory Peterson called one of St. George's rookeries "probably the greatest single bird cliff anywhere in North America." (Note, however, that only a dozen or so bird species actually breed on the islands; the rest are migrants.) Bird-watchers interested in adding to their life list may want to come early (mid-May–early June) for accidental Asian species that sometimes wander over from Siberia. Don't forget your bird book and binoculars!

ST. PAUL ISLAND

This fascinating island is approximately 17 miles long and 8 miles across. The old **St. Peter and Paul Church** is a focal point of life on St. Paul, and it has a lavishly ornate interior. It's right in the heart of this rough-edged town where the streets are gravel and foxes are a common sight.

There's only one place to stay, the 21-room **King Eider Hotel** (907/546-2477), where $125 per person gets you a room with two twin beds and a bath down the hall (four units have queen beds). The sitting area contains a guest computer and a TV, and Wi-Fi is available. Located in the airport "terminal," it's two miles away from town, but most visitors don't spend much time at the hotel since the tours are out all day. There are no restaurants in St. Paul, but Trident Seafoods serves three filling cafeteria-style meals daily: breakfast $9, lunch $14, and dinner $18.

There is also a small Alaska Commercial store with limited and expensive supplies, a tavern, two taxi companies, and vehicles from **North Star Truck Rental** (907/546-2645). Camping is not allowed on the island.

Getting There

The vast majority of visitors to St. Paul arrive on **St. Paul Island Tours** (907/278-2318 or 877/424-5637, www.alaskabirding.com). These trips include round-trip air transportation from Anchorage, lodging, transport around the island, and a guide with a good knowledge of birds, wildlife, history, and cultural traditions. Meals are extra, or you can bring your own food and use the hotel's microwave and fridge. Trips start at $1,656 per person for 3 days and 2 nights, up to $2,670 for 8 days and 7 nights. Be sure to schedule a buffer of several days since foggy weather sometimes prevents flights from landing for up to a week; bring heavy rain gear and good rubber boots. The tours are offered mid-May–August.

PenAir (907/243-2323 or 800/448-4226, www.penair.com) flies from Anchorage to St. Paul daily. Most flights are on a comfortable 30-passenger Saab turboprop, but it's still a long four-hour flight, much of it over open water. It can be harrowing, and planes are sometimes unable to land, forcing them to return. On Tuesday, Thursday, and Saturday PenAir also flies between St. Paul and St. George Islands.

ST. GEORGE ISLAND

St. George the Martyr Russian Orthodox Church is the most distinctive structure on St. George, though the very simple **St. George Tanaq Hotel** (907/859-2255 or 907/272-9886, www.stgeorgetanaq.com) is also a National Historic Landmark. Lodging here costs $169 per person (!) in rooms with twin beds and down-the-hall baths. Guest rooms include TVs, phones, and Wi-Fi, but reserve ahead to be certain of a bed, since there are only 10 of them. There are no restaurants or bars on the island, but you can buy food locally and cook it at the hotel's surprisingly nice kitchen. **St. George Island Canteen** has limited groceries at bush prices; better to bring your own from Anchorage. Camping is not allowed on St. George.

Getting There

PenAir (907/243-2323 or 800/448-4226, www.penair.com) flies from Anchorage to St. George on Tuesdays, Thursdays, and Saturdays. The four-hour flights are over open water. Fortunately, the plane often refuels in Dillingham, giving passengers a break. Planes also stop at St. Paul Island, so you can visit both islands if you're out this far. Local taxis are available to take you into town, and Tanaq rents pickup trucks for $125 per day.

WESTERN AND ARCTIC ALASKA

This is Alaska's true outback: far, far from the reach of civilization. The scattered settlements—Dillingham, Bethel, and Nome—are really more like pinpricks on the map. The vast distances between the towns make them difficult and expensive to reach, but also exotic and fascinating to visit.

Bristol Bay, on the southern end of the Bering Sea, is considered the world's most productive red salmon fishery. Dillingham, the main port town, is home to hundreds of salmon fishing boats and a multitude of sportfishing lodges. It's also the gateway to remote Wood-Tikchik State Park, the largest state park in the United States. Also nearby are the Walrus Islands, with an extraordinary walrus haul-out on Round Island. The village of Bethel occupies a low-lying lake-filled delta where the Kuskokwim and Yukon Rivers spread and finally empty into the Bering Sea. Yup'ik villages are scattered across the stark treeless plain. Farther north is Nome, a gold-rush town with an abundance of history and a network of roads across the beautiful rolling country.

The extremes of the Arctic make it hard to imagine how life survives. The too-brief summers can be gloriously beautiful, with a sun that never sets and luxuriant vegetation stretching in all directions, but winter brings a cold so bitter that even stepping outside for a few moments without proper protective clothing can be life-threatening. Visitors need to be well prepared before venturing away from the settlements. This is not a landscape to take lightly.

HIGHLIGHTS

Wood-Tikchik State Park: Sprawled across 1.6 million acres, the largest state park in the country encompasses a series of eight spectacular lakes backed by the rugged Wood River Mountains (page 468).

Walrus Islands State Game Sanctuary: Accessible by a three-hour boat ride from Togiak, this island is where hundreds of photogenic but ungainly walrus haul out. The remote location, often-stormy weather, and restrictions on visitation mean that only a few hardy people make it to this unique island (page 469).

Nome Back Roads: Fanning out in three directions from Nome are three wonderful dirt roads that take visitors to Native Alaskan villages, a hot springs, and even the rusting hulk of "The Last Train to Nowhere" (page 475).

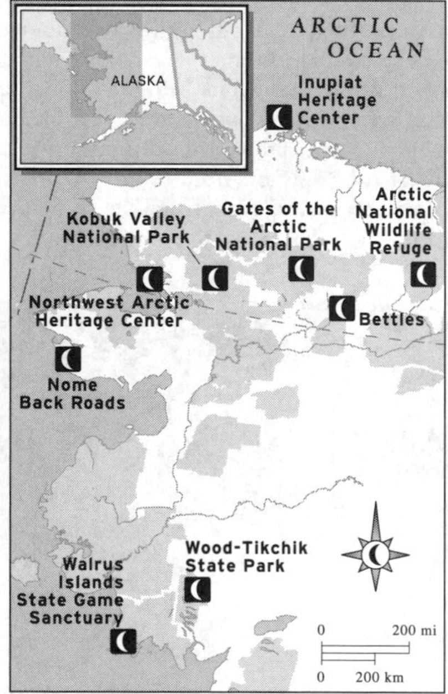

Northwest Arctic Heritage Center: This large, newly opened Park Service facility in Kotzebue provides an outstanding introduction to the northwest Arctic parks and Native peoples. (page 481).

Kobuk Valley National Park: This little-visited 1.7-million-acre park abuts the Kobuk River, with the amazing Great Kobuk Sand Dunes stretching across 25 square miles of Arctic wilderness (page 483).

Gates of the Arctic National Park: Covering more than 8 million acres of wild mountain lands in the Brooks Range, this very remote park is accessible by bush plane from surrounding villages. Hikers and rafters are on their own in a vast expanse of craggy ridges and glacially carved valleys (page 484).

Bettles: This miniscule Arctic settlement is best known as the access point for Gates of the Arctic National Park, but winter visitors find unparalleled northern lights. Two local lodges offer special aurora-viewing packages. (page 484).

Arctic National Wildlife Refuge: Home to 150,000 caribou, this refuge covers 8 million acres of North Slope wilderness threatened by oil development. Raft trips are the main access method for visitors (page 485).

Inupiat Heritage Center: Located in the North Slope town of Barrow, this living-history museum provides a great introduction to Eskimo traditions. While in Barrow, dip your toes in the Arctic Ocean, look for polar bears, or taste an enchilada at Pepe's North of the Border (page 489).

LOOK FOR TO FIND RECOMMENDED SIGHTS, ACTIVITIES, DINING, AND LODGING.

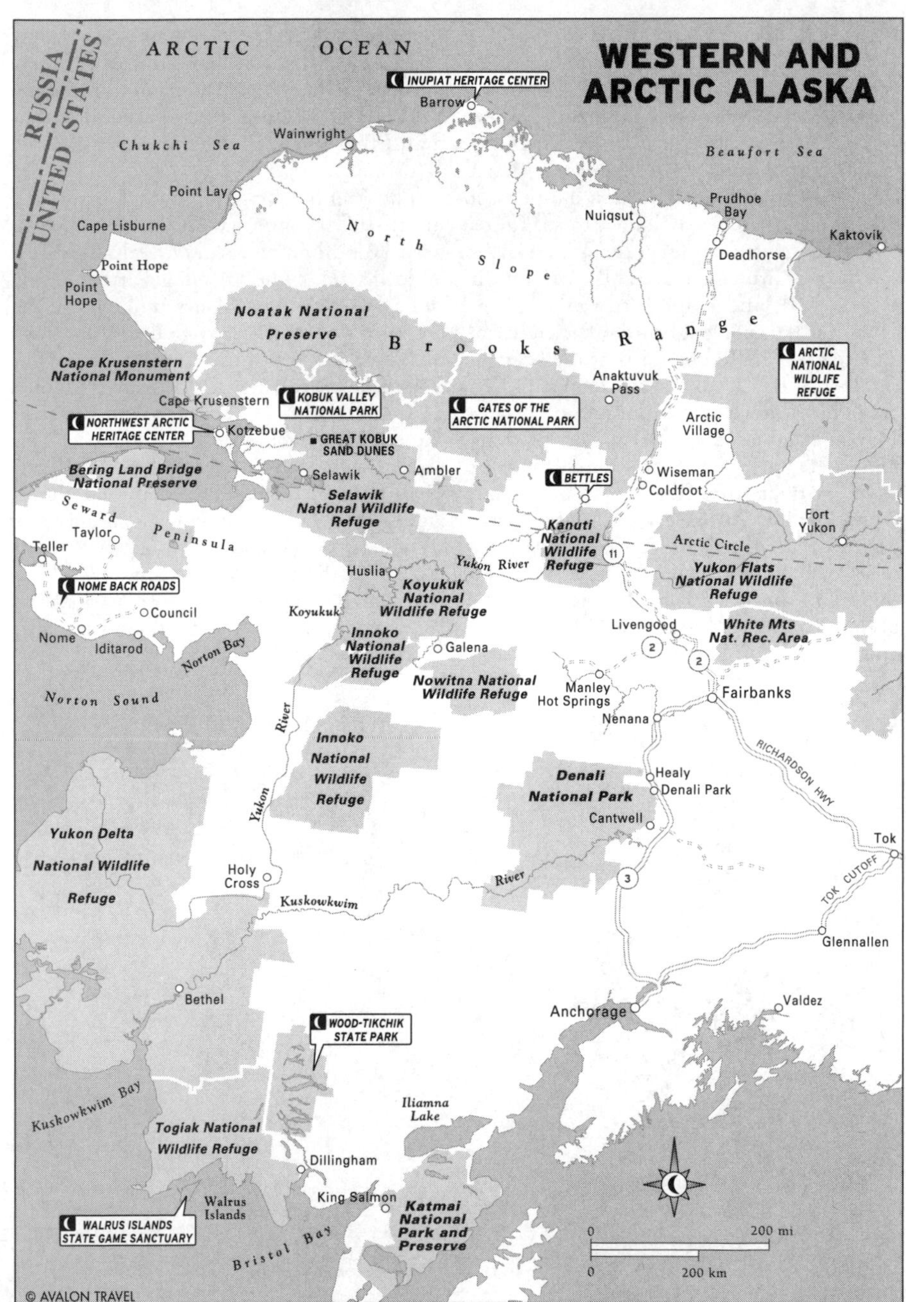
WESTERN AND ARCTIC ALASKA
ARCTIC OCEAN
RUSSIA
UNITED STATES
Chukchi Sea
Beaufort Sea
INUPIAT HERITAGE CENTER
Barrow
Wainwright
Point Lay
Cape Lisburne
Point Hope
Point Hope
North Slope
Nuiqsut
Prudhoe Bay
Deadhorse
Kaktovik
Brooks Range
Noatak National Preserve
Cape Krusenstern National Monument
Cape Krusenstern
KOBUK VALLEY NATIONAL PARK
GATES OF THE ARCTIC NATIONAL PARK
Anaktuvuk Pass
ARCTIC NATIONAL WILDLIFE REFUGE
Arctic Village
NORTHWEST ARCTIC HERITAGE CENTER
Kotzebue
GREAT KOBUK SAND DUNES
Bering Land Bridge National Preserve
Selawik
Ambler
Wiseman
Coldfoot
BETTLES
Selawik National Wildlife Refuge
Seward Peninsula
Taylor
Teller
Kanuti National Wildlife Refuge
Fort Yukon
Arctic Circle
Yukon River
Huslia
Yukon Flats National Wildlife Refuge
NOME BACK ROADS
Koyukuk National Wildlife Refuge
Council
Koyukuk
Nome
Iditarod
Norton Bay
Innoko National Wildlife Refuge
Galena
Livengood
White Mts Nat. Rec. Area
Nowitna National Wildlife Refuge
Manley Hot Springs
Fairbanks
Nenana
Norton Sound
Yukon River
Innoko National Wildlife Refuge
RICHARDSON HWY
Healy
Denali Park
Denali National Park
Cantwell
Yukon Delta National Wildlife Refuge
Holy Cross
Kuskowkwim River
Tok
TOK CUTOFF
Glennallen
Bethel
Anchorage
Valdez
WOOD-TIKCHIK STATE PARK
Kuskowkwim Bay
Iliamna Lake
Togiak National Wildlife Refuge
Dillingham
King Salmon
Walrus Islands
WALRUS ISLANDS STATE GAME SANCTUARY
Katmai National Park and Preserve
Bristol Bay
0 200 mi
0 200 km
© AVALON TRAVEL

PLANNING YOUR TIME

Getting into the bush is half the fun of any trip to Western and Arctic Alaska. This is a vast landscape where developments are few and access is almost entirely by air. Many visitors to Barrow arrive by Alaska Air jet for a one-day or overnight tour, but in most other areas visitors stay longer to soak up a bit of this grand country. It's quite expensive to get into the bush, and costs for air travel, food, and lodging can mount rapidly, so make sure you bring sufficient cash. The town of Dillingham sits at the heart of the Bristol Bay region (www.visitbristolbay.com), best known for the millions of sockeye salmon caught commercially. Many fishing lodges are sprinkled across the headwaters of major rivers that flow into the bay, and **Wood-Tikchik State Park**—the largest state park in the United States—encompasses a series of eight spectacular lakes each over 20 miles long and backed by the rugged slopes of the Wood River Mountains. West of here, and a three-hour boat ride from Togiak, are the **Walrus Islands State Game Sanctuary** and Round Island, where hundreds of these photogenic but ungainly masses of blubber haul out. Only a few hardy individuals (humans, that is) are allowed to visit the island at a time.

The Yup'ik village of Bethel sits at the mouth of the mighty Kuskokwim River, with 20-million-acre Yukon Delta National Wildlife Refuge on all sides. Farther north, the Seward Peninsula juts into the Bering Sea, positioning the old gold mining town of Nome just 190 miles from Siberia. The town is a fascinating mix of Native Alaskan and white cultural heritages, and serves as the endpoint each March for Alaska's "Last Great Race," the Iditarod Sled Dog Race. Gold mining still takes place around Nome, and massive dredges and other equipment are strewn across the tundra. Nome **back roads** fan out in three directions from town, leading through magnificent country to small villages, a hot spring, and even the rusting hulk of "The Last Train to Nowhere."

© DON PITCHER

children playing in the village of Bethel

Arctic Alaska is the real forbidden quarter, a place where winter rules much of the year but also where the summer sun never sets. Massive oil deposits at Prudhoe Bay drive the state's economy, and the town of Kotzebue serves as a hub for northwestern Alaska. The North Slope town of Barrow draws visitors to the **Inupiat Heritage Center** for a great intro to Eskimo traditions, along with the chance to dip their toes in the Arctic Ocean or taste an enchilada at Pepe's North of the Border. Spectacular **Gates of the Arctic National Park** covers more than 8 million acres of wild mountain lands in the Brooks Range, while **Arctic National Wildlife Refuge** is home to 150,000 caribou, several major rivers that attract adventurers, and the potential for oil, which attracts oil companies and politicians.

Dillingham and Vicinity

Dillingham (pop. 2,400) is the regional center for Bristol Bay, Alaska's largest sockeye salmon fishery. A large portion of the world's wild salmon catch comes from this enormous bay on the southern end of the Bering Sea. During the peak of the season, set nets line Dillingham beaches while gillnetters catch fish just offshore, and the town's four canneries run full blast. You won't, however, see the big fishing boats found elsewhere in Alaska, since commercial boats are limited to a maximum of 32 feet in length throughout Bristol Bay.

HISTORY

Dillingham's origins came from the first Russian fur traders who established a fort (Alexandrovski Redoubt) on the other side of Nushagak Bay in 1822. After the Americans took over, canneries were established in the area to process the enormous runs of red (sockeye) salmon up the Nushagak and Wood Rivers. When an influenza epidemic decimated the Native Alaskan villages around Nushagak Bay in the winter of 1918–1919, many of the survivors moved to Dillingham. The result is a place composed of Yup'iks, Aleuts, Russians, and Americans of other races. The local radio station, KDLG, still has Yup'ik-language broadcasts. Today, the town is almost wholly dependent on the rich salmon fisheries of Bristol Bay, with a mix of commercial fishing and dozens of sportfishing lodges. Proposed gold mines and offshore oil development could also be on the horizon.

SIGHTS

Although there are many sportfishing lodges in the area, Dillingham is not much of a tourist town; most people come here to work. For a one-stop visit to town, head to Seward and D Streets, where you'll find the **Sam Fox Museum** (907/842-5610, Mon.–Fri. 10 A.M.–5 P.M.), which also houses a small visitors center (907/842-5115, www.dillinghamak.com). The city library (907/842-5610, www.ci.dillingham.ak.us) is next door, with computers for Internet access.

The main attractions for visitors—if they aren't going fishing—are Wood-Tikchik State Park and Walrus Islands State Game Sanctuary. **Togiak National Wildlife Refuge** begins just three miles west of Dillingham and covers 4.3 million acres. It is a vital staging area for migrating waterfowl, especially brant, emperor geese, common eiders, and Steller's eiders. Stop by the refuge office in Dillingham (907/842-1063 or 800/817-2538, http://togiak.fws.gov) before heading out.

An enjoyable 24-mile dirt road leads out of Dillingham to the village of **Aleknagik** (pop. 200) where the state has a boat ramp on Lake Aleknagik. Wood-Tikchik Park begins at the upper end of this lake.

Dillingham's main event is the **Beaver Round-Up,** a five-day March party that features a championship dogsled race, dances, and the locally heralded Miss Dillingham pageant. The **4th of July Salmon Bake** is another fun event.

ACCOMMODATIONS

Add a 10 percent tax to all these lodging rates. **Bristol Inn** (104 Main St., 907/842-2240 or 800/764-9704, www.alaskaoutdoors.com/bristolinn, $180 s, $195 d, kitchenettes $187 s, $210 d) has a continental breakfast, Wi-Fi, and an airport shuttle.

Dillingham's most distinctive lodging place, **Thai Inn** (907/842-7378, www.thai-inn.com, $135 s, $150 d) is a huge downtown hilltop home. Several of the dozen guest rooms are decorated with hand-carved Thai pieces, giving it a decidedly un-Alaskan look. All rooms have private baths, fridges, microwaves, and Wi-Fi, and many include kitchens, 42-inch flat-screen TVs, and laundry. Breakfast (included) is served downstairs at Royal Orchid Café.

Beaver Creek B&B (907/842-7335 or 866/252-7335, www.dillinghamalaska.com, $185 d) has five houses and cabins in the area. All rooms include access to full kitchens, laundry facilities, free airport transport, and make-it-yourself breakfasts. Call well ahead for mid-summer reservations. The houses are four miles out of town, so you may want a rental car.

There is no camping in Dillingham, and much of the land out on the road is in Native Alaskan corporation or private hands. Showers are available at the boat harbor.

FOOD

In the heart of town, **Windmill Grille** (907/842-1205, Mon.–Fri. 11 A.M.–9 P.M., Sat. 4–9:30 P.M.) is open for lunch and dinner with pizzas ($20–40) that include the Windmill, a folded pizza, sandwiches ($15), and salads, along with seafood and steak ($15–25).

Despite the name, **Royal Orchid Café** (907/842-2665, daily 7 A.M.–2 P.M.) serves all-American fare for breakfast and lunch in an elegant setting within the Thai Inn. Other options are the **Muddy Rudder** (907/842-2634) downtown, and **Bristol Bay Eagle** (907/842-4453) near the boat harbor.

Espresso, Etc. (304 Main St., 907/842-5574) is the local mocha joint. Get groceries at **N&N Market** (907/842-5283, www.omnialaska.com) which has a deli, or the larger **Alaska Commercial Company** (907/842-5444, www.alaskacommercial.com).

GETTING THERE

The airport is a bit over two miles from Dillingham; ride into town on **Issama Cab** (907/842-4881) or **Punas Cab** (907/528-5588). A car is useful if you plan to spend any time in the Dillingham area, or want to head up the road to Aleknagik; rent one from **D & J Rentals** (907/842-2222).

Alaska Airlines (800/426-0333, www.alaskaair.com), **PenAir** (907/243-2323 or 800/448-4226, www.penair.com), and **Frontier Alaska** (907/266-8394 or 800/866-8394, www.frontierak.com) have daily flights between Anchorage and Dillingham all year. PenAir also serves many surrounding villages and towns.

Local air taxis include **Bay Air** (907/842-2570, www.bayair-alaska.com), **Fresh Water Adventures** (907/842-5060, www.freshwateradventure.com), **Shannon's Air Taxi** (907/842-2735), and **Tikchik Airventures** (907/842-5841, www.tikchikairventures.com). The dozens of regional fishing lodges keep them busy all summer. Freshwater Adventures flies a classic Grumman Goose, the belly-landing planes built in the 1940s.

WOOD-TIKCHIK STATE PARK

This 1.6-million-acre state facility—the largest state park in the country—is 300 miles southwest of Anchorage, and a half-hour floatplane flight from Dillingham. The park preserves a vast system of rivers and lakes, including two long chains of interconnected waterways. There are eight different lakes at least 20 miles long plus countless smaller ponds. These lakes offer some of the most awesome sportfishing to be found for trophy salmon, trout, Arctic char, and northern pike.

The east side of Wood-Tikchik is mostly flat wooded terrain, but to the west the rugged Wood River Mountains rise, some topping 5,000 feet. Canoeists or kayakers may want to float down such rivers as the Nuyakuk or the Tikchik, where the unsurpassed scenery is untouched by development. You could easily spend several weeks exploring this area, but be forewarned that there's lots of big open water, and storms can blow up. Also come prepared to battle the mosquitoes and other flying menaces.

Practicalities

For complete details on this remote park, contact Wood-Tikchik State Park headquarters in Anchorage (907/269-8698, www.alaskastateparks.org, year-round) or the Dillingham office (907/842-2641, late May–late Sept.).

Access is primarily by floatplane from Dillingham, but it's also possible to drive the 24 miles from Dillingham to the village of Aleknagik on Aleknagik Lake and then boat through a long series of connected lakes. There are no trails or other developed facilities within the park itself, but camping and hiking opportunities abound if you have the right gear and a boat to get around.

Most visitors to Wood-Tikchik stay at local fishing and hunting lodges, including **Alaska's Bearclaw Lodge** (907/842-4060 or 866/429-2327, www.bearclawlodge.com) and **Tikchik Narrows Lodge** (907/596-3511 summer, 360/379-2842 winter, www.tikchiklodge.com); the latter is especially recommended.

WALRUS ISLANDS STATE GAME SANCTUARY

The Walrus Islands are a cluster of seven small rocky points of land in northern Bristol Bay. One of them—Round Island—is famous as a haul-out spot for thousands of walrus during the summer; only the bulls come ashore here. The walrus masses form what author Tom Kizzia called "a writhing mat of wrinkled, rust-colored leather" on the rocky beach where they rest. There are also hundreds of thousands of nesting seabirds—black-legged kittiwakes, common murres, cormorants, and parakeet auklets—as well as tufted and horned puffins. Also on the island are inquisitive red foxes. Steller sea lions come ashore on one beach.

Practicalities

Contact the Alaska Department of Fish and Game (907/842-2334, www.wildlife.alaska.gov) for an information packet and permit application. You can apply as early as January 1, and it's a good idea to get your application in early to be sure of a place at the peak time (mid-June–July). The weather generally deteriorates after June. To keep human impacts to a minimum, only 12 permits ($50 pp) are issued for each five-day period, so you won't have a lot of neighbors, other than the birds and bulls. Two of the 12 permits are held open for those who apply within 10 days before a given time slot, so you might be able to get in at the last minute. Access to Round Island is difficult and expensive, but worth it for this once-in-a-lifetime experience.

To access Round Island you'll first need to fly to Dillingham from Anchorage (around $520 round-trip). **PenAir** (907/243-2323 or 800/448-4226, www.penair.com) and **Frontier Alaska** (907/266-8394 or 800/866-8394, www.frontierak.com) fly from Anchorage directly to the Native Alaskan village of Togiak, where Paul Markoff of **Togiak Outfitters** (907/493-5043, www.togiakoutfitters.com) provides transportation to the islands (2–3 hours each way) for $630 per person round-trip, including the permit. He operates a fast 22-foot boat, but the service is weather- and tide-dependent, and it's 30 miles of open ocean. He can also assist with transportation and lodging in Togiak.

You'll have to bring all your own camping gear, food, and supplies. The weather can be pretty wild—60-knot winds and pelting rain—so don't skimp on your tent and rain gear. Wooden tent platforms are available, but be sure to take long tent stakes—and some extras—to hold everything down. Also bring enough food to last a week longer than you'd expected. It rains probably 40 percent of the time, and the weather can occasionally close in for long periods, making it impossible to leave. Trails lead from the camping area to outstanding cliffs where you can look down on the walrus or across to nesting seabirds. Fish and Game has two research technicians on the island who will answer your questions; they aren't guides, however.

Bethel

Flying to Bethel (pop. 5,000) from Anchorage hammers home an appreciation of Alaska's vastness. The Alaska Range and Kuskokwim Mountains serve up a seemingly impenetrable set of summits for over 300 miles. Then it terminates abruptly in a range of hills that flattens into an enormous coastal plain. Far below, the land is pockmarked with thousands of ponds of all sizes, and the Kuskokwim River meanders its way toward the sea, past oxbows and brush-lined shores. The mixed Native Alaskan and immigrant town of Bethel sprawls along the wide Kuskokwim River some 80 miles from its mouth.

Bethel is one of the largest settlements in the Alaskan bush. It serves as a supply center, as well as a transportation and communication hub, for dozens of outlying villages. You're likely to meet many people fluent in both English and Yup'ik (the nightly TV news is in both languages) along with a surprising number of recent emigrants from Eastern Europe and Korea. The country is essentially flat tundra with willows along the river banks and thin black spruce forests farther upriver. In the summer, the Kuskokwim provides boat access to villages all along the river; when winter arrives, it becomes an ice road for settlements hundreds of miles upriver. This is certainly one of the most unique roads in the country. Each spring all commerce shuts down for a couple of weeks, when the river is too thin to drive on and the ice has not yet floated away in the big breakup.

Bethel is built on permafrost, so all buildings are constructed on stilts to prevent heat from thawing the ground and causing them to sink into a quagmire. Permafrost makes it very difficult to lay water lines, so water is trucked to holding tanks outside each home and business. This means you won't have a lot of water to waste on showers, and in some places the water is nearly undrinkable (this depends upon the source). This undrinkable water might partly explain the high sales of soda pop at local grocery stores, and makes a good excuse for the abundance of vodka in a town where alcohol cannot be legally sold.

SIGHTS

A trading post was established along the Kuskokwim River in the 1870s, followed a decade later by a Moravian Church mission. The town of Bethel—named for the scriptural directive "Arise, go to Bethel, and dwell there"—grew up around this mission and trading post. The old **Moravian Church,** built around 1885, is the most interesting and photogenic local structure.

The **Yup'iit Piciryarait Cultural Center** (907/543-1819), in the same building as the University of Alaska's Kuskokwim campus, contains a fascinating collection of old Yup'ik clothing and tools, along with photographic exhibits. There are seal-gut parkas, dolls, baskets, and beautiful carved ivory pieces.

Other than this, the primary sights are the town itself and the wild country that reaches for an eternity in all directions from Bethel. The **Yukon-Kuskokwim Delta Regional Hospital** is that strange yellow building you pass on the way into town from the airport. It looks like the old drawings of space stations once planned for Mars.

Hang around the Alaska Commercial Co. store for that most Bethel of all Bethel attractions, the legion of local taxi cabs—all waiting outside with their engines running while the Slavic, Albanian, and Korean drivers smoke cigarettes and talk. Imagine it as a scene from an old Western, except that the horses tied up out front have been replaced by taxis and the cowboys speak with an Eastern European or Asian accent.

Bethel lacks a visitors center, but for info try the **Bethel Chamber of Commerce** (907/543-2911, www.bethelakchamber.org) or the **Delta Discovery** website (www.deltadiscovery.com).

YUKON DELTA NATIONAL WILDLIFE REFUGE

The town of Bethel is encircled by this 20-million-acre wildlife refuge, the largest in the country. The refuge covers the widely spreading mouths of both the Yukon and Kuskokwim Rivers (The Y-K Delta), plus nearby Nunivak Island. Nearly all this land is a potholed mélange of tundra marshes, lakes, and streams. Yukon Delta National Wildlife Refuge is a vital area for waterfowl. The numbers are staggering: More than two million ducks, 750,000 geese and swans, plus another 100 million shorebirds nest here each summer. Most Outsiders come to the refuge to see the birds and other animals; most Yup'ik people come here to hunt and fish as they have since time immemorial.

Access to the refuge is by boat or floatplane. Hiking is difficult on this marshy terrain. The **visitors center** at refuge headquarters in Bethel (907/543-3151, http://yukondelta.fws.gov, Mon.–Fri. 8 A.M.–4:30 P.M., Sat. 1–4 P.M.) has wildlife displays and photographs. Staff occasionally guide summertime bird-watching tours.

Kuskokwim Wilderness Adventures (907/543-3900, www.kuskofish.com) guides camping, rafting, and dog-mushing trips in the Bethel area.

EVENTS

Bethel's primary winter event is the **Kuskokwim-300 Sled Dog Race** (907/543-3300, www.k300.org) held each January. It's a three-day mad dash up the frozen ice that attracts some of the fastest teams in the nation and even a few international entries. The **Cama'i Festival** in early April is a three-day Native Alaskan dance event with performers from all over Alaska and even Russia. This is a great time to buy Native Alaskan crafts.

SHOPPING

Ask around and you might find someone to sew one of the beautiful and distinctive parkas worn by Native Alaskan women, or to knit a garment out of musk ox wool, but be ready to part with a large amount of cash for either of these one-of-a-kind items. The finest Alaskan baskets come from the village of Hooper Bay, 100 miles northwest of Bethel.

ACCOMMODATIONS

Add a 6 percent lodging tax to rates listed below.

Allanivik Hotel (907/543-4305, www.allanivik.com, $135 s, $145 d) has comfortable rooms with private baths; Wi-Fi is available.

Bethel's largest lodging place is **Long House Bethel Hotel** (907/543-4612 or 866/543-4613, www.longhousebethelinn.com, $159–169 d). Wi-Fi is available, and some rooms contain fridges and microwaves.

Suite 881 (907/543-3883, www.suite881.net, $164 s, $184 d) is Bethel's newest, with eight modern rooms, laundry, flat-screen TVs, and Internet access.

Bentley's B&B (907/543-3552, $132–154 s, $158–178 d) has 35 rooms spread over six buildings. The less expensive rooms have shared baths, or you can pay a bit more for a private bath. A full breakfast and Wi-Fi are included.

Brown Slough B&B (907/543-4334 or 888/543-4334, www.bethelhotel.com, $115 s, $130 d) has two large and comfortable homes along the slough. One of these is a beautiful two-story log structure. Most of the eight guest rooms share baths, but one room has its own bath. All include a continental breakfast and Wi-Fi.

FOOD

Find good pizza, calzones, and Greek specialties (including gyros, shish kebab, and baklava) at **Dimitri's Restaurant** (907/543-3434). **Front St. Café** (907/543-3408) is probably the best overall dining choice in Bethel, with an ethnic mélange of Chinese, American, pizzas, and even Mexican food under one roof.

Located at Pacifica Guest House, **V.I.P. Restaurant** (907/543-4777) serves Korean, Japanese, and American meals three times a day. Out at the airport **Brother's Pizza & Subs** (907/543-3553) opens in the evening.

Get groceries and supplies from **Alaska**

Commercial Company (907/543-2661 or 800/478-2661) or **Swanson's** (907/543-3221, www.omnialaska.com).

Bethel is a "damp" town where booze cannot be sold but can be brought in for "personal use." This creates a situation ripe for bootlegging. More than a few locals import booze—especially vodka—to sell for a high markup ($50–70 for a fifth!) to others desperate for a drink. A few years back a man was caught with 108 bottles in his possession, but he managed to convince a jury that they were for the wedding of a long-lost daughter.

GETTING THERE AND AROUND

Bethel serves as the transportation hub for much of Western Alaska, and has the third-busiest flight service station in the state. **Alaska Airlines** (800/426-0333, www.alaskaair.com) and **Frontier Alaska** (907/266-8394 or 800/866-8394, www.frontiera.com) both provide daily year-round service between Anchorage and Bethel.

Three air-taxi companies offer scheduled flights or charters from Bethel to other bush villages: **Grant Aviation** (907/543-2000 or 888/359-4726, www.flygrant.com), **JP Air Service** (907/543-3279), and **Yukon Aviation** (907/543-3280, www.yukonaviation.com).

Rent cars from **Payless** (907/543-3058 or 800/729-5377). Oh, yes—if you want a cab, just look around; one is bound to be within a couple of hundred feet of any place in town.

Nome and Vicinity

If you make only one long flight to see bush Alaska, make it to fascinating Nome (pop. 3,500, of whom nearly 1,900 are Native Alaskans). The town sits on the Seward Peninsula on the edge of Norton Sound facing the Bering Sea, only 190 miles east of Siberia and 2,300 miles north of Seattle. Flying time is 90 minutes from Anchorage.

Nome was named when a cartographer marked its unnamed location on a map as "? Name," and a second mapmaker misread it as "C. [for Cape] Nome." Lying 150 miles south of the Arctic Circle, Nome is on roughly the same latitude as Fairbanks and shares similar hours of daylight as well as warmer temperatures than its Arctic coast cousins, Kotzebue and Barrow—although the mercury rests around 0°F in January and soars to a sizzling 60°F in the long days of July. Local motels advertise "Visit picturesque Nome this summer. Three days—no nights."

Like other Alaska bush settlements, Nome is far from pretty, with piles of junk strewn about the yards and more than a few drunks stumbling from the town's eight saloons. But it has more of a small-city feeling than Bethel or Kotzebue, with historic buildings, paved streets (some of them), and a real downtown. Although there are almost no trees in Nome, each winter the "Nome National Forest" sprouts as locals plant their former Christmas trees in the offshore pack ice. (People cut the trees near Teller each fall before the road closes for the winter.)

SIGHTS

Start out at the helpful **Nome Visitors Center** (daily 7 A.M.–8 P.M. late May–mid-Sept., Mon.–Fri. 8 A.M.–5 P.M. mid-Sept.–late May) on Front Street in the center of town, run by the Nome Convention and Visitors Bureau (907/443-6624 or 800/478-1901, www.visitnomealaska.com). The knowledgeable staff will point you in the right direction, and the scrapbooks, photo albums, and amazingly detailed handouts provide an excellent introduction to the area. Pick up the walking-tour brochure, mostly focusing on historical attractions such as the nearby dredges.

Step across the street to **city hall** with its

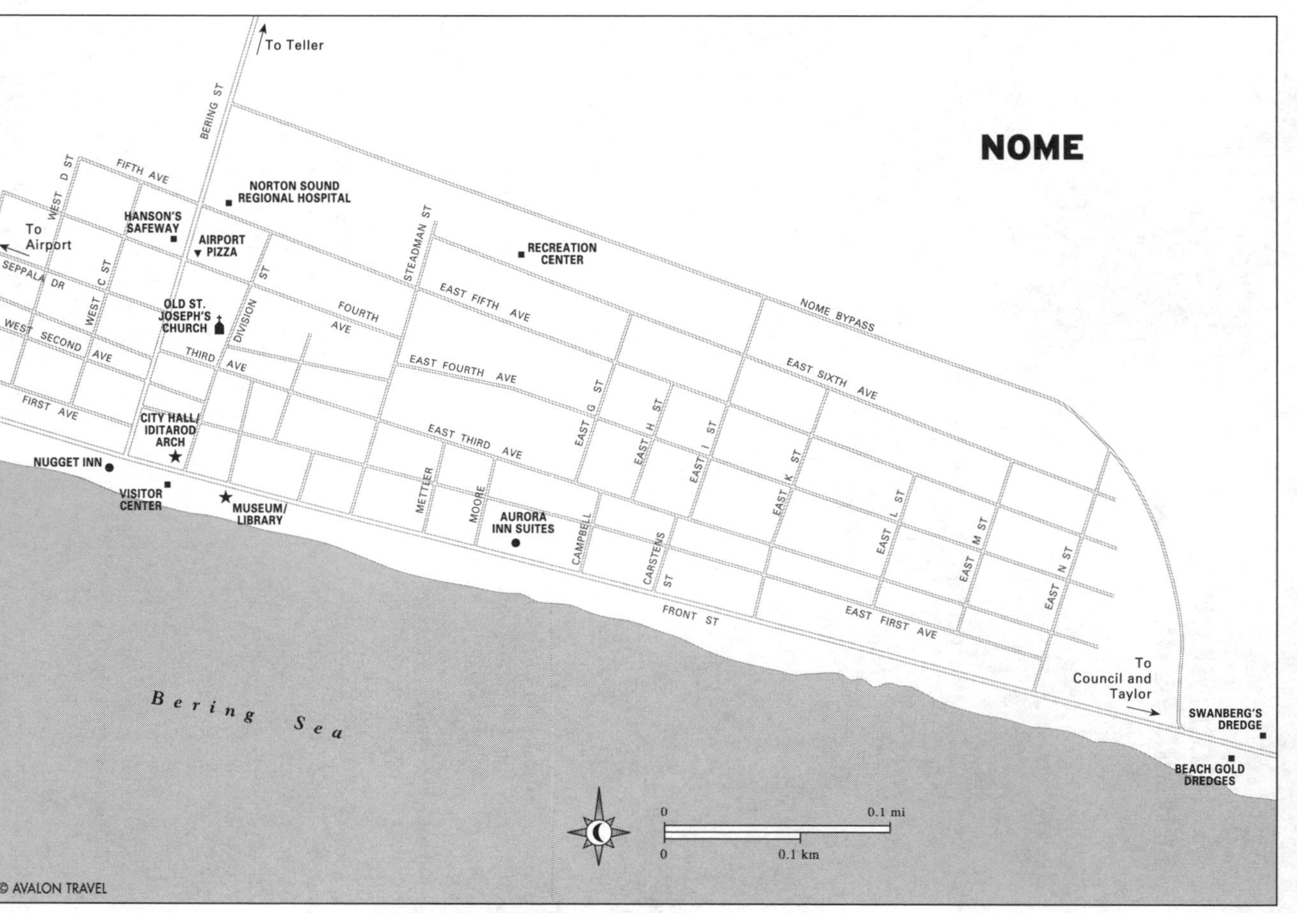

WESTERN ALASKA

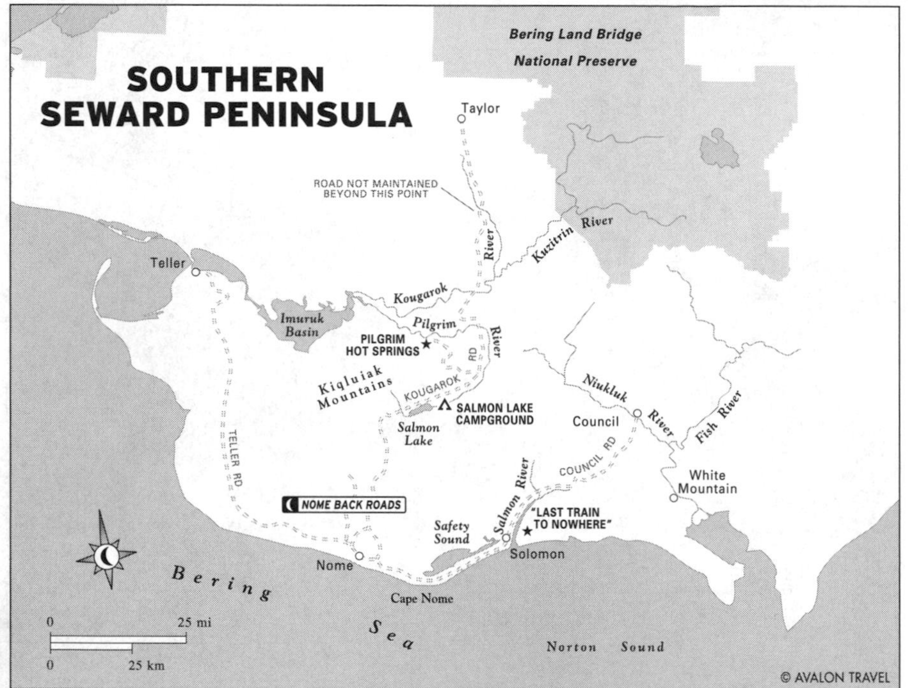

Victorian exterior. During the Iditarod Race, the massive **burled wooden arch** out front is moved over Front Street to mark the finish line.

The **Carrie McLain Museum** (907/443-6630, www.nomealaska.org/museum, daily 9 A.M.–5:30 P.M. June–early Sept., Tues.–Fri. noon–6 P.M. early Sept.–May) is in the basement of the library, a few doors east on Front Street. It houses a fascinating collection of historical photos from the gold-rush era, along with exhibits on Native Alaskan culture, sled-dog racing, the discovery of gold in 1898, the arrival of Wyatt Earp, and the rush of 40,000 miners to Nome in 1900.

Visit the National Park Service's **Bering Land Bridge Information Center** (179 Front St., 907/443-2522 or 800/471-2352, www.nps.gov/bela, Mon.–Fri. 8 A.M.–5 P.M.) for exhibits and videos. The staff has information on nearby Bering Land Bridge National Preserve and other national parks in the vicinity, including Cape Krusenstern, Noatak, and Kobuk Valley. Guided tundra hikes to nearby areas are offered occasionally in the summer.

Over on Division Street at 3rd Avenue is **Old St. Joseph's Catholic Church** (Mon.–Fri. 10 A.M.–2 P.M. summer), built in 1901 but closed in 1945. The building has been lovingly restored and is now used for local events. Take your photo at "America's largest gold pan" next to the church.

If you have a car or bike (or want a nice day hike), ride the 4.5-mile road to the 1,062-foot summit of **Anvil Mountain** behind Nome. World War II gun emplacements and an abandoned Cold War–era distant early warning station are on top, and on a clear day you'll be treated to views of the city, the Bering Sea, the Kigluaik Mountains, and the surrounding tundra.

NOME HISTORY

In 1898 the "three lucky Swedes," Jafet Lindberg, Erik Lindblom, and John Brynteson, discovered fabulous deposits of gold in Anvil Creek above present-day Nome. Word reached Dawson the next spring, and by fall 10,000 stampeders had arrived and set up tents on the beach, only to have them blown away by a fierce September storm that prompted a migration inland. There, more gold was found; in fact, placer deposits were carried by most streams that emptied into the Bering Sea. Twenty thousand prospectors crowded the coast by 1900, fully one-third of the white population in Alaska at the time. For a time it was the territory's largest city. A railroad had been built to Anvil Creek, which produced several dozen million-dollar claims. Some became rich, but many people who had bought one-way passage to the gold fields found themselves destitute, and the Army had to be brought in to get them home before the winter of 1901. Judge James Wickersham brought law and order to Nome in 1902 after the first judge was convicted of corruption. Several devastating fires and storms have destroyed most of Nome's historic downtown buildings, but a few of the original buildings survive.

In 1925 a diphtheria epidemic required emergency delivery of serum from Nenana, 650 miles overland by dogsled. Through the heroic efforts of mushers and dogs, the serum arrived in time to save many lives. This event is commemorated today in the famous Iditarod Sled Dog Race from Anchorage to Nome. The race takes place every March and turns Nome into a late-winter carnival.

During World War II, Nome was a major transfer point for lend-lease aircraft being sent to Russia from the United States. The planes were flown up to Alaska from the Lower 48 states, transferred to Russian pilots in Fairbanks, and then flown on to Nome and the Soviet Union. Almost 8,000 planes came through Nome 1942–1945, with most making it to the front for use in the war against Germany.

Today, Nome survives on small-scale gold mining, tourism, and as a regional center for the Seward Peninsula. Many visitors try their luck at panning for gold along the beaches here. Nome is a good place to buy ivory and other artwork in the various gift shops, along with imported crafts from Russia. Of course, the Iditarod Race focuses international attention on Nome every March.

Gold Fever

Gold dredges were once sprinkled all across the Seward Peninsula, and the last of these operated until 1995, when low gold prices and rising costs forced the last one to shut down. With a little exploration, you're sure to find some of the more than 100 old dredges that remain in the surrounding country. A number of these are within walking distance of Nome, but don't climb on them since they're unsafe. Closest is the **Swanberg Dredge** just east of town. Nearby is a small park with old mining equipment, including a steam shovel. Far more impressive is **Dredge No. 5,** a couple of miles north of town off the Teller Road. Offshore to the north of town is an enormous 14-story-tall dredge; it was the largest ever built.

Across the road from the Swanberg Dredge is a public beach where anyone can try their hand at panning for gold. The beach attracts an annual gathering of ambitious recreational miners who operate dredges throughout the summer months. It's hard work that involves a dry-suited diver operating a suction dredge atop a raft several hundred feet offshore. One local operation is even using a remote-controlled submarine (of sorts) to dredge. They're a pretty tight-lipped group, but they must be finding something since many return each summer, especially when gold prices spike as they did in the last few years.

NOME BACK ROADS

The real treat in Nome is the opportunity to explore this expansive, far-as-the-eye-can-see landscape. Over 250 miles of gravel roads fan out from town, taking you across the subarctic countryside around Seward Peninsula.

Wildlife—including musk ox, red foxes, wolves, moose, reindeer, and even a few grizzlies—can be seen, and the fishing is good for salmon, pike, grayling, whitefish, and Dolly Varden. Anglers will want to pick up the free *Nome Roadside Fishing Guide* from the visitors center before heading out.

Bird-watchers come from all over the nation to track down unusual bird species in the Nome area, including some that wander across the Bering Strait from Russia. The visitors center posts unusual sightings, and it has a bird checklist and brochure listing companies offering bird-watching trips. Also available at the visitors center is a brochure describing hiking routes.

In midsummer, the roads are lined with verdant tundra plants and a massive display of 200 species of flowers. Some have likened it to driving through Denali National Park but without anyone else there. The roads lead to the tiny settlements of Teller, Council, and Taylor, taking you past remnants from the gold rush—dredges, miners' cabins, and even an old train.

Air taxis from Nome provide flights to Bering Land Bridge National Preserve, where you will find popular Serpentine Hot Springs.

Kougarok Road

Also known as the Taylor Road, this exceptionally scenic route leads north along Nome River into the beautiful **Kigluaik Mountains,** a great place to explore on foot. The road parallels part of the historic Wild Goose Pipeline, built of metal hoops and redwood slats between 1905 and 1909 to carry water to Nome gold mines. The pipeline was never completed but is still intact in places. There's a free Bureau of Land Management (BLM) campground and picnic area at **Salmon Lake,** 40 miles out, and a hike-in shelter cabin in the Mosquito Pass area. Contact the BLM office in Nome (907/443-2177, www.blm.gov/ak) for the access route. A side trip to the old Catholic church and orphanage at **Pilgrim Hot Springs** is another option. The orphanage opened after the 1918 influenza epidemic killed many Eskimo parents in the area. The springs are not open to the public. Kougarok Road is not maintained beyond the Kougarok River bridge (Mile 85), although a trail continues to the village of Taylor.

Council Road

This gravel road heads east from Nome, following the shoreline of the Bering Sea for the first 30 miles before turning northeast. Eskimo fishing and hunting camps are all along this route. Bird-watchers flock to Safety Sound, a great place to watch for unusual species of ducks, swans, geese, and shorebirds.

At Mile 33, the road passes a favorite photographic stop, the rusting hulk of the **"Last Train to Nowhere."** The train consists of three locomotives and several cars from the Council City and Solomon River Railroad, begun in 1881. The engines originally served on the New York Elevated Railroad Company before they were shipped north in 1903, and they are the only such engines still in existence. The railroad was originally envisioned as part of a system that would connect Nome's gold fields with the Lower 48, but the vision died because of financial problems and wild storms that destroyed the tracks along the Bering Sea in 1907. At its maximum, the tracks only extended a distance of 35 miles.

The road ends at the Niukluk River (good fishing) near **Council,** 72 miles from Nome. It is possible to drive across the river at a fording point, but don't do so without help from locals. An alternative would be to have someone take you across by boat. One unusual aspect of the country around Council is the presence of trees, a real treat after all the open tundra elsewhere on the Seward Peninsula. The settlement of Council still has remnants of log cabins from the gold-rush era when the town was home to 10,000 people. Now it's a summer-home area for folks from Nome. Simple cabins are available at **Camp Bendelben** (907/443-2880).

Teller Road

It's a beautiful two-hour drive on this 73-mile gravel road that leads from Nome to the Eskimo village of **Teller** (pop. 250). Along the way you're

© DON PITCHER

the "Last Train to Nowhere"

likely to see reindeer herded by locals, along with musk ox and unusual bird species. Two stores in Teller have limited supplies.

ENTERTAINMENT AND EVENTS

Nome is a hard-drinking town with four liquor stores and six bars, including the surprisingly capacious **Board of Trade** (Front St., 907/443-2611). There's live music here most summer nights and during the Iditarod. The Board of Trade opened as the Dexter Saloon in 1901 under the proprietorship of gunslinger Wyatt Earp. Selling liquor and running gambling tables helped make Earp a very rich man; by the time he left Nome later that year, he had pocketed $80,000 in profits. Today, the gambling comes in the form of pull tabs and nightly bingo games.

Residents from outlying villages (all of which are dry) come to Nome to drink, and they do a very thorough job of it, as you will quickly see. Things can get pretty bad sometimes as the alcohol pours and the drunks get drunker. It could be worse, though—in the town's early days three-foot-thick urine "glaciers" were reported outside some saloons.

Nome's main attraction is the famous **Iditarod Trail Sled Dog Race** (www.iditarod.com). Beginning in Anchorage on the first Saturday in March, the race covers 1,049 miles to the finish point in Nome. It generally takes 10–12 days for the first team to reach Nome. Reserve far ahead to be sure of a motel room for the hectic finish. Everyone comes out to cheer the winning mushers and also-rans. The race ends under the burled arch that stands along Front Street.

Other March events include the **Iditarod Basketball Tournament.** With over 50 different high school boys' and girls' teams, this is said to be the largest in the nation. And, of course, there's the infamous **Bering Sea Ice Golf Classic,** which is played on the frozen sea off Nome, a place with hazards not common to most courses. It uses orange golf balls and green-dyed ice for the "greens." Another goofball event is the annual **Midnight Sun Polar Bear Swim** in the Bering Sea—assuming the ice is out. If you aren't so adventurous, there's always the indoor swimming pool at the high school. The Nome Convention and Visitors Bureau (907/443-6624 or 800/478-1901, www.visitnomealaska.com) has details on all these and other events.

SHOPPING

Check out Nome's gift shops for Eskimo dolls, carved ivory and soapstone, grass baskets, mukluks, and sealskin slippers. Good places to start are the **Arctic Trading Post** (907/443-2686), **Maruskiya's Gift Shop** (907/443-2955), and **Chukotka-Alaska** (907/443-4128 or 800/416-4128). The last two also sell handicrafts from Provideniya, Russia, just across the Bering Strait from Nome.

Get camping gear and other outdoor supplies from **Nome Outfitters** (120 W. 1st Ave., 907/443-2880 or 800/680-6663).

ACCOMMODATIONS

Nome's best-known hotel, **Nugget Inn** (907/443-2323 or 877/443-2323, www.nomenuggetinnhotel.com, $110 d) has tiny older guest rooms, but the exterior and lobby are full of character. You'll feel as though you just stepped back a century.

Aurora Inn & Suites (907/443-3838 or 800/354-4606, www.aurorainnome.com) has the finest lodging in Nome, with 56 bright and spacious guest rooms ($150 d), kitchenettes ($160–185 d), and apartments ($205–250 d). Amenities include a sauna, a guest computer, and Wi-Fi.

Extra Dry Creek B&B (907/443-7615, $125 s, $135 d) has a studio apartment unit with a kitchen, a bath, laundry, and Wi-Fi, along with breakfast ingredients.

At **Bering Sea B&B** (907/443-2936, $120 s, $140 d) two guest rooms share a bath, and a continental breakfast is included.

During the Iditarod each March, many locals open their homes for out-of-towners. The Nome Convention and Visitors Bureau (907/443-6624 or 800/478-1901, www.visitnomealaska.com) keeps a list, and their website has other lodging options.

CAMPING

Anyone can camp for free on the beach on the east side of Nome, but you'll need to get water from the visitors center and take showers at the recreation center. The abundant beach driftwood makes for great campfires. There's also a free Bureau of Land Management campground at **Salmon Lake,** 40 miles out on the Kougarok Road. Located in the mountains, it's worth the drive if you can afford a rental vehicle. There is good fishing for grayling, whitefish, and Dolly Varden too. It is also possible to camp on open tundra along the road system fanning out from Nome, but check first with the visitors center for a map of public lands since much of this is owned by Native Alaskans.

FOOD

Airport Pizza (406 Bering St., 907/443-7992 or 877/749-9270, www.airportpizza.com, Mon.–Fri. 7 A.M.–10 P.M., Sat.–Sun. 9 A.M.–10 P.M., dinner $17–38) serves pizzas by the slice or the pie, and is locally famous for fly-out pizzas shipped via air taxis to remote villages. But pizzas are only part of the menu here. You can get espresso from the drive-up window, big breakfasts, lunch sandwiches, burgers, and burritos, along with surprisingly good dinnertime pasta, steak, and seafood. Saturday night means prime rib, and there's a big-screen TV in the bar, with 15 microbrews on tap. Airport Pizza is the place in Nome.

For burgers and hearty breakfasts with the locals, head to **Polar Café** (204 Front St., 907/443-5191), or find Chinese meals at **Twin Dragon Restaurant** (100 Front St., 907/443-5552). **Husky Restaurant** (235 Front St., 907/443-1300) has Japanese and American meals, but sushi is the main attraction.

Arctic Trading Post (907/443-2686), across from the visitors center, serves espresso and also has regional books for sale. A **Subway** (135 E. Front St., 907/443-8100) is the only fast food chain in town.

Get groceries in town from **Hanson's Safeway** (4th Ave. and Bering St., 907/443-5454) or **Alaska Commercial Company** (on the north edge of Nome, 907/443-2243).

SERVICES

Find an ATM in the Wells Fargo on Front Street. The **Recreation Center** (208 E. 6th Ave., 907/443-5432) is three miles east of town next to the high school, and includes a swimming pool, racquetball courts, a weight room, a sauna, and even a bowling alley.

The **Kegoayah Kozga Library** (223 Front St., 907/443-6628, www.nomealaska.org/library, Mon.–Thurs. noon–8 P.M., Fri.–Sat. noon–6 P.M.) contains a rare books section, plus computers to check your email.

For emergencies, head to **Norton Sound Regional Hospital** (Bering St. and 5th Ave., 907/443-3311, www.nortonsoundhealth.org).

GETTING THERE AND AROUND

Alaska Airlines (907/443-2288 or 800/426-0333, www.alaskaair.com) has daily jet service into Nome from Anchorage and Kotzebue. **Frontier Alaska** (907/266-8394 or 800/866-8394, www.frontierak.com) flies between Fairbanks and Nome, with outbound service to surrounding villages and St. Lawrence Island; some of these are through its subsidiary, Hageland Aviation. **Bering Air** (907/443-5464 or 800/478-5422, www.beringair.com) also has bush flights from Nome. The Nome airport is 1.5 miles from town, a $6-per-person taxi ride from **Checker Cab** (907/443-5211).

Rent pickups, vans, or SUVs from **Stampede Ventures** (907/443-5252 or 800/354-4606, www.aurorainnome.com, $100 per day and up). Reserve ahead to be sure of finding a vehicle when you arrive. Gas prices in Nome are frequently twice those in Anchorage or the Lower 48.

Tours

Many visitors to Nome arrive as part of a see-the-Arctic package from **Alaska Airlines Vacations** (800/468-2248, www.alaskair.com/vacations). Tour options include a day trip to Nome ($574) or an overnight trip to Nome ($735 s, $1,308 d) with lodging. Both of these options also include local tours and round-trip air transportation from Anchorage.

For amusing and personalized tours of the Nome area, contact Richard Beneville of **Nome Discovery Tours** (907/443-2814, www.nomechamber.org/discoverytours, no credit cards). His background as an actor, dancer, and singer in New York may seem a bit out of place, but he's been in Alaska for decades and has deep knowledge of Nome and its fascinating history. A six-hour tour ($85 pp) includes town sights and also gets you out onto the tundra. There are also full-day slice-of-life trips to Teller ($150, highly recommended), Pilgrim Hot Springs, or Council.

ST. LAWRENCE ISLAND

This 100-mile-long island is about 160 miles southwest of Nome and just 36 miles from the Chukotsk Peninsula in Siberia. On a clear day, residents can see across the Bering Sea to the mountains of Siberia. The village of **Gambell** (pop. 550) is the primary settlement, home to Siberian Eskimo who have lived here for centuries. Most people speak Siberian Yup'ik as their primary language (though they also know English) and depend on subsistence hunting of bowhead and gray whales, seals, walrus, fish, birds, and even polar bears. The bones of whales are scattered around the village.

Because of its location, St. Lawrence Island is a good place to find unusual bird species, including Asian stragglers. Beautifully carved ivory and other crafts are available locally, but visitors should absolutely refuse to buy any Eskimo artifacts. Many of these priceless cultural relics have been looted from ancient village sites around the island by locals who pillage their own ancestors' graves for cash. Shame on them and on anyone who buys these items.

Bering Air (907/443-5464 or 800/478-5422, www.beringair.com) and **Frontier Alaska** (907/266-8394 or 800/866-8394, www.frontierak.com) both have daily service to St. Lawrence Island from Nome.

There is a well-stocked general store in Gambell, thanks to daily flights from Nome. **Sivuqaq Native Corporation** (907/985-5826) sets up local tours and lodging. Limited lodging is also available in the island's other village, **Savoonga** (pop. 630), where walrus-hide *umiak* boats are still used. There are no cars on St. Lawrence Island; folks get around by foot or four-wheeler.

The Arctic

In Arctic Alaska, settlements are far, far apart, and the land predominates. Geographically, it is a relatively simple area. The rugged Brooks Range parallels the Arctic Circle in a long arc across the state, descending on its northern margin to the treeless tundra of the North Slope. On the tundra are thousands of lakes and ponds, creating a vital nesting area for ducks, geese, swans, and shorebirds. Polar bears, grizzly bears, Arctic foxes, musk oxen, and other mammals are found in the Arctic, and vast herds of caribou make this their summer home, notably within the Arctic National Wildlife Refuge, which holds down the far northeast corner, bordered by the Arctic Ocean and Canada's Yukon Territory.

The Brooks Range encompasses both Noatak National Preserve and Gates of the Arctic National Park and Preserve, while other large public lands border the southern margins of these mountains: Kobuk Valley National Park, Cape Krusenstern National Preserve, and Selawik National Wildlife Refuge. Only one road connects the Arctic with the outside world: the **Dalton Highway,** which parallels the Trans-Alaska Pipeline from Livengood (north of Fairbanks) all the way to Deadhorse/Prudhoe Bay. It's almost 500 miles by car from Fairbanks to the Beaufort Sea/Arctic Ocean.

The People

Only two towns of any size are found in Arctic Alaska: Kotzebue and Barrow. Both are predominantly Inupiat Eskimo in population. Several national parks surround Kotzebue, and more parks and refuges encompass the Brooks Range, offering exciting possibilities for hikers and river runners in search of adventure. At the top of the continent on the Arctic Ocean lies Barrow, famous as the summertime land of the midnight sun, but also as the land where the sun does not rise for two straight months in winter. Prudhoe Bay, the source of Alaska's oil wealth, is also here, providing a temporary home for several thousand oilfield employees.

The Eskimo people who have made the Arctic their home for centuries have seen their culture undergo massive changes since their initial contact with Europeans 200 years ago. Christian missionaries brought new religions, attempted to obliterate all traces of their "pagan" beliefs, and forced them to take anglicized names. Other newcomers decimated the whales, seals, walrus, and other animals that were food for the Eskimo, and brought deadly diseases for which they had no immunity. Entire villages were killed by measles and influenza. In addition, the American culture of materialism and self-accomplishment contrasted sharply with traditions that emphasized getting along and working together. But perhaps the worst scourge the whites brought was alcohol. Even today, alcohol is a major factor in Alaska's high rate of suicide, drowning, and accidental deaths, particularly in the Arctic, where life is already so challenging. Visitors need to treat local people with sensitivity and respect, realizing that this is their land, not yours. If you show a genuine interest in people and their culture, you'll be rewarded with a far deeper understanding of their world. For an excellent introduction to the culture from an Eskimo perspective, see *The Epic of Qayaq: The Longest Story Ever Told by My People* by Lela Kiana Oman.

KOTZEBUE

The state's largest Native Alaskan settlement, Kotzebue (pop. 3,000) serves as a commercial hub for northwestern Alaska. The town covers a three-mile-long sandy spit at the tip of Baldwin Peninsula that has been occupied by Inupiat Eskimo for the last six centuries. Originally called Kikiktagruk ("almost an island"), today's name comes from Otto von Kotzebue, a Russian sailor who happened upon the village in 1816. Surrounding Kotzebue are

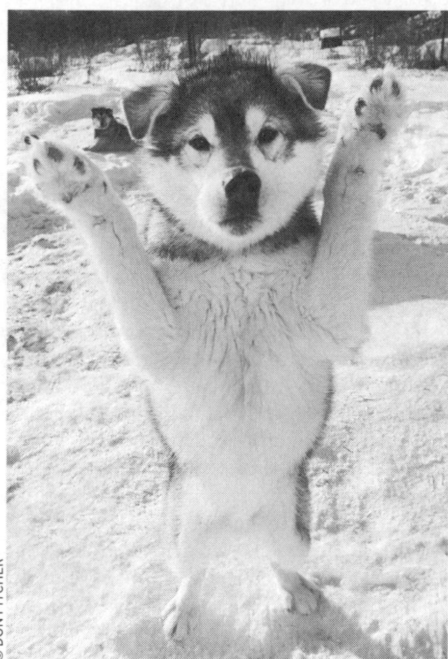
© DON PITCHER

sled dogs in Bettles

the shallow waters of Kotzebue Sound, and nearby are the mouths of the Noatak, Kobuk, and Selawik Rivers.

The Native Alaskans of Kotzebue lead a traditional lifestyle (with all the amenities, including snowmobiles and VCRs). It has the feeling of a large village, with a single paved road, rolling tundra, and open water. There are no trees, although the brush gets over your head in places. Just 30 miles north of the Arctic Circle, Kotzebue experiences endless sunlight for 36 days starting on June 3, but then suffers through an almost equal period of darkness around the winter solstice.

Northwest Arctic Heritage Center

New in 2009, the National Park Service's Northwest Arctic Heritage Center (907/442-3890 or 800/478-7252, www.nps.gov/kova, Mon.–Sat. 8 A.M.–5 P.M.) provides a focal point for the region. It covers Kobuk Valley National Park, Cape Krusenstern National Monument, Noatak National Preserve, and Bering Land Bridge. Built at a cost of $15 million (thank you, taxpayers), this 12,000-square-foot building houses exhibits on the natural world and Native Alaskan culture. Educational programs and Inupiaq dance performances may be offered. The center is located near the airport on 2nd Street.

Other Sights

Stroll around to absorb a bit of Kotzebue's Native Alaskan flavor. An interesting **cemetery** occupies several blocks in the center of town and includes colorfully decorated graves. Unfortunately, too many of these are from young people who died from suicide or alcohol-related accidents. Another cemetery occupies a hill overlooking town, and the same road continues out a couple of miles over the tundra to the town's water source. Walk south of Kotzebue past the airport to find a **fish camp** where several dozen structures are used for the drying and smoking of fish, seal, and walrus meat.

Red Dog Mine

Kotzebue's economy is dependent on the giant Red Dog Mine (907/426-2170, www.teckcominco.com), the largest zinc mine in the world and the employer of nearly 400 workers (many of them Native Alaskans). Located 100 miles north of town, Red Dog is owned by Teck Cominco, but the land belongs to the Northwest Alaska Native Association (NANA); both profit handsomely from the venture. The ore concentrate is trucked 45 miles from the mine to a port on the Chukchi Sea, where it is stored in an enormous warehouse (the largest building north of the Arctic Circle). Although mining takes place year-round, ore can only be shipped during the three-month summer, when the sea is ice-free.

Accommodations

Add a 12 percent tax to Kotzebue lodging rates. Stay at the modern (more or less) **Nullagvik Hotel** (907/442-3331, www.nullagvik.com,

$219 d), where Wi-Fi is an additional $10. A brand-new hotel is in the works here, but it probably won't open until 2014.

At **Bibber's B&B** (907/442-2693. $120 s, $150 d) a dozen guest rooms share six baths and three full kitchens, which are stocked with breakfast ingredients. Rooms have TVs and Wi-Fi.

There is no camping in Kotzebue, but you may be able to pitch a tent south of town past the airport along the beach. Many local people have summertime fish camps here, so ask around to make sure you aren't on someone's private space.

Food

Bayside Restaurant (907/442-3600) has decent Chinese food, along with sandwiches, steak, and halibut; it's probably your best choice in town.

Expensive groceries are available from **Alaska Commercial** (907/442-3285). Kotzebue is a "damp" town that doesn't allow alcohol sales, so bring your own from Anchorage.

Services

Native arts and crafts—especially carved ivory pieces and Eskimo dolls—are sold in the Nullagvik Hotel. An ATM is located at the Wells Fargo building (907/442-3258). **Maniilaq Health Center** (907/442-3321, www.maniilaq.org) is a large modern hospital with physicians on staff.

Getting There

Alaska Airlines (800/426-0333, www.alaskaair.com) has daily jet service to Kotzebue from Anchorage and Nome, while **Frontier Alaska** (907/266-8394 or 800/866-8394, www.frontierak.com) flies from Fairbanks to Kotzebue daily.

Scheduled flights to surrounding communities and air charters are available from **Bering Air** (907/442-3943 or 800/478-5422, www.beringair.com) and **Hageland Aviation/Frontier Alaska** (907/266-8394 or 800/866-8394, www.frontierak.com). You can also book air charters with **Northwestern Aviation** (907/442-3525, www.alaskaonyourown.com).

ARCTIC PARKS AND REFUGES

Four little-known national parks are found within a 100-mile radius of Kotzebue: Bering Land Bridge National Preserve, Cape Krusenstern National Monument, Kobuk Valley National Park, and Noatak National Preserve. Noatak and Kobuk abut Gates of the Arctic National Park, and the three combine to create a massive 16-million-acre wilderness, with another 2 million acres of wild country within Selawik National Wildlife Refuge immediately south of Kobuk Valley.

In addition to the Arctic National Wildlife Refuge, three other national wildlife refuges are at least partly inside the Arctic Circle. These include Selawik, Yukon Flats, and Kanuti National Wildlife Refuges. For details, contact the U.S. Fish and Wildlife Service in Anchorage (907/786-3542, http://alaska.fws.gov).

Bering Land Bridge

The 2.8-million-acre **Bering Land Bridge National Preserve** covers the northern Seward Peninsula 90 miles north of Nome and 50 miles south of Kotzebue. The area is considered a remnant of the land bridge that connected Siberia with Alaska during the last ice age. It served as a migratory corridor for people as well as animals, and the preserve has many archaeological sites, some of which date back 10,000 years or more.

Bering Land Bridge is vast; there are no roads that lead directly into it, and summer access is by small plane or boat. The preserve contains no trails and very few developed facilities, although several shelter cabins are available, along with a bunkhouse-style cabin at **Serpentine Hot Springs.** Next to the cabin is a bathhouse where you can soak in the mineral-laden waters. Unimproved trails lead up nearby ridges and to distinctive granite spires called tors. Other attractions include interesting lava flows near Imuruk Lake and volcanic craters. Get additional information from the Park Service office in Nome (907/443-2522 or 800/471-2352, www.nps.gov/bela).

Cape Krusenstern

The 660,000-acre Cape Krusenstern National Monument is northwest of Kotzebue, with access by boat or air charter. It contains significant archaeological sites on a series of 114 beach ridges that were formed over a period of 6,000 years. There are no developed facilities or trails within the national monument, but hikers enjoy the chance to look for a wide variety of waterfowl along with grizzlies, Dall sheep, and caribou. Park headquarters (907/442-3890 or 800/478-7252, www.nps.gov/cakr) is in Kotzebue.

Kobuk Valley National Park

The 1.7-million-acre Kobuk Valley National Park lies on the south side of the Baird Mountains 80 miles east of Kotzebue. The park is best known for the **Great Kobuk Sand Dunes** that cover 25 square miles near the Kobuk River, with some reaching to 250 feet in height. The dunes are a one-hour hike from the river, but the route can be obscure in places so be sure to get directions from the Park Service in Kotzebue (907/442-3890 or 800/478-7252, www.nps.gov/kova) before heading out.

You can fly directly to the dunes from Kotzebue via **Northwestern Aviation** (907/442-3525, www.alaskaonyourown.com) or **Bering Air** (907/442-3943 or 800/478-3943, www.beringair.com).

Two smaller areas of dunes dot the park, and the mountain passes are traversed by massive herds of caribou each spring and fall. In addition to the dunes, Kobuk Valley National Park offers pristine mountains and rivers, making it a destination for kayakers and canoeists. Most arrive by floatplane, flying from Bettles or Ambler into Walker Lake within Gates of the Arctic National Park. The 125-mile float trip to the village of Kobuk generally takes six days, or you can continue downriver all the way to Kiana. Contact the Park Service for more on running the river, and for a list of outfitters offering guided float trips.

© DON PITCHER

Great Kobuk Sand Dunes

There are no developed facilities within Kobuk Valley National Park itself, though several Native Alaskan villages dot the banks of the wide, slow-moving, and clear Kobuk River. *The Alaska River Guide* by Karen Jettmar provides details on floating its more challenging upper reaches.

Noatak National Preserve

The 6.6-million-acre Noatak National Preserve covers the enormous Noatak River drainage northeast of Kotzebue. Gates of the Arctic National Park is immediately east of Noatak National Preserve. Its northern edge is the crest of the DeLong Mountains, while to the south lie the Baird Mountains and Kobuk Valley National Park.

There are no developed trails or other facilities within the preserve. Most visitors float the river in kayaks or rafts, with the put-in point on the upper reaches. Fly in from Bettles or Kotzebue and get picked up in the village of

Noatak, approximately 350 miles away. Expect to take at least two weeks for this extraordinary and memorable trip. Contact the Park Service in Kotzebue (907/442-3890 or 800/478-7252, www.nps.gov/noat) for additional information. Karen Jettmar's *The Alaska River Guide* has details on floating the Noatak River.

Gates of the Arctic National Park

The central section of the Brooks Range is included within Gates of the Arctic National Park and Preserve, an 8.4-million-acre slice of majestic mountainous terrain. The park is famous for its deeply glaciated valleys, rugged summits—including the much-photographed **Arrigetch Peaks**—and abundant wildlife.

Park headquarters (4175 Geist Rd., Fairbanks, 907/457-5752, www.nps.gov/gaar, Mon.–Fri. 8 A.M.–4:30 P.M.) is in Fairbanks, and field offices include the **Coldfoot Ranger Station** (907/678-4227), **Bettles Ranger Station** (907/692-5494), and **Anaktuvuk Pass Ranger Station** (907/661-3520).

There are no roads or established trails within Gates of the Arctic, and the remote location and extreme climate of the Brooks Range require travelers to have strong wilderness skills. Before visiting the park, you will need to attend a backcountry orientation program at one of the ranger stations or at park headquarters. A small museum (907/661-3413, $5) in Anaktuvuk Pass has exhibits on Native Alaskan traditions and handicrafts.

Lodging facilities can be found on the park margins in Anaktuvuk Pass, Bettles, Coldfoot, and Wiseman.

Northern Alaska Tour Company (907/474-8600 or 800/474-1986, www.northernalaska.com) leads grueling 13-hour tours ($499 pp) from Fairbanks: van to Coldfoot, fly to Anaktuvuk Pass for a tour, and then fly back to Fairbanks. **Arctic Wild** (907/479-8203 or 888/577-8203, www.arcticwild.com) also guides visits to the Arrigetch Peaks.

Access to Gates of the Arctic is primarily by air out of Fairbanks, Bettles, Anaktuvuk Pass, or Coldfoot. **Bettles Air Service** (907/692-5111 or 800/770-5111, www.bettleslodge.com) and **Brooks Range Aviation** (907/692-5444 or 800/692-5443, www.brooksrange.com) have air charters from Bettles, and **Coyote Air Service** (907/678-5995 or 800/252-0603, www.flycoyote.com) flies out of Coldfoot.

Bettles

The tiny settlement of Bettles lies 35 miles north of the Arctic Circle and is renowned as a fall and winter destination for viewing the northern lights, with the most cloud-free skies of any Alaskan town. A Park Service ranger station here is open daily in the summer, and on weekdays the rest of the year. Dogsledding and snowmachining trips are available through the lodges.

Open year-round, **Bettles Lodge** (907/692-5111 or 800/770-5111, www.bettleslodge.com, $175 d shared bath, $195 d private bath) has a picturesque main lodge built in 1948, with a newer structure behind. For a taste of the North, the lodge offers summertime day trips ($500) from Fairbanks to Bettles that include the flight up and back, a boat tour, and a meal. Overnight summer trips start at $760 per person with airfare from Fairbanks. In fall and winter, the main attraction is aurora viewing, with a separate aurora-viewing cabin away from town. Winter packages (including air transport from Fairbanks, meals, and Arctic gear) begin at $780 per person for one night or $1,180 for two nights. The lodge includes a restaurant, a lounge, a gift shop, and even Wi-Fi. The simple restaurant is open for three meals daily, including $25 family-style dinners.

Spirit Lights Lodge (907/692-5252, www.spiritlightslodge.com) is a unique place where the focus is on winter, when "spirit lights" fill the night sky. Owners Annie and Bernard Browne are gracious hosts, providing creative home-cooked meals and the opportunity to rub shoulders with locals of all types. Three-day, three-night winter (Dec.–Mar.) packages are $1,300 per person, including round-trip airfare from Fairbanks, a comfortable suite with a kitchenette and a private bath, delicious meals, and use of snowshoes, skis,

© DON PITCHER

Spirit Lights Lodge in Bettles

and all the Arctic outerwear (including bunny boots) you'll need for nights of aurora-gazing. Space is limited, so call well ahead. In the summer months, the lodge rents suites ($150 d) and simple cabins that can sleep four guests ($100). Cabins have woodstoves and share a bath. Limited meals may be available in summer. Spirit Lights Lodge is highly recommended.

Everts Air Alaska (907/450-2350, www.evertsair.com) and **Wright Air Service** 9907/474-0502, www.wrightair.net) have scheduled flights between Fairbanks and Bettles. Two local air-taxi operators, **Bettles Air Service** (907/692-5111 or 800/770-5111, www.bettleslodge.com) and **Brooks Range Aviation** (907/692-5444 or 800/692-5443, www.brooksrange.com, summer only) fly onward to remote parts of the Brooks Range and Gates of the Arctic National Park.

Arctic National Wildlife Refuge

It doesn't get any wilder or more remote than this. The Arctic National Wildlife Refuge (ANWR, pronounced ANN-war) covers almost 20 million acres in the far northeastern part of Alaska, a landscape of flat and marshy coastal tundra, rolling hills, and tall glaciated peaks topping 8,000 feet. Other than a few summertime travelers in search of the ultimate wilderness experience, this treeless country has almost no human presence. There has, however, been intense pressure from the oil companies and their allies (including virtually all Alaskan politicians from both parties) to "unlock" this wilderness. The oil wealth that lies beneath ANWR is undoubtedly great, but the loss of this last great wilderness would be greater. The battle has pitched Native Alaskan people against each other—the Inupiat-owned Arctic Slope Regional Corporation is a big proponent of development (it stands to gain many millions of dollars in oil revenue)—but the Gwich'in people are adamantly opposed, fearing that development would destroy the vital caribou herds on which they depend.

The main reason people come to ANWR—other than to experience the stunning beauty of this place—is the wildlife. During the long

SAVING ANWR

An ongoing battle between developers and conservationists is whether to allow exploration and drilling for black gold within the 1.5-million-acre **Arctic National Wildlife Refuge** (ANWR). In a political compromise in 1980, the Alaska National Interest Lands Conservation Act called for a federal study to determine if oil and gas could be safely recovered within ANWR. Oil companies are concerned about the day when the North Slope reserves finally run dry, and claim that the pipeline's many years of operation have proven oil development and environmental protection are compatible on the North Slope. Also, improved technology has greatly refined development techniques, which further safeguard the wilderness. A poll of Alaskans would come down strongly in favor of opening the wildlife refuge to development, and only a handful of elected state politicians dare to stand up to the oil companies, which can pour many thousands of dollars into their (or an opponent's) campaigns. Oil money doesn't talk in Alaska politics – it yells.

Conservationists – along with a number of vocal Inupiat people from the tiny settlement of Arctic Village – have taken a strong stand against the development of ANWR, noting that any such development could imperil the 150,000-strong Porcupine caribou herd, a vital food source in their subsistence culture. In addition, they argue that this refuge is one of the few places on earth that protects a complete spectrum of Arctic ecosystems. The election of President Obama in 2008 signaled a major shift away from developing ANWR, but the final chapter has certainly not yet been written for one of the country's last great wildernesses.

and fierce winter, only the hardiest animals venture out of their dens, but in summer, the refuge erupts with life. (The ubiquitous mosquitoes are the best example of this; bring head nets and insect repellent.) Best-known are the annual migrations of the 150,000-strong **Porcupine caribou herd**—they are the reason the reserve was established—but also here are millions of nesting ducks, geese, swans, loons, and other birds. Large mammals include musk oxen, wolves, polar and grizzly bears, moose, and Dall sheep. Several major rivers drain ANWR on both sides of the Phillip Smith Mountains that split the refuge. The Sheenjek, Kongakut, Hulahula, and Wind Rivers are favorites of experienced kayakers and rafters.

Access to ANWR is by floatplane out of the surrounding settlements of Fort Yukon, Kaktovik, and Deadhorse. There are no developed facilities or trails within the refuge. Several companies offer expensive 10–12-day wilderness treks into ANWR down the Kongakut or Hulahula Rivers; recommended are **Alaska Discovery** (510/594-6000 or 800/586-1911, www.mtsobek.com), **Arctic Wild** (907/479-8203 or 888/577-8203, www.arcticwild.com), and **Chilkat Guides** (907/766-2491 or 888/292-7789, www.raftalaska.com).

For more on this magnificent wild place, contact the U.S. Fish and Wildlife Service in Fairbanks (907/456-0250 or 800/362-4546, http://arctic.fws.gov).

Kaktovik

The Inupiaq Eskimo village of Kaktovik (pop. 300) sits on Barter Island along the Beaufort Sea, just north of Arctic National Wildlife Refuge. The community hunts bowhead whales in September, and carcasses at the bone yard attract **polar bears,** making this a prime area to see these powerful creatures before they head back out on the sea ice. Up to 40 bears have been reported at peak times.

Kaktovik has a general store, along with clean and comfortable lodging at **Marsh Creek Inn** (907/640-5500, www.marsh-creekinn.com, $225 pp), where the room rate gets you lodging, three filling meals, and Wi-Fi. Guest rooms have twin beds, and some include private baths. Respected wildlife guide Robert Thompson of **Kaktovik Arctic Adventures** (907/640-6119, www.

kaktovikarcticadventures.com) leads polar bear viewing trips in the fall. **Frontier Alaska** (907/266-8394 or 800/866-8394, www.frontierak.com) has daily flights connecting Kaktovik with Fairbanks and Barrow.

Warbelow's Air Ventures (907/474-0518 or 800/478-0812, www.warbelows.com) has polar bear viewing trips from Fairbanks in September and October. These include round-trip airfare to Kaktovik, two days of guided day and night bear viewing, lodging, and meals at Marsh Creek Inn for $1,995; add $150 for an optional boat tour to watch bears along the shore. These trips can also be booked through **Polar Bears Alaska** (907/687-8120, www.polarbearsalaska.com).

Selawik National Wildlife Refuge

This large wetland covers more than two million acres along the Selawik River and its tributaries, and provides important habitat for caribou and other animals. The refuge is used by local people for subsistence hunting, fishing, and trapping, and it sees only a handful of visitors. Selawik River—a National Wild and Scenic River—is a Class I float trip from the headwaters to the village of Selawik. The Waring Mountains lie on the northern border of the refuge, and the Selawik Hills border the southern margin, providing hiking opportunities. Contact the refuge office in Kotzebue (907/442-3799 or 800/492-8848, http://selawik.fws.gov) for details.

BARROW

Located 350 miles north of the Arctic Circle, at 71 degrees latitude and 800 miles northeast of Nome, the small city of Barrow (pop. 4,400) is filled with paradoxes. Barrow has an $80 million high school with room for 2,000 students, plus a swimming pool, indoor track, and weight room. The grade school's indoor playground is useful in the winter, when typical temperatures often drop below -30°F outside; the town also has a first-rate hospital. Despite this, all the streets are unpaved, and yards are cluttered with old snowmachines, barking sled dogs, four-wheelers, skin boats, polar bear hides, and racks hung with dead ducks, caribou, and seal meat.

Barrow's population is predominantly Inupiat Eskimo, and many people still speak their indigenous language, but the taxi drivers are Filipinos, and many restaurants are owned by Koreans. One Native Alaskan woman I met sews gorgeous traditional Eskimo parkas and has dead eider ducks on her front porch, but she also spends a month or two lying on the beach in Hawaii each year.

Barrow receives 84 days of uninterrupted sunlight in summer, 67 days of darkness in winter. It sits on the edge of the Arctic Ocean, which remains virtually frozen 10 months of the year—an amazing sight in itself. Wintertime temperatures plummet far below zero, and the wind chill can push them as low as -80°F. Even in the summer, the weather is often chilly, wet, and windy. By mid-August it can be downright cold; be sure to bring warm clothes no matter when you visit. The dirt roads and wind also make for dusty (or muddy) conditions much of the summer.

Most visitors to Barrow arrive as part of a summertime package tour, some staying just a few hours, and others overnight. Few independent travelers visit the town since the cost of airfare alone is often higher than the tour price. Even fewer visitors get to see the events that are so important to Barrow—the whale hunts during the spring and the fall bowhead migrations. When a whale is brought in, the entire community comes out to help. Many assist in the butchering process, and the whale's fatty meat is shared. Afterward, the carcasses are dragged far out along Point Barrow to keep polar bears from wandering into town.

History

This stretch of coast was first mapped in 1826 by Captain Beech of the British Navy, who named it after Sir John Barrow, an English nobleman who encouraged and outfitted numerous Northwest Passage and polar expeditions. Whalers began arriving in the 1870s, and many of their ships became trapped in the ice; relief expeditions helped survey the North

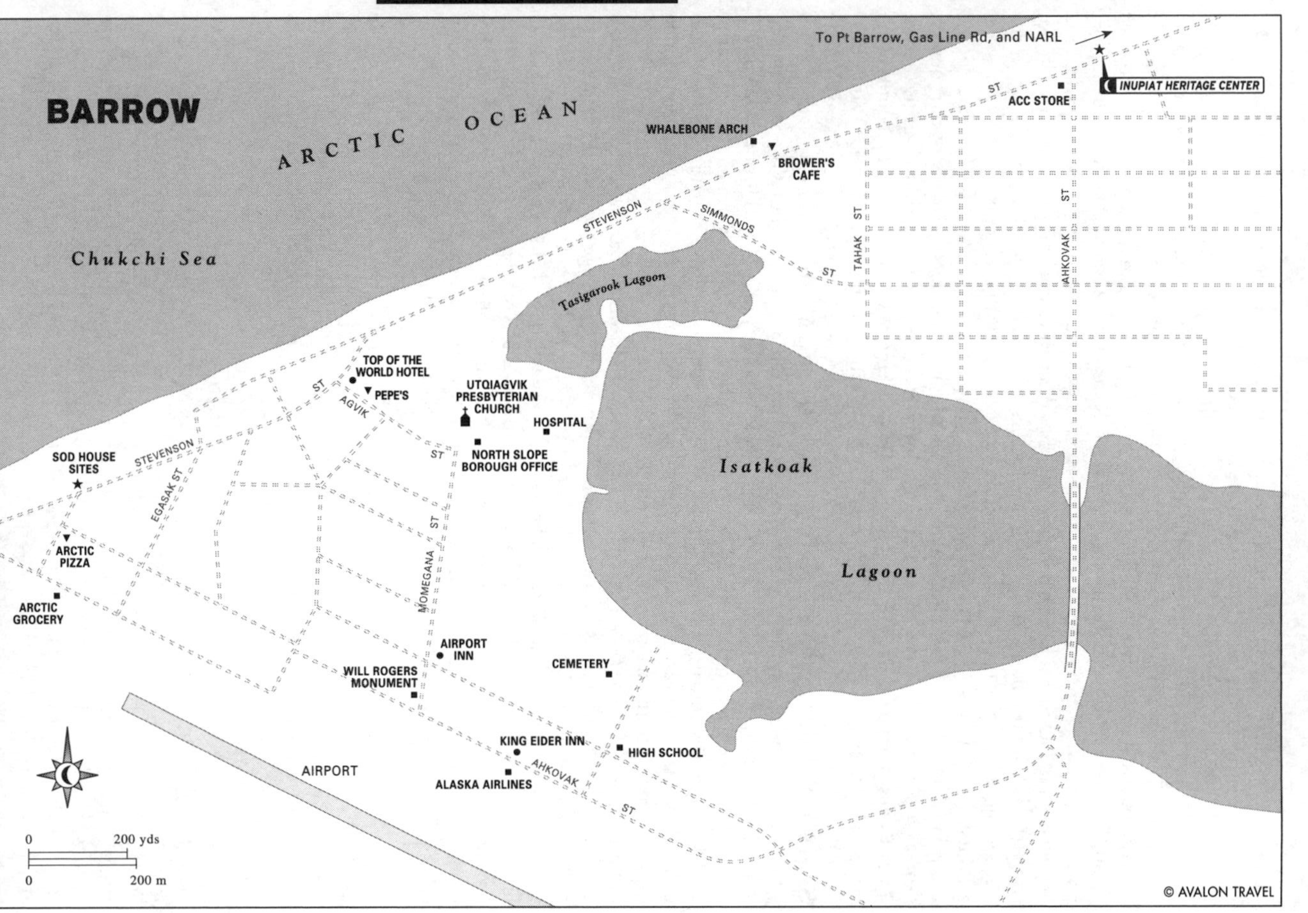
BARROW
ARCTIC OCEAN
Chukchi Sea
To Pt Barrow, Gas Line Rd, and NARL
INUPIAT HERITAGE CENTER
ACC STORE
WHALEBONE ARCH
BROWER'S CAFE
STEVENSON
SIMMONDS ST
TAHAK ST
AHKOVAK ST
Tasigarook Lagoon
Isatkoak Lagoon
TOP OF THE WORLD HOTEL
PEPE'S
AGVIK ST
UTQIAGVIK PRESBYTERIAN CHURCH
HOSPITAL
NORTH SLOPE BOROUGH OFFICE
SOD HOUSE SITES
STEVENSON
EGASAK ST
MOMEGANA ST
ARCTIC PIZZA
ARCTIC GROCERY
AIRPORT INN
WILL ROGERS MONUMENT
CEMETERY
KING EIDER INN
HIGH SCHOOL
AHKOVAK ST
ALASKA AIRLINES
AIRPORT
0
200 yds
0
200 m
© AVALON TRAVEL

Slope. The first plane reached Barrow in 1926, and famous bush pilot Wiley Post and humorist Will Rogers crashed and died here in 1935. Today, Barrow is the seat of the vast 88,000-square-mile North Slope Borough, and it has profited greatly from the oil pipeline—as can be seen in the modern buildings, services, and high wages.

One of the early white settlers was Charles D. Brower, who established a trading post at Barrow in 1884 and later married two Native Alaskan women. Their 14 children became important leaders in Barrow, and the big Brower family is still a vital part of the community. One part of town is even called Browerville.

Inupiat Heritage Center

The Inupiat Heritage Center (907/852-4594, www.nps.gov/inup, Mon.–Fri. 8:30 A.M.–5 P.M. year-round, $5 adults, $2 ages 14–17, children and seniors free) is a great place to learn about Inupiat Eskimo culture, particularly as it relates to whaling. Run by Ilisagvik College in coordination with the National Park Service, the heritage center houses artifacts, carved ivory, masks, dolls, sealskin boots, and a skin-covered boat. Fascinating dance and blanket-toss performances ($15) take place each afternoon in the summer.

Surprisingly, this facility is affiliated with the New Bedford Whaling National Historical Park in New Bedford, Massachusetts. More than 2,000 whaling voyages left New Bedford for Arctic waters during the late 19th and early 20th century, and many Inupiat Eskimo people participated in these commercial whaling ventures. In the winter, the center hosts today's whaling crews as they prepare their skin boats for the hunt.

A shop here sells Inupiat Eskimo baleen baskets, ivory carvings, and jewelry. Other places to find them include gift shops at the Top of the World Hotel and King Eider Inn, and the North Slope Borough Office. In addition, local artisans sell their works from tables at the AC Store entrance. Prices are a bit lower, and you're buying directly from the artist. The heritage center building also houses the **Tuzzy Consortium Library,** (907/ 852-4050 or 800/478-6916, www.tuzzy.org), where you can check your email.

Sights

Other than the Inupiat Heritage Center, Barrow's main attraction is simply the place and its people. Located on the Arctic Ocean (technically the town is on the Chukchi Sea; the Beaufort Sea lies just east of Point Barrow), it has long been occupied by the Inupiat. The remains of old houses made of whale bone and sod are visible on the shore at the west end of town, and they are fascinating to explore—but do not disturb any artifacts. Walk the eroding shoreline to the east past skin-covered wooden boats and a pair of arched whalebones at Brower's Cafe. More bones, along with a "milepost" sign, can be found outside historic **Utqiagvik Presbyterian Church,** established in 1898 and rebuilt after a fire in 1909. The **North Slope Borough Office** has a big bowhead whale skull out front, and inside are an impressive collection of artifacts that include parkas and carved walrus tusks. It also sells carved ivory, garments, and other items.

Wander around Barrow and you're bound to find something of interest. There's always a dead animal hanging in somebody's yard, and the sophisticated above-ground piping system is distinctively Arctic. (Barrow's gas comes from nearby fields and is very cheap, but water must be desalinated from brackish ponds.)

East of town is a mostly inactive Distant Early Warning (DEW) site and the old Naval Arctic Research Lab (NARL), now occupied by Ilisagvik Community College. More significant is the massive **Barrow Arctic Science Consortium** (www.arcticscience.org) facility, where researchers are studying global climate change and how rapid warming of the Arctic is affecting the ecosystem. The more you learn, the scarier it appears for such animals as polar bears and walrus.

Next to the airport, the **Barrow Visitors Center** is staffed daily 9 A.M.–5 P.M. mid-May–mid-September. For local information at other times, contact the **City of Barrow** (907/852-

5211, www.cityofbarrow.org). Outside the visitors center stands a monument to **Wiley Post and Will Rogers,** who died nearby in 1935. Another monument is at the actual crash site, 16 miles away and accessible only by foot or four-wheeler.

Gas Line Road extends 10 miles into the tundra from Barrow, providing good access for folks who want to wander or watch for birds. Barrow's excellent indoor **swimming pool** and recreation center are at the high school. The **Samuel Simmonds Memorial Hospital** (907/852-4611, www.arcticslope.org) provides emergency care.

Accommodations

Barrow has several places to stay. Largest and best-known is the **Top of the World Hotel** (907/852-3900 or 800/478-8520, www.tundratoursinc.com) where standard motel rooms run a budget-busting $210–230 s, $230–250 d. It's waterside location is unique in Barrow.

Barrow's newest and nicest place, **King Eider Inn** (907/852-4700 or 888/303-4337, www.kingeider.net, $189 s, $214 d, kitchenettes $199 s, $224 d, luxury suite $322 d), is right across from the airport (which can be noisy). Guests appreciate the Wi-Fi and guest computer.

The **Airport Inn** (907/852-2525 or 800/375-2527, $125 s or d) has clean and comfortable rooms with microwaves, fridges, Wi-Fi, and continental breakfasts. Some units include kitchenettes.

The least expensive option is the **Narl Hotel** (907/852-7800, $79 s, $98 d), where dorm-style rooms in an ATCO trailer have shared baths. This is primarily used by construction workers and scientists, and it's six miles out of town, so you'll need to pay $12 for a taxi ride. Eat next door at Ilisagvik College cafeteria (three meals per day year-round), with lots of grub for the cost. The Narl is often full in the summer.

Food

A longtime Barrow favorite, **Pepe's North of the Border** (907/852-8200, Sun. 9 A.M.–9 P.M., Mon.–Sat. 6 A.M.–10 P.M.) can be a tad expensive—a taco-enchilada combination plate is $19, and worth it. Or just order a bean burrito for $6 and fill up on chips and salsa. The menu also encompasses all-American breakfasts, burgers, sandwiches, seafood, and steaks for $10–30. In business since 1978, Pepe's is run by Fran Tate, who has filled this big fun place with the trappings of Mexico. And yes, the chefs really are from south of the border.

Another unexpected find in Barrow is **Osaka Sushi Bar** (907/852-4100), directly across from the Top of the World Hotel.

Sam & Lee's Restaurant (907/852-5555) has a filling lunchtime buffet and is open until 2 A.M., with breakfast available at any time. They're the only place open this late, and will also deliver via one of the local taxis. Also try **Brower's Cafe** (907/852-3456) on the other side of town in Browerville for Korean and American fare. Outside on the beach you'll see two arched whalebones and several skin boats.

Arctic Pizza (907/852-4222) has pizzas, and serves prime rib on Sunday nights, along with a mix of Italian, American, and Mexican food at other times. There's a big-screen TV for sports, and an upstairs with windows facing the Arctic Ocean. A much better bet—if you don't mind the lack of seating—is the oddly named **East Coast Pizza** (907/852-2100, Sun.–Thurs. 11 A.M.–11 P.M., Fri.–Sat. 11 A.M.–midnight), where owner/chef Vito Stojic serves fresh pizzas ($13–18), gyros, subs, and burgers. It's take-out only, but the best food in town.

For do-it-yourself meals, head to the **Alaska Commercial Store** (907/852-6711, www.alaskacommercial.com), where you'll find everything from ice cream to sofas. (And yes, they do sell refrigerators, even at the top of the world.) The AC also has a deli with espresso coffee and an ATM. But hold onto your wallet: Food prices are sky-high. Many of these items arrive by air—which explains the prices—but anything that won't spoil comes in aboard the barges that arrive during the brief ice-free period each August.

Getting There and Around

Alaska Airlines (800/426-0333, www.alaskaair.com) has daily jet service between Barrow and Fairbanks, and **Frontier Alaska** (907/266-8394 or 800/866-8394, www.frontierak.com) flies from Fairbanks. Frontier's subsidiary, Hageland Aviation, has scheduled flights out of Barrow to Prudhoe Bay and to a number of Arctic villages.

Alaska Airlines Vacations (www.alaskaair.com/vacations) offers excursions ($804 s, $1,378 d) from Fairbanks that include a tour and an overnight in Barrow at Top of the World Hotel. If you're really in a hurry, take a 12-hour quick trip ($574) from Fairbanks to Barrow and back with a tour of the town.

Northern Alaska Tour Company (907/474-8600 or 800/474-1986, www.northernalaska.com) has a package that duplicates the Alaska Air tours, and also offers a day-trip ($750) from Fairbanks to Barrow in a twin-engine Piper Chieftain. The flight is lower and more scenic, and it stops in Coldfoot for fuel, providing a taste of bush Alaska.

Tundra Tours (907/852-3900 or 800/478-8520, www.tundratoursinc.com) leads all-day tours that begin with a very informative bus tour around town and out to the end of the road near Point Barrow; the point itself is several more miles away. Following a lunch break, the tour shifts to the Inupiat Heritage Center for an introduction to the culture through dancing, drumming, and singing, followed by demonstrations of how traditional items are made and the opportunity to buy pieces from local artisans. The indoor blanket toss is always a highlight, but get your photos fast since they generally do just a couple of tosses. The cost is $105 per person, or combine a night's lodging at Top of the World Hotel with a day tour ($210 s, $295 d). Transportation to Barrow, of course, is extra.

Taxis are also available ($7 around town, $12 to NARL), or rent cars and pickups from **UIC Car Rental** (907/852-2700, www.ukpik.com). The **King Eider Inn** (907/852-4700 or 888/303-4337, www.kingeider.net) has vehicle rentals for guests.

BACKGROUND

The Land

The major physical features of western North America continue unbroken into that giant head of land that is Alaska. The Great Plains of the U.S. Midwest extend to become the Mackenzie Lowlands and the North Slope, while the Rocky Mountains form an inland spine from deep in Mexico to the Brooks Range. West of the Rockies, a high plateau runs from British Columbia north through the interiors of Yukon and Alaska, then west to the delta of the Yukon River, where it dips into the Bering Sea.

To the west of this plateau, two parallel chains and an intervening depression can be traced all the way from Mexico to Alaska. The Sierra Nevada of California become in turn the Cascades of Oregon and Washington, the Coast Mountains of British Columbia, the St. Elias and Wrangell Mountains, the Alaska Range, and finally the Aleutian Range, which then sinks into the Pacific just short of Asia. Closer to the ocean, California's Coast Range becomes the Olympic Mountains of Washington. Farther north, a string of islands from Vancouver to the Queen Charlottes and the Alexander Archipelago runs into the St. Elias Mountains, where the two chains unite into a jagged ice-capped knot. In Alaska they divide again as the Chugach and Kenai Mountains swing southwest toward Kodiak

© DON PITCHER

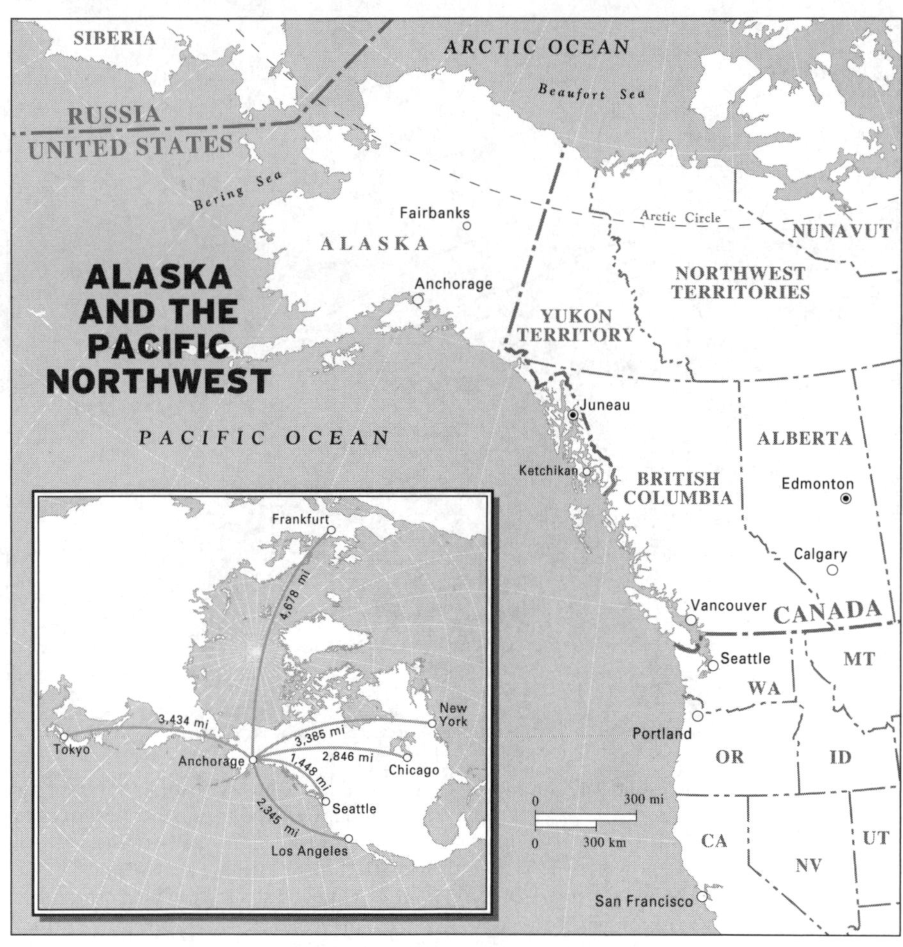

Island. Between these parallel chains is a 3,000-mile-long depression starting with California's Central Valley, then continuing with Puget Sound, the Inside Passage, the Susitna Basin in Southcentral Alaska, Cook Inlet, and Southwest Alaska's Shelikof Strait. Only four low-level breaks occur in the coastal mountains: the valleys of the Columbia, Fraser, Skeena, and Stikine Rivers. Most of the places described in this book are within or near this mighty barrier, which contains the highest peaks, the largest glaciers, and most of the active volcanoes in North America.

GEOLOGY

Plate Tectonics

Briefly, the huge Pacific plate (the ocean floor) is drifting slowly northeast. It collides with the North American plate, on which the continent rests, along an arc that stretches from the western Aleutians in the Gulf of Alaska to the Inside Passage—defining one section of the famous Pacific "Ring of Fire." This meeting of plates jams the ocean floor under the continental landmass and gives rise to violent geological forces: upthrusting mountains, extensive and large earthquakes,

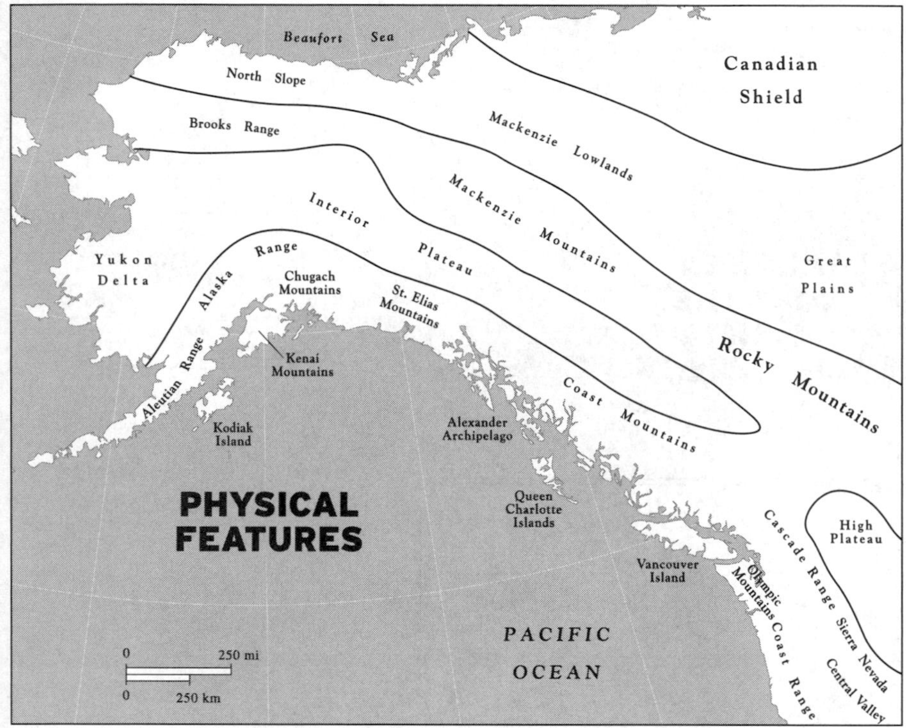

volcanic rumblings and eruptions, and movement along fault lines.

Somewhere in the mists of early geological time, a particularly persistent and powerful collision between the two plates caused the Brooks Range to rise; erosion has whittled its highest peaks to 8,000 feet, half their original height. Later, a similar episode thrust the Alaska Range into shape. The Pacific plate even today continues to nose under the continental plate in the vicinity of Yakutat (near where Southeast meets Southcentral Alaska). The force pushes Mt. Logan—Canada's highest peak—slowly upward. Learn more about the geological forces that shape Alaska at the University of Alaska Fairbanks **Geophysical Institute** website (www.gi.alaska.edu).

Earthquakes

One of the world's most seismically active regions, Alaska has withstood some of the most violent earthquakes and largest tidal waves ever recorded. In the last century, more than 80 Alaskan earthquakes registered higher than 7 on the Richter scale. The most destructive occurred at 5:35 P.M. on Good Friday, March 27, 1964, when the most powerful earthquake ever recorded in North America rocked Southcentral Alaska. This 9.2 magnitude quake (80 times bigger than the famous 1906 San Francisco earthquake, which is estimated at around 7.8) had a devastating impact on the region, flattening 75 homes and businesses in Anchorage, creating tsunamis that wiped out nearly every coastal village in Southcentral Alaska, and wreaking havoc all the way to California. The quake and its tsunamis killed 131 people. It was the second strongest in the 20th century; only a 9.5 magnitude quake in Chile in 1960 was larger.

© DON PITCHER

Mt. Redoubt steaming, west of Anchorage

Anyone who spends more than a few months in Southwest or Southcentral Alaska will probably feel at least one earthquake, and residents of the Aleutian Islands barely take notice of anything with a magnitude less than 6. The **Alaska Earthquake Information Center's** website (www.aeic.alaska.edu) provides detailed information on Alaskan earthquakes, including today's activity. For additional background on earthquakes in Alaska, visit the **USGS Earthquake Hazards Program** website (www.earthquake.usgs.gov).

Tsunamis

An earthquake deep below the ocean floor in the Gulf of Alaska or the open Pacific is especially dangerous to the coasts of Alaska and Hawaii, along with the west coast of Canada and the United States. The activity creates enormous tidal waves (tsunamis), which, although they are only 3–5 feet high in the open ocean, can travel at speeds exceeding 500 mph. Contrary to popular fears, a tsunami does not slam into the coast with 20 or 30 feet of water, washing away everything in its path like a flash flood. Instead, the water slowly inundates the land to a depth of 4–5 feet. Then, after a brief and chilling calm, the wave is sucked back out to sea in one vast undertow. Most of the destruction caused by the great Good Friday earthquake was of this nature, attested to by hair-raising pictures that you'll see in places like Valdez, Seward, and Kodiak. If you hear a tsunami warning, get to higher ground immediately. The **West Coast & Alaska Tsunami Warning Center** is based in Palmer, and its website (http://wcatwc.arh.noaa.gov) provides information on recent and historical tsunamis.

Volcanoes

Like its earthquakes, Alaska's major volcanoes are located along the Aleutian chain. In fact, 57 active volcanoes stretch along this arc, and most have been active in the last 300 years. The largest recorded eruption occurred when Novarupta blew its top in 1912, the most cataclysmic natural disaster since Krakatoa had cracked 30 years earlier.

There's always an active volcano somewhere in the state, especially in the Aleutians and along the Alaska Peninsula. The University of Alaska Fairbanks **Alaska Volcano Observatory** keeps track of volcanic activity, and its website (www.avo.alaska.edu) has details on current and historic eruptions.

Several volcanoes get particular attention because of their recent activity and proximity to major population centers: **Mt. Spurr** (78 miles west of Anchorage) erupted in 1992, **Mt. Augustine** (171 miles southwest of Anchorage) in 2005, and **Mt. Redoubt** (103 miles southwest of Anchorage) in 1989 and 2009. Each of these dumped ash in varying amounts on the region, closing schools and businesses, filling the air with ash (hazardous for people, electronics, and car engines), and creating havoc for air travel. The 1989 eruption of Mt. Redoubt nearly brought down a KLM jet when it flew into the ash cloud, causing all four engines to shut down. The plane dove two miles before the pilots were able to restart the engines

LAND OF SUPERLATIVES

Alaska boasts more superlative statistics than any other state in the country (itself a superlative). Consider: Alaska's total land area – 591,000 square miles (375 million acres) – is more than twice that of the next-largest state, Texas. A little more than four Alaskas could be jammed into the continental United States, while almost 300 Delawares could be jigsaw-puzzled into the 49th state. Mt. McKinley (also known as Denali), at 20,306 feet, is the highest point in North America; the Aleutian Trench, plunging to 25,000 feet below sea level, is one of the Pacific's deepest ocean troughs. Sitka, with more than 4,700 square miles within its boundaries, has the largest area of any North American city, and the North Slope Borough, at 88,000 square miles (slightly larger than Idaho), is the largest municipally governed entity in the world. Alaska's 45,000-mile coastline is longer than all the rest of the country's. Although only 3 percent of the state is covered in glaciers and ice fields (debunking the "frozen wasteland" myth – the most common misconception about Alaska), it still has more than 100 times more glacial area than the rest of North America. With all of 680,000 people, Alaska ranks third to last among the states in population, behind only Wyoming and Vermont. If Manhattan had the same population density, 17 people would live there. And if all the Manhattanites were transplanted to Alaska, they'd each have 125 acres.

and land safely in Anchorage. That same year, Redoubt generated a massive debris flow down the Drift River, inundating an oil terminal and threatening to spill oil into Cook Inlet.

GLACIATION

A glacier forms in areas of high precipitation and elevation where the snow is allowed to pile up to great depths, compacting the bottom layers into solid ice. The great weight above the bottom ice (along with the force of gravity) pushes it slowly downward like a giant frozen river, scooping out huge valleys and shearing off entire mountainsides. When the rate of advance is balanced by melt-off, the face of the glacier remains more or less stationary. If the glacier flows more quickly than its face melts, it advances; if it melts faster than it flows, the glacier recedes. Air bubbles are squeezed out of the glacier by this tremendous pressure, which makes glacial ice extremely dense. It's so compact that the higher frequencies of light cannot escape or penetrate it, which explains the dark-blue tinge. And because of its density, it also melts at fantastically slow rates; a small chunk or two will keep beer in a cooler chilled for a day or two.

Signs of the Glaciers

As you travel up the coast or hike in the national parks of the Interior, you'll soon start to recognize and identify glacial landforms. While rivers typically erode V-shaped valleys, glaciers gouge out distinctly U-shaped **glacial troughs.** Valleys and ridges branching from the main valley are sliced off to create **hanging valleys** and **truncated spurs.** A side valley that once carried a tributary glacier may be left as a **hanging trough;** waterfalls often tumble from these hanging valleys and troughs. Alpine glaciers scoop out the headwalls of their accumulation basins to form **cirques.** Bare jagged ridges between cirques are known as **arêtes.**

As a glacier moves down a valley it bulldozes a load of rock, sand, and gravel—known as **glacial till**—ahead of it, or carries it on top. Glacial till that has been dumped is called a **moraine. Lateral moraines** are pushed to the sides of glaciers, while a **terminal moraine** is deposited at the farthest point of the face's advance. A **medial moraine** is formed when two glaciers unite. These ribbonlike strips of rubble can be followed back to the point where the lateral moraines converge between the glaciers.

When looking at a glaciated landscape, watch for gouges and scrape marks on the bedrock, which indicate the direction of glacial

© DON PITCHER

Margerie Glacier, Glacier Bay National Park

flow. Watch too for **erratics,** huge boulders carried long distances and deposited by the glacier that often differ from the surround ing rock. Glacial runoff is often suffused with finely powdered till or **glacial flour,** which gives it a distinctive milky-white color; the abundance of this silt in glacial streams creates a twisting, braided course. With a little practice, you'll soon learn to recognize glacial features at a glance.

The vast majority of Alaska's glaciers, like those in many other parts of the world, are retreating as the global climate warms. In some cases, glaciers have drawn back many miles in the last few decades, exposing newly formed bays and producing massive outflows of icebergs. The 1989 *Exxon Valdez* oil spill was caused when the ship diverted to avoid ice from nearby Columbia Glacier; it didn't help, of course, that the captain was drunk. One of the few exceptions to the pattern of retreating glaciers is Hubbard Glacier near Yakutat, whose advance threatens to dam up a large bay, potentially changing the course of rivers. Learn more about glaciers and ongoing Alaska research at the **U.S. Geological Survey's** glacier and snow website (http://ak.water.usgs.gov/glaciology).

Permafrost

To picture permafrost, imagine a veneer of mud atop a slab of ice. In the colder places of the Lower 48, soil ecologists measure how much surface soil freezes in winter. In Alaska, they measure how much surface soil thaws in summer. True permafrost is ground that has stayed frozen for more than two years. To create and maintain permafrost, the annual average temperature must remain below freezing. The topsoil above the permafrost that thaws in the summer is known as the **active layer.** With the proper conditions, permafrost will penetrate downward until it meets heat from the earth's mantle. In the Arctic, permafrost begins a few feet below the surface and can extend 2,000–5,000 feet deep. This is known as **continuous permafrost,** which almost completely underlies the ground above the Arctic

Circle. **Discontinuous permafrost,** with permafrost in scattered patches, covers extensive parts of Alaska, particularly boggy areas covered by black spruce forests.

Frozen ground is no problem—until you need to dig in it. Russian engineers were the first to encounter industrial-scale problems with permafrost during the construction of the Trans-Siberian Railroad. In Alaska, gold mining, especially in deep-placer operations, often required up to two years of thawing hundreds of feet of permafrost before dredging could proceed. Today, houses frequently undermine their own permafrost foundations: Heat from the house thaws the ground, causing it—and the house above it—to sink. Similarly, road-building clears the insulating vegetation layer and focuses heat on the frozen layer, causing severe "frost heaving," the roller-coaster effect common to roads in Interior Alaska. In the 1970s, pipeline engineers had to contend with the possibility that the 145°F oil flowing through the pipe would have similarly detrimental effects on the permafrost, with potentially disastrous financial and ecological consequences. That's why more than half of the Trans-Alaska Pipeline is aboveground, supported by a specially designed and elaborate system of heat-reducing pipes and radiators. Today, there is increasing concern that warming global temperatures could have a devastating impact in the Arctic, causing permafrost to melt and greatly altering the ecosystem.

CLIMATE

Granted, over the course of a year, in any given location, Alaska's weather can be extreme and unpredictable. Because of the harshness of the winters, comfortable travel to many popular destinations is difficult early October–late April. Contrary to popular perception, however, the weather can also be quite pleasant. Alaska's spring, summer, and fall are not unlike these seasons in Minnesota. It's cool, it's warm; it's wet and dry; sometimes it's windy, sometimes it's muggy, sometimes it's foggy. For the latest outdoor forecast, visit the **National Weather Service's** Alaska website (www.arh.noaa.gov).

Extremes and Trends

It hit 100°F in the state once, in Fort Yukon in 1915. Fairbanks regularly breaks 90°F in July. It gets cold in Fort Yukon too, dropping as low as -78°F (Alaska's record low is -82°F, recorded in aptly named Coldfoot in 1989). *Any* wind at all at that temperature would make you feel even colder, if that's possible. Thompson Pass near Valdez gets quite a bit of snow, holding the records for the most in 24 hours (5 feet), a month (25 feet), and a year (81 feet). But Barrow, at the tip of the proverbial "frozen wasteland," got just three inches of snow in 1936–1937. An average of almost 13 feet of rain falls in Ketchikan every year—they call it "liquid sunshine." But again, one year Barrow squeaked by with only an inch.

Though Alaska retains the reputation of the Great Frozen North, a distinct warming trend has had a noticeable effect on the state. Temperatures warmed abruptly in the summer of 1977 and have remained unusually warm ever since, throughout all the seasons. For example, meteorologists report that in the Interior, only on rare occasions over the past 20 years has the mercury dropped much below -40°F. Also, the temperature of the permafrost has risen several degrees. For the latest research, visit the website of the University of Alaska Fairbanks **International Arctic Research Center** (www.iarc.uaf.edu).

Climatic Zones

It's possible to generalize about Alaskan weather and distinguish three climatic zones: coastal maritime, interior, and Arctic. The main factor affecting the southern coasts is the warm Japanese Current, which causes temperatures to be much milder than the norm at those latitudes. This current also brings continuous rain as humid Pacific air is forced up over the coastal mountains. For example, it rains in Juneau two out of three days. However, these mountains shield the Interior plateaus from the maritime air streams, so yearly precipitation there is low—a mere 15 inches. The Interior experiences great temperature extremes, from biting cold in winter to summer heat waves. The mountains also protect the coastal areas from cold—and hot—Interior air masses. The Arctic zone is characterized by cool, cloudy, and windy summers (averaging 50°F) and cold, windy winters—though not as cold as in the Interior.

Based at the University of Alaska Fairbanks, the **Alaska Climate Research Center** (http://climate.gi.alaska.edu) has detailed information on the state's climate, along with current weather conditions.

THE LIGHT AND THE DARK

If you plan to be in Alaska late May–late July, you can leave the flashlight at home. If you camped at the north pole for a week on either side of summer solstice, the sun would barely appear to move in the sky, frying you to a crisp from the same spot overhead, as if stuck in space. The Arctic Circle, at 67 degrees latitude, is usually defined as the line above which the sun doesn't set on June 21, nor rise on December 21.

Barrow lies at 71 degrees latitude, 4 degrees and roughly 270 miles north of the Arctic Circle. Here the sun doesn't dip below the horizon for 84 days, May 10–August 2. (You'll definitely see, and probably buy, the famous postcard with the time-lapse photograph showing the sun tracing a very mild curve: "going down" in the north-northwest, hovering above the horizon, and "coming up" in the north-northeast.)

Fairbanks, 140 miles south of the Arctic Circle, has 22 hours of direct sunlight on summer solstice, with the sky (if it's clear) going from a bright orange-blue to a sunset

THE PINEAL GLAND

Most Alaskan life-forms pack a year's worth of living into five months of light, then hibernate through seven months of dark and cold. This is not only a cliché; it's also a fact based on physiology – the physiology of the pineal gland, to be specific. This gland, shaped like a pinecone, sits on a short stem in the oldest and most mysterious section of the human brain. It's a lonely gland – a unique asymmetrical neuro-nub surrounded by large masses of advanced symmetrical tissue. Until recently, it was among the most obscure structures on the human neurological frontier; in fact, only a couple of decades ago it wasn't even considered a gland but was known only as the pineal "body."

This is somewhat surprising, since its function in other vertebrates has been understood for hundreds of years. In fish, reptiles, and birds, the pineal "eye" sits on a long stalk close to the brain's outer frontal section, right between the two regular eyes where a third eye would be. However, it's not connected to the eyes or any other sensory pathways; rather, the pineal gland is a simple efficient photoreceptor that senses and interprets the relative duration, intensity, and polarizing angles of light in the environment – making it the primary organ responsible for regulating internal circadian and seasonal rhythms. It tells fish how to navigate, birds when to migrate, and mammals when to sleep and reproduce.

How it works in other mammals is the key to understanding the gland's function in humans. Our gland produces a single (that we know of) hormone: melatonin. Melatonin circulates through the body and triggers two known reactions: drowsiness and reduced sex drive. What inhibits melatonin production? Light! The more sunlight – the greater its intensity and the steeper its angle – the less drowsiness and the stronger sex drive we feel. This helps explain many interesting general phenomena, such as why we sleep less deeply when it's not dark, the physiology of "spring fever," and why sex is better during the day. It also explains specific northern occurrences, such as why over two-thirds of Alaskan babies are conceived May-September (as opposed to November-February, as is commonly believed), and why you can do with a lot less sleep in Alaska in the summer.

purple to a sunrise pink and back to bright orange-blue. Even Ketchikan, at around 55 degrees latitude and probably the southernmost point on most Alaskan itineraries, enjoys more than 18 hours of daylight, with the starless dusk a paler shade of twilight. Similarly, in December Ketchikan receives six hours of pale daylight and Fairbanks only three, but at Barrow you wouldn't see the sun at all for nine weeks.

Why?

The explanation for the "midnight sun" lies in the tilted angle of the Earth's axis. Because the planet rotates off-center, the Arctic Circle leans toward the sun in summer, so a complete 24-hour rotation makes little difference in the angle at which the sun's rays strike the North Country. However, the rays do have to travel farther, and they strike Alaska at a lower angle, which you'll notice: The sun never gets nearly as high in the sky here as you're probably used to. Because of the low angle, the rays are diffused over a larger area, thus losing some intensity, which accounts for the cooler air temperatures. And since the sun seems to move across the sky at a low angle, it takes longer to "set" and "rise." In addition, the atmosphere refracts (bends) the sunbeams more dramatically closer to the poles, which causes the low light to linger even after the sun is down. This soft slanting light is often magical, with sharp shadows, muted colors, and silky silhouettes—a photographer's dream.

Northern Lights

The continual light is a novelty if you're traveling around Alaska for just a few weeks, but when you're there all summer, to paraphrase the commercial, "D-A-R-K spells relief." Stars? What a concept! Headlights? Oy vey! From early August, though, you start losing daylight quickly, to the tune of an hour a week in Fairbanks. Temperatures drop, berries and rose hips ripen, mushrooms sprout, and there's the possibility of experiencing one of life's all-time great thrills: God's light show, the aurora borealis.

The far-flung Eskimo had a variety of mythical explanations for the lights. Many believed that they represented the spirits of ancestors or animals, while others relegated the lights to malevolent forces. Prospectors preferred to think of them as vapors from rich ore deposits. The Japanese, however, have attributed the most romance to them: A marriage consummated under the lights will be especially fulfilling. Scientists have lately raised some controversy over particular aspects of the aurora, such as that the lights never dip below 40 miles above the earth (though many northerners swear they've seen the lights dancing along the ground); whether or not the lights manifest an electric sound is still a matter of some dissension, and even the experts who believe it don't know why. But these days everyone agrees that the sun, again, is responsible for the show.

When the solar surface sparks, the energy propels a wave of ionized particles (known as the "solar wind") through space. When these anxious ions encounter the gases in the earth's atmosphere, a madcap night of oxygen-nitrogen couples dancing begins. The sun's particles and the Earth's gases pair off, with the fastest ions grabbing the highest gases. The ensuing friction causes a red or yellow afterglow. The slower ions infiltrate the lower regions, and those encounters glow green and violet. The waving, shimmering, writhing ribbons of color cannot fail to excite your own ions and gases. For detailed information on northern lights and predictions of upcoming aurora activity, visit the website of the University of Alaska's **Geophysical Institute** (www.gedds.alaska.edu/auroraforecast). Other excellent websites include www.pfrr.alaska.edu/aurora and the kid-friendly www.alaskascience.com/aurora.htm. A number of lodges in the Fairbanks area have geared their winter season for people who come to view and photograph the northern lights, especially Chena Hot Springs Resort and Spirit Lights Lodge in Bettles. Many Fairbanks hotels will provide aurora wake-up calls on request.

Flora

VEGETATION ZONES

The vegetation of the Alaska Interior falls into four main categories: rain forest, boreal forest, taiga, and tundra. The lush coastal **rain forests** of Southeast Alaska are dominated by hemlock, spruce, and cedar. The Sitka spruce, Alaska's state tree, rivals California redwoods in height, age, beauty—and commercial value, of course. Sparser forests stretch across Southcentral Alaska, with spruce continuing through northern Kodiak Island but not farther west than the adjacent mainland. Dense thickets of alder and willow grow in the higher subalpine areas near the coast.

The **boreal forest** of the Interior lowlands consists primarily of scattered open stands of white spruce, paper birch, alpine fir, lodgepole pine, and balsam poplar (cottonwood). **Taiga,** the transition zone between boreal forest and tundra, is characterized by sparse and stunted black spruce, dwarf shrubbery (mostly the ubiquitous willow), and swampy areas known as "muskegs."

The lower-elevation **tundra,** also known as the "moist tundra," starts at the tree line, around 2,500 feet. There you find undergrowth similar to that of the taiga but without the trees. The higher-elevation alpine tundra consists of grasses, clinging mosses and lichens, and an abundance of tiny, psychedelically bright wildflowers, including the unforgettable forget-me-not (state flower), with gaze-catching petals of light blue.

TREE LINE

There are actually two tree lines in Alaska: One is determined by elevation, the other by latitude. Generally, the tree line descends in elevation as the latitude ascends. Although alder and poplar do survive in isolated stands near the Brooks Range, the Arctic region on the North Slope is mostly treeless tundra. Dwarf willow, alder, grasses, and moss give the tundra here the appearance of a shag carpet. This tundra belt continues along the shores of the Bering Sea to the Alaska Peninsula and Aleutian Islands. Southward, the Arctic vegetation is gradually replaced by Pacific coastal varieties.

FLOWERS

While you're hiking, an excellent book to have along is *Field Guide to Alaskan Wildflowers* by Verna E. Pratt. The photographs are good, the descriptions are usable, and the flowers are conveniently arranged by color.

Fireweed is a wildflower you'll come to know intimately during your travels in the North. It enjoys sunlight and grows profusely in open areas along roads and rivers. Given proper conditions, tall fireweed can grow to seven feet high. Its long stalk of pink flowers blossoms from bottom to top; sourdoughs claim they can predict the arrival and severity of winter by the speed with which fireweed finishes blooming.

forget-me-not, the Alaska state flower

In Southcentral and Interior Alaska, **prickly rose** is a common sight. The plant grows stems up to four feet high with sharp stickers. The flowers have five pink petals; the bright-red rose hips ripen in mid-August and contain highly concentrated vitamin C. Pop 'em in your mouth, suck off the slightly tart flesh, spit out the pips, and climb a mountain.

Three kinds of **primrose,** also a pinkish red, are another common sight on the tundra. Other red wildflowers of the tundra include **purple mountain saxifrage, moss campion,** and large bright-pink **poppies.**

White flowers include the **narcissus-flowered anemone,** similar to a **buttercup,** which also grows on the tundra. **Mountain avens** are easily recognizable—they look like white roses. A half-dozen kinds of white **saxifrage** are widespread throughout the state. Be careful of the local **water hemlock,** which is deadly poisonous. Similar is the **yarrow,** a medicinal herb with a disk of small white flowers and lacelike leaves. As soon as you identify **Labrador tea,** you'll notice it everywhere in the forest and taiga. **Cotton grass** looks exactly like its name. **Daisies** and **fleabane** complete this group of plants with white flowers.

Larkspur looks similar to fireweed, only it's a dark purple. It grows on a long stalk and a dwarf bush. **Monkshood** is a beautiful dark-blue flower of the buttercup family; **harebells** and **bluebells** are easily identified around Denali. Three kinds of **violets** grow in the boreal forest. Light-purple **lupine** flowers grow in 20-inch clusters. **Asters,** resembling purple daisies, bloom all over the Interior.

BERRIES

Berries are the only fruits that grow naturally in Alaska, and luckily the many varieties are abundant, several are edible, a few even taste good, and only one is poisonous. If you're into berry collecting, get to know poisonous **baneberry** immediately. A member of the crowfoot family, it grows mostly in the Southeast and the central Interior. The white berries look like black-eyed peas; they ripen to a scarlet red. **Juniper berries** grow throughout Alaska, but the **bog blueberries, Alaska blueberries,** and **huckleberries** are much tastier. Blueberries also grow on poorly drained, shady alpine slopes and are generally the first to ripen. **Salmonberries** turn a dark salmon-red in late summer, and are quite similar to raspberries.

Bunchberries are good tasting but have been known to upset a stomach or two. **Bog cranberries** are best after the first frost, especially when they're a deep purple—deliciously tart. **High-bush cranberries** are common but are best just before they're completely ripe. **Wild strawberries** are even better if you can get to them before the birds and rodents. The several kinds of **bearberries** (blue and red) are tasteless except to bears, and the **soapberry** will remind you of getting caught saying a dirty word as a kid. Pick up *Alaska Wild Berry Guide and Cookbook* for the complete lowdown on Alaska's berries.

MUSHROOMS

Approximately 500 species of mushrooms are found in Alaska, thrusting up from the fecund forests from Ketchikan to Katmai and the rich tundra from Kantishna to Kotzebue. Most of the mushrooms are harmless to humans, and are often edible; a handful are poisonous, such as varieties of **amanita** (especially the *muscaria,* or fly agaric) and **poison pax.** But if you learn to identify such common species as **hedgehogs** and **shaggy manes,** you'll enjoy happy hunting, mostly in July–August. For more information, see *Alaska's Mushrooms* by Harriette Parker.

FRANKENSTEIN CABBAGES

In 1941 the managers of the Alaska Railroad offered a $25 prize to the grower of the largest cabbage in the state, and since then cabbage growers have been competing. Usually the largest cabbages at the Tanana Valley State Fair (in Fairbanks in mid-August) weigh in at 65–70 pounds, but a world record was set in 2009 when a Wasilla man grew a 127-pound cabbage. Ten-pound celery, 3-pound beets, 2-pound turnips, and 1-pound carrots have also been blue-ribbon earners. Find them and more at the Alaska State Fair in Palmer at the end of August.

Fauna

If any aspect of Alaska embodies the image of the "last frontier," it's the state's animal kingdom. For millennia, Native Alaskan hunters, with their small-scale weapons and limited needs, had little impact on wildlife populations. Eskimo and Aleut villages subsisted comfortably on fish, small mammals, and one or two whales per year; the interior Athabascan bands did well on a handful of moose and caribou. This all changed in the mid-1700s with the coming of the Russians and Americans. Sea otters, fur seals, and gray whales were quickly hunted to the verge of extinction. By the 1850s the Alaskan musk ox had been annihilated. Wolves, in part because they preyed on the same game as humans, were ruthlessly hunted.

Conservation measures have nurtured their numbers, and today Alaska boasts one of the largest concentrations of animal populations remaining on earth. For example, there are nearly twice as many caribou in Alaska as there are people. There's a moose and a Sitka black-tailed deer for every three people. If 80,000 sheep strikes you as an impressive number, consider 40,000 grizzly bears. Bald and golden eagles are commonplace, and while the magnificent trumpeter swan was believed near extinction in the Lower 48, it was thriving in Alaska. Marine mammals, from orcas to the recovering otters, are common (though they have recently experienced major declines in the Aleutians and western Alaska), and Alaskan waters also contain fish and other sea creatures in unimaginable quantities.

Wildlife Viewing

Alaska's wildlife is a major draw for both visitors and residents. The state's vast stretches of wilderness contain abundant mammals, birds, and fish, including some of the largest and most magnificent animals in the world. Land mammals such as brown (grizzly) and black bears, caribou, moose, Dall sheep, wolves, and musk ox are the main attractions, but the state also has incomparable populations of birds, including such favorites as bald eagles, puffins, loons, and sandhill cranes. Marine mammals include seals, Steller sea lions, and sea otters, along with beluga whales, orca (killer) whales, humpback whales, gray whales, and others.

The *Alaska Wildlife Viewing Guide,* by Michelle Sydeman and Annabel Lund, is a useful introduction to finding wild animals. Visit the Alaska Department of Fish and Game's website (www.wildlifeviewing.alaska.gov) for details on dozens of species of Alaskan animals in their "Wildlife Notebook" series, and for descriptions of places to see wildlife. The state also produces regional wildlife viewing guides, along with excellent pamphlets covering various Alaskan towns and areas. Pick up copies in visitors centers around the state or find them on the website above.

In Alaska, wildlife may be encountered up close almost anywhere outdoors. Many animals are well prepared to defend their territories against intruders (you), and even the smallest can bite. Never attempt to feed or touch wildlife. It is seldom good for it, you, or those who follow. Any animal that appears unafraid or "tame" can be quite unpredictable, so keep your distance. One thing you don't have to worry about is snakes; there are none in Alaska. Surprisingly, however, there *are* frogs, even above the Arctic Circle.

LAND MAMMALS

Brown Bears

The brown bear, also called grizzly, is the symbol of the wild country and a measure of its wildness. Grizzlies once roamed all over North America. In 1800 there were over 100,000 of them; today, around 1,000 survive in the Lower 48. Ironically, the grizzly is the state animal of California, where it is now extinct. Things are very different in Alaska, where 40,000 of these magnificent creatures still inhabit the land.

Denali National Park offers some of the most accessible bear-viewing in the state. The

© DON PITCHER

brown bear

estimated 200 Denali grizzlies are still wild, mostly in their natural state. This is especially important for the continued education of the cubs, who are taught how to dig roots, find berries, catch ground squirrels, and take moose calves. However, Denali grizzlies are not afraid of people, and they are extremely curious; some have tasted canned beans, veggie burgers, and Oreo cookies. While no one has been killed by a grizzly at Denali, maulings have occurred, usually because of the foolishness of novice hikers and photographers or as a result of improper food storage. Take care, but don't be afraid to go hiking.

The natural grizzly diet is 80 percent vegetarian. They eat berries, willows, and roots, as well as preying on anything they can take: from ground squirrels to caribou, from foxes to small black bears. And they're challenged by nothing, except humans with high-powered weapons. Grizzlies are racehorse-fast and have surprising endurance; they need about 50 square miles for home territory and travel several miles each night. During the day they like to eat, sleep in the sun—often on snow patches—and entertain tourists on the shuttle buses.

Grizzlies are solitary creatures. Full-grown boars and sows are seen together only during mating season, in early summer. The gestation period is a little over five months, and the sows give birth in December to one to three cubs. The cubs are hairless, weigh one pound each, and remain blind for a week. They stay with the mother for over 2.5 years—two full summers. They're then chased away sometime before July of the third summer, when the sow is ready to mate again.

Contrary to popular belief, bears do not hibernate. They do sleep deeply in dens during the winter, sometimes for weeks. But they often get hungry, lonely, or restless, and step outside to forage for frozen roots, berries, and meat. Sometimes a bear will stay out all winter; that's the one that the Native Alaskans fear the most: the winter bear. Its fur tends to build up a thick layer of ice, rendering it nearly impenetrable, almost bulletproof. And of course, sows give birth in the deep winter, which they're certainly awake for.

Grizzlies and brown bears were once thought to be different species, but are now considered the same. The basic difference is in size, which is due to habitat. Grizzlies themselves are the world's largest land omnivores, growing to heights of 6–7 feet and weighing in at 500–600 pounds. However, they're the smaller of the two because they live in the Interior and feed mostly on vegetation. Brown bears are coastal, and with a rich source of fish protein, they have achieved near mythical sizes. Kodiak brown bears retain a reputation for being the largest, reaching heights of over 10 feet and weights of up to 1,400 pounds. On Admiralty Island in Southeast Alaska the brown bears are a bit smaller, but population densities are the highest anywhere: around one bear per square mile.

Hiking in bear country requires special precautions. A number of areas offer outstanding brown bear–viewing around Alaska; the most famous places are McNeil River, Katmai National Park, Pack Creek, and Kodiak Island.

Black Bears

Black bears are found in most forested parts of Alaska, though not on certain Southeast Alaskan islands. They are distinguished from grizzlies and brown bears by their size (much smaller), the shape of their face (much narrower), and the lack of a shoulder hump. Black bears are actually more dangerous to people than grizzlies: There have been more attacks and maulings in Alaska by black bears than by brown. Two places on Tongass National Forest offer a fine opportunity to watch black bears as they catch salmon: Anan Creek Bear Observatory near Wrangell and Margaret Creek Fish Ladder near Ketchikan.

Polar Bears

Polar bears dwell in northern and western Alaska, spending their lives wandering on pack ice (extensive areas of drifting ice) or along the coast. In winter, they wander south on the ice, sometimes even reaching the Kuskokwim River delta, but in the summer they are found out in the Chukchi Sea and Arctic Ocean. Global warming poses a serious threat to the long-term survival of this remarkable animal, and they are now officially listed as "threatened" under the Endangered Species Act. As the polar ice retreats, bears need to swim farther and farther to find ice where they can haul out and rest. Some polar bears may be able to survive by shifting to a shore-based existence in the summer, but the species faces a bleak future, no matter what Rush Limbaugh spouts.

Visitors to Alaska are highly unlikely to see a polar bear in the wild in the summer, but they can be found in the fall around whale carcasses at both Barrow and Kaktovik; locals provide bear viewing tours in both towns. The Alaska Zoo in Anchorage also has two polar bears. The best place to see and photograph polar bears in the wild is around Churchill in Manitoba, Canada (www.churchill.ca), where bear tourism is a thriving early winter business. Learn more about these endangered bears at the U.S. Fish and Wildlife Service website (http://alaska.fws.gov/fisheries/mmm).

Moose

The moose is the largest member of the deer family, and Alaska has the largest moose. A bull moose in his prime gets to be about 7 feet tall and weighs around 1,200 pounds, all from eating willow stems—about 30 pounds per day. They also eat aspen and birch, but willow is the staple of choice. The antlers, which are bone, are shed and renewed every year. Full-size antlers can weigh up to 70 pounds—that's mostly in September during the rut, or mating time. Bulls of near-equal rank and size butt their heads together to vie for dominance. You want to be really careful of bulls then; they are touchy. The cows have one or two calves, rarely three, in May, and that's when you want to be really careful of the cows too. The calves stay with the cow exactly one year; then she chases away the yearlings. Sometimes at the start of the summer season you'll spot a huge pregnant cow with a frisky yearling on her heels, and you've never seen a more hassled-looking expression on an animal's face. But that's family life.

Moose don't cover too much territory—about 30 miles a year, mostly in the forest, which provides natural defense against predators. The word *moose* comes from the Massachusetts Algonquian dialect and means "muncher of little twigs." By the way, the little flap of hair under the moose's chin is known as the "moostache." (Just kidding, it's really called the "dewlap.")

Harsh winters are deadly to moose. Deep snow and bitter cold can cause one in three moose in central Alaska to perish. Annually, hundreds of moose make their last stand along the snowless railroad tracks between Seward and Fairbanks and are killed by trains that don't stop for them. Hundreds of other starve to death. Those hit by cars along roadways are butchered and distributed to local people.

If Alaska moose are the world's largest, Kenai Peninsula moose are Alaska's largest. A Kenai moose holds the Alaskan record: at 10–11 years old, his antlers were just under 75 inches wide, he weighed 1,500–1,600 pounds, and he gave his life for Guinness.

Kenai National Wildlife Refuge was specifically established to protect moose, and these massive animals are a common sight along Kenai Peninsula roads at dusk. Other places to watch for moose are within the Anchorage bowl and in the Matanuska-Susitna Valley northeast of Anchorage. Drive with care, since moose can suddenly step onto the road without warning, and their massive bulk means that a collision could be fatal to both the moose and people in the vehicle.

Moose can be very aggressive, particularly in the winter months when food is scarce. A number of people have been killed by moose attacks, even in Anchorage. Always give moose a wide berth, especially if you're walking, on a bike or skis, or with a dog. If a moose appears ready to attack, quickly hide behind a tree, car, or other obstruction. Pepper spray may be effective if all else fails, or you can try to outrun a moose if you have no other options; they generally don't run far. If the moose knocks you down, curl up in a ball, protect your head with your hands, hold still, and say a few thousand Hail Marys.

Caribou

Caribou are travelin' fools. They're extremely flighty animals—restless, tireless, fast, and graceful. Run and eat, run and eat is pretty much all they do—oh, yeah, and reproduce. Reindeer, although of the same species, are smaller and often domesticated. Caribou are peaceful critters, and they'll outrun and outdistance their predators, mostly wolves, rather than fight. They like to travel in groups, unlike moose, which are loners. And they cover 10 times as much territory. Their herding and migrating imperatives are similar to those of the plains bison; they gather in large numbers and think nothing of running 50 miles, almost on a lark.

Caribou are extremely well adapted to their winter environment. They have huge nasal passages and respiratory systems in order to breathe the bitterly cold winter air. Thick fur covers almost every inch of their bodies; the fur itself is protected by large, hollow, oily guard hairs. This tends to make caribou look much larger than they really are; a good-sized bull weighs 400–500 pounds, a cow about half that. Caribou have the richest milk in the animal kingdom: It's 20 percent fat. They've also got huge prancing hooves, immortalized in the Santa Claus myth, which are excellent for running, swimming, disco dancing, and pawing at the snow to uncover the moss and lichens on which they subsist all through the harsh Arctic winter. The word *caribou* comes from the Maine Algonquian dialect and means "scraping hooves."

The caribou is the only member of the deer family whose females grow antlers. Babies are on their feet and nursing within an hour of birth, and at one week they can run 20 miles. If they can't, they'll most likely die, since the herd won't wait. But this helps to keep the herd healthy, controls population growth, and provides food for the carnivores.

Native Alaskans are among the caribou's natural predators. Historically, Native Alaskans ate the meat raw, roasted, and stewed. They ate all the organs, even the half-digested greens from the stomach. The little gobs of fat from behind the eyes were considered a delicacy. They used almost exclusively caribou hide for clothes, rugs, blankets, and tents. The leg skins were used to make mukluks; the long strands of stringy sinew provided sewing thread.

Nearly 1 million caribou roam across Alaska, with the largest herds in the Arctic, including within the Arctic National Wildlife Refuge. Caribou are commonly seen within Denali National Park and Preserve and along Interior and Southcentral Alaskan roads, including the Glenn Highway near Eureka, the Alaska Highway east of Tok, the Denali Highway, the Dalton Highway, and the Richardson Highway near Paxson.

Dall Sheep

Named for William H. Dall, one of the first people to survey the lower Yukon (1866), Dall sheep are sometimes called Alaska bighorn sheep, because the Rocky Mountain bighorn is a closely related species. Distinguished by their brilliant white color, the rams grow large curved horns, formed from a specialized skin structure made up of a compacted mass of hair and oil. The horns aren't shed; instead the sheep add another ring to them yearly, so the longer the horns, the older the ram, and the more dominant within the herd. The rams can weigh as much as 175 pounds; the ewes have small spiked horns and average 120 pounds.

Their habitat is the high alpine tundra, and they subsist on grasses, mosses, lichens, and flowers. Their bird's-eye view provides an excellent defense. They're also magnificent mountain climbers. Roughly 70,000 Dall sheep reside in the Chugach, Kenai, Alaska, and Wrangell mountain ranges. During summer, the rams migrate high into the ranges, leaving the prime lower grazing grounds for the ewes and lambs. It's natural that they migrate, the same way it's natural that they have predators. Their alpine tundra habitat is very fragile,

Dall sheep in Denali National Park

and it can take decades to regenerate after overgrazing. Migration and predation thus keep the flock healthy, control population growth, and guarantee the survival of the habitat.

Dall sheep inhabit mountain hillsides throughout much of Alaska. They are frequently seen on rocky slopes in Denali National Park, near Atigun Pass on the Dalton Highway, near Cooper Landing on the Kenai Peninsula, and along Turnagain Arm 20 miles south of Anchorage.

Wolves

Wolves have traditionally been one of the most misunderstood, misrepresented, and maligned mammals, in both fact and fable. We've come a long way from the days when it was believed that wolves were innately evil, with the visage of the devil himself, eating their hapless prey—or little girls in red hoods—alive. But it wasn't until the mid-1940s, when wildlife biologist Adolph Murie began a long-term and systematic study of the wolves in Mt. McKinley National Park, that all the misconceptions of the accepted lore about wolves began to change.

For three years Murie tramped mainly on the plains below Polychrome Pass and became extremely intimate with several wolf families. (His book, *The Wolves of Mount McKinley,* published in 1944, is still considered a classic natural history text.) Though Murie concluded that a delicate balance is established between predator and prey to their mutual advantage, declining Dall sheep populations, political pressure, and, indeed, tradition forced the park service to kill wolves, which were considered, against Murie's conclusions, to be the cause of the sheep decline. Typically, though, the wolf population was in just as dire straits as the sheep, and for several years no wolves were killed in the feds' traps because of their scarcity.

Since then, many researchers and writers have come to incisive conclusions about the wolf. It has been determined that their social systems—within the pack and with their prey—are amazingly complex and sophisticated. The alpha male and female are the central players in the pack, surrounded by 4–7 pups, yearlings, and other adults. The dominant female receives a long involved courtship from the dominant male (though he might not necessarily be the biological father of the pups). Territories can be as small as 200 square miles and as large as 800 square miles, depending on a host of influences.

Perhaps the most complex and fascinating aspect of wolf activity is the hunt. Barry Lopez, author of the brilliant *Of Wolves and Men,* argues persuasively that the individual prey is as responsible as the wolf for its own killing, in effect "giving itself to the wolf in ritual suicide." Lopez maintains that the eye contact between the wolf and its prey "is probably a complex exchange of information regarding the appropriateness of a chase and a kill." Lopez calls this the "conversation of death."

With the advent of radio collaring and tracking from airplanes, the movements of individual wolves and packs have continually surprised wildlife biologists. Wolves often travel 5–10 miles per hour for hours at a time. In a matter of days, an individual cut loose from a pack can wind up 500 miles away. Thus wolves are able to select and populate suitable habitats quickly.

Alaska's 7,500–10,000 wolves are thriving, even though roughly 15 percent of them are harvested yearly by trappers. They can be found all the way from the Southeastern panhandle to the Arctic slope, but are most common in Interior Alaska. Denali National Park offers travelers the best chance to see a wolf from the road system, but wolves may also be seen in other parts of the Alaska Range, in Brooks Range foothills, and in Wrangell–St. Elias National Park.

Captive wolves can be seen at the Alaska Zoo (www.alaskazoo.com) in Anchorage. A nonprofit organization, Wolf Song of Alaska (www.wolfsongalaska.org), has an education center in downtown Anchorage. A highly controversial state-sponsored hunting program has targeted wolves in some parts of the state to increase the survival of caribou and moose. The program includes the aerial killing of wolves and is widely opposed by environmental groups but applauded by some hunting organizations.

Elk

Elk—a relatively common sight in the western Lower 48—were also prevalent in Alaska 10,000 years ago but disappeared during the last ice age. In the mid-1920s, Alaskans decided that elk would be an attractive addition to the territory's big-game species, and a handful of Roosevelt elk were imported from Washington State. After a few years of island-hopping, the cervids (deer) were finally transplanted to their permanent home, Afognak Island off the north coast of Kodiak, and from there they apparently swam to Raspberry Island and Kodiak. Though the country was rugged—wet, windy, and choked with alder—the elk thrived in their new home, and some grew to 1,000 pounds. Within only 20 years (1950), 27 bulls were culled from the herd by resident hunters. Hunting continued up until the late 1960s, when a series of severe winters decimated the herds. Ten years of protection and mild winters allowed the herds to regenerate; today, 1,200 elk live on Afognak and Raspberry Islands, with a second small population on Etolin Island near Petersburg.

Musk Oxen

The musk ox is a stocky long-haired animal with a slight shoulder hump and a very short tail. Despite their name, musk oxen have no musk glands and are not oxen. The largest member of the sheep family, this shaggy prehistoric-looking creature was abundant in the North Country until it was hunted into extinction by the mid-1800s. In the 1930s, several dozen musk oxen were transplanted from Greenland to Nunivak Island in the Bering Sea. Like the elk on Afognak, the musk oxen on Nunivak thrived, and the resident Native Alaskans used the soft underwool to establish a small cottage industry knitting sweaters, scarves, and caps. And that's what it would have remained, a small cottage industry, if it hadn't been for Dr. John J. Teal, Jr., a student of Arctic explorer Vilhjalmur Stefansson. Stefansson recognized the potential of musk ox wool and inspired Teal to experiment with domesticating them. After spending 10 years with musk oxen on his farm in Vermont, Teal concluded that they were amiable, hardy, and easy to domesticate. So in 1964 he started the Musk Ox Project at the University of Alaska in Fairbanks.

In 1984 the project moved to a farm in the Matanuska Valley, where musk oxen are bred to produce *qiviut* (KEE-vee-oot), the soft underwool, which is renowned in Alaska for its insulation (eight times warmer by weight than sheep wool) and tactile (softer than the finest cashmere) properties. The *qiviut* is collected from the animals in the spring. The raw wool is sent to a mill in Rhode Island and then sold to Oomingmak (a Native Alaskan word for musk ox, meaning "bearded one"; www.qiviut.com), a co-op consisting of members in villages spread throughout western Alaska. Here the *qiviut* is knitted into garments, which are sold at retail outlets in Anchorage and at the farm near Palmer.

Today, wild musk oxen can be found on the Seward Peninsula near Nome, Nunivak and Nelson islands, the Yukon-Kuskokwim Delta, the North Slope near Prudhoe Bay, and the Arctic National Wildlife Refuge. The best places to see them up close are the Musk-Ox Farm in Palmer (www.muskoxfarm.org) and the Large Animal Research Station (www.uaf.edu/lars) at the University of Alaska in Fairbanks.

Lynx

Alaska's only native cat, the lynx is the northern version of the bobcat. Weighing around 20–30 pounds, these extremely secretive animals prey primarily on snowshoe hare, a species that undergoes an 8–11 year cycle of abundance. Lynx numbers fluctuate with those of hare but lag one or two years behind. When a hare population crashes, lynx numbers soon decline, and they sometimes travel up to 400 miles in search of food. Although snowshoe hare are an important prey for lynx, when they are scarce lynx hunt grouse, ptarmigan, squirrels, and rodents, and may even take larger animals such as caribou or Dall sheep.

Lynx are sometimes seen during long periods of summer daylight, especially in years when they are abundant. Lynx have large broad feet that function as snowshoes for winter hunting and traveling.

Mountain Goats

These members of the antelope family number 13,000–15,000 in Alaska. They have snow-white coats, shaggy heads, and black spiked horns up to a foot long, and they weigh in at 150–300 pounds. They mostly inhabit the coastal ranges and eastern Alaska Range and are frequently seen high on cliffs so precipitous that they would probably scare even Dall sheep.

Sitka Black-Tailed Deer

These small deer are found throughout Southeast Alaska, in Prince William Sound, and on Kodiak and Afognak Islands. Visitors to all these areas may occasionally see deer, but some of the largest populations are on Kodiak Island. The deer population averages more than 300,000 individuals but fluctuates widely, depending upon the severity of the winter. They're the second-most-prevalent game animal in Alaska behind caribou. They prefer a forest environment, but also roam high into the mountains for young shrubs and ripe berries in the late summer months. Males weigh 120 pounds, females 80 pounds.

Rodents

Ground squirrels and marmots are true hibernators: Unlike other mammals such as brown, grizzly, and polar bears, they sleep for six months straight in a deep coma. This separation between life and death is one of the thinnest lines in the animal world. A ground squirrel's heart slows to about six beats a minute, and its body temperature lowers to just above freezing, around 38°F. (In fact, a zoologist at the University of Alaska Fairbanks has found that the core temperature of the Arctic ground squirrel, the northernmost hibernator, can drop to as low as 26°F—six degrees below freezing! Of course, the squirrels don't freeze; they "supercool.")

The hibernating squirrel takes a breath every couple of minutes. It uses up half its body weight, since it isn't eating. If you stuck a needle in a hibernating ground squirrel's paw, it would take the animal about 10 minutes to begin to feel it.

Ground squirrels provide a large part of the grizzly and wolf diet, and that of scavenger birds' as well, since they're a common type of roadkill.

Marmots, similar to woodchucks, are sometimes mistaken for wolverines. They live in large rock outcroppings for protection and have a piercing whistle, which warns of approaching predators or other possible danger. Look for marmots around Polychrome Pass at Denali Park; ask the driver where exactly to see them.

Alaska has a number of other members of the rodent family: shrews, mice, voles, lemmings, and porcupines. Long-tailed and least weasels occupy a wide habitat in the taiga and tundra. Martens are another member of the weasel family, similar to, though much more aggressive than, mink; the pine marten is one of Alaska's most valuable fur-bearers. Wolverines are in attendance, though you'd be very lucky to see one. Red foxes are common in the Interior and Southcentral Alaska, and you're likely to see one at Denali Park; the white Arctic fox is a gorgeous animal, though you'll only see one in pictures.

MARINE MAMMALS

Marine mammals are found all along the Alaskan coast, from Ketchikan in the Southeast to Barrow on the Arctic Ocean. Sea otters are frequently found in harbors, bays, and inlets, particularly around kelp beds. Good places to look for whales, seals, sea otters, sea lions, porpoises, and other marine mammals are the Inside Passage, Prince William Sound, Kodiak Island, Kachemak Bay, and Kenai Fjords. The

Pribilof Islands serve as rearing and resting areas for thousands of northern fur seals, harbor seals, Steller sea lions, and walrus in the summer. Only Native Alaskans have the legal right to hunt marine mammals.

An Endangered Ecosystem?

In the last several decades, scientists have watched with increasing alarm as marine mammal populations plummeted in the North Pacific and the Bering Sea, particularly around the Aleutian Islands. Environmentalists blamed overfishing of pollock, while fishermen pointed the finger at long-term changes in ocean currents and temperatures. But recent evidence points in a different direction—whaling. After World War II, Japanese and Russian whalers developed lethal ways to hunt bowhead, sperm, and humpback whales, killing at least 500,000 of them before commercial whaling ended in the 1970s. These giant whales formed an important part of the diet for killer whales, and without this, the orcas turned to other food sources. As top predator in the ocean, killer whales apparently worked their way across the food chain, attacking fur and harbor seals in the 1970s, Steller sea lions in the 1980s and 1990s, and most recently an animal with very little meat, sea otters. If this is indeed the cause for the decline of these marine mammals, there is little that can be done to halt the damage. Overfishing (or in this case overwhaling) can have disastrous consequences for the oceans, and for animals and humans that depend on the fish.

The effects of commercial whaling continue to ripple through the ecosystem, but other problems pose even more serious threats in northern seas. **Global warming** is a particular problem for ice-dependent marine mammals such as walrus, ringed seals, spotted seals, and bearded seals. As Arctic ice retreats, the animals lose places to rest, give birth, and rear pups. In addition, polar bears (technically a marine mammal) are increasingly threatened by the loss of sea ice and the seals that provide food.

Ocean acidification has only recently been viewed as a serious problem. As the oceans absorb human-caused carbon dioxide, their pH decreases. If it drops too far, organisms such as clams, mussels, corals, and crabs are unable to form shells. In addition, many planktonic animals that provide food for salmon and other fish cannot survive, causing problems farther up the food chain. Learn more from the **Alaska Marine Conservation Council** (www.akmarine.org).

Sea Otters

A marine member of the weasel family, the sea otter had one characteristic that would seal its doom: a long, wide, beautiful pelt that's one of the warmest, most luxurious, and durable furs in existence. Otter fur catalyzed the Russian *promyshlenniki* to begin overrunning the Aleutians in the mid–late 18th century, sealing the doom of the Aleuts as well as the otters. In 1803, Alexander Baranov shipped 15,000 pelts back to eastern Russia. Up until the 1840s, otter hunting was the primary industry in the Pacific, and when the Americans bought Alaska in 1867, nearly 1 million otters had been killed in the northern Pacific.

During the extreme lawless period in the last quarter of the 19th century, the otters were annihilated. In 1906 schooners cruised the North Pacific for months without taking a single pelt. In 1910 a crack crew of 40 Aleut hunters managed to harvest 16 otters. In 1911 otters were added to the International Fur Seal Treaty, giving them complete protection from everybody. Small, isolated populations of otters had managed to survive in the western Aleutians, and their numbers have increased over the past century to roughly 100,000 today. Approximately 90 percent of the world's sea otter population can be found in coastal Alaska. The otters are doing fine in Southeast Alaska, but in the Aleutians they have declined precipitously over the last decade, partly because of predation from killer whales, and are now listed as a threatened species. For more on the current situation, visit the Fish and Wildlife Service's website (http://alaska.fws.gov/fisheries/mmm).

Steller Sea Lions

George Wilhelm Steller was the naturalist aboard Vitus Bering's 1742 exploration of Alaska, and the first European to step on Alaskan soil. Two marine mammals ended up with his name: the Steller's sea cow, a coldwater relative of the manatee; and the Steller seal lion. The sea cow was driven to extinction just 26 years later, a casualty of not being afraid of humans and the tasty flavor of its flesh. Today, the sea lion in much of Alaska is equally endangered.

Steller sea lions are pinnipeds—marine mammals with flippers, not feet. Males can weigh up to 2,000 pounds; females peak at 600 pounds. Sea lions eat several kinds of fish, but mostly pollock. They range across the North Pacific from northern Japan and Siberia all the way to California. These playful but powerful animals were abundant in western Alaskan waters until quite recently. In the 1960s, for example, an estimated 177,000 sea lions lived in the Gulf of Alaska and along the Aleutians. Commercial hunting was halted in the mid-1970s, but the population continued to drop by more than 80 percent. By 2000, a mere 34,000 survived. The western Alaska population was officially listed as endangered in 1997, while sea lion populations in Southeast Alaska and farther south to California are considered threatened.

Researchers are unsure why Steller sea lions are disappearing at such an alarming rate, and there are a multitude of possible causes—including overfishing, toxic chemicals, and predation by sharks and killer whales. Most likely it is some combination of factors, but if something isn't done, the Southwest Alaska population could be headed for extinction. Learn more about these fascinating animals—including the latest research—at the National Marine Fisheries Service's website (www.fakr.noaa.gov/protectedresources).

Whales

The largest summer marine visitors to Alaska are the whales. Each spring **gray whales** are seen migrating north from Baja California; in

Steller sea lions on a buoy near Juneau

© DON PITCHER
humpback whales near Juneau

the fall they return south. Also in the spring **humpback whales** move north from Hawaii. The humpback is easily distinguished by its humplike dorsal fin, large flippers, and huge tail, which shows as it dives. These 50-foot-long creatures often breach (jump) or beat the surface of the water with their tails, as if trying to send messages. Smaller (30-foot) **minke whales** are also common.

The **killer whale** (orca), which is not actually a whale but the largest of the dolphins (up to 24 feet long), travels in groups hunting fish and marine mammals. Its six-foot-high triangular dorsal fin and its black-and-white piebald pattern make it easily identifiable.

Whales can be spotted all along Alaska's thousands of miles of shoreline, but commercial whale-watching ventures are only found in Southeast Alaska, Prince William Sound, and the Kenai Peninsula. Larger towns in these areas all have charter-boat operators that lead trips combining whale-watching with other activities such as fishing, sea kayaking, photography, glacier viewing, or bird-watching. The Inside Passage's protected waterways are favorite haunts of humpback and killer whales during the summer months, particularly around Admiralty Island, within Glacier Bay National Park and Preserve, and near Sitka. Look for beluga whales in Turnagain Arm along the Seward Highway south of Anchorage. Boat tours of Prince William Sound depart from both Valdez and Whittier, providing a good opportunity to see occasional killer, minke, and humpback whales. Kenai Fjords National Park and Resurrection Bay—both accessible by boat tour from Seward—are popular places to spot killer whales and humpbacks, along with sea otters, seals, sea lions, and colonies of puffins. There's also a fair chance of seeing whales on the Kachemak Bay wildlife boat trips that depart from Homer.

For more information on whales in Alaska, visit the National Marine Fisheries Service's website (www.fakr.noaa.gov/protectedresources).

Fur Seals

The Alaska species of fur seal *(Callorhinus ursinus)* is a kind of "seal bear," as its Latin name suggests. The bulls grow up to 7 feet long and can weigh 400 pounds. Tens of thousands of these caterwauling creatures return to the Pribilof Islands yearly to breed. The dominant bulls arrive after eight months at sea in early June, and the noisy fight for the prime beach real estate often results in bloody bulls. The cows show up a couple of weeks later—small (80 pounds), submissive, and steeling themselves for a bloody bounce on the beach. A big stud bull might accumulate 60–70 cows in his harem, and it's exactly as debilitatingly profligate a scene as it sounds. The bulls don't eat, living only off their own fat all summer, and look like skid row derelicts by mid-August when they take off to the North Pacific to eat, sleep, and regain their strength.

The gestation period is one year, and the cows return to the same rookery to give birth. The pups swim away in late October and return after a couple of years as "bachelors." Between 2 and 7 years old, they play in the sand and surf until the young males have grown big and bad enough to have their way with the cows. For more information on fur seals, visit the National Marine Fisheries Service's website (www.fakr.noaa.gov/protectedresources).

Walrus

What the Pribilofs are to the fur seal, Round Island in northern Bristol Bay is to the Pacific walrus. Except here, it's a boys-only beach club; the females and babies remain in the northern Bering and Chukchi Seas, where they feed at the relatively shallow bottoms. Thousands of these giant 3,000-pound bulls cram themselves onto narrow beaches at the bottom of steep cliffs around the 1- by 2-mile island. It's an amazing sight, with the scrappy bulls ready to fight at the slightest affront; most of them are scarred from a multitude of old attacks, and broken or missing tusks are common. On the beach, walrus are ungainly, akin to Subaru-sized slugs. But in the water, these big fatties are slo-mo smooth.

As with other marine mammals in the Bering Sea, walrus populations have declined in recent years, though they have not suffered the precipitous declines of Steller sea lions and otters. There is, however, evidence that global warming is starting to impact walrus. The animals haul out onto sea ice to rest, but as the ice retreats, walrus have been forced to gather along the shore, limiting how far they can go for food and affecting the survival of young. Learn more about these fascinating animals at the U.S. Fish and Wildlife Service's website (http://alaska.fws.gov/fisheries/mmm).

BIRDS AND INSECTS

More than 400 species of birds can be found within Alaska, from tiny rufous hummingbirds to the nation's national emblem, the bald eagle. Because of Alaska's proximity to Siberia, many unusual species are sometimes seen, making islands in the Aleutians and within the Bering Sea of great interest to serious birders.

One of the rarest is the bristle-thighed curlew, with a population of just 5,000 worldwide—and its only breeding grounds are in Alaska. Eight of the curlews were banded in the Yukon Delta Wildlife Refuge in 1988, and one was subsequently seen on Caysan Island in the South Pacific, over 2,000 miles away. Many Asian species, such as the greenshank and the Siberian ruby-throat, only foray into the Americas as far as western Alaska.

Bird-Watching

Nome, the Pribilofs, and the Aleutians are popular destinations for birders looking to add to their life list. Excellent places to see nesting colonies of seabirds such as **puffins** and **kittiwakes** include Glacier Bay National Park and Preserve, Kachemak Bay near Homer, Kenai Fjords National Park near Seward, Fort Abercrombie State Park on Kodiak Island, Prince William Sound, the Pribilof Islands, and St. Lawrence Island.

Located on the edge of Fairbanks, **Creamer's Field** is a good place to view sandhill cranes, ducks, and geese during the spring and fall migrations. Also at Creamer's

Field is the **Alaska Bird Observatory,** which conducts songbird research and offers educational programs and birding reports for the area. Their website (www.alaskabird.org) has a "Birding Links" page with a multitude of websites for regional birding organizations. For additional information, contact the Alaska State office of the **Audubon Society** (907/276-7034, www.audubon.org/chapter/ak) or call the regional birding hotlines for the Anchorage area (907/338-2473), Interior Alaska (907/451-9213), and the Homer area (907/235-7337, www.birdinghomeralaska.org). Spring festivals in Homer (www.homeralaska.org/shorebird.htm) and Cordova (www.cordovachamber.com) provide fine opportunities to view and learn about shorebirds.

Eagles

As many eagles are found in Alaska as in the rest of the United States combined. **Bald eagles** are common sights along the coasts, but with their unmistakable white heads, seven-foot wingspans, and dive-bombing, salmon-snatching performances, the thrill of watching them is not quickly lost.

The highest concentrations of bald eagles can be found on Admiralty Island, in Prince William Sound, and along the Copper River Delta near Cordova. Admiralty has the largest nesting population of bald eagles in the world and is a great place to find them during the summer months. Over the winter you'll find upward of 3,000 eagles at the famous **Chilkat Bald Eagle Preserve,** and in spring a good place to look for eagles is the Stikine River near Wrangell.

Golden eagles, found throughout the Interior, come without the distinctive "baldness" but are no less magnificent for their size. Plentiful around Denali Park, golden eagles perched on the tundra, standing more than three feet tall, have been mistaken for everything from grizzly cubs to adolescent hikers.

The **white-tailed eagle** is an Asian raptor; Attu Island in the western Aleutians is its only North American habitat.

Trumpeter Swans

The world's largest waterfowl, these swans boast wingspans as wide as eagles (7 feet) and can weigh up to 40 pounds. They're pure white and so have figured prominently over the centuries in legends, drama, music, and metaphor. They fly as fast as 60 mph and as high as 10,000 feet on their migrations from Alaska to the Pacific Northwest for the winter (though a group of 500 overwinter in Alaska). They live to be 30 years old and have a hornlike call, which accounts for their common name.

In 1933, trumpeter populations hit an all-time low of 33 individuals in the Lower 48—having been hunted for their meat, down, and quills. But several thousand swans were seen by Alaskan bush plane biologists in the early 1950s, and by the early 1970s, trumpeters were removed from the Endangered Species list.

Today, of the nearly 12,000 swans in North America, about 10,000 spend their summers in Alaska, 2,000 of them in the Copper River delta. A great place to see them is on the road from Cordova to the Million Dollar Bridge.

Geese

The **Aleutian Canada goose** has made a remarkable comeback from the edge of extinction over the past several decades. Smaller than Canada geese, Aleutian geese were common throughout the islands up until the 20th century, when decades of fox farming nearly wiped out the species. Only a few hundred were left alive by the late 1960s on one fox-free island. Feral foxes were removed from a number of other Aleutians, and the geese were reintroduced; by 1990 their numbers had regenerated to the point (7,000) where they were removed from the ranks of the endangered and upgraded to "threatened."

Emperor geese are a distinctive black-throated bird, and nearly the entire population of 70,000 nest in Southwest Alaska, from the Aleutians to Kodiak.

Snow geese, on the other hand, are plentiful. Huge flocks totaling up to 100,000 birds migrate roughly 5,000 miles each year from central California through Alaska to their nesting grounds on Wrangel Island (in Russia).

Ptarmigan

The **willow ptarmigan** is the state bird, and one of the most popular targets of small-game hunters. Ptarmigan—willow, rock, and white-tailed—are similar to pheasant, quail, and partridge in the Lower 48. They reproduce in large quantities, molt from winter white to summer brown, and have a poor sense of self-preservation. The various Alaskan place-names containing "Chicken" usually refer to ptarmigan, which the namers had difficulty spelling.

Mosquitoes

The mosquito—contrary to popular belief—is not Alaska's state bird. But skeeters are nearly as much a symbol of the Great North as glaciers, totem poles, and the aurora borealis. Mosquito eggs hatch in water, so the boggy, muskegy, marshy forests and tundra, plus all the ponds, lakes, creeks, sloughs, and braided rivers of Alaska, provide the ideal habitat for these bothersome creatures. Alaska hosts around three dozen varieties of mosquitoes.

Mosquitoes hibernate in the winter and emerge starting in March–April. Peak season is late June–early July. The males don't alight or bite, but they do buzz around people's eyes, noses, and ears, which can be as annoying, if not more so, than the bites. The males live 6–8 weeks, feeding on plant juices; their sole purpose in life is to fertilize the eggs the females produce. They also feed birds and larger insects.

The females live long lives producing batches of eggs, up to 500 at a time. To nourish the eggs they feed on the blood of mammals, using a piercing and sucking mouth tube. The tube also injects an anticoagulant, which causes the itch and swelling from a bite. No Alaskan mosquitoes carry the diseases that tropical mosquitoes are known to, such as malaria, yellow fever, encephalitis, and elephantiasis.

Mosquitoes are most active at dawn and dusk. Windy conditions and low temperatures depress mosquito feeding and breeding. Mosquitoes are attracted to dark colors, carbon dioxide, warmth, and moisture. Mosquito repellent containing DEET (diethyl-meta-toluamide) is the most effective. A head net helps keep mosquitoes and other buggy critters away from your face and is a wise investment for anyone heading into remote parts of Interior Alaska or Kodiak Island. If you wear light-colored heavy clothing (the stinger can pierce light materials), camp in high and dry places that are apt to be breezy, and rub repellent on all exposed skin, you should be able to weather mosquito season without too much difficulty.

FISH

Get someone going on fishing in Alaska and you won't be able to shut him or her up or get a word in edgewise for the whole afternoon, guaranteed. The fisheries program in Alaska is extensive because commercial, sport, and recreational fishing are important to almost every state resident. Commercial fishing is Alaska's second-largest industry, and Alaska accounts for more than half of the nation's total seafood production. Sportfishing has always been popular but is playing a more important role in Alaska's economy as tourism increases. Below is a brief survey of the most popular fish in Alaska's 3 million lakes, 3,000 rivers, and 45,000 miles of coastline.

Salmon

Five kinds of salmon—king, red, pink, silver, and chum—all return to the same bend in the same little creek where they hatched to spawn and die, ending one of the most remarkable life cycles and feats of migration and single-minded endurance of any living creature. You'll be steeped in salmon lore if only by osmosis by the end of your trip, and you'll get more than your fill of this most delicious and pretty fish.

The **kings** (also known as chinooks) are the world's largest salmon, and the world's largest kings spawn in Alaskan waters. The average size for a king is 40–50 pounds. The world sport fish record is 97 pounds, and a few 100-pounders have been caught in commercial nets.

Kings generally spend 5–6 years in saltwater before returning to freshwater to spawn: the more years spent in the ocean, the larger the fish. They run mostly mid-May–mid-July.

Reds (sockeye) are the best-tasting salmon and the mainstay of the commercial fishing industry. They average 6–10 pounds and run in June–July.

Pinks (humpback) are the most plentiful, with massive runs of more than 150 million fish late June–early September. They're smallish, 3–4 pounds, with soft flesh and a mild taste; they're mostly canned (or caught by tourists).

Silvers (coho) seem to be the most legendary of the salmon for their speed, agility, and sixth sense. Their spawning growth rate is no less than fantastic, more than doubling their weight in the last 90 days of their lives. Silvers grow 7–10 pounds and run late, from late July all the way to November.

Chum (dog) are the least valued of the five Pacific salmon, even though they average 10–20 pounds, are extremely feisty, and are the most far-ranging, running way above the Arctic Circle. They're known as dog salmon because they've traditionally sustained working huskies, but chums remain popular with a hard-core group of sport anglers, who consider them terribly underrated. Surprisingly, they make some of the finest smoked fish.

Halibut

Halibut are Alaska's favorite monster fish and can grow so huge and strong that many anglers have an unsurpassed religious experience while catching one. "Chicken halibut" are the common 25–40 pounders, but 100- and 200-pounders are frequent sights in some ports; even 300-pounders are occasionally reeled in. The state-record halibut was a 464-pounder, more than 8 feet long, caught near Dutch Harbor in 1996. Even though halibut are huge and require 80-pound test line with 20-ounce lead sinkers, they're not the fiercest fighting fish, and just about anyone can catch one on a good day's charter from Homer, Seward, Kodiak, Whittier, Sitka, or Dutch Harbor. It has a very white flesh with a fine texture—many Alaskans regard it as the most flavorful (and least fishy-tasting) fish.

Smelt

The fattiest fish in northern waters is the Pacific Coast eulachon, also known as smelt, hooligans, and candlefish (legend claims that the dried fish are so fatty they can be wicked and lit like candles). These silver and white fish are roughly as long and slender as pencils, and they run in monumental numbers for three weeks in early summer from Northern California to the Pribilofs. A traditional source of oil, the females are dumped into pits or vats by the ton and left to rot for two weeks. Then freshwater is added, and the whole mess is boiled, during which the oil rises to the surface. After skimming, straining, filtering, and sterilizing, roughly 20 gallons of oil (reminiscent of cod-liver oil) can be processed from a ton of female smelt. The early males, in addition, are good tasting whether cooked, smoked, dried, or salted.

History

PREHISTORY

The Athabascan Indians of Canada have a legend that tells how, in the misty past, one of their ancestors helped a giant in Siberia slay a rival. The defeated giant fell into the sea, forming a bridge to North America. The forefathers of the Athabascans then crossed this bridge, bringing the caribou with them. Eventually the giant's body decomposed, but parts of his skeleton were left sticking above the ocean to form the Aleutian Islands.

In scientific terms, what probably happened was that low ocean levels—up to 450 feet below those at present—offered the nomadic peoples of northeastern Asia a 50-mile-long, 600-mile-wide land "bridge" over the Bering Sea. There is considerable controversy over exactly when humans crossed this isthmus, but it was certainly used at least 12,000 years ago, and perhaps considerably earlier.

One of the earliest records of humans in the Americas is a caribou bone with a serrated edge found at Old Crow in northern Yukon. Almost certainly used as a tool, the bone has been placed at 27,000 years old by carbon dating. The interior lowlands of Alaska and the Yukon Valley, which were never glaciated, provided an ice-free migration route. As the climate warmed and the great ice sheets receded toward the Rocky Mountains and the Canadian Shield, a corridor opened down the middle of the Great Plains, allowing movement farther south. (Recent scientific evidence suggests that ancient peoples also sailed or paddled along the coast from Asia to North America.)

The Athabascans

The Athabascans and other Paleo-Indians were the first people to cross the Bering land bridge. Their language is spoken today from Interior Alaska to the American Southwest (among Navajos and Apaches). Way back when (anywhere from 12,000 to 40,000 years ago), these people of the Interior followed the mastodon, mammoth, and caribou herds that supplied them with most of their necessities. Agriculture was unknown to them, but they did fashion basic implements from the raw copper found in the region. Eventually, certain groups found their way to the coast. The Athabascan-related Tlingits, for example, migrated down the Nass River near Prince Rupert and then spread north through Southeast Alaska. The rich environment provided them with abundant fish and shellfish, as well as with the great cedar logs from which they fashioned community houses, totem poles, and long dugout canoes.

The Eskimo

Eskimo or Inuit arrived from Asia some 4,500 years ago, migrating by boat along the coast of Alaska. Within 500 years their culture had spread across Arctic Canada and all the way to Greenland. Their language, which in Alaska is divided into the Inupiak dialect in the North and the Yup'ik and Alutiiq dialects in the south, is unrelated to any other in North America except that of the Aleuts.

Like the Tlingits, the Eskimo lived near the coast, along the migratory routes of the marine mammals they hunted in kayaks and umiaks. They also relied on caribou, birds, and fish. Their homes were partly underground and constructed of driftwood, antlers, whale bones, and sod. (The well-known snow-and-ice igloo was exclusive to indigenous people in Canada.) In the summer, skin tents were used at fish camps. The Eskimo did not use dogsleds until the coming of the Europeans.

The Aleut

Marine mammals and fish provided the Eskimo-related Aleuts with food, clothing, and household materials. The Aleut were famous for their tightly woven baskets. Before the 1740s arrival of the Russians, 25,000 Aleuts inhabited almost all of the Aleutian Islands, but by 1800 only about 2,000 survived. The ruthless Russian fur traders murdered and kidnapped the men, enslaved or abandoned the women,

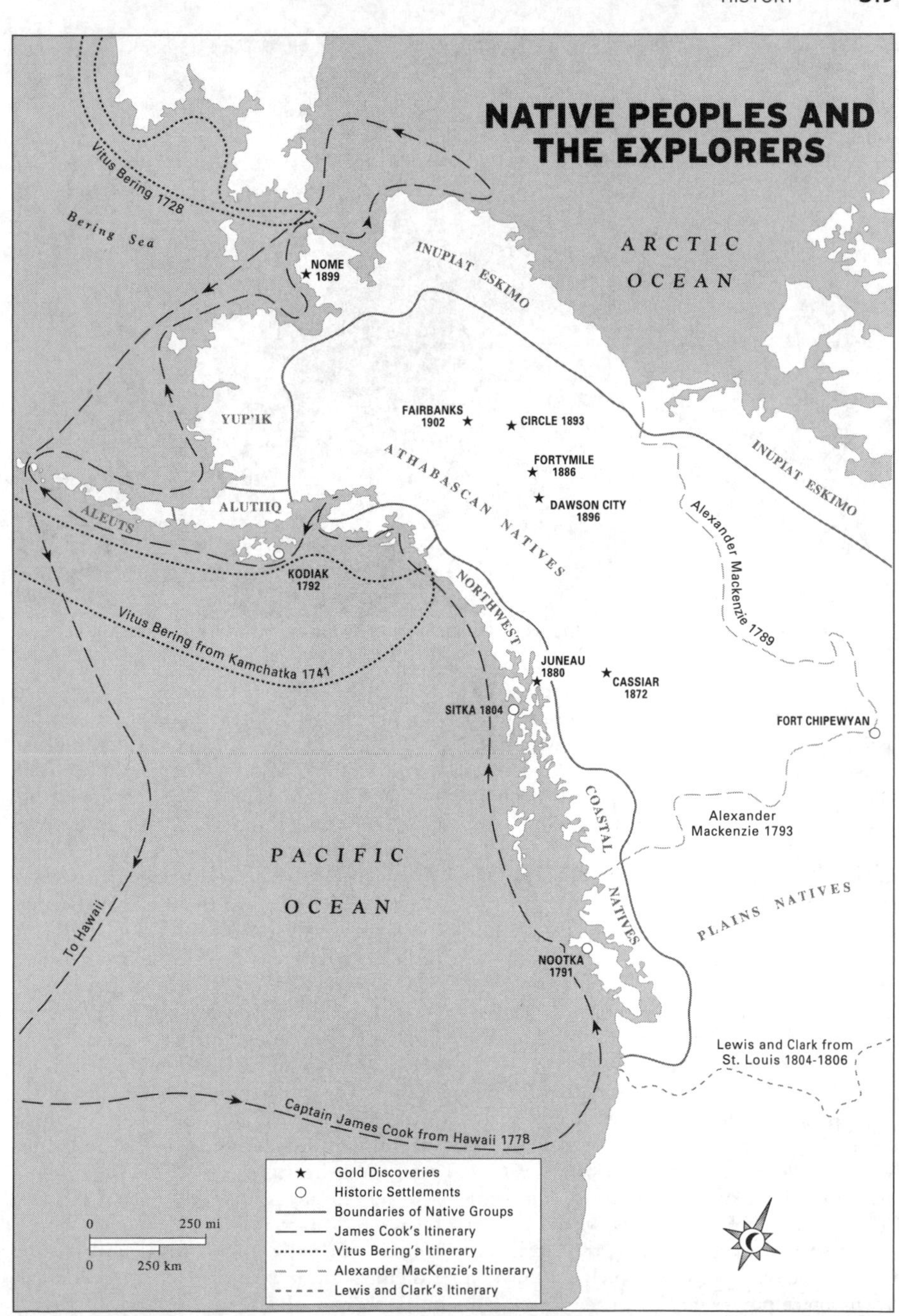
NATIVE PEOPLES AND THE EXPLORERS
Vitus Bering 1728
Bering Sea
NOME 1899
INUPIAT ESKIMO
ARCTIC OCEAN
YUP'IK
FAIRBANKS 1902
CIRCLE 1893
FORTYMILE 1886
DAWSON CITY 1896
ATHABASCAN NATIVES
INUPIAT ESKIMO
Alexander Mackenzie 1789
ALUTIIQ
ALEUTS
KODIAK 1792
NORTHWEST
Vitus Bering from Kamchatka 1741
JUNEAU 1880
CASSIAR 1872
SITKA 1804
FORT CHIPEWYAN
COASTAL NATIVES
Alexander Mackenzie 1793
PACIFIC OCEAN
PLAINS NATIVES
To Hawaii
NOOTKA 1791
Lewis and Clark from St. Louis 1804-1806
Captain James Cook from Hawaii 1778
Gold Discoveries
Historic Settlements
Boundaries of Native Groups
James Cook's Itinerary
Vitus Bering's Itinerary
Alexander MacKenzie's Itinerary
Lewis and Clark's Itinerary
0 250 mi
0 250 km

The Museum of the Aleutians in Unalaska/Dutch Harbor exhibits artifacts from original Native Alaskan cultures.

© DON PITCHER

and passed on their genes and diseases so successfully that today only 1,000 full-blooded Aleuts remain. The rest intermarried with the Russians, and scattered groups of their descendants are now found in the eastern Aleutians and the Pribilofs to the North.

EUROPEAN EXPLORATION

Vitus Bering

In the early 1700s, long before the New World colonists began manifesting their destiny by pushing the American frontier west to the Pacific coast, Russian *promyshlenniki* (explorers and traders) were already busy pushing their own frontier east to the Pacific. After these land conquerors had delineated Russia's inhospitable northeastern edges, they were followed by indomitable sea explorers who cast off from the coasts in search of answers to questions that had intrigued Europeans since Marco Polo's *Travels*—mainly, whether or not Asia was joined with America, the mysterious land to the east that was vaguely outlined on then-contemporary maps.

Danish-born Vitus Bering, a sailor in the Russian navy for nearly 20 years, set out in 1725 for Kamchatka Peninsula, Siberia, on orders from Peter the Great. It took him and his crew three years, dragging rigging, cable, and anchors 2,000 miles over trackless wilderness and suffering innumerable deprivations to reach the coast, where their real journey into the uncharted waters of the North Pacific would begin. Bering built his first boat, *Gabriel,* and sailed past St. Lawrence Island (south of present-day Nome) and the Diomedes, but fog prevented him from glimpsing North America. He returned and wintered in Kamchatka, sailed again in the spring, and charted most of the Kamchatka coast, but foul weather and a shortage of provisions again precluded exploring farther east.

Over the next 10 years, Bering shuttled between Moscow and his beloved coast, submitting patiently to royal politics and ridicule from the leading scientists and cartographers while planning and outfitting (though not commanding) a series of expeditions that charted the rest of the Siberian coast and Japan.

Finally, in 1741, at the age of 60, Bering undertook his remarkable voyage to America. Commanding the *St. Peter,* he sailed southeast from Kamchatka, came up south of the Aleutians, passed Kodiak, and sighted Mt. St. Elias on the mainland. By that time Bering, along with 31 members of his crew, was in the final throes of terminal scurvy. He died in December 1741 and was buried on what is now Bering Island, the westernmost of the Aleutians. Meanwhile, his lieutenant, Alexis Chirikov, commanding the *St. Paul,* had reached all the way to the site of Sitka. After much hardship, survivors from both ships made it back to Siberia—with a load of sea otter pelts. This bounty from the New World prompted a rush of Russian hunters and traders to Alaska.

Conflicting Claims

Reports of Russian advances alarmed the Spanish, who considered the entire west coast of North America theirs. Juan Pérez and Bruno de Heceta were ordered north from Mexico in 1774 and 1775. Spanish explorer Juan Francisco Quadra sailed as far north as Sitka in 1775 and 1779, but in the end, Spain failed to back up its claim with any permanent settlement north of San Francisco. It was Englishmen James Cook (in 1776–1780) and George Vancouver (in 1791–1792) who first carefully explored and charted this northern coast. In 1778, Cook landed on Vancouver Island, then sailed north all the way to what is now called Cook Inlet in Southcentral Alaska, in search of the Northwest Passage from the Atlantic. He continued to the Aleutians and entered the Bering Sea and the Arctic Ocean. A decade and a half later, Vancouver, aboard his ship HMS *Discovery,* charted the coast from California to Southeast Alaska and claimed the region for Britain. His was the first extensive exploration of Puget Sound and circumnavigation of Vancouver Island; his maps and charts of this confounding coast were so accurate that they were used for another 100 years.

Exploration by Land

Meanwhile, explorers were reaching the Pacific overland from bases in eastern Canada and the United States. In 1789 a Northwest Company trader, Alexander Mackenzie, paddled down the Mackenzie River to the Arctic Ocean. Four years later, in 1793, he became the first person to cross the entire continent by land, reaching the Pacific at Bella Coola, British Columbia. Other employees of the same aggressive Montreal-based company explored farther south. In 1808, Simon Fraser followed the Fraser River, stopping near the present site of the city of Vancouver; in 1810–1811 David Thompson traveled from the headwaters of the North Saskatchewan River to the mouth of the Columbia River, near present-day Portland. In 1803, after the United States purchased 827,000 square miles of territory west of the Mississippi River from France, President Thomas Jefferson ordered a military fact-finding mission into the area. Led by Lewis and Clark, a group of explorers paddled up the Missouri River to its headwaters and crossed to the Columbia, which they followed to the Pacific (1804–1806), helping to open vast expanses of western North America. American fur traders followed close behind. (The Alaskan interior was not properly explored, however, until the gold rush at the end of the 19th century.)

The Fur Trade

The excesses of the *promyshlenniki,* who had massacred and enslaved the Aleut, prompted the czar in 1789 to create the Russian America Company, headed by Grigori Shelikov, a fur trader and merchant who in 1784 had established the first permanent settlement in Alaska at Three Saints Bay on Kodiak Island. Alexander Baranov, a salesman in Siberia, was the first director of the company; he moved the settlement to present-day Kodiak town, and for the next 20 years Baranov *was* the law. One of the most powerful men in Alaskan history, he enslaved the remaining Aleuts, warred with the Panhandle Indians, initiated trade with the British, Spanish, and Americans, and sent his trading vessels as far away as Hawaii, Japan, and Mexico. Exhausting the resources of Kodiak and its neighborhood, he moved the company to Sitka, where, according to Merle Colby in his classic 1939 Works Progress Administration *Guide to Alaska,*

> *from his wooden "castle" on the hill surmounting the harbor he made Sitka the most brilliant capital in the new world. Yankee sailors, thrashing around the Horn, beating their way up the California coast, anchored at last in Sitka harbor and found the city an American Paris, its streets crowded with adventurers from half the world away, its nights gay with balls illuminated by brilliant uniforms and the evening dresses of Russian ladies.*

Except for the Tlingit Indians, who fought bitterly against Russian imperialism, Baranov's rule, extending from Bristol Bay in western Alaska to Fort Ross, California, was complete. His one last dream, of returning to Russia, was never fulfilled—on the voyage back to his homeland, Baranov died at the age of 72.

THE 19TH CENTURY

Political Units Form

In 1824 and 1825, Russia signed agreements with the United States and Britain, fixing the southern limit of Russian America at 54 degrees 40 minutes north latitude, near present-day Ketchikan. But the vast territory south of this line was left up for grabs. The American claim to the Oregon Territory around the Columbia River was based on its discovery by Robert Gray in 1792, and on the first overland exploration by Lewis and Clark. Britain based its claim to the region on its effective occupation of the land by the Northwest Company, which in 1821 merged with the Hudson's Bay Company. As American settlers began to inhabit the area, feelings ran high—President Polk was elected in 1846 on the slogan "Fifty-four Forty or Fight," referring to the proposed northern boundary between American and British territory in the Pacific Northwest. War between Britain and the United States was averted when both agreed to draw the boundary line to the Pacific along the 49th parallel, which remains to this day the Canada-U.S. border. Vancouver Island went to Britain, and the new Canadian nation purchased all the territorial holdings of the Hudson's Bay Company (Rupert's Land) in 1870. In 1871, British Columbia joined the Canadian Confederation on a promise from the leaders of the infant country of a railroad to extend there from the east.

The Russians Bail Out

The year 1863 was a difficult one for the Russian America Company. Back in the motherland, Russia's feudal society was breaking down, threatening the aristocracy's privileged status. In Alaska, competition from English and American whalers and traders was intensifying. Food was scarce, and supply ships from California were unreliable and infrequent. The worst, perhaps, was the dwindled numbers of fur seals and sea otters, hunted nearly to extinction over the past century. In addition, bad relations with Britain in the aftermath of the Crimean War (1853–1856) prompted Czar Alexander I to fear losing his far-flung Alaskan possessions to the British by force. Finally, the czar did not renew the company's charter, and the Russian America Company officially closed up shop.

Meanwhile, American technology was performing miracles. Western Union had laid two cables under the Atlantic Ocean from the United States to Europe, but neither had yet worked. So they figured, let's go the other way around the world: They proposed laying a cable overland through British Columbia, along the Yukon River, across the Bering Strait into Siberia, then east and south into Europe. In 1865, the Western Union Telegraph Expedition to Alaska, led by William Dall, surveyed the interior of Alaska for the first time, revealing its vast land and resources. This stimulated considerable interest in frontier-minded Washington, D.C. In addition, Czar Alexander's Alaska salesman, Baron Eduard de Stoeckl, was spending $200,000 of his own money to make a positive impression on influential politicians and journalists.

Secretary of State William H. Seward purchased Alaska on March 30, 1867, for the all-time bargain-basement price of $7.2 million—*two cents* per acre. The American flag was hoisted over Sitka on October 18, 1867. According to Ernest Gruening, first U.S. senator from Alaska:

> *A year later when the House of Representatives was called upon to pay the bill, skeptical congressmen scornfully labeled Alaska "Icebergia," "Walrussia," "Seward's Icebox," and "[President] Johnson's Polar Bear Garden." If American forces had not already raised the Stars and Stripes in Sitka, the House might have refused to pick up the tab.*

Stoeckl, meanwhile, reimbursed himself the $200,000 he'd invested and sent the other $7 million home to Alexander. Subsequently, Alaska faded into official oblivion for the next 15 years—universally regarded as a frozen wasteland and a colossal waste of money.

Organic Act of 1884

This act organized Alaska for the first time, providing a territorial governor and law enforcement (though not a local legislature or representation in Washington). President Chester Arthur appointed federal district court judges, U.S. attorneys, and marshals. From 1884 to 1900, only one U.S. judge, attorney, and marshal managed the whole territory, all residing in the capital, Sitka. The first three appointees to the court in Sitka were removed in disgrace amidst charges of "incompetence, wickedness, unfairness, and drunkenness." A succession of scandals dogged other federal appointees—and

PANNING FOR GOLD

Panning for gold is not only great fun, it's also a good way to get involved in the history of Alaska. Besides, there's the chance you'll find a nugget that will become a lifelong souvenir. You might even strike it rich! The amount of equipment required is minimal: an 18-inch plastic gravity-trap gold pan (buy one at any local surplus or sporting-goods store for a few dollars), tweezers and an eyedropper to pick out the gold flakes, and a small vial to hold them. Ordinary rubber gloves will protect your hands from icy creek water. An automobile oil dipstick bent at one end is handy for poking into crevices, and a small garden trowel helps dig out the dirt under rocks. Look for a gravel bar where the creek takes a turn, for larger rocks forming eddies during high water, for crevices in the bedrock, or for exposed tree roots growing near the waterline; these are places where gold will lodge. Try your luck on any of the old gold-rush creeks; tourist offices can often suggest likely areas. Stay away from commercial mining operations, and always ask permission if you're on someone's claim.

The principle behind panning is that gold, twice as heavy as lead, will settle to the bottom of your pan. Fill the pan half full of pay dirt you've scooped up from a likely spot and cover it with water. Hit the rim of the pan seven or eight times, or shake it back and forth. Break up lumps of dirt or clay with your hands and discard any rocks after rinsing them in the pan. Shake the pan again, moving it in a circular motion. Dip the front edge of the pan into the stream and carefully wash off excess sand and gravel until only a small amount of black sand remains. If you see gold specks too small to remove with tweezers, take the black sand out and let it dry. Later dump it on a clean sheet of paper and gently blow away the sand. The gold will remain. That's the basic procedure, though there are many ways to do it. It does take practice; ask a friendly sourdough for advice. Also, a number of spiked gold-panning facilities are found along the roads in Alaska – they are commercial, but good places to refine your technique.

that was only in Sitka; the vast Interior had no law at all until 1900, when Congress divided the territory into three legal districts, with courts at Sitka, Nome, and Eagle.

William H. Dall wrote of Alaska at that time as a place where "no man could make a legal will, own a homestead or transfer it, or so much as cut wood for his fire without defying a Congressional prohibition; where polygamy and slavery and the lynching of witches prevailed, with no legal authority to stay or punish criminals." Kipling's line, "There's never law of God or man runs north of 53," also refers to the young territory of Alaska. In contrast, Colby in his WPA guide commented that the gold-rush stampeders,

> *although technically without civil authority, created their own form of self-government. The miners organized "miners meetings" to enforce order, settle boundary disputes, and administer rough and ready justice. Too often this form of government failed to cope with [serious problems] yet the profound instinct of the American people for self-government and their tradition of democracy made local self-government effective until the creation of the Alaska Legislature in 1912.*

Gold!

Alaska's gold rush changed everything. After the California stampede of 1849, the search moved north. In 1858 there was a rush up the Fraser River to the Cariboo gold fields. In 1872, gold was found in British Columbia's Cassiar region. Strikes in Alaska and the Yukon followed one another in quick succession: at Juneau (1880), Fortymile (1886), Circle (1893), Dawson City (1896), Nome (1899), Fairbanks (1902), and Iditarod (1908).

A mobile group of men and women followed these discoveries on riverboats, dogsleds, and foot, creating instant outposts of civilization near the gold strikes. Gold also caused the Canadian and American governments to take a serious look at their northernmost possessions for the first time; the beginnings of Alaska's administrative infrastructure date from those times. Still, in 1896, when Siwash George Carmack and his two Athabascan brothers-in-law discovered gold where Bonanza Creek flowed into the Klondike River in Yukon Territory, this vast northern wilderness could barely be called "settled." Only a handful of tiny nonnative villages existed along the Yukon River from Ogilvie and Fortymile in western Yukon to Circle and Fort Yukon in eastern Alaska, and a single unoccupied cabin sat on a beach at the mouth of the Skagway River at the terminus of the Inside Passage.

But by the end of 1897, perhaps 20,000 stampeders had skirted the lone cabin on their way to the headwaters of the Yukon and the sure fortunes in gold that awaited them on the Klondike. The two trails from Skagway over the coastal mountains and on to the interior rivers proved to be the most "civilized" and successful routes to Dawson. But the fortune-frenzied hordes proceeded north, uninformed, aiming at Dawson from every direction on the compass. They suffered every conceivable hardship and misery, from which death (often by suicide) was sometimes the only relief. And those who finally burst through the barrier and landed at the Klondike and Dawson were already two years too late to partake of the "ready" gold.

But the North had been conquered by whites. And by the time the gold rush had spread to Nome, Fairbanks, Kantishna, Hatcher Pass, and Hope, Alaska could finally be called settled (if not civilized).

The consequences of this Anglo invasion were devastating for the people who had lived in this harsh land for thousands of years. Epidemics of measles, influenza, and pneumonia swept through the Native Alaskan communities, particularly in 1900 and 1918, sometimes killing every person in a village. Rescuers found entire families who had frozen to death because they did not have enough strength to keep the fire going. The impact of these deaths, combined with the sudden arrival of whites who introduced alcohol, depleted game and other food sources, and then brought Christianity as a replacement for indigenous beliefs, was profound. The consequences still ripple across Alaska, most notably in the form of rampant alcoholism, which is a factor in many Native Alaskan accidents and suicides.

THE 20TH CENTURY

In the first decade of the 20th century, the sprawling wilderness was starting to be tamed. The military set up shop at Valdez and Eagle to maintain law and order, telegraph cables were laid across the Interior, the Northwest Passage had been found, railroads were begun at several locations, vast copper deposits were being mined, and thousands of independent pioneer types were surviving on their own wits and the country's resources. Footpaths widened into wagon trails. Mail deliveries were regularized. Limited self-government was initiated: The capital moved to Juneau from Sitka in 1905; Alaska's first congressional delegate arrived in Washington in 1906; and a territorial legislature convened in 1912. A year later, the first people stood atop the south peak of Mt. McKinley, and the surrounding area was set aside as a national park in 1917. At that time, Alaska's white and Native Alaskan populations had reached equivalency, at around 35,000 each. Judge James Wickersham introduced the first statehood bill to the U.S. Congress in 1916, but Alaska drifted along in federal obscurity until the Japanese bombed Pearl Harbor.

War

It has been said that war is good for one thing: the rapid expansion of communications and mobility technology. Alaska proves that rule. In the early 1940s, military bases were established at Anchorage, Whittier, Fairbanks, Nome, Sitka, Delta, Kodiak, Dutch Harbor, and the tip of the Aleutians, which brought an immediate influx of military and support personnel and services. In addition, in 1942 alone, thousands of miles of road were punched through the trackless wilderness, finally connecting Alaska to the rest of the world: the 1,440-mile Alaska Highway from Dawson Creek, B.C., to Delta, Alaska; the 50 miles of the Klondike Highway from Whitehorse to Carcross; the 151-mile Haines Highway; and the 328-mile Glenn Highway from Tok to Anchorage, among others. At the war's peak, 150,000 troops were stationed in the territory; all told, the U.S. government spent almost $1 billion there during the war. After the war, as after the gold rush, Alaska's population increased dramatically, with service members remaining or returning. The number of residents nearly doubled between 1940 and 1950.

Statehood

The 1950s brought a boom in construction, logging, fishing, and bureaucracy to Alaska. The decade also saw the discovery of a large oil reserve off the western Kenai Peninsula in the Cook Inlet. The population continued to grow, yet Alaskans still felt like residents of a second-class colony of the United States and repeatedly asked for statehood status through the decade. Finally, on July 7, 1958, Congress voted to admit Alaska into the Union as the 49th state. On January 3, 1959, President Dwight D. Eisenhower signed the official proclamation—43 years after Judge James Wickersham had first introduced the idea.

In the 92 years between Alaska becoming a U.S. territory and becoming a state, much of the land was split up into Navy petroleum reserves, Bureau of Land Management parcels, national wildlife refuges, power projects, and the like to be administered by separate federal agencies, including national park, forest, and military services. By the time Alaska gained statehood in 1959, only 0.003 percent of the land was privately owned—mostly homesteads and mining operations—and just 0.01 percent had been set aside for Native Alaskan reservations, administered by the Bureau of Indian Affairs. The Statehood Act allowed Alaska to choose 104 million acres, but the issue of Native Alaskan land ownership was not considered, and it would take oil discoveries in the late 1960s to force redress for that injustice.

A little over five years after statehood, the

Good Friday earthquake struck Southcentral Alaska; at 9.2 on the Richter scale, it remains the largest earthquake ever recorded in North America. But Alaskans quickly recovered and rebuilt with the plucky determination and optimism that still characterize the young state.

Oil Changes Everything

Alaska entered the big time, experiencing its most recent boom, in 1968 when Atlantic Richfield discovered a 10 billion-barrel oil reserve at Prudhoe Bay. The following year, Alaska auctioned off leases to almost 500,000 acres of oil-rich country on the North Slope for $900 million, 10 times more money than all its previous leases combined. A consortium of oil company leaseholders immediately began planning the Trans-Alaska Pipeline to carry the crude from Prudhoe Bay to Valdez. But conservationists, worried about its environmental impact, and Native Alaskan groups, concerned about land-use compensation, filed suit, delaying construction for four years.

This impasse was resolved in 1971, when Congress passed the Alaska Native Claims Settlement Act (ANCSA), the most extensive compensation to any indigenous people in the history of the United States. It gave Alaska's aboriginal groups title to 44 million acres of traditional-use lands, plus $1 billion to be divided among all American citizens with at least 25 percent Athabascan, Eskimo, or Aleut blood. The act also created a dozen regional Native Alaskan corporations, a "13th Corporation" for Native Alaskans in the Lower 48, plus more than 200 village and urban Native Alaskan corporations.

The pipeline was built in 1974–1977. Again, after years of uncertainty, Alaska boomed, both in revenues and population. Since then, the state's economic fortunes have risen and fallen with the volatile price of oil.

Preserving the Wild Places

The ANCSA of 1971 had designated 80 million acres to be withdrawn from the public domain and set aside as national parks, wildlife refuges, and other preserves by 1978. In the mid–late 1970s, in the wake of the completion of the pipeline, this was the raging land issue, generally divided between fiercely independent Alaskans who protested the further "locking up" of their lands by Washington bureaucrats, and conservationists who lobbied to preserve Alaska's wildlife and wilderness. When Congress failed to act, President Jimmy Carter took a bold move that forever changed the way Alaskan lands are managed; he withdrew 114 million acres of Alaskan lands as national monuments on December 1, 1978. The withdrawal still rankles the state's right-wing politicians, who regard it as a criminal act that should be prosecuted.

Two years later, with the antienvironment Ronald Reagan waiting to take over the reins of power, Carter signed into law one of the most significant pieces of environmental legislation ever enacted, the Alaska National Interest Lands Conservation Act (ANILCA). The act set aside 106 million acres of federal property as "public-interest lands," to be managed by the National Park and National Forest Services, the Fish and Wildlife Service, and other agencies. These "d2 lands" (from section 17:d-2 of ANCSA) included the expansion of Mt. McKinley National Park (renamed Denali); the expansion of Glacier Bay and Katmai National Monuments, which became national parks; and the creation of Gates of the Arctic, Kobuk Valley, Wrangell–St. Elias, Kenai Fjords, and Lake Clark National Parks, plus the designation of numerous national monuments and preserves, scenic and wild rivers, and new wildlife refuges.

INTO A NEW CENTURY

The late 1990s were hard on Alaska, as oil prices dropped, pulp mills closed down, logging declined, and commercial fishing suffered from low prices and a market flooded with cheap farmed salmon from Chile, Norway, and British Columbia. But the first several years of the 21st century brought a reversal, with sky-high oil and gold prices, a big push to develop a natural gas pipeline across the state, increased tourism, higher prices for Alaska's wild salmon, and major political upheavals as FBI investigations threatened the oil industry's stranglehold on state government.

In 2006 voters did the unthinkable by voting to tax and regulate the cruise ship industry while simultaneously throwing out an incumbent governor (and former U.S. Senator), Frank Murkowski, and replacing him with an almost unknown politician named Sarah Palin. This was followed by a series of scandals in 2007–2008 that sent legislators to prison on corruption charges and eventually brought down Senator Ted Stevens. His conviction was later overturned, but not before voters had thrown him out of office in the 2008 election. For the first time in decades Alaska now has one Democrat (Mark Begich) in the U.S. Senate. Across the aisle is Republican Lisa Murkowski, first appointed to her seat in 2004 by her dad, Frank Murkowski. The lone representative, Republican Don Young, has been in office for decades, though his standing has been severely weakened by scandals.

Going Rogue

Even bigger news in 2008 was the sudden ascendancy of **Sarah Palin,** Alaska's then-governor. When John McCain brought her onto his ticket as the Republican vice presidential candidate, Palin garnered intense international attention—not all of it positive. She resigned in 2009 after 2.5 years in office, but as this was being written it appears obvious that she will remain a figure on the national stage. As an Alaskan, all I can say is: God help us all if she ever gets elected to any position of real power. It's difficult to imagine anyone less qualified for public office.

Government and Economy

GOVERNMENT

Like Delaware, Wyoming, Vermont, and North Dakota, Alaska has only one representative to the U.S. Congress, along with two senators. There are 20 state senators elected to four-year terms and 40 state representatives elected to two-year terms. They meet in the capitol in Juneau January–March. Local government is a mishmash of 16 first- and second-class boroughs, first- and second-class unincorporated villages, and tribal governments.

Alaskan politics start on the conservative end of the spectrum and head west from there to "I'll pull my gun out to show you how right-wing I am." The state has long been solidly Republican, but in 2008 corruption charges brought down some of the most powerful Republicans, all the way up to "Uncle Ted" Stevens, whose power and tenacity were legendary. He was replaced by moderate Democrat Mark Begich; the other U.S. Senator is Republican Lisa Murkowski. Representative Don Young remains in power, but it's probably only a matter of time until his questionable past actions catch up with him. As of 2009, Republicans have the governorship (Sean Parnell) and two of the three congressional seats, but the legislature was being run by a coalition of Democrats and Republicans. The big story, of course, is former Alaska governor Sarah Palin and her quixotic quest for the vice presidency in 2008. Stay tuned; Alaskans are suddenly in the political limelight, and you betcha they like it!

LAND USE AND MANAGEMENT

The vast majority of Alaska's 375 million acres is publicly owned, with less than 1 percent in private hands. Some 60 percent of this land is under federal management, with most of the rest in state or Native Alaskan corporation hands. Get complete details on Alaska's public lands from Alaska Public Lands Information Centers (www.alaskacenters.gov) in Anchorage (907/271-2737), Ketchikan, Tok, and Fairbanks.

National Park Service

In the federal scheme of things, the National Park Service gets all the glory. The national parks are the country's scenic showcases, and visitors come by the millions, usually to look, occasionally to experience. Denali National Park and Preserve—home to North America's highest mountain—is Alaska's most famous and overloved park, attracting well over 1 million tourists each year. Other well-known Alaskan national parks—Glacier Bay National Park and Preserve, Katmai National Park and Preserve, Kenai Fjords National Park, Klondike Gold Rush National Historical Park, Sitka National Historical Park, and Wrangell–St. Elias National Park and Preserve—are high on the list for travelers, and offer both visitors centers and various park activities. The other eight national parks and preserves (Aniakchak, Bering Land Bridge, Cape Krusenstern, Gates of the Arctic, Kobuk Valley, Lake Clark, Noatak, and Yukon-Charley Rivers) are so inaccessible that those with any facilities at all are prohibitively expensive for the average traveler, and the others are really no more than a name and a set of boundaries on the map.

People accustomed to national parks in the Lower 48 are surprised to find that very few trails run through Alaska's 15 parks. Most of the 54 million acres of national parkland are unforested and in the moist alpine tundra, where trails are not only unnecessary but largely detrimental to the ecology: As soon as the insulating ground cover is removed, the melting permafrost turns the trail into a muddy, impassable quagmire. Even in Denali, the only trails are around the park entrance and hotel area. Some parks (such as Denali, Glacier Bay, and Katmai) require backpacking permits; in the rest you're on your own. Several of the more accessible parks (Denali, Kenai Fjords, Klondike Gold Rush, Katmai, and Glacier Bay) have designated camping areas, but in the others you can pitch your tent on any level patch. For details on national parks in Alaska, request brochures from the National Park Service in Anchorage (907/271-2737, www.nps.gov/alaska).

Forest Service

In Alaska, the U.S. Forest Service manages the nation's two largest national forests: Tongass National Forest in Southeast Alaska and Chugach National Forest in Southcentral Alaska. These forests cover 23 million acres of land, much of which is forested, but also comprising high mountains, glaciers, lakes, large rivers, and wild coastlines. Two national monuments within the Tongass—Admiralty Island and Misty Fiords—are popular with travelers, and 19 wilderness areas cover 5.7 million acres in the Tongass.

Both Tongass and Chugach are popular recreation destinations, with hundreds of miles of hiking trails and a number of campgrounds (free–$16) and visitor centers. Also within these forests are more than 180 wilderness cabins ($25–50), a few of which are reachable by road or trail, with the others accessible only by floatplane or boat. You must reserve them well in advance through Recreation.gov (518/885-3639 or 877/444-6777, www.recreaton.gov, $10 fee). Brochures describing the cabins are available from Forest Service offices or from Alaska Public Lands Information Centers in Anchorage, Fairbanks, Tok, and Ketchikan.

For additional information, contact Tongass National Forest (907/586-7928, www.fs.fed.us/r10/tongass) and Chugach National Forest (907/271-3992, www.fs.fed.us/r10/chugach).

Fish and Wildlife Service

The Fish and Wildlife Service manages 16 different refuges covering more than 75 million acres in Alaska. Most of these are in remote regions that see little visitation (other than local subsistence hunters and fishermen), but they provide vital habitat for birds and other animals. The best-known Alaskan refuges are Arctic National Wildlife Refuge on the North Slope, Kenai National Wildlife Refuge on the Kenai Peninsula, and Kodiak National Wildlife Refuge on Kodiak Island. Kenai sees the most tourists and has a visitors center, hiking trails, canoe routes, and campgrounds. Kodiak has a visitors center plus a number of public-use cabins available for rent. A large new visitors center in Homer provides a great introduction to the Alaska Maritime National Wildlife Refuge, which sprawls across 2,500 Alaskan islands. The nation's largest refuge (20 million acres) is Yukon Delta National Wildlife Refuge in Western Alaska. For details on all 16 refuges, contact the Fish and Wildlife Service (907/786-3909, http://alaska.fws.gov).

Bureau of Land Management

Alaska's largest land-management agency (over 90 million acres) is the Bureau of Land Management (BLM, 907/271-5960, www.blm.gov/ak). Most BLM land is undeveloped, but three popular recreation sites—White Mountains National Recreation Area, Chena River State Recreation Area, and Steese Natural Conservation Area—feature a handful of hiking trails, campgrounds, and public cabins in the vicinity of Fairbanks.

State Lands

The State of Alaska owns 89 million acres—almost a quarter of the state—and manages this land for a variety of purposes, from mineral and oil development to state forests. The state manages more than 110 state parks and recreation areas spread over 3 million acres. Located in western Alaska, Wood-Tikchik State Park is the largest state park in the country, encompassing 1.5 million acres. More accessible—it's the most popular state park in Alaska—is Chugach State Park, which covers nearly 500,000 acres bordering Anchorage. Most of these state parks and recreation sites have trails and campgrounds. Camping fees are typically $10 per night, with some parks charging a $5 day-use fee. A number of state parks have public-use cabins for $65 per night.

For additional state park information call 907/269-8400 to request brochures and a statewide park map, or visit www.alaskastateparks.org. You can also use this website to check cabin availability; reservations are made at Department of Natural Resources public information offices in Anchorage or Fairbanks or at state park offices.

The Alaska Department of Fish and Game manages more than 30 state refuges, critical habitat areas, and wildlife sanctuaries, including the world-famous bear-viewing area at McNeil River and the Walrus Islands near Dillingham. It also jointly manages (with the Forest Service) the Pack Creek brown bear–viewing area on Admiralty Island. Also popular is Creamer's Field Migratory Waterfowl Refuge in Fairbanks. The agency issues sportfishing and hunting permits. For details on all its activities, contact the ADF&G (907/465-4180, www.state.ak.us/adfg).

Native Lands

Today, the 12 regional Native Alaskan corporations and more than 200 village and urban corporations created in 1971 by the ANCSA own some 37 million acres in Alaska. Much of this is closed to public access except with special permits; fees are commonly charged.

The ANCSA attempted to bring Native Alaskans into the mainstream of society, and it has succeeded in some ways while failing in others. Surprisingly, the corporations created by the act have become primary forces in logging, mining, and other developments around the state, in sharp contrast to the preserve-the-land policies that might have been anticipated. In parts of Southeast and Southcentral Alaska the Native Alaskan lands have been nearly all logged over; I know of one place where they logged almost within spitting distance of a Native Alaskan cemetery and historic clan house. (Of course, these developments are driven by money, since corporations need profits to survive and to pay dividends to their Native Alaskan shareholders.)

COST OF LIVING

No doubt about it—this place is expensive. Alaska ranks near the top in cost of living among all the states. Numerous factors conspire to keep prices high. Most consumer goods must be imported from the Lower 48, and transportation costs are tacked on along the way. In addition, the transportation and shipping rates within Alaska are similarly high, further inflating the cost of goods and services. In more remote regions especially, lack of competition coupled with steady demand ensures top-dollar prices. And let's not forget how long and cold and dark Alaskan winters are: The cost of heat and utilities is a hardship, and Alaska ranks first in per capita energy consumption in the United States.

Visitors to Anchorage and Fairbanks will be pleased to find that prices are not totally out of line with the Lower 48. Typical food prices in these two largest cities are around 25 percent higher than those in Portland, Oregon. Both cities have large discount-chain stores that help keep prices more reasonable. The big chains have also spread to Wasilla, Juneau, and Ketchikan, driving down prices in those areas (and squeezing local businesses).

Beyond these exceptions, the prices in the North are much higher than Outside, and are generally the worst in the most remote bush communities. Food costs in places such as Galena or Fort Yukon are more than twice those in Anchorage. Even in Homer—which is on the road system—food is 40 percent more expensive than in Anchorage. These financial realities apply to residents much more than to short-term visitors: If you're well prepared and you provision yourself adequately in the major commercial centers, any time spent in the bush shouldn't be too painful on the pocketbook.

MONEY FOR NOTHIN'

In 1976, with oil wealth about to come gushing out of the south end of the pipeline, voters approved a state constitutional amendment calling for a percentage of all oil and mineral revenues to be placed in a **Permanent Fund** (www.apfc.org). Money from this account can only be used for investment, not for state operating expenses, which explains why, during recent Alaskan recessions, when hundreds of state workers were laid off and state funds were severely cut back, billions of surplus dollars sat untouched in the fund. It's the only one of its kind in the country, the only state fund that pays dividends to residents, and the largest pool of public money in the country. In 2009—after the stock market tanked—it still totaled more than $33 *billion.*

A portion of the interest and capital gains income from these assets is distributed to all Alaska residents—even children—in a yearly Permanent Fund Dividend check sent out each October. In 1982, the first year of the dividend, each Alaskan received $1,000, but it didn't reach that level again until the stock market boom of the late 1990s, when it topped out at nearly $2,000. The 2009 payout was around $1,300 per person. All this sudden cash doesn't go unnoticed by local businesses, especially car dealers, furniture stores, and airlines, who put out a plethora of special deals as soon as the money hits the banks.

MAKING A LIVING

Employment

Anyone thinking of moving to Alaska to get rich is in for a rude awakening. For a number of years after the oil boom, Alaskans earned the most per capita of any state, but now Alaska ranks 33rd for income—and near the top for cost of living. The state's unemployment figures are usually several percentage points above the national average, even during the peak summer season.

Despite this, you can still come to Alaska and make a decent living; after all, most Alaskans came from somewhere else (only a third of Alaskans were born in the state—the second-lowest such percentage in the country). But the opportunities, it should be stressed, are limited. For example, almost a third of the people collecting a paycheck in Alaska work for federal, state, or local government. And the industry that accounts for 87 percent of state revenues (oil and gas) accounts for just 3 percent of employment. The real growth of late has come at the bottom end, in service jobs and retail sales, where your income would probably leave you officially listed with poverty status. So if a job as a Wal-Mart stocker is your dream, hop on the next flight to Anchorage.

For employment information, visit the Alaska Department of Labor's **Job Bank**

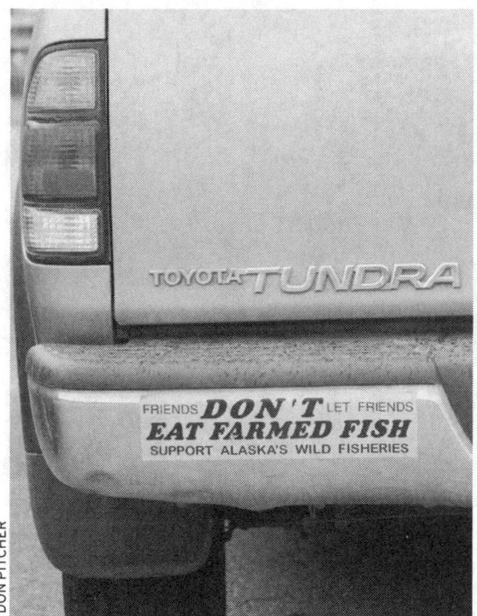

© DON PITCHER

Cordova bumper sticker

(www.jobs.state.ak.us), with an up-to-date listing of openings around the state. Here you'll find details on jobs in all sectors, including seasonal cannery work, state positions, and relocation information.

Fishing

Alaska's fisheries account for over half of the country's commercial fish production. Three-quarters of the value is in groundfish (pollock and cod) and salmon, the rest in shellfish, halibut, herring, and others. Alaska produces almost all of the U.S. canned-salmon stock (200 million pounds), and eight Alaskan ports are among the country's top 50 producers, with Dutch Harbor/Unalaska almost always in the top three, and Kodiak not far behind.

Alaska's fisheries are probably the most carefully managed in the country, with healthy stocks of wild salmon and halibut. Fish farming is illegal in Alaska, but farmed salmon from other areas flooded the market in the 1990s. Since then, there has been resurgence in demand for high-quality Alaskan wild salmon as consumers see problems caused by the farm-raised version—not to mention the difference in taste.

Learn more about Alaska's seafood industry (and get some good salmon and halibut recipes) from the **Alaska Seafood Marketing Institute** (www.alaskaseafood.org).

Agriculture

The percentage of Alaska's land used for farming is as minuscule as the percentage of Alaska's total economy that is accounted for by agriculture. Of the state's 375 million acres (17 million of it suitable for farming), only 910,000 acres are considered cultivable; of those, only 31,000 acres are occupied by crops. The Matanuska Valley (Palmer and Wasilla) and the Tanana Valley (Fairbanks and Delta) contain almost 90 percent of Alaska's usable farmland. Hay, potatoes, barley, and oats are the state's top agricultural products. Despite this, there has been a remarkable growth in small farms across Alaska, with summertime farmers markets from Sitka to Fairbanks.

In addition to legal crops, Alaska is famous for marijuana, and that crop is widely regarded as the state's biggest moneymaker. Cannabis-growing operations (most are indoor operations) are especially big in the Matanuska Valley, where the potent Matanuska Thunder F— gains the favor of potheads everywhere. A measure to legalize pot failed in 2004, but medical marijuana was approved by the voters several years earlier.

Gold and Minerals

Thirty million ounces of gold were taken from Alaska between 1880 and 1980. Today, the Fort Knox Mine near Fairbanks is Alaska's biggest gold producer, extracting 1,000 ounces of gold per day. Another major gold mine is scheduled to open near Delta Junction in 2005, and other large hard-rock mines are near Galena and McGrath, while small placer mines are common across Alaska.

Zinc is the state's most valuable mineral, mined at the enormous Red Dog Mine, 90 miles north of Kotzebue. The largest zinc mine in the world, it produces 575,000 tons of zinc

© DON PITCHER

touring the historic AJ Mine in Juneau

and 100 million tons of lead per year. Coal is mined at Usibelli, near Denali National Park, and deposits of jade, molybdenum, chromite, nickel, platinum, and uranium are known, though the cost of mining in remote Alaska limits these ventures.

One highly controversial mine does not yet exist. Located in the upper reaches of the Bristol Bay watershed (home to the world's most productive red salmon fisheries) is an enormous gold, copper, and molybdenum deposit known as **Pebble Creek.** The mining company talks of valuations in the hundreds of *billions* of dollars, and a massive open pit mine has been proposed on the site. It is opposed, however, by an unlikely coalition that includes fishers, Native Alaskan corporations, environmentalists, and wealthy lodge owners. Get their version at www.renewableresourcescoalition.org, and the mining company's story at www.pebblepartnership.com.

Oil and Gas

Everything that moves in Alaska is lubricated with oil, primarily North Slope crude. Without oil, the Alaskan economy would stiffen, shatter, and disappear into thin air. Oil and gas revenues account for 87 percent of the state's tax revenue. Alaska is so addicted to oil revenue that when the price of a barrel of oil drops by $1, the budget must be adjusted by $150 million. Though the industry accounts for just 3 percent of the total workforce, the average annual salary for these workers is $100,000. Few elected officials would dare speak out against the oil companies; they all know who pays the tab when election bills come in, and they don't want that cash going to their opponents.

At more than 350 million barrels of oil per year, Alaska accounts for around 17 percent of the nation's oil production, second only to Texas. Peak production was in 1988, when 738 million barrels of Prudhoe crude flowed through the pipeline. The Prudhoe Bay oilfield, the largest in North America and 18th in the world, had produced 14 billion barrels by 2003, but production continues to decline.

Enormous quantities of natural gas lie

beneath the North Slope, and proposals have been made to build a gas pipeline paralleling the existing oil line, or to develop a gas-to-liquids technology so that the gas can be sent down the existing oil pipeline. Higher gas prices and increased demand may finally lead to its development within the next decade. In addition to the North Slope, both oil and gas are produced from offshore wells in Cook Inlet. The natural gas is used in Anchorage and Kenai, but production has declined in recent years.

Tourism

Tourism is Alaska's third-largest industry, behind petroleum production and commercial fishing. It's also the second-largest employer, accounting for thousands of seasonal jobs. More than 1 million visitors travel to Alaska each year, 90 percent of them arriving May–September from the continental United States and Canada. Approximately half of all visitors (including business travelers) travel independently; the rest come up on cruise ships and package tours.

Native Corporations

Native corporations are major players in Alaska's economy, and they also have large investments (we're talking billions of dollars) spread all over the nation. The corporations include **Arctic Slope Regional Corporation** (www.asrc.com), **Cook Inlet Regional Corporation (CIRI)** (www.ciri.com), **Chugach Alaska Corporation** (www.chugach-ak.com), **Doyon, Limited** (www.doyon.com), and **NANA Regional Corporation** (www.nana.com). Doyon, with more than 12 million acres, is the largest corporate landholder in the nation.

All of these companies are involved in tourism ventures around Alaska, but CIRI and NANA especially have major investments in tour companies, hotels, and other facilities. Another company that travelers to Southeast Alaska will certainly come into contact with is the Juneau-based village **Goldbelt Corporation** (www.goldbelt.com), which runs the Mt. Roberts Tram, a hotel, and various other operations. If you travel in the North, you'll probably spend time in a Native Alaskan–owned facility or on one of their tour boats or buses.

The People

As of 2009, Alaska's population was 680,000. Of this, roughly 16 percent were of Native Alaskan descent. The nonnative population is predominantly white, with a small percentage of black, Hispanic, Asian, and Pacific Islanders. The Hispanic and Asian populations are growing rapidly in Alaska, and visitors to bush towns are often surprised to find that many of the restaurants are owned by Korean Americans, the cab drivers may be from the former Yugoslavia, and the cannery workers come from the Philippines or Mexico. Of course, the cruise ships that ply Inside Passage waters are staffed by workers from all over the globe. Anchorage has by far the most diverse population; more than one-third of its residents are Hispanic, Asian, black, or Native Alaskan.

Joe Average

According to statistics, the "typical" Alaskan is a 32-year-old white male. I think I know him: He's single, has a college degree, lives in Anchorage, works for Federal Express, hunts caribou with his buddies each fall, drives a big Ford pickup, owns a four-wheeler and snowmachine (they call them snowmobiles Outside), and is likely to be seen at Chilkoot Charlie's most Friday nights. (By the way, the bald guy who gained notoriety as "Joe the Plumber" in the 2008 presidential election campaign was a former resident of Alaska.) The state has the second-highest percentage of kids under 18 of any state; only Utah is higher.

In Anchorage and the other large Alaskan cities, the ratio of men to women is almost equal, but the state as a whole has one of the highest male-to-female ratios in the nation: 104 males to 100 females (compared with 95 males to 100 females Outside). Of course, you should also know the old and all-too-accurate adage: Alaska, where the odds are good, but the goods are odd.

Alaska is the largest state but the third-least populous (behind Wyoming and Vermont), resulting in the lowest population density—1.0 people per square mile (compare this to Wyoming, which has the second smallest at 4.7, or New Jersey, the most crowded at 1,042). It's also second to last in the number of people born in-state (34 percent); Florida is last at 31 percent. Alaska takes last place in its percentage of farm workers (0.1 percent).

ALASKAN NATIVES

Southeast Natives

One of Alaska's only Indian reservations is at Metlakatla, near Ketchikan. A group of nearly 1,000 **Tsimshian** people relocated here in 1887 from their traditional homeland, slightly south near Prince Rupert, as a result of disagreements between William Duncan, the tribe's missionary, and his church superiors. These indigenous people are thus the only ones not included in the ANCSA. Similarly, about 800 **Haida** people live on southern Prince of Wales Island at the southeastern tip of Alaska, the northern extent of the Haida homeland.

The **Tlingit** (KLINK-it) Indians are the traditional dwellers of Southeast Alaska, related to the Interior Athabascans. Blessed with an incredible abundance of food, fuel, furs, and tools, the Tlingits evolved a sophisticated and complex society, religion, and artistry. The primary social unit was the community house, which typically sheltered 50–100 people. Huge trunks of cedar and spruce provided the house posts, often carved and painted with the clan's totemic symbols; slaves were put in the post holes to cushion the connection between totem and earth. One had to stoop to pass through the single door; no windows punctuated the long structure. Ten or so of these clan houses made up a village, and a number of neighboring villages made up a

© DON PITCHER

statue commemorating The First Unknown Family, Golden Heart Park in Fairbanks

tribe. But these distinctions held little importance to the Tlingits, who felt connected genetically only to members of the same clan.

All marriages occurred between clans; marrying within the clan was considered incestuous. Descent was matrilineal: Children belonged to the mother's clan, and a man's heirs were his sisters' children. Therefore the pivotal male relationship was between uncle and nephews. At the age of 10, boys went to live with an uncle, who taught them the ways of the world. The uncle arranged the boy's marriage to a girl of another clan, who remained with her mother until the wedding. The dowry price was usually a number of blankets; the Tlingits were famous for their weaving and embroidery. Feasts known as "potlatch" honored the dead while feting the living. The Tlingits knew how to party. Often the potlatch continued for days or even weeks, during which the host fed, clothed, and entertained a neighboring, usually wealthier, clan, then "gave away" the clan's most valuable possessions to them. It was understood that the hosted clan would reciprocate eventually, with an even greater degree of festivity and generosity.

The Tlingits had an intensely animistic belief system in which everything, from glaciers to fish hooks, had a spirit. Tlingit shamans were virtually omnipotent, alternately controlling and beseeching *yek,* or karma, on behalf of the tribe. They also professed a complete understanding of the afterlife, "on authority of men who died and came back." Tlingit arts were expressed by men who carved totems for house posts, through the potlatch and other important events, and by women who wove exquisite blankets. Unlike the Aleut, the Tlingits were fierce warriors who were never completely conquered by the invading Russians, going head-to-head and hand-to-hand every inch of the way until they settled into an uneasy coexistence.

Athabascans

Nomadic hunters and migrants, the Athabascans are related to the Tlingit of Southeast Alaska and the Navajo and Apache of the American Southwest. They subsisted on salmon and the Interior's mammals, mostly caribou and moose. They passed the cruel winters in tiny villages of no more than six houses, with a *kashim,* or community center, as the focal point. They ice-fished and trapped in the dark, using dogsleds as transportation. Their arts were expressed primarily in beautifully embroidered clothing and beadwork. The men remained constantly occupied with survival tasks—finding food, building houses, maintaining gear. When the first white explorers and traders arrived in the early 19th century, the Athabascans immediately began to trade with them, learning the new cultures and in turn educating the newcomers in local customs and skills, not the least of which was dogsledding.

A tiny separate group of indigenous people, the **Eyaks** are found on the coast of Alaska between Cordova and Yakutat and have distinct links to both the Athabascans to the north and Tlingits to the east.

Aleuts

As the Athabascans were almost entirely land-based people, the Aleuts were almost entirely dependent on the sea. Clinging to the edge of tiny, treeless, windswept Aleutian Islands, they lived in small dwellings made of sealskin-covered frames, with fireplaces in the middle and steam baths attached on the sides. They made sea otter skins into clothing and processed walrus and seal intestines into parkas. Their kayaks (called *bidarka*) were made of marine mammal skins stretched over a wooden or whalebone frame. Basketry was their highest artistic achievement, and their dances were distinctly martial, with masks, rattles, and knives.

When the Russians invaded the Aleutians in the mid-1700s like furies from hell, around 25,000 Aleuts inhabited almost all the Aleutian Islands and the southern portion of the Alaska Peninsula. Within 50 years, over half had died through violence, starvation, or disease. Most of the rest became slaves and were dispersed around the New World to hunt the sea otter and fight for the Russians. In fact, Aleuts traveled as far south as Catalina Island off the Southern California coast, wiping out the Gabrieliño Indians there, along with the entire otter population, in 1810. Many of the women served as concubines to the Russian overlords, further diluting the Aleut lineage. Today, most Aleuts carry only half or a quarter Aleut blood; only 1,000 are considered full-blooded.

Eskimo

The term *Eskimo* comes from the French Canadian *Esquimau,* which in turn is derived from the Algonquin *askimowew,* which means "eaters of raw fish." Although the term is not at all derogatory, the Native Alaskans of these regions often prefer to use more specific titles: the **Yup'ik** peoples of Southwest Alaska, the **Inupiat** peoples of the Arctic and circumpolar region, and the **Alutiiq** peoples of Kodiak Island, the Alaska Peninsula, and parts of the Kenai Peninsula and Prince William Sound. In addition, remote St. Lawrence Island

CAPSULE ALASKAN GLOSSARY

A type of pidgin called "Chinook" evolved in the Pacific Northwest in the 18th century. The language first developed in interactions between the large, powerful Chinook nation (hence the name "Chinook") of the Columbia River, which did business with white traders, and the Nootka people, who held a monopoly on the shells from which the shell money of the Pacific was manufactured. After Europeans arrived, Chinook adopted words from English and French; it became indispensable to traders in Alaska through the entire 19th century. Of the 500 words in the Chinook vocabulary, a few are still used today.

Some of the Alaskan words below have been borrowed from indigenous tongues; the rest derive from the colorful frontier slang of explorers, traders, trappers, prospectors, fishers, roughnecks, and travel writers.

- ***akutak*** – Yup'ik word for Native Alaskan ice cream: a combination of whipped berries, seal oil, and snow
- **Alaskan malamute** – a particular breed of working dog used to pull sleds
- **Alcan** – nickname for the Alaska Highway
- **Arctic Circle** – an imaginary line, roughly corresponding to 67 degrees north latitude, that the sun remains entirely above on summer solstice and entirely below on winter solstice
- **Aurora** – goddess of dawn
- **aurora borealis** – the scientific term for the northern lights
- ***baidarka*** – an Aleut kayak covered with animal skins
- **baleen** – also known as whalebone, these stiff flexible whale's "teeth" are woven into baskets by Eskimo men
- ***banya*** – Russian in origin; a small sauna in which rocks surround a woodstove, and are sprinkled with water for a steam bath; common on Kodiak Island and along the Bering Sea
- ***barabara*** – traditional Aleut or Eskimo shelter, made of driftwood and a sod roof
- **blanket toss** – originally a means of spotting game on the tundra, a Native Alaskan event in which 6-8 people use a large blanket to toss the "spotter" high in the air and catch him; now part of most festivals, and demonstrated for tourists in Barrow and Kotzebue
- **breakup** – the period in late April or early May when the river ice suddenly fractures and begins to flow downstream; a particularly muddy, slushy time of year
- **bunny boot** – see *vapor-barrier boots*
- **bush** – Borrowed from Africa and Australia, this term generally designates remote areas off the road system, particularly in Interior, Western, and Arctic Alaska
- **cabin fever** – Alaska-size claustrophobia due to the extreme cold and dark of winter
- **cache** – pronounced "cash," a log hut built on tin-wrapped stilts used to store food and supplies beyond the reach of animals
- **Chain, The** – nickname for the Aleutian Islands
- ***cheechako*** – meaning "just arrived," used to describe newcomers and visitors, especially those who haven't spent a winter in Alaska or received a dividend check; some sourdoughs view anyone not born in the state as a cheechako
- **chinook** – a strong warm wind originating in Prince William Sound; can be particularly destructive in hillside sections of Anchorage
- **chum** – a kind of salmon; also known as dog salmon, after its primary consumers
- **Eskimo** – from French Canadian *Esquimau*, a word derived originally from northern Algonquin *askimowew*, which means "eater of raw fish"

- **fish wheel** – an ingenious mechanism that uses the current of a river or stream for power to scoop fish into a tank
- **freeze-up** – the time of year, mostly in Northwest and Arctic regions, when bodies of water are frozen and seaports are icebound
- ***gussuk*** – derogatory Eskimo term for a white person
- **honey bucket** – in much of bush Alaska, the local sewage system: a five-gallon plastic bucket used as a toilet. The untreated waste is often dumped into rivers in the summer or onto river ice in winter (for natural "flushing" when the ice breaks up in the spring). Because of the obvious health hazards – not to mention the smell – the state has been trying to bring sewage-treatment facilities to small villages.
- **hooch** – shortened version of the Chinook word *hootchenoo,* meaning home-distilled spirits
- **husky** – the generic term for a sled dog. A toy poodle hooked up to a sled is technically a husky – for the brief moment before it's eaten by a large **Siberian husky.** Like the malamute, the Siberian husky is a singular breed famous for strength and intelligence.
- **icefog** – caused by an inversion in which warm air traps cold air near the surface, which keeps getting colder and colder until the water vapor in the air freezes, creating floating ice crystals; Fairbanks is notorious for its wintertime icefog
- **iceworm** – originally a joke by sourdoughs on cheechakos, the joke was ultimately on the sourdoughs – iceworms actually exist, and you can see specimens in the museum in Juneau and at the Portage Glacier visitors center
- **Iditarod** – Famous 1,000-mile dogsled race from Anchorage to Nome; takes place in early March. One explanation of the name comes from the term *rod,* a measurement of work accomplished in the gold fields; thus the word is actually a sentence: "I did a rod." Another holds that the name evolved from the name of an Ingalik Indian village reported as "Khadilotden." It was then reported by the USGS as "Haidilatna," and finally anglicized as Iditarod.
- **igloo** – Native Alaskans' shelters are never igloos made of ice (see *barabara*), except in extreme emergencies
- **Inside Passage** – another name for Southeast Alaska; it refers to the many protected waterways of this island archipelago
- **Inupiak** – a northern Eskimo dialect used by Inupiat peoples
- **iron dog** – snowmobile
- **iron ranger** – collection boxes at state and federal campgrounds
- ***kuspuk*** – parka worn by Eskimo women, often with a small backpack-like pouch for carrying babies
- **liquid sunshine** – Ketchikan's euphemism for rain
- **Lower 48** – an Alaskan term used to refer to the contiguous continental United States
- **moose nuggets** – small, round, brown moose droppings, bravely made into jewelry by enterprising (usually bankrupt) local artisans
- **mukluk** – boot made by Eskimo women, with tough sealskin soles, reindeer-hide uppers, fur and yarn trim, sewn together with caribou sinew
- ***muktuk*** – an Eskimo delicacy of the rubbery outer layer of whale skin and fat; very chewy, served raw or pickled
- **mush** – popularized by Sgt. Preston of the Yukon, this command means "Let's go!" to

(continued on next page)

CAPSULE ALASKAN GLOSSARY (continued)

anxious dog teams everywhere; originally a Chinook term adapted from the French *marchons*

- **muskeg** – swampy areas covered by moss and scrub
- **native** – the preferred term for Alaska's original inhabitants
- **no-see-ums** – tiny biting flies that plague Alaska after mosquito season
- ***nunatak*** – lonely rock peak jutting out above ice fields
- **Outside** – anywhere other than Alaska, primarily used in reference to the Lower 48
- **Panhandle** – nickname for Southeast Alaska
- **permafrost** – permanently frozen ground, with a layer of topsoil that thaws during the summer
- **petroglyphs** – stone-age carvings on rock faces
- **poke** – a miner's moosehide bag full of gold dust and nuggets
- **potlatch** – A Native Alaskan party to celebrate any occasion. Often the hosts would give away all their possessions to their guests. This exercise in the detachment from all worldly goods was also an exercise in gaining more, as the event conferred on the guests the obligation to host a bigger potlatch with better gifts.
- ***promyshlenniki*** – early Russian explorers and traders
- ***pushky*** – from Russian, the colloquial term for cow parsnip, a common plant that can cause caustic skin burns, particularly on a sunny day; most commonly used on Kodiak Island and in Southcentral Alaska
- ***qiviut*** – underwool of musk ox, supposedly eight times lighter, warmer, and more expensive than wool
- **ruff** – fur edge on a parka hood, often of wolf guard hairs
- **salt chuck** – a narrow constriction at the end of a lagoon, where the direction of the water flow depends on the tides (out at low, in at high); mainly used in Southeast Alaska.
- **shitcicle** – the pile of excrement that gathers in bush outhouses each winter in the form of an inverted icicle; when it gets too close to the top, someone has the unpleasant job of knocking it down
- ***skookum*** – Chinook, meaning "strong" or "worthy"
- **Slope** – The gently sloping tundra around Prudhoe Bay; also known as the North Slope; Slope workers are almost always employed by the oil companies
- **snowmachine** – snowmobile
- **solstice** – first day of summer (June 21) or winter (December 21)
- **sourdough** – a mixture of flour, water, sugar, and yeast, allowed to ferment before being used to make bread or hotcakes; an old-timer
- **squaw candy** – dried or smoked salmon
- ***surimi*** – processed seafood product manufactured from bottom fish (usually pollock) in Kodiak, Unalaska, and other Alaskan ports; used in "crab" salads and cocktails, as well as in less expensive sushi
- **taiga** – from a Russian word meaning "land of little sticks," which describes the transition zone between the boreal forest and treeless tundra
- **Taku wind** – sudden gusts of up to 100 mph that sweep down on Juneau from the nearby ice fields
- **termination dust** – the first snowfall that coats mountaintops at the end of summer, a sign that Alaska's many seasonal workers are about to be terminated

- **tree line** – the elevation (in Alaska, 2,500 feet) and latitude (generally following the Arctic Circle) above which no trees grow
- **tundra** – from another Russian word, meaning "vast treeless plain;" used to describe nearly 30 percent of Alaska's land area
- ***ulu*** – a shell-shaped Eskimo knife that tourists buy in record numbers and airlines disallow in hand luggage
- ***umiak*** – an open skin-covered Eskimo boat used in the hunting of whales and other sea mammals
- **visqueen** – thin clear plastic sheeting
- **XtraTufs** – high-top rubber boots ubiquitous on Southeast Alaskan feet
- **Yup'ik** – dialect of the Bering Coast Eskimo

contains **Siberian Yup'ik** peoples. All four groups speak distinct dialects of the same basic language.

In traditional Eskimo culture there was a strong sense of community; their society was mostly leaderless, with every able member responsible for contributing to the struggle for survival. The line between personal and communal property was fuzzy at best, and theft did not exist. Everything was shared, including (claim some anthropologists) wives. All justice was determined by what was deemed best for the community. Marriages too were so determined.

A boy entered adulthood after his first kill, and the event was celebrated by a large feast. A girl was considered grown as soon as she began menstruating, which was accompanied by a two-week ritual. The man-child selected a bride, paid a minimal price, and unceremoniously set up house in a hut similar to the Aleuts'—a bone-and-brush framework covered with moss and grass. Igloos made of snow and ice were used only as temporary shelters on the trail (and mostly by central Canadian indigenous people). Fuel was derived from whale oil and driftwood. They ate meat almost exclusively: fish, whale, walrus, caribou, and birds. Also like their relatives the Aleut, they used skin and hides for clothing and boating. Masks are the most visible form of Eskimo art, but their aesthetic touch marks almost everything they make.

The Russians had little impact on the remote Eskimo, but their introduction to Western ways by the Boston whalers around the 1850s was swift and brutal. Many Eskimo quickly succumbed to whiskey, and Native Alaskan men were shanghaied while unconscious to labor on the white whalers' ships. They learned about prostitution (renting the women) and slavery (selling them). They learned how to use firearms and casually kill each other, usually in a drunken fit. They acquired syphilis, white sugar, canned food, and money.

An encounter between the Eskimo of St. Lawrence Island and a single whaling vessel in 1880, described by Colby in his classic *Guide to Alaska* (1939), sums up the scene:

> *The master sent members of his crew ashore with bottles of grain alcohol, [for which] the Native Alaskans traded ivory, whalebone, and furs. The officers and crew selected a harem from the young women of the village, and paid them in alcohol. When the whaling vessel left, the entire village of 450 Native Alaskans was dead-drunk and beggared, for they had even cut up their skin boats to trade for liquor. Around them were plenty of hair seal and walrus, but by the time the village had sobered and collected weapons the game was gone. Only about twenty-five villagers survived.*

The whaling years ended just before the gold rush began, but the ruin of the Eskimo culture was almost total. Gradually, with the help of missionaries and legislators, the Eskimo in the late 19th century turned to reindeer herding, which began to provide income, food, and skins. Today, an estimated 34,000 Eskimo live in Alaska, having doubled their number over the past 50 years. The Eskimo people live in an arc stretching from Siberia to Greenland.

NATIVE ARTS AND CRAFTS

Not unlike most other aboriginal cultures, Native Alaskan arts and crafts were intricately intertwined with animism, religious ceremony, and utility. Each group worked with its abundant natural resources to produce all the necessities of a lifestyle in which subsistence, religion, and artistic expression were inseparable.

Alaskan tourism and Native Alaskan crafts have gone hand in hand since the first Russian stepped ashore. When John Muir arrived in Wrangell by steamer in 1890, he wrote,

> *There was a grand rush on shore to buy curiosities and see totem poles. The shops were jammed and mobbed, high prices paid for shabby stuff manufactured expressly for tourist trade. Silver bracelets hammered out of dollars and half dollars by Indian smiths are the most popular articles, then baskets, yellow cedar toy canoes, paddles, etc. Most people who travel look only at what they are directed to look at. Great is the power of the guidebook-maker, however ignorant.*

A similar observation holds today, especially in the shops selling made-in-China Alaskan trinkets or carved-in-Bali totem poles and masks. When buying Native Alaskan handicrafts from anyone other than the artist, always look for the **Silver Hand** logo that identifies the work as an authentic Native Alaskan piece. Get details from the Alaska State Council on the Arts (907/269-6610 or 888/278-7424, www.eed.state.ak.us/aksca/native.htm). Good places to buy Native Alaskan crafts are the various museum gift shops or directly from the artisans, if you visit remote villages.

Ivory

The Inupiat Eskimo of northern coastal Alaska are renowned for their use of ivory, harvested only by Native Alaskans from the tusks and teeth of walrus, as well as ivory from woolly mammoths and giant mastodons uncovered by miners or erosion. The ivory is carved, also known as "scrimshawed," and made into various implements. Today you'll see ivory jewelry, *ulu* handles, cribbage boards, and the like. The use of ivory for handicrafts is severely restricted by federal regulations established to protect the walrus. Native carvers can carve on ivory obtained from walrus killed for subsistence food, and nonnatives can legally carve on fossilized ivory (darker-colored ivory that was buried in the ground). But don't make the mistake of buying an ivory piece and then taking it through Canada, unless you have a written permit from the Convention on Trade in Endangered Species (www.cites.org). Avoid border confiscations and other legal problems by mailing your pieces home. You won't have any problems carrying them onboard an aircraft, unless your plane lands outside the United States.

Baskets

All Native Alaskan groups used available resources to fashion baskets for storage, carrying, and cooking. Birch-bark baskets, often lashed with spruce roots, were made by the forest Athabascans. The coastal Haida, Tlingit, and Tsimshian Indians used the bark of big cedar trees. They also made entire baskets of spruce roots, occasionally weaving in maidenhead ferns for decoration. The Yup'ik and Aleut indigenous people of Western Alaska are known for small, delicate baskets fashioned from coastal rye grass. They also process baleen, the long strips of cartilage-like teeth that hang from the upper jaw of whales, and weave the strips into baskets.

The finest examples of the different baskets are displayed in the largest Alaskan museums;

commercial baskets sell for anywhere from $40 for simple birch-bark trays to several thousand dollars for large baleen baskets.

Masks

Each Native Alaskan culture had its traditional mask-making technology and its complex ceremonial uses for masks. Eskimo mask art and ritual were among the most highly developed in the world. Masks, like totems, represented the individual animals and birds that were worshipped, and each mask was believed to embody the spirit, or *inua,* of the animal. The masks of the Athabascans were worn by dancers, accompanied by a tribal choir, to dramatize the tribe's relationship to animal spirits as well as to entertain guests at feasts. Some believe Aleut masks symbolized the faces of ancient inhabitants of the western Alaska archipelago, though these people were only distantly related to the Aleut, if at all.

The use of masks has declined in Native Alaskan cultures, and the art of mask-making isn't as prevalent today as it's said to have been before contact with the Western world. But you will see commercial masks in Native Alaskan galleries and gift shops around the North; these bear a close resemblance to those of long ago.

Totems

Totem poles were the largest and most dramatic of the Native Alaskan arts and social images, though today, totemic images are reproduced in every medium and size. Typical totemic characterizations include highly stylized wolves, whales, bears, ravens, eagles, and beavers, as well as mythological monsters, human ancestors, and religious spirits. These images are a common sight in gift shops all over Alaska.

Other Pieces

Fur parkas are the quintessential Eskimo garment and are available in remote villages and at shops in Anchorage and Fairbanks. The finest of these are custom-made and cost a small fortune; ask locally for the best seamstresses. Beautifully crafted **dolls** are a hallmark of Eskimo artists who typically use furs and other local materials. Other distinctively Alaskan items include **dance fans, beadwork,** and handcrafted silver or jade **jewelry.**

ESSENTIALS

Getting There and Around

BY AIR

Anchorage International Airport (www.anchorageairport.com) is the hub for air travel into Alaska, although there are nonstop flights into Fairbanks, Juneau, and Ketchikan from the Lower 48 states, plus a few international flights directly into Fairbanks.

The state's flagship carrier, **Alaska Airlines** (800/426-0333, www.alaskaair.com), has jet service to all the larger cities and towns in Alaska, as well as throughout the United States and all the way to Mexico.

Regional Airlines

Alaska Airlines serves most larger towns around the state, including such far-flung places as Barrow, Nome, Bethel, Kodiak, and Dillingham. **Frontier Alaska** (907/266-8394 or 800/866-8394, www.frontierak.com) is the largest in-state airline. As Frontier, the company has hubs in both Anchorage and Fairbanks, with service between the two cities several times a day, plus flights to Aniak, Barrow, Dillingham, and many bush villages, and from Allakaket to Wainwright. Their subsidiary **Era Aviation** (booked via the Frontier Alaska phone numbers and website) has daily service from Anchorage to Bethel, Cordova, Homer, Kenai, Kodiak, and Valdez. A second subsidiary, **Hageland Aviation,** serves

© DON PITCHER

© DON PITCHER

Alaska Airlines, the state's flagship carrier

a variety of bush communities from Nome and Kotzebue.

PenAir (907/243-2323 or 800/448-4226, www.penair.com) flies from Anchorage to Aniak, Cold Bay, Dillingham, Dutch Harbor, Iliamna, King Salmon, McGrath, Pribilof Islands, Sand Point, and Unalakleet. **Arctic Circle Air** (907/842-3870 or 888/214-2364, www.arcticcircleair.com) serves Cordova, Iliamna, St. Marys, Unalakleet, and Yakutat from Anchorage, and Galena, Tanana, Anaktuvuk Pass, Arctic Village, and Eagle from Fairbanks. **Grant Aviation** (907/243-3592 or 888/359-4726, www.flygrant.com) connects Anchorage with Homer and Kenai. **Wings of Alaska** (907/789-0790, www.wingsofalaska.com) serves northern Southeast Alaska, including Juneau, Gustavus, Skagway, Haines, Hoonah, and Kake.

BY BUSH PLANE

Flying in a real live Alaska bush plane is a spectacular way to see the state, and it's also the only practical way to access the vast majority of Alaska's roadless areas. You will never forget your first flight over Alaska, whether it's a floatplane heading to Misty Fiords National Monument or a tiny Super Cub taking you to a remote Arctic camp. These airlines have regularly scheduled, though expensive, flights to towns and attractions that either have no public ground transportation or simply can't be reached overland—which accounts for more than three-quarters of the state. For many people who live in Alaska's bush, these planes provide a lifeline of mail, food, and supplies. The planes seat 2–12 passengers, and they fly for the regular fare no matter how many passengers are aboard (if the weather is cooperating).

But if you're heading to a really remote cabin, fjord, river, glacier, or park, that's when you'll encounter the famous Alaskan bush pilots, with their equally famous charter rates, which can make Alaska Airlines' fares look like the bargain of the century. Still, you'll have quite a ride—landing on tiny lakes with pontoons, on snow or ice with skis, on gravel bars with big fat tires, loaded to the gills with people, equipment, extra fuel, tools, mail, supplies, and anything else under the sun. Make sure you agree on all the details beforehand—charges, drop-off and pickup times and locations, emergency and alternative procedures, and tidal considerations. Never be in much of a hurry; time is told differently up here, and many variables come into play, especially the weather. If you're well prepared for complications and have a flexible schedule and a loose attitude, one of these bush hops will no doubt be among your most memorable experiences in Alaska, worth every penny and minute that you spend.

As far as what you can expect to pay, most flightseeing operations have preset itineraries and prices. Some companies flying out of the larger towns also have set rates to some of the more popular destinations. However, for most drop-off trips, you pay for the ride according to engine hours, both coming and going. So if your destination is a spot that's an hour from the airstrip, you pay for four hours of engine time (an hour out and an hour back, twice).

Safety in the Air

Before you head out into the wild blue yonder, there are a few things you should know. Alaska has far more than its share of fatal airplane crashes every year, generally 3–4 times the national average for small planes. These have happened to even the best pilots flying for even the most conscientious companies, but certain operators cut corners in safety and allow their pilots to fly under risky weather conditions. You can't avoid all risks, of course, but you can improve your odds by taking a few precautions of your own.

First and foremost, you should choose your pilot and flight service with care. Just because someone has a pilot's license and is flying in Alaska doesn't mean that he or she is a seasoned bush pilot. You're well within your rights to ask about the pilot's qualifications, and about time spent flying *in Alaska.* The oft-repeated saying is, "There are old pilots and there are bold pilots, but there are no old bold pilots." Given a choice, you want an "old" one—not so much in chronological years, but one that has been flying in and out of the bush for a good long time. Ask locally about the air safety record of the various companies. Also ask which companies have the contracts with the Forest Service or other federal agencies, since they tend to be ones that aren't allowed to take chances. You can also search the Web for accident statistics for a specific company at the **National Transportation Safety Board's** website (www.ntsb.gov).

Even if you're just going on a 30-minute flightseeing tour, wear clothing appropriate for the ground conditions. Unplanned stops because of weather or mechanical problems aren't unusual. Warm comfortable hiking clothes, rain gear, and lightweight boots or sturdy shoes make reasonable bush plane apparel.

Weather is a major limiting factor in aviation. Small planes don't operate on airline-type schedules, with arrivals and departures down to the minute. Leave yourself plenty of leeway when scheduling trips, and don't pressure your pilot to get you back to the airstrip so you won't miss your bus, boat, train, dogsled ride, or salmon bake. More than one crash has been the result of subtle or not-so-subtle pressure by clients to fly when it was against the pilot's better judgment. Never pressure a pilot to fly, and always try to act as a second pair of eyes to look for any signs of danger, such as other aircraft in the vicinity.

Before taking off, your pilot should brief all passengers on the location of safety and survival equipment and airsickness bags, how to exit during an emergency landing (or crash), and the location and function of the Emergency Locator Transmitter (ELT) and survival kit. Ear protection may also be supplied, as most small planes are quite noisy. Just in case, buy a set of foam earplugs at a sporting-goods store before you go to the airport. They cost under $1, weigh nothing, and are perfectly adequate for aircraft noise levels.

You'll probably be asked how much you weigh (don't be coy—lives are at stake) and told where you should sit. Weight and balance are critical in little planes, so don't whine about not getting to sit up front if you're told otherwise. Many companies place severe restrictions on how much gear they carry, charging excess baggage fees over a certain limit (sometimes less than 50 pounds).

Gear stowage can be a challenge in small planes, especially when transporting people who are heading out on long expeditions. Don't even think of showing up at the airfield with hard-sided luggage. Internal-frame backpacks, duffel bags, and other soft, easily compressed and stowed items are much easier to handle. Don't strap sleeping bags and other gear onto the outside of a pack. Lots of small items are much easier to arrange and find homes for than a few bulky things. Also, if you're carrying a canister of red pepper spray to deter bears, tell the pilot beforehand and follow directions for stowage. Pilots don't want the stuff inside the cabin (imagine what might happen if it went off in this enclosed space), but they'll store it in a float if the plane is so equipped, or you may be able to strap it to a strut with duct tape.

Whenever you fly, leave a flight route, destination, expected departure and arrival times, and a contact number for the flight service with a reliable friend. Then relax and enjoy the scenery. Flying in Alaska is a tremendous experience, one that relatively few people get to enjoy, and in spite of all the cautionary notes above, it is still a generally safe and reliable way to get to and see the wilderness.

FERRY SERVICE

Ferries plying the Inside Passage from Bellingham to Skagway cruise up an inland waterway and through fjords far wilder than Norway's, surpassing even a trip down the coast of Chile to Punta Arenas. One difference is that the North American journey is cheaper and more easily arranged than its South American or Scandinavian counterparts. Another difference is the variety of services, routes, and destinations for this 1,000-mile historic cruise. Ferries operated by the **Alaska Marine Highway** (907/465-3941 or 800/642-0066, www.dot.state.ak.us/amhs) are the core of Inside Passage travel.

There are two primary state ferry networks: one from Bellingham, Washington, or Prince Rupert, British Columbia, and throughout Southeast Alaska; the other through Southcentral Alaska from Cordova all the way to Dutch Harbor in the Aleutians. In addition, a ferry sails between Whittier and Juneau twice monthly in the summer, linking the two regions.

The **Inter-Island Ferry Authority** (907/826-4848 or 866/308-4848, www.interislandferry.com) operates a passenger and vehicle ferry between Ketchikan and Prince of Wales Island.

British Columbia Ferries (250/386-3431 or 888/223-3779, www.bcferries.com) sails Canada's Inside Passage from Port Hardy at the northern tip of Vancouver Island to Prince Rupert on the B.C. mainland's north coast.

Alaska Marine Highway

One of the first actions of the newly created Alaska State government in 1959 was to establish a state ferry system. Originally it consisted of just a single boat, but after passage of a 1960 state bond, three new ships were built and more have been added over the years. The newest additions are two high-speed ferries (high-speed when they are operating, which can be half the time): the *Fairweather* in Southeast Alaska and the *Chenega* for Prince William Sound. All state ferries carry both passengers and vehicles, and offer food service. The larger ferries also have cabins, showers, storage lockers, gift shops, pay phones, and cocktail lounges.

Ferries generally stop for 1–2 hours in the larger towns, but less than 1 hour in the smaller villages. You can usually go ashore while the vessel is in port. Most ferry terminals open only 1–2 hours before ship arrivals, closing upon their departure. A baggage cart transports luggage from the terminal to the ship if you want to save your back a bit. There is a limit of 100 pounds of luggage per person, but this is only enforced if you are way over the limit and the ship is full.

Life Onboard

The ferries have a relaxed and slow-paced atmosphere; it's impossible to be in a hurry here.

Many travelers think of the ferry as a floating motel—a place to dry off, wash up, rest up, sleep, and meet other travelers while at the same time moving on to new sights and new adventures. Ferry food is reasonably priced and quite good, but many budget travelers stock up on groceries before they board. The hot water is free in the cafeteria if you're trying to save bucks by bringing along Cup-O-Noodles and instant oatmeal.

Most ferries have Forest Service or Fish & Wildlife Service interpreters on board in the summer, showing videos, giving talks, and answering questions about trails and campgrounds. Feature movies are shown on the video monitors every day.

Staterooms or Solarium?

Staterooms offer privacy, as well as a chance to get away from the hectic crowding of midsummer. These cabins have two or four bunk beds, and some also include private baths; other folks use the baths and showers down the hall.

If you don't mind hearing others snoring or talking nearby, you can save a bundle and make new friends with fellow voyagers. There's generally space to stretch out a sleeping bag in the recliner lounge (an inside area with airline-type seats), as well as in the solarium—a covered and heated area high atop the ship's rear deck. The solarium has several dozen deck chairs to sit and sleep on, and it can get so popular that at some embarkation points there's a mad dash to grab a place. To be assured of a deck chair, get in line five hours ahead of time if you're coming aboard in Bellingham in midsummer. When the weather is good you're also likely to see the rapid development of a tent city on the rear deck, often held down with duct tape (sold in gift shops on board).

Getting Tickets

The ferries operate year-round. Get schedules and make reservations by calling 907/465-3941 or 800/642-0066 or online at www.dot.state.ak.us/amhs. Reservations for the summer can be made as early as December, and travelers taking a vehicle should book as early as possible to be sure of a space. Before you get ready to board, call the local ferry terminal to make sure the ferry is on schedule; often they are running behind, and the too-frequent breakdowns can totally change departure times.

Although there is usually space for walk-on passengers, it's a smart idea to make advance reservations for ferries out of Bellingham, especially for cabins. Reservations are required for anyone with a vehicle and are generally available six months in advance. The ferry system charges an extra fee to carry bicycles, canoes, kayaks, and inflatable boats.

CRUISE SHIPS

For many people, particularly retirees, cruise ships offer a luxury way to see Alaska. A multitude of ships ply the Inside Passage and Gulf of Alaska waters, carrying 900,000 people each summer—half of all travelers to the state. Cruises make it easy for travelers to explore the Inside Passage while enjoying good food and cozy accommodations.

Cruise ship tourism has proven to be a mixed blessing for Alaska. True, it does bring in millions of dollars to the state, and towns such as Skagway are almost totally given over to cruise ships, but the ships also dump hundreds of thousands of gallons of wastewater into Alaska's pristine waterways, pollute the air, and cause major disruptions in local communities. In 2006, Alaskan voters were angry enough to slap a $50 head tax and various restrictions on the industry.

If you're traveling by cruise ship, you will be inundated with suggested shore excursions offered through the ship. There are advantages to booking through your ship, but they do take a cut and the prices are often substantially higher than you would pay if you booked the trip yourself. Readers of this book will have a good idea of the offerings, but visit www.shoretrips.com to see some of the available options and their costs.

The Ships

Most ships depart from Vancouver, British Columbia, but some cruises also leave from

© DON PITCHER
cruise ship in Chilkoot Inlet near Haines

Seattle or San Francisco. The largest vessel can hold more than 3,000 passengers, and some offer impressive buffets, luxurious atrium lobbies, private stateroom verandas, health spas, and lounges with live music and casinos. Not all ships are large and glitzy, however. The smallest "expedition" ships may hold just a few dozen passengers. On these, the emphasis is on education and ecotourism. Many of the smaller ships also have professional naturalists on board and act as "mother ships" for short sea kayaking or hiking trips. Not surprisingly, expedition ships are considerably more expensive than the giant cruise liners.

Large Ships

Any good travel agent or online travel site can set up an Alaska cruise, or you can book your own by contacting the companies directly. A good overall place to begin an exploration of cruise ship travel is the website of the **Cruise Lines International Association** (www.cruising.org). It has links to all the major players, plus general information. For specifics on Alaska cruising, visit www.alaskacruisingreport.com. Other useful websites include www.cruisecritic.com, www.cruisereviews.com, www.cruise-chat.com, and www.cruisemates.com; www.cruisecritic.com is especially useful if you're looking for cheap cruises.

The large ships that visit Alaska are operated by **Carnival Cruise Lines** (888/227-6482, www.carnival.com), **Celebrity Cruises** (800/647-2251, www.celebritycruises.com), **Crystal Cruises** (888/799-4625, www.crystalcruises.com), **Disney Cruise Line** (888/352-2500, www.disneycruise.com), **Holland America Line** (206/281-3535 or 877/724-5425, www.hollandamerica.com), **Norwegian Cruise Lines** (866/234-7350, www.ncl.com), **Princess Cruises** (800/776-6237, www.princess.com), **Regent Seven Seas** (877/505-5370, www.rssc.com), and **Royal Caribbean International** (866/562-7625, www.royalcaribbean.com). **Silversea Cruises** (877/215-9986, www.silversea.com) operates the smallest of the large ships with space for 300 or so passengers. These are the ultimate luxury ships if you really want to feel pampered.

Smaller Cruise Ships

You don't have to join these megaships to see Alaska by sea. A number of companies offer smaller ships (under 100 passengers) for a more intimate look at the state. Of course, these are also considerably more expensive than ships that pack folks into every nook and cranny. Companies with small cruise ships include **Cruise West** (206/441-4757 or 888/851-8133, www.cruisewest.com) and **Lindblad Expeditions** (212/765-7740 or 800/397-3348, www.expeditions.com).

Even smaller boats provide the ultimate in luxury for groups of 6–8 people. Good expedition companies include **Alaska Sea Adventures** (907/772-4700 or 888/772-8588, www.yachtalaska.com), **Alaska Sailing Charters** (907/723-0883 or 866/486-1732, www.alaskasailingcharters.com), **Alaska Yacht Adventures** (907/789-1978 or 800/725-3913, www.alaskayachtcharters.

com), **All Aboard Yacht Charters** (360/898-7300 or 800/767-1024, www.alaskacharters.com), **American Safari Cruises** (888/862-8881, www.amsafari.com), **Alaska on the Home Shore** (360/592-2375 or 800/287-7063, www.homeshore.com), **Discovery Voyages** (800/324-7602, www.discoveryvoyages.com), **Dolphin Charters** (510/527-9622 or 800/472-9942, www.dolphincharters.com), and **Maple Leaf Adventures** (888/599-5323, www.mapleleafadventures.com).

Costs and Itineraries

Prices for cruises have dropped in recent years as more and larger ships have moved into the Alaskan market. The bargain deals are typically early or late in the summer season and can be amazingly cheap at times. Cruises typically last 7–12 days and are either taken as a round-trip tour of the Inside Passage or a one-way cruise that encompasses both the Inside Passage and towns along the Gulf of Alaska. It is also possible to add in a land tour, either as part of a hurried seven-day ship-and-bus package or as an add-on to the cruise. The add-on option often includes time in Southcentral and Interior Alaska and might start with a trip through the Inside Passage followed by a bus tour from Skagway to Fairbanks, a train trip to Denali National Park, and then on to Anchorage, where you fly home. Many other cruise options exist; contact the individual companies for details.

TRAIN

Except for the White Pass & Yukon Route excursion between Skagway and Fraser, and the kids' choo-choos around Pioneer Park in Fairbanks and at Alaska Live Steamers in Wasilla, Alaska's only train is the **Alaska Railroad** (907/265-2494 or 800/544-0552, www.alaskarailroad.com). The railroad runs 470 miles between Seward and Fairbanks with a seven-mile spur between Portage and Whittier; it is the only state-owned railroad in the United States. The train—historic and a bit exotic—is also much roomier and slower than a tour bus but is about the same price (and is occasionally even on time). Dining service is available, and helpful tour guides are on board in the summer months. In addition, some of the trains will make flag stops to pick up hikers or people living in the Alaskan bush.

Two daily expresses (mid-May–mid-Sept.), one northbound and one southbound, run between Anchorage and Fairbanks for $210 one-way. Anchorage to Denali costs $146, and Fairbanks to Denali is $64. The train also connects Seward with Anchorage ($75) and Anchorage with Whittier ($65) daily in the summer. The railroad has luxurious double-deck "GoldStar" cars ($85 extra to Denali) and a variety of package tours that combine train rides with boat trips and other activities. Princess Tours and Holland America Tours/Gray Line hook double-decker superdome coaches to the end of the express trains in the summer.

REGIONAL BUSES

There is no regular bus service between the Lower 48 and Alaska, but you *can* get there from here. **Greyhound Canada** (604/482-8747 or 800/661-8747, www.greyhound.ca) covers much of Canada, reaching north to Whitehorse in Yukon. From there, you'll need to hop aboard an **Alaska Direct Bus Line** (907/277-6652 or 800/770-6652, www.alaskadirectbusline.com) van to Tok, Anchorage, and Fairbanks. Service is three times a week in the summer, twice weekly the rest of the year. Reservations are recommended.

Alaska/Yukon Trails (907/479-2277 or 888/770-7275, www.alaskashuttle.com) runs a daily summer-only service connecting Anchorage with Talkeetna, Denali, and Fairbanks, plus three-times-a-week runs from Fairbanks to Delta Junction, Tok, Chicken, Dawson City, and Whitehorse.

Several other companies have van service in Southcentral and Interior Alaska: **Denali Overland Transportation** (907/733-2384 or 800/651-5221, www.denalioverland.com), **Alaska Park Connection** (907/245-0200 or 800/266-8625, www.alaskacoach.com), **Seward Bus Lines** (907/563-0800 or 888/420-

7788, www.sewardbuslines.net), **Homer Stage Line** (907/235-2252, www.homerstageline.com), and **Girdwood Shuttle** (907/783-1900, www.girdwoodshuttle.com).

Green Tortoise

This is more than just a bus ride—it's a vacation and a cultural experience in itself. The buses have bunks that convert to seats and tables in the day, and passengers enjoy communal meals. One of the best things about these trips is the people—alternative travel attracts good company. This is a friendly, unprivate way to travel, although it is not inexpensive.

Green Tortoise (415/956-7500 or 800/867-8647, www.greentortoise.com) has several trips each summer to Alaska, and each bus holds 36 passengers and 2 drivers. Book no later than March to ensure a space. Some trips leave from San Francisco and wind up in Anchorage; others start and end in Anchorage.

Despite the casual approach, Green Tortoise buses are reliable and have a good safety record. The company also runs bus trips all over the country and even to Central America.

CARS

Getting to Alaska by car is the most flexible means of mobility. You can start anywhere, and once there, you can go anywhere there's a road, anytime you feel like it, stopping along the way for however long you decide. The roads in the North Country are especially fun, and you have some of them almost to yourself. On a few roads you'll rarely see another car. It's very open, unconfined, and uninhibiting—a large part of the spell of the North.

One essential for Alaskan drivers of all types is ***The Milepost,*** a fat annual book that's packed with mile-by-mile descriptions for virtually every road within or to Alaska (including, of course, the Alcan). The book is sold everywhere in Alaska—even at Costco—and is easy to find in Lower 48 bookstores or online at www.themilepost.com. Warning: Don't believe everything you read in *The Milepost;* much of the text is paid ads for specific businesses—watch for the small notice.

The Alaska Highway

You can drive all the way up and back, or put the car on the ferry one way. The Alaska Highway (nicknamed the **Alcan**) has been dramatically upgraded from the early days when you had to carry extra fuel and four spare tires, when you had to protect your headlights and windshield with chicken wire, and when facilities were spaced 250 miles apart. Today, the entire road is paved, gas stations are about every 50 miles, and roadhouses and hotels are numerous. Still, this road is 1,442 miles through somewhat inhospitable wilderness. Frost heaves and potholes are not uncommon. Mechanics are few and far between, and parts are even scarcer. Gas prices are no laughing matter, especially on the Canadian side, where they're typically almost double those in the Lower 48 states. If you're coming from anywhere east of Idaho or Alberta, you can hit Mile 0 of the Alaska Highway through Edmonton without having to backtrack east at all. But if you're heading north from the West Coast, or through the Canadian Rockies, you'll probably wind up in Prince George and have to head east a bit to Dawson Creek (the starting point).

You can also head west out of Prince George on the Yellowhead Highway and take the **Cassiar Highway** north from Meziadin Junction to just west of Watson Lake in Yukon Territory. This 458-mile paved road is scenically stunning, but services are a little less frequent than on the Alaska Highway.

Go Prepared

A few commonsense preparations can eliminate all but the most unexpected problems. A credit card (preferably Visa or MasterCard) is essential, especially if you don't want to worry about changing money on either side of the border. You can expect to get hit hard by gas prices along the Alcan and in the more remote stretches within Alaska. But along the main Interior and Southcentral Alaska thoroughfares, prices are often only a few cents higher than Outside. Finally, by driving the whole way in one direction and putting the car on

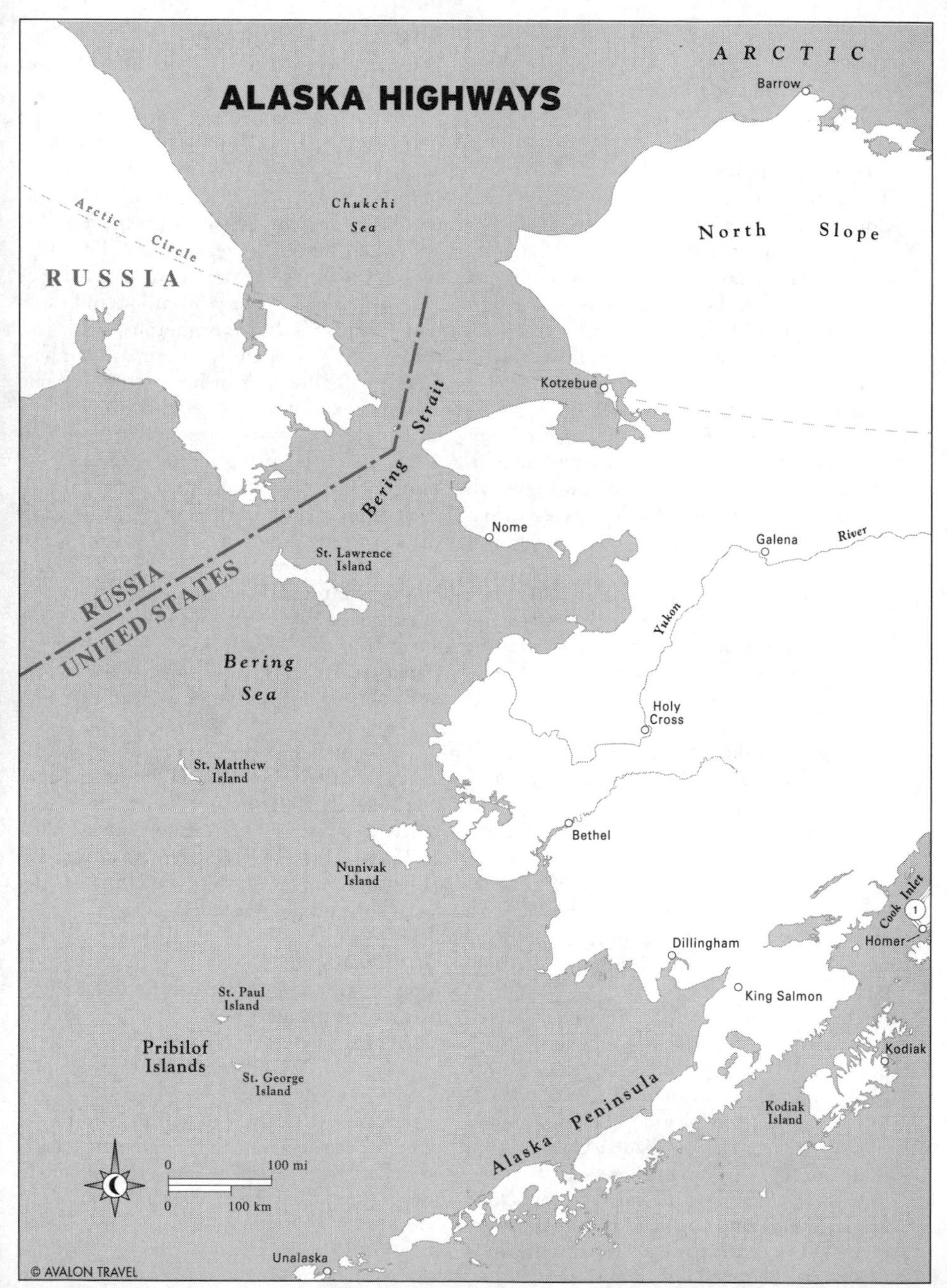
ALASKA HIGHWAYS
ARCTIC
Barrow
Chukchi Sea
North Slope
Arctic Circle
RUSSIA
Kotzebue
Bering Strait
Nome
Galena
River
St. Lawrence Island
RUSSIA
UNITED STATES
Yukon
Bering Sea
Holy Cross
St. Matthew Island
Bethel
Nunivak Island
Cook Inlet
1
Homer
Dillingham
King Salmon
St. Paul Island
Pribilof Islands
St. George Island
Kodiak
Kodiak Island
Alaska Peninsula
0
100 mi
0
100 km
Unalaska
© AVALON TRAVEL

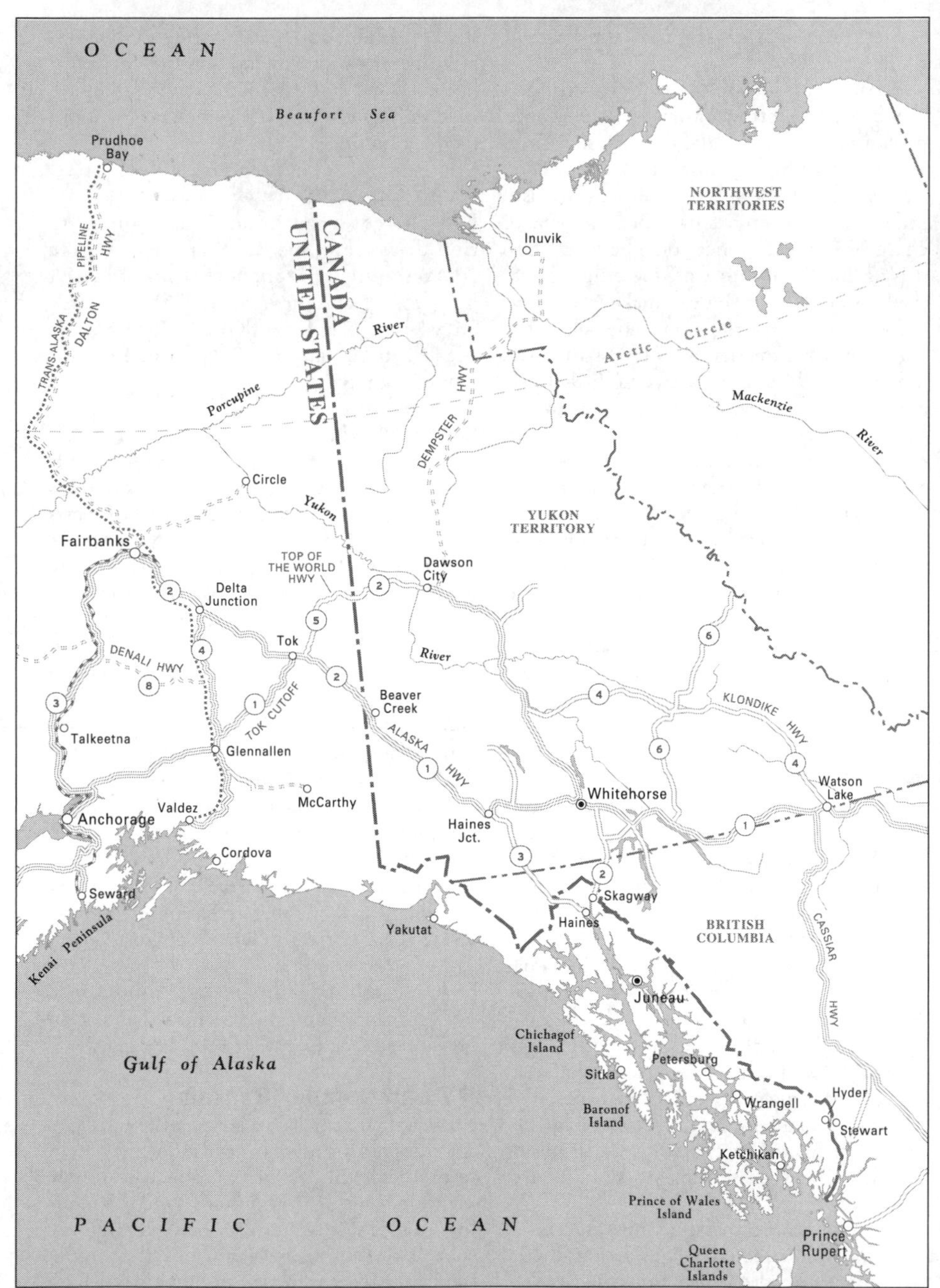
OCEAN
Beaufort Sea
Prudhoe Bay
PIPELINE
HWY
TRANS-ALASKA
DALTON
CANADA
UNITED STATES
NORTHWEST TERRITORIES
Inuvik
River
Arctic Circle
Porcupine
HWY
DEMPSTER
Mackenzie
River
Circle
Yukon
YUKON TERRITORY
Fairbanks
TOP OF THE WORLD HWY
Dawson City
Delta Junction
Tok
River
DENALI HWY
Beaver Creek
TOK CUTOFF
KLONDIKE HWY
Talkeetna
Glennallen
ALASKA HWY
McCarthy
Whitehorse
Watson Lake
Anchorage
Valdez
Haines Jct.
Cordova
Seward
Skagway
Haines
Yakutat
BRITISH COLUMBIA
CASSIAR HWY
Kenai Peninsula
Juneau
Chichagof Island
Gulf of Alaska
Petersburg
Sitka
Baronof Island
Wrangell
Hyder
Stewart
Ketchikan
Prince of Wales Island
PACIFIC OCEAN
Prince Rupert
Queen Charlotte Islands

the ferry in the other, you can take different routes up and back.

A reliable car is a must. Get the car carefully serviced before setting out; when you ask your mechanic, "Will it make it to Alaska?" you won't be kidding. If you get stuck somewhere, there might not be another mechanic for 100 miles. And tow trucks have been known to charge $5 *per mile.* Since you'll be tempted to drive hundreds of miles off the beaten track, the best investment you can make in your car is five good tires. Bring a pressure gauge and check the tires frequently. A few spare hoses (and hose tape) and belts take up little room and can come in very handy. Spare gas and oil filters are also useful because of the amount of dust on the gravel roads in the dry months. Water is an absolute necessity; carry at least a five-gallon jug. Also, if you have a mobile phone, it may prove useful not only for keeping in touch with friends at home but also for emergencies. Service is good in the major cities and most towns, but it can be spotty or nonexistent elsewhere. Take tools and jumper cables even if you don't know how to use them. Someone usually comes along who doesn't have tools but knows what to do.

Winter Travel

During the winter months, travelers to Alaska need to take special precautions. Always call ahead for road and avalanche conditions before heading out. Studded snow tires and proper antifreeze levels are a necessity, but you should also have on hand a number of emergency supplies including tire chains, a shovel and a bag of sand in case you get stuck, a first-aid kit, booster cables, signal flares, a flashlight, a lighter and a candle, a transistor radio, nonperishable foods (granola bars, canned nuts, or dried fruit), a jug of water, an ice scraper, winter clothes, blankets, and a sleeping bag. The most valuable tool may well be a **cell phone** to call for help—assuming you're in an area with reception.

If you become stranded in a blizzard, stay in your car. You're more likely to be found, and the vehicle provides shelter from the weather. Run the engine and heater sparingly, occasionally opening a downwind window for ventilation. Don't run the engine if the tailpipe is blocked by snow or you may risk carbon monoxide poisoning.

Road Updates

For current road conditions, construction delays, and more, contact the **Alaska Department of Transportation** online at http://511.alaska.gov, or dial 511 toll-free anywhere in Alaska or 866/282-7577 outside Alaska. In Yukon, call 877/456-7623 or visit www.511yukon.ca.

Car Rentals

An increasingly popular way to see Alaska is by flying into the state and renting a car. This provides travelers with flexibility, and the costs have dropped in recent years. Rental cars are available in all the larger towns, but they are generally cheapest out of Anchorage, where most of the major car rental companies have airport booths. For long rentals, it's always best to get a car away from the airport, where the taxes are higher. In the peak summer season you should reserve up to two months in advance to get the best rates and to be assured of finding any car at all when you arrive.

If you plan to rent a car for an extended period, it's probably worth your while to check travel websites such as www.travelocity.com to see which company offers the best rates. When reserving a car, be sure to mention if you have an AAA card or are a member of Costco; you can often save substantially on the rates. Also be sure to ask about driving restrictions, since most car rental companies prohibit their use on gravel roads such as the one to McCarthy.

RV and Camper Rentals

Recreational vehicles are among the most despised sights on Alaskan roads, but they seem to proliferate like rabbits as soon as the snow melts each spring. Motor homes are infamous for cruising slowly down the Seward Highway south of Anchorage, wagging a tail of impatient cars for a mile or more behind. Many snowbirds drive up to Alaska for the summer in their RVs, fleeing to Arizona for the winters. Other folks fly into Anchorage, Fairbanks, or Whitehorse and rent one of these land yachts.

Despite these criticisms, RVs can be a decent choice if the price of gas is not out of sight and if you can cram enough folks inside to cut your costs. But for just two people they are a profligate and environmentally disastrous investment.

PACKAGE TOURS

A 7–21-day whirlwind trip around Alaska is available from dozens of tour packagers. All will book you onto one of a variety of cruise ships up the Inside Passage, reserve your hotel rooms, roll you between them on motor coaches and railcars, and offer options for local and overnight side trips. Many are escorted by tour guides, and some even include all meals in the price. Many people choose this route for convenience, comfort, and security, though they certainly pay for what they get. The companies change and their offerings vary from year to year, so your best bet is to work through a travel agent who specializes in Alaska tours.

The two largest Alaska tour companies are **Holland America Tours/Gray Line of Alaska** (907/277-5581 or 888/452-1737, www.graylinealaska.com) and **Princess Tours** (206/336-6000 or 800/835-8907, www.princess.com). Both are also major players in the cruise travel industry, and many cruise ship travelers simply add on a land segment to their voyage. **Cruise West** (800/580-0651, www.cruisewest.com) also sets up a wide variety of trips that include small-ship cruises and tours. Other tour options include **Alaska Airlines Vacations** (800/468-2248, www.alaskaair.com), **Alaska Bound** (231/439-3000 or 888/252-7527, www.alaskabound.com), **Alaska Travel Adventures** (907/783-2928 or 800/334-8730, www.alaskaadventures.com), **Alaska Tour & Travel** (907/245-0200 or 800/208-0200, www.alaskatravel.com), **Knightly Tours** (206/938-8567 or 800/426-2123, www.knightlytours.com), and **Tauck Tours** (800/788-7885, www.tauck.com).

Specialty Tours

For adventure travel tours, contact **Backcountry Safaris** (907/222-1632 or 877/812-2159, www.alaskakayak.com), **CampAlaska Tours** (907/376-9438 or 800/376-9438, www.campalaska.com), **Get Up and Go Alaska Tours** (907/245-0795 or 888/868-4147, www.getupandgotours.com), **Adventure Alaska Tours** (907/782-3730 or 800/365-7057, www.adventurealaskatours.com), or **Denali Treking Company** (907/733-2566, www.alaskahiking.com). **Joseph Van Os Photo Safaris** (206/463-5383, www.photosafaris.com) leads photo trips around Alaska, with an emphasis on wildlife.

Bird-watchers should point their spotting scopes toward **Wilderness Birding Adventures** (907/694-7442, www.wildernessbirding.com) for extended trips to remote parts of the state, and **St. Paul Island Tours** (907/278-2318 or 877/424-5637, www.alaskabirding.com) for trips to the Pribilofs. **Alaska Birding Tours** (907/262-5218 or 800/725-3327, www.alaskabirdingtours.com) guides Kenai Peninsula birding trips. Other recommended companies include **Victor Emanuel Nature Tours** (800/328-8368, www.ventbird.com) and **Wings Birding Tours** (520/320-9868 or 888/293-6443, www.wingsbirds.com).

For bicycle tours around Alaska, check out **Alaskabike** (907/245-2175, www.alaskabike.com), **Alaska Backcountry Bike Tours** (907/746-5018 or 866/354-2453, www.mountainbikealaska.com), or **Backroads** (510/527-1555 or 800/462-2848, www.backroads.com).

ALASKA PASS

The Alaska Pass (206/463-6777 or 800/248-7598, www.alaskapass.com) is a good option if you plan to travel using a combination of ferries, trains, and buses. Passes are available for varying lengths of time, and you can either buy one that allows travel every day (not a good idea if you want to do something more than sit on a bus or ferry) or one that lets you travel a certain number of days out of the total. The latter cost $799 adults or $400 kids for a

12-day pass that includes 8 travel days; or $979 adults or $475 kids for a 21-day pass that includes 12 travel days.

BICYCLE

Inveterate cyclists have a love affair with bike riding that makes the relationship between car and driver look like a one-night stand. If you're indifferent to or can overcome the hardships (hills, trucks, rain and wind, bugs, time, security considerations, and sore muscles), the advantages of bikes are unassailable. They're free to operate, nonpolluting, easy to maintain, and great exercise. They also slow down the world and attract the immediate friendly and curious attention of the locals.

Almost all of the bus companies, ferries, and railways will carry your bike as accompanied baggage for a nominal amount, although a few want you to have it in a box. Most airlines also accept bicycles as luggage, as long as they're boxed before check-in (you will pay an extra charge). Before you buy a ticket, compare prices, then ask each airline about taking a bicycle.

Alaska can be just as hard on bikes as on cars, however, if not harder. Fifteen-speed mountain bikes are recommended to handle the rough roads better. Know how to fix your own bike, and take along a good repair kit, as bicycle shops are few and far between. At the minimum, you should have spare tubes and tires, a patch kit, a pump, extra cables, a spare chain, and a chain tool. Carry your gear in saddlebag panniers lined with plastic bags. Fenders are nice in wet weather. Warm waterproof clothing is essential, particularly rain pants, a poncho, a rain hat, a wool shirt, wool socks, and waterproof shoes. Bicycling gloves, shorts, and clear goggles are also necessary. You could buy everything you need in Anchorage.

Short-distance bicycles are available for rent in every major town and are an excellent way to see the local sights, especially in fair weather.

Cycling Information

The Anchorage-based **Arctic Bicycle Club** (907/566-0177, www.arcticbike.org) organizes road races, mountain bike races, and tours, and its website is an excellent source for anyone interested in cycling in Alaska. Useful books are *Alaska Bicycle Touring Guide* by Pete Praetorius and Alys Culhane and *Mountain Bike Alaska: 49 Trails in the 49th State* by Richard Larson. A few companies offer guided cycling trips around Alaska.

Tips for Travelers

VISAS AND OFFICIALDOM

Immigration officials are trained to be suspicious, particularly in this post–September 11 world. Expect heightened security measures at all border crossings, and even when boarding state ferries. Get a passport for each member of your family; you'll probably need it. Never argue or get angry with an official—it doesn't help, and they have the law on their side. The best approach is just to be as polite as possible.

Entry into the United States

All international travelers now need a passport to enter the United States; even U.S. citizens crossing the border from Canada into Alaska need passports or a similar document such as an enhanced driver's license or trusted-traveler card. Most Western Europeans and Commonwealth residents can usually easily obtain a six-month travel visa from U.S. consulates, and citizens of some countries can get visas at the border. You must have an onward or return ticket. No vaccinations are required, and you can bring an unlimited amount of money (over US$5,000 must be registered). Be aware that you might wind up crossing the Canada-U.S. border four times in each direction (Lower 48 into British Columbia or Alberta, back into Southeast Alaska, then into

Yukon, then back into mainland Alaska). If you're an overseas visitor, make sure you understand the requirements for *reentering* the United States. Regulations seem to be in a constant state of flux, so get the latest border info from **U.S. Customs and Border Protection** by visiting www.customs.gov.

Entry into Canada

No visa is required for visitors from Western Europe, most Commonwealth countries, or the United States. Americans and citizens of other countries can enter Canada only with a passport. For children, bring a passport or birth certificate. Travelers under age 18 must be accompanied by or have written permission from a parent or guardian to enter Canada. Handguns and automatic weapons are not allowed into Canada, even if you're simply driving through to Alaska or the Lower 48. A U.S. driver's license is acceptable in Canada, but international licenses are required for residents of other countries. Get details at the **Canada Border Services Agency** (www.cbsa-asfc.gc.ca).

TIME ZONES

Alaska is divided into two time zones, but nearly all of the state—from Southeast Alaska to the western tip of the mainland—is on Alaska time, one hour earlier than Pacific time or four hours earlier than the East Coast. The western Aleutians are on Hawaii time, two hours earlier than Pacific time. British Columbia and Yukon are on Pacific time. So when you go from Prince Rupert to Ketchikan, Dawson to Eagle, or Beaver Creek to Tok, you gain an hour; from Skagway to Whitehorse you lose an hour.

CONDUCT AND CUSTOMS

As you explore, remember that northerners are fiercely independent people who value their privacy. They can also be overwhelmingly hospitable if you treat them with respect. Never put up your tent in or near a village without first asking permission. When visiting a Native Alaskan village or any small isolated community, look people straight in the eye and be the first to say hello. Remember, you are the intruder, so you should be the one to make the effort to put them at ease.

Under no circumstances should you walk into a small settlement, fish camp, or other personal area and immediately start photographing people. This is rude and may well get folks angry. Most people are happy to pose for a photo if you simply take the time to talk and express a genuine interest in them and their lives. But if they say no, just move on. There may also be times when it is best simply to leave before tempers flare, particularly when people have been drinking heavily (an all-too-common experience in some villages), or when their politics stray to the don't-tread-on-me fringe.

ACCESSIBLE ALASKA

Because of the undeveloped character of Alaska, much of the state is not readily accessible to those with disabilities. This is particularly true in parts of bush Alaska, where even having a flush toilet may be a luxury, and entering small aircraft is a major challenge. Despite this, many towns and cities—particularly those that see an influx of seniors as cruise ship passengers each summer—have made great strides in recent years. Even in remote areas, some Forest Service and State of Alaska cabins have wheelchair ramps, outsized outhouses, and fishing platforms. In addition, quite a few trails around Alaska have been built for wheelchairs, including popular ones in Ketchikan, Juneau, and Anchorage. Hotels, buses, trains, cruise ships, tour boats, and ferries throughout the state all have some sort of accommodation for travelers in wheelchairs or with limited mobility.

A good place for travelers with disabilities is **Access Alaska** (907/248-4777 or 800/770-4488, www.accessalaska.org), a nonprofit independent-living center in Anchorage that can assist travelers with specific needs, including wheelchair-accessible hotels and restaurants, along with accessible horseback rides and river trips. Other independent-living centers are in

Fairbanks (907/479-7940 or 800/770-7940) and Juneau (907/586-4920).

In Anchorage, **Hertz** (800/654-3131, www.hertz.com) has rental cars with hand controls, and **Alaska Cab** (907/563-5353) offers lift-equipped van service.

TRAVELING WITH CHILDREN

Long a destination for seniors and couples, Alaska is increasingly popular with families, and even the cruise lines have gotten into the act with all sorts of kid-friendly activities and childcare onboard the larger vessels. Disney Cruise Line began trips to Alaska in 2010, opening another option. The small adventure cruise ships are primarily the domain of couples, and children can get in the way or become bored. They're welcome on all state ferries, but parents need to keep a close watch due to the onboard hazards. Fortunately, the leisurely pace, engaging scenery, good food, naturalist talks, and free movies make the traveling easier.

Anyone traveling with kids today should consider bringing a portable DVD player, a laptop computer, or an iPhone with a stock of movies and games for those times when Mom and Dad want the kids just to quiet down. And don't forget the headphones so you don't need to hear *Finding Nemo* again.

Most attractions and activities have lower rates for children, and some also offer one-size-fits-all family rates. Be sure to get your children into the great outdoors since that's really what Alaska is all about. The long bus ride into Denali National Park can be challenging for little ones, but the chance to see bears, moose, and wolves makes the trip worthwhile for everyone. Of special interest is the Park Service's **Junior Ranger Program,** in which children attend a nature program, hike a trail, or complete other activities. They're rewarded with an official Junior Ranger patch and are sworn in. It's always a big hit, but your kids may later try to arrest you if you get too close to a ground squirrel.

Be sure to set aside time for a special kid-friendly place such as the Anchorage Zoo, the kiddie train rides at Pioneer Park in Fairbanks, the Alaska SeaLife Center in Seward, the Mt. Roberts Tram in Juneau, or the one place all children love—H2Oasis Indoor Water Park in Anchorage.

Many tours are open to children, but the more hazardous ones (including helicopter flights, sea kayaking, white-water rafting, and zip-lines) impose age restrictions. Children are accepted in most Alaskan lodging places, but they will not do well in certain wilderness lodges or bed-and-breakfasts.

TRAVELING WITH PETS

In general, travelers visiting Alaska should leave their pets at home. Dogs may be good hiking companions, but if not kept under control they could bring a bear charging in your direction. Most hotels do not allow pets, and even those that do typically tack on an extra charge for the privilege. Folks driving up the Alaska Highway—particularly RVers—frequently bring along a small dog or cat, but a current rabies certificate is required when crossing into Canada.

GAY AND LESBIAN TRAVELERS

Openly gay individuals may feel uncomfortable in politically conservative Alaska, so discretion may be wise, especially in rural areas such as Glennallen, where Rush Limbaugh is regarded as a socialist. Anchorage, not surprisingly, is the primary center for gays and lesbians in Alaska. The nonprofit group Identity Inc. runs a **Gay and Lesbian Community Center** (336 E. 5th Ave., 907/929-4528, www.identityinc.org), promotes the PrideFest event (www.anchoragepride.com) each June, and operates a help line. Two Anchorage bars—**Mad Myrna's** (530 E. 5th Ave., 907/276-9762, www.alaska.net/~madmyrna) and **The Raven** (708 E. 4th Ave., 907/276-9672)—are favorite meeting places. **Out North Contemporary Art House** (1325 Primrose St., 907/279-8200, www.outnorth.org) sometimes presents plays with a gay and lesbian slant, and several Anchorage B&Bs promote themselves for gay travelers and couples.

SENIORS

Alaska is a very popular summer destination for seniors traveling by cruise ship or RV, and for a surprising number of retirees who move to the state. Alaska Marine Highway ferries offer half-price senior discounts on certain smaller vessels in the summer and on most wintertime sailings. Most museums and some restaurants have discounted rates for those over age 65, and visitors to national parks can get an America the Beautiful Senior Pass that allows entry to all parks for a one-time charge of $10.

Travelers over age 55 should consider joining an **Exploritas** (formerly Elderhostel, www.exploritas.com) educational adventure, with dozens to choose from in Alaska. **AARP** (www.aarp.org) also has discounted Alaskan trips and other benefits.

WILDERNESS SAFETY TIPS

The most important part of enjoying—and surviving—the backcountry is to be prepared. Know where you're going; get maps, camping information, weather, and trail conditions from a ranger before setting out. Don't hike alone. Two are better than one, and three are better than two; if one gets hurt, one person can stay with the injured person and one can go for help. Bring more than enough food so hunger won't cause you to continue when weather conditions say stop. Tell someone where you're going and when you'll be back.

Always carry the **essentials:** a map, a compass, a water bottle, a first-aid kit, a flashlight, matches or a lighter, and fire starter (Vaseline and cotton balls work great), a knife, extra clothing (a full set, in case you fall in a stream), rain gear, extra food, and sunglasses—especially if you're hiking on snow. Many travelers now also carry along a GPS unit to stay oriented. Cell phones are popular but often don't work in remote areas. Satellite phones are the ultimate safety toy, but they are a pricey addition to your trip.

Check your ego at the trailhead; stop for the night when the weather gets bad, even if it's 2 P.M., or head back, and don't press on when you're exhausted—tired hikers are sloppy hikers, and even a small injury can be disastrous in the woods.

Hypothermia

Anyone who spends much time in the outdoors will discover the dangers of exposure to cold, wet, and windy conditions. Even at temperatures well above freezing, hypothermia—the reduction of the body's inner core temperature—can prove fatal.

In the early stages, hypothermia causes uncontrollable shivering, followed by a loss of coordination, slurred speech, and then a rapid descent into unconsciousness and death. Always travel prepared for sudden changes in the weather. Wear clothing that insulates well and that holds its heat when wet. Wool and polypro are far better than cotton, and clothes should be worn in layers to provide better heat trapping and a chance to adjust to conditions more easily. Always carry a wool hat, since your head loses more heat than any other part of your body. Bring a waterproof shell to cut the wind. Put on rain gear *before* it starts raining; head back or set up camp when the weather looks threatening; eat candy bars, keep active, or snuggle with a friend in a down bag to generate warmth.

If someone in your party begins to show signs of hypothermia, don't take any chances, even if the person denies needing help. Get the victim out of the wind, strip off his clothes, and put him in a dry sleeping bag on an insulating pad. Skin-to-skin contact is the best way to warm a hypothermic person, and that means you'll also need to strip and climb in the sleeping bag. If you weren't friends before, this should heat up the relationship! Do not give the victim alcohol or hot drinks, and do not try to warm the person too quickly since it could lead to heart failure. Once the victim has recovered, get medical help as soon as possible. Actually, you're far better off keeping close tabs on everyone in the group and seeking shelter *before* exhaustion and hypothermia set in.

Frostbite

Frostbite is a less serious but quite painful problem for the cold-weather hiker; it is caused by

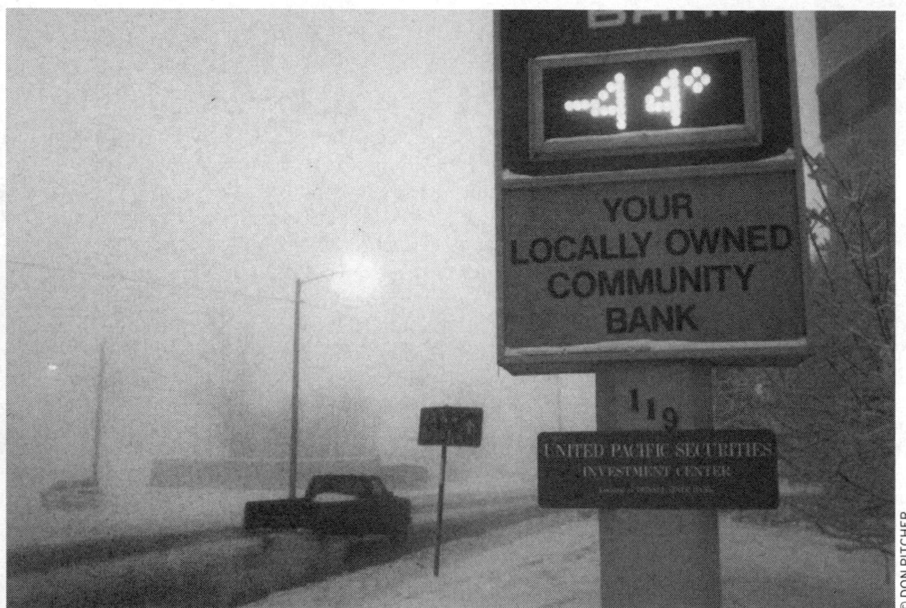

44 degrees below zero in Fairbanks

direct exposure or by heat loss because of wet socks and boots. Frostbitten areas will look white or gray and feel hard on the surface, softer underneath. The best way to warm the area is with other skin: Put your hand under your arm, your feet on your friend's belly. Don't rub it with snow or warm it near a fire. In cases of severe frostbite, in which the skin is white, quite hard, and numb, immerse the frozen area in water warmed to 99–104°F until it's thawed. Avoid refreezing the frostbitten area. If you're a long way from medical assistance and the frostbite is extensive, it's better to keep the area frozen and get out of the woods for help; thawing is very painful, and it would be nearly impossible to walk on a thawed foot.

Beaver Fever

Although lakes and streams in Alaska may appear clean, you could be risking a debilitating sickness by drinking the water without treating it first. The protozoan *Giardia lamblia* is found throughout the state, spread by both humans and animals (including beavers). The disease is curable with drugs, but it's always best to carry safe drinking water on any trip, or to boil any water taken from creeks or lakes. Bringing water to a full boil for one minute is sufficient to kill *Giardia* and other harmful organisms. Another option—most folks choose this one—is to use a water filter (available in camping stores). Note, however, that these may not filter out other organisms such as *Campylobacter jejuni,* bacteria that are just 0.2 microns in size. Chlorine and iodine are not always reliable, taste foul, and can be unhealthy.

CRIME

Alaska has a surprisingly high violent-crime rate; the most recent figures put the state at 10th in the nation in terms of violent crimes, with 588 such crimes per 100,000 residents. Part of this is due to simple demographics, since Alaska has the second-highest percentage of young people in the nation, but it is also a reflection of the impact of alcohol abuse. Alaska has a sexual-assault rate more than twice the national average, and the child sexual-assault rate is a shocking six times the national average.

The good news is that crime has dropped in recent years, especially in Anchorage, where many of the worst incidents have taken place. In general you're quite safe traveling in Alaska, though you should take the standard precautions, such as not leaving belongings in an unlocked vehicle and not walking around certain Anchorage neighborhoods after dark. Also, it's wise to avoid situations where people have been drinking heavily, even in bush Alaska. To be honest, after 25 years in the North, my only experience with crime took place when gear was stolen from me in Prince Rupert, British Columbia, and (equally shocking) in my hometown of Homer. I'm not saying crime doesn't exist, but many Alaskan towns are so safe that folks leave their doors unlocked and their keys in the cars.

Information and Services

MONEY

Unless otherwise stated, all prices in this handbook are in U.S. dollars. Tipping (usually 15 percent of the bill) is expected at most sit-down eating places fancier than snack bars or take-away counters. Tourism employees, fishing guides, and others providing personal service often depend on tips for their real income.

I travel almost exclusively using credit cards and an ATM card, but a few people still prefer traveler's checks. The major **credit cards**—especially Visa and MasterCard—are accepted almost everywhere in the larger towns. This is probably the easiest way to travel, especially if you can get airline mileage credit at the same time. Note, however, that credit cards may not be accepted by businesses in bush Alaska, so call ahead if you aren't traveling with cash or traveler's checks.

You'll find **ATMs** in all the larger towns and increasingly even in the more remote settlements. For locations, head to www.mastercard.com and www.visa.com/atms.

Traveler's checks from American Express, Bank of America, or Visa are accepted by most businesses; but don't arrive with traveler's checks in non-U.S. currency since they're only accepted at a few banks. In some remote villages, even traveler's checks may not be accepted.

Some Canadian and U.S. cash will make your first few hours in the neighboring country less of a hassle. Note that there are no exchange facilities at the borders; Canadians take U.S. dollars at a poor rate, while Alaskan businesses often refuse Canadian dollars (they do, however, take the coins at an equal value with U.S. coins). Most Wells Fargo offices in Anchorage and some other cities will exchange Canadian dollars, Japanese yen, and euros for U.S. dollars.

COMMUNICATIONS AND MEDIA

Newspapers

Newspapers are becoming thinner with each passing year as the Internet cuts into their business. Alaska's unofficial state newspaper is the ***Anchorage Daily News,*** and its website (www.adn.com) contains current stories, news blogs, classified ads, upcoming events, weather, and video. The company also produces a thick and free *Alaska Visitors Guide* that can be found in the larger visitors centers or online at www.alaska.com.

The state's other two midsize daily papers are the ***Fairbanks Daily News-Miner*** (www.newsminer.com) and the ***Juneau Empire*** (www.juneauempire.com).

The ***Anchorage Press*** (www.anchoragepress.com) is a free weekly newspaper available from racks all around Anchorage. Weekly newspapers come out in most of the state's midsize towns.

Alaska Magazine (907/272-6070, www.alaskamagazine.com) is available at grocery checkouts and magazine racks across Alaska, and in many Lower 48 magazine shops. Like the *Milepost* and *Juneau Empire, Alaska Magazine* is owned by a Georgia-based media conglomerate, Morris Communications.

Radio

Commercial radio stations are in all the larger towns, and the state is blessed to have the **Alaska Public Radio Network** (www.aprn.org), one of the finest public radio networks in the country. Anchorage's **KSKA** (91.1 FM, www.kska.org) is the flagship station, but many Alaskan towns have their own versions, including Ketchikan's KRBD (www.krbd.org) and Barrow's KBRW (www.kbrw.org). Anchorage's noncommercial **KNBA** (90.3 FM, www.knba.org) is one of the only Native Alaskan–owned radio stations in the nation, and it broadcasts some of the best music programming in Alaska. Two other notable stations are **KBBI** (890 AM, www.kbbi.org) in Homer and **KTNA** (88.5 FM, www.ktna.org) in Talkeetna.

Post Offices

Post offices are generally open 9 A.M.–5 P.M. Monday–Friday, though a few open their doors on Saturday. Anchorage's airport post office is open 24 hours a day year-round. When post offices are closed, their outer doors usually remain open, so you can go in to buy stamps from the machines. Many grocery store checkout counters also sell books of stamps at no markup.

Phones and Email

Telephone service is excellent to all the major towns and cities in Alaska, though you may experience a delay in some remote areas, and the wilderness lodges often depend on radio or satellite phones. Cellular phone coverage is variable, and not all systems work even when services exist, so contact your carrier for a coverage map ahead of your trip.

Alaska is surprisingly well wired, and even the most remote towns now have some sort of online connection. Nearly every library in Alaska (except Ketchikan) has at least one computer where you can check your email or surf the Web for free, though you may need to wait in line or sign up ahead of time. In addition, nearly all towns now have commercial businesses where you can rent computers by the hour for the same purpose. Wireless Internet (Wi-Fi) is becoming the norm for Alaskan hotels and bed-and-breakfasts, along with many local businesses. It's even available on some state ferries. Visit www.free-hotspot.com for updated listings around the state.

MAPS AND TOURIST INFORMATION

Readers of this book willing to expend a little energy will certainly be able to set up a travel itinerary that covers their own interests, but if you want to leave the arranging to others, you may want to contact one of the many itinerary planners who specialize in Alaska. These could be as close as your local travel agent, or one of the online information sources such as www.alaska.com or www.alaskaone.com. For a human touch from those in the know, try **Viking Travel** (907/772-3818 or 800/327-2571, www.alaskaferry.com), **Alaska Tours** (907/277-3000, www.alaskatours.com), **Alaska Ferry Adventures** (907/235-7099 or 800/382-9229, www.akmhs.com), or **Homer Travel & Tours** (907/235-7751 or 800/478-7751, www.alaskahomertravel.com).

A great starting point when planning a trip to Alaska is the official ***Alaska State Vacation Planner,*** produced annually through a joint partnership between the state and private businesses. It's distributed by the Alaska Travel Industry Association (907/929-2200, www.travelalaska.com). Find chambers of commerce around the state at www.alaskachamber.com.

Members of the American Automobile Association (AAA, www.aaa.com) should request an Alaska *TourBook* and *CampBook* plus detailed maps. Overseas visitors who belong to an affiliated club in their home country can obtain these materials for free by showing their membership card at an AAA office in any large city.

Recreation

EXPLORING THE LAND

Hiking and Camping

Hiking and camping are the preferred outdoor recreations for the majority of Alaskans and visitors. These pastimes are available to practically anybody, from 3-month-old infants to 93-year-old great-grannies. Here, you don't have to be in particularly good shape, you don't need a big bank balance, and you don't have to have the latest high-tech equipment. Most public land is open to free camping, though there are restrictions in the more populous areas.

For the size of the Alaskan outdoors, there are very few trails, but it's easy just to pick a direction, especially in the vast taiga and tundra, and go. Also, the perpetual daylight during hiking season allows for additional deviation from normal hiking-camping cycles, providing further freedom. And the definite possibility of encountering a variety and abundance of wildlife is an incalculable bonus. For more information about hiking, contact the **Alaska Public Lands Information Centers** (www.alaskacenters.gov) in Anchorage, Fairbanks, Ketchikan, and Tok.

Mountaineering

A number of organizations guide mountaineering expeditions in Alaska. For specific destinations, visit the Park Service or Forest Service websites for a list of permitted guides. Good wilderness guiding companies include **Alaska Mountaineering School** (907/733-1016, www.climbalaska.org), **Alaska Mountain Guides & Climbing School** (907/766-3366 or 800/766-3396, www.alaskamountainguides.

PHOTOGRAPHY IN ALASKA

Hand in hand with hiking and camping goes photography – of the gorgeous scenery, the fauna and flora, and the special light. Professional photographers can have a literal field day in Alaska, because the ideal light conditions – at dawn and sunset everywhere else – continue throughout the long days of low light and long angles in the boreal region. Casual photographers are satisfied with automatic point-and-shoot, disposable, and cheap digital cameras, though none of these do justice to the grandness of Alaska.

A good starting setup would include a 28-105 zoom lens and a 100-300 zoom lens; longer and more expensive lenses (400 or 500 mm) are needed for serious wildlife work. A flash helps to fill in shadow areas on sunny days. A tripod is highly recommended, though some professional lenses have image stabilization to make it easier to hand-hold lenses at slower shutter speeds. ISO 200 film is fine for most purposes, but you may need higher speed (ISO 400-1200) for low-light situations.

Digital photographers need to plan ahead, especially for trips into backcountry areas where extra batteries and backup storage devices are vital. Small laptop computers or iPhones are perfect for storing your images, checking for any problems, and sending emails while on the road.

A couple of caveats are in order. A common cause of wildlife incidents is photographers either getting too close or having a false sense of security behind the camera. Your backcountry common sense should remain intact with or without a camera in front of you. Besides, there are times and places not to use a camera – mostly in order not to separate you from a given experience, but also in Native Alaskan villages without permission. In addition, many museums prohibit the use of flashes or tripods, and Russian Orthodox churches sometimes prohibit cameras or video.

The author's blog (www.donpitcher.com/blog) has additional advice for digital photographers, including links to helpful photo websites.

com), **Alaska Discovery** (510/594-6000 or 800/586-1911, www.akdiscovery.com), and **NOLS** (907/745-4047, www.nols.edu). A good online source for info on Alaska climbing opportunities is www.akclimber.com.

Mountain Biking

The most popular mountain biking trails are in the Anchorage area and include many miles of paths (both paved and unpaved) along the shore and within a couple of city parks. Paved biking paths can also be found paralleling portions of the Seward Highway south of Anchorage, and in Fairbanks, Homer, Valdez, Juneau, and other cities. Many Forest Service trails are open to mountain biking, but some of these are muddy and challenging to ride. Especially popular is the Resurrection Pass Trail on the Kenai Peninsula.

The Anchorage-based **Arctic Bicycle Club** (907/566-0177, www.arcticbike.org) organizes road races, mountain bike races, and tours. Its website is an excellent source for anyone interested in cycling in Alaska, with links to bike shops and references to helpful books.

Flightseeing

Even if you don't go backpacking while you're in Alaska, treat yourself at least once to a small plane or helicopter ride over some spectacular country. The flight from Talkeetna to Denali National Park is always a highlight—particularly with a landing on the Ruth Glacier. Flights over Glacier Bay from Juneau, Haines, or Skagway will leave you hyperventilating for two days. And you won't believe how grand Columbia Glacier really is on the flight over it from Anchorage or Valdez.

Bird-Watching

The **National Audubon Society** (www.audubon.org/chapter/ak) has chapters in Anchorage (907/338-2473 birding hotline, www.anchorageaudubon.org), Juneau (www.juneau-audubon-society.org), and Fairbanks (907/451-9213 birding hotline, www.arcticaudubon.org). In

© DON PITCHER

bikes in Talkeetna

Homer, visit www.birdinghomeralaska.org or call 907/235-7337 for unusual Kachemak Bay birds. All these websites provide details on local birding hot spots across the state. In Fairbanks, the **Alaska Bird Observatory** (907/451-7059, www.alaskabird.org) conducts research on migratory birds and has banding demonstrations. Their website features links to most other Alaska birding organizations and online sites.

FISHING

Alaska is world-famous for its fish and fishing. More than half of the country's commercial seafood production comes from the state, and sportfishing is a favorite activity of both Alaska residents and visitors. Fishing options are equally vast in Alaska, where undeveloped areas stretch for hundreds of miles and the population is clustered onto a tiny portion of the land. The state is speckled with more than 1 million lakes—including some of the largest in the nation—along with 34,000 miles of pristine coastline and 42 Wild and Scenic Rivers.

The **Alaska Department of Fish and Game**'s website (www.adfg.state.ak.us) has details on sportfishing, including descriptions of the various species, fishing regulations, news, and an abundance of other fish facts.

Alaska Fishing by Rene Limeres and Gunnar Pedersen is a comprehensive guide to fishing in Alaska, with detailed information on the when, where, and how to catch fish, along with natural history and other details. Locals, as always, are the best advice-givers about fishing techniques, spots, and regulations, and they might even share some secrets.

Popular Alaskan Fish

Salmon are the primary attraction for many sport anglers, and all five species of Pacific salmon are found in Alaska. Steelhead and rainbow trout, which are also salmonid, are famous for their beautiful coloration and fighting spirit. Rainbows are found in many streams and lakes around the state; the larger steelhead are the sea-run form.

Dolly Varden, also known as Arctic char, are a sea-run trout that flourish in many Alaska rivers. Arctic grayling occur in lakes and streams across the state, particularly in Interior Alaska and the Alaska Peninsula. The fish have a large and distinctive sail-like dorsal fin, and they put up a big fight when hooked. Other important freshwater fish species include lake trout, brook trout (an introduced species), northern pike, sheefish, and whitefish.

Pacific halibut is a large flatfish that is commonly caught in saltwater, particularly in Southeast and Southcentral Alaska. Halibut sometimes reach the proverbial barn-door size, and it isn't uncommon to see ones that weigh in excess of 200 pounds. Many Alaskans consider halibut the best-tasting fish in the state. In addition to salmon caught in saltwater, other popular ocean-caught sport fish include rockfish and lingcod.

Catching 'Em

Fishing is not only great fun, it's the way to bag some super meals. All you need are a breakdown or retractable rod, a variety of hooks, flies, spinners, spoons, sinkers, line (4–8-pound for freshwater, 12–30-pound for saltwater, depending on what you're after), and a reel. All but the rod will fit in a small plastic case. For bait, get a small bottle of salmon eggs for freshwater, shrimp for saltwater. Have a filet knife to clean the fish. While fishing, watch for protected areas with deadfalls or rocks where fish like to hide. You'll have the best luck in the early morning or late evening, or on cloudy days when the sun leaks out to shimmer on the water. So as not to attract bears, keep your catch on a stringer well downstream.

Fishing Regulations

Fishing licenses are required. In Alaska, 1-day nonresident sportfishing licenses cost $20, 3-day $35, and 14-day $80. If you plan to catch king salmon, all these fees increase to $30, $55, and $130, respectively. The Alaskan license is valid in national parks.

Fishing licenses are sold in most outdoor stores and by charter fishing operators. Ask for brochures outlining local fishing regulations

ALASKA SALMON

Five species of wild Pacific salmon are found in Alaskan waters. All are anadromous – spending time in both fresh and salt water – and all five species also have at least two common names, making them confusing to newcomers. The yearly return of adult salmon is a major event for wildlife in many parts of Alaska, as quiet little streams suddenly erupt in a frenzy of life and death. Commercial fishers search out the migrating schools in the ocean as they prepare to head up rivers and creeks to spawn. Anglers line the riverbanks, hoping to catch a big king or coho. Bears pace the creeks, ready to pounce on salmon in the shallow water. Foxes, eagles, ravens, gulls, and magpies wait for the salmon to weaken or die before feeding on them. Mergansers and smaller birds such as dippers eat the eggs, as do such fish as Dolly Varden and rainbow trout. Crab and halibut move into the areas near creek mouths, eating salmon carcasses that wash downstream.

Female salmon spawn in creeks and rivers during late summer throughout much of Alaska, digging holes ("redds") in the gravel with their tails before laying hundreds of small red eggs. The males fight for position to fertilize the eggs as soon as they are laid. Shortly after spawning the salmon die, and their carcasses create a stench that permeates late-summer evenings. But these carcasses also add important nutrients to the system that are used by the plankton that form the basis of the food chain. The plankton in turn is eaten by the young salmon fry that emerge from the eggs, thus helping to complete this never-ending cycle of life and death.

King (Chinook) Salmon

The largest of all Pacific salmon, the king commonly exceeds 30 pounds (the sport-caught record is 97 pounds), and is the most highly prized and one of the best-tasting sport fish in Alaska. The most famous place to catch kings is the Kenai River in Southcentral Alaska, but some of the finest kings head up the Copper River near Cordova.

Sockeye (Red) Salmon

Much smaller (6–10 pounds), and difficult to catch on spinning rods, sockeye are considered the best-tasting salmon. They turn bright red with an olive-green head when ready to spawn. Sockeye are the most important fish in the Bristol Bay and Kodiak areas, but for

when you buy your license. Check open and closed seasons, bag limits, and the like to avoid trouble with the law. For the whole thing—spelled out in minute bureaucratic detail—request a copy of the regulations booklet from the **Alaska Department of Fish and Game** (907/465-4180, www.adfg.state.ak.us).

Fishing Derbies

Many Alaskan towns have salmon or halibut fishing derbies in the summer. If one is going on when you visit, it may be worth your while to buy a derby ticket before heading out on the water. The prize money gets into the thousands of dollars for some of these events, and more than a few anglers tell of the big one that would have made them rich if they'd only bought a derby ticket first. Some of the biggest fishing derbies are in Seward, Homer, and Juneau.

Guided Fishing

Local knowledge is one of the best ways to be assured of a successful Alaska fishing trip. By using a charter or guide service, you're likely to have a more productive sportfishing excursion. Fishing guides can be found in most Alaskan communities, some offering float trips accessible by car and others going to more remote fly-in destinations. Charter fishing boats are available at coastal locations, particularly in Southeast and Southcentral Alaska and along the Kenai Peninsula.

Particularly important charter boat

sport anglers, the most famous sockeye river is the Kenai, where "combat fishing" reigns in midsummer.

Coho (Silver) Salmon

The silvery cohos generally weigh 7-10 pounds and are a beautiful and powerful fish that can be caught in both fresh and saltwater. They are another favorite of anglers, and they have a delicate flavor.

Chum (Dog) Salmon

Chum are also quite large (5-15 pounds) but are not considered as tasty as kings, sockeye, or coho. Spawning time turns them into grotesque monsters with huge doglike teeth. The name "dog salmon" may also refer to their use as food for dogsled teams in central Alaska. Chum are a very important food source in villages along the Yukon River.

Pink (Humpback) Salmon

The smallest (3-4 pounds) and most abundant salmon in Alaska are the pinks. "Humpie" runs sometimes turn creeks into a seething mass of spawning fish. They are considered a "trash fish" by many Alaskans, but are fine to eat when caught in saltwater before they have started to change. Once they reach freshwater, however, they develop prominently humped backs and grotesque jaws. Pinks are the major commercial fish in Southeast Alaska and Prince William Sound, and they are the mainstay of many canneries.

CATCHING SALMON

When salmon move from the ocean into their spawning streams, their bodies undergo rapid changes that reduce the quality of the meat. The freshest and brightest salmon are found in the ocean or lower reaches of the rivers rather than farther upstream. If you want to try your luck at fishing, purchase a 14-day nonresident fishing license for $80, or a 3-day nonresident license for $35. Licenses are available in sporting goods stores throughout Alaska. Before heading out, pick up a copy of the latest fishing regulations, or visit the Alaska Department of Fish and Game website (www.adfg.state.ak.us).

Many travelers carry a small collapsible fishing pole to save on space. These work well with trout and smaller salmon, but may not survive an encounter with a 10-pound silver and certainly won't handle a 35-pound king.

fishing towns include Homer, Seward, Kodiak, Valdez, Cordova, Juneau, Sitka, and Ketchikan. Charter boat trips typically last either a half-day or all day. Remote fishing lodges are widespread throughout the state, offering top-quality sportfishing with all of the amenities; find them in the *Alaska State Vacation Planner* or online at www.travelalaska.com. Note that it's common to tip fishing guides, particularly if they're especially helpful or if you land a big one. There's no standard amount, but a 10 percent tip would certainly be appreciated.

For information on fishing charters, available from every seaport in the state, check the local chamber of commerce websites or pick up brochures when you get into town.

ON THE WATER

Boating

Alaska's waters offer an endless range of boating opportunities, and in many coastal towns, particularly in Southeast Alaska, there are almost as many boats as cars. Boats are also important in inland parts of Alaska, particularly along major waterways such as the Yukon and Kuskokwim Rivers, where they provide a vital means of traversing undeveloped country. Skiff rentals are available in the larger coastal towns for those who want to head out on their own to explore or fish. Dozens of companies offer boat tours or charter-boat fishing trips throughout the state, in vessels ranging from 13-foot aluminum skiffs to luxury motor yachts offering multiday ecotours.

WILD OR FARMED?

Alaska is world-renowned for its wild salmon, and careful management ensures that the fish will still be there for future generations. Unfortunately, fishers have not fared so well. Many struggle to make their boat payments while others have simply given up on their life's work and are now back in school learning a new trade.

Since 1980 the worldwide market share of wild-caught salmon has gone from 99 percent to less than 40 percent today. The reason for this abrupt change is the rise of salmon farming, primarily in Chile, Norway, the United Kingdom, and British Columbia. The state of Alaska prohibits salmon aquaculture to protect both its wild-fish stocks and the 10 percent of state jobs coming from fishing. Unfortunately, the British Columbia government was considerably less farsighted, and more than 120 fish farms dot B.C. waters, along with another eight in the state of Washington.

Pen-raised fish are cheap, available year-round, and of consistent quality, making them perfect for corporations feeding a global market. But they have had a disastrous impact on both commercial fishers and the environment. Farmed salmon are more susceptible to diseases such as sea lice (which can then spread to wild fish), the huge concentrations of fish pollute local areas with waste, and they are a nonnative species: Atlantic salmon. This last issue becomes a real problem when they escape, and hundreds of thousands have done so over the years, competing with the five species of wild Pacific salmon, spawning in the region's streams, and showing up in fishing nets across Alaska.

And what about the fish? Pen-raised fish are fed pellets of fishmeal, fish oil, and vitamins, plus heavy doses or antibiotics, not to mention the coloring added to their diet to make their meat pink instead of gray. Diseases have proven to be a serious problem, especially in Chile, where infectious salmon anemia virtually wiped out the salmon farming industry in 2008.

Wild salmon taste far better, are not dyed, and have more of the omega-3 fatty acids that help protect your health. So the next time you see salmon at your local grocery store, ask if it's farmed Atlantic salmon or wild Pacific salmon. The farmed version will certainly be cheaper, but what is the real cost?

Learn more about Alaska's wild salmon and other fish from the **Alaska Seafood Marketing Institute** website (www.alaskaseafood.org).

River Rafting

White-water rafting trips are offered by numerous adventure-travel outfitters around the state. Several of the more reasonable, short, and accessible trips include floats down the Sixmile Creek south of Anchorage, Nenana River at Denali, Kenai River at Sterling, Susitna River near Talkeetna, Mendenhall River near Juneau, Sheridan River near Cordova, and the Lowe River outside of Valdez. A large number of float-trip companies and wilderness outfitters offer overnight, several day, and up to three-week-long trips, particularly within Wrangell–St. Elias National Park. Check the list in the state's *Alaska Vacation Planner* (www.travelalaska.com) for names and addresses. Those looking to do it by themselves should buy Karen Jettmar's excellent *Alaska River Guide.*

Sea Kayaking

Sea kayaks are quiet and fairly stable, providing an outstanding way to explore hidden Alaskan coves or to watch wildlife. Because of this, kayaking has increased in popularity in recent years, both for independent travelers who rent a kayak and for those who choose a package trip with a professional guiding company.

Kayaks originated as skin-covered boats crafted by the Eskimo of Alaska and Siberia, but today's versions are built from more modern materials. Most sea kayaks have a hard outer shell of plastic or fiberglass, but folding kayaks, made with wooden or aluminum

© DON PITCHER

kayaking class in Homer

supports and waterproof covers, are also available. The latter can be folded into relatively compact packages, making them useful for travelers heading into remote areas accessible only by floatplane.

Companies offering sea kayak rentals and tours are in Southeast Alaska (Glacier Bay, Gustavus, Haines, Juneau, Ketchikan, Petersburg, Sitka, Skagway, and Wrangell), Kenai Peninsula (Homer, Seldovia, and Seward), Prince William Sound (Cordova, Valdez, and Whittier), Southwest Alaska (Kodiak, King Salmon, and Unalaska), and Western Alaska (Dillingham).

Canoeing

Canoeing is a common activity on lakes and rivers in Alaska. Two canoe routes (Swanson River Route and Swan Lake Route) connect lakes within the Kenai National Wildlife Refuge, and another route links lakes across Admiralty Island National Monument. The Yukon River is a popular float trip, with many people starting in either Whitehorse or Dawson City and floating to the town of Eagle (or beyond). The country around Fairbanks is also very popular with canoeists who enjoy the relatively gentle Chena River. Canoe rentals are available in all these areas.

Sailing

Alaska has a small but active community of sailing enthusiasts, with sailboats in coastal towns from Ketchikan to Kodiak. Resurrection Bay near Seward generally offers the state's top wind conditions, and companies there offer day trips, sailing lessons, and bareboat charters. Other popular sailing areas (they have relatively dependable winds) are around Prince William Sound and in Kachemak Bay near Homer.

Surfing

Surprisingly, surfing is growing in popularity in Alaska. It will never be a particularly common sight, but many coastal towns—including Yakutat, Kodiak, Sitka, Homer, and Unalaska—have a few hard-core souls

FESTIVALS AND EVENTS

The biggest events in Alaska revolve around the sun and snow. A number of Alaskans, especially those who live in the Interior and the north, believe that the purpose of summer solstice is to compress all the partying encouraged by the light and heat of summer into a single 24-hour period. Fairbanks has at least three "Midnight Sun" activities on solstice. The summer is also the time for town and citywide celebrations, such as Golden Days in Fairbanks, the Little Norway Festival in Petersburg, and Colony Days in Palmer. There are fishing derbies in the waters off the coastal towns, and athletic competitions, such as triathlons and mountain races, everywhere.

The most famous winter festivals are Anchorage's Fur Rendezvous and the Iditarod. Every town has some sort of winter carnival that frequently includes dog mushing, a snow sports competition, and accompanying arts and crafts fairs.

Typically, the major public holidays are also a cause for celebration, including Memorial Day (last Mon. in May), July 4th (Independence Day), Labor Day (last Mon. in Sept.), Thanksgiving Day (last Thurs. in Nov.), Christmas, and New Year's Eve. The happiest days of the year, though, are in mid-October when the big Permanent Fund dividend checks show up in the mailboxes of state residents.

January
Kodiak – Russian Orthodox Starring Ceremony; Bethel – Kuskokwim 300; Seward – Polar Bear Jump Off; Anchorage – Anchorage Folk Festival

February
Anchorage – Fur Rendezvous; Cordova – Iceworm Festival; Fairbanks – Yukon Quest Sled Dog Race; Wrangell – Tent City Festival

March
Anchorage, Nome, and Wasilla – Iditarod Trail Sled Dog Race; Dillingham – Beaver Roundup Festival; Fairbanks – World Ice Art Championships; Kodiak – Pillar Mountain Golf Classic; Nome – Bering Sea Ice Golf Classic

who head out when conditions are right. The state's best-known area is Yakutat in Southeast Alaska, where miles of uncrowded black-sand beaches attract surfers. Surfing supplies can be found in Yakutat and Kodiak. Homer is also an increasingly popular destination for kitesurfers, with good winds most afternoons.

Hot Springs

Alaska is a thermally active region, a fact attested to by its more than 100 hot spring sites, of which roughly a dozen are accessible and developed. Accessible, in Alaska, is a relative term: Possibly the most accessible hot spring in the state is at Chena, 60 miles east of Fairbanks on a paved road. Also accessible near Fairbanks is Manley Hot Springs, over 150 hard dirt-road miles. Circle Hot Springs, a similar distance from Fairbanks, is no longer open to the public. Other popular hot springs are in Southeast Alaska: White Sulphur and Tenakee on Chichagof Island west of Juneau, Chief Shakes near Wrangell, and Baranof on Baranof Island. Contact the Alaska Department of Natural Resources for its map of thermally active areas in Alaska.

WINTER SPORTS

Skiing and Snowboarding

Downhill ski and snowboard areas are near Anchorage (Alyeska Resort, Hilltop Ski Area, and Alpenglow), Juneau (Eaglecrest), and Fairbanks (Moose Mountain and Skiland). The largest of these is Alyeska (www.alyeskaresort.com), with 500 skiable acres, 60 trails, a 60-passenger aerial tram, 8 chair lifts, and 2 pony lifts.

Cross-country skiing (both classic and skate) is very popular in Alaska, particularly in Anchorage, where many miles of lighted

April
Bethel – Camai Dance Festival; Girdwood – Alyeska Spring Carnival; Juneau – Alaska Folk Festival

May
Cordova – Copper River Delta Shorebird Festival; Haines – Great Alaska Craftbeer & Homebrew Festival; Homer – Kachemak Bay Shorebird Festival and K-Bay SeaFest; Kodiak – Crab Festival; Nome – Memorial Day Polar Bear Swim; Petersburg – Little Norway Festival

June
Anchorage – Mayor's Midnight Sun Marathon, Elmendorf Open House and Air Show, Taste of Anchorage; Fairbanks – Midnight Sun Baseball Game, Yukon 800 Boat Race; Haines – Kluane to Chilkat International Bike Relay; Palmer – Colony Days; Sitka – Summer Music Festival

July
Delta Junction – Deltana Fair; Eagle River – Bear Paw Festival; Fairbanks – Golden Days, World Eskimo-Indian Olympics; Girdwood – Girdwood Forest Fair; Homer – KBBI Concert on the Lawn; Seward – Mt. Marathon Race; Talkeetna – Moose Dropping Festival

August
Fairbanks – Tanana Valley Fair; Haines – Southeast Alaska State Fair; Ketchikan – Blueberry Arts Festival; Ninilchik – Kenai Peninsula State Fair; Palmer – Alaska State Fair; Seward – Silver Salmon Derby; Talkeetna – Bluegrass Festival; Valdez – Gold Rush Days

September
Kodiak – State Fair and Rodeo; Kenai, Valdez, Whittier, Wrangell – Silver Salmon Derby

October
Anchorage – Alaska Federation of Natives Convention; Sitka – Alaska Day Festival

November
Anchorage – Great Alaska Shootout; Haines – Alaska Bald Eagle Festival; Sitka – Whalefest

December
Kodiak – Harbor Stars Boat Parade; Talkeetna – Winterfest

and groomed trails are available throughout the winter. Anchorage may well have the finest cross-country skiing of any American city, and a number of the nation's best Olympic skiers come from here. The city's main cross-country ski areas are in Kincaid Park, Hillside Ski Area, and the Tony Knowles Coastal Trail. Additional groomed ski trails are around Fairbanks, Homer, Juneau, Palmer, Eagle River, Seward, and Valdez. The **Nordic Skiing Association of Anchorage** (907/276-7609, www.anchoragenordicski.com) is Alaska's largest cross-country association, and its website has links to the state's other Nordic skiing groups.

Dog Mushing

Dogsledding has a rich history in Alaska, and sled dog races are a major winter staple across much of the state. The most famous are the **Iditarod Trail Sled Dog Race** (www.iditarod.com) from Anchorage to Nome in March and the **Yukon Quest International Sled Dog Race** (www.yukonquest.com) between Fairbanks and Whitehorse in February. A number of companies offer wintertime dogsled tours, some of which are timed to coincide with the Iditarod or Yukon Quest.

During the summer months, visitors can ride on wheeled sleds behind teams of dogs, providing a chance to get the feel of the real thing. These very popular rides—some led by Iditarod mushers—are offered in Fairbanks, Seward, Skagway, Wasilla, and Denali. In addition, summertime dogsled tours take place on glaciers near Juneau, Skagway, and Seward. Tourists are flown up to the glacier by helicopter and given a chance to ride along as the dogs head across the ice and snow. It's a unique—but very expensive—experience.

PACK THE ESSENTIALS

The following items assume that your trip to Alaska takes place in the summer months. If you plan to travel before May or after September, additional winter supplies will certainly be needed. In general, plan on cool and wet weather for your trip, but also throw in a pair of short pants for those hot Fairbanks afternoons.

Even if you arrive in Alaska without the correct gear, almost anything you need is available in the larger towns, and in Anchorage the prices are really not much higher than in Lower 48 cities. In addition, the larger cities typically have at least one place that rents outdoor gear such as tents and stoves.

In addition to the items listed below, travelers to Southeast Alaska and other rainy parts of the state should bring rubber boots and heavy-duty rain gear. You may want to wait to purchase these because local shops carry higher quality gear than is generally available outside Alaska.

A **cell phone** can be especially useful if you want to stay in contact with friends and family while traveling, but coverage varies, so check with your service provider for specifics. And of course, don't forget your camera!

Clothing Essentials

- light water-resistant coat (Gore-Tex works well)
- sweater or wind-block jacket
- lightweight gloves
- long johns
- walking shoes
- hiking boots
- hiking socks
- liner socks
- rain pants
- warm cap
- swimsuit
- sunglasses

Camping Essentials

- 50 feet of line
- camp stove and fuel bottle
- compass
- cooking pot
- day pack
- first-aid kit
- fishing tackle (or get this in Alaska)
- insect repellent
- internal-frame backpack
- jackknife or Leatherman tool (a better option)
- plastic bags
- plate, cup, spoon, and fork
- sewing kit
- sleeping bag
- small towel
- sunscreen
- tent and ground cloth
- Thermarest pad
- water bottle
- water filter
- waterproof matches and lighter

Snowmobiling

Snowmobiling—or snowmachining, as it's called in Alaska—is both a bush necessity in the winter and a favorite of the motor-head crowd in urban centers. The **Alaska State Snowmobile Association** (www.aksnow.org) has additional info on their website. Rentals and tours are available in Anchorage and Fairbanks.

SPECTATOR SPORTS

The **Alaska Baseball League** (www.alaska-baseballleague.org) consists of six semiprofessional teams: Mat-Su Miners, Kenai Peninsula Oilers, Alaska Goldpanners of Fairbanks, Anchorage Bucs, Anchorage Glacier Pilots, and Fairbanks Athletes in Action. The teams include talented college players from throughout the country who come to Alaska to play in June and July. Alaska Baseball League teams play each other, along with Outside teams from the West Coast and Hawaii, with the top teams ending up at the National Baseball Congress World Series in Wichita, Kansas. Alaskan teams have won these World Series many times, and quite a few famous players have spent a summer on Alaska turf, including Mark McGwire, Tom Seaver, Graig Nettles, and Dave Winfield.

Hockey is very big in Alaska, especially in Anchorage and Fairbanks, where overachiever dads push their kids onto the ice by age four. The **Alaska Aces** (www.alaskaaces.com) play professional hockey in the minor-league West Coast Hockey League, and both the University of Alaska Anchorage (UAA) and the University of Alaska Fairbanks (UAF) have nationally competitive hockey teams.

In bush Alaska, no sport is bigger than basketball, and any visitor who can play well stands a good chance of immediately being accepted by the locals. There's intense competition among high school teams at the state level, and both UAA and UAF have their own basketball squads. The state's biggest basketball event is the **Great Alaska Shootout** (www.shootout.net) held in Anchorage each November and featuring eight college teams.

RESOURCES

Suggested Reading

An excellent place to find Alaskan books is through the **Alaska Natural History Association** (907/274-8440, www.alaskanha.org). You can order several hundred nature books, maps, calendars, guides, and other titles online or through their print catalog.

A number of the books listed below are out of print, but you can find many of them in regional libraries, or check the Web for special orders. Two recommended sources for rare and out-of-print Alaskan books are Anchorage's **Title Wave Books** (907/278-9283 or 888/598-9283, www.wavebooks.com) and Juneau's **The Observatory** (907/586-9676, www.observatorybooks.com).

ART AND LITERATURE

Bancroft-Hunt, Norman. *People of the Totem: The Indians of the Pacific Northwest.* New York: Peter Bedrick Books, 1989. A beautifully illustrated history of the art of Tlingit and other Northwest peoples. Out of print.

Bodett, Tom. *As Far as You Can Go Without a Passport.* New York: Perseus Publishing, www.perseusbooks.com, 1986. A collection of wry, bring-a-smile-to-your-face Alaska tales. Bodett's other books include *The End of the Road* and *Small Comforts.* Out of print.

Jans, Nick. *The Last Light Breaking.* Anchorage: Alaska Northwest Books, www.gacpc.com, 1993. A beautifully written collection of essays about life in the Eskimo village of Ambler.

Jans, Nick. *A Place Beyond.* Anchorage: Alaska Northwest Books, www.gacpc.com, 1996. Another fine collection of stories by one of Alaska's most observant writers.

Kizzia, Tom. *The Wake of the Unseen Object.* Lincoln, NE: University of Nebraska Press, www.nebraskapress.unl.edu, 1998. A lovingly written journey through the wild heart of today's Alaskan bush. Filled with insights into the clashing cultures of indigenous and white America.

Krakauer, Jon. *Into the Wild.* New York: Random House, www.randomhouse.com, 1997. Now a Hollywood movie, this is the tale of Chris McCandless, a young man whose 1992 death in the bush north of Denali does not merit the attention it received. The story is loved by many Outsiders, but viewed with disdain by many Alaskans.

London, Jack. *The Call of the Wild.* This gripping tale of a sled dog's experience along the gold rush trail was Jack London's most successful rendering of the spirit of the North. Reprint editions are available from several publishers.

Lopez, Barry. *Arctic Dreams.* New York: Random House, www.randomhouse.com, 2001. A wonderful exploration of the Arctic, with a mixture of scientific information and environmental thinking. Highly recommended.

Lopez, Barry. *Of Wolves and Men.* New York: Scribner, www.galegroup.com/scribners, 1982. An excellent discussion of the hunter-hunted dynamic.

Marshall, Robert. *Alaska Wilderness: Exploring the Central Brooks Range.* Berkeley, CA: University of California Press, www.uscpress.edu, 1983. A thrilling account of the author's exploration of the Central Brooks Range.

McGinniss, Joe. *Going to Extremes.* New York: Plume, 1989. One man's journey to Alaska leads him to a series of characters as diverse as the state itself. This reissue of a 1980 book, though quite dated, is still popular with travelers.

McPhee, John. *Coming into the Country.* New York: Noonday Press, 2003. Even though it was actually written in the 1970s, this remains perhaps the best portrayal of Alaskan bush lifestyles ever written. It's the book you'll still see folks reading on the long ferry ride north.

Muir, John. *Stickeen.* Berkeley, CA: Heyday Books, www.heydaybooks.com, 1990. Originally published almost a century ago, this classic dog short story offers a vastly different take on Glacier Bay than that seen by the cruise ship tourists.

Schooler, Lynn. *Blue Bear: A True Story of Friendship, Tragedy and Survival in the Alaskan Wilderness.* New York: Harper-Collins Publishers, www.harpercollins.com, 2002. This beautifully crafted memoir chronicles Schooler's life and how it was changed by Michio Hoshino, the renowned wildlife photographer killed by a grizzly in 1996.

Service, Robert. *Collected Poems.* New York: Putnam Publishing, www.penguingroup.com, 1989. No one has ever better captured the flavor of northern life than the poet Robert Service.

Stewart, Hilary. *Looking at Indian Art of the Northwest Coast.* Seattle: University of Washington Press, www.washington.edu/uwpress, 2003. A concise analysis of the art forms of this powerful culture.

Stewart, Hilary. *Looking at Totem Poles.* Seattle: University of Washington Press, www.washington.edu/uwpress, 2003. Details on the history and art of more than 100 totem poles in Alaska and British Columbia.

Walker, Spike. *Working on the Edge.* New York: St. Martin's Press, www.stmartins.com, 2003. Harrowing tales from the edge of the abyss—working the king-crab boats of the Bering Sea in the boom years of the 1970s and early 1980s, when the financial stakes were almost as high as the risks to life. Read it before you even consider working on a crab boat.

DESCRIPTION AND TRAVEL

Alaska Almanac. Anchorage: Alaska Northwest Books, www.gacpc.com, published annually. A rich source of useful information about the state, all in one compact volume.

Alaska Atlas & Gazetteer. Freeport, ME: DeLorme Mapping, www.delorme.com, 2004. This large book of up-to-date topographic maps is a wise investment if you plan to explore the more remote parts of Alaska. Very easy to use.

Alaska Wilderness Guide. Augusta, GA: Morris Communications, www.morris.com, 2001. A good source for general information on all of Alaska's villages and cities, as well as its many wild places.

Colby, Merle. *A Guide to Alaska.* New York: MacMillan, 1939. Written over half a century ago, this Federal Writers' Project guide to Alaska has never been surpassed. Out of print, but can be found in a good library.

Hempstead, Andrew. *Moon Western Canada.* Berkeley, CA: Avalon Travel Publishing, www.moon.com, 2010. Like this book, Andrew Hempstead's titles are part of the Moon Handbooks series. He provides excellent advice for travelers in British Columbia and Yukon, Alaska's neighbors to the east.

Howard, Jim. *Guide to Sea Kayaking in Southeast Alaska: The Best Trips and Tours from Misty Fjords to Glacier Bay.* Old Saybrook, CT: Globe Pequot Press, www.globepequot.com, 1999. This book describes 41 Southeast Alaska kayak trips.

Jettmar, Karen. *Alaska's Glacier Bay.* Anchorage: Alaska Northwest Books, www.gacpc.com, 1997. A good little sourcebook for park information.

Jettmar, Karen. *The Alaska River Guide.* Anchorage: Alaska Northwest Books, www.gacpc.com, 1998. Filled with vital information for anyone planning to float the more than 100 rivers in Alaska.

Kelley, Mark. *Glacier Bay National Park Alaska.* Juneau: Mark Kelley Photography, www.markkelley.com, 2000. A beautiful coffee-table book by Southeast Alaska's foremost photographer.

Larson, Richard. *Mountain Bike Alaska—49 Trails in the 49th State.* Anchorage: Glacier House Publications, 1991. An outdated but reasonably complete look at mountain biking in Alaska.

The Milepost. Augusta, GA: Morris Communications, www.themilepost.com, published annually. For motorists, this publication—in existence for more than 60 years—is the best guidebook to Alaska. The highway maps and description make it a must if you're driving north. Although the information is accurate and comprehensive, specific listings of hotels, bars, and restaurants are limited to advertisers, and the ads don't tell the whole story.

Moore, Terris. *Mt. McKinley: The Pioneer Climbs.* Seattle: The Mountaineers, www.mountaineers.org, 1981. An exciting history of the challenge to climb North America's highest mountain.

Nienhueser, Helen, and John Wolfe Jr. *55 Ways to the Wilderness in Southcentral Alaska.* Seattle: The Mountaineers, www.mountaineers.org, 2002. A compact trail guide, complete with maps, photos, and descriptions of the best the region has to offer.

Praetorius, Pete, and Alys Culhane. *Alaska Bicycle Touring Guide.* Juneau: Denali Press, 1992. The best source for cyclists planning a trip around Alaska and Yukon.

Quick, Daniel L. *Kenai Canoe Trails.* Anchorage: Todd Publications, 1997. A very helpful guide to canoe routes within Kenai National Wildlife Refuge.

Romano-Lax, Andromeda. *How to Rent a Public Cabin in Southcentral Alaska.* Berkeley, CA: Wilderness Press, www.wildernesspress.com, 2003. An enjoyable and detailed guide to dozens of Forest Service and state park cabins.

Shepherd, Shane, and Owen Wozniak. *50 Hikes in Alaska's Chugach State Park.* Seattle: The Mountaineers, www.mountaineers.org, 2001. An informative guide to hiking in the second-largest state park in the country.

Skillman, Don. *Adventure Kayaking: Trips in Glacier Bay.* Berkeley, CA: Wilderness Press, www.wildernesspress.com, 1998. A helpful guide to sea kayaking around Glacier Bay.

Wayburn, Peggy. *Adventuring in Alaska.* San Francisco: Sierra Club Books, www.sierraclub.org/books, 1998. A guide to the remote wilderness regions of Alaska and how to get there.

HISTORY

Adney, Tappan. *Klondike Stampede.* Vancouver, Canada: University of British Columbia Press, www.ubcpress.ubc.ca, 1995. The best and most readable book on Alaska's gold rush.

Berton, Pierre. *The Klondike Fever.* New York: Perseus Books, www.perseusbooks.com, 2003. Originally published in 1958, this remains the definitive account of the gold rush.

Chevigny, Hector. *Lord of Alaska.* Portland, OR: Binford & Mort, 1971. Biography of Alexander Baranof, manager of the Russian-American Company 1791–1817. Out of print.

Cohen, Stan. *The Forgotten War.* Missoula, MT: Pictorial Histories Publishing, 1993. A pictorial history of World War II in Alaska and northwestern Canada.

Greiner, James. *Wager with the Wind: The Don Sheldon Story.* New York: St. Martin's Press, www.stmartins.com, 1982. The true story of one of the state's most famous bush pilots.

Heller, Herbert L. *Sourdough Sagas.* Cleveland: World Publishing, 1967. Colorful tales of mishap and adventure among Alaska's prospecting pioneers. Out of print.

Morgan, Murray. *One Man's Gold Rush: A Klondike Album.* Seattle: University of Washington Press, www.washington.edu/uwpress, 1995. A feast of gold-rush photography.

Muir, John. *Travels in Alaska.* Written in 1915, this is Muir's classic narration of his experiences on the Stikine River and at Glacier Bay during 1879, 1880, and 1890. Several publishers offer reprints.

Neufeld, David, and Frank Norris. *Chilkoot Trail, Heritage Route to the Klondike.* Whitehorse, Yukon: Lost Moose Publishing, 1996. A fascinating book about the gold rush, filled with black-and-white photos.

Okun, S. B. *The Russian-American Company.* Cambridge, MA: Harvard University Press, 1951. This translation from the Russian gives a different view of Alaska in the period up to 1867. Out of print.

Oman, Lela Kiana. *The Epic of Qayaq: The Longest Story Ever Told by My People.* Seattle: University of Washington Press, www.washington.edu/uwpress, 1995. The story of the Inupiat people of the Kobuk Valley as told in stories passed down though the generations. Beautifully illustrated. The author is a respected elder in Nome.

Sherwood, Morgan B. *Exploration of Alaska, 1865–1900.* Fairbanks: University of Alaska Press, www.uaf.edu/uapress, 1992. This reprint of the 1965 book details the opening of the Interior.

Wilson, Graham, and Clelie Rich, editors. *The Klondike Gold Rush: Photographs from 1896–1899.* Whitehorse, Yukon: Wolf Creek Books, 2003. An excellent collection of historical photos from the Klondike gold rush.

NATURAL HISTORY

Hulten, Eric. *Flora of Alaska and Neighboring Territories.* Stanford, CA: Stanford University Press, www.sup.org, 1968. A huge manual of vascular plants—highly technical, but easy to consult.

Matsen, Brad. *Ray Troll's Shocking Fish Tales.* Anchorage: Alaska Northwest Books, www.gacpc.com, 1993. Illustrated by Ray Troll, outrageous fish artist par excellence, this book offers a mix of scientific and philosophical ramblings about creatures of the sea. Great fun.

Murie, Adolph. *A Naturalist in Alaska.* Tucson: University of Arizona Press, www.uapress.arizona.edu, 1990. This reprint of a 1961 classic still offers excellent insight into the fauna of Alaska.

Murie, Adolph. *The Wolves of Mount McKinley.* Seattle: University of Washington Press, www.washington.edu/uwpress, 1985. Another Murie classic, originally published in 1944.

O'Clair, Rita M., Robert H. Armstrong, and Richard Carstensen. *The Nature of Southeast Alaska.* Anchorage: Alaska Northwest Books, www.gacpc.com, 2003. See the world through the naturalists' eyes in this beautifully illustrated guide to the lives of animals and plants in Southeast Alaska.

Sydeman, Michelle, and Annabel Lund. *Alaska Wildlife Viewing Guide.* Old Saybrook, CT: Globe Pequot Press, www.globepequot.com, 1996. A small helpful guide to the state's animals.

Walker, Tom. *River of Bears.* Stillwater, MN: Voyageur Press, 1993. The story of the McNeil River and the bears that have made it a favorite of photographers. Photos by Larry Aumiller, the Fish and Game employee who guides hundreds of visitors each summer. Out of print.

Wynne, Kate. *Guide to Marine Mammals of Alaska.* Fairbanks: University of Alaska, 1997. An outstanding easy-to-use guide to the whales, seals, porpoises, sea lions, and other sea mammals around Alaska. Perfect for anyone riding the ferryboats or heading out on a wildlife tour. Out of print.

Internet Resources

The Internet is a great source of information on Alaska. The following is a tiny sample; a quick Web search will turn up a multitude of additional websites for your area of interest.

Alaska Travel Industry Association
www.travelalaska.com

This organization distributes the official *Alaska State Vacation Planner.*

State of Alaska
www.state.ak.us

The State of Alaska website has links to state agencies and tourism sites.

Chamber of Commerce
www.alaskachamber.com

Links to all Alaskan chambers of commerce are included (but you may have to search a bit).

Alaska State Parks
www.alaskastateparks.org

Find details on Alaska's state parks and recreation areas on this useful site.

National Park Service
www.nps.gov/akso

The National Park Service's Alaska website has details on Denali, Glacier Bay, Wrangell–St. Elias, Katmai, and 11 other national parks in Alaska.

Alaska Department of Fish and Game
www.wildlife.alaska.gov

The Fish and Game website is a good starting place for details on sportfishing and wildlife viewing around Alaska.

Public Lands Information Centers
www.alaskacenters.gov

Four Alaska Public Lands Information Centers are scattered around the state; their website offers an overview of federal lands in Alaska.

U.S. Fish and Wildlife Service
http://alaska.fws.gov

Head here for details on the Fish and Wildlife Service, which manages 16 refuges across the state, including Kodiak National Wildlife Refuge and Arctic National Wildlife Refuge.

Alaska Marine Highway System
www.dot.state.ak.us/amhs

Visit this website for current Alaska Marine Highway ferry schedules and fares.

511.Alaska.gov
http://511.alaska.gov

Especially useful for winter travel in Alaska, this site has details on road conditions, winter travel tips, highway construction updates, and more.

Recreation.gov
www.recreation.gov

Head here to book any Forest Service cabin in Alaska, plus a handful of other public cabins and campgrounds around the state.

Alaska Climate Research Center
http://climate.gi.alaska.edu

This site includes climatic data, current weather conditions, and Alaskan forecasts.

University of Alaska Fairbanks Geophysical Institute
www.gedds.alaska.edu/auroraforecast

Head here for northern lights activity in Alaska, with predictions for tonight and several days ahead.

Alaska Wilderness Recreation and Tourism Association
www.awrta.org

Find a complete listing of Alaskan environmental groups, with links to their websites.

Alaska.com
www.alaska.com

This website is a great resource, with tons of links. It's operated by the *Anchorage Daily News,* whose website, www.adn.com, has current Alaska news, fishing info, and much more.

Community and Regional Affairs
www.dced.state.ak.us/dca

The Alaska Community Database offers trivia on 350 cities and towns around the state. Maps and photos are also featured.

Don Pitcher
www.donpitcher.com and www.donpitcher.com/blog

Author Don Pitcher's website includes links to most websites found in this book, and his blog provides a taste of life on the last frontier.

Index

A

C

D

E

F

H

I

J

K

P

QR

S

T

U

XYZ